WHERE YOUR MONEY GOES

The 1994–95 Green Book

U.S. House of Representatives
Committee on Ways and Means

BRASSEY'S
Washington • London

First Brassey's edition 1994

This book was originally prepared for the use of members of the U.S. House of Representatives Committee on Ways and Means and was published by the U.S. Government Printing Office in 1994 as the *1994 Green Book*.

Library of Congress Cataloging-in-Publication Data

Where your money goes: the 1994–95 green book/U.S. House of
   Representatives, Committee on Ways and Means.—1st Brassey's ed.
      p.   cm.
    Includes index.
    ISBN 0–02–881130–5
    1.   Economic assistance.   Domestic—United States.   2.
  Entitlement spending—United States.   3. United States Congress
  House Committee on Ways and Means.   I. United States.
  Congress.   House.   Committee on Ways and Means. II.
  Background material and data on major programs within the
  jurisdiction of the Committee on Ways and Means.
  HC110.P63W523   1994
  336.3'9'0973—dc20

                                        94–37042
                                            CIP

10 9 8 7 6 5 4 3 2 1

Printed in the United States of America

LETTER OF TRANSMITTAL

COMMITTEE ON WAYS AND MEANS,
U.S. HOUSE OF REPRESENTATIVES,
Washington, D.C., July 15, 1994.

Hon. SAM M. GIBBONS,
Acting Chairman, Committee on Ways and Means,
House of Representatives, Washington, D.C.

DEAR MR. CHAIRMAN: Since 1981, the Committee on Ways and Means has published the annual "Green Book," which presents background material and statistical data on the major entitlement programs within the Committee's jurisdiction: Social Security, Medicare, Unemployment Compensation, Trade Adjustment Assistance, Aid to Families with Dependent Children, Child Support Enforcement, Supplemental Security Income, the Title XX Social Services Block Grant program, Child Welfare, Foster Care, Adoption Assistance, and Child Care programs.

While initially intended for the use of the Members of the Committee and their staffs, this document has become a valuable resource for Members of Congress, Congressional staff, government officials at the Federal, State and local level, academicians, public policy analysts, as well as the general public.

On behalf of the staff, I am pleased to transmit to you and the other Members of the Committee on Ways and Means, the 1994 edition (the 14th edition) of the Green Book. The Green Book integrates a description of each program within the jurisdiction of the Committee with current data regarding the population served by the program, an analysis of interactions with other major programs, and historical background information.

The staff wishes to express its appreciation to the many individuals and organizations who contribute annually to the publication of the Green Book. At the risk of failing to mention some individuals, the staff wishes to recognize the following organizations and individuals for their contribution to this year's edition of the Green Book.

1. The Congressional Research Service of the Library of Congress and the following individuals:

Melvina Ford, Section 18;
Molly Forman, Sections 12 and 18;
Tom Gabe, Appendices A, G, and H;
Janet Kline, All the health sections;
Bill Krouse, Section 18;
Ann Lourdeman, Section 18;
Carolyn Merck, Section 15;
Jennifer Neisner, Sections 7, 10, and 18;
Richard Price, All the health sections;

Joe Richardson, Section 18;
Carmen Solomon, Sections 6, 10, 11, and 18;
Karen Spar, Section 14;
Anne Stewart, Sections 12 and 18;
Jim Storey, Section 7 and Appendix F;
2. The Congressional Budget Office and the following individuals:
Wayne Boyington, Appendix J;
Karin Carr, Appendix J;
Leslie Griffin, Appendix J;
Richard Kasten, Section 16;
Carla Pedone, Section 18;
Murray Ross, Appendix H;
Frank Sammartino, Section 16;
Bob Williams, Section 16 and Appendix H;
3. The Department of Health and Human Services;
4. The Department of Labor;
5. The Social Security Administration;
6. The Census Bureau of the Department of Commerce;
7. The Prospective Payment Assessment Commission;
8. The Physician Payment Review Commission;
9. The Pension Benefit Guaranty Corporation;
10. The staff of the Railroad Retirement Board;
11. The staff of the Joint Committee on Taxation; and
12. The staff of the House Budget Committee.

Many members of the Committee's majority staff made a major contribution to the preparation and publication of this document. Richard Hobbie, Staff Director of the Subcommittee on Human Resources, edited the 1994 Green Book and Joseph Grant of the Subcommittee on Oversight staff assisted him. Victoria Jacobs of the Subcommittee on Human Resources staff coordinated and managed the production of the 1994 Green Book. Other members of the Committee's majority staff who deserve special recognition are: Yvette Chocolaad, Corrie Hess, and Sherri Wood of the Subcommittee on Human Resources staff, Kathryn Olson and Katherine Rourke of the Subcommittee on Social Security staff, Helene Krasnoff, Ellen Magrini, Kathleen Pakos, and Kristen Panerali of the Subcommittee on Health staff, Kathleen O'Connell of the Tax staff, Mary Jane Wignot of the Subcommittee on Trade staff, and George Whittle.

Any suggestions which improve this document are welcomed and will be reflected in subsequent editions of this publication.

Sincerely,

JANICE MAYS,
Chief Counsel and Staff Director.

PREFACE

The staff of the Committee on Ways and Means, with assistance from many individuals at the Congressional Research Service, the Congressional Budget Office, the Department of Health and Human Services, the Department of Labor, the Social Security Administration, the Census Bureau of the Department of Commerce, the Prospective Payment Assessment Commission, the Physician Payment Review Commission, the Pension Benefit Guaranty Corporation, the Railroad Retirement Board, the Joint Committee on Taxation, and the House Budget Committee, has prepared this document for the members of the Committee to use in evaluating the programs under the Committee's jurisdiction, and analyzing possible revisions to such programs.

This year's edition of the Green Book emphasizes descriptive information, and contains a new section-by-section index in the back to facilitate the locating of subtopics.

This document is divided into 18 sections and 10 appendices:

The majority of the sections describe programs within the jurisdiction of the Committee. One section describes other major Federal assistance programs not within the jurisdiction of the Committee on Ways and Means and one section describes tax expenditures and other tax provisions related to retirement, health, poverty, employment, and disability. These sections present summary tables indicating the relative size and recent growth of the individual programs, and extensive information on program eligibility, payment, financing, participant characteristics, interactions with other programs, and history.

The appendices provide background data on topics indirectly related to these programs.

The appendices include: health status, utilization, and expenditures of the elderly; national health expenditures and health insurance coverage; Medicare reimbursement to hospitals and physicians; data on unemployment and employment; demographic and economic characteristics of families with children and the elderly; poverty and antipoverty effectiveness; economic, population, immigration, income and fiscal data; and, budget tables.

CONTENTS

PART 1

DESCRIPTION OF PROGRAMS WITHIN THE JURISDICTION OF THE COMMITTEE ON WAYS AND MEANS PROVIDING BENEFITS OR SERVICES TO INDIVIDUALS

Section 1. The Old-Age and Survivors Insurance Program (OASI)

The old-age and survivors insurance (OASI) program provides monthly benefits to retired workers and their dependents and to survivors of insured workers. Old-age retirement benefits were provided for retired workers by the original Social Security Act of 1935, and benefits for dependents and survivors were provided by the 1939 amendments. The disability insurance (DI) cash benefits program, enacted in 1956, and the hospital insurance (HI) program, enacted in 1965, are closely related to the old-age and survivors insurance program. (These related programs are discussed in later sections.)

GENERAL

A worker builds protection under these programs through employment that is covered by the Social Security system. Coverage is generally compulsory. However, employees of State and local governments who are members of a public retirement system are covered on a voluntary group basis.[1] Currently, an estimated 96 percent of the Nation's paid work force is covered either voluntarily or mandatorily.

Contributions for wage and salaried workers are made under the Federal Insurance Contributions Act (FICA, chapter 21 of the Internal Revenue Code). Contributions are based on earnings up to the annual maximum taxable wage base ($60,600 in 1994 for OASDI and no limit for HI). The employee contribution is withheld from wage and salary payments to employees and is matched by employers. Self-employed persons are covered by the Self-Employment Contributions Act (SECA, chapter 2 of the Internal Revenue Code). They pay contributions on their net earnings annually up to the same maximum as employees, but at a rate that is equal to the combined employee-employer tax rate. However, the self-employed may deduct 7.65 percent from their net earnings before computing their Social Security tax and may also deduct half of their Social Security tax as a business expense for income tax purposes.

Revenue from the OASI portion of the tax is credited automatically to the Old-Age and Survivors Insurance Trust Fund. In addition, the revenue derived from the taxation of a portion of Social Security retirement and survivors' benefits is credited to the OASI trust fund. The trust fund is the source of payment for: (1) monthly benefits when the worker retires or dies (including a financial interchange with the railroad retirement system), and (2) adminis-

---

[1] State and local coverage is voluntary for the OASI and DI programs for those employees who are members of a public retirement system. However, it became mandatory for HI purposes for persons hired by State or local governments on or after April 1, 1986. Once a State or local government entity joins the system, it cannot opt out.

trative expenses for the program. A discussion of OASDI administrative costs may be found in section 3.

BENEFITS

Summary

Monthly cash benefits under OASI are paid as a matter of earned right to workers who are insured for benefits and to their eligible dependents and survivors. Generally, benefit amounts paid both to the insured worker and to the insured worker's dependents or survivors are related to the past earnings of the insured worker. An individual may be entitled to benefits as a worker based on his own earnings history and also to benefits as a dependent of another worker. However, the amount of the benefit is adjusted so that, in effect, only the larger of the two benefits is paid.

In December 1993, there were 42.2 million beneficiaries in the OASI and DI programs who were in current-payment status. Monthly benefits paid out were $25.7 billion.

Table 1–1 summarizes various types of beneficiaries and average benefit amounts. Table 1–2 shows total OASI and DI benefits paid in past years.

TABLE 1–1.—OASDI CASH BENEFITS IN CURRENT-PAYMENT STATUS AND NEW AWARDS, DECEMBER 1993

	Number in current payment (thousands)	Percent of beneficiary population	Average monthly benefit	Number of new awards (in thousands)	Average new award
Total monthly beneficiaries	42,246	100.0	$607	4,001	$530
Retired workers	26,104	61.8	674	1,661	647
Wives and husbands of retired workers	3,094	7.3	347	291	315
Children of retired workers	436	1.0	297	107	277
Disabled workers	3,726	8.8	642	635	638
Wives and husbands of disabled workers	273	.6	156	75	158
Children of disabled workers	1,255	3.0	173	399	158
Widowed mothers and fathers	289	.7	448	56	435
Surviving children	1,836	4.3	443	311	436
Widows and widowers ...	5,077	12.0	630	434	624
Disabled widow(er)s	147	.3	434	32	431
Parents	5	.01	547	(1)	545
Special age-72	2	0	183	(1)	145

1 Fewer than 500.

Source: Office of Research and Statistics, Social Security Administration.

TABLE 1–2.—TOTAL OASDI BENEFITS PAID

[In millions]

Year	Total	OASI	DI
1937	$1	$1	....
1940	35	35	....
1950	961	961	....
1960	11,245	10,677	$568
1970	31,863	28,796	3,067
1980	120,511	105,074	15,437
1985 [1]	186,196	167,360	18,836
1990 [1]	247,796	222,993	24,803
1991 [1]	268,098	240,436	27,662
1992 [1]	419,325	254,939	31,091

[1] Unnegotiated checks not deducted.

Source: Social Security Bulletin, Annual Statistical Supplement, 1992, table 4.A4.

Brief history

The 1935 Social Security Act provided monthly benefits to retired workers age 65 and over and a lump-sum death benefit to the estate of these workers. The monthly benefits were to first be paid beginning January 1, 1942. The 1939 Social Security Amendments provided benefits to dependents—wives aged 65 and over and children under age 16 (changed to 18 in 1946)—of retired workers, and to survivors—widows aged 65, mothers with eligible child in care, children under age 16, and dependent parents—of deceased workers. In addition the 1939 Amendments provided that these benefits first be paid in 1940.

Benefits that have been added in the retirement and survivors programs since 1939 include: retired women aged 62–64 (1956); retired men aged 62–64 (1961); widows aged 60–64 (1956 and 1965); widowers aged 60 and over (1950, 1961, and 1972); and disabled widows age 50 and over (1967).

In 1956, benefits were extended to disabled workers aged 50–64 and to disabled children of retired, disabled, or deceased workers age 18 and over, if they became disabled prior to age 18 (changed to disabled prior to age 22 in 1973). The 1958 Amendments provided benefits to dependents of disabled workers on the same basis as dependents of retired workers. Benefits for disabled workers under age 50 were provided in 1960.

Monthly cash benefits have been increased on an ad hoc basis 10 times prior to the first automatic cost-of-living adjustment which was incorporated in the act by the Social Security Amendments of 1972. Beginning with the 1975 increase, benefits have been automatically adjusted to keep pace with inflation. Since 1975, there have been increases annually except during calendar year 1983, when the adjustment was delayed 6 months (see table 1–12).

Description of major benefit types

Child's benefit. Under the OASI program, a monthly benefit is payable to an unmarried child or eligible dependent grandchild of a retired worker or a deceased worker who was fully or currently insured at death if the child or grandchild is: (1) under age 18; (2) a full-time elementary or secondary student under age 19; (3) a disabled person aged 18 or over whose disability began before age 22. A grandchild is eligible for benefits on a grandparent's earnings record if the child was adopted by the grandparent. If adopted by the surviving spouse of that grandparent, the child would be eligible if he or she lived with *or* received one-half support from the grandparent prior to the grandparent's death. Even in cases where the child has not been adopted by the grandparent (or his or her surviving spouse), if the child's parents became disabled or died before the grandparent became entitled to benefits or died, the child would be eligible if he or she had lived with *and* relied on the grandparent for one-half support prior to the grandparent's entitlement or death.

Lump-sum death benefit. A lump-sum payment is payable upon the death of a fully or currently insured worker to the surviving spouse who was living with the deceased worker or was eligible to receive monthly cash survivor benefits upon the worker's death. If there is no eligible spouse, the lump-sum death payment is payable to any child of the deceased worker who is eligible to receive monthly cash benefits as a surviving child. If there is no surviving spouse and no children of the worker eligible for monthly benefits, then the lump-sum death payment is not paid. The payment amount is $255.

Minimum benefit. The minimum benefit is the smallest benefit (before actuarial reduction or earnings test reduction) payable to a worker or his or her survivors/dependents. In 1977, the minimum benefit was frozen at $122 per month for all workers who reached age 62 or became disabled after 1978 and all survivors of workers who died after 1978. Legislation in 1981 eliminated the minimum benefit for all persons becoming eligible for benefits in January 1982 or later (except for certain members of religious orders who have taken a vow of poverty; such persons who became eligible in 1982–91 are exempt from the new law). These persons have their benefits computed under the regular benefit computation rules. Persons eligible for benefits prior to January 1, 1982 are able to continue receiving the minimum benefit, which is subject to annual cost-of-living adjustments.

Mother's or father's benefit. A monthly benefit is payable to a widow (widower) or surviving divorced mother (father) if: (1) the deceased worker on whose account the benefit is paid was fully or currently insured at time of death and (2) the widow (widower) or surviving divorced mother (father) has one or more entitled children of the worker in her care. These payments continue as long as the youngest child being cared for is under age 16 or disabled.

Parent's benefit. This is a monthly benefit payable to a dependent parent, age 62 or over, of a deceased fully insured worker.

Retired-worker (old-age) benefit. This is a monthly benefit payable to a retired worker aged 62 or over who is fully insured.

"Special age-72" benefit. This is a monthly benefit payable to certain persons born before January 2, 1900, who do not have sufficient quarters of coverage to qualify for a retired-worker benefit. The benefit is payable only for months in which the individual is a resident of the 50 States, the District of Columbia, or the North-

ern Mariana Islands and receives no public assistance cash payments or SSI payments. It is reduced by the amount of any government pension (except workers' compensation and veterans' service-connected compensation) that the individual is receiving or is eligible to receive. When husband and wife are both eligible for these benefits, a full benefit is paid to each spouse.

Special minimum benefit. This is a benefit that is not based on the worker's average monthly wage or average indexed monthly earnings, but instead on his/her length (years) of covered employment. It is designed to help those who worked in covered employment for many years but had low earnings. The amount of the special minimum is computed by multiplying the number of years of coverage in excess of 10 and up to 30 by $11.50 for monthly benefits payable in 1979, with automatic cost-of-living increases applicable to years 1979 and later. The number of years of coverage equals the number obtained by dividing total creditable wages in 1937–50 by $900 (not to exceed 14), plus the number of years after 1950 and before 1991 for which the worker is credited with at least 25 percent of the annual maximum taxable earnings. For this purpose for years after 1978, annual maximum taxable earnings are defined as the "old-law" taxable earnings base (i.e., the hypothetical earnings base that would be in effect if the ad hoc increases in the base enacted in 1977 were disregarded). In addition, for years after 1990, a year of coverage is earned if the worker is credited with at least 15 percent of the "old-law" taxable earnings base. The special minimum benefit is not subject to the delayed-retirement-credit provisions.

Spouse's benefit. This is a monthly benefit payable to a spouse or divorced spouse of a retired worker under one of the following conditions: (1) currently married spouse is aged 62 or older or is caring for one or more of the worker's entitled children who are disabled or have not reached age 16; or (2) divorced spouse is aged 62 or older, is not married, and the marriage to the worker had lasted 10 years before the divorce became final. A divorced spouse may be entitled independently of the worker's retirement under certain circumstances.

Widow's or widower's benefit. This is a monthly benefit payable to a widow(er) or surviving divorced spouse of a worker fully insured at the time of death if he or she is unmarried, or remarriage occurred after the widow(er)'s first eligibility for benefits; and (a) is aged 60 or older or (b) aged 50–59 and has been disabled throughout a waiting period of 5 consecutive calendar months that began no later than 7 years after the month the worker dies or after the end of her entitlement to benefits as a widowed mother.

BENEFIT ELIGIBILITY: INSURED STATUS

Benefits can only be paid to workers, their dependents or survivors if the worker is "insured" for these benefits. Insured status is measured in terms of "quarters of coverage."

Prior to 1978, one quarter of coverage was earned for each calendar quarter in which a worker was paid $50 or more in wages for covered employment (except for agricultural labor). Since the beginning of 1978 the crediting of quarters of coverage has been on an annual rather than a quarterly basis. In 1978, a worker earned one quarter of coverage, up to a total of four, for each $250 of annual earnings reported from covered employment or self-employment. The amount of annual earnings needed for a quarter of coverage is subject to annual automatic increases, effective in January of each year, in proportion to increases in average wages in the economy. In 1994, the amount is $620 for workers.

For the purpose of the OASI program, there are two types of insured status: "fully insured" and "currently insured." Workers are fully insured for benefits for themselves and for their families if they have one quarter of coverage (earned at any time after 1936) for every four quarters elapsing after 1950, or the year of reaching age 21, if later, up to the year in which they reach age 62, become disabled, or die. Fully insured status is required for eligibility for all types of benefits except certain survivor benefits. A person must have at least six quarters of coverage to be fully insured. A person with 40 quarters of coverage is fully insured for life.

Workers are currently insured if they have six quarters of coverage during the thirteen calendar quarters ending with the quarter in which they died. Currently insured status by itself provides that the worker's surviving family members are eligible for child's, mother's, father's and lump-sum death benefits.

TABLE 1–3.—AMOUNT OF COVERED EARNINGS NEEDED TO EARN ONE QUARTER OF COVERAGE SINCE 1978

Year	Amount
1978	$250
1979	260
1980	290
1981	310
1982	340
1983	370
1984	390
1985	410
1986	440
1987	460
1988	470
1989	500
1990	520
1991	540
1992	570
1993	590
1994	620
1995	[1] 640
1996	[1] 660
1997	[1] 680
1998	[1] 710
1999	[1] 740

[1] Based on economic assumptions in the President's FY 1995 Budget.

Source: Office of the Actuary, Social Security Administration.

BENEFIT COMPUTATION

The amount of a monthly benefit award is determined by first computing an insured worker's average monthly wage (AMW) or—in the case of most workers who attain age 62, become disabled, or die after 1978—average indexed monthly earnings (AIME). The AMW is used in computing benefits under the old (pre-1979) benefit formula, and the AIME is used in computing benefits under the new (post-1978) benefit formula enacted in 1977. The AMW or AIME is linked (by a table or by a formula, respectively, in the law) to the monthly retirement benefit payable at that worker's normal retirement age. This amount is called the primary insurance amount (PIA). Benefits for dependents and survivors are calculated as a percentage of the insured worker's PIA. The calculated amounts may be subject to minimum levels, and all benefits are subject to maximum limits. Benefits payable to workers, spouses, widows, and widowers who choose to retire before their normal retirement age are subject to an actuarial reduction. Benefits payable to workers who choose to retire after their normal retirement age are subject to increase through the delayed retirement credit, as are the benefits payable to their widows and widowers. The delayed retirement credit is 1 percent per year for workers age 65 before 1982 and 3 percent per year for workers age 65 before 1990. Starting in 1990, the delayed retirement credit increases by one-half of 1 percent every other year until it reaches 8 percent for workers reaching age 65 after 2007.

The normal retirement age

The normal retirement age is the earliest age at which unreduced retirement benefits can be received. The normal retirement age is presently age 65, but will be gradually increased to age 67 beginning in 2000.[2] For persons reaching age 62 in 2000, the normal retirement age will be increased by 2 months—to age 65 and 2 months. In each succeeding year, the normal retirement age will be increased by 2 additional months until it reaches age 66 for persons attaining age 62 in 2005. The normal retirement age will then remain at age 66 for persons attaining age 62 through 2016. Beginning with persons attaining age 62 in 2017, the normal retirement age will again increase by 2 months each year, until it reaches age 67 for persons attaining age 62 in 2022 and later. Table 1–5 shows the schedule of increases in the normal retirement age.

Average wage index

The Social Security Administration average wage index (AWI) is the national average of total wages. It is adjusted to be consistent with the AWI series before 1978. (Prior to 1978, the AWI was four times the average taxable wages reported to SSA for the first calendar quarter.) For years prior to 1991, the AWI was based on wages subject to income taxes, as reported on W-2 forms filed by employers. For years beginning in 1991, contributions to certain deferred compensation plans, while not subject to income tax, are in-

---

[2] Changes in the normal retirement age are a result of the Social Security Amendments of 1983 (P.L. 98–21).

cluded in the AWI as a result of Public Law 101–239 (OBRA 1989). These contributions (i.e., 401(k) or salary-reduction retirement plan contributions) were added to the earnings basis for calculation of the AWI because they are subject to Social Security taxation in the same way as cash earnings. The AWI for any given calendar year is calculated by multiplying the prior year's AWI by the increase in average earnings (as described above) that occurred between those two years.

The increase in national average wages, as measured by the SSA AWI, is used to index a worker's earnings under the "wage-indexed" (AIME) benefit computation method and to automatically adjust certain wage-indexed program amounts (e.g., the maximum taxable earnings base, the retirement earnings test exempt amounts and the "bend points" in the formulas for determining primary insurance amounts and maximum family benefits).

Average indexed monthly earnings (AIME)

The AIME is a dollar amount that represents the average monthly earnings, adjusted for the change in the average of total wages[3] in the economy (the SSA AWI), that was received by the worker during a number of years of his covered employment. Indexing creates an earnings record that reflects the value of the individual's earnings relative to national average earnings in the indexing year. The indexing year is the second year before the year in which the worker attains age 62 or, if earlier, becomes disabled or dies. Earnings in and after the indexing year are counted at their nominal value.

There are four steps in the calculation of the AIME: (1) indexing the worker's earnings for each year after 1950 by dividing the worker's posted earnings for the year being indexed by the average wages of all workers in that same year and multiplying this result by the average earnings in the indexing year; (2) determining the number of computation years—the number of years after 1950 (or the year of attainment of age 21, if later) and up to the year the worker attains age 62, becomes disabled, or dies, minus dropout years, generally 5 (minimum number of computation years is 2); (3) selecting the actual computation years, based on highest indexed earnings, from any years after 1950; and (4) dividing the sum of earnings in the computation years by the total number of months in the computation years.

The indexed earnings histories (rounded to whole dollars) are illustrated in table 1–4 for three different workers retiring in 1994 at age 62. The actual earnings for the three workers are shown in the first three columns. These are multiplied by the indexing factor (column 4) to arrive at indexed earnings (last 3 columns of table 1–4). The indexing factor for 1954 is average wages when an individual turned 60 ($22,935.42) divided by average wages for 1954 ($3,155.64). The lowest 5 years of indexed earnings may be dropped. For example, a lifelong full-time worker who had maximum-creditable earnings would be able to drop earnings in 1954, 1962, 1963, 1964, and 1965, and would have total indexed earnings

---

[3] Total wages includes wages that are not taxable for Social Security purposes (e.g., noncovered earnings and earnings above the taxable earnings base).

of $1,421,412 (see table 1–4). Dividing this by the number of months in the computation period (35 years×12 months=420 months) results in an average indexed monthly earnings (AIME) of $3,384. The corresponding AIME's for the average and low (defined as 45 percent of average wages) earners are $1,912 and $860, respectively.

TABLE 1–4.—EARNINGS HISTORIES FOR HYPOTHETICAL WORKERS AGE 62 IN 1994

[Rounded to nearest dollar]

Year	Nominal earnings			Indexing factor	Indexed earnings		
	Low [1]	Average [2]	Maximum [3]		Low [1]	Average [2]	Maximum [3]
1954	1,420	3,156	3,600	7.2681	[4] 10,321	[4] 22,935	[4] 26,165
1955	1,486	3,301	4,200	6.9471	[4] 10,321	[4] 22,935	29,178
1956	1,590	3,532	4,200	6.4929	[4] 10,321	[4] 22,935	27,270
1957	1,639	3,642	4,200	6.2980	[4] 10,321	[4] 22,935	26,451
1958	1,653	3,674	4,200	6.2430	[4] 10,321	[4] 22,935	26,220
1959	1,735	3,856	4,800	5.9483	10,321	22,935	28,552
1960	1,803	4,007	4,800	5.7237	10,321	22,935	27,474
1961	1,839	4,087	4,800	5.6121	10,321	22,935	26,938
1962	1,931	4,291	4,800	5.3445	10,321	22,935	[4] 25,654
1963	1,978	4,397	4,800	5.2166	10,321	22,935	[4] 25,040
1964	2,059	4,576	4,800	5.0118	10,321	22,935	[4] 24,056
1965	2,096	4,659	4,800	4.9231	10,321	22,935	[4] 23,631
1966	2,222	4,938	6,600	4.6443	10,321	22,935	30,653
1967	2,346	5,213	6,600	4.3993	10,321	22,935	29,035
1968	2,507	5,572	7,800	4.1164	10,321	22,935	32,108
1969	2,652	5,894	7,800	3.8915	10,321	22,935	30,354
1970	2,784	6,186	7,800	3.7075	10,321	22,935	28,918
1971	2,924	6,497	7,800	3.5301	10,321	22,935	27,535
1972	3,210	7,134	9,000	3.2150	10,321	22,935	28,935
1973	3,411	7,580	10,800	3.0257	10,321	22,935	32,678
1974	3,614	8,031	13,200	2.8559	10,321	22,935	37,698
1975	3,884	8,631	14,100	2.6574	10,321	22,935	37,469
1976	4,152	9,226	15,300	2.4858	10,321	22,935	38,033
1977	4,401	9,779	16,500	2.3453	10,321	22,935	38,697
1978	4,750	10,556	17,700	2.1727	10,321	22,935	38,457
1979	5,166	11,479	22,900	1.9980	10,321	22,935	45,753
1980	5,631	12,513	25,900	1.8329	10,321	22,935	47,471
1981	6,198	13,773	29,700	1.6652	10,321	22,935	49,457
1982	6,539	14,531	32,400	1.5783	10,321	22,935	51,138
1983	6,858	15,239	35,700	1.5050	10,321	22,935	53,729
1984	7,261	16,135	37,800	1.4215	10,321	22,935	53,731
1985	7,570	16,823	39,600	1.3634	10,321	22,935	53,990
1986	7,795	17,322	42,000	1.3241	10,321	22,935	55,611
1987	8,292	18,427	43,800	1.2447	10,321	22,935	54,518
1988	8,700	19,334	45,000	1.1863	10,321	22,935	53,382
1989	9,045	20,100	48,000	1.1411	10,321	22,935	54,772
1990	9,463	21,028	51,300	1.0907	10,321	22,935	55,953
1991	9,815	21,812	53,400	1.0515	10,321	22,935	56,151
1992	10,321	22,935	55,500	1.0000	10,321	22,935	55,500
1993	[5] 10,589	[5] 23,532	57,600	1.0000	[5] 10,589	[5] 23,532	57,600

[1] Worker with earnings equal to 45 percent of the SSA average wage index.
[2] Worker with earnings equal to the SSA average wage index.
[3] Worker with earnings equal to the Social Security maximum taxable earnings. [4] Dropout years.
[5] Estimate based on economic assumptions in the President's FY 1995 Budget.
Source: Office of the Actuary, Social Security Administration.

Average monthly wage (AMW)

The AMW, which is used in computing benefits under the old pre-1979 benefit formula, is computed by: (1) determining the number of computation years—the number of years after 1950 (or the year of attainment of age 21, if later) and up to the year the worker attains age 62 (age 65 for men born before January 2, 1911, and the later of age 62 or the year 1975 for men born after January 1, 1911), onset of disability or death, minus dropout years, generally 5 (minimum number of computation years is 2); (2) selecting the actual computation years, based on highest nonindexed earnings, from any years after 1950; and (3) dividing the sum of nonindexed earnings in the computation years by the total number of months in the computation years.

Primary insurance amounts (PIA)

The monthly benefit amount payable to a retired worker who begins to receive benefits at his normal retirement age is his PIA rounded to the next lower dollar, if not already a multiple of $1. The PIA is used as a base for computing all benefits which are payable on the basis of that worker's earnings record.

The method of determining the PIA generally depends on whether an AIME or an AMW was computed for the worker. (This, of course, depends on the worker's date of birth.) If an AMW has been computed for the worker, the PIA is determined through reference to benefit tables which are updated annually. Under a transitional guarantee provision of the 1977 amendments (which is applicable only to workers who attain age 62 in 1979–83), the PIA is determined on the basis of the frozen 1978 benefit table if it is higher than under the AIME method.

Other methods for determining a PIA also exist, and PIA's based on different methods must be compared to select the highest one. This highest PIA actually determines the worker's benefits. The most common of these other PIA's is the special minimum PIA. This PIA is designed to assist workers with long-term low earnings.

In cases where an AIME has been computed, the PIA is determined by applying the "primary benefit formula" to the AIME. For a worker reaching age 62 in 1994, the PIA equals 90 percent of the first $422 of AIME, 32 percent of the next $2,123 of AIME, and 15 percent of the AIME above $2,545. Applying this formula to the AIME's of the three example workers results in PIA's of $519.90 for the low-wage worker, $856.90 for the average-wage worker, and $1,185.00 for the maximum-wage worker. (For the low-wage worker, the 1994 special minimum PIA of $505.30 is less than the AIME-based PIA of $519.90, and therefore is not used to determine his or her benefits.) The numbers $422 and $2,545 are often referred to as "bend points" of the PIA formula. These are adjusted each year by the change in average wages. After the year of initial eligibility (age 62 for retired worker benefits), the PIA is increased each year for the increase in the Consumer Price Index (CPI). Thus, the PIA's of $519.90, $856.90, and $1,185.00 would be in effect for January through November 1994, and will be increased by the cost-of-living adjustment that will increase benefits beginning December 1994 under current law.

The PIA is recomputed each year if a worker over age 62 has earnings that were not included in the original computation. However, the PIA is only changed to reflect these earnings if they result in an increased PIA; additional earnings can never result in a decrease in the PIA.

BENEFIT AMOUNTS

The monthly benefit amount payable to a retired worker who begins to receive benefits at the normal retirement age is the PIA rounded to the next lower dollar, if not already a multiple of $1.

Workers attaining age 62 before 2000 (the year in which the retirement age begins to increase) who retire before age 65 will receive a benefit with an actuarial reduction. Retirement after normal retirement age results in an actuarial increase in the benefit payable.

TABLE 1–5.—INCREASES IN NORMAL RETIREMENT AGE AND DELAYED RETIREMENT CREDITS, WITH RESULTING BENEFIT, AS A PERCENT OF PRIMARY INSURANCE AMOUNT [PIA], PAYABLE AT SELECTED AGES, FOR PERSONS REACHING AGE 62 IN 1986 OR LATER

Year of birth	Age 62 attained in—	"Normal retirement age"	Credit for each year of delayed retirement after normal retirement age	Benefit, as a percent of PIA, beginning at age— 62	65	66	67	70
1924	1986	65	3	80	100	103	106	115
1925–26	1987–88	65	3½	80	100	103½	107	117½
1927–28	1989–90	65	4	80	100	104	108	120
1929–30	1991–92	65	4½	80	100	104½	109	122½
1931–32	1993–94	65	5	80	100	105	110	125
1933–34	1995–96	65	5½	80	100	105½	111	127½
1935–36	1997–98	65	6	80	100	106	112	130
1937	1999	65	6½	80	100	106½	113	132½
1938	2000	65, 2 mo	6½	79⅙	98 8/9	105 5/12	111 11/12	131 5/12
1939	2001	65, 4 mo	7	78⅓	97 7/9	104⅔	111⅔	132⅔
1940	2002	65, 6 mo	7	77½	96⅔	103½	110½	131½
1941	2003	65, 8 mo	7½	76⅔	95 5/9	102½	110	132½
1942	2004	65, 10 mo	7½	75⅚	94 4/9	101¼	108¾	131¼
1943–54	2005–16	66	8	75	93⅓	100	108	132
1955	2017	66, 2 mo	8	74⅙	92 2/9	98 8/9	106⅔	130⅔
1956	2018	66, 4 mo	8	73⅓	91 1/9	97 7/9	105⅓	129⅓
1957	2019	66, 6 mo	8	72½	90	96⅔	104	128
1958	2020	66, 8 mo	8	71⅔	88 8/9	95 5/9	102⅔	126⅔
1959	2021	66, 10 mo	8	70⅚	87 7/9	94 4/9	101⅓	125⅓
1960 or later	2022 or later	67	8	70	86⅔	93⅓	100	124

Source: Social Security Bulletin, October 1984/Vol. 47, No. 10, p. 11.

After the year 2000, the minimum age of eligibility for reduced benefits will remain unchanged at age 62 (age 60 for widows and widowers). However, there will be increases in the amount of reduction for early retirement. The amount of reduction will be $\frac{5}{9}$ of 1 percent for each of the first 36 months of early retirement (as under present law), and $\frac{5}{12}$ of 1 percent for each month in excess of 36. Thus, for persons attaining age 62 during 2005–16, for whom the normal retirement age will be 66, the reduced benefit payable at age 62 will be 75 percent of the PIA. For persons attaining age 62 in 2022 and later, for whom the normal retirement age will be 67, the reduced benefit payable at age 62 will be 70 percent of the PIA. (See table 1–5.) There will be no increase in the maximum reduction for widow(er)s.

Auxiliary benefit amounts are also based on the worker's PIA. Table 1–6 lists major types of benefits with the percent of the insured worker's PIA which is paid.

TABLE 1–6.—PERCENTAGE OF PRIMARY INSURANCE AMOUNT (PIA) PAID FOR DEPENDENT'S AND SURVIVOR'S BENEFITS

Type of monthly benefit	Percent of PIA
Dependents: [1]	
Wives, husbands—age 65	[3] 50.0
Mothers, fathers, children, grandchildren	50.0
Survivors: [1]	
Widows, widowers—age 65 [2]	[3] 100.0
Dependent parent—age 62	82.5
Widows, widowers, disabled—age 50	71.5
Mothers, fathers, children	75.0

[1] Subject to maximum family benefit limitation.
[2] Subject to general limitation that survivor cannot get a higher benefit than deceased worker would be getting if alive.
[3] These percentages decrease as the normal retirement age increases beginning in the year 2000.

REPLACEMENT RATES

Frequently Social Security benefits are discussed in terms of how much of a person's preretirement earnings the benefits represent. Benefits expressed as a percent of earnings are called replacement rates. The following table shows replacement rates based on the PIAs of hypothetical workers who retired at normal retirement age after full-time careers with steady earnings equal to: (1) 45 percent of average earnings in the economy (as recorded through the Social Security average wage index), (2) 100 percent of average earnings in the economy, and (3) the maximum earnings taxable each year for FICA and SECA tax purposes.

TABLE 1–7.—SOCIAL SECURITY REPLACEMENT RATES, 1940–2040 [1]

[In percent]

Year of birth	Year of attaining normal retirement age	Replacement rates [2]		
		Low earner [3]	Average earner [4]	Maximum earner [1]
1875	1940	39.4	26.2	16.5
1885	1950	33.2	19.7	21.2
1895	1960	49.1	33.3	29.8
1900	1965	45.6	31.4	32.9
1905	1970	48.5	34.3	29.2
1910	1975	[5] 59.9	42.3	30.1
1911	1976	60.1	43.7	32.1
1912	1977	61.0	44.8	33.5
1913	1978	63.4	46.7	34.7
1914	1979	64.4	48.1	36.1
1915	1980	68.1	51.1	32.5
1916	1981	72.5	54.4	33.4
1917	1982	[6] 65.8	[6] 48.7	[6] 28.6
1918	1983	[5] 63.5	45.8	26.3
1919	1984	[5] 62.6	42.8	23.7
1920	1985	[5] 61.1	40.9	22.8
1921	1986	[5] 60.3	41.1	23.1
1922	1987	[5] 59.5	41.2	22.6
1923	1988	[5] 58.4	40.9	23.0
1924	1989	[5] 57.9	41.6	24.1
1925	1990	[5] 58.2	43.2	24.5
1935	1991	57.1	42.4	25.6
1944	2010	56.0	41.7	27.1
1954	2020	56.0	41.7	27.8
1963	2030	55.7	41.5	27.6
1973	2040	55.7	41.5	27.5

[1] Earnings equal to the maximum wage taxable for Social Security purposes.
[2] Total monthly benefits payable for year of entitlement at normal retirement age expressed as percent of earnings in year prior to entitlement for workers with steady career earnings. Normal retirement age will rise starting with workers who attain age 62 in 2000 and will ultimately reach age 67 for workers attaining age 62 in 2022 and later. Projections for 1993 and later are based on the intermediate II assumptions of the 1993 OASDI Trustees' Report.
[3] Earnings equal to 45 percent of the "SSA average index."
[4] Earnings equal to the "SSA average wage index."
[5] Special minimum benefit.
[6] "Transition guarantee" under 1977 amendments.

Source: Office of the Actuary, Social Security Administration.

BENEFIT REDUCTION AND INCREASE

Social Security benefits may be reduced, withheld or increased for several reasons, chiefly on account of early retirement or delayed retirement, and on account of earnings in excess of the exempt amount provided in the law ($8,040 in 1994 for beneficiaries under age 65, and $11,160 for beneficiaries age 65–69). In addition, there is an overall limit on the total amount of benefits which can be paid at one time on the basis of any one earnings record.

Actuarial reduction. This is the reduction in the monthly benefit amount payable: (a) on entitlement at ages 62–64 if the beneficiary is a retired worker, a spouse of a retired or disabled worker (with entitlement not dependent on having a child beneficiary in his/her care), or a divorced spouse; (b) on entitlement at age 60–64 if the beneficiary is a widow, widower, or a surviving divorced spouse; or (c) on entitlement, in case of disability, at ages 50–59 if the beneficiary is a widow, widower, or surviving divorced spouse.

At the time of award, the following reductions in benefit amount are made for:

A *retired-worker beneficiary*—5/9 of 1 percent for each month of entitlement before age 65 (maximum reduction of 20 percent);

A *wife or husband beneficiary*—25/36 of 1 percent for each month of entitlement before age 65 (maximum reduction of 25 percent);

A *widow(er) including surviving divorced spouse*—19/40 of 1 percent for each month of entitlement between age 60 (maximum reduction of 28.5 percent) and age 65. Disabled widow(er)s ages 50 to 59 receive 71.5 percent of the PIA.

The benefit continues to be paid at a reduced rate even after age 65, except that the reduced rate is refigured at age 65 for all beneficiaries and also at age 62 for a widow, widower, and a surviving divorced spouse to omit months for which the reduced benefits were not paid. Data on benefits paid to new retired workers in 1993 indicates that 72 percent of all such benefits were actuarially reduced (70 percent for men, 75 percent for women). Table 1–8 presents information on the number of workers retiring in a given year who file for actuarially reduced benefits.

TABLE 1-8.—NUMBER OF SOCIAL SECURITY RETIRED-WORKER NEW BENEFIT AWARDS AND PERCENT RECEIVING REDUCED BENEFITS BECAUSE OF ENTITLEMENT BEFORE AGE 65, AS OF DECEMBER OF GIVEN YEAR

[Number in millions]

Year [1]	Total		Men		Women	
	Number	Percent	Number	Percent	Number	Percent
1956	0.9	12	0.6	([2])	0.4	31
1960	1.0	21	.6	([2])	.4	60
1965	1.2	49	.7	43	.4	60
1970	1.3	63	.8	57	.5	72
1975	1.5	73	.9	69	.6	79
1980	1.6	76	.9	73	.7	80
1985	1.7	74	1.0	70	.7	79
1986	1.7	74	1.0	71	.7	79
1987	1.7	74	1.0	71	.7	79
1988	1.6	74	.9	70	.7	78
1989	1.7	73	1.0	69	.7	78
1990	1.7	74	1.0	71	.7	78
1991	1.7	72	1.0	69	.7	76
1992	1.7	72	1.0	69	.7	76
1993	1.7	72	1.0	70	.7	75

[1] Data for 1985-90 based on a 1-percent sample; data for earlier years and for 1991-93 based on 100 percent.
[2] Reduced benefits were not available to men until 1961. They were not available to women until 1956.

Source: Office of Research and Statistics, Social Security Administration.

Delayed retirement credit (DRC). A credit for delayed retirement is due a worker for each month the worker: (1) was fully insured, (2) had attained normal retirement age (currently, age 65) but was not yet age 70, and (3) did not receive benefits because the worker had not filed an application or was working. Each monthly credit serves as a basis for increasing the monthly benefit (unless the benefit is based on a special minimum PIA) by $\frac{1}{12}$ of 1 percent for workers who attained age 62 before 1979 and by $\frac{1}{4}$ of 1 percent for workers attaining age 62 from 1979 through 1986. The increase is applicable to the worker's monthly benefits amount but not to the PIA. Hence, auxiliary benefits are generally not affected. The exception is that a surviving spouse (including divorced) receiving widow(er)'s benefits is entitled, for months after May 1978, to the same increase that had been applied to the benefit of the deceased worker or for which the worker was eligible for at the time of death.

As a result of the Social Security Amendments of 1983, beginning with workers who attain age 65 in 1990 (i.e., age 62 in 1987) the increment for delaying retirement past the normal retirement age will increase by $\frac{1}{2}$ of 1 percent every second year until reaching 8 percent per year of delayed retirement for workers attaining age 65 after 2007. (See Table 1-5.)

Maximum family benefit. The maximum monthly amount that can be paid on a worker's earnings record varies with the PIA. For benefits payable on the earnings records of retired and deceased workers, the maximum varies between 150 and 188 percent of the PIA. No more than the established maximum can be paid to a family regardless of the number of beneficiaries entitled on that earnings record. The family maximum is computed by adding fixed percentages of dollar amounts which are part of the PIA. For the family of a worker who becomes age 62 or dies in 1994, the total amount of benefits payable to them will be limited to:

150 percent of the first $539 of PIA, plus;
272 percent of PIA from $539 through $779, plus;
134 percent of PIA from $779 through $1,016, plus;
175 percent of PIA over $1,016.

The dollar amounts in this benefit formula (i.e. the "bend points") are adjusted annually by the same index used to update the bend points in the primary benefit formula.

Whenever the total of the individual monthly benefits payable to all the beneficiaries entitled on one earnings record exceeds the maximum, each dependent's or survivor's benefit is proportionately reduced to bring the total within the maximum.

In computing the total of the individual monthly benefits for entitlements based on a single earnings record, a benefit payable to a divorced spouse or to a surviving divorced spouse is not included.

Retirement test. The retirement test is a provision in the law that reduces benefits for nondisabled recipients who earn income from work above a certain amount.

The test has been modified many times over the years. In 1994, the law provides that beneficiaries under age 65 may earn $8,040 a year in wages or self-employment income without their benefits being affected. Beneficiaries age 65–69 can earn $11,160 a year. For beneficiaries under age 65 who have earnings in excess of these amounts, $1 of benefits is lost for each $2 of earnings. For beneficiaries age 65–69, the reduction rate is $1 of benefits lost for every $3 of earnings in excess of the exempt amount. The exempt amounts are adjusted each year to rise in proportion to average wages in the economy. The test does not apply to beneficiaries age 70 and over (they receive full benefits regardless of the level of their earnings). In the first year of entitlement—and last year for dependent beneficiaries—the so-called "grace year"—a monthly test of earnings also applies, if it is more advantageous than the annual test of earnings. Under the monthly test, a beneficiary may receive benefits for any month in which his or her earnings do not exceed one-twelfth of the annual exempt amount regardless of annual earnings. However, under this monthly test, if earnings in a month exceed one-twelfth of the annual exempt amount, no benefit is paid for that month. The monthly test is used only when it is more beneficial to the individual. For the self-employed, benefits are paid for any month in which the individual does not perform "substantial services" in his or her trade or business.

Retired workers whose benefits are not paid due to the retirement test for one or more months are compensated through future increases in their benefit amount. For workers under age 65, their actuarial reduction factor is reduced. Beneficiaries age 65–69 get a DRC for each month benefits were not paid.

Examples:

1. John—Age 63 with $4,000 in annual benefits before the retirement test is applied:

Earnings in 1994	$9,040
Exempt amount for under age 65	8,040
Excess over exempt amount	1,000
Benefit reduction=50 percent of excess	500
Benefits John will receive in 1994	3,500

2. Ida—Age 67 with $4,000 in annual benefits before the retirement test is applied:

Earnings in 1994	11,760
Exempt amount for 65 and older	11,160
Excess over exempt amount	600
Benefit reduction=33⅓ percent of excess	200
Benefits Ida will receive in 1994	3,800

The test does not apply to pensions, rents, dividends, interest, and other types of "unearned" income. These forms of income were exempted in order to encourage savings for retirement as supplements to Social Security.

History of the retirement test. The retirement test was part of the original plan that led to Social Security. The 1935 report of the Committee on Economic Security appointed by President Franklin D. Roosevelt recommended that no benefits be paid before a person had "retired from gainful employment." Initially, the Social Security Act provided that benefits would not be paid for any month in which the individual had received "wages with respect to regular employment." Before any benefits were payable under the program, Congress modified this provision in the Social Security Amendments of 1939. No benefits would be paid for any month in which wages from covered employment were $15 or more. This arrangement prevailed until 1950.

The 1950 amendments extended Social Security coverage to the bulk of nonfarm self-employed workers. It was claimed that many self-employed people never retired and therefore would never receive benefits. As a result, the 1950 act exempted persons age 75 and over from the test. In addition, in the first of many actions to increase the amount of earnings permitted, allowable monthly income from wages was increased from $14.99 to $50.

Over the years, the earnings limits, the age limits, and the formulae for reducing benefits have been changed many times. Starting with the 1954 amendments, benefits were no longer totally withheld if the retiree had earnings above the exempt amount. Instead, a reduced benefit was payable. In addition, the 1954 act exempted persons age 72 and over from the test.

The 1972 amendments reduced benefits by $1 for every $2 of earnings above the exempt amount. The 1972 amendments also provided that, beginning in 1975, the exempt amounts would be "indexed" to rise at the same rate as wage growth. To compensate workers who did not receive benefits between ages 65 and 72, including those who did not because of the retirement test, the amendments established the delayed retirement credit.

In the consideration of major Social Security legislation in 1977, there was considerable pressure to eliminate the retirement test for persons over age 65. As a compromise, the limit on earnings was raised for persons age 65 and older, and since then two different exempt amounts have applied for those under age 65 and those age 65–69. The 1977 amendments also lowered from 72 to 70 the age at which the test would no longer apply, to be effective in 1982 (subsequent legislation postponed the effective date to 1983). In response to criticism that it discriminated in favor of workers who had substantial but irregular employment (e.g., teachers), Congress also eliminated the monthly test except for the first year of retirement. In 1980, Congress extended the monthly test to the year a dependent beneficiary became ineligible for benefits.

TABLE 1-9.—RETIREMENT TEST EXEMPT AMOUNTS

Year	Under age 65	Age 65 and over [2]
1975	$2,520	$2,520
1976	2,760	2,760
1977	3,000	3,000
1978	3,240	4,000
1979	3,480	4,500
1980	3,720	5,000
1981	4,080	5,500
1982	4,440	6,000
1983	4,920	6,600
1984	5,160	6,960
1985	5,400	7,320
1986	5,760	7,800
1987	6,000	8,160
1988	6,120	8,400
1989	6,480	8,880
1990	6,840	9,360
1991	7,080	9,720
1992	7,440	10,200
1993	7,680	10,560
1994	8,040	11,160
1995	[1] 8,280	[1] 11,400
1996	[1] 8,520	[1] 11,760
1997	[1] 8,880	[1] 12,240
1998	[1] 9,240	[1] 12,720
1999	[1] 9,600	[1] 13,320

[1] Based on economic assumptions in the President's FY 1995 Budget.
[2] In 1955–82, retirement earnings test did not apply at ages 72 and over; beginning in 1983, it does not apply at ages 70 and over.

Source: Office of the Actuary, Social Security Administration.

As part of major legislation restoring financial integrity to Social Security in 1983, Congress made two liberalizations affecting persons who continue to work after attaining retirement age. The first provided that beginning in 1990 beneficiaries who have attained the normal retirement age will lose only $1 in benefits for each $3 in earnings above the exempt amount. The second increased the delayed retirement credit (DRC). Prior to the increase, the DRC was equal to ¼ of 1 percent for each month (3 percent a year) beyond the normal retirement age that a person did not receive benefits. Under the 1983 provision, the DRC will increase gradually to ⅔ percent a month over the period 1990 to 2009 (8 percent a year).

As a result of a legislative change in the Deficit Reduction Act of 1984, the Social Security Administration requests earlier reports of earnings from beneficiaries who are most likely to have earnings in excess of the exempt amount. These beneficiaries may thus have their benefits ceased in the actual year of excess earnings, rather than receiving overpayments which must then be recouped later.

Work effort and the retirement test. The Congressional Budget Office, in its May 23, 1991 testimony before the Committee on Ways and Means Subcommittee on Social Security, made the following comments regarding the work-response of seniors to the retirement test:

> Eliminating the earnings test would increase work effort among some people aged 65 through 69, but the overall impact would be small. This conclusion is based on three considerations. First, the earnings test is only one of many factors that determine work effort. Among other factors likely to influence a worker's decision to retire are the level of Social Security and private pension benefits that would be received, the employment of a spouse, the availability of suitable work, and the health of the worker.

> Second, the empirical research that is available provides little support for the notion that older workers would increase their work effort significantly. . . . A widely cited study . . . found no evidence that liberalizing the earnings test in the 1970's precipitated large-scale reentry into the labor force. . . . [Another study that examined workers age 62 through 69 projected that] workers whose earnings are already above the limit might increase their hours by as much as 20 percent if the test were eliminated, but noted that such workers account for a very small share of this age group. In addition, workers whose earnings are high enough that they lose all of their Social Security benefits under the current earnings test might reduce their work effort in response to the increase in their total incomes from eliminating the test.

> Finally, it is noteworthy that more than half of all workers begin collecting benefits as soon as they become eligible at age 62, even though they will receive reduced benefits throughout their retirement. A sizeable number of older workers clearly prefer retirement to continued employment, even though the 20 percent higher benefits they could obtain by delaying retirement until age 65 would compensate them for receiving three fewer years of benefits.

Impact of the retirement test. Social Security Administration actuaries estimate that, in 1992, some 7 million persons age 65–69 were entitled to Social Security retired-worker benefits. Of these, 90 percent were unaffected by the earnings test: 73 percent had no earnings at all, and 17 percent had earnings under the exempt amount. Only 10 percent of those age 65–69 had earnings in excess of the retirement test exempt amount.

Those who are affected by the retirement test, and who would therefore gain from its elimination, are generally better off economically than the rest of the population aged 65 through 69. Research by the Congressional Budget Office shows that almost half of individuals age 65–69 with family incomes of $50,000 or more in 1989 were affected by the retirement test. By contrast, of those with no earnings or earnings below the threshold, more than half had incomes below $25,000. Table 1–10 shows the distribution by family income of those affected by the retirement test.

The Social Security Administration estimates the net cost of repealing the retirement test for individuals age 65 through 69 at more than $5 billion per year, or $22.9 billion for fiscal years 1995–99. Social Security Administration actuaries estimate that only 10 percent of the cost of these benefits would be offset by additional taxes paid and administrative savings.

Chart 1–1 shows the distribution of additional benefits among earner families if the retirement test were repealed. Half of the additional $27.4 billion in benefits—nearly $14 billion—would go to those with family incomes above $63,500 in 1992. Only 5 percent of the additional benefits would go to those with family incomes below $28,000.

CHART 1–1. DISTRIBUTION OF ADDITIONAL BENEFITS UNDER ELIMINATION OF THE RETIREMENT EARNINGS TEST, 1992

[In percent]

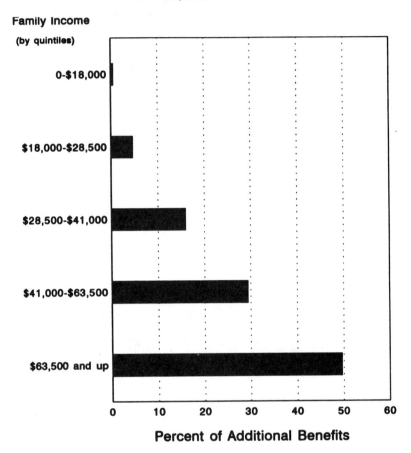

Family income is of earner families only.
Source: SSA Office of Research and Statistics

TABLE 1–10.—DISTRIBUTION IN 1989 OF PEOPLE AGED 65–69 ELIGIBLE TO RECEIVE SOCIAL SECURITY BENEFITS, BY FAMILY INCOME AND EARNINGS

[In percent]

Annual family income	Entire group	With no earnings	Earnings under limit	Earnings over limit
Under $15,000	32	37	31	3
$15,000 to $24,999	23	24	27	13
$25,000 to $31,999	12	12	12	11
$32,000 to $49,999	17	15	18	29
$50,000 and over	16	12	12	45
All incomes	100	100	100	100

Notes.—Details may not add to totals because of rounding. Income is distinct from earnings: earnings are wages, salaries, and income from self-employment, and are only part of total income. Excludes new retirees.

Source: Congressional Budget Office tabulations of data from March 1990 Current Population Survey.

Withholding. This is the suspension of benefit payments until the conditions causing deductions are known to have ended. Reasons for withholding benefits include: (1) earnings by a beneficiary (or any dependent drawing benefits on his earnings record) under age 70 from either covered or noncovered employment which exceeds the annual allowable amount (the retirement test); (2) failure of a spouse under age 62 or mother or father beneficiary to have an entitled child in her care; (3) for special age-72 beneficiaries, receipt of public assistance or supplemental security income (SSI) payments or government pensions; (4) the payee is not determined; and (5) administrative reasons.

Some of the administrative reasons for withholding benefits are: (a) refusal of beneficiary to accept checks for personal reasons; (b) beneficiary's residence in certain foreign countries; and (c) under certain conditions, an alien beneficiary's residence outside the United States for more than 6 full consecutive calendar months.

Suspension of monthly benefit payments does not affect eligibility for hospital insurance benefits under Medicare (although Medicare is generally not available for treatment outside the United States).

BENEFITS FOR RECIPIENTS OF PENSIONS FROM NONCOVERED EMPLOYMENT

The public pension offset. Social Security benefits payable to spouses of retired, disabled, or deceased workers are generally reduced to take account of any public pension the spouse receives as a result of work in a government job (Federal, State, or local) not covered by Social Security. The amount of the reduction is equal to two-thirds of the government pension. The offset does not apply to workers whose government job is covered by Social Security on the last day of the person's employment.

Generally, Federal workers hired before 1984 are part of the Civil Service Retirement System (CSRS) and are not covered by Social Security. Federal workers hired after 1983 are covered by the

Federal Employee's Retirement System Act of 1986 (FERS), which includes coverage by Social Security. The FERS law provided employees covered by the CSRS the opportunity from July 1, 1987, to December 31, 1987, to make a one-time election to join FERS and thereby obtain Social Security coverage. Thus, a CSRS employee who switched to FERS during this period immediately became exempt from the government pension offset.[4] Federal workers who subsequently joined FERS need to have 5 years of coverage under FERS after December 31, 1987, to be exempt from the offset.

The "windfall" benefit. Under the so-called "windfall" benefit provision of the Social Security Amendments of 1983, Social Security benefits are generally reduced for workers who also have pensions from work that was not covered by Social Security (e.g., work under the Federal Civil Service Retirement System). Under the regular, weighted benefit formula, benefits are determined by applying a percentage to average indexed monthly earnings. For workers eligible in 1994, benefits equal 90 percent of the first $422 of average indexed monthly earnings, 32 percent of earnings from $422 to $2,545, and 15 percent of earnings above $2,545. The formula applicable to those with pensions from noncovered employment substitutes 40 percent for the 90 percent factor in the first bracket. (The second and third factors remain the same.) The resulting reduction in the worker's Social Security benefit is limited to one-half the amount of the noncovered pension. The new law was phased in over a 5-year period and affects those first eligible for both Social Security benefits and noncovered pensions after 1985.

Workers who have 30 years or more of substantial Social Security coverage are fully exempt from this treatment. For workers who have 21–29 years of coverage, the percentage in the first bracket in the formula increases by 5 percentage points for each year over 20, as shown in the table below:

TABLE 1–11.—WINDFALL BENEFIT FORMULA FACTORS

Years of Social Security coverage	First factor in formula (percent)
20 or fewer	40
21	45
22	50
23	55
24	60
25	65
26	70
27	75
28	80
29	85
30 or more	90

---

[4] This period was extended administratively to June 30, 1988.

Automatic Benefit Adjustments

Benefit increases for Social Security and SSI recipients are based on increases in the cost of living as measured by the Bureau of Labor Statistics' Consumer Price Index (CPI). The CPI used for this purpose is the CPI for Urban Wage Earners and Clerical Workers (CPI-W). As a result of a provision contained in the Omnibus Budget Reconciliation Act of 1986, it is no longer necessary for the rise in the CPI to exceed 3 percent in order to trigger the annual cost-of-living adjustment (COLA). A COLA will now be provided in any year in which there is a measurable (0.1 percent) increase in consumer prices. If there was a year of price deflation and no COLA was provided, then a 2-year change in the CPI of at least 0.1 percent would be needed before a COLA is provided.

Prior to 1984, the change in the CPI was measured from the first calendar quarter of the base year to the first calendar quarter of the current year. The benefit increases in 1984 and later years are based on the CPI increase from the third quarter of the base year through the third quarter of the year in which the benefit increase becomes effective. In addition, benefit increases beginning with the January 1986 check are based upon a price index in which the housing component is measured on a rental equivalence basis.

If the assets of the combined OASI and DI trust funds represent less than a 20 percent reserve ratio and wages increase at a rate lower than inflation, the automatic benefit increase will be based on wage growth rather than inflation.

The Secretary of Health and Human Services (HHS) is required by law to publish the amount of the increase in the Federal Register within 45 days after the close of the measuring period. The benefit increase is effective in December and first appears in benefit checks received in January, i.e., 3 months after the close of the measuring period. (Prior to 1983 the benefit adjustment was effective in June and payable in July.)

For example, since a benefit increase was effective in 1992, that year became the base for the 1993 benefit increase. The CPI for the third quarter of 1992 was 138.8. This was the arithmetical average of the CPI for July, August and September 1992.

Month in 1992:	*CPI-W*
July	138.4
August	138.8
September	139.1
Total	416.3

The average CPI-W for the 3rd quarter of 1992 is thus:

$$416.3/3 = 138.8 \text{ (rounded to the nearest 0.1)}$$

The CPI for the third quarter of 1993 was 142.4. This was the arithmetical average of the CPI for July, August and September 1993.

Month in 1993:	*CPI-W*
July	142.1
August	142.4
September	142.6
Total	427.1

The average CPI–W for the third quarter of 1993 is thus:

$$427.1/3=142.4 \text{ (rounded to the nearest } 0.1)$$

The percentage increase in the CPI from the third quarter of 1992 to the third quarter of 1993 is:

$$(142.4-138.8)/138.8=2.6$$

Thus, the benefit increase for December 1993 was 2.6 percent (and was reflected in the January 1994 checks).

The benefit increase is always rounded to the nearest 0.1 percent. It applies to all types of beneficiaries.

TABLE 1–12.—HISTORICAL COMPARISON OF AVERAGE WAGE INCREASES TO BENEFIT INCREASES AND CHANGES IN CPI, 1965–93

[In percent]

Calendar year	Increase in wages [1]		Increase in CPI [2]		Increase in benefits [3]	
	Over prior year	Cumulative from each year to 1993	Over prior year	Cumulative from each year to 1993	Over prior year	Cumulative from each year to 1993
1965	1.8	405.1	1.6	348.3	7.0	442.8
1966	6.0	376.5	3.2	334.6	0.0	442.8
1967	5.6	351.4	2.8	322.9	0.0	442.8
1968	6.9	322.3	4.2	306.0	13.0	380.4
1969	5.8	299.3	5.4	285.1	0.0	380.4
1970	5.0	280.4	5.7	264.4	15.0	317.7
1971	5.0	262.2	4.4	249.1	10.0	279.7
1972	9.8	229.9	3.4	237.5	20.0	216.4
1973	6.3	210.4	6.2	217.9	0.0	216.4
1974	5.9	193.0	11.0	186.5	11.0	185.1
1975	7.5	172.6	9.1	162.7	8.0	164.0
1976	6.9	155.1	5.7	148.4	6.4	148.1
1977	6.0	140.6	6.5	133.3	5.9	134.3
1978	7.9	122.9	7.7	116.6	6.5	120.0
1979	8.7	105.0	11.4	94.4	9.9	100.2
1980	9.0	88.1	13.4	71.4	14.3	75.1
1981	10.1	70.9	10.3	55.5	11.2	57.5
1982	5.5	61.9	6.0	46.6	7.4	46.6
1983	4.9	54.4	3.0	42.4	[4] 3.5	41.7
1984	5.9	45.8	3.5	37.6	3.5	36.9
1985	4.3	39.9	3.5	32.9	3.1	32.8
1986	3.0	35.9	1.6	30.8	1.3	31.1
1987	6.4	27.7	3.6	26.3	4.2	25.8
1988	4.9	21.7	4.0	21.5	4.0	20.9
1989	4.0	17.1	4.8	15.9	4.7	15.5
1990	4.6	11.9	5.2	10.2	5.4	9.6
1991	3.7	7.9	4.1	5.8	3.7	5.7
1992	5.2	2.6	2.9	2.8	3.0	2.6
1993	[5] 2.6	....	2.8	....	[6] 2.6	....

[1] Average annual wages used to index earnings records.

[2] Increase in annual average CPI–W.

[3] Legislated benefit increases through 1975 and increases based on CPI thereafter. After 1975, the CPI and benefit increases are different because they reflect the change in prices measured over different periods of time.

[4] As a result of the Social Security Amendments of 1983, COLA's are provided on a calendar year basis, with the benefit increase payable in January rather than July. The July 1983 COLA was delayed to January 1984. This delay and a change in the computation period led to 6 months of 1983 (first quarter–third quarter) not being accounted for in any COLA increase—a period during which the CPI increased 2.4 percent.

[5] Preliminary.

[6] Effective December 1993, payable January 3, 1994.

Source: Office of the Actuary, Social Security Administration.

TAXATION OF SOCIAL SECURITY (OASDI) BENEFITS FOR HIGHER INCOME PERSONS

Beneficiaries with income above certain thresholds are required to include a portion of their Social Security benefits (and railroad retirement tier 1 benefits) in their taxable income. The Social Security Act Amendments of 1983 required beneficiaries with incomes of more than $25,000 if single and $32,000 if married to include up to 50 percent of their benefits in taxable income, beginning in 1984. The Omnibus Budget Reconciliation Act of 1993 required beneficiaries with incomes of more than $34,000 if single and $44,000 if married to include up to 85 percent of their benefits in their taxable income, beginning in 1994. For these purposes, "income" is defined as Adjusted Gross Income plus tax-exempt bond interest plus one-half of Social Security benefits.

The following worksheet shows the steps involved in determining how much of a beneficiary's Social Security benefits are taxable. The examples which follow illustrate the results of applying this worksheet.

WORKSHEET FOR DETERMINING THE TAXABLE PORTION OF SOCIAL SECURITY BENEFITS

1. Enter yearly Social Security benefits ...._____
2. Divide line 1 by 2 ...._____
3. Enter Adjusted Gross Income plus tax-free interest ...._____
4. Add line 2 and line 3 ...._____
5. Enter: $25,000 if single or head of household; $32,000 if married filing jointly; $0 if married filing separately ...._____
6. Subtract line 5 from line 4 ...._____
   (If result on line 6 is zero or a negative number, stop; no benefits are taxable.)
7. Divide line 6 by 2 ...._____
8. Enter smaller of amounts on line 2 or line 7 ...._____
9. Enter amount on line 4 ...._____
10. Enter: $34,000 if single or head of household; $44,000 if married filing jointly; $0 if married filing separately ...._____
11. Subtract line 10 from line 9 ...._____
    (If result on line 11 is zero or a negative number, stop; amount on line 8 is amount of benefits taxable.)
12. Multiply line 11 by 0.85 ...._____
13. Enter smallest of: amount on line 8; $4,500 if single or head of household; $6,000 if married filing jointly; $0 if married filing separately ...._____
14. Add amounts on line 12 and line 13 ...._____
15. Multiply line 1 by 0.85 ...._____
16. Enter smaller of amounts on line 14 or line 15 ...._____
    (Amount on line 16 is total amount of benefits taxable.)

Source: Congressional Research Service.

Examples:

	Single	Single	Married	Married	Married
Total income (including Social Security)	$27,000	$35,000	$38,000	$50,000	$80,000
Social Security benefits .	12,000	7,000	12,000	12,000	18,000
Amount of benefits taxable	0	3,250	0	6,000	15,300
Percent of benefits taxable	0	46	0	50	85
Income tax liability on all benefits taxable ...	0	559	0	900	4,284

The proceeds from the taxation of Social Security benefits under the 1983 law are credited to the OASDI trust funds, except that the additional taxes resulting from the OBRA 1993 provision are credited to the HI trust fund.

For calendar year 1995, CBO projects that 23 percent of Social Security beneficiaries will be affected by the taxation of benefits (see table 1–14).

TABLE 1–13.—TAXATION OF SOCIAL SECURITY BENEFITS; TAX AMOUNTS BY TRUST FUNDS CREDITED AND AS A PERCENT OF TOTAL OASDI BENEFIT PAYMENTS

[Dollars in millions]

Fiscal year	Total OASDI benefits	Taxes credited to trust funds from the taxation of OASDI benefits			Taxes credited to trust funds as percent of OASDI benefits		
		OASDI	HI	Total	OASDI	HI	Total
Past experience:							
1984 ..	$173,603	$2,275	....	$2,275	1.3	....	1.3
1985 ..	183,959	3,368	....	3,368	1.8	....	1.8
1986 ..	193,869	3,558	....	3,558	1.8	....	1.8
1987 ..	202,430	3,307	....	3,307	1.6	....	1.6
1988 ..	213,907	3,390	....	3,390	1.6	....	1.6
1989 ..	227,150	3,772	....	3,772	1.7	....	1.7
1990 ..	243,275	3,081	....	3,081	1.3	....	1.3
1991 ..	263,104	5,921	....	5,921	2.3	....	2.3
1992 ..	281,650	6,237	....	6,237	2.2	....	2.2
1993 ..	298,176	6,161	....	6,161	2.1	....	2.1
Projected: [1]							
1994 ..	313,842	5,695	$1,642	7,337	1.8	0.5	2.3
1995 ..	330,583	6,610	4,219	10,828	2.0	1.3	3.3
1996 ..	348,429	7,007	4,488	11,496	2.0	1.3	3.3
1997 ..	367,470	7,429	4,752	12,181	2.0	1.3	3.3
1998 ..	387,465	7,900	5,030	12,930	2.0	1.3	3.3
1999 ..	408,632	8,402	5,312	13,714	2.1	1.3	3.4

[1] Based on economic assumptions in the President's FY 1995 budget.

Note.—Tax amounts, as shown above for past years, are the amounts collected through the Federal income tax system (including adjustments for actual experience in prior years) plus taxes withheld from the OASDI benefits of certain nonresident aliens.

Source: Office of the Actuary, Social Security Administration.

TABLE 1-14.—EFFECT OF TAXING SOCIAL SECURITY BENEFITS BY INCOME CLASS, 1995

[Numbers of persons in thousands; dollars in millions]

Level of individual or couple income[1]	Persons age 65 and over			All recipients					
	Number	Number affected by taxation[2]	Percent affected by taxation[2]	Number of Social Security beneficiaries[3]	Number affected by taxation[3]	Percent affected by taxation[3]	Aggregate amount of Social Security benefits	Aggregate amount of taxes on benefits	Taxes as percent of benefits
Less than $10,000	6,480	0	0.0	8,430	0	0.0	46,605	0	0.0
$10,000 to $15,000	4,522	0	0.0	5,398	0	0.0	42,991	0	0.0
$15,000 to $20,000	3,746	0	0.0	4,472	0	0.0	36,802	0	0.0
$20,000 to $25,000	3,258	0	0.0	3,743	0	0.0	31,701	0	0.0
$25,000 to $30,000	2,833	98	3.5	3,309	135	4.1	28,486	13	0.0
$30,000 to $40,000	4,138	1,048	25.3	4,895	1,316	26.9	42,489	386	0.9
$40,000 to $50,000	2,417	1,908	78.9	2,825	2,394	84.7	24,557	1,084	4.4
$50,000 to $60,000	1,376	1,238	90.0	1,584	1,559	98.5	14,337	1,441	10.0
$60,000 to $75,000	1,238	1,112	89.8	1,391	1,378	99.1	12,976	2,081	16.0
$75,000 to $100,000	1,036	926	89.4	1,042	1,039	99.7	9,618	2,194	22.8
$100,000 to $200,000	886	793	89.5	867	865	99.8	8,015	1,985	24.8
At least $200,000	337	259	76.7	270	266	98.5	2,659	811	30.5
All	32,268	7,383	22.9	38,228	8,952	23.4	301,235	9,994	3.3

[1] Cash income (based on income of tax filing unit), plus capital gains realizations.
[2] Some elderly individuals do not receive Social Security benefits and are thus not affected by taxation of benefits.
[3] Includes beneficiaries under and over age 65.

Note.—Aggregate benefits and revenues are understated by about 10 percent because of benefits paid abroad, deaths of recipients before March interview, and exclusion of institutionalized beneficiaries. The number of beneficiaries is also understated.

Source: Congressional Budget Office simulations based on data from the Current Population Survey.

CHARACTERISTICS OF BENEFICIARY POPULATION

Table 1–15 provides detailed information on the numbers of various OASDI beneficiaries, the average amount of monthly benefits by type of beneficiary for new awards and for all beneficiaries currently receiving payments.

TABLE 1–15.—NUMBER OF PERSONS RECEIVING VARIOUS TYPES OF OASDI BENEFITS BY AGE, SEX, AND AVERAGE MONTHLY BENEFIT AMOUNTS, DECEMBER 1992

[Based on a 10-percent sample]

Beneficiaries	Number (thousands)	Percent of total beneficiaries	Average monthly benefit	Percentage of total benefits
Retired workers	25,746	62.0	$653	68.8
Retired men	13,474	32.5	735	40.5
Retired women	12,272	29.6	562	28.2
Disabled workers	3,473	8.4	626	8.9
Disabled men	2,221	5.4	696	6.3
Disabled women	1,252	3.0	501	2.6
Spouses of retired workers	3,115	7.5	337	4.3
Wives of retired workers	3,085	7.4	338	4.3
Wives with entitled children	83	.2	227	.1
Without entitled children 62 and over	3,003	7.2	341	4.2
Husbands of retired workers	29	.1	211	(1)
Spouses of disabled workers	272	.7	156	.2
Wives of disabled workers	264	.6	157	.2
Wives with entitled children	204	.5	137	.1
Without entitled children 62 and over	61	.1	224	.1
Husbands of disabled workers	7	(1)	112	(1)
Children of (retired, deceased or disabled) workers	3,400	8.4	325	4.5
Children of retired workers	432	1.1	285	.5
Minor children of retired workers (0–17)	238	.6	252	.3
Student children of retired workers (18 and 19)	12	(1)	320	(1)
Disabled children of retired workers (18 and over)	182	.4	326	.2
Children of deceased workers	1,810	4.5	433	3.2
Minor children of deceased workers (0–17)	1,340	3.4	427	2.3

TABLE 1–15.—NUMBER OF PERSONS RECEIVING VARIOUS TYPES OF OASDI BENEFITS BY AGE, SEX, AND AVERAGE MONTHLY BENEFIT AMOUNTS, DECEMBER 1992—Continued

[Based on a 10-percent sample]

Beneficiaries	Number (thousands)	Percent of total beneficiaries	Average monthly benefit	Percentage of total benefits
Student children of deceased workers (18 and 19)	54	.1	503	1
Disabled children of deceased workers (18 and over)	416	1.0	439	7
Children of disabled workers	1,159	2.9	170	8
Minor children of disabled workers (0–17)	1,091	2.7	165	7
Student children of disabled workers (18 and 19)	26	.1	264	(1)
Disabled children of disabled workers (18 and over)	42	(1)	251	(1)
Widowed mothers and fathers ...	294	.7	437	5
Total widowed mothers	278	.7	445	.5
Total widowed fathers	16	(1)	294	(1)
Widows and widowers (nondisabled)	5,056	12.5	608	12.6
Total widows (nondisabled)	5,021	12.4	609	12.5
Total widowers (nondisabled)	36	.1	444	.1
Widows and widowers (disabled)	132	.3	424	.2
Total widows (disabled)	129	.3	427	.2
Total widowers (disabled) .	2	....	285	....
Parents total	5	(1)	538	(1)
Special age 72 (primary)	4	(1)	178	(1)
Total OASI beneficiaries	36,593	88.2	602	90.1
Total DI beneficiaries	4,903	11.8	492	9.9
Total OASDI beneficiaries	41,497	100.0	589	100.0

[1] Less than 0.1%.

Note.—Columns may not add due to rounding.

Source: Office of Research and Statistics, Social Security Administration.

TABLE 1–16.—1994 SUMMARY SOCIAL SECURITY INFORMATION

Tax rate:

Employee and employer each	7.65 percent (6.20 percent—OASDI, 1.45 percent—HI).
Self-employed	15.30 percent (12.40 percent—OASDI, 2.9 percent—HI).
OASDI contribution and benefit base	$60,600.
Limitation on earnings subject to HI tax was repealed, effective 1994.	
Earnings required for a quarter of coverage.	$620.
Earnings required for a year of coverage:	
Under the special minimum provision [1].	$6,750.
Under the windfall elimination provision [2].	$11,250.
Retirement test exempt aearnings limits:	
Age 65–69	$11,160 annual, $930 monthly.
Under age 65	$8,040 annual, $670 monthly.

Bend points:

PIA

90 percent of first $422 of AIME, plus 32 percent of AIME over $422 through $2,545, plus 15 percent of AIME over $2,545.

Maximum Family Benefit

150 percent of first $539 plus 272 percent of PIA over $539 through $779, plus 134 percent of PIA over $779 through $1,016, plus 175 percent of PIA over $1,016.

Benefit examples for worker retiring in 1994 at age 65:

	January 1994 PIA	Replacement rate (percent)
Low earner [3]	$505.30	57.4
Average earner [4]	829.80	42.4
Maximum earner [5]	1,147.50	24.0

[1] Amount is 15 percent of the "old-law" base—the contribution and benefit base that would be in effect without passage of the 1977 amendments.
[2] Amount is 25 percent of the "old-law" base.
[3] Earnings equal to 45 percent of average wages.
[4] Average earnings level: 1992, $22,935.42; 1993 (est.) $23,532.
[5] Earnings equal to the maximum earnings taxable for OASDI program: 1992, $55,500; 1993, $57,600.

Source: Office of the Actuary, Social Security Administration.

TABLE 1–17.—MONTHLY BENEFIT AMOUNTS FOR SELECTED BENEFICIARY FAMILIES WITH FIRST ELIGIBILITY IN 1993, BY AVERAGE INDEXED MONTHLY EARNINGS FOR SELECTED WAGE LEVELS, EFFECTIVE DECEMBER 1993

Beneficiary family	Worker with yearly earnings equal to—		
	Federal minimum wage [1]	Average wage [2]	Maximum taxable earnings [3]
RETIRED WORKER FAMILIES [4]			
Average indexed monthly earnings	$926.00	$1,820.00	$3,154.00
Primary insurance amount	542.60	836.00	1,146,00
Maximum family benefit	833.80	1,525.90	2,004.80
Monthly benefit amount:			
Retired worker claiming benefits at age 62: [4]			
Worker alone	434.00	668.00	916.00
Worker with spouse claiming benefits at age 62 [4]	637.00	981.00	1,345.00
SURVIVOR FAMILIES [5]			
Average indexed monthly earnings	861.00	1,824.00	4,256.00
Primary insurance amount	521.30	837.40	1,315.60
Maximum family benefit	781.90	1,527.70	2,301.60
Monthly benefit amount:			
Survivors of worker deceased at age 40: [5]			
1 surviving child	390.00	628.00	986.00
Widowed mother or father and 1 child	780.00	1,256.00	1,972.00
Widowed mother or father and 2 children	780.00	1,527.00	2,301.00
DISABLED WORKER FAMILIES [6]			
Average indexed monthly earnings	900.00	1,821.00	3,652.00
Primary insurance amount	534.00	836.40	1,222.60
Disability maximum family benefit [7]	784.80	1,254.60	1,833.90
Monthly benefit amount:			
Disabled worker age 50: [6]			
Worker alone	534.00	836.00	1,222.00
Worker, spouse, and 1 child	784.00	1,254.00	1,832.00

[1] Annual earnings are calculated by multiplying the Federal minimum hourly wage (currently $4.25) by 2,080 hours.

[2] Worker earned the national average wage in each year used in the computation of the benefit.

[3] Worker earned the maximum amount of wages that can be credited to a worker's Social Security record in all years used in the computation of the benefit.

[4] Assumes the worker began to work at age 22, retired at age 62 in 1993 with maximum reduction, and had no prior period of disability.

[5] Assumes the deceased worker began to work at age 22, died in 1993 at age 40, had no earnings in that year, and had no prior period of disability.

[6] Assumes the worker began to work at age 22, became disabled at age 50, and had no prior period of disability.

[7] The 1980 Amendments to the Social Security Act provide for different family maximum amount for disability cases. For disabled workers entitled after June 1980, the maximum is the smaller of (1) 85 percent of the worker's AIME (or 100 percent of the PIA, if larger) or (2) 150 percent of the PIA.

LEGISLATIVE CHANGES MADE IN THE 97TH CONGRESS

The 97th Congress made numerous changes in the OASDI program. The major changes were included in the Omnibus Budget Reconciliation Act of 1981 (Public Law 97–35). Table 1–18 lists these changes and contains Congressional Budget Office estimates of their budgetary impact made at that time.

TABLE 1–18.—CONGRESSIONAL BUDGET OFFICE ESTIMATES FOR LEGISLATIVE CHANGES MADE IN OASDI DURING 1981 (JANUARY 1982 ESTIMATES), FISCAL YEARS 1982–84

[In millions of dollars]

	Fiscal year—		
	1982	1983	1984
Elimination of minimum benefit for future beneficiaries	−81	−180	−210
Elimination of benefits for postsecondary students	−567	−1,580	−2,033
Restrictions on payment of lump-sum death benefits	−200	−210	−215
Modification of month of initial entitlement for certain workers and their dependents	−190	−220	−240
Temporary extension of earnings limitation to include all persons aged less than 72	−380	−120	0
Termination of mother's and father's benefits when youngest child attains age 16	−30	−88	−496
Modification of rounding rules	−79	−272	−314
Cost reimbursement for provision of earnings information	−1	−2	−5
Revision of reimbursements for vocational rehabilitation services	−87	−86	−73
Modify worker's compensation offset to: (1) Apply offset to certain other public disability benefits-megacap; (2) apply offset to benefits of workers aged 62 to 64; and (3) begin offset in first month of dual benefit payment	−87	−122	−156
Extension of coverage to first 6 months of sick pay (revenue increase)	−534	−762	−828
Total OASDI	−2,236	−3,642	−4,570

LEGISLATIVE CHANGES MADE IN THE 98TH CONGRESS

The 98th Congress made extensive changes in OASDI programs in the Social Security Amendments of 1983 (Public Law 98–21), enacted to restore the financial status of the Social Security trust funds. Table 1–19 outlines the estimated outlay and revenues effects of the 1983 amendments under the alternative II–B assumptions of the 1983 Trustees' report. At the time, it was estimated that in the period 1983 through 1989 the OASDI and HI trust funds would receive $166.2 billion and $33.6 billion in additional financing, respectively. Table 1–20 shows the estimated long-range effects of the 1983 amendments, under 1983 assumptions.

TABLE 1–19.—ESTIMATED AMOUNTS OF CHANGES IN OASDI RECEIPTS AND BENEFIT PAYMENTS RESULTING FROM THE 1983 SOCIAL SECURITY AMENDMENTS, CALENDAR YEAR 1983–89

[In billions of dollars]

Provision	Calendar year—							Total, 1983–89
	1983	1984	1985	1986	1987	1988	1989	
Increase tax rate on covered wages and salaries	....	8.6	0.3	....	....	14.5	16.0	39.4
Increase tax rate on covered self-employment earnings	....	1.1	3.1	3.0	3.2	3.7	4.4	18.5
Cover all Federal elected officials and political appointees	....	(1)	(1)	(1)	(1)	(1)	(1)	.1
Cover new Federal employees	....	.2	.7	1.2	1.8	2.4	3.1	9.3
Cover all nonprofit employees	....	1.3	1.5	1.8	2.1	2.6	3.0	12.4
Total for new coverage	....	1.5	2.2	3.0	3.9	5.0	6.1	21.8
Prohibit State and local government terminations	....	.1	2.	.4	6.	8.	1.1	3.2
Accelerate collection of State and local taxes	....	.6	(1)	(1)	.1	.1	.1	1.0
Modify general fund financing basis for non-contributory military service credits	18.4	−.4	−.4	−.3	−.4	−.4	−.4	16.1
Provide reimbursements from general fund for unnegotiated checks	1.3	.1	.1	.1	.1	.1	.1	1.6
Delay benefit increases 6 months	3.2	5.2	5.4	5.5	6.2	6.7	7.3	39.4
Continue benefits on remarriage	....	(2)	(2)	(2)	(2)	(2)	(2)	−.1
Modify indexing of deferred survivors' benefits	....	....	(2)	(2)	(2)	(2)	(2)	(2)
Raised disabled widow(er)'s benefits to 71.5 percent of PIA	....	−.2	−.2	−.2	−.2	−.3	−.3	−1.4
Pay divorced spouses whether or not worker has retired	....	....	(2)	(2)	(2)	(2)	(2)	−.1
Eliminate "windfall" benefits for individuals receiving pensions from non-covered employment	....	....	....	(3)	(3)	(3)	.1	.1
Offset spouses benefits by up to two-thirds of noncovered Government pension (public pension offset)	(2)	(2)	(2)	(2)	(2)	(2)	(2)	(2)
Expand use of death certificates to stop benefits	(3)	(3)	(3)	(3)	(3)	(3)	(3)	.1
Impose 5-year residency requirement for certain aliens	....	....	(3)	(3)	(3)	(3)	(3)	.1
Tax one-half of benefits for high income beneficiaries	....	2.6	3.2	3.9	4.7	5.6	6.7	26.6
All other changes	(2)	(2)	(2)	(2)	(2)	(2)	(2)	−.1
Total for all changes	22.8	19.2	13.9	15.3	18.0	35.8	41.2	166.2

[1] New additional taxes of less than $50 million.
[2] Additional benefits of less than $50 million.
[3] Reduction in benefits of less than $50 million.

Note.—Based on 1983 alternative II–B assumptions. Estimates shown for each provision include the effects of interaction with all preceding provisions. Totals do not always equal the sum of components due to rounding. Positive figures represent additional income or reduction in benefits. Negative figures reductions in income or increases in benefits.

Source: Office of the Actuary, Social Security Administration, 1983.

TABLE 1–20.—ESTIMATED LONG-RANGE OASDI COST EFFECTS OF THE SOCIAL SECURITY AMENDMENTS OF 1983

Provision	Effect as percent of payroll		
	OASI	DI	OASDI
Present law prior to amendments:			
Average cost rate	13.04	1.34	14.38
Average tax rate	10.13	2.17	12.29
Actuarial balance	−2.92	+.83	−2.09
Changes included in titles I and III of the amendments: [1]			
Cover new Federal employees	+.26	+.02	+.28
Cover all nonprofit employees	+.09	+.01	+.10
Prohibit State and local terminations	+.06	+.00	+.06
Delay benefit increases 6 months	+.28	+.03	+.30
Eliminate "windfall" benefits	+.04	+.00	+.04
Raise delayed retirement credits	−.10	....	−.10
Tax one-half of benefits	+.56	+.05	+.61
Accelerate tax rate increase	+.03	....	+.03
Increase tax rate on self-employment	+.17	+.02	+.19
Adjust self-employment income	−.02	−.00	−.03
Change DI rate allocation	+.81	−.81	....
Continue benefits on remarriage	−.00	−.00	−.00
Pay divorced spouse of nonretired	−.01	−.00	−.01
Modify indexing of survivor's benefits	−.05	....	−.05
Raise disabled widow's benefits	−.01	....	−.01
Modify military credits financing	+.01	+.00	+.01
Credit unnegotiated checks	+.00	+.00	+.00
Tax certain salary reduction plans	+.03	+.00	+.03
Modify public pension offset	−.00	−.00	−.00
Suspend auxiliary benefits for certain aliens	+.00	+.00	+.00
Modify earnings test for those aged 65 and over [2]	−.01	....	−.01
All other provisions of titles I and III	−.00	−.00	−.00
Subtotal for the effect of the above provisions [3]	+2.07	−.68	+1.38
Remaining deficit after the above provisions	−.85	+.15	−.71
Additional change relating to long-term financing (title II): [4]			
Raise normal retirement age to 67	+.83	−.12	+.71
Total effect of all of the provisions [5]	+2.89	−.80	+2.09
After the amendments:			
Actuarial balance	−.03	+.03	−.00
Average income rate	11.47	1.42	12.89
Average cost rate	11.50	1.39	12.89

[1] The values of each of the individual provisions listed from title I and title III represent the effect over present law and do not take into account interaction with other provisions with the exception of the provision relating to the earnings test.

[2] Estimates from modifying the earnings test take into account interaction with the provision raising delayed retirement credits.

[3] The values in the subtotal for all provisions included in title I and title III take into account the estimated interactions among these provisions.

[4] The values for each of the provisions of title II take into account interaction with the provisions included in title I and title III.

[5] The values for the total effect of the amendments take into account interactions among all of the provisions.

Source: Social Security Bulletin, July 1983. The above estimates are based on preliminary 1983 Trustees' Report Alternative II–B assumptions. Individual estimates may not add to totals due to rounding and/or interaction among proposals.

LEGISLATIVE CHANGES MADE IN THE 99TH CONGRESS

Several legislative changes were made in the Social Security program in the 99th Congress. The Consolidated Omnibus Reconciliation Act of 1985 (Public Law 99–272) included a variety of minor and technical legislative changes in Social Security. Additionally, Public Law 99–272 contained provisions to: (a) exempt wages paid to retired Federal judges, performing active duty, for purposes of FICA taxation and the Social Security earnings limitation; and (b) to protect certain Social Security beneficiaries who receive overpayments through the electronic direct deposit system.

The Omnibus Budget Reconciliation Act of 1986 (Public Law 99–509) included two significant Social Security provisions. The first eliminated the requirement that the annual rise in the Consumer Price Index must exceed 3 percent in order for a cost-of-living adjustment to be paid to Social Security beneficiaries. The new law required that a cost-of-living adjustment be paid in any year in which there was a measurable increase in consumer inflation. Second, Public Law 99–509 removed from the States the responsibility for collecting and depositing with the Federal Government Social Security contributions on behalf of their political subdivisions. All State and local entities now deposit their Social Security contributions directly to the Federal Government on a time schedule that parallels the treatment of private employers.

The Emergency Deficit Reduction and Balanced Budget Act of 1985 (Public Law 99–177) contained a provision to remove the receipts and disbursements of the Social Security trust funds from the unified budget effective in fiscal year 1986, and to restrict consideration of legislative changes in Social Security as part of the congressional budget process. It also contained measures to bring the Federal budget into balance by fiscal year 1991, and under those measures, Social Security income and outgo was to be used in calculating the Federal deficit. However, the benefits were made exempt from any automatic cuts required to reduce the deficit. Moreover, the act contained provisions making it difficult for Social Security changes to be brought up in the congressional budget process by permitting the raising of "points of order" against such measures.

LEGISLATIVE CHANGES MADE IN THE 100TH CONGRESS

Extend FICA tax to certain earnings.—

Armed Services reservists.—FICA taxes were extended to "inactive duty training" (generally weekend training drill sessions).

Agricultural workers.—Wages paid to an employee who received less than $150 in annual cash remuneration by an agricultural employer were subject to FICA if the employer paid more than $2,500 in the year to all employees, provided the employee: (1) is a hand harvest laborer and is paid on a piece-rate basis in an operation which has been customarily recognized as having been paid on a piece-rate basis in the region of employment, (2) commutes daily from his or her permanent residence, and (3) has been employed in agriculture less than 13 weeks during the preceding calendar year.

Individuals aged 18–21.—FICA taxes were extended to services performed by individuals between the ages of 18 and 21 who are employed in their parent's trade or business.

Spouses.—FICA taxes were extended to services performed by an individual in the employ of his or her spouse's trade or business.

Tips.—The employer's share of FICA taxes was extended to include all cash tips (up to the Social Security wage base).

Phase-out of reduction in windfall benefits.—The phase-out of the reduction of benefits for workers with noncovered pensions was changed from 25 through 30 years of Social Security coverage to 20 through 30 years.

Treatment of group-term life insurance wages under FICA.—Employer-provided group-term life insurance was included in wages for FICA tax purposes if such insurance were includable for gross income tax purposes, effective January 1, 1988.

Correction in government pension offset.—Federal employees who switch from the Civil Service Retirement System (CSRS) to the Federal Employees' Retirement System (FERS) on or after January 1, 1988 were exempted from the government pension offset only if they had 5 or more years of Federal employment covered by Social Security after December 31, 1987.

Continuation of disability benefits pending appeal.—The existing provision for continued payment of disability benefits during the administrative appeal process was extended through 1989.

Lengthening the extended period of eligibility for disability benefits.—The extended period of eligibility during which a disability beneficiary who returns to work may become automatically reentitled to benefits was lengthened from 15 months to 36 months. Medicare eligibility was not continued beyond the period provided under current law.

Payment of attorneys' fees.—The administrative policy which permitted administrative law judges to authorize attorneys' fees of up to $3,000 without approval by an SSA regional office was reinstated.

LEGISLATIVE CHANGES MADE IN THE 101ST CONGRESS

Continuation of disability benefits during appeal.—The provision permitting disability insurance beneficiaries to elect to have their benefits continued during appeal was made permanent.

Payment of benefits to a child adopted after a parent's entitlement to retirement or disability benefits or adopted by a surviving spouse.—A child adopted after a worker became entitled to retirement or disability benefits was made eligible for child's insurance benefits regardless of whether he or she was living with and dependent on the worker prior to the worker's entitlement. A child adopted by the surviving spouse of a deceased worker was made eligible for benefits regardless of whether he or she had been receiving support from anyone other than the worker and the worker's spouse, as long as the child either lived with the worker or received one-half support from the worker in the year preceding the worker's death.

Repeal of carryover reduction in retirement or disability insurance benefits due to receipt of widow(er)'s benefits before age 62.—The carryover reduction applied to retirement or disability benefits received by widow(er)s who collected widow(er)'s benefits before age 62 was eliminated.

Improvements in Social Security Administration services and beneficiary protections.—A number of improvements were made in SSA procedures regarding correction of earnings records; standards applicable in determinations of fault, good faith and good cause; same-day interviews on time-sensitive matters; notices sent to blind Social Security beneficiaries; legal representatives of claimants; and the avenues of recourse open to potential applicants who lose benefits because SSA provides them with inaccurate or incomplete information. In addition, SSA was required to issue a report on options for increasing its use of foreign language notices. Conforming changes were also made in the Supplemental Security Income program as applicable.

Earnings and benefit statements.—SSA was required, upon request, to provide individuals with a statement of their earnings and contributions and an estimate of their future benefits. Beginning in 1995, these statements will be provided to all individuals who attain age 60. Beginning in October 1999, these statements will be provided annually to all workers covered under Social Security.

Inclusion of certain deferred compensation in the calculation of average wages under the Social Security Act.—Contributions to deferred compensation plans, including amounts deferred in 401(k) plans, were included in the determination of average wages for Social Security purposes.

Treatment of refunds by employers under the Medicare Catastrophic Coverage Act of 1988 for FICA and other purposes.—Refunds provided to individuals by employers under the maintenance-of-effort provision of the Medicare Catastrophic Coverage Act of 1988 were excluded from wages for FICA, FUTA, and railroad retirement and railroad unemployment insurance tax purposes. In addition, the Secretary of the Treasury was given authority to prescribe the manner in which the refunds were to be reported.

Extension of Social Security coverage exemption for members of certain religious faiths.—The exemption from Social Security coverage for workers who are members of certain religious groups was extended to: (a) qualifying employees of partnerships in which each partner holds a religious exemption from Social Security coverage, and (b) qualifying employees of churches and church-controlled nonprofit organizations who would otherwise be covered as self-employed for purposes of Social Security taxation.

Prohibition against termination of coverage of U.S. citizens and residents employed abroad by a foreign affiliate of an American employer.—American employers were prohibited from terminating the Social Security coverage of U.S. citizens and residents employed abroad in their foreign affiliates.

Extension of disability insurance program demonstration project authority.—The authority of the Secretary of HHS to conduct work incentive demonstration projects was extended for three additional years.

Inclusion of employer cost of group-term life insurance in compensation under the Railroad Retirement Tax Act.—Employer-paid premiums for group-term life insurance coverage in excess of

$50,000 were made subject to the railroad retirement payroll tax, bringing the treatment of such premiums into conformity with their treatment under the Social Security Act.

Inclusion of deferred compensation arrangements, including 401(k) plans, in compensation under the Railroad Retirement Tax Act.—Contributions to 401(k) deferred compensation plans were made subject to the railroad retirement payroll tax, bringing the treatment of such contributions into conformity with their treatment under the Social Security Act.

Codification of the Rowan *decision with respect to railroad retirement.*—Except for meals and lodging provided for the convenience of the employer, it was stipulated that nothing in Internal Revenue Service (IRS) regulations defining wages for purposes of the income tax is to be construed as requiring a similar definition for purposes of the railroad retirement payroll tax, thus conforming the Railroad Retirement Tax Act to the Social Security Act.

Extension of general fund transfers to railroad retirement tier II trust fund.—The transfer of proceeds from the income taxation of railroad retirement Tier II benefits from the general fund of the Treasury to the railroad retirement trust fund was extended to October 1, 1992.

Social Security coverage of State and local employees not covered by a public retirement system.—Employees of State and local governments (excluding students who are employed by public schools, colleges or universities) who are not covered by a public retirement system were covered by Social Security and Medicare (i.e., Old-Age, Survivors, and Disability Insurance (OASDI) and Hospital Insurance (HI); effective after July 1, 1991.

Budgetary treatment of Social Security trust funds.—The Social Security trust funds (OASDI Trust Funds) were removed from the calculation of the deficit under the Gramm-Rudman-Hollings law beginning with fiscal year 1991; thus, Social Security was taken "off budget." The trust funds were protected by points of order in the House and Senate against legislation which would reduce trust fund balances.

Improvement of the definition of disability applied to disabled widow(er)s.—The stricter definition of disability that was previously applied only to widow(er)s was repealed. Instead, a disabled widow(er) was made subject to the same definition of disability as already applied to disabled workers.

Improvements in the OASDI and supplemental security income (SSI) representative payee system.—The representative payee system was improved by: (a) requiring the Secretary of Health and Human Services (the Secretary) to conduct a more extensive investigation of the representative payee applicant; (b) providing stricter standards in determining the fitness of the representative payee applicant to manage benefit payments on behalf of the beneficiary; and (c) directing the Social Security Administration to make recommendations regarding the application of stricter accounting procedures to certain high-risk representative payees.

In addition, certain community-based nonprofit social service agencies providing representative payee services of last resort were allowed to collect a fee from an individual's Social Security or SSI benefit for expenses incurred in providing such services.

Streamlining of the attorney fee payment process.—The process by which SSA reviews and approves any fee charged by an attorney representing a claimant before the agency was reformed. The existing fee petition process was generally replaced by a streamlined procedure under which fees are paid up to a limit of 25 percent of past-due benefits not to exceed $4,000, unless the attorney, claimant, or administrative law judge objects. The fee petition was retained in cases for which the fee requested exceeds the limits, or if the determination made on the claim is not favorable.

Improvements in SSA services and beneficiary protections.—The Secretary was required to carry out a demonstration to test ways to improve procedures for providing service by telephone. In addition, when a claimant who is denied benefits reapplies, rather than appealing, based on inaccurate or misleading information from SSA, the failure to appeal would not constitute a basis for denial of the second application. New requirements were also established for improvements in notices regarding title II and title XVI benefits.

Restoration of telephone access to the local offices of SSA.—SSA was required to reestablish telephone access to its local offices at the level generally available on September 30, 1989, the day before it established a national 800 number and cut off access to local offices serving 40 percent of the population.

Creation of a rolling 5-year trial work period for all disabled beneficiaries.—Effective January 1, 1992, the trial work period was liberalized so that a disabled beneficiary would exhaust this period only after completing 9 trial work months in any rolling 60-month period. In addition, beneficiaries would receive a new trial work period for each period of eligibility.

Continuation of benefits on account of participation in a non-State vocational rehabilitation program.—Beneficiaries who medically recover while participating in an approved non-State vocational rehabilitation program were granted the same benefit continuation rights as those who medically recover while participating in a State-sponsored program.

Limitation on new entitlement to special age-72 payments.—The provision precluded the unintended payment of so-called "Prouty benefits," which were enacted in 1966 to help workers who were too old to earn sufficient quarters of coverage to qualify for regular benefits. Because of subsequent amendments to the law, it was theoretically possible for some workers to qualify for Prouty benefits after 1990, even though, when enacted, they were not expected to be paid to anyone who reached age 72 after 1971.

Elimination of advance tax transfer.—The Social Security trust funds were credited with tax receipts as they were collected throughout the month, rather than in advance (at the first of the month), as under previously existing law. However, the advance tax-transfer mechanism (enacted to help meet the Social Security funding emergency that existed prior to the 1983 amendments) was retained as a contingency to be used if the trust funds drop to such a low level that it is needed in order to pay current benefits.

Repeal of retroactive benefits for certain categories of individuals.—Retroactive benefits were eliminated for two categories of individuals eligible for reduced benefits: (a) those with dependents entitled to unreduced benefits, and (b) those with preretirement earnings over the amount allowed under the retirement test who had used the retroactive benefits to charge off their excess earnings.

Consolidation of old computation methods.—A number of little-used, pre-1968 benefit computation formulas were eliminated.

Suspension of dependents' benefits when a disabled worker is in an extended period of eligibility.—Current SSA practice regarding the nonpayment of benefits to a disabled worker's dependents when that worker is in an extended period of eligibility and is not receiving monthly Social Security benefits was codified.

Payment of benefits to a deemed spouse and a legal spouse.—Eligibility requirements for payment of benefits to a "deemed spouse"—a spouse whose marriage is found to be invalid—were changed so that the entitlement of the worker's legal spouse would no longer terminate payment of benefits to a deemed spouse.

Creation of a vocational rehabilitation demonstration project.—SSA was required to carry out a demonstration project testing the advantages and disadvantages of permitting disabled Social Security beneficiaries to select a qualified vocational rehabilitation provider, either public or private, from which to receive services aimed at enabling them to obtain work and leave the disability rolls.

Use of Social Security number by certain legalized aliens.—Certain aliens who were granted amnesty under the provisions of the Immigration Reform and Control Act of 1986 were exempted from criminal penalties for fraudulent use of a Social Security card. The exemption did not apply to those individuals who sold Social Security cards, possessed cards with intent to sell, or counterfeited or possessed counterfeited cards with the intent to sell.

Reduction in amount of wages needed to earn a year of coverage toward the special minimum benefit.—Effective in 1991, the amount of earnings needed to earn a year of coverage toward the special minimum benefit (designed to assist long-term, low-wage workers) was reduced from 25 percent of the "old law" contribution and benefit base ($10,725 in 1993), to 15 percent of the base ($6,435 in 1993).

Charging of earnings of corporate directors.—A provision of previous law that treated a corporate director's earnings as taxable when the services to which they are attributable were performed was repealed. A director's earnings continue to be treated as received when the services are performed for purposes of the Social Security retirement test.

Collection of employee Social Security tax on group-term life insurance.—In cases where an employer continues to provide taxable group-term life insurance to an individual who has left his employment, the former employee was required to pay the employee portion of the Social Security tax directly.

Waiver of the 2-year waiting period for certain divorced spouses.—The 2-year waiting period for independent entitlement to divorced spouse benefits was waived in cases where the worker was entitled to benefits prior to the divorce.

Pre-effectuation review of favorable decisions by the Social Security Administration.—The percentage of favorable decisions made by State disability determination services that must be reviewed by

SSA was reduced from 65 percent of all such decisions to 50 percent of allowances and as many continuances as are required to maintain a high level of accuracy in such decisions. The reviews are to be targeted on those cases most likely to contain errors.

Recovery of overpayments from former Social Security beneficiaries through tax refund offset.—SSA was permitted to recover overpayments from former beneficiaries through arrangements with the Internal Revenue Service (IRS) to offset the former beneficiary's tax refund.

LEGISLATIVE ACTION DURING THE 102D CONGRESS

No amendments to title II of the Social Security Act were made during the 102d Congress.

LEGISLATIVE ACTION DURING THE 103D CONGRESS

No amendments to title II of the Social Security Act were made during the first session of the 103d Congress.

Section 2. Disability Insurance Program

The disability insurance (DI) program provides monthly cash benefits for disabled workers under age 65 and their dependents. Benefits were provided to disabled workers age 50 or older by the 1956 Social Security Amendments; benefits for their dependents were provided by the 1958 Social Security Amendments; and benefits to disabled workers under age 50 were provided by the 1960 amendments.

GENERAL

Many provisions of the DI program are identical to those of the OASI program. For example, all workers who are covered by OASI are also covered by DI. Contributions are made under the same provision of the Internal Revenue Code and are made on the same wage base.

The DI portion of the OASDI tax is allocated to the Disability Insurance Trust Fund, which is the source of payment for monthly benefits to disabled workers and their dependents and for administrative expenses of the program. In addition, the revenue derived from the taxation of disability benefits is credited to the trust fund.

The purpose of both OASI and DI benefits is to replace income lost when the wage-earner is no longer able to work. However, significant differences exist between the two programs, primarily because of the different nature of the event insured. The OASI program insures a worker, his dependents and survivors against loss of income due to the worker's retirement or death. The DI program insures against the loss of income due to the worker's physical or mental disability. In addition, the OASI program is administered solely by Federal employees in Federal installations, whereas the DI program is administered both through Federal Social Security offices and State disability determination services staffed by State employees.

BENEFITS

Summary

In general, DI monthly cash benefits are paid and computed on the same basis as in the OASI program. Benefit amounts are related to the past earnings of the insured worker. Medicare is provided to disabled workers, widow(er)s, or adult children after they have been entitled to disability benefits for 24 months.

In December 1993 there were 5.2 million DI beneficiaries in current-payment status. The total monthly benefits paid out were $2.6 billion. Table 2–1 summarizes various types of beneficiaries of the DI program currently receiving benefits, average benefit amounts, and the number of new awards during 1993.

TABLE 2–1.—DISABILITY CASH BENEFITS: NUMBER IN CURRENT PAYMENT STATUS AND AVERAGE BENEFIT AMOUNT (DECEMBER 1992) AND NUMBER OF BENEFITS AWARDED DURING THE YEAR AND AVERAGE BENEFIT AMOUNT, 1993

	Current payment		New awards	
	Number (in thousands)	Average payment	Number (in thousands)	Average payment
Disabled workers	3,726	$642	635	$638
Wives and husbands of workers	273	156	75	158
Children of disabled workers	1,255	173	399	158

Source: Office of Research and Statistics, Social Security Administration.

Description of major benefit types

Disabled-worker benefit.—A monthly benefit payable to a disabled worker under age 65 insured for disability.

Spouses' benefit.—Monthly benefit payable to a spouse or divorced spouse of a disabled worker under one of the following conditions: (1) wife or husband (a) is aged 62 or older, or (b) has 1 or more entitled children of the worker who are disabled or under age 16 in his or her care; or (2) divorced wife (husband) is aged 62 or older and her (his) marriage to worker lasted 10 years before the divorce became final.

Child's benefit.—A monthly benefit payable to an unmarried child or eligible grandchild of a disabled worker who is under age 18 or a full-time elementary or secondary student under age 19.

Disabled adult child's benefit.—A monthly benefit payable to a disabled person aged 18 or over—a son or daughter or eligible grandson or granddaughter of a retired, deceased, or disabled worker—whose disability began before age 22.

Disabled widow (or widower).—A widow or widower may qualify for benefits on the deceased spouse's work record at age 50 through age 59. Effective January 1991, the definition of disability a widow or widower must meet to qualify for disability benefits is the same as that for a worker.

Definition of disability

Generally, disability is defined as an inability to engage in substantial gainful activity by reason of a physical or mental impairment. The impairment must be medically determinable and expected to last for not less than 12 months or to result in death. Claimants may be determined to be disabled only if, due to such an impairment, they are unable to engage in any kind of substantial gainful work, considering their age, education, and work experience, which exists in the national economy. The work need not exist in the immediate area in which the claimant lives, nor must a specific job vacancy exist for the individual. Moreover, no showing is required that the worker would be hired for the job if he or she applied.

There is a special definition and eligibility requirements for persons who are blind.

Waiting period

An initial 5-month waiting period is required before DI benefits are paid. Benefits are payable for the 6th month. However, benefits may be paid for the 1st full month of disability to a worker who becomes disabled within 60 months (for a disabled widow or widower the period is 84 months) after termination of DI benefits from an earlier period of disability.

Insured status

Workers are *insured for disability* if they are fully insured and, except for persons who are blind or disabled before age 31, have a total of at least 20 quarters of coverage during the 40-quarter period ending with the quarter in which the worker became disabled. Workers who are disabled before age 31 must have total quarters of coverage equal to half the calendar quarters which have elapsed since the worker reached age 21, ending in the quarter in which the worker became disabled. However, a minimum of 6 quarters is required.

BENEFIT COMPUTATION

DI benefits are computed in the same manner as old age and survivors benefits except that the number of years of earnings which is excluded when determining the benefit amount is less than 5 for workers under age 47. (The number of drop-out years allowed increases with the age of the insured worker at disablement.) The amount of the monthly benefit is based on the insured worker's primary insurance amount (PIA).

The following table lists major disability benefits with the percentage of the insured worker's PIA.

TABLE 2–2.—TYPE OF MONTHLY BENEFIT

	Percent of PIA
Disabled worker (any age)	100
Dependents of disabled worker:[1] Wife or husband (age 62), mother, father, children and grandchildren	50
Survivors:[1] Disabled (age 50–59), widows or widowers	71.5

[1] Subject to maximum family benefit limitation.

Substantial gainful activity

The Secretary of HHS[1] has specific regulatory authority to prescribe the criteria for determining when earnings derived from employment demonstrate an individual's ability to engage in substantial gainful activity (SGA).

The Secretary has published regulations specifying the monetary amounts which indicate substantial gainful activity. Effective January 1, 1990, the SGA earnings level was raised to $500 a month

---

[1] Throughout the remainder of this section when Secretary is used, it is the Secretary of Health and Human Services.

(net of impairment-related work expenses). Table 2–3 shows SGA amounts since 1968.

TABLE 2–3.—MONTHLY SGA AMOUNTS

Year	SGA
July 1968–73	$140
1974–75	200
1976	230
1977	240
1978	260
1979	280
1980–89	300
1990–94	500

Work incentives

The law provides a 45-month period for disabled beneficiaries to test their ability to work without losing their entitlement for benefits. The period consists of (1) a "trial work period" (TWP) which allows disabled beneficiaries to work for up to 9 months (within a 5-year period)[2] with no effect on their disability or (if eligible) Medicare benefits, and (2) a 36-month "extended period of eligibility," during the last 33 of which disability benefits are suspended for any month in which the individual is engaged in SGA. Medicare coverage continues so long as the individual remains entitled to disability benefits and, depending on when the last month of SGA occurs, may continue for 3 to 24 months after entitlement to disability benefits ends. When Medicare entitlement ends because of the individual's work activity, but he or she is still medically disabled, he or she may purchase Medicare protection.

If beneficiaries medically recover to the extent they no longer meet the definition of disability, disability and Medicare benefits are terminated regardless of the trial work period or extended period of disability provisions. However, persons who contest this determination may choose to continue to receive disability benefits (subject to recovery) and Medicare benefits while their appeal is being reviewed, until a decision is rendered by an administrative law judge.

DI maximum family benefit

The maximum monthly amount of DI family benefits which is payable on a disabled worker's earnings record for workers who first become entitled after June 1980, is the smaller of 85 percent of the worker's average indexed monthly earnings or 150 percent of the worker's primary insurance amount. However, in no case can the benefit be reduced below 100 percent of the worker's primary insurance amount.

---

[2] Only one TWP is allowed in any one period of disability. The TWP is completed only if the 9 months are within a 60-month period. By regulation, earnings of more than $200 a month constitute "trial work."

Offset for other public disability benefits

When a disabled worker under age 65 qualifies on the basis of total or partial disability (whether or not permanent) for benefits that are provided by Federal, State and local governments and worker's compensation, the Social Security benefits payable to him and his family are reduced by the amount, if any, that the total monthly benefits payable under the two or more programs exceed 80 percent of his average current earnings before he became disabled. Needs-tested benefits, Veterans' Administration disability benefits, and benefits based on public employment covered by Social Security are not subject to the provision. A worker's average current earnings for this purpose are the larger of (a) the average monthly earnings used for computing his Social Security benefits, or (b) his average monthly earnings in employment or self-employment covered by Social Security during the 5 consecutive years of highest covered earnings after 1950, or (c) the average monthly earnings during the calendar year of highest covered earnings during a period consisting of the year in which disability began and the preceding 5 years without regard to the limitations which specify a maximum amount of earnings creditable for Social Security benefits. The combined payments after the reduction are never less than the total amount of the DI benefits payable before the reduction. In addition, the Social Security benefit after the reduction is increased by the full amount of the cost-of-living increase as applied to the unreduced benefit. Every 3 years the original amount of benefits subject to reduction is redetermined to reflect changes in average wage levels. If increases in the average national wages would result in a higher benefit than that payable based on the original computation, the benefit is increased effective January of the redetermination year.

The offset begins in the month during which concurrent entitlement begins under a Federal or State law.

The offset of the Social Security disability benefit will not be made if the State worker's compensation law provides for an offset against Social Security disability benefits. However, this waiver of the offset only applies where the State program began offsetting on or before February 18, 1981.

DETERMINATION OF DISABILITY

State agency determinations of disability

Disability determinations are made by State agencies that agree to make such determinations and substantially comply with the regulations of the Secretary. The Secretary is required to issue regulations specifying, in such detail as he or she deems appropriate, performance standards and administrative requirements and procedures to be followed in performing the disability determination function "in order to assure effective and uniform administration of the disability insurance program throughout the United States." Certain operational areas are cited as "examples" of what the regulations may specify. These include such items as the nature of the administrative structure, the physical location of and relationship among agency staff units, performance criteria and fiscal control procedures.

The law also provides that if the Secretary finds that a State agency is substantially failing to make disability determinations consistent with his regulations, the Secretary shall, not earlier than 180 days following his findings, terminate State administration and make the determinations himself. The law also allows for termination by the State. The State would be required to continue to make disability determinations for not less than 180 days after notifying the Secretary of its intent to terminate. Thereafter, the Secretary would be required to make the determinations.

Determining disability: Application of law and regulations

The adjudication of claims is accomplished on a sequential basis. The first step is to determine whether the individual is engaging in substantial gainful activity (SGA). Under current administrative practice, if a person is actually earning more than $500 a month (net of impairment-related work expenses) he or she ordinarily will be considered to be engaging in SGA. By law, this limit is $930 a month for disabled blind individuals in 1994. If it is determined that the individual is engaging in SGA, a finding is made that he or she is not disabled without consideration of medical factors. If an individual is found not to be engaging in SGA, the severity and duration of the impairment are explored. If the impairment is determined to be "not severe" (i.e., it does not significantly limit the individual's capacity to perform work), the individual is denied.[3] If the impairment is "severe," a determination is made as to whether the impairment "meets" or "equals" the medical listings published in regulations by SSA[4] and whether it will last for 12 months. If it neither "meets" nor "equals" the listing (which will result in an allowance) but meets the 12-month duration rule, a determination is then made of whether the claimant is able to carry out his former occupation. If he can, he is denied benefits; if he cannot, the nonmedical factors come into play.

At this stage, because of a judicial opinion and subsequent administrative and legislative ratification, the burden of proof switches to the Government to show that the individual can, considering his impairment, age, education, and work experience, engage in some other kind of substantial gainful activity which exists in the national economy. Such work, however, does not have to exist in the immediate area in which he lives and a specific job vacancy does not have to be available to him. Work in the national economy is defined in the law as work which exists in significant numbers either in the region where such individual lives or in several regions of the country.

---

[3] It is important to note that the "severity" step became very controversial in the 1980s, with several Federal circuit courts ruling that SSA's procedures violate the intent of the law that every claimant receive an individual determination based on medical and vocational factors. However, in a 1987 decision, the Supreme Court, while raising a number of concerns about SSA's procedures, upheld the Agency's application of the "severity" test at this stage of the sequential process. *Bowen* v. *Yuckert*, No. 85–1409, June 8, 1987.

[4] The Listing of Impairments contains over 100 examples of medical conditions that would ordinarily prevent an individual from engaging in any gainful activity. Each listing describes a degree of severity such that an individual who is not working and has such an impairment is considered unable to work by reason of the medical impairment. The listing describes specific medically acceptable clinical and laboratory findings and signs which establish the severity of the impairments. An impairment or combination of impairments is said to "equal the listings" if the medical findings for the impairment are at least equivalent in severity and duration to the listed findings of a listed impairment.

SSA has developed a vocational "grid" designed to reduce the subjectivity and lack of uniformity in applying the vocational factor. The grid regulations embody in a formula certain worker characteristics such as age, education, and past work experience, in relation to the individual's residual functional capacity (RFC) to perform work-related physical and mental activities. If the claimant has a particular level of residual work capability—characterized by the terms Sedentary, Light, Medium, Heavy and Very Heavy—an automatic finding of "disabled" or "not disabled" is required when applied to various combinations of age, education, and work experience.

Federal review of State determination

The Secretary may, on his own motion, review any determination by a State agency.

The law requires that the Secretary review 50 percent of the disability allowances and a sufficient number of other determinations to ensure a high degree of accuracy.

Periodic review of individuals receiving disability benefits

The 1980 Disability Amendments required that the Social Security Administration reexamine every individual on the rolls who is determined to be nonpermanently disabled for benefit eligibility at least once every 3 years. Where there is a finding of permanency, the Secretary may reexamine at such times as is determined to be appropriate. These reviews are in addition to the administrative eligibility review procedures existing prior to the 1980 amendments. Legislation enacted in late 1982 provided authority for the Secretary to slow down the rate of continuing eligibility reviews mandated by the 1980 amendments.

Medical improvement standard

The 1984 Disability Benefits Reform Act amended the law to require that in continuing eligibility review cases, benefits may be terminated only if the Secretary finds that there has been medical improvement in the person's condition and that the individual is now able to engage in substantial gainful activity. There are several statutory exceptions to this standard, which are described in greater detail in the "Recent Legislation" section of this chapter.

Medical evidence

An individual is not considered under a disability unless he furnishes such medical and other evidence as the Secretary may require.

Under the law, the Secretary will generally reimburse physicians or hospitals for supplying medical evidence in support of claims for DI benefits. The Secretary also pays for medical examinations that are needed to adjudicate the claim.

Attorneys' fees and representation

Attorneys and other individuals who represent disability claimants on appeal and who wish to charge a fee for their services must have the fee approved by the Social Security Administration (SSA). Under the law in effect through June 30, 1991, representatives must submit a fee petition detailing the number of hours spent on the claim and requesting a specific fee.

The Omnibus Budget Reconciliation Act of 1990 (Public Law 101–508) generally replaced the fee petition process (effective July 1, 1991) with a streamlined process in which SSA will approve any fee agreement jointly submitted by the claimant and the representative if the claimant is successful in his or her appeal for benefits and if the agreed-upon fee does not exceed 25 percent of past-due benefits, but not to exceed $4,000.

As under previous law, the Secretary withholds 25 percent of the past-due benefits of a claimant represented by an attorney and pay the attorney the approved fee directly.

A court which renders a decision favorable to a claimant for social security benefits is permitted to set a reasonable fee for the attorney who represented the claimant before the court. The fee cannot exceed 25 percent of the past-due benefits that result from the court's decision. The Secretary may certify for payment to the attorney, out of the total of the past-due benefits, the amount of the fee set by the court.

VOCATIONAL REHABILITATION

The Social Security Act requires that persons applying for a determination of disability be promptly referred to State vocational rehabilitation agencies for necessary rehabilitation services. The act provides for withholding of benefits for refusal, without good cause, to accept rehabilitation services available under a State plan approved under the Vocational Rehabilitation Act in such amounts as the Secretary shall determine.

Public Law 97–35 eliminated reimbursement from the trust funds to the State vocational rehabilitation agencies for rehabilitation services except in cases where the services have resulted in the beneficiary's performance of substantial gainful activity (SGA) for a continuous period of at least 9 months. Such a 9-month period could begin while the individual is under a vocational rehabilitation program and may also coincide with the trial work period or the individual's waiting period for benefits. The services must be performed under a State plan for vocational rehabilitation services under title I of the Rehabilitation Act. In the case of any State that is unwilling to participate or does not have a plan that meets the requirements of the Vocational Rehabilitation Act, the Commissioner of Social Security may provide such services by agreement or contract with other public or private agencies, organizations, institutions or individuals. The determination that the vocational rehabilitation services contributed to the successful return of the individual to SGA, and the determination of the amount of costs to be reimbursed, are made by the Commissioner of Social Security in accordance with criteria formulated by him. Payments under this provision can be made in advance or by way of reimbursement, with necessary adjustments for overpayments or underpayments.

DISABILITY CLAIMS AND APPEALS STRUCTURE

The Social Security appeals and case review process is a complex multilayered structure that is inextricably linked with the disability determination process. Since about 94 percent of the hearing requests in fiscal year 1993 involve disability claims (both Social Security and supplemental security income), the process described will be for that type of claim. The application for disability benefits is made at the Federal Social Security district office where the claimant is interviewed and the sources of medical evidence are recorded. After determining whether the applicant meets the insured status requirements, the case is then sent to the State agency which, operating as an agent of the Social Security Administration, makes the initial determination of disability. If a claimant or terminated beneficiary is dissatisfied with an initial denial or termination of disability benefits by the State agency, he can request a reconsideration within 60 days of receipt of the notice of denial. The reconsideration is also carried out by the State agency, but by personnel other than those who made the initial determination. If upon reconsideration the claimant is again denied benefits, he will be given a hearing before an administrative law judge (ALJ), providing he files a request within 60 days of receipt of the notice of denial. If the claim is denied by the ALJ, the claimant has 60 days to request review by the Appeals Council. The Appeals Council may also, on its own motion, review a decision within 60 days of the ALJ's decision. The 1980 Disability Amendments required the Secretary to review a percentage of ALJ hearing decisions, and this review is being conducted by the Appeals Council.

The Appeals Council may review, affirm, modify or reverse the decision of the ALJ, or it may remand it to the ALJ for further development. The claimant is notified in writing of the final action of the Appeals Council, and is informed of his right to obtain further review by commencing a civil action within 60 days in a United States district court.

Under current law, as amended by the 1984 Disability Benefits Reform Act, DI beneficiaries whose benefits have been terminated for medical reasons, e.g., recovery or improvement in the medical condition that was the basis for the disability, can elect to continue to receive disability and Medicare benefits through the hearing stage of the appeals process. The disability benefits are subject to recovery, however, if the initial termination decision is upheld as the final decision of the Secretary.

Table 2–4 shows the number of cases allowed and appealed at various levels of appeal for application decisions and Continuing Disability Reviews (CDRs) processed by State agencies. Table 2–5 presents information for fiscal years 1979 through 1993 of the number of cases which are reviewed and reversed at the ALJ level. Table 2–6 presents information on the number of continuing disability reviews—title II cases—that were conducted in fiscal years 1977–93. Note that due to a sharp increase in initial claims, the number of CDRs processed has declined in recent years from a high of 291,000 in 1988 to 49,000 in 1993.

TABLE 2–4. DISABILITY DETERMINATIONS AND APPEALS, FISCAL YEAR 1993

TITLE II, TITLE XVI AND CONCURRENT TITLE II AND XVI DECISIONS FOR DISABILITY
CLAIMS BY WORKERS, WIDOWS, WIDOWERS AND DISABLED ADULT CHILDREN 1/

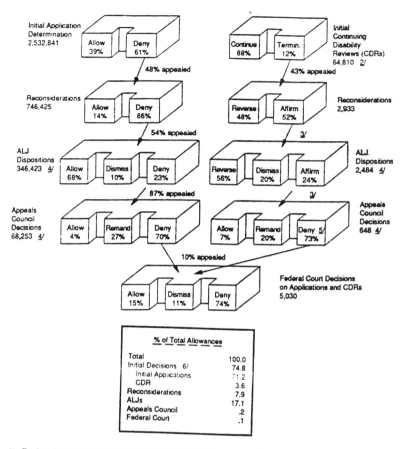

% of Total Allowances	
Total	100.0
Initial Decisions 6/	74.8
Initial Applications	71.2
CDR	3.6
Reconsiderations	7.9
ALJs	17.1
Appeals Council	.2
Federal Court	.1

1/ The data relate to workloads processed in fiscal year 1993, but include some cases where the initial level decision was made in a prior period. The data include determinations on initial applications as well as continuing disability reviews (both periodic reviews and medical diary cases).
2/ Includes non-State CDR mailer continuations. Also includes 8,500 CDRs where there was "no decision." The continuance and termination rates are computed without the "no decision" cases.
3/ Many ALJ dispositions and AC decisions are based on DDS determinations from a previous year. Therefore, a percent appealed is not provided.
4/ Includes ALJ decisions not appealed further by the claimant but reviewed by the Appeals Council on its "own motion" authority.
5/ Includes affirmations, denials and dismissals of requests for review, own motion and reopening cases.
6/ Initial determinations plus CDRs.

Source: Social Security Administration

TABLE 2–5.—ADMINISTRATIVE LAW JUDGE FAVORABLE RATES—DISABILITY INSURANCE [1] INITIAL DENIALS AND TERMINATIONS,[2] FISCAL YEARS 1979–93

Fiscal year	Dismissed	Unfavorable	Favorable	Total	Percent favorable
Initial denials:					
1979	6,332	31,485	48,934	86,751	56.4
1980	7,093	31,703	56,733	95,529	59.4
1981	15,141	59,930	98,129	173,200	56.7
1982	15,403	67,481	91,865	174,749	52.6
1983	14,334	65,626	79,427	159,387	49.8
1984	15,075	63,381	88,301	166,757	53.0
1985	14,806	61,161	92,118	168,085	54.8
1986	28,792	44,223	78,737	151,752	51.9
1987	15,271	58,412	98,180	171,863	57.1
1988	18,213	58,788	111,748	188,749	59.2
1989	19,695	54,284	122,070	196,049	62.3
1990	19,297	45,264	127,707	192,268	66.4
1991 [3]	19,880	44,594	144,945	209,419	69.2
1992 [3]	19,665	48,407	166,661	234,733	71.0
1993 [3]	20,190	47,579	171,508	239,277	71.7
Terminations:					
1979	1,401	4,078	8,052	13,531	59.5
1980	1,431	4,197	9,909	15,537	63.8
1981	2,623	6,945	16,685	26,253	63.6
1982	4,670	17,502	37,306	59,478	62.7
1983	9,247	37,284	73,821	120,352	61.3
1984	25,681	22,590	56,327	104,598	53.9
1985	4,176	2,415	3,126	9,717	32.2
1986	1,095	2,129	2,014	5,238	38.4
1987	812	1,954	2,014	4,780	42.1
1988	1,031	2,807	3,426	7,264	47.2
1989	1,220	3,482	4,882	9,584	50.9
1990	1,166	2,940	4,695	8,801	53.3
1991 [3]	1,007	2,140	3,935	7,082	55.6
1992 [3]	812	1,642	2,812	5,266	53.4
1993 [3]	720	1,281	2,079	4,080	51.0

[1] Includes title II and concurrent title II/title XVI disability cases and concurrent title II/title XVI aged cases.
[2] Includes all termination cases regardless of the basis for termination.
[3] Final data.

Source: Office of Hearings and Appeals, Social Security Administration.

TABLE 2–6.—CONTINUING DISABILITY REVIEWS (CDR) INITIAL DECISIONS: TITLE II DIS-ABLED WORKERS, DISABLED WIDOWS AND WIDOWERS, AND DISABLED CHILDREN CESSATIONS AND CONTINUATIONS, FISCAL YEARS 1977–93

	Cessations		Continuations		Total cases		
	Number	Per-cent	Number	Per-cent	Cessa-tions and continu-ations	Total disabled persons	Percent re-viewed
1977	41,475	38.7	65,745	61.3	107,220	[1] 3,322,230	3.2
1978	38,847	46.4	44,804	53.6	83,651	3,447,767	2.4
1979	45,216	48.1	48,868	51.9	94,084	3,457,837	2.7
1980	44,273	46.8	50,227	53.2	94,550	3,454,010	2.7
1981	80,956	47.9	87,966	52.1	168,922	3,413,602	4.9
1982	179,857	44.8	221,325	55.2	401,182	3,263,354	12.3
1983	182,074	41.7	254,424	58.3	436,498	3,226,888	13.5
1984 [2]	31,927	24.6	97,752	75.4	129,679	3,249,367	4.0
1985 [2]	475	14.6	2,785	85.4	3,260	3,332,870	.1
1986	2,554	5.6	42,805	94.4	45,359	3,261,768	1.4
1987	20,343	12.4	143,712	87.6	164,055	3,433,524	4.8
1988	33,565	11.5	257,377	88.5	290,942	3,492,762	8.3
1989	24,102	9.2	237,722	90.8	261,824	3,559,840	7.4
1990 [3]	15,154	10.5	129,026	89.5	144,180	3,678,509	3.9
1991 [4]	5,697	12.5	39,749	87.5	45,446	3,866,645	1.2
1992	6,923	15.0	39,291	85.0	46,214	4,165,133	1.1
1993 [5]	4,886	9.9	44,316	90.1	49,202	4,457,500	1.1

[1] In current pay at end of fiscal year.

[2] The decline in the number of reviews in 1984 and 1985 was due to the national moratorium on reviews pending enactment and implementation of the new legislation with revised criteria for CDR's (enacted in fiscal year 1984, regulations promulgated late fiscal year 1985).

[3] The decline in CDR processing in 1990 was due to the unanticipated processing of approximately 40,000 class action court cases.

[4] The continued decline in CDR processing is due to the increase in the initial claims workloads.

[5] Includes non-State CDR mailer continuations.

Source: Office of Disability, Social Security Administration.

RECENT EXPERIENCE IN THE DISABILITY PROGRAM

DI awards and beneficiaries

Over the past 15 years, the DI program has experienced a period of sharp cost curtailment followed by a rebound in growth. The number of DI beneficiaries (disabled workers and their dependents) on the rolls peaked at 4.9 million in May 1978. The beneficiary population then declined sharply to 3.8 million in July 1984. Thereafter, the number of beneficiaries rose steadily, again reaching 5.3 million in January 1994.

Similarly, the number of new DI benefit awards declined from 592,000 in 1975 to approximately 299,000 in 1982. As shown in table 2–7, with the exception of a dip in 1987 and 1988, awards then rose steadily, reaching a high of 637,000 in 1992 before falling slightly to about 635,000 in 1993. (The large 1992 increase is partially attributable to SSA's short-term measures for dealing with increased DI applications. By increasing the volume of applications processed, these measures resulted in both increased awards and increased denials.)

The incidence of disability (number of awards per 1,000 insured workers) fell from an all-time high of 7.1 in 1975 to an all-time low of 2.9 in 1982. In 1993, this rate stood at 5.1 percent.

Tables 2-7 and 2-8 show the number of DI awards and applications, award rates, and the number of beneficiaries for selected fiscal years.

Backlogs and applicant waiting times

In recent years, the combination of increasing workloads and reduced staff has left the State Disability Determination Services unable to keep pace with their workloads.[5] As shown in table 2-9, backlogs of pending claims have risen sharply, subjecting qualified applicants to long waits for benefits. Between 1988 and 1992, applications pending at the DDSs rose from 323,000 to 725,000, causing claimants to wait 50 percent longer, or three months instead of two, for an eligibility decision.

TABLE 2-7.—DISABLED WORKERS' APPLICATIONS, AWARDS AND RATIO OF AWARDS TO APPLICATIONS AND AWARDS PER 1,000 INSURED WORKERS FOR SELECTED YEARS, 1960-93

	Number of applications (in thousands)	Total awards	Awards as a percent of applications	Awards per 1,000 insured workers
1960	418.6	207,805	50	4.5
1965	532.9	253,499	48	4.7
1970	868.2	350,384	40	4.8
1971	924.4	415,897	45	5.6
1972	947.8	455,438	48	6.0
1973	1,066.9	491,616	46	6.3
1974	1,330.2	535,977	40	6.7
1975	1,285.3	592,049	46	7.1
1976	1,232.2	551,460	45	6.5
1977	1,235.2	568,874	46	6.5
1978	1,184.7	464,415	39	5.2
1979	1,187.8	416,713	35	4.4
1980	1,262.3	396,559	31	4.0
1981	1,161.3	345,254	30	3.4
1982	1,020.0	298,531	29	2.9
1983	1,017.7	311,491	31	3.0
1984	1,035.7	357,141	34	3.4
1985	1,066.2	377,371	35	3.5
1986	1,118.4	416,865	37	3.8
1987	1,108.9	415,848	37	3.7
1988	1,017.9	409,490	40	3.6
1989	984.9	425,582	43	3.7
1990	1,067.7	467,977	44	3.9
1991	1,208.7	536,434	44	4.4
1992	1,335.1	636,637	48	5.2
1993	1,425.8	635,238	45	5.1

Source: Office of the Actuary, Social Security Administration.

---

[5] Between 1984 and 1990, DDS staff was cut by 19 percent—from 14,500 to 11,800.

In its budget proposal for fiscal year 1995, SSA projected that its backlog of initial disability claims would continue to rise sharply, increasing from 720,000 to 1,102,000 during 1995. Table 2–9 shows disability backlogs and applicant waiting times since 1988.

TABLE 2–8.—NUMBER OF DISABILITY INSURANCE BENEFICIARIES FOR SELECTED YEARS: 1960–93

[Current payment status, December]

	Disabled workers	Spouses	Children	Total
Year:				
1960	455,371	76,599	155,481	687,451
1965	988,074	193,362	557,615	1,739,051
1970	1,492,948	283,447	888,600	2,664,995
1975	2,488,774	452,922	1,410,504	4,352,200
1980	2,861,253	462,204	1,358,715	4,682,172
1981	2,776,519	428,212	1,251,543	4,456,274
1982	2,603,713	365,883	1,003,869	3,973,465
1983	2,568,966	308,060	935,904	3,812,930
1984	2,596,535	303,984	921,285	3,821,804
1985	2,656,500	305,528	945,141	3,907,169
1986	2,727,386	300,592	965,301	3,993,279
1987	2,785,885	290,895	967,944	4,044,724
1988	2,830,284	280,821	963,195	4,074,300
1989	2,895,364	271,488	961,975	4,128,827
1990	3,011,294	265,890	988,797	4,265,981
1991	3,194,938	266,219	1,051,883	4,513,040
1992	3,467,783	270,674	1,151,239	4,889,696
1993	3,725,966	272,759	1,254,841	5,253,566

Source: Office of Research and Statistics, Social Security Administration.

TABLE 2–9.—DISABILITY BACKLOGS AND APPLICANT WAITING TIMES

[Claims pending and weeks of work on hand at the State Disability Determination Services (DDSs)]

Year	Total claims pending at end of year	Weeks of work on hand [1]
1988	323,000	8.4
1989	479,000	10.0
1990	538,000	11.3
1991	693,000	14.3
1992	725,000	12.1
1993	717,398	10.7

[1] The number of weeks of work pending in the DDSs provides the best approximation of the amount of time an applicant must wait for an eligibility decision.

Source: National Council of Disability Determination Directors.

CHARACTERISTICS OF DI BENEFICIARIES

Tables 2–10 and 2–11 present data on the demographic, social, and medical characteristics of the disabled population over time. For instance, table 2–10 shows the increase in the receipt of benefits by women, which reflects larger societal trends in female workforce participation. Table 2–10 also indicates the higher levels of educational attainment that characterize the present disabled population in comparison to that of 1970.

GAO STUDY OF TERMINATED BENEFICIARIES: 1981–84

In response to a request from the House Ways and Means Subcommittee on Social Security, the General Accounting Office (GAO) issued a report in November 1989, which compared the health, employment, and financial status of Disability Insurance (DI) beneficiaries with that of denied applicants and beneficiaries removed from the rolls during 1981–84. Based on written and oral interviews with a random sample of these individuals, the GAO found that:

1. Most DI beneficiaries removed from the rolls between 1981 and 1984 have been reinstated. However, of those who were not, nearly half are not working.—As of 1987, 63 percent of the beneficiaries who were determined ineligible for benefits during SSA's 1981–84 review had been reinstated to the disability benefit rolls. Another 4 percent had begun to receive Social Security retirement benefits, and 7 percent had died. Altogether, only about 26 percent of those found ineligible remained terminated; 58 percent of these terminated individuals (or 15 percent of those earlier found ineligible) had returned to work.

2. Denied applicants continue to have employment problems.—About 58 percent of the applicants who were denied benefits in 1984 and were not receiving benefits as of 1987 reported they were not working. Over two-thirds of these nonworking denied applicants had been out of work for at least 3 years, and 54 percent said they did not expect to ever work again. Of the denied applicants who were working at the time of GAO's survey, 71 percent said that because of their health, they were limited in the kind or amount of work that they could do. Over 40 percent were earning less in 1986 than they were before applying for disability.

3. Both DI beneficiaries and denied applicants who are not working report poor health.—GAO assessed the survey respondents' health status on the basis of their self-perceptions and reported abilities to perform the activities of daily living and personal care. Although the health status reported by denied applicants was slightly better than that of the allowed population, both generally reported poor health. In addition, self-reported health status differed significantly between the denied who worked and those who did not. After separating the denied into working and nonworking groups, the self-reported health status of the nonworking denied group closely resembled that reported by the allowed population; and both

TABLE 2–10.—PERCENT DISTRIBUTION BY AGE, SEX AND EDUCATION OF TITLE II DISABLED WORKER BENEFICIARIES ALLOWED BENEFITS IN SELECTED CALENDAR YEARS 1970–93, COMPARED WITH ADULT U.S. POPULATION IN 1990

Characteristics	Year allowed benefits												Adult U.S. population[1]
	1970	1975	1979	1982	1985	1987	1988	1989	1990	1991	1992	1993	
Total percent	100.0	100.0	100.0	100.0	100.0	100.0	100.0	100.0	100.0	100.0	100.0	100.0	100.0
Age:													
Under 35	9.0	11.0	13.6	14.4	16.8	17.1	15.2	16.2	15.7	15.7	16.8	16.2	46
35 to 44	11.0	10.0	11.5	12.3	15.0	16.0	16.5	17.9	18.7	19.6	20.4	20.9	24
45 to 54	26.0	26.0	27.2	26.5	25.7	22.9	23.3	24.7	24.7	25.1	25.6	26.8	16
55 to 59	24.0	23.0	27.0	27.2	23.9	20.8	20.6	20.4	19.9	19.5	18.5	18.6	7
60 and over	30.0	30.0	20.6	19.6	18.7	23.2	24.4	20.9	21.0	20.1	18.7	17.6	7
Median age (years)	56.0	55.6	53.4	53.1	51.7	53.0	53.3	52.1	51.9	51.4	50.5	50.3	32.9
Sex:													
Male	74	68	69	70	67	66	66	64	64	64	63	62	49
Female	26	32	31	30	33	34	34	36	36	36	37	38	51
Education (years of school completed):													
No schooling[2]	2	1	1	1	2	1	1	1	1	1	1	1	1
Elementary school (1 to 8)	44	37	29	26	23	18	18	17	16	16	12	11	9
High school	46	52	55	56	59	57	59	60	62	62	50	45	45
9 to 11	23	24	23	22	22	19	20	19	19	19	15	14	11
12	23	28	32	34	37	38	39	41	43	43	35	31	34
Some college	9	10	12	14	14	16	15	17	17	17	14	12	45
Unknown	0	0	3	3	2	8	7	5	5	5	23	31	0

[1] Derived from 1990 census. Figures for age based on population aged 18 to 64. Figures for education based on persons aged 25 and over.
[2] Also includes special schools for handicapped.

Source: Office of Disability, Social Security Administration.

TABLE 2–11.—PERCENT DISTRIBUTION BY DISABLING CONDITION OF TITLE II DISABLED WORKER BENEFICIARIES ALLOWED BENEFITS IN SELECTED CALENDAR YEARS 1970–93

Disabling condition and mobility	Year allowed benefits											
	1970	1975	1979	1982	1985	1987	1988	1989	1990	1991	1992	1993
Total percent [1]	100	100	100	100	100	100	100	100	100	100	100	100
Disabling condition:												
Infective and parasitic diseases [2]	3	1	1	1	1	1	0	1	6	6	7	7
Neoplasms	10	10	14	17	15	12	16	18	17	16	13	15
Allergic, endocrine system, metabolic and nutritional diseases	4	3	3	4	5	5	3	3	3	4	5	5
Mental, psychoneurotic and personality disorders	11	11	11	11	18	23	22	22	23	24	25	26
Diseases of the nervous system and sense organs	6	7	8	9	8	8	8	9	9	8	8	7
Circulatory system	31	32	28	25	19	17	18	17	16	15	14	15
Respiratory system	7	7	6	7	5	5	5	5	5	5	4	5
Digestive system	3	3	2	2	2	1	2	2	2	2	2	2
Skeletal musculo	15	17	17	16	13	14	14	11	12	13	13	12
Accidents, poisonings and violence	8	6	6	6	4	5	5	4	4	4	4	3
Other/unknown	2	3	3	2	11	9	7	9	5	5	5	5

[1] Due to rounding, may not add to 100 percent.
[2] Beginning in 1990, AIDS/HIV cases are included in this category.

Source: Office of Disability, Social Security Administration.

were significantly worse than that of the working denied. For example:

—80 percent of the nonworking denied group and 78 percent of the allowed population perceived their health as fair to poor, with about 44 percent of both stating they were in poor health; in contrast, only 13 percent of the working denied said they were in poor health;

—40 percent of the nonworking denied group and 51 percent of the allowed population said they had to depend on others for at least one personal care activity, such as dressing, eating, or getting in and out of bed; only 12 percent of the working denied needed any help; and

—71 percent of the nonworking denied group and 76 percent of the allowed population could be classified as having severe functional limitations; in comparison, only 41 percent of the working denied could be so classified.

4. DI beneficiaries' impairments differed from those of denied applicants.—The denied applicants (both working and nonworking) reported back problems as the impairment that limited them the most; the allowed population most often reported mental and heart problems.

5. Both the allowed and denied populations reported serious financial problems.—The median family income reported by the nonworking denied was about $6,500 in 1986. Total family income was below Census's poverty level for 61 percent of this group, and 35 percent depended on government programs other than Social Security (mainly public assistance) for half or more of their total family income.

Despite receiving DI benefits, 33 percent of the allowed population said they lacked enough income to get along; 43 percent reported income that is below the poverty level. At the time of GAO's survey in 1987, a significant proportion of the denied groups were without medical insurance coverage. Twenty-nine percent of the working denied and 25 percent of the nonworking denied reported no medical insurance coverage. Most of those without insurance said they had been without it since 1984 or earlier.

LEGISLATIVE CHANGES, 1984–93

98TH CONGRESS: THE DISABILITY BENEFITS REFORM ACT OF 1984

Public Law 98–460, the Disability Benefits Reform Act of 1984, made several substantial changes in the standards for review of disability beneficiaries, and in other provisions of the program as well. The following is a summary of the law.

1. Medical improvement standard

Public Law 98–460 established a medical improvement standard under which the Secretary may terminate disability benefits on the basis that the person is no longer disabled only if:

(1) There is substantial evidence demonstrating that (a) there has been any medical improvement in the individual's impairment or combination of impairments (other than medical improvement which is not related to the person's ability to

work), (b) the individual is now able to engage in substantial gainful activity (SGA); or

(2) There is substantial evidence consisting of new medical evidence and a new assessment of RFC which demonstrates that although there is no medical improvement, (a) the person has benefited from advances in medical or vocational therapy or technology related to ability to work, and (b) that he or she is now able to perform SGA; or

(3) There is substantial evidence that although there is no medical improvement (a) the person has benefited from vocational therapy and (b) the beneficiary can now perform SGA; or

(4) There is substantial evidence that, based on new or improved diagnostic techniques or evaluations, the person's impairment or combination of impairments is not as disabling as it was considered to be at the time of the prior determination, and that therefore the individual is able to perform SGA; or

(5) There is substantial evidence either in the file at the original determination or newly obtained showing that the prior determination was in error; or

(6) There is substantial evidence that the original decision was fraudulently obtained; or

(7) If the individual is engaging in SGA (except where he or she is eligible under section 1619), fails without good cause to cooperate in the review or follow prescribed treatment or cannot be located.

In making the determination, the Secretary was required to consider the evidence in the file as well as any additional information concerning the claimant's current or prior condition secured by the Secretary or provided by the claimant.

Determinations under this provision had to be made on the basis of the weight of the evidence, and on a neutral basis with regard to the individual's condition, without any inference as to the presence or absence of disability based on the previous finding of disability.

Effective date: Applied only with respect to the following categories:

(1) Determinations by the Secretary made after the date of enactment;

(2) Cases pending at any level of the administrative process on the date of enactment;

(3) Cases of individual litigants pending in Federal court on the date the conference report was filed;

(4) Cases of named plaintiffs in class action suits pending on that date;

(5) Cases of unnamed plaintiffs in class action suits certified prior to that date; and

(6) Cases where a request for judicial review was made on a decision of the Secretary made during the 60 days preceding enactment.

Cases in categories (3), (4), (5), and (6) had to be remanded to the Secretary for review under this standard. Individuals in (5) were to be sent a notice via certified mail informing them that they had 120 days after the date of receipt of the notice to request a review under the medical improvement standard.

No class action could be certified after the date the conference report was filed which raised the issue of medical improvement with respect to an individual whose benefits were terminated prior to that date.

Persons whose cases were remanded to the Secretary were to receive benefits pending the Secretary's decision and appeal of that decision if they so elected. If found eligible, any person whose case was remanded under this provision was to receive benefits retroactive to the date they were last found ineligible.

2. *Evaluation of pain*

The Secretary of HHS was required, in conjunction with the National Academy of Sciences, to conduct a study concerning the questions of using subjective evidence of pain in determining whether a person is under a disability, and the state of the art of preventing, reducing or coping with pain. This study was completed and a report was submitted to the House Committee on Ways and Means and the Senate Committee on Finance in 1986. While making many recommendations, it basically supported the existing treatment of allegations of pain in disability determinations.

The provision also established a statutory standard for considering pain which was in effect until December 31, 1986.

3. *Multiple impairments*

In determining whether a person's impairment or impairments are of a sufficient medical severity to be the basis of a finding of eligibility for benefits, the Secretary was required to consider the combined effect of all of the person's impairments, whether or not any one impairment would alone be severe enough to qualify the person for benefits. The provision became effective for all determinations made on or after 30 days after enactment.

4. *Moratorium on mental impairment reviews*

A moratorium was imposed on reviews of all cases of mental impairment disability until the mental impairment criteria in the Listing of Impairments were revised to realistically evaluate the person's ability to engage in SGA in a competitive workplace environment. The moratorium applied to all cases on which an administrative or judicial appeal was pending on or after June 7, 1983. All persons claiming benefits based on mental impairment disability who received an unfavorable initial or continuing disability decision after March 1, 1981 were permitted to reapply for benefits within 12 months of enactment. The revised criteria were published in 1985.

5. *Pretermination notice*

The Secretary was required to initiate demonstration projects on providing face-to-face interviews for (1) pretermination continuing disability cases and (2) for all initial denial cases, in lieu of face-to-face evidentiary hearings at reconsideration, to be done in at least five States with a report due to the House Committee on Ways and Means and the Senate Committee on Finance on April

1, 1986. The Secretary was also required to notify individuals, upon initiating a periodic eligibility review, that termination of benefits could be the result of the review, and that medical evidence may be provided. Although these studies have been completed, the report has not yet been submitted to Congress.

6. Continuation of benefits during appeal

This provision provided for continuation of disability and Medicare benefits during appeal for all continuing disability review cases through the decision of the ALJ, at the election of the individual. Where the ALJ's decision is adverse to the individual, the disability benefits were to be repaid. The provision was made permanent for SSI disability recipients, and applied to DI beneficiaries through December 1987. The Omnibus Budget Reconciliation Act of 1987 extended the provision for DI beneficiaries through December 1988; the 1988 tax technical corrections bill extended the provisions through December 1989; and the Omnibus Budget Reconciliation Act of 1989 extended them through December 1990.

7. Qualifications of medical professionals

This provision required the Secretary to make every reasonable effort, in cases based on mental impairments, to insure that a qualified psychiatrist or psychologist completes the medical portion of the case review and of the residual functional capacity assessment before any determination is made that an individual is not disabled. The Secretary was given the authority to contract directly for such services if the State agency is unable to do so.

8. Standards for consultative examinations/medical evidence

The Secretary was required to promulgate regulations regarding consultative examinations, including when they should be obtained, the type of referral to be made, and the procedures for monitoring the referral process. Further, the Secretary was required to make every effort to obtain necessary medical evidence from the treating physician before evaluating medical evidence from any other source, and to consider all evidence in the case record and development of complete medical history over at least the preceding 12-month period.

9. Administrative procedure and uniform standards

As required, regulations were published setting forth uniform standards for DI and SSI disability determinations under section 553 of the Administrative Procedure Act, to be binding at all levels of adjudication.

10. Nonacquiescence

While the conference agreement dropped both the House and Senate provisions relating to the Secretary's acquiescence with Court rulings, the intent was not to endorse the practice of "nonacquiescence." The conferees noted that questions had been raised about the constitutional basis of the practice, that many of the conferees had strong concerns about the practice, and that a policy of nonacquiescence should be followed only where steps have been taken or are intended to be taken to receive a review of the disputed issue in the Supreme Court. The conferees also urged the Secretary to seek a resolution of the nonacquiescence issue in the Supreme Court.

In January 1990, SSA issued regulations relating to its adherence with circuit court decisions which are in conflict with SSA's policies. Their key provisions are that: (a) SSA will apply a circuit court decision that conflicts with SSA policy, within the circuit and at all levels of administrative adjudication, unless the Government decided to appeal the decision; and (b) SSA will publish in the Federal Register an Acquiescence Ruling explaining how adjudicators should apply the circuit court decision. SSA will also publish all other Social Security Rulings in the Federal Register.

11. Payment of costs of rehabilitation services

The provision permitted reimbursement to State agencies for costs of VR services provided to individuals receiving DI benefits under section 225(b) of the Social Security Act who medically recover while in VR, whether or not the person worked at SGA for 9 months, and whether or not the person failed to cooperate in the program.

12. Direction for Quadrennial Social Security Advisory Council

The provision required the next quadrennial advisory council (as required in the Social Security Act) to study the medical and vocational aspects of disability using ad hoc panels of experts where appropriate. The study was to include alternative approaches to work evaluation for SSI recipients, effectiveness of VR programs, and other disability program policies, standards, and procedures. The Council issued its report in March of 1988.

13. Staff attorneys

The Secretary was to report, within 120 days of enactment, to the House Committee on Ways and Means and the Senate Committee on Finance, on the actions taken by the Secretary to establish positions which enable staff attorneys to gain the qualifying experience and quality of experience necessary to compete for ALJ positions. Statement of managers stated that it was assumed, given U.S. Office of Personnel Management (OPM) actions at the time, that statutory requirements for establishing specific positions were not required, and the Secretary was urged to take all reasonable steps to see that the OPM actions resulted in SSA staff attorneys becoming qualified for GS–15 ALJ positions.

14. SSI benefits for persons working despite impairment

This provision extended sections 1619 (a) and (b) through June 30, 1987, and required the Secretaries of HHS and Education to establish training programs for staff personnel in SSA district offices and State VR agencies, and disseminate information to SSI applicants, recipients, and potentially interested public and private organizations. Sections 1619 (a) and (b) were made permanent in 1986.

15. Frequency of continuing eligibility reviews

The Secretary was required to promulgate regulations establishing standards for determining the frequency of continuing eligibility reviews. Final regulations were to be issued within 6 months and during that period no individual could be subjected to more than one periodic review.

16. Representative payees for Social Security and SSI beneficiaries

The Secretary was required to (1) evaluate qualifications of prospective payees prior to or within 45 days following certification, (2) establish a system of annual accountability monitoring where payments are made to someone other than a parent or spouse living in the same household with the beneficiary, and (3) report to Congress on implementation, and annually on the number of cases of misused funds and disposition of such cases.

LEGISLATIVE CHANGES IN THE 100TH CONGRESS

Public Law 100–203, the Budget Reconciliation Act of 1987

1. *Continuation of benefits during appeal.*—The existing provision for continued payment of disability benefits during the administrative appeal process was extended through 1988.

2. *Lengthening of the extended period of eligibility for disability benefits.*—The extended period of eligibility during which a disability beneficiary who returns to work may become automatically reentitled to benefits, was lengthened from the current 15 months to 36 months. Medicare eligibility is not continued beyond the period provided under current law.

3. *Payment of attorneys' fees.*—The administrative policy which permits ALJs to authorize attorneys' fees of up to $3,000 without approval by an SSA regional office was reinstated.

Public Law 100–647, the Technical and Miscellaneous Revenue Act of 1988

1. *Continuation of benefits during appeal.*—The existing provision for continued payment of benefits was again extended, through 1989.

2. *Interim benefits in cases of delayed final decisions.*—Interim benefits will be paid to individuals who have received a favorable decision from an administrative law judge but whose cases are under review by the Appeals Council and the Council has not rendered a decision within 110 days. These interim payments are not subject to recovery as overpayments if the final determination is unfavorable.

LEGISLATIVE CHANGES IN THE 101ST CONGRESS

Public Law 101–239, the Omnibus Budget Reconciliation Act of 1989

1. *Continuation of benefits during appeal.*—The existing provision for continued payment of benefits was again extended, through 1990.

2. *Extension of disability insurance program demonstration authority.*—The authority of the Secretary to waive compliance with

the benefit requirements of titles II and XVIII for the purpose of conducting work incentive demonstration projects was extended for 3 years, through June 9, 1993.

3. *Representation of claimants.*—Effective June 1, 1991, the Secretary would be required to maintain an electronically retrievable list of claimants' legal representatives.

Public Law 101–508, the Omnibus Budget Reconciliation Act of 1990

1. *Continuation of benefits during appeal.*—The existing provision for continued payment of benefits during appeal was made permanent.

2. *Improvement of the definition of disability applied to disabled widow(er)s.*—The stricter definition of disability that was previously applied only to widow(er)s was repealed. Instead, a disabled widow(er) is subject to the same definition of disability as is already applied to disabled workers.

3. *Creation of a rolling five-year trial work period for all disabled beneficiaries.*—Effective January 1, 1992, the current trial work period will be liberalized so that a disabled beneficiary will exhaust this period only after completing 9 trial work months in any 60-month period. In addition, the provision prohibiting a TWP for beneficiaries, who qualified for disability benefits without serving a waiting period, was repealed.

4. *Continuation of benefits on account of participation in a non-State vocational rehabilitation program.*—Beneficiaries who medically recover while participating in an approved non-State vocational rehabilitation program are granted the same benefit continuation rights as those who medically recover while participating in a State-sponsored program.

5. *Pre-effectuation review of favorable decisions by the Social Security Administration.*—The percentage of favorable decisions made by State disability determination services that must be reviewed by SSA was reduced from 65 percent of all such decisions to 50 percent of allowances and a sufficient number of other determinations to maintain a high level of accuracy in such decisions. The reviews are to be targeted on those cases most likely to contain errors.

6. *Vocational rehabilitation (VR) demonstration projects.*—The Secretary is required to conduct demonstration projects permitting disabled beneficiaries to select a public or private rehabilitation provider which would furnish rehabilitation services aimed at enabling them to engage in substantial gainful activity and to leave the disability rolls. Legislative changes in the 103d Congress no legislative changes to the disability insurance program were made in the first session of the 103d Congress.

LEGISLATIVE CHANGES IN THE 102D CONGRESS

No legislative changes to the disabilty insurance program were made in the 102d Congress.

LEGISLATIVE CHANGES IN THE 103D CONGRESS

No legislative changes to the disability insurance program were made in the first session of the 103d Congress.

Section 3. Social Security Financing

OVERVIEW

This section presents an overview of the financing of the old-age, survivors, and disability insurance (OASDI) trust funds and provides a summary of the short- and long-term projections for the financial solvency of these funds.

CURRENT LAW FINANCING

The Social Security programs, or old-age, survivors, and disability insurance and hospital insurance trust funds (OASDHI), are primarily financed through the payroll tax and from income taxes paid on Social Security benefits. The payroll tax is imposed on covered earnings up to a specific dollar amount. Workers who earn more than the maximum taxable earnings base do not pay FICA (Federal Insurance Contributions Act) or SECA (Self-Employed Contributions Act) tax on their earnings above the base. Table 3-1 shows income to the OASI and DI trust funds for selected years.

Most of current income to the system goes out directly to meet current benefit obligations. Benefit outlays are made under a permanent appropriation, equal to the amount to which beneficiaries are entitled based on their earnings records, and are not limited to the amount of revenue credited to the trust fund from contributions and interest. If, as occurred in the early 1980's, yearly income is insufficient to cover benefit payments, reserves are used to make up the difference.

Any funds collected in excess of the amount needed to make benefit payments are credited to the trust funds as reserves, in the form of Government securities. These reserves serve as a cushion against temporary shortfalls in revenues or large increases in outlays due to economic fluctuations; the reserves also provide interest income to the trust funds. As a result of the Social Security Amendments of 1983, OASDI reserves are projected to build rapidly in the next quarter century.

The payroll tax is levied on earnings in employment covered by Social Security, with portions of the total tax rate allocated by law to each of the three trust funds (OASI, DI and HI). All persons who work in covered employment pay this mandatory tax on their earnings up to a maximum dollar amount (known as the maximum taxable earnings base, or wage base). Employers pay an equal tax for these workers. Beginning in 1991, two separate wage bases were made effective, one for the OASDI tax and another for the HI tax. As a result of the Omnibus Budget Reconciliation Act of 1993, the wage base for the HI portion of the payroll tax was eliminated beginning in 1994.

Prior to 1984, self-employed workers paid a tax rate which was less than the combined employee-employer rate. Effective in 1984,

(72)

self-employed workers began to pay Social Security taxes that were equivalent to the combined employer-employee rate and to receive a partial credit against that tax through 1989. Effective in 1990 and thereafter, the credit was replaced with a system designed to achieve parity between employees and the self-employed. Under this system:

1. The base of the self-employment tax is adjusted downward to reflect the fact that employees do not pay FICA tax on the value of the employer's FICA tax. The base is equivalent to net earnings from self-employment (up to the taxable wage base) less 7.65 percent.

2. A deduction is allowed for income tax purposes, for half of SECA liability, to allow for the fact that employees do not pay income tax on the value of the employer's FICA tax.

TABLE 3–1.—INCOME TO THE OASI AND DI TRUST FUNDS FOR SELECTED FISCAL YEARS

[Dollars in millions]

	Fiscal year [1]						
	1970	1975	1980	1985	1990	1994 [2]	1998 [2]
OASI:							
Net contributions	$29,955	$56,017	$97,608	$175,305	$261,506	$309,518	$386,793
Income from taxation of benefits	....	....	....	3,151	2,924	5,392	7,461
Payments from the general fund	442	447	557	105	34	10	3
Net interest	1,350	2,292	1,886	1,321	14,143	28,388	43,088
Total	31,746	58,757	100,051	179,881	278,607	343,308	437,345
DI:							
Net contributions	4,141	7,356	16,805	16,876	27,291	33,158	41,448
Income from taxation of benefits	....	....	....	218	158	303	439
Payments from the general fund	16	52	118				
Net interest [3]	223	512	453	890	766	685	–1,274
Total	4,380	7,920	17,376	17,984	28,215	34,146	40,613
Grand total—OASI and DI	36,126	66,677	117,427	197,865	306,822	377,454	477,958

[1] Under the Congressional Budget Act for 1974, fiscal years 1977 and later consist of the 12 months ending on September 30 of each year. Fiscal years prior to 1977 consist of the 12 months ending on June 30 of each year.
[2] Based on President Clinton's fiscal year 1995 budget assumptions.
[3] Assets of the DI Trust Fund are estimated to be exhausted in 1996. For projection purposes, it is assumed that the DI Trust Fund could borrow money, to be repaid with interest, on the same terms that it normally would invest positive trust fund balances.

Source: Office of the Actuary, Social Security Administration.

Under current law, as of January 1994, the employer and employee each pay an OASDI tax equal to 6.20 percent of the first $60,600 of earnings and an HI tax equal to 1.45 percent on all earnings. (Self-employed persons pay 15.30 percent.) In general, increases in the wage base are automatic, based on the increase in average wages in the economy (excluding self-employment earnings) each year.[1] (The Omnibus Reconciliation Act of 1989 raised the wage base beyond the automatic increase by including certain types of "deferred compensation," such as contributions to section 401(k) retirement plans, in the calculation of the average wages.)

Tables 3–2, 3–3, and 3–4 show payroll tax rates, annual wage bases and maximum annual contributions.

---

[1] Increases in the wage base are triggered whenever cost-of-living adjustments are granted to Social Security beneficiaries and are effective on a calendar year basis.

TABLE 3–2.—PAYROLL TAX RATES FOR EMPLOYEES AND EMPLOYERS AND WAGE BASE LEVELS

Calendar years	OASDI wage base [1]	Tax rates (percent) for employer and employee, each			
		Total	OASI	DI	HI
1937–49	$3,000	1.000	1.000	....	....
1950	3,000	1.500	1.500	....	....
1951–53	3,600	1.500	1.500	....	....
1954	3,600	2.000	2.000	....	....
1955–56	4,200	2.000	2.000	....	....
1957–58	4,200	2.250	2.000	0.250	....
1959	4,800	2.500	2.250	0.250	....
1960–61	4,800	3.000	2.750	0.250	....
1962	4,800	3.125	2.875	0.250	....
1963–65	4,800	3.625	3.375	0.250	....
1966	6,600	4.200	3.500	0.350	0.350
1967	6,600	4.400	3.550	0.350	0.500
1968	7,800	4.400	3.325	0.475	0.600
1969	7,800	4.800	3.725	0.475	0.600
1970	7,800	4.800	3.650	0.550	0.600
1971	7,800	5.200	4.050	0.550	0.600
1972	9,000	5.200	4.050	0.550	0.600
1973	10,800	5.850	4.300	0.550	1.000
1974	13,200	5.850	4.375	0.575	0.900
1975	14,100	5.850	4.375	0.575	0.900
1976	15,300	5.850	4.375	0.575	0.900
1977	16,500	5.850	4.375	0.575	0.900
1978	17,700	6.050	4.275	0.775	1.000
1979	22,900	6.130	4.330	0.750	1.050
1980	25,900	6.130	4.520	0.560	1.050
1981	29,700	6.650	4.700	0.650	1.300
1982	32,400	6.700	4.575	0.825	1.300
1983	35,700	6.700	4.775	0.625	1.300
1984	37,800	7.000	5.200	0.500	1.300
1985	39,600	7.050	5.200	0.500	1.350
1986	42,000	7.150	5.200	0.500	1.450
1987	43,800	7.150	5.200	0.500	1.450
1988	45,000	7.510	5.530	0.530	1.450
1989	48,000	7.510	5.530	0.530	1.450
1990	51,300	7.650	5.600	0.600	1.450
1991	53,400	7.650	5.600	0.600	1.450
1992	55,500	7.650	5.600	0.600	1.450
1993	57,600	7.650	5.600	0.600	1.450
1994	60,600	7.650	5.600	0.600	1.450
1995–99	(2)	7.650	5.600	0.600	1.450
2000+	(2)	7.650	5.490	0.710	1.450

[1] The maximum amount of taxable earnings for the HI program is the same as that for the OASDI program for 1966–90. Separate HI taxable maximums of $125,000, $130,200, and $135,000 were applicable to the years 1991–93, respectively. After 1993, the limitation on taxable earnings for the HI program does not apply.

[2] Increases automatically with increases in the average wage index. The CBO estimates that the OASDI wage base will be $60,600 in 1995; $62,100 in 1996; $63,900 in 1997; $66,900 in 1998; and $72,000 in 1999.

Source: Office of the Actuary, Social Security Administration.

TABLE 3–3.—PAYROLL TAX RATES FOR SELF-EMPLOYED INDIVIDUALS, 1980 AND AFTER

Calendar year	OASI	DI	OASDI com-bined	HI	OASDHI combined
1980	6.2725	.7775	7.05	1.05	8.10
1981	7.0250	.9750	8.00	1.30	9.30
1982	6.8125	1.2375	8.05	1.30	9.35
1983	7.1125	.9375	8.05	1.30	9.35
1984	10.4000	1.0000	11.40	2.60	[1] 14.00
1985	10.4000	1.0000	11.40	2.70	[1] 14.10
1986–87	10.4000	1.0000	11.40	2.90	[1] 14.30
1988–89	11.0600	1.0600	12.12	2.90	[1] 15.02
1990–99	11.2000	1.2000	12.40	2.90	15.30
2000 and after	10.9800	1.4200	12.40	2.90	15.30

[1] Excludes tax credits for the self-employed which equaled 2.7 percent in 1984, 2.3 percent in 1985, and 2.0 percent for the years 1986 through 1989. See text for explanation of change in tax treatment of the self-employed.

78

TABLE 3–4.—MAXIMUM ANNUAL CONTRIBUTION, 1937–94

| Calendar years | Employee taxes | | | | Self-employed total |
	Total	OASI	DI	HI	
1937–49	$390.00	$390.00	....	....	....
1950	45.00	45.00	....	....	....
1951–53	162.00	162.00	....	....	$243.00
1954	72.00	72.00	....	....	108.00
1955–56	168.00	168.00	....	....	252.00
1957–58	189.00	168.00	$21.00	....	283.50
1959	120.00	108.00	12.00	....	180.00
1960–61	288.00	264.00	24.00	....	432.00
1962	150.00	138.00	12.00	....	225.60
1963–65	522.00	486.00	36.00	....	777.60
1966	277.20	231.00	23.10	$23.10	405.90
1967	290.40	234.30	23.10	33.00	422.40
1968	343.20	259.35	37.05	46.80	499.20
1969	374.40	290.55	37.05	46.80	538.20
1970	374.40	284.70	42.90	46.80	538.20
1971	405.60	315.90	42.90	46.80	585.00
1972	468.00	364.50	49.50	54.00	675.00
1973	631.80	464.40	59.40	108.00	864.00
1974	772.20	577.50	75.90	118.80	1,042.80
1975	824.85	616.88	81.08	126.90	1,113.90
1976	895.05	669.38	87.98	137.70	1,208.70
1977	965.25	721.88	94.88	148.50	1,303.50
1978	1,070.85	756.68	137.18	177.00	1,433.70
1979	1,403.77	991.57	171.75	240.45	1,854.90
1980	1,587.67	1,170.68	145.04	271.95	2,097.90
1981	1,975.05	1,395.90	193.05	386.10	2,762.10
1982	2,170.80	1,482.30	267.30	421.20	3,029.40
1983	2,391.90	1,704.68	223.13	464.10	3,337.95
1984	2,532.60	1,862.15	179.05	491.40	4,271.40
1985	2,791.80	2,059.20	198.00	534.60	4,672.80
1986	3,003.00	2,184.00	210.00	609.00	5,166.00
1987	3,131.70	2,277.60	219.00	635.10	5,387.40
1988	3,379.50	2,488.50	238.50	652.50	5,859.00
1989	3,604.80	2,654.40	254.40	696.00	6,249.60
1990	3,924.45	2,872.80	307.80	743.85	7,848.90
1991	4,085.10	2,990.40	320.40	774.30	8,170.20
1992	4,245.75	3,108.00	333.00	804.75	8,491.50
1993	4,406.40	3,225.60	345.60	835.20	8,812.80
1994	4,635.90	3,393.60	363.60	878.70	9,271.80

Note.—In 1984 only, an immediate credit of 0.3 percent of taxable wages was allowed against the OASDI contribution paid by employees. Credits of 2.7 percent, 2.3 percent, and 2.0 percent were allowed against the combined OASDI and HI taxes on net earnings from self-employment in 1984, 1985, and 1986–89, respectively. Figures in table are reduced to reflect this credit.

Source: Office of the Actuary, Social Security Administration.

COVERAGE

In 1940, approximately 24 million persons worked in employment covered by the Social Security system. Over the years, major categories of workers were brought under the system, such as State and local government employees (on a voluntary basis), regularly employed farm and domestic workers, members of the armed services, and self-employed professionals such as physicians and lawyers. In 1993, about 135 million workers and an estimated 96 percent of all jobs in the United States were covered under Social Security. The present-law Social Security wage base is updated automatically according to wage increases in the economy. In 1993, an estimated 86 percent of all earnings from jobs covered by Social Security were taxable.

TABLE 3–5.—CIVILIAN WORKERS COVERED BY SOCIAL SECURITY SYSTEM, 1939–92

[In millions]

Year	Paid civilian employees [1]	OASDI coverage	Percent covered	OASDHI coverage	Percent covered
1939 [2]	43.6	24.0	55.1	24.0	55.1
1944 [2]	51.2	30.8	60.2	30.8	60.2
1949 [2]	56.7	34.3	60.5	34.3	60.5
1955	62.8	51.8	82.5	51.8	82.5
1960	64.6	55.7	86.2	55.7	86.2
1961	65.3	56.1	85.9	56.1	85.9
1962	66.4	57.3	86.3	57.3	86.3
1963	67.6	58.5	86.5	58.5	86.5
1964	69.3	60.1	86.7	60.1	86.7
1965	71.6	62.7	87.6	62.7	87.6
1966	73.6	64.9	88.2	64.9	88.2
1967	74.4	65.7	88.3	65.7	88.3
1968	75.9	67.1	88.4	67.1	88.4
1969	78.0	68.6	87.9	68.6	87.9
1970	77.8	69.9	89.9	69.9	89.9
1971	79.6	71.7	90.1	71.7	90.1
1972	82.6	74.7	90.4	74.7	90.4
1973	85.6	77.6	90.6	77.6	90.6
1974	85.4	77.3	90.5	77.3	90.5
1975	86.0	77.9	90.6	77.9	90.6
1976	89.2	81.0	90.9	81.0	90.9
1977	93.5	85.1	91.0	85.1	91.0
1978	97.0	88.4	91.2	88.4	91.2
1979	99.4	90.7	91.3	90.7	91.3
1980	98.9	89.3	90.3	89.3	90.3
1981	99.0	90.2	91.1	90.2	91.1
1982	98.3	89.8	91.4	89.8	91.4
1983	102.2	93.6	91.6	96.0	94.0
1984	105.5	97.9	92.7	100.3	95.0
1985	107.7	100.0	92.9	102.4	95.1
1986	110.2	104.1	94.4	106.5	96.6
1987	113.3	107.5	94.8	110.0	97.1
1988	115.6	109.8	95.0	112.4	97.3
1989	117.4	111.7	95.2	114.4	97.4
1990	117.0	111.3	95.2	114.1	97.5
1991	116.3	111.0	95.5	113.3	97.5
1992	117.8	112.7	95.7	114.8	97.5

[1] Includes paid employees and self-employed for all years.
[2] Monthly average for these years, all other years as of December.

Source: Office of Research and Statistics, Social Security Administration.

TABLE 3–6.—CIVILIAN WAGES COVERED BY OASDI SYSTEM, 1950–92 [1]

[Dollars in billions]

Year	Total earnings	Earnings in covered employment		Total earnings in covered employment	Covered earnings as a percent of total earnings	Taxable earnings	Taxable earnings as a percent of total earnings in covered employment
		Employed	Self-employed				
1950	186.1	109.8	....	109.8	59.0	87.5	79.7
1955	257.4	171.6	24.5	196.1	76.2	157.5	80.3
1960	324.9	236.0	29.2	265.2	81.6	207.0	78.1
1965	428.8	311.4	40.3	351.7	82.0	250.7	71.3
1970	631.7	483.6	48.0	531.6	85.2	415.6	78.2
1975	940.1	717.2	70.4	787.6	83.8	664.7	84.4
1976	1,037.2	797.2	76.8	874.7	84.3	737.7	84.3
1977	1,140.4	879.5	80.6	960.1	84.2	816.6	85.0
1978	1,288.6	998.9	93.7	1,092.6	84.8	915.6	83.8
1979	1,437.1	1,122.0	100.2	1,222.2	85.0	1,067.0	87.3
1980	1,548.4	1,231.0	97.8	1,328.8	85.8	1,180.7	88.9
1981	1,696.5	1,352.0	98.9	1,450.9	85.5	1,294.1	89.2
1982	1,764.0	1,418.0	98.6	1,516.6	86.0	1,365.3	90.0
1983	1,870.8	1,502.0	113.2	1,615.2	86.3	1,454.1	90.0
1984	2,086.0	1,671.5	129.3	1,800.8	86.3	1,608.8	89.3
1985	2,246.2	1,794.5	142.3	1,936.8	86.2	1,722.6	88.9
1986	2,389.2	1,921.0	160.8	2,081.8	87.1	1,844.4	88.6
1987	2,571.4	2,057.1	179.9	2,237.0	87.0	1,960.0	87.6
1988 [2]	2,767.3	2,224.7	208.1	2,432.8	87.9	2,088.4	85.8
1989 [2]	2,933.7	2,367.8	221.0	2,588.8	88.2	2,241.1	86.6
1990 [2]	3,108.4	2,507.5	213.0	2,720.5	87.5	2,367.8	86.9
1991 [2]	3,191.3	2,583.0	187.1	2,770.1	86.8	2,418.9	87.3
1992 [2]	3,387.4	2,692.0	204.8	2,896.8	85.5	2,529.9	87.3

[1] Sum of wages and salaries and proprietors' income with inventory valuation and capital consumption adjustments, as estimated by the Bureau of Economic Analysis in the National Income and Product Accounts.

[2] Preliminary.

Source: Social Security Bulletin, Annual Statistical Supplement, 1993, and Office of Research and Statistics, Social Security Administration.

While coverage is compulsory for most types of employment, approximately 4.3 million workers were exempt from coverage under Social Security in 1993. The majority of these noncovered workers were and still are in the Federal Government and in State and local governments. Beginning January 1, 1983, Federal employees were covered under the Medicare portion of the Social Security tax, and all Federal employees hired after 1983 are covered under the OASDI portion as well. In 1990, about 67 percent of State and local government workers (13.5 million out of 20.3 million jobs), were covered by Social Security. Beginning January 1, 1984, all employees of nonprofit organizations became covered, and terminations of

Social Security coverage by State government entities were no longer allowed.[2] State and local employees hired after March 31, 1986 are mandatorily covered under the Medicare program and must pay HI payroll taxes. Beginning July 1, 1991, State and local employees who were not members of a public retirement system were mandatorily covered under Social Security. This requirement was contained in the 1990 Omnibus Budget Reconciliation Act (OBRA).

While the most recent year for which actual data are available is 1990, the Social Security Administration estimates that in 1993, 21.5 million individuals will work at some time during the year for a State or local government, and the wages of 77 percent of these individuals will be covered by Social Security. Some 2.2 million of the 16.6 million covered State and local workers are estimated to have been covered as a result of OBRA 1990. Table 3–8 shows State-by-State data on State and local government jobs covered in 1990.

TABLE 3–7.—SOCIAL SECURITY COVERAGE, 1990

[In millions]

Occupational group	Number of employees	Covered	
		Number	Percent
Specifically exempt from OASDI coverage:			
Federal Civilian employees	4.3	2.5	58.1
Voluntary coverage:			
State and local government	20.2	13.5	66.8
Industry and commerce	92.6	92.4	99.8
Nonprofit	7.9	7.8	98.7
Farm	1.2	1.0	83.3
Domestic	1.0	0.5	50.0
Self-employed	10.6	8.1	76.4

[2] Terminations were prohibited as of April 1983.

TABLE 3–8.—ESTIMATES OF SOCIAL SECURITY COVERAGE OF WORKERS WITH STATE AND LOCAL GOVERNMENT EMPLOYMENT, 1990

[Based on 1-percent sample; numbers in thousands]

State	All workers [1]	Covered workers	Percent covered
Total	20,254	13,538	67
Alabama	339	309	91
Alaska	81	30	37
Arizona	360	321	89
Arkansas	181	166	92
California	2,185	743	34
Colorado	310	105	34
Connecticut	251	151	60
Delaware	60	44	73
Florida	971	776	80
Georgia	560	443	79
Hawaii	94	59	63
Idaho	101	102	101
Illinois	981	461	47
Indiana	428	356	83
Iowa	270	235	87
Kansas	249	222	89
Kentucky	300	225	75
Louisiana	350	74	21
Maine	104	47	45
Maryland	393	347	88
Massachusetts	473	19	4
Michigan	784	643	82
Minnesota	401	256	64
Mississippi	220	200	91
Missouri	381	286	75
Montana	84	72	86
Nebraska	160	144	90
Nevada	82	21	26
New Hampshire	88	77	88
New Jersey	578	544	94
New Mexico	165	129	78
New York	1,673	1,343	80
North Carolina	562	501	89
North Dakota	69	61	88
Ohio	828	25	3
Oklahoma	263	238	90
Oregon	259	231	89
Pennsylvania	733	673	92
Rhode Island	73	44	60
South Carolina	310	276	89
South Dakota	70	64	91

TABLE 3–8.—ESTIMATES OF SOCIAL SECURITY COVERAGE OF WORKERS WITH STATE AND LOCAL GOVERNMENT EMPLOYMENT, 1990—Continued

[Based on 1-percent sample; numbers in thousands]

State	All workers [1]	Covered workers	Percent covered
Tennessee	390	308	79
Texas	1,275	638	50
Utah	158	142	90
Vermont	54	51	94
Virginia	498	463	93
Washington	398	335	84
West Virginia	155	138	89
Wisconsin	439	343	78
Wyoming	63	57	90

[1] Includes seasonal and part-time workers for whom State and local government employment was not the major job.

Source: Social Security Administration Office of Research and Statistics.

SOCIAL SECURITY ADMINISTRATIVE EXPENSES

The costs of administering the Social Security retirement and disability programs are financed from the Social Security trust funds, subject to annual appropriations. Traditionally these costs are low, comprising between 1 and 2 percent of annual benefit payments. During fiscal year 1993, they amounted to $3.0 billion.

These trust-fund financed administrative funds comprised 51 percent of the Social Security Administration's 1993 administrative budget. The agency received another 14 percent from the Medicare trust funds, as well as 35 percent from general revenues for administration of Supplemental Security Income (SSI). This brought SSA's total administrative budget to $4.8 billion (excluding the special appropriation for disability and automation investment).

While Social Security benefit payments were taken off-budget in 1990, the budgetary treatment of administrative expenses remains controversial. On the one hand, the Office of Management and Budget interprets the 1990 statute as applying to benefit payments only; and it has placed administrative costs under the budgetary cap on domestic discretionary spending. The Congressional Budget Office, on the other hand, interprets the 1990 statute as applying to all Social Security trust funds payments, including both benefits and administrative expenses. Legislation mandating that OMB comply with the CBO interpretation has been introduced in the 103d Congress.

TABLE 3–9.—NET ADMINISTRATIVE EXPENSES IN MILLIONS OF DOLLARS AND AS A PERCENTAGE OF BENEFIT PAYMENTS, FISCAL YEARS 1989–93

Fiscal year	Total administrative expenses	OASI trust fund benefit payments	DI trust fund benefit payments	Total benefit payments
1989	2,407	.8	3.3	1.1
1990	2,280	.7	3.0	.9
1991	2,535	.7	2.9	1.0
1992	2,668	.7	2.8	.9
1993	2,955	.8	2.8	1.0

Source: Social Security Office of the Actuary.

CURRENT SHORT-RANGE STATUS OF THE TRUST FUNDS

An assessment of the short-range status of the trust funds depends heavily on the economic assumptions underlying the estimates because both the revenues and expenditures of the program are tremendously affected by general economic trends such as unemployment, wage growth, and inflation. Table 3–10 presents short-term projections of the financial status of the trust funds under the assumptions contained in the Congressional Budget Office baseline.

Status of OASDI trust funds

Under the President's budget as well as CBO baseline assumptions, the combined OASDI trust funds will continue the growth begun in 1984 throughout the 5-year projection period incorporated in the President's and CBO's forecasts. Under CBO's assumptions, the annual excess of revenues over benefit outlays (sometimes called the "surplus") will reach almost $100 billion by 1999. Throughout the 1990's, and for some period into the next century, the favorable demographic pattern of a large baby-boom generation at peak earning years combined with the retirement of the relatively small generation born during the Depression should ensure large trust fund reserves.

For the combined OASDI funds, the trust fund reserve ratio is estimated to increase from 114 percent at the beginning of 1994 to 127 percent for 1995, and then continue to increase each year thereafter, reaching 182 percent by 1999.

TABLE 3–10.—CURRENT LAW PROJECTIONS OF THE OLD-AGE AND SURVIVORS INSUR-
ANCE AND DISABILITY INSURANCE TRUST FUND OUTLAYS, INCOME, AND BALANCES
UNDER CBO'S BASELINE ECONOMIC ASSUMPTIONS

[By fiscal year, in billions of dollars]

	Fiscal year—						
	1993	1994	1995	1996	1997	1998	1999
Old-age survivors insurance:							
Total outlays	270	282.6	296.2	311.4	324.7	339.7	355.5
Income	319.3	348.4	371.3	393.8	417.5	442.9	488.8
Year-end balance	355.7	421.4	496.5	578.8	871.6	774.7	887.9
Start-of-year balance as a percent of outlays [1]	113	126	142	159	178	198	218
Disability insurance:							
Total outlays	34.6	38.2	41.5	45.0	48.5	52.1	55.9
Income	32.1	34.7	36.3	37.9	39.4	40.8	42.1
Year-end balance	10.3	6.8	1.6	−5.5	−14.6	−25.9	−39.7
Start-of-year balance as a percent of outlays [1]	37	27	10	4	−11	−28	−45
Combined OASI and DI:							
Total outlays	304.6	320.8	337.7	356.4	373.2	391.9	411.4
Income	351.4	383.1	407.6	431.7	456.8	483.7	510.8
Year-end balance	388.0	428.2	498.1	573.4	657.0	748.8	848.3
Start-of-year balance as a percent of outlays [1]	105	114	127	140	164	168	182

[1] Start-of-year balances are computed as the balances at the end of the previous fiscal year. Beginning in 1996, they also include advanced tax transfers on October 1 for the DI trust fund.

Source: Based on Congressional Budget Office January 1994 baseline economic assumptions.

Budgetary treatment of OASDI trust funds

Social Security and other Federal programs that operate through trust funds were counted officially in the Federal budget beginning in fiscal year 1969. This was done administratively by President Johnson. At the time Congress did not have a budget-making process. In 1974, Congress began setting budget goals annually through passage of budget resolutions. Like the budgets the President prepared, these resolutions reflected a unified budget approach that included trust fund programs such as Social Security in the budget totals. Although Social Security continued to be counted in the budget throughout the 1970s and 1980s, measures were enacted in 1983, 1985, and 1987 making the program a more visible component of the budget and imposing potential procedural hurdles for budgetary bills containing Social Security changes. Most significant among them was the Balanced Budget and Emergency Deficit Control Act of 1985 (P.L. 99–177), which incorporated the original Gramm-Rudman-Hollings deficit-reduction procedures and contained specific provisions setting forth the budgetary treatment of the OASDI trust funds. The act required that the OASDI trust funds be taken off-budget beginning in fiscal year 1986. (The 1983 Social Security Amendments had previously required that the funds be taken off budget in fiscal year 1993.) However, the act also required that the income and outgo of the OASDI trust funds be taken into account in determining if Federal spending had to be cut to meet the Gramm-Rudman-Hollings deficit-reduction goals.

This meant that the OASDI trust funds would be counted in the budget figures throughout the period in which Gramm-Rudman-Hollings was in force which originally was fiscal years 1986–91, but was extended for 2 years—to fiscal year 1993—by the Balanced Budget and Emergency Deficit Control Reaffirmation Act of 1987 (P.L. 100–119).

Other provisions of the balanced budget act exempted OASDI benefits from automatic reductions, or so-called sequestration. Thus, while OASDI income and outgo were counted to determine the size of the Federal deficit, OASDI benefits were not subject to automatic reduction if the deficit was too high.[3] The act further included provisions making it "out of order" for either the House or Senate to take up changes in OASDI as part of a budget reconciliation measure. Separate votes in each body—suspending or otherwise altering the rules under which the respective bodies operate—were required to make consideration of any proposed OASDI change permissible. In the Senate, this would require approval by three-fifths of its members.

Social Security also was affected by restrictions in the Act on bringing up legislative changes that would violate budget resolution totals or separate spending and revenue allocations for programs under the jurisdiction of each committee made subsequent to passage of budget resolutions. Social Security was affected by these restrictions in the same way as other programs and tax provisions; points of order (so-called sections 302 and 311 objections) could be raised against legislation involving revenue reductions or spending increases that violated the budget resolution totals or subsequent spending allocations by committees for the first year to which the budget resolution applied. These, too, could be overridden only by a vote of three-fifths of the Senate.

The Omnibus Budget Reconciliation Act of 1990 (P.L. 101–508) made major changes in the Federal budget process. Among them was the removal of the Social Security trust funds from all Federal budget calculations, including calculations of budget deficits and surpluses. As a result, OASDI no longer affects or is affected by limitations caused by Federal deficits or the budget process in general (with the exception of administrative expenses).

The 1990 law established specific dollar limits on discretionary spending (mostly annual appropriations) and a so-called pay-as-you-go requirement for direct spending (mostly entitlement programs) and revenues. For fiscal years 1991–95, these new limits and the pay-as-you-go requirement replaced the overall deficit-reduction targets established under the former Gramm-Rudman-Hollings procedures. As under the old law, if any spending limit or the pay-as-you-go rule is violated, the President may be required to issue sequestration orders bringing spending down to the prescribed limits.

Social Security spending and revenues are excluded from these new limits and overall targets, with the exception of administrative expenditures, which, under an OMB interpretation, are incor-

---

[3] However, administrative expenses of the Social Security Administration were subject to sequestration.

porated in a limit on discretionary domestic spending.[4] Social Security is also exempt from sequestration orders, as it was under the old law (again, with the exception of administrative expenses).

Finally, the new law continues the old law provision (section 310(g)) that permits points of order against reconciliation bills that contain Social Security measures.

OASDI tax receipts are expected to exceed benefits and other expenses continuously over the budget forecast period, i.e., the next 5 years. Barring a major recession, the excess receipts should grow substantially. What this means is that, with all other things held constant, surplus OASDI receipts would have offset a substantial portion of the deficits the Government incurs with respect to its other activities if Social Security had continued to be counted in the budget. The following table and chart show how the removal of the operations of the OASDI trust funds from the budget calculations affects CBO's 5-year forecast of Federal budget deficits.

---

[4] Under the law prior to passage of the Budget Enforcement Act of 1990, Social Security administrative expenses were subject to sequestration if Gramm-Rudman-Hollings deficit targets were exceeded. The 1990 law states that Social Security is not to be counted as budget authority or outlays for purposes of the Gramm-Rudman deficit reduction law (which the new law amends). However, it also lists Social Security among the programs subject to the discretionary domestic spending limit. One interpretation of this is that Social Security administrative expenses, as discretionary spending, are subject to the domestic discretionary limit. An alternative interpretation is that the provision excluding Social Security from all aspects of the budget law exempts these expenses from the discretionary limit. The inconsistency appears to give OMB latitude to make either interpretation.

TABLE 3–11.—PROJECTED FEDERAL BUDGET DEFICITS, INCLUDING AND EXCLUDING OASDI TRUST FUNDS IN THE CALCULATION

[By fiscal year, in billions of dollars]

Fiscal year	1994	1995	1996	1997	1998	1999
Projected budget deficit:						
Including OASDI	228	180	180	192	187	213
Excluding OASDI	290	249	255	275	279	312
Increase in projected deficit from excluding OASDI	82	70	75	84	92	99

Note.—Details may not add to totals due to rounding.

Source: Congressional Budget Office based on January 1994 economic assumptions.

CHART 3–1. FEDERAL BUDGET DEFICITS WITH AND WITHOUT OASDI

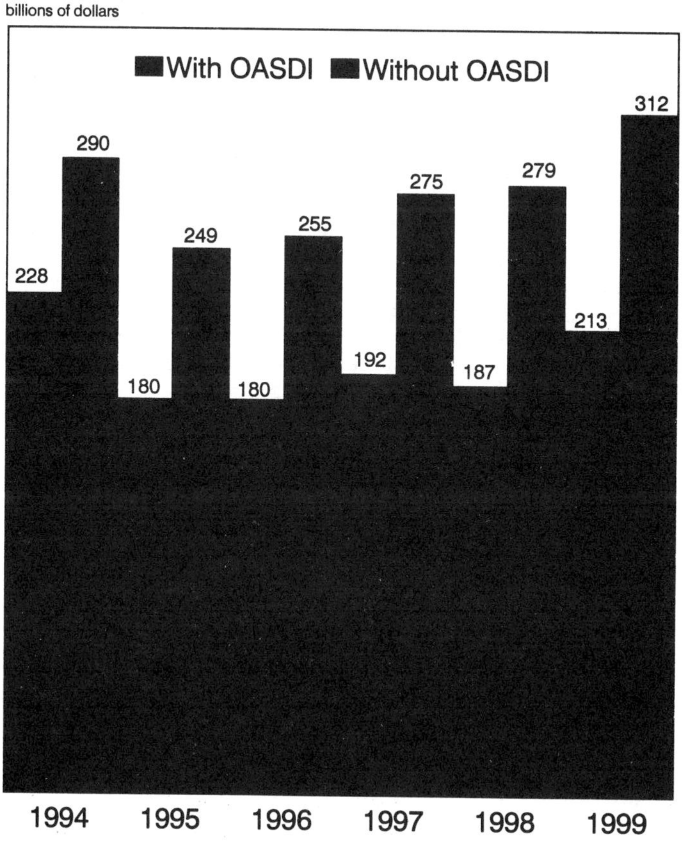

billions of dollars

Source: CRS, based on CBO baseline forecast, March 1994

NEW PROCEDURES TO PROTECT THE TRUST FUNDS

Since the fiscal constraints of the budget process no longer apply to Social Security, the 1990 budget law established separate rules for the House and Senate that make it difficult to bring measures to a floor vote if they would weaken the financial condition of the program.

In the House, a point of order can be raised against a bill that includes more than $250 million in Social Security spending increases or revenue reductions over a 5-year period, unless the bill also contains offsetting spending reductions or tax increases that bring its net impact within the limit. In determining whether a bill falls within the $250 million limit, any costs from prior legislation (i.e., enacted in the current or previous 4 years) that fall within the 5-year budgeting period would be counted. Also, a point of order can be raised against a measure that would increase long-range (75 year) program costs or reduce long-range revenues by at least 0.02 percent of taxable payroll.

In the Senate, budget resolutions must set specific amounts for Social Security income and outgo for the first fiscal year to which the budget resolution applies and cumulative amounts for a 5-year period. These amounts must be completely separate from budget resolution totals. Further, the Social Security income and outgo recommended in budget resolutions reported by the Senate Budget Committee cannot narrow the difference between Social Security income and outgo projected under current law. (Doing so could draw an objection). Once a conference agreement on a budget resolution is reached, allocations made to the Finance Committee must include a Social Security outlay allocation. Budget Act points of order can then be raised against Social Security bills that would cause outlays to be increased or revenues to be reduced (without offsetting changes) from those reflected in the budget resolution and Finance Committee allocation. Overriding such an objection requires a vote of three-fifths of the Senate.

THE IMPACT OF THE OASDI SURPLUSES ON THE FINANCIAL CONDITION OF THE GOVERNMENT

As attention is increasingly drawn to the surplus OASDI receipts, questions have emerged about how the money is actually used. The basic concern is that the money was intended to be invested in the OASDI trust funds, to be set aside for future years, and not to be used to finance other Government spending today. However, the issue is a complex one and is often confusing and poorly described.

Part of the confusion arises from a lack of understanding that OASDI taxes are not deposited in trust funds and OASDI benefits are not paid from trust funds. OASDI taxes are deposited in the Federal Treasury like other taxes and become part of the general pool of funds through which the Government functions. Airport and highway taxes, civil service retirement contributions, Medicare receipts, and many other forms of dedicated Federal revenues—*all of which have corresponding trust funds*—are treated likewise. The trust funds themselves receive credit for the revenues when the Government receives them, usually in the form of postings of non-marketable, interest-bearing Federal securities. Conversely, when the Government makes expenditures for trust fund programs, the money is paid from the Treasury, and the securities posted to the trust funds are reduced by a corresponding amount. Simply stated, the OASDI trust funds are given IOUs when OASDI taxes are received by the Treasury, and those IOUs are taken back when the Treasury makes expenditures on the program's behalf. This handling of OASDI's finances goes back to the inception of the program and has not been altered by the inclusion or exclusion of the OASDI trust funds in or from the Federal budget.

In effect, whether or not OASDI is counted as part of the Federal budget, OASDI taxes will continue to be deposited in the Federal Treasury and the trust funds will continue to receive credit for them as they are collected. Moreover, this credit will continue to give the Treasury Department "authority," or what might be described as a "permanent appropriation," to spend for OASDI.[5]

The more fundamental issue about the use of surplus OASDI taxes revolves around perceptions of how the existence of this money will influence Congress and the administration in making future fiscal policy decisions for the Government as a whole. Since surplus OASDI taxes are deposited in the Federal Treasury, there is no way of knowing their ultimate use. In the course of fiscal policymaking, three basic uses can be made of the money: (1) It can be spent on other programs; (2) it can cause other taxes to be lower than they otherwise would be; or (3) it can cause Government borrowing from financial markets to be lower.[6]

It is sometimes stated, ipso facto, that surplus OASDI taxes cause the Government to borrow less from financial markets. However, this perspective represents an oversimplification. The law has always dictated that OASDI trust funds be credited with Federal securities to reflect OASDI tax receipts, but it has never dictated how the surplus receipts themselves are to be used by the Federal Government. The outcome—*what happens to the money*—basically depends on what one assumes fiscal policymakers would decide about spending and taxation for the Government overall if the surplus OASDI taxes were not levied. If levying them influences Congress to avoid cutting spending elsewhere or raising other taxes, Government borrowing from financial markets is not being reduced.

The Government has the potential to increase savings in the economy by reducing the amount of borrowing it does in financial markets. However, this outcome depends on its ability to reduce the difference between its overall income and outgo. It is the Government's net deficit overall that determines how much is really being borrowed from financial markets, not a surplus arising in one of its accounts. All other things held constant, cutting Social Security taxes or increasing Social Security spending would impede efforts to reduce Federal borrowing from financial markets in the same way as any other tax reductions or spending increases, and

---

[5] Meaning that as long as there are securities posted to the OASDI trust funds, the Treasury Department can continue to make OASDI expenditures.

[6] While the Government is said to "borrow" these surplus receipts, technically, it is crediting one of its accounts and debiting another—i.e., borrowing money from itself.

thereby curtail efforts by the Government to increase savings in the economy.

The long-range impact of the OASDI surpluses

In their 1994 report, the Social Security trustees projected that surplus OASDI taxes would continue until the early years of the post-World War II baby-boom generation's retirement—i.e., until sometime between 2010 and 2015. After that, OASDI taxes would fall short of expenditures indefinitely. The program then would have to draw on the IOUs accumulated in its trust funds, and the Government would have to make good on them. In essence, beginning sometime between 2010 and 2015, the Government would no longer have the benefit of surplus OASDI taxes and, in fact, would have to find other resources to cover the trust funds' IOUs. How these resources will be obtained poses a major long-range fiscal policy question. Although the OASDI trust funds would have grown substantially—reaching approximately $1.3 trillion in 2015 as measured in constant 1994 dollars—and would continue to provide authority for the Treasury Department to keep spending for the program until almost the middle of the next century, the trust funds themselves will not provide the resources to pay the benefits. They simply give the Social Security system a claim on other Government resources. What this means in practice is that when the trust funds' IOUs are needed because OASDI tax receipts fall below expenditures, the Government will have to raise other taxes, curtail other expenditures, or increase its borrowing from the public.

CHART 3–2. PROJECTED SIZE OF SOCIAL SECURITY TRUST FUNDS

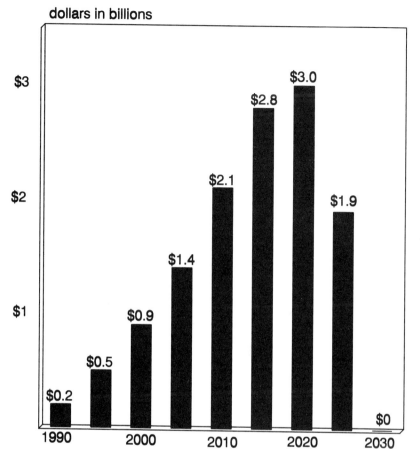

dollars in billions

Source: 1994 trustees' report, intermediate assumptions

CHART 3–3. SOCIAL SECURITY INCOME AND COST RATES, 1995–2065

FIGURE II.F3.—ESTIMATED OASDI INCOME RATES AND COST RATES BY
ALTERNATIVE, CALENDAR YEARS 1984-2070

[As a percentage of taxable payroll]

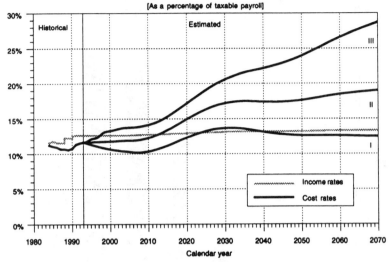

Economists argue that if the surplus OASDI taxes arising over the next two decades were to result in a reduction in Government borrowing from the public, more money would exist in investment markets, which could lead to greater economic growth. If this were to occur, extracting resources from the economy in the future to honor the OASDI claims would not necessarily be burdensome. Said another way, if one accepts the premise that reductions in the unified budget deficit today will lead to economic growth by increasing the amount of resources available for investment, then surplus OASDI taxes today could aid in building a higher economic base in the future from which to draw the resources to pay future OASDI benefits.

Even if fiscal policy decisions do lead to enhanced savings, and the Nation's growth rate is augmented in the coming decades, OASDI costs would grow automatically with the economy. In essence, larger OASDI claims would accompany greater economic growth (since that growth would manifest itself in higher wages and entitlement to larger benefits). Further, the post-World War II baby-boom generation and future retirees will raise financial demands across the board, not just for OASDI, as the ratio of workers to retirees falls in the next century. The goods and services to be consumed by society cannot be stockpiled in advance, and the economy will have to adjust. Whether this would be a mild or severe adjustment is largely conjecture, but the manner in which retirement claims are accumulated (publicly or privately) does not necessarily determine it. It may revolve just as much on how the future elderly feel about retiring versus working. No matter how much nominal wealth can be cashed in to produce given levels of retirement income, the amount of goods and services that can be furnished will depend heavily on the proportion of the population able and willing to do the furnishing.

LONG RANGE STATUS OF THE TRUST FUNDS

OASDI trust funds

Because the Social Security program has been designed as a contributory system in which those who pay the taxes supporting it are considered to be earning the right to future benefits, Congress has traditionally required long-range estimates of the program's actuarial balance and has set future tax rates with a view to assuring that the income of the program will be sufficient to cover its outgo. Under current procedures, the long-range actuarial analysis of the cash benefits program covers a 75-year period—this would generally be long enough to cover the anticipated retirement years of those currently in the work force.

The long-range status of the Social Security trust funds is ordinarily expressed in terms of "percent of taxable payroll" rather than in dollar amounts. This permits a direct comparison between the tax rate actually in the law and the cost of the program. For example, if the program is projected to have a deficit of "1 percent of taxable payroll," this means that the Social Security tax rates now in the law would have to be increased by 0.5 percent points for employee and employer, each, in order to pay for the benefits due under present law. (Alternatively, the program could be brought back into balance by an equivalent reduction in benefit outgo or by a combination of revenue increases and outgo reductions.) If the program is projected to have a deficit of 1.5 percent of taxable payroll and expenditures are projected to be 10 percent of taxable payroll, then, under the given set of assumptions, 15 percent (1.5 divided by 10) of expenditures could not be met with that tax schedule. In 1994, the total taxable payroll is estimated to be $2.8 trillion so that in 1994 terms, 1.5 percent of payroll represented about $42 billion.

In the short range, the financial soundness of each of the trust funds can be assessed by considering the size of the trust fund balance, in absolute terms and as a percentage of the annual expenditures, and whether the balance is growing or declining. In the long range, the traditional measure of financial soundness has been the actuarial balance of the system. The actuarial balance is defined as the difference between the total summarized income rate and the total summarized cost rate.

Projections of the long-range financial condition of the Social Security programs are affected by three basic types of factors: (1) demographic factors, such as rates of fertility, life expectancy, and labor force participation, which determine how many workers there will be in the society in relation to nonworking beneficiaries; (2) economic factors such as unemployment, productivity, and inflation; and (3) factors specifically related to the Social Security program, such as benefit levels, total number of covered workers, and percent of eligible workers drawing early retirement benefits.

In projecting the long-term condition of the OASDI trust funds, the actuaries at the Social Security Administration employ three sets of alternative economic and demographic assumptions. Alternative I is based on optimistic assumptions, alternative II on moderate assumptions, and alternative III on pessimistic assumptions. In general, alternative II is considered the most balanced estimate of long-term solvency.

It is clear that these factors cannot be predicted with any certainty as far into the future as 75 years, and the long-range projections should not be taken as absolute predictions of deficits or surpluses in the funds.

Beginning with the 1988 trustees report, the Social Security trustees used an alternative method of determining actuarial balance. Under the "present value" method, interest earnings on the fund are more fully recognized. Calculations were based on the present value of future income, outgo and taxable payroll by discounting the future annual amounts at an assumed rate of interest.

Traditionally, the trustees based their conclusion about the long-range actuarial condition of the program on the "closeness" of the income and cost rates *when averaged over a 75-year period.* If the income rate was between 95 and 105 percent of the cost rate over this projection period, the system was said to be in close actuarial balance.

The 1991 trustees report incorporated a more refined measure of actuarial soundness "designed to reveal problems occurring at any time during the" 75-year measuring period. The 5 percent "tolerance" (i.e., the amount of acceptable actuarial deficit) was retained in measuring the program's actuarial soundness for the 75-year period as a whole, but less tolerance is now permitted for shorter periods of valuation. The spread between income and outgo is evaluated throughout the measuring period in reaching a conclusion of whether close actuarial balance exists, with the amount of acceptable deviation gradually declining from 5 percent for the full 75-year period to 0 (or no acceptable deviation) for the first 10-year segment of the measuring period. (To meet the short-range test of financial adequacy, the reserve balance at the end of the first 10-year segment must be at or higher than 100 percent of annual expenditures, which condition is consistent with the 10-year segment of the long-range test of close actuarial balance, and also must be expected to reach that level within the first 5 years and then remain there.) Under this new test, if income were at least 95 percent of the cost level for the 75-year period as a whole, the trust fund still could be deemed to be out of close actuarial balance if income and outgo were too small, compared to cost, for shorter segments of the measuring period.

Under this new measure, the trustees concluded in their 1994 report, as they did in their 1991, 1992, and 1993 reports, that OASDI is not in close actuarial balance over the long run.

1994 TRUSTEES' REPORT

The 1994 Trustees Report was released just prior to the publication of the 1994 Greenbook. Following are highlights of the 1994 report, accompanied by tables showing projections for the trust funds.

• In the short range, the assets of the OASI and DI Trust Funds, if combined, would be expected to increase under intermediate assumptions from the current level of $378.3 billion, or 116 percent of annual expenditures, to $1,048 billion, or 197 percent of annual expenditures, at the beginning of the year 2003.

• The OASI Trust Fund is expected to increase rapidly during the next 10 years, from 129 percent of annual expenditures at the beginning of 1994 to about 259 percent of annual expenditures at the beginning of the year 2003, based on the intermediate assumptions.

• The assets of the DI Trust Fund are expected to decline steadily from $9.0 billion at the end of 1993 until the fund is exhausted in 1995, unless corrective legislation is enacted promptly to strengthen the financing of the DI program. The Board of Trustees is again recommending a reallocation of contribution rates between the OASI and DI Trust Funds, to remedy the expected financial shortfalls in the DI Trust Fund.

• In the long range, income and expenditures are generally expressed as a percentage of the total amount of earnings subject to taxation under the OASDI program (referred to as "taxable payroll"). Summarized income and cost rates over the 75-year long-range period are determined through present-value calculations and by taking into account actual beginning fund balances and targeted ending fund balances (or reserves) of 100 percent of annual expenditures.

Overall, for the period 1994–2068, the difference between the summarized income and cost rates for the OASDI program is a deficit of 2.13 percent of taxable payroll based on the intermediate assumptions. This is a substantial increase over the estimated deficit of 1.46 percent of taxable payroll shown in the 1993 Annual Report for the period 1993–2067, based on the intermediate assumptions. The increase in the deficit is attributable to a number of factors, including an increase in the estimated level of future average benefits, a decrease in the assumed ultimate level of average real-wage gains in the future, an increase in the assumed ultimate levels of disability incidence rates, and the change in the 75-year projection period to include the relatively large annual deficit for the year 2068.

• On a combined basis, the OASDI program is not in close actuarial balance over the next 75 years. In addition, the individual OASI and DI Trust Funds are not in close actuarial balance. These results are the same as those shown in the 1993 Annual Report.

• Income from OASDI payroll taxes represents 12.4 percent of taxable payroll. Since the tax rate is not scheduled to change in the future under present law, OASDI payroll tax income as a percentage of taxable payroll remains constant at 12.4 percent. Adding the OASDI income from the income taxation of benefits to the income from payroll taxes yields a total "income rate" of 12.6 percent. This rate is estimated to increase gradually to 13.3 percent of taxable payroll by the end of the 75-year projection period based on the intermediate assumptions. The growth is attributable, in part, to increasing proportions in both the number of beneficiaries and the amount of their benefits subject to taxation in the future. These proportions will increase because the income thresholds, above which benefits are taxable, are not indexed to future increases in average prices or average income.

• OASDI expenditures for benefit payments and administrative expenses currently represent about 11.6 percent of taxable payroll. This "cost rate" is estimated to remain below the corresponding income rate for the next 19 years, based on the intermediate assumptions. With the retirement of the "baby-boom" generation starting in about 2010, OASDI costs will increase rapidly relative to the taxable earnings of workers. By the end of the 75-year projection period, the OASDI cost rate is estimated to reach 18.9 percent under the intermediate assumptions, resulting in an annual deficit of about 5.6 percent.

• Under the intermediate assumptions, the excess of OASDI tax revenues over expenditures for the next 19 years, together with interest earnings on the trust funds, will result in a rapid accumulation of assets for the combined OASI and DI Trust Funds during this period. However, total income is estimated to fall short of expenditures beginning in 2019 and continuing thereafter, under the intermediate assumptions. In this circumstance, trust fund assets would be redeemed to cover the difference. The assets of the combined OASI and DI Trust Funds are estimated to be depleted under present law in 2029 based on the intermediate assumptions.

TABLE 3–12.—MAXIMUM TRUST FUND RATIOS AND YEAR OF EXHAUSTION FOR THE OASI, DI AND COMBINED TRUST FUNDS UNDER ALTERNATIVE ASSUMPTIONS

	OASI	DI	Combined
Alternative I:			
Maximum trust fund ratio (percent)	1,014	23	882
Year attained	2070	1994	2070
Year of exhaustion	....	1995	....
Alternative II:			
Maximum trust fund ratio (percent)	361	23	241
Year attained	2014	1994	2012
Year of exhaustion	2036	1995	2029
Alternative III:			
Maximum trust fund ratio (percent)	180	22	131
Year attained	2007	1994	1998
Year of exhaustion	2023	1995	2014

Source: 1994 OASDI Trustees' report.

TABLE 3–13.—ESTIMATED INCOME RATES AND COST RATES UNDER ALTERNATIVE II OF THE 1994 TRUSTEES' REPORT, CALENDAR YEARS 1994–2070

[As a percentage of taxable payroll]

Calendar year	OASI			DI			Combined		
	Income rate	Cost rate	Balance	Income rate	Cost rate	Balance	Income rate	Cost rate	Balance
1994	11.42	10.24	1.18	1.21	1.40	−0.19	12.63	11.64	0.98
1995	11.39	10.21	1.19	1.21	1.47	−.26	12.60	11.67	.93
1996	11.42	10.19	1.23	1.21	1.52	−.31	12.63	11.71	.92
1997	11.42	10.15	1.27	1.21	1.57	−.35	12.63	11.72	.92
1998	11.42	10.12	1.30	1.21	1.62	−.41	12.64	11.74	.90
1999	11.42	10.09	1.34	1.21	1.67	−.45	12.64	11.75	.88
2000	11.20	10.06	1.14	1.43	1.71	−.27	12.64	11.77	.87
2001	11.21	10.05	1.15	1.43	1.75	−.32	12.64	11.80	.84
2002	11.21	10.04	1.16	1.44	1.79	−.36	12.64	11.83	.81
2003	11.21	10.03	1.18	1.44	1.83	−.40	12.64	11.86	.78
2005	11.23	9.99	1.25	1.44	1.90	−.46	12.67	11.89	.78
2010	11.31	10.24	1.07	1.44	2.03	−.59	12.75	12.27	.48
2015	11.40	11.31	.09	1.45	2.10	−.66	12.85	13.42	−.56
2020	11.50	12.82	−1.31	1.45	2.14	−.69	12.96	14.96	−2.01
2025	11.60	14.15	−2.55	1.45	2.21	−.76	13.05	16.36	−3.31
2030	11.67	15.03	−3.36	1.46	2.20	−.74	13.13	17.22	−4.10
2035	11.71	15.37	−3.66	1.46	2.15	−.69	13.17	17.52	−4.35
2040	11.73	15.27	−3.54	1.46	2.15	−.69	13.19	17.42	−4.23
2045	11.74	15.18	−3.44	1.46	2.24	−.78	13.20	17.42	−4.22
2050	11.77	15.35	−3.58	1.46	2.29	−.83	13.23	17.64	−4.41
2055	11.80	15.75	−3.95	1.46	2.32	−.86	13.26	18.07	−4.81
2060	11.83	16.19	−4.35	1.46	2.29	−.83	13.30	18.48	−5.18
2065	11.86	16.49	−4.64	1.46	2.28	−.81	13.32	18.77	−5.45
2070	11.87	16.71	−4.84	1.46	2.29	−.83	13.34	19.00	−5.67

Note.—Totals do not necessarily equal the sums of rounded components.

Source: 1994 OASDI Trustees' report.

TABLE 3–14.—ESTIMATED TRUST FUND RATIOS UNDER ALTERNATIVE II OF THE 1994 TRUSTEES' REPORT, CALENDAR YEARS 1994–2070

[In percent]

Calendar year	OASI	DI	Combined
1994	129	23	116
1995	143	8	126
1996	157	(1)	136
1997	173	(1)	146
1998	188	(1)	156
1999	204	(1)	165
2000	219	(1)	173
2001	233	(1)	182
2002	246	(1)	189
2003	259	(1)	197
2005	286	(1)	211
2010	346	(1)	239
2015	359	(1)	231
2020	316	(1)	180
2025	238	(1)	96
2030	139	(1)	(1)
2035	28	(1)	(1)
2040	(1)	(1)	(1)
2045	(1)	(1)	(1)
2050	(1)	(1)	(1)
2055	(1)	(1)	(1)
2060	(1)	(1)	(1)
2065	(1)	(1)	(1)
2070	(1)	(1)	(1)
Trust fund is estimated to be exhausted in	2036	1995	2029

[1] The trust fund is estimated to have been exhausted by the beginning of this year. The last line of the table shows the specific year of trust fund exhaustion.

Note.—The OASDI ratios shown for years after a given fund is estimated to be exhausted are theoretical and are shown for informations purposes only.

Source: 1994 OASDI Trustees' report.

TABLE 3–15.—ESTIMATED OPERATIONS OF THE COMBINED OASI AND DI TRUST FUNDS IN CONSTANT 1994 DOLLARS[1] UNDER ALTERNATIVE II, CALENDAR YEARS 1994–2070

[In billions]

Calendar year	Income ex- cluding in- terest	Interest in- come	Total in- come	Outgo	Assets at end of year
1994	$347.0	$30.4	$377.4	$324.8	$430.9
1995	357.5	32.2	389.7	332.0	475.4
1996	365.4	34.2	399.6	338.9	521.0
1997	372.1	36.3	408.4	345.6	566.8
1998	378.1	38.5	416.6	352.1	612.3
1999	384.4	40.7	425.1	358.5	657.1
2000	390.9	42.9	433.8	364.8	701.5
2001	397.3	45.2	442.5	371.5	745.5
2002	403.5	47.7	451.2	378.6	789.5
2003	410.4	50.1	460.6	385.9	833.8
2005	426.6	55.3	481.9	401.2	925.9
2010	467.0	68.7	535.7	450.2	1,159.8
2015	504.1	76.6	580.8	527.3	1,273.6
2020	537.8	68.2	606.1	622.3	1,106.4
2025[2]	570.9	38.2	609.0	716.9	578.8

[1] The adjustment from current to constant dollars is by the CPI.
[2] Estimates for later years are not shown because the combined OASI and DI Trust Funds are estimated to become exhausted in 2029 under alternative II and in 2014 under alternative III.

Note.—Totals do not necessarily equal the sums of rounded components.

Source: 1994 OASDI Trustees' Report.

TABLE 3–16.—ESTIMATED COST OF OASDI AND HI SYSTEMS AS PERCENT OF GDP
UNDER ALTERNATIVE II, 1994–2070

[In percent]

Calendar year	OASDI	HI	OASDI and HI
Alternative II:			
1994	4.83	1.60	6.43
1995	4.82	1.66	6.47
1996	4.82	1.71	6.53
1997	4.82	1.76	6.58
1998	4.82	1.82	6.64
1999	4.82	1.89	6.71
2000	4.82	1.95	6.77
2001	4.82	2.01	6.84
2002	4.83	2.07	6.90
2003	4.83	2.13	6.97
2005	4.83	2.24	7.08
2010	4.96	2.48	7.44
2015	5.38	2.84	8.22
2020	5.95	3.22	9.16
2025	6.44	3.64	10.08
2030	6.71	4.04	10.75
2035	6.76	4.33	11.09
2040	6.66	4.47	11.14
2045	6.60	4.55	11.15
2050	6.62	4.59	11.21
2055	6.72	4.66	11.38
2060	6.80	4.77	11.57
2065	6.84	4.90	11.74
2070	6.86	5.03	11.89
Summarized rates: [1]			
25-year: 1994–2018	5.22	2.39	7.61
50-year: 1994–2043	5.80	3.10	8.90
75-year: 1994–2068	6.02	3.51	9.53

[1] Summarized rates are calculated on the present-value basis including the value of the trust funds on January 1, 1994 and the cost of reaching and maintaining a target trust fund level equal to 100 percent of annual expenditures by the end of the period.

Note.—Totals do not necessarily equal the sums of rounded components.

Source: 1994 Annual Report of the Board of Trustees of the Federal Old-Age and Survivors Insurance and Disability Insurance Trust Funds.

ECONOMIC AND DEMOGRAPHIC ASSUMPTIONS

The following tables provide specific information concerning the economic and demographic assumptions which underlie the Social Security trustees' 1994 short and long-run financial projections.

TABLE 3–17.—ECONOMIC ASSUMPTIONS IN THE 1994 TRUSTEES REPORT, 1960–2070

Calendar year	Average annual percentage change in—			Real-wage differential [3] (percent)	Average annual unemployment rate [4] (percent)
	Real GDP [1]	Average wages in covered employment	Consumer Price Index [2]		
Historical data:					
1960–64	3.9	3.4	1.3	2.1	5.7
1965–69	4.4	5.4	3.4	2.0	3.8
1970–74	2.4	6.3	6.1	.2	5.4
1975	−.8	6.7	9.1	−2.4	8.5
1976	4.9	8.7	5.7	3.0	7.7
1977	4.5	7.3	6.5	.8	7.1
1978	4.8	9.7	7.7	2.0	6.1
1979	2.5	9.8	11.4	−1.6	5.8
1980	−.5	9.0	13.4	−4.4	7.1
1981	1.8	9.8	10.3	−.5	7.6
1982	−2.2	6.5	6.0	.5	9.7
1983	3.9	5.1	3.0	2.1	9.6
1984	6.2	7.3	3.5	3.8	7.5
1985	3.2	4.3	3.5	.8	7.2
1986	2.9	5.1	1.6	3.5	7.0
1987	3.1	4.7	3.6	1.1	6.2
1988	3.9	4.8	4.0	.8	5.5
1989	2.5	4.3	4.8	−.5	5.3
1990	1.2	[5] 4.8	5.2	−.4	5.5
1991	−.7	[5] 3.8	4.0	−.2	6.7
1992	2.6	[5] 5.2	2.9	2.3	7.4
1993	[5] 2.9	[5] 2.4	2.8	−.5	6.8
Intermediate assumptions:					
1994	3.2	2.7	2.7	.0	6.3
1995	2.8	4.8	3.2	1.6	6.2
1996	2.6	4.3	3.3	1.0	6.0
1997	2.4	4.3	3.4	1.0	6.0
1998	2.2	4.3	3.5	.9	6.0
1999	2.2	4.6	3.7	.9	6.0
2000	2.1	4.8	3.9	.9	6.0
2001	2.0	4.8	4.0	.8	5.9
2002	2.0	5.0	4.0	1.0	5.9
2003	2.0	5.1	4.0	1.1	5.9

TABLE 3–17.—ECONOMIC ASSUMPTIONS IN THE 1994 TRUSTEES REPORT, 1960–2070—Continued

Calendar year	Average annual percentage change in—			Real-wage differen- tial [3] (per- cent)	Average annual unemploy- ment rate [4] (percent)
	Real GDP [1]	Average wages in covered employ- ment	Consumer Price Index [2]		
2010	1.7	5.1	4.0	1.1	6.0
2020	1.3	5.0	4.0	1.0	6.0
2030	1.3	5.0	4.0	1.0	6.0
2040	1.2	5.0	4.0	1.0	6.0
2050	1.2	5.0	4.0	1.0	6.0
2060	1.2	5.0	4.0	1.0	6.0
2070	1.2	5.0	4.0	1.0	6.0

[1] The real GDP (gross domestic product) is the value of total output of goods and services, expressed in 1987 dollars.

[2] The Consumer Price Index is the annual average value for the calendar year of the Consumer Price Index for Urban Wage Earners and Clerical Workers (CPI–W).

[3] The real-wage differential is the difference between the percentage increases, before rounding, in (1) the average annual wage in covered employment, and (2) the average annual Consumer Price Index.

[4] Through 2003, the rates shown are unadjusted civilian unemployment rates. After 2003, the rates are total rates (inclduing military personnel), adjusted by age and sex based on the estimated total labor force for July 1, 1992.

[5] Preliminary.

Source: 1994 Trustees Report.

TABLE 3–18.—PROJECTED EARNINGS FOR HYPOTHETICAL WORKERS

Year	Low [1]	Average [2]	Maximum [3]
1994	$10,840	$24,090	$60,600
1995	11,338	25,196	62,100
1996	11,811	26,246	63,600
1997	12,308	27,352	66,600
1998	12,832	28,516	69,300
1999	13,407	29,794	72,300

[1] Worker with earnings equal to 45 percent of the SSA average wage index.

[2] Worker with earnings equal to the SSA average wage index.

[3] Worker with earnings equal to the Social Security maximum taxable earnings.

Source: Office of the Actuary, Social Security Administration.

TABLE 3–19.—MAJOR LONG-TERM DEMOGRAPHIC ASSUMPTIONS

[1994 trustees' report alternative II assumptions]

Calendar year	Total fertility rate [1]	Age-sex-adjusted death rate [2] (per 100,000)	Life expectancy [3]			
			At birth		At age 65	
			Male	Female	Male	Female
1995	2.04	761.6	72.3	79.2	15.4	19.2
2000	2.01	731.0	73.0	79.7	15.6	19.4
2005	1.98	701.1	73.8	80.2	15.8	19.5
2010	1.95	678.4	74.3	80.5	16.0	19.7
2015	1.92	659.2	74.7	80.9	16.3	19.9
2020	1.90	641.0	75.0	81.2	16.5	20.2
2025	1.90	623.8	75.3	81.5	16.7	20.4
2030	1.90	607.3	75.6	81.8	16.9	20.6
2035	1.90	591.6	75.9	82.1	17.1	20.9
2040	1.90	576.7	76.2	82.3	17.3	21.1
2045	1.90	562.4	76.5	82.6	17.5	21.3
2050	1.90	548.8	76.8	82.9	17.7	21.5
2055	1.90	535.7	77.1	83.2	17.9	21.7
2060	1.90	523.3	77.4	83.5	18.1	21.9
2065	1.90	511.4	77.6	83.7	18.3	22.1
2070	1.90	500.0	77.9	84.0	18.5	22.3

[1] The total fertility rate for any year is the average number of children who would be born to a woman in her lifetime if she were to experience the birth rates by age observed in, or assumed for, the selected year, and if she were to survive the entire child-bearing period. The ultimate total fertility rate is assumed to be reached in 2018.

[2] The age-sex-adjusted death rate is the crude rate that would occur in the enumerated total population as of April 1, 1980, if that population were to experience the death rates by age and sex observed in, or assumed for, the selected year.

[3] The life expectancy for any year is the average number of years of life remaining for a person if that person were to experience the death rates by age observed in, or assumed for, the selected year.

TABLE 3–20.—COVERED WORK FORCE—NUMBER OF BENEFICIARIES AND DEPENDENCY RATES

	1960	1980	2000	2020	2040
Total population (in millions)	190	235	285	325	349
Covered workers	73	112	147	161	166
Beneficiaries (OASI and DI)	14	35	47	68	84
Aged dependency ratio [1]	.173	.195	.210	.279	.372
Total dependency ratio [2]	.904	.749	.691	.701	.791
Worker/beneficiary ratio	5.1	3.2	3.1	2.4	2.0

[1] Ratio of persons aged 65 and over to the number of persons aged 20–64.

[2] Ratio of non-working-age to working-age population—population under 20 plus population 65 and over divided by population 20–64.

Source: 1994 Trustees Report.

SENSITIVITY OF LONG-RANGE PROJECTIONS

Long-range estimates of the financial status of the OASDI trust funds are extremely sensitive to the basic social, economic, and demographic variables that underpin the projections. Slight variations in assumptions about future demographic or economic trends can lead to substantially different financial projections, and thus any longer term estimate is necessarily very uncertain. In general terms, the income to the funds crucially depends on long-run trends in covered wages paid to employees, which in turn depends on many fundamental economic and demographic factors, such as real wage growth in the economy, fluctuations in the size of the work force, productivity, and overall rates of fertility and immigration. The expenditures of the program depend on the amount of benefits that are paid, which is of course affected by the level of consumer inflation, changes in mortality rates and life expectancy, disability incidence, and work and retirement patterns among the elderly population.

As a way of illustrating the sensitivity of long-term projections to variations in basic assumptions, table 3–21 presents data on the effects of varying assumptions about real wage growth in the alternative II estimates. This table is based on the premise that all other alternative II demographic and economic assumptions are held constant. (Under alternative II, the real wage growth assumption is 1.0 percent.)

TABLE 3–21.—ESTIMATED OASDI SUMMARIZED INCOME RATES, COST RATES, AND ACTUARIAL BALANCES, BASED ON ALTERNATIVE II WITH VARIOUS REAL-WAGE ASSUMPTIONS

[As a percentage of taxable payroll]

Valuation period	Ultimate percentage increase in wages—CPI [1]		
	4.5–4.0	5.0–4.0	5.5–4.0
Summarized income rate:			
25-year: 1994–2018	13.39	13.35	13.31
50-year: 1994–2043	13.29	13.24	13.19
75-year: 1994–2068	13.30	13.24	13.19
Summarized cost rate:			
25-year: 1994–2018	13.25	12.85	12.45
50-year: 1994–2043	15.09	14.53	13.97
75-year: 1994–2068	15.97	15.37	14.77
Balance:			
25-year: 1994–2018	+.14	+.50	+.86
50-year: 1994–2043	−1.80	−1.29	−.79
75-year: 1994–2068	−2.67	−2.13	−1.58

[1] The first value in each pair is the assumed ultimate annual percentage increase in average wages in covered employment. The second value is the assumed ultimate annual percentage increase in the Consumer Price Index. The difference between the two values is the real-wage differential.

Source: 1994 Trustees' Report.

Section 4. Railroad Retirement System

The railroad retirement system is a federally legislated program which provides retirement, disability and survivor annuities to workers whose employment was connected with the railroad industry for at least 10 years. The system, in existence since 1936, was substantially modified by the Railroad Retirement Act of 1974 (RRA) which provided for closer coordination with the Social Security system. Credits are primarily secured by employment in the railroad industry, although any Social Security credits earned during employees' work careers are included in the benefit computation. Benefits are financed through a combination of employee, employer, and Federal Government contributions.

TABLE 4–1.—MONTHLY RAILROAD RETIREMENT CASH BENEFITS IN CURRENT-PAYMENT STATUS, NOVEMBER 1993

	Number	Percent of total	Average monthly benefit
Total monthly benefits	840,600	100.0	$763
Retired workers	337,100	40.1	1,033
Disabled workers [1]	33,200	3.9	1,284
Spouses of retired and disabled workers	202,600	24.1	430
Divorced spouses	3,500	0.4	261
Aged widows and widowers	226,100	26.9	630
Disabled widow(er)s	6,800	0.8	568
Widowed mothers and fathers	1,800	0.2	775
Remarried widow(er)s	5,900	0.7	421
Divorced widow(er)s	7,800	0.9	450
Children	15,700	1.9	552
Parents	100	([2])	478

[1] Under age 65.
[2] Less than 0.05 percent.

Note.—Includes tier 1, tier 2, and vested dual benefits. Excludes 179,800 supplemental employee annuities averaging $44. Total includes fewer than 50 survivor option annuities averaging $79, payable under laws in effect before August 1946.

Source: Railroad Retirement Board.

Retirement and survivor benefit payments during fiscal year 1993 totaled $7,872 million. These payments were made to 898,000 beneficiaries. Retired employee and spouse annuitants constituted 615,000 of these beneficiaries and received $5,896 million. Survivor beneficiaries received a total of $1,976 million, consisting of $1,969 million in monthly benefits and $7 million in lump-sum payments. Information on the number of beneficiaries and average benefit amounts for November 1993 is shown in table 4–1.

JURISDICTION

In the House of Representatives, the jurisdiction over the railroad retirement system is divided between two standing committees. Under the rules of the House, the Energy and Commerce Committee has jurisdiction over "railroads, including railroad labor, railroad retirement and unemployment, except revenue measures related thereto." That committee, therefore, has jurisdiction over the Railroad Retirement Act which contains the substantive legislation relating to railroad retirement legislation. The Committee on Ways and Means has jurisdiction over all revenue measures, including the Railroad Retirement Tax Act (Chapter 22 of the Internal Revenue Code of 1986). Within the Committee on Ways and Means jurisdiction over employment taxes and trust fund operations relating to the railroad retirement system lies within the Subcommittee on Social Security.

HISTORICAL DEVELOPMENT

In the final quarter of the 19th century, railroad companies were among the largest in America. It was in the rail industry that the first industrial pension was established in 1874. By the mid-1920's more than 80 percent of all rail workers were covered by pension plans.

In the early 1930's these pension plans began to face enormous financial problems. The commercial success of the rail industry peaked in the period between 1900 and 1920, and rail employment decreased significantly in the 1920's.

Rail pension plans were for the most part poorly constructed. There was no regulation of plan terminations, which were frequent. Pension funds were chronically underfinanced, and most could not stand the financial exigencies of the depression.

These problems plus a tradition of Federal regulation of the railroads led to the enactment of the Railroad Retirement Act of 1934.

The original railroad retirement system was structured to provide annuities to retirees based on rail earnings and length of service. Benefits were disbursed for retirees at age 65, although workers with 30 years of service could retire at 60, with a reduction in payments. The original disability provisions were very stringent. Little was provided for dependents, and nothing for spouses.

Throughout its history, the railroad retirement system has been modified many times by Congress. In the late 1940's and 1950's benefits were liberalized, and the railroad retirement system was brought into closer conformity with Social Security. For instance, in 1946, benefits were extended to survivors, based on combined railroad and Social Security covered employment. This extension represented a concern for the social goal of providing income security in old age, or social insurance, rather than simply rewarding career performance.

In the 1970's and 1980's, the railroad retirement system encountered recurrent financial crises as a result of employment declines in the industry, inflation, and the increase in the number of beneficiaries. Major legislation was enacted in 1974, 1981, 1983, and 1987 to prevent the system from becoming insolvent.

The Railroad Retirement Solvency Act of 1983 (Public Law 98–76) increased payroll taxes on employers and employees, deferred cost-of-living increases, reduced early retirement benefits, subjected benefits to Federal income taxes, and provided other measures designed to improve railroad retirement financing. Without the enactment of this legislation, the Railroad Retirement Board would have been required to substantially reduce benefit payments in 1983. Since enactment, the trust funds have accumulated a reserve of over $12 billion.

The Omnibus Budget Reconciliation Act of 1987 (P.L. 100–203) increased tier 2 tax rates in January 1988 by a total of 2 percent: 1.35 percent on employers and 0.65 percent on employees. In addition, the law extended for 1 year, until October 1, 1989, the time during which revenues from Federal income taxes on tier 2 railroad retirement benefits may be transferred from the general fund of the U.S. Treasury to the Railroad Retirement Account for use in paying benefits.

The continuing decline in rail employment has raised questions concerning the practicality of relying on payroll tax funding in the next century. Consequently, the Committee on Ways and Means included in the 1987 reconciliation bill a provision which established a Commission on Railroad Retirement Reform to conduct a comprehensive study of the issues pertaining to the long-term financing of the railroad retirement system. The Commission consisted of seven members representing railroads, including commuter railroads, labor, and the public, and it made its final report in September 1990. A listing of the Commission's findings and recommendations is reproduced under "Financial Status of the Railroad Retirement Account" at the end of this section.

Railroad retirement amendments were included with railroad unemployment insurance amendments in the Technical and Miscellaneous Revenue Act of 1988 (P.L. 100–647). This legislation assured repayment of the Railroad Unemployment Insurance Account's debt to the Railroad Retirement Account by extending a temporary unemployment insurance tax until the debt was fully repaid with interest in 1993. Public Law 100–647 also eased work restrictions and the crediting of military service in certain cases and provided more equitable treatment of severance pay for railroad retirement purposes.

The Omnibus Budget Reconciliation Act of 1989 (P.L. 101–239) included a number of railroad retirement and Social Security provisions which affected payroll taxes and benefits beginning in 1990. The law increased the amount of earnings subject to Social Security and railroad retirement payroll taxes by including contributions to 401(k) deferred compensation plans in the measure of average wages, which is used to index the wage base. It also extended for 1 additional year, until October 1, 1990, the time during which revenues from Federal income taxes on tier 2 railroad retirement benefits may be transferred to the Railroad Retirement Account for use in paying benefits.

The Omnibus Budget Reconciliation Act of 1990 (P.L. 101–508) further extended the date of this transfer until October 1, 1992, and also permanently exempted supplemental annuities from reductions under Gramm-Rudman.

The Omnibus Budget Reconciliation Act of 1993 (P.L. 103–66) made all Social Security and railroad retirement tier I earnings subject to the Medicare payroll tax, and, for those with higher incomes, made a larger amount of Social Security and railroad retirement tier I benefits subject to Federal income tax. In addition, bills to extend the income tax transfer on a permanent basis were proposed in the 103d Congress in 1993–94.

ANNUITY STRUCTURE

The 1974 Railroad Retirement Act established three benefit components. The ongoing benefit system was divided into two "tiers," one of which approximates Social Security (tier 1), and the other, an industry staff retirement benefit (tier 2). The third component, a vested dual benefit, preserved certain benefits for employees who had qualified for both railroad retirement and Social Security benefits prior to the 1974 Act.

Tier 1

These benefits are based on the Social Security formula, using the employee's combined railroad earnings and non-railroad Social Security covered earnings up to the Social Security maximum wage base. The tier 1 benefit is roughly equal to what the Social Security benefit would have been had the worker's railroad employment been covered by the Social Security program. Because the railroad retirement tier 1 benefit is based on both Social Security and railroad employment, any Social Security benefit to which the railroad retirement system beneficiary is also entitled is subtracted from the tier 1 benefit amount. Tier 1 benefits are adjusted for the cost-of-living by the same percentage as Social Security benefits.

Tier 2

Tier 2 benefits are based on the employee's service in the railroad industry alone and are payable in addition to the tier 1 benefit amount. For current retirees, the tier 2 benefit is equal to seven-tenths of 1 percent of the employee's average monthly earnings in the 60 months of highest earnings, times the total number of years of railroad service, less 25 percent of any employee vested dual benefit also payable. Tier 2 benefits are automatically adjusted annually at a rate equal to 32.5 percent of the Social Security automatic cost-of-living adjustment.

Dual benefit payments

One of the chief purposes of the Railroad Retirement Act of 1974 was to coordinate railroad retirement and Social Security benefit payments to eliminate certain dual benefits considered to be a "windfall" for persons receiving benefits under both systems.

This "windfall" was a result of the fact that the total benefit these retirees received from both systems was higher than the benefit they would have received if their benefit was based on their total career earnings but paid only under railroad retirement. The total benefit was higher in these cases since the Social Security benefit formula favors workers who have low average earnings throughout their careers. Low career average earnings result from a career of low wages or from a relatively short career in Social Security covered employment. Workers who spend a period of time in employment not covered by Social Security, such as railroad employment, receive the benefit of this "tilt" in the benefit formula, even though they may very well not have had low career earnings.

As a result of the 1974 Act, "windfall" benefits were eliminated for any railroad employees not qualified for such benefits as of January 1, 1975. They were generally preserved for those individuals who were vested under both the railroad retirement and Social Security systems before 1975. These vested dual benefits are financed out of the general revenue fund through an annual appropriation rather than from the Social Security or railroad retirement trust funds, and are subject to reduction during any year in which the appropriation is less than required for full benefit payments. The fiscal year 1993 appropriation was $294,030,000 including income tax transfers. The fiscal year 1994 appropriation was $277,000,000, including income tax transfers. Currently paid to about 22 percent of the Railroad Retirement Board's beneficiaries, the average vested dual benefit is $125 per month.

Supplemental annuities

These are provided under the 1974 Act equal to $23 for 25 years of service plus $4 for each additional year up to a maximum of $43 per month. However, as a result of the 1981 Omnibus Budget Reconciliation Act, employees first hired after October 1, 1981 are not eligible for supplemental annuities when they retire.

Lump-sum death benefits

Lump-sum death benefits are paid when there is no person eligible for a monthly survivor benefit in the month in which the worker died. Generally, 10 years of railroad service and a current connection with the railroad industry are required. For employees with 10 or more years of railroad service before 1975, the amount is based on the 1937 Act. For all other railroad workers, the amount is equivalent to that which would be paid under the Social Security Act (unless survivor benefits are paid).

A residual lump-sum payment is, in effect, a refund of the employee's pre-1975 railroad retirement taxes plus an allowance in lieu of interest, less benefits already paid. This payment is not made as long as monthly benefits are payable either at the time of the employee's death or in the future. However, a widow(er) or parent under age 60 can waive rights to future monthly benefits in order to receive a residual payment.

PROGRAM DATA

Table 4–2 provides data concerning all railroad retirement benefits paid in selected fiscal years 1950–93. Table 4–3 presents data on new awards for November 1993.

TABLE 4–2.—TOTAL BENEFIT PAYMENTS AND NUMBER OF BENEFICIARIES, BY FISCAL YEAR

Fiscal year	Benefit payments (in millions) [1]			Beneficiaries (in thousands) [2]		
	Total	Retire-ment	Survivor	Total	Retire-ment	Survivor
1950	$301.6	$248.2	$53.4	458	272	189
1955	549.7	424.5	125.2	700	452	252
1960	925.7	711.5	214.2	873	584	299
1965	1,117.7	834.0	283.7	980	650	340
1970	1,593.5	1,177.0	416.5	1,051	702	366
1975	3,060.3	2,222.4	837.9	1,094	733	380
1980	4,730.6	3,389.8	1,340.8	1,084	731	367
1981	5,286.6	3,779.9	1,506.7	1,074	726	363
1982	5,725.5	4,097.9	1,627.6	1,067	722	359
1983	6,041.1	4,354.2	1,686.9	1,056	715	357
1984	6,099.8	4,417.8	1,682.0	1,040	705	351
1985	6,250.9	4,539.3	1,711.6	1,023	694	343
1986	6,329.5	4,608.1	1,721.4	1,007	684	339
1987 [3]	6,520.3	4,773.6	1,746.7	994	675	333
1988	6,675.9	4,915.0	1,760.9	981	666	328
1989	6,938.5	5,140.9	1,797.6	967	659	322
1990	7,194.6	5,357.0	1,837.6	951	650	315
1991	7,490.8	5,593.2	1,897.6	932	638	307
1992	7,693.9	5,754.0	1,939.9	913	626	301
1993	7,872.3	5,896.0	1,976.2	898	615	298

[1] Retirement benefits include tier 1 and tier 2 employee and spouse benefits, employee and spouse vested dual benefits, and supplemental employee annuity payments. Survivor benefits include tier 1 and tier 2 benefits, vested dual benefits and lump-sum payments. Total benefits include hospital insurance benefits for services in Canada.

[2] Number of beneficiaries represents all individuals paid benefits in that year. In the total number for each year, beneficiaries are counted only once, even though they may have received more than one type of benefit. In fiscal year 1993, about 15,000 individuals received both retirement and survivor benefits. Figures are partly estimated.

[3] Benefits paid for fiscal years beginning 1987 are not strictly comparable to those for prior years due to a change in accounting systems.

TABLE 4–3.—NUMBER AND AVERAGE AMOUNT OF NEW AWARDS BY BENEFICIARY TYPE, NOVEMBER 1993

	Number	Average amount
Employee annuities:		
Retired	776	$1,288
Disability (under age 65)	230	1,415
Supplemental	510	41
Spouse annuities	893	464
Divorced spouse annuities	51	274
Survivor benefits:		
Aged widows and widowers	773	766
Disabled widows and widowers	21	618
Widowed mothers and fathers	15	816
Divorced and remarried widows	108	454
Children	71	646
Parents	....	....
Insurance lump sums	403	862
Residual payments	5	4,015
Total	3,856	....

Source: Railroad Retirement Board.

FINANCING THE RAILROAD RETIREMENT SYSTEM

Railroad retirement and survivor benefits are financed by five sources of income. These are (1) payroll taxes on railroad earnings paid by covered employees and employers up to a certain maximum wage base; (2) income from the Social Security financial interchange; (3) appropriations from general revenues; (4) income from investments; and (5) a cents-per-hour tax levied on carriers only.

Payroll Taxes

The primary source of income to the railroad retirement account is payroll taxes levied on covered employers and their employees which are imposed on wages below an annual maximum amount, known as the "wage base." Currently, both employers and employees pay a "tier 1" tax which is equivalent to the combined Social Security (Old-Age, Survivors and Disability Insurance) and Hospital Insurance (part A of Medicare) tax rate. In addition, a "tier 2" tax is paid by both rail employers and employees. The 1994 annual tier 1 and tier 2 wage bases are $60,600 and $45,000, respectively. Beginning in 1994, there is no wage base for the hospital insurance portion of the tax (1.45 percent on employers and employees, each). Thus, this tax is imposed on all wages.

The scheduled tax rates for both tier 1 and tier 2 are shown in table 4–4.

The tier 1 wage base is equal to the Social Security wage base and automatically increases with wage growth in the economy.

TABLE 4–4.—SCHEDULED TAX RATES FOR TIER 1 AND TIER 2, SELECTED YEARS

	Tier 1		Wage base	Tier 2		Wage base	Combined [1]	
	Employer	Employee		Employer	Employee		Employer	Employee
1975	5.85	5.85	$14,100	9.5	0	$14,100	15.35	5.85
1980	6.13	6.13	25,900	9.5	0	20,400	15.63	6.13
1985	7.05	7.05	39,600	13.75	3.50	29,700	20.80	10.55
1986	7.15	7.15	42,000	14.75	4.25	31,500	21.90	11.40
1987	7.15	7.15	43,800	14.75	4.25	32,700	21.90	11.40
1988	7.51	7.51	45,000	16.10	4.90	33,600	23.61	12.41
1989	7.51	7.51	48,000	16.10	4.90	35,700	23.61	12.41
1990	7.65	7.65	51,300	16.10	4.90	38,100	23.75	12.55
1991	7.65	7.65	[2] 53,400	16.10	4.90	39,600	23.75	12.55
1992	7.65	7.65	[2] 55,500	16.10	4.90	41,400	23.75	12.55
1993	7.65	7.65	[2] 57,600	16.10	4.90	42,900	23.75	12.55
1994	7.65	7.65	60,600	16.10	4.90	45,000	23.75	12.55
1995 [3]	7.65	7.65	62,100	16.10	4.90	46,200	23.75	12.55
1996 [3]	7.65	7.65	63,900	16.10	4.90	47,400	23.75	12.55
1997 [3]	7.65	7.65	66,600	16.10	4.90	49,500	23.75	12.55
1998 [3]	7.65	7.65	69,300	16.10	4.90	51,600	23.75	12.55
1999 [3]	7.65	7.65	72,300	16.10	4.90	54,000	23.75	12.55

[1] These rates apply only up to the tier 2 maximum wage base.
[2] The wage base for the 1.45 percent hospital insurance tax, included in the 7.65 percent tier 1 rate, is $125,000 in 1991, $130,200 in 1992, $135,000 in 1993, and no limit in 1994 and later.
[3] 1995–99 wage bases are projected.

The tier 2 wage base is equal to what the Social Security wage base would have been without regard to the ad hoc increases in the wage base which were provided by the Social Security Amendments of 1977 (P.L. 95–215).

Financial Interchange

The railroad retirement system and the Social Security programs have been coordinated financially since 1951. The purpose of the financial interchange is to place the Social Security trust funds in the same position they would have been in if railroad employment had been covered under Social Security since its inception.

Generally, under the interchange, for a given fiscal year there is computed the revenue that would have been collected by the Social Security trust funds if railroad employment had been covered directly by Social Security. This amount is netted against the amount of benefits Social Security would have paid to railroad beneficiaries based on railroad and nonrailroad earnings during that period. Where Social Security benefits that would have been paid exceed income to the trust funds that would have been due, the excess, plus an allowance for interest and administrative expenses, is transferred from the Social Security trust funds to the Railroad Retirement Board's Social Security Equivalent Benefit Account. If income exceeds benefits, the transfer would be from the RRB's Social Security Equivalent Benefit Account to the Social Security trust funds. Before 1985, transfers were to or from the Railroad Retirement Account.

The determination of the amount to be transferred through the financial interchange for a given fiscal year is made no later than June of the year following the close of the preceding fiscal year. Table 4–5 shows the actual operation of the financial interchange for selected years as it relates to each of the three major Social Security trust funds.

In order to make available to the RRB's Social Security Equivalent Benefit Account funds from the forthcoming financial interchange on a more current basis, the Railroad Retirement Solvency Act of 1983 provided for transfers from general Treasury funds to the RRB's Social Security Equivalent Benefit Account for each month an amount equal to the Social Security level benefits paid from the account during the month less the Social Security level taxes received by the account in that month. The amount so transferred for a particular month is repaid when the Social Security system makes reimbursement for that month under the financial interchange program.

TABLE 4–5.—AMOUNTS TRANSFERRED TO OR FROM (−) THE SOCIAL SECURITY EQUIV-ALENT BENEFIT ACCOUNT [1] AND THE VARIOUS SOCIAL SECURITY TRUST FUNDS IN SELECTED FISCAL YEARS 1954 THROUGH 1993

[In millions of dollars]

	OASI	DI	HI	Total
Fiscal year:				
Through June 30,				
1954	− 21.1			− 21.1
1955	− 7.4			− 7.4
1960	318.4	− 4.9		313.5
1965	435.6	23.6		459.3
1970	578.8	10.4	− 63.5	525.7
1975	981.8	28.5	− 132.5	877.8
1980	1,442.0	− 12.1	− 244.3	1,185.6
1981	1,584.9	29.4	− 276.5	1,337.9
1982	1,793.3	26.4	− 351.4	1,468.2
1983	2,250.8	27.8	− 357.7	1,920.9
1984	2,404.0	21.6	− 350.6	2,075.0
1985	2,310.2	42.7	− 371.4	1,981.5
1986	2,585.1	67.7	− 364.4	2,288.4
1987	2,557.3	56.9	− 368.0	2,246.2
1988	2,790.0	61.3	− 363.8	2,487.5
1989	2,845.3	88.2	− 378.8	2,554.7
1990	2,969.3	79.9	− 367.4	2,681.8
1991	3,374.6	82.1	− 352.2	3,104.5
1992	3,148.4	58.0	− 374.5	2,831.9
1993	3,352.5	82.8	− 400.5	3,034.9
Total	49,977.2	1,065.7	− 6,211.9	44,831.1

[1] Before 1985, transfers were to or from the Railroad Retirement Account.

Source: Railroad Retirement Board.

General revenue appropriations

Vested dual benefits are funded solely through general revenue appropriations. The Congress authorized such funding in the 1974 act through the year 2000. The total appropriated for the first 18 fiscal years for which these benefits were payable, 1976–93, was $6,120 million.

The Omnibus Budget Reconciliation Act of 1981 (Public Law 97–35) established a Dual Benefits Payments Account. Each year an amount which is appropriated for the payment of vested dual benefits is placed into this account. If the amount which is appropriated is insufficient to pay the full vested dual benefits to all eligible beneficiaries for a full year, the Railroad Retirement Board is authorized to prorate payments from the dual benefits account so that the amounts paid do not exceed the amounts appropriated.

In addition to amounts transferred to the Dual Benefits Payments Account through the regular appropriations process, the Railroad Retirement Solvency Act of 1983 provided for the appropriation of approximately $1.7 billion to the Railroad Retirement Account in three installments paid on January 1, 1984, 1985, and 1986. These three appropriations were to reimburse the Railroad Retirement Account for prior shortfalls in the annual appropriations. The actual amounts received, including interest, totaled $2,128 million. This amount is not included in the figure given above for total appropriations, 1976–93.

Income from investments

Funds not needed immediately for benefit payments are invested in interest-bearing securities. During fiscal year 1993, the Railroad Retirement Account and Social Security Equivalent Benefit Account received $827 million in investment income. This represents an annualized interest yield of 6.52 percent.

Cents-per-hour tax

A cents-per-hour tax is used to fund the supplemental annuity benefit. This tax is levied solely on employers. The rate, 30¢ per workhour in January 1994, is determined quarterly by the Railroad Retirement Board and is set at a level necessary to fund the benefit on a pay-as-you-go basis.

INCOME TAXATION OF RAILROAD RETIREMENT BENEFITS

Prior to 1984, railroad retirement benefits, with the exception of supplemental annuities, were not subject to Federal income taxation. However, as a result of the Railroad Retirement Solvency Act (Public Law 98–76) and the Social Security Act Amendments of 1983 (Public Law 98–21), tier 1, tier 2, and vested dual benefits received after December 31, 1983, are subject to taxation. The taxation provisions were subsequently amended by the Consolidated Omnibus Budget Reconciliation Act of 1985, the Tax Reform Act of 1986, and the Omnibus Budget Reconciliation Act (OBRA) of 1993. Under current law, the Social Security equivalent portions of tier 1 benefits are taxed in a manner identical to Social Security benefits. The proceeds derived from the taxation under pre-OBRA 1993 rules of those tier 1 benefits which are equivalent to Social Security benefits are deposited in the Social Security Equivalent Benefit Account and credited to the Social Security trust funds through adjustments in the financial interchange. The additional income taxes attributable to OBRA 1993 are deposited in the Hospital Insurance trust fund. Tier 1 benefits in excess of Social Security equivalent levels (including early retirement benefits payable at ages 60–61 and occupational disability annuities) and tier 2 benefits are taxed in a manner identical to private and public service pensions and the proceeds were deposited in the Railroad Retirement Account through fiscal year 1992, after which legislative authority for the tier 2 tax transfer expired. Vested dual benefits are taxed like private and public service pensions with the proceeds derived deposited in the Dual Benefits Payments Account.

FINANCIAL STATUS OF THE RAILROAD RETIREMENT ACCOUNT

One of the most important factors affecting the financial status of the railroad retirement system is the level of employment in the industry. The recent history of industry employment is shown in chart 4–1 and table 4–6 below.

TABLE 4–6.—RAILROAD INDUSTRY EMPLOYMENT, 1940–93

	Number (thousands)
1940	1,195
1945	1,085
1950	1,421
1955	1,239
1960	909
1965	753
1970	640
1975	548
1976	540
1977	546
1978	542
1979	554
1980	532
1981	503
1982	440
1983	395
1984	395
1985	372
1986	342
1987	320
1988	312
1989	308
1990	296
1991	285
1992	276
1993	271

Source: Railroad Retirement Board.

CHART 4–1.—RAILROAD INDUSTRY EMPLOYMENT, 1940–93

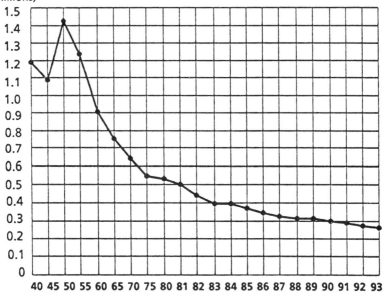

Employment (millions) vs. Year

While the trust funds currently have a reserve of over $12 billion, the continuing decline in railroad employment has periodically raised questions concerning the financing of the railroad retirement system after the year 2000. Section 502 of the Railroad Retirement Solvency Act of 1983 requires a report each year on the railroad retirement system's actuarial status, and financing recommendations when appropriate. Because of the decline in employment, the Railroad Retirement Board's Chief Actuary recommended in his 1987 report that a commission be established to study the advisability of instituting a tax on operating revenues to fund a portion of the cost of railroad retirement benefits, and that such a study should solicit the views of railroad labor, railroad management and other interested parties. He also recommended that tier 2 taxes be increased until any tax adjustments recommended by the commission become effective.

Under the 1987 budget law, the Commission's study was to take into account—

(1) the possibility of restructuring the financing of railroad retirement benefits through increases in the tier 2 tax rate, increases in the tier 2 tax wage base, the imposition of a tax on operating revenues, revisions in the investment policy of the railroad retirement pension fund, and establishing a privately funded and administered railroad industry pension plan;

(2) the economic outlook for the railroad industry, and the nature of the relationships between the railroad retirement system, levels of railroad employment and compensation, and the performance of the rail sector;

(3) the ability of the system under current law to pay benefits to current and future retirees and other beneficiaries;

(4) the financial relationship of the system to the railroad unemployment insurance system, the Social Security system, and the General Fund; and

(5) any other matters which the Commission considers would be necessary, appropriate, or useful to the Congress in developing legislation to reform the system.

The 1987 budget law also increased tier 2 payroll tax rates in January 1988 by a total of 2 percent, and allowed revenues from Federal income taxes on tier 2 railroad retirement benefits to be returned to the railroad retirement system until October 1, 1989; later legislation extended the date to October 1, 1990, and then to October 1, 1992.

In June 1991, the Railroad Retirement Board transmitted to Congress its 18th triennial actuarial valuation of the railroad retirement program's assets and liabilities, which projected income and outgo under four employment assumptions. The valuation concluded that, barring a sudden, unanticipated, large drop in railroad employment, the railroad retirement system will experience no cash flow problems for at least 20 years. The long-term stability of the system, however, depends on actual railroad employment levels over the coming years. Subsequent annual financial projections yielded similar conclusions.

Findings of the Commission on Railroad Retirement Reform

The following list of major findings and recommendations is reprinted from the press release which accompanied the Commission on Railroad Retirement Reform's September 1990 final report.

1. The Railroad Retirement system is financially sound in the intermediate-term.

2. It is quite probable that the Railroad Retirement system is financially sound over the long-range future (the next 75 years).

3. Tier 2 of the railroad retirement system has elements of both a social insurance program and a private-pension tier for railroad employees. The system is actuarially sound as the term is applied to a social insurance program.

4. Based on its review, the Commission concluded that, on balance, the future of the national economy appears to be favorable over the next decade for the freight railroad sector.

5. Employment projection D used in the 17th Actuarial Valuation [of the Railroad Retirement Board] is the most reasonable and predictive of the five projections. In fact, this projection appears to be on the low side.

6. The Railroad Retirement Tax Act should be amended to substitute a partial-pegged-payroll tax for the current employment-based employer tax. If this alternative tax basis is adopted, the statute should clearly indicate that these tax payments are to be recorded as period expenses when paid.

7. If the partial-pegged-payroll tax is not adopted, and if contracting-out increases as a problem, causing reduced employment, serious consideration should be given to imposing an excise tax on contracting-out, either as a tax on all outlays or limited to "traditional" railroad services.

8. The current temporary transfers of income-tax revenue on tier 2 and unrecompensed tier 1 benefits should be continued on a permanent basis.

9. The Commission recommends the development of alternative retirement systems for newly hired railroad employees only, and proposes transition rules to encourage the development of satisfactory individual company and/or multiemployer pension plans for such new employees.

10. The early-retirement provisions of the Railroad Retirement Act should be phased out to provide eventual retirement-age requirements which are the same as those under Social Security.

11. The "notch" in the early-normal-retirement-age reduction factor should be changed in an actuarially correct manner.

12. The occupational-disability annuity provisions of the Railroad Retirement Act should be amended to provide that, effective for disabilities occurring on or after January 1, 1994, the duration for receipt of such benefits is to be limited to 24 months.

13. In conjunction with the phase-out of the early-retirement provisions and modification of the occupational-disability annuity eligibility, the Railroad Retirement Act should be amended to conform the provisions for tier 1 benefits to the benefits provided under the Social Security Act for those individuals who become entitled or eligible on or after the effective date.

14. The Railroad Retirement Act should be changed so as to restore the previous cross-reference to the Federal Insurance Contributions Act for determining tier 1 tax rates. [The cross-reference was restored by the 1990 Omnibus Budget Reconciliation Act.]

15. A further increase in the current tier 2 tax rates is not needed if the present benefit structure remains unchanged. The current procedure of regular financial reporting by the Railroad Retirement Board, with recommendations for adjustments to the tax rates if necessary, is an efficient and adequate mechanism for any future corrective action.

16. Increasing the tier 2 taxable compensation base is not recommended.

17. The Railroad Retirement Tax Act should be amended to allow individual employers to assume the employee tier 2 tax, and such payments made by the employer should not be included as compensation for RRTA or income tax purposes.

18. The financial relationship of the Railroad Retirement Account and the General Fund through the Dual Benefits Payments Account is appropriate and should be continued.

19. The proposal in the fiscal year 1991 budget of the United States to modify the current method of calculating the appropriation for the dual-benefits payments should be rejected because it would be an abrogation of past agreements and because it lacks a sound rationale.

20. No change in the financial interchange relationship between the Railroad Retirement Account and the Social Security system is recommended.

21. The Railroad Retirement Account and the Social Security Equivalent Benefit Account should be combined (as the Railroad Retirement Account), and should no longer be maintained as separate accounting entities.

22. No change in the relationship between the Railroad Unemployment Insurance Account and the Railroad Retirement Account is recommended.

23. Concerning the investment management of the Railroad Retirement Account: (1) The statutory formula for determining the monthly rate of interest to be earned by the Account on par value special issues of the U.S. Treasury should be changed from one based on notes of at least 3 years to maturity, to all "marketable interest-bearing obligations" of at least 4 years to maturity; (2) The current statutory investment authority should be continued; and (3) If the partial-pegged-payroll tax alternative is not adopted, and the balance in the Railroad Retirement Account increases to a more than adequate level (e.g., 3 or 4 years of anticipated outgo), Congress should consider granting the Board more flexible investment authority, so as to include private-sector investments.

24. Tier 1 benefits should be extended to the divorced-spouse categories of beneficiaries which are now excluded from receiving such benefits.

25. The Railroad Retirement Act should be amended to require the simultaneous filing of employee and spouse annuities to which an individual is entitled.

26. The Railroad Retirement Act should be amended to provide that all future benefit changes in the Social Security Act shall apply to tier 1 benefit provisions of the Railroad Retirement Act.

27. The Railroad Retirement Act should be amended to provide that coverage should apply to all interurban passenger railroads which receive any direct or indirect Federal funding for their operations or construction, regardless of whether or not they operate between states.

28. No separate special tax-treatment should be provided for passenger railroads.

Section 5. Medicare

Medicare, authorized under title XVIII of the Social Security Act, is a nationwide health insurance program for the aged and certain disabled persons. It consists of two parts: the hospital insurance (part A) program and the supplementary medical insurance (part B) program.

ELIGIBILITY

Most Americans age 65 or older are automatically entitled to protection under part A. Persons age 65 or older who are not "fully insured" (i.e., not eligible for monthly Social Security or railroad retirement cash benefits) may obtain coverage, providing they pay the full actuarial cost of such coverage. For those who are not automatically entitled to part A benefits, the full monthly premium, as of January 1, 1994, is $245. Also eligible, after a 2-year waiting period, are people under age 65 who are receiving monthly Social Security benefits on the basis of disability and disabled railroad retirement system annuitants. (Dependents of the disabled are not eligible.) Most people who need a kidney transplant or renal dialysis because of chronic kidney disease are, under certain circumstances, entitled to benefits under part A regardless of age.

Part B of Medicare is voluntary. All persons age 65 or older (whether "insured" or not) may elect to enroll in the supplementary medical insurance program by paying the monthly premium. Persons eligible for part A by virtue of disability or chronic kidney disease may also elect to enroll in part B. The premium, as of January 1, 1994, is $41.10 per month.

NUMBER OF BENEFICIARIES

In fiscal year 1994, approximately 32.1 million aged and 4.1 million disabled will have protection under part A. Of those, it is estimated that 7.0 million aged and 0.9 million disabled will actually receive reimbursed services. In fiscal year 1994, 31.4 million aged and 3.7 million disabled will be enrolled in part B. About 26.7 million of the aged and 3.0 million of the disabled will receive part B reimbursed services.

(123)

TABLE 5–1.—NUMBER OF AGED AND DISABLED ELIGIBLE ENROLLEES AND BENEFICIARIES, AND AVERAGE AND TOTAL MEDICARE BENEFIT PAYMENTS

[Persons in thousands]

	Fiscal year										Projected average annual growth (percent)		
	1975 (actual)	1980 (actual)	1985 (actual)	1990 (actual)	1991 (actual)	1992 (actual)	1993 [1] (estimate)	1994 [1] (estimate)	1995 [1] (estimate)	1996 [1] (estimate)	1975–85	1985–90	1990–96
Part A:													
Persons enrolled (monthly average):													
Aged	21,795	24,571	27,123	29,801	30,456	30,808	31,630	32,054	32,432	32,763	2.2	1.9	1.6
Disabled	2,047	2,968	2,944	3,270	3,380	3,561	3,833	4,094	4,389	4,683	3.7	2.1	6.2
Total	23,842	27,539	30,067	33,071	33,836	34,369	35,463	36,148	36,821	37,446	2.3	1.9	2.1
Beneficiaries receiving reimbursed services:													
Aged	4,906	5,943	6,168	6,070	6,110	6,710	6,820	6,960	7,100	7,230	2.3	-0.3	3.0
Disabled	456	721	672	680	700	735	805	865	935	1,000	4.0	0.2	6.6
Total	5,362	6,664	6,840	6,750	6,810	7,445	7,625	7,825	8,035	8,230	2.5	-0.3	3.4
Average annual benefit per person enrolled: [2][3]													
Aged	$326	$853	$1,563	$1,971	$2,007	$2,324	$2,539	$2,800	$3,009	$3,260	17.0	4.7	8.7
Disabled	$345	$948	$1,806	$2,139	$2,177	$2,527	$2,665	$2,861	$3,024	$3,232	18.0	3.4	7.1
Total	$327	$863	$1,587	$1,987	$2,024	$2,345	$2,553	$2,807	$3,010	$3,257	17.1	4.6	8.6
Part B:													
Persons enrolled (average):													
Aged	21,504	24,422	27,049	29,426	29,910	30,471	30,982	31,354	31,697	32,000	2.3	1.7	1.4
Disabled	1,835	2,698	2,672	2,907	3,023	3,163	3,383	3,656	3,954	4,244	3.0	1.7	6.5
Total	23,339	27,120	29,721	32,333	32,933	33,634	34,365	35,010	35,651	36,244	2.4	1.7	1.9
Beneficiaries receiving reimbursed services:													
Aged	11,311	16,034	20,199	23,820	24,115	25,603	25,994	26,682	27,355	27,968	6.0	3.4	2.7
Disabled	797	1,669	1,933	2,184	2,276	2,522	2,772	3,031	3,326	3,620	9.3	2.5	8.8
Total	12,108	17,703	22,132	26,004	26,391	28,125	28,766	29,713	30,681	31,588	6.2	3.3	8.3
Average annual benefit per person enrolled: [2]													
Aged	$153	$347	$705	$1,250	$1,342	$1,403	$1,474	$1,593	$1,781	$1,957	16.5	12.1	7.8
Disabled	$259	$615	$1,021	$1,602	$1,758	$1,847	$1,994	$1,863	$2,005	$2,181	14.7	9.4	5.3
Total	$161	$374	$733	$1,282	$1,380	$1,445	$1,525	$1,621	$1,806	$1,983	16.3	11.8	7.5

[1] Represents current law. Does not include regulations or legislative proposals.
[2] Does not include administrative cost.
[3] Includes Part A catastrophic benefits beginning in fiscal year 1989. There are no catastrophic benefits after fiscal year 1990.

Source: Health Care Financing Administration, Division of Budget.

TABLE 5–2.—BENEFIT PAYMENTS BY SERVICE UNDER MEDICARE PART A AND PART B FISCAL YEARS 1975, 1980, 1993, 1995 AND 1996

[In millions of dollars]

Fiscal year:	1975		1980 (per-cent)	1985 (per-cent)	1990		1993		1995 (est.)[1]		1996 (est.)[1]		Projected average annual growth (percent)		
	Percent	Amount			Percent	Amount	Percent	Amount	Percent	Amount	Percent	Amount	1975–85	1985–90	1990–96[1]
Part A:															
For inpatient hospital services	70.5	$9,947	67.4	65.0	55.2	$59,208	52.5	$75,021	50.1	$87,833	49.6	$96,110	16.3	5.5	8.4
For skilled nursing facility services	1.9	273	1.2	0.8	2.7	2,843	3.5	5,027	3.8	6,598	3.7	7,093	7.3	38.9	16.5
For home health services	0.9	133	1.5	2.7	3.1	3,352	6.7	9,529	8.6	15,074	8.9	17,217	30.5	11.9	31.4
For hospice services	0.0	0	0.0	0.0	0.3	318	0.7	958	0.8	1,341	0.8	1,538	NA	NA	30.0
Total benefit payments	73.3	10,353	70.1	68.6	61.3	65,721	63.3	90,535	63.3	110,846	62.9	121,958	16.5	6.6	10.9
Part B:															
For physician services	21.7	3,067	23.0	24.1	27.0	$28,968	23.6	33,800	22.9	$40,150	22.6	$43,762	18.5	11.5	7.1
For outpatient services	3.7	529	5.3	5.6	7.8	8,365	8.3	11,916	8.5	14,833	8.7	16,915	22.2	16.4	12.5
For other medical and health services	1.2	169	1.6	1.6	3.9	4,165	4.7	6,682	5.4	9,393	5.8	11,205	20.6	30.4	17.9
Total benefit payments	26.7	3,765	29.9	31.4	38.7	41,498	36.7	52,398	36.7	64,376	37.1	71,882	19.2	13.7	9.6
Total	100.0	14,118	100.0	100.0	100.0	107,219	100.0	142,934	100.0	175,222	100.0	193,840	17.3	9.1	10.4

[1] Represents projections of current law.

Source: Health Care Financing Administration, Division of Budget.

TABLE 5–3.—BENEFIT PAYMENTS BY SERVICE UNDER MEDICARE PART A AND PART B, FISCAL YEARS 1975 THROUGH 1995

[In millions of dollars]

	1975	1976	1977	1978	1979	1980	1981	1982	1983	1984
Part A										
For inpatient hospital services	9,947	11,742	14,265	16,687	19,068	22,860	27,841	32,788	36,108	39,193
For skilled nursing facility services	273	308	351	355	371	392	398	453	538	548
For home health service	133	217	289	357	433	524	655	1,102	1,456	1,716
For hospice services	0	0	0	0	0	0	0	0	4	4
Total benefit payments	10,353	12,267	14,905	17,399	19,872	23,776	28,894	34,343	38,102	41,461
Part B										
For physician services	2,874	3,437	4,286	4,954	5,947	7,282	8,860	10,649	12,889	14,582
For radiology and pathology services	193	251	313	373	449	531	654	743	609	615
For outpatient service	529	727	965	1,194	1,457	1,803	2,213	2,867	3,345	3,530
For other medical and health services	169	257	303	331	406	528	618	547	644	746
Total benefit payments	3,765	4,672	5,867	6,852	8,259	10,144	12,345	14,806	17,487	19,473
Total	14,118	16,939	20,772	24,251	28,131	33,920	41,239	49,149	55,589	60,934

	1985	1986	1987	1988	1989	1990	1991	1992	1993	1994 [1]	1995 [1]
Part A											
For inpatient hospital services	45,218	46,283	47,264	48,969	52,442	59,208	60,491	69,145	75,021	81,627	87,833
For skilled nursing facility services	550	577	630	742	2,327	2,843	2,512	3,645	5,027	6,152	6,598
For home health service	1,908	1,939	1,815	2,010	2,251	3,352	4,995	6,985	9,529	12,533	15,074
For hospice services	34	68	104	137	211	318	479	808	958	1,138	1,341
Total benefit payments	47,710	48,867	49,813	51,858	57,231	65,721	68,477	80,584	90,535	101,450	110,846
Part B											
For physician services	16,223	18,553	21,926	24,243	26,176	28,968	31,127	32,304	33,800	35,868	40,150
For radiology and pathology services	565	[2]	[2]	[2]	[2]	[2]	[2]	[2]	[2]	[2]	[2]
For outpatient service	3,917	4,937	5,793	6,466	7,321	8,365	9,234	10,671	11,916	12,985	14,833
For other medical and health services	1,103	1,679	2,218	2,973	3,370	4,165	5,153	5,620	6,682	7,899	9,393
Total benefit payments	21,808	25,169	29,937	33,682	36,867	41,498	45,514	48,595	52,398	56,752	64,376
Total	69,518	74,036	79,750	85,540	94,098	107,219	113,991	129,179	142,934	158,202	175,222

[1] Represents estimates of current law. Does not include legislative proposals. Includes catastrophic benefits, in fiscal years 1989 and 1990.
[2] Not available. Physician services for fiscal years 1986 through 1994 include radiology and pathology services.

Source: Health Care Financing Administration, Division of Budget.

TABLE 5-4.—HISTORICAL AND PROJECTED AMOUNTS OF PART A (HOSPITAL INSURANCE) AND PART B (SMI) DEDUCTIBLE, COINSURANCE AND PREMIUMS[1]

For benefit periods beginning in calendar year	Inpatient hospital[2]			Skilled nursing facility 21st thru 100th day coinsurance per day[5]	HI monthly premium[6]			SMI deductible	SMI premium	
	First 60 days deductible	61st thru 90th day coinsurance per day[3]	60 lifetime reserve days (nonrenewable) coinsurance per day[4]		Effective date	Full amount	Reduced amount		Effective date	Amount
1966	$40	$10	(7)	(7)	....	....	NA	$50	7/66	$3.00
1967	40	10	(7)	$5.00	....	....	NA	50		3.00
1968	40	10	$20	5.00	....	....	NA	50	4/68	4.00
1969	44	11	22	5.50	....	....	NA	50		4.00
1970	52	13	26	6.50	....	....	NA	50	7/70	5.30
1971	60	15	30	7.50	....	....	NA	50	7/71	5.60
1972	68	17	34	8.50	....	....	NA	50	7/72	5.80
1973	72	18	36	9.00	7/73	$33	NA	60	8 9/73	6.30
1974	84	21	42	10.50	7/74	36	NA	60	7/74	6.70
1975	92	23	46	11.50	7/75	40	NA	60		6.70
1976	104	26	52	13.00	7/76	45	NA	60	7/76	7.20
1977	124	31	62	15.50	7/77	54	NA	60	7/77	7.70
1978	144	36	72	18.00	7/78	63	NA	60	7/78	8.20
1979	160	40	80	20.00	7/79	69	NA	60	7/79	8.70
1980	180	45	90	22.50	7/80	78	NA	60	7/80	9.60
1981	204	51	102	25.50	7/81	89	NA	60	7/81	11.00
1982	260	65	130	32.50	7/82	113	NA	75	7/82	12.20
1983	304	76	152	38.00		113	NA	75		12.20
1984	356	89	178	44.50	1/84	155	NA	75	1/84	14.60
1985	400	100	200	50.00	1/85	174	NA	75	1/85	15.50
1986	492	123	246	61.50	1/86	214	NA	75	1/86	15.50
1987	520	130	260	65.00	1/87	226	NA	75	1/87	17.90
1988	540	135	270	67.50	1/88	234	NA	75	1/88	24.80

1989	9 560	NA	NA	1/89	10 25.50	156	NA	75	1/89	31.90
1990	592	148	296	1/90	74.00	175	NA	75	1/90	28.60
1991	628	157	314	1/91	78.50	177	NA	100	1/91	29.90
1992	652	163	326	1/92	81.50	192	NA	100	1/92	31.80
1993	676	169	338	1/93	84.50	221	NA	100	1/93	36.60
1994	696	174	348	1/94	87.00	245	184	100	1/94	41.10
1995 11	720	180	360	1/95	90.00	264	185	160	1/95	46.10
1996 11	748	187	374	1/96	93.50	285	186	100	1/96	42.80
1997 11	788	197	394	1/97	98.50	307	185	100	1/97	47.10
1998 11	836	209	418	1/98	104.50	332	183	100	1/98	52.10
1999 11	884	221	442	1/99	110.50	359	197	100	1/99	53.80

[1] For services furnished on or after January 1, 1982, the coinsurance amounts are based on the inpatient hospital deductible for the year in which the services were furnished. For services furnished prior to January 1, 1982, the coinsurance amounts are based on the inpatient hospital deductible applicable for the year in which the individual's benefit period began.

[2] For care in psychiatric hospital—190 day lifetime limit.

[3] Always equal to ¼ of inpatient hospital deductible through 1988, and for 1990 and later, eliminated for 1989.

[4] Always equal to ½ of inpatient hospital deductible through 1988, and for 1990 and later, eliminated for 1989.

[5] Always equal to ⅛ of inpatient hospital deductible through 1988 and for 1990 and later. For 1989 it was equal to 20 percent of estimated Medicare covered average cost per day.

[6] Not applicable prior to July 1973. Applies to aged individuals who are not fully insured, and to certain disabled individuals who have exhausted other entitlement. The reduced amount is available to aged individuals who are not fully insured but who have, or whose spouse has or had, at least 30 quarters of coverage under title II of the Social Security Act. The reduced amount is 75% of the full amount in 1994, 70% in 1995, 65% in 1996, 60% in 1997 and 55% in 1998 and thereafter.

[7] Not covered.

[8] For August 1973 the premium was $6.10.

[9] In 1989, the HI deductible was applied on an annual basis, not a benefit period basis (unlike the other years).

[10] In 1989, the SNF coinsurance was on days 1–8 of the 150 days allowed annually; for the other years it is on days 21–100 of 100 days allowed per benefit period.

[11] Administration projections under current law using fiscal year 1995 budget assumptions.

Note.—In addition to the deductible and coinsurance amounts shown in the table, the first 3 pints of blood are not reimbursed by Medicare. Currently there is no deductible or coinsurance on home health benefits. From January 1973 to June 30, 1982, there was a $60 annual deductible and prior to July 1, 1981, benefits were limited to 100 visits per benefit period under part A and 100 visits per calendar year under part B. Special limits apply to certain benefits: (1) Outpatient physican services for mental illness; 50 percent of approved charges, up to a maximum of $250 in benefits per year; July 1, 1966, through December 31, 1987; $450 in benefits per year, January 1, 1988, through December 31, 1988; $1,100 in benefits per year, January 1, 1989, through December 31, 1989; beginning January 1, 1990, the limit was removed; (2) physical and occupational therapy services furnished by physical therapists in independent practice: maximum annual approved charges July 1, 1973, through December 31, 1981, $80 per year; January 1, 1982, through December 31, 1989, $400 per year; and January 1, 1983, through December 31, 1989, $500 per year; January 1, 1990, and thereafter $750 per year.

Source: Health Care Financing Administration, Office of the Actuary, Office of Medicare and Medicaid Cost Estimates.

COVERAGE

Most individuals establish entitlement to part A on the basis of work in employment covered by either the Social Security or railroad retirement systems. Certain employment is excluded from Social Security (including part A hospital insurance) taxation.

The Tax Equity and Fiscal Responsibility Act of 1982 extended the hospital insurance tax to Federal employment effective with respect to wages paid on or after January 1, 1983. Beginning January 1, 1983, Federal employment is included in determining eligibility for protection under Medicare part A. A transitional provision allows individuals who were in the employ of the Federal Government both before and during January 1, 1983, to have their prior Federal employment considered as employment for purposes of providing Medicare coverage. Newly hired employees of State and local governments hired after March 31, 1986, are liable for the HI tax.

BENEFITS

Part A of Medicare will pay for:

1. *Inpatient hospital care.*—All reasonable expenses for the first 60 days minus a deductible ($696 in calendar year 1994) in each benefit period. For days 61–90, a coinsurance amount ($174 in calendar year 1994) is deducted. When more than 90 days are required in a benefit period, a patient may elect to draw upon a 60 day lifetime reserve. A coinsurance amount ($348 in calendar year 1994) is also deducted for each reserve day.

2. *Skilled nursing facility care.*—Up to 100 days (following hospitalization) in a skilled nursing facility for persons in need of continued skilled nursing care and/or skilled rehabilitation services on a daily basis. After the first 20 days, there is a daily coinsurance ($87 in calendar year 1994).

3. *Home health care.*—Home health visits provided to persons who need skilled nursing care, physical therapy, or speech therapy on an intermittent basis.

4. *Hospice care.*—Hospice care services provided to terminally ill Medicare beneficiaries with a life expectancy of 6 months or less up to a 210-day lifetime limit. A subsequent period of hospice coverage is allowed beyond the 210-day limit if the beneficiary is recertified as terminally ill.

Part B of Medicare generally pays 80 percent of the approved amount (fee schedule, reasonable charges, or reasonable cost) for covered services in excess of an annual deductible ($100). Services covered include the following:

1. *Doctor's services.*—Including surgery, consultation, and home, office and institutional visits. Certain limitations apply for services rendered by dentists, podiatrists and chiropractors and for the treatment of mental illness.

2. *Other medical and health services.*—Laboratory and other diagnostic tests, X-ray and other radiation therapy, outpatient services at a hospital, rural health clinic services, home dialysis supplies and equipment, artificial devices (other than dental), physical and speech therapy, and ambulance services.

3. *Home health services.*—Unlimited number of medically necessary home health visits for persons not covered under part A.

The 20 percent coinsurance and $100 deductible do not apply for such benefits.

Table 5–4 illustrates the deductible, coinsurance and premium amounts for both part A and part B services from the inception of Medicare.

ADMINISTRATION

Responsibility for administration of the Medicare program has been delegated by the Secretary of Health and Human Services to the Administrator of the Health Care Financing Administration (HCFA). Much of the day-to-day operational work of the program is performed by "intermediaries" and "carriers" which have responsibility for reviewing claims for benefits and making payments.

In general, hospitals and other providers paid under part A of Medicare can nominate, subject to HCFA's approval, a national, State, or other public or private agency to serve as a fiscal intermediary between themselves and the Federal Government.

The Secretary enters into contracts with insurance organizations to serve as carriers. The carrier must perform its obligations under the contract efficiently and effectively and must meet such requirements as to financial responsibility, legal authority, and other matters as the Secretary finds pertinent. The carrier must ensure that payments made to providers under part B on a reasonable cost or reasonable charge basis (as may be applicable) are reasonable.

Medicare administrative costs in fiscal year 1993 amount to approximately 1.9 percent of total program outlays.

Hospitals

The Social Security Amendments of 1983 (Public Law 98–21) altered the way in which Medicare pays hospitals. From the inception of the program, Medicare had paid hospitals on a "reasonable cost" basis. Effective October 1, 1983, Medicare began paying under a prospective payment system. Medicare payments for inpatient operating costs of hospitals are determined in advance and made on a per discharge basis. A fixed amount per case is paid based upon the type of case or "diagnosis-related group" (DRG) into which the case is classified.

The payment system is not applied to direct medical education costs and certain other costs. Certain hospitals are excluded from the system: psychiatric, long-term care, children's cancer and rehabilitation hospitals. Excluded hospitals continue to be paid based on reasonable costs subject to certain rate of increase limitations.

Additional payments are made for extraordinarily costly cases, for the indirect costs of medical education, and for hospitals serving a disproportionate share of low income patients. An adjustment is made for the wage level in the area in which the hospital is located. In addition, there are certain other exceptions and adjustments including those for sole community providers, national and regional referral centers, and cancer treatment centers.

The prospective payment system was phased in over 4 years from payments based on an individual hospital's historical costs to payments based on the new payment rates. In addition, the system was phased in from payments representing nine regional payment levels to one national payment level for each DRG. There are separate payment levels for large urban, other urban, and rural areas. OBRA 1990 (P.L. 101–508) included a phaseout of the other urban/rural payment differential designed to eliminate the different payment levels for other urban and rural hospitals by fiscal year 1995. Once the phaseout is complete, there will be two payment levels for large urban and other hospitals.

Hospitals and other institutional providers receiving payment under Medicare part A submit bills on behalf of the beneficiary and agree to accept the program's payment as payment in full. In general, providers are permitted to charge beneficiaries only the deductible and coinsurance amounts authorized by law.

Physicians

Medicare part B provides insurance coverage for physician services and for certain other medical services. To be entitled to benefits under Medicare part B, individuals must enroll in part B and pay a monthly premium.

Payments are made for services covered under part B after an annual deductible requirement of $100 has been satisfied. Payment is set at 80 percent of the Medicare fee schedule or other payment amount. Beneficiaries are responsible for the remaining 20 percent as coinsurance. A few services are exempt from deductible and coinsurance requirements.

Beginning January 1, 1992, a new physician payment system is being phased in over 5 years. It is based on a fee schedule that assigns relative values to services. Relative values reflect three things: physician work (time, skill and intensity involved in the service), practice expenses, and malpractice costs. These relative values are adjusted for geographic variations in the costs of practicing medicine. These adjusted relative values are then converted into a dollar payment amount by a conversion factor.

Medicare payment is made either on an "assigned" or "unassigned" basis. By accepting assignment, physicians agree to accept the Medicare approved amount as payment in full. Thus, if assignment is accepted, beneficiaries are not liable for any out-of-pocket costs other than standard deductible and coinsurance payments. In contrast, if assignment is not accepted, beneficiaries may be liable for charges in excess of the Medicare approved charge, subject to certain limits. This is known as balance billing.

Medicare's participating physician program was established in 1984 to provide beneficiaries with the opportunity to select physicians who have agreed to accept assignment on all services provided during a 12-month period. Nonparticipating physicians continue to be able to accept or refuse assignment on a claim-by-claim basis. A number of incentives are provided to encourage physicians to sign participation agreements. These include: higher payment levels, more rapid claims payment, and widespread distribution of participating physician directories.

TABLE 5–5.—PARTICIPATING INSTITUTIONS AND ORGANIZATIONS (JUNE 1984, 1989, 1990, 1991, 1992 AND 1993)

	1984	1989	1990	1991	1992	1993
Hospitals	6,675	6,508	6,520	6,487	6,457	6,417
Short stay	6,038	5,582	5,549	5,480	5,427	5,343
Long stay	637	926	971	1,007	1,030	1,074
Skilled nursing facilities	5,952	8,198	8,937	9,674	10,589	11,308
Home health agencies	4,684	5,546	5,730	5,826	6,175	6,828
Independent laboratories	3,801	4,613	4,879	4,926	7,526	7,547
Clinical laboratory independent act (CLIAs)	....	....	....	....	....	159,172
Outpatient physical therapy providers	791	1,082	1,195	1,317	1,435	1,618
Portable X-ray suppliers	269	418	443	462	473	493
Rural health clinics	420	484	551	692	899	1,106
Comprehensive outpatient rehabilitation facilities	48	170	186	193	207	222
Ambulatory surgical centers	155	1,096	1,197	1,335	1,476	1,626
Hospices	108	703	825	1,057	1,199	1,395
Facilities providing services to renal disease beneficiaries	1,335	1,888	1,992	2,130	2,269	2,410
Hospitals certified as both renal transplant and renal dialysis centers	147	164	166	168	166	164
Hospitals certified as renal transplant centers	16	50	52	58	65	65
Hospital dialysis facilities	117	163	174	198	212	217
Non-hospital renal dialysis facilities	645	1,121	1,217	1,320	1,430	1,558
Dialysis centers only	359	332	1,882	331	337	347
Inpatient care	51	58	52	55	59	59
Hospital and skilled nursing facility beds:						
Hospitals	1,144,142	1,103,359	1,104,574	1,101,823	1,096,647	1,089,196
Short stay	1,023,465	973,013	970,480	966,577	960,616	951,433
Long stay	530,403	130,346	134,094	135,246	136,031	137,763
Skilled nursing facilities	530,403	492,999	508,585	567,199	597,234	616,633

Source: Health Care Financing Administration, BDMS, Decision Support Division.

Beginning in 1993, nonparticipating physicians are not allowed to charge more than 115 percent of Medicare's allowed amount for any service. Medicare's allowed amount for nonparticipating physicians is set at 95 percent of that for participating physicians. Thus, nonparticipating physicians are only able to bill 9.25 percent (115 percent times 95 percent) over the approved amount recognized for participating physicians.

The limits and participation differentials that now apply to physicians would be extended to other providers and practitioners when billing for a service covered under the physician fee schedule.

To provide incentives for physicians to get involved in efforts to stem expenditure increases, the law requires the calculation of annual Medicare volume performance standards (MVPSs), which are standards for the rate of expenditure growth. The relationship of actual expenditures to the MVPS is one factor used in determining the annual update in the conversion factor in a subsequent year.

A program to measure outcomes and effectiveness of the new system has been established. (Additional information concerning physician payment is included in appendix E.)

Table 5–5 above shows the number of participating institutions and organizations.

END STAGE RENAL DISEASE PROGRAM

The Medicare program covers individuals who suffer from end stage renal disease, if they are (1) fully insured for old age and survivor insurance benefits, or (2) are entitled to monthly social security benefits, or (3) are spouses or dependents of individuals described in (1) or (2). Such persons must be medically determined to be suffering from end stage renal disease and must file an application for benefits. Approximately 7 percent of the population suffering from end stage renal disease (ESRD) do not meet any of these requirements and thus is not covered for Medicare renal benefits.

Benefits for qualified end stage renal disease beneficiaries include all part A (hospital insurance) and part B (supplementary medical insurance) medical items and services. ESRD beneficiaries are automatically enrolled in the part B portion of Medicare and must pay the monthly premium for such protection.

Table 5–6 shows estimates of expenditures, number of beneficiaries, and the average expenditure per person from 1974 through 1999. Total projected program expenditures for Medicare end stage renal disease program for fiscal year 1993 are estimated at $6.7 billion. In fiscal year 1993, there were an estimated 184,257 beneficiaries, including successful transplant patients, and also including persons entitled to Medicare on the basis of disability who also have ESRD.

When the ESRD program was created, it was assumed that program enrollment would level out at about 90,000 enrollees by 1995. That mark was passed several years ago, and no indication exists that enrollment will stabilize soon.

TABLE 5–6.—ESRD MEDICARE BENEFICIARIES AND PROGRAM EXPENDITURES

[Expenditures in millions]

Fiscal year	Expenditures (HI & SMI)	HI beneficiaries	Per person
1974	$229	15,993	$14,319
1975	361	22,674	15,921
1976	512	28,941	17,691
1977	641	35,889	17,861
1978	800	43,482	18,398
1979	1,010	52,636	19,188
1980	1,250	55,509	22,519
1981	1,472	61,930	23,769
1982	1,651	69,552	29,738
1983	1,994	78,642	25,355
1984	2,336	87,929	26,567
1985	2,824	97,200	29,053
1986	3,159	106,633	29,625
1987	3,475	116,937	29,717
1988	3,909	127,487	30,662
1989	4,601	139,132	33,069
1990	5,093	152,541	33,388
1991	5,654	164,354	34,401
1992	6,124	174,454	35,104
1993	6,662	184,257	36,156
1994	7,266	194,201	37,415
1995	7,960	204,310	38,960
1996	8,754	214,564	40,799
1997	9,617	224,926	42,756
1998	10,580	235,351	44,954
1999	11,657	245,806	47,424

Note: Estimates for 1979–99 are subject to revision by the Office of the Actuary, Office of Medicare and Medicaid Cost Estimates; projections for 1994–99 are under the fiscal year 1995 budget assumptions.

Source: Office of the Actuary, Health Care Financing Administration, Department of Health and Human Services, for fiscal years 1979–99.

Table 5–7 shows that new enrollment grew an average annual rate of 9.7 percent from 1986 to 1991. Most of the growth in program participation is attributable to growth in the numbers of elderly people receiving services and growth in the numbers of more seriously ill people entering treatment. Table 5–7 shows the greatest rate of growth in program participation is in people over age 75, at 15.7 percent, followed by the second highest rate of growth in people ages 65 to 74 years old. This age group exhibited a growth rate of 12.2 percent. The largest rate of growth in primary causes of people entering ESRD treatment was diabetes. People with diabetes frequently have multiple health problems, making treatment for renal failure more difficult.

TABLE 5–7.—MEDICARE END STAGE RENAL DISEASE PROGRAM NEW ENROLLMENTS BY AGE AND PRIMARY DIAGNOSIS: 1986–91

Age and primary diagnosis	1986	1987	1988	1989	1990	1991	Average annual percent change	Percent change 1990–91
Number of new enrollees:								
Total	32,061	35,081	38,151	42,885	46,658	50,831	9.7	8.9
Age:								
Under 15 years	420	430	403	405	461	454	1.6	−1.5
15–24 years	1,188	1,247	1,268	1,315	1,271	1,242	0.9	−2.3
25–34 years	2,992	2,852	3,087	3,413	3,438	3,485	3.1	1.4
35–44 years	3,659	3,989	4,340	4,704	5,133	5,501	8.5	7.2
45–54 years	4,450	4,893	5,390	5,904	6,230	6,753	8.7	8.4
55–64 years	7,217	7,885	8,456	9,108	9,819	10,587	8.0	7.8
65–74 years	7,937	8,972	9,669	11,302	12,682	14,097	12.2	11.2
75 years and over	4,198	4,813	5,538	6,734	7,624	8,712	15.7	14.3
Diagnosis:								
Diabetes	9,434	10,488	11,717	14,214	15,939	18,249	14.1	14.5
Glomerulonephritis	4,717	4,958	5,228	5,643	5,779	5,810	4.3	0.5
Hypertension	8,049	9,221	10,325	12,161	13,278	14,633	12.7	10.2
Polycystic-kidney disease	1,225	1,248	1,250	1,275	1,402	1,474	3.8	5.1
Interstit Nephritis	1,355	1,240	1,233	1,378	1,371	1,497	2.0	9.2
Obstructive Nephropathy	846	839	872	954	916	985	3.1	7.5
Other	1,879	2,016	2,182	2,596	2,788	3,456	13.0	24.0
Unknown	2,349	2,804	2,657	2,443	2,408	2,693	2.8	11.8
Missing	2,207	2,267	2,687	2,221	2,777	2,034	−1.6	−26.8

Source: Health Care Financing Administration, Bureau of Data Management and Strategy: Data from the Program Management and Medical Information System, April 1993 update.

The rates of growth in older and sicker patients entering treatment for end stage renal disease indicate a shift in physician practice patterns. In the past, most of these people would not have entered dialysis treatment because their age and severity of illness made successful treatment for renal failure less likely. Although the reasons that physicians have begun treating older and sicker patients are not precisely known, it is clear that these practice patterns have, and will continue, to result in steady growth in the numbers of patients enrolling in Medicare's end stage renal program.

End stage renal disease is invariably fatal without treatment. Treatment for the disease takes two forms: transplantation and dialysis. Although the capability to perform transplants had existed since the 1950's, problems with rejection of transplanted organs limited its application as a treatment for renal failure. The 1983 introduction to the market of a powerful and effective immunosuppressive drug, cyclosporine, resulted in a dramatic increase in the numbers of transplants being performed and the success rate of transplantation.

Table 5–8 indicates that the number of transplants in 1992 was more than double the number performed in 1980. Despite the significant increases in the number and success of kidney transplants, transplantation will not be the treatment of choice for all ESRD patients. A chronic, severe shortage of kidneys available for transplantation now limits the number of patients who can receive transplants. Even absent a shortage of organs, some patients are not suitable candidates for transplants because of their age, severity of illness or other complicating conditions. And some ESRD patients do not want an organ transplant.

For all of these reasons, dialysis is likely to remain the primary treatment for end stage renal disease. Dialysis is an artificial method of performing the kidney's function of filtering blood to remove waste products. There are two types of dialysis: hemodialysis and peritoneal dialysis. In hemodialysis, still the most common form of dialysis, blood is removed from the body, filtered and cleansed through a dialyzer, sometimes called an artificial kidney machine, before being returned to the body. Peritoneal dialysis does not require use of a machine. Instead, filtering takes place inside the body by inserting dialysate fluid through a permanent surgical opening in the peritoneum (abdominal cavity). Toxins filter into the dialysate fluid and are then drained from the body through the surgical opening. To be effective, both types of dialysis generally need to be performed several times a week, usually three times.

TABLE 5–8.—TOTAL KIDNEY TRANSPLANTS PERFORMED IN MEDICARE CERTIFIED U.S. HOSPITALS

Calendar year	Total trans-plants	Living donor		Cadaveric donor	
		Number	Percent	Number	Percent
1979	4,189	1,186	28	3,003	72
1980	4,697	1,275	27	3,422	73
1981	4,883	1,458	30	3,425	70
1982	5,358	1,677	31	3,681	69
1983	6,112	1,784	29	4,328	71
1984	6,968	1,704	24	5,364	76
1985	7,695	1,876	24	5,819	76
1986	8,976	1,887	21	7,089	79
1987	8,967	1,907	21	7,060	79
1988	8,932	1,760	20	7,116	80
1989	8,899	1,893	21	7,006	79
1990	9,796	2,091	21	7,705	79
1991	10,026	2,382	24	7,644	76
1992	10,115	2,536	25	7,579	75

Source: HCFA, BDMS, OSDM, Division of Special Programs.

Since 1983, Medicare has reimbursed outpatient maintenance dialysis on the basis of a fixed rate which is adjusted to reflect the proportion of patients dialyzing at home. Separate rates are established for hospitals and for independent, or free-standing, facilities. Both rates were originally derived from audited costs; both are divided into nonlabor and labor components. The labor component is adjusted by a wage index to reflect differences in wages. In addition, the hospital rate contains two additional adjustments which result in slightly higher rates. One adjustment consists of a 5 percent add-on to the overall rate to account for possible data collection errors, and the second adjustment consists of a $2.10 add-on per treatment to account for hospitals' additional overhead. The fixed rate is paid for each treatment.

When this rate structure was implemented in 1983, HCFA estimated that the average payment for independent facilities would be around $127 per treatment and the average payment to hospitals would be approximately $131. In 1986, HCFA proposed to lower the rates, based on 1983 audit data which showed declining costs. The rates HCFA proposed to implement would have resulted in an average rate of $115.40 for independent facilities and an average rate of $119.70 for hospital-based facilities. OBRA 1986 preempted the implementation of these rates by reducing each rate by $2.00. In OBRA 1989, Congress required that these rates be maintained until October 1, 1990. OBRA 1990 increased rates by $1, effective January 1, 1991. The current average payment rate for hospital renal facilities is $130 per treatment and the average payment rate for independent renal facilities is $126 per treatment.

The effect of a dialysis rate that has been either fixed or declining since 1983 is less real spending per enrollee on dialysis services. Adjusting for inflation, dialysis reimbursement rates were nearly 65 percent lower in 1991 than they were in 1974. Considerable evidence documents increasing efficiency and lower costs associated with dialysis, but concerns that the rates have adversely affected quality and access to care remain. In OBRA 1987, Congress authorized the Institute of Medicine to conduct a comprehensive study of the ESRD program and the effects of the composite rate.

The Institute of Medicine (IOM) study required by OBRA 1987 was submitted to Congress in April 1991. As part of its mandate, the IOM examined several indicators of quality (mortality, morbidity, and dialysis staffing patterns). The IOM also examined the dialysis rate structure, commented on its implications for quality, and made a number of recommendations regarding ESRD dialysis rates. It found no conclusive evidence linking the composite rate to declining quality of care, as measured by mortality and morbidity. Nevertheless, the IOM suggested that there might be an indirect effect on quality of care due to the composite rate structure. It recommended modifications to the current rate structure, including updating the rates yearly and rebasing the rate structure after a comprehensive quality assurance program is established. It also recommended against further reductions in the composite rate and against rebasing the rate using current audit data because, in its opinion, current costs may not include all services providers deem medically appropriate.

Recent changes

Dialysis payment rates.—OBRA 1989 mandated the continuance of the dialysis rates then in effect until October 1, 1990. In addition, it required the Secretary to follow standard regulatory procedures when proposing rate changes. OBRA 1990 increased the dialysis rates in effect on September 30, 1990, by $1 for services provided on or after January 1, 1991.

OBRA 1990 also directed the Prospective Payment Assessment Commission (ProPAC) to conduct a study to determine the costs, services and profits associated with various dialysis treatment modalities. The Commission was also required to make recommendations to Congress by June 1, 1992, on methods and levels of reimbursement for dialysis services. In its June 1992 report, ProPAC indicated that it has adopted an incremental approach to evaluating payment method and level and developing an update. The Commission will evaluate several options for unit of payment, including looking at larger bundles of services across longer time periods, recalculating base rates using more recent data, and using site of service and modality to determine payment.

In addition to this study, OBRA 1990 directed ProPAC to make a recommendation to Congress on an appropriate factor to be used in updating payments for services. ProPAC is to submit its recommendations to Congress by March 1 of each year for the succeeding fiscal year. In its March 1994 Report to Congress, ProPAC did not recommend an increase in payments for dialysis services.

Limitation of method II payments for home dialysis.—In January 1989, HCFA proposed to limit payments (called method II payments) to suppliers who deal directly with Medicare beneficiaries rather than providing supplies through an approved Medicare dialysis facility. HCFA's proposed rule was in response to information that one supplier received monthly payments nearly twice as high as facilities received for dialyzing patients, either in-facility or at home. These rules were not implemented.

Subsequently, the General Accounting Office conducted a study of method II payments. GAO concluded that the differential in payments between method I (payments to dialysis facilities for home dialysis patients) and method II suppliers was not justified. Shortly after GAO's report was released, Congress incorporated GAO's recommendations by enacting a payment limit on method II payments in OBRA 1989. The new limit is 100 percent of the median dialysis rate paid to hospital-based facilities. In the case of home patients on continuous cycling peritoneal dialysis (CCPD), the limit is 130 percent of the median hospital-based dialysis rate. The payment limit took effect on February 1, 1990.

Staff-assisted home dialysis demonstration project.—In response to continuing congressional concerns about some home dialysis patients' needs for staff assistance after the limitation on method II payments was imposed, OBRA 1990 established a 3-year demonstration project to determine whether Medicare coverage of staff assistants could be both cost effective and safe for patients. The demonstration was to begin within 9 months of OBRA 1990's enactment for a maximum of 800 participants. The law defines staff assistant services as including: technical assistance with operating the hemodialysis machine and care of patients during home dialysis; and administration of medications in patients' homes. Home dialysis staff assistants must meet minimum requirements specified by the Secretary and any State requirements applicable in the State where the staff assistant practices.

The law establishes rather stringent patient eligibility criteria designed to assure that the demonstration is limited to patients whose health problems are exacerbated by travel to a dialysis facility and whose family members are not able to assist them with home dialysis.

Payments to an ESRD provider or dialysis facility participating in the demonstration project are to be prospectively determined by the Secretary, made on a per treatment basis, and paid as an add-on to the dialysis rate. OBRA 1990 provides detailed instructions on calculating the payment rate for staff assistants. The payment structure is designed to prevent duplicate payments for labor costs, since the dialysis rate structure already includes labor costs associated with providing in-facility dialysis.

OBRA 1990 provided funding of $4 million in each of fiscal years 1991 and 1992 for the demonstration; $3 million in fiscal year 1993; $2 million in fiscal year 1994; and $1 million in fiscal year 1995. The Secretary is directed to submit a preliminary report on the status of the demonstration by December 1, 1992, and a final report by December 31, 1995. The final report is to evaluate the demonstration project and include recommendations regarding eligibility criteria and cost-control mechanisms for providing Medicare coverage of home dialysis aides.

Reimbursement for epoetin.—On June 1, 1989 the U.S. Food and Drug Administration (FDA) approved marketing of a drug used to treat anemia associated with chronic renal failure. The drug, epoctin, is a genetically engineered copy of a protein (erythropoietin or EPO) that the body uses to stimulate production of red blood cells. EPO is used as a substitute for transfusions. Medicare began reimbursing for the drug for chronic renal failure patients with a specified level of anemia in 1989. Chronic renal failure patients may include those not on dialysis or transplant patients as long as they have the specified level of anemia.

In a break with longstanding policy, Medicare's reimbursement rate for EPO was negotiated in advance of FDA approval and was set at about 80 percent of the anticipated market price. Concern about the eventual costs that EPO would add to ESRD expenditures played a major role in HCFA negotiation of a Medicare reimbursement rate below market price.

Reimbursement for the drug varies by the setting in which it is administered. If administered in an approved ESRD facility (either a hospital or an independent facility), payment is made as an add-on to the dialysis rate. For each administration of the drug of less than 10,000 units, the additional payment was initially set at $40. For patients requiring more than 10,000 units, a payment of $30 was initially made, which was an addition to the $40 payment. The maximum payment was $70.

Physicians receiving monthly capitation payments for providing services to ESRD patients are reimbursed for drug costs but are not given any additional reimbursement for administering the drug. However, they are reimbursed an additional $2 per treatment for supplies, such as syringes. HCFA suggested that reimbursement for actual drug costs be based on drug prices reported in the Drug Topics red book, blue book or Medispan manuals, although, as a matter of practice, some carriers reimburse drug costs based on actual invoices.

Prior to implementing Medicare coverage of EPO, budget estimators had no reliable basis on which to estimate the number of ESRD patients who would use it. HCFA's preliminary estimate was that about 25 percent (25,000 to 30,000) of dialysis patients would use it in the first year of coverage, but that approximately 80 percent (75,000 to 80,000) of dialysis patients would use it by 1994 or 1995. The total yearly costs of providing the drug per user were estimated at $5,600, with Medicare paying $4,480 and the remaining $1,120 paid by other insurers or beneficiaries.

Medicare claims for dialysis patients processed for December 1991 indicate that the dose per treatment averaged about 3,399 units. A total of 75,845 ESRD patients received EPO that month. Medicare payments for EPO in December 1991 were $35.2 million.

OBRA 1990 revised payments made to dialysis facilities for EPO by establishing payment rates per 1,000 unit increments; abolishing the $70 payment cap; and indexing EPO payment rates for subsequent years. Effective January 1, 1991, payments to dialysis facilities for EPO were limited to $11 per 1,000 unit increments, rounded to the nearest 100 units. OBRA 1993 mandated a reduction in EPO payments to $10 per 1,000 units, rounded to the nearest 100 units (or $1 per 100 units) effective January 1, 1994.

OBRA 1990 also extended coverage for self-administration of EPO to home dialysis patients if they are competent to administer it without medical or other supervision. The Secretary is to develop methods and standards to determine who is competent to self-administer the drug. Payments for EPO on behalf of home dialysis patients who self-administer EPO are made on the same basis as payments to facilities. This includes payments to suppliers on behalf of method II patients. Coverage for self-administration of EPO became effective for services provided on or after July 1, 1991. OBRA 1993 permitted all dialysis patients to self-administer EPO.

Medicare spending for ESRD services

Table 5–9 shows overall per capita Medicare spending by type of ESRD patient from 1986–91. There are four types of ESRD patients: (1) dialysis patients, (2) transplant patients, (3) functioning graft (successful transplant) patients, and (4) graft failure (failed transplant) patients. Dialysis patients are those on dialysis during the year in question. Transplant patients are those who received a transplant during that year. Functioning graft patients are recipients of successful transplants performed during a previous year, and graft failure patients are those who received a transplant during a prior year, but whose transplants failed during the year in question.

Per capita spending for ESRD patients averaged $31,899 in 1991 for patients who had at least 1 full year of Medicare entitlement in the prior year. Thus, these expenditure data exclude patients for whom Medicare was a secondary payer. Spending varied significantly by type of patient. Patients with successful transplants had the lowest average annual expenditures at $7,098, followed by dialysis patients at $35,652. Patients whose transplants failed had higher annual costs at $43,373. The highest costs were reported for patients who had a transplant during the year in question; their 1991 per capita costs were reported at $97,252. If their transplants are successful over the long run, however, these patients are ultimately less expensive to serve because they no longer need either expensive acute care or chronic dialysis services.

TABLE 5–9.—MEDICARE END STAGE RENAL DISEASE PROGRAM EXPENDITURES BY PATIENT TREATMENT GROUP, EXCLUDING MEDICARE SECONDARY PAYER PATIENTS:[1] 1986–91

Treatment group	1986	1987	1988	1989	1990	1991	Average annual percent change 1986–91
Total number of patients	99,769	108,474	120,431	132,734	145,664	160,805	10.0
Expenditures (per person):							
Total	$24,957	$25,501	$25,852	$27,726	$29,480	$31,899	5.0
Inpatient	11,087	11,190	11,384	12,436	12,989	14,067	4.9
Outpatient	8,999	9,057	8,936	8,927	9,860	10,601	3.3
Physician/supplier	4,737	5,122	5,393	6,192	6,358	6,821	7.6
Other[2]	134	132	139	171	272	410	25.1
Dialysis							
Number of patients	78,228	83,751	92,595	101,816	111,435	122,843	9.4
Expenditures (per patient):							
Total	$26,700	$27,891	$28,674	$31,023	$33,039	$35,652	6.0
Inpatient	10,443	10,890	11,403	12,712	13,198	14,098	6.2
Outpatient	10,810	11,040	10,946	10,967	12,165	13,133	4.0
Physician/supplier	5,296	5,812	6,167	7,148	7,361	7,942	8.4
Other[2]	152	149	159	196	315	480	25.9
Transplant							
Number of patients	3,876	3,729	3,767	3,768	4,351	4,648	3.7

TABLE 5–9.—MEDICARE END STAGE RENAL DISEASE PROGRAM EXPENDITURES BY PATIENT TREATMENT GROUP, EXCLUDING MEDICARE SECONDARY PAYER PATIENTS:[1] 1986–91—Continued

Treatment group	1986	1987	1988	1989	1990	1991	Average annual percent change 1986–91
Expenditures: Total	$68,036	$70,559	$71,334	$75,892	$81,339	$97,252	7.4
Inpatient	51,731	53,128	52,899	56,586	61,236	75,697	7.9
Outpatient	8,270	8,597	8,905	8,890	9,695	10,365	4.6
Physician/supplier	7,936	8,731	9,412	10,292	10,274	10,897	6.5
Other[2]	99	104	117	124	193	293	24.2
Functioning Graft							
Number of patients	16,627	19,721	22,720	25,524	28,260	31,623	13.7
Expenditures: Total	$6,160	$6,184	$6,124	$6,697	$6,885	$7,098	2.9
Inpatient	4,120	3,935	3,800	4,119	4,201	4,319	0.9
Outpatient	694	754	780	829	826	842	3.9
Physician/supplier	1,287	1,431	1,480	1,671	1,736	1,778	6.7
Other[2]	59	65	65	78	122	159	21.9
Graft Failure							
Number of patients	1,038	1,273	1,349	1,626	1,618	1,691	10.3
Expenditures: Total	$33,802	$35,541	$37,415	$39,739	$39,330	$43,373	5.1

Inpatient	19,416	20,534	21,898	23,398	22,324	24,722	5.0
Outpatient	8,293	8,572	8,476	8,390	9,304	9,810	3.4
Physician/supplier	5,932	6,333	6,932	7,806	7,541	8,538	7.6
Other[2]	161	103	109	145	161	303	13.5

[1] Expenditures were calculated only for persons who had at least one full year of Medicare entitlement prior to the observation year. Thus, any patients for whom Medicare was a secondary payer were not included.

[2] Other includes skilled nursing facility and home health services.

Source: Health Care Financing Administration, Bureau of Data Management and Strategy: Data from the Program Management and Medical Information System, and the Medicare Automated Data Retrieval System, April 1992 update, 1986–91.

HOME HEALTH

The hospital insurance (part A) and the supplementary medical insurance (part B) programs cover home health visits for persons who need skilled nursing care on an intermittent basis or physical therapy or speech therapy. Persons must also be homebound. The home health benefit is not subject to deductibles or copayments. When an individual is covered under parts A and B of the Medicare program, the individual will generally receive payment for home health services under part A of the program. In 1992, Medicare covered an average of 57 home health visits for persons who qualified for the benefit.

Beginning in 1990, the Medicare home health benefit became again one of the fastest growing parts of the Medicare program. In 1990, reimbursements for home health increased by 49 percent, and in 1993, they increased by 36 percent. As table 10 indicates, home health payments are projected to increase significantly through at least 1996.

Reimbursement to home health agencies is based on Medicare rules for reasonable cost reimbursement. However, home health agencies are required to use the cost per visit by type of service for apportioning costs. Under this method, the total allowable costs of all visits for each type of service (skilled nursing, home health aide, etc.) is divided by the total number of visits by type of service. These average cost per visit amounts are multiplied by the number of covered Medicare visits for each type of service. The products represent the cost Medicare will recognize by type of service, subject to home health agency cost limits.

In 1986, Public Law 99–509 established the current methodology for determining home health care limits. These are set at 112 percent of the mean of the labor-related and nonlabor per unit costs for each type of service provided by freestanding home health agencies. The limits are then applied on an aggregate basis to all the visits made by the agency, with appropriate adjustments for the special costs of hospital-based agencies.

As a result of OBRA 1993 cost limits applicable to home health services will not be updated for cost reporting periods beginning on or after July 1, 1994, and before July 1, 1996. In addition, additional payments for the administrative cost of hospital-based home health agencies will be eliminated for cost reporting periods beginning after fiscal year 1993.

TABLE 5–10.—TOTAL MEDICARE HOME HEALTH BENEFIT PAYMENTS [1]

[In millions of dollars]

Fiscal year	Reimbursements			Change from prior year	Visits per 1,000 enrollees [2]	Average charge per visit [2]
	Part A	Part B	Total			
1969	NA	NA	$69	....	232	$13
1970	NA	NA	82	18.8	222	14
1971	NA	NA	78	– 4.9	164	16
1972	NA	NA	82	5.1	168	17
1973	NA	NA	89	8.5	189	18
1974	NA	NA	147	65.2	211	21
1975	NA	NA	208	41.5	271	24
1976	NA	NA	331	59.1	347	27
1977	NA	NA	429	29.6	419	29
1978	NA	NA	529	23.3	464	32
1979	NA	NA	628	18.7	515	34
1980	NA	NA	756	20.4	577	36
1981	NA	NA	889	17.6	713	40
1982	NA	NA	1,167	31.3	1,024	44
1983	NA	NA	1,480	26.8	1,227	47
1984	NA	NA	1,744	17.8	1,344	50
1985	$1,908	$40	1,948	11.7	1,329	55
1986	1,939	32	1,971	1.2	1,256	58
1987	1,815	35	1,850	– 6.1	1,153	61
1988	2,010	46	2,056	11.1	1,144	64
1989	2,251	56	2,307	12.2	1,313	64
1990	3,352	75	3,427	48.5	1,889	64
1991	4,995	62	5,057	47.6	2,219	69
1992	6,986	75	7,061	39.6	3,717	59
1993	9,529	101	9,630	36.4	4,660	61
1994	12,533	121	12,654	31.4	5,702	63
1995	15,074	140	15,214	20.2	6,446	65
1996	17,217	162	17,379	14.2	6,898	68
1997	19,127	188	19,315	11.1	7,045	72
1998	20,518	217	20,735	7.4	7,108	76
1999	21,932	250	22,182	7.0	7,166	79

[1] Based on fiscal year 1995 President's budget assumptions. HCFA revises historical estimates slightly with the added data available each year.
[2] Based on Part A alone.

NA=Not available.

Source: Health Care Financing Administration, Division of Budget.

HOSPICE CARE

Public Law 97–248 authorized Medicare part A coverage for hospice care services provided to individuals who are entitled to Medicare part A benefits and who are certified to be terminally ill. In 1986, the Congress in Public Law 99–272 made the hospice benefit a permanent part of the Medicare program effective April 7, 1986.

On December 16, 1983, the Health Care Financing Administration (HCFA), published regulations to implement the hospice provisions of Public Law 97–248. Among other things, the regulations establish requirements for eligibility, covered benefits, services, reimbursement procedures, and the conditions a hospice must meet to be approved for participation in the Medicare program.

Part A beneficiaries may elect to receive hospice care in lieu of most other Medicare benefits for up to two periods of 90 days each, a subsequent period of 30 days, and an additional extension period if elected.

The statute provides that payment to hospice providers be equal to the costs which are reasonable and related to the cost of providing hospice care, or which are based on such other tests of reasonableness as the Secretary may prescribe, subject to a "cap amount." The cap amount for a beneficiary for a year was established at $6,500, adjusted annually by the medical component of the CPI. The cap for the period November 1, 1992 through October 31, 1993 is $12,248.

HCFA has implemented a prospective payment methodology for hospice care. Under this methodology, hospices are paid one of four predetermined rates for each day a Medicare beneficiary is under the care of the hospice. The rates vary according to the level of care furnished to the beneficiary. Total reimbursement to a hospice for care furnished to the Medicare beneficiary will vary by the length of the patient's period in the hospice program as well as by the characteristics of the services (intensity and site) furnished to the beneficiary.

Four basic payment categories are used for reimbursing hospices. The payment rates are national rates which are adjusted by the Bureau of Labor Statistics wage index for an area. The published payment rates are:

(a) *Routine home care day.*—Routine home care day is a day on which an individual who has elected to receive hospice care is at home and is not receiving continuous home care. The routine home care rate is paid for every day a patient is at home and under the care of the hospice regardless of the volume or intensity of the services provided on any given day as long as less than 8 hours of care are provided. Currently, this rate is $88.65.

(b) *Continuous home care day.*—A continuous home care day is a day on which an individual who has elected to receive hospice care receives hospice care consisting predominantly of nursing care on a continuous basis at home. Home health aide or homemaker services or both may also be provided on a continuous basis. Continuous home care is furnished only during brief periods of crisis and only as necessary to maintain the terminally ill patient at home. Home care must be provided for a period of at least 8 hours before it would be considered to fall within the category of continuous home care. Payment for continuous home care will vary depending on the number of hours of continuous services provided. Currently this rate is $517.43 for 24 hours or $21.56 per hour.

(c) *Inpatient respite care day.*—An inpatient respite care day is one on which the individual who has elected hospice care receives care in an approved facility on a short-term (not more than 5 days at a time) basis for the respite of his caretakers. Currently this rate is $91.70.

(d) *General inpatient care day.*—A general inpatient care day is one on which an individual who has elected hospice care receives general inpatient care in an inpatient facility for pain control or acute or chronic symptom management which cannot be managed in other settings. Care may be provided in a hospital, skilled nursing facility or inpatient unit of a freestanding hospice. Currently this rate is $394.39.

Public Law 101–239 required that the payment rates be increased by the hospital market basket percentage increase each fiscal year. As a result of OBRA 1993 the payment rates will be increased by the hospital market basket percentage increase minus 2.0 percentage points in fiscal year 1994, market basket minus 1.5 percentage points in fiscal years 1995 and 1996, and market basket minus 0.5 percentage points in fiscal year 1997.

TABLE 5–11.—ESTIMATES OF HOSPICE PROGRAM DATA

	Admissions	Days per admission	Cost per hospice day	Cost per admission	Total cost (outlays in millions)
Fiscal year:					
1984	2,200	29	$62	$1,800	$4
1985	11,000	33	66	2,200	34
1986	28,012	37	66	2,442	68
1987	68,721	41	74	3,034	104
1988	84,770	44	74	3,256	137
1989	89,008	48	74	3,552	211
1990	105,209	60	85	5,100	318
1991	122,179	61	93	5,686	479
1992	131,041	62	97	6,033	808
1993	153,490	62	101	6,281	958
1994	171,589	64	104	8,885	1,138
1995	192,185	64	107	6,880	1,341
1996	217,123	64	111	7,090	1,538
1997	244,331	64	115	7,357	1,758
1998	271,484	64	120	7,669	1,997
1999	298,423	65	125	8,119	2,248

Note: Fiscal year 1984 through fiscal year 1992 are actuals; fiscal year 1993 through fiscal year 1999 are estimates.

Source: CBO estimates.

SKILLED NURSING FACILITY

Medicare's part A hospital insurance program covers 100 days of skilled nursing facility (SNF) care for persons who can demonstrate a need for daily skilled nursing care for a condition related to a prior hospitalization. The first 20 days of SNF care are paid in full by the program. Days 21 through 100 are subject to a copayment of $87 a day in 1994. In 1992 Medicare covered an average of 27.5 days of care for those persons who qualified for the benefit.

In general, SNFs are reimbursed on the basis of reasonable costs subject to certain limits. For SNFs, limits are applied to the per diem routine service costs (nursing, room and board, administrative, and other overhead) of a facility. Capital-related and ancillary costs, such as physical therapy and drugs, are excluded from the cost limits. Separate limits are established for SNFs on the basis of whether they are freestanding or hospital-based facilities and whether they are located in urban or rural areas. Freestanding SNF cost limits are set at 112 percent of the average per diem labor-related and nonlabor costs. Hospital-based SNF cost limits are set at the limit for freestanding SNFs, plus 50 percent of the difference between the freestanding limit and 112 percent of the average per diem routine service costs of hospital-based SNFs. OBRA 1993 provides that the per-diem cost limits applied to payment for SNF services will not be changed for cost reporting periods beginning during fiscal years 1994 and 1995. Additional payments for excess overhead costs allocated to hospital-based facilities are eliminated, effective for cost reporting periods beginning on or after October 1, 1993.

Public Law 99–272 established a prospective payment rate system for certain SNFs that elect such payment for cost reporting periods beginning on or after October 1, 1986. SNFs providing less than 1,500 days of care per year to Medicare patients in the preceding year would have the option of being paid a prospective payment rate set at 105 percent of the regional mean for all SNFs in the region. The rate is calculated separately for urban and rural areas and the prospective per diem rate also reflects wage differences between urban and rural areas within each region. These rates cannot exceed the per diem cost limit that would otherwise be applicable to that facility and cannot exceed its cost limit adjusted for capital costs.

Proprietary skilled nursing facilities (SNFs) receive, in addition to payments for the costs of providing services, a return on equity payment, which provides the investors in the facility a return on their investment equivalent to what they would have earned if they had invested the same amount in specified government securities. SNFs are the only providers still receiving Medicare return on equity payments. OBRA 1993 eliminated Medicare payment to SNFs for return on equity, applicable to portions at cost reporting periods beginning on or after October 1, 1993.

Several important changes occurred in the SNF program during 1988 and 1989. First, in April 1988, HCFA issued a new manual to the carriers that was designed to clarify the SNF eligibility requirements. Increases in monthly SNF outlays and anecdotal information strongly suggested that the manual clarifications increased eligibility. Before this manual was issued, monthly outlays for Medicare SNF's were approximately $60 million per month. By the end of 1988, they had risen to almost $100 million per month.

Second, in June 1988 the Medicare Catastrophic Coverage Act of 1988 was enacted. The Medicare catastrophic legislation (1) removed the requirement that a Medicare beneficiary had to be in the hospital for at least 3 days prior to entering a SNF, (2) instituted a daily coinsurance payment in 1989 of $25.50 for the first 8 days (formerly no copayments were required for the first 20 days), (3) eliminated the coinsurance a beneficiary would have to pay after 8 days (formerly copayments of one-eighth of the hospital deductible of $70 in 1989 were required for days 21–100), and (4) changed the number of days that a person could receive the benefit from 100 days per spell of illness to 150 days per year. These changes were effective January 1, 1989. Monthly SNF spending rose rapidly from $97 million in January 1989 to $280 million in November 1989. Congress subsequently repealed all the legislative changes made in the SNF benefit when it repealed the Medicare Catastrophic Coverage Act.

TABLE 5–12.—SKILLED NURSING FACILITY DATA

Fiscal year	Number of SNF facilities	Total covered days of care (thousands)	Total interim reimbursement (thousands)	Interim reimbursement per day
1977	4,461	9,757.7	314,148	32
1978	4,982	9,231.1	317,472	34
1979	5,055	8,642.0	329,388	38
1980	5,155	8,701.0	358,508	41
1981	5,295	8,678.2	393,939	45
1982	5,510	8,696.2	425,251	49
1983	5,760	9,277.4	465,341	50
1984	6,183	9,546.9	489,722	51
1985	6,725	9,114.1	509,714	56
1986	7,065	8,175.6	515,444	63
1987	7,148	7,501.8	560,521	75
1988	7,379	11,152.5	857,142	77
1989	8,201	30,172.9	3,046,642	101
1990	8,937	23,986.5	1,966,545	82
1991	10,061	22,368.2	2,253,113	101
1991 [1]	11,309	26,843.9	3,253,306	121

[1] Data are considered preliminary.

Source: Data derived from Medicare Decision Support System (MSS), Current Utilization Series Table 8, 09/30/93 Update.

Table 5–12 shows the impact of the 1989 expansions: the number of participating facilities, covered days of care, and total reimbursement all increased in 1989. While covered days of care and reimbursements have declined since the repeal of the expansions, they have not returned to their pre-1989 levels. A report of the Office of the Inspector General, DHHS, points to the continued impact of the revised coverage guidelines; SNFs reluctance to abandon their decisions to participate or expand their certified beds after having invested resources to do so; and high demand for skilled nursing home care.

DURABLE MEDICAL EQUIPMENT

Current Medicare law does not provide an inclusive definition of durable medical equipment (DME). Section 1861(n) of the Social Security Act specifies that DME includes "* * * iron lungs, oxygen tents, hospital beds, wheelchairs (including power-operated vehicles) * * * used in a patient's home, including an institution used as his home * * *" DME also includes "medical supplies (including catheters, catheter supplies, ostomy bags, and supplies related to ostomy care, but excluding drugs and biologicals)".[1] In addition to items specified in the law, a wide variety of DME is covered under Medicare part B.

CURRENT REIMBURSEMENT FOR DURABLE MEDICAL EQUIPMENT

Medicare pays for DME on the basis of a fee schedule enacted in the Omnibus Budget Reconciliation Act of 1987. Prior to OBRA 1987, reimbursement for DME was made on the basis of reasonable costs to hospital outpatient departments and other providers, such as skilled nursing facilities, and reasonable charges to other part B suppliers. The fee schedule became effective January 1, 1989.

Under the fee schedule, reimbursement is of the lesser of 80 percent of the actual charge for the item or the fee schedule amount. Within the fee schedule, there are five categories of DME. Each category has separate reimbursement principles, although the principles for some categories are similar. The five categories are as follows: (1) inexpensive or other routinely purchased durable medical equipment, which is defined as equipment costing less than $150 or which is purchased at least 75 percent of the time; (2) items requiring frequent and substantial servicing; (3) customized items, which is defined as equipment constructed or modified substantially to meet the needs of an individual patient; (4) other items of durable medical equipment (frequently referred to as the "capped rental" category); and (5) oxygen and oxygen equipment.

In addition to these five categories, prosthetics and orthotics were also included in the DME fee schedule prior to the enactment of the Omnibus Budget Reconciliation Act of 1990. Section 1861(s)(9) of the Social Security Act defines prosthetics and orthotics as "leg, arm, back and neck braces, and artificial legs, arms and eyes." As with DME, this definition is not inclusive.

OBRA 1990 established reimbursement principles for prosthetics and orthotics under a separate section of law. Although a new section of law was created for prosthetics and orthotics, the reimbursement principles established remained identical to those under the DME fee schedule, except that prosthetics and orthotics were exempted from the DME reimbursement changes made in OBRA 1990. (The following discussion of DME reimbursement principles includes prosthetics and orthotics.)

Table 5–13 shows total Medicare allowed payment amounts for DME in calendar year 1992.

---

[1] Section 1861(m)(5) of the Social Security Act.

TABLE 5–13.—ALLOWED AMOUNTS FOR SELECTED DURABLE MEDICAL EQUIPMENT (DME) CALENDAR YEAR 1991 AND 1992

[In millions of dollars]

Category	Allowed amounts	
	1991	1992
Capped rental [1]	$461	$468
Customized items [2]	7	9
Oxygen [3]	739	1,093
Prosthetics/orthotics [4]	553	785
Inexpensive/routinely purchased [5]	137	181
Items requiring frequent maintenance [6]	144	181
Other [7]	349	135
Total	2,390	2,856

[1] Items of DME on a monthly rental basis not to exceed a period of continuous use of 15 months.

[2] Items unsuitable for grouping together for profiling due to unique nature (custom fabrication, etc.). Payment based on individual adjudication. Amount is incomplete because it only represents HCPCS E1220. Other items are not coded in HCPCS.

[3] Oxygen and oxygen equipment paid based on a monthly rate per beneficiary. Payment not made for purchased equipment except where installment payments continue.

[4] These items include other prosthetic and orthotic devices (except for items included in the categories "Customized Items" and "Items Requiring Frequent Maintenance," transcutaneous electrical nerve stimulators, parenteral/enteral nutritional supplies and equipment, and intraocular lenses). Devices in this category paid on lump sum purchase basis.

[5] Inexpensive defined as equipment for which the purchase price does not exceed $150. Routinely Purchased defined as equipment that is acquired 75 percent of the time by purchase.

[6] Paid on a rental basis until medical necessity ends.

[7] This category includes medical and surgical supplies, additional ostomy supplies, enteral formulae and enteral medical supplies, orthotic devices, and vision services which were reported using procedure codes (e.g., temporary codes and local codes) not included on the list of codes for categories 1–6 (above) provided by the Health Care Financing Administration (HCFA), Bureau of Policy Development.

Source: Health Care Financing Administration (HCFA), Bureau of Data Management and Strategy. Data from the part B Medicare Annual Data System. Codes for the categories above provided by HCFA, Bureau of Policy Development, OSDM, DPPS.

CHART 5–1. MEDICARE REIMBURSEMENT FOR DURABLE MEDICAL EQUIPMENT

	Inexpensive or routinely purchased DME	Items requiring frequent and substantial servicing	Customized items	Other items of DME (capped rental)	Prosthetics and orthotics	Oxygen and oxygen equipment
Examples of items	Commode chairs, electric heat pads, IV poles, bed rails, vaporizers, blood glucose monitors, pacemaker monitors, seat lift chairs.	Ventilators, internal positive pressure breathing (IPPB) machines, ventilators, excluding ventilators that are either continous airway pressure devices or intermittent assist devices with continuous airway pressure devices.	Customized wheelchairs adapted specifically for an individual.	Hospital beds, infusion pumps, walkers, wheelchairs (including power-driven chairs).	Artificial limbs, ostomy supplies.	Liquid and gaseous and various types of oxygen equipment.
Fee schedule basis ...	Average charge for purchase or rental.	Average reasonable charge.	Determined by the carrier on an individual basis.	Average of purchase prices on assigned claims, reduced by the percentage by which averge charges is lower than average purchase prices.	Average reasonable charge for purchase.	Average reasonable charge for purchase.

National floors and ceilings.	Floor = 85% of median of local payment amounts; ceiling = 100% of same. Effective: 1994.	Floor = 85% of median of local payment amounts; ceiling = 100% of same. Effective: 1994.	No	Floor = 85% of median of local payment amounts; ceiling = 100% of same. Effective: 1994.	Floor = 85% of average of national purchase prices; ceiling = 125% of same. Effective: 1992. Subsequent year: limits are 90% and 120%.	Floor = 85% of the median of all local monthly payment rates; ceiling = 100% of same. Effective 1994.
1993 update	CPI–U 0	CPI–U 0	Not applicable	CPI–U 0	CPI–U 0	CPI–U 0
1994 update			Not applicable			
Other provisions		Reasonable lifetime		Reasonable lifetime; limit on rental payments = 120% of purchase price.		
Base period	July 1, 1986 to June 30, 1987, updated by the CPI–U to Dec. 1987.	July 1, 1986 to June 30, 1987, updated by the CPI–U to Dec. 1987.	Not applicable	Base period for purchase prices—July 1, 1986 to Dec. 30, 1986, updated by the CPI–U to Dec. 1987. Base period for reasonable charges—Apr. 1, 1988—Dec. 31, 1988.	July 1, 1986 to June 30, 1987.	Jan. 1, 1986 to Dec. 30, 1986, reduced by 5%, and updated by the CPI–U to Dec. 1987.

CHART 5–1. MEDICARE REIMBURSEMENT FOR DURABLE MEDICAL EQUIPMENT—Continued

	Inexpensive or routinely purchased DME	Items requiring frequent and substantial servicing	Customized items	Other items of DME (capped rental)	Prosthetics and orthotics	Oxygen and oxygen equipment
Rent or purchase	Rental or purchase .	Rental only	Purchase only	Rental with option to purchase in first month for power-driven chairs; for other items, option to purchase is offered in the 10th continuous rental month.	Purchase only	Not applicable—monthly payment amount made.
Regional or national limits.	Phased-in national limits, beginning in 1991 and fully implemented in 1993.	Phased-in national limits, beginning in 1991 and fully implemented in 1993.	Not applicable	Phased-in national limits, beginning in 1991 and fully implemented in 1993.	Phased-in regional limits beginning in 1992 and fully implemented in 1994. Effective January 1, 1994 national limits would apply to ostomy supplies, trachestomy supplies and urologicals.	Phased-in national limits beginning in 1991 and fully implemented in 1993.

Medicare law specifies detailed reimbursement principles for DME.[2] Chart 5–1 gives examples of each category of equipment, shows the key components of the fee schedule, and describes how these components affect each category of equipment. The following discussion provides more explanation about these components.

Fee schedule basis

The basis for determining the fee schedule is established in law for each type of equipment. For items requiring frequent and substantial servicing, prosthetics and orthotics, and oxygen and oxygen equipment, the average Medicare *reasonable* charge is the basis from which fee schedules payments are calculated. Under reasonable charge reimbursement, payment is set at the lowest of the actual charge, the customary charge, the prevailing charge in the locality, or the inflation indexed charge (IIC) for that item.

For customized items, carriers are permitted to determine the appropriate payment amount without regard to average or reasonable charges.

The fee schedule basis for "capped rental" equipment is more complicated than for other categories. Originally, the basis for determining fee schedule payments for capped rental equipment was the average of submitted purchase prices on assigned claims during the base period.[3] OBRA 1990 altered this provision by setting the basis equal to the average of the purchase prices submitted for assigned claims submitted during the base time period, increased by the update factor, minus the percentage by which the average of the reasonable charges for submitted claims is lower than the average of purchase prices submitted for items during the last 9 months of 1988.

Implementation of this provision was originally slated for January 1, 1991, but was delayed until June 1991 because of questions about the validity of claims data. Payment limits were implemented retroactively to May 1, 1991. This provision was included in OBRA 1990 because of Congressional concerns that the fee schedule basis for capped rental items was too high and thus resulted in excessive Medicare payments for these items.

Base time period

Current law specifies the time period used to calculate the basis of the fee schedule for each category of equipment. The most common base period is from July 1, 1986 to June 30, 1987, updated by the Consumer Price Index for Urban consumers (CPI–U) to December 1987.

Rental or purchase

Some categories of DME may only be rented, some may only be purchased, and some may be either rented or purchased. Inexpensive or routinely purchased DME may be rented or purchased. Items requiring frequent and substantial servicing must be rented

---

[2] The DME fee schedule is contained in section 1834(a) of the Social Security Act; reimbursement principles for prosthetics and orthotics are specified in section 1834(h).

[3] In the case of assigned claims, the supplier agrees to accept 80 percent of the Medicare fee schedule payment as payment in full. The beneficiary is liable for 20 percent coinsurance, but not for any amount by which the supplier's charge exceeds the fee schedule amount.

because they need regular maintenance to function properly and avoid risk to beneficiaries' health. Customized items may only be purchased because they are specifically fitted for an individual and cannot be used by anyone else. Since oxygen is a consumable item, it cannot be rented. Medicare does not reimburse for purchase of oxygen equipment; rental for equipment is included in the monthly payment for oxygen.

Other items of DME are rented with an option to purchase at different times, depending on the equipment. For power-driven wheelchairs, beneficiaries are given the option to purchase in the first month of rental. If beneficiaries exercise the option to purchase power-driven wheelchairs, payment for purchase is made on a lump-sum basis. For other items in this category, beneficiaries are given the option to purchase in the tenth month of continuous rental. If beneficiaries opt to purchase, title is transferred to them after the thirteenth month of continuous rental.[4] For all items in this category of DME, reimbursement for rental is limited to 15 continuous months.

Regional or national limits on payment

Beginning in 1993, most categories of DME are subject to national limits on payments. The national limits replace regional limits enacted in OBRA 1987.

Customized items and prosthetics and orthotics are generally not subject to these limits. Customized items are not subject to any payment limits, while prosthetics and orthotics are subject to regional payment limits, beginning in 1992, and fully implemented in 1994. OBRA 1993, however, imposed national limits on ostomy supplies, tracheostomy supplies and urologicals effective January 1, 1994.

Payment floors and ceilings

The national limits on payments contain upper and lower limits (referred to as ceilings and floors) on payments. The ceiling was originally equal to 100 percent of the weighted average of local payment amounts and the floor is equal to 85 percent of the weighted average of local payment amounts. These limits took effect in 1991. OBRA 1993 changed the basis for the ceilings and floor to median effective January 1, 1994.

The floors and ceilings applied to the regional payment limits for prosthetics and orthotics vary somewhat from those used for national payment limits. The limits did not take effect until 1992. In 1992, the floor for prosthetics and orthotics was the same—85 percent of the weighted average of the local payment amount, but the ceiling is higher—125 percent of the weighted average. In addition, the limits differ in 1993 and subsequent years, when they are set at 90 and 120 percent of the weighted average of local payment amounts.

---

[4] The same cycle of payments for maintenance and servicing applies to both rented and purchased equipment in this category.

Update to the fee schedule

The 1994 fee schedule update for most categories of DME was the CPI–U or 3.0 percent. The update is applied to fee schedule payments set during the base period, rather than to more current charge data.

The 1993 payment update for prosthetics and orthotics was the CPI–U or 3.0 percent. As a result of OBRA 1993 prosthetics and orthotics will not receive an update in 1994 and 1995. One piece of prosthetic and orthotic equipment, a transcutaneous electrical nerve stimulator (TENS), was subject to a 15-percent reduction in fee schedule payments from April 1, 1990, through December 30, 1990. TENS devices were subjected to an additional 15 percent reduction in 1991. OBRA 1993 reduced payment by an additional 30 percent effective January 1, 1994.

Other provisions

Useful lifetime for rental items.—As enacted in OBRA 1987, payment for categories of equipment that could only be rented was made on a monthly basis. In the case of items requiring frequent and substantial servicing, monthly rental payments continued as long as the equipment was needed. In the case of capped rental items, monthly payments were made for 15 months, after which one payment was made every subsequent 6 months for maintenance and servicing of the item. In both cases, no provision was made for replacement of the item.

OBRA 1990 permitted the Secretary to establish a useful lifetime for these types of equipment, and to establish a new cycle of monthly payments for capped rental items. A useful lifetime of 5 years was established, unless the Secretary determines that 5 years is not appropriate for an individual item. In that case, the Secretary is to establish an alternative reasonable lifetime. When the reasonable lifetime has been reached, or the carrier determines that an item is lost or irreparably damaged, the item is replaced.

Limitation on payment amounts for capped rental items.—Prior to OBRA 1990, monthly payments for capped rental items were made for a 15-month period, with total payments for an item limited to 150 percent of the purchase price. Each monthly payment was equal to 10 percent of the purchase price. OBRA 1990 limited monthly rental payments for these items to 120 percent of the purchase price, with monthly payments equal to 10 percent of the purchase price for the first 3 months, and 7.5 percent of the purchase price for the next 12 months.

ADMINISTRATION OF THE FEE SCHEDULE

Consolidation of administration

On June 18, 1992, the Health Care Financing Administration (HCFA) published a final rule regarding DME claims payments. The rule establishes four regional carriers to process all claims for DME and prosthetics and orthotics. HCFA argues that, as a result of this consolidation, greater efficiency in claims processing will be achieved, and variance in coverage policy and utilization parameters will be greatly reduced.

In addition, the rule also requires that the responsibility for processing claims for beneficiaries residing within each regional area would be allocated to the regional carrier for that area. This change will eliminate the ability of suppliers to engage in "carrier shopping," that is, filing claims in those carrier areas that have higher payment rates.

Consolidation of claims processing for DME and prosthetics and orthotics was phased in beginning October 1, 1993 and is scheduled to be completed by July 1, 1994. The process will be on a state-by-state basis with the larger States being incorporated into the system during the final stages.

The rule also proposes minimum standards that suppliers must meet before obtaining a Medicare billing number. A supplier must receive and fill orders from its own inventory or inventory in other companies with which it has contracted to fill such orders. In addition, a supplier must be responsible for delivering Medicare covered items to beneficiaries, honoring any warranties, answering any questions or complaints the beneficiaries might have, maintaining and repairing rental items and accepting returns of substandard or unsuitable items from beneficiaries.

Overused items

OBRA 1990 required the Secretary to develop a list of DME items frequently subject to unnecessary utilization; the list must include seat-lift mechanisms; transcutaneous electrical nerve stimulators (TENS); and motorized scooters. Carriers are directed to determine, in advance, whether payment will be made for items on the Secretary's list. Thus, DME suppliers must obtain carriers' approval before providing items on the list to Medicare beneficiaries.

Certificates of medical necessity

All DME must be prescribed by a physician in order to be reimbursed by Medicare. Instead of a physician's prescription, carriers may require completion of a certificate of medical necessity (CMN) to document that an item is reasonable and medically necessary. OBRA 1990 prohibited DME suppliers from distributing completed or partially completed CMNs and established penalties for suppliers who knowingly and willfully distribute forms in violation of the prohibition.

The purpose of this provision was to prohibit DME suppliers from directly marketing DME items to Medicare beneficiaries by providing them with completed CMNs for them to submit to their physicians. Requiring physicians to complete CMNs will also encourage them to take a more active role in considering their patients' needs for DME, while simultaneously reducing DME suppliers' ability to influence DME acquisition.

This provision was to be implemented January 1, 1991, but was not implemented until December 1991 because of administrative difficulties.

Inherent reasonableness

The Secretary is permitted to increase or decrease Medicare payments in cases where the payment amount is "* * * grossly excessive or grossly deficient and not inherently reasonable." The Secretary's authority to make these payment adjustments is generally referred to as inherent reasonableness authority.

In order to make a payment adjustment, the Secretary must demonstrate that the payment meets several criteria of inherent reasonableness specified by law. In addition, the Secretary must publish a notice in the Federal Register outlining his proposal to reduce or increase payment amounts, the proposed methodology for adjusting the payment amount, and the potential impact of the payment adjustment. The Secretary is also required to provide a 60-day public comment period and to publish a final determination in the Federal Register. The final determination must include an explanation of the factors and data the Secretary took into consideration in making the determination.

According to HCFA, the Secretary rarely uses inherent reasonableness authority because the requirements are too stringent and the notice requirements too burdensome to permit easy imposition of inherent reasonableness adjustments. Moreover, the Secretary was prohibited, by law, from making inherent reasonableness adjustments to the DME fee schedule prior to January 1, 1991.

MEDICARE PAYMENTS FOR SERVICES IN HOSPITAL OUTPATIENT DEPARTMENTS

Medicare outpatient hospital services are reimbursed under Medicare part B. Services provided in outpatient hospital settings and included in expenditure data for this service setting are: emergency room services, clinic, laboratory, radiology, pharmacy, physical therapy, ambulance, operating room services, end stage renal disease services, durable medical equipment, and other services such as computer axial tomography and blood. Services rendered by physicians in outpatient hospital settings are not included in these expenditure data.

Prior to 1983, hospital outpatient services, excluding physicians' services, were paid for on a reasonable cost basis. Some services, such as emergency services, are still reimbursed on a reasonable cost basis. However, Congress has enacted a number of provisions that have altered the ways hospital outpatient departments are paid for their services and placed limits on others. For example, outpatient dialysis services are paid on the basis of a fixed composite rate; clinical laboratory services are paid on the basis of a fee schedule; x-ray services are subject to a limit on payments; and ambulatory surgical facility fees for surgeries performed in hospital outpatient departments are based on a weighted average of the hospital's costs and the prevailing fee that would be paid to a freestanding ambulatory surgical facility in the area.

Payments for services delivered in outpatient hospitals were $9.7 billion in calendar year 1992. Payments to outpatient hospitals constituted approximately 20 percent of all Medicare part B payments in 1992 and about 8 percent of total Medicare payments (parts A and B). Table 5–14 provides information on the number of part B enrollees, covered charges, aggregate reimbursements and reimbursements per enrollee for hospital outpatient services from 1974 to 1992. Table 5–15 shows the percent distribution of Medicare hospital outpatient charges, by type of service for 1992.

TABLE 5–14.—MEDICARE HOSPITAL OUTPATIENT CHARGES AND REIMBURSEMENT BY TYPE OF ENROLLMENT AND YEAR SERVICE INCURRED: SELECTED YEARS 1974–92

Type of enrollment and year of service	Number of SMI [1] enroll-ees in thousands	Covered charges in thousands	Program payments		
			Amount in thousands	Per enrollee	Percent of charges
All beneficiaries:					
1974	23,166,570	$535,296	$323,383	$14	60.4
1976	24,614,402	974,708	630,323	26	64.7
1978	26,074,085	1,384,067	923,658	35	66.7
1980	27,399,658	2,076,396	1,441,986	52	69.4
1982	28,412,282	3,164,530	2,203,260	78	69.6
1984	29,415,397	5,129,210	3,387,146	115	66.0
1986	30,589,728	8,115,976	4,881,605	160	60.1
1987	31,169,960	9,623,763	5,600,094	180	58.2
1988	31,617,082	11,833,919	6,371,704	201	53.8
1989	32,098,770	14,195,252	7,160,586	223	50.4
1990	32,635,800	18,346,471	8,171,088	250	44.5
1991	33,239,840	22,016,673	8,612,320	259	39.1
1992	33,956,460	26,209,063	9,703,004	286	37.0
		Average annual rate of growth			
1974–89	2.2	24.4	22.9	20.3	−1.9
1974–84	2.4	25.4	26.5	23.4	0.9
1984–92	1.8	22.6	14.1	12.1	−7.0
Aged:					
1974	21,421,545	394,680	220,742	10	55.9
1976	22,445,911	704,569	432,971	19	61.5
1978	23,530,893	1,005,467	648,249	28	64.5
1980	24,680,432	1,517,183	1,030,896	42	69.9
1982	25,706,792	2,402,462	1,645,064	64	68.5
1984	26,764,150	4,122,859	2,679,571	100	65.0
1986	27,862,737	6,529,273	3,809,992	137	58.4
1987	28,382,203	7,859,038	4,436,787	156	56.5
1988	28,780,154	9,790,273	5,098,546	177	52.1
1989	29,216,027	11,855,127	5,767,589	197	48.6
1990	29,691,180	15,384,510	6,563,454	221	42.7
1991	30,183,480	18,460,835	6,842,329	227	37.1
1992	30,722,080	21,856,012	7,593,513	247	34.7
		Average annual rate of growth			
1974–89	2.1	25.5	24.3	22.0	−0.9
1974–84	2.3	26.4	28.4	25.9	1.5
1984–92	1.7	23.2	13.9	12.0	−7.5
Disabled:					
1974	1,745,019	140,617	102,641	57	70.8
1976	2,168,467	270,139	197,352	91	73.1
1978	2,543,162	378,600	275,409	108	72.7
1980	2,719,226	559,213	411,090	152	73.5
1982	2,705,490	762,068	558,195	206	73.2
1984	2,651,247	1,006,351	707,575	267	70.3

TABLE 5–14.—MEDICARE HOSPITAL OUTPATIENT CHARGES AND REIMBURSEMENT BY TYPE OF ENROLLMENT AND YEAR SERVICE INCURRED: SELECTED YEARS 1974–92—Continued

Type of enrollment and year of service	Number of SMI [1] enrollees in thousands	Covered charges in thousands	Program payments		
			Amount in thousands	Per enrollee	Percent of charges
1986	2,726,991	1,586,703	1,071,613	393	67.5
1987	2,787,757	1,764,726	1,163,307	417	65.9
1988	2,836,928	2,043,646	1,273,158	449	62.3
1989	2,882,743	2,340,124	1,392,897	483	59.5
1990	2,944,620	2,961,961	1,607,634	546	54.0
1991	3,056,360	3,555,838	1,769,991	579	49.8
1992	3,234,380	4,353,051	2,109,491	695	48.5
Average annual rate of growth					
1974–89	3.4	20.6	19.0	15.3	−1.2
1974–84	4.3	21.8	21.3	16.7	−0.1
1984–92	2.5	20.1	14.6	12.7	−4.5

[1] 1974 is the first full year of coverage for disabled beneficiaries under Medicare.

Source: Health Care Financing Administration, Bureau of Data Management and Strategy: Data from the Medicare Decision Support System; Data developed by the Office of Research and Demonstrations.

TABLE 5–15.—PERCENT DISTRIBUTION OF HOSPITAL OUTPATIENT CHARGES UNDER MEDICARE, BY TYPE OF SERVICE, 1992

	Percent of charges
Radiology	19.2
Laboratory	9.7
Operating room	12.6
End stage renal disease	9.3
Pharmacy	6.8
Emergency room	3.5
Clinic	1.9
Physical therapy	4.0
Medical supplies	9.9
All other [1]	23.0

[1] Includes computerized axial tomography, durable medical equipment, blood, etc.

Source: Health Care Financing Administration, Bureau of Data Management and Strategy: Data from the Medicare Decision Support System.

From 1984 to 1992, hospital outpatient reimbursements grew 14.6 percent a year.

Recent legislative changes

Capital.—OBRA 1989 reduced payments for capital costs for outpatient services paid on a reasonable cost basis or a blend of reasonable costs and charges by 15 percent for portions of cost-reporting periods *beginning* in fiscal year 1990. This reduction also applied to capital related to services reimbursed on a blended amount; these services include radiology, diagnostic procedures and outpatient surgery. However, in the case of blends or limits based on blends, the reduction applied only to the cost portion of the blended amount. Outpatient capital costs of sole community hospitals were exempt from this reduction.

OBRA 1990 reduced reimbursement for capital costs for outpatient hospital services and the cost portion of outpatient hospital services paid on the basis of a blended amount for payments attributable to portions of cost-reporting periods *occurring during* fiscal year 1991 by 15 percent. These payments will be reduced by 10 percent for portions of cost-reporting periods *occurring during* fiscal years 1992, 1993, 1994, and 1995. Sole community hospitals and rural primary care hospitals are exempt from these reductions. OBRA 1993 extended the 10 percent reduction through fiscal year 1998.

Services paid on a cost-related basis.—OBRA 1990 also reduced payment for services paid on a cost-related basis, other than capital costs, by 5.8 percent of the recognized costs for payments attributable to cost-reporting periods occurring during fiscal years 1991, 1992, 1993, 1994, and 1995. The reduction is also applied to cost portions of blended payment limits for ambulatory surgery and radiology services. Sole community hospitals and rural primary care hospitals are exempt from the reduction. OBRA 1993 extended the 5.8 percent reduction through fiscal year 1998.

Prospective payment proposal.—OBRA 1990 also directed the Secretary to develop a proposal to replace the current payment system for hospital outpatient services with a prospective payment system. The Secretary is to consider the following factors in developing the proposal: (1) the need to provide for appropriate limits on increases in Medicare expenditures; (2) the need to adjust prospectively determined rates to account for changes in a hospital's outpatient case mix; (3) providing hospitals with incentives to control the costs of providing outpatient services; (4) the feasibility and appropriateness of including payment for outpatient services not currently paid on a cost-related basis under Medicare (including clinical diagnostic laboratory tests and dialysis services) in the system; (5) the need to increase payments to hospitals that treat a disproportionate share of low-income patients; teaching hospitals; and hospitals located in geographic areas with high wages and wage-related costs; (6) the feasibility and appropriateness of bundling services into larger units, such as episodes or visits, in establishing the basic unit for making payments under the system; and (7) the feasibility and appropriateness of varying payments on the basis of whether services are provided in a freestanding or hospital-based facility.

The law also required the Administrator of Health Care Financing Administration to submit research findings regarding prospective payments for hospital outpatient services to specified committees of Congress by January 1, 1991. The Secretary was directed to submit his proposal to Congress by September 1, 1991. As of January 1994, that report had not been submitted to Congress. The Prospective Payment Assessment Commission (ProPAC) was to submit its analysis and comments on the proposal by March 1,

1992. ProPAC recommended implementation of a prospective payment system for all providers of outpatient services, including hospitals, physicians' office-based services, and freestanding ambulatory surgical centers. The Commission also recommended adjusting the payment rate to reflect justifiable cost differences such as wages and case mix.

Eye and eye and ear specialty hospitals.—OBRA 1990 also changed the reimbursement blend for ambulatory surgery services provided in eye, and eye and ear specialty hospitals meeting specified conditions. Prior to OBRA 1990, payment for these services was based on a blend that consists of 75 percent of the hospital's costs and 25 percent of the applicable freestanding ambulatory surgical center rate. However, the blend was scheduled to change to 50/50 for cost-reporting periods beginning after fiscal year 1990. OBRA 1990 extended use of the 75/25 blend to services provided in cost-reporting years beginning before January 1, 1995.

UTILIZATION AND QUALITY CONTROL PEER REVIEW PROGRAM

The Medicare utilization and quality control peer review organization program was established by Congress under the Tax Equity and Fiscal Responsibility Act of 1982 (TEFRA, P.L. 97–35). Building on the former professional standards review organizations, the new peer review organizations (PROs) were charged by the 1982 law with reviewing services furnished to Medicare beneficiaries to determine if the services met professionally recognized standards of care and were medically necessary and delivered in the most appropriate setting. Major changes were made to the PRO program by the Social Security Act Amendments of 1983 (P.L. 98–21) and subsequent budget reconciliation acts. Most PRO review is focused on inpatient hospital care. However, there is limited PRO review of ambulatory surgery, postacute care, and services received from Medicare HMOs.

There are currently 53 PRO areas, incorporating the 50 States, Puerto Rico, and the territories. Organizations eligible to become PROs include physician-sponsored and physician-access organizations. In limited circumstances, Medicare fiscal intermediaries may also be eligible. Physician-sponsored organizations are composed of a substantial number of licensed physicians practicing in the PRO review area (e.g., a medical society); physician access organizations are those which have available to them sufficient numbers of licensed physicians so that adequate review of medical services can be assured. Such organizations obtain PRO contracts from the Secretary of HHS, through a competitive proposal process. Each organization's proposal is evaluated by HCFA for technical merit using specific criteria that are quantitatively valued. Priority is given to physician-sponsored organizations in the evaluation process. By October 1993, all 53 PROs were operating under the fourth round of contracts (also referred to as the "fourth scope of work").

In general, each PRO has a medical director and a staff of nurse reviewers (usually registered nurses), data technicians, and other support staff. In addition, each PRO has a board of directors, comprised of physicians and, generally, representatives from the State medical society, hospital association, and State medical specialty societies. OBRA 1986 (P.L. 99–509) requires each board to have a consumer representative. Because the board is usually consulted before a case is referred by the PRO to the HHS inspector general for sanction, it assumes a major role in the PRO review process. Each PRO also has physician advisors who are consulted on cases in which there is a question regarding the nurse reviewer's referral. Only physician advisors can make initial determinations about services furnished or proposed to be furnished by another physician.

PROs are paid by Medicare on a cost basis for their review work. Spending for the PROs in fiscal year 1993 totaled $214 million; in 1994, spending is expected to be $325 million. (Spending varies considerably from year to year depending on where the PROs are in their contract cycles. HCFA projections for fiscal year 1995 are $218 million.) Funds for the PRO program are apportioned each year from the Medicare HI and SMI trust funds in an amount that is supposed to be sufficient to finance PRO program requirements. This is the same manner as transfers are made for payment of Medicare services provided directly to beneficiaries. HCFA is bound by law to follow the apportionments in the running of the PRO program; as such, the apportionments determine contract specifications and serve as a device to control spending.

The PRO review process combines both utilization and quality review. In conducting utilization review, the PRO checks that the services provided to a Medicare patient were necessary, reasonable, and appropriate to the setting in which they are provided. Although some utilization review is done on a prospective basis, the bulk of the reviews are done retrospectively, i.e., after the hospitalization has occurred. When a PRO determines that the services provided were unnecessary or inappropriate (or both), it issues a payment denial notice. The provider(s), physician(s), and the patient are given an opportunity to request reconsideration of the determination.

In general, the PRO checks for indications of poor quality of care as it is conducting utilization review. If a PRO reviewer detects a possible problem, then further inquiry is made into the case. If it is determined that the care was of poor quality, the PRO must take steps to correct the problem. Specific sanctions are required if the PRO determines that the care was grossly substandard or if the PRO has found that the provider or the physician has a pattern of substandard care. In addition, under section 9403 of COBRA (P.L. 99–272), as amended by P.L. 101–239, authority exists for the PROs to deny payments for substandard quality of care but this provision has not been implemented.

Each of the contracts between HHS and the PROs must contain certain similar elements outlined in a document known as the Scope of Work. Under the third and previous scopes of work, PRO review was centered on case-by-case examinations of individual medical records, selected primarily on a sample basis, basically using local clinical criteria. This approach to medical review has been criticized by the Institute of Medicine and others as being costly, confrontational, and ineffective. The fourth scope of work incorporates a new review strategy called the Health Care Quality Improvement Initiative. PROs are required to use explicit, more nationally uniform criteria to examine patterns of care and outcomes using detailed clinical information on providers and patients. Instead of focusing on unusual deficiencies in care, the PROs are instructed to focus on persistent differences between actual indications of care and outcomes from those patterns of care and outcomes considered achievable. HCFA believes that this approach will encourage a continual improvement of medical practice in a way that will be viewed by physicians and providers as educational and not adversarial.

CBO BASELINE MEDICARE PROJECTIONS

The supplementary medical insurance (SMI) baseline is constructed following the Medicare volume performance standard (the standard) guidelines established in OBRA 1989 and amended in OBRA 1990 and OBRA 1993. The standard is a prospectively set target for growth in physicians' services. Actual growth is then compared to the standard and physicians' fees are adjusted to reflect the difference between the standard and actual growth. For example, the 1990 standard was set at 9.1 percent for all physicians' services. The actual growth in 1990 expenditures for physicians' services was 10.0 percent. Therefore, the 1992 Medicare Economic Index (MEI) was reduced by the difference (0.9 percent) subject to a maximum reduction of 2 percentage points.

For years after 1991, a default process was established to set a standard in the absence of congressional action. A standard was calculated for all physicians' services and for surgical and nonsurgical services separately. Surgical services are defined as surgical services performed by surgical specialists. Nonsurgical services are all other physicians' services including independent laboratory services. If the default becomes the standard, then the update for each category of physicians' services would be adjusted by the difference between growth in expenditures and the standard for each category.

The default standard is the product of (1) the increase in fees for physician services, (2) the increase in average enrollment (or non-HMO enrollees), (3) the average annual increase in the volume and intensity of services for the past 5 years, (4) the percentage increase or decrease caused by legislation or regulation, and (5) 1 minus the standard factor stated in the law. The standard factor is 1.5 percentage points in 1992 and 2 percentage points in 1993.

The 1992 standard was 6.5 percent for surgical services, 11.2 percent for nonsurgical services, and 10 percent for all physician services. The 1993 standard was 8.4 percent for surgical services, 10.8 percent for nonsurgical services and 10 percent for all services.

OBRA 1993 increased the performance standard factor to 3.5 percentage points in fiscal year 1994 and 4 percentage points thereafter. It also created a new primary care category. The fiscal year 1994 standard is 8.6 percent for surgical services, 10.5 percent for primary care services, 9.2 percent for other nonsurgical services, and 9.3 percent for all physicians services.

TABLE 5-16.—CBO PROJECTIONS FOR MEDICARE PROGRAM COMPONENTS BASELINE

[Outlays by fiscal year, in billions of dollars]

	1993	1994	1995	1996	1997	1998	1999
Medicare Part A: Hospital Insurance (HI)							
Total HI outlays	$91.6	$102.0	$111.8	$120.8	$131.4	$143.1	$156.9
Annual growth rate		11.3	9.6	8.1	8.8	8.9	9.7
Hospitals	74.8	81.0	87.9	94.3	102.2	111.3	122.4
Annual growth rate		8.3	8.5	7.3	8.4	8.9	10.0
PPS hospitals	64.8	69.2	74.5	78.5	83.8	90.1	98.1
Non-PPS hospitals/units	10.1	11.9	13.4	15.8	18.4	21.2	24.3
Hospice	1.0	1.1	1.3	1.5	1.8	2.1	2.4
Annual growth rate		18.5	16.0	16.4	16.8	15.9	16.4
Home health	9.5	11.7	13.6	15.3	17.0	18.6	20.3
Annual growth rate		23.6	16.5	12.3	11.2	9.5	8.7
Skilled nursing facilities	5.3	6.6	7.4	8.1	8.8	9.5	10.1
Annual growth rate		24.4	12.4	9.0	8.5	7.6	7.2
Other part A (PROs)	0.2	0.3	0.2	0.2	0.2	0.2	0.2
Annual growth rate		50.0	-33.3	0.0	0.0	0.0	0.0
Administration (subject to appropriation)	0.9	1.2	1.3	1.3	1.4	1.4	1.5
Annual growth rate		38.8	5.3	4.8	4.6	4.4	4.3
General part A information							
Indirect teaching payments	3.3	3.6	3.9	4.1	4.5	4.8	5.3
Direct medical education payments	1.7	1.7	1.8	1.9	2.0	2.2	2.3
Disproportionate share payments	3.0	3.3	3.5	3.8	4.1	4.4	4.8
Inpatient capital payments	7.7	8.5	9.4	10.3	11.2	12.3	13.4
HI trust fund income	97.1	106.6	118.6	125.9	131.7	138.1	143.8
HI trust fund surplus	5.5	4.6	6.8	5.1	0.3	-5.0	-13.1
HI trust fund balance (EOY)	126.1	130.7	137.5	142.5	142.8	137.8	124.7
Other part A information							
HI deductible (in CY dollars)	$676	$696	$720	$748	$784	$824	$868
Part A FY enrollment (millions)	35.5	36.1	36.8	37.4	38.0	38.5	39.0
PPS market basket increase FY%	4.1	4.3	4.7	4.6	4.3	4.2	4.2
PPS update factor (average)	2.7	2.0	2.6	2.6	3.8	4.2	4.2

	$221	$245	$262	$276	$295	$317	$340
Monthly premium (in CY dollars)	$221	$245	$262	$276	$295	$317	$340
Premium receipts (FT billions)	$0.5	$0.6	$0.7	$0.8	$0.8	$0.9	$1.0
Medicare Part B: Supplementary Medical Insurance (SMI)							
Total SMI outlays	54.3	60.9	68.7	77.5	87.5	98.2	110.1
Annual growth rate		12.2	12.9	12.8	12.9	12.2	12.1
Physicians	28.5	30.2	33.4	36.8	40.6	44.3	47.8
Annual growth rate		6.2	10.7	10.2	10.3	8.9	8.1
DME and P & O suppliers	2.2	2.4	2.7	3.0	3.3	3.7	4.0
Annual growth rate		9.9	11.1	10.7	10.9	9.7	9.0
Laboratories[1]	4.2	4.7	5.3	6.0	6.7	7.5	8.4
Annual growth rate		11.7	12.7	12.4	12.5	12.1	11.9
Outpatient hospital	9.6	11.0	12.7	14.8	17.2	19.8	23.1
Annual growth rate		14.4	15.5	16.3	15.8	15.6	16.6
Other part B	7.9	10.8	12.6	14.9	17.7	20.8	24.5
Annual growth rate		37.4	16.7	18.3	18.4	17.7	17.9
Administration (subject to appropriation)	1.8	1.7	1.9	2.0	2.0	2.1	2.2
Annual growth rate		-10.2	12.6	4.9	4.6	4.3	4.3
Other part B information							
SMI deductible (in dollars)	$100	$100	$100	$100	$100	$100	$100
MEI update (calendar year)	2.2	2.3	2.9	2.8	2.7	2.6	2.5
Physician update (calendar year)[2]	1.4	9.3	5.2	3.2	1.4	-2.4	-2.5
Laboratory update (calendar year)	3.0	0.0	0.0	3.0	3.0	3.1	3.1
DME update (calendar year)	3.1	2.7	2.9	2.9	3.1	3.1	3.1
Premium information							
Monthly premium (in dollars)	$36.60	$41.10	$46.10	$43.30	$51.00	$57.10	$58.90
Premium receipts (in billions)	14.7	16.8	19.2	19.0	21.5	24.7	27.8
FY enrollment (in millions)	34.3	34.9	35.6	36.2	36.7	37.2	37.6
Total medicare disbursements	145.9	162.8	180.5	198.3	218.9	241.3	267.1
Total function 570—Medicare (disbursements net of premiums)	130.7	145.5	160.6	178.5	196.6	215.7	238.3

[1] Laboratory spending reflects services provided in physician offices, outpatient hospital departments and independent laboratories. In previous years the CBO fact sheet has shown spending for independent laboratories only.

[2] Based on the current volume performance standard, we assume an upward adjustment to the MEI in fiscal years 1995 and 1996, and a downward adjustment to the MEI in fiscal years 1997, 1998 and 1999.

Source: Congressional Budget Office.

MEDICARE AS SECONDARY PAYER

Under current law, Medicare is a secondary payer under specified circumstances when beneficiaries are covered by other third-party payers. Medicare is secondary payer to workers' compensation, automobile, medical, no-fault, and liability insurance.

Medicare is also secondary payer to certain employer health plans covering aged and disabled beneficiaries and for end stage renal disease (ESRD) beneficiaries during the first 18 months of a beneficiary's entitlement to Medicare on the basis of ESRD.

Table 5–17 shows savings attributable to these Medicare secondary payer provisions. In fiscal year 1985, combined Medicare part A and part B savings were $750 million. By fiscal year 1993, the total savings equaled $2.9 billion.

TABLE 5–17.—MEDICARE SAVINGS ATTRIBUTABLE TO SECONDARY PAYER PROVISIONS, BY TYPE OF CIRCUMSTANCE

[In millions of dollars, by fiscal year]

	Workers compensation	Working aged	ESRD	Automobile	Disability	Total
1988:						
Part A	$110.1	$786.7	$88.4	$149.6	$275.5	$1,410.3
Part B	18.1	313.8	20.2	22.3	93.5	467.9
Total	128.2	1,100.5	108.6	171.9	369.0	1,878.2
1989:						
Part A	99.4	867.7	75.0	179.6	399.3	1,621.0
Part B	27.5	337.1	25.1	28.2	137.0	554.9
Total	126.9	1,204.8	100.1	207.8	536.3	2,175.9
1990:						
Part A	120.9	981.6	144.1	220.1	498.4	1,965.1
Part B	21.6	325.8	21.5	26.4	123.2	518.5
Total	142.5	1,307.4	165.6	246.5	621.6	2,483.6
1991:						
Part A	107.4	932.7	144.9	235.6	526.6	1,947.2
Part B	21.2	417.5	40.2	26.6	186.2	691.7
Total	128.6	1,350.2	185.1	262.2	712.8	2,638.9
1992:						
Part A	118.9	1,044.9	140.8	233.9	600.9	2,139.4
Part B	17.3	398.3	37.4	34.5	182.9	670.4
Total	136.2	1,443.2	178.2	268.4	783.8	2,809.8
1993:						
Part A	100.4	1,073.1	133.6	239.6	657.8	2,204.5
Part B	11.3	392.2	32.8	28.9	192.3	657.5
Total	111.7	1,465.3	166.4	268.5	850.1	2,862.0

Source: Health Care Financing Administration.

FINANCING

Background

The Medicare part A Hospital Insurance Trust Fund (HI) finances inpatient hospital, skilled nursing facility, home health and other institutional services. The part B Supplementary Medical Insurance Trust Fund (SMI) finances principally physician and hospital outpatient services.

The Hospital Insurance Trust Fund is financed primarily through Social Security payroll tax contributions paid by employers, employees and the self-employed. The payroll tax rate for HI for calendar year 1994 is 1.45 percent on all earnings in covered employment. (The OASDI earnings base for 1994 is $60,600.) An equal contribution rate is paid by the employer. Table 5–18 shows the contribution rates and maximum taxable earnings for both HI and the old-age, survivors and disability insurance (OASDI) programs.

TABLE 5–18.—CURRENT LAW SOCIAL SECURITY PAYROLL TAX RATES FOR EMPLOYERS AND EMPLOYEES EACH AND TAXABLE EARNINGS BASES

Calendar year	Employee and employer rates, each (percent)			HI taxable earnings base	Maximum HI tax
	OASDI combined	HI	OASDHI combined		
1977	4.95	0.90	5.85	$16,500	$148.50
1978	5.05	1.10	6.05	17,700	194.70
1979	5.08	1.05	6.13	22,900	240.45
1980	5.08	1.05	6.13	25,900	271.95
1981	5.35	1.30	6.65	29,700	386.10
1982	5.40	1.30	6.70	32,400	421.20
1983	5.40	1.30	6.70	35,700	464.10
1984	5.70	1.30	7.00	37,800	491.40
1985	5.70	1.35	7.05	39,600	534.60
1986	5.70	1.45	7.15	42,000	609.00
1987	5.70	1.45	7.15	43,800	635.10
1988	6.06	1.45	7.51	45,000	652.50
1989	6.06	1.45	7.51	48,000	696.00
1990	6.20	1.45	7.65	51,300	743.85
1991	6.20	1.45	7.65	[1] 125,000	1,812.50
1992	6.20	1.45	7.65	130,200	1,887.90
1993	6.20	1.45	7.65	135,000	1,957.50
1994	6.20	1.45	7.65	[2] none	no limit
1995	6.20	1.45	7.65	none	no limit
1996	6.20	1.45	7.65	none	no limit

[1] The Omnibus Budget Reconciliation Act of 1990 created a separate taxable earnings base for HI. Prior to 1991, the OASDI and HI bases were the same.
[2] The Omnibus Budget Reconciliation Act of 1993 eliminated the taxable earnings base for HI for 1994 and later.

As table 5–19 demonstrates, the bulk of the financing for HI is derived from payroll taxes. In 1993, $400 million was transferred from the railroad retirement fund. This is the estimated amount that would have been in the fund if railroad employment had always been covered under the Social Security Act.

HI benefits are provided to certain uninsured persons who became 72 before 1968. Such payments are made initially from the HI Trust Fund, with reimbursement from the general fund of the Treasury for the costs, including administrative expenses, of the payments. $367 million in 1993 and $506 million in 1994 was transferred to HI on this basis.

Certain persons not eligible for HI protection either on an insured basis or on the uninsured basis described in the previous paragraph may obtain protection by enrolling in the program and paying a monthly premium ($225 or $184 in 1994) as explained on Table 5–4. This accounts for an estimated $779 million of financing in fiscal year 1994.

Sections 217(g) and 229(b) of the Social Security Act, prior to modification by the Social Security Amendments of 1983, authorized annual reimbursement from the general fund of the Treasury to the HI Trust Fund for costs arising from the granting of deemed wage credits for military service prior to 1957, according to quinquennial determinations made by the Secretary of Health and Human Services. These sections, as modified by the Social Security Amendments of 1983, provided for a lump sum transfer in 1983 for costs arising from such wage credits. In addition, the lump sum transfer included combined employer-employee HI taxes on the noncontributory wage credits for military service after 1965 and before 1984. After 1983, HI taxes on military wage credits are credited to the fund on July 1 of each year. The Social Security Amendments of 1983 also provided for (1) quinquennial adjustments to the lump sum amount transferred in 1983 for costs arising from pre-1957 deemed wage credits and (2) adjustments as deemed necessary to any previously transferred amounts representing HI taxes on noncontributory wage credits. In 1993, this accounts for $81 million of income to the HI trust fund.

The remaining $10,679 million in 1993 of receipts consisted almost entirely of interest on the investments of the trust fund.

TABLE 5-19.—INCOME TO THE HOSPITAL INSURANCE AND SUPPLEMENTARY MEDICAL INSURANCE TRUST FUNDS FOR SELECTED FISCAL YEARS, 1970-99

[In millions of dollars]

	1970	1975	1980	1985	1990	Fiscal year[1]						Percent of total 1995 financing
						1991	1992	1993	1994[2]	1995[2]	1999[2]	
Hospital insurance:												
Payroll taxes	4,785	11,291	23,244	46,490	70,655	74,655	80,978	83,147	92,106	101,472	127,184	57.7
Transfers from railroad retirement account	64	132	244	371	367	352	374	400	401	406	396	0.2
Reimbursement for uninsured persons	617	481	697	766	413	605	621	367	506	462	174	0.3
Premiums from voluntary enrollment[3]	0	6	17	38	113	367	484	622	779	864	1,271	0.5
Payments for military wage credits	11	48	141	86	107	4 -1,011	86	81	80	68	64	0.0
Transfer from SMI Trust Fund[5]								1,805				0.0
Tax on Social Security Benefits									1,638	4,193	5,285	2.4
Interest on investment and other income	137	609	1,072	3,182	7,908	8,969	10,133	10,679	10,718	10,762	8,403	6.1
Total[6]	5,614	12,568	25,415	50,933	79,563	83,938	92,677	97,101	106,228	118,227	142,777	67.2
Supplementary medical insurance:												
Premiums[7]	936	1,887	2,928	5,524	8 11,494	11,807	12,748	14,683	16,802	19,192	24,101	10.0
General revenues	928	2,330	6,932	17,898	33,210	34,730	38,684	44,227	38,148	36,955	78,173	21.0
Transfer to HI Trustfund[5]								-1,805	0	0	0	0
Interest and other income	12	105	415	1,155	8 1,434	1,629	1,717	1,889	1,966	1,539	815	0.9
Total[6]	1,876	4,322	10,275	24,577	8 46,138	48,166	53,149	58,994	57,686	57,686	103,689	32.8
Grand total	7,490	18,890	35,690	75,510	8 125,701	132,104	145,826	156,095	163,144	175,913	245,866	100.0

[1] Fiscal years 1970 and 1975, consist of the 12 months ending on June 30 of each year. [2] Administration projections under current law using fiscal year 1995 budget assumptions. [3] Medicaid payment of Medicare premiums is required on behalf of certain underpoverty persons on Medicaid, and over 65 years of age but not eligible for Medicare, effective January 1, 1989 according to the Medicare Catastrophic Coverage Act of 1988. [4] Includes the lump sum general revenue adjustment of $1,100 million as provided for by section 151 of Public Law 98-21. [5] Part B premiums paid into SMI Trust Fund for Medicare Catastrophic benefits; P.L. 102-394 required these funds to be transferred to the HI Trust Fund. [6] Totals do not necessarily equal sums of rounded components. [7] Includes SMI catastrophic premiums and supplemental catastrophic premium refund in fiscal year 1990. [8] Includes the impact of the Medicare Catastrophic Coverage Act of 1988 (Public Law 100-360).

Source: 1994 Annual Reports of the Board of Trustees of the Federal Hospital Insurance and Supplementary Medical Insurance Trust Funds for 1970-94; current law using fiscal year 1995 budget assumptions for 1994-99.

Part B, which is voluntary, is financed from premiums paid by the aged, disabled and chronic renal disease enrollees and from general revenues. The premium rate is derived annually based upon the projected costs of the program for the coming year. Under prior law, the premium rate was changed on July 1 of each year. The Social Security Amendments of 1983 (Public Law 98–21) moved the premium increase date to January 1 of each year to coincide with the changed date for the annual Social Security cash benefit cost-of-living (COLA) increase.

Ordinarily, the premium rate is the lower of: (1) an amount sufficient to cover one-half of the costs of the program for the aged or (2) the current premium amount increased by the percentage by which cash benefits were increased under the COLA provisions of the Social Security program. Premium income, which originally financed half of the costs of part B, declined—as a result of this formula—to less than 25 percent of total program income.

The Tax Equity and Fiscal Responsibility Act of 1982 (Public Law 97–248), temporarily suspended the COLA limitation for 2 years—calendar years 1984 and 1985. During this period, enrollee premiums were allowed to increase to amounts necessary to produce premium income equal to 25 percent of program costs for elderly enrollees. The Deficit Reduction Act of 1984 (Public Law 98–369) extended the TEFRA provision through calendar years 1986 and 1987. The 1987 reconciliation bill (Public Law 100–203) extended the provision through 1989 and the 1989 reconciliation bill extended the provision through 1990. The Omnibus Reconciliation Act of 1990 set the premium rates in law for each of the years 1991–95. The revenue generated by these premium amounts were estimated to be sufficient to pay approximately 25 percent of program costs for these years. The flat premium for 1994 is $41.10 per month. OBRA 1993 again set the premium equal to 25 percent of program costs, without specifying the dollar amount, for 1996–98.

FINANCIAL STATUS OF THE TRUST FUNDS

The Hospital Insurance Trust Fund balances are dependent upon the income to the HI Trust Fund primarily through payroll taxes exceeding the outlays for Medicare benefits and administrative costs. Outlays are affected by increases in inpatient hospital expenditures which have been rising at a faster rate than the income to the HI Trust Fund. Table 5–20 shows the annual percentage increase in Medicare outlays from fiscal year 1967 to fiscal year 1993 and the Congressional Budget Office (CBO) and HCFA projections from 1994 to 1999.

TABLE 5–20.—MEDICARE OUTLAYS, FISCAL YEARS 1967–99

	Part A[1]		Part B		Total	
	Dollars (in millions)	Percent increase (over prior year)	Dollars (in millions)	Percent increase (over prior year)	Dollars (in millions)	Percent increase (over prior year)
1967	2,597	....	799	....	3,396	....
1968	3,815	46.9	1,532	91.7	5,347	57.4
1969	4,758	24.7	1,840	20.1	6,598	23.4
1970	4,953	4.1	2,196	19.3	7,149	8.4
1971	5,592	12.9	2,283	4.0	7,875	10.2
1972	6,276	12.2	2,544	11.4	8,820	12.0
1973	6,842	9.0	2,637	3.7	9,479	7.5
1974	8,065	17.9	3,283	24.5	11,348	19.7
1975	10,612	31.6	4,170	27.0	14,782	30.3
1976 [1]	12,579	18.5	5,200	24.7	17,779	20.3
1977	15,207	20.9	6,342	22.0	21,549	21.2
1978	17,862	17.5	7,356	16.0	25,218	17.0
1979	20,343	13.9	8,814	19.8	29,157	15.6
1980	24,288	19.4	10,737	21.8	35,025	20.1
1981	29,260	20.5	13,228	23.2	42,488	21.3
1982	34,864	19.2	15,560	17.6	50,424	18.7
1983	38,624	10.8	18,311	17.7	56,935	12.9
1984	42,108	9.0	20,372	11.3	62,480	9.7
1985	48,654	15.5	22,730	11.6	71,384	14.3
1986	49,685	2.1	26,218	15.3	75,903	6.3
1987	50,803	2.3	30,837	17.6	81,640	7.6
1988	52,730	3.8	34,947	13.3	87,677	7.4
1989 [2]	58,238	10.4	38,317	9.6	96,555	10.1
1990 [2]	66,687	14.5	43,022	12.3	109,709	13.6
1991	69,642	4.4	47,024	9.3	116,666	6.3
1992	81,971	17.7	50,285	6.9	132,256	13.4
1993	91,604	11.8	54,254	7.9	145,858	10.3
CBO projections [3]						
1994	101,901	11.2	60,879	12.2	162,780	11.6
1995	111,474	9.4	65,699	12.8	180,173	10.7
1996	120,382	8.0	77,522	12.8	197,904	9.8
1997	131,007	8.8	87,534	12.9	218,541	10.4
1998	142,810	9.0	98,205	12.2	241,015	10.3
1999	166,971	....	....	....	....	....
HCFA projections [3]						
1994	102,892	12.3	58,490	7.8	161,382	10.6
1995	112,258	9.1	66,144	13.1	178,402	10.5
1996	123,359	9.9	73,665	11.4	197,024	10.4
1997	135,197	9.6	81,825	11.1	217,022	10.2
1998	147,664	9.2	90,981	11.2	238,645	10.0
1999	161,540	9.4	101,552	11.6	263,092	10.2

[1] In the transition quarter from July to October 1976 (when the beginning of the Federal fiscal year was changed), outlays were $4,805 million. These outlays do not appear in the table.
[2] Includes Catastrophic outlays beginning in fiscal year 1989. There are no catastrophic outlays after fiscal year 1990.
[3] Projections under current law.

Source: 1993 Annual Report of the Board of Trustees: HI Trust Fund and SMI Trust Fund, HCFA Office of the Actuary. For 1991 through 1999, HCFA Division of Budget and CBO.

Supplementary medical insurance

Because the Supplementary Medical Insurance (SMI) Trust Fund is financed through beneficiary premiums and the general revenues, it does not face the prospect of depletion as does the HI Trust Fund. However, the rapidly rising cost of health care is placing a heavy burden on the SMI Trust Fund—causing beneficiary premiums to rise and increasing the Federal deficit.

HI trust fund income, outlays, and balance

Table 5–21 shows the projections of the Congressional Budget Office and the administration for the HI Trust Funds with respect to income, outlays and balances for the years 1993 through 1999.

TABLE 5–21.—PROJECTIONS FOR THE HOSPITAL INSURANCE TRUST FUND, FISCAL YEARS 1993–99 TOTAL OUTLAYS, INCOME, AND END-OF-YEAR BALANCES, UNDER CBO AND ADMINISTRATION BASELINE ASSUMPTIONS, PRESENT LAW

[By fiscal year, in billions of dollars]

	1993 [1]	1994	1995	1996	1997	1998	1999
Total outlays	91.2	102.0	111.8	120.8	131.4	143.1	156.8
Income	92.1	101.6	118.5	125.9	131.7	138.1	143.8
Net additions	5.5	4.5	6.5	5.1	.3	5.0	(13.1)
End-of-year balance	127.4	130.7	137.5	142.8	142.8	137.8	124.7
Beginning-of-year balance, as percent of outlays	132	124	117	114	108	100	88

[1] Actuals.

Note: Components may not add to totals due to rounding.

Source: Congressional Budget Office, and HCFA Division of Budget.

Sensitivity of HI Trust Funds balances to different outlay growth assumptions

Table 5–22 presents alternative projections of Hospital Insurance (HI) Trust Fund outlay growth through 2009. All of these projections assume the economic projections underlying the baseline path. The alternatives all are arranged in the table from least to most growth. Hospital outlays are projected to grow by 1 or 2 percent less and 1 or 2 percent more than the baseline in each year. These changes could be due to variations in hospital rate increases, admission patterns, intensity or change in case mix, or technology changes. The percentage refers to entire hospital outlays and not just those outlays covered by the prospective payment system.

Income to the trust fund is the same (except for interest which varies by size of trust fund balance) in each projection. Under the least growth alternative, expenditures are $143 billion in fiscal year 1998 compared to $149 billion in the baseline projection. Trust fund balances are $34 billion greater in this alternative.

TABLE 5–22.—ALTERNATIVE PROJECTIONS OF HOSPITAL INSURANCE OUTLAY GROWTH AND YEAR-END BALANCES

[By fiscal year, in billions of dollars]

	1993[1]	1994	1995	1996	1997	1998	1999	2000
2 percent lower HI outlay growth:								
Outlays	$91.5	$100.1	$107.8	$114.3	$122.1	$130.4	$140.5	$150
End-of-year balance[2]	125.1	132.5	143.6	155.8	155.7	175.5	183.1	188
1 percent lower HI outlay growth:								
Outlays	91.6	101.1	109.7	117.5	126.7	138.6	148.5	150
End-of-year balance[2]	126.1	131.5	140.5	149.2	154.9	157.4	154.4	147
Baseline:								
Outlays	91.5	102.0	111.8	120.8	131.4	143.1	156.9	170
Income	87.1	106.5	115.6	125.8	131.7	138.1	143.8	150
Yearly surplus	5.5	4.6	6.8	5.1	0.3	(5.0)	(13.1)	(21)
End-of-year balance[2]	126.1	130.7	137.5	142.5	142.8	137.8	124.7	104
1 percent higher HI outlay growth:								
Outlays	81.5	102.9	113.8	124.1	136.3	149.7	185.7	181
End-of-year balance[2]			134.3	135.7	130.3	117.7	94.1	50
2 percent higher HI outlay growth:								
Outlays	91.5	103.8	115.8	127.5	141.3	156.6	174.9	193
End-of-year balance[2]	125.1	128.8	131.2	128.9	118.0	97.2	62.6	14

179

TABLE 5–22.—ALTERNATIVE PROJECTIONS OF HOSPITAL INSURANCE OUTLAY GROWTH AND YEAR-END BALANCES—Continued

	2001	2002	2003	2004	2005	2006	2007
2 percent HI outlay growth:							
Outlays	159	170	181	193	206	220	235
End-of-year balance [2]	191	191	187	179	165	145	118
1 percent HI outlay growth:							
Outlays	171	184	198	214	230	248	268
End-of-year balance [2]	134	115	88	52	4	(56)	(129)
Baseline:							
Outlays	184	200	218	235	267	280	305
Income	155	160	165	170	174	177	181
Yearly surplus	(29)	(40)	(52)	(87)	(83)	(102)	(123)
End-of-year balance [2]	75	35	(18)	(84)	(170)	(275)	(403)
1 percent higher HI outlay growth:							
Outlays	198	217	238	251	287	315	345
End-of-year balance [2]	13	(49)	(128)	(228)	(352)	(504)	(688)
2 percent higher HI outlay growth:							
Outlays	213	235	251	289	320	354	393
End-of-year balance [2]	(52)	(137)	(245)	(380)	(549)	(755)	(1,004)

TABLE 5–22.—ALTERNATIVE PROJECTIONS OF HOSPITAL INSURANCE OUTLAY GROWTH AND YEAR-END BALANCES—Continued

	2008	2009	2010	2011	2012	2013	2014	2015
2 percent lower HI outlay growth:								
Outlays	252	270	289	311	336	363	393	424
End-of-year balance[2]	83	37	(20)	(91)	(179)	(287)	(416)	(575)
1 percent lower HI outlay growth:								
Outlays	289	313	339	358	401	437	477	520
End-of-year balance[2]	(218)	(324)	(451)	(602)	(782)	(995)	(1,248)	(1,544)
Baseline:								
Outlays	332	363	397	434	478	526	579	637
Income	185	188	191	195	198	201	204	208
Yearly surplus	(148)	(175)	(205)	(240)	(280)	(325)	(375)	(431)
End-of-year balance[2]	(557)	(744)	(965)	(1,228)	(1,542)	(1,912)	(2,347)	(2,855)
1 percent higher HI outlay growth:								
Outlays	381	420	463	512	568	631		
End-of-year balance[2]	(910)	(1,175)	(1,490)	(1,863)	(2,305)	(2,826)	(3,439)	(4,155)
2 percent higher HI outlay growth:								
Outlays	437	486	540	602	675	758	847	950
End-of-year balance[2]	(1,304)	(1,662)	(2,089)	(2,595)	(3,186)	(3,905)	(4,740)	(5,719)

[1] Actuals.

[2] Projections for fiscal years 1994 through 1999 assume economic and technical assumptions used in CBO baseline. Projections for fiscal years 1999–2015 are made by using the average of the growth rates for outlays and revenues in the last 2 years of CBO's baseline estimate. Outlay growth rates were further adjusted for changes in projected part A enrollment.

Note: Totals may not add due to rounding.

Source: Congressional Budget Office.

TABLE 5–23.—ACTUARIAL BALANCES OF THE HOSPITAL INSURANCE PROGRAM, UNDER
ALTERNATIVE SETS OF ASSUMPTIONS

[In percent]

	Alternative		
	I	II	III
Projection periods			
1993–2017:			
Summarized tax rate [1]	2.90	2.90	2.90
Summarized cost rate [2]	3.99	5.01	6.36
Actuarial balance [3]	−1.09	−2.11	−3.46
1993–2042:			
Summarized tax rate [1]	2.90	2.90	2.90
Summarized cost rate [2]	4.52	6.84	10.81
Actuarial balance [3]	−1.62	−3.94	−7.91
1993–2067:			
Summarized tax rate [1]	2.90	2.90	2.90
Summarized cost rate [2]	4.94	8.01	13.51
Actuarial balance [3]	−2.04	−5.11	−10.61
25-year subperiods			
1993–2017:			
Summarized tax rate [1]	2.90	2.90	2.90
Summarized cost rate [4]	3.99	4.94	6.18
Actuarial balance [3]	−1.09	−2.04	−3.28
2018–2042:			
Summarized tax rate [1]	2.90	2.90	2.90
Summarized cost rate [4]	5.15	9.04	16.08
Actuarial balance [3]	−2.25	−6.14	−13.18
2043–2067:			
Summarized tax rate [1]	2.90	2.90	2.90
Summarized cost rate [4]	6.08	11.48	21.96
Actuarial balance [3]	−3.18	−8.58	−19.06

[1] As scheduled under present law.

[2] Expenditures for benefit payments and administrative costs for insured beneficiaries, on an incurred basis, expressed as a percentage of taxable payroll, computed on the present value, including the cost of attaining a trust fund balance at the end of the period equal to 100 percent of the following year's estimated expenditures, and including an offset to cost due to the beginning trust fund balance.

[3] Difference between the summarized tax rate (as scheduled under present law) and the summarized cost rate.

[4] Expenditures for benefit payments and administrative costs for insured beneficiaries, on an incurred basis, expressed as a percentage of taxable payroll, computed on the present-value basis. Includes neither the trust fund balance at the beginning of the period nor the cost of attaining a non-zero trust fund balance at the end of the period.

Source: Table 1.D.3 in the 1993 Annual Report of the Board of Trustees of the Federal Hospital Insurance Trust Fund.

Long-range estimates

Long-range estimates for the next 75 years (1993–2067) are shown in table 5–23 for the HI program under all three alternative assumptions shown in the 1993 HI Trustees' report. As in the case of the OASDI program, annual expenditures are expressed as a percentage of taxable earnings. The income rate is simply the combined scheduled HI tax rate for employees and employers.

The average deficit over the next 25-year period is 2.11 percent of taxable earnings under alternative II assumptions. Over the next 75 years, is 5.11 percent of taxable earnings, that is, the cost rate is more than 175 percent higher than the tax rate now scheduled in the law for the future. In other words, the tax rate would have to be increased by 175 percent or program costs would have to be reduced by nearly 65 percent to restore actuarial solvency.

MEDICARE HISTORICAL DATA

Tables 5–24 through 5–38 present detailed historical data on the Medicare program. Tables 5–24 through 5–26 present detailed enrollment data. Table 5–27 describes the percentage of Medicare enrollees participating in a State buy-in agreement. Tables 5–28 and 5–29 show the distribution of Medicare payments by type of coverage and type of service. Tables 5–30 and 5–31 show the number of persons served and average reimbursement amounts per person and per enrollee. Tables 5–32–36 present the use of inpatient hospital services, skilled nursing facility services, home health agency services and beneficiaries under the ESRD program. Table 5–37 presents Medicare utilization and reimbursement by State and table 5–38 shows the number of Medicare enrollees in prepaid health plans.

TABLE 5–24.—NUMBER OF MEDICARE ENROLLEES, BY TYPE OF COVERAGE AND TYPE OF ENTITLEMENT, FOR SELECTED YEARS

Type of entitlement and coverage	Number of Medicare enrollees as of July 1 (in thousands)															Average annual percent rate of growth		
	1968	1975	1980	1981	1982	1983	1984	1985	1986	1987	1988	1989	1990	1991	1992	1968–75	1975–84	1984–92
Total:																		
HI[1] and/or SMI[2]	19,821	24,959	28,478	29,010	29,494	30,026	30,456	31,083	31,750	32,411	32,980	33,579	34,203	34,870	35,579	3.3	1.9	2.0
Total HI	19,770	24,640	28,067	28,590	29,069	29,587	29,996	30,589	31,216	31,853	32,413	33,040	33,719	34,429	35,153	3.2	1.9	2.0
HI only	1,016	1,054	1,079	1,069	1,082	1,052	1,040	1,094	1,160	1,241	1,363	1,481	1,574	1,633	1,645	0.5	0.3	5.9
Total SMI	18,805	23,905	27,400	27,941	28,412	28,975	29,416	29,989	30,590	31,170	31,617	32,099	32,629	33,237	33,933	3.5	1.9	1.8
SMI only	51	318	411	420	425	439	460	493	534	558	567	539	484	441	425	29.9	3.3	-1.0
Aged:																		
HI and/or SMI	19,821	22,790	25,515	26,011	26,540	27,109	27,571	28,176	28,791	29,380	29,879	30,409	30,948	31,485	32,010	2.0	1.7	1.9
Total HI	19,770	22,472	25,104	25,591	26,115	26,670	27,112	27,683	28,257	28,822	29,312	29,869	30,464	31,043	31,584	1.8	1.7	1.9
HI only	1,016	845	835	829	833	816	807	865	928	996	1,098	1,192	1,263	1,300	1,297	-2.6	-0.2	6.1
Total SMI	18,805	21,945	24,680	25,182	25,707	26,292	26,765	27,311	27,863	28,382	28,780	29,216	29,686	30,185	30,712	2.2	1.8	1.7
SMI only	51	318	411	420	425	439	459	493	534	558	557	539	484	441	425	29.9	3.3	-1.0
All disabled:																		
HI and/or SMI	(4)	2,168	2,963	2,999	2,954	2,918	2,884	2,907	2,959	3,031	3,102	3,171	3,255	3,385	3,568	NA	3.5	2.7
Total HI	(4)	2,168	2,963	2,999	2,954	2,918	2,884	2,907	2,959	3,031	3,101	3,171	3,255	3,385	3,568	NA	3.5	2.7
HI only	(4)	209	244	239	249	235	233	229	232	243	265	288	311	333	348	NA	2.0	5.1
Total SMI	(4)	1,959	2,719	2,759	2,705	2,682	2,651	2,678	2,727	2,788	2,837	2,883	2,943	3,052	3,220	NA	3.7	2.5
SMI only[3]																		
End stage renal disease only:																		
HI and/or SMI	(4)	13	28	27	27	28	30	31	39	47	53	58	65	69	72	NA	8.5	11.6
Total HI	(4)	13	28	27	27	28	30	31	39	47	53	58	65	69	69	NA	8.5	11.6
HI only	(4)	1	1	1	2	2	2	2	3	3	4	5	6	6	7	NA	8.0	17.0
Total SMI	(4)	12	27	26	26	26	28	29	36	44	49	54	59	62	65	NA	9.0	11.1
SMI only[3]																		

[1] Hospital insurance. [2] Supplementary medical insurance. [3] Disabled and ESRD only must have HI to be eligible for SMI coverage. [4] Medicare disability entitlement began in 1973.

Source: Health Care Financing Administration, Bureau of Data Management and Strategy, "Annual Program Statistics" and unpublished data.

184

TABLE 5-25.—GROWTH IN NUMBER OF AGED MEDICARE ENROLLEES, BY SEX AND AGE, FOR SELECTED YEARS

Sex and age	Number of enrollees (in thousands)													Average annual percent growth rate			Total aged population 1992[1]	Enrollees as percent of total aged population 1992
	1968[1]	1975[1]	1980	1981	1982	1984	1986	1987	1988	1989	1990	1991	1992	1968–75	1975–82	1982–92		
All persons	19,496	22,548	25,515	26,011	26,540	27,571	28,791	29,380	29,879	30,409	30,948	31,485	32,011	2.1	2.4	1.9	32,285	99.2
65–69	6,551	7,642	8,459	8,570	8,652	8,784	9,163	9,358	9,469	9,659	9,695	9,690	9,692	2.2	1.8	1.1	9,977	97.1
70–74	5,458	5,950	6,756	6,888	7,022	7,300	7,564	7,647	7,752	7,775	7,951	8,163	8,373	1.2	2.3	1.8	8,483	98.7
75–79	3,935	4,313	4,809	4,931	5,064	5,327	5,573	5,692	5,792	5,931	6,058	6,175	6,261	1.3	1.9	2.1	6,415	97.6
80–84	2,249	2,793	3,081	3,112	3,185	3,382	3,559	3,659	3,764	3,856	3,957	4,085	4,166	3.1	1.9	2.7	4,150	100.4
85 and over	1,303	1,850	2,410	2,510	2,617	2,778	2,932	3,024	3,102	3,187	3,286	3,393	3,519	5.1	5.1	3.0	3,259	108.0
Males	8,177	9,201	10,268	10,454	10,653	11,044	11,525	11,762	11,967	12,187	12,416	12,650	12,886	1.7	2.1	1.9	13,045	98.8
65–69	2,944	3,420	3,788	3,843	3,881	3,942	4,109	4,196	4,245	4,331	4,352	4,358	4,374	2.2	1.8	1.2	4,475	97.7
70–74	2,322	2,504	2,841	2,898	2,958	3,088	3,214	3,255	3,308	3,323	3,406	3,505	3,604	1.1	2.4	2.0	3,651	98.7
75–79	1,596	1,669	1,854	1,903	1,956	2,061	2,160	2,211	2,257	2,321	2,382	2,441	2,485	0.6	2.3	2.4	2,553	97.3
80–84	864	1,005	1,062	1,068	1,093	1,161	1,221	1,257	1,296	1,330	1,369	1,411	1,454	2.2	1.2	2.9	1,457	99.8
85 and over	450	604	722	741	764	793	822	843	861	881	906	934	968	4.3	3.4	2.4	909	106.5
Females	11,319	13,347	15,247	15,557	15,887	16,526	17,266	17,619	17,912	18,222	18,532	18,835	19,125	2.4	2.5	1.9	19,240	99.4
65–69	3,606	4,222	4,671	4,727	4,771	4,842	5,054	5,162	5,224	5,328	5,343	5,332	5,317	2.3	1.8	1.1	5,503	96.6
70–74	3,136	3,446	3,914	3,990	4,064	4,212	4,350	4,393	4,444	4,452	4,545	4,657	4,769	1.4	2.4	1.6	4,833	98.7
75–79	2,338	2,644	2,954	3,028	3,108	3,266	3,414	3,481	3,534	3,610	3,676	3,734	3,776	1.8	2.3	2.0	3,862	97.8
80–84	1,386	1,788	2,019	2,043	2,092	2,222	2,339	2,402	2,468	2,526	2,588	2,653	2,713	3.7	2.3	2.6	2,693	100.7
85 and over	853	1,248	1,689	1,769	1,853	1,985	2,110	2,181	2,241	2,306	2,380	2,459	2,551	5.6	5.8	3.2	2,349	108.6

[1] Total aged population data reflect U.S. residents.

Source: Health Care Financing Administration, Bureau of Data Management and Strategy, unpublished data; and U.S. Department of Commerce, Bureau of the Census.

TABLE 5–26.—GROWTH IN NUMBER OF DISABLED MEDICARE ENROLLEES WITH HI COVERAGE, BY TYPE OF ENTITLEMENT AND AGE, FOR SELECTED YEARS

Type of entitlement and age	Number of enrollees										Average annual percent growth rate		
	1975	1980	1981	1982	1984	1988	1989	1990	1991	1992	1975–82	1982–88	1982–92
All disabled persons	2,058,424	2,425,231	2,998,949	2,415,646	2,884,410	3,101,482	3,170,917	3,254,983	3,385,439	3,568,625	2.3	4.3	4.0
Under age 35	238,070	193,392	383,503	195,918	388,240	471,129	478,422	483,262	494,285	512,495	-2.7	15.7	10.1
35 to 44	251,142	258,374	385,139	268,948	422,207	572,408	609,974	654,953	711,364	762,759	1.0	13.4	11.0
45 to 54	508,345	572,823	654,700	532,020	584,214	670,131	705,616	741,193	790,435	874,797	.7	3.9	5.1
55 to 64	1,060,967	1,400,642	1,575,607	1,418,762	1,489,749	1,397,814	1,376,905	1,375,575	1,389,355	1,419,574	4.2	-0.2	-0.0
All disabled workers	1,638,662	2,396,897	2,439,446	2,388,299	2,309,866	2,456,135	2,510,319	2,579,097	2,693,502	2,856,517	5.5	0.5	1.8
Under age 35	100,439	184,619	195,000	187,514	193,094	249,291	253,918	257,760	268,392	286,466	9.3	4.9	4.3
35 to 44	164,439	253,186	269,765	264,036	290,395	414,749	445,291	482,071	530,417	576,549	7.0	7.8	8.1
45 to 54	426,451	565,846	558,519	525,384	485,378	552,442	581,969	612,692	657,358	731,713	3.0	0.8	3.4
55 to 64	947,333	1,393,246	1,416,162	1,411,365	1,340,999	1,239,653	1,229,141	1,226,574	1,237,335	1,216,769	5.9	-2.1	-1.1
Adults disabled as children	324,864	409,072	427,513	439,293	459,620	519,009	531,445	542,416	553,388	566,336	4.4	2.8	2.6
Under age 35	153,708	173,689	180,167	181,752	186,003	207,331	209,017	208,901	208,536	208,710	2.4	2.2	1.4
35 to 44	84,508	105,092	110,617	117,056	126,252	146,460	152,197	158,725	165,569	170,363	4.8	3.8	3.8
45 to 54	71,484	80,381	83,135	84,332	87,380	99,444	103,777	107,092	110,279	117,333	2.4	2.8	3.4
55 to 64	45,164	49,910	53,594	56,153	59,985	65,774	66,454	67,698	69,004	69,930	3.2	2.7	2.2
Widows and widowers	83,771	110,785	105,091	99,269	85,227	73,101	70,688	68,793	69,753	74,157	2.5	-5.0	-2.9
Under age 35	1	0	1	0									-100.0
35 to 44													
45 to 54	7,445	7,576	6,523	5,806	4,608	5,685	5,658	5,615	6,112	7,399	-3.5	-.4	2.5
55 to 64	76,325	103,208	98,567	93,462	80,618	67,416	65,030	63,178	63,641	66,758	2.9	-5.3	-3.3
End-stage renal disease only	11,127	28,334	26,899	27,347	29,697	53,237	58,465	64,677	68,796	71,615	13.7	11.7	10.1
Under age 35	3,729	8,773	8,336	8,404	9,143	14,507	15,487	16,601	17,357	17,299	12.3	9.5	7.5
35 to 44	2,187	5,188	4,756	4,912	5,559	11,199	12,486	14,157	15,378	15,847	12.3	14.7	12.4
45 to 54	2,966	6,977	6,523	6,636	6,848	12,560	14,212	15,794	16,686	18,352	12.2	11.2	10.7
55 to 64	2,245	7,396	7,284	7,397	8,147	14,971	16,280	18,125	19,375	20,117	18.6	12.5	10.5

Source: Health Care Financing Administration, Bureau of Data Management and Strategy, unpublished data.

TABLE 5–27.—MEDICARE ENROLLMENT: NUMBER AND PERCENTAGE OF INDIVIDUALS ENROLLED IN SUPPLEMENTARY MEDICAL INSURANCE (SMI) UNDER BUY-IN AGREEMENTS, BY TYPE OF BENEFICIARY AND BY YEAR OR 1992 AREA OF RESIDENCE

Year or area of residence [1]	All persons		Aged		Disabled	
	Number in thousands	Percent of SMI enrolled	Number in thousands	Percent of SMI enrolled	Number in thousands	Percent of SMI enrolled
Year:						
1968	1,648	8.8	1,648	8.8	NA	NA
1975	2,846	12.0	2,483	11.4	363	18.7
1980	2,954	10.9	2,449	10.0	504	18.9
1981	3,257	11.7	2,659	10.6	598	21.7
1982	2,791	9.8	2,288	8.9	503	18.6
1983	2,654	9.3	2,177	8.4	477	18.1
1984	2,601	8.9	2,127	8.0	474	18.2
1985	2,670	9.0	2,164	8.0	505	19.2
1986	2,776	9.2	2,222	8.0	554	20.9
1987	2,985	9.6	2,337	8.2	648	23.2
1988	3,033	9.6	2,341	8.1	691	24.4
1989	3,351	10.4	2,549	8.7	802	27.8
1990	3,604	11.0	2,714	9.1	890	30.2
1991	3,766	10.4	2,817	8.7	949	27.8
1992	4,055	11.4	2,972	9.3	1,083	30.3
Area of residence [1]						
All areas	4,055	11.4	2,972	9.3	1,083	30.3
United States	4,053	11.6	2,970	9.5	1,083	31.3
Alabama	108	17.8	84	16.0	24	29.3
Alaska	6	21.4	4	16.7	2	50.0
Arizona	35	6.5	25	5.1	10	20.0
Arkansas	73	18.1	57	16.2	16	30.2
California	697	20.4	527	17.0	170	53.0
Colorado	41	10.7	29	8.5	12	30.0
Connecticut	30	6.2	18	4.0	12	32.4
Delaware	5	5.4	3	3.6	2	22.2
District of Columbia	13	16.7	10	14.1	3	42.9
Florida	222	9.0	175	7.7	47	25.8
Georgia	142	18.4	109	16.4	33	31.1
Hawaii	14	10.3	11	8.7	3	33.3
Idaho	10	7.2	7	5.5	3	25.0
Illinois	111	7.0	75	5.2	36	25.2
Indiana	68	8.6	47	6.7	21	25.3
Iowa	45	9.7	31	7.2	14	37.8
Kansas	32	8.6	23	6.7	9	31.0
Kentucky	84	15.2	60	12.8	24	28.9
Louisiana	98	17.8	74	15.6	24	30.8
Maine	25	13.2	17	10.1	8	38.1
Maryland	54	9.5	40	7.7	14	28.6
Massachusetts	98	10.9	68	8.4	30	36.1
Michigan	102	8.0	64	5.6	38	27.0

TABLE 5–27.—MEDICARE ENROLLMENT: NUMBER AND PERCENTAGE OF INDIVIDUALS ENROLLED IN SUPPLEMENTARY MEDICAL INSURANCE (SMI) UNDER BUY-IN AGREEMENTS, BY TYPE OF BENEFICIARY AND BY YEAR OR 1992 AREA OF RESIDENCE— Continued

Year or area of residence [1]	All persons		Aged		Disabled	
	Number in thousands	Percent of SMI enrolled	Number in thousands	Percent of SMI enrolled	Number in thousands	Percent of SMI enrolled
Minnesota	46	7.6	30	5.4	16	32.7
Mississippi	95	25.1	75	23.5	20	34.5
Missouri	62	7.7	42	5.8	20	24.4
Montana	10	8.1	6	5.5	4	30.8
Nebraska	14	5.8	8	3.6	6	33.3
Nevada	11	6.8	8	5.5	3	20.0
New Hampshire	5	3.4	3	2.3	2	15.4
New Jersey	105	9.3	78	7.5	27	29.3
New Mexico	26	13.5	20	11.8	6	27.3
New York	275	10.8	197	8.5	78	31.7
North Carolina	139	14.7	107	12.9	32	27.4
North Dakota	5	5.0	3	3.2	2	25.0
Ohio	131	8.2	96	6.7	35	21.1
Oklahoma	55	11.8	43	10.8	12	27.3
Oregon	34	7.6	24	5.9	10	26.3
Pennsylvania	140	7.0	93	5.0	47	28.5
Rhode Island	12	7.4	8	5.4	4	26.7
South Carolina	89	19.0	67	16.6	22	34.4
South Dakota	10	8.8	7	6.7	3	33.3
Tennessee	127	17.6	93	14.8	34	36.2
Texas	265	13.8	212	12.2	53	29.3
Utah	12	7.0	7	4.5	5	33.3
Vermont	9	11.7	6	8.6	3	37.5
Virginia	89	11.7	66	9.8	23	27.4
Washington	61	9.5	41	7.0	20	33.9
West Virginia	33	10.4	23	8.5	10	21.3
Wisconsin	71	9.7	44	6.6	27	39.7
Wyoming	4	7.3	3	6.0	1	20.0
Puerto Rico [2]	0	0.0	0	0.0	0	0.0
Guam and Virgin Islands [3]	1	11.8	1	12.5	0	6.3

[1] State of residence is not necessarily State that bought coverage.
[2] No State buy-in agreement.
[3] Data for these areas combined to prevent disclosure of confidential information.

Source: Health Care Financing Administration, Bureau of Data Management and Strategy, "HCFA Statistics" and unpublished data.

188

TABLE 5–28.—DISTRIBUTION OF MEDICARE BENEFIT PAYMENTS, BY TYPE OF COVERAGE AND TYPE OF SERVICE, AND BY YEAR OR TYPE OF ENROLLEE

| Type of coverage and type of service | Amount and distribution of payments for all enrollees, calendar year— | | | | | | | | | | | | | |
| | 1975 | | 1980 | | 1981 | | 1982 | | 1983 | | 1984 | | 1985 | |
	Amount	Per-cent	Amount	Per-cent	Amount	Per-cent	Amount	Per-cent	Amount	Per-cent	Amount	Per-cent	Amount	Per-cent
Total payments (millions)	15,588	100.0	35,686	100.0	43,442	100.0	51,086	100.0	57,443	100.0	62,870	100.0	70,391	100.0
Hospital insurance	11,315	72.6	25,051	70.2	30,329	69.8	35,631	69.7	39,337	68.5	43,209	68.7	47,444	67.4
Inpatient	10,877	69.8	24,116	67.6	29,161	67.1	33,947	66.5	37,252	64.9	40,878	65.0	44,940	63.8
Skilled nursing facility	254	1.6	395	1.1	410	0.9	484	0.9	543	0.9	543	0.9	548	0.8
Home health agency	104	0.7	540	1.5	758	1.7	1,200	2.3	1,542	2.7	1,779	2.8	1,913	2.7
Hospice	0	0	0	0	0	0	0	0	0	0	8	0.0	43	0.1
Supplementary medical insurance	4,273	27.4	10,635	29.8	13,113	30.2	15,455	30.3	18,106	31.5	19,661	31.3	22,947	32.6
Physicians'	3,416	21.9	8,187	22.9	10,086	23.2	11,893	23.3	14,062	24.5	15,434	24.5	17,312	24.6
Outpatient hospital	643	4.1	1,897	5.3	2,406	5.5	2,994	5.9	3,385	5.9	3,452	5.5	4,319	6.1
Home health agency	95	0.6	234	0.7	193	0.4	54	0.1	25	0.1	30	0.0	38	0.1
Group practice plan	80	0.5	203	0.6	274	0.6	335	0.7	410	0.7	464	0.7	720	1.0
Independent laboratory	39	0.3	114	0.3	154	0.4	179	0.4	224	0.4	281	0.4	558	0.8

TABLE 5–28.—DISTRIBUTION OF MEDICARE BENEFIT PAYMENTS, BY TYPE OF COVERAGE AND TYPE OF SERVICE, AND BY YEAR OR TYPE OF ENROLLEE—Continued

Type of coverage and type of service	Amount and distribution of payments for all enrollees													
	1986		1987		1988		1989		1990		1991		1992	
	Amount	Per-cent	Amount	Per-cent	Amount	Per-cent	Amount	Per-cent	Amount	Per-cent	Amount	Per-cent	Amount	Per-cent
Total payments (millions)	75,844	100.0	80,162	100.0	86,317	100.0	98,097	100.0	108,518	100.0	118,653	100.0	132,951	100.0
Hospital insurance	49,605	65.4	49,342	61.6	52,347	60.6	59,803	61.0	66,050	60.9	71,317	60.1	83,691	62.9
Inpatient	47,008	62.0	46,905	58.5	49,265	57.1	54,227	55.3	59,383	54.7	62,640	52.8	71,000	53.4
Skilled nursing facility	575	0.8	635	0.8	848	1.0	2,879	2.9	2,620	2.4	2,632	2.2	4,051	3.0
Home health agency	1,945	2.6	1,690	2.1	2,078	2.4	2,465	2.5	3,689	3.4	5,484	4.6	7,760	5.8
Hospice	77	0.1	112	0.1	156	0.2	238	0.2	358	0.3	561	0.5	880	0.7
Supplementary medical insurance	26,239	34.6	30,820	38.4	33,970	39.4	38,294	39.0	42,468	39.1	47,336	39.9	49,260	37.1
Physicians'	19,213	25.3	22,618	28.2	24,372	28.2	27,056	27.6	29,609	27.3	32,313	27.2	32,394	24.4
Outpatient hospital	5,157	6.8	5,916	7.4	6,549	7.6	7,676	7.8	8,482	7.8	9,783	8.2	10,990	8.3
Home health agency	31	0.0	40	0.0	47	0.1	60	0.1	74	0.1	65	0.1	71	0.1
Group practice plan	1,113	1.5	1,361	1.7	2,019	2.3	2,308	2.4	2,827	2.6	3,531	3.0	3,933	3.0
Independent laboratory	725	1.0	885	1.1	983	1.1	1,194	1.2	1,476	1.4	1,644	1.4	1,872	1.4

Source: Health Care Financing Administration, Bureau of Data Management and Strategy and Office of the Actuary, unpublished data.

TABLE 5–29.—DISTRIBUTION OF MEDICARE BENEFIT PAYMENTS, BY TYPE OF COVERAGE AND TYPE OF SERVICE, AND BY TYPE OF ENROLLEE, 1992

| | Calendar year 1992 payments by type of enrollee | | | | | |
| | All enrollees | | Aged | | Disabled | |
	Amount (in millions)	Percentage distribution	Amount (in millions)	Percentage distribution	Amount (in millions)	Percentage distribution
Total payments (millions)	132,951	100.0	117,532	100.0	15,419	100.0
Hospital insurance	83,691	62.9	74,325	63.2	9,366	60.7
Inpatient	71,000	53.4	62,338	53.0	8,662	56.2
Skilled nursing facility	4,051	3.0	3,907	3.3	144	0.9
Home health agency	7,760	5.8	7,244	6.2	516	3.3
Hospice	880	0.7	836	0.7	44	0.3
Supplementary medical insurance	49,260	37.1	43,207	36.8	6,053	39.3
Physicians'	32,394	24.4	29,169	24.8	3,225	20.9
Outpatient hospital	10,990	8.3	8,740	7.4	2,250	14.6
Home health agency	71	0.1	71	0.1	0	0.0
Group practice plan	3,933	3.0	3,541	3.0	392	2.5
Independent laboratory	1,872	1.4	1,686	1.4	186	1.2

Source: Health Care Financing Administration, Bureau of Data Management and Strategy and Office of the Actuary, unpublished data.

TABLE 5–30.—PERSONS SERVED AND REIMBURSEMENTS FOR AGED MEDICARE ENROLLEES, BY TYPE OF COVERAGE AND BY YEAR OR 1992 DEMOGRAPHIC CHARACTERISTICS

Year, period, or 1992 characteristic	Hospital insurance and/or supplementary medical insurance			Hospital insurance			Supplementary medical insurance		
	Persons served per 1,000 enrollees	Reimbursements		Persons served per 1,000 enrollees	Reimbursements		Persons served per 1,000 enrollees	Reimbursements	
		Per person served	Per enrollee		Per person served	Per enrollee		Per person served	Per enrollee
Year:									
1968	397.8	$670.08	$266.56	204.0	$934.42	$190.67	394.8	$203.94	$80.51
1975	527.9	1,054.63	556.78	220.9	1,855.38	409.78	536.0	295.91	158.60
1980	637.7	1,790.51	1,141.84	240.0	3,378.53	810.77	652.3	545.42	355.77
1981	655.0	2,024.49	1,325.97	243.4	3,877.39	943.84	669.5	613.13	410.47
1982	641.4	2,439.38	1,564.65	250.7	4,461.53	1,118.69	653.8	732.53	478.92
1983	660.2	2,610.80	1,723.69	250.9	4,803.71	1,205.13	672.2	825.26	554.77
1984	685.7	NA	NA	239.6	NA	NA	698.9	NA	NA
1985	722.1	2,762.06	1,994.59	218.8	6,167.28	1,349.60	739.1	933.25	689.79
1986	731.7	2,870.05	2,099.93	213.0	6,528.36	1,390.28	750.8	1,012.17	759.95
1987	754.1	3,025.22	2,281.19	209.8	6,902.60	1,448.33	775.9	1,147.95	890.64
1988	767.8	3,177.60	2,439.87	207.5	7,514.76	1,559.23	792.5	1,192.41	944.96
1989	784.9	3,444.86	2,703.90	206.1	8,196.19	1,688.96	812.8	1,338.10	1,087.56
1990	801.6	3,578.43	2,868.57	209.0	8,519.97	1,780.60	831.6	1,398.86	1,163.29
1991	800.1	3,905.65	3,124.82	211.8	9,348.53	1,980.26	830.0	1,473.27	1,222.80
1992	794.4	4,193.90	3,331.60	213.0	10,126.3	2,157.2	823.4	1,522.9	1,254.0
Annual percentage change in period:									
1968 to 1975	4.1	6.7	11.1	1.1	10.3	11.5	4.5	5.5	10.2
1975 to 1985	3.2	10.1	13.6	−0.1	12.8	12.7	3.3	12.2	15.8
1985 to 1992	2.8	11.0	14.1	−1.9	14.7	12.5	3.0	13.9	17.3
Age:									
65 and 66 years	747.9	$2,850.26	$2,131.65	132.5	$9,778.39	$1,295.25	811.0	$1,147.25	$930.46
67 and 68 years	709.7	3,414.87	2,423.50	143.0	10,319.07	1,475.46	753.1	1,367.88	1,030.12
69 and 70 years	743.2	3,599.13	2,674.74	159.9	10,241.04	1,637.48	775.5	1,431.25	1,109.94
71 and 72 years	758.9	3,910.35	2,967.44	176.0	10,507.15	1,848.89	780.7	1,513.47	1,181.60
73 and 74 years	799.5	4,144.01	3,312.95	198.0	10,485.84	2,076.62	813.9	1,587.84	1,292.42
75 to 79 years	831.0	4,635.29	3,851.76	235.6	10,550.66	2,485.48	842.7	1,694.16	1,427.75

TABLE 5–30.—PERSONS SERVED AND REIMBURSEMENTS FOR AGED MEDICARE ENROLLEES, BY TYPE OF COVERAGE AND BY YEAR OR 1992 DEMOGRAPHIC CHARACTERISTICS—Continued

Year, period, or 1992 characteristic	Hospital insurance and/or supplementary medical insurance			Hospital insurance			Supplementary medical insurance		
	Persons served per 1,000 enrollees	Reimbursements		Persons served per 1,000 enrollees	Reimbursements		Persons served per 1,000 enrollees	Reimbursements	
		Per person served	Per enrollee		Per person served	Per enrollee		Per person served	Per enrollee
80 to 84 years	860.3	4,966.50	4,272.89	288.9	9,969.93	2,880.67	871.6	1,683.09	1,467.05
85 years and over	882.4	5,337.27	4,709.47	357.0	9,424.71	3,364.45	921.2	1,582.57	1,457.79
Sex:									
Male	754.3	4,677.45	3,527.97	215.6	10,669.68	2,300.06	790.1	1,669.79	1,319.38
Female	821.5	3,894.72	3,199.36	211.3	9,750.52	2,060.40	845.3	1,432.36	1,210.78
Race:									
White	803.0	4,124.04	3,311.48	213.7	9,965.58	2,129.90	829.5	1,500.23	1,244.39
All other	732.5	4,877.32	3,572.67	211.8	11,457.45	2,426.51	775.7	1,747.96	1,355.95
Census region:									
Northeast	830.2	4,525.56	3,757.30	218.5	11,224.99	2,452.61	859.2	1,622.32	1,393.85
North Central	824.9	3,873.28	3,195.13	218.7	9,503.69	2,078.32	843.7	1,378.56	1,163.12
South	826.7	4,235.65	3,501.53	234.0	9,670.71	2,262.99	846.6	1,533.64	1,298.44
West	697.8	4,251.20	2,966.66	170.4	11,177.96	1,904.55	715.9	1,606.35	1,149.92

Note.—Data for 1992 are considered preliminary.

Source: Health Care Financing Administration, Bureau of Data Management and Strategy, "Annual Medicare Program Statistics."

TABLE 5–31.—PERSONS SERVED AND REIMBURSEMENTS FOR DISABLED ENROLLEES, BY TYPE OF COVERAGE AND BY YEAR OR 1992 DEMOGRAPHIC CHARACTERISTICS

Year, period, or 1992 characteristic	Hospital insurance and/or supplementary medical insurance			Hospital insurance			Supplementary medical insurance		
	Persons served per 1,000 enrollees	Reimbursements		Persons served per 1,000 enrollees	Reimbursements		Persons served per 1,000 enrollees	Reimbursements	
		Per person served	Per enrollee		Per person served	Per enrollee		Per person served	Per enrollee
Year:									
1968	NA	NA	NA	NA	NA	NA	NA	NA	NA
1975	449.5	$1,548.09	$695.83	219.2	$2,076.58	$455.20	471.4	$564.95	$266.32
1980	594.1	2,544.04	1,511.34	245.7	3,798.09	933.16	633.8	994.18	630.06
1981	615.2	2,880.99	1,772.39	251.4	4,400.27	1,106.16	655.9	1,103.92	724.04
1982	608.9	3,431.26	2,089.35	256.9	5,109.65	1,312.85	650.5	1,303.37	847.90
1983	628.8	3,658.08	2,300.24	257.7	5,549.82	1,430.30	670.1	1,412.07	946.23
1984	639.5	NA	NA	242.6	NA	NA	683.5	NA	NA
1985	668.8	3,855.22	2,578.24	227.9	7,223.96	1,646.25	715.5	1,414.04	1,011.70
1986	681.0	4,032.05	2,745.64	226.3	7,622.94	1,724.99	729.0	1,518.86	1,107.32
1987	695.7	3,993.70	2,778.14	219.4	7,610.01	1,669.66	747.8	1,611.42	1,205.10
1988	703.7	4,114.84	2,895.52	209.3	8,372.64	1,752.76	760.0	1,643.77	1,249.35
1989	721.3	4,530.89	3,268.36	208.0	9,481.76	1,971.89	785.0	1,816.65	1,426.08
1990	734.3	4,702.65	3,452.97	208.9	9,846.77	2,056.60	803.5	1,921.76	1,544.18
1991	728.5	5,069.61	3,693.15	208.7	10,634.43	2,218.91	799.0	2,046.50	1,635.16
1992	729.3	5,351.81	3,903.33	208.9	11,278.42	2,355.73	799.4	2,145.26	1,714.91
Annual percentage change in period:									
1968 to 1975	NA	NA	NA	NA	NA	NA	NA	NA	NA
1975 to 1985	4.05	9.55	13.99	0.39	13.28	13.72	4.26	9.61	14.28
1985 to 1992	1.24	4.80	6.10	-1.24	6.57	5.25	1.60	6.14	7.83

TABLE 5–31.—PERSONS SERVED AND REIMBURSEMENTS FOR DISABLED ENROLLEES, BY TYPE OF COVERAGE AND BY YEAR OR 1992 DEMOGRAPHIC CHARACTERISTICS—Continued

Year, period, or 1992 characteristic	Hospital insurance and/or supplementary medical insurance			Hospital insurance			Supplementary medical insurance		
	Persons served per 1,000 enrollees	Reimbursements		Persons served per 1,000 enrollees	Reimbursements		Persons served per 1,000 enrollees	Reimbursements	
		Per person served	Per enrollee		Per person served	Per enrollee		Per person served	Per enrollee
Age:									
Under 35 years	706.9	$5,425.42	$3,835.41	199.1	$11,566.96	$2,303.03	766.9	$2,190.43	$1,679.83
35 to 44 years	688.7	5,099.80	3,512.47	185.7	11,181.41	2,075.86	760.1	2,108.41	1,602.53
45 to 54 years	703.5	5,316.64	3,740.06	196.3	11,241.57	2,206.84	777.8	2,202.85	1,713.36
55 to 59 years	732.0	5,560.89	4,070.48	216.5	11,392.43	2,466.48	803.8	2,215.65	1,780.94
60 to 64 years	805.9	5,407.53	4,358.09	244.1	11,160.37	2,723.92	874.3	2,051.32	1,793.54
Sex:									
Male	682.6	5,304.28	3,620.77	196.6	11,423.79	2,245.59	751.4	2,040.09	1,532.94
Female	805.1	5,417.11	4,361.16	228.8	11,076.07	2,534.18	875.9	2,289.19	2,005.20
Race:									
White	727.8	4,900.77	3,566.59	202.1	10,868.66	2,196.28	800.0	1,903.04	1,522.51
All other	735.3	6,702.86	4,928.56	230.0	12,353.36	2,840.81	799.5	2,872.19	2,296.19
Census region:									
Northeast	755.8	5,775.08	4,364.60	210.4	12,699.79	2,672.11	831.5	2,267.46	1,885.46
North Central	737.0	4,947.12	3,646.04	207.6	10,818.63	2,245.69	805.6	1,920.02	1,546.76
South	756.4	5,286.27	3,998.42	229.9	10,547.60	2,424.58	805.8	2,100.26	1,692.44
West	694.1	5,842.26	4,055.22	182.3	12,933.15	2,357.77	751.9	2,468.12	1,855.80

NA—Not available.

Note.—Data for 1992 are considered preliminary.

Source: Health Care Financing Administration, Bureau of Data Management and Strategy, "Annual Medicare Program Statistics."

TABLE 5–32.—USE OF INPATIENT HOSPITAL SERVICES BY MEDICARE ENROLLEES, BY TYPE OF ENROLLEE AND TYPE OF HOSPITAL: CALENDAR YEAR 1991 [1]

Type of enrollee and type of hospital	Bills [2]		Covered days of care			Reimbursements in dollars		
	Number in thousands	Per enrollees	Number in thousands	Per bill	Per 1,000 enrollees	Amount in millions	Per bill	Per enrollee
All enrollees:								
All hospitals	11,426	328	95,569	8.4	2,741	62,122	5,437	1,782
Short-stay	10,917	313	90,381	8.3	2,592	60,255	5,519	1,728
Long-stay	509	15	5,188	10.2	149	1,867	3,665	54
Psychiatric ..	287	8	2,660	9.3	76	726	2,529	21
All other	222	6	2,527	11.4	72	1,141	5,130	33
Aged:								
All hospitals	9,982	317	83,786	8.4	2,661	54,981	5,508	1,746
Short-stay	9,679	307	80,450	8.3	2,555	53,644	5,543	1,704
Long-stay	304	10	3,337	11.0	106	1,337	4,401	42
Psychiatric ..	104	3	1,041	10.0	33	310	2,981	10
All other	200	6	2,295	11.5	73	1,027	5,140	33
Disabled:								
All hospitals	1,444	426	11,783	8.2	3,480	7,140	4,945	2,109
Short-stay	1,238	366	9,931	8.0	2,933	6,610	5,338	1,953
Long-stay	206	61	1,852	9.0	547	530	2,578	157
Psychiatric ..	183	54	1,619	8.8	478	416	2,272	123
All other	23	7	232	10.2	68	114	5,047	34

[1] Preliminary data. Detail may not add due to rounding.
[2] Discharges not available by type of hospital.

Note.—Only services rendered by inpatient hospitals are included.

Source: Health Care Financing Administration, Bureau of Management and Strategy, unpublished data.

TABLE 5-33.—USE OF SHORT-STAY HOSPITAL SERVICES BY AGED MEDICARE ENROLLEES, BY FISCAL YEAR OR 1991 DEMOGRAPHIC CHARACTERISTICS

Calendar year, period, or 1991 characteristic	Aged hospital insurance enrollees (in thousands) [1]	Discharges		Total days of care			Total charges (in millions)	Total charges		
		Number (in thousands)	Per 1,000 enrollees	Number (in thousands)	Per discharge	Per 1,000 enrollees		Per discharge	Per covered day of care	Per enrollee
Year:										
1975	22,472	7,285	324	81,592	11.2	3,631	11,853	1,627	145	527
1980	25,104	9,051	361	96,772	10.7	3,855	28,114	3,106	291	1,120
1982	26,115	9,817	376	100,431	10.0	3,846	40,875	4,164	407	1,565
1984	27,112	9,705	358	86,062	8.9	3,174	46,964	4,839	546	1,732
1985	27,683	8,918	322	76,926	8.6	2,779	47,371	5,312	616	1,711
1986	28,257	8,917	316	77,240	8.7	2,733	52,623	5,901	681	1,862
1987	28,822	9,000	312	79,804	8.9	2,769	60,900	6,767	763	2,113
1988	29,312	9,146	312	80,938	8.8	2,761	69,920	7,645	864	2,385
1989	29,869	9,026	302	79,784	8.8	2,671	78,204	8,664	980	2,618
1990	30,948	9,351	302	82,179	8.8	2,655	102,544	10,966	1,248	3,313
1991	31,043	9,645	311	82,743	8.6	2,665	118,882	12,326	1,437	3,830
Annual percentage change in period:										
1975–82	2.2	4.4	2.1	3.0	−1.6	0.8	19.3	14.4	15.9	16.8
1982–91	1.9	−0.2	−2.1	−2.1	−1.7	−4.0	12.6	12.8	15.0	10.5
Age:										
65–69 years	9,571	NA	NA	NA	NA	NA	NA	NA	NA	NA
70–74 years	8,050	NA	NA	NA	NA	NA	NA	NA	NA	NA
75–79 years	6,078	NA	NA	NA	NA	NA	NA	NA	NA	NA
80–84 years	3,990	NA	NA	NA	NA	NA	NA	NA	NA	NA
85 years or over	3,354	NA	NA	NA	NA	NA	NA	NA	NA	NA

Sex:											
Male	12,523	NA	NA	NA	NA	NA	NA	NA	NA	NA	NA
Female	18,520	NA	NA	NA	NA	NA	NA	NA	NA	NA	NA
Race:[2]											
White	26,948	NA	NA	NA	NA	NA	NA	NA	NA	NA	NA
All other	3,066	NA	NA	NA	NA	NA	NA	NA	NA	NA	NA
Census region:											
Northeast	6,793	NA	NA	NA	NA	NA	NA	NA	NA	NA	NA
North central	7,688	NA	NA	NA	NA	NA	NA	NA	NA	NA	NA
South	10,388	NA	NA	NA	NA	NA	NA	NA	NA	NA	NA
West	5,555	NA	NA	NA	NA	NA	NA	NA	NA	NA	NA

[1] As of July 1.
[2] Excludes unknown race.

Source: Health Care Financing Administration, Bureau of Data Management and Strategy.

TABLE 5-34.—USE OF SKILLED NURSING FACILITY SERVICES AND PERCENTAGE CHANGE, BY TYPE OF MEDICARE ENROLLEE, AND CALENDAR YEAR OR PERIOD, OR 1991 DEMOGRAPHIC CHARACTERISTIC

Type of enrollee and year, period, or 1991 characteristic	Number of SNF facilities [1]	HI aged enrollees in thousands [2][3]	Persons served		Covered days of care			Reimbursements			
			Number in thousands	Per 1,000 enrollees	Number in thousands	Per person served	Per enrollee	Amounts in millions	Per person served	Per enrollee	Per day
Year:				**Aged**							
1969 [3]	4,786	20,014	394	19.7	17,520	45	0.9	$311	$790	$16	$18
1975	3,932	22,472	260	11.5	8,585	33	0.4	233	896	10	27
1981	5,295	25,591	243	9.5	8,373	34	0.3	361	1,486	14	43
1982	5,510	26,115	244	9.3	8,549	35	0.3	388	1,591	15	45
1983	5,760	26,670	257	9.6	9,007	35	0.3	413	1,612	16	46
1984	6,183	27,112	290	10.7	9,309	32	0.3	458	1,581	17	49
1985	6,725	27,683	304	11.0	8,615	28	0.3	464	1,525	17	54
1986	7,065	28,257	294	10.4	7,867	27	0.3	474	1,613	17	60
1987	7,148	28,822	283	9.8	7,139	25	0.2	524	1,853	18	73
1988	7,683	29,312	371	12.7	10,681	29	0.4	811	2,184	28	76
1989	8,688	29,869	613	20.5	28,522	47	1.0	2,806	4,580	94	98
1990	9,008	30,464	615	20.2	22,873	37	0.8	1,886	3,068	62	82
1991	9,674	31,043	648	20.9	21,415	33	0.7	2,151	3,321	69	100
Annual percentage change in period:											
1969 to 1975	-3.2	1.9	-6.7	-8.5	-11.2	-4.8	-12.9	-4.7	2.1	-6.6	7.3
1975 to 1981	5.1	2.2	-1.1	-3.2	-0.4	0.7	-2.5	7.6	8.8	5.3	8.1
1981 to 1986	5.9	2.0	3.9	1.8	-1.2	-4.9	-3.2	5.6	1.6	3.5	6.9
1986 to 1991	6.5	1.9	17.1	15.0	22.2	4.3	19.9	35.3	15.5	32.8	10.8
Age:											
65 to 69 years		9,571	51	5.3	NA	NA	NA	172	3,367	18	NA
70 to 74 years		8,050	87	10.8	NA	NA	NA	298	3,420	37	NA
75 to 79 years		6,078	129	21.2	NA	NA	NA	438	3,407	72	NA
80 to 84 years		3,990	153	38.4	NA	NA	NA	508	3,312	127	NA

85 years or over	....	3,354	227	67.8	NA	NA	NA	734	3,230	219	NA
Sex:											
Male	....	12,523	209	16.7	NA	NA	NA	682	3,006	54	NA
Female	....	12,523	209	16.7	NA	NA	NA	147	3,096	12	NA
Race:[4]											
White	....	26,948	582	21.6	NA	NA	NA	1,917	3,025	71	NA
All other	....	3,067	48	15.8	NA	NA	NA	177	3,536	58	NA
Census region:											
Northeast	1,954	6,793	116	17.0	4,839	42	0.7	373	3,227	55	77
North Central	2,569	7,688	210	27.3	6,599	31	0.9	613	2,918	80	93
South	2,479	10,388	178	17.2	5,940	33	0.6	566	3,173	54	95
Disabled											
Year:											
1975	3,932	2,168	8	3.9	289	34	0.1	9	1,049	4	30
1980	5,155	2,963	9	2.9	319	38	0.1	13	1,571	5	42
1982	5,510	2,954	8	2.6	296	38	0.1	14	1,762	5	46
1983	5,760	2,918	8	2.7	305	38	0.1	15	1,856	5	48
1984	6,183	2,884	9	3.1	314	35	0.1	15	1,675	5	47
1985	6,725	2,907	10	3.5	305	30	0.1	17	1,681	6	57
1986	7,065	2,959	10	3.5	295	29	0.1	19	1,872	6	65
1987	7,148	3,031	10	3.3	272	27	0.1	21	2,154	7	79
1988	7,683	3,101	13	4.2	401	31	0.1	33	2,529	11	81
1989	8,688	3,171	23	7.4	1,437	61	0.5	143	6,107	45	100
1990	9,008	3,255	23	7.1	1,022	44	0.3	85	3,696	26	83
1991	9,674	3,385	23	6.7	825	36	0.2	87	3,846	26	106
Annual percentage change in period:											
1975–80	5.6	6.4	0.3	-5.8	2.0	1.7	-4.2	8.7	8.4	2.1	6.6
1980–85	5.5	-0.4	3.9	4.3	-0.9	-4.6	-0.5	5.3	1.4	5.7	6.3
1985–91	6.2	2.6	14.0	11.2	18.1	3.5	15.1	30.9	14.8	27.6	10.9
Age:											
Under 35 years	....	494	1	2.7	NA	NA	NA	6	4,590	12	NA
35 to 44 years	....	711	3	3.9	NA	NA	NA	12	4,467	17	NA
45 to 54 years	....	790	5	6.0	NA	NA	NA	19	3,929	24	NA

TABLE 5–34.—USE OF SKILLED NURSING FACILITY SERVICES AND PERCENTAGE CHANGE, BY TYPE OF MEDICARE ENROLLEE, AND CALENDAR YEAR OR PERIOD, OR 1991 DEMOGRAPHIC CHARACTERISTIC—Continued

Type of enrollee and year, period, or 1991 characteristic	Number of SNF facilities[1]	HI aged enrollees in thousands[2][3]	Persons served		Covered days of care			Reimbursements			
			Number in thousands	Per 1,000 enrollees	Number in thousands	Per person served	Per enrollee	Amounts in millions	Per person served	Per enrollee	Per day
55 to 59 years	....	568	5	8.1	NA	NA	NA	18	3,853	31	NA
60 to 64 years	....	821	9	11.2	NA	NA	NA	32	3,507	39	NA
Sex:											
Male	....	2,111	12	5.9	NA	NA	NA	48	3,868	23	NA
Female	....	1,274	10	8.4	NA	NA	NA	39	3,818	30	NA
Race:[4]											
White	....	2,547	18	6.9	NA	NA	NA	65	3,711	26	NA
All other	....	773	5	6.0	NA	NA	NA	20	4,361	26	NA
Census region:											
Northeast	1,954	647	3	5.4	149	48	0.2	11	3,618	17	76
North Central	2,569	797	7	9.3	252	37	0.3	23	3,400	29	93
South	2,479	1,266	7	5.6	239	36	0.2	24	3,614	19	101
West	1,997	565	6	10.0	182	31	0.3	28	4,764	50	154

[1] Number serving either aged or disabled Medicare enrollees, as of January 1991.
[2] As of July 1.
[3] Regions exclude residence unknown and territories.
[4] Excludes unknown race.

Source: Health Care Financing Administration, Bureau of Data Management and Strategy, unpublished data.

TABLE 5–35.—VISITS, CHARGES, AND REIMBURSEMENTS FOR HOME HEALTH AGENCY SERVICES AND PERCENTAGE CHANGES BY CALENDAR YEAR OR PERIOD, OR DEMOGRAPHIC CHARACTERISTICS

Calendar year, period, or 1992 characteristic [2]	Visits		Charges [1]			Reimbursements					
	Number in millions	Per 1,000 enrollees	Total amount in millions	Amount in millions for visits	Amount per visit	Amount (in millions)			Average annual percentage change in total	Total per visit	Total per enrollee
						HI	SMI	Total			
Year:											
1969	9	424	$88	NA	NA	$52	$26	$78	....	$9	$4
1975	11	431	226	211	20	152	63	215	18.4	20	9
1980	23	792	775	739	33	490	176	666	25.4	30	23
1983	38	1,253	1,689	1,627	43	1,405	22	1,427	28.9	38	48
1984	41	1,358	2,026	1,912	46	1,677	27	1,704	19.4	41	56
1985	40	1,303	2,152	1,979	49	1,766	31	1,797	5.4	44	58
1986	39	1,229	2,214	2,125	54	1,781	36	1,817	1.1	47	57
1987	37	1,138	2,236	2,127	58	1,774	39	1,813	−0.2	49	56
1988	38	1,156	2,472	2,358	62	1,916	44	1,960	8.1	51	59
1989	47	1,404	3,233	3,106	66	2,368	57	2,426	23.8	51	72
1990	70	2,045	5,007	4,841	69	3,626	69	3,695	52.3	53	108
1991	99	2,852	7,348	5,342	71	5,281	61	5,342	44.6	54	153
1992	134	3,759	10,377	10,034	75	7,367	80	7,477	39.4	56	209

TABLE 5–35.—VISITS, CHARGES, AND REIMBURSEMENTS FOR HOME HEALTH AGENCY SERVICES AND PERCENTAGE CHANGES BY CALENDAR YEAR OR PERIOD, OR DEMOGRAPHIC CHARACTERISTICS—Continued

Calendar year, period, or 1992 characteristic [2]	Visits		Charges [1]			Reimbursements					
	Number in millions	Per 1,000 enrollees	Total amount in millions	Amount in millions for visits	Amount per visit	Amount (in millions)			Average annual percentage change in total	Total per visit	Total per enrollee
						HI	SMI	Total			
Annual percentage change in period:											
1969 to 1975	4.0	0.3	17.1	NA	NA	19.7	15.8	18.4	....	13.9	14.2
1975 to 1983	16.9	14.3	28.6	29.1	10.0	32.1	−12.4	26.7	....	8.4	23.8
1983 to 1992	15.1	13.0	22.3	22.4	6.4	20.2	15.5	20.2	3.5	4.4	17.9
Type of enrollee:											
Aged	118	3,676	9,132	8,830	....	6,483	71	6,553	....	56	205
Disabled	16	4,497	1,245	1,204	....	884	9	894	....	56	251
Sex:											
Male	NA	NA	NA	NA	NA	NA	NA	NA	NA	NA	NA
Female	NA	NA	NA	NA	NA	NA	NA	NA	NA	NA	NA
Race: [2]											
White	NA	NA	NA	NA	NA	NA	NA	NA	NA	NA	NA
All other	NA	NA	NA	NA	NA	NA	NA	NA	NA	NA	NA

[1] Excludes durable medical equipment and supplies, except for drugs and biologicals, furnished by home health agencies.
[2] Data for 1992 as of September 1993.

Source: Health Care Financing Administration, Bureau of Data Management and Strategy, unpublished data.

TABLE 5–36.—SELECTED UTILIZATION AND REIMBURSEMENT DATA FOR END-STAGE RENAL DISEASE, AND KIDNEY TRANSPLANT PROGRAMS FOR SELECTED CALENDAR YEARS

Program and key program variables	1975	1983	1984	1985	1986	1987	1988	1989	1990	1991
End stage renal disease program:[1] Beneficiaries:										
Number	12,702	27,847	29,397	30,876	38,970	47,222	53,247	58,409	64,692	68,807
Percentage change[2]	....	1.8	5.6	5.0	26.2	21.2	12.8	9.8	10.6	6.4
Expenditures:										
Total (in millions)	$361	$1,898	$2,381	$2,680	$3,108	$3,441	$3,851	$4,528	$5,262	$6,154
Percentage change[2]	....	23.1	25.4	12.6	16.0	10.7	11.9	17.6	16.2	17.0
Expenditures per beneficiary:										
Amount (in dollars)[3]	$16,185	$21,228	$22,245	$23,479	$24,957	$25,501	$25,852	$27,726	$29,480	$31,899
Percentage change[2]	....	3.4	4.8	5.5	6.3	2.2	1.4	8.4	6.3	8.2
New beneficiaries during year:										
Number	6,763	6,738	7,532	9,372	14,696	15,570	17,416	19,340	19,913	20,140
Percentage change[2]	....	0.0	11.8	24.4	56.8	5.9	11.9	11.0	3.0	1.1
Kidney transplant program:[4] Total transplants:										
Number of patients[5]	3,730	6,112	6,968	7,695	8,976	8,967	8,932	8,899	9,796	10,026
Percentage change[2]	....	14.1	14.0	10.4	16.6	-0.1	-0.4	-0.4	10.1	2.4
Kidney transplanted from living donors:[6]										
Number	NA	1,784	1,704	1,876	1,887	1,907	1,816	1,893	2,091	2,382
Percentage of total transplants	....	31.9	27.0	26.5	22.9	23.0	-4.8	4.2	21.3	13.9
Number of beneficiaries losing entitlement because of 3-year limitation	NA	NA	NA	NA	NA	NA	NA	NA	NA	NA

[1] Persons entitled solely because of end stage renal disease.
[2] For intervals of more than one year, rate shown is average annual rate of change.
[3] Not adjusted for PPS pass-throughs.
[4] Transplants in Medicare-certified U.S. hospitals.
[5] Transplant count includes non-Medicare patients.
[6] Includes transplants to non-Medicare patients.

NA—Not available.

Source: Health Care Financing Administration, Bureau of Data Management and Strategy, and OACT.

TABLE 5–37.—MEDICARE UTILIZATION AND REIMBURSEMENT: NUMBER OF AGED PERSONS SERVED UNDER HOSPITAL INSURANCE AND/OR SUPPLEMENTARY MEDICAL INSURANCE PER 1,000 ENROLLED, AMOUNT REIMBURSED PER PERSON SERVED, AND PERCENTAGE CHANGE, BY CENSUS DIVISION AND STATE, FOR SELECTED CALENDAR YEARS

	Persons served per 1,000 enrolled					Annual percent change				Reimbursement per person served					Annual percent change			
	1967	1985	1990	1991	1992³	1967–92	1985–90	1990–91	1991–92	1967	1985	1990	1991	1992³	1967–91	1985–90	1990–91	1991–92
Total, all areas¹	366.5	722.1	801.6	800.1	794.4	3.1	2.1	−0.2	−0.7	$592	$2,762	$3,578	$3,906	$4,194	8.2	5.3	9.2	7.4
United States²	370.9	731.2	810.5	808.8	802.7	3.1	2.1	−0.2	−0.8	593	2,772	3,592	3,921	4,212	8.2	5.3	9.2	7.4
New England	380.4	767.4	829.0	831.3	830.9	3.2	1.6	0.3	0.0	680	2,708	3,573	4,074	4,364	7.7	5.7	14.0	7.1
Maine	330.1	756.1	868.8	871.3	872.8	4.0	2.8	0.5	0.2	586	2,369	2,744	3,068	3,292	7.1	3.0	11.8	7.3
New Hampshire	391.6	739.7	810.5	812.5	829.4	3.0	1.8	0.2	2.1	467	2,374	2,974	3,240	3,511	8.4	4.6	8.9	8.4
Vermont	411.7	742.8	841.0	853.0	843.9	2.9	2.5	1.4	−1.1	515	1,990	2,569	3,017	3,154	7.6	6.0	13.5	4.5
Massachusetts	394.2	766.5	813.6	813.5	809.0	2.9	1.2	0.0	−0.6	708	2,971	4,029	4,541	4,896	8.1	6.3	12.7	7.8
Rhode Island	375.4	829.6	853.6	844.8	836.4	3.3	0.6	−1.0	−1.0	625	2,619	3,236	3,756	4,315	7.8	4.3	16.1	14.9
Connecticut	390.9	764.1	838.1	846.0	851.4	3.2	1.9	0.9	0.6	711	2,570	3,511	4,151	4,310	7.6	6.4	18.2	3.8
Middle Atlantic	388.1	768.2	834.7	831.7	830.0	3.1	1.7	−0.4	−0.2	578	2,771	3,933	4,249	4,581	8.7	7.3	8.0	7.8
New York	406.9	765.7	830.4	823.3	809.2	2.8	1.6	−0.9	−1.7	610	2,533	4,119	4,382	4,596	8.6	10.2	6.4	4.9
New Jersey	399.0	759.8	826.7	827.3	836.4	3.0	1.7	0.1	1.1	526	2,650	3,483	3,958	4,551	8.8	5.6	13.6	15.0
Pennsylvania	365.0	776.4	844.7	844.8	852.5	3.5	1.7	0.0	0.9	533	3,147	3,948	4,245	4,579	9.0	4.6	7.5	7.9
East North Central	350.2	725.9	834.4	837.0	833.8	3.5	2.8	0.3	−0.4	614	2,906	3,595	3,817	4,042	7.9	4.3	6.2	5.9
Ohio	353.6	718.4	846.3	846.3	846.7	3.6	3.3	0.0	0.0	585	2,792	3,824	3,977	4,053	8.3	6.5	4.0	1.9
Indiana	343.7	672.2	837.0	836.3	820.1	3.5	4.5	−0.1	−1.9	545	2,510	3,234	3,443	3,927	8.0	5.2	6.5	14.1
Illinois	339.2	693.4	788.1	792.9	792.1	3.5	2.6	0.6	−0.1	703	3,313	3,760	4,078	4,332	7.6	2.6	8.5	6.2
Michigan	379.5	804.3	871.4	872.9	881.3	3.4	1.6	0.2	1.0	532	2,991	3,749	3,973	4,117	8.7	4.6	6.0	3.6
Wisconsin	354.7	736.9	843.2	851.4	828.3	3.5	2.7	1.0	−2.6	639	2,527	2,877	3,066	3,404	6.8	2.6	6.6	11.0
West North Central	363.2	693.4	979.7	797.1	805.5	3.2	2.8	−0.1	1.1	558	2,627	3,108	3,620	3,494	7.6	3.4	4.9	7.2
Minnesota	389.0	624.8	682.5	694.9	711.3	2.4	1.8	1.8	2.4	601	2,447	3,101	3,235	3,308	7.3	4.9	4.3	2.3
Iowa	365.9	715.3	850.6	847.2	853.0	3.4	3.5	−0.4	0.7	505	2,282	2,753	2,914	3,161	7.6	3.8	5.8	8.5
Missouri	364.8	712.0	816.6	813.4	821.1	3.3	2.8	−0.4	0.9	544	3,118	3,514	3,624	3,986	8.2	2.4	3.1	10.0
North Dakota	441.2	730.7	853.4	839.1	850.3	2.7	3.2	−1.7	1.3	492	2,466	2,949	3,089	3,358	8.0	3.6	4.7	8.7
South Dakota	358.0	694.2	815.1	812.1	815.9	3.3	3.3	−0.4	0.5	514	2,281	2,714	2,894	3,037	7.5	3.5	6.6	4.9
Nebraska	352.5	634.2	808.8	799.4	810.2	3.4	5.0	−1.2	1.4	540	2,449	2,719	2,935	2,942	7.3	2.1	7.9	0.2
Kansas	365.3	765.4	850.0	848.0	848.3	3.4	2.1	−0.2	0.0	540	2,553	3,144	3,346	3,679	7.9	4.3	6.4	10.0
South Atlantic	350.5	740.4	827.7	825.0	825.8	3.5	2.3	−0.3	0.1	554	2,531	3,438	3,837	4,203	8.4	6.3	11.6	9.5
Delaware	368.2	770.9	843.6	840.3	870.7	3.5	1.8	−0.4	3.6	552	2,612	3,526	3,430	3,910	7.9	6.2	−2.7	14.0

Maryland	349.4	757.6	838.3	836.4	845.2	3.6	2.0	-0.2	1.1	564	2,975	4,190	4,563	5,113	9.1	7.1	8.9	12.1
District of Columbia	452.8	739.4	772.7	771.4	762.6	2.1	0.9	-0.2	1.1	570	3,774	5,019	5,476	6,035	9.9	5.9	9.1	10.2
Virginia	317.3	729.7	848.5	857.2	844.8	4.0	3.1	1.0	-1.4	516	1,976	3,127	3,438	3,590	8.2	9.6	9.9	4.4
West Virginia	342.2	692.0	828.6	834.7	844.4	3.7	3.7	0.7	1.2	489	2,575	3,197	3,601	3,907	8.7	4.4	12.6	8.5
North Carolina	324.0	727.9	852.3	862.8	858.9	4.0	3.2	1.2	-0.5	515	1,982	2,799	3,172	3,428	7.9	7.1	13.3	8.1
South Carolina	296.2	680.6	832.2	834.1	845.5	4.3	4.1	0.2	1.4	523	2,340	2,689	3,049	3,288	7.6	2.8	13.4	7.88
Georgia	320.2	743.5	843.8	840.6	849.8	2.6	2.6	-0.4	1.1	474	2,479	3,456	3,987	4,466	9.3	6.9	15.4	12.0
Florida	420.9	759.1	805.8	793.1	791.4	1.2	1.2	-1.6	-0.2	588	2,773	3,709	4,148	4,566	8.5	6.0	11.8	10.1
East South Central	332.1	698.1	846.9	853.8	843.2	3.8	3.9	0.8	-1.2	489	2,570	3,413	3,831	4,249	9.0	5.8	12.2	10.9
Kentucky	365.9	671.9	837.3	834.7	837.2	3.4	4.5	-0.8	0.3	458	2,395	3,424	3,657	3,923	9.0	7.4	6.8	7.3
Tennessee	354.8	678.7	853.4	859.9	836.6	3.5	4.7	0.8	-2.7	502	2,816	3,402	3,911	4,425	8.9	3.9	15.0	13.1
Alabama	322.7	743.8	848.9	854.6	858.6	4.0	2.7	0.7	0.5	490	2,502	3,596	3,958	4,420	9.1	7.5	10.1	11.7
Mississippi	283.2	699.9	845.1	868.6	840.0	4.4	3.8	2.8	-3.3	471	2,480	3,122	3,717	4,098	9.0	4.7	19.1	10.3
West South Central	374.8	687.4	825.0	829.6	817.6	3.2	3.7	0.6	-1.4	504	2,811	3,624	3,955	4,291	9.0	5.2	9.1	8.5
Arkansas	319.3	715.4	862.9	870.3	841.3	4.0	3.8	0.9	-3.3	466	2,550	3,155	3,640	3,821	8.9	4.3	15.4	5.0
Louisiana	343.4	653.5	821.1	832.4	828.0	3.6	4.7	1.4	-0.5	446	3,167	4,368	4,683	4,977	10.3	6.6	7.2	6.3
Oklahoma	416.1	677.8	878.3	887.6	828.0	2.8	5.3	1.1	-5.7	486	2,482	3,127	3,467	3,933	8.5	4.7	10.9	13.4
Texas	393.7	693.2	805.1	806.4	807.4	2.9	3.0	0.2	0.1	522	2,860	3,652	3,951	4,288	8.8	5.0	8.2	8.5
Mountain	417.1	716.6	772.7	770.5	740.3	2.3	1.5	-0.3	-3.9	560	2,637	3,992	3,471	3,720	7.9	4.5	5.4	7.2
Montana	416.5	679.7	823.5	842.8	805.8	2.7	3.9	2.3	-4.4	505	2,348	3,000	3,201	3,295	8.0	5.0	6.7	2.9
Idaho	408.8	714.5	862.5	875.9	830.4	2.9	3.8	1.6	-5.2	467	2,384	2,556	2,723	3,213	7.6	1.4	6.5	18.0
Wyoming	395.0	681.7	782.7	764.3	786.7	2.8	2.8	-2.4	2.9	432	2,804	3,182	2,999	3,267	8.4	2.6	-5.8	8.9
Colorado	475.4	704.0	740.8	753.3	723.9	1.7	1.0	1.7	-3.9	578	2,521	3,223	3,496	3,907	7.8	5.0	8.5	11.8
New Mexico	377.6	689.8	736.4	732.8	731.0	2.7	1.3	-0.5	-0.2	513	2,462	3,154	3,156	3,258	7.9	5.1	0.1	3.2
Arizona	431.7	758.1	774.3	760.2	704.3	2.0	0.4	-1.8	-7.4	612	2,896	3,692	3,876	4,008	8.0	5.0	5.0	3.4
Utah	346.0	713.1	808.2	799.4	799.4	3.4	2.5	-1.1	0.0	580	2,225	2,799	3,128	3,350	7.3	4.7	11.8	7.1
Nevada	414.9	688.9	721.2	711.2	703.7	2.1	0.9	-1.4	-1.1	532	3,243	3,903	4,006	4,376	8.8	3.8	2.6	9.2
Pacific	468.9	739.7	713.8	699.2	681.9	1.5	-0.7	-2.0	-2.5	630	6,153	3,853	4,305	4,467	8.3	-8.9	11.7	3.8
Washington	433.0	731.1	760.8	758.5	755.9	2.3	0.8	-0.3	-0.3	507	2,522	3,218	3,576	3,790	8.5	5.0	11.1	6.0
Oregon	392.6	716.2	707.8	694.6	680.0	2.2	-0.2	-1.9	-2.1	583	2,459	2,833	3,051	3,360	7.1	2.9	7.7	10.1
California	490.7	745.7	710.3	692.7	671.8	1.3	-1.0	-2.5	-3.0	653	3,379	4,138	4,661	4,794	8.5	4.1	12.6	2.9
Alaska	307.2	678.4	759.0	781.6	784.3	3.8	2.3	3.0	0.3	376	3,554	4,007	4,325	4,303	10.7	2.4	7.9	-0.5
Hawaii	407.4	709.3	589.9	583.9	574.9	1.4	-3.6	-1.0	-1.5	572	2,334	3,095	3,100	3,480	7.3	5.8	0.2	12.3

[1] Consists of United States, Puerto Rico, Virgin Islands, and other outlying areas.
[2] Consists of 50 States, District of Columbia, and residence unknown.
[3] Preliminary data.

Source: Health Care Financing Administration, Bureau of Data Management and Strategy, "Annual Medicare Program Statistics," and unpublished data.

TABLE 5–38.—MEDICARE: SUMMARY OF RISK AND COST CONTRACTS BY CATEGORY DATA AS OF JANUARY 1, 1994

Current contract summary	Number of contracts	Percent	Number of enrollees
TEFRA risk contracts:			
Model:			
IPA	74	69	916,482
Group	20	19	339,631
Staff	14	12	588,645
Ownership:			
Profit	67	62	1,296,877
Non-profit	41	38	547,881
TEFRA cost contracts: [1]			
Model:			
IPA	16	62	123,332
Group	3	12	12,073
Staff	7	26	24,971
Ownership:			
Profit	8	31	35,610
Non-profit	18	69	124,766
Percent of total medicare beneficiaries			5.6

[1] Does not include cost enrollees remaining in risk plans.

Note.—Data as of January 1994. IPA is the Individual Practice Association.

Source: Health Care Financing Administration.

Section 6. SSI Program Description

The Supplemental Security Income (SSI) program is a means-tested, federally administered income assistance program authorized by title XVI of the Social Security Act. Established by the 1972 amendments to the Social Security Act (Public Law 92–603) and begun in 1974, SSI provides monthly cash payments in accordance with uniform, nationwide eligibility requirements to needy aged, blind and disabled persons. The SSI program replaced the former Federal grants to the States for old-age assistance, aid to the blind and aid to the permanently disabled. These grants continue in Guam, Puerto Rico and the Virgin Islands. SSI, however, operates in the Commonwealth of the Northern Mariana Islands.

Table 6–1 summarizes the trends in the SSI program since its inception in 1974:

(1) The number of recipients on SSI has risen from nearly 4 million in 1974 to nearly 6 million in December 1993. The number of SSI recipients declined early in the program as the number of aged individuals on SSI declined, but that trend reversed in the mid-1980s as rapid growth in disabled recipients outstripped the minimal change in the elderly and blind SSI populations. From 1984 through 1993, the disabled population on SSI grew at an annual average rate of about 9.2 percent.

(2) Total annual benefits paid under the SSI program rose at an average rate of 7.9 percent from about $5.3 billion in 1974 to $23.6 billion in 1993. After adjusting for inflation, however, total annual benefits rose by an annual average rate of 2.2 percent.

(3) The monthly Federal benefit rates for individuals and couples rose from $140 and $210 in 1974 to $446 and $669 in 1994, respectively. Nearly all of these changes resulted from the statutory indexation of the Federal benefit rates to the Consumer Price Index (CPI).

(4) The proportion of SSI recipients receiving Social Security benefits declined from nearly 53 percent in 1974 to about 40 percent in 1993. The fraction of SSI recipients receiving some other type of unearned income rose from about 11 percent in 1974 to 13 percent in 1993, and the fraction with earnings jumped from about 3 percent in 1974 to more than 4 percent in December 1993.

(5) The Federal benefit rate as a percent of the appropriate poverty level for individuals has ranged from 72 to 77 percent and is currently 75 percent; for couples it has ranged from 86 to 91 percent and is currently at 89.5 percent. Most States supplement the Federal benefit for at least some participants.

(6) The SSI program pays benefits to children who are blind or have other disabilities. Some of the increases in participation since 1991 reflect the revised definition of disability for

(207)

children as a result of the Supreme Court's decision in the *Sullivan* v. *Zebley* case.

BASIC ELIGIBILITY

To qualify for SSI payments, a person must satisfy the program criteria for age, blindness or disability. The aged are defined as persons 65 years and older. The blind are individuals with 20/200 vision or less with the use of a correcting lens in the person's better eye, or those with tunnel vision of 20 degrees or less. Disabled individuals are those unable to engage in any substantial gainful activity by reason of a medically determined physical or mental impairment expected to result in death or that has lasted, or can be expected to last, for a continuous period of at least 12 months.

Also, a child under age 18 who has an impairment of comparable severity with that of an adult may be considered disabled. On February 20, 1990, the Supreme Court affirmed the Court of Appeals (Third Circuit) decision in *Sullivan* v. *Zebley*. As a result, SSA is completing a reevaluation of childhood disability claims for SSI benefits which were denied because the child's functional limitations were not considered in making the decision on the severity of the impairment. Federal regulations that revise the disability evaluation and determination process for SSI claims of disabled children (i.e., implementing the *Zebley* decision) were issued in February 1991.

A person also must be needy, i.e., have limited income and resources (discussed later) to be eligible for SSI. However, disabled SSI recipients whose incomes exceed the limits because of earnings but who continue to be medically disabled, may continue to be eligible for Medicaid. In addition, to qualify for SSI, a person must (1) be a U.S. citizen or an immigrant lawfully admitted for permanent residence or otherwise permanently residing in the United States under color of law and, (2) be a resident of the United States or the Northern Mariana Islands, or a child of military personnel stationed outside the United States.

TABLE 6–1.—SUPPLEMENTAL SECURITY INCOME SUMMARY

[Selected calendar years 1974–93]

Item	1974	1978	1980	1984	1986	1988	1990	1991	1992	1993
Recipients: [1]										
Total	3,996,064	4,216,925	4,142,017	4,029,333	4,269,184	4,463,869	4,817,127	5,118,470	5,566,189	5,984,300
Aged	2,285,909	1,967,900	1,807,776	1,530,289	1,473,428	1,433,420	1,454,041	1,464,684	1,471,022	1,474,852
Blind	74,616	77,135	78,401	80,524	83,115	82,864	83,686	84,549	85,400	85,456
Disabled	1,635,539	2,171,890	2,255,840	2,418,522	2,712,641	2,947,585	3,279,400	3,569,237	4,009,767	4,424,022
Number with Section 1619(a)	NA	NA	NA	406 (8/84)	992 (1/86)	19,920	[2]13,994	15,531	17,603	18,597
Number with Section 1619(b)	NA	NA	NA	6,804	8,106	15,625	23,517	26,852	31,649	34,293
Annual Payments (In millions):										
Total	$5,246	$6,552	$7,940	$10,372	$12,081	$13,786	$16,599	$18,534	$22,238	$23,991
Federal Benefits	3,833	4,881	5,866	8,281	9,498	10,734	12,894	14,765	18,247	20,722
Federal Admin. State Supp	1,264	1,491	1,848	1,792	2,243	2,671	3,239	3,231	3,435	3,270
State Admin. State Supp	149	180	226	299	340	381	466	538	[3]556	564
Annual Payments (In millions of 1992 dollars)	$14,929	$14,099	$13,519	$14,006	$15,465	$16,350	$17,818	$19,092	$22,238	$23,841
Monthly Federal Benefits Rates:										
Individuals	$140.00	$177.80	$208.20	$314.00	$336.00	$354.00	$386.00	$407.00	$422.00	$434.00
Couples	210.00	266.70	312.30	472.00	504.00	532.00	579.00	610.00	633.00	652.00
Average Federal SSI payments: [1]										
All Recipients	$95.11	$111.98	$143.35	$196.16	$215.40	$227.49	$261.47	$286.03	$329.74	$317.41
Aged Individuals	78.48	91.22	112.45	143.24	151.38	159.36	175.29	186.28	195.86	204.45
Aged Couples	93.02	120.48	157.56	221.98	246.07	273.18	322.82	414.26	448.61	478.42
Average Federally administered: [1]										
State supplementation	$70.92	$75.00	$99.15	$97.61	$115.41	$122.68	$139.79	$130.55	$118.08	$108.50
Income of Recipients Percent with: [1]										
Social Security benefits	52.7	51.7	51.0	49.6	48.9	47.8	45.9	44.3	41.3	40.1
Other unearned income	10.5	11.5	11.0	11.2	12.1	12.4	13.0	14.1	14.5	13.4
Earnings	2.8	3.1	3.2	3.5	3.9	4.4	4.7	4.6	4.4	4.3
Average amount of: [1]										
Social Security benefits	$130.01	$156.50	$196.94	$250.61	$263.29	$286.49	$318.57	$329.19	$335.72	$338.85
Other unearned income	61.10	66.93	74.35	84.56	86.40	85.92	98.13	94.71	91.96	100.44
Earnings	80.00	99.32	106.95	126.47	142.17	173.09	195.64	206.86	207.55	210.22

TABLE 6–1.—SUPPLEMENTAL SECURITY INCOME SUMMARY—Continued

[Selected calendar years 1974–93]

Item	1974	1978	1980	1984	1986	1988	1990	1991	1992	1993
Poverty Thresholds (Age 65 and over):										
Individual	$2,364	$3,127	$3,949	$4,979	$5,255	$5,674	$6,268	$6,532	$6,729	$6,930
Couple	2,982	3,944	4,983	6,282	6,630	7,158	7,905	8,241	8,489	8,741
Federal Benefit Rate as a percent of Poverty:										
Individual	74.1	72.7	72.3	75.6	76.7	74.9	73.9	74.8	75.3	75.2
Couple	88.1	86.4	86.0	90.2	91.2	89.2	87.9	88.8	89.5	89.5

[1] December data.
[2] The decrease in 1619(a) participants in 1990 was caused by the increase in the substantial gainful activity level to $500 monthly.
[3] Fiscal year 1992 data.

Source: Social Security Bulletin, Annual Statistical Supplement, and unpublished data.

Further, since SSI payments are reduced by other income, applicants and recipients must apply for any other money benefits due them. The Social Security Administration works with recipients and helps them get any other benefits for which they are eligible.

Persons who are disabled because of drug addiction or alcoholism must accept appropriate treatment for their addictions as a condition of SSI eligibility. Additionally, except for children of military personnel, persons outside of the United States for a month are not eligible for SSI. Blind or disabled children of military personnel who accompany their parents to overseas duty stations may be eligible for SSI if they were eligible in the month before they left the United States.

People who get SSI checks can get Social Security checks, too, if they are eligible for them. However, a person cannot get SSI payments and participate in the AFDC program. If a parent or child is eligible under both programs, the parent can choose whichever best suits the family.

Residents of public institutions for a full calendar month are ineligible for SSI unless one of the following exceptions applies:

1. The public institution is a medical treatment facility and Medicaid pays more than 50 percent of the cost of care.

2. The individual is residing in a publicly operated community residence which serves no more than 16 residents. Such a facility must provide an alternative living arrangement to a large institution and be residential (i.e., not a correctional, educational or medical facility).

3. The public institution is a public emergency shelter for the homeless. Such a facility provides food, a place to sleep, and some services to homeless individuals on a temporary basis. Payments to a resident of a public emergency shelter for the homeless are limited to no more than 6 months in any 9-month period.

4. The individual is in a public institution primarily to receive educational or vocational training. To qualify, the training must be an approved program and must be designed to prepare an individual for gainful employment.

5. The individual was eligible for SSI under one of the special provisions of section 1619 of the Social Security Act (see section on Special SSI Benefits, Medicaid Services, and Related Provisions for the Working Disabled) in the month preceding the first full month of residency in a medical or psychiatric institution which agrees to permit the individual to retain benefit payments. Payment may be made for the first full month of institutionalization and the subsequent month.

6. A physician certifies that the recipient's stay in a medical facility is likely not to exceed 3 months and the recipient needs to continue to maintain and provide for the expenses of the home to which he may return. Payments may be made for up to the first 3 months of institutionalization.

ELIGIBILITY OF SSI RECIPIENTS FOR SOCIAL SECURITY

SSI law requires that SSI applicants file for all other benefits for which they may be entitled. Since its inception SSI has been viewed as the "program of last resort." That is, after evaluating all other income, SSI pays what is necessary to bring an individual to the statutorily prescribed income "floor." As of September 1993, 40.7 percent of all SSI recipients also received Social Security benefits (65 percent of aged SSI recipients). Social Security benefits are the single highest source of income for SSI recipients. The SSI program considers Social Security benefits unearned income and thus counts all but $20 monthly in determining the SSI benefit amount.

ELIGIBILITY OF SSI RECIPIENTS FOR AFDC

An *individual* cannot receive both SSI payments and AFDC benefits and, if eligible for both, must choose which benefit to receive. Generally, the AFDC agency encourages individuals to file for SSI and, once the SSI payments start, the individual is removed from the AFDC filing unit.

ELIGIBILITY OF SSI RECIPIENTS FOR MEDICAID

States have three options as to how they treat SSI recipients in relation to Medicaid eligibility. Section 1634 of SSI law allows the Social Security Administration to enter into agreements with States to cover all SSI recipients with Medicaid eligibility. SSI recipients are not required to make a separate application for Medicaid under this arrangement. Thirty-one States and the District of Columbia chose this option, and SSI recipients in these States account for approximately 79 percent of all SSI recipients nationwide.

Under the second option, States elect to provide Medicaid eligibility for all SSI recipients, but only if the recipient completes a separate application with the State agency which administers the Medicaid program. The seven States of Alaska, Idaho, Kansas, Nebraska, Nevada, Oregon, and Utah and the Commonwealth of the Northern Mariana Islands affecting about 2.4 percent of SSI recipients nationwide, have elected this option.

The third and most restrictive option is known as the "209(b)" option, under which States may impose Medicaid eligibility criteria which are more restrictive than SSI criteria, so long as the criteria chosen are not more restrictive than the State's approved Medicaid State plan in January 1972. The 209(b) States may be more restrictive in defining blindness or disability, and/or more restrictive in their financial requirements for eligibility, and/or require a Medicaid application with the State. However, aged, blind, and disabled SSI recipients who are Medicaid applicants must be allowed to spend-down in 209(b) States, regardless of whether or not the State has a medically needy program. Twelve States use the 209(b) option for Medicaid coverage of aged, blind, and disabled SSI recipients. About 18.3 percent of the SSI recipient population nationwide lives in these 209(b) States. The 12 States that use this option are:

Connecticut	Minnesota	North Dakota
Hawaii	Missouri	Ohio
Illinois	New Hampshire	Oklahoma
Indiana	North Carolina	Virginia

An amendment included in the 1986 SSI disability amendments (P.L. 99–643) required, effective July 1, 1987, that 209(b) States continue Medicaid coverage for individuals in section 1619 status if they had been eligible for Medicaid for the month preceding their becoming eligible under section 1619.

The same legislation required States to provide for continued Medicaid coverage for those individuals who lose their eligibility for SSI on or after July 1, 1987 when their income increases because they become newly eligible for Social Security benefits as an adult who became disabled as a child (disabled adult child) or because of an increase in their benefits as an adult who became disabled as a child. "Disabled adult children" who otherwise would be eligible for SSI continue to be considered SSI recipients for Medicaid purposes. Protection against loss of Medicaid also is provided for certain blind or disabled individuals who lose their SSI benefits when they qualify for Social Security disabled widow or widower's benefits beginning as early as age 50. The Omnibus Budget Reconciliation Act of 1990 provides that such individuals, who otherwise would continue to qualify for SSI on the basis of blindness or disability, will be deemed to be SSI recipients for purposes of Medicaid eligibility until they become eligible for Medicare Hospital Insurance. This provision has been effective since January 1, 1991.

ELIGIBILITY OF SSI RECIPIENTS FOR FOOD STAMPS

Except in California, which has converted food stamp benefits to cash that is included in the State supplementary payments, SSI recipients may be eligible to receive food stamps. SSI beneficiaries living alone or in a household where all other members of the household receive or are applying for SSI benefits can file for food stamps at an SSA office. If all household members receive SSI, they do not need to meet the food stamp program financial eligibility standards to participate in the program because they are categorically eligible. However, SSI beneficiaries living in households where other household members do not receive or are not applying for SSI benefits are referred to the local food stamp office to file for food stamps. These households must meet the net income eligibility standard of the food stamp program to be eligible for food stamp benefits.

The interaction with the food stamp program has important financial implications for a State which desires to increase the income of its SSI recipients by $1. Because food stamps are reduced by $0.30 for each additional $1 of SSI income including State supplements, the State must expend $1.43 to obtain an effective $1 increase in SSI recipients' total income.

INCOME EXCLUSIONS

Under the program, $20 of monthly income from virtually any source (such as Social Security benefits, but *not* need-tested income such as veterans' pensions) is excluded from countable income (total income minus exclusions). In addition, the first $65 of monthly earned income plus one-half of remaining earnings are excluded. Income received in sheltered workshops and work activity centers is considered earned income and qualifies for earned income exclusions. Table 6–2 shows the maximum income that an individual and couple can have and still remain eligible for Federal SSI benefits under the regular Federal SSI benefit standards—taking into account these income exclusions.

Work-related expenses are disregarded in the case of blind applicants or recipients and impairment-related work expenses are disregarded in the case of disabled applicants or recipients.

The SSI program also does not count income and/or resources that are set aside as part of an approved plan to achieve self-support (PASS). A PASS is an income and/or resource exclusion that allows a person who is blind or disabled to set aside income and/or resources for a work goal. The money set aside can be used to pay for such items or services as education, vocational training, or starting a business.

SSI law requires that an SSI applicant or recipient apply for all other benefits for which they are eligible. For example, in September 1993, 65 percent of the aged, 32 percent of the disabled, and 37 percent of the blind receiving SSI were also Social Security recipients.

The value of any in-kind assistance is counted as income unless such in-kind assistance is specifically excluded by statute. Generally, in-kind assistance provided by or under the auspices of a federally assisted program, or by a State or local government (for example, nutrition, food stamps, housing or social services), will not be counted as income. As described later, if an SSI applicant or recipient is living in the household of another and receiving in-kind support and maintenance from him or her, the SSI benefit standard for such an individual will be reduced by one-third of the Federal SSI benefit standard. By regulation, the Social Security Administration has also provided that the value of any in-kind support and maintenance received (other than in the case of those receiving in-kind assistance by reason of living in another's household), is presumed to be equal to one-third of the Federal SSI benefit standard plus $20. The individual can rebut this presumption. If it is determined that the actual value is less than the one-third amount, the lower actual value will be counted as unearned income.

In-kind support and maintenance provided by a private nonprofit organization to aged, blind, or disabled individuals is excluded under the SSI program if the State determines that the assistance is provided on the basis of need. Another exclusion from income is certain types of assistance provided to help meet home energy needs. Assistance provided to an aged, blind, or disabled individual for the purpose of meeting home energy costs either in cash or in kind and which is furnished by a home heating oil or gas supplier or by a utility company is to be excluded. Assistance for home energy costs provided in-kind by a private nonprofit organization is also excluded.

As countable income increases, a recipient's SSI benefit amount decreases. Ineligibility for SSI occurs when countable income equals the Federal benefit standard plus the amount of applicable federally administered State supplementation.

TABLE 6–2.—MAXIMUM INCOME FOR ELIGIBILITY FOR FEDERAL SSI BENEFITS, 1994

	Receiving only Social Security		Receiving only wage income	
	Monthly	Annually	Monthly	Annually
Individual	$466	$5,592	$977	$11,724
Couple	689	8,268	1,423	17,076

Source: Supplemental Security Income, Social Security Administration.

RESOURCES

SSI eligibility is restricted to qualified persons who have countable resources not exceeding $2,000, or $3,000 in the case of married couples. The Deficit Reduction Act of 1984 (P.L. 98–369) increased the countable assets limit by $100 a year for an individual and $150 a year for a couple, beginning in calendar year 1985 and each year through calendar year 1989. Prior to January 1, 1985, the assets limit for an individual was $1,500 and $2,250 for a couple.

In determining countable resources, a number of items are not included, such as the individual's home; and, within reasonable limits set by the Secretary of Health and Human Services: household goods, personal effects, an automobile, and a burial space for the individual, spouse, and members of the immediate family. Regulations place a limit of $2,000 in equity value on excluded household goods and personal effects and exclude the first $4,500 in current market value of an auto (100 percent of the auto's value if it is used to obtain medical treatment or for employment or has been modified for use by or transportation of a handicapped person or is necessary to perform essential daily activities because of distance, climate or terrain). The value of property which is used in a person's trade, or business, or by the person as an employee is also excluded. The value of certain other property that produces income, goods or services essential to a person's self-support may be excluded within limits set by the Secretary in regulations. SSI and Social Security retroactive benefit payments may not be considered as a resource for a period of 6 months after the month in which the retroactive benefit is received. Resources set aside under a PASS are also excluded.

The cash surrender value of life insurance policies if the total face value of all policies on an individual's life is $1,500 or less are not counted toward the $2,000 or $3,000 countable resources limit. The entire cash surrender value of life insurance policies if the total face value of all policies on an individual's life is greater than $1,500 counts toward the resources limit, but may be excludable under one of the other resource provisions.

An individual and spouse may have excluded up to $1,500 each of burial funds. However, the $1,500 maximum amount is reduced by the face value of any excluded life insurance policies and the value of any irrevocable burial contracts, trusts or arrangements. If left to accumulate, interest earned on excluded burial funds and burial spaces is not countable as either income or resources for SSI purposes.

Current law provides that as of July 1, 1988, an individual who gives away or sells any nonexcludable resource for less than fair market value will no longer be subject to a penalty for such a transfer. However, such a transfer may make the individual ineligible for certain Medicaid covered nursing services. SSA must notify individuals of the penalty and provide information upon request to the States regarding transfers of resources.

The Deficit Reduction Act of 1984 (P.L. 98–369) requires the Internal Revenue Service to furnish the Social Security Administration with certain nonwage information about SSI recipients. The IRS information consists primarily of reports of interest payments submitted to IRS by financial institutions but also includes income from dividends, unemployment compensation, etc. The purpose of the provision was to assist in alerting the Social Security Administration of the potential ownership by SSI recipients of bank accounts in excess of the SSI countable resources limit. In fiscal year 1987, computer matches between IRS tax files and SSI records resulted in 239,000 such matches. Only cases involving IRS reports of interest income of $51 or more were examined. The resulting savings to the SSI program were $64 million. As a result of the Social Security Administration's evaluation of these cases, the tolerance level was lowered to $41 beginning with fiscal year 1988 and 398,000 matches were identified. In fiscal year 1989, the matches totaled 508,000. SSA has evaluated and adjusted the tolerance levels several times over the years. Effective October 1993, the tolerance level for income from resources—e.g., interest and dividends—is $60. The tolerance level for other nonwage income not from resources—e.g., unemployment compensation and pensions—is $1,000. Also, a special tolerance was developed for cases that had been matched before; if the current year's resources are less than $10 more than the prior year's resource indicators, the IRS report is not examined. All match information is sent to Social Security offices for verification of the information. For fiscal year 1993 there were about 413,000 matches. (The results of a study which will include an estimate of savings for the 1993 matches is not expected until the summer of 1994.)

Prior to the 1984 Deficit Reduction Act, if in any month a recipient's assets exceeded the asset limit, the individual was ineligible for benefits in that month and the entire amount of the benefit paid for that month was considered an overpayment subject to recovery. Effective 1984, SSI law provides that in cases where there is an overpayment based on an excess of assets of $50 or less, the recipient is deemed to be without fault for purposes of waiving the overpayment and the overpayment is not recovered unless the Secretary finds that the failure to report the excess was knowing and willful on the part of the recipient.

An individual may receive SSI benefits for a limited time even though he has certain nonliquid property that, if counted, would make him ineligible. These benefits are conditioned upon the disposal of the property, and are subject to recovery as overpayments when the property is sold. The 1987 Budget Reconciliation Act provides, in addition, for the exclusion of real property, for so long as it cannot be sold, because it is jointly owned and sale would cause undue hardship to the joint owner due to loss of housing; has legal impediments to its sale; or where reasonable efforts to sell it have been unsuccessful.

SSI BENEFITS

Individuals and couples applying for or receiving SSI benefits are determined to be eligible or to remain eligible if their countable income does not exceed certain levels, and they meet all other eligibility requirements.

Federal SSI benefit standard

The Federal SSI benefit standard for an individual for 1994 is $446 a month and $669 for a couple. As is discussed later, most States supplement the Federal SSI benefit. The result is a combined Federal SSI/State supplemented benefit against which countable income is compared in determining eligibility and benefit amount. However, many States limit their supplementation to certain categories of individuals based on specific indicators of need—especially special housing needs. In December 1993, 348,335 persons, or 5.8 percent of all SSI recipients, were eligible for benefits only because (federally-administered) State supplementation increased the benefit.

The Federal SSI benefits are indexed to the Consumer Price Index (CPI) and by the same percentage as Social Security benefits. This occurs through a reference in the SSI law to the Social Security cost-of-living adjustment (COLA) provision. Prior to the Social Security Amendments of 1983 (Public Law 98–21), the SSI and Social Security cost-of-living increases occurred in benefits paid in July. Public Law 98–21 delayed the Social Security and SSI COLA's from July 1983 to January 1984. However, in lieu of a COLA increase in the SSI benefit standard in July 1983, the Federal SSI benefit was increased in July, 1983, by $20 a month for an individual and $30 a month for a couple. Table 6–3 shows the Federal SSI benefit from the beginning of the SSI program until the present time.

Living in the household of another

The SSI law provides that if an SSI applicant or recipient is "living in another person's household and receiving support and maintenance in-kind from such person," the Federal SSI benefit applicable to such individual or couple is two-thirds of the regular Federal SSI benefit. As shown in table 6–3, the Federal SSI benefit in 1994 for those determined to be living in the household of another is $297.34 for an individual and $446 for a couple.

TABLE 6–3.—FEDERAL SSI BENEFIT LEVELS

[In dollars]

Date	Medic-aid institution	Own household			Household of another		
		Single	Couple	Essential person	Single	Couple	Essential person
Initial	25.00	130.00	195.00	65.00	86.67	130.00	43.34
Jan. 1974	25.00	140.00	210.00	70.00	93.34	140.00	46.67
July 1974	25.00	146.00	219.00	73.00	97.34	146.00	48.67
July 1975	25.00	157.70	236.60	78.90	105.14	157.74	52.60
July 1976	25.00	167.80	251.80	84.00	111.87	167.87	56.00
July 1977	25.00	177.80	266.70	89.00	118.54	177.80	59.34
July 1978	25.00	189.40	284.10	94.80	126.27	189.40	63.20
July 1979	25.00	208.20	312.30	104.20	138.80	208.20	69.47
July 1980	25.00	238.00	357.00	119.20	158.67	238.00	79.47
July 1981	25.00	264.70	397.00	132.60	176.47	264.67	88.40
July 1982	25.00	284.30	426.40	142.50	189.54	284.27	95.00
July 1983	25.00	304.30	456.40	152.50	202.87	304.27	101.67
Jan. 1984 [1]	25.00	314.00	472.00	157.00	209.34	314.67	104.67
Jan. 1985	25.00	325.00	488.00	163.00	216.67	325.34	108.67
Jan. 1986	25.00	336.00	504.00	168.00	224.00	336.00	112.00
Jan. 1987	25.00	340.00	510.00	170.00	226.67	340.00	113.34
Jan. 1988	25.00	354.00	532.00	177.00	236.00	354.67	118.00
Jan. 1989	30.00	368.00	553.00	184.00	245.34	368.67	122.67
Jan. 1990	30.00	386.00	579.00	193.00	257.34	386.00	128.67
Jan. 1991	30.00	407.00	610.00	204.00	271.34	406.67	136.00
Jan. 1992	30.00	422.00	633.00	211.00	281.34	422.00	140.67
Jan. 1993	30.00	434.00	652.00	217.00	289.34	434.67	144.67
Jan. 1994	30.00	446.00	669.00	223.00	297.34	446.00	148.67

[1] Cost-of-living adjustments to Federal SSI benefit levels are rounded to the next lower whole dollar beginning with the increase effective January 1984.

Source: Office of Research and Statistics, Social Security Administration.

Regulations specify the criteria for determining when this reduced benefit applies. It does not apply to an individual who owns or rents; buys food separately; eats meals out rather than eating with the household; or pays a pro rata share of the household's food and shelter expenses.

In September 1993, 5.3 percent, or about 313,100 SSI recipients, had their benefits determined on the basis of this "one-third reduction" benefit standard. Sixty-five percent of those recipients were receiving benefits on the basis of disability (see table 6–4).

Of the 26 States and the District of Columbia that provide optional supplements to the Federal SSI benefit, 9 States and the District of Columbia provide the same amount of supplementation for those whose Federal SSI benefit amount is determined on the basis of the "one-third reduction." Eight States provide a higher State supplementation for such recipients; in six States the amount of State supplementation is less; two States provide no supplementation for those recipients; and one State's supplementation varies depending upon need.

Medicaid institution/personal needs allowance

When an individual enters a hospital or other medical institution in which more than half of the bill is paid by the Medicaid program, his or her monthly SSI benefit standard is reduced to $30, beginning with the first full calendar month the individual is in such institution. This Personal Needs Allowance (PNA) is intended to take care of small personal expenses, with the cost of maintenance and medical care being provided through Medicaid. The Federal PNA benefit of $25 was increased to $30 a month on July 1, 1988—the first increase since the SSI program began in 1974. The annual cost-of-living increase for SSI does not apply to the personal needs allowance. The 1987 Budget Reconciliation Act does, however, provide that if a physician certifies that a person's stay in such a medical institution is not likely to exceed 3 months and the person needs to continue to maintain a home to which he or she may return, the SSI benefits will not be reduced and he or she will continue to receive the full SSI benefit for up to the first 3 months of institutionalization.

Approximately 165,400 or 2.8 percent of SSI recipients received benefits in September, 1993, on the basis of this personal needs allowance. For those individuals whose income from non-SSI sources exceeds the $30 benefit standard (including those who previously, when they were not living in a medical institution, were receiving some SSI because their Social Security benefits were less than the regular SSI benefit), Medicaid regulations require States to allow such individuals (and other non-SSI Medicaid eligibles) to retain no less than $30 a month of their income as a "personal needs allowance" when their income is applied, along with Medicaid reimbursement, to pay for their institutional medical care.

Sixteen State programs have exercised their option to supplement this Federal SSI benefit. Prior to the 1985 Budget Reconciliation Act, SSI regulations would not allow for Federal administration of the State supplements of these payments. An amendment included in that legislation now requires the Social Security Administration, at the request of a State, to administer such State supplementary payments. As of December 1993, California, the District of Columbia, Maine, Massachusetts, Michigan, New Jersey, New York, Rhode Island, and Vermont had opted for Federal administration. Approximately 24 States allow some or all of those individuals affected by the Medicaid personal needs allowance regulations to retain more than $30 a month.

Another benefit affecting some persons involves Federal payments to an individual who was transferred to SSI from a former State program of aid to the aged, blind or disabled. The Federal benefits of these persons are increased by up to $223 monthly in 1994 to take into account an "essential person" living in the household. An essential person is generally an ineligible spouse or relative whose needs were considered in determining the requirements of an eligible individual under the former State program but who is not eligible for SSI. Some States have categories of State supplementation similar to the "essential persons" category for individuals transferred from the pre-SSI program.

TABLE 6–4.—NUMBER AND PERCENTAGE DISTRIBUTION OF PERSONS RECEIVING FED-
ERALLY ADMINISTERED PAYMENTS, BY REASON FOR ELIGIBILITY AND FEDERAL SSI
BENEFIT STANDARD/LIVING ARRANGEMENT, SEPTEMBER 1993

Federal benefit standard/living arrangement [1]	Total	Reason for eligibility		
		Aged	Blind	Disabled
Total number	5,907,605	1,473,531	85,885	4,348,189
Total percent	100.0	100.0	100.0	100.0
Federal SSI benefit standard	91.9	90.5	91.4	92.4
Living in the household-of-another Federal SSI benefit standard	5.3	7.0	5.6	4.7
Medicaid institution/personal needs allowance Federal SSI benefit standard	2.8	2.6	3.0	2.8

[1] As used for determination of Federal SSI payment standard.
Source: Office of Research and Statistics, Social Security Administration.

DEEMING OF INCOME AND RESOURCES

The income of an ineligible spouse who lives with an adult SSI
applicant or recipient is considered in determining the eligibility
and amount of payment to the individual. The income of the parents of a child under the age of 18 who is blind or disabled is also
considered in determining the eligibility and payment for the child.
However, effective June 1, 1990, children with disabilities who are
eligible for Medicaid at home under State home care plans, who
previously received SSI personal needs allowances while in medical
institutions, and who otherwise would be ineligible for SSI because
of their parents' income or resources, can receive the $30 monthly
personal needs allowance that would be payable if they were institutionalized, without regard to their parents' income and resources.
The law also provides that deeming of income and resources shall
occur "except to the extent determined by the Secretary to be in-
equitable under the circumstances".

By regulation, the Secretary of HHS has provided that in determining the amount of the income of the ineligible spouse or parent
to be deemed to the SSI applicant or recipient, the needs of the
spouse or parent and other children in the household are taken
into account. In addition, the SSI earned and unearned income exclusions are applied in determining the amount of income to be
deemed to the SSI applicant or recipient. If the combined countable
income of an SSI applicant and an ineligible spouse does not exceed
the SSI benefit standard for an eligible couple in that State (including any federally-administered State supplementary payment), the
SSI applicant would be eligible to receive an SSI and/or State supplementary benefit.

For example, in a State with no State supplementation the deeming procedure would work as follows in the case of an ineligible
spouse earning $520 per month living with an eligible individual
with $200 of Social Security benefits:

Unearned income of eligible individual	$200.00
Less $20 exclusion	−20.00
Countable unearned income	180.00
Earned income of ineligible individual	520.00
Less $65 earned income disregard	−65.00
Less one-half of remaining earnings ($455)	−227.50
Countable earned income	227.50
Plus countable unearned income	180.00
Couple's total countable income	407.50
SSI payment standard for couples	669.00
Less countable income	−407.50
Benefit payable to eligible individual	261.50

Thus the benefit for the eligible individual will be $261.50. Without deeming, the individual would have received $266 [$446 − ($200 less $20 exclusion)]. The $20 exclusion can only be used once and is first applied to unearned income, which in this example is the $200 of Social Security income.

An individual's resources are deemed to include those of the ineligible spouse (or in the case of a child under the age of 18, those of the parents) with whom the individual is living. Under the Secretary's regulations, in determining the amount of the spouse's or parents' resources that can be deemed, all applicable exclusions are applied. In the case of a child, only the value of the parents' resources that exceeds the applicable limits ($2,000 for a single parent, and $3,000 for two parents) is deemed to the child.

In a study conducted in December 1989, there were about 92,700 cases in which deeming reduced benefits. Some 71,180 were spouse-to-spouse and 21,520 were parent-to-child cases. This does not take into account, however, the number of individuals who were not eligible because of the deeming provision.

In determining the eligibility of aliens applying for SSI, the income and resources of their sponsors are considered. After income and resources allowances for the needs of the sponsors and income allowances for their dependents, the remainder is deemed available for the support of the alien applicant. Prior to January 1, 1994, the remainder was deemed available for a 3-year period after the alien's entry into the United States. Effective January 1, 1994, through September 30, 1996, the remainder is deemed available for a 5-year period after the alien's entry into the United States. Under current law, the deeming period will revert to 3 years again on October 1, 1996. This provision does not apply to those who become blind or disabled after admission as a permanent resident, to refugees, and to persons granted political asylum.

OVERPAYMENTS

A provision in the 1984 Deficit Reduction Act established a limit on the rate that overpayments made to SSI recipients can be recovered. SSI law limits the amount of adjustment or recovery in any month to the lesser of: (1) the amount of the benefit for that month; or (2) an amount equal to 10 percent of the countable income (plus the SSI payment) of the individual (or couple) for that month. This limitation does not apply if there is fraud in connection with the overpayment. The recipient may request a different rate at which benefits may be withheld to recover the overpayment.

STATE SUPPLEMENTATION

State supplementary payments are required by law to maintain income levels of former public assistance recipients transferred to the Federal SSI program. In February 1994, approximately 3,400 recipients or less than 0.1 percent of all recipients were receiving payments based in part or solely because of this provision. States have the option to choose to supplement the Federal SSI benefit standard for both former public assistance recipients and other SSI recipients. At the present time, all but eight States and jurisdictions provide some form of optional State supplementation. Those are: Arkansas, Georgia, Kansas, Mississippi, Commonwealth of the Northern Mariana Islands, Tennessee, Texas, and West Virginia. States (or local jurisdictions) may elect to administer their supplementary payments themselves or may contract with the Social Security Administration for Federal administration. Seventeen States and the District of Columbia have contracted with the Social Security Administration to administer the State optional supplementation program. Since the SSI program began in 1974, six States have shifted from Federal to State administration of their optional State supplementation program.

Administrative fees

The Omnibus Budget Reconciliation Act of 1993 amended the State supplementation provision to provide for State payment for Federal administration of State supplementary payments. For fiscal year 1994 (i.e., from October 1, 1993 through September 30, 1994), a State with federally administered supplementary payments pays the Secretary an administration fee of $1.67 per payment. The rate per payment changes to $3.33 for fiscal year 1995, and $5.00 for fiscal year 1996 and each succeeding year, or a different rate deemed appropriate for the State by the Secretary.

State SSI supplement levels over time

Throughout the entire period from July, 1975, to January, 1994, 23 States have continuously provided supplemental SSI payments to aged individuals living independently, and 21 States continuously supplemented SSI payments to aged couples living independently.

During the period of July, 1975, to January, 1994, no State increased supplements faster than inflation for aged individuals living independently (see table 6–5).

The District of Columbia, South Dakota, Utah, and Wyoming all began supplementing SSI payments to individuals between 1975 and 1980.

Among the States which have supplemented SSI payments for aged couples living independently, only Alaska and Minnesota have kept their supplemental increases equivalent to or higher than inflation (see table 6–6). Other States have allowed inflation to erode the purchasing power of supplements or have reduced them in the face of State fiscal problems.

Approximately 44 percent of SSI recipients receive a State supplement. For those SSI recipients, other than those receiving a State supplement because they are living in some type of group living arrangement, the amount of State supplement ranges from $1 a month to $374 a month for an individual. At present, 26 States and the District of Columbia supplement the Federal standard for individuals living independently.

TABLE 6–5.—STATE SSI SUPPLEMENTS FOR AGED INDIVIDUALS WITHOUT COUNTABLE INCOME LIVING INDEPENDENTLY [1]

State	July 1975	July 1980	Jan. 1985	Jan. 1988	Jan. 1990	Jan. 1991	Jan. 1992	Jan. 1993	Jan. 1994	Percent change (constant dollars) 1975–94 [1]
Alaska [2]	$142	$235	$261	$305	$331	$349	$362	$374	$374	−2
California	101	164	179	221	244	223	223	186	157	−42
Colorado	27	55	58	58	58	45	56	56	56	−23
Connecticut [3]	NA	NA	NA	393	366	359	325	[3] NA	NA	NA
District of Columbia	0	15	15	15	15	15	15	15	15	NA
Hawaii	17	15	5	5	5	5	5	5	5	−89
Idaho	63	74	78	73	73	70	70	65	45	−74
Illinois [3]	NA	NA	NA	NA	NA	NA	NA	NA	NA	NA
Maine	10	10	10	10	10	10	10	10	10	−63
Massachusetts	111	137	129	129	129	129	129	129	129	−57
Michigan	12	24	27	30	30	31	14	14	14	−57
Minnesota [4]	31	34	35	35	75	81	81	81	81	−3
Nebraska	67	75	61	43	38	24	30	28	28	−85
Nevada	55	47	36	36	36	36	36	36	36	−76
New Hampshire	12	46	27	27	27	27	27	27	27	−17
New Jersey	24	23	31	31	31	31	31	31	31	−52
New York	61	63	61	72	86	86	86	86	86	−48
Oklahoma	27	79	60	64	64	64	64	60	60	−18
Oregon	17	12	2	2	2	2	2	2	2	−96
Pennsylvania	20	32	32	32	32	32	32	32	32	−41
Rhode Island	31	42	54	59	64	64	67	64	64	−24
South Dakota	0	15	15	15	15	15	15	15	15	NA
Utah	0	10	10	9	6	6	5	5	1	NA
Vermont	29	41	53	58	63	65	65	57	55	−30
Washington [5]	36	43	38	28	28	28	28	28	28	−71
Wisconsin	70	100	100	103	103	103	92	93	85	−55
Wyoming	0	20	20	20	20	20	20	10	10	NA
Median	31	43	36	36	37	36	32	31	31	−63

[1] The percentage change in constant dollars was computed by inflating July 1975 to January 1994 by the CPI–U price index. The July 1975 index value is 54.2 and the January 1994 value is 146.2.

[2] 1975 and 1980—less if shelter costs less than $35 monthly.

[3] State decides benefit on a case-by-case basis.

[4] State has two geographic payment levels—Hennepin County and the remainder of Minnesota. Level shown is for Hennepin County, the area with the largest number of SSI recipients.

[5] State has two geographic payment levels—highest levels are shown in table. Sum paid in King, Pierce, Kitsap, Snohomish, and Thurston Counties.

Source: Office of Supplemental Security Income, Social Security Administration, and Committee on Ways and Means staff calculations.

TABLE 6–6.—STATE SSI SUPPLEMENTS FOR AGED COUPLES WITHOUT COUNTABLE INCOME LIVING INDEPENDENTLY

State	July 1975	July 1980	Jan. 1985	Jan. 1988	Jan. 1990	Jan. 1991	Jan. 1992	Jan. 1993	Jan. 1994	Percent change (constant dollars) 1975–94 [1]
Alabama	$9	0	0	0	0	0	0	0	0	− 100
Alaska [2]	183	$338	$371	$444	$484	$510	$528	$544	$544	+ 10
California	251	389	448	534	588	557	557	488	440	− 35
Colorado	133	229	278	292	309	293	323	328	323	− 10
Connecticut [3]	NA	NA	NA	602	525	522	461	[3] NA	NA	NA
District of Co-lumbia	0	30	30	30	30	30	30	30	30	NA
Hawaii	28	24	9	9	9	9	9	9	9	− 88
Idaho	49	80	46	44	45	44	45	40	21	− 84
Illinois [3]	NA	NA	NA	NA	NA	NA	NA	NA	NA	NA
Maine	15	15	15	15	15	15	15	15	15	− 63
Massachusetts	173	214	202	202	202	202	202	202	202	− 57
Michigan	18	36	40	45	45	46	21	21	21	− 57
Minnesota [4]	38	44	66	66	88	132	129	126	126	+ 23
Nebraska	67	114	89	66	65	34	48	39	39	− 78
Nevada	106	90	74	74	74	74	74	74	74	− 74
New Hampshire	0	42	21	21	21	21	21	21	21	NA
New Jersey	13	12	25	25	25	25	25	25	25	− 29
New York	76	79	76	93	102	103	103	102	102	− 50
Oklahoma	54	158	120	128	128	128	128	120	102	− 18
Oregon	17	10	0	0	0	0	0	0	0	− 100
Pennsylvania	30	49	49	49	49	49	49	49	49	− 39
Rhode Island	59	79	102	111	120	121	127	120	120	− 25
South Dakota	0	15	15	15	15	15	15	15	15	NA
Utah	0	20	20	18	12	12	11	10	5	NA
Vermont	61	76	96	106	115	118	118	110	103	− 37
Washington [5]	40	44	37	22	22	22	22	22	22	− 80
Wisconsin	105	161	161	166	166	166	146	146	134	− 53
Wyoming	0	40	40	40	40	40	40	19	19	NA
Median	57	63	66	66	65	49	49	30	39	− 75

[1] The percentage change in constant dollars was computed by inflating July 1975 to January 1994 by the CPI–U price index. The July 1975 index value is 54.2 and the January 1994 value is 146.2.

[2] 1975 and 1980—less if shelter costs less than $35 monthly.

[3] State decides benefit on a case-by-case basis.

[4] State has various geographic payment levels. Level shown is for Hennepin County, the area with the largest number of SSI recipients.

[5] State has two geographic payment levels—highest levels are shown in table. Sum paid in King, Pierce, Kitsap, Snohomish, and Thurston Counties.

Source: Office of Supplemental Security Income, Social Security Administration.

MAXIMUM SSI AND FOOD STAMP BENEFITS FOR INDIVIDUALS LIVING INDEPENDENTLY

Table 6–7 for individuals living independently and table 6–8 for couples illustrate the maximum potential payment from Federal SSI, State supplements and food stamps for persons with no income, by State. These tables assume that the elderly individual or couple receive an excess shelter deduction of $207 (the maximum for nonelderly) and an excess medical cost deduction of $13 in the food stamp program. Approximately 64 percent of the elderly in the food stamp program take a shelter deduction, and it is estimated that approximately 17 percent of the elderly are allowed a deduction that exceeds the excess shelter expense ceiling for nonelderly or nondisabled households ($207 per month). However, since only 13 percent of the elderly claim a medical cost deduction, the $13 average of medical cost deductions averaged over all elderly recipients was chosen. Since only 17 percent of all elderly claimed more than the shelter cost deduction ceiling, the shelter deduction ceiling was chosen.

TABLE 6–7.—MAXIMUM POTENTIAL SSI AND FOOD STAMP BENEFITS FOR AGED INDIVIDUALS LIVING INDEPENDENTLY, JANUARY 1994 [1]

State	Maximum SSI benefit	Food stamp benefit [2]	Combined benefits	
			Monthly	Annual
Alabama	$446	$83	$529	$6,348
Alaska	820	79	899	10,788
Arizona	446	83	529	6,348
Arkansas	446	83	529	6,348
California	603	[3] 0	603	7,236
Colorado	502	66	568	6,816
Connecticut	[4] NA	NA	NA	NA
Delaware	446	83	529	6,348
District of Columbia	461	79	540	6,480
Florida	446	83	529	6,348
Georgia	446	83	529	6,348
Hawaii	451	187	638	7,656
Idaho	[5] 491	76	567	6,804
Illinois	[6] NA	NA	NA	NA
Indiana	446	83	529	6,348
Iowa	446	83	529	6,348
Kansas	446	83	529	6,348
Kentucky	446	83	529	6,348
Louisiana	446	83	529	6,348
Maine	456	80	536	6,432
Maryland	446	83	529	6,348
Massachusetts	575	44	619	7,428
Michigan	460	79	539	6,468
Minnesota	[7] 527	59	586	7,032
Mississippi	446	83	529	6,348
Missouri	446	83	529	6,348
Montana	446	83	529	6,348

TABLE 6–7.—MAXIMUM POTENTIAL SSI AND FOOD STAMP BENEFITS FOR AGED INDIVIDUALS LIVING INDEPENDENTLY, JANUARY 1994 [1]—Continued

State	Maximum SSI benefit	Food stamp benefit [2]	Combined benefits	
			Monthly	Annual
Nebraska	474	75	549	6,588
Nevada	482	72	554	6,648
New Hampshire	473	75	548	6,576
New Jersey	477	74	551	6,612
New Mexico	446	83	529	6,348
New York	532	57	589	7,068
North Carolina	446	83	529	6,348
North Dakota	446	83	529	6,348
Ohio	446	83	529	6,348
Oklahoma	506	65	571	6,852
Oregon	448	82	530	6,360
Pennsylvania	478	73	551	6,612
Rhode Island	510	64	574	6,888
South Carolina	446	83	529	6,348
South Dakota	461	79	540	6,480
Tennessee	446	83	529	6,348
Texas	446	83	529	6,348
Utah	447	83	530	6,360
Vermont	[8]501	67	568	6,816
Virginia	446	83	529	6,348
Washington	[9]474	75	549	6,588
West Virginia	446	83	529	6,348
Wisconsin	531	57	588	7,056
Wyoming	456	80	536	6,432

[1] In most States these maximums apply also to blind or disabled SSI recipients who are living in their own households; but some States provide different benefit schedules for each category.

[2] For one-person households, maximum food stamp benefits from Oct. 1993 through Sept. 1994 are $112 in the 48 contiguous States and the District of Columbia, $147 in Alaska (urban areas, benefit levels in rural Alaska are increased by about 50 percent to account for higher food prices in such areas), and $187 in Hawaii.

For the 48 contiguous States and D.C., the calculation of benefits assumes: (1) a "standard" deduction of $131 per month; (2) an excess shelter deduction of $207 per month (the maximum allowable for nonelderly, nondisabled households); and (3) an excess medical expense deduction of $13 monthly (estimated from 1991 medical expense information). If smaller excess shelter costs were assumed, food stamp benefits would be smaller. For Alaska and Hawaii, higher deduction levels were used, as provided by law ($595 and $493, respectively, for combined standard and excess shelter allowance).

[3] SSI recipients in California are ineligible for food stamps. California provides increased cash aid in lieu of stamps.

[4] Individual budget process.

[5] State disregards $20 of SSI payment in determining the State supplementary payment.

[6] State decides benefits on case-by-case basis.

[7] Payment level for Hennepin County. State has two geographic payment levels—one for Hennepin County and the other for the remainder of the State.

[8] State has two geographic payment levels—highest are shown in table.

[9] Sum paid in King, Pierce, Kitsap, Snohomish, and Thurston Counties.

Source: Table prepared by the Congressional Research Service (CRS) on the basis of data from the Social Security Administration.

TABLE 6–8.—MAXIMUM POTENTIAL SSI AND FOOD STAMP BENEFITS FOR AGED
COUPLES LIVING INDEPENDENTLY, JANUARY 1994 [1]

State	Maximum SSI benefit	Food stamp benefit [2]	Combined benefits	
			Monthly	Annual
Alabama	$669	$110	$779	$9,348
Alaska	1,213	85	1,298	15,576
Arizona	669	110	779	9,348
Arkansas	669	110	779	9,348
California	1,109	[3]0	1,109	13,308
Colorado	992	13	1,005	12,060
Connecticut	[4]NA	NA	NA	NA
Delaware	669	110	779	9,348
District of Columbia	699	101	800	9,600
Florida	669	110	779	9,348
Georgia	669	110	779	9,348
Hawaii	678	287	965	11,580
Idaho	[5]690	110	800	9,600
Illinois	[6]NA	NA	NA	NA
Indiana	669	110	779	9,348
Iowa	669	110	779	9,348
Kansas	669	110	779	9,348
Kentucky	669	110	779	9,348
Louisiana	669	110	779	9,348
Maine	684	106	790	9,480
Maryland	669	110	779	9,348
Massachusetts	871	50	921	11,052
Michigan	690	104	794	9,528
Minnesota	[7]795	72	867	10,404
Mississippi	669	110	779	9,348
Missouri	669	110	779	9,348
Montana	669	110	779	9,348
Nebraska	708	98	806	9,672
Nevada	743	88	831	9,972
New Hampshire	690	104	794	9,528
New Jersey	694	103	797	9,564
New Mexico	669	110	779	9,348
New York	771	79	850	10,200
North Carolina	669	110	779	9,348
North Dakota	669	110	779	9,348
Ohio	669	110	779	9,348
Oklahoma	789	74	863	10,356
Oregon	669	110	779	9,348
Pennsylvania	718	95	813	9,756
Rhode Island	789	74	863	10,356
South Carolina	669	110	779	9,348

TABLE 6–8.—MAXIMUM POTENTIAL SSI AND FOOD STAMP BENEFITS FOR AGED COUPLES LIVING INDEPENDENTLY, JANUARY 1994 [1]—Continued

State	Maximum SSI benefit	Food stamp benefit [2]	Combined benefits	
			Monthly	Annual
South Dakota	684	106	790	9,480
Tennessee	669	110	779	9,348
Texas	669	110	779	9,348
Utah	674	109	783	9,396
Vermont	[8] 772	79	851	10,212
Virginia	669	110	779	9,348
Washington	[9] 691	103	794	9,528
West Virginia	669	110	779	9,348
Wisconsin	803	70	873	10,476
Wyoming	688	104	792	9,504

[1] In most States these maximums apply also to blind or disabled SSI recipients who are living in their own households; but some States provide different benefit schedules for each category.

[2] For two-person households, maximum food stamp benefits from Oct. 1993 through Sept. 1994 are $206 in the 48 contiguous States and the District of Columbia, $271 in Alaska (urban areas, benefit levels for rural Alaska are about 50 percent higher to account for high food prices in such areas), and $343 in Hawaii.

For the 48 contiguous States and D.C., the calculation of benefits assumes: (1) a "standard" deduction of $131 per month, (2) an excess shelter deduction of $207 per month (the maximum allowable for nonelderly, nondisabled households); and (3) an excess medical expense deduction of $13 monthly (estimated from 1991 medical expense information). If smaller excess shelter costs were assumed, food stamp benefits would be smaller. For Alaska and Hawaii, higher deduction levels were used, as provided by law ($595 and $493, respectively, for combined standard and excess shelter allowance).

[3] SSI recipients in California are ineligible for food stamps. California provides increased cash aid in lieu of stamps.

[4] Individual budget process.

[5] State disregards $20 monthly of SSI income in determining the State supplementary payment amounts.

[6] State decides benefits on case-by-case basis.

[7] Payment level for Hennepin County. State has two geographic payment levels—one for Hennepin County and one for the remainder of the State.

[8] State has two geographic payment levels—highest levels are shown in table.

[9] Sum paid in King, Pierce, Kitsap, Snohomish, and Thurston Counties.

Source: Table prepared by the Congressional Research Service (CRS) on the basis of data from the Social Security Administration.

State supplementation for special housing needs

A significant number of the aged, disabled and blind population receiving SSI cannot live alone because of mental or physical limitations and have a need for housing which involves services beyond room and board. These services often include supervision for daily living and protective services for the mentally retarded, chronically mentally ill, or the frail or confused elderly. Such nonmedical supervised and/or group living arrangements generally cost more than the Federal SSI benefit needs standard of $446 a month and often more than the combined Federal and SSI State supplementation for those classified as living independently.

All but 10 of the 50 States and the District of Columbia have Federal or State administered State supplementation which is specifically directed at covering the additional cost of providing housing in a protective, supervised, or group living arrangement.

These living arrangements are identified by a variety of terms including: adult foster care homes; domiciliary care homes; congregate care; group homes for the mentally retarded and a variety of other terms. The amount of supplementation by the State also varies a great deal. For example, in the State of Maryland under a State-administered supplementation program, a "specialized and intensive supervision" group living facility has a State supplementation of $702 a month in addition to the Federal benefit level of $446. The total Federal and State SSI payment in a month is $1,148. In one State the State supplementation is less than $2 a month for those who need little supervision and care. However, in some States, the cost of supervised group living care is also partially met by direct State funding of the staff. In a number of States, the State makes payments for nonmedical group care directly to private residential facilities based on a rate negotiated by the State with each facility. In such cases, there is often a "personal needs allowance" payment made directly to or on behalf of the residents of the facility.

COMPARISON OF SSI PAYMENT LEVELS TO POVERTY THRESHOLDS

Table 6–9 compares the Federal SSI benefit for a single individual to the Bureau of the Census poverty threshold. Both the poverty threshold and the benefit level are indexed to the Consumer Price Index. (The percentage increase for the poverty threshold and the SSI benefit increase varies slightly because of a difference in the method of calculation.) As a result of Public Law 98–21, the SSI benefit levels were increased by $20 per month for individuals and $30 per month for couples in July 1983. They were further increased by 3.5 percent in January 1984. This explains why SSI benefits, in relation to the poverty level, increased to approximately 75 percent in 1984 and 1985 compared to 71 percent in the 1975 to 1982 period. In 1993, benefit levels were 75.2 percent of the poverty level.

Table 6–10 presents the same information for a couple. The SSI benefit for a couple is approximately 90 percent of the poverty threshold.

CHARACTERISTICS OF THE SSI POPULATION

As shown in table 6–12, in September 1993, 5.908 million persons received federally administered SSI payments. Of these, 1.474 million received federally administered payments on the basis of being aged, 4.348 million on the basis of being disabled, and 85,885 on the basis of blindness. However, approximately 636,391 of those receiving benefits on the basis of disability or blindness were over the age of 65. Table 6–12 also indicates that approximately 3.4 million of those receiving federally administered SSI payments only receive Federal SSI payments, 2.2 million receive a combination of federally financed and State financed payments, and 346,271 receive State financed supplementation only.

TABLE 6-9.—COMPARISON OF COMBINED BENEFITS TO POVERTY THRESHOLDS FOR ELIGIBLE INDIVIDUALS RECEIVING SSI; SSI AND SOCIAL SECURITY; AND SSI, SOCIAL SECURITY AND FOOD STAMPS FOR SELECTED YEARS: 1975 TO 1994

	Calendar year—									
	1975	1980	1984	1986	1988	1990	1991	1992	1993	1994
Poverty threshold	2,572	3,941	4,980	5,255	5,672	6,268	6,532	6,729	6,930	[1]7,117
Federal SSI benefits:										
Dollars per year	1,822	2,677	3,768	4,032	4,248	4,632	4,884	5,064	5,208	5,352
Percent of poverty	70.8	72.3	75.6	76.7	74.9	73.9	74.8	75.3	75.2	75.2
Federal SSI and Social Security:										
Dollars per year	2,062	2,917	4,008	4,272	4,488	4,872	5,124	5,304	5,448	5,592
Percent of poverty	80.2	74.0	80.5	81.3	79.1	77.7	78.4	78.8	78.6	78.6
Federal SSI, Social Security, and food stamps:[2]										
Dollars per year	2,350	3,345	4,294	4,488	4,848	5,318	5,580	5,820	5,952	6,144
Percent of poverty	91.4	84.9	86.2	85.4	85.5	84.8	85.4	86.5	85.9	86.3

[1] Projected on basis of CBO projected increases in the consumer price index.
[2] In computing the food stamp benefit for 1975, average deductions among all elderly households are assumed. For later years, the applicable standard deduction plus average shelter and medical deductions among all elderly households is assumed.

Source: Congressional Research Service.

232

TABLE 6–10.—COMPARISON OF COMBINED BENEFITS TO POVERTY THRESHOLDS FOR ELIGIBLE COUPLES RECEIVING SSI; SSI AND SOCIAL SECURITY; AND SSI, SOCIAL SECURITY AND FOOD STAMPS FOR SELECTED YEARS: 1975 TO 1994

	Calendar year—									
	1975	1980	1984	1986	1988	1990	1991	1992	1993	1994
Poverty threshold	3,232	4,954	6,280	6,628	7,156	7,906	8,238	8,489	8,741	[1]8,977
Federal SSI benefits:										
Dollars per year	2,734	4,016	5,664	6,048	6,384	6,948	7,320	7,596	7,824	8,028
Percent of poverty	84.6	81.1	90.2	91.2	89.2	87.9	88.9	89.5	89.5	89.4
Federal SSI and Social Security:										
Dollars per year	2,974	4,256	5,904	6,288	6,624	7,188	7,560	7,836	8,064	8,268
Percent of poverty	92.0	86.0	94.0	94.9	92.6	90.9	91.8	92.3	92.3	92.1
Federal SSI, Social Security, and food stamps: [2]										
Dollars per year	3,430	4,906	6,393	6,696	7,200	7,935	8,340	8,700	8,880	9,084
Percent of poverty	106.1	99.0	101.8	101.0	100.6	100.4	101.2	102.5	101.6	101.2

[1] Projected on basis of CBO projected increases in the consumer price index.
[2] In computing the food stamp benefit for 1975, average deductions among all elderly households are assumed. For later years, the applicable standard deduction plus average shelter and medical deductions among all elderly households is assumed.

Source: Congressional Research Service.

Table 6–13 shows the trends in the numbers of persons receiving federally administered SSI payments from December, 1975, through September, 1993, both by reason for eligibility and by age categories. There was a steady decline in the number of SSI recipients from 1975 until 1983. However, in the last 9 years the number of SSI recipients has increased from about 3.9 million to more than 5.9 million.

Characteristics of adult SSI recipients receiving benefits on the basis of disability or blindness

Major disabling diagnosis.—As shown in table 6–11, of the SSI disabled ages 18–64, 23.7 percent were eligible on the basis of mental retardation; and 32.2 percent on the basis of other mental disorders. Therefore, over one-half of all SSI disabled recipients are eligible on the basis of a mental disability. The next three largest categories are: diseases of the nervous system and sense organs— 8.8 percent; diseases of musculoskeletal and connective tissues—8.7 percent; and diseases of the circulatory system—6.8 percent. Related to the nature of the impairments of the SSI disabled is the fact that in December 1993, 1,145,700 or 30.6 percent of the adult disabled or blind receiving SSI benefits had a representative payee. Representative payees are individuals, agencies or institutions selected by the Social Security Administration to receive and use SSI payments on behalf of the SSI recipient when it has been found necessary by reason of the mental or physical limitations of the recipient.

Age.—When a person who is receiving SSI on the basis of blindness or disability becomes age 65, the Social Security Administration does not convert the individual to eligibility on the basis of age. As shown in table 6–14, 17 percent of the SSI adult population receiving benefits on the basis of disability are age 65 or over (28.2 percent of the blind were age 65 or over).

Sex.—In January 1994, 55 percent of those receiving SSI benefits on the basis of disability and 56.4 percent on the basis of blindness were women (table 6–15).

Race.—In January 1994, 57.6 percent of those receiving SSI on the basis of disability were white; 31.2 percent were black; 7.9 percent were other races; and in 3.4 percent of the cases, race was not reported (table 6–15).

Other income.—In September 1993, 32.4 percent of the disabled and 36.9 percent of the blind received Social Security benefits. Table 6–16 shows the number of SSI recipients with other sources of unearned income.

Of the blind and disabled receiving SSI, 5.2 percent had earned income in September 1993 (table 6–16).

Characteristics of SSI recipients receiving benefits on the basis of age

Age.—In September 1993, as shown in table 6–14, of those SSI recipients receiving benefits on the basis of age, i.e., age 65 or older, 35.9 percent were 80 years of age or older.

Sex.—In January 1994, as shown in table 6–15, 73.8 percent of those receiving benefits on the basis of age were women.

Race.—As shown in table 6–15, 55.4 percent of those receiving SSI on the basis of age were white; 22.0 percent were black; 19.4 percent were other races; and in 3.1 percent of the cases, race was not reported.

Other income.—65.1 percent of the SSI recipients receiving benefits on the basis of age also received Social Security benefits. Only 2.1 percent had earned income.

Characteristics of children receiving SSI payments

In June 1993, 732,000 blind and disabled children were eligible for SSI payments. These children made up 12.6 percent of the over 5.8 million SSI recipients in June, and represent a fast growing segment of the SSI population. By comparison, in December 1980 payments were made to almost 229,000 blind and disabled children (5.5 percent of the 4.1 million recipients in that month).

To be eligible for SSI payments as a child, an individual must be under age 18 (or under 22 if he or she is a full time student), unmarried, and must meet the SSI disability or blindness, citizenship/residency, and income and resources criteria [applicable to adults].

In June 1993, almost 61 percent of the SSI children were 12 years old or less, and an estimated 20 percent of the children were under age 6. About 28 percent, an estimated 199,000 children were between the ages of 13 and 17. Child recipients are more likely to be boys than girls, by about three or two. Approximately 46 percent are nonwhite.

Three-quarters of the children live in their parents' home. Less than 2 percent are patients in a medical facility where more than half of the cost of their care is covered by the Medicaid program. Another 18 percent live in other hospitals, nursing homes, residential schools, foster care, or independently.

About 29 percent of the children had some type of unearned income. The three major types of unearned income were: in-kind support and maintenance (8.2 percent), Social Security benefits (8.1 percent), and support from absent parents (7.2 percent). In addition, about 10 percent of the children had income "deemed" from their parents.

More than half (61 percent) of the SSI children were medically eligible based on a mental disorder, and most of these (43 percent) were mentally retarded. The only other diagnostic category of any size was diseases of the nervous system and sense organs, which included all of the approximately 9,000 blind children on SSI in June 1993.

TABLE 6–11.—DISABILITY DIAGNOSIS OF SSI AND SECTION 1619 DISABILITY
RECIPIENTS: JUNE 1993 [1]

[Percentage distribution by diagnostic group]

Diagnostic group	Supplemental Security Income—SSI		
	All SSI disabled 18–64 yrs.[1]	SSI sec. 1619(a) participants[2]	SSI sec. 1619(b) participants[2]
Individuals	2,614,310	18,597	34,293
Total percent	100.0	100.0	100.0
Infectious and parasitic diseases	1.9	0.9	1.5
Neoplasms	1.7	1.3	1.8
Endocrine, nutritional, and metabolic disorders	4.1	2.5	2.6
Mental disorders (other than mental retardation)	28.1	26.5	28.1
Mental retardation	28.2	43.7	35.8
Diseases of:			
Nervous system and sense organs[2] .	11.0	13.7	14.6
Circulatory system	6.1	2.0	2.7
Respiratory system	2.8	0.8	0.8
Digestive system	0.7	0.3	0.5
Musculoskeletal system	7.6	2.6	4.4
Congenital anomalies	1.7	0.9	0.7
Injuries	3.2	2.6	3.7
Other	2.9	2.2	2.8

[1] Information on diagnosis of SSI disabled recipients under age 65 is from the December 1992 SSI 10-percent disability file. Information on diagnosis for section 1619 recipients is available from SSI source files. Percentages shown are based on 12,786 section 1619(a) participants, and 22,749 section 1619(b) participants.

[2] Most of these section 1619(b) participants who are classified as blind individuals are included in this category. A few section 1619(b) blind participants have a primary impairment other than diseases of the eye and are coded in other categories in this table. Also, there are a few participants classified as having diseases of the eye who are not blind, whose impairment does not meet the definition of blindness, and are classified as disabled.

Source: Social Security Administration, OSSI.

TABLE 6–12.—NUMBER OF PERSONS RECEIVING FEDERALLY ADMINISTERED PAYMENTS, TOTAL AMOUNT AND AVERAGE MONTHLY AMOUNT, BY SOURCE OF PAYMENT AND CATEGORY, SEPTEMBER 1993

Source of payment	Total	Aged	Blind	Disabled
	Number of persons			
With—				
Federally administered payments [3]	5,907,605	1,473,531	[1] 85,885	[2] 4,348,189
Federal payment only .	3,406,549	792,980	44,084	2,569,485
Both Federal and State supplementation	2,154,785	528,979	34,415	1,591,391
State supplementation only	346,271	151,572	7,386	187,313
Total with—				
Federal payment [4]	5,561,334	1,321,959	78,499	4,160,876
State supplementation [5]	2,501,056	680,551	41,801	1,778,704
	Amount of payments [in thousands]			
Total	2,036,914	345,961	30,984	1,659,968
Federal payments	1,762,015	267,490	24,401	1,470,123
State supplementation	274,899	78,471	6,583	189,845
	Average monthly amount			
Total	$344.80	$234.73	$360.76	$381.76
Federal payments	316.83	202.34	310.84	353.32
State supplementation	109.91	115.31	157.48	106.73

[1] Includes an estimated 21,609 persons age 65 or older.

[2] Includes an estimated 614,782 persons age 65 or older.

[3] All persons with Federal SSI payments and/or federally administered State supplementation.

[4] All persons with a Federal SSI payment whether receiving a Federal payment only or both a Federal and State supplementation.

[5] All persons with federally administered State supplementation whether receiving State supplementation only or both a Federal SSI payment and a State supplementation.

Source: Office of Research and Statistics, Social Security Administration.

TABLE 6–13.—SSI: NUMBER OF PERSONS RECEIVING FEDERALLY ADMINISTERED SSI PAYMENTS, BY CATEGORY AND AGE: DECEMBER 1975, SEPTEMBER 1983, 1986, 1988, 1989, 1990, 1991, 1992, AND 1993

[In thousands]

Reason for eligibility and by age categories	Dec. 1975	Sept. 1983	Sept. 1986	Sept. 1988	Sept. 1989	Sept. 1990	Sept. 1991	Sept. 1992	Sept. 1993
Total	4,314	3,898	4,232	4,434	4,570	4,764	5,050	5,486	5,908
Reason for eligibility:									
Aged	2,307	1,528	1,476	1,434	1,439	1,452	1,463	1,478	1,474
Blind	74	79	83	83	83	84	85	86	86
Under 18	3	6	7	7	7	7	7	8	8
18 to 21	4	5	5	4	4	4	4	4	4
22 to 64	46	45	48	49	49	50	51	52	52
65 and over	22	23	23	22	22	22	22	22	22
Disabled	1,933	2,292	2,673	2,917	3,048	3,229	3,502	3,921	4,348
Under 18	104	191	231	247	256	287	366	511	683
18 to 21	90	122	138	136	139	143	150	167	186
22 to 64	1,559	1,517	1,787	1,987	2,091	2,218	2,393	2,637	2,864
65 or over	179	462	517	548	563	579	592	606	615
Age:									
Under 18	107	197	238	254	263	294	373	518	691
18 to 21	93	127	143	140	143	147	154	171	190
22 to 64	1,605	1,562	1,835	2,036	2,140	2,269	2,445	2,690	2,917
65 and over	2,508	2,013	2,016	2,003	2,023	2,051	2,078	2,107	2,110

Source: Office of Research and Statistics, Social Security Administration.

TABLE 6–14.—NUMBER AND PERCENTAGE DISTRIBUTION OF SSI RECIPIENTS RECEIVING FEDERALLY ADMINISTERED PAYMENTS, BY CATEGORY AND AGE, SEPTEMBER 1993

Age	Total	Aged	Blind	Disabled
Children:				
Total number	737,150	....	9,285	727,865
Total percent	100.0	....	100.0	100.0
Under 5	16.4	....	15.7	16.4
5 to 9	28.2	....	27.2	28.3
10 to 14	32.7	....	28.9	32.7
15 to 17	16.5	....	15.9	16.5
18 to 21 [1]	6.2	....	12.4	6.2
Adults:				
Total number	5,170,455	1,473,531	76,600	3,620,324
Total percent	100.0	100.0	100.0	100.0
18 to 21	2.8	....	3.9	3.9
22 to 29	9.0	....	13.4	12.6
30 to 39	13.9	....	16.4	19.6
40 to 49	12.6	....	14.7	17.7
50 to 59	13.4	....	14.5	18.8
60 to 64	7.5	....	8.8	10.5
65 to 69	11.3	21.0	8.5	7.4
70 to 74	10.1	24.1	6.4	4.5
75 to 79	7.6	19.0	5.0	3.1
80 or older	11.7	35.9	8.3	2.0

[1] Persons aged 18–21 can be classified as either children or adults depending on their student status.

Source: Office of Research and Statistics, Social Security Administration.

TABLE 6–15.—NUMBER AND PERCENTAGE DISTRIBUTION OF ALL PERSONS RECEIVING FEDERALLY ADMINISTERED PAYMENTS, BY CATEGORY, RACE, AND SEX, JANUARY 1994

Race and sex	Total	Aged	Blind	Disabled
Total number	5,948,900	1,465,300	85,500	4,398,100
Total percent	100.0	100.0	100.0	100.0
Race:				
White	57.1	55.4	57.4	57.6
Black	28.9	22.0	26.8	31.2
Other	10.8	19.4	11.3	7.9
Not reported	3.3	3.1	4.4	3.4
Sex and race:				
Men	40.3	26.2	43.6	45.0
White	22.6	13.9	24.6	25.4
Black	11.7	4.8	11.9	14.0
Other	4.5	6.7	4.9	3.7
Not reported	1.6	.8	2.2	1.8
Women	59.6	73.8	56.4	55.0
White	34.5	41.5	32.9	32.2
Black	17.1	17.2	14.9	17.1
Other	6.3	12.7	6.4	4.2
Not reported	1.7	2.3	2.2	1.5

Source: Office of Research and Statistics, Social Security Administration.

In summary, the trends in the nature of the SSI population show the following:

—A steady decline in the number of persons receiving SSI benefits on the basis of old age.

—An increase from 107,000 in December 1975 to 737,150 in September 1993 of the number of disabled and blind children under 18 receiving SSI benefits.

—A sharp increase of 1,354,000 between 1983 and 1993 in the number of persons ages 22–64 receiving benefits on the basis of disability or blindness.

TABLE 6–16.—NUMBER OF PERSONS RECEIVING FEDERALLY ADMINISTERED PAYMENTS AND NUMBER WITH CONCURRENT INCOME AND AVERAGE MONTHLY AMOUNT, BY CATEGORY AND TYPE OF INCOME, SEPTEMBER 1993

Type of income	Total	Reason for eligibility		
		Aged	Blind	Disabled
Total number	5,907,605	1,473,531	85,885	4,348,189
Number				
Social Security benefits	2,402,028	959,733	31,673	1,410,622
Other unearned income	828,619	325,950	11,029	491,640
Earned income	262,236	30,589	6,175	225,472
Average monthly income				
Social Security benefits	$330.48	$336.21	$345.30	$326.25
Other unearned income	97.62	76.75	95.68	111.50
Earned income	213.59	200.52	520.31	206.96

Source: Office of Research and Statistics, Social Security Administration.

TABLE 6–17.—NUMBER OF PERSONS RECEIVING FEDERALLY ADMINISTERED SSI PAYMENTS AND UNEARNED INCOME (OTHER THAN SOCIAL SECURITY) AND AVERAGE MONTHLY UNEARNED INCOME, BY TYPE OF INCOME, SEPTEMBER 1993

Type of income	Number [1]	Average [2]
Total	828,619	$97.62
Veterans' benefits	121,647	149.74
Railroad retirement	5,225	307.54
Black lung benefits	1,766	293.99
Employment pensions	46,914	112.26
Worker's compensation	4,110	292.68
Support and maintenance in kind	212,242	99.86
Support from absent parents	56,849	148.57
Asset income	241,251	10.10
Assistance based on need	58,145	71.20
Other [3]	80,470	221.96

[1] With unearned income other than social security benefits.
[2] Monthly amount of unearned income.
[3] Includes military, civil service pension, and demonstration projects.

Source: Office of Research and Statistics, Social Security Administration.

SSI PARTICIPATION RATES

Table 6–18 shows Federal SSI participation among the elderly and the total population using various measures. The numerator in the first three columns is the sum of columns two and four in table 6–21. In other words, the number of SSI aged participants includes the disabled population over age 65. Column one simply divides the SSI aged participants by the total number of elderly. That rate declined from 11.1 percent in 1975 to 6.5 percent in 1992, primarily as a result of increasing incomes among the aged and decreasing participation among low-income elderly. Column two presents the number of elderly SSI recipients divided by the number of poor elderly. This rate has declined from 76 percent in 1975 to 54 percent in 1982. Between 1982 and 1984, this percentage increased, perhaps as a result of outreach efforts mandated by the 1983 Social Security Amendments (P.L. 98–21). After 1984, the rate declined to 56.5 percent in 1987, increased to 60.1 percent in 1989, and declined to 53 percent in 1992. This is a gross measure of participation, in that it does not control for other SSI eligibility factors, such as assets or the undercounting of income. Column three shows the number of SSI aged recipients as a percentage of the number of poor elderly before means-tested transfers.

The final column of table 6–18 shows the number of Federal SSI participants as a percentage of the total population. The numerator for this calculation is the first column of table 21. As shown in the table, the percentage of the entire population receiving SSI benefits has declined from 2.0 percent in 1975 to 1.7 percent for the 1982 to 1985 time period. It has since increased to 2.3 percent in 1993 and is projected to increase to 2.5 percent by 1994.

TABLE 6–18.—SSI PARTICIPATION RATES

[In percent]

	Among all elderly	Among elderly poor	Among pretransfer elderly poor	Among entire population
1975	11.1	75.6	NA	2.0
1976	10.3	72.4	NA	1.9
1977	9.8	74.1	NA	1.9
1978	9.4	71.5	NA	1.9
1979	9.0	61.3	68.7	1.8
1980	8.7	57.5	64.7	1.8
1981	8.1	55.0	63.3	1.8
1982	7.5	53.6	62.3	1.7
1983	7.3	55.2	61.9	1.7
1984	7.3	61.2	66.3	1.7
1985	7.1	58.7	64.5	1.7
1986	6.9	57.9	63.4	1.8
1987	6.8	56.5	64.7	1.8
1988	6.6	57.6	64.3	1.8
1989	6.5	60.1	64.6	1.9
1990	6.6	56.3	63.3	1.9
1991	6.8	55.0	61.1	2.0
1992	6.5	52.7	NA	2.2
1993 [1]	6.6	NA	NA	2.3
1994 [1]	6.7	NA	NA	2.5

[1] Projected.

NA—Not available.

Note.—The denominator for columns 1 and 4 is in table 15, appendix N, the denominator for column 3 is shown in table 3 of appendix J, and the denominator for column 3 is in table 19 of appendix J.

Source: Staff of the Committee on Ways and Means.

Table 6–19 shows the percentage of a given State's population receiving SSI benefits for selected years. Table 6–20 shows the percentages of a State's total, aged, and disabled populations between the ages of 18 and 64 receiving SSI benefits for both 1979 and 1993, respectively. The percentage of the population receiving SSI has been calculated by dividing the average number of monthly Federal SSI recipients in each State for each of the selected years by the State's population in July of those selected years. Likewise, percentages for the aged and disabled have been calculated by dividing a State's average number of monthly recipients in each program by that State's aged and disabled population in July 1979 and 1993.

As shown in table 6–19, the total percentage of the popultion receiving SSI benefits increased to 2.26 percent in 1993 from 2 percent in 1975. However, between these years, the percentage of the population receiving SSI benefits declined to 1.74 percent in 1985 (a 13 percent decline) and has since risen to 2.26 percent of the population in 1993.

As shown in table 6–20 the proportion of adult SSI recipients aged 18–64 in this total population rose from 1.26 to 1.90 percent.

TABLE 6–19.—SSI RECIPIENCY RATES BY STATE

[In percent]

State	1975	1985	1990	1991	1992	1993
Alabama	3.98	3.29	3.29	3.35	3.43	3.64
Alaska	0.81	0.65	0.84	0.87	0.90	0.96
Arizona	1.24	1.04	1.22	1.33	1.42	1.54
Arkansas	4.09	3.14	3.23	3.34	3.47	3.66
California	3.09	2.59	2.93	3.03	3.10	3.14
Colorado	1.37	0.93	1.14	1.23	1.29	1.38
Connecticut	0.76	0.83	0.98	1.05	1.10	1.19
Delaware	1.19	1.21	1.21	1.23	1.27	1.34
District of Columbia	2.23	2.51	2.67	2.83	3.00	3.21
Florida	1.86	1.62	1.71	1.82	1.90	2.06
Georgia	3.27	2.56	2.46	2.51	2.55	2.65
Hawaii	1.08	1.08	1.25	1.27	1.30	1.40
Idaho	1.06	0.84	1.03	1.10	1.21	1.28
Illinois	1.22	1.18	1.55	1.67	1.78	2.00
Indiana	0.83	0.87	1.09	1.17	1.26	1.39
Iowa	1.00	0.96	1.18	1.23	1.29	1.37
Kansas	1.05	0.87	0.99	1.05	1.14	1.26
Kentucky	2.83	2.65	3.11	3.27	3.42	3.71
Louisiana	3.90	2.87	3.15	3.29	3.49	3.84
Maine	2.31	1.89	1.93	1.97	2.03	2.17
Maryland	1.17	1.16	1.25	1.30	1.35	1.44
Massachusetts	2.30	1.91	1.98	2.12	2.23	2.40
Michigan	1.31	1.35	1.54	1.61	1.71	1.93
Minnesota	1.00	0.78	0.92	0.99	1.05	1.17
Mississippi	5.21	4.28	4.42	4.56	4.68	4.98
Missouri	2.10	1.58	1.66	1.75	1.83	1.96
Montana	1.12	0.92	1.25	1.33	1.38	1.44
Nebraska	1.06	0.88	0.99	1.05	1.09	1.19
Nevada	1.00	0.85	0.95	0.98	1.04	1.14
New Hampshire	0.67	0.62	0.62	0.68	0.71	0.77
New Jersey	1.11	1.23	1.36	1.44	1.52	1.66
New Mexico	2.29	1.83	2.08	2.19	2.25	2.39
New York	2.24	2.00	2.31	2.46	2.60	2.85
North Carolina	2.71	2.21	2.24	2.33	2.36	2.47
North Dakota	1.25	0.96	1.17	1.25	1.30	1.34
Ohio	1.22	1.19	1.44	1.55	1.63	1.84
Oklahoma	3.03	1.81	1.92	1.97	2.02	2.13
Oregon	1.12	0.95	1.11	1.18	1.24	1.35
Pennsylvania	1.24	1.39	1.60	1.69	1.77	1.90
Rhode Island	1.72	1.62	1.74	1.83	1.91	2.05
South Carolina	2.84	2.60	2.59	2.61	2.67	2.80
South Dakota	1.32	1.19	1.45	1.53	1.62	1.72
Tennessee	3.24	2.71	2.87	2.98	3.06	3.22
Texas	2.23	1.57	1.73	1.81	1.87	2.00
Utah	0.76	0.53	0.73	0.79	0.84	0.94
Vermont	1.93	1.76	1.79	1.89	1.99	2.08
Virginia	1.53	1.49	1.54	1.61	1.67	1.76
Washington	1.46	1.09	1.27	1.34	1.39	1.50
West Virginia	2.37	2.24	2.63	2.78	2.91	3.17
Wisconsin	1.44	1.50	1.75	1.83	1.88	2.04
Wyoming	0.67	0.45	0.76	0.85	0.92	1.04
Total [1]	2.00	1.74	1.94	2.03	2.11	2.26

[1] The total number of SSI recipients used to calculate the total recipiency rate includes a certain number of recipients whose State is unknown. For 1975, 1985, 1990, 1991, 1992, and 1993, the numbers of unknown (in thousands) respectively were 256, 14, 0, 96, 71, and 91.

Source: Social Security Administration and Committee staff. Percentages are calculated as the average number of monthly SSI recipients over the total population of each State in July of the selected year.

TABLE 6–20.—SSI RECIPIENCY RATES BY STATE, AND PROGRAM TYPE, FOR 1979 AND 1993

[In percent]

State	Total recipiency rate			Adult recipiency rate [1]			Aged recipiency rate		
	1979	1993	Percent change 1979–93	1979	1993	Percent change 1979–93	1979	1993	Percent change 1979–93
Alabama	3.55	3.64	2.5	1.83	2.69	47.0	21.01	11.35	−46.0
Alaska	0.77	0.96	24.7	0.54	0.89	64.8	14.04	6.41	−54.3
Arizona	1.11	1.54	38.7	0.89	1.44	61.8	4.98	3.52	−29.3
Arkansas	3.50	3.66	4.6	1.87	2.67	42.8	17.05	9.74	−42.9
California	3.02	3.14	4.0	2.05	2.44	19.0	16.43	13.76	−16.3
Colorado	1.10	1.38	25.5	0.77	1.26	63.6	6.68	3.76	−43.7
Connecticut	0.75	1.19	58.7	0.63	1.15	82.5	2.70	2.49	−7.7
Delaware	1.19	1.34	12.6	0.94	1.17	24.5	5.43	3.19	−41.3
District of Columbia	2.28	3.21	40.8	1.92	2.72	41.7	8.56	8.08	−5.6
Florida	1.78	2.06	15.7	1.14	1.51	32.5	6.21	4.90	−21.1
Georgia	2.87	2.65	−7.7	1.89	2.05	8.5	17.73	10.44	−41.1
Hawaii	1.05	1.40	33.3	0.69	1.03	49.3	7.57	5.95	−21.4
Idaho	0.79	1.28	62.0	0.64	1.25	95.3	3.78	2.38	−37.0
Illinois	1.08	2.00	85.2	0.95	1.98	108.4	4.25	3.77	−11.3
Indiana	0.75	1.39	85.3	0.61	1.37	124.6	3.32	2.18	−34.3
Iowa	0.89	1.37	53.9	0.62	1.37	121.0	3.50	2.25	−35.7
Kansas	0.89	1.26	41.6	0.63	1.23	95.2	3.47	2.15	−38.0
Kentucky	2.54	3.71	46.1	1.79	3.49	95.0	12.54	8.92	−28.9
Louisiana	3.35	3.84	14.6	2.03	2.99	47.3	20.14	11.37	−43.5

	1.95	2.17	11.3	1.39	2.02	45.3	8.58	5.52	−35.7
Maine									−35.7
Maryland	1.15	1.44	25.2	0.94	1.22	29.8	5.40	4.45	−17.6
Massachusetts	2.24	2.40	7.1	1.28	2.14	67.2	10.80	6.08	−43.7
Michigan	1.26	1.93	53.2	1.07	1.95	82.2	5.85	3.59	−38.6
Minnesota	0.81	1.17	44.4	0.55	1.14	107.3	3.71	2.55	−31.3
Mississippi	4.49	4.98	10.9	2.42	3.65	50.8	26.01	16.47	−36.7
Missouri	1.76	1.96	11.4	1.10	1.80	63.6	7.89	4.07	−48.4
Montana	0.89	1.44	61.8	0.72	1.54	113.9	3.79	2.50	−34.0
Nebraska	0.88	1.19	35.2	0.64	1.16	81.3	3.38	2.18	−35.5
Nevada	0.84	1.14	35.7	0.53	0.97	83.0	5.87	3.50	−40.4
New Hampshire	0.58	0.77	32.8	0.44	0.77	75.0	2.53	1.55	−38.7
New Jersey	1.14	1.66	45.6	0.86	1.34	55.8	4.69	4.46	−4.9
New Mexico	1.97	2.39	21.3	1.37	1.97	43.8	12.36	8.27	−33.1
New York	2.12	2.85	34.4	1.59	2.27	42.8	8.26	8.36	1.21
North Carolina	2.40	2.47	2.9	1.58	1.84	16.5	13.60	8.13	−40.2
North Dakota	0.99	1.34	35.4	0.57	1.24	117.5	5.05	3.18	−37.0
Ohio	1.11	1.84	65.8	0.99	1.90	91.9	4.17	2.76	−33.8
Oklahoma	2.32	2.13	−8.2	1.33	1.73	30.1	11.62	5.99	−48.5
Oregon	0.86	1.35	57.0	0.70	1.38	97.1	3.28	2.52	−23.2
Pennsylvania	1.40	1.90	35.7	1.12	1.79	59.8	4.96	3.51	−29.2
Rhode Island	1.59	2.05	28.9	1.08	1.83	69.4	6.43	4.80	−25.3
South Carolina	2.69	2.80	4.1	1.78	2.13	19.7	16.96	9.59	−43.5
South Dakota	1.14	1.72	50.9	0.72	1.57	118.1	4.99	3.66	−26.7
Tennessee	2.86	3.22	12.6	1.87	2.76	47.6	14.77	9.02	−38.9
Texas	1.89	2.00	5.8	0.95	1.39	46.3	12.69	8.83	−30.4
Utah	0.55	0.94	70.9	0.51	1.04	103.9	3.03	1.97	−35.0

TABLE 6–20.—SSI RECIPIENCY RATES BY STATE, AND PROGRAM TYPE, FOR 1979 AND 1993—Continued

[In percent]

State	Total recipiency rate			Adult recipiency rate [1]			Aged recipiency rate		
	1979	1993	Percent change 1979–93	1979	1993	Percent change 1979–93	1979	1993	Percent change 1979–93
Vermont	1.77	2.08	17.5	1.31	1.97	50.4	8.08	5.32	−34.2
Virginia	1.50	1.76	17.3	1.02	1.37	34.3	8.52	5.99	−29.7
Washington	1.16	1.50	29.3	0.98	1.56	59.2	4.83	3.18	−34.2
West Virginia	2.13	3.17	48.8	1.86	3.19	71.5	7.95	5.63	−29.2
Wisconsin	1.44	2.04	41.7	0.96	1.91	99.0	6.54	4.20	−35.8
Wyoming	0.42	1.04	147.6	0.29	1.06	265.5	2.74	2.08	−24.1
Total [1]	1.85	2.26	22.2	1.26	1.90	50.8	8.98	6.44	−28.3

[1] All adult recipients ages 18–64.

Source: Social Security Administration and Committee staff. Percentages are calculated as the average number of monthly SSI recipients, adult SSI recipients aged 18–64, and aged SSI recipients over the total population, aged 18–64 population, and aged population of each State in July 1979 and July 1993; respectively. Due to the need to recalculate percentages of adult SSI recipients aged 18–64, it was necessary to base the 1979 calculations on the number of December 1979 SSI recipients.

NUMBER OF RECIPIENTS: 1970–93

Table 6–21 illustrates the changes in the number of individuals receiving assistance under the federally administered SSI program and prior programs. The total number of individuals receiving assistance was 3.1 million in 1970; this increased to 4.3 million in 1975 and declined to 3.9 million in 1982. Since then, the number of SSI recipients has grown each year. In 1993, there were over 5.9 million SSI recipients. The number of aged receiving SSI has declined sharply since 1975 from 2.3 million (or 2.5 million if disabled over age 65 are counted as aged) to 1.5 million individuals in 1993 (2.1 million if disabled over 65 are counted). The number of blind or disabled receiving assistance increased sharply from 1.0 million in 1970 to roughly 4.3 million in 1993 (3.8 million if persons over age 65 are excluded).

New SSI eligibility criteria for disabled children

Under SSI law, a child under age 18 who has an impairment of comparable severity with that of an adult may be considered disabled. On February 20, 1990, the Supreme Court ruled in *Sullivan* v. *Zebley* that the Social Security Administration was improperly determining the eligibility of disabled children for the SSI program. Prior to the *Zebley* decision, for both adults and children, an applicant's condition was compared to a listing of impairments. If it met or equalled a listing, the disability criteria for SSI was met. However, children were evaluated only against the listing, while adults whose condition did not meet or equal a listing were given an individual functional assessment (called a residual functional capacity assessment) to determine disability. In the *Zebley* case, the Supreme Court held that determinations of children's eligibility for SSI also must take into account functional limitations.

The court order defined the *Zebley* class entitled to readjudication and, possibly, retroactive benefits as all title XVI childhood disability claimants who have received a less than favorable decision of the Secretary or whose claims for SSI childhood disability were terminated on or after January 1, 1980, through February 11, 1991, based on medical grounds. January 1, 1980, was the compromise date agreed to by both parties. The plaintiffs supported offering readjudication to all children denied benefits on medical grounds since the beginning of the SSI program in 1974, while the Social Security Administration advocated a retroactive period starting on the date *Zebley* was filed, July 12, 1983. The closing date of the retroactive class, February 11, 1991, is the date on which the Social Security Administration published the revised regulation for determining disability in children.

TABLE 6–21.—NUMBER OF PERSONS RECEIVING FEDERALLY ADMINISTERED SSI PAYMENTS, 1974–99; AND ADULT ASSISTANCE UNDER PRIOR PROGRAMS, 1970–73

[In thousands]

| Year [1] | Total [2] | Aged [3] | Blind or disabled | | Federal SSI [6] | State supplemental only |
			Total [4]	65 and older [5]		
1970	3,098	2,082	1,016	....	....	....
1971	3,172	2,024	1,148	....	....	....
1972	3,182	1,934	1,248	....	....	....
1973	3,173	1,820	1,353	....	....	....
1974	3,996	2,286	1,710	([7])	([8])	([8])
1975	4,314	2,307	2,007	201	3,893	421
1976	4,236	2,148	2,088	249	3,799	437
1977	4,238	2,051	2,187	302	3,778	460
1978	4,217	1,968	2,249	344	3,755	462
1979	4,150	1,872	2,278	386	3,687	462
1980	4,142	1,808	2,334	419	3,682	460
1981	4,019	1,678	2,341	443	3,590	429
1982	3,858	1,549	2,309	462	3,473	384
1983	3,901	1,515	2,386	485	3,590	311
1984	4,029	1,530	2,499	507	3,699	331
1985	4,138	1,504	2,634	525	3,799	339
1986	4,269	1,473	2,796	540	3,922	348
1987	4,385	1,455	2,930	560	4,019	366
1988	4,464	1,433	3,030	573	4,089	375
1989	4,593	1,439	3,154	587	4,206	387
1990	4,817	1,454	3,363	605	4,412	405
1991	5,118	1,465	3,654	615	4,730	389
1992	5,566	1,471	4,095	628	5,202	364
1993	6,011	1,475	4,536	680	5,664	347
1994 [9]	6,525	1,478	5,047	757	6,172	353
1995 [9]	7,025	1,481	5,544	831	6,665	360
1996 [9]	7,503	1,487	6,016	902	7,135	368
1997 [9]	7,954	1,493	6,461	969	7,579	375
1998 [9]	8,383	1,498	6,885	1,033	8,001	382
1999 [9]	8,792	1,503	7,289	1,093	8,404	388

[1] Data are for December of each year.

[2] All persons with Federal SSI payments and/or Federally administered State supplementation; 1974–1994. For 1970–1973, the total is the number of recipients under the Old-Age Assistance and Aid to the Blind and Aid to the Permanently and Totally Disabled Programs.

[3] For 1970–1973, this column is the number of recipients under the Old-Age Assistance program.

[4] For 1970–1973, this column is the number of recipients under the Aid to the Blind and Aid to the Permanently and Totally Disabled Programs.

[5] For 1974–1999, this is the number of age 65 or older individuals who first received SSI benefits because of being blind or disabled.

[6] All persons with Federal SSI payments include those receiving Federal payments only or both Federal SSI and Federally administered State supplementation.

[7] Data not available for December 1974. In January 1974, there were 87,000 blind and disabled recipients aged 65 or older.

[8] Data not available.

[9] For 1994–1999, data are projections based on the President's budget estimates of December 1993.

Source: Office of Supplemental Security Income, Social Security Administration.

TABLE 6–22.—NUMBER OF PERSONS RECEIVING SSI PAYMENTS, BY STATE, DECEMBER 1993

State	Federally administered [1]				State administered total [5]
	Total	Aged	Blind	Disabled	
Total [1]	5,984,330	1,474,852	85,456	4,424,022	314,030
Alabama [2]	155,734	42,496	1,611	111,627	3,001
Alaska [2]	5,909	1,204	109	4,596	4,726
Arizona [2]	63,033	12,985	817	49,231	694
Arkansas	90,582	23,335	1,186	66,061	....
California	994,213	335,845	22,602	635,766	....
Colorado [2]	51,055	9,556	514	40,985	31,377
Connecticut [2]	40,233	7,597	525	32,111	29,155
Delaware	9,696	1,684	124	7,888	....
District of Columbia	18,836	3,453	204	15,179	....
Florida [3]	292,769	93,638	3,260	195,871	14,237
Georgia	186,808	47,024	2,648	137,136	....
Hawaii	16,967	6,898	159	9,910	....
Idaho [2]	14,477	2,000	142	12,335	2,985
Illinois [2]	244,950	35,029	2,526	207,395	60,055
Indiana [2]	81,976	10,247	1,135	70,594	1,128
Iowa	39,379	6,581	1,015	31,783	....
Kansas	32,997	4,904	395	27,698	....
Kentucky [2]	145,668	26,702	1,881	117,085	6,367
Louisiana	170,483	36,302	2,293	131,888	....
Maine	27,817	6,366	284	21,167	....
Maryland [3]	73,529	16,462	810	56,257	1,132
Massachusetts	148,615	47,117	4,519	96,979	....
Michigan	192,390	25,162	2,178	165,050	....
Minnesota [2]	54,881	10,255	761	43,865	21,339
Mississippi	134,318	35,951	1,563	96,804	....
Missouri [2]	105,042	19,227	1,113	84,702	11,283
Montana	12,406	1,781	129	10,496	....
Nebraska [2]	19,523	3,379	253	15,891	6,619
Nevada	16,789	5,350	547	10,892	....
New Hampshire [2]	8,980	1,389	96	7,495	5,804
New Jersey	134,285	34,800	1,176	98,309	....
New Mexico [2]	39,993	9,823	620	29,550	281
New York	536,018	139,921	3,944	392,153	....
North Carolina [2]	174,526	45,289	2,602	126,635	17,951
North Dakota [4]	8,600	1,982	95	6,523	267
Ohio	214,038	23,022	2,543	188,473	....
Oklahoma [2]	69,954	16,968	977	52,009	65,298
Oregon [2]	42,571	7,036	636	34,899	16,743
Pennsylvania	236,354	42,841	2,811	190,702	....
Rhode Island	21,309	5,011	224	16,074	....
South Carolina [2]	103,812	26,262	1,794	75,756	4,330
South Dakota [3]	12,515	2,652	148	9,715	217
Tennessee	167,590	36,889	1,995	128,706	....
Texas [4]	370,719	126,703	5,558	238,458	....
Utah	18,199	2,157	307	15,735	....

TABLE 6–22.—NUMBER OF PERSONS RECEIVING SSI PAYMENTS, BY STATE, DECEMBER 1993—Continued

State	Federally administered [1]				State administered total [5]
	Total	Aged	Blind	Disabled	
Vermont	12,176	2,243	123	9,810	....
Virginia [2]	117,809	29,363	1,603	86,843	6,694
Washington	81,634	12,558	890	68,186	....
West Virginia [4]	60,202	8,369	736	51,097	....
Wisconsin	106,198	20,110	1,201	84,887	....
Wyoming [2]	5,154	710	60	4,384	2,347
Other:					
N. Mariana Islands	532	213	14	305	....

[1] Includes fewer than 200 cases not distributed by State.
[2] Data for Federal SSI payments only. State has state-administered supplementation.
[3] Data for Federal SSI payments and Federally administered state supplementation only, State also has state-administered supplementation.
[4] Data for Federal SSI payments only, State supplementary payments not made.
[5] Represents September 1993 data.

Source: Office of Research and Statistics and Office of Supplemental Security Income, Social Security Administration.

Impact of the Sullivan v. Zebley decision

In March 1991, the district court approved a settlement agreement that established an eligible class under Zebley back to January 1980. Implementation of this settlement required an intensive effort to locate children who were denied benefits from January 1, 1980, to February 11, 1991. Notices were sent to approximately 452,000 individuals. Of this number, close to 321,700 have responded accounting for about 71 percent of potential class members. According to SSA, when the additional recipients who filed new claims or were processed as a result of the Zebley case or related childhood disability regulations were added to the rolls, the number of blind/disabled childhood recipients increased by 86,000 in fiscal year 1991 and 169,000 in fiscal year 1992 and 146,600 in fiscal year 1993.

Presumptive SSI eligibility for persons with AIDS and HIV

SSI law permits benefits to be paid to a person applying for SSI benefits on the basis of disability or blindness before a formal determination of disability or blindness has been made when available information indicates a high probability that the person is disabled or blind and the person is otherwise eligible.

Section 1631(a)(4)(B) of the Social Security Act provides that the Secretary of the Department of Health and Human Services may pay up to 6 months of SSI benefits to a person applying for SSI based on disability or blindness prior to the determination of the individual's disability or blindness if the individual is presumptively disabled or blind and otherwise eligible. A finding of presumptive disability or blindness may be made at the Social Security field offices only for specified impairment categories (because the field office employees generally are not trained disability adjudicators); however, at the State agencies (where there are disability adjudicators) they may be made for any impairment category.

On February 11, 1985, acquired immunodeficiency syndrome (AIDS), as defined by the Centers for Disease Control, was added (pursuant to interim Federal regulations) to the impairment categories, thus allowing field offices to find presumptive disability for persons claiming they had AIDS. These regulations were scheduled to expire February 11, 1988, but were extended until December 31, 1989; and in 1989 they were extended until December 31, 1991. In December 1991, a new more liberal regulation was implemented. Under the new procedures, the Social Security field offices may make a finding of presumptive disability for any individual with the human immunodeficiency virus (HIV) whose disease manifestations are of listing-level severity, not only to those who have been diagnosed with AIDS.

ELIGIBILITY OF DRUG ADDICTS AND ALCOHOLICS FOR SSI

The SSI program has the authority to award SSI disability payments on the grounds of drug addiction or alcoholism. Under the SSI program an individual is considered to be a medically determined drug addict or alcoholic only if (1) he or she is disabled (as defined by SSI law), and (2) drug addiction or alcoholism is a contributing factor to such disability. The presence of a condition diagnosed or defined as addiction to alcohol or drugs does not by itself qualify an individual for SSI benefits.

Section 1631(a)(2)(A) of the Social Security Act requires SSI recipients disabled because of drug addiction or alcoholism to have a representative payee; section 1611(e)(3)(A) of the Social Security Act requires these recipients to participate in an approved treatment program when available and appropriate; and section 1611(e)(3)(B) of the Social Security Act requires recipients to allow their participation in the treatment program to be monitored by agencies under contract to SSA.

SSI provisions relating to drug addicts and alcoholics were contained in the original SSI law (P.L. 92–603). Initially the Senate sought to exclude these individuals from SSI by putting them in a separate program. Members of Congress thought that these drug addicts and alcoholics would need more than the cash payments that SSA could provide, that they would need treatment, case management, and close monitoring so that they would not use SSI benefits to "feed their addiction." The requirement for representative payees grew out of this latter concern.

According to data from a 1991 Department of Health and Human Services' inspector general report, about 20,000 persons diagnosed as disabled drug addicts and alcoholics are receiving SSI benefits. About 40 percent of these recipients were determined to be disabled only after appealing their case to an Administrative Law Judge. More than half of this caseload live in either California or Illinois, three-fourths of the caseload is male, 41 percent are white and 37 percent are black, and most of the recipients are addicted to alcohol rather than drugs. Although 99 percent of the recipients have the required representative payee (usually a family member),

SSA provides very little monitoring and does not know whether the majority (66 percent) of the recipients are in treatment.[1]

In December 1993, there were about 79,000 disabled drug addicts and alcoholics on the SSI rolls.

In 1991, SSA entered into a collaboration with the Department of Health and Human Services' Public Health Services' Substance Abuse and Mental Health Services Administration to improve referral and monitoring of treatment for SSI recipients who are drug addicts and alcoholics. As a result, SSA has established referral and monitoring services contracts with agencies in 32 States and the District of Columbia to perform numerous specified tasks to ensure both better service to SSI recipients and greater management oversight. SSA plans to have similar contracts in place in the remaining States by the end of fiscal year 1994. SSA increased funding for referral and monitoring activities from $4 million in fiscal year 1993 to $20 million in fiscal year 1994 and $36 million in fiscal year 1995—an 80 percent increase—which will allow them to serve about 69,000 SSI drug addict and alcoholic recipients in fiscal year 1995.

SPECIAL SSI BENEFITS, MEDICAID SERVICES, AND RELATED PROVISIONS FOR THE WORKING DISABLED

Earned income disregards.—Since SSI began in 1974, the law has required that a portion of the earned income of SSI recipients be disregarded in determining the eligibility for and the amount of SSI benefits payable. In determining SSI eligibility and/or benefit amount, the first $65 of monthly earned income (or, up to the first $85 if the recipient has no unearned income) plus one-half of the remaining earnings are disregarded. In addition, any work-related expenses are disregarded in the case of blind persons and impairment-related work expenses are disregarded in the case of disabled persons. Also, income and/or resources set aside under a PASS are excluded. Earned income disregards were included in the pre-SSI federally assisted State programs for the aged, blind, and disabled.

Eliminating work disincentives.—Prior to the enactment of the section 1619 program in 1980, on a temporary 3-year basis (and continued for an additional two years as a demonstration project), a disabled SSI recipient who worked faced a substantial risk of losing SSI benefits and frequently, Medicaid. Work was treated the same way it was under the Social Security disability insurance (SSDI) program: after a trial work period, work at the substantial gainful activity (SGA) level ($500 or more of earnings per month; $300 per month before January 1990) led to the loss of disability status even if the individual's total income and resources were within SSI program limits. Loss of SSI disability status caused loss of Medicaid eligibility as well. (Many States provide automatic Medicaid coverage to all recipients of Federal SSI payments. Nearly all States follow the SSI definition of disability to establish Medicaid eligibility.) Thus, disabled individuals who could work or, at least, could have tried to work had a disincentive to work because

---

[1] U.S. Department of Health and Human Services. Office of Inspector General. *Social Security Policies Concerning Drug Addicts and Alcoholics.* July 1991.

of their fear of losing their SSI benefits or often more importantly their eligibility for health services under Medicaid.

Summary of section 1619 provisions intended to remove work disincentives for the disabled

Section 1619(a) of SSI law, enacted as a permanent provision of law in 1986, provides for the continuation of cash benefits for those SSI recipients who are receiving benefits on the basis of disability even if their earnings are at or above the SGA level and as long as there is not a medical improvement in the disabling condition. The amount of their cash benefits is gradually reduced as their earnings increase under the income disregard formula until their countable earnings reach the SSI benefit standard or what is known as the "breakeven point." In a State with no supplementation, as shown in table 6–2, this earned income eligibility limit is $977 per month in 1994 for a person who has no unearned income. People who receive the special SSI benefits continue to be eligible for Medicaid on the same basis as regular SSI recipients. States have the option of supplementing the Federal benefits standard for those entitled to benefits under this provision. The "breakeven point" increases $2 for every $1 of State supplementation above the Federal SSI benefit standard.

Under section 1619(b), blind and disabled individuals can continue to be eligible for Medicaid even if their earnings take them past the SSI income disregard "breakeven point." In some 209(b) States, workers may lose Medicaid eligibility before attaining 1619(b) status, if they did not have Medicaid coverage the month before section 1619 status began, thus making this provision inoperable for those workers. This special eligibility status, under which the individual is considered a blind or disabled individual receiving SSI benefits for purposes of Medicaid eligibility, applies as long as the individual: (1) continues to be blind or have a disabling impairment; (2) except for earnings, continues to meet all the other requirements for SSI eligibility; (3) would be seriously inhibited from continuing to work by the termination of eligibility for Medicaid services; and (4) has earnings that are not sufficient to provide a reasonable equivalent of the benefits (SSI, State supplementary payments, Medicaid and publicly funded attendant care) that would have been available if he or she did not have those earnings.

In making an initial determination under the fourth criterion, SSA decided to compare the individual's gross earnings to a "threshold" amount. The threshold amount is the amount of gross earnings, after the monthly $20 general income, $65 earned income and one-half of the remainder exclusions are applied, that it would take to reduce to zero the Federal SSI benefit and State supplementary payment for an individual with no other income or exclusions living in his or her own household plus the average Medicaid expenditures for disabled SSI cash recipients for the State of residence. If the individual's earnings exceed the threshold, an individualized threshold is calculated which considers the person's actual Medicaid use, the State supplement rate for the person's actual living arrangement, and the value of publicly funded attendant care available to the person in the absence of his or her earnings. In determining a person's income to compare to the individualized threshold, any applicable exclusions are deducted from his or her earnings, including work expenses if the person is blind, impairment-related work expenses, and income set aside under a plan for achieving self-support.

In other words, Medicaid eligibility continues until the individual's earnings reach a higher plateau which takes into account the person's ability to afford medical care as well as his or her normal living expenses, or he or she medically recovers.

Under the provisions of Public Law 99–643, which was effective July 1, 1987, a disabled individual also has the ongoing protection of being able to be reinstated to eligibility for cash assistance benefits under regular SSI or 1619(a), or Medicaid only eligibility under 1619(b) if his or her work attempt fails or the physical or mental disability makes the ability to work very erratic. This protection is not indefinite, but SSA, under the provisions of Public Law 99–643, will not terminate the disability status of an individual for 12 months after his or her most recent eligibility for regular SSI or eligibility under section 1619(a) or 1619(b). However, if the individual recovers medically a new application and new disability determination would be required to establish a new period of eligibility.

SSI Outreach Activities

The 1983 Social Security Amendments (P.L. 98–21) mandated the Social Security Administration (SSA) to conduct two separate outreach activities aimed at the aged population. The first was a one-time mailing of alerts to those aged individuals and couples whose Social Security benefits were less than the Supplemental Security Income (SSI) eligibility levels. Between February and July 1984, over 7.6 million notices were mailed as part of this one-time alert. SSA used a mail survey questionnaire to evaluate the effects of this alert process. As a result of the one-time outreach effort, there were approximately 160,000 field office contacts. These contacts resulted in 79,000 applications for SSI payments and 58,000 awards, with an average monthly SSI payment of $60 to supplement these recipients' Social Security benefits. Most of the people who did not contact SSA after receiving the alert reported that they felt that they were ineligible because of too many resources or too much income.

The second outreach activity is an ongoing effort to notify two groups of Social Security beneficiaries: those about to reach age 65; and disabled individuals who have been receiving Social Security benefits for 21 consecutive months and will soon be eligible for Medicare. Beginning in July 1983, and continuing each month, approximately 110,000 aged and disabled Social Security beneficiaries receive an SSI alert which accompanies the Medicare enrollment notice. Eighty percent of the alerts go to retired beneficiaries, with the remainder sent to disability beneficiaries. The trend in SSI monthly aged awards showed a marked change when this mailing began. SSA estimates that about 2,000 additional aged awards per month have resulted from the ongoing alerts since July 1983.

As a result of these two outreach efforts, the decline in the aged SSI population was temporarily reversed, resulting in a high of 2,083,633 aged recipients in September 1984. Since that date, the aged SSI population has begun to decrease, although at a slower rate than that experienced before the outreach.

The Omnibus Budget Reconciliation Act of 1989 established a permanent outreach program for disabled and blind children. In addition, beginning in 1989, SSA made SSI outreach an ongoing agency priority. The goal of SSA's SSI outreach strategy is to reduce the barriers that prevent or discourage potentially SSI-eligible individuals from participating in the program. Common barriers include lack of information or understanding about the program, perceived stigma from participating in the program, the complexity of the application process, and homelessness.

SSA seeks to overcome these barriers by providing better information about the program, alleviating any stigma surrounding the program, and making the program more accessible to potentially eligible persons. SSA tries to overcome these barriers both directly and through cooperative efforts with other government and private sector organizations that have contacts with local SSA field officers.

In fiscal year 1990, Congress mandated SSA to expand the scope of its SSI outreach activities and provided funding for SSA to conduct an SSI Outreach Demonstration project. To this end, Congress appropriated funding for cooperative agreements as follows: fiscal year 1990—$3 million; fiscal year 1991—$6 million; fiscal year 1992—$6 million; and fiscal year 1993—$6 million. To date, SSA has funded 82 diverse cooperative agreements targeting a variety of populations such as African-Americans, Native Americans, the homeless, the mentally ill, and people infected with HIV. SSA is in the process of awarding additional cooperative agreements which will allow it to continue testing innovative outreach methods and fill research gaps in target populations from the earlier awards.

Congress also mandated that SSA spend no less than five percent of the funding on an independent evaluation of the demonstration program. In fiscal year 1991, SSA awarded a contract for such evaluation and a cross-project comparison to develop models for effective outreach. Completed projects are in various phases of evaluation. Exemplary models will be publicized and replicated.

At the regional, State and local levels, SSA field components have implemented many creative outreach activities. SSA has established a vehicle called the Resource Information Center for collecting, sharing, and providing updates to the entire SSA field structure about these outreach efforts being conducted in regional and field offices.

At the national level, SSA has established a network of liaisons with a number of other Federal agencies that serve low-income people to improve access to the SSI program and other benefits and services. These agencies include the Department of Veterans' Affairs, Department of Agriculture, and five other Federal agencies operating under the auspices of the Federal Interagency Coordinating Council which target young children with disabilities.

SSI AND THE HOMELESS

SSA has implemented specific legislation and developed outreach programs and administrative initiatives to better meet the needs of the homeless, who may be eligible for SSI. This was prompted by evidence that approximately 30 to 40 percent of the residents of emergency homeless shelters are chronically mentally ill, and are former residents of mental institutions.

These initiatives are designed to address the special problems related to the homeless: they are often difficult to locate and contact; they have limited ability to find information needed to apply for benefits; and they are often reluctant to follow through with the claims process or are incapable of doing so. While many of the chronically mentally ill live with family or have other ongoing contact with those who can assist them with daily living activities, the homeless, mentally ill are more likely to have very limited contact with family or others who could assist them in obtaining housing or applying for benefits.

Legislative changes enacted to address the issue of homelessness include not counting in-kind support or maintenance provided by a private nonprofit organization as income under the SSI program if determined by the State to be based on need, and allowing temporary residents of public emergency shelters to receive SSI benefits for up to 6 months in any 9-month period. SSA also has statutory authority to provide emergency advance payments in amounts up to the full SSI monthly benefit standard to individuals applying for SSI who are presumptively eligible and who have a financial emergency and payments for up to 6 months to presumptively blind and presumptively disabled individuals.

SSA has also provided assistance to the homeless by instituting several administrative initiatives. For example, in many areas of the country local field offices regularly visit homeless shelters, clinics, and hospitals to take and expedite SSI applications. SSA has also instituted special procedures on disability applications filed by homeless claimants. For example, for most applications SSA defers the nonmedical development of a claim until the States' Disability Determination Services make a favorable medical determination. However, to facilitate prompt payment to homeless claimants, SSA initiates full claims development at the time of application.

SSA has identified homelessness as one barrier to filing for SSI benefits and, in response, has initiated a wide range of outreach activities aimed at this population. For example, local field offices have established ongoing programs where local social service agencies, soup kitchens, shelters, and churches screen homeless people for possible SSI eligibility, refer them to SSA, and help them through the application process. Many of SSA's SSI outreach demonstration programs deal specifically with the homeless or concentrate on the homeless in addition to other target populations, especially individuals who suffer from mental illness or AIDS.

In August 1991, SSA began a joint project with the Department of Veterans Affairs (VA), which has two successful programs dealing with homeless, mentally ill veterans. One pilot project involves stationing SSA and State Disability Determination Services staff in VA sites to work as a team with VA clinicians to take and process applications. Another pilot involves the creation of a new position which combines SSA and State Disability Determination Services functions into one "specialist" position. The specialists also work as a team with VA clinicians. This project has shown promising results in finding and delivering benefits to eligible homeless veterans.

"Immediate payments."—Beginning in October 1985, local social security offices were given the authority to make "immediate payments" for certain Social Security and SSI cases when it is found that benefits are due but unpaid and even an expedited Treasury payment would result in deprivation of food and/or shelter or endangerment of health. "Immediate" usually means while the beneficiary waits or the next day at the latest. The payments are made using bankdrafts prepared by the SSA field office. Payments are limited to a maximum per beneficiary of $400 or the amount due, whichever is less, in a 30-day period. The person's eligibility for benefits must be verified by the local office. During fiscal year 1993, 38,294 immediate payments were issued under this procedure. The total amount of these payments equaled $12,666,732 for an average of $330 per payment.

"Prerelease Procedure."—The prerelease procedure helps institutionalized individuals return to community living. Some individuals are medically ready to be released from an institution but are financially unable to support themselves. The prerelease procedure allows such individuals to apply for SSI payments and food stamps several months in advance of their anticipated release based on their probable future living arrangements so benefits can commence quickly after release. A formal prerelease agreement can be developed between an institution and the local Social Security office. However, an individual can file an application for SSI under prerelease without the existence of such an agreement.

SSI MODERNIZATION PROJECT

In 1990, the Social Security Commissioner established the SSI Modernization Project to determine the effectiveness of the SSI program. The Project's 21 outside experts published their final report in September 1992, drawing on extensive public testimony and comment. The report included more than 50 options for program improvement, many of which would require legislation and all of which would involve substantial cost. Provisions dealing with some of the issues addressed by the experts were introduced in both the 102d and 103d Congress, but none has passed. In October 1993, the House Committee on Ways and Means Subcommittee on Human Resources held an oversight hearing on SSI and heard testimony on the Modernization Project Report. In light of the need to achieve a balance in relation to efforts aimed at reducing a budget deficit and reforming health care and welfare, many legislators viewed SSI modernization legislation as too costly and expansive. The subcommittee held a subsequent hearing on the Modernization Project in March 1994.

SSI PROGRAM COSTS

Table 6–23 shows the total expenditures for the SSI program in each State, including not only the federally administered Federal and State supplementation payments but also the State administered State supplementation payments. Table 6–24 shows the total (Federal- and State-administered) State supplementation payments for SSI for fiscal years 1985 through 1993.

TABLE 6–23.—SUPPLEMENTAL SECURITY INCOME: TOTAL PAYMENTS, FEDERAL SSI PAY-
MENTS, AND FEDERALLY ADMINISTERED AND STATE ADMINISTERED STATE SUPPLE-
MENTARY PAYMENTS, FISCAL YEAR 1993

[In thousands of dollars]

| State | Total | Federal SSI [1] | State supplementation | |
			Federally adminis-tered [2]	State adminis-tered
Total	$24,173,827	$20,311,676	$3,298,496	$563,655
Alabama	530,650	528,567	....	2,083
Alaska	33,259	20,287	....	[4] 12,972
Arizona	230,533	227,404	....	[4] 3,129
Arkansas	299,216	299,216	([3])	....
California	5,075,783	2,863,453	2,212,330	....
Colorado	235,044	179,987	....	[4] 55,057
Connecticut	241,274	144,438	....	96,836
Delaware	32,578	31,831	747	....
District of Co-lumbia	71,473	66,574	4,899	....
Florida	1,039,971	1,021,363	([3])	18,608
Georgia	608,535	608,516	19	....
Hawaii	68,756	57,690	11,066	....
Idaho	55,464	51,252	....	[4] 4,212
Illinois	1,073,690	1,007,854	....	[4] 65,836
Indiana	307,664	303,847	....	3,817
Iowa	130,027	127,168	2,859	....
Kansas	114,553	114,553	([3])	....
Kentucky	551,082	535,769	....	15,313
Louisiana	692,553	692,549	4	....
Maine	77,619	70,386	7,233	....
Maryland	281,598	275,329	32	6,237
Massachusetts ...	583,542	435,676	147,866	....
Michigan	762,089	699,406	62,683	....
Minnesota	238,243	184,383	....	[4] 53,860
Mississippi	474,366	474,355	11	....
Missouri	391,369	365,503	....	[4] 25,866
Montana	41,784	40,882	902	....
Nebraska	72,526	65,821	....	6,705
Nevada	57,682	54,096	3,586	....
New Hampshire..	38,217	29,705	....	8,512
New Jersey	521,269	449,304	71,965	....
New Mexico	137,027	136,698	....	329
New York	2,369,189	1,893,160	476,029	....
North Carolina	646,659	551,214	....	95,445
North Dakota	27,072	25,852	....	1,220

TABLE 6–23.—SUPPLEMENTAL SECURITY INCOME: TOTAL PAYMENTS, FEDERAL SSI PAY-
MENTS, AND FEDERALLY ADMINISTERED AND STATE ADMINISTERED STATE SUPPLE-
MENTARY PAYMENTS, FISCAL YEAR 1993—Continued

[In thousands of dollars]

State	Total	Federal SSI [1]	State supplementation	
			Federally adminis-tered [2]	State adminis-tered
Ohio	840,617	840,589	28	....
Oklahoma	265,811	229,254	....	36,557
Oregon	171,232	151,063	....	[4] 20,169
Pennsylvania	979,698	869,751	109,947	....
Rhode Island	77,093	60,996	16,097	....
South Carolina ...	351,169	338,792	....	12,377
South Dakota	42,334	41,653	10	671
Tennessee	560,825	560,825	([3])	....
Texas	1,220,944	1,220,944	....	....
Utah	67,627	66,749	878	....
Vermont	44,866	34,939	9,927	....
Virginia	402,297	384,980	....	17,317
Washington	322,619	295,811	26,808	....
West Virginia	232,666	232,666	....	....
Wisconsin	461,094	328,333	132,761	....
Wyoming	17,137	16,610	....	527
N. Mariana Islands	2,178	2,178	....	....

[1] Includes $1.5 million not distributed by State.
[2] Total reduced by 197,000 due to adjustments not yet identified and credited by State.
[3] Amount not shown; negative adjustment exceeds amount paid.
[4] Estimated data.

Source: Office of Research and Statistics, Social Security Administration.

TABLE 6-24.—STATE SSI SUPPLEMENTATION PAYMENTS FOR EACH FISCAL YEAR 1985–93

[In thousands of dollars]

State	1985	1986	1987	1988	1989	1990	1991	1992	1993
Total	$2,234,846	$2,496,275	$2,835,516	$3,006,796	$3,308,277	$3,589,348	$3,750,812	$3,987,110	$3,862,151
Alabama	15,003	13,659	11,606	10,436	7,964	6,594	6,394	3,845	2,083
Alaska	12,970	12,970	12,970	12,970	12,970	12,972	12,972	12,972	12,972
Arizona	2,194	2,668	3,045	3,309	2,691	2,560	3,129	3,129	3,129
Arkansas	30	28	32	20	14	15	12	8	0
California	1,288,260	1,466,079	1,729,305	1,862,170	2,038,339	2,274,296	2,303,637	2,433,459	2,212,330
Colorado	47,474	38,320	35,416	24,132	41,035	42,649	50,002	53,309	55,057
Connecticut	31,200	36,578	46,577	54,584	74,257	67,670	98,838	94,725	96,836
Delaware	457	671	703	730	725	708	721	750	747
Dist. of Columbia	4,106	4,202	4,265	4,538	4,498	4,365	4,278	4,694	4,899
Florida	8,174	9,718	11,314	11,309	12,609	14,656	18,055	18,899	18,608
Georgia	13	8	19	18	10	16	9	12	19
Hawaii	3,598	3,740	3,893	4,263	6,799	10,885	10,314	10,698	11,066
Idaho	4,023	4,136	4,205	4,205	4,205	4,212	4,212	4,212	4,212
Illinois	44,491	51,197	56,856	59,573	55,716	57,137	65,756	64,241	65,836
Indiana	1,191	1,744	2,666	3,619	3,099	3,285	3,405	3,563	3,817
Iowa	1,620	1,908	2,098	2,204	2,275	2,408	2,508	2,672	2,859
Kansas	32	27	34	25	21	21	17	12	0
Kentucky	9,947	9,795	10,109	10,467	10,473	11,611	14,801	15,492	15,313
Louisiana	51	42	47	33	23	25	19	12	4
Maine	5,372	5,413	7,454	7,540	7,452	7,494	7,371	7,325	7,233
Maryland	4,238	5,252	5,505	6,159	6,159	6,155	6,520	6,542	6,269
Massachusetts	109,994	109,452	112,561	120,010	114,691	117,113	124,761	137,516	147,866
Michigan	62,824	66,338	68,779	69,833	72,369	74,682	72,561	61,636	62,683
Minnesota	17,024	19,818	22,850	24,667	40,641	43,924	48,933	55,224	53,860
Mississippi	33	29	35	27	26	22	19	12	11
Missouri	6,027	5,132	4,410	4,009	3,102	2,808	8,476	26,158	25,866
Montana	805	834	844	839	842	864	910	909	902
Nebraska	5,325	5,348	5,457	5,454	6,550	5,793	5,334	6,175	6,705
Nevada	2,421	2,531	2,594	2,704	2,771	2,928	3,029	3,184	3,586

New Hampshire	7,740	7,326	6,501	5,865	9,662	6,843	7,675	7,948	8,512
New Jersey	46,675	48,124	49,996	50,446	59,291	53,697	57,328	64,765	71,965
New Mexico	226	216	280	248	270	263	307	333	329
New York	225,075	277,035	305,678	317,504	366,972	388,150	410,081	440,374	476,029
North Carolina	36,449	41,091	47,963	52,745	58,989	63,135	75,066	91,925	95,445
North Dakota	1,183	1,518	1,406	1,480	1,549	1,390	1,291	1,408	1,220
Ohio	1	35	37	31	30	34	31	31	28
Oklahoma	30,187	31,380	32,894	34,045	33,414	34,168	35,055	36,012	36,557
Oregon	9,781	9,767	10,342	11,843	15,419	17,946	20,169	20,169	20,169
Pennsylvania	65,203	69,186	75,502	74,670	76,565	79,571	84,668	94,971	109,947
Rhode Island	8,842	9,402	9,848	10,263	10,816	11,729	12,973	14,967	16,097
South Carolina	3,932	4,812	4,927	5,004	9,785	8,897	11,994	11,685	12,377
South Dakota	499	591	636	587	590	567	620	652	681
Tennessee	6	0	6	1	4	4	1	1	0
Texas¹	0	0	0	0	0	0	0	0	0
Utah	820	872	855	1,086	981	808	898	959	878
Vermont	6,709	7,236	7,684	7,841	8,346	8,685	9,374	10,299	9,927
Virginia	11,267	12,164	12,846	14,432	15,949	15,296	16,863	16,782	17,317
Washington	20,022	17,443	19,424	18,058	18,994	19,915	21,558	24,043	26,808
West Virginia¹	0	0	0	0	0	0	0	0	0
Wisconsin	71,733	80,288	86,363	90,642	95,205	100,276	107,543	118,063	132,761
Wyoming	199	216	218	226	296	279	326	440	527

¹ Texas and West Virginia do not pay State supplementation.

Source: Social Security Administration.

Table 6–25 illustrates the total amount of Federal and State benefit payments from calendar years 1970 to 1987 and fiscal years 1988 to 1999. From 1970 to 1973, these were the benefits under the old-age assistance, aid to the blind, and aid to the permanently and totally disabled programs. In fiscal year 1993, Federal benefit payments totaled $20,312 billion and State payments totaled $3,862 billion.

TABLE 6–25.—FEDERAL AND STATE BENEFIT PAYMENTS UNDER SSI AND PRIOR ADULT ASSISTANCE PROGRAMS, CALENDAR YEARS 1970–87 AND FISCAL YEARS 1988–99 [1]

[Outlays in millions of dollars]

Year [2]	Total	Total constant 1993 dollars	Federal payments	Total State payments	State payments		SSI administrative costs (fiscal year)
					Federally administered	State administered	
1970	2,939	10,870	1,801	1,138			
1971	3,206	11,360	(3)	(3)			
1972	3,392	11,645	1,993	1,398			
1973	3,418	11,047	1,987	1,432			
1974	5,246	15,270	3,833	1,413	1,264	149	[4] 285
1975	5,878	15,678	4,314	1,565	1,403	162	399
1976	6,066	15,298	4,512	1,554	1,388	166	500
1977	6,306	14,933	4,703	1,603	1,431	172	NA
1978	6,552	14,420	4,881	1,671	1,491	180	539
1979	7,075	13,984	5,279	1,796	1,590	207	610
1980	7,941	13,829	5,866	2,074	1,848	226	668
1981	8,593	13,565	6,518	2,076	1,839	237	718
1982	8,981	13,355	6,907	2,074	1,798	276	779
1983	9,404	13,549	7,423	1,981	1,711	270	830
1984	10,372	14,325	8,281	2,091	1,792	299	864
1985	11,060	14,750	8,777	2,283	1,973	311	953
1986	12,081	15,818	9,498	2,583	2,243	340	1,022
1987	12,951	16,360	10,029	2,922	2,563	359	976
1988	14,375	17,631	11,368	3,007	2,645	362	975
1989	14,707	17,214	11,399	3,308	2,881	427	1,051
1990	16,095	17,946	12,507	3,589	3,159	431	1,075
1991	17,979	19,083	14,228	3,751	3,235	516	1,257
1992	21,258	21,899	17,270	3,987	3,431	556	1,538
1993	24,173	24,173	20,312	3,862	3,298	564	1,467
1994 [4]	28,628	27,871	24,475	4,153	3,545	608	1,690
1995 [4]	29,955	28,355	26,085	3,870	3,215	655	1,956
1996 [4]	30,591	28,104	26,985	3,606	2,900	706	1,620
1997 [4]	36,310	32,363	32,465	3,845	3,085	760	1,798
1998 [4]	39,754	34,366	35,915	3,839	3,020	819	1,808
1999 [4]	43,623	35,425	39,430	3,833	2,950	883	1,832

[1] Payments and adjustments during the respective year but not necessarily accrued for that year.

[2] 1970–1973 refers to Old-Age Assistance, Aid to the Blind and Aid to the Permanently and Totally Disabled; 1974–99 refers to Supplemental Security Income.

[3] Data not available.

[4] Estimated.

Source: Office of SSI, and Office of Budget, Social Security Administration.

Section 7. Unemployment Compensation

OVERVIEW

The Social Security Act of 1935 (Public Law 74–271) created the Federal-State unemployment compensation (UC) system. It has two main objectives: (1) to provide temporary and partial wage replacement to involuntarily unemployed workers who were recently employed; and (2) to help stabilize the economy during recessions. The U.S. Department of Labor oversees the system, but each State administers its own program. Because Federal law defines the District of Columbia, Puerto Rico, and the Virgin Islands as "States" for the purposes of unemployment compensation, there are 53 State programs.

The Federal Unemployment Tax Act of 1939 (Public Law 76–379) and titles III, IX, and XII of the Social Security Act form the framework of the system. The Federal Unemployment Tax Act (FUTA) imposes a 6.2 percent gross tax rate on the first $7,000 paid annually by covered employers to each employee. Employers in States with programs approved by the Federal Government and with no delinquent Federal loans may credit 5.4 percentage points against the 6.2 percent tax rate, making the minimum, net Federal unemployment tax rate 0.8 percent. Since all States have approved programs, 0.8 percent is the Federal tax rate that generally applies. This Federal revenue finances administration of the system, half of the Federal-State extended benefits program, and a Federal account for State loans. The States are supposed to use the revenue turned back to them by the 5.4 percent credit to finance their regular State programs and half of the Federal-State extended benefits program.

In 1976, Congress passed a temporary surtax of 0.2 percent of taxable wages to be added to the permanent FUTA tax rate (Public Law 94–566). Thus, the current 0.8 percent FUTA tax rate has two components: a permanent tax rate of 0.6 percent, and a temporary surtax rate of 0.2 percent. Under the Omnibus Budget Reconciliation Act of 1987 (Public Law 100–203), the 0.2 percent surtax was extended for 3 years through 1990. The Omnibus Budget Reconciliation Act of 1990 (Public Law 101–508) extended it again through 1995. The Emergency Unemployment Compensation Act of 1991 (Public Law 102–164) extended the temporary surtax through 1996. Most recently, the Omnibus Budget Reconciliation Act of 1993 (Public Law 103–66) extended the surtax through 1998.

TABLE 7–1.—UNEMPLOYMENT COMPENSATION PROGRAM STATISTICS

	Fiscal years											
	1983	1984	1985	1987	1988	1989	1990	1991	1992	1993	1994 (estimated)	1995 (projected)[1]
Total civilian unemployment rate (percent)	10.1	7.8	7.2	6.4	5.6	5.3	5.4	6.5	7.3	7.0	7.0	6.7
Insured unemployment rate (percent)[2]	4.3	2.9	2.9	2.5	2.2	2.1	2.3	3.1	3.1	2.7	2.7	2.5
Coverage (millions of individuals)	86.3	89.9	93.5	98.0	101.2	104.3	106.1	105.1	104.9	106.3	108.1	110.0
Average weekly benefit amount (current dollars)	120	119	123	134	140	145	154	163	167	172	177	182
In 1994 dollars[3]	179	171	170	176	176	174	176	178	177	177	177	177
State unemployment compensation:												
Beneficiaries (millions of individuals)	9.9	7.6	8.4	7.5	6.8	7.0	8.1	10.2	9.6	7.8	8.5	8.5
Regular benefit exhaustions (millions of individuals)	4.6	2.8	2.5	2.5	1.9	1.9	2.2	3.2	3.9	3.3	2.7	2.5
Regular benefits paid (billions of dollars)	20.8	13.3	14.3	15.0	13.2	13.5	16.8	24.4	25.6	22.1	22.7	22.6
Extended benefits (State share: billions of dollars)	1.21	.03	.03	.04	.04	(6)	.03	.01	.02	.00	.05	.07
State tax collections (billions of dollars)	14.4	19.0	20.0	19.1	18.3	17.3	16.0	15.3	17.6	21.0	21.6	22.0
State trust fund impact (income-outlays: billions of dollars)[4]	−7.62	+5.70	+5.65	+4.11	+5.12	+3.80	−.88	−9.13	−8.03	−1.11	−1.22	−.61
Federal unemployment compensation accounts:												
Federal tax collections (billions of dollars)[5]	3.58	5.02	4.44	5.08	5.50	4.45	5.36	5.33	5.41	[7]4.23	5.44	5.54
Outlays: Federal extended benefits share plus Federal supplemental benefits (billions of dollars)	6.80	3.01	1.27	.04	.04	(6)	.03	.01	11.15	13.17	3.73	.74
State administrative costs (billions of dollars):												
Unemployment Insurance Service	1.70	1.58	1.58	1.56	1.61	1.71	1.74	1.95	2.49	2.54	2.47	2.40
Employment Service	.72	.76	.92	.90	.95	1.00	1.01	1.05	1.02	1.08	1.09	1.10
Total administrative costs	2.42	2.31	2.50	2.46	2.56	2.71	2.75	3.00	3.51	3.62	3.56	3.50

[1] Based on President Clinton's 1995 budget.   [2] The average number of workers claiming State unemployment compensation benefits as a percent of all workers covered.   [3] Adjusted using CPI–U.   [4] Excludes interest earned.   [5] Net of reduced credits.   [6] Less than $5 million.   [7] Reflects a book adjustment of minus $967 million.

Source: Office of Research, Legislation and Program Policies/ETA/UIS/DOL, Division of Actuarial Services.

The Federal Unemployment Tax Act (FUTA) generally determines covered employment. FUTA also imposes certain requirements on the State programs, but the States generally determine individual qualification requirements, disqualification provisions, eligibility, weekly benefit amounts, potential weeks of benefits, and the State tax structure used to finance all of the regular State benefits and half of the extended benefits.

The Social Security Act provides for the administrative framework. Title III authorizes Federal grants to the States for administration of the State UC laws. Title IX authorizes the various components of the Federal Unemployment Trust Fund. Title XII authorizes advances or loans to insolvent State UC programs.

BENEFITS

Coverage

In order to qualify for benefits, an unemployed person usually must have worked recently for a covered employer for a specified period of time and for a certain amount of wages. About 109 million individuals are covered by UC. This is 98 percent of all wage and salary workers or 90 percent of all employed persons.

The Federal Unemployment Tax Act (FUTA) covers certain employers that State laws also must cover for employers in the States to qualify for the 5.4 percent Federal credit. Since employers in the States would lose this credit and their employees would not be covered if the States did not have this coverage, all States cover the following groups: (1) Except for nonprofit organizations, State-local governments, certain agricultural labor, and certain domestic service, FUTA covers employers who paid wages of at least $1,500 during any calendar quarter or who employed at least one worker in at least 1 day of each of 20 weeks in the current or prior year; (2) FUTA covers agricultural labor for employers who paid cash wages of at least $20,000 for agricultural labor in any calendar quarter or who employed 10 or more workers in at least 1 day in each of 20 different weeks in the current or prior year. In addition, section 3306(c)(1) of FUTA exempts certain alien farmworkers until January 1995; and (3) FUTA covers domestic service employers who paid cash wages of $1,000 or more for domestic service during any calendar quarter in the current or prior year.

FUTA requires coverage of nonprofit organization employers of at least four workers for 1 day in each of 20 different weeks in the current or prior year and State-local governments without regard to the number of employees. Nonprofit and State-local government organizations are not required to pay Federal unemployment taxes; they may choose instead to reimburse the system for benefits paid to their laid-off employees.

TABLE 7-2.—INSURED UNEMPLOYMENT AS A PERCENT OF TOTAL UNEMPLOYMENT

Year	Jan.	Feb.	Mar.	Apr.	May	June	July	Aug.	Sept.	Oct.	Nov.	Dec.	Avg.
1967	52	52	54	54	50	30	39	41	33	33	35	47	43
1968	57	50	52	50	45	26	34	38	33	34	38	48	42
1969	54	54	52	48	43	27	35	36	31	33	40	51	41
1970	57	54	52	53	53	36	42	45	42	44	48	53	48
1971	58	58	61	59	56	42	45	48	44	46	47	55	52
1972	56	58	56	52	49	36	41	38	33	34	38	47	45
1973	51	46	46	44	43	31	36	37	34	38	38	48	41
1974	53	54	57	60	55	40	43	44	40	42	48	60	50
1975	66	73	77	81	79	72	77	79	73	74	76	80	76
1976	78	75	76	73	72	58	66	66	60	59	60	63	67
1977	67	66	66	66	59	46	52	49	47	48	49	57	56
1978	54	54	50	47	44	36	39	42	35	37	34	43	43
1979	48	48	47	47	42	33	39	38	37	38	40	49	42
1980	52	51	53	52	49	45	49	49	55	49	50	54	50
1981	54	50	48	46	40	35	37	37	36	34	38	41	41
1982	47	44	48	49	45	40	42	42	43	48	49	47	45
1983	50	53	51	53	53	40	39	36	34	33	39	41	44
1984	40	38	38	36	34	30	31	31	30	31	31	38	34
1985	40	41	41	39	32	28	30	30	28	27	32	37	34
1986	38	36	37	35	32	29	32	32	29	30	32	37	33
1987	37	37	38	35	31	28	30	29	28	26	29	34	32
1988	37	37	37	35	31	28	30	29	27	27	30	34	32
1989	35	35	40	37	30	29	33	33	29	31	29	38	33
1990	40	42	44	41	37	33	36	34	32	34	34	40	37
1991	47	46	48	49	41	37	39	37	35	34	38	51	42
1992	56	54	59	59	54	46	48	48	49	50	50	51	52
1993	50	48	51	52	48	43	47	48	47	44	46	49	48

Source: USDOL/ETA/UIS, Division of Actuarial Services.

States may cover certain employment not covered by FUTA, but most States have not expanded FUTA coverage significantly. The excluded coverage involves: (1) self-employment; (2) certain agricultural labor and domestic service; (3) service for relatives; (4) service of patients in hospitals; (5) certain student interns; (6) certain alien farmworkers; (7) certain seasonal camp workers; and (8) railroad workers.

The number of covered workers receiving unemployment compensation

Although the UC system covers 90 percent of all employed persons, table 7–2 shows that on average only 48 percent of unemployed persons were receiving UC benefits in 1993. This compares with a peak of 81 percent of the unemployed receiving UC benefits in April 1975 and a low point of 26 percent in October 1987. Despite high unemployment during the early 1980's, there was a downward trend in the proportion of unemployed persons receiving regular State benefits until the mid-1980's. The proportion receiving UC rose sharply in December 1991 due to the temporary EUC program. The yearly average exceeded 50 percent in 1992 for the first time since 1980.

In May 1988, Mathematica Policy Research (MPR), under contract to the U.S. Department of Labor, released a study on the decline in the proportion of unemployed receiving benefits during the 1980's. This analysis did not find a single cause for the decline but instead found statistical evidence that the following factors contributed to the decline in UC claims (the figures in parentheses show the share of the decline attributed to each factor):

—the decline in the proportion of unemployed from manufacturing industries (4–18 percent);

—geographic shifts in composition of the unemployed among regions of the country (16 percent);

—changes in State program characteristics (22–39 percent):

—increase in the base period earnings requirements (8–15 percent);

—increase in income denials for UC receipt (10 percent); and

—tightening up other nonmonetary eligibility requirements (3–11 percent);

—changes in Federal policy such as partial taxation of UC benefits (11–16 percent);

—changes in unemployment as measured by the CPS (1–12 percent).

The group of unemployed most likely to be insured are job losers. Chart 7–1 shows the number of unemployment compensation claimants measured as a percentage of the number of job losers. This coverage ratio remained fairly stable from 1968 through 1979. Over that 12-year span, there were from 90 to 110 recipients of regular State UC for every 100 job losers. This ratio fluctuated somewhat over the business cycle, but it was otherwise quite stable.

Beginning in 1980, the ratio of UC recipients to job losers fell sharply, reaching an all-time low in 1983 when there were fewer than 60 regular UC recipients for every 100 job losers. After 1983, the coverage ratio has increased somewhat, so that there were about 75 regular UC claimants for every 100 job losers in 1990. However, the ratio declined again with the 1990–91 recession.

CHART 7–1. RATIO OF INSURED UNEMPLOYMENT TO JOB LOSERS (YEARLY AVERAGES), 1968–93

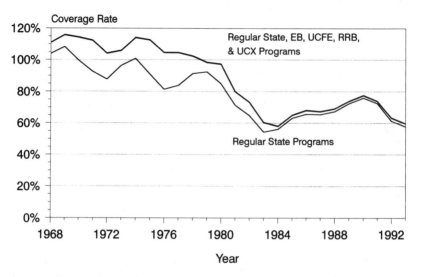

Note.—Insured unemployment data includes the Virgin Islands and Puerto Rico, but the data for job losers do not include these territories.

Source: Chart prepared by CRS based on data from the Economic Report of the President, 1994, and U.S. Department of Labor.

Eligibility

States have developed diverse and complex methods for determining UC eligibility. In general there are three major factors: (1) the amount of recent employment and earnings; (2) demonstrated ability and willingness to seek and accept suitable employment; and (3) certain disqualifications related to a claimant's most recent job separation or job offer refusal.

Monetary qualifications

Table 7–3 shows the State monetary qualification requirements in the base year for the minimum and maximum weekly benefit amounts, and for the maximum total potential benefits. The base year is a recent 1-year period that most States (48) define as the first 4 of the last 5 completed calendar quarters before the unemployed person claims benefits. Most States require employment in at least 2 calendar quarters of the base year. Qualifying wages for the minimum weekly benefit amount vary from $130 in Hawaii to $5,400 in Montana. For the maximum weekly benefit amount, the range is $4,650 in Nebraska to $27,144 in Colorado. The range of qualifying wages for the maximum total potential benefit, which is the product of the maximum weekly benefit amount and the maximum potential weeks of benefits, is from $5,320 in Puerto Rico to $30,600 in Washington.

TABLE 7–3.—MONETARY QUALIFICATION REQUIREMENTS FOR MINIMUM AND MAXIMUM WEEKLY BENEFIT AMOUNTS AND MAXIMUM TOTAL POTENTIAL BENEFITS IN 1994 [1]

State	Required total earnings in base year			Minimum work in base year (quarters) [3]
	For minimum weekly benefit	For maximum weekly benefit	For maximum potential benefits [2]	
Alabama	$1,032	$7,896	$12,869	2Q
Alaska	1,000	22,250	22,250	2Q
Arizona	1,500	6,919	14,429	2Q
Arkansas	1,215	13,462	19,812	2Q
California	1,125	9,542	11,958	....
Colorado	1,000	27,144	27,144	....
Connecticut	600	12,680	12,680	2Q
Delaware	966	12,190	12,190	....
District of Columbia	1,950	13,065	17,420	2Q
Florida	400	10,000	26,000	2Q
Georgia	1,350	9,250	19,238	2Q
Hawaii	130	8,762	8,762	2Q
Idaho	1,430	7,638	19,858	2Q
Illinois	1,600	12,285	12,285	2Q
Indiana	2,500	5,000	15,786	2Q
Iowa	1,090	6,066	16,458	2Q
Kansas	1,860	7,500	19,500	2Q
Kentucky	1,500	19,283	19,283	2Q
Louisiana	1,200	6,788	17,428	2Q
Maine	2,287	6,643	15,444	2Q
Maryland	900	8,028	8,028	2Q
Massachusetts	2,400	9,750	27,083	....
Michigan	1,340	11,320	19,810	2Q
Minnesota	1,250	9,912	23,790	2Q
Mississippi	1,200	6,600	12,870	2Q
Missouri	1,500	5,833	13,650	2Q
Montana	5,400	21,700	21,700	2Q
Nebraska	1,200	4,650	12,009	2Q
Nevada	600	8,625	17,940	2Q
New Hampshire	2,800	24,500	24,500	2Q
New Jersey	2,460	11,567	20,242	2Q
New Mexico	1,285	6,402	8,537	2Q
New York	1,600	11,980	11,980	2Q
North Carolina	2,324	14,664	21,996	2Q
North Dakota	2,795	15,080	19,302	2Q
Ohio	1,702	9,520	12,376	2Q

TABLE 7–3.—MONETARY QUALIFICATION REQUIREMENTS FOR MINIMUM AND MAXIMUM WEEKLY BENEFIT AMOUNTS AND MAXIMUM TOTAL POTENTIAL BENEFITS IN 1994 [1]— Continued

State	Required total earnings in base year			Minimum work in base year (quarters) [3]
	For minimum weekly benefit	For maximum weekly benefit	For maximum potential bene-fits [2]	
Oklahoma	4,160	8,888	15,405	2Q
Oregon	1,000	22,720	22,720	2Q
Pennsylvania	1,320	13,080	13,080	2Q
Puerto Rico	280	5,320	5,320	2Q
Rhode Island	1,780	10,065	22,389	2Q
South Carolina	900	7,917	15,834	2Q
South Dakota	1,288	7,728	13,104	2Q
Tennessee	1,560	9,620	19,240	2Q
Texas	1,480	9,065	23,589	2Q
Utah	1,900	9,672	23,881	2Q
Vermont	1,628	9,405	9,405	....
Virginia	3,250	10,400	20,800	2Q
Virgin Islands	1,287	8,229	16,458	2Q
Washington	1,825	8,500	30,600	....
West Virginia	2,200	26,500	26,500	2Q
Wisconsin	1,380	7,290	15,795	2Q
Wyoming	1,650	8,700	18,333	2Q

[1] Based on benefits for total unemployment. Amounts payable can be stretched out over a longer period in the case of partial unemployment.

[2] Based on maximum weekly benefit amount paid for maximum number of weeks. Total potential benefits equal a worker's weekly benefit amount times this potential duration.

[3] Number of quarters of work in base year required to qualify for minimum benefits. "2Q" denotes that State directly or indirectly requires work in at least 2 quarters of the base year. States without an entry have the minimum work requirement specified as a wage amount.

Source: U.S. Department of Labor.

Since the beginning of 1993, 12 States increased the required earnings in the base year to qualify for the minimum weekly benefit amount. Thirty-four States increased and one decreased the qualification requirement for the maximum weekly benefit amount. Thirty-six States increased their qualification requirements for maximum potential benefits.

Ability to work and availability for work

All State laws provide that a claimant must be: (1) able to work; and (2) available for work. A claimant must meet these conditions continually to receive benefits.

Only minor variations exist in State laws setting forth the requirements concerning "ability to work." A few States specify that a claimant must be mentally and physically able to work.

"Available for work" is often translated to mean being ready, willing, and able to work. In addition to registration for work at a local employment office, most State laws require that a claimant seek work actively or make a reasonable effort to obtain work. Generally, a person may not refuse an offer of, or referral to, "suitable work" without good cause.

"Suitable work" is generally work in a claimant's customary occupation which meets certain health, safety, moral, and labor standards. Most State laws list certain criteria by which the "suitability" of a work offer is to be tested. The usual criteria include the degree of risk to a claimant's health, safety, and morals; the physical fitness and prior training, experience, and earnings of the person; the length of unemployment and prospects for securing local work in a customary occupation; and the distance of the available work from the claimant's residence. Generally, as the length of unemployment increases, the claimant is required to accept a wider range of jobs.

In addition, Federal law requires States to deny benefits provided under the extended benefit program to any individual who fails to accept any work that is offered in writing or is listed with the State employment service, or who fails to apply for any work to which he or she is referred by the State agency, if the work is within the person's capabilities, pays wages equal to the highest of the Federal or any State or local minimum wage, pays a gross weekly wage that exceeds the person's average weekly unemployment compensation benefits plus any supplemental unemployment compensation (usually private) payable to the individual, and is consistent with the State definition of "suitable" work in other respects. Public Law 102–318 suspended these provisions, however, from March 7, 1993, until January 1, 1995. In addition, the Advisory Council on Unemployment Compensation recommended the repeal of these provisions in its interim report of February 1994.

States must refer extended benefits claimants to any job meeting these requirements. If the State, based on information provided by the individual, determines that the individual's prospects for obtaining work in his or her customary occupation within a reasonably short period are good, the determination of whether any work is "suitable work" is made in accordance with State law rather than the above.

There are certain circumstances under which Federal law provides that State and extended benefits may not be denied. A State may not deny benefits to an otherwise eligible individual for refusing to accept new work under any of the following conditions: (1) if the position offered is vacant directly due to a strike, lockout, or other labor dispute; (2) if the wages, hours, or other conditions of the work offered are substantially less favorable to the individual than those prevailing for similar work in the locality; (3) if, as a condition of being employed, the individual would be required to join a company union or to resign from or refrain from joining any bona fide labor organization. Further, benefits may not be denied solely on the grounds of pregnancy. The State is prohibited from canceling wage credits or totally denying benefits except in cases of misconduct, fraud, or receipt of disqualifying income.

There are also certain conditions under which Federal law requires that benefits be denied. For example, benefits must be denied to professional and administrative employees of educational institutions during summer (and other vacation periods) if they have a reasonable assurance of reemployment; to professional athletes between sport seasons; and to aliens not legally admitted to work in the United States.

Disqualifications

The major causes for disqualification from benefits are not being able to work or available for work, voluntary separation from work without good cause, discharge for misconduct connected with the work, refusal of suitable work without good cause, and unemployment resulting from a labor dispute. Disqualification for one of these reasons may result in a postponement of benefits for some prescribed period, a cancellation of benefit rights, or a reduction of benefits otherwise payable.

Of the 16.1 million "monetarily eligible" initial UC claims in 1993, 23.7 percent were disqualified. This figure subdivides into 4.7 percent not being able to work or available for work, 6.5 percent voluntarily leaving a job without good cause, 4.2 percent being fired for misconduct on the job, 0.2 percent refusing suitable work, and 8.0 percent committing other disqualifying acts. The total disqualification rate ranged from a low of 8.8 percent in Tennessee to a high of 117.9 percent in Nebraska, with Colorado the next highest at 68.9 percent. (Note that a claimant can be disqualified for any week claimed, so it is possible for a claimant to be disqualified more times than the total number of that claimant's initial claims in the benefit year.)

Federal law requires that benefits provided under the extended benefits program will be denied to an individual for the entire spell of his or her unemployment if he or she was disqualified from receiving State benefits because of voluntarily leaving employment, discharge for misconduct, or refusal of suitable work. These benefits will be denied even if the disqualification were subsequently lifted with respect to the State benefits prior to reemployment. The person could receive these benefits, however, if the disqualification were lifted because he or she became reemployed and met the work or wage requirement of State law. Public Law 102–318 suspended these provisions, however, from March 7, 1993, until January 1, 1995. The Advisory Council on Unemployment Compensation is required to study these provisions and make recommendations by February 1, 1995.

Ex-service members

The Emergency Unemployment Compensation Act of 1991 (Public Law 102–164) provided that ex-members of the military are treated the same as other unemployed workers with respect to the waiting period for benefits and benefit duration. Before this 1991 action, Congress had placed restrictions on benefits for ex-service members.

The Omnibus Budget Reconciliation Act of 1981 (Public Law 97–35) limited unemployment benefits to individuals who: (1) had 365 or more days of military service; (2) were discharged or released under honorable conditions; (3) did not resign or voluntarily leave the service (i.e., they were not eligible for reenlistment); and (4) were not released or discharged "for cause" as defined by the Department of Defense. The requirements applied to individuals who left Federal military service on or after July 1, 1981, but only for weeks of unemployment that began on or after August 13, 1981, the date of enactment of Public Law 97–35.

The Miscellaneous Revenue Act of 1982 (Public Law 97–362) modified the above eligibility requirements for ex-service members. Federal unemployment benefits became payable to unemployed ex-service members who: (1) were separated under honorable conditions (and, in the case of officers, did not resign for the good of the service); and (2) had completed the first full term of active service they agreed to serve. Ex-service members who were separated prior to completing their first full term of active service could qualify for unemployment compensation benefits if they separated under honorable conditions: (1) for the convenience of the Government under an early release program; (2) because of medical disqualification, pregnancy, parenthood, or any service-incurred injury or disability; (3) because of hardship; or (4) if they had served for 365 continuous days, because of personality disorder or inaptitude. In addition to these eligibility requirements, ex-service members had to wait 4 weeks from the date of their separation from the service before they could receive benefits. The maximum number of weeks of benefits an ex-service member could receive based on employment in the military was 13.

Pension offset

The Unemployment Compensation Amendments of 1976 (Public Law 94–566) required all States to reduce an individual's unemployment compensation benefits by the amount of any governmental or private pension or retirement pay received by the individual. Public Law 96–364 modified this offset requirement.

Under current law, States are required to make the offset only in those cases in which the work-related pension was maintained or contributed to by a "base period" or "chargeable" employer. Entitlement to, and the amount and duration of, unemployment benefits are based on work performed during this State-specified base period. A "chargeable" employer is one whose account will be charged for unemployment compensation received by the individual. However, the offset must be applied to Social Security benefits without regard to whether base period employment contributed to that entitlement.

States are allowed to reduce the amount of the offset by an amount consistent with any contribution the employee made toward the pension. For example, this allows States to limit the offset to one-half of the amount of a social security pension received by an individual who qualifies for unemployment benefits.

Taxation of unemployment insurance benefits

The Tax Reform Act of 1986 (Public Law 99–514) made all unemployment compensation taxable after December 31, 1986. The Revenue Act of 1978 first made a portion of unemployment compensation benefits taxable beginning January 1, 1979. Generally, the unemployment insurance benefits subject to Federal tax under the 1978 law were equal to the lower of: (1) the amount of unemployment compensation, or (2) one-half the excess of adjusted gross income, unemployment insurance payments, and excludable disability income over $20,000 for single taxpayers and over $25,000 for married taxpayers filing jointly. Beginning January 1, 1983, these amounts were changed to $12,000 for single taxpayers and $18,000 for married taxpayers filing jointly.

Table 7–4 illustrates the effect of taxing all unemployment compensation benefits for calendar year 1995. This table understates the impact of taxation because total unemployment compensation benefits reported on the current population survey (CPS) are equal to only about two-thirds of benefits actually paid out. Because of underreporting of unemployment compensation benefits in the CPS and underestimates of benefits paid in 1995, taxes collected on benefits probably will be about twice as high as the $3.1 billion in table 7–4.

TABLE 7–4.—ESTIMATED EFFECT OF TAXING UNEMPLOYMENT COMPENSATION BENEFITS, BY INCOME CLASS, 1995

Level of individual or couple income [1]	Number of recipients of unemployment compensation (in thousands)	Number affected by taxation of benefits (in thousands)	Percentage affected by taxation	Total amount of unemployment compensation benefits (in millions of dollars)	Total amount of taxes on benefits (in millions of dollars)	Taxes as a percent of total benefits
Less than $10,000	1,335	667	50.0	2,056	142	6.9
$10,000 to $15,000 ...	978	809	82.7	1,761	211	12.0
$15,000 to $20,000 ...	1,182	1,122	94.9	2,075	347	16.7
$20,000 to $25,000 ...	948	925	97.6	1,939	374	19.3
$25,000 to $30,000 ...	863	848	98.3	1,804	344	19.1
$30,000 to $40,000 ...	1,324	1,307	98.7	2,654	456	17.2
$40,000 to $50,000 ...	1,041	1,041	100.0	1,919	329	17.1
$50,000 to $100,000 .	1,559	1,559	100.0	3,344	760	22.7
At least $100,000	168	163	97.1	546	159	29.1
All	9,399	8,438	89.8	18,052	3,122	17.3

[1] Cash income (based on income of tax filing unit) plus capital gains realizations.

Note.—Aggregate unemployment compensation benefits on the CPS are equal to only about two-thirds of total benefits paid out. The number of recipients is also understated on the CPS.

Source: Congressional Budget Office, based on data from the Current Population Survey (CPS).

Amount and duration of weekly benefits

In general, the States set weekly benefit amounts as a fraction of the individual's average weekly wage up to some State-determined maximum. The total maximum duration available under permanent law is 39 weeks. The regular State programs usually provide up to 26 weeks. The permanent Federal-State extended benefits program provides up to 13 additional weeks in States where unemployment rates are relatively high. An additional 7 weeks is available under a new optional trigger enacted in 1992, but only 8 States have adopted this trigger as of June 30, 1994. The temporary emergency unemployment compensation program, which operated through April 30, 1994, provided either 7 or 13 additional weeks of benefits. A State offering this program could not have offered the permanent extended benefit program simultaneously, however.

The State-determined weekly benefit amounts generally replace between 50 and 70 percent of the individual's average weekly pretax wage up to some State-determined maximum. The average weekly wage is often calculated only from the calendar quarter in the base year in which the claimant's wages were highest. The State-determined maximum weekly benefit amounts generally vary between 50 and 70 percent of the average weekly covered wage in each State. Individual wage replacement rates tend to vary inversely with the claimant's average weekly pretax wage, with high wage earners receiving lower wage replacement rates. Thus, the national average weekly benefit amount as a percent of the average weekly covered wage was only 37 percent in the quarter ending September 30, 1993.

Table 7–5 shows the minimum and maximum weekly benefit amounts and potential duration for each State program. In fiscal year 1993, the national average weekly benefit amount was $173 and the average duration was 15.6 weeks, making the average total benefits $2,699. The minimum weekly benefit amounts for 1994 vary from $5 in Hawaii to $73 in Washington. The maximum weekly benefit amounts range from $133 in Puerto Rico to $487 in Massachusetts.

TABLE 7–5.—AMOUNT AND DURATION OF WEEKLY BENEFITS FOR TOTAL UNEMPLOYMENT UNDER THE REGULAR STATE PROGRAMS

State	1994 weekly benefit amount [1]		1993 average weekly benefit	1994 potential duration (weeks)		1993 average duration (weeks)
	Minimum	Maximum		Minimum	Maximum	
Alabama	$22	$165	$126	15	26	9
Alaska	44–68	212–284	161	16	26	17
Arizona	40	185	147	12	26	16
Arkansas	45	254	148	9	26	13
California	40	230	152	14	26	18
Colorado	25	261	183	13	26	13
Connecticut	15–22	317–367	210	26	26	16
Delaware	20	265	173	24	26	14
District of Columbia	50	335	215	20	26	22
Florida	10	250	165	10	26	15
Georgia	37	185	144	9	26	10
Hawaii	5	337	247	26	26	18
Idaho	44	235	151	10	26	12
Illinois	51	235–311	194	26	26	18
Indiana	50	170–192	138	14	26	13
Iowa	31–38	211–259	168	11	26	12
Kansas	62	250	184	10	26	16
Kentucky	22	229	147	15	26	12
Louisiana	10	181	118	8	26	17
Maine	35–52	198–297	153	21	26	14

TABLE 7–5.—AMOUNT AND DURATION OF WEEKLY BENEFITS FOR TOTAL
UNEMPLOYMENT UNDER THE REGULAR STATE PROGRAMS—Continued

State	1994 weekly benefit amount [1]		1993 average weekly benefit	1994 potential duration (weeks)		1993 average duration (weeks)
	Minimum	Maximum		Minimum	Maximum	
Maryland	25–33	223	181	26	26	16
Massachusetts	14–21	325–487	229	10	30	16
Michigan	42	293	210	15	26	12
Minnesota	38	305	203	10	26	15
Mississippi	30	165	123	13	26	14
Missouri	45	175	142	11	26	14
Montana	54	217	135	8	26	13
Nebraska	20	154	131	20	26	12
Nevada	16	230	172	12	26	15
New Hampshire	32	196	137	26	26	11
New Jersey	69	347	228	15	26	18
New Mexico	39	197	143	19	26	18
New York	40	300	188	26	26	20
North Carolina	22	282	158	13	26	11
North Dakota	43	232	148	12	26	13
Ohio	42	238–319	180	20	26	15
Oklahoma	16	237	161	20	26	14
Oregon	66	285	169	5	26	16
Pennsylvania	35–40	329–337	197	16	26	17
Puerto Rico	7	133	88	26	26	17
Rhode Island	41–51	310–387	204	15	26	16
South Carolina	20	203	141	15	26	11
South Dakota	28	168	128	18	26	11
Tennessee	30	185	129	12	26	12
Texas	41	245	177	9	26	16
Utah	17	248	175	10	26	13
Vermont	36	209	156	26	26	16
Virginia	65	208	162	12	26	14
Virgin Islands	32	211	162	13	26	18
Washington	73	340	180	16	30	17
West Virginia	24	280	161	26	26	14
Wisconsin	46	243	161	12	26	12
Wyoming	40	220	159	12	26	15

[1] A range of amounts is shown for those States that provide dependents' allowances.

Source: U.S. Department of Labor.

Most States vary the duration of benefits with the amount of earnings the claimant has in the base year. Nine States provide the same duration for all claimants. The minimum durations range from 5 weeks in Oregon to 26 weeks in 9 States. The maximum duration is 26 weeks in 51 States. Two States have maximum durations longer than 26 weeks, up to 30 weeks in Massachusetts and Washington.

Since the beginning of 1993, nine States increased their minimum weekly benefit amounts. Thirty-three States raised their maximum weekly benefit amounts. One State lowered its minimum potential duration.

EXTENDED BENEFITS

The Federal-State extended benefits program provides one-half of a claimant's total State benefits up to 13 weeks in States with an activated program, for a combined maximum of 39 weeks of regular and extended benefits. Weekly benefit amounts are identical to the regular State UC benefits for each claimant, and Federal funds pay half the cost. The program activates in a State under two conditions: (1) if the State's 13-week average insured unemployment rate (IUR) in the most recent 13 weeks is at least 120 percent of the average of its 13-week IUR's in the last 2 years for the same 13-week calendar period and its current 13-week average IUR is at least 5.0 percent; or (2) at State option, if its current 13-week average IUR is at least 6.0 percent. All but 12 State programs have adopted the second, optional condition. The 13-week average IUR is calculated from the ratio of the average number of insured unemployed persons under the regular State programs in the last 13 weeks to the average covered employment in the first 4 of the last 6 completed calendar quarters.

States have the option of electing an alternative trigger authorized by the Unemployment Compensation Amendments of 1992 (P.L. 102–318). This new trigger is based on a 3-month average total unemployment rate (TUR) using seasonally adjusted data. If this TUR average exceeds 6.5 percent and is at least 110 percent of the same measure in either of the prior 2 years, a State can offer 13 weeks of EB. If the average TUR exceeds 8 percent and meets the same 110-percent test, 20 weeks of EB can be offered. Analysis of historical data shows that this TUR trigger would have made EB more widely available than did the IUR trigger. As of June 30, 1994, the TUR trigger has been authorized by 8 States (Alaska, Connecticut, Kansas, Maine, Oregon, Rhode Island, Vermont, and Washington). Extended benefits were activated using the TUR trigger in October 1993 in Oregon (for 13 weeks) and Washington (for 20 weeks), and in March 1994 in Maine (20 weeks).

BENEFIT EXHAUSTION

Due to the limited duration of UC benefits, some individuals exhaust their benefits. For the regular State programs, 3.3 million individuals exhausted their benefits in fiscal year 1993, or 39 percent of claimants who began receiving UC during the 12 months ending March 31, 1993. These exhaustions raise the question of whether new policies are needed to reduce the exhaustion rate or ameliorate financial hardships caused by the cessation of benefits.

A study of exhaustees was completed in September 1990 by Mathematica Policy Research, Inc., under contract to the U.S. Department of Labor.[1] The purpose of this study was to examine the characteristics and behavior of exhaustees and nonexhaustees and to explore the implications of this information. The UC exhaustees

---

[1] Corson, Walter and Dynarski, Mark. A Study of Unemployment Insurance Recipients and Exhaustees: Findings from a National Survey. U.S. Department of Labor, Unemployment Insurance Service. Occasional Paper 90–3. September 1990.

study was designed to provide nationally representative estimates of the characteristics of exhaustees and nonexhaustees. The samples were chosen from individuals who began collecting benefits during the period October 1987 through September 1988. Overall, 1,920 exhaustees and 1,009 nonexhaustees were interviewed.

The study's authors reached three general conclusions:

—A large proportion of UI recipients expected to be recalled to their previous jobs. The unemployment spells of these job-attached workers were considerably shorter than those of workers who suffered permanent job losses, and few job-attached workers exhausted their UI benefits. The practice of exempting job-attached workers from administrative work-search requirements is sensible under these circumstances. Workers who were not job-attached—in particular, workers who were dislocated from their previous jobs or who had low skill levels— were likely to experience long unemployment spells, and a significant proportion of these workers exhausted their UI benefits. For this group, administrative work-search requirements are sensible. Targeting reemployment services to this group may also be a reasonable strategy for reducing periods of joblessness.

—The work disincentive effect was not a dominant factor in explaining the exhaustion of UI benefits. Most workers who exhausted their benefits were still unemployed more than a month after receiving their final payment, and a majority were still unemployed two months after receiving their final payment. Moreover, workers who found jobs after exhausting their UI benefits were generally receiving lower wages than on their prior jobs. Under these circumstances, extending the potential duration of UI benefits may reduce the financial hardships of exhaustion considerably, while creating only mild disincentive effects for some workers.

—State exhaustion rate trigger mechanisms would not be clearly superior to the State Insured Unemployed Rate (IUR) triggers in targeting extended benefits to areas with high cyclical unemployment. Substate trigger mechanisms for extended benefits would do a poor job of targeting extended benefits to local areas with high structural unemployment.

SUPPLEMENTAL BENEFITS

The extended benefits (EB) program was enacted to provide unemployment benefits to workers who had exhausted their regular benefits during periods of high unemployment. Before enactment of a permanent EB program, Congress authorized two temporary programs. First, a voluntary program was authorized by the Temporary Unemployment Compensation (TUC) Act of 1958 (P.L. 85–441). TUC was signed into law on June 4, 1958; it expired on April 10, 1959 (June 30, 1959, for Federal employees and veterans). TUC was established in response to the 1957–58 recession. It offered States interest-free loans if they increased the duration of benefits to UI recipients by 50 percent (up to a maximum of 13 weeks) after they had exhausted their regular benefits. A total of 17 States participated, while 5 other States enacted their own EB programs. Between June 1958 and July 1959 slightly over 2 million claimants received benefits totalling $600 million under TUC.

The second temporary EB program was authorized by the Temporary Extended Unemployment Compensation (TEUC) Act of 1961 (P.L. 87–6). TEUC was enacted on March 24, 1961; it expired on June 30, 1962. The program was financed through the Unemployment Trust Fund by a temporary increase in the net Federal unemployment tax. All States were required to participate. UI recipients who had exhausted their regular benefits could receive up to 50 percent of their regular benefits for up to 13 weeks, provided that the combined total duration of regular and extended benefits did not exceed 39 weeks. A total of 2.8 million claimants received benefits totaling $817 million during the 15 months of this program.

The Federal-State Extended Unemployment Compensation Act of 1970 (P.L. 91–373) authorized a permanent mechanism for providing extended benefits. Under the original program, UI recipients who had exhausted their regular benefits could receive EB if: (1) the national seasonally adjusted insured unemployment rate reached at least 4.5 percent for 3 consecutive months; or (2) their State's insured unemployment averaged at least 4 percent for 13 consecutive weeks and was at least 120 percent higher than the average insured unemployment rate for the corresponding 13 weeks during the preceding 2 years. As with TEUC, UI recipients who exhausted their regular benefits receive 50 percent of their regular benefits for up to 13 weeks of EB, provided that the total duration did not exceed 39 weeks. EB rules were amended by the Omnibus Budget Reconciliation Act (OBRA) of 1981 (P.L. 97–35) and the Unemployment Compensation Amendments of 1992 (P.L. 102–318).

On three occasions temporary programs have provided supplemental benefits to UI recipients who had exhausted both their regular and extended benefits during periods of severe unemployment.

The Emergency Unemployment Compensation Act of 1971 (P.L. 92–224) was enacted on December 29, 1971, and was originally scheduled to expire on September 30, 1972. This program was financed by the Federal Government through the Extended Unemployment Compensation Account (EUCA), from which non-interest-bearing repayable advances were made available to the States. A State became eligible when its insured unemployment rate was at least 6.5 percent, unless it failed to meet a requirement that the average of the current 13-week insured unemployment rate be at least 120 percent of the average of the rates for the same 13-week periods for the last 2 years. UI recipients who exhausted their regular and extended benefits were eligible to receive benefits for up to half of the duration of their regular benefits or 13 weeks, whichever was less. P.L. 92–329 extended this act for 6 months, until it expired on March 31, 1973.

The Emergency Unemployment Compensation Act of 1974 (P.L. 93–572) was enacted on December 31, 1974, and created the Federal Supplemental Benefits (FSB) program. FSB was authorized in response to the 1974–75 recession. Initially, funds for the program came from non-interest-bearing repayable advances from the general fund, which Congress expected the Unemployment Trust Fund to repay from EUCA after the recession. UI recipients who exhausted their regular and extended benefits could receive up to 13 weeks of FSB. States became eligible if they met either the national or State insured unemployment rates specified in the Federal-State Unemployment Compensation Act of 1970 for EB eligibility. FSB was extended 3 times.

The Tax Reduction Act of 1975 (P.L. 94–12) doubled the potential duration of FSB to 26 weeks, allowing a UI recipient to receive benefits under the regular, extended, and FSB programs for up to 65 weeks. These additional benefits were financed by the Federal Government and were to expire on January 1, 1976. The Emergency Compensation and Special Unemployment Assistance Extension Act of 1975 (P.L. 94–45) extended FSB to March 31, 1977. Among other provisions, this law abolished the national trigger for State FSB eligibility. The Emergency Unemployment Compensation Extension Act of 1977 (P.L. 95–19) reduced FSB to a potential duration of 13 weeks. The Act provided that, after April 1, 1977, FSB would be financed through non-repayable advances from Federal general revenue. It also extended FSB to October 31, 1977, when the program finally expired.

The Tax Equity and Fiscal Responsibility Act (TEFRA) of 1982 (P.L. 97–248) established the Federal Supplemental Compensation (FSC) program in response to the 1982 recession. TEFRA was enacted on September 3, 1982, and FSC was scheduled to expire on March 31, 1983. The program provided benefits to UI recipients who had exhausted their regular and extended benefits on or after June 1, 1982, for up to 6, 8, or 10 weeks of benefits. FSC claimants received the same weekly sums as under the regular Federal-State UI program. The FSC program was extended and modified six times.

The Surface Transportation Assistance Act of 1982 (P.L. 97–424) was enacted on January 6, 1983. The act provided that the duration of FSC benefits would be 16, 14, 12, 10, or 8 weeks, depending on conditions within a State. The expiration date of March 31, 1983, was left unchanged. P.L. 98–13, which was enacted on March 29, 1983, continued the program past the expiration date pending completion of the Social Security Amendments of 1983, which contained a 6-month extension. That measure (P.L. 98–21), enacted on April 20, 1983, extended FSC retroactively from April 1, 1983, to September 30, 1983. This act provided for basic FSC benefits for 14, 12, 10, or 8 weeks, depending on the unemployment conditions within a State. It also provided additional FSC benefits of 10, 8, or 6 weeks to individuals who exhausted their basic FSC benefits on or before April 1, 1983. Additional FSC benefits were equal to three-fourths of the basic FSC benefits payable in a State.

FSC was extended three more times. P.L. 98–118, enacted on October 11, 1983, extended FSC to October 18, 1983. The Federal Supplemental Compensation Amendments of 1983 (P.L. 98–135), enacted on October 24, 1983, extended FSC until March 31, 1985. This legislation provided basic FSC benefits for up to 14, 12, 10, or 8 weeks and provided additional FSC benefits for up to 5, 4, or 2 weeks, depending on the unemployment conditions within a State. P.L. 99–15, enacted on April 4, 1985, extended the FSC program until June 30, 1985, when it finally expired.

The Emergency Unemployment Compensation Act of 1991 (P.L. 102–164) enacted on November 15, 1991, and amended by P.L.

102–182 on December 4, 1991, authorized a temporary emergency unemployment compensation (EUC) program to provide additional weeks of assistance through June 13, 1992. The EUC program effectively superseded EB.

The EUC program entitled people whose regular UC benefit years expired on or after March 1, 1991, to extra weeks of assistance. The program as amended provided 20 weeks of benefits in States with an adjusted insured unemployment rate (AIUR) of at least 5 percent or a 6-month average total unemployment rate (TUR) of at least 9 percent. Beneficiaries in other States received 13 weeks of benefits. (The AIUR is the IUR used to trigger EB, adjusted to include regular benefit exhaustees in a State for the most recent 3 months for which data are available.)

Congress authorized EUC with an additional 13 weeks of benefits for eligibles in all States by enacting Public Law 102–244 on February 7, 1992. Thus, EUC could pay benefits for up to 26 or 33 weeks, depending on the State. The program was set to expire on July 4, 1992. Benefit durations were to return to the original 13 or 20 weeks after June 13, 1992.

Another extension of EUC was enacted on July 3, 1992 (P.L. 102–318). It reduced the available benefits to 20 or 26 weeks and extended the program through March 6, 1993. A third extension, enacted on March 4, 1993 (P.L. 103–6), extended EUC for new claims filed through October 2, 1993. Finally, EUC was extended by P.L. 103–152 on November 25, 1993, retroactive to October 3, 1993, for new claims filed on or before February 5, 1994. Benefit payments to claimants were made through April 30, 1994. Benefits were reduced to 7 or 13 weeks, depending on a State's unemployment rate.

Benefits under EUC were originally financed from spending authority in the Extended Unemployment Compensation Account (EUCA) of the Unemployment Trust Fund. However, depletion of EUCA led Congress to fund EUC from Federal general revenue from July 1992 until October 1993. States that qualified for EB while EUC was in effect could elect to trigger off EB. This reduced the State funding burden, since 50 percent of EB costs are financed from State UC accounts while EUC was entirely federally funded.

As of the week beginning January 9, 1994, 13 weeks of benefits were available from EUC in 4 States (Alaska, California, Puerto Rico, and West Virginia). (Washington and Oregon were offering EB based on the optional TUR trigger.) All other States had 7 weeks available from EUC.

Table 7–6 shows for each State the number of EUC claims during the week ending December 18, 1993, and average weekly benefits during December 1993. Nationally, claims totaled 1.0 million, with three States (California, New York and Pennsylvania) accounting for more than one-third of them. The average weekly EUC benefit nationwide was $173, the same as the U.S. average for the regular UC program.

TABLE 7–6.—NUMBER OF CLAIMS, AVERAGE WEEKLY BENEFITS AND BENEFITS PAID IN
THE EUC PROGRAM BY STATE

State	No. of continued claims, week ending Dec. 18, 1993	Average weekly benefit, December 1993	Total benefits paid Nov. 15, 1991 through Feb. 5, 1994 (millions) [1]
U.S. total	971,639	173	$26,210
Alabama	8,821	120	158
Alaska	5,452	166	110
Arizona	7,031	141	168
Arkansas	7,992	[2]153	145
California	241,394	158	4,127
Colorado	6,781	[3]182	159
Connecticut	17,745	204	752
Delaware	1,649	173	41
District of Columbia	5,105	212	127
Florida	53,991	161	1,038
Georgia	11,919	146	330
Hawaii	3,046	259	97
Idaho	3,455	151	68
Illinois	42,627	188	1,134
Indiana	5,763	129	164
Iowa	6,974	161	130
Kansas	5,363	181	146
Kentucky	10,900	147	188
Louisiana	9,787	123	160
Maine	6,518	155	184
Maryland	18,361	173	444
Massachuesetts	25,055	234	1,200
Michigan	29,775	201	1,303
Minnesota	10,044	196	278
Mississippi	5,952	120	124
Missouri	17,063	142	361
Montana	2,456	138	36
Nebraska	1,843	127	25
Nevada	2,807	167	126
New Hampshire	1,594	138	70
New Jersey	42,866	220	2,036
New Mexico	2,257	142	55
New York	92,292	192	3,543
North Carolina	14,408	146	368
North Dakota	1,496	148	23
Ohio	29,599	179	867
Oklahoma	4,666	169	133

TABLE 7–6.—NUMBER OF CLAIMS, AVERAGE WEEKLY BENEFITS AND BENEFITS PAID IN
THE EUC PROGRAM BY STATE—Continued

State	No. of continued claims, week ending Dec. 18, 1993	Average weekly benefit, December 1993	Total benefits paid Nov. 15, 1991 through Feb. 5, 1994 (millions) [1]
Oregon	6,482	165	350
Pennsylvania	64,550	193	2,009
Puerto Rico	18,250	89	188
Rhode Island	10,037	200	264
South Carolina	8,503	138	185
South Dakota	289	122	4
Tennessee	11,443	125	273
Texas	42,978	170	1,209
Utah	2,392	172	56
Vermont	2,103	154	50
Virginia	10,761	156	278
Virgin Islands	[4]112	NA	([5])
Washington	10,753	166	490
West Virginia	7,450	167	158
Wisconsin	9,920	166	260
Wyoming	769	161	19

[1] Data are incomplete for some States.
[2] Data for October 1993.
[3] Data for November 1993.
[4] Data for week ending Nov. 27, 1993.
[5] Less than $500,000.

NA—Not available.

Source: U.S. Dept of Labor.

Table 7–7 shows the monthly trend in EUC continuing claims
and first payments. The number entering the program remained
fairly steady from February 1992 through November 1992 at about
300,000 a month, but entrants exceeded that total for all but one
of the next 9 months. The total number of active claims varied between 1.4 and 1.7 million from January 1992 through April 1993
but fell below 1.0 million in December 1993.

TABLE 7-7.—EMERGENCY UNEMPLOYMENT COMPENSATION CLAIMS

[In thousands]

Month	First payments [1]	Continuing claims (end of month) [1]
1991:		
November	114	635
December	1,051	1,196
1992:		
January	447	1,505
February	320	1,651
March	310	1,655
April	308	1,675
May	264	1,683
June	271	1,483
July	282	1,411
August	302	1,416
September	309	1,467
October	321	1,501
November	294	1,660
December	386	1,466
1993:		
January	471	1,486
February	321	1,479
March	378	1,374
April	347	1,437
May	297	1,286
June	328	1,329
July	389	1,447
August	388	1,353
September	293	1,300
October	137	1,032
November	65	1,283
December	383	922

[1] Reports were not received from all States for every month. Nonreporting was highest in November 1991.

Source: U.S. Department of Labor.

Table 7-8 shows outlay estimates for EUC at different points in time. The January 1993 budget baseline estimate of $18.2 billion for fiscal years 1992 and 1993, prepared before the March 1993 extension of EUC, greatly exceeded the earlier estimates: $12.8 billion in OMB's July 1992 Midsession Review; $8.3 billion by OMB when the laws were enacted; $12.0 billion by CBO when the laws were enacted. The growth in the estimate of $5.4 billion from July 1992 to January 1993 was attributed by the Department of Labor to three factors: exhaustions from the regular State program were unexpectedly near record levels; claimants were staying on EUC longer than expected; and large numbers of claimants eligible for both regular benefits and EUC were choosing EUC.

After the issuance of the January 1993 baseline estimate, the further extension of EUC into fiscal year 1994 occurred. The estimated cost raised the total estimated cost at time of enactment to $18.6 billion (CBO) and $14.8 billion (OMB). The Clinton administration's budget released in February 1994 estimated the total cost of EUC benefits to be $28.0 billion for the 3 years.

TABLE 7–8.—EUC OUTLAYS FOR FISCAL YEARS 1992–94

[In billions of dollars]

	Fiscal years			Total
	1992	1993	1994	
Estimates at time of enactment				
By OMB:				
Public Law 102–164, Public Law 102–182	3.0	(0.1)	0	2.9
Public Law 102–244	2.5	.3	0	2.8
Public Law 102–318	.6	2.0	0	2.6
Public Law 103–6	0	3.1	2.3	5.4
Public Law 103–152	0	0	1.1	1.1
Total	6.1	5.3	3.4	14.8
By CBO:				
Public Law 102–164, Public Law 102–182	4.3	(1)	0	4.3
Public Law 102–244	2.7	.6	0	3.3
Public Law 102–318	1.0	3.4	0	4.4
Public Law 103–6	0	3.2	2.3	5.5
Public Law 103–152	0	0	1.1	1.1
Total	8.0	7.2	3.4	18.6
OMB fiscal year 1993 Midsession review, July 1992	9.7	3.1	0	12.8
OMB fiscal year 1994 baseline, January 1993	11.1	7.1	0	18.2
OMB fiscal year 1994 Clinton budget, April 1993	11.1	12.3	2.1	25.5
OMB fiscal year 1994 Midsession review, July 1993	11.1	12.7	1.8	25.6
OMB fiscal year 1995 baseline, January 1994	11.1	13.2	3.7	28.0

[1] Less than $50,000,000.

Source: Office of Management and Budget, Congressional Budget Office.

HYPOTHETICAL WEEKLY BENEFIT AMOUNTS FOR VARIOUS WORKERS IN THE REGULAR STATE PROGRAMS

Table 7–9 illustrates benefit amounts for various full-year workers in regular State programs for January 1994. Column A of the table is for a full-time worker earning the minimum wage; column B is for a worker earning $6 per hour, while column C shows benefit amounts for a worker earning $9 per hour. Column D is for a part-time worker earning the minimum wage and working 20 hours per week. The weekly benefit amount for the full-time minimum wage worker varies from $77 to $176. The maximum amount a worker can receive in these examples (column C) in each State varies considerably, from $120 to $340 per week.

TABLE 7–9.—WEEKLY STATE BENEFIT AMOUNTS FOR VARIOUS FULL-YEAR WORKERS IN JANUARY 1994

	Hypothetical worker [1]			
	A	B	C	D
Alabama	165	165	165	92
Alaska	106	134	232	70
Arizona	88	125	185	44
Arkansas	85	120	180	45
California	82	105	142	46
Colorado	101	144	216	50
Connecticut	95	130	210	52
Delaware	96	135	203	48
District of Columbia	90	125	195	0
Florida	85	120	180	42
Georgia	88	124	185	44
Hawaii	106	149	223	53
Idaho	85	120	180	0
Illinois	101	141	237	59
Indiana	98	134	192	54
Iowa	100	141	234	50
Kansas	93	132	198	59
Kentucky	105	148	222	52
Louisiana	77	109	164	38
Maine	110	151	228	60
Maryland	93	130	211	47
Massachusetts	85	120	230	43
Michigan	NA	NA	NA	NA
Minnesota	85	120	180	42
Mississippi	85	120	165	42
Missouri	99	140	175	49
Montana	88	124	187	44
Nebraska	92	128	154	48
Nevada	88	124	187	44
New Hampshire	98	123	164	0
New Jersey	109	154	248	0
New Mexico	85	120	180	42
New York	85	120	180	43
North Carolina	85	120	180	42
North Dakota	85	120	180	0
Ohio	85	120	180	0
Oklahoma	88	124	187	44
Oregon	110	156	234	60
Pennsylvania	95	132	197	52
Puerto Rico	85	120	133	43

TABLE 7–9.—WEEKLY STATE BENEFIT AMOUNTS FOR VARIOUS FULL-YEAR WORKERS IN JANUARY 1994—Continued

	Hypothetical worker [1]			
	A	B	C	D
Rhode Island	102	144	236	51
South Carolina	85	120	180	42
South Dakota	85	120	168	42
Tennessee	169	185	185	84
Texas	89	125	188	45
Utah	86	120	180	43
Vermont	98	138	208	0
Virginia	88	124	187	0
Virgin Islands	85	120	180	42
Washington	176	249	340	88
West Virginia	93	131	198	46
Wisconsin	88	124	187	0
Wyoming	88	124	187	44

[1] Hypothetical workers:
  A. $4.25/hr. wage; 40 hrs./wk.; 52 wks./yr.; nonworking spouse; no children.
  B. $6.00/hr. wage; 40 hrs./wk.; 52 wks./yr.; nonworking spouse; no children.
  C. $9.00/hr. wage; 40 hrs./wk.; 52 wks./yr.; nonworking spouse; 2 children.
  D. $4.25/hr. wage; 20 hrs./wk.; 52 wks./yr.; nonworking spouse; no children.

NA—Not available. Michigan computes benefits based on after-tax wages.

Source: U.S. Department of Labor.

THE UNEMPLOYMENT TRUST FUND

The Federal unified budget accounts for all Federal-State UC outlays and taxes in the Federal Unemployment Trust Fund. The Unemployment Trust Fund has 59 accounts. The accounts consist of 53 State UC benefit accounts, the Railroad Unemployment Insurance Account, the Railroad Administration Account, and four Federal accounts. (The railroad accounts are discussed in section 8 of this document.)

The four Federal accounts in the trust fund are: (1) the Employment Security Administration Account (ESAA), which funds administration; (2) the Extended Unemployment Compensation Account (EUCA), which funds the Federal half of the Federal-State extended benefits program; (3) the Federal Unemployment Account (FUA), which funds loans to insolvent State UC programs; and (4) the Federal Employee Compensation Account (FECA), which funds benefits for Federal civilian and military personnel authorized under 5 U.S.C. 85. Federal unemployment taxes finance the ESAA, EUCA, and FUA, but general revenues finance the FECA. Present law authorizes interest-bearing loans to ESAA, EUCA, and FUA from the general fund. The three accounts may receive noninterest-bearing advances from one another to avoid insufficiencies.

Financial Condition of the Unemployment Trust Fund

Federal Accounts.—At the end of fiscal year 1993, the Employment Security Administration Account (ESAA) had reached its fiscal year 1993 ceiling of $1.4 billion; the Extended Unemployment Compensation Account (EUCA) balance was below its ceiling of $8.4 billion by $7.5 billion; the Federal Unemployment Account (FUA) fell short of its $13.9 billion ceiling by $9.0 billion.

Under the administration's fiscal year 1995 budget assumptions, the EUCA balance will continue to fall well short of its ceiling throughout the 5-year projection period. By the end of fiscal year 1999, FUA would be short by only $0.6 billion, however.

State Accounts.—The State accounts had recovered substantially from the financial problems that began in the 1970's and continued through the early 1980's, but the 1990–91 recession reversed that trend. Table 7–10 shows that the State accounts at the beginning of 1994 held $28.8 billion, which still represents a marked improvement over the negative balance of nearly $3 billion in 1982.

The balances in the State accounts are about the same as the balances in the early 1970's after adjusting for inflation, before serious financial problems began for most States. However, State reserve ratios (trust fund balances divided by total wages paid in the respective States during the year) show that a number of State accounts are at risk of financial problems in major recessions. The third column from the right margin of table 7–10 shows that these State ratios are only 43 percent of their levels in 1970. Two States (Massachusetts and Missouri) presently have outstanding Federal loans to their accounts.

For the third quarter of calendar year 1993, the second-to-last column of table 7–10 shows for each State the "High-Cost Multiple," the ratio of the State's reserve ratio to its highest cost rate. The highest cost rate is determined by choosing the highest ratio of costs to total covered wages paid in a prior year. States with high-cost multiples of at least 1.0 have reserves that could withstand a recession as bad as the worst one they have experienced previously. States with high-cost multiples below 1.0 have been at significant risk of insolvency during recessions.

Thirty-two States had high-cost multiples below 1.0. Twenty-six States had high-cost multiples below 0.8, and 17 States had high-cost multiples below 0.5. Based on this measure, those States in the worst financial shape were Arkansas, California, Connecticut, the District of Columbia, Illinois, Maine, Maryland, Massachusetts, Michigan, Minnesota, Missouri, New York, Ohio, Pennsylvania, Rhode Island, Texas, and West Virginia.

TABLE 7–10.—FINANCIAL CONDITION OF STATE UNEMPLOYMENT COMPENSATION PROGRAMS

States	Net reserves (end of calendar year) [In millions of dollars]					Reserve ratios [Percent]					1993/ 1970	High-cost mul-tiple[1]	Rank
	1970	1975	1979	1982	1993[1]	1970	1975	1979	1982	1993[1]			
Total	11,903	3,070	8,583	(2,645)	28,821	3.11	0.53	0.91	−0.24	1.33	43	0.57	......
Alabama	130	(2)	118	9	577	2.96	0	.98	.06	2.04	69	.94	23
Alaska	35	75	65	134	227	5.51	3.07	2.78	2.94	4.47	81	1.03	19
Arizona	119	67	226	215	376	4.25	1.35	2.36	1.66	1.36	32	.55	36
Arkansas	49	2	24	(77)	133	2.26	.04	.37	0	.89	39	.33	41
California	1,219	546	2,738	2,708	2,700	2.91	.88	2.51	1.83	.96	33	.41	37
Colorado	91	47	137	(4)	387	2.54	.70	1.11	0	1.24	49	.98	22
Connecticut	252	(232)	(267)	(252)	1	0.08	0	0	0	0	0	0	52
Delaware	22	0	(30)	(35)	228	1.72	0	0	0	3.18	185	1.18	15
District of Columbia	74	(3)	(44)	(57)	8	3.22	0	0	0	.08	2	.04	51
Florida	268	80	665	865	1,562	2.60	.42	2.13	1.89	1.58	61	.86	25
Georgia	340	268	447	397	1,087	4.74	2.28	2.28	1.49	1.88	40	.88	24
Hawaii	44	5	79	108	323	2.90	.23	2.24	2.43	3.18	110	1.20	13
Idaho	46	54	93	29	241	5.16	3.21	3.20	.85	3.64	71	1.15	17
Illinois	401	(31)	(460)	(2,069)	936	1.55	0	0	0	.81	52	.30	43
Indiana	326	198	418	63	1,020	3.13	1.31	1.69	.23	2.12	68	1.19	14
Iowa	125	63	155	(63)	641	3.19	.96	1.45	0	3.29	103	1.25	11
Kansas	84	135	238	142	659	3.00	2.65	2.75	1.29	3.13	104	1.59	5
Kentucky	175	137	159	(121)	404	4.21	1.95	1.36	0	1.65	39	.59	35
Louisiana	146	141	238	(102)	681	2.91	1.58	1.51	0	2.51	86	.81	26
Maine	39	2	0	(4)	50	2.86	0	0	0	.63	22	.22	47

TABLE 7-10.—FINANCIAL CONDITION OF STATE UNEMPLOYMENT COMPENSATION PROGRAMS—Continued

States	Net reserves (end of calendar year) [In millions of dollars]					Reserve ratios [Percent]					1993/ 1970	High-cost mul-tiple [1]	Rank
	1970	1975	1979	1982	1993 [1]	1970	1975	1979	1982	1993 [1]			
Maryland	213	29	273	220	235	3.26	.29	1.83	1.11	.60	18	.27	46
Massachusetts	378	(99)	132	436	(154)	3.04	0	0	1.23	0	0	0	52
Michigan	491	(286)	112	(2,186)	421	2.49	0	.25	0	.50	20	.14	49
Minnesota	119	(35)	70	(288)	241	1.76	0	.41	0	.57	32	.29	45
Mississippi	85	90	231	257	402	3.87	2.25	3.47	3.12	2.86	74	1.45	7
Missouri	264	95	296	(64)	7	3.03	.75	1.47	0	.02	1	.09	50
Montana	26	8	16	9	101	3.33	.57	0	.27	1.94	58	.64	34
Nebraska	55	29	81	72	170	2.87	.84	1.58	1.14	1.53	53	1.02	20
Nevada	39	5	95	122	237	3.20	.22	2.31	2.02	1.79	56	.65	32
New Hampshire	55	29	82	75	166	4.62	1.56	2.42	1.60	1.79	39	.71	29
New Jersey	448	(348)	(507)	(423)	2,049	2.76	0	0	0	2.38	86	.71	29
New Mexico	40	33	80	101	263	3.45	1.61	2.14	1.98	3.02	88	1.84	3
New York	1,693	574	403	819	327	3.76	1.02	.51	.78	.18	5	.18	48
North Carolina	414	342	564	400	1,490	5.22	2.71	2.71	1.52	2.69	52	1.04	18
North Dakota	13	22	21	11	53	2.53	1.94	1.13	.46	1.58	62	.67	31
Ohio	693	294	513	(1,658)	852	3.01	.91	1.02	0	.92	31	.30	43
Oklahoma	55	27	177	108	438	1.69	.46	1.56	.62	2.19	130	1.60	4
Oregon	122	24	320	161	1,068	3.39	.40	3.00	1.37	4.73	140	1.47	6
Pennsylvania	852	(86)	(1,091)	(2,145)	1,153	3.53	0	0	0	1.20	34	.36	38
Puerto Rico	85	(26)	(33)	(47)	747	4.90	0	0	0	8.91	182	2.12	2
Rhode Island	75	(41)	(96)	(76)	115	4.34	0	0	0	1.54	35	.35	40
South Carolina	166	95	195	50	476	4.61	.95	1.96	.40	1.89	41	.65	32
South Dakota	8	20	16	9	49	3.81	1.96	.95	.43	1.29	34	1.24	12
Tennessee	212	200	264	15	676	3.57	1.95	1.63	.08	1.67	47	.77	28
Texas	337	231	396	142	543	1.90	.71	.65	0	.37	19	.33	41

Utah	51	32	67	.10	356	3.55	1.22	1.43	.16	2.92	82	1.44	8
Vermont	26	(25)	(21)	(27)	181	3.72	0	0	0	4.43	119	1.36	9
Virginia	218	122	103	14	555	3.41	1.08	.56	.06	1.05	31	.80	27
Virgin Islands	NA	NA	(7)	46	52	NA	NA	0	0	7.60	NA	3.33	1
Washington	226	(67)	297	(3)	1,782	3.73	0	1.66	.70	4.23	113	1.00	21
West Virginia	108	78	39	150	156	4.07	1.70	.56	0	1.53	38	.38	39
Wisconsin	322	121	465	(144)	1,251	4.29	.99	2.37	0	3.02	70	1.17	16
Wyoming	19	31	69	(413)	122	4.29	3.02	3.15	1.44	4.11	96	1.36	9

[1] Data are for the third quarter of calendar year 1993.

Source: U.S. Department of Labor, Employment and Training Administration, Unemployment Insurance Service, Division of Actuarial Services, UI Data Summary, 3d quarter, calendar year 1993, Dec. 1993. U.S. Department of Labor, Employment and Training Administration, Unemployment Insurance Financial Handbook Data.

Table 7–11 summarizes the beginning balances in the unemployment trust fund accounts for selected fiscal years. At the start of fiscal year 1994, the four Federal accounts and the 53 State benefit accounts had a total balance of $37.0 billion. In real terms this represents a decline of 25 percent compared to 1971. This decline in real dollars in the State accounts from 1971 does not allow for the further erosion implied by the 53-percent increase in the labor force over this time period. A better measure is the ratio of the 1993 to 1970 reserve ratios in table 7–10, which shows that aggregate reserves in 1993 were only a little more than two-fifths of their level in 1970.

TABLE 7–11.—BEGINNING-OF-YEAR BALANCES IN UNEMPLOYMENT TRUST FUND ACCOUNTS FOR SELECTED FISCAL YEARS

[In millions of dollars]

Account	1971	1976	1980	1983	1994
Employment security administration .	65	365	572	545	2,123
Extended unemployment compensation	0	116	764	483	877
Federal unemployment (reserve for State loans)	575	9	567	599	4,948
Federal employee compensation	(1)	(1)	(1)	24	206
State unemployment compensation [2]	12,409	6,145	8,272	720	28,821
Total: Nominal dollars	13,049	6,635	10,175	2,371	36,975
Total: Real dollars [3]	49,572	18,394	20,755	3,569	36,975

[1] There was no separate account for Federal employee compensation for this year.
[2] Figures are net of loans from Federal funds.
[3] Real dollars are obtained using CPI–U for the preceding fiscal years.

Source: U.S. Department of Labor, Unemployment Insurance Service, Division of Actuarial Services.

The Federal unemployment tax

Total unemployment taxes on employers for a full-time, full-year worker earning the average wage in covered employment in 1992 is estimated to have averaged $260, or 13 cents per hour. The Federal portion is $56, or 3 cents per hour, and the average State portion is $204, or 10 cents per hour. Employer taxes vary substantially, however, depending on the State taxable wage base, State tax schedules, and Federal credits.

The Federal Unemployment Tax Act (FUTA) currently imposes a minimum, net Federal payroll tax on employers of 0.8 percent on the first $7,000 paid annually to each employee. The gross FUTA tax rate is 6.2 percent, but employers in States meeting certain Federal requirements and having no delinquent Federal loans are eligible for a 5.4 percent credit, making the minimum, net Federal tax rate 0.8 percent.

Chart 7–2 shows the historical trend in the Federal taxable wage base from 1940 to 1992. The wage base was held constant at $3,000 until 1971, but has been increased three times since then. The chart also shows the erosion of the taxable wage base during the 1950's and 1960's relative to wage growth. If the taxable wage base had been indexed for wage growth since 1940, the wage base would have been over $50,000 in 1992 instead of only $7,000.

Chart 7–3 depicts the historical trends in the statutory and effective Federal unemployment tax rates. The effective tax rate equals FUTA revenue as a percent of total covered wages. Although the statutory tax rate doubled from 0.4 percent in the late 1960's to 0.8 percent in the late 1980's, the effective tax rate has fluctuated between 0.2 and 0.3 percent in most of those years.

CHART 7–2. FEDERAL UC TAXABLE ANNUAL WAGE BASE IN CURRENT AND WAGE-ADJUSTED DOLLARS, 1940–92

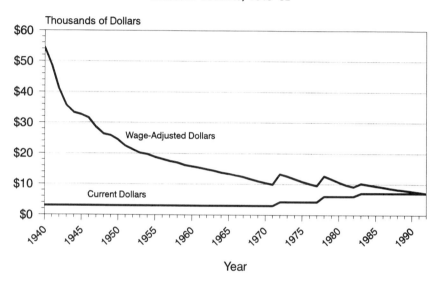

Source: Chart prepared by the Congressional Research Service (CRS) based on data from the U.S. Department of Labor (DoL).

CHART 7–3. HISTORY OF FEDERAL UNEMPLOYMENT TAX RATE, 1954–93

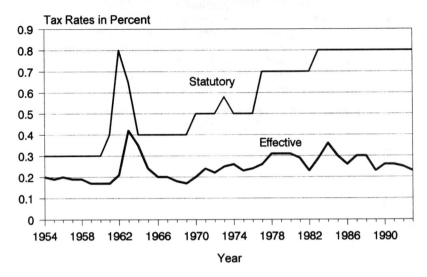

Source: Chart prepared by the Congressional Research Service (CRS) based on data from the U.S. Department of Labor (DoL).

CHART 7–4. FLOW OF FUTA FUNDS UNDER EXISTING FEDERAL STATUTES

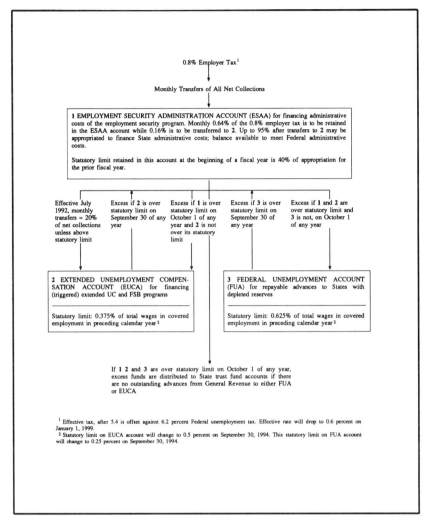

0.8% Employer Tax [1]

Monthly Transfers of All Net Collections

1 EMPLOYMENT SECURITY ADMINISTRATION ACCOUNT (ESAA) for financing administrative costs of the employment security program. Monthly 0.64% of the 0.8% employer tax is to be retained in the ESAA account while 0.16% is to be transferred to 2. Up to 95% after transfers to 2 may be appropriated to finance State administrative costs; balance available to meet Federal administrative costs.

Statutory limit retained in this account at the beginning of a fiscal year is 40% of appropriation for the prior fiscal year.

| Effective July 1992, monthly transfers = 20% of net collections unless above statutory limit | Excess if 2 is over statutory limit on September 30 of any year | Excess if 1 is over statutory limit on October 1 of any year and 2 is not over its statutory limit | Excess if 3 is over statutory limit on September 30 of any year | Excess if 1 and 2 are over statutory limit and 3 is not, on October 1 of any year |

2 EXTENDED UNEMPLOYMENT COMPEN-SATION ACCOUNT (EUCA) for financing (triggered) extended UC and FSB programs

Statutory limit: 0.375% of total wages in covered employment in preceding calendar year [2]

3 FEDERAL UNEMPLOYMENT ACCOUNT (FUA) for repayable advances to States with depleted reserves

Statutory limit: 0.625% of total wages in covered employment in preceding calendar year [2]

If 1 2 and 3 are over statutory limit on October 1 of any year, excess funds are distributed to State trust fund accounts if there are no outstanding advances from General Revenue to either FUA or EUCA

[1] Effective tax, after 5.4 is offset against 6.2 percent Federal unemployment tax. Effective rate will drop to 0.6 percent on January 1, 1999.
[2] Statutory limit on EUCA account will change to 0.5 percent on September 30, 1994. This statutory limit on FUA account will change to 0.25 percent on September 30, 1994.

State unemployment taxes

The States finance their programs and half of the permanent extended benefits program with employer payroll taxes imposed on at least the first $7,000 paid annually to each employee.[2] States have adopted taxable wage bases at least as high as the Federal level because they otherwise would lose the 5.4 percent credit to employers on the difference between the Federal and State taxable wage bases. Table 7–12 shows that, as of January 1994, 41 States had taxable wage bases higher than the Federal taxable wage base, ranging up to $25,000 in Hawaii.

[2] Alaska, New Jersey, and Pennsylvania also tax employees directly.

Although the standard State tax rate is 5.4 percent, State tax rates based on unemployment experience can range from zero on some employers in 15 States up to a maximum as high as 10 percent in 3 States.

Estimated national average State tax rates on taxable wages and total wages for 1993 were 2.3 and 0.9 percent, respectively. Estimated average State tax rates on taxable wages ranged from 0.5 percent in South Dakota to 4.8 percent in New York and Pennsylvania. Estimated average State tax rates on total wages varied from 0.2 percent in South Dakota to 2.1 percent in Rhode Island.

TABLE 7–12.—STATE UNEMPLOYMENT TAX BASES AND RATES

State	1994 tax base	1994 experience rates [1]		Estimated 1993 average tax rates as a percent of—	
		Minimum	Maximum	Taxable wages	All wages
U.S. average	NA	NA	NA	2.3	0.9
Alabama	$8,000	0.14	6.74	1.6	.6
Alaska	23,800	1.0	6.5	2.0	1.3
Arizona	(2)	.1	5.4	1.5	.4
Arkansas	9,000	0	6.0	3.0	1.3
California	(2)	.1	5.4	3.6	.9
Colorado	10,000	0	5.4	1.3	.5
Connecticut	9,000	.5	6.4	3.4	.9
Delaware	8,500	.1	8.0	2.6	.8
District of Columbia	9,500	.1	7.4	4.0	1.0
Florida	(2)	.1	5.4	1.8	.6
Georgia	8,500	.01	8.64	1.6	.6
Hawaii	25,000	0	5.4	1.0	.7
Idaho	20,400	.1	6.8	1.8	1.2
Illinois	9,000	.2	6.4	2.9	1.0
Indiana	(2)	.2	5.7	1.2	.4
Iowa	13,900	0	9.0	1.6	.8
Kansas	8,000	.025	5.4	2.4	.9
Kentucky	8,000	.3	10.0	2.1	.8
Louisiana	8,500	.3	6.0	1.9	.6
Maine	(2)	.5	7.5	3.8	1.3
Maryland	8,500	.1	8.3	2.9	1.0
Massachusetts	10,800	.6	9.3	3.9	1.6
Michigan	9,500	0	10.0	4.1	1.4
Minnesota	15,100	.1	9.0	1.8	.9
Mississippi	(2)	.1	6.4	2.1	1.0
Missouri	8,500	0	8.7	2.3	.8
Montana	15,100	0	6.4	1.4	.9
Nebraska	(2)	0	5.4	1.2	.4

TABLE 7–12.—STATE UNEMPLOYMENT TAX BASES AND RATES—Continued

State	1994 tax base	1994 experience rates [1]		Estimated 1993 average tax rates as a percent of—	
		Minimum	Maximum	Taxable wages	All wages
Nevada	15,900	.3	5.4	1.5	.8
New Hampshire	8,000	.01	6.5	2.2	.7
New Jersey	17,200	.4	6.47	1.2	.5
New Mexico	13,100	.1	5.4	1.5	.7
New York	(2)	0	6.4	4.8	1.1
North Carolina	13,200	.01	5.7	1.0	.5
North Dakota	13,000	.1	5.4	1.4	.8
Ohio	8,750	.1	6.5	2.9	1.0
Oklahoma	10,700	.1	6.2	1.2	.4
Oregon	19,000	.9	5.4	2.6	1.6
Pennsylvania	8,000	.3	9.2	4.8	1.5
Puerto Rico	(2)	1.0	5.4	2.9	1.0
Rhode Island	16,400	.8	8.4	3.7	2.1
South Carolina	(2)	.19	5.4	1.8	.6
South Dakota	(2)	0	9.5	.5	.2
Tennessee	(2)	.1	10.0	2.0	.7
Texas	9,000	0	6.0	1.3	.5
Utah	16,200	.1	8.0	1.0	.6
Vermont	8,000	.4	8.4	2.7	1.0
Virginia	8,000	0	6.2	1.2	.4
Virgin Islands	22,000	.1	9.5	1.5	1.2
Washington	19,900	.36	5.4	2.3	1.4
West Virginia	8,000	0	7.5	3.0	1.1
Wisconsin	10,500	0	8.9	2.2	1.0
Wyoming	11,400	0	8.5	2.1	1.0

[1] Actual rates could be higher if State has an additional tax.
[2] The 1994 tax base is $7,000 except as otherwise shown in this column.

NA—Not applicable.

Note.—This table shows State unemployment tax levels. It does not include the Federal unemployment tax.

Source: Department of Labor.

Table 7–13 shows recent State data on unemployment compensation covered employment, wages, taxable wages, the ratio of taxable to total wages, and average weekly wages. The ratio of taxable wages to total wages varied from 0.19 in the District of Columbia to 0.64 in Montana.

TABLE 7–13.—12-MONTH AVERAGE EMPLOYMENT AND WAGES COVERED BY
UNEMPLOYMENT COMPENSATION (UC) FOR PERIOD ENDING DECEMBER 1992

State	Covered employment (thousands)	Total wages (millions)	Taxable wages (millions)	Ratio of taxable wages to total wages	Average weekly total wages
United States	105,168	$2,684,987	$776,547	0.29	$491
Alabama	1,576	34,368	10,709	.31	419
Alaska	222	6,983	3,265	.47	605
Arizona	1,487	34,003	9,214	.27	440
Arkansas	915	18,130	6,181	.34	381
California	12,174	350,578	79,343	.23	554
Colorado	1,521	37,574	12,601	.34	475
Connecticut	1,479	48,207	9,478	.20	627
Delaware	331	8,762	2,328	.27	509
District of Columbia	426	14,825	2,864	.19	670
Florida	5,241	119,920	33,723	.28	440
Georgia	2,836	68,335	20,581	.30	463
Hawaii	511	12,885	7,042	.55	484
Idaho	404	8,207	4,356	.53	390
Illinois	5,015	139,200	37,826	.27	534
Indiana	2,442	57,369	14,884	.26	452
Iowa	1,194	24,764	10,236	.41	399
Kansas	1,060	23,001	9,182	.40	417
Kentucky	1,403	30,343	9,149	.30	416
Louisiana	1,546	34,163	10,415	.30	425
Maine	486	10,396	2,814	.27	411
Maryland	1,907	50,372	11,533	.23	508
Massachusetts	2,672	78,990	25,668	.32	568
Michigan	3,790	103,635	28,254	.27	526
Minnesota	2,083	52,381	19,808	.38	484
Mississippi	909	17,159	5,501	.32	363
Missouri	2,196	51,140	12,947	.25	448
Montana	292	5,496	3,542	.64	362
Nebraska	712	14,313	3,920	.27	387
Nevada	624	15,299	7,387	.48	471
New Hampshire	465	11,406	2,803	.25	471
New Jersey	3,292	105,631	37,999	.36	617
New Mexico	551	11,216	4,534	.40	392
New York	7,465	241,143	42,898	.18	621
North Carolina	3,047	67,127	27,834	.41	424
North Dakota	247	4,597	1,777	.39	357
Ohio	4,613	112,559	31,706	.28	469

TABLE 7–13.—12-MONTH AVERAGE EMPLOYMENT AND WAGES COVERED BY UNEM-
PLOYMENT COMPENSATION (UC) FOR PERIOD ENDING DECEMBER 1992—Continued

State	Covered employment (thousands)	Total wages (millions)	Taxable wages (millions)	Ratio of taxable wages to total wages	Average weekly total wages
Oklahoma	1,147	24,316	8,883	.37	408
Oregon	1,224	28,422	13,557	.48	446
Pennsylvania	4,819	123,170	31,288	.25	492
Puerto Rico	858	12,068	4,088	.34	271
Rhode Island	409	9,833	4,136	.42	462
South Carolina	1,455	30,738	8,812	.29	406
South Dakota	281	4,936	1,513	.31	337
Tennessee	2,131	47,849	13,368	.28	432
Texas	6,945	172,414	52,620	.31	477
Utah	701	15,039	6,668	.44	413
Vermont	241	5,367	1,518	.28	429
Virginia	2,609	62,976	17,929	.28	464
Virgin Islands	44	984	482	.49	428
Washington	2,127	53,837	24,658	.46	487
West Virginia	594	12,986	3,789	.29	420
Wisconsin	2,255	51,607	17,531	.34	440
Wyoming	191	3,967	1,403	.35	400

Source: UI data summary, 2d quarter calendar year 1993, Sept. 1993.

ADMINISTRATIVE FINANCING AND ALLOCATION

State unemployment compensation administrative expenses are Federally financed. A portion of revenue raised by the Federal Unemployment Tax Act (FUTA) is designated for administration and to maintain a system of public employment offices.

FUTA revenue flows into three Federal accounts in the Unemployment Trust Fund: (1) the Employment Security Administration Account (ESAA), (2) the Extended Unemployment Compensation Account (EUCA), and (3) the Federal Unemployment Account (FUA). Authorized by title IX of the Social Security Act, ESAA finances administrative costs associated with Federal and State unemployment compensation and employment services.

Under current law, 80 percent of FUTA revenue is allocated to ESAA and 20 percent to EUCA. FUA receives funds indirectly if they overflow from ESAA and EUCA. Funds for administration are limited to 95 percent of the estimated annual revenue that is expected to flow to ESAA from the FUTA tax. Funds for administration may be augmented by three-eighths of the amount in ESAA at the beginning of the fiscal year, or $150 million, whichever is less, if the rate of insured unemployment is at least 15 percent higher than it was over the corresponding calendar quarter in the immediately preceding year.

Title III of the Social Security Act authorizes payment to each State with an approved unemployment compensation law such amounts as are deemed necessary for the proper and efficient administration of such law during the fiscal year. Allocations are based on: (1) the population of the State; (2) an estimate of the number of persons covered by the State unemployment insurance law; (3) an estimate of the cost of proper and efficient administration of such law; and (4) such other factors as the Secretary of Labor finds relevant.

Subject to the limit of available resources, the allocation of State grants for administration is the summation of resources derived in two major areas, the Unemployment Insurance Service (UI) and the Employment Service (ES). Each area has its own allocation methodology subject to general constraints set forth in the Social Security Act and the Wagner-Peyser Act.

Each year, as part of the development of the President's Budget, the Department of Labor, in conjunction with the Department of Treasury, estimates revenue expected from FUTA and the appropriate amount to be available for administration (and the Federal share of extended benefits). The estimate of FUTA revenues is based on several factors: (1) a wage base of $7,000 per employee; (2) a tax rate of 0.8 percent (0.64 percentage point for administration and 0.16 percentage point for extended benefits); (3) the administration's projection of the level of unemployment and the growth in wages; and (4) the level of covered employment subject to FUTA. Additionally, a determination is made based on the administration's forecast for unemployment as to whether the rate will increase by at least 15 percent.

Each year the President's Budget sets forth an estimate of national unemployment in terms of the volume of unemployment claims per week. This is characterized as average weekly insured unemployment (AWIU). A portion of AWIU is expressed as "base" and the remainder as "contingency." At the present time, the base is set at the level of resources required to process an average weekly volume of 2.0 million weeks of unemployment.

Resources available to each State to administer its unemployment compensation program (i.e., process claims and pay benefits) are provided from either "base" funds or "contingency" funds. At the beginning of the fiscal year, only the base funds are allocated, while contingency funds are allocated on a needs basis as workload materializes. Base funds are distributed to the State for use throughout the fiscal year and are available regardless of the level of unemployment (workload) realized. If a State processes workloads in excess of the base level, it receives contingency funds determined by the extent of the resources required to process the additional workload.

The allocation of the base UI grant funds to each State is made by:

(1) Projecting the workloads that each State is expected to process.

These projections are then adjusted so that the sum across States for each workload item is equal to the budgeted base workload.

(2) Determining the staff required to process each State's projected workload.

The staff requirements are computed by multiplying the projected workloads by minutes per unit (MPU) and dividing the result by the number of work minutes per staff year for each State. The MPUs were derived from work measurement studies conducted in each State that establish the number of minutes required to perform specific tasks. The MPUs developed from the studies are necessarily reduced so that the total of computed staff years for each workload item across States equals the staff years available in the appropriation. The MPUs are reduced according to a complex mathematical formula that takes into account workload volume and the range of MPUs.

(3) Multiplying the final staff-year allocations for each State by the cost per staff year (i.e., State salary and benefit level) to determine dollar funding levels.

(4) Allocating overhead resources (administrative and management staff and nonpersonal services) using a methodology driven by the program staff years developed in the UI base allocation.

Each Department of Labor regional office may redistribute resources among the States in its area with national office approval.

In Public Law 102–164, Congress required the Department of Labor to study the allocation process and recommend improvements. Public Law 102–318 extended the time the Department has to complete this study until December 31, 1994.

RECENT MAJOR LEGISLATION

Major Federal laws passed by Congress since 1981 and their key provisions are as follows:

The Omnibus Budget Reconciliation Act of 1981 (Public Law 97–35) imposed interest charges up to 10 percent per annum under certain conditions on loans obtained by State UC programs after April 1, 1982. It also reduced the extended benefits program by an estimated $3 to $4 billion in fiscal year 1983. The primary changes that resulted in this reduction were: (A) elimination of the national trigger under the extended benefits program; (B) raising the State trigger to 5 percent, and 120 percent, or 6 percent; and (C) excluding claims for extended benefits from the calculation of the insured unemployment rate used for the extended benefit trigger.

The Tax Equity and Fiscal Responsibility Act of 1982 (Public Law 97–248) increased the taxable wage base from $6,000 to $7,000 and raised the minimum, net Federal unemployment tax rate to 0.8 percent in 1983. It also raised the gross tax and credit rates in 1985 to 6.2 and 5.4 percent, respectively. This left the minimum, net Federal rate unaffected but raised the maximum, potential, net tax rate in States with delinquent loans from 3.4 to 6.2 percent. The Act also created the temporary Federal supplemental compensation program, which authorized 6 to 10 additional weeks of benefits through March 31, 1983. This act also rounded UC benefits to the lowest dollar, extended the Reed Act, modified the treatment of school employees, and reduced the thresholds for taxation of unemployment compensation to $12,000 for single filers and $18,000 for married couples filing jointly.

The Social Security Amendments of 1983 (Public Law 98–21) extended the Federal supplemental compensation program through September 30, 1983, providing a maximum of 8 to 14 weeks of benefits. It also established conditions under which States could defer the payment of interest on loans from the Federal Unemployment Account and qualify for reduced FUTA credit reductions.

The Tax Reform Act of 1986 (Public Law 99–514) made all unemployment compensation subject to taxation under the Federal personal income tax.

The Omnibus Budget Reconciliation Act of 1987 (Public Law 100–203) extended the 0.2 percent FUTA surtax for 3 years through 1990.

The Omnibus Budget Reconciliation Act of 1990 (Public Law 101–508) extended the 0.2 percent FUTA surtax for 5 years through 1995.

The Emergency Unemployment Compensation Act of 1991 (Public Law 102–164) established temporary extended benefits through July 4, 1992. It returned to States the option of covering nonprofessional school employees between school terms and restored benefits for ex-military members to the same duration and waiting period applicable to other unemployed workers. It extended the 0.2 percent FUTA surtax for 1 year through 1996.

The Unemployment Compensation Amendments of 1992 (Public Law 102–318) extended EUC for claims filed through March 6, 1993, and reduced the benefit periods to 20 and 26 weeks. The law also gave claimants eligible for both EUC and regular benefits the right to choose the more favorable of the two. States were authorized, effective March 7, 1993, to adopt an alternative trigger for the Federal-State EB program. This trigger is based on a 3-month average total unemployment rate (TUR) and can activate either a 13- or a 20-week benefit period depending on the rate.

The Emergency Unemployment Compensation Amendments of 1993 (Public Law 103–6) extended EUC for claims filed through October 2, 1993. The law also authorized funds for automated State systems to identify permanently displaced workers for early intervention with reemployment services.

The Unemployment Compensation Amendments of 1993 (Public Law 103–152) extended EUC for claims filed through February 5, 1994, and set the benefit periods at 7 and 13 weeks. It repealed a provision passed in 1992 that allowed claimants to choose between EUC and regular State benefits. It required States to implement a system to identify UI claimants most likely to need job search assistance to avoid long-term unemployment.

INTERIM RECOMMENDATIONS OF THE ADVISORY COUNCIL ON UNEMPLOYMENT COMPENSATION—FEBRUARY 1994

Purpose of the Extended Benefits program

The scope of the Extended Benefits program should be expanded to enhance the capacity of the Unemployment Insurance system to provide assistance for long-term unemployed workers as well as short-term unemployed workers. Those individuals who are long-term unemployed should be eligible for extended Unemployment Insurance benefits, provided they are participating in job search activities or in education and training activities, where available and suitable, that enhance their re-employment prospects. To maintain the integrity of the Unemployment Insurance income support system, a separate funding source should be used to finance job search and education and training activities for long-term unemployed workers.

The trigger for extended benefits

The Council is unanimous in the view that there is a pressing need to reform the Extended Benefits program.

The majority of the Council recommends that the Extended Benefits program should trigger on when a state's seasonally adjusted total unemployment rate (STUR) exceeds 6.5 percent as measured before the Current Population Survey redesign. Two members of the Council recommend that each state should have the choice of using either the STUR trigger of 6.5 percent with a threshold requirement of 110 percent above either of the 2 previous years, or an IUR or AIUR trigger set at 4 percent with a threshold requirement of 120 percent over the previous 2 year period.

The Council hopes Congress can implement these reforms promptly. Although the Council has reservations about the inefficient targeting of emergency benefits, Congress should extend the existing Emergency Unemployment Compensation for a 6 month period to provide a bridge program until these Extended Benefits reforms can be implemented.

Neither substate nor regional data should be used for the purpose of determining whether or not Extended Benefits are available within a given area.

Financing extended benefits reform

If additional revenue is required to implement the Council's recommendations, such revenue should be generated by a modest increase in the FUTA taxable wage base, to $8,500.

Work search test under extended benefits

The Federal requirement that individuals who are receiving Extended Benefits must accept a minimum wage job if one is offered, or become ineligible for benefits, should be eliminated. Each State should be allowed to determine an appropriate work search test, based on the conditions of its labor market.

FUTA taxation of alien agricultural workers

As of January 1, 1995, the wages of alien agricultural workers (H2–A workers) should be subject to FUTA taxes.

Section 8. Railroad Unemployment Compensation System

The railroad unemployment compensation (RRUC) system has been in existence since 1938. Railroad workers were initially covered by the unemployment provisions of the Social Security Act of 1935. The Railroad Unemployment Insurance Act (Public Law 75–722) was passed in 1938 to provide a uniform unemployment insurance system for all railroad workers, regardless of the State in which they worked or lived. This was done largely because of administrative problems at that time in handling claims for railroad workers who earned wages in a number of different States and as a result of the railroad unions' desire that individuals throughout the industry be treated the same for purposes of unemployment compensation.

The Technical and Miscellaneous Revenue Act of 1988 (Public Law 100–647) increased the railroad unemployment and sickness daily benefit rate, indexed future benefit rates, qualifying earnings requirements and the contribution base to national wage levels, established a waiting period for benefits, and included other measures to improve the railroad unemployment insurance system's financing.

The Emergency Unemployment Compensation Act of 1991, as amended in November 1993 (Public Laws 102–164 and 103–152), providing temporary extended State unemployment benefits, also provided temporary extended benefits under the Railroad Unemployment Insurance Act.

BENEFITS AND ELIGIBILITY REQUIREMENTS

A new benefit year for unemployment and sickness benefits begins every July 1. To qualify in the benefit year beginning July 1, 1994, a worker must have base year railroad earnings of at least $2,025 in the preceding calendar year, not counting earnings over $810 per month. Under the indexing provisions of the law reflecting growth in average national wages, a worker must have base year earnings of $2,100 in calendar year 1994 not counting earnings of more than $840 per month, to qualify in the benefit year beginning July 1, 1995. If the base year was the first year of railroad service, the worker also must have worked in 5 months of that year.

No benefits are payable for the first claims for unemployment and sickness in a benefit year. This generally results in a 2-week waiting period. A claimant is normally paid for days of unemployment or sickness over 4 in 14-day registration periods.

TABLE 8–1.—RAILROAD UNEMPLOYMENT AND SICKNESS INSURANCE PROGRAM STATISTICS

							Benefit year ending in							1994 (est.)	1995 (est.)
	1970	1975	1980	1985	1986	1987	1988	1989	1990	1991	1992	1993		
Insured unemployment (percent)[1]	11	12	17	18	20	18	14	10	9	9	8	7	6.5	6.5
Coverage (thousands of qual. employees)	748	640	609	459	445	420	393	366	349	336	322	311	302	294
Unemployment: (average daily benefit):														
Current dollars	12.61	12.68	24.94	24.98	24.97	[2]24.76	[3]24.75	N/A	[4]30.16	30.85	30.97	32.86	N/A	N/A
In 1990 dollars[5]	40.30	30.13	40.10	30.18	29.42	28.37	27.22	N/A	30.16	N/A	N/A	N/A	N/A	N/A
Sickness: (average daily benefit):														
Current dollars	12.66	12.69	24.97	24.99	24.98	[2]24.71	[3]24.76	N/A	[4]30.25	30.81	30.98	32.84	N/A	N/A
In 1990 dollars[5]	40.46	30.16	40.15	30.19	29.44	28.32	27.23	N/A	30.25	N/A	N/A	N/A	N/A	N/A
Number of beneficiaries:														
Unemployment (thousands)	79.2	77.9	101.6	81.7	87.6	75.2	54.4	35.2	29.9	30.5	26.4	20.7	19.6	19.1
Sickness (thousands)	91.4	67.4	76.8	51.6	49.5	45.2	41.7	33.7	28.2	25.6	23.6	21.8	21.1	20.6
Benefit exhaustions, normal benefits:														
Unemployment (thousands)[6]	6.3	4.8	11.2	16.1	17.4	17.0	10.6	6.6	5.6	5.9	5.9	4.3	N/A	N/A
Sickness (thousands)	16.8	7.9	9.5	8.0	8.8	9.1	8.4	7.6	6.1	5.4	5.3	4.6	N/A	N/A
Amount paid:														
Unemployment (millions)[7]	35.0	37.5	112.7	125.8	140.4	118.6	85.8	60.8	57.2	60.1	55.1	49.2	46.2	49.2
Sickness (millions)	57.9	29.6	60.0	43.8	47.4	55.7	24.8	32.1	32.6	32.6	12.0	21.5	22.5	24.0
Total tax collection:														
Benefits account (millions)	122.7	109.4	173.3	223.1	213.2	192.6	186.9	181.9	192.5	165.7	134.7	66.0	22.3	4.2
Administration (millions)	8.2	7.3	12.9	15.2	14.2	12.9	12.7	13.9	17.2	17.4	20.5	14.8	17.9	17.9
Outlays:														
Benefits (millions)[6]	93.0	67.1	172.7	169.6	187.8	174.3	110.6	92.9	89.8	92.7	67.1	70.7	68.7	73.2
Administration (millions)	6.6	7.3	11.2	14.8	15.2	14.3	14.2	13.5	14.6	14.5	16.8	16.1	16.1	17.9
Account balance (millions)[8]	81.3	113.9	40.8	50.8	85.7	98.8	135.7	223.8	188.4	288.0	368.8	212.4	194.8	134.6

[1] Unemployment beneficiaries divided by qualified employees; does not include sickness insurance beneficiaries. [2] Benefit amounts for registration periods beginning on August 1 through September 17, 1986, were reduced 7.4 percent under the Gramm-Rudman-Hollings Act. [3] Benefit amounts for claims processed on or after November 20 were reduced 8.5 percent under the Gramm-Rudman-Hollings Act. [4] Benefit amounts for registration periods beginning on or after October 1, 1989, were originally reduced by 5.3 percent under the Gramm-Rudman-Hollings Act. On February 10, 1990, the final fiscal year 1990 Gramm-Rudman-Hollings sequestration rate of 1.7 percent was implemented for all days of unemployment and sickness after September 30, 1989. Refund payments were issued on February 13, 1990. Cumulative averages do not reflect these refunds. [5] Calculated using the fiscal year CPI–X1 price index. [6] Excludes supplemental extended benefits financed from general revenues. [7] Includes benefits under title V of the Emergency Unemployment Compensation Act of 1991, as amended, which has provided extended unemployment benefits, regardless of years of service. [8] Account balances do not reflect amounts due the Railroad Retirement Account. Benefit payments were restored to previous levels in late December 1987 and refunds of previously withheld amounts were made in the first week of January. Loans were repaid in full with a $180.2 million cash repayment from the Railroad Unemployment Insurance Account on June 29, 1993.

TABLE 8–2.—BENEFITS UNDER THE RAILROAD UNEMPLOYMENT INSURANCE SYSTEM

Qualifying wages:	
Base year 1992	$1,962.50
Base year 1993	$2,025.00
Base year 1994	$2,100.00
Daily benefit rate: Basic rate	60 percent of daily rate of pay.
Maximum:	
Benefit year 1993–94	$33.00
Benefit year 1994–95	$36.00
Minimum guarantee	$12.70
Maximum normal benefits:[1]	
For 14-day period:	
Benefit year 1993–94	$330
Benefit year 1994–95	$360
For benefit year:	
Duration	130 compensable days.
Amount: [1]	
Benefit year 1993–94	$4,290
Benefit year 1994–95	$4,680
Maximum extended benefits: [2]	
10–14 years' service:	
Duration	65 compensable days.
Amount:	
Benefit year 1993–94	$2,145
Benefit year 1994–95	$2,340
15 or more years' service:	
Duration	130 compensable days.
Amount:	
Benefit year 1993–94	$4,290
Benefit year 1994–95	$4,680

[1] Not to exceed the employee's taxable earnings in the base year counting earnings up to $1,014 a month for benefit year 1993–94 (base year 1992) and $1,046 a month for benefit year 1994–95 (base year 1993).

[2] Title V of the Emergency Unemployment Compensation Act of 1991, as amended in 1993, through April 30, 1994, provided extended unemployment benefits, regardless of years of service, to workers who exhausted prior benefit rights by certain dates. Claimants with less than 10 years of service are subject to base year earnings limitations.

Note.—Some net sickness benefits payments are somewhat less than the above amounts since they are subject to tier I railroad retirement taxes.

Source: Railroad Retirement Board.

The maximum daily benefit payable in the benefit year which began July 1993 is $33; and for biweekly claims, maximum benefits can total $330. The maximum daily benefit rises to $36 and maximum benefits for biweekly claims rise to $360 in the benefit year which begins July 1994. As a result of sequestration under the Balanced Budget and Emergency Deficit Control Act, unemployment and sickness benefits have been reduced periodically since 1986. In fiscal year 1990 maximum biweekly benefits were initially reduced from $310 to $293.57. The Omnibus Budget Reconciliation Act of fiscal year 1990 revised the biweekly rate to $304.73. Budget reconciliation legislation has precluded reductions since then.

The program offers "normal" benefits and two categories of "extended" benefits. The duration of benefits varies by worker. Qualified workers can receive normal benefits for up to 130 days or 26 weeks, but the total may not exceed their creditable wages in the base year. Two groups of workers may get extended benefits:

(1) Workers with at least 15 years of railroad service may get up to 130 additional days, or up to an additional 26 weeks of benefits beyond the normal 26 weeks; and

(2) Workers with at least 10 but fewer than 15 years of railroad service may receive up to 65 additional days or 13 additional weeks.

However, under the 1991 Emergency Unemployment Compensation Act providing extended State unemployment benefits, as amended in 1993, through April 30, 1994, claimants who exhaust their rail unemployment insurance benefits by certain dates may be eligible under certain conditions for temporary extended benefits payable by the Board, even though they have less than 10 years of service.

The average duration of benefits fluctuates with the unemployment rate. In the 1940 through 1993 period, it ranged from 7.4 to 19.1 weeks and averaged 12.1 weeks.

In 1946, a program of cash sickness benefits was established for railroad workers as part of the unemployment compensation system. Sickness benefits are financed out of the same employer paid payroll taxes used to finance unemployment compensation benefits. A qualified railroad worker may receive sickness benefits if he files a "statement of sickness" signed by a doctor and mailed within 7 days of the first day for which a day of sickness is claimed.

A rail worker who is unemployed due to a strike not in violation of the Railway Labor Act of 1926 can receive unemployment compensation benefits after a 14 day waiting period. Unemployment benefits cannot be paid to individuals participating in a strike that is in violation of the Railway Labor Act, and is therefore "illegal." Individuals who are unemployed due to an "illegal" strike, but who are not actually participating in the strike, are eligible for unemployment compensation benefits but are subject to the 14 day waiting period.

Total expenditures for unemployment and sickness payments were $71 million in benefit year 1992–93, which was 0.6 percent of total wages paid by the industry during the same period. This compares to a peak of 5.1 percent in 1959. It is also much lower than in benefit year 1983, a recession year, when the figure was 3.9 percent. Since the beginning of sickness benefits, unemployment benefits have comprised over two-thirds of total payments. In 1993, unemployment benefits accounted for 70 percent of the total.

Benefit payments vary directly with the insured unemployment rate, covered employment, average weekly benefit amount, and average duration of benefits. The insured unemployment rate is the percentage of workers qualified under the RRUC program who drew benefits in a particular benefit year. The railroad insured unemployment rate has been high and volatile since the beginning of the RRUC program, averaging 14 percent. Since 1946 it has ranged from a relatively low 7 percent to 30 percent in benefit year 1982–83.

Changes in covered employment have short-run and long-run effects on the RRUC program. In the short run, when layoffs cause employment to decline, the insured unemployment rate and benefits paid increase. In the long run, when employers have fewer workers to lay off, benefits decline and the program shrinks. Since the peak of 1,680,000 workers in calendar year 1945, railroad employment declined to 271,000 in 1993. Two-thirds of this decline occurred in the 21 years between 1945 and 1966. In the 27 years since then, the remaining one-third of the decline occurred. In other words, the average annual decline through 1966 was 45,000, but after 1966 it was 17,000.

TAXES

The railroad unemployment and sickness benefit programs are financed by payroll taxes on railroad employers. The employees do not pay railroad unemployment taxes. The taxable earnings base in calendar year 1994 is the first $840 of each employee's monthly earnings. The earnings base is indexed each year by a rate which is equal to approximately two-thirds of the annual rate of increase in the maximum base for railroad retirement tier 1 taxes.

Experience-based tax rates, phased in on a partial basis in 1991 and 1992, became fully effective in 1993 with a minimum of 0.65 percent and a maximum of 12 percent. The maximum rate in future years could be 12.5 percent if a maximum surcharge is in effect.

Railroad unemployment taxes are collected by the Railroad Retirement Board. Of each year's tax receipts, an amount equal to 0.65 percent of taxable payroll is set aside for administration. Excess funds allocated but not needed for administration are transferred to the Railroad Unemployment Insurance Account at the end of each fiscal year.

The Railroad Unemployment Insurance and Railroad Unemployment Insurance Administration Accounts are part of the Federal Unemployment Trust Fund. This trust fund has 53 State UC program accounts, 4 Federal accounts, and the 2 railroad accounts.

Since 1959, the railroad unemployment trust fund has been able to borrow funds from the railroad pension fund when employer taxes have not been sufficient to cover the costs of unemployment and sickness benefits. The RRUC program became depleted for the first time in 1960 after a long decline from peak reserves of nearly 18 percent of total annual wages in 1948. By 1963, it owed the retirement account $314 million, or 5.9 percent of total annual wages paid in the industry that year. The program gradually recovered during the 1960s until it had positive reserves again in 1974. The reserves were depleted again in 1976 through 1978 and loans were again required beginning in 1981.

A rapid decline in 1981 and 1982 in railroad employment resulted in substantial borrowing from the pension system which reached a peak level of over $850 million at the end of 1986. This debt was repaid in full with a $180.2 million cash repayment from the Railroad Unemployment Insurance Account on June 29, 1993. Interest on the loan during the debt period was charged at the average rate earned by U.S. Treasury securities held by the retirement account so that the retirement account did not lose any investment earnings as a result of the loan.

Financial measures to assist the Railroad Unemployment Insurance Account were included in the Railroad Retirement Solvency Act enacted August 12, 1983.

The Solvency Act raised the taxable limit on monthly earnings and the base-year qualifying amount. The waiting period for benefits during strikes was increased from 7 to 14 days. A temporary repayment tax on railroad employers began July 1, 1986, to initiate repayment of the loans made by the Railroad Retirement Account.

The 1983 legislation also mandated the establishment of a Railroad Unemployment Compensation Committee to review the unemployment and sickness benefit programs and submit a report to Congress. The Committee reviewed all aspects of the railroad unemployment insurance system, in particular repayment of the system's debt to the Railroad Retirement Account, and the viability of transferring railroad unemployment benefit payments to State programs.

The Consolidated Omnibus Budget Reconciliation Act of April 1986 (Public Law 99–272) amended the temporary unemployment insurance loan repayment tax beginning July 1, 1986, continued authority for borrowing by the Railroad Unemployment Insurance Account from the Railroad Retirement Account, and provided a contingency surtax on rail employers if further borrowing took place.

The 1988 Technical and Miscellaneous Revenue Act railroad unemployment insurance amendments were based on the recommendations of the Railroad Unemployment Compensation Committee. The 1988 amendments improved financing by indexing the tax base to average national wages and experience rating employer contributions. Repayment of the unemployment system's debt to the retirement system was assured by fixing the loan repayment tax at 4 percent of the contribution base, remaining in force at that rate until the debt was fully repaid with interest on June 29, 1993.

A contingency surtax (3.5 percent) effective in the event of further borrowing by the Railroad Unemployment Insurance Account, was eliminated in 1991. Instead, a surcharge will be added to employers' unemployment insurance taxes for a calendar year if the balance in the unemployment insurance account on the previous June 30 goes below $100 million. The surcharge rate would be 1.5, 2.5, or 3.5 percent depending on how low the balance had fallen. If a 3.5 percent surcharge goes into effect for a given year, the maximum rate for any employer would be 12.5 percent rather than 12 percent. If the account balance on the preceding June 30 is above $250 million, the excess will be refunded to the employers in the form of a rate reduction for the year through a pooled credit.

The 1988 amendments require the Board to make annual financial reports to Congress beginning July 1989 on the status of the unemployment insurance system. The reports must include any recommendations for financing changes which might be advisable, specifically with regard to rates of employer contributions.

The unemployment insurance financial report was submitted in June 1993 before the loan was repaid. It stated that experience-based contribution rates, phased in during 1991 and 1992, would keep the system solvent, even under the most pessimistic employment assumptions, that maximum benefit rates increase 42 percent, from $33 to $47, from 1992 to 2002 and that average employer contribution rates are at or near the minimum of 0.65 percent in 1993–95. The report also indicated that no new loans will be required during the 10-year projection period (fiscal years 1993–2002). The Board therefore recommended no changes to the system at that time. However, given the cash outlay subsequently applied to the repayment of the prior loans, subsequent estimates indicate that new loans in small amounts could, under pessimistic assumptions, possibly be required during part of the projection period.

The costs of the temporary extended unemployment benefits provided under the Emergency Unemployment Compensation Act were $4.2 million in fiscal year 1993 and are expected to be $1.0 million in fiscal year 1994.

Section 9. Trade Adjustment Assistance

The Trade adjustment assistance (TAA) programs were first established under the Trade Expansion Act of 1962 for the purpose of assisting in the special adjustment problems of workers and firms adversely affected by Federal policies to reduce import restrictions. As a result of limited eligibility and usage of the programs, criteria and benefits were liberalized under Title II of the Trade Act of 1974, Public Law 93–618.

The Omnibus Budget Reconciliation Act of 1981 (OBRA 81), Public Law 97–35, reformed the program for workers as proposed by the Administration. Under the program prior to October 1, 1981, income support payments were a supplement to State unemployment insurance (UI) and were paid concurrently during weeks the worker was eligible for UI. A fundamental change under the 1981 amendments made trade readjustment allowance (TRA) benefits a continuation of the UI program once UI benefits are exhausted. These and other amendments, particularly in program eligibility and benefits, were intended to reduce program cost significantly and to shift its focus from income compensation for temporary layoffs to a return to work through training and other adjustment measures for the long-term or permanently unemployed. The OBRA 81 also made relatively minor modifications in the program for firms. Most amendments became effective on October 1, 1981. Both programs were extended at that time for 1 year, to terminate on September 30, 1983.

Public Law 98–120 (H.R. 3813 as amended by the Senate), approved on October 12, 1983, extended the worker and firm TAA programs for 2 years until September 30, 1985. Sections 2671–2673 of the Deficit Reduction Act of 1984, Public Law 98–369, included three provisions (sections 3, 6, and 8 of H.R. 3391 as passed by the House on September 15, 1983) which amended the program for workers to increase the availability of worker training allowances and the level of job search and relocation benefits, and amended the program for firms to increase the availability of industrywide technical assistance.

The termination date of the worker and firm TAA programs was further extended under temporary legislation in the first session of the 99th Congress (Public Laws 99–107, 99–155, 99–181, and 99–189) until December 19, 1985. The Consolidated Omnibus Budget Reconciliation Act of 1985 (COBRA 85), Public Law 99–272, approved April 7, 1986, reauthorized the TAA programs for workers and firms for 6 years retroactively from December 19, 1985, until September 30, 1991, with amendments.

Sections 1421–1430 of Public Law 100–418, the Omnibus Trade and Competitiveness Act of 1988 (OTCA 88), enacted on August 23, 1988, made significant amendments in the worker TAA program, particularly concerning the eligibility criteria for cash benefits, funding, and administration. A training requirement as a condition for income support to encourage and enable workers to obtain early reemployment became effective under the OTCA 88 amendments as of November 21, 1988, replacing a 1986 amendment that instituted a job search requirement as a condition for receiving cash benefits. The amendments also expanded TAA coverage of workers and firms, contingent upon the imposition of an import fee to fund program costs. The OTCA 88 extended TAA program authorization for an additional 2 years until September 30, 1993.

Section 136 of the "Customs and Trade Act of 1990," Public Law 101–382, approved August 20, 1990, extended the completion and reporting period for the supplemental wage allowance demonstration projects for workers required by the 1988 amendments. No other amendments affecting the TAA programs were enacted in the 101st Congress or in the first session of the 102d Congress. Section 106 of Public Law 102–318, to extend the emergency unemployment compensation program, provided for weeks of active military duty in a reserve status (including service during Operation Desert Storm) to qualify toward the minimum number of weeks of prior employment required for TAA eligibility. No other changes were made to the program during the 102d Congress.

Section 13803 of the Omnibus Budget Reconciliation Act (OBRA 1993) of 1993, Public Law 103–66, approved August 10, 1993, reauthorized the TAA programs for workers and firms for an additional 5 years through fiscal year 1998, with assistance to terminate on September 30, 1998. Section 13803 of the OBRA 1993 also reduced the level of the "cap" on training entitlement funding from $80 million to $70 million for fiscal year 1997 only.

Sections 501 through 506 of the North American Free Trade Agreement (NAFTA) Implementation Act, Public Law 103–182, approved December 8, 1993, set forth the "NAFTA Worker Security Act", establishing the NAFTA transitional adjustment assistance program as a new subchapter D (section 250) under chapter 2 of Title II of the Trade Act of 1974.

TRADE ADJUSTMENT ASSISTANCE PROGRAM FOR WORKERS

Trade adjustment assistance for workers under sections 221 through 250 of the Trade Act of 1974, as amended, consists of trade readjustment allowances (TRA), employment services, training and additional TRA allowances while in training, and job search and relocation allowances for certified and otherwise qualified workers. The program is administered by the Employment and Training Administration (ETA) of the Department of Labor through State agencies under cooperative agreements between each State and the Secretary of Labor. ETA processes petitions and issues certifications or denials of petitions by groups of workers for eligibility to apply for TAA. The State agencies act as Federal agents in providing program information, processing applications, determining individual worker eligibility for benefits, issuing payments, and providing reemployment services and training opportunities.

Certification requirements

A two-step process is involved in the determination of whether an individual worker will receive trade adjustment assistance: (1)

certification by the Secretary of Labor of a petitioning group of workers in a particular firm as eligible to apply; and (2) approval by the State agency administering the program of the application for benefits of an individual worker covered by a certification.

The process begins by a group of three or more workers, their union, or authorized representative filing a petition with the ETA for certification of group eligibility. To certify a petitioning group of workers as eligible to apply for adjustment assistance, the Secretary must determine that three conditions are met:

 1. A significant number or proportion of the workers in the firm or subdivision of the firm have been or are threatened to be totally or partially laid off;

 2. Sales and/or production of the firm or subdivision have decreased absolutely; and

 3. Increased imports of articles like or directly competitive with articles produced by the firm or subdivision of the firm have "contributed importantly" to both the layoffs and the decline in sales and/or production.

The OTCA 88 amendments expanded the potential eligibility coverage also to include workers in any firm or subdivision of a firm that engages in exploration or drilling for oil or natural gas.

TABLE 9–1.—NUMBER OF PETITIONS INSTITUTED AND CERTIFIED AND ESTIMATED NUMBER OF WORKERS PETITIONING AND CERTIFIED FOR TRADE ADJUSTMENT ASSISTANCE FROM 1975 THROUGH 1993

Calendar year	Cases instituted		Cases certified		
	Petitions	Estimated workers	Petitions	Per-cent [1]	Estimated workers
1975	528	210,988	121	50	54,843
1976	1,014	218,544	430	46	143,579
1977	1,289	227,562	411	38	143,716
1978	1,732	171,315	854	42	164,416
1979	2,119	320,714	844	41	221,481
1980	5,347	1,027,277	935	29	585,392
1981	1,134	132,222	260	9	32,992
1982	1,030	170,155	254	20	20,004
1983	959	164,096	482	35	57,094
1984	504	43,812	337	52	15,758
1985	1,392	123,736	491	60	32,098
1986	1,774	166,077	829	39	74,017
1987	1,535	190,881	682	39	86,283
1988	1,948	180,190	658	52	70,486
1989	1,458	142,422	848	41	69,199
1990	1,466	151,724	574	40	62,813
1991	1,479	144,849	585	39	56,444
1992	1,448	120,614	721	50	48,772
1993	1,207	135,880	527	43	69,416
Total	29,363	4,043,058	10,843	37	2,008,803

[1] Estimated percent of petitioning workers certified under completed cases; figures are not precise but indicate the trend.

TABLE 9–2.—ESTIMATED NUMBER OF WORKERS CERTIFIED BY MAJOR INDUSTRIES, 1975–93

	Thousands
Total estimated number of workers certified, 1975–93	2,009
Certifications by major industries:	
Automobiles	782
Apparel	273
Steel	175
Footwear	112
Electronics	103
Oil and gas	74
Fabricated metal products	56
Textiles	39

Source: Department of Labor.

The Secretary is required to make the eligibility determination within 60 days after a petition is filed. A certification of eligibility to apply for TAA covers workers who meet the requirements and whose last total or partial separation from the firm or subdivision before applying for benefits occurred within 1 year prior to the filing of the petition.

State agencies must give written notice by mail to each worker to apply for TAA where it is believed the worker is covered by a certification of eligibility and must publish notice of each certification in newspapers of general circulation in areas where certified workers reside. State agencies must also advise each adversely affected worker, at the time that worker applies for UI, of TAA program benefits and the procedures, deadlines, and qualifying requirements for applying, advise each such worker to apply for training before or at the same time that worker applies for TRA benefits, and promptly interview each certified worker and review suitable training opportunities available.

Qualifying requirements for trade readjustment allowances

In order to receive entitlement to payment of a trade readjustment allowance for any week of unemployment, an individual must be an adversely affected worker covered by a certification, file an application with the State agency, and meet the following qualifying requirements:

1. The worker's first qualifying separation from adversely affected employment occurred within the period of the certification applicable to that worker, i.e., on or after the "impact date" in the certification (the date on which total or partial layoffs in the firm or subdivision thereof began or threatened to begin, but never more than 1 year prior to the date of the petition), within 2 years after the date the Secretary of Labor issued the certification covering the worker, and before the termination date (if any) of the certification.

2. The worker was employed during the 52-week period preceding the week of the first qualifying separation at least 26 weeks at wages of $30 or more per week in adversely affected employment with a single firm or subdivision of a firm. A week of employment includes the week in which layoff occurs and up to 7 weeks of em-

ployer-authorized vacation, sickness, injury, maternity, or military service for training, or service as a full-time union representative. Weeks of disability covered by workers' compensation and, as amended in 1992, weeks of active duty in a military reserve status may also count toward the 26-week minimum.

3. The worker was entitled to unemployment insurance, has exhausted all rights to any UI entitlement, including any extended benefits (EB) or Federal supplemental compensation (FSC) (if in existence), and does not have an unexpired waiting period for any UI.

4. The worker must not be disqualified for EB with respect to the particular week of unemployment by reason of the work acceptance and job search requirements under section 202(a)(3) of the Federal-State Extended Unemployment Compensation Act of 1970. All TRA claimants in all States are subject to the provisions of the EB "suitable work" test under that Act (i.e., must accept any offer of suitable work, actively engage in seeking work, and register for work) after the end of their regular UI benefit period as a precondition for receiving any weeks of TRA payments. The EB work test does not apply to workers enrolled or participating in a TAA-approved training program; the test does apply to workers for whom TAA-approved training is certified as not feasible or appropriate.

5. The worker must be enrolled in, or have completed following separation from adversely affected employment within the certification period, a training program approved by the Secretary of Labor in order to receive basic TAA payments, unless the Secretary has determined and submitted a written statement to the individual worker certifying that approval of training is not "feasible or appropriate" (e.g., training is not available that meets the criteria for approval, funding is not available to pay the full training costs, there is a reasonable prospect that the worker will be reemployed by the firm from which separated). No cash benefits may be paid to a worker who, without justifiable cause, has failed to begin participation or has ceased participation in an approved training program until the worker begins or resumes participation, or to a worker whose waiver of participation in training is revoked in writing by the Secretary.

Cash benefit levels and duration

A worker is entitled to TRA payments for weeks of unemployment beginning the later of (a) the first week beginning more than 60 days after the filing date of the petition that resulted in the certification under which the worker is covered (i.e., weeks following the statutory deadline for certification), or (b) the first week after the worker's first total qualifying separation.

The TRA cash benefit amount payable to a worker for a week of total unemployment is equal to, and a continuation of, the most recent weekly benefit amount of unemployment insurance payable to that worker preceding that worker's first exhaustion of UI following the worker's first total qualifying separation under the certification, reduced by any Federal training allowance and disqualifying income deductible under UI law.

The maximum amount of *basic* TRA benefits payable to a worker for the period covered by any certification is 52 times the TRA payable for a week of total unemployment minus the total amount of UI benefits to which the worker was entitled in the benefit period in which the first qualifying separation occurred (e.g., a worker receiving the normal 26 weeks of UI benefits could receive 26 weeks of basic TRA benefits thereafter; a worker receiving 39 weeks of UI regular and extended benefits could receive a maximum 13 weeks of basic TRA benefits). UI and TRA payments combined are limited to a maximum 52 weeks in all cases involving extended compensation benefits (i.e., a worker who received 52 or more weeks of unemployment benefits would not be entitled to basic TRA). TRA benefits are not payable to workers participating in on-the-job training.

The 1988 amendments essentially restored the movable 2-year eligibility period for collecting basic TRA in effect prior to the 1981 amendments (i.e., restored eligibility to the most recent rather than from the first qualifying separation). The eligibility period for collecting basic TRA is the 104-week period that immediately follows the week in which a total qualifying separation occurs. If the worker has a subsequent total qualifying separation under the same certification, the eligibility period for basic TRA moves from the prior eligibility period to 104 weeks after the week in which the subsequent total qualifying separation occurs.

A worker may receive up to 26 *additional* weeks of TRA benefits after collecting basic benefits (up to a total maximum of 78 weeks of UI and TRA benefits combined) if that worker is participating in approved training, in order to assist in completing such training. To receive the additional benefits, the worker must apply for the training program within 210 days after certification or first qualifying separation, whichever date is later. Additional benefits may be paid only during the 26-week period that follows the last week of entitlement to basic TRA, or that begins with the first week of training if the training begins after the exhaustion of basic TRA.

A worker participating in approved training continues to receive basic and additional TRA payments during breaks in such training if the break does not exceed 14 days, if the worker was participating in the training before the beginning of the break, resumes participation in the training after the break ends, and the break is provided for in the training schedule. Weeks when TRA is not payable because of this break provision count against the eligibility periods for both basic and additional TRA.

TABLE 9–3.—TOTAL OUTLAYS FOR TRADE READJUSTMENT ALLOWANCES, NUMBER OF RECIPIENTS, AVERAGE WEEKLY PAYMENTS AND DURATION, FISCAL YEARS 1976 THROUGH 1993

Fiscal year	Total outlays (millions)	Total number of recipients (thousands)	Average weekly payment per recipient
1975 (4th quarter)	$71	47	$58
1976 [1]	79	62	47
1977	148	111	57
1978	257	155	68
1979	256	132	70
1980	1,622	532	126
1981	1,440	281	140
1982	103	30	119
1983	37	30	120
1984	35	16	139
1985	40	20	133
1986	118	40	144
1987	208	55	155
1988	186	47	165
1989	125	24	175
1990	93	19	164
1991	116	25	169
1992 [2]	43	9	163
1993 (preliminary)	51	10	157

[1] Fiscal year 1976 is the first full year of experience under the program as amended by the Trade Act of 1974.

[2] The 1992 figures for TRA recipients and outlays are abnormally low because of Extended Unemployment Compensation (EUC) payments that were made to eligible workers in lieu of TRA payments. Average duration figures for 1992 are not available.

Note.—The above figures relate only to trade readjustment allowances; administrative expenses and outlays for employment services, training, and job search and relocation allowances are not included.

Source: Department of Labor.

Training and other employment services, job search and relocation allowances

Training and other employment services and job search and relocation allowances are available through State agencies to certified workers whether or not they have exhausted UI benefits and become eligible for TRA payments.

Employment services consist of counseling, vocational testing, job search and placement, and other supportive services, provided for under any other Federal law.

Training, preferably on-the-job, shall be approved for a worker if the following six conditions are met:

(1) There is no suitable employment available;

(2) The worker would benefit from appropriate training;

(3) There is a reasonable expectation of employment following training completion;

(4) Approved training is reasonably available from government agencies or private sources;

(5) The worker is qualified to undertake and complete such training; and

(6) Such training is suitable for the worker and available at a reasonable cost.

If training is approved, the worker is entitled to payment of the costs from the Secretary directly or through a voucher system, unless they have been paid or are reimbursable under another Federal law. On-the-job training costs are payable only if such training is not at the expense of currently employed workers. Remedial education is a separate and distinct approvable training program.

Approved training is an entitlement in any case where the six criteria for approval are reasonably met, up to an $80 million statutory ceiling ($70 million in fiscal year 1997) on annual fiscal year training costs (including job search and relocation allowances and subsistence payments) payable from TAA funds. Up to this limit, workers are entitled to have the costs of approved training paid on their behalf. If the Secretary foresees that the $80 million ceiling will be exceeded in any fiscal year, the Secretary can decide how remaining TAA funds shall be apportioned among the States for the balance of that year.

Costs of approved TAA training may be paid solely from TAA funds, solely from other Federal or State programs or private funds, or from a mix of TAA and public or private funds, except if the worker in the case of a nongovernmental program would be required to reimburse any portion of the costs from TAA funds. Duplicate payment of training costs is prohibited, and workers are not entitled to payment of training costs from TAA funds to the extent these costs are paid or shared from other sources. Training may still be approved if the fiscal year TAA funding entitlement limit is reached if the training costs are paid from outside sources.

Supplemental assistance is available to defray reasonable transportation and subsistence expenses for separate maintenance when training is not within the worker's commuting distance, equal to the lesser of actual per diem expenses or 50 percent of the prevailing Federal per diem rate for subsistence and prevailing mileage rates under Federal regulations for travel expenses.

Job search allowances are available to certified workers who cannot obtain suitable employment within their commuting area, are totally laid off, and who apply within 1 year after certification or last total layoff, whichever is later, or within 6 months after concluding training. The allowance for reimbursement is equal to 90 percent of necessary job search expenses, based on the same increased supplemental assistance rates described above, up to a maximum amount of $800. The Secretary of Labor is required to reimburse workers for necessary expenses incurred to participate in an approved job search program.

TABLE 9–4.—TRAINING, JOB SEARCH, AND RELOCATION ALLOWANCES: TOTAL NUMBER OF WORKERS AND OUTLAYS, FISCAL YEARS 1976 THROUGH 1993

Fiscal year	Total number			Total outlays (millions)
	Entered training	Job searches	Relocations	
1975 (4th quarter)	463	158	44	....
1976	823	23	26	$2.7
1977	4,213	277	191	4.0
1978	8,337	1,072	631	12.8
1979	4,456	1,181	855	13.5
1980	1 9,475	931	629	6.0
1981	1 20,366	1,491	2,011	2.4
1982	5,844	697	662	19.4
1983	11,299	696	3,269	36.0
1984	6,821	799	2,220	17.0
1985	7,424	916	1,692	30.2
1986	12,229	1,276	2,292	28.6
1987	22,888	1,709	1,537	49.9
1988	9,538	1,156	1,347	54.4
1989	17,042	863	989	62.6
1990	18,057	565	1,245	57.6
1991	20,093	525	759	64.9
1992	18,582	594	751	70.2
1993	19,454	796	1,961	80.0
Total	210,471	14,881	22,782	617.2

1 Of total workers entering training, 5,640 (59 percent) in 1980 and 18,940 (94 percent) in 1981 self-financed their training costs.

Source: Department of Labor.

Relocation allowances are available to certified workers totally laid off at time of relocation who have been able to obtain an offer of or actual suitable employment only outside their commuting area, who apply within 14 months after certification or last total layoff, whichever is later, or within 6 months after concluding training, and whose relocation takes place within 6 months after application or completion of training. The allowance is equal to 90 percent of reasonable and necessary expenses for transporting the worker, family, and household effects, based on the same increased supplemental assistance rates described above, plus a lump sum payment of three times the worker's average weekly wage up to a maximum amount of $800.

Funding

Federal funds, as an appropriated entitlement from general revenues under the Federal Unemployment Benefit Account (FUBA) under the ETA in the Department of Labor, cover the portion of the worker's total entitlement represented by the continuation of UI benefit levels in the form of TRA payments, as well as payments for training and job search and relocation allowances, and State related administrative expenses. Funds made available under grants to States defray expenses of employment services and other administrative expenses. For fiscal year 1994, $189.9 million is appropriated for trade readjustment allowances, training, and job search and relocation allowances, and related administrative expenses.

The States are reimbursed from Treasury general revenues for benefit payments and other costs incurred under the program. A penalty under section 239 of the Trade Act of 1974 provides for reduction by 15 percent of the credits for State unemployment taxes which employers are allowed against their liability for Federal unemployment taxes if a State has not entered into, or has not fulfilled its commitments, under a cooperative agreement.

NAFTA WORKER SECURITY ACT

Subchapter D of chapter 2 (section 250) of title II of the Trade Act of 1974 establishes a NAFTA transitional adjustment assistance program for workers who may be adversely impacted by the NAFTA. Import-impacted workers may also petition for assistance under TAA, but cannot obtain benefits under both programs. Assistance under subchapter D shall terminate after the earlier of September 30, 1998, or the date on which legislation establishing a program providing all dislocated workers with comprehensive assistance substantially similar to the assistance provided under subchapter D becomes effective.

A group of workers (including workers in any agricultural firm or subdivision of an agricultural firm) shall be certified as eligible to apply for adjustment assistance under subchapter D if the Secretary determines that a significant number or proportion of the workers in the firm or subdivision of the firm have become or are threatened to become totally or partially separated, and either:

1. Sales and/or production of the firm or subdivision have decreased absolutely, imports from Mexico or Canada of articles like or directly competitive with articles produced by such firm or subdivision have increased, and the increase in imports contributed importantly to the workers' separation or threat of separation and to the decline in the sales or production of the firm or subdivision; or

2. There has been a shift in production by the workers' firm or subdivision to Mexico or Canada of articles like or directly competitive with articles produced by the firm or subdivision.

The Administration intends to supplement the NAFTA program through administrative action to provide assistance to workers in secondary firms that supply or assemble products directly affected by the NAFTA, as well as to family farmers and farm workers adversely affected by the NAFTA who do not meet the eligibility requirements under the program.

A group of workers or their union or other duly authorized representative may file a petition for certification of eligibility to apply for adjustment assistance under subchapter D with the Governor of the State in which the worker's firm or subdivision is located. Upon receipt of the petition, the Governor shall notify the Secretary of Labor. Within 10 days thereafter, the Governor shall make a preliminary finding as to whether the petition meets the certification criteria and transmit the petition, together with a statement of the finding and reasons therefor, to the Secretary for action. If the preliminary finding is affirmative, the Governor shall ensure that rapid response and basic readjustment services authorized under other Federal law are made available to the workers.

Within 30 days after receiving the petition, the Secretary must determine whether the petition meets the certification criteria. Upon an affirmative determination, the Secretary shall issue to workers covered by the petition a certification of eligibility to apply for comprehensive assistance. Upon denial of certification, the Secretary shall review the petition to determine if the workers meet the requirements of the TAA program for certification.

Certified workers under the NAFTA program receive employment services, training, trade readjustment allowances, and job search and relocation allowances in the same manner and to the same extent as workers covered under a TAA certification, with the following exceptions: (1) the total amount of payments for training costs for any fiscal year shall not exceed $30 million; (2) with respect to TRA benefits, the authority of the Secretary of Labor to waive the training requirement does not apply with respect to payments under subchapter D; and (3) to receive TRA benefits, the worker must also be enrolled in a training program approved by the Secretary by the later of the last day of the 16th week of the worker's initial UI benefit period or the last day of the 6th week after the week in which the Secretary issues a certification covering the worker. In extenuating circumstances, the Secretary may extend the time for enrollment for not more than 30 days.

The NAFTA program took effect on January 1, 1994, the date the NAFTA entered into force for the United States. No worker can be certified as eligible to receive assistance under subchapter D whose last total or partial separation occurred before January 1, except for those workers whose last layoff occurred after December 8 (the date of enactment of the NAFTA Implementation Act) and before January 1 who would otherwise be eligible to receive assistance under subchapter D.

TRADE ADJUSTMENT ASSISTANCE PROGRAM FOR FIRMS

Sections 251–264 of the Trade Act of 1974, as amended, contain the procedures, eligibility requirements, benefits and their terms and conditions, and administrative provisions of the trade adjustment assistance program for firms adversely impacted by increased import competition. The program is administered within the Department of Commerce by the Economic Development Administration. Amendments in 1986 under the COBRA 86 eliminated financial assistance (direct loan or loan guarantee) benefits, increased government participation in technical assistance, and expanded the criteria for firm certification.

Program benefits consist exclusively of technical assistance for petitioning firms which qualify under a two-step procedure: (1) certification by the Secretary of Commerce that the petitioning firm is eligible to apply, and (2) approval by the Secretary of Commerce of the application by a certified firm for benefits, including the firm's proposal for economic adjustment.

To certify a firm as eligible to apply for adjustment assistance, the Secretary must determine that three conditions are met:

1. A significant number or proportion of the workers in the firm have been, or are threatened to be, totally or partially laid off;

2. Sales and/or production of the firm have decreased absolutely, or sales and/or production that accounted for at least 25 percent of total production or sales of the firm during the 12 months preceding the most recent 12-month period for which data are available have decreased absolutely; and

3. Increased imports of articles like or directly competitive with articles produced by the firm have "contributed importantly" to both the layoffs and the decline in sales and/or production.

Potential eligibility coverage includes firms that engage in exploration or drilling for oil or natural gas.

A certified firm may file an application with the Secretary of Commerce for benefits at any time within 2 years after the date of the certification of eligibility. The application must include a proposal by the firm for its economic adjustment. The Secretary may furnish technical assistance to the firm in preparing its petition for certification and/or in developing a viable economic adjustment proposal.

The Secretary approves the firm's application for assistance only if he determines that its adjustment proposal (1) is reasonably calculated to make a material contribution to the economic adjustment of the firm; (2) gives adequate consideration to the interests of the workers in the firm; and (3) demonstrates that the firm will make all reasonable efforts to use its own resources for economic development.

Benefits

Technical assistance may be given to implement the firm's economic adjustment proposal in addition to, or in lieu of, precertification assistance or assistance in developing the proposal. It may be furnished through existing government agencies or through private individuals, firms, and institutions (including private consulting services), or by grants to intermediary organizations, including 12 regional Trade Adjustment Assistance Centers (TAACs). The Federal Government may bear the full cost of technical assistance to a firm in preparing its petition for certification. However, the Federal share cannot exceed 75 percent of the cost of assistance furnished through private individuals, firms, or institutions for developing or implementing an economic adjustment proposal. Grants may be made to intermediate organizations to defray up to 100 percent of their administrative expenses in providing technical assistance.

The Secretary of Commerce also may provide technical assistance of up to $10 million annually per industry to establish industrywide programs for new product or process development, export development, or other uses consistent with adjustment assistance objectives. The assistance may be furnished through existing agencies, private individuals, firms, universities, and institutions, and by grants, contracts, or cooperative agreements to associations, unions, or other nonprofit organizations of industries in which a substantial number of firms or workers have been certified.

Funding

Funds to cover all costs of the program are subject to annual appropriations to the Economic Development Administration of the Department of Commerce from general revenues. For fiscal year 1994, a total of $10.0 million has been appropriated to the program.

Section 10. Aid to Families With Dependent Children and Related Programs (Title IV-A)

BACKGROUND AND ELIGIBILITY

Aid to dependent children was established by the Social Security Act of 1935 as a cash grant program to enable States to aid needy children without fathers. Renamed Aid to Families with Dependent Children (AFDC), the program provides cash welfare payments for (1) needy children who have been deprived of parental support or care because their father or mother is absent from the home continuously, is incapacitated, is deceased or is unemployed, and (2) certain others in the household of such child. Currently all 50 States, the District of Columbia, Guam, Puerto Rico, and the Virgin Islands operate an AFDC program. Although 1988 legislation provided that American Samoa could participate in the AFDC program, as of April 1994 it had not chosen to do so.

States define "need," set their own benefit levels, establish (within Federal limitations) income and resource limits, and administer the program or supervise its administration. Federal funds currently pay from 50 to about 80 percent of the AFDC benefit costs in a State (55 percent on average) and 50 percent of administrative costs.

Table 10–1 summarizes the trends of several key elements in the AFDC program from 1970 to 1993. Between 1970 and 1993, the number of recipients has increased 91 percent, from 7.4 million in 1970 to 14.1 million in 1993. The number of families has increased over the same time period 163 percent, from 1.9 million to 5.0 million. AFDC benefit expenditures have increased 44 percent, after adjusting for inflation, from $15.5 billion in 1970 to $22.3 billion in 1993. Administrative costs remained almost the same in both 1970 and 1993, after adjusting for inflation, at nearly $3.0 billion. AFDC administrative costs were 19 percent of AFDC benefit payments in 1970 and 13 percent in 1993. After accounting for inflation, the average monthly AFDC benefit per family was $676 in 1970 and $373 in 1993, a 45 percent reduction.

(324)

TABLE 10-1.—SUMMARY OF KEY AFDC PROGRAM ELEMENTS

[In dollars, except for caseload numbers]

	1970	1975	1980	1985	1988	1990	1991	1992	1993
Total AFDC									
Benefit expenditures (millions)	4,082	8,153	11,540	14,580	16,663	18,539	20,356	22,240	22,286
1993[1]	15,496	22,586	20,700	19,627	20,437	20,671	21,606	22,911	22,286
Federal share (millions)	2,187	4,625	6,448	7,817	9,125	10,149	11,165	12,252	12,270
1993[1]	8,303	12,813	11,566	10,523	11,192	11,316	11,850	12,621	12,270
Administrative cost (millions)	758	1,082	1,479	1,779	2,353	2,661	2,673	2,764	2,956
1993[1]	2,878	2,997	2,653	2,395	2,886	2,967	2,837	2,847	2,956
Federal share (millions)	572	552	750	890	1,194	1,358	1,373	1,422	1,518
1993[1]	2,171	1,529	1,345	1,198	1,464	1,514	1,457	1,465	1,518
Average monthly numbers (thousands):									
Families	1,909	3,269	3,574	3,692	3,748	3,974	4,375	4,769	4,981
Recipients	7,429	11,067	10,597	10,813	10,920	11,460	12,595	13,625	14,144
Children	5,494	7,821	7,220	7,165	7,326	7,755	8,515	9,225	9,539
Average family size	4.0	3.2	3.0	3.0	3.0	2.9	2.9	2.9	2.9
Average montly benefit per family	178	208	269	329	370	389	388	389	373
1993[1]	676	576	483	443	454	434	412	401	373
AFDC-Basic and AFDC-UP									
Benefit expenditures (millions), 1993:[1]									
Total AFDC	15,496	22,586	20,700	19,627	20,437	20,671	21,606	22,911	22,286
AFDC-Basic	14,620	21,583	19,457	17,532	18,695	19,021	19,667	20,728	19,990
AFDC-UP	877	1,003	1,243	2,095	1,742	1,650	1,939	2,183	2,298
Average monthly families (thousands):									
Total AFDC	1,909	3,269	3,574	3,692	3,748	3,974	4,375	4,769	4,981
AFDC-Basic	1,831	3,168	3,433	3,431	3,538	3,770	4,107	4,447	4,622
AFDC-UP	78	101	141	261	210	204	268	322	359
Average monthly benefit per family—1993:[1]									
Total AFDC	676	576	483	443	454	434	412	401	373
AFDC-Basic	665	568	472	426	440	420	399	388	360
AFDC-UP	937	827	735	669	691	674	603	565	533

[1] Adjusted for inflation using CPI–U (fiscal year).

Note: AFDC benefit expenditures have not been reduced by child support enforcement collections and do not include foster care payments; AFDC enrollment figures do not include foster care children.

Source: Department of Health and Human Services, Administration for Children and Families and Congressional Research Service.

Regardless of the method used to express the need standard, the Social Security Act requires that the standard be uniformly applied within the State or locality to all families in similar circumstances. While participating States must comply with the terms of the Federal legislation, the AFDC program is voluntary, and States traditionally have been at liberty to pay as little or as much in benefits as they choose. In addition to State variations in AFDC eligibility and benefit levels, the benefit levels vary primarily by family size and sometimes by shelter costs.

Eligibility for AFDC ends on a child's 18th birthday, or at State option upon a child's 19th birthday if the child is a full-time student in a secondary or technical school and may reasonably be expected to complete the program before he or she reaches age 19.

While optional prior to October 1, 1990, States that operate AFDC programs are now required to offer AFDC to children in two-parent families who are needy because of the unemployment of one of their parents (AFDC–UP). Eligibility for AFDC–UP is limited to those families in which the principal wage earner is unemployed but has a history of work. States that did not have an unemployed parent program as of September 26, 1988 may limit benefits under the AFDC–UP program to as few as 6 months in any 13-month period.

The Family Support Act of 1988 (Public Law 100–485) substantially revised the education and training requirements of the AFDC program. As of October 1, 1990, States are required to have a job opportunities and basic skills training (JOBS) program. The new program is designed to help needy families with children avoid long-term welfare receipt. The JOBS program replaces the work incentive (WIN) and WIN demonstration programs, and incorporates other work requirements of previous law. In addition, the JOBS program must include an educational component. States are required to enroll virtually all able-bodied persons whose youngest child is at least age 3, provided State resources are available.

Families receiving AFDC are automatically eligible for Medicaid. The Family Support Act also requires that States provide transitional Medicaid benefits for those who lose AFDC eligibility as a result of increased hours of, or increased income from, employment or as a result of the loss of earnings disregards.

The Family Support Act requires that States guarantee child care if it is decided that child care is necessary for an individual's employment or participation in education or training activities (including participation in the JOBS program) approved by the State, and requires that transitional child care be provided for families who lose AFDC eligibility as a result of increased hours of, or increased income from, employment or as a result of the loss of earnings disregards.

The AFDC statute also includes entitlement funds to the States to provide child care to families who are not receiving AFDC who need such care in order to work and would otherwise be at risk of becoming eligible for AFDC.

Finally, Federal law requires AFDC mothers to assign their child support rights to the State and to cooperate with welfare officials in establishing the paternity of a child and in obtaining support payments from the father.

TREATMENT OF INCOME AND RESOURCES

Federal AFDC law requires that all income received by an AFDC recipient or applicant be counted against the AFDC grant except that income explicitly excluded by definition or deduction. Moreover, AFDC law requires that certain persons be considered part of the AFDC assistance unit and that part of the income of certain other persons be counted in determining the AFDC eligibility status and benefit amount.

In 1981, Congress required that a portion of the income of a stepparent be counted in determining AFDC eligibility and benefit amounts. However, in a few States (7 as of October 1, 1990), State law requires that all stepparents assume the legal responsibility of a natural or adoptive parent. In those States all of the stepparent's income must be counted in determining the AFDC eligibility status and/or benefit amount of the children and spouse.

In 1984, a standard definition of the AFDC assistance unit was established for the first time. Under this requirement, the parent(s) of a dependent child and any dependent brothers or sisters who are in the home are to be included in the AFDC unit, with eligibility and benefits based on the income and circumstances of this family unit. SSI recipients, stepsiblings, and children receiving foster care maintenance payments or adoption assistance are excluded from this requirement. In addition, if a minor who is living in the same home as her parents applies for aid as the parent of a needy child, a portion of the income of the minor's parents is to be counted as available to the filing unit.

The law also requires that income from a nonrecurring earned or unearned lump sum payment that exceeds the monthly AFDC need standard must be taken into account in determining AFDC eligibility and/or benefit amount. Lump sum payments in excess of the State's need standard—for the given family size—renders a family ineligible for AFDC for a period of time equal to the lump sum payment divided by the State's monthly need standard.

Unearned income

States are required by Federal law and/or regulations to disregard certain income in determining the eligibility and benefits of families applying for or receiving AFDC. Unearned income not counted by the AFDC program includes the following: the first $50 of current monthly child support payments received by the family, certain Department of Education grants and loans to undergraduate students for educational purposes, loans and grants, such as scholarships, obtained and used under conditions that preclude their use for current living costs, the value of Department of Agriculture donated foods, benefits received from Child Nutrition programs or nutrition programs for the elderly, payments to VISTA workers, some payments to certain Indian tribes, any amounts paid by a State welfare agency from State-only funds to meet the needs of AFDC children, if the payments are made under a statutorily-established State program that has been continuously in effect since before January 1, 1979, payments for supporting services or reimbursement of out-of-pocket expenses made to volunteers serving as foster grandparents, senior health aides, or senior companions, and Agent Orange settlement payments.

Earned income

States are required by Federal law to disregard certain earned income when determining the amount of benefits to which a recipient family is entitled. States must disregard all the earned income of each dependent child receiving AFDC who is a full-time student or a part-time student who is not a full-time employee and is attending a school, college, university, or vocational training course. States may, for a period of 6 months, disregard all or part of the earned income of a dependent child who is a full-time student and who is applying for AFDC, if and only if the earnings of such child are excluded for such month in determining the family's total income pursuant to the 185 percent gross income eligibility test. States also have the option of disregarding all or any part of income derived from Job Training Partnership Act (JTPA) programs by a dependent child applying for or receiving AFDC (there is a 6-month limit on the disregard of earned income, and no limit on unearned income).

With respect to self-employment, "earned income" is defined by Federal regulations as the "total profit from a business enterprise, farming, etc., resulting from a comparison of the gross receipts with the "business expenses," i.e., expenses directly related to producing the goods or services and without which the goods or services could not be produced. However, under AFDC regulations, items such as depreciation, personal business and entertainment expenses, personal transportation, purchase of capital equipment and payments on the principal of loans for capital assets or durable goods are not considered business expenses.

Before OBRA of 1981, in order to provide a financial incentive for recipients to seek and maintain employment, Federal law required the deduction of an initial $30 in monthly earnings plus one-third of remaining earnings, plus work expenses (any expenses, including child care costs, reasonably attributable to the earning of income). When making an initial determination of eligibility, however, only work expenses were disregarded.

Amendments in OBRA of 1981 changed the order in which the disregards were applied, limited the disregard for work expenses to $75 per month, capped the child care disregard at $160 per month per child, and specified that the HHS Secretary could lower these sums for part-time work. The $30 plus one-third disregard was limited to a period of 4 consecutive months; recipients who left AFDC and then returned could not again qualify for this disregard for 12 months. States were prohibited from paying AFDC to any family with a *gross* income above 150 percent of the State's standard of need and were required to assume that working AFDC recipients received a monthly earned income tax credit (EITC), if they appeared eligible for it and regardless of when or if the credit was actually available. Under prior law, the EITC was counted only when received; most AFDC recipients did not receive the EITC on a monthly basis. These changes substantially reduced the amount of earnings a recipient could have and remain eligible for an AFDC payment.

In 1984, Congress further revised these disregards. The gross income limit was increased to 185 percent of the State standard of need, the work expense disregard of $75 per month was applied to both full- and part-time workers, and the $30 disregard—originally a part of $30 and one-third—was extended for an additional 8 months beyond the 4-month limit on the one-third deduction. The 1984 legislation also returned to prior law policy with respect to the earned income tax credit: it was to be counted only when actually received.

The Family Support Act of 1988 revised the treatment of earned income effective October 1, 1989. The work expense disregard is $90 per month, the maximum child care expense allowance is $175 per month per child ($200 for children under age 2), and the child care disregard is now calculated after other disregard provisions have been applied. Furthermore, States are now required to disregard the earned income tax credit in determining eligibility for and benefits under the AFDC program.

Table 10–2 illustrates the impact of the 1981, 1984 and 1988 changes on a mother with two children working full-time at a low wage. Two AFDC benefit standards are illustrated: $680 represents the AFDC payment standard for a family of three in a high benefit State and $366 is the payment standard for a three-person family in the median State (January 1994 data).

Several States use a method of paying AFDC that allows working families to retain a greater portion of their AFDC grant as earnings increase. This method of payment, commonly referred to as "fill-the-gap," provides greater financial incentives for families to work than the standard payment method. Under the standard payment method, the AFDC grant is determined by subtracting countable income (e.g., earnings less disregards) from the State's payment standard. (States' AFDC payment standard may be less than the State's AFDC "need standard"—the amount a State recognizes as essential for a family to meet basic and special needs.) Some States having AFDC payment standards below their need standard allow families to fill part or all of the gap between the payment and need standard with earnings, before reducing the AFDC grant. Other States set a maximum payment below the payment standard, allowing families to only "fill-the-gap" up to the payment standard. Many States having AFDC payment standards below their need standard do not use a fill-the-gap policy—they begin to reduce the AFDC grant dollar for dollar, for earnings in excess of the standard earnings disregards. In January 1994, ten States were using some form of "fill-the-gap": Mississippi, Tennessee, Kentucky, North Carolina, Georgia, Utah, South Dakota, Colorado, Wyoming, and Maine. Working mothers in these States have higher net income at equivalent earnings than mothers living in States with similar AFDC payment levels that do not use a "fill-the-gap" payment method.[1]

---

[1] This information on "fill-the-gap" payment was taken from an upcoming report: Library of Congress, Congressional Research Service, Work Incentives and Disincentives in the Welfare System. Gabe, Tom and Gene Falk.

TABLE 10–2.—CALCULATION OF MONTHLY AFDC BENEFITS FOR A WORKER WITH LOW EARNINGS UNDER PRE-OBRA, OBRA, AND CURRENT LAW

	Pre-OBRA (1979)	OBRA (1981)		DEFRA (1984)			Current law (FSA) (1988)		
		First 4 months	After 4 months	First 4 months	After 4 months	After 12 months	First 4 months	After 4 months	After 12 months
Income:									
Gross earnings	581	581	581	581	581	581	581	581	581
EITC	....	+32	+32	....	....	....	....	....	....
Gross income	581	613	613	581	581	581	581	581	581
Disregards:									
Initial disregards [1]	−30	−105	−75	−105	−105	−75	−120	−120	−90
One-third of rest	−184	(2)	(2)	(2)	(2)	(2)	−154	(2)	(2)
Child care	−100	−100	−100	−100	−100	−100	−100	−100	−100
One-third of rest	(2)	−136	(2)	−125	(2)	(2)	(2)	(2)	(2)
Other expenses	[3]−70	(2)	(2)	(2)	(2)	(2)	(2)	(2)	(2)
Total disregards	384	341	175	330	205	175	374	220	190
Net countable income	197	272	438	251	376	406	207	361	391
AFDC benefits:									
$680 payment standard	483	408	242	429	304	274	473	319	289
$366 payment standard	169	94	0	115	0	0	159	45	0

[1] Pre-OBRA: $30 disregard. OBRA: Standard work expense deduction of $75 plus $30 in first 4 months. DEFRA: Standard work expense deduction of $75 plus $30 disregard in first 12 months. FSA: Standard work expense deduction of $90 plus $30 disregard in first 12 months.

[2] Not applicable.

[3] Itemized work expenses including payroll deductions and transportation.

[4] To receive an AFDC check, the benefit amount must equal at least $10.

Note.—EITC is only counted in the years that it is shown.

Resources

Allowable resources are limited, by Public Law 97–35, to $1,000 (or such lower amount as the State may determine) equity value (i.e., market value minus any encumbrances) per family, excluding the home and one automobile if the family member's ownership interest does not exceed a limit chosen by the Secretary of Health and Human Services. In addition, States must disregard from countable resources burial plots and funeral agreements for members of the assistance unit. Also, for a limited time, States must exclude real property the family is making a "good faith" effort to sell, but only if the family agrees to repay benefits. HHS regulations set $1,500 or a lower level set by the State as the equity value limit for the automobile and permit States to exclude from countable resources "basic items essential to day to day living," such as clothing and furniture. Previous regulations permitted States to adopt a counted resource limit as high as $2,000 per family member, but allowed States to consider the home and auto as counted resources.

Neither law nor Federal regulations mention capital equipment as being exempt from the resource requirement. Notwithstanding this, families with a self-employed caretaker relative are potentially eligible for AFDC benefits. The Characteristics of State Plans indicates that about half of the States specifically exclude from the resource limitation farm machinery, livestock, and tools and equipment essential to employment, livelihood, or income.

MONTHLY REPORTING AND RETROSPECTIVE BUDGETING

AFDC eligibility and benefits are determined monthly. Public Law 97–35 required States to determine *eligibility* on the basis of the family's circumstances in the current month. *Payment amounts* were to be determined "retrospectively"—on the basis of the family's countable income and resources in the preceding month (or, at the discretion of the Secretary of Health and Human Services, the second preceding month). In addition, States were to require recipients to provide monthly reports on income, family composition, and resources. However, the Secretary could waive this requirement if the State demonstrated that it would be cost-beneficial to do so. The only categories of recipients that could not be exempted were those with earned income or a recent work history.

In 1984, Public Law 98–369 revised these monthly reporting and retrospective budgeting requirements. Retrospective budgeting was mandatory only for cases which file a monthly report. Monthly reporting was required for cases with earned income or a recent work history and whenever cost effective.

The Omnibus Budget Reconciliation Act of 1990 gave States the option of specifying which categories of AFDC families, if any, have to file monthly reports. Further, States now have the option to choose to apply retrospective budgeting to any one or more of the categories to whom the reporting requirement applies.

AFDC BENEFITS UNDER THE UNEMPLOYED PARENTS PROGRAM

The original Social Security Act permitted States to give AFDC only to needy children in one-parent homes, unless the second parent was incapacitated. Then, as now, most AFDC children lived in fatherless homes. For the first 25 years of the program, if a father lost his job and his family became needy, State AFDC programs were forbidden to help the family so long as the father lived at home. In 1961, in an antirecession measure, the law was changed so that families with jobless fathers at home could qualify for AFDC. Since May of that year States were permitted to give AFDC to needy children of unemployed parents.

Effective October 1, 1990, all States that operate AFDC programs are required to provide AFDC to two-parent families who are needy because of the unemployment of the principal wage earner. (The requirement did not take effect until October 1, 1992, for American Samoa, Puerto Rico, Guam, and the Virgin Islands.) The requirement is repealed September 30, 1998.

States that had an AFDC–UP program as of September 26, 1988, are required to continue operating the program without any time limit on eligibility. Other States have the option to impose such a time limit. In exercising this option, a State may not deny AFDC to a family unless the family has received AFDC under the unemployed parents program in at least 6 of the preceding 12 months. As of July 1992, the following States have time limits on eligibility: Arizona, Arkansas, Colorado, Florida, Georgia, Idaho, Louisiana, Nevada, South Dakota, Texas, Utah, Virginia, and Wyoming.

Like other AFDC families, families receiving AFDC cash assistance in the unemployed parents program are automatically eligible for Medicaid. The Family Support Act of 1988 requires States electing time-limited benefits to provide Medicaid to all members of the family without any time limitation.

At the inception of the AFDC–UP program, States defined "unemployment," and some included in the program families in which the principal wage earner worked as much as 35 hours a week. Since 1971, Federal regulations have specified that an AFDC parent must work fewer than 100 hours in a month to be classified as unemployed, unless hours are of a temporary nature for intermittent work and the individual met the 100-hour rule in the two preceding months and is expected to meet it the following month. The Family Support Act of 1988 authorizes eight State or local demonstrations to test a definition of unemployment that is easier to meet than the present 100-hour rule, including (if any State or locality so requests) at least one demonstration that tests the elimination of the 100-hour rule or any other Federal durational standard. Projects are currently underway in California, Wisconsin, and Utah to demonstrate and evaluate alternative definitions of unemployment.

Attachment to the labor force is one condition of eligibility for AFDC–UP. The principal earner must: (1) have 6 or more quarters of work in any 13-calendar-quarter period ending within 1 year prior to application for assistance; or (2) have received or been eligible to receive unemployment compensation within 1 year prior to application for assistance. A quarter of work is a quarter in which an individual earns at least $50 or in which the individual participated in the JOBS program. At State option, attendance in elementary or secondary school, vocational or technical training, or participation in JTPA, may be substituted for up to 4 of the 6 required quarters of work. Participation in the WIN program and CWEP prior to October 1990 also count toward the quarter of work requirement.

INTERACTION BETWEEN AFDC AND OTHER PROGRAMS

Medicaid

States must provide Medicaid to families receiving cash assistance under AFDC. Several recent acts require that States extend this categorically needy Medicaid coverage, at regular Federal matching rates, to other groups. The most important of these groups include (1) pregnant women, and children up to age 6, with family incomes up to 133 percent of the poverty level; (2) children born on or after October 1, 1983, with family incomes below the Federal poverty level (this provision is phased in to cover all children up to age 19 by the year 2002); and (3) certain persons whose family income and resources are below the AFDC standards but who fail to qualify for AFDC for other reasons, such as family structure (these include first-time pregnant women). At their option, States may provide coverage to pregnant women and infants with incomes at or below 185 percent of the Federal poverty level.

When families lose AFDC eligibility, categorical Medicaid eligibility also frequently ends, except under those circumstances outlined above, or if the family qualifies for transitional Medicaid benefits established under Public Law 100–485, the Family Support Act of 1988, which took effect April 1, 1990. As a result of this act, States are required to extend Medicaid coverage for 12 months to families who leave cash assistance due to earnings. During the first 6 months of coverage, the States must provide each family the same Medicaid coverage that the family had while receiving AFDC. States are not permitted to impose premiums for this coverage. States do have a "Medicaid wrap-around" option, under which they may use Medicaid funds to pay a family's expenses for premiums, deductibles and coinsurance for any health care coverage offered by the employer of the caretaker relative. The employer coverage would then be treated by the Medicaid program as a third party liability.

During the second 6 months of coverage, the States have a number of options. First, they may limit the scope of the Medicaid coverage to acute care benefits, dropping nursing home coverage and other nonacute benefits. Second, States may impose a monthly premium on families with incomes, less necessary child care expenses, in excess of 100 percent of the Federal poverty level. The monthly premium on these families could not exceed 3 percent of gross income. Premiums would be determined on the basis of quarterly reports from families on earnings and child care costs. Third, States have the option of offering families the choice of (1) basic Medicaid coverage (either the same as offered to cash assistance beneficiaries or the more limited acute care package) or (2) one or more types of alternative coverage. These alternative coverages could include enrollment in an employer group health plan, a State employee plan, a State health plan for the uninsured, or a health maintenance organization. Families would always have a choice of staying with their basic Medicaid coverage, although they could not elect both the basic Medicaid and one of the alternative coverages. With respect to the basic Medicaid coverage, States would have the same "Medicaid wrap-around" option as during the first 6-month period. In general, transitional coverage would terminate if a family no longer had a child, failed to report earnings on a quarterly basis, failed to pay any required premium, or fradulently obtained cash assistance benefits.

Effective October 1, 1990, States are required to extend cash assistance benefits to two-parent families where the principal earner is unemployed (AFDC–UP). States that have an AFDC–UP program as of September 26, 1988, are required to continue operating such programs without any time limit on eligibility. Other States will have the option to limit cash assistance benefits to as few as 6 months in any 13-month period. States are required to provide full Medicaid coverage to all members of these families even in months when cash assistance benefits are not paid because of a State-established time limit.

In the mid-1980s, States sought to cover pregnant women and children under the Medicaid program. However, they did not want to raise AFDC benefit levels in order to cover them. Congress thus passed legislation giving States the option of covering pregnant women and children and linking their eligibility to the poverty guidelines rather than receipt of AFDC. To prevent States from reducing AFDC benefits (because the targeted populations could be covered irrespective of the AFDC program), Public Law 100–360 prohibited the Secretary of Health and Human Services from approving a State's Medicaid plan if the State reduced its AFDC payment levels below those that were in effect on May 1, 1988.

Food stamps

Most AFDC families are also eligible for and participate in the food stamp program, which provides an important in-kind supplement to the cash assistance paid under AFDC. Although food stamp benefits are not counted in determining AFDC eligibility, the food stamp program does consider AFDC payments to be countable income and reduces the food stamp benefit by $0.30 for each dollar of countable cash income. This interaction between AFDC and the food stamp program has important financial implications for a State which desires to increase the income of its AFDC recipients. Because food stamps are reduced by $0.30 for each additional $1 of AFDC income, the State must expend $1.43 to obtain an effective $1 increase in AFDC recipients' total income. For a State with a 50 percent matching rate, the State must expend $0.72 of State-only funds to actually obtain a $1 increase in recipient income. This would be the typical situation for an AFDC recipient with no earnings.

Table 10–3 illustrates the interaction of various programs for a mother with two children at various earning levels. The example assumes the family lives in Pennsylvania. Calculations are made after the mother has been working for 4 months and lost the disregard of one-third of "residual" earnings (those remaining after subtraction of a $120 standard allowance).

TABLE 10–3.—EARNINGS AND BENEFITS FOR A MOTHER WITH TWO CHILDREN WITH DAYCARE EXPENSES—AFTER 4 MONTHS ON JOB (JANUARY 1994)—(PENNSYLVANIA)

| Earnings | EITC | AFDC [1] | Food stamps [2] | Medicaid | Taxes | | | Work expenses [4] | "Disposable" income |
					Social Security	Federal income [3]	State income		
0	0	$5,052	$2,496	Yes	0	0	0	0	[5] $7,548
$2,000	$600	4,892	2,184	Yes	$153	0	0	$600	[5] 8,923
$4,000	1,200	3,292	2,304	Yes	306	0	0	1,200	[5] 9,290
$5,000	1,500	2,492	2,364	Yes	383	0	0	1,500	[5] 9,473
$6,000	1,800	1,692	2,424	Yes	459	0	0	1,800	[5] 9,657
$7,000	2,100	892	2,484	Yes	536	0	0	2,100	[5] 9,840
$8,000	2,400	0	2,568	Yes [6]	612	0	0	2,400	[5] 9,956
$9,000	2,528	0	2,388	Yes [7]	689	0	$4	2,700	[5] 10,523
$10,000	2,528	0	2,208	No [7]	765	0	34	3,000	10,937
$15,000	1,820	0	1,308	No [8]	1,148	0	174	4,200	12,606
$20,000	936	0	0	No	1,530	$58	314	5,200	13,834
$30,000	0	0	0	No	2,295	1,718	594	5,400	19,993
$50,000	0	0	0	No	3,825	5,569	1,154	5,400	34,052

[1] Assumes these deductions: $120 monthly standard allowance (which would drop to $90 after 1 year on the job) and child care costs equal to 20 percent of earnings, up to maximum of $350 for 2 children.

[2] Assumes these deductions: 20 percent of earnings, $131 monthly standard deduction and child care costs equal to 20 percent of wages, up to maximum of $320 for 2 children.

[3] Head of household rates in effect for 1994. The dependent care tax credit reduces tax liability at earnings of $15,000 and above.

[4] Assumed to equal 10 percent of earnings up to maximum of $100 monthly, plus child care costs equal to 20 percent of earnings up to a maximum of $350 for 2 children.

[5] In addition, the benefits from Medicaid could be added, but are not, since the extent to which they increase disposable income is uncertain.

[6] Family would qualify for Medicaid because the mother, by law, would be deemed still an AFDC recipient, even though no AFDC would be paid; her calculated benefit would be below the minimum amount ($10 monthly) payable.

[7] Family would qualify for Medicaid for 12 months after leaving AFDC under the 1988 Family Support Act. State must offer Medicaid to all children up to age 6 whose family income is not above 133 percent of the Federal poverty guideline (ceiling of $16,385 for a family of 3 in 1994) and to children over age 6 born after September 1, 1983 (up to age 10⅓ in January 1994), whose family income is below the poverty guideline ($12,320 for a family of 3).

[8] After losing her Medicaid transitional benefits, to regain eligibility, mother must spend down on medical expenses to State's medically needy income limit ($5,604 in January 1994).

Source: Congressional Research Service.

CHART 10–1. DISPOSABLE INCOME AT VARIOUS WAGE LEVELS FOR A FAMILY OF THREE WITH CHILD CARE EXPENSES, PENNSYLVANIA, JANUARY 1994

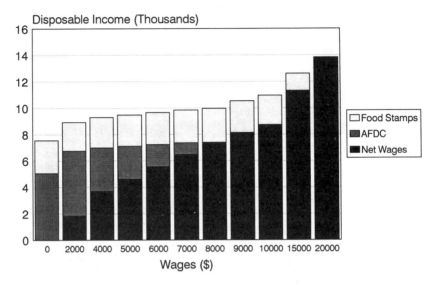

[1] Net wages equal earnings plus EITC minus taxes and work expenses.

Source: Committee on Ways and Means.

Child support enforcement

Federal law requires AFDC families (and applicants), as a condition of eligibility for aid, to assign their support rights to the State, to cooperate with the State in establishing the paternity of a child born outside of marriage, and to cooperate with the State in obtaining support payments. Families receiving AFDC benefits automatically qualify (free of charge) for CSE services. Their cases are referred to the CSE agency. The provision requiring the AFDC applicant or recipient to assign to the State her rights to support covers both current support and any arrears which have accrued, and lasts as long as the family receives AFDC. When the family no longer receives AFDC, the mother or caretaker relative regains her right to collect support, but if there are arrears, the State may claim those arrears up to the amount paid out as AFDC benefits.

Child support payments made on behalf of a child receiving AFDC are supposed to be paid to the CSE agency rather than directly to the family. If the child support collection is insufficient to disqualify the family from receiving AFDC payments, the family receives its full monthly AFDC grant plus (pursuant to the 1984 Deficit Reduction Act) the first $50 of the child support payment made in the child's behalf for that month. In several States where the need standard exceeds the maximum payment, additional amounts of child support are disregarded. The remainder of that monthly child support payment is distributed to reimburse the State and Federal Governments in proportion to their assistance to the family. If the family's income, including the child support payment, is sufficient to make the family ineligible for AFDC payments, the family's AFDC benefits are ended, and future child support payments are paid directly from the noncustodial parent to the family. (The Federal share of child support collections paid on behalf of AFDC children is used first to pay incentives to States on their AFDC and non-AFDC collections. The remainder is used to offset Federal AFDC benefit costs. Neither Federal law nor regulations stipulate the use of the States share of AFDC child support collections.)

As noted above, some States are required to provide monthly supplemental payments to AFDC recipients who have less disposable income now than they would have had in July 1975 because child support is paid to the CSE agency instead of directly to the family. States required to pay supplemental payment are often referred to as "fill-the-gap" States. These States pay less assistance than their full AFDC need standard, and allow recipients to use child support income to make up all or part of the difference between the payment made by the State and the State's need standard.

Section 402(a)(28) of the Social Security Act requires States that had a fill-the-gap policy in 1975 and currently have such a policy, to add to the AFDC benefit all or part of the child support collection (the amount which would have caused no reduction in the AFDC benefit if it had been paid directly to the family).

Information obtained from the Office of Child Support Enforcement (June 1990) indicates that seven States that had fill-the-gap policies in July 1975 also have them now and thus must follow the benefit calculation rules of section 402(a)(28) when taking account of child support collections for AFDC families. They are: Georgia, Maine, Mississippi, South Carolina, Tennessee, Virginia, and Wyoming. Another 13 jurisdictions which had fill-the-gap policies in July 1975, no longer have them.

SSI and Social Security

In AFDC, Social Security benefits are treated as unearned income and thus AFDC benefits are reduced by $1 for each $1 of OASDI benefits. SSI benefits received by a potential member of an AFDC family are treated differently. This member (both a child or an adult receiving SSI benefits) is not regarded as a part of the AFDC unit. Thus his needs are not taken into account in determining the AFDC benefit level. At the same time, the income and resources of the SSI recipient are also ignored in determining the AFDC benefit.

JOB OPPORTUNITIES AND BASIC SKILLS (JOBS) TRAINING PROGRAM AND SUPPORTIVE SERVICES

The Family Support Act of 1988 established a new employment, education and training program for recipients of AFDC. This new program, called the Job Opportunities and Basic Skills (JOBS) training program, replaces the work incentive (WIN) program and other provisions of prior law.

Purpose and administration

The purpose of the JOBS program is to assure that needy families with children obtain the education, training and employment that will help them avoid long-term welfare dependence. Each State is required to have a JOBS program, under a State plan approved by the Secretary of the Department of Health and Human Services (HHS). States were required to implement the program no later than October 1, 1990. No later than October 1, 1992, the program must be available in every subdivision of the State where it is feasible to operate the program. Table 10–4 provides information on JOBS programs in the States, based on JOBS State plans as of January 1994. As the first column of the table shows, all 50 States, the District of Columbia, and the territories (Guam, Puerto Rico and the Virgin Islands) met the implementation date requirement for JOBS, and many implemented the program early. The table also shows that, as of January 1994, all of the jurisdictions were implementing the program statewide.

The JOBS program is administered at the Federal level by the Assistant Secretary for Children and Families in HHS, and at the State level by the State welfare agency. The State welfare agency may offer services and activities directly, or through arrangements or contracts with Job Training Partnership Act (JTPA) administrative entities, State and local educational agencies and with other public agencies or private organizations (including community-based organizations).

Assessment, employability plan, case management, and orientation

The State must make an initial assessment of the education, child care and other supportive service needs as well as the skills, prior work experience, and employability of each JOBS participant, and, on the basis of the assessment, develop an employability plan for the participant. The State agency may require the participant to enter into an agreement with the State that specifies the participant's obligations under the program, and the activities and services to be provided by the State. Table 10–4 shows that 8 States chose to require such an agreement (January 1994 data).

The State agency may assign a case manager to each participant and the participant's family. The case manager must be responsible for assisting the family to obtain needed services to ensure effective participation in the JOBS program. Table 10–4 shows that only 2 States—Iowa and Oklahoma—chose not to assign a case manager.

The State agency is required to provide certain information about the JOBS program and supportive services to applicants and recipients. For example, the agency must inform applicants and recipients of AFDC of the opportunities for which they are eligible under the JOBS program, the obligation of the State agency, and the rights, responsibilities and obligations of participants. The agency must provide detailed information about day care services and must inform applicants and recipients of all other supportive services, including transitional health care benefits (see separate section on supportive services).

Services and activities

A range of services and activities must be offered by each State under the JOBS program; however, States are not required to operate the JOBS program uniformly in all parts of the State. The services and activities a State must offer include: (1) education activities, including high school or equivalent education, basic and remedial education to achieve a basic literacy level, and education for individuals with limited English proficiency; (2) job skills training; (3) job readiness activities; (4) job development and job placement; and (5) supportive services (see separate section on supportive services).

States are required to offer two of the following four activities: (1) group and individual job search; (2) on-the-job training; (3) work supplementation programs; and (4) community work experience (CWEP) programs or any other work experience program approved by the Secretary. In addition to these activities, States may also offer postsecondary education to JOBS participants. Table 10–4 shows which of these activities the individual States are offering, as of January 1994.

When an individual age 20 or over who does not have a high school diploma (or equivalent) is required to participate in the JOBS program, the State agency must include education services as a component unless (1) the individual demonstrates a basic literacy level, or (2) the employability plan identifies a long-term employment goal that does not require a high school diploma.

Following is a more detailed discussion of the Federal requirements for job search, CWEP, and work supplementation programs.

Job search.—States may require AFDC applicants and recipients to participate in a job search program beginning at the time of application. States may require up to 8 weeks of job search for applicants, and may, in addition, require up to 8 weeks of job search for AFDC recipients each year. This means that in the first year, up to 16 weeks of job search may be required, with 8 weeks per year thereafter. Additional job search activities may not be required by the State of an individual unless they are in combination with some other education, training or employment activity which is designed to improve the individual's prospects for employment. In no event may a State require an individual to participate in more than 3 weeks of job search before the State conducts an employability assessment for that individual. Finally, job search cannot be treated for any purpose as an activity under the JOBS program if an individual has participated in job search for 4 out of the preceding 12 months.

Community work experience.—The purpose of a CWEP program is to provide experience and training for individuals not otherwise able to obtain employment. CWEP programs must be designed to improve the employability of participants through actual work experience and training and to enable individuals employed under CWEP programs to move into regular employment. CWEP programs must be limited to projects which serve a useful, public purpose in fields such as health, social service, environmental protection, education, urban and rural development and redevelopment, welfare, recreation, public facilities, public safety and day care.

A State electing to operate a CWEP program must ensure that the maximum number of hours that any individual may be required to work under the CWEP program is no greater than the number of hours derived by dividing the total AFDC benefit by the Federal minimum wage (or, if greater, the State minimum wage). Any AFDC benefit amount for which the State receives reimbursement through child support collection cannot be taken into account in determining the maximum number of hours that individuals may be required to work.

After an individual has been assigned to a CWEP position for 9 months, the individual cannot be required to continue in that assignment unless the maximum number of hours of work is no greater than the cash benefit (excluding child support) divided by the rate of pay for individuals employed in the same or similar occupations by the same employer at the same site.

At the conclusion of each CWEP assignment, but, in any event, after each 6 months of participation in CWEP, the State agency must provide a reassessment, and revision, as appropriate, of the individual's employability plan.

Work supplementation.—Under a work supplementation program, a State reserves the amount that would have been payable to an AFDC family and uses the amount instead to provide and subsidize a job for the family. Recipients may be placed in jobs offered by private as well as nonprofit employers. The work supplementation is an alternative to an AFDC payment. Under JOBS, States may make work supplementation either mandatory or voluntary, and States are required to provide Medicaid to work supplementation participants.

States operating a work supplementation program may adjust the level of their AFDC standard of need in order to carry out the program, and need standards may vary from one area of the State to another. Need standards may also vary among recipient categories, to the extent that the State determines the variation to be appropriate on the basis of the ability of the recipient to participate in the work supplementation program. States are able to make further adjustments to amounts paid to different categories of AFDC recipients participating in work supplementation in order to offset increases in benefits from non-AFDC means-tested programs.

States are permitted to reduce or eliminate the amount of earned income disregards for families participating in a work supplementation program, and are permitted to offer the $30 plus one-third earned income disregard for up to 9 months for participants.

Federal funding under the program is limited for each participant to the aggregate of 9 months worth of the maximum AFDC grant (unreduced by earned income disregards or changes to the need standard) the participant family otherwise would have received were it not participating in the work supplementation program and had no income (or less if the person participates for fewer than 9 months).

Participation requirements

To the extent resources are available, a State must require nonexempt AFDC recipients to participate in the JOBS program. Exempt applicants and recipients may participate on a voluntary basis. Exempt recipients would be those who are: (1) ill, incapacitated, or of advanced age; (2) needed in the home because of the illness or incapacity of another family member (who need not be a member of the AFDC unit); (3) the parent or other relative of a child under age 3 who is personally providing care for the child (or, if provided in the State plan, any age that is less than 3 but not less than 1); (4) employed 30 or more hours a week; (5) a child under age 16 or attending, full time, an elementary, secondary or vocational school; (6) a woman who is in at least the second trimester of pregnancy; or (7) residing in an area where the program is not available. Table 10–3 shows that most States exempt recipients with a child under age 3 who are providing care for the child.

The 1988 law includes certain limitations on participation. The parent of a child under age 6 (but older than the age for an exemption) who is personally providing care for the child may be required to participate only if child care is guaranteed and required participation is limited to no more than 20 hours per week. In the case of an AFDC–UP family, the exemption relating to age of child may apply to only one parent, except that the State may require both parents to participate if child care is guaranteed.

There are certain special requirements under JOBS related to education. To the extent the JOBS program is available and State resources permit, a State must require a custodial parent under age 20 who has not completed high school (or the equivalent), including a parent who is not otherwise required to participate in JOBS solely because of the exclusion relating to providing care for a young child, to participate in an educational activity. Even though such a parent is providing care for a child under 6 years of age, the State agency may require the parent to participate in the educational activity on a full-time basis. Alternative work or training activities may be provided if the parent fails to make progress in an educational activity, or if an educational assessment determines that participation in an educational activity is inappropriate. Participation in alternative activities is limited to 20 hours per week.

If an individual is attending school or a course of vocational training, not less than half time, at the time he or she would otherwise begin to participate in the JOBS program, and making satisfactory progress, the attendance may meet the participation requirement for the individual, but the costs of the school or training are not eligible for Federal reimbursement.

Certain minimum participation standards are established for fiscal years 1990 through 1995 for the AFDC caseload. States face a reduced Federal match if those participation standards are not met. In fiscal year 1990, at least 7 percent of the nonexempt caseload in each State must participate in the JOBS program in any month. The minimum participation rates in subsequent years are 7 percent in fiscal year 1991, 11 percent in fiscal years 1992–1993, 15 percent in fiscal year 1994, and 20 percent in fiscal year 1995.

At least one parent in each AFDC–UP family must participate at least 16 hours a week in a work activity, but, with respect to CWEP, not more hours than the minimum wage equivalent based on the welfare payment less the portion of the payment reimbursed to the State by child support. Participation must be in work supplementation, community work experience or other work experience program, on-the-job training, or a State-designed work program approved by the Secretary. The percentage of AFDC–UP families required to meet this work requirement is 40 percent in fiscal year 1994, 50 percent in fiscal year 1995, 60 percent in fiscal year 1996, and 75 percent in fiscal year 1997 and fiscal year 1998 (calculated so that, on average, these percentages of the caseload would be participating in each month of the year). A State may substitute participation in an educational program in the case of a parent under age 25 who has not completed high school.

Targeting of JOBS funds

As described in detail later, Federal matching for JOBS program costs is available as a capped entitlement. The JOBS program includes incentives for States to target funds toward certain populations. States face a reduced Federal match unless 55 percent of JOBS funds is spent on the following populations: (1) families in which the custodial parent is under age 24 and has not completed high school or has little or no work experience in the preceding year; (2) families in which the youngest child is within 2 years of being ineligible for assistance because of age; (3) families who have received assistance for 36 or more months during the preceding 60-month period; and (4) applicants who have received AFDC for any 36 of the 60 months immediately preceding application. Volunteers must be given first consideration within target groups.

Funding of JOBS and supportive services

Federal matching for JOBS program costs is available as a capped entitlement limited to $600 million in fiscal year 1989, $800 million in fiscal year 1990, $1 billion in fiscal year 1991, 1992 and 1993, $1.1 billion in fiscal year 1994, $1.3 billion in fiscal year 1995, and $1.0 billion a year thereafter. The Federal match is 90 percent for expenditures up to the amount allotted to the States for the WIN program in fiscal year 1987. Of additional amounts, the Federal match is at the Medicaid rate, with a minimum Federal match of 60 percent, for nonadministrative costs and for personnel costs for full-time staff working on the JOBS program. The match for other administrative costs is 50 percent. The Federal match for JOBS is reduced to 50 percent unless (1) 55 percent of funds are spent on certain target populations, and (2) the States meet participation rate requirements. The entitlement cap for JOBS is allocated as follows: States receive an amount equal to their WIN allotment for fiscal year 1987 ($126 million for all States) and the remainder is allocated on the basis of each State's relative number of adult recipients of AFDC. Federal program funds may not be used to supplant non-Federal funds for existing services and activities.

Child care during participation in JOBS and for employment is reimbursed as a separate, open-ended entitlement at the Medicaid matching rate. Transportation and other work-related expenses are reimbursed at a rate of 50 percent and are included among those expenditures subject to the JOBS entitlement cap.

Table 10–5 provides information on Federal allocations to the States for the JOBS program for fiscal years 1991 through 1993, along with information on the amount of these funds States have expended and obligated. The table also includes information on federally reimbursed expenditures for child care. According to HHS, total Federal and State expenditures for the JOBS program (not including child care) equaled $1.006 billion for fiscal year 1992.

Supportive and transitional services

State agencies must guarantee child care for a recipient if the care is necessary for the individual to work. In addition, the State must guarantee child care for education and training activities, including participation in the JOBS program, if the State approves the activity and determines that the individual is participating satisfactorily. The State agency must also guarantee child care to the extent the care is necessary for an individual's employment in any case where a family has ceased to receive AFDC assistance as a result of increased hours of, or increased income from, employment or as a result of the loss of earnings disregards. Transitional child care is limited to a period of 12 months after the last month for which the family actually received AFDC assistance. (AFDC child care assistance programs are described in more detail in section 12.)

The State must provide payment or reimbursement for necessary transportation and other work-related expenses, including other work-related supportive services, that the State determines are necessary to enable an individual to participate in JOBS. Federal matching is 50 percent subject to the overall JOBS funding cap (see section on Federal and State expenditures for JOBS). There is no Federal limit on the amount of reimbursement with respect to an individual.

TABLE 10–4.—SUMMARY OF JOBS PROGRAMS FROM STATE PLANS: JANUARY 1994 [1]

State	Name of program	Optional components [2]	Exemption from participation if child under age— [3]	Allow postsecondary education? Any limits?	Assign case manager?	Require agency participant contract?
Alabama	JOBS	OJT, alt. work exp., JS ..		Yes; 2 year limit	Yes	No
Alaska	JOBS	OJT, alt. work exp., JS, other ed. & training.		Yes; 30 consecutive months limit.	Yes	No
Arizona	JOBS	OJT, CWEP, JS	2	Yes; 2 year limit	Yes	No
Arkansas	Project Success	Alt. work exp., JS	1	Yes; 4 year limit	Yes	No
California	GAIN	OJT, work supp., CWEP, JS.		Yes; 2 year limit	Yes	Yes
Colorado	New Directions	OJT, work supp., CWEP, JS.	1	Yes; 24 month limit	Yes	No
Connecticut	JOBS	OJT, JS	2	Yes; 2 years; 3 years for certified programs.	Yes	No
Delaware	First Step	OJT, CWEP, JS		Yes	Yes	No
District of Columbia	ARC	OJT, alt. work exp., JS		Yes; 2 year limit	Yes	No
Florida	Project Independence	OJT, work supp., CWEP, alt. work exp., JS.		Yes; 4 year limit	Yes	No
Georgia	PEACH	OJT, CWEP, alt. work exp., JS.		Yes; 28 month limit	Yes	No
Guam	JOBS	OJT, CWEP, JS		Yes	Yes	No
Hawaii	JOBS	OJT, CWEP, alt. work exp., alt. education, JS, other ed. & training.		Yes	Yes	No
Idaho	JOBS	OJT, alt. work exp., JS, other ed. & training.		Yes; 4 year limit	Yes	No

State	Program	Education/training activities		Postsecondary education		
Illinois	Project Chance	OJT, work supp., CWEP, alt. work exp., JS, other ed. & training.		Yes; no limits	Yes	No
Indiana	IMPACT: JOBS	OJT, CWEP, JS		Yes	Yes	No
Iowa	Promise JOBS	OJT, CWEP, alt. work exp., JS, other training.		Yes; 30 month limit for 2 year degree program; 40 month limit for 3 or 4 year programs.	No	No
Kansas	Kan Work in 23 counties; minimal JOBS in balance of State.	OJT, CWEP, JS, other training.		Yes; up to BA/BS	Yes	No
Kentucky	JOBS	OJT, CWEP, alt. work exp., JS.		Yes; limited to 6 semesters for 2 and 3 year programs; 8 semesters for 4 year programs.	Yes	No
Louisiana	Project Independence	OJT, CWEP, JS	1	Yes; 4 year limit	Yes	Yes
Maine	ASPIRE/JOBS	OJT, JS, other ed. & training.		Yes; limited to 6 semesters for AA degree, 12 semesters for BA degree.	Yes	Yes
Maryland	Project Independence	OJT, alt. work exp., JS, work supp., other ed. & training.		Yes	Yes	No
Massachusetts	Mass JOBS	OJT, work supp., JS		Yes; limited to 3 years for 2-year degree, voc-tech programs; 6 years for 4-year programs.	Yes	No

TABLE 10-4.—SUMMARY OF JOBS PROGRAMS FROM STATE PLANS: JANUARY 1994 [1]—Continued

State	Name of program	Optional components [2]	Exemption from participation if child under age—[3]	Allow postsecondary education? Any limits?	Assign case manager?	Require agency participant contract?
Michigan	MOST	OJT, work supp, CWEP, JS.	1	No	Yes	No
Minnesota	Project STRIDE	OJT, work supp, CWEP alt. work exp., JS.		Yes	Yes	No
Mississippi	JOBS	OJT, alt. work exp., JS, other training.		Yes; 4 year limit, 3 year vocational.	Yes	No
Missouri	FUTURES	OJT, CWEP, JS, other ed. & training.		Yes	Yes	No
Montana	JOBS	OJT, work supp., JS, CWEP, alt. work exp.		Yes	Yes	Yes
Nebraska	JOBS	OJT, CWEP, alt. work exp., JS.	1	Yes	Yes	No
Nevada	JOBS	OJT, CWEP, JS		No	Yes	No
New Hampshire	JOBS	OJT, CWEP, JS		Yes	Yes	No
New Jersey	REACH	OJT, work supp, CWEP, JS, other ed. & training.	2	Yes	Yes	No
New Mexico	Project Forward	OJT, CWEP, alt. work exp., JS, other ed. & training.		Yes	Yes	No
New York	JOBS	OJT, work supp., CWEP, JS, other ed. & training.		Yes, 2 year limit	Yes	No
North Carolina	JOBS	OJT, CWEP, JS		Yes	Yes	No
North Dakota	JOBS	OJT, CWEP, JS		Yes	Yes	No

State	Program					
Ohio	JOBS	OJT, work supp., CWEP, alt. work exp., JS.		Yes; 2 year limit	Yes	No
Oklahoma	Education, Training and Employment.	OJT, work supp., alt. work exp., JS, other ed. & training.	1	Yes; 5 year limit	No	No
Oregon	JOBS	OJT, work supp., CWEP, alt. work exp., JS, other training.	1	No	Yes	No
Pennsylvania	New Directions	OJT, CWEP, alt. work exp., JS, other ed. & training.		Yes	Yes	No
Puerto Rico	PASOS	OJT, alt. work exp., work supp., JS, other ed. & training.		Yes	Yes	No
Rhode Island	Pathways to Independence.	Work supp., OJT, JS		Yes; 24 month limit	Yes	No
South Carolina	Work Support Program	OJT, alt. work exp., JS, other ed. & training.		Yes; 4 year limit	Yes	No
South Dakota	FIND	OJT CWEP, JS	1	Yes	Yes	No
Tennessee	JOBS/WORK	OJT, alt. work exp., JS ..		Yes; 4 year limit	Yes	No
Texas	JOBS	OJT, alt. work exp., JS ..		Yes; 2 year limit	Yes	No
Utah	JOBS	OJT, alt. work exp. (WEAT), JS.		Yes; with limits	Yes	Yes
Vermont	Reach Up	OJT, work supp., CWEP, JS.		Yes; 3 year limit for AA certificate, 5 years for BA degree.	Yes	No
Virgin Islands	JOBS/HOPE	OJT, CWEP, work supp., JS.	2	Yes; with limits	Yes	Yes
Virginia	JOBS	OJT, work supp., alt. work exp., JS, other ed. & training.		Yes	Yes	No

TABLE 10–4.—SUMMARY OF JOBS PROGRAMS FROM STATE PLANS: JANUARY 1994 [1]—Continued

State	Name of program	Optional components [2]	Exemption from participation if child under age— [3]	Allow postsecondary education? Any limits?	Assign case manager?	Require agency participant contract?
Washington	JOBS/FIP	OJT, alt. work exp., CWEP, work supp., JS.		Yes; with limits	Yes	No
West Virginia	JOBS	CWEP, OJT, JS		Yes; 2 year limit	Yes	No
Wisconsin	JOBS	CWEP, OJT, work supp., JS, alt. work exp., other training.	2	Yes; 2 year limit	Yes	Yes
Wyoming	Wyoming Opportunities for Work (WOW) Program.	OJT, alt. work exp, JS		Yes; 4 year limit for AA & vocational; 6 year limit for BA.	Yes	Yes

[1] Information based on State JOBS Plan, filed for the biennium beginning October 1, 1992.
[2] All States include a Job Search component.
[3] Unless otherwise noted, State follows basic statutory approach and exempts the parent of a child under age 3.

Note.—Optional components can include Job Search, Alternative Work Experience, On the Job Training (OJT), Community Work Experience Program (CWEP), Work Supplementation, Other Education, and other activities.

Source: ACF/OFA/Division of JOBS Program of Department of Health and Human Services.

TABLE 10–5.—FEDERAL ALLOCATIONS AND EXPENDITURES FOR THE JOBS PROGRAM

[By fiscal year; in millions of dollars]

States	Jobs—total authorization 1993 [1]	Indians set-aside 1993 [2]	Awarded to States 1993 [3]	Total obligated 1993 [5]	Total obligated 1992 [5]	Total obligated 1991 [5]	Total expended 1993 [4]	Title IV-A child care 1993	Title IV-A child care 1992
Alabama	9.4	....	8.8	9.3	6.2	4.3	9.0	9.9	5.4
Alaska	2.8	0.9	1.8	1.8	1.7	1.4	1.8	1.6	1.4
American Samoa	0.1	....	....					....	....
Arizona	11.7	1.2	5.7	5.8	4.0	3.0	5.6	8.6	6.1
Arkansas	5.0	....	5.0	5.0	5.3	5.5	4.3	1.8	1.6
California	157.2	0.4	96.8	96.8	94.0	108.3	85.2	19.4	18.0
Colorado	10.5	(6)	6.7	6.7	5.9	5.3	6.7	5.3	4.0
Connecticut	12.1	....	6.1	6.1	7.4	9.2	6.1	7.4	6.4
Delaware	2.1	....	2.0	2.1	1.7	1.4	1.6	2.7	2.0
District of Columbia	4.7	....	4.7	4.7	3.6	3.2	4.7	3.1	3.1
Florida	38.5	....	15.9	15.9	14.4	13.4	15.4	19.9	16.6
Georgia	25.9	....	15.8	10.3	10.3	8.0	10.3	25.2	16.8
Guam	0.4	....	0.2	0.2	0.2	0.2	0.2	....	....
Hawaii	4.1	....	4.1	4.1	5.0	1.7	4.1	0.2	0.2
Idaho	2.4	(6)	2.3	2.3	2.3	2.3	2.3	1.1	1.0
Illinois	49.1	....	25.9	25.9	20.5	19.2	20.8	12.3	7.2
Indiana	14.8	....	8.1	8.1	5.7	3.9	8.1	6.3	3.4
Iowa	8.4	....	5.8	5.9	5.8	5.5	5.9	2.5	1.8
Kansas	6.5	(6)	6.4	6.4	5.7	4.5	6.4	6.9	5.2
Kentucky	17.6	....	14.8	13.7	11.5	8.3	13.2	11.0	8.7
Louisiana	16.5	....	16.5	16.5	15.4	7.9	16.5	9.0	6.6
Maine	5.8	(6)	3.7	3.7	3.4	3.6	3.7	0.9	0.7
Maryland	16.7	....	14.1	14.1	16.8	14.1	11.4	15.0	10.9
Massachusetts	24.4	....	20.5	20.5	20.6	21.5	19.5	27.0	22.1
Michigan	55.4	0.1	35.2	35.2	28.7	21.1	35.2	22.1	15.5
Minnesota	15.8	0.9	11.7	11.7	11.5	9.5	11.5	13.9	11.3
Mississippi	10.8	(6)	10.8	10.8	9.4	1.5	3.2	3.4	2.4
Missouri	18.9	....	9.8	9.8	6.3	3.1	9.8	13.3	7.8
Montana	2.9	0.4	2.5	2.5	2.5	1.8	2.5	1.8	2.1
Nebraska	3.5	(6)	2.7	2.7	3.1	2.2	2.7	8.1	6.5
Nevada	2.3	(6)	1.2	1.2	1.0	0.7	1.2	1.0	0.8
New Hampshire	2.3	....	2.3	2.3	2.0	1.6	2.9	2.4	2.2
New Jersey	27.0	....	27.0	21.0	24.9	25.7	21.0	9.0	8.0
New Mexico	6.7	0.7	1.6	1.6	1.2	1.2	1.6	3.9	2.1
New York	85.3	(6)	85.2	85.2	85.8	52.4	58.6	56.1	46.7
North Carolina	22.4	(6)	17.7	17.7	14.9	8.0	17.7	38.0	23.6
North Dakota	1.7	0.4	1.2	1.3	1.2	1.2	0.9	1.7	1.9
Ohio	58.7	....	44.6	58.6	49.0	44.2	50.8	36.1	19.3
Oklahoma	9.3	0.1	6.9	6.7	6.3	5.6	6.7	16.5	13.7
Oregon	11.4	(6)	11.4	11.4	11.2	10.3	11.4	8.9	7.8
Pennsylvania	44.9	....	34.5	34.7	31.2	29.1	22.7	25.0	15.8
Puerto Rico	13.1	....	9.5	9.6	7.1	1.7	9.4	....	....
Rhode Island	4.8	....	4.2	4.8	4.2	3.6	4.4	3.6	3.2
South Carolina	8.8	....	5.0	5.4	4.6	3.8	4.7	3.9	2.2
South Dakota	1.7	0.5	1.2	1.3	1.3	1.0	0.9	1.2	1.1
Tennessee	18.4	....	5.0	7.8	7.2	2.6	5.6	20.0	13.2
Texas	48.2	....	37.2	37.2	33.6	23.2	33.9	33.5	31.2
Utah	4.5	(6)	4.5	4.5	4.0	3.7	4.1	8.8	7.7
Vermont	3.2	....	2.9	2.9	2.6	2.0	2.9	2.0	1.7
Virgin Islands	0.3	....	0.3	0.3	0.3	0.3	0.3	....	....
Virginia	13.6	....	9.1	9.1	7.2	6.0	9.1	10.5	8.4
Washington	24.4	0.5	19.9	23.9	20.1	12.0	16.7	23.2	17.0
West Virginia	10.7	....	9.8	9.8	8.6	4.8	9.8	4.7	3.2
Wisconsin	20.7	0.3	20.4	20.4	21.6	23.4	20.4	10.7	10.2
Wyoming	1.6	(6)	1.5	1.5	1.4	1.0	1.2	2.1	2.1
Totals	1,000.0	7.1	728.5	738.8	681.4	564.0	646.6	582.5	437.9

[1] JOBS—total authorization: Total federal funds available for the JOBS program for fiscal year 1993.   [2] Indian set-aside: Ratio of adult recipients in a tribal service area to the State's total of adult recipients multiplied by the State's total allocation.   [3] Excludes the Indian set-aside.   [4] Total expended: The amount of funds that left the State's treasury through September 30, 1993, for the program.   [5] Total obligated: The amount of funds obligated by the State by September 30, 1993. For example, if a contract is signed by the State to provide services based on a set fee, the amount owed for those services is an obligation. That obligation becomes an expenditure only when the invoice for the services is actually paid.   [6] Denotes allocations and expenditures of less than $50,000.

Note.—Data are up to date as of February 23, 1994. Table is based on best available data reported by States.

Source: Administration for Children and Families.

Table 10–6 shows the average monthly percent of JOBS participants in various components by State in fiscal year 1991. The numbers reveal a great deal of variation in the emphasis States place on different JOBS program components.

Table 10–7 examines the average monthly expenditures in various components of the JOBS program by State. This table shows a considerable degree of variation among States in the amount of money spent on individual JOBS components.

TABLE 10–6.—AVERAGE MONTHLY PERCENTAGE OF JOBS PARTICIPANTS BY STATE AND COMPONENT—FISCAL YEAR 1992

State	Total partici-pants	Job entry	High school	As-signed higher ed.	Self init. higher ed.	Voca-tional training	Job skills train-ing	Job readi-ness	Job de-velop	Assess emp. plan	Job search	OJT	Work supp.	CWEP	Other
Alabama	5,472	7.1	29.0	1.6	10.4	5.4	5.9	2.3	0.2	27.4	9.7	0.3	0.0	0.0	0.9
Alaska	596	1.8	18.6	11.7	7.9	0.0	3.2	39.6	0.0	9.2	6.9	0.7	0.0	0.0	0.3
Arizona	2,336	9.1	19.1	3.7	4.6	7.1	8.6	0.6	1.3	11.6	30.7	0.7	0.0	2.8	0.0
Arkansas	3,660	0.0	22.2	8.8	0.0	10.9	7.8	6.4	0.9	10.8	4.8	0.5	0.0	0.0	27.9
California	60,567	6.5	43.3	1.3	7.3	6.4	11.3	5.1	0.9	14.5	2.7	1.1	0.8	3.2	0.0
Colorado	5,183	6.8	18.4	16.1	5.9	2.0	8.4	3.6	0.0	16.0	8.8	0.4	0.0	12.8	0.0
Connecticut	5,714	7.0	36.1	8.7	11.1	9.7	5.2	5.3	1.8	6.0	5.4	1.8	0.0	0.0	0.1
Delaware	722	3.2	7.5	0.8	11.8	3.6	2.2	0.0	15.4	51.4	5.5	0.1	0.0	0.0	13.6
District of Col	2,424	1.2	11.9	0.0	0.0	8.6	10.2	1.0	0.0	36.1	4.5	0.2	0.0	1.9	8.8
Florida	13,750	14.4	20.9	7.0	0.6	2.0	0.3	1.3	0.3	14.7	37.1	0.2	0.0	0.4	1.0
Georgia	9,077	6.5	29.0	20.7	8.4	2.0	3.0	6.0	0.1	12.8	9.0	0.4	0.0	2.0	0.3
Guam[1]															
Hawaii	252	2.0	32.9	27.0	1.6	0.0	4.4	18.3	0.4	6.7	0.0	0.0	0.0	5.6	1.2
Idaho	726	9.1	16.3	3.2	9.9	12.5	11.6	10.3	0.4	14.9	4.8	0.4	0.0	0.0	6.6
Illinois	19,180	2.8	25.5	16.2	1.7	1.6	9.7	7.4	0.0	5.7	20.3	0.0	0.0	1.5	7.6
Indiana	4,428	7.0	31.9	10.3	8.3	14.4	2.9	8.3	1.2	9.9	3.1	0.1	0.0	2.7	0.0
Iowa	5,667	1.6	15.0	10.9	3.6	1.4	9.1	6.2	0.0	40.3	8.4	0.1	0.1	0.2	3.2
Kansas	3,520	8.9	29.5	14.2	13.0	6.5	3.3	2.2	1.1	8.3	4.4	0.4	0.0	4.3	2.9
Kentucky	2,761	0.0	26.7	8.1	37.2	5.7	8.0	3.8	0.0	3.9	3.5	0.3	0.0	0.7	0.0
Louisiana	5,624	3.6	41.9	2.2	2.3	8.7	17.8	4.1	0.0	13.6	5.1	0.5	0.0	0.4	0.0
Maine	2,261	3.8	18.1	22.9	0.1	0.2	1.5	12.4	0.5	32.2	6.9	0.0	0.0	0.0	1.5
Maryland	6,219	6.6	16.1	3.4	1.7	1.4	11.1	15.5	17.4	17.2	4.7	0.3	0.1	0.0	4.5
Massachusetts	16,910	25.9	14.7	10.3	0.0	0.0	17.2	3.4	0.6	7.4	20.4	0.0	0.0	0.0	0.0
Michigan	41,941	7.1	20.5	0.1	24.2	15.4	3.3	3.1	2.4	15.3	4.6	0.2	0.1	3.9	0.0
Minnesota	9,785	6.6	16.1	14.9	0.0	0.0	29.5	3.1	6.8	4.6	17.9	0.5	0.0	0.0	0.0
Mississippi	1,852	5.2	39.1	5.5	5.4	1.9	11.1	4.6	0.9	12.1	8.0	1.0	0.3	3.7	1.2
Missouri	3,914	3.6	19.6	7.0	12.1	10.0	11.7	3.0	0.0	17.0	11.9	0.3	0.0	0.1	3.6
Montana	2,124	24.1	9.1	6.6	2.7	1.4	4.4	6.7	1.6	10.5	17.9	1.3	0.0	8.1	3.6
Nebraska[1]															

TABLE 10–6.—AVERAGE MONTHLY PERCENTAGE OF JOBS PARTICIPANTS BY STATE AND COMPONENT—FISCAL YEAR 1992—Continued

State	Total partici- pants	Job entry	High school	As- signed higher ed.	Self init. higher ed.	Voca- tional training	Job skills train- ing	Job readi- ness	Job de- velop	Assess emp. plan	Job search	OJT	Work supp.	CWEP	Other
Nevada	921	6.4	23.1	0.0	2.7	11.3	5.4	1.1	0.0	21.6	9.1	0.1	0.0	19.1	0.0
New Hampshire	1,414	0.8	22.2	40.8	1.4	0.0	3.7	2.8	0.0	0.8	20.4	0.1	0.0	0.0	7.0
New Jersey	13,609	5.6	29.0	6.6	0.2	0.0	18.0	6.3	0.0	24.2	7.7	0.1	0.2	1.9	0.3
New Mexico	4,970	6.9	22.9	17.3	1.8	2.9	14.1	0.0	0.0	16.9	12.5	0.1	0.0	4.2	0.5
New York	32,796	2.6	22.3	5.7	7.6	35.2	5.0	4.5	4.5	2.4	0.3	0.3	0.7	4.4	0.0
North Carolina	6,895	5.3	25.3	17.9	7.4	2.0	7.0	12.0	0.0	18.0	1.6	0.2	0.0	3.3	0.0
North Dakota	2,494	17.2	8.1	23.3	2.4	0.6	12.9	20.6	0.0	9.5	3.3	0.5	0.0	2.3	0.0
Ohio	46,620	2.8	28.0	16.5	1.2	0.2	3.8	1.9	1.2	21.4	7.2	0.0	0.1	15.6	0.0
Oklahoma	9,478	8.1	18.8	4.4	34.4	6.1	8.9	1.9	0.1	3.2	4.3	0.0	0.0	8.6	1.2
Oregon	7,408	11.9	17.0	0.0	0.0	5.8	9.2	9.5	0.0	17.3	25.6	0.0	0.0	0.0	3.8
Pennsylvania	21,435	3.7	17.3	4.6	2.2	0.0	44.6	10.4	0.0	9.8	4.2	0.1	0.0	2.7	0.4
Puerto Rico	3,532	5.3	6.7	9.4	7.0	13.3	13.3	2.2	1.6	3.0	1.5	0.7	0.1	0.0	2.5
Rhode Island	2,978	2.7	20.1	22.6	29.3	1.7	16.9	1.2	0.3	3.0	1.5	0.0	0.2	0.0	0.5
South Carolina	8,533	6.7	28.8	4.9	1.3	0.8	6.8	1.8	0.0	10.8	34.9	0.3	0.0	0.0	3.2
South Dakota	880	18.0	8.3	13.0	24.0	10.0	0.9	0.8	0.0	3.0	12.4	1.0	0.0	8.7	0.0
Tennessee	4,810	4.8	36.3	19.3	6.5	0.5	9.1	5.4	0.0	13.8	2.1	0.8	0.0	0.2	1.1
Texas	20,641	7.5	18.6	2.8	3.1	4.5	3.3	3.2	0.0	46.7	9.9	0.4	0.0	0.0	0.0
Utah	6,394	32.3	12.0	11.8	2.4	2.1	10.4	3.6	0.0	14.7	7.0	0.0	0.0	3.0	0.0
Vermont	2,012	0.0	11.6	24.7	0.8	0.0	4.7	4.0	0.0	7.7	38.6	0.3	0.0	7.6	0.0
Virgin Islands	547	3.7	29.3	0.0	0.7	0.7	1.1	0.0	1.8	13.7	40.8	0.0	0.0	5.5	2.7
Virginia	8,118	6.0	23.7	14.8	4.2	2.3	7.7	3.4	8.0	9.5	10.5	0.2	018	0.0	9.3
Washington	17,054	6.1	17.5	15.2	7.0	2.6	7.6	1.4	0.1	29.4	10.9	0.4	0.3	0.3	1.1
West Virginia	6,763	7.3	6.4	2.6	2.9	0.5	0.0	0.9	0.1	69.2	2.1	0.3	0.0	4.5	3.1
Wisconsin	18,578	15.1	15.9	7.9	16.5	0.0	3.2	4.2	0.0	10.2	14.8	0.5	1.0	3.3	7.2
Wyoming	422	5.7	5.0	7.3	12.3	0.2	3.8	4.7	0.0	11.4	18.2	0.9	0.0	0.0	30.3
U.S. total	483,417	7.2	24.5	8.2	6.7	6.3	9.5	4.5	1.4	16.5	9.4	0.4	0.1	3.7	1.5

¹ Data not reported.

TABLE 10–7.—PERCENTAGE DISTRIBUTION OF JOBS IV–F COMPONENT/ACTIVITY EXPENDITURES (STATE AND FEDERAL) [1]

[Fiscal year 1992; in percent]

State	Assess./emploly. plan	Education	Job skills	Job readiness	Post secondary	Job search	OJT	Work supp.	CWEP	Other	Job dvpmnt/placemnt	Self-initiated education	Self-initiated training	Total component expenditures
Alabama	38	27	10	5	3	7	(4)	0	0	4	1	3	2	$7,427,743
Alaska	26	14	6	8	6	6	1	0	0	17	2	2	1	1,443,703
Arizona	17	69	9	0	0	5	0	0	0	0	0	0	0	1,726,660
Arkansas	38	20	2	8	3	5	0	0	0	14	0	6	4	6,063,886
California	27	30	13	7	0	3	1	0	4	0	5	0	0	114,205,782
Colorado	0	3	0	0	62	3	23	0	11	0	0	0	0	1,100,054
Connecticut	(2)	(2)	(2)	(2)	(2)	(2)	(2)	(2)	(2)	(2)	(2)	(2)	(2)	(2)
Delaware	37	16	12	1	11	6	(4)	0	1	24	0	16	0	1,978,916
District of Columbia	21	12	11	1	0	11	(4)	0	1	5	14	1	5	3,798,960
Florida	30	22	6	7	1	17	1	(4)	(4)	0	10	1	(4)	20,877,410
Georgia	2	36	4	5	47	3	(4)	0	2	0	1	0	0	4,497,555
Hawaii	16	24	4	11	42	(4)	1	0	2	0	3	1	0	142,879
Idaho	36	18	1	21	0	10	0	0	0	11	0	0	0	3,015,168
Illinois	14	38	10	4	16	10	(4)	0	2	3	3	2	0	23,887,515
Indiana	30	17	24	11	5	5	1	0	0	4	4	0	0	3,550,914
Iowa	28	12	18	7	20	8	0	0	(4)	5	1	0	0	7,839,488
Kansas [3]	20	80	0	0	0	0	0	0	1	0	0	0	0	1,402,625
Kentucky	29	33	15	7	6	6	1	(4)	0	0	0	0	0	6,207,953
Louisiana	16	48	12	8	1	4	(4)	0	(4)	6	4	1	0	11,281,195
Maine	7	27	2	9	37	8	1	0	0	2	5	(4)	(4)	4,361,927
Maryland	35	18	16	16	3	3	(4)	0	0	2	4	0	0	15,717,482
Massachusetts	17	27	29	5	3	19	0	(4)	0	0	0	0	0	28,250,889

TABLE 10–7.—PERCENTAGE DISTRIBUTION OF JOBS IV–F COMPONENT/ACTIVITY EXPENDITURES (STATE AND FEDERAL) [1]—Continued

[Fiscal year 1992; in percent]

State	Assess./emploly. plan	Education	Job skills	Job readiness	Post-secondary	Job search	OJT	Work supp.	CWEP	Other	Job dvpmnt/placemnt	Self-initiated education	Self-initiated training	Total component expenditures
Michigan	14	3	28	23	0	16	2	0	0	0	14	0	0	2,634,092
Minnesota	16	22	28	4	13	16	1	0	(4)	0	0	0	0	13,022,486
Mississippi	52	23	6	3	3	6	4	0	0	2	2	2	0	2,702,526
Missouri	46	6	5	10	4	11	(4)	0	(4)	2	2	8	7	7,391,960
Montana	16	12	14	17	4	19	2	0	12	0	0	2	1	2,280,659
Nebraska	4	16	3	52	6	18	0	0	0	1	0	1	0	3,642,160
Nevada	20	22	19	2	0	8	2	0	20	0	0	1	6	1,301,326
New Hampshire	4	21	1	25	20	11	6	0	0	9	3	0	0	1,307,100
New Jersey	13	27	23	11	0	22	(4)	1	1	2	1	0	0	15,047,965
New Mexico	6	28	19	6	17	4	(4)	0	(4)	4	0	4	3	1,168,240
New York	38	26	5	7	4	2	1	1	6	0	8	1	2	76,922,828
North Carolina	7	34	10	12	21	1	1	0	3	0	0	12	0	24,659,100
North Dakota	40	6	12	11	10	5	6	0	(4)	0	0	(4)	0	986,193
Ohio	27	14	4	4	8	11	(4)	(4)	8	6	5	2	0	68,673,814
Oklahoma	16	26	10	5	2	11	(4)	1	0	14	13	(4)	1	3,348,017
Oregon	8	25	8	27	0	26	1	0	0	4	6	0	(4)	10,819,307
Pennsylvania	6	22	40	10	6	6	1	0	3	1	6	1	0	39,922,098
Rhode Island	7	26	15	4	28	5	(4)	12	0	0	2	1	(4)	5,226,935
South Carolina	25	26	3	10	4	11	0	0	0	13	8	1	(4)	5,016,687
South Dakota	69	2	2	1	8	11	2	0	4	0	0	2	0	794,221
Tennessee	15	45	9	7	16	2	1	1	(4)	0	0	1	5	5,644,179
Texas	27	30	3	11	4	9	(4)	0	0	0	5	5	6	41,745,481
Utah	25	14	12	8	8	24	(4)	0	0	6	3	0	0	3,129,151
Vermont	0	100	0	0	0	0	0	0	0	0	0	0	0	87,681
Virginia	21	30	12	6	10	10	(4)	1	0	9	0	1	0	9,648,182
Washington	37	16	9	3	12	8	1	1	(4)	3	3	4	2	18,750,258

West Virginia	20	29	1	26	0	14	4	0	5	0	0	1	0	9,975,705
Wisconsin	34	14	5	10	9	16	2	2	6	(4)	2	1	(4)	25,805,311
Wyoming	2	12	8	2	18	16	(4)	0	0	21	0	18	2	2,212,815
Guam	87	2	(4)	6	3	(4)	2	0	0	0	(2)	0	0	265,161
Puerto Rico	(2)	(2)	(2)	(2)	(2)	(2)	(2)	(2)	(2)	(2)	0	(2)	(2)	(2)
Virgin Islands	59	15	26	0	0	0	0	0	0	0	0	0	0	187,472
United States	25	25	12	10	6	8	1	(4)	3	3	4	2	1	673,097,814

[1] These expenditures include: (1) actual IV–F administrative expenditures associated with program components/activities and supportive services (excluding child care) and (2) actual program costs (excluding supportive services program costs).   [3] State did not report any data for the fourth quarter.   [4] Less than .5 percent.
[2] State did not report data for any quarter.

Source: DHHS/Administration for Children and Families/Office of Family Assistance.

Table 10–8 examines State level of effort with respect to partici- pation in the JOBS program. The first four columns present data that the States reported to DHHS. Column 5 shows the percentage of the AFDC caseload that is not exempt from JOBS participation requirements. As with many of the previous tables there is a lot of variation among States. In Mississippi only 20 percent of AFDC families were subject to JOBS participation requirements (7 per- cent in Hawaii and 20 percent in Tennessee), whereas in Montana 90 percent of AFDC families were required to participate in the JOBS program. Column 6 displays countable JOBS participants (i.e., those who met the 20-hour rule requirement) as a percentage of persons required to participate in the JOBS program. Although column 6 closely approximates the JOBS participation rate for each State, Federal law specifies the exact methodology States must use to derive their participation rates. This methodology is more com- plex than simply dividing the number of countable JOBS partici- pants by the number of non-exempt AFDC adult recipients (which is how column 6 was calculated). The reader should use the data presented in table 10–8 with caution. These data have not been re- viewed for accuracy and appear to overstate participation in the JOBS program, given that States have testified that they may have trouble meeting the 15 percent participation rate in fiscal year 1994 and the 20 percent rate in fiscal year 1995.

According to a May 1993 report by the General Accounting Office (GAO), "JOBS participation rates data are not accurate nor com- parably derived across States." The GAO report asserts that DHHS officials have been aware of the participation rate data problems in the four States surveyed by GAO and in at least 20 other States as well. The report says that DHHS officials responded that inad- equate resources have prevented them from validating the proc- esses States use to ensure the accuracy and completeness of the State's data.

JOBS: A Status Report

Federal law requires that States enroll at least 11 percent of non-exempt AFDC families in their JOBS program during fiscal year 1992 and fiscal year 1993 (up from 7 percent in fiscal year 1991). In addition, effective October 1, 1992, States were required to implement the JOBS program statewide. Approximately 16 per- cent of adult non-exempt AFDC recipients were counted as partici- pants of the JOBS program during fiscal year 1992 (see table 10– 8). As of May 1993, information from DHHS indicates that all ju- risdictions have implemented the JOBS program statewide.

To meet these new requirements, most States had to expand their JOBS program for fiscal year 1993. Some 34 States increased funding for their JOBS program; 6 States reduced funding (Arkan- sas, Connecticut, Maryland, Massachusetts, Nebraska, and Wyo- ming); and 4 States froze funding (Delaware, Guam, Idaho, and Minnesota). To "draw down" the $1 billion available in Federal funding for the JOBS program, States must provide matching funds. Due to tight State budgets, only about 70 percent of the eli- gible Federal funds were claimed by States in fiscal year 1993. Only 16 States claimed their full allocation of Federal JOBS funds.

TABLE 10–8.—JOBS PARTICIPATION: STATE LEVEL OF EFFORT, FISCAL YEAR 1992

[Data based on monthly averages from October 1991–September 1992]

State	Total adult recipients		Total JOBS participants		Percent of AFDC adults mandatory for JOBS	Countable JOBS participants, as a percent of mandatories
	AFDC	JOBS Mandatories	Active	Countable		
	(1)	(2)	(3)	(4)	(5)	(6)
Alabama [1]	41,219	10,721	5,472	3,188	26	30
Alaska	11,676	2,577	596	452	22	18
Arizona [1]	54,593	13,524	2,336	1,491	25	11
Arkansas	21,690	7,933	3,680	1,928	37	24
California [2]	704,723	276,199	60,687	33,991	39	12
Colorado [1]	40,875	28,531	5,193	4,765	70	17
Connecticut	51,902	31,729	5,714	7,512	61	24
Delaware	8,525	3,496	722	638	41	18
District of Columbia	17,827	9,032	2,424	1,054	51	12
Florida [1]	184,262	48,315	13,750	7,488	26	15
Georgia [1]	119,752	46,438	9,077	5,751	39	12
Guam	1,325	375	NR	13	28	3
Hawaii [1]	16,738	1,124	252	113	7	10
Idaho [1]	6,450	1,346	726	522	21	39
Illinois	215,774	122,492	19,180	13,780	57	11
Indiana [1]	66,222	26,031	4,426	1,578	39	6
Iowa	35,559	11,374	5,687	1,309	32	12
Kansas	27,962	15,542	3,520	3,117	56	20
Kentucky [1]	82,362	19,502	2,761	3,962	24	20
Louisiana [1]	78,261	25,727	5,624	3,314	33	13
Maine	25,764	14,269	2,261	1,296	55	9
Maryland	71,996	36,285	6,219	3,670	50	10
Massachusetts	101,762	50,525	16,910	16,323	50	32
Michigan	233,293	130,704	41,941	22,009	56	17
Minnesota	66,722	19,520	9,785	3,181	29	16

TABLE 10–8.—JOBS PARTICIPATION: STATE LEVEL OF EFFORT, FISCAL YEAR 1992—Continued

[Data based on monthly averages from October 1991–September 1992]

State	Total adult recipients		Total JOBS participants		Percent of AFDC adults mandatory for JOBS	Countable JOBS participants, as a percent of mandatories
	AFDC	JOBS Mandatories	Active	Countable		
	(1)	(2)	(3)	(4)	(5)	(6)
Mississippi [1]	49,608	9,711	1,852	1,289	20	13
Missouri [1]	86,353	24,623	3,914	3,441	29	14
Montana [1]	11,495	10,339	2,124	1,772	90	17
Nebraska	15,564	6,338	NR	4,891	41	77
Nevada [1]	9,851	2,732	921	398	28	15
New Hampshire	10,358	4,145	1,414	1,027	40	25
New Jersey	111,740	62,316	13,609	8,890	56	14
New Mexico [1]	30,844	8,673	4,970	2,254	28	26
New York	374,431	169,721	32,798	24,549	45	14
North Carolina	103,944	39,980	6,895	5,543	38	14
North Dakota	6,404	2,369	2,494	725	37	31
Ohio	260,048	139,504	46,620	26,280	54	19
Oklahoma	42,866	30,057	8,478	9,634	70	32
Oregon	39,823	19,215	7,408	4,123	48	21
Pennsylvania	197,360	91,265	21,435	12,101	46	13
Puerto Rico [1]	62,068	18,450	3,532	3,484	30	19
Rhode Island	20,477	12,879	2,978	1,784	63	14
South Carolina	39,979	13,922	8,533	2,289	35	16
South Dakota	6,017	2,067	860	519	34	25
Tennessee	86,605	17,750	4,910	3,485	20	20
Texas [1]	229,610	104,537	20,841	12,026	46	12
Utah	17,346	14,601	6,394	5,074	84	35
Vermont	11,290	5,766	2,012	820	51	14
Virginia	59,443	21,612	8,118	3,855	36	18
Virgin Islands	966	380	547	99	39	26

Washington	97,557	34,876	17,054	10,889	36	31
West Virginia	45,256	23,327	6,763	3,017	52	13
Wisconsin	79,301	41,811	16,578	13,380	53	32
Wyoming	6,332	2,174	422	675	34	31
Total	4,400,166	1,888,450	483,417	310,754	43	16

¹ JOBS Program is not statewide as of June 3, 1992.   ² State approved to use a sample to estimate the number of AFDC recipients required to participate in JOBS for fiscal year 1992.   NR—Data not reported.

Note.—These data should be used with caution. The first four columns from which the other columns are derived, represent State data that were not reviewed or audited for accuracy.

Source: Administration for Children and Families, DHHS.

TITLE IV–A EMERGENCY ASSISTANCE

The Social Security Act permits States, at their option, to operate an Emergency Assistance program for needy families with children (whether or not eligible for AFDC) if the assistance is necessary to avoid the destitution of the child or to provide living arrangements in a home for the child. The statute authorizes 50 percent Federal matching for emergency assistance furnished for a period not in excess of 30 days in any 12-month period. Regulations state that Federal matching is available for emergency assistance authorized by the State during one period of 30 consecutive days in any 12 consecutive months, including payments which are to meet needs which arose before the 30-day period or are for such needs as rent which extend beyond the 30-day period.

In fiscal year 1993, 40 jurisdictions operated an Emergency Assistance program. Table 10–9 presents the average monthly caseload and total fiscal year payments for jurisdictions participating in the program. Table 10–10 provides historical data on total payments.

As of October 1, 1990, according to State plans on file with the Department of Health and Human Services (DHHS), most EA programs covered natural disasters (23 jurisdictions), such as floods, fires, and storms, and unspecified crisis threatening family or living arrangements (21 jurisdictions). Other qualifying causes for emergency aid specified by various States included (in order of frequency): eviction, potential eviction, or foreclosure; homelessness; utility shut-off or loss of heating energy supply or equipment; civil disorders or crimes of violence; child or spousal abuse; loss of employment or strike; health hazards/risks to health and safety; emergency medical needs; and illness, accident, or injury.

Note that AFDC regulations also allow States to include in their State standards of need provision for meeting "special needs" of AFDC applicants and recipients. The State plan must specify the circumstances under which payments will be made for special needs.

During the mid 1980s, some States began using AFDC special needs funds and/or emergency assistance funds to house otherwise homeless families in hotels. Moreover, a few States were found to be using emergency assistance (EA) funds for more than the 30-day limit specified in law. Placement of a family in a hotel, a last resort that costs an average of more than $1,000 a month, has been controversial, and several reports have found dangerous and squalid conditions in some such "welfare hotels."

In response, DHHS issued a proposed rule (published in the Federal Register on December 14, 1987) restricting use of AFDC-special needs for housing expenses, and reconfirming the 30-day limit on EA expenditures. The DHHS proposed regulation would have (1) established an "unambiguous" time limit on the use of EA funds and (2) prohibited States from adopting, either as a special or basic need, an AFDC shelter allowance that varied by type of residence (e.g., apartment or hotel). On December 22, 1987, Congress passed legislation that prohibited, until October 1, 1988, the DHHS from taking any action on the proposed EA and AFDC-special needs regulations. The moratorium on promulgation of the regulation was intended to give Congress an opportunity to determine whether and how the current AFDC statute should be amended to respond to the problems of homeless families. The Stewart B. McKinney Homeless Assistance Amendments Act of 1988 extended the moratorium until October 1, 1989, required DHHS to issue a report on recommendations for statutory and regulatory changes in AFDC-special needs and the EA program with respect to improving the responsiveness of those programs to the emergency needs of AFDC-eligible families, and eliminated the use of such funds to provide families shelter in commercial or transient facilities. The report was sent to Congress July 3, 1989, with a proposal to issue a final regulation which would prohibit reimbursement under the EA program for assistance for periods beyond 30 consecutive days in a 12-month period (while continuing to allow EA funds for past-due rent and utility costs and for first month's rent and security deposit). The proposal also would delete from the Department's previously proposed rule the provision precluding States from establishing AFDC shelter allowances that vary by type of residence. In addition, the report stated that the Department would develop legislative proposals to prohibit the use of Federal AFDC and EA matching funds for welfare hotels. The 1989 OBRA prohibited the Secretary from implementing any final EA or AFDC-special need regulations before October 1, 1990. The 1990 OBRA extended this prohibition until October 1, 1991.

TABLE 10–9.—EMERGENCY ASSISTANCE: TOTAL CASELOAD AND PAYMENTS (FEDERAL AND STATE) FOR SELECTED FISCAL YEARS 1985–93

State	Average monthly caseload				Total fiscal year payments (in thousands)				Monthly dollar payment per family	
	1985 [1]	1990	1992	1993 [2]	1985	1990	1992	1993 [2]	1985	1993
Arizona	0	0	122	191	0	0	$1,193	$3,675	0	$1,603
Arkansas	48	0	NA	0	$58	0	197	2,557	$101	0
California	734	450	0	0	41,554	$40,956	[3] 247	0	4,718	0
Colorado	0	0	852	0	0	0	2,602	24	0	0
Delaware	194	202	161	112	232	417	320	419	100	312
District of Columbia	968	1,682	1,780	1,499	2,381	9,591	2,995	21,276	205	1,183
Florida	0	2,095	848	921	0	8,828	3,633	3,884	0	351
Georgia	854	1,704	1,094	1,454	7,405	5,029	4,205	9,529	723	546
Hawaii	0	0	90	25	0	0	745	371	0	1,237
Illinois	1,161	1,998	1,724	1,177	2,295	3,218	4,799	4,152	165	294
Iowa	0	0	430	435	0	0	1,701	1,759	0	337
Kansas	159	197	206	218	394	515	514	637	206	244
Maine	304	259	461	347	1,007	1,184	1,158	749	276	180
Maryland	1,784	2,000	2,084	2,169	2,445	5,060	4,945	7,156	114	275
Massachusetts	4,584	5,336	3,721	4,058	17,678	58,970	37,850	45,676	321	938
Michigan	4,211	5,656	1,372	1,490	10,067	20,432	13,926	23,767	199	1,329
Minnesota	1,165	1,849	1,755	1,913	5,624	10,427	10,028	11,268	402	491
Missouri	0	0	NA	0	0	0	758	2,418	0	0
Montana	72	60	75	39	386	162	270	227	446	485
Nebraska	181	253	186	172	646	1,641	1,110	1,396	297	676
Nevada	0	52	0	19	0	147	0	117	0	513
New Hampshire	0	46	244	329	0	386	882	1,214	0	307
New Jersey	601	3,820	6,577	8,678	2,171	50,902	52,271	53,268	301	512
New York	4,473	12,724	14,580	14,750	37,543	126,878	84,364	542,806	699	3,067
North Carolina	0	1,482	2,303	2,293	0	4,235	5,449	5,464	0	199

North Dakota	0	0	0	335	0	0	0	1,335	0	332
Ohio	5,037	4,330	4,011	3,921	11,778	6,339	7,767	8,600	195	183
Oklahoma	803	2,197	2,699	2,205	2,548	4,325	5,832	3,591	264	136
Oregon	1,312	1,758	1,532	1,567	3,415	4,869	4,246	4,763	217	253
Pennsylvania	32	1,512	525	702	92	4,705	2,636	5,157	239	612
Puerto Rico	1,069	538	354	489	247	126	250	192	33	33
South Carolina	0	0	0	0	0	0	0	545	0	0
South Dakota	0	0	0	63	0	0	0	359	0	475
Utah	0	106	120	120	0	257	620	320	0	222
Vermont	302	395	304	298	364	1,395	1,414	1,450	100	405
Virgin Islands	0	NA	NA	0	0	4	0	0	0	0
Virginia	18	15	43	43	63	57	89	42	290	81
Washington	727	511	537	610	3,327	2,437	2,731	3,087	381	422
West Virginia	1,202	1,201	1,225	1,194	1,521	1,529	1,764	1,819	105	127
Wisconsin	44	889	799	818	197	2,437	3,246	3,174	372	323
Wyoming	466	196	94	217	1,129	482	232	2,001	202	768
U.S. total	32,500	55,514	52,906	54,869	156,565	377,942	266,989	788,668	401	1,198

[1] Expenditure data for fiscal year 1985 does not include prior quarter adjustments.
[2] Data for fiscal year 1993 are preliminary.
[3] Represents prior year claims.

NA—Data not available.

Source: Office of Financial Management, Administration for Children and Families.

364

TABLE 10–10.—TOTAL FEDERAL AND STATE PAYMENTS UNDER THE EMERGENCY
ASSISTANCE PROGRAM, SELECTED FISCAL YEARS 1970–93

[In millions]

	Amount
Fiscal year:	
1970	$14
1975	70
1980	109
1985	157
1986	175
1987	203
1988	256
1989	310
1990	378
1991	306
1992	631
1993	789

Source: Office of Financial Management, Administration for Children and Families.

SECTION 1115 DEMONSTRATION PROJECTS—WAIVERS FROM AFDC LAW

Section 1115 of the Social Security Act authorizes the Secretary of the DHHS to waive specified requirements of the Social Security Act pertaining to the AFDC program in order to enable a State to carry out any experimental, pilot, or demonstration projects that the Secretary judges likely to help in promoting the objectives of the program. Since about 1990, States have sought to offset the huge expansion in the AFDC rolls by implementing proposals designed to change the behavior of AFDC recipients and/or by cutting benefits. Several States have linked AFDC receipt to desired behaviors such as regular school attendance, getting children immunized, and marriage. Some have tried to constrain AFDC costs by cutting benefits, providing smaller benefits to new State entrants, and by denying benefit increases to mothers that have additional children while on AFDC.

Since 1990, about 20 States have received waivers from one or more AFDC rules.

CHILD CARE FOR FAMILIES AT RISK OF AFDC RECEIPT

The Omnibus Budget Reconciliation Act of 1990 increased funding for the existing AFDC child care program to provide $300 million for fiscal year 1991 and thereafter to the States to provide child care services to low-income, non-AFDC families that (1) need such care in order to work and (2) would otherwise be at risk of becoming eligible for AFDC.

Capped entitlement funds would be allocated on the basis of child population. Rules relating to Federal matching rates, reimbursement, standards and fee schedules would match the same rules as apply for child care for AFDC families, except that all child care providers that receive funds must be licensed, regulated, or registered.

The At-Risk program is described in more detail in section 12.

AFDC BENEFIT LEVELS AND TRENDS

Each State establishes a "need standard" (the income the State decides is essential for basic consumption items) and a "payment standard" (100 percent or less of the need level). Benefits are generally computed by subtracting countable income from the State's payment standard.

Maximum payments

Maximum AFDC payments vary sharply from State to State, as shown by tables 10–11 and 10–12. State payments for AFDC families of three with no countable income in January 1994 ranged from $120 in Mississippi to $923 in Alaska. Table 10–11 presents the gross income limit, the need standard, the maximum monthly potential AFDC and food stamp benefits for a one-parent family of three persons, as of January 1994, combined AFDC and food stamp benefits as a percent of the Census Bureau poverty threshold for a 3-person family, and AFDC benefits as a percent of the poverty threshold.

The food stamp benefits are calculated by deducting from the family's AFDC benefit (the only cash income of the family) the maximum deductions allowed under food stamps for a nonaged, nondisabled family: a total of $338. This consists of a standard deduction of $131, given in all households, plus a deduction of $207 for excess shelter costs.

If the family qualified only for the standard deduction, its food stamp benefits would be cut in most States by about $62. Table 10–11 shows combined maximum potential benefits of $689 to a Maine AFDC family of 3, including $271 in food stamps. The same family would receive only $626 in combined benefits, including $208 in food stamps, if it were credited only with the standard deduction. Food stamp program data show that most AFDC families do qualify for a deduction of some shelter costs.

As table 10–14 illustrates, during 1993, 11 jurisdictions increased AFDC payments. Forty jurisdictions had no payment increases. Three jurisdictions decreased benefits. As a result of these changes, the median State benefit for a family of three decreased from $367 to $366 per month in nominal dollars.

TABLE 10–11.—GROSS INCOME LIMIT, NEED STANDARD, AND MAXIMUM MONTHLY PO-
TENTIAL BENEFITS, AFDC AND FOOD STAMPS, ONE-PARENT FAMILY [1] OF THREE PER-
SONS, JANUARY 1994

State	Gross income limit (185 percent of need standard)	100 percent of "need"	Maximum AFDC grant [2]	Food stamp benefit [3]	Combined benefits	Combined benefits as a percent of 1993 poverty threshold [4]	AFDC benefits as a percent of 1993 poverty threshold [4]
Alabama	$1,245	$673	$164	$295	$459	48	17
Alaska	1,804	975	923	285	1,208	101	77
Arizona	1,783	964	347	292	639	67	36
Arkansas	1,304	705	204	295	499	52	21
California	1,323	715	607	214	821	86	63
Colorado	779	421	356	289	645	67	37
Connecticut	1,258	680	680	192	872	91	71
Delaware	625	338	338	295	633	66	35
District of Columbia	1,317	712	420	270	690	72	44
Florida	1,833	991	303	295	598	62	32
Georgia	784	424	280	295	575	60	29
Hawaii	2,109	1,140	712	422	1,134	103	65
Idaho	1,833	991	317	295	612	64	33
Illinois	1,647	890	[5]367	291	658	69	38
Indiana	592	320	288	295	583	61	30
Iowa	1,571	849	426	268	694	72	44
Kansas	794	429	[5]429	284	713	74	45
Kentucky	973	526	228	295	523	55	24
Louisiana	1,217	658	190	295	485	51	20
Maine	1,023	553	418	271	689	72	44
Maryland	938	507	[5]366	295	661	69	38
Massachusetts	1,071	579	579	222	801	83	60
Michigan (Washtenaw County)	1,086	587	[5]489	249	738	77	51
Michigan (Wayne County)	1,019	551	[5]459	258	717	75	48
Minnesota	984	532	532	236	768	80	55
Mississippi	681	368	120	295	415	43	13
Missouri	1,565	846	292	295	587	61	30
Montana	945	511	401	276	677	71	42
Nebraska	673	364	364	287	651	68	38
Nevada	1,293	699	348	292	640	67	36
New Hampshire	3,049	1,648	550	231	781	81	57
New Jersey	1,822	985	[5]424	276	700	73	44
New Mexico	660	357	357	289	646	67	37
New York (Suffolk County)	1,301	703	[5]703	201	904	94	73
New York (New York City)	1,067	577	[5]577	239	816	85	60
North Carolina	1,006	544	272	295	567	59	28
North Dakota	757	409	409	273	682	71	43
Ohio	1,626	879	[5]341	295	636	66	36

TABLE 10–11.—GROSS INCOME LIMIT, NEED STANDARD, AND MAXIMUM MONTHLY PO-TENTIAL BENEFITS, AFDC AND FOOD STAMPS, ONE-PARENT FAMILY [1] OF THREE PER-SONS, JANUARY 1994—Continued

State	Gross income limit (185 percent of need standard)	100 percent of "need"	Maximum AFDC grant [2]	Food stamp benefit [3]	Combined benefits	Combined benefits as a percent of 1993 poverty threshold [4]	AFDC benefits as a percent of 1993 poverty threshold [4]
Oklahoma	871	471	324	295	619	65	34
Oregon	851	460	[5] 460	293	753	78	48
Pennsylvania	1,136	614	421	270	691	72	44
Rhode Island	1,025	554	[5] 554	268	822	86	58
South Carolina	814	440	200	295	495	52	21
South Dakota	908	491	417	271	688	72	43
Tennessee	788	426	185	295	480	50	19
Texas	1,062	574	184	295	479	50	19
Utah	1,021	552	414	272	686	72	43
Vermont	2,079	1,124	638	205	843	88	67
Virginia	727	393	354	290	644	67	37
Washington	2,142	1,158	[5] 546	258	804	84	57
West Virginia	919	497	249	295	544	57	26
Wisconsin	1,197	647	517	241	758	79	54
Wyoming	1,247	674	360	288	648	68	38
Guam	611	330	330	436	766	80	34
Puerto Rico	666	360	180	0	180	NA	19
Virgin Islands	555	300	240	380	620	65	25
Median AFDC State [6]	938	507	366	295	661	69	38

[1] In most States these benefit amounts apply also to 2-parent families of 3 (where the second parent is incapacitated or unemployed). Some, however, increase benefits for such families.

[2] In States with area differentials, figure shown is for area with highest benefit.

[3] Food stamp benefits are based on maximum AFDC benefits shown and assume deductions of $338 monthly ($131 standard household deduction plus $207 maximum allowable deduction for excess shelter cost) in the 48 contiguous States and D.C. In the remaining four jurisdictions these maximum allowable food stamp deductions are assumed: Alaska, $582; Hawaii, $480; Guam, $513; and Virgin Islands, $267. If only the standard deduction were assumed, food stamp benefits would drop by about $62 monthly in most of the 48 contiguous States and D.C. Maximum food stamp benefits from October 1993 through September 1994 are $295 for a family of three except in these 4 jurisdictions, where they are as follows: Alaska, $388; Hawaii, $492; Guam, $436; and Virgin Islands, $380.

[4] Except for Alaska and Hawaii, this column is based on the Census Bureau's 1993 poverty threshold for a family of three persons, $11,521, converted to a monthly rate of $960. For Alaska, this threshold was increased by 25 percent; for Hawaii, by 15 percent.

[5] In these States part of the AFDC cash payment has been designated as energy aid and is disregarded by the State in calculating food stamp benefits. Illinois disregards $18. Kansas disregards $57. Maryland disregards $43. New Jersey disregards $25. New York disregards $53. Ohio disregards $14. Oregon disregards $118. Rhode Island disregards $127.85. Washington disregards $86.

[6] With respect to maximum AFDC benefit among 50 States and D.C.

Note.—Puerto Rico does not have a food stamp program, instead a cash nutritional assistance payment is given to recipients.

Source: Table prepared by CRS from information provided by a telephone survey of the States.

TABLE 10–12.—MAXIMUM AFDC BENEFITS, BY FAMILY SIZE, JANUARY 1994 [1]

State	1-person family	2-person family	3-person family	4-person family	5-person family	6-person family
Alabama	$111	$137	$164	$194	$225	$252
Alaska* [2]	514	821	923	1,025	1,127	1,229
Arizona [3]	204	275	347	418	489	561
Arkansas	81	162	204	247	286	331
California	299	490	607	723	824	926
Colorado [2][4]	214	280	356	432	512	590
Connecticut* [5]	430	549	680	792	893	999
Delaware*	201	270	338	407	475	544
District of Columbia	265	330	420	513	591	695
Florida [3]	180	241	303	364	426	487
Georgia	155	235	280	330	378	410
Hawaii	418	565	712	859	1,006	1,153
Idaho	205	251	317	382	448	513
Illinois [2][6]	212	268	367	414	485	545
Indiana [2]	139	229	288	346	405	463
Iowa	183	361	426	495	548	610
Kansas*	267	352	429	497	558	619
Kentucky	162	196	228	285	333	376
Louisiana [7]	72	138	190	234	277	316
Maine [2]	198	312	418	526	632	739
Maryland	162	286	366	441	511	562
Massachusetts*	392	486	579	668	760	854
Michigan:						
(Washtenaw County) [8]	305	401	489	593	689	822
(Wayne County) [8]	276	371	459	563	659	792
Minnesota* [2]	250	437	532	621	697	773
Mississippi	60	96	120	144	168	192
Missouri	136	234	292	342	388	431
Montana [2][3]	235	318	401	484	567	650
Nebraska*	222	293	364	435	506	577
Nevada [2]	229	288	348	408	468	527
New Hampshire	414	481	550	613	673	754
New Jersey	162	322	424	488	552	616
New Mexico*	209	283	357	431	504	578
New York:						
(Suffolk County)* [9]	446	576	703	824	949	1,038
(New York City)* [9]	352	468	577	687	800	884
North Carolina	181	236	272	297	324	349
North Dakota* [2]	221	333	409	501	569	628
Ohio	203	279	341	421	493	549
Oklahoma [2]	200	251	324	402	470	538
Oregon* [2]	310	395	460	565	660	755
Pennsylvania [10]	215	330	421	514	607	687
Rhode Island* [11]	327	449	554	632	710	800
South Carolina	118	159	200	240	281	321
South Dakota	293	368	417	464	512	560
Tennessee	95	142	185	226	264	305
Texas [2]	75	158	184	221	246	284

TABLE 10–12.—MAXIMUM AFDC BENEFITS, BY FAMILY SIZE, JANUARY 1994 [1]—
Continued

State	1-person family	2-person family	3-person family	4-person family	5-person family	6-person family
Utah	240	332	414	484	551	607
Vermont [12]	437	536	638	717	804	860
Virginia [13]	220	294	354	410	488	518
Washington	349	440	546	642	740	841
West Virginia [3]	145	201	249	312	360	413
Wisconsin [14]	248	440	517	617	708	766
Wyoming [3]	195	320	360	390	450	510
Guam*	151	258	330	417	497	592
Puerto Rico [15]	132	156	180	204	228	252
Virgin Islands	120	180	240	300	360	420
Median State [16]	212	294	366	435	511	577

*These States pay 100 percent of the need standard.

[1] Maximum benefit paid for a family of given size with zero countable income. Family members include 1 adult caretaker.

[2] Alaska, Colorado, Illinois, Indiana, Maine, Minnesota, Montana, North Dakota, Oklahoma, Oregon, and Texas also have a children-only schedule.

[3] Arizona, Florida, Montana, West Virginia and Wyoming have 2 payment schedules, 1 that includes shelter expenses and 1 that does not.

[4] Colorado no longer has separate payment schedules for winter months and nonwinter months.

[5] Connecticut has 3 rent regions. Data shown are from rent region A which has the highest rents.

[6] Illinois divides itself into 3 distinct areas with regard to payment schedules. Data shown are from the Cook County area, which includes Chicago.

[7] Louisiana has 2 payment schedules—1 for urban areas, from which our data were taken, and 1 for rural areas.

[8] Michigan has varied shelter maximums. Shown are benefits for Washtenaw County (Ann Arbor) and Wayne County (Detroit).

[9] New York has payment schedules for each social service district. Shown are the Suffolk County and New York City amounts. The figures include energy payments.

[10] Pennsylvania has four regions. The figures in the table are from region 1, which has the highest benefits.

[11] Rhode Island no longer has separate payment schedules for winter months and nonwinter months.

[12] Vermont has a base amount plus a shelter maximum that depends on whether the recipient is living inside or outside of Chittenden County. The largest amount paid to a recipient with no other income equals 60.6 percent of the base amount plus 60.6 percent of the shelter allowance. The shelter maximum for families living in Chittenden County is $400 per month, for those living outside Chittenden County the shelter maximum is $325 monthly.

[13] Virginia has 3 payment schedules. The figures shown are from area 3 which has the highest benefits.

[14] Wisconsin has 2 regions—1 for urban areas, from which our data were taken, and one for rural areas.

[15] Puerto Rico pays 50 percent of need plus 50 percent of rent as paid. The figures assume rent at $20 a month. Officials estimate that $20 is the average amount allowed for rent.

[16] Among 50 States and D.C.

Source: Prepared by Congressional Research Service on the basis of a telephone survey of the States.

Need and payment standards

To receive AFDC payments, a family must pass two income tests: first, a gross income test, and second, a counted ("net") income test. The gross income test is 185 percent of the State's need standard for the relevant family size; and it applies to both applicants and enrollees. This was increased by Congress from 150 percent of the need standard by Public Law 98–369 in 1984. No one with gross income that *exceeds* 185 percent of the need standard can receive AFDC. For applicants, the counted income test is 100 percent of the need standard, and it determines whether the family is deemed to be in "need" (see tables 10–11 and 10–12).

However, to be eligible for an actual payment, the family's counted income also must be below the State's payment standard, which in 35 jurisdictions is below the need standard.

Further, a $10 minimum payment rule imposed by Public Law 97–35 requires that counted income be at least $10 below the payment standard for an actual payment to be made.

Table 10–13 shows the change in the AFDC need standard in selected years, from July 1970 to January 1994, by State. The increase in the median State from July 1970 to July 1975 (a period of 5 years) was 20 percent and from July 1975 to July 1980 it was 15 percent. From July 1980 to January 1994 (a period of 13½ years), the increase was 80 percent. Between July 1970 and January 1994, the Consumer Price Index (CPI) rose an estimated 275 percent, as compared to a 150 percent increase in the AFDC need standard.

Many States increased their need standards (but often not actual benefit levels) after passage of the gross income limit in 1981.

Trends

Table 10–14 presents information on how the maximum AFDC benefit for a 3-person family with no income has grown from July 1970 to January 1994 by State. In current dollars, the maximum benefit of the median State climbed 28 percent from July 1970–July 1975, 23 percent from July 1975–July 1980, and 27 percent from July 1980–January 1994 (a period of 13½ years).

In constant dollars (after adjustment for inflation), benefit levels failed to keep pace with inflation. The median decline in benefit levels adjusted for inflation from 1970 to 1994 was 47 percent.

TABLE 10–13.—AFDC NEED STANDARD FOR A THREE-PERSON FAMILY BY STATE FOR SELECTED YEARS

	July 1970[1]	July 1975	July 1980	January 1985[2]	January 1988[2]	January 1989[2]	January 1990[2]	January 1991[2]	January 1992[2]	January 1993[2]	January 1994[2]
Alabama	$184	$180	$192	$384	$384	$571	$578	$603	$637	$673	$673
Alaska	350	350	457	719	779	809	846	891	924	923	975
Arizona	212	233	233	233	621	621	621	621	928	964	964
Arkansas	149	245	234	234	695	705	705	705	705	705	705
California	351	316	480	555	633	663	694	694	694	703	715
Colorado	193	217	290	421	421	421	421	421	421	421	421
Connecticut	283	346	475	546	601	623	649	680	680	680	680
Delaware	245	245	266	287	319	333	333	338	338	338	338
District of Columbia	229	286	394	654	712	712	712	712	712	712	712
Florida	189	195	195	400	775	807	838	880	928	965	991
Georgia	177	193	193	366	366	376	414	424	424	424	424
Hawaii	226	428	468	468	515	557	964	1,012	1,067	1,109	1,140
Idaho	238	345	371	554	554	554	554	554	554	554	991
Illinois	232	261	288	657	713	740	777	811	844	867	890
Indiana	272	307	307	307	320	320	320	320	320	320	320
Iowa	247	309	360	497	497	497	497	497	849	849	849
Kansas	243	321	345	373	409	427	409	409	422	429	429
Kentucky	208	185	188	197	207	218	526	526	526	526	526
Louisiana	172	164	402	538	632	658	658	658	658	658	658
Maine	277	277	415	510	573	632	652	652	573	553	553
Maryland	249	259	270	433	497	522	548	562	522	497	507
Massachusetts	268	259	379	439	510	539	539	539	539	539	579

TABLE 10–13.—AFDC NEED STANDARD FOR A THREE-PERSON FAMILY BY STATE FOR SELECTED YEARS—Continued

	July 1970[1]	July 1975	July 1980	January 1985[2]	January 1988[2]	January 1989[2]	January 1990[2]	January 1991[2]	January 1992[2]	January 1993[2]	January 1994[2]
Michigan (Washtenaw County)	NA	NA	NA	592	576	608	611	622	587	587	587
Michigan (Wayne County)	219	333	425	557	540	572	575	586	551	551	551
Minnesota	256	330	417	524	532	532	532	532	532	532	532
Mississippi	202	241	220	286	368	368	368	368	368	368	368
Missouri	285	325	312	312	312	312	312	312	312	312	846
Montana	221	201	259	401	434	434	434	453	478	497	511
Nebraska	281	279	310	350	350	364	364	364	364	364	364
Nevada	269	279	285	285	550	550	550	550	620	620	699
New Hampshire	262	308	346	378	486	496	506	516	516	1,513	1,648
New Jersey	302	310	360	385	424	424	424	424	424	985	985
New Mexico	167	197	220	258	264	264	264	310	324	324	357
New York (Suffolk County)	NA	NA	NA	579	665	665	703	703	703	703	703
New York (New York City)	279	332	394	474	539	539	577	577	577	577	577
North Carolina	168	183	192	446	532	532	544	544	544	544	544
North Dakota	232	283	334	371	371	386	386	401	401	401	409
Ohio	207	346	346	627	685	712	739	776	817	853	879
Oklahoma	179	217	282	282	471	471	471	471	471	471	471
Oregon	229	369	282	386	412	420	432	444	460	460	460
Pennsylvania	265	296	332	614	614	614	614	614	614	614	614
Rhode Island	229	278	340	479	503	517	543	554	554	554	554
South Carolina	162	178	187	187	388	403	419	440	440	440	440
South Dakota	264	289	321	329	366	366	377	385	404	476	491

Tennessee	179	179	179	246	353	365	387	412	426	426	426
Texas	198	155	155	494	574	574	574	574	574	574	574
Utah	223	327	480	685	693	502	516	537	537	537	552
Vermont	287	402	670	852	889	930	973	1,029	1,112	1,122	1,124
Virginia	240	298	344	363	393	393	393	393	393	393	393
Washington	258	315	458	768	835	872	907	983	1,014	1,125	1,158
West Virginia	220	275	275	275	497	497	497	497	497	497	497
Wisconsin	214	383	522	628	647	647	647	647	647	647	647
Wyoming	246	240	315	360	360	360	360	674	674	674	674
Guam	NA	NA	261	265	265	265	330	330	330	330	330
Puerto Rico	108	108	102	180	180	180	180	180	160	360	360
Virgin Islands	NA	131	209	209	209	300	300	300	300	300	300
Median State [3]	232	279	321	401	503	522	539	544	544	554	579

[1] Data on 3-person families were not published or reported before 1975. Thus, the 1970 data were derived by reducing the reported 4-person need standard by the proportional difference between 3- and 4-person AFDC need standards as shown in the July 1975 DHEW reports.

[2] CRS survey data.

[3] Among 50 States and the District of Columbia.

NA—Not available.

Note.—Table compiled by the Congressional Research Service (CRS) on the basis of data from the Department of Health and Human Services and, where noted, from CRS itself.

These changes in maximum AFDC benefit levels are summarized in table 10–14 below. The median State's maximum AFDC benefit (guarantee) for a family of three rose in nominal terms from $184 in fiscal year 1970 to $366 in fiscal year 1994. In constant dollars, however, the median State's guarantee declined 47 percent.

Most AFDC families are eligible also for food stamps (until 1979 all were). As real AFDC benefits declined in the last dozen years, food stamp benefits rose to offset part of their losses. However, combined AFDC-food stamp benefits for a 3-person family without countable income on average dropped from $900 (1993 dollars) in July 1972, when food stamps operated under uniform national rules, to $658 (1993 dollars) in July 1993. This 27 percent drop was almost wholly due to shrinkage in AFDC benefit levels. Food stamp maximum benefits were virtually unchanged in real terms, since they were adjusted for food price inflation in all years except 1982 and 1993.

TABLE 10-14.—AFDC MAXIMUM BENEFIT FOR A THREE-PERSON FAMILY, BY STATE FOR SELECTED YEARS

	July 1970[1]	July 1975	July 1980	January 1985[2]	January 1987[2]	January 1990[2]	January 1991[2]	January 1992[2]	January 1993[2]	January 1994[2]	Percent change, 1970-94[3]
Alabama	$65	$108	$118	$118	$118	$118	$124	$149	$164	$164	−33
Alaska	328	350	457	719	749	846	891	924	923	923	−25
Arizona	138	163	202	233	293	293	293	334	347	347	−33
Arkansas	89	125	161	164	192	204	204	204	204	204	−39
California	186	293	473	555	617	694	694	663	624	607	−13
Colorado	193	217	290	346	346	356	356	356	356	356	−51
Connecticut	283	346	475	546	590	649	680	680	680	680	−36
Delaware	160	221	266	287	310	333	338	338	338	338	−44
District of Columbia	195	243	286	327	364	409	428	409	409	420	−43
Florida	114	144	195	240	264	294	294	303	303	303	−29
Georgia	107	123	164	208	256	273	280	280	280	280	−30
Hawaii	226	428	468	468	468	602	632	666	693	712	−16
Idaho	211	300	323	304	304	315	315	315	315	317	−60
Illinois	232	261	288	341	342	367	367	367	367	367	−58
Indiana	120	200	255	256	256	288	288	288	288	288	−36
Iowa	201	294	360	360	381	410	426	426	426	426	−43
Kansas	222	321	345	373	403	409	409	422	429	429	−48
Kentucky	147	185	188	197	197	228	228	228	228	228	−59
Louisiana	88	128	152	190	190	190	190	190	190	190	−42
Maine	135	176	280	370	405	453	453	453	453	418	−17
Maryland	162	200	270	313	345	396	406	377	359	366	−40
Massachusetts	268	259	379	396	491	539	539	539	539	579	−42
Michigan (Wayne County)	219	333	425	468	473	516	525	459	459	459	−44
Minnesota	256	330	417	524	532	532	532	532	532	532	−45

TABLE 10–14.—AFDC MAXIMUM BENEFIT FOR A THREE-PERSON FAMILY, BY STATE FOR SELECTED YEARS—Continued

	July 1970[1]	July 1975	July 1980	January 1985[2]	January 1987[2]	January 1990[2]	January 1991[2]	January 1992[2]	January 1993[2]	January 1994[2]	Percent change, 1970-94[3]
Mississippi	56	48	96	96	120	120	120	120	120	120	−43
Missouri	104	120	248	263	279	289	292	292	292	292	−25
Montana	202	201	259	332	354	359	370	390	390	401	−47
Nebraska	171	210	310	350	350	364	364	364	364	364	−43
Nevada	121	195	262	233	285	330	330	372	348	348	−23
New Hampshire	262	308	346	378	397	506	516	516	516	550	−44
New Jersey	302	310	360	385	404	424	424	424	424	424	−63
New Mexico	149	169	220	258	258	264	310	324	324	357	−36
New York City	279	332	394	474	497	577	577	577	577	577	−45
North Carolina	145	183	192	223	259	272	272	272	272	272	−50
North Dakota	213	283	334	371	371	386	401	401	401	409	−49
Ohio	161	204	263	290	302	334	334	334	341	341	−44
Oklahoma	152	217	282	282	310	325	341	341	324	324	−43
Oregon	184	337	282	386	397	432	444	460	460	460	−33
Pennsylvania	265	296	332	364	382	421	421	421	421	421	−58
Rhode Island	229	278	340	479	503	543	554	554	554	554	−35
South Carolina	85	96	129	187	199	206	210	210	200	200	−37
South Dakota	264	289	321	329	366	377	385	404	404	417	−58
Tennessee	112	115	122	138	155	184	195	185	185	185	−56
Texas	148	116	116	167	184	184	184	184	184	184	−67
Utah	175	252	360	363	376	387	402	402	402	414	−37
Vermont	267	322	492	558	572	662	679	673	659	638	−36
Virginia	225	268	310	327	354	354	354	354	354	354	−58
Washington	258	315	458	476	492	501	531	531	546	546	−44

West Virginia	114	206	206	206	249	249	249	249	249	249	−42
Wisconsin	184	342	444	533	544	517	517	517	517	517	−25
Wyoming	213	235	315	360	360	360	360	360	360	360	−55
Guam	NA	NA	261	265	265	330	330	330	330	330	NA
Puerto Rico	43	43	44	90	90	90	90	180	180	180	+12
Virgin Islands	NA	131	209	171	171	240	240	240	240	240	NA
Median State[4]	184	235	288	332	354	364	367	372	367	366	−47

[1] Data on 3-person families were not published or reported before 1975. Thus, the 1970 data were derived by reducing the reported 4-person maximum benefit amount by the proportional difference between 3- and 4-person AFDC maximum benefit as shown in the July 1975 DHEW reports.

[2] CRS survey data.

[3] Real percentage change, calculated assuming a January 1994 CPI–U value of 146.2 relative to the July 1970 value of 39.0.

[4] Among 50 States and the District of Columbia.

NA—Not available.

Note.—Table compiled by CRS on the basis of data from DHHS and, where noted, from CRS itself.

TABLE 10–15.—HISTORICAL TRENDS IN AVERAGE PAYMENT PER RECIPIENT AND PER FAMILY; AND MAXIMUM AND MEDIAN BENEFITS FOR A FAMILY OF FOUR; FOR SELECTED YEARS FROM 1970 TO 1993 [1]

AFDC payments	1970	1975	1980	1985	1986	1987	1989	1991	1992	1993
Average monthly benefit per family	178	210	274	339	352	359	381	388	383	377
In constant 1993 dollars [2]	663	564	480	455	464	457	444	412	394	377
Average monthly benefit per person	46	63	94	116	120	123	131	135	134	133
In constant 1993 dollars [2]	171	169	165	156	158	156	153	143	138	133
Median State benefit in July for a family unit of 4 with no income [1]	221	264	350	399	415	420	432	435	435	435
In constant 1993 dollars [2]	823	709	614	536	547	534	503	462	448	435

[1] Among 50 States and the District of Columbia.
[2] The constant dollar numbers were calculated using the CPI–U.
Note.—AFDC benefit amounts have not been reduced by child support enforcement collections.

Source: Family Support Administration and the Congressional Research Service.

TABLE 10—16.—INCOME LEVELS AT WHICH AFDC ELIGIBILITY ENDS FOR A FAMILY OF 3, BY STATE AND PERIOD OF RECEIPT, JANUARY 1994 [1][2]

	185 percent of need standard	Payment standard	AFDC maximum benefit	First 4 months			After 12 months		
				Effective eligibility level	Eligibility level as a percent of—		Effective eligibility level	Eligibility level as a percent of—	
					Poverty level	Minimum wage		Poverty level	Minimum wage
Alabama	$1,245	$164	$164	366	38	50	254	26	34
Alaska	1,804	923	923	1,505	125	204	1,013	84	137
Arizona	1,783	347	347	641	67	87	437	46	59
Arkansas	1,304	204	204	426	44	58	294	31	40
California	1,323	607	607	1,031	107	140	697	73	95
Colorado	779	421	356	752	78	102	511	53	69
Connecticut	1,258	680	680	1,140	119	155	770	80	104
Delaware	625	338	338	627	65	85	428	45	58
District of Columbia	1,317	420	420	750	78	102	510	53	69
Florida	1,833	303	303	575	60	78	393	41	53
Georgia	784	424	280	756	79	103	514	54	70
Hawaii	2,109	712	712	1,188	108	161	802	73	109
Idaho	1,833	317	317	596	62	81	407	42	55
Illinois	1,647	367	367	671	70	91	457	48	62
Indiana	592	288	288	552	58	75	378	39	51
Iowa	1,571	426	426	759	79	103	516	54	70
Kansas	794	429	429	764	80	104	519	54	70
Kentucky	973	526	228	909	95	123	616	64	84
Louisiana	1,217	190	190	405	42	55	280	29	38
Maine	1,023	553	418	950	99	129	643	67	87
Maryland	938	366	366	669	70	91	456	48	62
Massachusetts	1,071	579	579	989	103	134	669	70	91
Michigan (Wayne County)	1,019	459	459	809	84	110	549	57	74

TABLE 10-16.—INCOME LEVELS AT WHICH AFDC ELIGIBILITY ENDS FOR A FAMILY OF 3, BY STATE AND PERIOD OF RECEIPT, JANUARY 1994 [1] [2]—Continued

	185 percent of need standard	Payment standard	AFDC maximum benefit	First 4 months			After 12 months		
				Effective eligibility level	Eligibility level as a percent of—		Effective eligibility level	Eligibility level as a percent of—	
					Poverty level	Minimum wage		Poverty level	Minimum wage
Minnesota	984	532	532	918	96	125	622	65	84
Mississippi	681	368	120	672	70	91	458	48	62
Missouri	1,565	292	292	558	58	76	382	40	52
Montana	945	401	401	722	75	98	491	51	67
Nebraska	673	364	364	666	69	90	454	47	62
Nevada	1,293	348	348	642	67	87	438	46	59
New Hampshire	3,049	550	550	945	98	128	640	67	87
New Jersey	1,822	424	424	756	79	103	514	54	70
New Mexico	660	357	357	656	68	89	447	47	61
New York (New York City)	1,067	577	577	986	103	134	667	69	91
North Carolina	1,006	544	272	936	98	127	634	66	86
North Dakota	757	409	409	734	76	100	499	52	68
Ohio	1,626	341	341	632	66	86	431	45	58
Oklahoma	871	324	324	606	63	82	414	43	56
Oregon	851	460	460	810	84	110	550	57	75
Pennsylvania	1,136	421	421	752	78	102	511	53	69
Rhode Island	1,025	554	554	951	99	129	644	67	87
South Carolina	814	200	200	420	44	57	290	30	72
South Dakota	908	417	417	746	78	101	507	53	69
Tennessee	788	426	185	759	79	103	516	54	70
Texas	1,062	184	184	396	41	54	274	29	37
Utah	1,021	414	414	741	77	101	504	53	68

Vermont	2,079	638	638	1,077	112	146	728	76	99
Virginia	727	354	354	651	68	88	444	46	60
Washington	2,142	546	546	939	98	127	636	66	86
West Virginia	919	249	249	494	51	67	339	35	46
Wisconsin	1,197	517	517	896	93	122	607	63	82
Wyoming	1,247	590	360	1005	105	136	680	71	92
Guam	611	330	330	615	64	83	420	44	57
Puerto Rico	296	180	180	390	41	53	270	28	37
Virgin Islands	555	240	240	480	50	65	330	34	45

[1] These calculations assume no child care expenses and work expenses of $90 per month. The breakevens for 5–12 months can be obtained by adding $30 to the breakeven for "After 12 months." The calculations are also based on a 1993 poverty level of $11,521 ($960 per month) for a family of three, and a 1993 minimum wage salary of $8,840 ($737 per month).

[2] Income level at which Medicaid eligibility ends. Because of minimum payment rule, actual AFDC benefits may end at a slightly different income level.

Source: Congressional Research Service.

AFDC benefits for special needs

In general, the AFDC need standard provides for basic consumption items such as food, clothing, shelter, fuel and utilities, personal care items, and household supplies that are essential to recipients. The need standard may also provide for special (recurrent or nonrecurrent) needs, such as special dietary requirements, pregnancy allowance, training and/or educational expenses, expenses caused by catastrophe or eviction, etc.

"Special needs," which may be recurring or nonrecurring, are usually defined as those needs that are recognized by the State as essential for some persons but not for all, and therefore must be determined on an individual basis. They are part of the total "need standard" used to measure AFDC eligibility and determine benefits amount for those families for whom such special needs items are appropriate. Federal funds pay at least 50 percent of each State's AFDC benefit expenditures which include funds spent on special need items, and about 54 percent of U.S. total AFDC benefit costs. (The Federal Government also pays one-half the cost of each State's AFDC administrative costs.) Note that AFDC benefit amount information included elsewhere in this section does not take into account payments related to special needs.

The first mention of special needs in Federal regulations occurred on July 17, 1968. These were interim regulations. Final regulations, with identical AFDC-special needs language, were published and took effect on January 29, 1969. Title 45, section 233.20(a)(2)(v) of the U.S. Code of Federal Regulations (1987), unchanged from the 1969 regulations, requires States to specify in their AFDC State plan a statewide standard, expressed in dollars, to be used in determining need of applicants and recipients and the amount of the benefit payment. Further, if the State includes "special need" items in its standard, it must describe them and the circumstances under which they will be taken into account. Regulations require that special needs in a State standard be considered for all AFDC applicants or recipients who require them, except that work expenses and child care/dependent care costs resulting from work, job search, or participation in a community work experience program cannot be defined as special needs.

As of October 1, 1990, according to State plans on file with the Department of Health and Human Services, 32 jurisdictions included special need items in their State standard. Examples of the special need items specified by States follow: child care that was not related to employment; training and/or educational expenses; special transportation; pregnancy allowance; special clothing and clothing replacement; expenses caused by catastrophe or eviction; excess shelter, fuel, or utilities costs; repair of property, appliances, or furnishings; special diets; telephone or special telephone services; fees and/or deposits; funeral and burial expenses; temporary shelter; and moving and/or storage expenses. Additional/excess cost of shelter, fuel, or utilities, pregnancy allowance, and child care costs (not employment related), were the most frequently cited special need items. As inferred above, 22 jurisdictions specified *no* special need items. New York specified the most special needs items, 19, followed by California and Connecticut which both specified 10 items.

FEDERAL AND STATE FUNDING OF AFDC BENEFIT PAYMENTS AND
ADMINISTRATIVE COSTS

AFDC benefit payments and administrative costs

The Federal share of a State's AFDC benefit payments is determined by the matching formula specified for Medicaid in title XIX of the Social Security Act (States may choose an alternate formula, but none do so). The Federal Medicaid matching rate is inversely related to State per capita income; thus, Federal matching for AFDC benefit payments varies from State to State, ranging from 50 percent in States with high per capita incomes to close to 80 percent in Mississippi, a State with relatively low per capita income. Table 10–17 provides State-specific information on the Federal share of AFDC benefit payments.

For the outlying areas—Guam, Puerto Rico and the Virgin Islands—75 percent Federal matching is provided for AFDC benefits, but the law imposes a ceiling on total Federal funds for AFDC and several other programs. The ceilings are as follows: Puerto Rico, $82 million; Guam, $3.8 million; and the Virgin Islands, $2.8 million.

The Federal Government pays 50 percent of the costs of administering the AFDC program in all States.

Some States require their localities to finance a portion of the non-Federal share of benefit payments (see table 10–18), and the non-Federal share of administrative costs (see table 10–19).

Table 10–20 provides information on total Federal and State benefit payments under the single parent and unemployed parent programs for fiscal years 1970 through 1993, and DHHS projections for fiscal years 1994 through 1999 (for State-level data on benefit payments, see table 10–23). Table 10–21 breaks these data down into their Federal and State shares, and also includes information on administrative costs for the AFDC program.

TABLE 10–17.—FEDERAL SHARE OF AFDC BENEFITS PAYMENTS,[1] SELECTED FISCAL
YEARS 1984 THROUGH 1995

[In percent]

State	1984–85 [2]	1988	1990	1992	1994	1995
Alabama	72.14	73.29	73.21	72.93	71.22	70.45
Alaska	50.00	50.00	50.00	50.00	50.00	50.00
Arizona	61.21	62.12	60.99	62.61	65.90	66.40
Arkansas	73.65	74.21	74.58	75.66	74.46	73.75
California	50.00	50.00	50.00	50.00	50.00	50.00
Colorado	50.00	50.00	52.11	54.79	54.30	53.10
Connecticut	50.00	50.00	50.00	50.00	50.00	50.00
Delaware	50.00	51.90	50.00	50.12	50.00	50.00
District of Columbia	50.00	50.00	50.00	50.00	50.00	50.00
Florida	58.41	55.39	54.70	54.69	54.78	56.28
Georgia	67.43	63.84	62.09	61.78	62.47	62.23

TABLE 10–17.—FEDERAL SHARE OF AFDC BENEFITS PAYMENTS,[1] SELECTED FISCAL YEARS 1984 THROUGH 1995—Continued

[In percent]

State	1984–85 [2]	1988	1990	1992	1994	1995
Guam (Federal funds limited) [3]	75.00	75.00	75.00	75.00	75.00	75.00
Hawaii	50.00	53.71	54.50	52.57	50.00	50.00
Idaho	67.28	70.47	73.32	73.24	70.92	70.14
Illinois	50.00	50.00	50.00	50.00	50.00	50.00
Indiana	59.93	63.71	63.76	63.85	63.49	63.03
Iowa	55.24	62.75	62.52	65.04	63.33	62.62
Kansas	50.67	55.20	56.07	59.23	59.52	58.90
Kentucky	70.72	72.27	72.95	72.82	70.91	69.58
Louisiana	64.65	68.26	73.12	75.44	73.49	72.65
Maine	70.63	67.08	65.20	62.40	61.96	63.30
Maryland	50.00	50.00	50.00	50.00	50.00	50.00
Massachusetts	50.13	50.00	50.00	50.00	50.00	50.00
Michigan	50.70	56.48	54.54	55.41	56.37	56.84
Minnesota	52.67	53.98	52.74	54.43	54.65	54.27
Mississippi	77.63	79.65	80.18	79.99	78.85	78.58
Missouri	61.40	59.27	59.18	60.84	60.64	59.86
Montana	64.41	69.40	71.35	71.70	71.05	70.81
Nebraska	57.13	59.73	61.12	64.50	61.98	60.40
Nevada	50.00	50.25	50.00	50.00	50.31	50.00
New Hampshire	59.45	50.00	50.00	50.00	50.00	50.00
New Jersey	50.00	50.00	50.00	50.00	50.00	50.00
New Mexico	69.39	71.52	72.25	74.33	74.17	73.31
New York	50.88	50.00	50.00	50.00	50.00	50.00
North Carolina	69.54	68.68	67.46	66.52	65.14	64.71
North Dakota	61.32	64.87	67.52	72.75	71.13	68.73
Ohio	55.44	59.10	59.57	60.63	60.83	60.69
Oklahoma	58.47	63.33	68.29	70.74	70.39	70.05
Oregon	57.12	62.11	62.95	63.55	62.12	62.36
Pennsylvania	56.04	57.35	56.86	56.84	54.61	54.27
Puerto Rico (Federal funds limited) [3]	75.00	75.00	75.00	75.00	75.00	75.00
Rhode Island	58.17	54.85	55.15	53.29	53.87	55.49
South Carolina	73.51	73.49	73.07	72.66	71.08	70.71
South Dakota	68.31	70.43	70.90	72.59	69.50	68.06
Tennessee	70.66	70.64	69.64	68.41	67.15	66.52
Texas	54.37	56.91	61.23	64.18	64.18	63.31
Utah	70.84	73.73	74.70	75.11	74.35	73.48
Vermont	69.37	66.23	62.77	61.37	59.55	60.82
Virgin Islands (Federal funds limited) [3]	75.00	75.00	75.00	75.00	75.00	75.00

TABLE 10–17.—FEDERAL SHARE OF AFDC BENEFITS PAYMENTS,[1] SELECTED FISCAL YEARS 1984 THROUGH 1995—Continued

[In percent]

State	1984–85[2]	1988	1990	1992	1994	1995
Virginia	56.53	51.34	50.00	50.00	50.00	50.00
Washington	50.00	53.21	53.88	54.98	54.24	51.97
West Virginia	70.57	74.84	76.61	77.68	75.72	74.60
Wisconsin	56.87	58.98	59.28	60.38	60.47	59.81
Wyoming	50.00	57.96	65.95	69.10	65.63	62.87

[1] The Federal share of the AFDC program is calculated by the same formula used to determine the Federal share of medicaid costs except in States that elect an alternate formula or have no medicaid program. Texas chose the alternate formula until July 1, 1983. Arizona used the alternate formula until the first quarter of fiscal year 1983, when it was deemed qualified to use the medicaid formula for the first time.

[2] Effective Oct. 1, 1983, through Sept. 30, 1985.

[3] Public Law 96–272 made permanent the 75-percent matching rate for AFDC effective Oct. 1, 1979. For medicaid the matching rate remains 50 percent.

Source: Department of Health and Human Services, Administration for Children and Families.

TABLE 10–18.—FINANCING OF NON-FEDERAL SHARE OF BENEFIT PAYMENTS, FOR
STATES USING STATE AND LOCAL FUNDS, AS OF OCTOBER 1993

	Percent State funds	Percent local funds
California [1]	95.0	5.0
Colorado	57.3	42.7
Indiana	60.0	40.0
Minnesota [2]	85.0	15.0
Montana [3]	77.5	22.5
New Jersey	75.0	25.0
New York [4]	50.0	50.0
North Carolina [5]	50.0	50.0
North Dakota [5]	75.0	25.0
Ohio [6]	36.1	4.0
Wisconsin [7]	100.0	....

[1] Counties pay up to 100 percent of some types of emergency assistance costs.

[2] Counties finance 90 percent of the non-Federal costs of the emergency assistance program.

[3] For all cases in State-administered counties and Indian cases in State-supervised counties, State funds only.

[4] For persons with State residence. For persons without State residence, for persons eligible for public assistance and care under AFDC and who are released from a State mental hygiene facility after a stay of 5 or more years, and for Indians living on reservations, State pays 100 percent of assistance.

[5] State pays 100 percent for Indians living on reservations.

[6] Percentage of total costs before deduction of Federal share.

[7] State pays State costs and up to 100 percent of local costs. Localities pay foster care and institutional costs in excess of State appropriations.

Source: "Characteristics of State Plans for AFDC," Administration For Children and Families.

TABLE 10–19.—FINANCING OF NON-FEDERAL SHARE OF COSTS OF ADMINISTRATION, FOR STATES USING STATE AND LOCAL FUNDS, AS OF OCTOBER 1993

	Percent State funds	Percent local funds
Arkansas	100% in 50 counties; lesser proportion in 25 counties.	25 counties participate in maintenance costs.
California [1]	100% of State costs; 70% of local costs.	30% of local costs.
Colorado	60%	40%
Indiana	100% of State costs, plus up to 50% of specified local costs.	50% or more of specified local costs.
Iowa	100% of State and district costs.	100% of local costs.
Maryland	100% of State budgeted positions.	100% of local and nonbudgeted positions.
Minnesota	Varies with appropriations	Varies with State appropriations.
Mississippi	Varies according to county population.	Varies according to county population.
Montana [2]	50%.	50%.
Nebraska	Varies	Local funds used for some travel, rent, and equipment.
New Jersey	100% of State costs	100% of local costs.
New York	50% (or 100% for Indians living on reservations).	50%.
North Carolina	100% of State costs and varying proportion of local costs, based on prior actual expenditures.	Portion of local costs not covered by State appropriation.
North Dakota	100% of State costs	100% of local costs if able.
Ohio	45.5% [3]	4.5%.
South Dakota	100% of State costs	100% of local costs.
Virginia	60%	40%.
Wisconsin	100% of State costs and up to 100% of local costs.	Any costs in excess of State appropriation.

[1] Counties pay 100 percent of non-Federal share of costs for emergency assistance cases involving removal of a child from the home.
[2] State pays all administrative costs in State-administered counties.
[3] Percentage of total cost before deduction of Federal share (50.0%).

Source: State Plans for AFDC, Administration For Children and Families.

TABLE 10–20.—FEDERAL AND STATE AFDC BENEFIT PAYMENTS UNDER THE SINGLE PARENT AND UNEMPLOYED PARENT PROGRAMS: FISCAL YEARS 1970 TO 1999

[In millions of dollars]

Fiscal year	Single parent [1]	Unemployed parent	Child support collections [2]	Total, columns (1) and (2) minus (3) [3]	Column (4) expressed in 1993 constant dollars [4]
	(1)	(2)	(3)	(4)	(5)
1970	3,851	231	0	4,082	14,535
1971	4,993	412	0	5,405	18,380
1972	5,972	422	0	6,394	20,996
1973	6,459	414	0	6,873	21,676
1974	6,881	324	0	7,205	20,972
1975	7,791	362	0	8,153	21,586
1976	8,825	525	286	9,064	22,464
1977	9,420	617	423	9,614	22,180
1978	9,624	565	472	9,717	21,063
1979	9,865	522	597	9,790	19,485
1980	10,847	693	593	10,947	19,587
1981	11,769	1,075	659	12,185	19,825
1982	11,601	1,256	771	12,086	18,372
1983	12,136	1,471	865	12,742	18,526
1984	12,759	1,612	983	13,388	18,670
1985	13,024	1,556	901	13,679	18,397
1986	13,672	1,563	951	14,284	18,753
1987	14,807	1,516	1,071	15,252	19,455
1988	15,243	1,420	1,197	15,466	18,953
1989	15,889	1,350	1,287	15,952	18,656
1990	17,059	1,480	1,416	17,123	19,077
1991	18,529	1,827	1,603	18,753	19,890
1992	20,121	2,119	1,822	20,418	21,019
1993	19,990	2,298	1,937	20,351	20,351
1994 [5]	20,462	2,223	2,132	20,553	19,982
1995 [5]	21,009	2,188	2,376	20,821	19,709
1996 [5]	21,763	2,168	2,619	21,312	19,642
1997 [5]	22,615	2,173	2,845	21,943	19,692
1998 [5]	23,453	2,183	3,085	22,551	19,708
1999 [5]	24,396	2,207	3,325	23,278	NA

[1] Includes payments to two-parent families where one adult is incapacitated.
[2] Total AFDC collections (including collections on behalf of foster care children) less payments to recipients.
[3] Net AFDC benefits—Gross benefits less those reimbursed by child support collections.
[4] Adjusted based on the CPI–XI index by Committee staff.
[5] Administration projection under current law.

NA—Not available.

Source: Office of Financial Management, Administration for Children and Families.

TABLE 10–21.—TOTAL, FEDERAL, AND STATE AFDC EXPENDITURES: FISCAL YEARS 1970 TO 1999

[In millions of dollars]

Fiscal year	Federal share		State share		Total	
	Benefits	Administrative	Benefits	Administrative	Benefits	Administrative
1970	2,187	[1] 572	1,443	186	4,082	[1] 881
1971	3,008	271	2,469	254	5,477	525
1972	3,612	[2] 240	2,942	241	6,554	NA
1973	3,865	313	3,138	296	7,003	610
1974	4,071	379	3,300	362	7,371	740
1975	4,625	552	3,787	529	8,412	1,082
1976	5,258	541	4,418	527	9,676	1,069
1977	5,626	595	4,762	583	10,388	1,177
1978	5,701	631	4,890	617	10,591	1,248
1979	5,825	683	4,954	668	10,779	1,350
1980	6,448	750	5,508	729	11,956	1,479
1981	6,928	835	5,917	814	12,845	1,648
1982	6,922	878	5,934	878	12,857	1,756
1983	7,332	915	6,275	915	13,607	1,830
1984	7,707	876	6,664	822	14,371	1,698
1985	7,817	890	6,763	889	14,580	1,779
1986	8,239	993	6,996	967	15,235	1,960
1987	8,914	1,081	7,409	1,052	16,323	2,133
1988	9,125	1,194	7,538	1,159	16,663	2,353
1989	9,433	1,211	7,807	1,206	17,240	2,417
1990	10,149	1,358	8,390	1,303	18,539	2,661
1991	11,165	1,373	9,191	1,300	20,356	2,673
1992	12,252	1,422	9,988	1,342	22,240	2,764
1993	12,270	1,518	10,016	1,438	22,286	2,956
1994 [3]	12,470	1,564	10,215	1,493	22,685	3,057
1995 [3]	12,756	1,597	10,441	1,558	23,197	3,155
1996 [3]	13,160	1,637	10,771	1,619	23,931	3,256
1997 [3]	13,631	1,682	11,157	1,682	24,788	3,365
1998 [3]	14,097	1,741	11,539	1,741	25,636	3,483
1999 [3]	14,629	1,802	11,974	1,802	26,603	3,605

[1] Includes expenditures for services.
[2] Administrative expenditures only.
[3] Administration projection under current law.

NA—Not available.

Note.—Benefits do not include emergency assistance payments or reimbursement from child support enforcement collections. Foster care payments are included from 1971 to 1980. Beginning in fiscal year 1984, the cost of certifying AFDC households for food stamps are shown in the food stamp appropriation, U.S. Department of Agriculture. Administrative costs include Child Care administration, Work Program, ADP, FAMIS, Fraud Control, SAVE and other State and local administrative expenditures.

Source: Office of Financial Management, Administration for Children and Families.

AFDC CASELOAD DATA

Table 10–22 presents State-specific information on caseloads and benefit payments under the AFDC single parent and unemployed parent programs. Average monthly benefits per AFDC family were $373 in fiscal year 1993. Table 10–23 provides similar information for the unemployed parents program only.

Table 10–24 presents data on the average monthly number of families and individuals receiving AFDC benefits since 1970. The table includes information on families and individuals in both the single parent and unemployed parent programs. In fiscal year 1993, the average monthly family enrollment in the combined programs was almost 5.0 million, and 359 thousand of these families were in the unemployed parent program. The table also includes historical information on the average monthly benefit under the combined programs.

The number of AFDC families rose more than 50 percent from 1971 to 1981, reaching a high of 3.9 million (monthly average) in 1981. In 1982, after OBRA took effect, the number dropped 8 percent, but in 1983 it rose 2.3 percent. Enrollment in 1993 reached an all time high and is projected to increase steadily (but at a much slower rate) over the next 5 years to 5.6 million in 1999.

Table 10–25 presents State-by-State data on total AFDC expenditures for the years 1985–93.

Table 10–26 shows the number of total AFDC recipients and the number of child recipients for 1970 to 1993, and shows these numbers as percentages of the total population and the poverty population, respectively. As a percentage of the total population, AFDC recipients declined by over one-half a percentage point from the mid-1970s to 1989. Between 1989 and 1991, the percentage of the population receiving AFDC increased significantly but is still below the early 1970 levels. The percentage of children receiving AFDC remained relatively constant at around 11 percent between 1972 and 1989, hitting a low of 10.75 percent in 1982. In 1990, the percentage rose to almost 12 percent and is expected to increase to a little over 13 percent in 1993. As a percentage of children in poverty, child AFDC recipients have fallen from a high of 80.5 percent in 1973 to a low of 49.6 percent in 1982, and have risen to 59.9 percent in 1990.

TABLE 10–22.—AVERAGE MONTHLY NUMBER OF AFDC FAMILIES AND RECIPIENTS, TOTAL BENEFIT PAYMENTS AND ADMINISTRATIVE COSTS, AND AVERAGE PAYMENT PER FAMILY AND RECIPIENT, FISCAL YEAR 1993 (PRELIMINARY DATA)

State	Total assistance payments (millions)	Average monthly caseload (thousands)	Average monthly recipients (thousands)	Average payment per Family	Average payment per Recipient	Total administrative costs (in millions)[1]	Annual administrative cost per AFDC family[2]
Alabama	$95.5	52	140	$154	$57	$20.6	$399
Alaska	110.6	12	36	762	253	8.9	736
Arizona	268.7	70	197	320	114	35.9	513
Arkansas	59.8	27	73	187	69	12.9	485
California	5,855.0	859	2,463	568	198	499.4	581
Colorado	164.0	43	123	322	111	24.8	584
Connecticut	386.3	57	162	562	199	27.5	480
Delaware	39.7	11	28	290	119	6.4	561
District of Columbia	112.6	25	67	378	141	27.9	1,125
Florida	804.7	254	695	264	97	125.8	495
Georgia	432.1	141	398	255	90	56.7	401
Guam	9.2	2	5	511	142	1.7	1,133
Hawaii	143.4	18	56	653	214	9.3	508
Idaho	28.5	8	21	301	112	8.3	1,051
Illinois	882.9	231	689	318	107	77.1	333
Indiana	224.8	73	212	257	88	41.0	562
Iowa	163.3	37	101	371	135	17.7	482
Kansas	125.9	30	88	347	119	22.3	738
Kentucky	210.0	83	225	211	78	39.0	471
Louisiana	176.9	90	263	164	56	20.5	228
Maine	117.1	24	67	408	145	6.4	268
Maryland	316.5	80	221	329	119	71.8	895
Massachusetts	749.9	114	325	546	192	70.5	616
Michigan	1,190.1	230	688	432	144	168.6	734
Minnesota	384.0	64	192	499	167	57.5	897
Mississippi	86.9	60	172	120	42	13.3	221
Missouri	283.8	90	262	263	90	34.0	378
Montana	49.1	12	35	350	118	9.1	778
Nebraska	65.6	17	48	327	113	12.0	719
Nevada	44.0	13	35	282	104	10.3	792
New Hampshire	56.0	11	30	424	158	6.7	609
New Jersey	538.2	126	349	356	128	145.9	1,159
New Mexico	119.1	31	95	317	104	11.0	351
New York	2,658.4	433	1,197	512	185	556.1	1,285
North Carolina	353.4	131	335	225	88	57.7	441
North Dakota	28.1	7	19	360	127	3.7	569
Ohio	980.5	258	719	317	114	104.3	404
Oklahoma	172.0	49	138	296	104	38.8	800
Oregon	202.4	43	118	396	143	38.2	897
Pennsylvania	917.7	205	608	372	126	106.2	517
Puerto Rico	76.8	61	190	105	34	14.4	237

TABLE 10–22.—AVERAGE MONTHLY NUMBER OF AFDC FAMILIES AND RECIPIENTS, TOTAL BENEFIT PAYMENTS AND ADMINISTRATIVE COSTS, AND AVERAGE PAYMENT PER FAMILY AND RECIPIENT, FISCAL YEAR 1993 (PRELIMINARY DATA)—Continued

State	Total assistance payments (millions)	Average monthly caseload (thousands)	Average monthly recipients (thousands)	Average payment per		Total administrative costs (in millions) [1]	Annual administrative cost per AFDC family [2]
				Family	Recipient		
Rhode Island	134.2	22	62	504	181	6.2	279
South Carolina ..	118.0	53	147	184	67	18.9	355
South Dakota	25.0	7	20	289	104	3.6	500
Tennesee	219.8	108	311	170	59	37.4	347
Texas	532.3	279	782	159	57	79.9	287
Utah	78.0	18	53	353	124	16.0	870
Vermont	65.7	10	29	548	192	5.0	500
Virgin Islands ...	3.5	1	4	243	77	0.8	667
Virginia	231.2	74	194	261	99	44.7	607
Washington	605.5	101	288	498	175	67.4	665
West Virginia	121.6	41	119	245	85	7.0	169
Wisconsin	441.2	80	237	460	155	46.3	579
Wyoming	26.5	7	18	340	121	3.7	569
U.S. total	22,286	4,981	14,144	373	131	2,955.5	593

[1] Administrative costs include Child Care administration, Work Program, ADP, FAMIS, Fraud Control, SAVE, and other State and local administrative expenditures.

[2] Average annual administrative cost per family.

Source: Office of Financial Management, Administration for Children and Families.

TABLE 10–23.—AFDC–UP RECIPIENTS OF CASH PAYMENTS AND AMOUNTS OF PAYMENTS BY STATE, FISCAL YEAR 1993 (PRELIMINARY DATA)

State	UP money payments (thousands)	Average monthly number of families	Average monthly number of recipients	Average monthly payment per—	
				Family	Recipient
Alabama	$386	495	1,948	$65	$17
Alaska	21,211	2,026	9,293	872	190
Arizona	4,730	1,318	5,548	299	71
Arkansas	1,458	399	1,688	305	72
California	1,148,349	141,584	576,161	676	166
Colorado	3,667	1,309	3,363	233	91
Connecticut	17,269	2,200	9,293	654	155
Delaware	476	121	500	328	79
District of Columbia	1,343	173	862	647	130
Florida	25,507	6,120	24,020	347	88
Georgia	3,801	1,019	4,237	311	75
Guam	1,006	111	614	755	137
Hawaii	8,308	887	4,269	781	162
Idaho	2,096	472	1,982	370	88
Illinois	44,223	10,036	43,593	367	85
Indiana	15,114	3,858	16,751	326	75
Iowa	11,357	2,200	9,069	430	104
Kansas	12,081	2,450	10,297	411	98
Kentucky	28,603	9,000	36,281	265	66
Louisiana	2,794	1,091	4,802	213	48
Maine	17,765	2,656	11,152	557	133
Maryland	4,838	967	4,211	417	96
Massachusetts	45,435	6,525	27,773	580	136
Michigan	184,379	31,585	134,236	486	114
Minnesota	49,817	6,936	32,680	599	127
Mississippi	263	158	623	139	35
Missouri	20,053	5,142	22,104	325	76
Montana	6,148	1,163	5,113	441	100
Nebraska	6,065	1,283	5,524	394	91
Nevada	1,397	357	1,495	326	78
New Hampshire	2,941	548	2,332	447	105
New Jersey	24,161	4,676	19,644	431	102
New Mexico	8,859	1,779	8,272	415	89
New York	116,487	17,063	70,715	569	137
North Carolina	9,815	3,057	12,098	268	68
North Dakota	2,583	489	2,154	440	100
Ohio	11,531	23,939	96,869	388	96
Oklahoma	3,315	698	2,945	396	94
Oregon	21,240	3,929	16,038	450	110

TABLE 10–23.—AFDC–UP RECIPIENTS OF CASH PAYMENTS AND AMOUNTS OF PAYMENTS BY STATE, FISCAL YEAR 1993 (PRELIMINARY DATA)—Continued

State	UP money payments (thousands)	Average monthly number of families	Average monthly number of recipients	Average monthly payment per—	
				Family	Recipient
Pennsylvania	52,701	10,471	44,864	419	98
Rhode Island	4,823	703	2,867	572	140
South Carolina	1,984	867	3,398	191	49
South Dakota	119	31	153	320	65
Tennssee	11,365	4,494	13,474	211	70
Texas	19,739	7,836	33,251	210	49
Utah	1,031	192	853	447	101
Vermont	9,589	1,427	5,781	560	138
Virginia	2,878	767	3,237	313	74
Washington	118,554	16,051	68,095	616	145
West Virginia	29,272	8,171	32,778	299	74
Wisconsin	54,023	7,995	38,693	563	116
Wyoming	816	185	755	368	90
U.S. total	2,297,765	359,009	1,488,748	533	129

Source: Office of Financial Management, Administration for Children and Families.

TABLE 10–24.—HISTORICAL TRENDS IN AFDC ENROLLMENTS AND AVERAGE PAYMENTS

Fiscal year	Average monthly number of (in thousands)					Average monthly benefit	
	Families [1]	Recipients [1]	Children [1]	Unemployed parent families	Unemployed parent recipients	Family	Recipient
1970	1,909	7,429	5,494	78	420	$178	$46
1971	2,532	9,556	6,963	143	726	180	48
1972	2,918	10,632	7,698	134	639	187	51
1973	3,123	11,038	7,965	120	557	187	53
1974	3,170	10,845	7,824	95	434	194	57
1975	3,342	11,067	7,928	101	451	210	63
1976	3,561	11,339	8,156	135	593	226	71
1977	3,575	11,108	7,818	149	659	242	78
1978	3,528	10,663	7,475	127	567	250	83
1979	3,493	10,311	7,193	113	504	257	87
1980	3,642	10,597	7,320	141	612	274	94
1981	3,871	11,160	7,615	209	881	277	96
1982	3,569	10,431	6,975	232	976	300	103
1983	3,651	10,659	7,051	272	1,144	311	106
1984	3,725	10,866	7,153	287	1,222	322	110
1985	3,692	10,813	7,165	261	1,131	339	116
1986	3,747	10,995	7,294	253	1,101	352	120
1987	3,784	11,065	7,381	236	1,035	359	123
1988	3,748	10,920	7,326	210	929	370	127
1989	3,771	10,935	7,370	193	856	381	131
1990	3,974	11,460	7,755	204	899	389	135
1991	4,375	12,595	8,515	268	1,148	388	135
1992	4,769	13,625	9,225	322	1,348	389	136
1993	4,981	14,144	9,539	359	1,489	373	131
1994 [2]	5,055	14,336	9,681	346	1,433	374	132
1995 [2]	5,148	14,551	9,859	338	1,398	376	133
1996 [2]	5,252	14,809	10,058	331	1,365	380	135
1997 [2]	5,363	15,093	10,271	327	1,344	385	137
1998 [2]	5,460	15,344	10,456	323	1,326	391	139
1999 [2]	5,575	15,649	10,677	321	1,316	398	142

[1] Includes unemployed parent families and, for 1971–81, foster care children.
[2] Administration projection under current law.

Note.—AFDC benefit amounts have not been reduced by child support collections.

Source: Office of Financial Management, Administration for Children and Families.

TABLE 10–25.—TOTAL AFDC BENEFIT EXPENDITURES, FISCAL YEARS 1985–93 [1]

[In millions]

	1985	1986	1987	1988	1989	1990	1991	1992	1993	Percent real change 1985–93 [2]
Alabama	$70.6	$68.3	$64.8	$62.1	$61.1	$61.5	$67.5	$85.1	$95.5	0
Alaska	42.1	46.0	51.0	53.7	54.8	59.5	76.8	96.3	110.6	95
Arizona	65.3	78.6	93.9	103.3	117.0	138.4	177.8	242.6	268.7	206
Arkansas	41.3	48.4	49.8	53.3	55.4	57.0	60.0	61.1	59.8	8
California	3,364.3	3,573.6	3,869.2	4,091.0	4,436.5	4,954.9	5,519.8	5,828.3	5,855.0	29
Colorado	100.2	106.6	117.5	125.1	131.0	136.7	149.9	162.5	164.0	22
Connecticut	223.2	223.4	221.0	218.4	241.4	295.2	347.2	376.9	386.3	29
Delaware	26.4	24.7	24.2	24.2	25.1	28.7	32.6	37.3	39.7	12
District of Columbia	76.6	76.5	77.7	76.2	77.5	84.0	97.5	102.4	112.6	9
Florida	247.9	261.3	291.7	318.1	354.6	417.5	515.1	733.1	804.7	141
Georgia	197.9	222.8	243.8	265.8	289.3	320.7	376.4	420.3	432.1	62
Guam	2.7	4.1	3.6	3.3	3.1	5.0	7.1	7.8	9.2	153
Hawaii	78.6	73.3	68.4	77.2	89.1	98.8	107.9	125.3	143.4	36
Idaho	19.2	19.3	20.2	19.3	18.4	19.5	22.2	24.0	28.5	10
Illinois	869.1	885.8	872.9	814.8	786.5	838.7	892.2	882.6	882.9	−25
Indiana	153.2	147.5	146.2	167.3	162.2	169.9	193.2	218.2	224.8	9
Iowa	159.6	169.7	166.4	155.0	149.0	152.4	160.2	164.3	163.3	−24
Kansas	85.1	91.2	96.4	97.3	104.3	105.1	108.7	119.2	125.9	10
Kentucky	138.1	104.4	137.6	142.9	155.4	179.1	204.1	213.1	210.0	13
Louisiana	154.1	161.5	172.8	182.2	184.8	188.0	188.1	181.8	176.9	−15

Maine	78.1	84.0	82.4	79.8	86.1	101.3	113.2	118.3	117.1	11
Maryland	121.6	249.7	250.3	250.2	265.5	295.8	330.4	333.3	316.5	93
Massachusetts	416.8	470.8	515.3	557.9	592.2	630.3	665.6	750.9	749.9	34
Michigan	1,197.9	1,247.8	1,201.0	1,231.4	1,226.4	1,211.3	1,184.1	1,162.0	1,190.1	−26
Minnesota	308.3	322.3	334.4	337.8	343.4	355.0	370.7	387.0	384.0	−7
Mississippi	60.7	74.0	80.7	85.3	84.9	86.3	87.9	88.8	86.9	6
Missouri	195.3	208.6	212.7	214.7	220.0	228.0	250.6	273.9	283.8	8
Montana	32.1	36.8	40.4	41.4	40.6	40.4	42.0	45.7	49.1	14
Nebraska	58.3	61.5	60.4	56.3	56.6	58.6	61.2	65.3	65.6	−16
Nevada	11.7	15.7	16.3	20.4	24.2	27.2	32.1	41.0	44.0	179
New Hampshire	20.4	19.6	18.1	21.1	24.3	31.8	45.3	54.5	56.0	104
New Jersey	251.3	509.0	482.8	458.7	440.1	451.4	488.7	[2] 515.7	538.2	59
New Mexico	51.1	51.3	55.9	56.2	55.0	60.6	86.2	105.9	119.1	73
New York	2,021.4	2,098.6	2,097.9	2,140.1	2,153.7	2,254.4	2,480.9	2,927.2	2,658.4	−2
North Carolina	160.9	137.6	191.0	205.6	220.5	246.7	303.6	335.3	353.4	63
North Dakota	18.2	19.9	20.9	21.9	24.0	24.3	25.0	27.5	28.1	15
Ohio	759.9	803.5	810.1	805.3	826.6	877.2	935.1	984.0	980.5	−4
Oklahoma	87.8	100.2	111.5	118.5	124.3	132.1	152.2	169.2	172.0	46
Oregon	106.5	120.4	119.1	128.1	137.5	145.2	177.2	200.1	202.4	41
Pennsylvania	750.6	388.8	750.9	746.8	738.5	798.3	827.3	906.1	917.7	−9
Puerto Rico	N.A.	33.0	66.4	66.7	70.6	71.5	75.2	76.9	76.8	N.A.
Rhode Island	73.4	78.8	80.9	81.6	85.8	99.0	117.2	128.4	134.2	36
South Carolina	89.5	103.2	102.7	91.2	91.3	95.7	107.4	119.2	118.0	−2
South Dakota	17.8	14.5	21.2	21.0	21.6	21.7	23.6	25.2	25.0	4
Tennessee	89.3	99.9	117.0	125.4	142.0	167.9	196.6	205.8	219.8	83
Texas	227.7	280.5	319.5	344.1	367.5	415.9	473.3	516.5	532.3	74
Utah	50.8	54.5	60.5	61.3	63.5	64.1	70.7	75.5	78.0	14
Vermont	38.2	39.5	41.2	40.2	41.4	48.1	54.6	67.0	65.7	28
Virgin Islands	N.A.	2.1	2.6	2.3	2.9	2.9	3.3	3.5	3.5	N.A.
Virginia	169.6	178.9	173.3	168.6	168.4	177.4	199.6	224.8	231.2	1

TABLE 10-25.—TOTAL AFDC BENEFIT EXPENDITURES, FISCAL YEARS 1985-93 [1]—Continued

[In millions]

	1985	1986	1987	1988	1989	1990	1991	1992	1993	Percent real change 1985-93 [2]
Washington	343.6	375.2	399.5	401.4	420.7	437.9	485.8	605.9	605.5	31
West Virginia	85.3	109.0	110.0	106.9	110.0	110.0	113.6	120.1	121.6	6
Wisconsin	556.4	443.8	568.7	505.9	454.2	440.4	447.1	453.3	441.2	−41
Wyoming	14.2	15.8	18.1	18.7	18.8	19.3	24.9	27.2	26.5	39
U.S. total	14,580.2	15,235.4	16,322.6	16,663.3	17,240.0	18,538.5	20,356.2	22,223.5	22,286.0	14

[1] Data for fiscal years 1985-89 do not include prior quarter adjustments.
[2] Percent change between 1985 and 1993 adjusted for inflation using CPI-X1.

Source: Office of Financial Management, Administration for Children and Families.

TABLE 10–26.—NUMBER OF AFDC RECIPIENTS, AND RECIPIENTS AS A PERCENTAGE OF VARIOUS POPULATION GROUPS

[In thousands]

Calendar year	Total AFDC recipients[1]	AFDC child recipients[1]	Total population ages 0–17[2]	AFDC recipients as a percent of total population[2]	AFDC child recipients as a percent of total child population	AFDC recipients as a percent of prewelfare poverty population[3]	AFDC child recipients as a percent of children in poverty[4]
1970	8,303	6,104	69,759	4.07	8.75	NA	58.5
1971	10,043	7,303	69,806	4.86	10.46	NA	69.2
1972	10,736	7,766	69,417	5.13	11.19	NA	75.5
1973	10,738	7,763	68,762	5.08	11.29	NA	80.5
1974	10,621	7,684	67,984	4.98	11.30	NA	75.7
1975	11,131	7,952	67,164	5.17	11.84	NA	71.6
1976	11,098	7,850	66,250	5.10	11.85	NA	76.4
1977	10,856	7,632	65,461	4.94	11.66	NA	74.2
1978	10,387	7,270	64,773	4.68	11.22	NA	73.2
1979	10,140	7,057	64,106	4.52	11.01	54.5	68.0
1980	10,599	7,295	63,684	4.66	11.45	49.2	63.2
1981	10,893	7,397	63,212	4.75	11.70	47.1	59.2
1982	10,161	6,767	62,812	4.39	10.77	40.6	49.6
1983	10,569	6,967	62,566	4.52	11.14	41.9	50.1
1984	10,645	7,017	62,483	4.51	11.23	43.6	52.3
1985	10,672	7,074	62,624	4.49	11.30	45.0	54.4
1986	10,850	7,206	62,866	4.52	11.46	46.6	56.0
1987	10,841	7,240	63,056	4.47	11.48	46.7	56.4
1988	10,915	7,328	63,247	4.46	11.59	48.5	58.8
1989	10,799	7,287	63,456	4.38	11.48	47.6	57.9
1990	11,699	7,922	64,185	4.69	12.34	48.0	59.0
1991	12,728	8,601	65,145	5.05	13.20	49.1	60.0
1992	[5]13,623	[5]9,224	66,163	5.34	13.94	NA	63.1

[1] Annual numbers. In calculating the number of AFDC recipients, data for Guam, Puerto Rico, and the Virgin Islands was subtracted from the total AFDC population. Data for these territories was not available for 1970–76, so an estimate was used based on the ratio in later years (1977–87) of the number of recipients in these areas to the total number of recipients.

[2] Population numbers represent U.S. resident population, not including Armed Forces overseas.

[3] Poverty population is determined by the number of people whose income (cash income plus social insurance plus Social Security before taxes and means-tested transfers) falls below the appropriate poverty threshold. This information can be found in appendix J, table 20, 1992 Green Book.

[4] This information can be found in appendix J, table 2, 1992 Green Book.

[5] Recipient estimates assume the same number of AFDC recipients in Guam, Puerto Rico, and the Virgin Islands in 1992 and 1993 as existed in 1991.

NA—Poverty population data is not available for this time period.

Characteristics of AFDC Families

This section describes the characteristics of AFDC families, using two main sources of data. For years through 1979, the sources were individual surveys of similar design specially conducted to gather information from agency case files. For 1982 and later years, data were derived from information collected from cases within the National Integrated Quality Control System's (NIQCS) monthly sample of cases.

Table 10–27 shows that the share of AFDC families with earnings fell 42 percent from March 1979 to 1992, from 12.8 percent to 7.4 percent. The share of families with no reported income other than AFDC climbed from 80.6 percent in 1979 to 86.8 percent in 1983, and fell to 78.9 percent by 1992. Moreover (table 10–33), the average amount of income deemed to members of the AFDC assistance unit tripled, from $63 per family in March 1979 to $186 in 1992.

Table 10–27 also shows the trend in other selected characteristics of AFDC families from 1969 to 1992. During this period, the average family size decreased from 4.0 persons to 2.9, the percent of families participating in the food stamp program increased, and the share of AFDC households with nonrecipient members climbed slightly.

Table 10–27 indicates that the share of AFDC families with no more than two children rose from 49.6 percent in 1969 to 72.7 percent in 1992, and the percentage of families reporting no father in the home rose from 84.7 percent in 1979 to 89.4 percent in 1992.

TABLE 10-27.—AFDC CHARACTERISTICS, 1969–92

	May 1969	January 1973	May 1975	March 1979	1983[1]	1986[1]	1988[1]	1990[1]	1992[1]
Average family size (persons)	4.0	3.6	3.2	3.0	3.0	3.0	3.0	2.9	2.9
Number of child recipients (percent of AFDC cases):									
One	26.6	NA	37.9	42.3	43.4	42.7	42.5	42.2	42.5
Two	23.0	NA	26.0	28.1	29.8	30.8	30.2	30.3	30.2
Three	17.7	NA	16.1	15.6	15.2	15.9	15.8	15.8	15.5
Four or more	32.5	NA	20.0	13.9	10.1	9.8	9.9	9.9	10.1
Unknown		NA			1.5	.8	1.7	1.4	.7
Basis for eligibility (percent children):									
Parents present:									
Incapacitated	[2]11.7	10.2	7.7	5.3	3.4	3.2	3.7	3.6	4.1
Unemployed	24.6	4.1	3.7	4.1	8.7	7.4	6.5	6.4	8.2
Parents absent:									
Death	[2]5.5	5.0	3.7	2.2	1.8	1.9	1.8	1.6	1.6
Divorce or separation	[2]43.3	46.5	48.3	44.7	38.5	36.3	34.6	32.9	30.0
No marriage tie	[2]27.9	31.5	31.0	37.8	44.3	48.9	51.9	54.0	53.1
Other reason	[2]3.5	3.6	4.0	5.9	1.4	2.4	1.6	1.9	2.0
Unknown					1.7				.9
Education of mother (percent of mothers):[3]									
8th Grade or less	29.4	NA	16.7	9.5	NA	4.8	5.5	5.8	4.9
1–3 years of HS	30.7	NA	31.7	20.8	NA	14.3	14.7	16.5	18.8
High School Degree	16.0	NA	23.7	18.8	NA	17.3	17.5	19.3	22.4
Some College	2.0	NA	3.9	2.7	NA	3.4	3.9	5.7	6.8
College Graduate	.2	NA	.7	.4	NA	.5	.6	.4	.5
Unknown	21.6	NA	23.3	47.8	NA	59.7	58.3	52.3	46.6
Age of mother (percent of mothers):[3]									
Under 20	6.6	NA	8.3	[4]4.1	[4]3.6	[4]3.3	[4]3.4	7.9	7.6
20 to 24	16.7	NA	[5]	[6]28.0	[6]28.6	[7]33.6	[7]32.2	23.8	24.5
25 to 29	17.6	NA	[5]	21.4	23.8	[8]20.0	[8]19.4	24.6	23.3
30 to 39	30.4	NA	27.9	27.2	27.9	30.1	31.5	32.0	32.7
40 or over	25.0	NA	17.6	15.4	15.7	13.0	13.4	11.7	11.8
Unknown	3.6	NA	3.0	4.0	0.3				.1
Ages of children (percent of recipient children):									
Under 3	14.9	NA	16.5	18.9	22.5	21.9	21.1	24.2	24.6
3 to 5	17.6	NA	18.1	17.5	20.1	21.1	21.0	21.5	21.7
6 to 11	36.5	NA	33.7	33.0	31.5	32.4	33.3	27.5	32.4

TABLE 10-27.—AFDC CHARACTERISTICS, 1969-92—Continued

	May 1969	January 1973	May 1975	March 1979	1983[1]	1986[1]	1988[1]	1990[1]	1992[1]
12 and over	31.0	NA	30.9	29.8	25.5	24.3	22.4	21.3	21.2
Unknown	......	NA	.8	.9	.3	.1	1.3	.0	.0
Mother's employment status (percent):[3]									
Full-time job	8.2	9.8	10.4	8.7	1.5	1.6	2.2	2.5	2.2
Part-time job	6.3	6.3	5.7	5.4	3.4	4.2	4.2	4.2	4.2
Presence of income (percent families):									
With earnings	NA	16.3	14.6	12.8	5.7	7.5	8.4	8.2	7.4
No non-AFDC income	56.0	66.9	71.1	[9]80.6	[9]86.8	[9]81.3	[9]79.6	[9]80.1	[9]78.9
Median months on AFDC since most recent opening	23.0	27.0	31.0	29.0	26.0	27.0	26.3	23.0	22.5
Race (percent parents)[10]									
White	NA	38.0	39.9	40.4	41.8	39.7	38.8	38.1	38.9
Black	45.2	45.8	44.3	43.1	43.8	40.7	39.8	39.7	37.2
Hispanic	NA	13.4	12.2	13.6	12.0	14.4	15.7	16.6	17.8
Native American	1.3	1.1	1.1	1.4	1.0	1.3	1.4	1.3	1.4
Asian	NA	NA	.5	1.0	1.5	2.3	2.4	2.8	2.8
Other and unknown	4.8	1.7	2.0	.4	NA	1.4	1.9	1.5	2.0
Incidence of households (percent):									
Living in public housing	12.8	13.6	14.6	NA	10.0	9.6	9.6	9.6	9.2
Participating in food stamp or donated food program	52.9	68.4	75.1	75.1	83.0	80.7	84.6	85.6	87.3
Including nonrecipient members	33.1	34.9	34.8	NA	36.9	36.7	36.8	37.7	38.9
Father's relationship to youngest child (percent):									
No father	NA	NA	NA	84.7	89.8	91.2	91.6	92.0	89.4
Natural father	NA	NA	NA	9.6	NA	NA	NA	NA	NA
Adoptive father	NA	NA	NA	.0	NA	NA	NA	NA	NA
Stepfather	NA	NA	NA	5.6	NA	NA	NA	NA	NA

[1] Data are for the Federal fiscal year October through September. All percentages are based on the average monthly caseload during the year. Hawaii and the territories are not included in 1983. Data for 1986 include Hawaii, but not the territories. Data after 1986 include the territories and Hawaii.   [2] Calculated on the basis of total number of families.   [3] For years after 1983, data are for adult female recipients.   [4] Under age 19.   [5] The percentage for 20 to 29 year olds was 43.1.   [6] The ages were 19-24 in 1979, 1983 and 1990.   [7] In 1986 and 1988 this age group was 19 to 25.   [8] In 1986 and 1988 this age group was 26-29.   [9] State collected child support directly beginning in 1975, removing one source of non-AFDC income.   [10] For 1983, 12.6 percentage points where race was unknown were allocated proportionately across all categories.

NA—Not available.

Source: Office of Family Assistance, Administration for Children and Families, and Congressional Budget Office.

Table 10–28 indicates that the share of families who received benefits for more than 5 years (since the most recent opening of their case) did not change dramatically during the 1980's, and has dropped in 1990, 1991, and 1992.

TABLE 10–28.—EMPLOYMENT STATUS OF AFDC MOTHERS AND TENURE OF AFDC FAMILIES [1]

	Percent of total caseload							
	March 1979 [2]	May 1982	1983 [3]	1986 [3]	1988 [3]	1990 [3]	1991 [3]	1992 [3]
Employment status of mother (or other caretaker): [4]								
No mother (caretaker)	8.3	12.2	8.7					
Full-time work, 30 or more hours per week	[5]8.0	[5]1.3	1.5	1.6	2.1	2.5	2.2	2.2
Part-time work, fewer than 30 hours per week	[5]5.0	[5]4.3	3.4	4.2	4.2	4.2	4.2	4.2
Incapacitated	6.0	NA	4.1	3.4	3.8			
At school or training	2.6	NA	2.0	1.9	2.2	11.5	12.5	16.1
On layoff	.5	NA	.8	.2	.2	.2	.1	.2
Seeking work	9.1	NA	NA	27.3	27.6	[6]10.5	[6]11.2	[6]11.8
Other—needed at home or not actively seeking work	60.5	82.2	64.8	58.3	55.5	[7]68.6	[7]68.8	[7]65.1
Unknown						2.6	.8	.6
Number of months on AFDC since most recent opening (percent of cases):								
1 to 6 months	16.4	20.0	18.9	17.2	18.2	19.8	20.4	19.0
7 to 12 months	12.5	12.4	13.1	12.6	13.2	14.4	14.8	15.2
13 to 24 months	16.7	16.2	16.6	17.2	17.3	18.4	19.2	19.3
25 to 36 months	11.4	12.6	12.0	11.8	11.2	11.9	12.2	12.8
37 to 60 months	15.3	14.2	15.4	14.9	15.0	13.7	12.8	14.1
61 plus months	26.9	23.5	23.7	25.9	24.9	21.7	20.5	19.6
Unknown	.8	1.1	.3	.4	.2	.01	.1	.1

[1] See text about difference in data sources for 1979, and 1982 and later years.
[2] Source: Committee staff tabulation of March 1979 AFDC recipients' data base.
[3] Fiscal year average monthly. 1983 does not include Hawaii or the territories. 1986 data do not include the territories. 1988–1992 data include the territories and Hawaii.
[4] Since 1986, the data are percent of female adult recipients.
[5] Full-time work, 35 hours or more per week; part-time work, fewer than 35 hours per week.
[6] For 1990–1992, unemployed, not on layoff or strike.
[7] For 1990–1992, not employed, not participating in any educational or training activities.

NA—Not available.

Source: Department of Health and Human Services.

Table 10–29 presents data on income sources of AFDC families. It indicates that the share of AFDC families with earnings from the mother (or other caretaker relative) or from the spouse of the caretaker relative declined from 12.6 percent in March 1979 to 7.4 percent in 1992. Further, according to the table, the average monthly amount earned dropped in nominal terms from $382 to $330 for mothers with earnings, and stay relatively constant in nominal dollars from $323 to $307 for fathers (or spouses of caretaker relatives) with earnings. These changes resulted primarily from provisions of OBRA 1981, which reduced eligibility for AFDC among families with earnings.

TABLE 10-29.—INCOME SOURCES OF AFDC FAMILIES,[1] SELECTED YEARS

Income source	Percentage of caseload with income type							Average amount for those with income type						
	March 1979	May 1982	Fiscal year					March 1979	May 1982	Fiscal year				
			1986[3]	1988[3]	1990[3]	1991[3]	1992[3]			1986[3]	1988[3]	1990[3]	1991[3]	1992[3]
Earned income:														
Mother (or caretaker relative)	12.0	5.3	6.2	7.0	6.9	6.7	6.1	$382	$261	$264	$276	$318	$324	$330
Father (or spouse of caretaker relative)	.6	.4	1.0	1.1	1.1	1.1	1.1	323	244	271	316	332	307	325
Children (14+)	.1	(⁴)	.3	.3	.3	.2	.2	206	398	323	299	301	348	358
Other adults	.1	NA	.2	.2	.1	.1	.1	265	NA	420	450	285	338	252
Public service	.1	NA	NA	NA	NA	NA	NA	246	NA	NA	NA	NA	NA	NA
OASDI	3.1	2.5	2.0	2.5	2.4	2.3	2.1	134	145	207	211	235	211	226
Veterans' benefits	.4	NA	.2	.2	.2	.1	.1	128	NA	139	122	135	114	182
Other government income	.4	.4	.3	.3	.3	.5	.7	143	134	131	109	105	159	96
Unemployment compensation	.7	1.0	.7	.6	.6	.9	.9	238	255	289	285	310	359	354
Workmen's compensation	.1	(⁴)	.1	.1	.1	.1	.1	237	200	299	267	396	542	348
Deemed income	.2	.3	.1	.1	.2	.2	.2	63	159	153	143	132	253	186
Contributions from other persons	.6	.9	NA	1.3	1.5	1.7	1.6	72	79	NA	92	105	109	109
Other cash income	1.9	2.5	⁵ 2.0	⁵ 2.0	⁵ 2.0	⁵ 2.3	⁵ 4.2	81	251	128	83	105	67	162
SSI (Federal)	NA	NA	3.0	1.9	1.1	1.1	1.3	NA	NA	334	369	442	410	436
Other public assistance or State SSI	NA	NA	1.1	.8	.6	.6	.3	NA	NA	374	299	299	311	315
In-kind income	.4	NA	NA	NA	⁶.0	NA	NA	71	NA	NA	NA	⁶ 125	NA	NA
Total	19.4	NA	18.7	20.4	19.9	19.9	21.1	299	NA	228	....	239	238	246

[1] See text about differences in data sources for 1979, 1982, and subsequent years.
[2] Source: Committee staff tabulation of March 1979 AFDC recipients' data base.
[3] Fiscal year average monthly. 1986 data do not include the territories. 1988–92 data include both Hawaii and the territories.
[4] Less than 0.05 percent.
[5] Includes Federal SSI, State SSI, general assistance, income from assets and property and other unearned income.
[6] EITC.

NA—Not available.

Source: ACF, Department of Health and Human Services.

TABLE 10-30.—INCOME OF AFDC FAMILIES NOT COUNTED BY THE PROGRAM,[1] SELECTED YEARS

Disregards	Percent of caseload with disregard							Average amount for those with disregard						
	March 1979[2]	May 1982	Fiscal year					March 1979	May 1982	Fiscal year				
			1986[3]	1989[3]	1990[3]	1991[3]	1992[3]			1986[3]	1989[3]	1990[3]	1991[3]	1992[3]
Optional $5 disregard	1.1	(4)	(4)	(4)	(4)	(4)	(4)	$6	(4)	(4)	(4)	(4)	(4)	(4)
$30 and one-third of earned income[5]	12.5	2.5	3.8	4.0	4.0	4.0	3.8	147	$62	$76	83	92	89	89
Child care	3.9	1.3	1.5	1.7	1.2	1.6	1.4	101	86	106	119	128	132	153
Other work expenses	8.4	5.2	6.2	6.9	6.7	6.8	6.3	95	54	76	77	89	92	92
Cases with child care and other work expenses[6]	3.0	NA	NA	NA	NA	NA	NA	100	NA	NA	NA	NA	NA	NA
Child support	.1	(7)	3.0	5.1	4.9	4.5	4.7	93	NA	8 47	8 48	8 48	8 48	8 48
Other	1.6	.4	NA	NA	NA	NA	NA	77	100	NA	NA	NA	NA	NA
Total	13.8	NA	6.3	7.0	6.8	7.0	6.4	250	NA	146	153	171	172	177

[1] See text about differences in data sources for March 1979, 1982, and subsequent years.
[2] Source: Committee staff tabulation of March 1979 AFDC recipients' data base.
[3] Average monthly for fiscal years.
[4] Repealed by 1981 law.
[5] Limited to 4 months' duration by 1981 law; however, 1984 law extended $30 disregard to 12 months.
[6] In these cases, there was insufficient information in the data file to distinguish between child care and other work expenses.
[7] Less than 0.05 percent.
[8] Average amount of $50 child support passthrough.

NA—Not available.

Note.—The child support pass through is not included in the total amount disregarded. It is part of unearned income rather than earned income.

Source: ACF, Department of Health and Human Services.

The AFDC recipient population is not a homogenous group of families or individuals, as illustrated in table 10–31. The table subdivides the 1992 AFDC caseload into seven mutually exclusive and exhaustive groups. Column one of the table contains data on the entire caseload. Column two of the table describes the AFDC units with no adult recipients. They represent 14.7 percent of the AFDC units and 11.5 percent of total payments. The average payment per case was $285 per month.

Columns 3–6 represent characteristics of the more typical AFDC units—one adult with children. The one adult caseload was split into four groups based on the reason for deprivation of the youngest child. Column three includes those cases with one adult for whom the reason for AFDC eligibility is that the other adult is absent because they are not married; these represent 48 percent of AFDC units.

The final two columns (columns seven and eight) of the table present characteristics of cases with two adult recipients. Column eight represents those cases where one parent is incapacitated, and column seven presents data on the unemployed parents (AFDC–UP) program caseload. In total, they represent a little over 7.0 percent of the total caseload and receive about 10.6 percent of the total payments. The cases where one parent is incapacitated tend to be older, as demonstrated by both the age of the mother and the age of the youngest child.

Tables 10–32 through 10–35 present selected 1992 characteristics of the AFDC population by State. Table 10–32 presents selected demographic characteristics, including the number of persons in the AFDC unit and household, the percent of units with household members not in the unit, the percent of units with no adult recipients and with one adult recipient, and the percentage distribution of the units by age of youngest child and race of parent. Table 10–33 presents selected income characteristics, including the percent of units with earned income, unearned income, and various income disregards. This table also supplies the average monthly amount of these sources of income for those receiving them. Finally, table 10–33 provides information on the percent of units participating in the food stamp program. Table 10–34 provides a detailed percentage distribution of AFDC units by shelter arrangement. Table 10–35 provides a detailed percentage distribution of AFDC units by the reason for deprivation of the youngest child.

TABLE 10-31.—1992 AFDC CHARACTERISTICS BY UNIT TYPE [1]

	Total	One adult					Two adult		Unknown
		No adult	Not married	Divorced or legally separated	Not legally separated or divorced	Other reasons	Unemployed parent	Other	
Number of units (in thousands)	4,769	669	2,289	527	560	240	263	75	116
Percent of total	100.0	14.7	48.0	11.0	11.7	5.0	5.5	1.6	2.4
Average monthly payment	$374	$285	$367	$381	$405	$372	$568	$464	
Percent of total dollars paid out	100.0	11.5	48.3	11.5	13.0	5.1	8.6	2.0	
Average number in assistance unit	2.9	1.7	2.9	2.9	3.2	2.7	4.6	4.3	
Food Stamps:									
Percent participating	87.3	64.3	91.7	90.5	92.3	86.3	96.1	84.2	
				Percentage Distribution					
Number of recipients:									
One	9.3	56.1	0	0	0	17.6	0	0	
Two	37.0	26.0	46.3	40.4	32.0	35.9	0	1.4	
Three	27.9	11.2	29.2	35.9	36.2	21.8	25.7	29.7	
Four	15.2	4.8	14.8	16.1	20.2	13.4	30.4	28.7	
Five	6.6	1.2	6.0	5.6	7.9	6.3	21.4	21.9	
Six	2.5	0.4	1.9	1.4	2.5	3.2	12.2	12.4	
Seven or more	1.5	0.3	1.0	0.5	1.1	1.7	10.4	5.8	
Number of nonrecipients:									
Zero	57.6	1.2	67.8	66.6	71.1	41.2	80.8	80.2	
One	19.8	43.6	14.4	17.7	13.8	33.9	10.9	11.5	
Two	10.7	24.2	8.3	9.2	7.9	13.1	4.5	3.5	
Three	5.3	12.2	4.5	3.5	3.8	5.7	1.5	1.2	
Four or more	6.5	18.8	5.0	3.0	3.4	6.2	2.2	3.6	
Shelter:									
Owns or buying	4.4	6.0	1.9	6.8	4.3	8.3	9.9	18.9	
Homeless/emergency shelter	0.1	0.1	0.2	0.0	0.1	0.1	0.0	0.0	
Public housing	9.1	6.3	11.4	7.2	7.7	8.6	5.0	5.5	
HUD rent subsidy	12.1	6.3	14.2	14.7	12.1	8.5	8.4	6.8	
Other subsidy	1.7	1.0	2.0	2.0	1.5	1.6	1.5	1.7	
Private housing	63.5	67.5	60.8	62.0	66.2	65.4	71.1	63.2	

TABLE 10-31.—1992 AFDC CHARACTERISTICS BY UNIT TYPE [1]—Continued

	Total	One adult					Two adult		
		No adult	Not married	Divorced or legally separated	Not legally separated or divorced	Other reasons	Unemployed parent	Other	Unknown
Rents free	1.8	1.8	2.2	1.7	1.1	1.6	0.5	0.1	
Group quarters	7.3	10.9	7.4	5.6	7.1	5.9	3.5	3.7	
Number of child recipients:									
Zero	0	0	0	0	0	0	0.1	0	
One	43.7	54.7	46.3	40.4	32.1	46.9	25.9	25.2	
Two	30.7	27.4	29.9	35.9	36.2	25.0	30.3	31.9	
Three	15.5	11.2	14.8	16.1	20.2	14.4	21.4	23.6	
Four or more	10.0	6.8	9.0	7.6	11.6	13.7	22.4	19.4	
Race of caretaker:									
White	39.0	25.8	30.8	69.7	43.8	46.2	62.2	53.8	
Black	37.3	36.4	50.9	14.0	28.0	26.1	7.4	8.0	
Hispanic	17.6	31.7	13.6	12.7	22.9	14.4	13.6	24.5	
Asian	2.8	1.9	1.4	1.6	2.2	9.7	13.1	10.5	
American Indian	1.4	1.4	1.4	1.2	0.9	1.6	2.8	0.9	
Unknown	1.9	2.7	1.9	0.9	2.2	2.0	0.8	2.2	
Age of youngest child in AFDC unit:									
Under 3	42.4	30.9	51.6	14.1	38.4	48.3	52.5	41.9	
3 to 5	21.4	18.0	21.6	24.2	24.0	15.8	23.3	16.1	
6 to 11	23.3	28.5	18.9	39.3	25.2	18.9	15.7	23.5	
12 to 15	9.4	15.3	6.0	16.6	9.2	11.0	6.5	13.2	
16 to 18	3.6	7.3	1.9	5.8	3.1	6.1	2.0	5.3	
Unknown	0	0	0	0	0	0	0.1	0	
Number of months continuously on AFDC:									
6 or less	18.9	17.1	16.1	18.6	24.7	26.7	28.9	22.1	
7 to 12	15.0	15.6	14.1	14.7	17.7	12.5	19.0	14.1	
13 to 18	10.9	10.5	10.6	12.2	12.4	8.8	10.5	13.0	
19 to 24	8.4	8.3	8.9	8.4	8.1	5.7	7.9	9.7	
25 to 36	12.9	12.9	13.7	12.3	11.6	12.9	10.1	11.4	
37 to 48	8.3	7.9	8.7	9.3	6.8	9.6	5.3	7.6	
49 to 60	5.8	5.7	6.4	5.9	4.3	5.3	5.0	5.7	

61 to 120		10.8	11.1	13.7	10.6	14.4	14.4		13.7
121 to 180		4.5	1.9	2.9	2.7	3.5	4.9		4.2
181 and up		1.2	0.3	1.9	1.0	0.8	2.2		1.8
Age of female adult recipient:									
11 to 18		0.6	3.9	6.3	1.7	0.7	4.9	NA	3.8
19 to 21		8.6	10.9	14.0	8.9	3.8	17.5	NA	13.7
22 to 25		9.3	18.3	17.5	17.9	12.1	22.2	NA	19.5
26 to 29		17.3	19.4	10.9	20.2	19.6	18.7	NA	18.6
30 to 34		18.2	19.7	15.7	23.4	28.1	18.5	NA	20.3
35 to 39		18.9	14.4	11.2	13.7	19.3	10.4	NA	12.5
40 and up		26.3	13.5	24.5	14.2	16.4	7.9	NA	11.5
Unknown—		0.8	0	0	0	0	0	NA	0
AFDC female adults employment status:									
Employed full-time		1.5	1.4	1.7	2.7	3.5	2.1	NA	2.3
Employed part-time		3.9	3.6	2.7	3.8	5.0	2.8	NA	3.3
Employed other		0.9	1.5	0.8	0.8	1.5	0.9	NA	1.0
Not employed		85.3	77.8	83.5	79.7	74.9	83.0	NA	81.2
Unemployed		8.5	15.8	11.2	13.1	15.1	11.2	NA	12.2
Percent with non-AFDC income	24.3	29.3	37.3	28.3	21.9	34.2	20.3	3.2	21.1
Average monthly amount of income	$307	$413	$364	$284	$257	$219	$214	$206	$246
Percent with earned income	8.5	10.9	20.7	6.0	8.8	12.0	6.7	0.1	7.4
Average monthly earned income	$309	$341	$338	$322	$358	$344	$326	$345	$335
Percent of earned income disregarded	47.2	44.5	43.2	46.2	52.2	51.0	58.9	39.7	52.7
Percent with unearned income	16.8	21.7	20.4	23.1	14.3	25.1	14.7	3.1	15.0
Average amount of unearned income	$288	$387	$321	$263	$175	$134	$148	$199	$181
Percent with countable assets	14.1	30.4	36.4	22.5	16.1	29.5	13.5	6.5	16.5
Income of persons not in assistance unit:									
Percent with income	43.0	20.7	22.6	56.6	20.6	30.2	22.0	93.8	50.0
Average monthly amount	$486	$714	$611	$584	$479	$607	$543	$526	$537
Percent with earned income	1.3	1.3	3.4	3.3	4.1	10.9	5.4	8.8	6.6
Percent with public assistance income	32.1	18.9	15.8	50.8	13.1	14.5	13.7	92.5	43.8
Percent with other unearned income	12.4	0.7	4.5	14.6	5.5	7.7	5.8	16.9	10.5

[1] Characteristics information was not always available for 100 percent of cases. The number of missing cases, to the extent there were any with respect to a particular characteristic, was small as a percent of the AFDC family caseload (usually below 3 percent).

Source: Administration for Children and Families, HHS.

TABLE 10–32.—SELECTED DEMOGRAPHIC CHARACTERISTICS OF AFDC UNITS, BY STATE, OCTOBER 1991–SEPTEMBER 1992

State	Average number in unit	Average number in household of unit	Percent of units			Percentage distribution by age of youngest child [1]			Percentage distribution by race of natural/adoptive parent [1][2]				
			With household members not in unit	With no adult recipient	With 1 adult recipient	0-2 yrs.	3-5 yrs.	6 or more yrs.	White	Black	His-panic	Asian	Native American
U.S. total	2.9	3.8	42.3	14.8	77.4	42.0	21.2	35.9	38.9	37.2	17.8	2.8	1.4
Alabama	2.8	4.1	54.8	19.5	78.1	43.0	18.4	37.6	24.8	74.5	0.2	0.3	0.1
Alaska	2.8	3.4	26.3	8.0	80.0	39.7	22.0	37.7	53.1	9.4	2.9	2.0	31.7
Arizona	2.8	4.4	63.0	16.8	79.5	46.6	20.3	32.5	36.1	8.9	37.0	0.8	16.7
Arkansas	2.8	4.2	61.2	20.5	77.8	42.9	20.6	36.4	40.4	58.9	0.3	0.2	0.2
California	2.9	4.4	59.9	25.5	60.2	43.7	22.3	33.7	30.7	17.2	35.6	10.0	1.3
Colorado	2.9	3.3	25.2	10.0	84.7	44.8	23.3	31.5	42.8	13.5	40.8	1.6	1.1
Connecticut	2.8	3.4	35.5	10.7	86.1	41.8	20.2	37.7	33.8	30.5	34.5	0.6	1.1
Delaware	2.8	3.4	33.1	20.6	75.0	42.5	21.6	35.7	26.6	65.9	6.9	0.0	0.0
District of Columbia	2.7	4.2	62.1	16.5	82.5	50.2	17.2	31.8	0.0	98.7	0.8	0.4	0.3
Florida	2.8	3.8	51.2	18.6	79.5	45.2	22.1	32.3	33.4	50.8	15.3	0.4	0.0
Georgia	2.8	3.8	47.6	16.0	82.4	41.3	21.3	37.2	25.2	73.5	0.8	0.3	0.1
Hawaii	3.2	3.4	12.4	7.4	79.4	43.2	21.8	34.1	23.3	0.7	0.9	68.2	0.0
Idaho	2.8	3.2	28.5	12.8	83.2	46.9	20.9	31.6	84.6	0.6	10.1	0.3	4.5
Illinois	3.0	3.9	41.8	10.3	85.4	44.9	20.5	34.1	28.9	60.7	9.9	0.5	0.1
Indiana	2.9	3.7	43.8	9.1	86.7	40.1	22.6	36.3	52.8	36.6	2.2	0.1	0.1
Iowa	2.8	3.3	27.7	11.0	81.3	42.3	21.0	36.5	84.6	11.9	1.3	1.0	0.9
Kansas	3.0	3.8	37.8	10.6	76.7	45.5	21.5	32.8	65.7	27.4	4.5	1.4	1.0
Kentucky	2.7	3.7	49.6	14.2	74.2	33.6	19.6	46.7	81.2	18.2	0.0	0.4	0.1
Louisiana	3.0	4.5	61.0	16.9	82.1	40.3	21.2	38.0	18.0	80.5	0.7	0.4	0.2
Maine	2.9	3.4	29.1	4.2	81.0	40.1	20.6	39.0	98.2	0.6	0.4	0.4	0.6
Maryland	2.7	3.5	44.1	11.4	86.7	41.8	21.8	36.4	27.7	68.3	1.2	0.5	0.1
Massachusetts	2.8	3.2	24.4	8.9	84.8	43.5	22.0	34.1	51.8	16.4	24.0	3.8	0.0
Michigan	3.0	3.3	23.0	5.7	85.4	45.4	20.0	33.8	48.9	47.2	2.7	0.4	0.7
Minnesota	3.0	3.6	31.4	7.6	80.3	39.0	21.9	37.8	62.6	18.2	3.1	8.1	7.7
Mississippi	2.9	4.4	59.8	18.4	80.9	39.2	19.4	41.1	17.3	82.1	0.0	0.3	0.2
Missouri	3.0	3.8	40.7	8.1	84.4	44.5	20.5	35.1	54.5	44.2	0.7	0.5	0.0
Montana	2.9	3.2	20.9	6.7	81.4	39.8	20.1	39.8	68.9	0.3	1.7	0.6	28.2
Nebraska	2.8	3.6	42.1	19.8	73.0	49.3	19.6	30.7	64.6	23.5	4.9	2.3	4.7
Nevada	2.6	2.8	19.0	19.0	78.5	52.4	17.1	30.1	54.9	30.2	10.6	1.1	3.3

New Hampshire	2.7	2.9	20.0	13.6	79.0	39.0	23.9	36.0	84.8	2.3	1.9	0.3	0.0
New Jersey	2.9	3.1	18.8	15.8	79.8	43.7	22.1	33.8	23.8	49.3	26.0	0.7	0.0
New Mexico	2.9	3.2	19.6	12.8	78.8	38.4	19.0	41.6	20.7	4.8	59.1	0.0	15.1
New York	2.8	3.1	18.6	8.5	84.5	37.9	22.6	34.6	22.5	35.8	32.8	0.5	0.2
North Carolina	2.6	3.9	58.3	17.3	80.5	42.2	20.9	36.6	29.3	67.2	0.6	0.2	2.8
North Dakota	2.9	3.2	17.6	5.8	87.8	43.9	21.4	34.7	60.4	0.6	0.6	0.0	38.4
Ohio	2.9	3.7	42.4	12.8	75.6	41.1	18.4	38.9	59.1	38.4	2.1	0.2	0.0
Oklahoma	2.9	3.6	35.2	10.8	86.5	39.5	19.9	40.4	58.5	28.9	2.2	0.4	9.9
Oregon	2.9	3.9	48.6	10.7	80.1	46.5	22.6	30.7	86.3	6.1	4.3	1.5	1.6
Pennsylvania	3.0	3.3	22.2	9.1	81.1	39.2	24.9	35.5	48.1	41.3	9.0	1.2	0.2
Rhode Island	2.8	3.4	29.6	8.7	85.6	42.1	21.9	34.8	60.8	14.5	13.9	10.3	0.1
South Carolina	2.9	4.2	55.5	21.3	76.3	42.2	20.8	36.6	21.4	78.0	0.2	0.0	0.0
South Dakota	2.7	3.7	50.8	20.1	78.3	39.0	24.6	36.3	48.2	0.3	0.0	0.0	51.4
Tennessee	2.7	3.7	47.6	13.5	82.3	39.7	19.9	39.5	48.1	51.0	0.2	0.6	0.0
Texas	2.9	3.8	47.1	18.4	78.3	43.4	19.0	37.6	24.5	33.7	41.0	0.6	0.2
Utah	2.9	3.3	25.3	10.7	86.0	40.0	24.1	35.8	78.6	2.8	11.5	1.7	5.4
Vermont	3.0	3.4	30.1	5.3	70.5	37.3	20.7	40.8	97.2	1.6	0.6	0.3	0.3
Virginia	2.7	3.9	55.3	18.2	78.9	42.1	22.0	35.9	32.2	64.7	1.7	1.4	0.0
Washington	2.8	3.7	44.1	13.8	70.9	43.6	21.0	35.0	71.6	9.3	7.9	5.7	4.8
West Virginia	3.0	3.6	35.8	10.9	66.5	35.8	20.3	43.5	88.7	7.5	0.2	0.1	0.0
Wisconsin	3.0	3.8	42.5	12.3	77.6	46.7	19.1	34.0	48.7	37.2	6.2	4.4	3.1
Wyoming	2.8	3.3	27.2	8.3	87.8	39.5	19.2	41.5	75.4	3.9	10.4	0.0	10.4
Guam	3.5	5.1	46.6	3.8	87.8	60.3	18.7	20.8	1.2	0.6	0.3	97.6	0.0
Puerto Rico	3.2	4.1	44.2	10.5	76.0	19.6	21.9	58.4	0.1	0.0	99.7	0.0	0.0
Virgin Islands	3.6	4.4	36.6	10.6	87.0	42.5	20.2	37.4	1.0	32.9	18.8	0.0	0.0

[1] Percentages will not add to total as "unknown" and "other" not included.   [2] All race categories are mutually exclusive.

Source: Administration for Children and Families, U.S. Department of Health and Human Services.

TABLE 10-33.—SELECTED INCOME CHARACTERISTICS OF AFDC UNITS, BY STATE, OCTOBER 1991–SEPTEMBER 1992

State	Units with earned income		Units with unearned income		Units with income disregarded for child care		Units that have $30 plus one-third disregard		Percent of units participating in the food stamp program[2]
	Percent of total units	Average monthly amount (dollars)[1]	Percent of total units[1]	Average monthly amount (dollars)[1]	Percent of units with earned income	Average monthly amount (dollars)[1]	Percent of units with earned income	Average monthly amount (dollars)[1]	
Alabama	3.1	167.58	13.0	73.55	22.6	79.75	32.3	72.83	90.7
Alaska	16.9	440.51	16.3	534.98	17.1	130.50	60.9	134.42	62.9
Arizona	7.0	264.83	3.7	180.22	18.6	118.94	65.7	89.62	93.3
Arkansas	6.2	210.25	20.2	172.17	21.0	141.62	61.3	77.64	86.1
California	7.5	387.43	16.2	263.47	18.7	183.61	44.0	71.95	82.9
Colorado	8.6	309.22	11.9	165.31	22.1	143.44	45.3	81.98	89.8
Connecticut	5.9	374.49	17.4	170.03	15.3	219.60	45.8	130.12	89.2
Delaware	10.3	236.73	15.0	99.71	5.8	107.50	57.3	133.21	87.5
District of Columbia	1.5	539.93	5.4	321.05	40.0	192.03	86.7	135.38	89.8
Florida	4.9	387.06	10.7	113.51	34.7	182.96	71.4	108.09	91.2
Georgia	7.6	309.44	27.0	121.14	25.0	113.33	60.5	90.91	85.9
Hawaii	14.0	525.90	9.2	258.57	8.6	112.29	52.1	133.57	91.7
Idaho	12.8	255.39	22.9	109.95	24.2	138.00	60.9	125.04	89.1
Illinois	5.3	302.89	12.0	198.89	35.8	220.25	39.6	88.81	95.3
Indiana	6.9	266.62	25.1	115.89	29.0	120.46	65.2	68.86	90.6
Iowa	19.1	307.01	23.2	103.08	30.9	136.74	35.6	96.79	89.4
Kansas	11.5	290.95	13.0	111.99	5.2	71.29	57.4	86.24	88.9
Kentucky	12.6	334.21	16.0	148.70	26.2	139.02	54.8	74.16	89.9
Louisiana	3.5	200.98	17.6	110.30	20.0	126.50	68.6	71.10	94.5
Maine	18.0	386.91	79.9	263.38	35.6	139.11	42.2	132.59	93.6
Maryland	4.0	330.98	12.6	85.71	30.0	129.56	55.0	110.37	92.0
Massachusetts	4.0	281.96	19.7	192.60	10.0	102.60	45.0	88.96	39.2
Michigan	13.2	361.98	18.7	184.53	9.8	132.52	41.7	83.20	94.1
Minnesota	13.8	312.71	24.9	154.20	22.5	110.38	50.0	104.49	90.8
Mississippi	11.3	261.25	23.0	94.98	16.8	107.46	38.9	71.83	33.4
Missouri	5.7	253.36	19.0	148.23	19.3	123.23	52.6	78.39	92.2
Montana	16.9	303.79	14.5	174.22	20.7	201.92	62.1	104.69	86.6
Nebraska	14.2	289.75	7.5	182.35	8.5	135.71	57.0	91.24	90.4
Nevada	4.1	322.73	29.1	96.03	19.5	100.00	85.4	124.92	78.8
New Hampshire	8.1	342.92	21.0	159.49	3.7	216.00	51.9	91.92	85.5

New Jersey	2.7	339.03	3.6	368.07	22.2	122.14	51.9	91.65	88.4
New Mexico	9.3	222.52	8.1	194.75	12.9	85.75	62.4	67.12	90.0
New York	4.3	349.60	11.3	213.73	20.9	242.77	34.9	85.38	93.1
North Carolina	11.6	350.43	23.8	134.05	19.8	110.29	60.3	110.31	76.7
North Dakota	16.2	251.75	36.7	111.61	21.6	159.92	56.8	75.59	89.9
Ohio	7.0	352.86	17.1	118.16	14.3	126.54	68.6	105.42	91.9
Oklahoma	5.4	248.69	7.4	218.80	0.0	0.00	68.5	71.94	90.6
Oregon	12.2	281.04	23.2	129.93	26.2	100.43	55.7	89.46	93.4
Pennsylvania	5.9	319.00	6.1	272.92	22.0	118.94	54.2	86.07	92.5
Rhode Island	5.8	320.11	13.1	200.56	10.3	116.00	58.6	38.07	95.5
South Carolina	8.3	359.64	18.3	182.81	22.9	122.03	68.7	106.47	86.7
South Dakota	13.7	263.65	45.1	131.72	23.4	120.10	70.1	66.73	82.1
Tennessee	11.2	402.38	13.4	289.21	16.1	147.50	69.6	109.84	92.6
Texas	5.6	213.77	6.5	114.50	12.5	135.17	50.0	66.67	95.2
Utah	14.8	328.48	16.0	120.97	9.5	97.67	62.2	103.83	90.2
Vermont	12.8	383.34	20.4	161.51	2.3	100	60.9	119.24	94.0
Virginia	5.2	300.58	9.9	176.82	13.5	143.37	59.6	68.05	86.9
Washington	9.1	346.87	14.6	259.16	7.7	180.94	45.1	99.84	87.3
West Virginia	3.2	216.92	20.4	98.12	0.0	0.00	28.1	54.57	93.6
Wisconsin	16.1	354.01	23.7	131.52	28.0	148.39	62.7	81.15	86.6
Wyoming	26.2	377.08	13.0	205.42	0.0	0.00	53.4	101.37	93.8
Guam	3.0	413.80	10.4	183.09	10.0	100	70.0	152.00	82.8
Puerto Rico	0.5	78.67	2.3	94.74	0.0	0.00	40.0	47.00	0.0
Virgin Islands	0.7	103.00	5.8	108.41	0.0	0.00	100.0	48.5	90.1
U.S. total	7.4	335.11	15.0	181.02	18.9	152.93	51.4	89.27	87.3

[1] Average amount for those with the income source or income disregard.
[2] Unknown category was distributed proportionately within States reporting proportions of unknown.
NA—Not available.
Source: Administration for Children and Families, U.S. Department of Health and Human Services.

TABLE 10-34.—AFDC FAMILIES BY TYPE OF SHELTER ARRANGEMENT—OCTOBER 1991–SEPTEMBER 1992

[In percent except total families]

State	Total families	Homeless shelter/ emergency housing	Owns or is buying	Rents in public housing	Rent subsidy—		Rents in private housing with no subsidy	Shares group quarters	Rents free	Unknown
					HUD	Other				
U.S. total	4,768,572	.1	4.4	9.2	12.1	1.7	63.1	1.7	7.2	.5
Alabama	50,631	.1	5.2	22.5	10.8	.9	29.3	2.1	29.0	*
Alaska	10,807	.3	7.1	15.1	6.0	7.1	52.6	.3	11.4	*
Arizona	63,598	.1	3.5	7.0	10.5	1.3	62.7	.2	14.6	*
Arkansas	26,769	.1	5.2	11.6	24.1	.6	26.4	3.8	28.2	*
California	806,086	*	1.1	1.6	6.4	.7	88.9	1.1	.2	*
Colorado	42,081	.1	2.8	7.1	17.8	7.2	58.0	6.0	1.0	*
Connecticut	55,499	.7	1.0	14.1	20.7	2.4	52.9	4.9	3.3	*
Delaware	10,661	.3	7.2	10.6	24.1	.6	54.1	2.2	.9	*
District of Columbia	22,566	1.6	3.3	17.8	24.0	6.0	36.8	7.9	*	2.6
Florida	221,205	.1	2.5	8.4	7.9	.4	75.8	.7	4.2	*
Georgia	135,972	.1	5.3	16.8	10.8	1.8	46.1	3.5	11.6	4.1
Hawaii	16,530	.2	4.7	11.7	18.5	1.2	43.5	10.7	9.5	*
Idaho	7,335	.6	4.5	3.6	27.7	3.4	44.4	5.6	9.2	1.1
Illinois	228,625	.2	2.0	11.2	7.7	1.1	71.1	1.1	5.5	*
Indiana	69,134	*	3.6	8.0	14.0	5.0	61.2	.5	6.2	1.5
Iowa	37,158	*	8.3	1.3	23.1	1.0	60.5	2.2	3.6	*
Kansas	28,741	*	3.7	8.5	13.1	.6	66.4	.7	6.7	.3
Kentucky	83,133	*	13.6	10.3	11.4	.7	51.7	*	12.4	*
Louisiana	92,200	*	5.4	13.8	13.0	1.6	35.7	3.4	27.0	*
Maine	23,919	*	15.5	15.1	15.1	7.7	40.0	2.2	4.2	.2
Maryland	79,807	.1	1.1	9.1	13.9	1.6	73.9	.2	.2	*
Massachusetts	111,448	.2	1.6	11.9	21.2	8.4	54.5	1.8	.3	*
Michigan	225,609	.1	10.2	1.9	7.7	2.0	73.4	.2	4.0	.7
Minnesota	63,656	*	10.5	15.0	17.4	7.2	44.7	.6	2.8	1.8
Mississippi	60,810	*	7.7	9.8	17.2	1.3	25.8	*	38.1	.1

Missouri	85,176	.5	6.0	4.8	20.1	1.0	57.5	.7	9.3	.1
Montana	10,909	*	6.4	31.4	16.0	4.9	38.4	1.7	1.2	*
Nebraska	16,551	*	6.3	6.0	26.0	4.2	50.7	4.0	2.8	*
Nevada	11,867	*	*	*	26.6	.8	49.5	.8	22.3	2.3
New Hampshire	10,499	.3	3.5	10.3	5.5	5.2	68.1	4.5	.3	*
New Jersey	125,847	.3	1.5	5.2	9.4	4.0	72.7	5.9	1.1	*
New Mexico	28,764	.1	13.3	12.3	19.9	4.2	38.7	5.5	5.9	*
New York	397,172	.3	1.0	16.3	10.5	1.9	68.3	.6	1.1	*
North Carolina	121,427	.2	1.0	14.3	9.5	.5	68.0	1.9	4.7	*
North Dakota	6,394	*	6.9	5.8	48.0	9.0	19.9	5.5	4.9	*
Ohio	264,271	.1	4.4	12.0	14.3	1.9	59.3	1.1	7.1	.2
Oklahoma	46,837	*	3.9	2.2	31.1	1.6	38.0	4.5	18.5	*
Oregon	41,460	.1	2.9	4.4	17.5	2.0	71.3	.4	1.4	.2
Pennsylvania	200,699	*	3.7	13.4	6.4	.2	71.9	3.0	1.2	*
Rhode Island	21,288	.1	2.3	9.6	20.1	.6	58.4	5.4	3.5	.1
South Carolina	49,710	.2	6.9	7.9	19.4	.1	36.6	*	28.8	*
South Dakota	7,223	*	6.4	3.5	21.4	1.5	39.3	5.1	8.9	.1
Tennessee	95,179	*	5.6	17.7	12.6	1.0	53.5	.8	8.7	*
Texas	265,819	.1	7.6	7.6	18.8	.1	32.1	2.5	31.2	.2
Utah	17,882	*	1.9	2.2	20.3	1.7	68.0	3.0	2.8	*
Vermont	10,047	*	9.4	15.4	7.5	.6	57.1	6.9	3.1	19.7
Virginia	70,677	.1	1.7	7.3	19.6	.9	43.2	.4	7.1	.1
Washington	96,407	.3	5.3	9.3	11.9	1.6	69.4	.8	1.3	.1
West Virginia	40,469	*	13.0	6.9	18.2	.2	42.5	2.6	16.4	*
Wisconsin	81,680	.2	4.2	4.8	11.0	2.0	70.2	4.5	3.2	.3
Wyoming	6,625	.3	11.7	22.8	14.2	1.0	42.5	4.7	2.6	*
Guam	1,283	*	1.8	.6	32.0	5.0	7.1	.9	52.5	.1
Puerto Rico	61,375	*	32.3	20.4	5.6	2.5	19.9	2.7	16.6	4.1
Virgin Islands	1,053	*	4.5	64.0	1.4	.3	11.3	.7	13.7	

*Less than .05 percent.

Source: Administration for Children and Families, U.S. Department of Health and Human Services.

TABLE 10-35.—AFDC FAMILIES BY REASON FOR DEPRIVATION OF THE YOUNGEST CHILD, OCTOBER 1991–SEPTEMBER 1992

[In percent except total families]

State	Total families	Parent deceased	Parent incapacitated	Parent unemployed	Parent absent					
					Divorced or legally separated	Not legally separated	Paternity Established	Paternity Not established	Other	Unknown
U.S. total	4,768,572	1.5	3.6	7.0	12.6	14.6	23.6	32.7	1.5	1.6
Alabama	50,631	1.1	5.0	2.5	10.8	10.2	22.9	43.8	2.3	1.6
Alaska	10,807	2.0	2.0	12.0	25.4	11.4	16.3	24.3	4.3	1.1
Arizona	63,598	1.4	3.3	1.9	13.1	15.9	17.5	42.9	1.7	1.1
Arkansas	26,769	1.3	3.0	1.7	16.8	9.4	34.8	31.7	1.0	.4
California	806,086	1.1	5.4	17.1	12.0	17.4	13.3	29.1	1.9	.4
Colorado	42,081	.5	3.5	3.6	19.7	11.8	15.2	40.6	1.5	.7
Connecticut	55,499	1.2	.9	3.2	10.2	11.3	39.8	29.0	2.7	.5
Delaware	10,661	.9	4.4	1.9	7.5	8.1	40.6	33.4	2.2	.9
District of Columbia	22,566	2.3	1.3	5.2	1.1	4.5	17.0	64.3	1.5	1.7
Florida	221,205	1.8	1.0	2.4	10.7	20.6	24.4	35.9	2.2	.5
Georgia	135,972	1.8	3.3	.6	13.4	13.4	57.5	8.7	.6	.5
Hawaii	16,530	2.2	9.0	5.0	13.1	14.9	24.5	29.9	.5	.9
Idaho	7,335	2.8	5.3	8.4	22.6	14.8	19.3	20.7	3.6	.8
Illinois	228,625	.6	.9	3.9	9.0	9.7	14.8	57.7	1.0	1.3
Indiana	69,134	1.1	4.4	2.0	19.4	8.6	33.9	28.1	1.0	1.5
Iowa	37,158	1.9	3.8	5.6	25.1	9.9	25.0	27.3	.4	.9
Kansas	28,741	1.0	2.9	8.0	21.8	13.2	17.2	30.8	3.4	.3
Kentucky	83,133	1.9	12.0	9.6	16.7	14.5	16.0	28.3	.5	.4
Louisiana	92,200	2.2	3.1	.8	7.0	12.1	16.8	54.0	1.9	1.3
Maine	23,919	2.0	5.5	12.2	22.7	13.3	23.9	17.7	.4	.7
Maryland	79,807	1.9	1.7	1.9	4.9	11.1	52.1	24.0	.7	.5
Massachusetts	111,448	2.8	3.1	5.1	10.4	15.0	25.9	34.2	1.3	.8

State										
Michigan	225,609	1.5	1.7	8.2	15.1	6.9	30.2	32.1	1.1	1.3
Minnesota	63,656	1.5	2.8	10.8	21.9	6.6	39.6	13.8	1.1	1.9
Mississippi	60,810	1.7	2.6	.2	6.4	18.1	21.8	48.5	.5	.2
Missouri	85,176	1.3	3.2	6.5	14.4	13.2	25.6	33.3	1.6	1.0
Montana	10,909	1.7	4.4	9.9	23.8	12.5	19.8	25.3	.9	.3
Nebraska	16,551	.9	2.6	7.2	20.2	12.5	13.7	35.8	.2	1.2
Nevada	11,867	2.2	.5	5.4	11.1	20.4	13.3	40.5	*	.8
New Hampshire	10,499	.3	3.9	5.2	20.6	23.2	21.0	23.5	1.3	1.0
New Jersey	125,847	1.9	.3	4.6	6.2	10.8	36.9	37.6	.8	.8
New Mexico	28,764	2.2	3.9	5.8	17.4	15.2	16.2	35.9	.6	1.7
New York	397,172	1.7	2.0	4.2	8.3	18.6	32.6	20.2	.9	9.3
North Carolina	121,427	1.8	2.5	1.8	8.6	13.6	37.5	31.1	1.1	.5
North Dakota	6,394	.9	1.7	5.2	27.5	8.7	34.7	19.4	*	.6
Ohio	264,271	1.5	2.9	11.0	17.0	10.3	13.6	37.4	2.5	2.0
Oklahoma	46,837	.8	3.7	1.2	22.5	18.6	16.5	35.0	1.2	.5
Oregon	41,460	.8	2.7	8.5	19.4	15.9	23.4	27.0	1.4	.6
Pennsylvania	200,699	1.4	4.1	4.1	9.3	12.5	27.0	38.3	1.0	1.3
Rhode Island	21,288	.9	3.7	3.4	17.0	19.2	23.0	30.4	.5	1.3
South Carolina	49,710	.3	2.4	1.5	6.4	21.9	18.1	48.1	*	1.2
South Dakota	7,223	1.0	2.2	.3	25.2	3.2	26.8	37.4	2.6	1.3
Tennessee	95,179	1.8	5.6	2.5	14.1	17.2	20.8	33.8	1.8	1.1
Texas	265,819	2.5	3.4	2.9	12.4	20.8	11.0	43.8	2.4	.8
Utah	17,882	.9	3.1	1.6	26.6	19.3	20.3	23.3	.8	.3
Vermont	10,047	1.6	7.8	13.8	26.3	5.3	26.3	16.0	.6	2.2
Virginia	70,677	1.3	3.5	1.2	8.2	17.2	26.2	40.4	.9	1.1
Washington	96,407	.9	4.1	15.2	16.9	16.3	16.4	24.2	3.0	.5
West Virginia	40,469	1.5	7.7	21.0	19.2	16.5	10.3	21.9	1.2	.6
Wisconsin	81,680	1.5	5.0	9.6	15.1	5.8	30.0	25.4	2.0	.6
Wyoming	6,625	1.0	1.0	3.9	41.5	9.6	11.7	29.0	.5	1.3
Guam	1,283	3.0	4.7	2.7	9.5	4.5	30.9	39.2	.9	.6
Puerto Rico	61,375	2.5	14.2	(¹)	16.1	19.5	40.8	4.8	1.8	.2
Virgin Islands	1,053	.3	3.8	.7	9.9	3.4	60.6	20.2	(¹)	.3

¹ Less than .05 percent.

Source: U.S. Department of Health and Human Services.

THE AFDC QUALITY CONTROL SYSTEM

Description of AFDC QC system

The AFDC quality control system has two goals: correcting faults in program administration that contribute to erroneous payments and reducing the extent of misspent benefit dollars. To these ends, it attempts to: (1) measure the extent and dollar value of "errors" in administration; (2) identify the types and causes of error; and (3) specify and monitor corrective actions taken to eliminate or reduce errors. Sanctions are also imposed on States whose error rates are above the national average.

The "errors" identified and measured in the quality control system range from simple arithmetical mistakes, to incomplete or inaccurate reporting of income, to outright recipient fraud. Although quality control error rates and the information behind them do give a picture of the extent to which improper payments are being made and help administering agencies pinpoint areas where improvement is needed, only part of the error rate can be attributed to recipient fraud. In fact, "agency-caused" errors make up nearly half the errors typically identified in quality control surveys, and "recipient-caused" errors may often be simple mistakes in understanding what is required or failure to provide correct information on a timely basis.

The AFDC quality control system and sanction rules were completely revised under the Omnibus Budget Reconciliation Act of 1989 (P.L. 101–239), beginning for fiscal year 1991.

The new system:

(1) Imposes penalties on States whose payment error rates are above the national average.

(2) Establishes penalties based on a sliding scale which reflect the degree to which a State's error rate exceeds the national average.

(3) Takes into account both overpayments and underpayments that are made to AFDC recipients, and gives States an incentive to improve their overpayment recoveries and AFDC child support collection programs.

(4) Establishes a new Quality Control Review Panel to assure that quality control review cases that are in dispute between States and the Federal Government are resolved in a uniform and fair manner.

(5) Retains the Departmental Appeals Board to resolve all other issues in dispute between the States and the Federal Government.

Error measurement. The core of the quality control system is the quality control case survey. The system annually compiles the results of a statistically valid sample of cases. Each selected case is subjected to a thorough review by quality control personnel, including a full field investigation. This review identifies payments to ineligibles, overpayments, underpayments, the type of error made, the responsibility (recipient versus administering agency) for the error, and, to a limited degree, incorrect denials of aid. Error "rates" are then established for that review period for each State: "caseload" error rates indicate the proportion of ineligible cases, overpaid cases, underpaid cases, and, in some cases, improperly denied cases in the sample caseload; "payment" error rates indicate the extent of erroneous payments as a proportion of total dollars paid out to the sampled caseload.

Before the official error rate is determined, States may challenge the Federal review decisions by requesting reconsideration of any decisions on cases that are different from their own ("difference" cases) by a Quality Control Review Panel. Decisions by the Quality Control Review Panel are on the record and are not appealable to the Departmental Appeals Board. Decisions on difference cases may not be appealed to the court until and unless any disallowance becomes final. A disallowance becomes final if a State does not appeal the disallowance determination to the Departmental Appeals Board, or, if the State does appeal, once the Board has made a decision.

In establishing a State's error rate, certain types of errors are excluded: (1) errors based on failure to carry out properly changes in Federal legislation for a period of 6 months after the effective date of the legislation or the issuance of interim final or final regulations, whichever is later (however, States would not be relieved of the obligations to implement new legislation); (2) errors resulting from a State agency's correct use of erroneous information received from Federal agencies; (3) errors resulting from a State agency's action based on written Federal policies (e.g., Federal written advisories made in response to State inquiries); (4) errors due to circumstances (defined as those resulting in a declaration of a state of emergency by the Governor or the President); and (5) errors due to monthly reporting that do not affect the amount of payment. The following errors are among those that are counted: lack of a Social Security number in the file (unless an application for a number has been filed) and failure to assign child support rights.

The decision as to whether a case is in error is made by comparison against permissible State practice (i.e., policies consistent with the approved State plan). However, if the State plan is inconsistent with Federal regulations, Federal regulations prevail if the Secretary has informed the State of the inconsistency. If a change in State law is required, the Secretary may allow a reasonable time for the State to make the required change. A case which is at variance with Federal law and regulations because of compliance with a court order is reviewed against the court order.

The Secretary, in consultation with the States, is required to establish regulations setting forth the time period in which reviews must be completed and findings must be reported; the time period in which difference cases must be resolved; the time period in which error rates must be issued; and the sample size necessary to obtain a statistically valid error rate. To enable the Department of HHS to meet these regulatory timetables, the Secretary must insure that there will be adequate staff to perform required functions, and must report annually to the Senate Committee on Finance and the House Committee on Ways and Means as to whether the time-tables have been met. If a State fails to complete its reviews on a timely basis, the Secretary may conduct the reviews on his own initiative and will charge the State for any costs incurred in making the reviews.

Determination of disallowances.—In general, the Federal Government provides matching funds for all approvable State expenditures except for those in excess of the error tolerance level. The error tolerance level is the national average error rate or 4 percent, whichever is higher, computed by determining the overpayment error rate for each State and determining the average for all States.

Disallowances for States with error rates above the error tolerance level will be assessed on a sliding scale, reflecting the degree to which the State's error rate exceeds the error tolerance level. For example, a State with an error rate of 7.8 percent is 20 percent above a 6.5 percent national average tolerance level and would owe 20 percent of the sanction on the entire amount of its overpayments above the tolerance level (20 percent × 1.3 percent × the Federal share of benefits). In no case, however, would a State be required to repay more than 100 percent of its overpayments above the tolerance level.

Any sanction amount owed by a State is due upon issuance by the Secretary of the notice to the State of a disallowance. The State may pay immediately, or the Secretary and the State may negotiate an agreement under which repayment may be made over a period of up to 2½ years. Interest will accrue beginning 45 days after the date the State receives the notice of the disallowance. If a subsequent appeal is decided in the State's favor, the Federal Government will repay all State payments with interest.

Before repayment to the Federal Government, several adjustments must be made.

(1) If a State's error rate for underpayments is below the national average, its repayment amount will be reduced by reducing its overpayment error rate. For example, if the underpayment rate is 0.1 percentage point below the national average, the overpayment error rate would be reduced by 0.1 percentage point. This reduction could be applied to any penalty due for the measurement year or for either of the following 2 years. The Secretary is required to conduct a study and report to Congress on negative case actions—improper denials and terminations.

(2) A State's repayment amount will also be reduced by a percentage equal to the percentage improvement in its AFDC child support collection rate (the number of AFDC cases for which a child support collection is made over the total number of AFDC cases) measured against the average collection rate for the State in the preceding 3 years, or the percentage by which the State's AFDC child support collection rate exceeds the national average, whichever is greater.

(3) The amount to be repaid will be further reduced to reflect overpayments recovered by the State.

Appeal procedures.—If a State decides to appeal its disallowance to the Departmental Appeals Board, it must do so within 60 days of the notice of disallowance. In deciding whether to uphold the disallowance or any portion of it, the Board must conduct a thorough review of the issues and take into account all relevant evidence. With respect to difference cases, the Departmental Appeals Board will adopt the decision of the Quality Control Review Panel.

If an appeal is not completed by the Board within 90 days, interest will be suspended until the appeal is completed. A State may appeal a decision by the Departmental Appeals Board (including a decision adopted by the Board with respect to a difference case) to Federal district court within 90 days of the decision by the Board. Court review shall be on the record established in the Departmental Appeals Board review in accordance with the standard of review prescribed by section 706(2) (A) through (E) of title 5 of the United States Code.

HYPOTHETICAL EXAMPLE OF QUALITY CONTROL DISALLOWANCE COMPUTATION

[Assumes: State overpayment rate: 8%, underpayment rate: 2.8%; National overpayment rate: 6%, underpayment rate: 3.0%]

1. Calculation of State error rate:

a. National underpayment rate	3.0%
(less) State underpayment rate	2.8%
Underpayment "bonus"	0.2%
b. State overpayment rate	8.0%
(less) Underpayment "bonus"	0.2%
"Error rate"	7.8%

2. Calculation of "basic" disallowance:

State's AFDC payments	$10,000,000
(times) Federal match rate	50%
Gross Federal cost	$5,000,000
(times) Excess error rate (7.8% is 1.8 percentage points above 6% national average)	1.8%
Excess erroneous payment	$90,000
(times) Percent by which error rate exceeds national average. (7.8% is 30% above 6%)	30%
"Basic" disallowance	$27,000

3. Adjustment for overpayment recoveries:

Overpayment recoveries (Federal share)	$5,000
(times) State error rate above national average (1.8%) as a percent of total State error rate (7.8%). (1.8% is 23% of 7.8%)	23%
Overpayment adjustment	$1,150

4. Adjustment for child support improvement:

a. Percent by which AFDC child support collection rate (e.g. 16%) exceeds national AFDC child support collection rate (e.g. 12%). (16% is 33% higher than 12%)	33%
b. Percent by which AFDC child support collection rate (e.g. 16%) exceeds State average over 3 prior years (e.g. 14%). (16% is 14% higher than 14%)	14%
c. "Basic" disallowance from step 2	$27,000
(less) Overpayment adjustment (step 3)	$1,150
Adjusted disallowance	$25,850
(times) Child support adjustment percent (higher of 4.a. or 4.b.)	33%
Child support adjustment	$8,530

5. Final calculation:

Adjusted disallowance (4.c.)	$25,850
(less) Child support adjustment	$8,530
Final disallowance amount	$17,320

Effective date; treatment of disallowances for prior years.—The new quality control system is effective beginning with fiscal year 1991. All disallowances for error rates determined for years prior to 1991 were waived permanently under the provisions of OBRA 1989.

Administration

In the AFDC program, the quality control system is operated by State quality control staff under Federal instructions and guidelines. A State's error rate is determined by using findings from both the State's full sample and a Federal subsample. The cost of operating quality control systems is carried as a regular administrative cost and is shared by the States and Federal Government, just as any other administrative expense.

Corrective action

The basic goal of quality control systems is to reduce, over time, the extent and cost of errors in program administration. As part of the system, "corrective action plans" for error reduction are regularly formulated based on the findings of the quality control sample surveys. Corrective actions can range from personnel policy changes or new computer systems, to substantive changes in eligibility rules or procedures for verifying information provided by recipients. Very often, "error-prone" profiles are drawn up from the results of quality control surveys to assist administrators in identifying cases to which particular attention should be paid.

Recent quality control statistics

Table 10–36 summarizes national overpayment error rates for the AFDC program over recent quality control review periods. Table 10–37 provides a State-by-State comparison of fiscal year 1991 overpayment and underpayment error rates. Table 10–38 depicts the estimated sanction amounts and estimated collection schedule, according to the Department of Health and Human Services. Table 10–39 provides information on negative case actions, improper denials and terminations of aid.

TABLE 10–36.—SUMMARY OF NATIONAL OVERPAYMENT DOLLAR ERROR RATES UNDER THE AFDC PROGRAM

October 1979–March 1980	8.3
April 1980–September 1980	7.3
October 1980–March 1981	8.3
April 1981–September 1981	7.0
October 1981–March 1982	7.2
April 1982–September 1982	6.6
October 1982–March 1983	6.2
April 1983–September 1983	6.8
October 1983–March 1984	6.2
April 1984–September 1984	5.7
Fiscal year 1985	6.1
Fiscal year 1986	7.1
Fiscal year 1987	6.3
Fiscal year 1988	6.8
Fiscal year 1989	5.7
Fiscal year 1990	6.0
Fiscal year 1991	[1] 5.0

[1] This is the lowest national overpayment error rate achieved under the AFDC–QC system.

Note: Overpayment errors include payments made to ineligible families but do not include underpayments.

Source: Department of Health and Human Services.

TABLE 10–37.—AFDC—QUALITY CONTROL PAYMENT ERROR RATES

[In fiscal year 1991]

State	Overpayment		Underpayment rate
	State	Rate	
U.S. Total	....	4.96	0.80
Alabama	40	6.29	0.77
Alaska	8	2.88	1.31
Arizona	52	8.31	1.18
Arkansas	20	3.76	0.75
California	15	3.49	0.54
Colorado	5	2.67	1.72
Connecticut	6	2.74	0.34
Delaware	42	6.68	0.19
District of Columbia	38	5.98	1.01
Florida	54	9.66	1.21
Georgia	12	3.37	0.88
Guam	49	7.55	1.88
Hawaii	10	3.18	0.68
Idaho	25	4.17	1.50
Illinois	33	4.99	0.54
Indiana	36	5.80	0.42
Iowa	34	5.22	0.44
Kansas	27	4.36	0.35
Kentucky	9	3.10	0.72
Louisiana	47	7.14	0.78
Maine	11	3.27	0.06
Maryland	45	6.88	0.54
Massachusetts	23	3.99	0.66
Michigan	24	4.14	0.86
Minnesota	7	2.80	0.56
Mississippi	48	7.47	0.94
Missouri	35	5.27	0.49
Montana	28	4.36	1.08
Nebraska	46	6.89	0.37
Nevada	22	3.97	0.45
New Hampshire	18	3.74	1.77
New Jersey	29	4.69	0.29
New Mexico	31	4.92	1.05
New York	44	6.73	2.08
North Carolina	17	3.68	0.86
North Dakota	3	1.65	0.42
Ohio	53	8.36	0.77
Oklahoma	21	3.86	0.82
Oregon	19	3.74	0.37
Pennsylvania	32	4.92	0.18
Puerto Rico	39	6.10	1.25
Rhode Island	14	3.46	0.16
South Carolina	41	6.56	0.90
South Dakota	1	1.18	1.05
Tennessee	43	6.71	0.31
Texas	50	8.02	0.63
Utah	16	3.64	0.57
Vermont	4	1.96	0.22
Virgin Islands	2	1.49	0.00
Virginia	13	3.39	0.31
Washington	37	5.83	0.51
West Virginia	51	8.17	0.53

TABLE 10–37.—AFDC—QUALITY CONTROL PAYMENT ERROR RATES—Continued

[In fiscal year 1991]

State	Overpayment		Underpayment rate
	State	Rate	
Wisconsin	30	4.77	0.82
Wyoming	26	4.27	0.68

Source: Administration for Children and Families, U.S. Department of Health and Human Services.

TABLE 10–38.—ESTIMATED AFDC SANCTION AMOUNTS AND COLLECTION SCHEDULE

	HHS estimated error rate	HHS estimated sanction amounts (in millions)	HHS projected schedules for collecting sanctions
Fiscal year:			
1991	5.0	5.0	0
1992	5.0	38.3	0
1993	5.0	38.2	0
1994	5.0	38.6	60.7
1995	4.9	38.5	50.8
1996	4.8	38.7	38.6
1997	4.7	39.1	38.5
1998	4.7	40.3	38.7
1999	4.7	41.6	39.1

Source: Office of Financial Management, Administration for Children and Families.

TABLE 10–39.—DATA ON AFDC QUALITY CONTROL NEGATIVE CASE ACTIONS

[Fiscal year 1991]

State	Total number of negative case actions	Negative case action error rates		Total number of incorrect negative case actions	
		Eligibility requirements	Advance notice/hearing requirements only	Eligibility requirements	Advance notice/hearing requirements only
United States [1] .	3,676,280	2.22	1.90	81,760	69,675
Alabama	31,838	1.29	1.29	410	410
Alaska	10,231	2.02	0.00	207	0
Arizona	83,793	1.53	0.87	1,281	732
Arkansas	37,332	0.32	1.29	120	480
California	650,379	1.84	3.31	11,955	21,520
Colorado	67,928	0.26	1.54	174	1,045
Connecticut	30,134	0.00	0.00	0	0
Delaware	8,480	0.00	1.10	0	93
Dist. of Col	23,764	0.00	2.56	0	609
Florida	129,656	10.23	2.70	13,266	3,504
Georgia	135,835	3.07	1.41	4,169	1,911
Guam	765	2.65	1.59	20	12
Hawaii	11,985	0.00	1.62	0	194
Idaho	17,383	4.00	1.78	695	309
Illinois	169,933	1.69	0.56	2,880	960
Indiana	36,036	2.17	4.04	783	1,455
Iowa	20,854	2.74	0.46	571	95
Kansas	21,805	1.63	0.54	356	119
Kentucky	56,447	0.94	1.88	529	1,058
Louisiana	71,146	1.11	0.28	793	198
Maine	17,197	1.55	0.00	266	0
Maryland	35,100	0.66	2.30	231	808
Massachusetts	64,445	0.76	0.50	487	325
Michigan	167,383	4.00	1.27	6,695	2,123
Minnesota	46,310	1.42	2.49	659	1,154
Mississippi	32,068	2.40	0.40	770	128
Missouri	52,088	2.05	2.39	1,067	1,244
Montana	4,316	0.57	6.25	25	270
Nebraska	7,731	1.05	1.05	81	81
Nevada	15,580	1.41	0.00	219	0
New Hampshire	14,205	0.83	0.83	118	118
New Jersey	59,059	0.00	0.00	0	0
New Mexico	29,155	3.38	0.42	984	123
New York	259,518	0.39	1.16	1,006	3,018
North Carolina	78,021	0.94	0.47	733	366
North Dakota	5,554	2.40	0.00	133	0
Ohio	87,383	3.74	6.78	3,267	5,921
Oklahoma	42,621	0.00	0.00	0	0
Oregon	31,159	0.00	4.90	0	1,526
Pennsylvania	148,649	1.77	4.82	2,625	7,158
Puerto Rico	24,222	1.15	4.60	278	1,114
Rhode Island	11,224	1.57	0.52	176	59

TABLE 10–39.—DATA ON AFDC QUALITY CONTROL NEGATIVE CASE ACTIONS—
Continued

[Fiscal year 1991]

State	Total number of negative case actions	Negative case action error rates		Total number of incorrect negative case actions	
		Eligibility require-ments	Advance no-tice/hearing require-ments only	Eligibility require-ments	Advance no-tice/hearing require-ments only
South Carolina	53,663	5.45	3.03	2,927	1,626
South Dakota	7,915	1.05	0.53	83	42
Tennessee	61,096	1.86	1.60	1,137	975
Texas	384,185	3.92	0.51	15,057	1,943
Utah	23,783	1.86	0.93	442	221
Vermont	12,185	0.00	0.96	0	117
Virgin Islands	N/A	N/A	N/A	N/A	N/A
Virginia	73,054	0.52	1.81	379	1,325
Washington	103,548	1.19	1.58	1,230	1,640
West Virginia	26,280	1.49	4.98	392	1,307
Wisconsin	74,787	2.70	0.00	2,016	0
Wyoming	7,072	0.97	3.38	68	239

[1] Weighted average excluding the Virgin Islands.

N/A—Data not available.

THE OMNIBUS BUDGET RECONCILIATION ACT (OBRA) OF 1993

On August 10, 1993, the Omnibus Budget Reconciliation Act of 1993 (P.L. 103–66) was signed into law. The provisions of the Act pertaining to the AFDC program are summarized below.

Limit all AFDC administrative cost matching rates to 50 percent. OBRA 93 reduces the 90-percent matching rate for automated systems to 50 percent, reduces the 75-percent matching rate for fraud control programs to 50 percent, and reduces the 100-percent matching rate for immigration verification systems to 50 percent.

Increase in disregard of stepparents income. OBRA 93 increases the earnings disregard for stepparents to $90 monthly, from $75 monthly. This amount of earnings is not to be counted in determining the eligibility or benefit amounts of AFDC applicants and recipients.

THE OMNIBUS BUDGET RECONCILIATION ACT (OBRA) OF 1990

On November 5, 1990, the Omnibus Budget Reconciliation Act of 1990 (P.L. 101–508) was signed into law. The provisions of the Act pertaining to the AFDC program are summarized below.

State option to require monthly reporting and retrospective budgeting. OBRA 90 gives States the option of specifying from which categories of families, if any, monthly reports will be required. States also may choose to apply retrospective budgeting procedures to any one or more of the categories to whom the reporting requirement applies.

Treatment of foster care maintenance payments and adoption assistance. OBRA 90 requires that State and/or local foster care maintenance payments not be counted in determining the family's income or resources. Similarly, State and/or local adoption assistance payments are not to be counted, unless the family would benefit from their inclusion.

Eliminating the term "legal guardian." OBRA 90 deletes all references in AFDC law to legal guardians.

Reporting of child abuse and neglect. OBRA 90 mandates State agencies to report, to an appropriate agency, known or suspected instances of child abuse and neglect of children receiving AFDC, foster care, or adoption assistance.

Permissible uses of AFDC information. OBRA 90 allows title IV–E foster care and adoption assistance programs to access information about AFDC applicants and recipients.

Moratorium on final regulations for emergency assistance. OBRA 90 extends the prohibition of issuance of final regulations, and the prohibition on modifying current policy, to October 1, 1991.

Allow good cause exemption for child care transition benefits. OBRA 90 corrects an oversight of previous law by applying the good cause exemption to transitional child to make it consistent with the exception that applies to AFDC cash benefits.

Technical correction to the JOBS program regarding failure to participate. OBRA 90 repeals penalty language that denied AFDC to children of a principal earner who fails to participate in the JOBS program without good cause. Thus, the children of such parents continue to receive benefits.

Technical correction regarding AFDC–UP eligibility requirements. OBRA 90 amended previous law to allow participation in WIN and CWEP prior to October 1, 1990, to count toward the quarter of work requirement for AFDC–UP eligibility.

Technical correction to community development demonstration. OBRA 90 amends previous law to specify that DHHS can enter into agreements with up to 10 nonprofit organizations each year.

GAO study of JOBS funding for Indian Tribes. OBRA 90 directs GAO to conduct a study of the implementation of the JOBS program with respect to Indian Tribes and Alaska Native organizations.

THE FAMILY SUPPORT ACT OF 1988

Summary of provisions

On October 13, 1988, the Family Support Act of 1988 (Public Law 100–485) was signed into law. The major elements of the JOBS, child care transition, and Medicaid transition programs are summarized in table 10–40.

TABLE 10–40.—IMPORTANT ELEMENTS OF JOBS AND THE TRANSITIONAL CHILD CARE AND MEDICAID PROGRAMS

Important elements of JOBS:

Funding provisions .... Federal match rates: 90 percent for $126 million (equal to 1987 WIN funding); AFDC benefit match rate with a floor of 60 percent for most expenditures (the highest state benefit match in 1993 will be 79 percent); AFDC benefit match rate for child care; 50 percent for most administrative costs and other services.
Entitlement caps (excluding child care).

[Fiscal year, in millions of dollars]

1989	600
1990	800
1991	1,000
1992	1,000
1993	1,000
1994	1,100
1995	1,300
1996 and after	1,000

Work-related activities .... States must include these activities: education, job skills training, job readiness, job development and job placement.
States must include two of the following activities: group and individual job search, on-the-job training, work supplementation, community work experience or other approved work experience.

Priority groups .... States must spend 55 percent of their funds on:
(1) Recipients or applicants who have received AFDC for any 36 of the preceding 60 months.
(2) Parents under age 24 who have not completed high school or had little or no work experience in the preceding year.
(3) Members of families whose youngest child is within two years of being ineligible for AFDC.
States must give priority to volunteers within these three groups.

Participation requirements:

[Fiscal year, in percent]

General:	
1990 [1]	7
1991	7
1992	11
1993	11
1994	15
1995	20
AFDC–UP:	
1994	40
1995	50
1996	60
1997	75
1998	75

Important elements of the Transitional Child Care Program:

Funding provisions .... Uncapped entitlement at AFDC benefit match rate (50 percent to 79 percent).

Eligibility	Families who leave AFDC because of increased earnings, hours of work, or loss of the earnings disregards. Families must have received AFDC in at least three of the preceding six months. No income limits.
Benefits	Direct child care services, vouchers, cash, reimbursements, or other arrangements adopted by state agency. Care must meet state and local standards. Last for 12 months.
Maximum payments	Reimbursements are limited to actual costs, up to local market rates. States may set payment maximums below market rates. These caps may not be less than the AFDC child care disregards of $175 a month for children two years and older and $200 a month for children under age two unless local market rates are lower than these levels.
Family copayments	Vary with family's ability to pay as determined by states in sliding scale formulas.
Effective dates	Program begins April 1, 1990. Program ends September 30, 1998.

Important elements of the Transitional Medicaid Program:

Funding provisions	Uncapped entitlement at Medicaid match rate (50 percent to 79 percent).
Eligibility	Families who leave AFDC because of increased earnings, hours of work, or loss of the earnings disregards. Families must have received AFDC in at least three of the preceding six months. Families whose average gross monthly earnings (less necessary child care expenses) are below 185 percent of the poverty thresholds.
Benefits	Last for 12 months. Second six months are contingent on payment of a premium, which is at state option.
Premiums	States allowed to charge a premium after six months to families whose average gross monthly earnings (less necessary child care expenses) are above the poverty thresholds. Premiums limited to no more than 3 percent of a family's average gross monthly earnings.
Effective dates	Program begins April 1, 1990. Program ends September 30, 1998.

[1] There is no penalty for not meeting the 1990 requirements.

Source: Congressional Budget Office.

Impact of the Family Support Act of 1988

Table 10–41 shows CBO's estimated costs of the Family Support Act at the time of enactment. New Federal Government costs were estimated to total $3.3 billion over the 5-year period from fiscal years 1989 through 1993. The act included funding provisions primarily dealing with the recovery of debts owed the Federal Government and changes in the dependent care credit under the income tax system. Revenues and receipts from the funding provisions balanced the added spending and left the projected Federal deficit essentially unchanged over the 5 years. Also, as shown in table 10–41, the bill was projected to add a cost of $0.7 billion to State and local governments, one-fifth of Federal Government costs.

TABLE 10–41.—COST SUMMARY OF MAJOR PROVISIONS OF FAMILY SUPPORT ACT OF 1988

[Fiscal year, in millions]

	1989	1990	1991	1992	1993	Total 1989–93
Federal costs (CBO estimates):						
JOBS Program:						
Establish JOBS	33	242	357	277	167	1,076
Add mandatory participation rates	....	....	45	75	45	165
Other	0	1	7	6	2	18
Transitional assistance:						
Reimburse child care for 12 months after leave AFDC	....	25	205	245	260	735
Provide Medicaid for 12 months after leave AFDC	....	5	105	155	165	430
AFDC–UP Program:						
Mandate AFDC–UP [1]	....	....	315	397	441	1,153
Child support enforcement:						
Mandate income withholding	....	....	−25	−55	−90	−170
Mandate child support guidelines	....	−25	−70	−115	−160	−370
Other	5	12	56	38	30	141
Miscellaneous:						
Expand earnings disregards	....	30	45	45	45	165
Other	24	23	−16	−30	−39	−38
Total outlays	62	313	1,024	1,038	866	3,305
Revenues (Joint Committee on Taxation estimates):						
IRS debt collection	400	400	400	400	400	2,000
Restrict child care tax credit to children < 13 (current law < 15)	9	86	90	93	97	375
Taxpayer id no. required of service provider to obtain child care credit	37	102	121	132	137	529
Other	27	90	97	105	111	430
Total revenues	473	678	708	730	745	3,334
State and local costs:						
JOBS Program:						
Establish JOBS	−4	−63	−133	−158	−169	−527
Add mandatory participation rates	....	....	30	50	35	115
Other	0	0	1	1	1	3
Transitional assistance:						
Reimburse child care for 12 months after leave AFDC	....	15	120	145	150	430
Provide Medicaid for 12 months after leave AFDC	....	5	85	125	135	350
AFDC–UP Program:						
Mandate AFDC–UP [1]	....	....	232	294	323	849
Child support enforcement:						
Mandate income withholding	....	....	−25	−65	−105	−195
Mandate child support guidelines	....	−35	−85	−135	−180	−435
Other	−1	−2	18	−3	−22	−10
Miscellaneous:						
Expand earnings disregards	....	47	57	57	62	223
Other	13	−6	−29	−38	−40	−99
Total outlays	8	−39	271	273	190	704

[1] Includes two related provisions, one of which allows States to amend the "quarters of work" rule and a second which requires demonstrations of the 100-hour rule.

Source: Congressional Budget Office and Joint Committee on Taxation.

CBO recently received available data on actual spending under the Family Support Act and the following compares actual spending with CBO's 1988 estimates in two areas.

Job Opportunities and Basic Skills Training Program (JOBS). In 1988, CBO estimated that not all of the States would spend enough to draw down the full amount of available Federal funds. According to CBO, Federal outlays would reach $345 million in 1990 and $600 million in 1991. Actual outlays were $264 and $546 million, respectively. In 1991, spending totaled only 55 percent of the $1 billion in available funds.

Aid to Families with Dependent Children for Unemployed Parents (AFDC–UP). For fiscal year 1991, an average 22,000 AFDC–UP cases in States that had not previously had AFDC–UP programs received benefits each month, at an estimated annual cost to the Federal Government of about $50 million. This cost is significantly below CBO's estimated cost of $150 million in AFDC benefit payments at the time the Family Support Act was passed. In addition, Medicaid costs for these families in 1991 were overestimated in 1988.

The major source of the error is in the projection of the number of participating families. CBO estimated that 65,000 families would participate, about three times the actual number. One element is that participating families were probably overestimated primarily because of an assumed participation rate that was too high. The participation rate is the proportion of families eligible for program benefits who participate in the program. CBO assumed a participation rate of 55 percent, slightly below the participation rate that prevailed in the AFDC–UP program in the early 1980's. Participation rates in the States that had to implement an AFDC–UP program, however, turned out to be lower on average than rates in other States. Also, participation rates have been estimated to vary widely across States in the AFDC–UP program, from barely 1 percent to over 90 percent, for reasons no one understands. In March 1991, only two of the new AFDC–UP States—Kentucky and Texas—had more than 5,000 families receiving AFDC–UP; 11 of the States had fewer than 500 families receiving benefits.

THE OMNIBUS BUDGET RECONCILIATION ACT (OBRA) OF 1987

In December of 1987, Congress enacted H.R. 3545, the Omnibus Budget Reconciliation Act of 1987 (Public Law 100–203). This new law includes four AFDC amendments, which are summarized below:

1. Fraud control under AFDC program.—Effective April 1, 1988, authorizes 75 percent Federal funding for the costs of a State's fraud control program.

2. Assistance to Homeless Families.—Prohibits the Secretary of Health and Human Services, prior to October 1, 1988, from taking any action that would have the effect of implementing, in whole or in part, the proposed regulations published in the *Federal Register* on December 14, 1987. These regulations would have restricted the use of AFDC emergency assistance funds for homeless families and would have limited States' authority to make payments for special needs of AFDC recipients. The moratorium on promulgation of regulations is intended to give Congress an opportunity to determine whether and how the current AFDC statute should be amended to respond to the problems of homeless families.

3. Washington State Demonstration Program.—Allows the State of Washington to conduct a demonstration of its proposed Family Independence Program.

4. New York State Demonstration Program.—Allows the State of New York to test a child support supplement demonstration program as an alternative to the present AFDC program.

THE DEFICIT REDUCTION ACT OF 1984

In June of 1984, Congress enacted H.R. 4170, the Deficit Reduction Act of 1984 (Public Law 98–369). This new law, which took effect on October 1, 1984, includes 22 AFDC amendments and an income and asset verification amendment which affected several programs, and are summarized below:

1. Gross income limitation.—Under prior law, eligibility for AFDC was limited to families with gross incomes at or below 150 percent of the State standard of need. The act increases the gross income limitation to 185 percent of the State standard of need.

2. Work expense deduction.—Under prior law, States were required to disregard the first $75 of monthly earnings for full-time work expenses; a lower deduction applied to part-time workers. The act requires States to disregard the first $75 monthly for full and part-time workers.

3. Continuation of $30 disregard.—Under prior law, the $30 plus one-third of remaining earnings disregard was limited to 4 months. The act retains the 4-month limit on the one-third disregard but extends the $30 disregard for an additional 8 months for a total of 12 months.

4. Work transition status.—Under prior law, a family who lost AFDC eligibility due to the 4-month limit on the earnings disregard, simultaneously lost categorical eligibility for Medicaid. The act provides that families who lose AFDC because of the termination of the earnings disregard will be eligible for 9 months of Medicaid coverage. At State option, an additional 6 months of Medicaid coverage can be provided. In addition, families who lost AFDC eligibility prior to enactment of the work transition will also be eligible for Medicaid under certain specified circumstances.

5. Clarification of earned income provisions.—The act clarifies that the term "earned income" as used in the AFDC program means the gross amount of earnings, prior to the taking of payroll or other deductions.

6. Burial plots, funeral agreements and certain property.—Under prior law, burial plots and funeral agreements were counted toward the $1,000 asset limit. The act exempts from the AFDC resources limitation, burial plots and funeral agreements. An AFDC policy on real property that is similar to SSI policy is also established.

7. Federal matching for Community Work Experience Program (CWEP) expenses.—Under prior law, States were required to reimburse a CWEP participant for necessary transportation and other expenses. Federal matching for this reimbursement was by regulation, limited to $25 per month. The act requires States to reimburse a CWEP participant for costs incurred if the State is unable to provide directly any transportation or day care services. Reimbursement of day care expenses is limited to those determined by the State to be reasonable, necessary and cost effective up to $160 per month per child.

8. *Retrospective budgeting and monthly reporting.*—Under prior law, monthly reporting and retrospective budgeting were required for all AFDC cases; however, the Secretary of Health and Human Services could waive the monthly reporting requirement if it was not cost effective to require the report. The act mandates retrospective budgeting for cases filing a monthly report. Monthly reporting is required when cost effective; cases with earned income and recent work history must report monthly.

9. *Earned income tax credit (EITC).*—Under prior law, States were required to assume that an individual was receiving the earned income tax credit on an advance basis regardless of when or if it was received. The act requires States to count the EITC only when actually received.

10. *Demonstrations of one-stop service delivery.*—The act authorizes from 3 to 5 Federally-assisted demonstration projects designed to test the effectiveness and efficiency of integrating the delivery of human services.

11. *Work requirements for pregnant women.*—The act adds to those who are exempt from work registration, any woman who is in the third trimester of pregnancy.

12. *Recalculation of lump sum income.*—Under prior law, States could only recalculate ineligibility due to receipt of lump sum income if a life threatening circumstance occurred. The act allows States to recalculate the ineligibility period under other specified circumstances. Ineligibility may be recalculated if: (1) an event occurs which would have changed the amount of AFDC paid; (2) the income becomes unavailable for reasons beyond the family's control; and/or (3) the family incurs, becomes responsible for and pays medical bills which offset the lump sum income.

13. *Overpayment recoupment.*—Under prior law, States were required to attempt to recover all benefit overpayments. The act permits States to waive overpayment recovery when it is not cost effective. States will be permitted to automatically waive overpayments of less than $35. Larger overpayments must be collected unless the State determines, after attempting to collect the overpayment, that the cost to collect would exceed the amount owed.

14. *Protective payments.*—Under prior law, States were required to make protective payments to a third party when a parent on AFDC failed to meet certain statutory procedural requirements. The act permits States to make the payment to the parent if, after all reasonable efforts have been made, a suitable protective payee cannot be found.

15. *Eligibility requirements for aliens.*—Under prior law the income of an individual who sponsors a non-refugee alien was deemed to be available to the alien for 3 years after entry into the United States. The act establishes a similar policy for aliens who are sponsored by organizations or agencies.

16. *Fugitive felons.*—The act permits States to disclose the current address of an AFDC recipient if a law enforcement agency provides the correct social security number and demonstrates that the recipient is a fugitive felon.

17. Payment schedule for back claims.—The act establishes a payment schedule for court-ordered reimbursements and certain other back claims owed by the Federal Government to the States that have been allowed or are pending.

18. Work supplementation program.—The act modifies the existing work supplementation program to provide additional flexibility to States in operating grant diversion programs in which all or part of the AFDC grant can be used to subsidize a job.

19. Disregard of in-kind income.—The act extends, until October 1, 1987, the disregard of certain in-kind assistance provided on the basis of need.

20. Standard filing unit/child support payments.—There was no requirement in prior law that parents and all siblings be included in the AFDC unit. The act requires States to include in the filing unit the parents and all minor siblings living with a dependent child who applies for or receives AFDC. In addition, a monthly disregard of $50 of child support received by a family is established.

21. CWEP work for Federal agencies.—The act permits Federal agencies or offices to serve as community work experience program (CWEP) sites under the same requirements as apply to other sites.

22. Earned income of full-time students.—For purposes of applying the gross income limitation, the act allows States to disregard the income of an AFDC child who is a full-time student.

23. Income and eligibility verification procedures.—Under present law, IRS wage information furnished by employers to IRS is available to State welfare agencies for use in their AFDC and food stamp programs, and to the Social Security Administration for administering the SSI program. However, IRS unearned income information (filed by a financial institution or corporation with respect to payments to individuals in the form of interest, dividends, etc.) is not available to Federal and State agencies for use in the administration of these programs. Quarterly wage information from the unemployment compensation program is available to State welfare agencies in most States.

Public Law 98–369 provides for the IRS to disclose return information with respect to unearned income to Federal, State, or local agencies administering AFDC, SSI, Medicaid, food stamps, and the cash assistance programs administered in Puerto Rico, Guam, and the Virgin Islands.

Disclosure can only be made to agencies that meet the requirements to safeguard this confidential information against disclosure, and verification of the unearned income information is required prior to taking action to reduce or terminate benefits.

The provision also replaces existing statutory provisions relating to use (for purposes of AFDC) of return and other wage information and use of social security numbers, by adding a new section to the Social Security Act requiring States to have in effect an income and eligibility verification system for use in administering the AFDC, Medicaid, unemployment compensation, and food stamp programs (and the adult assistance programs in the territories). State agencies must request and make use of: (1) wage and other income information available under the Internal Revenue Code; and (2) quarterly wage information. Each State is required as of September 30,

1988, to maintain a quarterly wage reporting system, although not necessarily through its unemployment compensation system.

The income and eligibility system requires use of standardized data formats to facilitate exchange of information, for the purpose of identifying and reducing ineligibility and incorrect payments.

THE OMNIBUS BUDGET RECONCILIATION ACT (OBRA) OF 1981

The Omnibus Budget Reconciliation Act of 1981 (OBRA) imposed a gross income limit for AFDC eligibility (150 percent of a State's need standard), capped the deduction for child care costs ($160 monthly per child), set a standard deduction for other work expenses ($75 monthly), and ended the work incentive disregard for working recipients after their first 4 months on a job. These provisions affected AFDC parents with jobs by reducing or ending their benefits. They also had potential effects on welfare mothers without jobs by reducing the gains possible from work, and on nonwelfare mothers with low earnings. Under previous law, a person in the latter group could increase total income by decreasing or ending earnings, enrolling in AFDC, and then resuming work. OBRA also required States to count part of the income of a stepparent as available to an AFDC child.

Former HHS Assistant Secretary Rubin reported in testimony that 408,000 families lost eligibility and 299,000 lost benefits as a result of the OBRA changes. The changes saved the Federal and State governments about $1.1 billion in 1983. This implies an average loss in benefits per family of $1,555 per year.

GAO evaluation of the 1981 amendments

At the request of the House Ways and Means Committee, the U.S. General Accounting Office conducted an in-depth evaluation of the effect of the 1981 amendments on individual AFDC families in five cities: Boston, Dallas, Memphis, Milwaukee, and Syracuse. GAO examined case records, analyzed 10 years of HHS program data, and interviewed former working AFDC recipients more than a year after their termination from AFDC due to the 1981 amendments.

Findings include:
—Once the declines in caseload and outlays stabilized, OBRA had decreased the national AFDC-basic monthly caseload by 493,000 cases and monthly outlays by $93 million. However, because the caseload rose faster than predicted after this point, long-term effects are less certain.
—Working AFDC recipients who lost eligibility due to the OBRA cuts were more likely to be non-white, younger than those who remained on AFDC (28–33) and had been working for their current employer between 1.7 and 3.4 years.
—Recipients who lost AFDC eligibility suffered a substantial loss of income which they could not make up by increased earnings or other means. The average *monthly* income loss for working single parent families who lost AFDC eligibility was $186 in Memphis, $229 in Dallas, $180 in Milwaukee, $151 in Syracuse, and $115 in Boston.
—A large number of families interviewed had fallen below the poverty level after the OBRA changes were implemented.

This ranged from a high of 85.5 percent of families below poverty in Memphis to a low of 28 percent of the Milwaukee families interviewed in poverty.

—Lack of health coverage was common among these former AFDC recipients. In Dallas, 59.2 percent of those families who lost AFDC did not have any health coverage. In Memphis, 45 percent, in Boston 27.5 percent, in Syracuse, 17.1 percent and in Milwaukee, 13.9 percent had no health coverage at all. Private health insurance coverage was more common in high AFDC benefit States.

—Families terminated from AFDC were more likely to face increased emergency situations. In several sites, significantly more families had to forgo medical treatment or were refused medical and/or dental treatment because they could not pay. It was also more common for these families to run out of food before the end of the month, have to seek food from a church or charity group, or need to borrow $50 or more from friends or relatives to meet expenses. In all but one site, those terminated from AFDC said they are eating worse now than before.

LENGTH OF TIME ON WELFARE AND TURNOVER WITHIN THE AFDC CASELOAD

LENGTH OF TIME ON WELFARE

Average length of time on welfare.—A 1983 study of AFDC families [2] using annual data, found that although most "spells" of AFDC are relatively short, most persons enrolled in the program at any point in time are in the midst of spells that last at least 8 years. As the first two columns of table 10–42 illustrate, the study reported that 50 percent of AFDC spells lasted less than 2 years and 62 percent lasted less than 4 years. At the same time, the study reported that 50 percent of the persons enrolled at a point in time were in the midst of very long episodes (8 or more years) of AFDC receipt, and such long-term recipients used most of the resources of the program.

The 1983 study has since been updated by one of its authors, because it understated the extent of long-term welfare dependence by neglecting to take into account the fact that multiple spells of welfare receipt are common (about one-third of all welfare spells are followed by subsequent spells). Accounting for multiple spells alters the distribution of total expected time on welfare, as the last two columns of table 10–42 illustrate. The fact remains, however, that while a significant percent of all persons on welfare will be enrolled for less than 2 years (30 percent) or less than 4 years (50 percent), a majority of persons enrolled in AFDC at a point in time are in the midst of what will be long periods of welfare receipt (65 percent).

---

[2] Bane, Mary Jo, and Ellwood, David T., The Dynamics of Dependence: The Routes to Self-Sufficiency. Prepared for the U.S. Department of Health and Human Services under contract No. HHS–100–82–0038, June 1983. (Prepared by Urban Systems Research and Engineering, Inc., Cambridge, Mass.)

TABLE 10–42.—DISTRIBUTION OF LENGTH OF TIME ON AFDC

[In percent]

Expected time on AFDC	Single spell analysis		Multiple spell analysis	
	Persons beginning a spell	Persons on AFDC at a point in time	Persons beginning first AFDC spell	Persons on AFDC at a point in time
1 to 2 years	48	14	30	7
3 to 4 years	14	10	20	11
5 to 7 years	20	25	19	17
8 or more years	17	50	30	65
All	100	100	100	100

This seemingly paradoxical finding that there are large differences between point-in-time and ever-began estimates of welfare dependency highlights a crucial element of welfare dynamics that is characteristic of the dynamics of spells of poverty and unemployment as well. The differences in the estimates occur because the probability of being on welfare (or being poor or unemployed) at a given time is necessarily higher for longer-term recipients than for those who have shorter welfare spells. Thus, the point-in-time welfare sample is a biased sample of *all* persons who have ever received welfare.

An example of spells of hospitalization will help to establish this point. Consider a 13-bed hospital in which 12 beds are occupied for an entire year by 12 chronically ill patients, while the other bed is used by 52 patients, each of whom stays exactly 1 week. On any given day, a hospital census would find that about 85 percent of patients (12/13) were in the midst of long spells of hospitalization. Nevertheless, viewed over the course of a year, short-term use clearly dominates: out of the 64 patients using hospital services, about 80 percent (52/64) spent only 1 week in the hospital. Exactly the same dynamic accounts for the results with regard to welfare experience. One of the most important lessons from the longitudinal evidence is that while the welfare population at any point in time is composed predominantly of long-term users, the typical recipient is a short-term user.

Recent research seems to indicate that studies based on annual data, such as the 1983 Bane and Ellwood (and 1986 Ellwood) study on welfare dynamics, underestimate the movement on and off the AFDC program and overestimate long-term welfare dependence. A study by Pavetti[3] compares the 1983 Bane/Ellwood data with annual National Longitudinal Survey of Youth (NLSY) data and monthly NLSY data. Pavetti concludes that while the use of monthly data does change the general findings (1983) of Banes and Ellwood, monthly data *"produces a distribution with many more short spells of welfare [and] fewer long spells,"* Table 10–43 displays

---

[3] "The Dynamics of Welfare and Work: Exploring the Process By Which Young Women Work Their Way Off Welfare" [by] Pavetti, LaDonna A. John F. Kennedy School of Government, Harvard University. Draft, October 1992, revised chapter 1993.

Pavetti's findings and indicates that 70 percent of all recipients who begin a spell of welfare will have spells that last for 2 years or less; only 7 percent of recipients who begin a spell of welfare receipt will have a spell that will last for more than 8 years. Bane and Ellwood's 1983 data in column 2 of the table show that 48 percent of AFDC recipients who begin a spell of AFDC receipt are expected to stay on the program for 2 years or less, and nearly 15 percent are expected to stay on the program for more than 8 years. (In 1986, Ellwood revised the report to take account of multiple spells of AFDC receipt; see earlier discussion.) The finding of the three States, California, Minnesota, and Washington, which have conducted cohort studies using monthly data, support the work done by Pavetti.[4]

TABLE 10–43.—DISTRIBUTION OF AFDC SPELLS

Spell length in years [1]	Persons beginning a spell			Completed spell distribution for persons on AFDC at a point in time [2]		
	Bane/ Ellwood (1983)	NLSY annual	NLSY monthly	Bane/ Ellwood (1983)	NLSY annual	NLSY monthly
1 (5.3)	29.0	26.0	56.0	6.2	6.3	11.0
2 (18.6)	19.2	20.7	14.1	8.2	10.0	9.7
3 (30.6)	8.8	13.9	8.1	5.6	10.0	9.2
4 (43.9)	5.2	11.4	6.3	4.4	11.0	10.4
5 (55.2)	6.8	6.2	3.3	7.3	7.4	6.7
6 (67.7)	10.6	3.7	2.0	13.5	5.4	4.9
7 (80.4)	3.1	3.1	1.7	4.6	5.2	5.2
8 (92.0)	2.6	2.6	1.5	4.5	4.9	5.0
Over 8	14.8	12.3	7.0	45.7	39.9	37.8
Total	100.0	99.9	100.0	100.0	100.1	100.0
Average	4.7	4.2	2.3	10.0	8.4	7.2

[1] The number in parentheses in this column represents the average spell length in months for persons who completed a spell of welfare during this year. For example, the average spell length for spells that lasted between 1 and 12 months was 5.3 months; the average spell length for spells that lasted between 13 and 24 months was 18.6 months. I observe very few spells that last longer than 8 years. Therefore, I assume that the average length of spells that last longer than 8 years is 90 percent of the full width of the interval.

[2] These distributions assume a no-growth steady state for the AFDC population.

Source: The Dynamics of Welfare and Work: Exploring the Process by Which Young Women Work Their Way Off Welfare [by] Pavetti, LaDonna A. John F. Kennedy School of Government, Harvard University, Draft, revision of chapter 2, p. 18. 1993.

---

[4] The reader should note that the Bane/Ellwood study measured years in which the family received at least the equivalent of 1 month of the maximum AFDC grant per family size, rather than years of continuous AFDC receipt. Further, the State cohort studies define exits differently; using monthly data, California defined an exit as being off AFDC for at least 1 month, while Washington defined it as being off AFDC for at least 3 months.

Subgroup analysis of length of time on welfare.—Tables 10–44 and 10–45 present data on the length of time on welfare for various subgroups of the population. Table 10–44 is based on ever-began estimates of welfare receipt which take into account multiple spells. This table shows that the most powerful predictor of long-term welfare receipt is marital status. Single women average 9 years of AFDC receipt, and 39 percent are predicted to receive AFDC for 10 or more years. Race and work experience also seem to distinguish themselves among different subgroups of AFDC recipients. Blacks and those who did not work in the 2 years prior to their first receiving welfare are estimated to average over 8 years of AFDC receipt, and nearly one-third of each group are expected to receive AFDC for 10 or more years. Education may well be another important grouping: high school graduates seem to fare better than dropouts. However, these education-related estimates are less reliable because the sample size with less than 9 years of education is very small.

Table 10–45 presents another approach to evaluating length of time on welfare. It takes a sample of the entire 1970 population, and chronicles welfare receipt patterns for the next 10 years. Eighty-five percent of this 1970 sample lived in families in which no AFDC income was received in the following 9 year period, 1970–1979. Fewer children (81 percent) received no AFDC. This table also presents data on individuals for whom AFDC and Food Stamps together constituted 50 percent of their family's annual income. Only 4 percent of all nonwhite Americans and 0.2 percent of all white Americans in this group were on welfare 8 to 10 years out of the total 10-year period. Note that these data do not describe the welfare receipt patterns of the population in anything but this 10-year window. Years of welfare receipt prior to and after this period are not accounted for. Thus, these data represent a lower bound estimate of long-term receipt. Table 10–46 shows similar patterns for the 1980–89 time period.

TABLE 10–44.—PERCENTAGE OF AFDC RECIPIENTS WITH VARIOUS CHARACTERISTICS AND AVERAGE TOTAL DURATIONS OF AFDC RECEIPT

Recipient characteristics at time of first spell beginning	Percent of all first-time recipients (new beginnings)	Percent of recipients at any point in time [1]	Average number of years of AFDC receipt	Percent who will have AFDC spells of 10 or more years
Age:				
Under 22	30.0	35.9	8.23	32.8
22 to 30	40.7	41.9	7.08	25.8
31 to 40	11.8	8.8	5.15	15.0
Over 40	17.6	13.4	5.23	15.8
Race/ethnicity:				
White	55.2	47.7	5.95	19.6
Black	40.1	47.4	8.14	32.0
Other	4.8	4.8	6.94	25.5
Years of education:				
Under 9	9.7	9.6	6.81	24.5
9 to 11	37.6	41.9	7.65	29.2
Over 11	52.7	48.5	6.33	21.8
Marital status:				
Single	29.5	40.0	9.33	39.3
Divorced	28.1	20.2	4.94	13.7
Separated	32.3	31.9	6.80	24.4
Widowed	8.4	5.3	4.37	10.2
Number of children:				
0 to 1	43.4	48.7	7.71	29.7
2 to 3	42.8	37.3	6.04	20.1
Over 3	13.8	13.7	6.83	24.5
Age of youngest child:				
Under 3	51.3	60.4	8.09	31.9
3 to 5	22.5	22.3	6.79	24.2
6 to 10	19.7	12.9	4.51	11.3
Over 10	6.5	4.4	4.71	12.4
Work experience:				
Worked in the last 2 years	65.8	59.6	6.53	23.0
Did not work in the last 2 years	34.2	39.8	8.00	31.2
Disability status:				
No disability	81.6	81.4	6.85	24.8
Disability limits work	18.4	18.6	6.97	25.0

[1] These figures assume that the AFDC caseload is a "steady state."

Source: David T. Ellwood. "Targeting Would-Be Long-Term Recipients of AFDC," Table IV–1. Simulation model estimates are based on the 15-year panel study of income dynamics. For each individual who began a first spell on or after the third sample year of the PSID, probabilities are predicted for exiting from first spell, for recidivism, and for exiting from later spells, based on logic models.

TABLE 10–45.—WELFARE DEPENDENCY, 1970–79, BY TWO DEFINITIONS OF DEPENDENCY

[In percent]

Years on welfare	Fraction living in households in which at least $1 of AFDC was received by head or wife			Fraction living in households in which AFDC of head and wife plus food stamps was at least 50 percent of total family income		
	All	Children, age 0 to 5 in 1970	Women, age 18 to 55 in 1970	All	Children, age 0 to 5 in 1970	Women, age 18 to 55 in 1970
All races:						
0 years	84.8	80.5	85.7	92.5	88.4	92.7
1 to 2 years	7.5	7.7	6.6	3.7	4.7	3.3
3 to 7 years	5.5	7.8	5.2	3.0	5.4	3.1
8 to 10 years	2.2	4.0	2.4	.7	1.6	.8
Total	100.0	100.0	100.0	100.0	100.0	100.0
White:						
0 years	89.9	86.8	90.7	95.7	93.3	95.8
1 to 2 years	5.7	6.3	5.0	2.6	3.3	2.2
3 to 7 years	3.4	4.8	3.1	1.8	3.1	1.8
8 to 10 years	1.1	2.2	1.3	.2	.3	.2
Total	100.0	100.0	100.0	100.0	100.0	100.0
Nonwhite:						
0 years	57.2	52.5	57.8	75.6	66.3	75.4
1 to 2 years	17.2	13.9	16.1	10.3	11.3	9.5
3 to 7 years	17.1	21.6	17.5	10.4	15.4	11.1
8 to 10 years	8.6	12.1	8.7	3.8	6.8	3.9
Total	100.0	100.0	100.0	100.0	100.0	100.0

Table reads: 85.0 percent of the population lived in households in which no AFDC income was received during the 1970–79 period.

Source: Special tabulations of the Panel Study of Income Dynamics by Greg J. Duncan and Kavitha Sitaram.

TABLE 10–46.—WELFARE DEPENDENCY, 1980–89, BY TWO DEFINITIONS OF DEPENDENCY

[In percent]

Years on welfare	Fraction living in households in which at least $1 of AFDC was received by head or wife			Fraction living in households in which AFDC of head and wife plus food stamps was at least 50 percent of total family income		
	All	Children age 0 to 5 in 1980	Women, age 18 to 55 in 1980	All	Children age 0 to 5 in 1980	Women, age 18 to 55 in 1980
All races:						
0 years	88.2	80.2	86.3	93.6	87.7	92.8
1 to 2 years	5.5	8.1	6.2	3.1	5.6	3.4
3 to 7 years	4.3	6.3	5.6	2.3	3.6	2.8
8 to 10 years	2.0	5.4	2.6	.9	3.1	1.1
Total	100.0	100.0	100.0	100.0	100.0	100.0
White:						
0 years	92.6	88.2	92.2	96.1	92.3	96.0
1 to 2 years	3.9	5.1	4.1	2.2	4.6	2.1
3 to 7 years	2.6	3.8	2.7	1.3	2.1	1.4
8 to 10 years	.9	2.7	1.2	.3	1.0	.3
Total	100.0	100.0	100.0	100.0	100.0	100.0
Nonwhite:						
0 years	66.3	41.8	65.7	81.2	65.2	81.3
1 to 2 years	13.8	22.4	13.5	7.6	10.8	7.5
3 to 7 years	12.6	18.1	13.0	7.4	11.1	7.5
8 to 10 years	7.2	17.7	7.7	3.7	12.8	3.7
Total	100.0	100.0	100.0	100.0	100.0	100.0

Table reads: 88.2 percent of the population lived in households in which no AFDC income was received during the 1980–89 period.

Source: Special tabulation of the Panel Study of Income Dynamics by Greg J. Duncan and Kavitha Sitaram.

TABLE 10–47.—LONG-TERM WELFARE DEPENDENCY, 1970–79 AND 1980–89

[In percent]

Fraction living in households in which AFDC of head and wife plus food stamps was at least 50 percent of total family income

Individuals on welfare for 8 to 10 years	Women, age 18 to 55 in 1970	Women, age 18 to 55 in 1980	Children, age 0 to 5 in 1970	Children, age 0 to 5 in 1980
All races	0.7	2.6	1.6	3.1
White	.2	1.2	.3	1.0
Nonwhite	3.8	7.7	6.8	12.8

Source: Special tabulations of the Panel Study of Income Dynamics by Greg J. Duncan and Kavitha Sitaram. Table prepared by Committee staff.

INTERGENERATIONAL WELFARE RECEIPT

Researchers have held great interest in identifying possible intergenerational effects of welfare receipt,[5] particularly the extent that children growing up in welfare-recipient households are more likely to receive welfare when they become adults. Theories of poverty have often included an intergenerational component which has led to the belief that a similar process occurs with welfare use.

Two perspectives pervade the culture-of-poverty theories—a cultural perspective and a structural perspective. The cultural perspective supports the existence of a welfare "culture" that shapes the values and attitudes of children raised in dependent homes, either through early parental socialization or from more general childhood experiences that guide development into adulthood. The structural view holds that the values and attitudes of children being raised in dependent homes or in neighborhoods with high concentrations of welfare families are not significantly different from those of other children. Instead, these children develop different values and attitudes as they encounter the same kinds of structural impediments to jobs and marriages (such as discrimination or poor employment opportunities) that blocked their parents.

The data necessary to sort out these two explanations do not exist for the United States. However, descriptive intergenerational information can help to provide a more accurate perspective on the patterns of AFDC receipt. It must be kept in mind, though, that these data fail to adjust for other aspects of parental background and environment that may also affect the likelihood of AFDC receipt. Children from AFDC-dependent homes generally have fewer parental resources available to them, live in worse neighborhoods, and go to lower quality schools. All of these factors could have an effect on their chance of receiving AFDC that is independent of the effect of their parents' AFDC receipt.

The results of two studies are presented below. The first, by Martha S. Hill and Michael Ponza (1984), uses data from the Panel Study of Income Dynamics. The study found that most daughters in families that received welfare did not receive welfare as young adults. As table 10–48 illustrates, only 19 percent of black daugh-

---

[5] Borrowed heavily from Duncan, Greg J., Martha S. Hill, and Saul D. Hoffman, "Welfare Dependence Within and Across Generations," Science, Vol. 239, January 29, 1988.

ters and 26 percent of white daughters in "highly dependent" welfare families became "highly dependent" themselves. It is also interesting to note that fully 42 percent of the black daughters and 27 percent of the white daughters who grew up in families with high welfare receipt received no welfare as young adults.

At the same time, the data also show a higher incidence of welfare receipt among women with some welfare backgrounds (defined as both high and low welfare dependence). From this perspective, young women who grew up in welfare families were more than twice as likely to receive welfare themselves as young adults whose parents received no welfare assistance—58 percent versus 27 percent, respectively. The numbers also remain high when subdivided by race (see table 10–48).

A second study, conducted by Greg Duncan and colleagues (1988), shows similar results to the Hill and Ponza study. Duncan's data, taken from a 19-year longitudinal study of American families, surveyed a sample of daughters whose parents' economic status was observed while the daughters were between the ages of 13 and 15, and later when they were between the ages of 21 and 23 years. For each of the two 3-year periods, "AFDC dependence" was defined in terms of whether AFDC income was not reported in any of the years (no dependence), in one or two years (moderate dependence), or in all three years (high dependence) (table 10–49).

Despite the stereotype that high welfare receipt is routinely passed from mother to child, the data showed that a majority of daughters who grew up in highly dependent homes did not share the fate of their parents. Only one out of five (20 percent) of the daughters from high welfare receipt families were themselves highly dependent on AFDC in their early 20s; and more than three out of five (64 percent) of the daughters with welfare backgrounds received no AFDC during the 3-year period.

TABLE 10–48.—INTERGENERATIONAL TRANSMISSION OF WELFARE DEPENDENCY

[In percent]

Parental welfare status	Status of daughters as young adults			Some welfare dependence	Number of observations
	Received no welfare	Low welfare dependence	High welfare dependence		
Received no welfare:					
Black	53	33	14	47	108
White	79	19	2	21	354
All women	73	22	5	27	462
Low welfare dependence:					
Black	31	49	20	69	130
White	63	31	5	36	75
All women	42	42	15	57	205
High welfare dependence:					
Black	42	39	19	58	92
White	27	47	26	73	25
All women	41	41	21	61	117
Some welfare dependence:					
Black	36	45	19	64	222
White	54	35	11	45	100
All women	42	42	16	58	322

Note.—"High welfare dependence" is defined as receiving at least 25 percent of average family income as cash welfare payments. "Some welfare dependence" accounts for all women with either low or high welfare dependence.

Source: Reanalysis by the Committee on Ways and Means staff based on data from: Hill, Martha S., and Ponza, Michael. "Does Welfare Dependency Beget Dependency?" Institute for Social Research, mimeo, Fall 1984.

However, Duncan's data, like Hill and Ponza's data, also showed a higher likelihood of welfare receipt among women with welfare backgrounds. The fraction of daughters from highly dependent homes who themselves become highly dependent (20 percent) is much greater than the fraction of daughters from nonrecipient families who become highly dependent (only 3 percent). And while more than three out of five of the daughters who grew up in AFDC-dependent homes received no AFDC themselves, more than nine-tenths of those who grew up in nonrecipient families received no AFDC in their early adult years.

TABLE 10–49.—INTERGENERATIONAL PATTERNS OF AFDC RECEIPT

Dependence of parents (percent)	Dependence of daughters (percent)				Unweighted number of cases
	No	Moderate	High	Total	
No	91	6	3	100	811
Moderate	62	22	16	100	127
High	64	16	20	100	147

Source: Duncan, Greg J., Martha S. Hill, and Saul D. Hoffman, "Welfare Dependence Within and Across Generations," Science, Vol. 239, January 29, 1988.

TURNOVER WITHIN THE AFDC CASELOAD

To further understand the dynamics of welfare receipt, data are available which describe which events in an individual's life provide the explanation for beginnings and endings of spells of AFDC receipt.

Beginnings of AFDC spells.—As table 10–50 illustrates, three-fourths of all spells in the PSID data set began with a relationship change that created a female-headed family with children. Almost half the AFDC spells started after a wife became a female family head (by loss of the male head and his earnings due to absence, divorce, separation, death). Another 30 percent began when a never-married, divorced, or separated woman acquired a child.

In contrast to changes in family composition, changes in earnings were a relatively minor cause of resorting to welfare. Only 15 percent of AFDC spells could be traced to a drop in family earnings.

Endings of AFDC spells.—The most common route out of AFDC was by way of a change in family structure. Some 46 percent of endings occurred this way—35 percent when a female head became a wife and 11 percent when the household no longer contained a child under 18.

Increased earnings were much more significant in ending AFDC than decreased earnings were in starting it. Some 26 percent of endings occurred this way—21 percent when the female head herself earned more money and 5 percent when another member of the family increased earnings.

A more recent analysis (Pavetti, 1993) indicates that 46 percent of exits from the AFDC program occur because of work, rather than the 21 percent estimated by Bane and Ellwood (1983). Pavetti maintains that most of the difference in the estimates is caused by the use of monthly versus annual data. The Pavetti study also indicates that by the end of 5 years about two-thirds of all women who leave AFDC for work return to the AFDC program. Pavetti's study also indicates that 11 percent exit AFDC because of marriage, re-marriage, or reconciliation; the 1983 Bane/Ellwood study indicated that marriage was the most common route out of welfare, with 35 percent of recipients exiting that way.

Poverty status.—About 40 percent of those who ended AFDC spells were poor after their exit. About 52 percent of those whose AFDC eligibility ended because they no longer had an eligible child were poor in the following year. For those who earned their way off AFDC, about 32 percent were poor in the year after their welfare spell; their poverty reflected the sub-poverty gross income eligibility limits of AFDC in many States.

TABLE 10–50.—EVENTS ASSOCIATED WITH THE BEGINNINGS AND ENDINGS OF AFDC SPELLS

Beginnings	Percent	Endings	Percent
Divorce/separation	45	Marriage	35
Childless, unmarried woman becomes a female head with children.	30	Children leave parental home ...	11
Earnings of female head fell	12	Earnings of female head increased.	21
Earnings of others in family fell	3	Earnings of others in family increased.	5
Other income fell	1	Transfer income increased	14
Other (including unidentified) ...	9	Other (including unidentified) ...	14
All	100	All	100

Sources: "Beginnings": Bane and Ellwood (1983), p. 18, using PSID data. "Endings": Ellwood (1985), p. 46, using PSID data.

WELFARE AND OTHER SOURCES OF SUPPORT FOR ADOLESCENT MOTHERS

Young mothers, like all young adults, are in the process of making a transition from childhood to adulthood and eventual self-sufficiency. In this process, the young mother relies on a changing mix of private resources and, in many cases, public assistance to support herself and her family.

One of the subgroups at greatest risk for long-term welfare receipt is comprised of young never-married women who enter the AFDC program when their child is less than 3 years old. For example, it is estimated that over 40 percent of never-married women who enter the AFDC system at age 25 or less with a child less than 3 years old will spend 10 years or more on AFDC.[6] This subsection provides data on the number of teenage mothers in the United States and the proportion receiving AFDC, and presents data on some of the dynamics of their welfare receipt.

Number of Teenage Mothers.—There are several different estimates of the number of teenage mothers in the United States. Probably the best estimates are based on data from the National Center for Health Statistics (NCHS). These are shown in table 10–51 for 1983.

---

[6] Ellwood, David T. "Targeting 'Would-Be' Long-Term Recipients of AFDC," prepared for the U.S. Dept. of Health and Human Services under contract No. 100–84–0059, June 1986. (Prepared by Mathematica Policy Research, Inc.)

TABLE 10–51.—NUMBER OF TEENAGE MOTHERS IN THE UNITED STATES BY CURRENT AGE AND AGE AT BIRTH OF FIRST CHILD, 1983

Current age	Total	Unmarried at time of first birth	Age at first birth	Total	Unmarried at time of first birth
Under 15	10,234	9,583	Under 15	58,860	54,320
15	33,798	30,215	15	117,811	100,792
16	82,425	68,889	16	195,333	151,725
17	162,949	127,065	17	227,039	160,670
18	256,161	183,695	18	195,041	124,142
19	361,801	633,231	19	113,284	61,029
Total	907,368	652,678		907,368	652,678

Source: Based on data from NCHS annual natality reports, 1978–83.

Preliminary NCHS data indicate that the number of teenage mothers equaled 907,368 in 1983, of which 652,678 were unmarried.

Private Sources of Income.—A young mother has three potential sources of private income: her parents or relatives, the father of her children, and her own earnings. The private resources that a young mother has access to depend heavily on her marital status and living arrangements. Although the marital status and living arrangements of young mothers tend to change over time, more than 90 percent of young mothers in the Current Population Survey (March 1986 and 1987) fell into one of three combinations: 42 percent were married and living with their husbands and children; 28 percent were single and living with their parents or other relatives; and 21 percent were single and living with their children in their own homes. Each of these groups rely on different sources of income for their economic well-being.

Those mothers living at home or with relatives likely benefit from the household income and may, in some cases, contribute to the family's income themselves. Young mothers living alone appear to be less able to support themselves and their children than older mothers who delayed childbearing.

Young mothers may also receive support from their husband or the absent father of their children. The amount of support available from husbands varies by the husbands' characteristics—such as age, employment status, and level of educational attainment. Studies suggest that roughly half of absent fathers maintain contact with their children and that many provide both financial aid and in-kind resources such as food, clothing, and child care, particularly during the first few years after their children are born. Some absent fathers also pay court-mandated child support payments, although mothers who were never married are much less likely to receive such aid—and get smaller payments when they do—than are their counterparts who were previously married. Furthermore, the low levels of support provided by some absent fathers may be related to their own inadequate resources. These fathers tend to have less education, to have higher unemployment rates, and to rely on parents or other relatives for their own support.

The Dynamics of Welfare Receipt Among Teenage Mothers.—Because adolescent mothers often have limited private resources, many of them receive public assistance, primarily AFDC, during their first few years of motherhood.

Data from AFDC quality control records indicate that in 1983 the average monthly number of teenage mothers receiving AFDC was 236,000. Of these teenage mothers on AFDC, 199,000 were unmarried. Data from AFDC records suggest that by 1986, the number of teenage mothers had fallen to roughly 213,000, of which 172,000 were unmarried. Of these teenage mothers on AFDC in 1986, 52.3 percent were 19, 31.1 percent were 18, 10.5 percent were 17, 4.4 percent were 16, and the remainder were 15 and younger.

An examination of data from the National Longitudinal Survey of Youth (NLSY) reveals patterns of young mother's entries into and exits from the AFDC program. Table 10–52 describes the probability that an adolescent mother will begin to receive AFDC within the first 48 months after the birth of her first child.[7] Of these adolescents who had their first child between 1979 and 1985,[8] about 27 percent reported receiving welfare at some point within the 12 months following the birth of that child. This proportion increased slightly to 30 percent in the fourth year (37 to 48 months after birth).

Adolescent mothers who were unmarried at the time of the birth of their first child were much more likely to receive welfare than were those teenage mothers who were married when they gave birth. Approximately 48 percent of the unmarried mothers received welfare for at least one month in the first year after the birth of their first child, compared with roughly 7 percent of those who were married when they gave birth.

Both groups of young mothers were slightly more likely to receive welfare 13 to 24 months after giving birth than in the first 12 months after birth. As might be expected, mothers who were unmarried when they gave birth continued to be much more likely to receive welfare—namely, 49 percent of the unmarried mothers reported at least one month of welfare receipt 13 to 24 months after giving birth compared with about 8 percent of the married adolescents.

Although the differences in the recipiency rates of the two marital status groups are likely to be due to a number of factors, it is useful to recognize that marriage directly affects the eligibility of the young mother. Married couples are likely to have higher incomes than are unmarried adolescent mothers and thus are less likely to need or to qualify for benefits. In addition, many States did not operate AFDC–UP programs during this period; therefore, married couples, where the principal earner was unemployed, could not receive AFDC benefits.

---

[7] In this table, adolescent mothers are defined as those who were between the ages of 15 and 19 when they had their first child. The mothers examined here had their first children between 1979 and 1985.

[8] Through the AFDC-Unemployed Parent (AFDC–UP) program, States had the option to provide benefits to married couples where the principal earner is unemployed. In 1983, for example, 29 States did not provide AFDC–UP benefits—meaning that a married couple would not be eligible for assistance unless one was incapacitated. The Family Support Act of 1988 now requires States to operate an AFDC–UP program.

Mothers who were 15 to 17 years old when they gave birth were slightly more likely to report being on welfare in the first 12 months after birth (29 percent) than were 18- to 19-year-old mothers (26 percent). This difference becomes larger during the subsequent 12 months (13 to 24 months after giving birth), when the proportion of younger adolescent mothers who report receiving welfare in at least one month increased to 32 percent, while that of older adolescent mothers stayed fairly steady at 25 percent.

TABLE 10–52.—ADOLESCENT MOTHERS RECEIVING AFDC

[In percent]

Characteristics of mother	Time between birth and receipt of AFDC (months)			
	0 to 12	13 to 24	25 to 36	37 to 48
All	27	28	29	30
Marital status at birth of first child:				
Married	7	8	12	14
Unmarried	48	49	50	49
Age at birth of first child all mothers:				
15 to 17	29	32	39	38
18 to 19	26	25	23	24
Mothers who were unmarried when they first gave birth:				
15 to 17	45	49	57	52
18 to 19	51	49	42	44
Race:				
All mothers:				
White	21	21	22	23
Black	42	46	50	47
Mothers who were unmarried when they first gave birth:				
White	52	49	45	47
Black	46	51	56	52

Source: Congressional Budget Office tabulations of data from the National Longitudinal Survey of Youth (1979–1985).

Notes.—Adolescent mothers are defined as all women who first gave birth when they were between the ages of 15 and 19.

These findings are based on relatively small samples and therefore should be taken as indicative of general patterns of behavior rather than as precise estimates, particularly for the period furthest from the birth.

The differences in the welfare recipiency patterns of adolescent mothers of different ages could be due to a number of factors. In particular, they are likely to be partially due to marital status differences between the two groups—the younger mothers in this sample were much less likely to be married than were older mothers. Other factors that might play a role include differences in living arrangements and in the likelihood of having a subsequent birth.

Section 11. Child Support Enforcement Program

BACKGROUND

The enactment of the Child Support Enforcement (CSE) program in 1975 represented a major new commitment on the part of the Congress to address the problem of nonsupport of children. Although prior to that time the Social Security Act had included provisions which were aimed at improving the collection of support on behalf of children, these provisions had not proved to be effective. The 1975 amendments were aimed at strengthening in a very significant way the efforts of the Federal and State Governments to improve the enforcement of child support obligations.

The 1975 legislation (Public Law 93–647) added a new part D to title IV of the Social Security Act. The statute, as amended, authorizes Federal matching funds to be used for enforcing the support obligations owed by noncustodial parents to their children and the custodial parent, locating absent parents, establishing paternity, and obtaining child and spousal support. Basic responsibility for administering the program is left to the States, but the Federal Government plays a major role in funding, monitoring and evaluating State programs, providing technical assistance, and in certain instances, in giving direct assistance to the States in locating absent parents and obtaining support payments from them. The program requires the provision of child support enforcement services for both welfare and nonwelfare families and requires States to publicize frequently, through public service announcements, the availability of child support enforcement services, together with information about the application fee and a telephone number or address to be used to obtain additional information.

PROGRAM TRENDS

Table 11–1 summarizes child support enforcement program trends since 1978. In 1993, $2.2 billion was spent to collect $9.0 billion. A sum of $3.98 was collected for every $1 of administrative expense. This was up by 38 percent from the low point of only $2.89 per dollar of administrative expense in 1982. Also, 553,000 paternities were established; 4,481,000 absent parents were located; 1,038,000 support obligations were established; collections were made for an average of 2,827,000 cases, 241,880 families were removed from AFDC because of child support collections; and 12.0 percent of AFDC payments were saved as a result of child support enforcement.

Table 11–2 compares various measures of the effectiveness of the child support enforcement program between administrative data and census data. The first four rows of table 11–2 are from the Office of Child Support Enforcement and illustrate huge increases in total constant dollar collections, the number of absent parents located, and paternities and awards that were established between 1978 and 1989.

The bottom portion of the table based on census data presents an entirely different picture of the effectiveness of the child support enforcement program. For example, rather than having total real collections increase by 165 percent, it shows that total real collections increased by only 26 percent between 1978 and 1989. Other measures of effectiveness from census data illustrate a similar picture.

One possible explanation for this different picture is that the official child support enforcement statistics are capturing collections that were being made anyway. Since income from census survey data tends to be underreported on household surveys, the truth may lie somewhere in between. To receive AFDC, mothers must assign their support rights to the AFDC agency. As a result, another problem with survey data is that AFDC mothers included in the CPS survey are asked only to report child support received and are not supposed to report any portion of their AFDC grant as child support, except for the $50 pass-through.

The terms in table 11–2 from the Census are defined as follows. The term "demographically eligible" includes all women who are living with children under 21 years of age whose natural fathers are not living in the household. This includes ever-divorced (including remarried) or currently separated women. The percent with awards are the women with court-ordered payments. The reason the percent "supposed to receive payment" is different from the percent with awards is that some mothers awarded payments were not due them for the year in question.

DEMOGRAPHIC TRENDS

A sizable and growing proportion of American households are families that consist only of a mother and her children. Between 1970 and 1992, the number of female-headed families with children under 18 increased 164 percent; the number of such two-parent families declined by 4 percent. As a result, by 1992 nearly one out of every four children under 18 in the United States lived in a family where the mother was never married or the father was not living with his child or children because of death, divorce, or separation. An unprecedented number of children live in single-parent homes, many without adequate or any support from the other parent.

TABLE 11-1.—PROGRAM OPERATIONS, SUMMARY OF NATIONAL (FEDERAL AND STATE) STATISTICS, FISCAL YEARS 1978–93

[Numbers in thousands, dollars in millions]

	1978	1980	1982	1984	1985	1986	1987	1988	1989	1990	1991	1992	1993
Total child support collections	$1,047	$1,478	$1,770	$2,378	$2,696	$3,246	$3,917	$4,605	$5,241	$6,010	$6,886	$7,965	$8,909
In 1993 dollars[1]	$2,282	$2,574	$2,585	$3,219	$3,523	$4,137	$4,854	$5,483	$5,955	$6,505	$7,095	$7,951	$7,951
Total AFDC collections[2]	$472	$603	$786	$1,000	$1,092	$1,225	$1,349	$1,486	$1,593	$1,750	$1,984	$2,259	$2,417
Federal	$311	$246	$311	$402	$341	$369	$413	$449	$458	$533	$626	$738	$777
State	$148	$274	$354	$448	$415	$424	$473	$525	$563	$620	$700	$789	$847
Total non-AFDC collections	$575	$874	$984	$1,378	$1,604	$2,019	$2,569	$3,119	$3,648	$4,260	$4,902	$5,706	$6,493
Total administrative expenditures	$312	$466	$612	$723	$814	$941	$1,066	$1,171	$1,363	$1,606	$1,804	$1,995	$2,241
Federal	$236	$349	$459	$507	$571	$633	$750	$804	$938	$1,061	$1,212	$1,343	$1,517
State	$76	$117	$153	$216	$243	$308	$316	$366	$426	$545	$593	$652	$724
Federal incentive payments to States and localities	$54	$72	$107	$134	$145	$158	$185	$222	$266	$264	$278	$299	$339
Average number of AFDC cases in which a collection was made	458	503	597	647	684	582	609	621	658	701	755	831	873
Average number of non-AFDC cases in which a collection was made	249	243	448	547	654	786	934	1,083	1,247	1,363	1,555	1,749	1,954
Number of parents located	454	643	779	875	878	1,046	1,145	1,388	1,628	2,062	2,577	3,706	4,481
Number of paternities established	111	144	173	219	232	245	269	307	339	393	472	516	553
Number of support obligations established	315	374	462	573	669	731	812	871	938	1,022	[4]821	894	1,038
Percent of AFDC assistance payments recovered through child support collections	(3)	5.2	6.8	7.0	7.3	8.6	9.1	9.8	10.0	10.3	10.7	11.4	12.0
Total child support collections per dollar of total administrative expenses	$3.35	$3.17	$2.89	$3.29	$3.31	$3.45	$3.68	$3.93	$3.84	$3.74	$3.82	$3.99	$3.98

[1] Adjusted for inflation using fiscal CPI. [2] AFDC collections are divided into State/Federal shares and incentives are taken from the Federal share thereby reducing the Federal amounts. [3] Not available. [4] Data beginning in 1991 exclude modifications of support orders.

Source: Office of Child Support Enforcement.

TABLE 11–2.—COMPARISON OF MEASURES OF IV–D EFFECTIVENESS WITH CENSUS
CHILD SUPPORT DATA, 1978–89

Measure	Year					Percent change, 1978–89
	1978	1983	1985	1987	1989	
From program statistics:						
Total collections (1989 dollars in billions)[1]	$2.0	$2.5	$3.1	$4.3	$5.3	165
Parents located (thousands)	454	831	878	1,145	1,624	258
Paternities established (thousands)	111	208	232	269	339	205
Awards established (thousands)	315	496	669	812	936	197
From Census surveys:						
Total collections (1989 dollars in billions)[1]	$8.9	$8.8	$8.3	$10.9	$11.2	26
IV–D collections as percent of total collections	23	28	37	39	47	104
Of demographically eligible, percent with awards	59	58	61	59	58	−2
Of demographically eligible, percent supposed to receive payment	48	46	50	51	50	4
Of demographically eligible, percent who received some payment	35	35	37	39	37	6
Of mothers supposed to receive payment, percent who received full amount	49	50	48	51	51	4
Percent of poor female-headed families with child support or alimony	[2]18.6	NA	NA	26.0	26.9	[3]45
Child support and alimony as a percent of total income received by poor female-headed families	[2]4.7	NA	NA	5.5	5.8	[3]23
Percent of female-headed families with child support or alimony	[2]33.9	NA	NA	35.8	37.4	[3]10
Child support and alimony as a percent of total income received by female-headed families	[2]7.4	NA	NA	6.8	7.7	[3]4

[1] Constant (1989) dollars using CPI.   [2] 1979 data.   [3] Percentage change 1979 to 1989.   NA—Not available.

Note.—Demographically eligible means women with own children under 21 years of age living with them from an absent father.

Sources: U.S. Bureau of the Census, Child Support and Alimony, Current Population Reports, Series P–23, 1978, No. 112; 1983, No. 141; 1985, No. 152; 1987, No. 67; and 1989, No. 173.

In 1992, nearly 46 percent of the 8.2 million families maintained solely by the mother with children under 18, had incomes below the poverty threshold. Almost 11 percent of the mothers of these poor children worked full-time, full-year.

In 1992, 17.6 million children (under 18) lived with only one parent, 114 percent more than in 1970. Even though the total number of children under 18 years old in the United States declined from 69.2 million in 1970 to 66 million in 1992, the number of children affected by divorce, separation, and unmarried status of mother continued to rise. Almost 27 percent of all children lived in a one-parent family in 1992, compared with 12 percent in 1970. A 1985 current population survey indicated that about 15 percent of children living in two-parent married-coupled families were living with a step-parent.

Of the 17.6 million children living with one parent, 88 percent lived with their mothers and 12 percent with their fathers. Between 1970 and 1992 the number of children living with only their fathers grew by 192 percent (from 748,000 to 2,182,000). The proportion of all children who lived with only their fathers rose from 1.1 percent to 3.3 percent.

The largest number of children in one-parent families had a parent who was divorced, followed by children whose parents were never married. In 1992, of the children who lived only with one parent, 37 percent had a parent who was divorced, 24 percent had a parent who was separated, and 34 percent had a parent who had never been married. The number of children living with a divorced parent has almost tripled since 1970, but the number with a never-married parent grew nearly elevenfold.

THE PROCESS OF CHILD SUPPORT ENFORCEMENT

Local family and domestic courts and administrative agencies handle the establishment and enforcement of child support obligations according to Federal, State, and local laws. Working with the parents and considering the best interests of the children, the courts decide which parent will have custody of the children, the amount of the child support obligation of the noncustodial parent, the rights of access to the children by the noncustodial parent, and how the support obligation will be enforced.

The federally mandated child support enforcement program provides services aimed at locating absent parents, establishing paternity, establishing a support obligation, and enforcing the support obligation. The child support enforcement program does not provide services aimed at other issues between parents, such as property settlement, custody, and access to the children. These issues are handled by local courts with the help of private attorneys.

Any parent who needs help in locating an absent parent, establishing paternity, establishing a support obligation, or enforcing a support obligation may apply for services. Parents receiving benefits under the Aid to Families with Dependent Children (AFDC) program, the federally assisted foster care program or the Medicaid program automatically receive services. Services are free to such recipients, but others are charged up to $25 for services. States can charge fees on a sliding scale, pay the fee out of State funds or recover the fees from the noncustodial parent.

When a parent applies for child support enforcement services, the following information aids the process: the name and address of the noncustodial parent; the absent parent's Social Security number; children's birth certificates; the child support order; the divorce decree or separation agreement; the name and address of the most recent employer of the noncustodial parent; the names of friends and relatives or organizations to which the noncustodial parent might belong; information about income and assets; and any other information about absent parents that might help the locating process. Once this information is provided, it is used in strictest confidence.

If the child support enforcement program cannot locate the noncustodial parent with the information provided by the custodial parent, it must try to locate the noncustodial parent through the State parent locator service. The State uses various information such as telephone directories, motor vehicle registries, tax files, and employment data. The State also can ask the Federal Parent Locator Service (FPLS) to locate the noncustodial parent. The FPLS can access data from the Social Security Administration, the Internal Revenue Service, the Selective Service System, the Department of Defense, the Veterans' Administration, and the National Personnel Records Center.

Under the Family Support Act of 1988 (P.L. 100–485), States are required to initiate the establishment of paternity for all children under the age of 18, including those for whom an action to establish paternity was previously dismissed because of the existence of a statute of limitations of less than 18 years. The act also sets paternity establishment standards for the States, and encourages them to create simple civil procedures for establishing paternity in contested cases. All parties to a contested case may be required to submit to genetic testing. The Federal Government pays 90 percent of the laboratory costs, and States may charge persons not receiving AFDC for the cost of establishing paternity.

Under the Family Support Act of 1988, a State must use its child support award guidelines in establishing the child support obligation of the noncustodial parent. Also, the State must review and adjust individual awards every 3 years under certain circumstances beginning October 13, 1993. Some States base their guidelines on net income and others on gross income. Some States factor in health care, day care, and extraordinary expenses while other States allow for deviation from the guideline if an extraordinary expense is shown. States generally use one of three basic types of guidelines to determine award amounts. "Income shares," which is based on the combined income of both parents is used in 32 States; "percentage-of-income," which is based on the number of eligible children, which is then used to determine a percentage of the noncustodial parents' income to be paid in child support is used in 17 States; and "Melson-Delaware," which provides a minimum self-support reserve for parents before the cost of rearing the children is prorated between the parents to determine the award amount is used in 3 States.

Local courts and child support enforcement agencies attempt to collect child support when the noncustodial parent does not pay. Under the Family Support Act of 1988, the State must impose wage withholding on the noncustodial parent in all newly issued or modified child support enforcement program cases. As of October 1, 1990, wage withholding will apply to all other newly issued child support orders beginning in 1994. Other techniques for enforcing support include regular billings, delinquency notices, liens on property, seizure and sale of property, reporting arrearages to credit agencies, garnishment of wages, and offsetting of State and Federal income taxes.

States might bring charges of criminal nonsupport against noncustodial parents if they cannot collect, or they might use civil or criminal contempt-of-court charges. These court proceedings usually involve much time because of court backlogs, delays, and continuances. Once a court decides the case, noncustodial parents often have been given probation or suspended sentences, and lower support payments and only partial payment of arrearages. To combat problems associated with court delays, the statute requires States to implement expedited processes under the State judicial system or State administrative processes for obtaining and enforcing support orders and at State option for establishing paternity.

The most difficult child support orders to enforce are the interstate cases. States are required to cooperate in interstate child support enforcement, but problems arise from the additional autonomy of the local courts. Family law has been under the jurisdiction of State and local governments, and citizens fall under the jurisdiction of the courts where they live.

If the noncustodial parent lives out of State, the primary tool for interstate enforcement is the Uniform Reciprocal Enforcement of Support Act (URESA). All States have their own URESA laws. Under these laws, the child support enforcement official or private attorney files a two-State petition with the enforcement agency or a court in another State. Where the URESA provisions in the two States are compatible, the law can be used effectively. However, many of these laws are out of date and incompatible, which makes interstate child support enforcement relatively ineffective.

The National Conference of Commissioners on Uniform State Laws originally drafted a model URESA in 1950. Since then, amendments have been made in 1952, 1958, and 1968. The Family Support Act of 1988 authorized a commission to study problems in interstate child support enforcement. One of the Commission's recommendations to Congress is to replace URESA with UIFSA, the Uniform Interstate Family Support Act, a model State law for handling child support cases drafted by the National Conference of Commissioners on Uniform State Laws.

Child support awards

In 1989, of the 10.0 million women who had children present under the age of 21 from a noncustodial father, 42 percent never were awarded child support rights (nor had an agreement to receive child support payments) and, thus, were dependent for income on sources other than the father. For poor mothers, the proportion without child support awards was even higher at 57 percent (see table 11–4).

TABLE 11-3.—CHILD SUPPORT PAYMENTS IN 1978, 1981, 1983, 1985, 1987, AND 1989

[Women as of spring 1979, 1982, 1984, 1986, 1988, and 1990. Child support payments for women with own children under 21 years of age present from an absent father; alimony payment for ever-divorced women]

	Number (thousands)						Percent distribution					
	1978	1981	1983	1985	1987	1989	1978	1981	1983	1985	1987	1989
Total	7,094	8,387	8,690	8,808	9,415	9,955	100.0	100.0	100.0	100.0	100.0	100.0
Awarded [1]	4,196	4,969	5,015	5,396	5,554	5,748	59.1	59.2	57.7	61.3	59.0	57.7
Supposed to receive payments	3,424	4,043	3,995	4,381	4,829	4,953	48.3	48.2	46.0	49.7	51.3	49.8
Not supposed to receive payments ..	772	926	1,020	1,015	725	795	10.9	11.0	11.7	11.5	7.7	8.0
Not awarded [1]	2,898	3,417	3,675	3,411	3,861	4,207	40.9	40.7	42.3	38.7	41.0	42.3
Supposed to receive payments	3,424	4,043	3,995	4,381	4,829	4,953	100.0	100.0	100.0	100.0	100.0	100.0
Actually received payments	2,455	2,902	3,037	3,243	3,676	3,725	71.6	71.8	76.0	74.0	76.1	75.2
Received full amount	1,675	1,888	2,018	2,112	2,475	2,546	48.9	46.7	50.5	48.2	51.3	51.4
Received partial amount	779	1,014	1,019	1,131	1,201	1,179	22.8	25.1	25.5	25.8	24.9	23.8
Did not receive payments	969	1,140	958	1,138	1,153	1,228	28.4	28.2	24.0	26.0	23.9	24.8

[1] Award status as of spring 1979, 1984, 1986, 1988, and 1990.

Source: U.S. Bureau of the Census. Current Population Reports, Series P-23, No. 112 Child Support and Alimony 1978, No. 141 Child Support and Alimony 1983 (advance report), No. 152 Child Support and Alimony 1985 (advance report), No. 167 Child Support and Alimony: 1987, and No. 173 Child Support and Alimony: 1989. Washington, U.S. Government Printing Office.

TABLE 11–4.—CHILD SUPPORT PAYMENTS FOR ALL WOMEN, WOMEN ABOVE THE POVERTY LEVEL, AND WOMEN BELOW THE POVERTY LEVEL, SELECTED YEARS 1978–89

[Child support payments for women with own children under 21 years of age present from an absent father as of spring 1979, 1982, 1984, 1986, 1988, and 1990]

	1978	1981	1983	1985	1987	1989
All women:						
Total (in thousands)	7,094	8,387	8,690	8,808	9,415	9,955
Percent awarded [1]	59.1	59.2	57.7	61.3	59.0	57.7
Percent actually received payment	34.6	34.6	34.9	36.8	39.0	37.4
Percent received full payment	23.6	22.5	23.2	24.0	26.3	25.6
Women above poverty level:						
Total (in thousands)	5,121	5,821	5,792	6,011	6,224	6,749
Percent awarded [1]	67.3	67.9	65.3	71.0	66.5	64.6
Percent actually received payment	41.1	41.4	42.6	44.1	44.8	43.1
Women below poverty level:						
Total (in thousands)	1,973	2,566	2,898	2,797	3,191	3,206
Percent awarded [1]	38.1	39.7	42.5	40.4	44.3	43.3
Percent actually received payment	17.8	19.3	19.6	21.3	27.7	25.4
Aggregate payment (in billions of dollars): [2]						
Child support due	12.6	13.7	12.5	12.6	15.9	16.3
Child support received	8.1	8.4	8.8	8.3	10.9	11.2
Aggregate child support deficit	4.5	5.3	3.7	4.3	5.0	5.1

[1] Award status as of spring 1979, 1982, 1984, 1986, 1988, and 1990.
[2] In 1989 dollars.

Source: U.S. Bureau of the Census. Current Population Reports, Series P–60, No. 173 Child Support and Alimony: 1989, Washington, U.S. Government Printing Office.

Approximately 5.7 million women with children under age 21 (58 percent) had been awarded child support or had an agreement to receive child support payments, but only 5.0 million (50 percent) of the women were actually "supposed to receive" child support in 1989. The rights of the remaining 8 percent were no longer in force because the father who owed payments had died, the children had grown past the age of eligibility for payments, or because of another reason.

Many of the women who were awarded child support payments did not receive the full amount they were due. In 1989, about half (51 percent) of the 5.0 million women owed child support payments received the full amount, about 24 percent of the women received less than they were owed, and 25 percent received no payment at all. Table 11–5 shows that average amount of child support for women who *received* payments in 1989 was $2,995, about 19 percent of their average total income. In 1978, the average amount of child support was $1,800, about 20 percent of the woman's income.

TABLE 11–5.—CHILD SUPPORT PAYMENTS AWARDED AND RECEIVED IN 1989—WOMEN WITH CHILDREN PRESENT, BY SELECTED CHARACTERISTICS

[Women with own children under 21 years of age present from an absent father as of spring 1990]

Characteristics of women	Total (thousands)	Percent awarded child support payments [1]	Supposed to receive child support in 1989			
			Total (thousands)	Actually received support in 1989		
				Percent	Mean child support	Mean income
ALL WOMEN						
Total	9,955	57.7	4,953	75.2	$2,995	$16,171
Current Marital Status						
Married [2]	2,531	79.0	1,685	72.1	2,931	14,469
Divorced	3,056	76.8	2,123	77.0	3,322	19,456
Separated	1,352	47.9	527	79.7	3,060	14,891
Widowed [3]	65	(B)	34	(B)	(B)	(B)
Never married	2,950	23.9	583	73.2	1,888	9,495
Race and Spanish Origin						
White	6,905	67.5	4,048	76.5	3,132	16,632
Black	2,770	34.5	791	69.7	2,263	13,898
Spanish origin [4]	1,112	40.6	364	69.8	2,965	14,758
Years of School Completed						
Less than 12 years	2,372	36.9	741	66.7	1,754	8,201
High school: 4 years	4,704	62.0	2,470	76.4	2,698	13,535
College:						
1 to 3 years	1,988	65.0	1,139	76.6	3,338	18,462
4 years or more	891	74.5	603	77.9	4,850	30,872
WOMEN BELOW POVERTY						
Total	3,206	43.3	1,190	68.3	1,889	5,047
Current Marital Status						
Married [2]	176	72.2	106	67.0	2,275	4,351
Divorced	820	70.4	525	66.3	2,112	5,581
Separated	612	47.1	221	74.2	1,717	4,917
Widowed	8	(B)	4	(B)	(B)	(B)
Never Married [3]	1,590	24.5	334	68.6	1,553	4,543
Race						
White	1,763	54.6	827	67.8	1,972	5,010
Black	1,314	29.2	325	69.8	1,674	5,174
Spanish origin [4]	536	33.0	148	63.5	1,824	4,958

[1] Award status as of spring 1989.
[2] Remarried women whose previous marriage ended in divorce.
[3] Widowed women whose previous marriage ended in divorce.
[4] Persons of Spanish origin may be of any race.

Note.—B base less than 75,000.

Source: U.S. Bureau of the Census. Series P–23, No. 173, Child Support and Alimony: 1989.

Of the 10 million women with children by a noncustodial father, 25 percent were remarried, 45 percent were divorced or separated, and 30 percent were never married. About 32 percent had incomes below the poverty level. Of these poor women, only 43 percent had agreements to receive child support and were due payments in 1989. Another 6 percent had agreements but were not due payments in 1989 (see table 11–5). Of the poor mothers who were supposed to receive child support payments in 1989, 68 percent (813,000) actually received payments, while 32 percent did not.

For women who actually received child support payments in 1989, the amount of payment tended to be higher than average for divorced women, white women, and women who had gone to college for at least a year. Those with lower than average payment amounts included never-married women, black women, and women who had not completed 12 years of school (see table 11–5).

Only 24 percent of women who had never married were awarded child support payments; compared with 77 percent of divorced women, 79 percent of remarried women and 48 percent of women who were separated. Moreover, among the 5.0 million women who were supposed to receive child support, the percentages of those who actually received payments were: 73 percent of never-married mothers, 72 percent of remarried mothers, 80 percent of separated mothers, and 77 percent of divorced mothers.

Of the 3.7 million women who actually received child support payments in 1989, 44 percent were divorced, 33 percent were remarried, 11 percent were separated, and 11 percent were single (never married). The women who had never married received, on the average, the lowest amount of child support payments. Among women who were poor despite having been awarded child support, the percentages differed. Of the 813,000 poor women who received child support payments in 1989, 43 percent were divorced, 9 percent were remarried, 20 percent were separated, and 28 percent were never married.

Black mothers and mothers of Spanish origin living apart from the father of their children were much less likely than their white counterparts to be awarded child support. Almost 68 percent of white mothers were awarded child support payments, compared with 35 percent of black mothers, and 41 percent of mothers of Spanish origin. Further, both black and Spanish-origin mothers received smaller payments, on the average, than did white mothers.

Mothers who were not high school graduates were less likely than the average to be awarded child support, and their support payments were on the average much smaller than those of mothers who had completed more than 12 years of school.

In addition, the age of the woman was related to the awarding of child support payments. Women aged 30 to 39 were the most likely to be awarded child support. Women 40 years of age and older were the most likely to actually receive payments and they received, on average, higher support payments. Women under age 30 were the least likely to be awarded payments, and those who were awarded support received smaller payments, on average, than older women.

Another factor related to child support was the number of children the mother had with her in the absence of their father. Women with two children were the most likely to receive support.

SERVICES FOR AFDC AND NON-AFDC CASES

Each State's child support plan must provide that the child support agency will undertake to secure support for an AFDC child whose rights to support have been assigned to the State. This includes nearly all AFDC children, since assignment of rights to support is a condition of eligibility for AFDC benefits. The State must also provide in its plan that it will undertake to establish the paternity of an AFDC child who is born out of wedlock. These requirements apply in all cases except where, in accordance with standards established by the Secretary, the State finds that to apply them would be against the best interests of the child. For families whose AFDC eligibility ends due to the receipt of (or an increase in) child support, States must continue to provide child support enforcement services, without imposing the application fee. This policy was established by Public Law 98–378, the Child Support Enforcement Amendments of 1984.

With respect to non-AFDC families, the law provides that the State must make available, once an application is filed with the State agency, the child support collection and paternity determination services which are provided under the plan for AFDC families. The State must charge non-AFDC families an application fee of up to $25. The amount of the maximum allowable fee may be adjusted periodically by the Secretary of the Department of Health and Human Services to reflect changes in administrative costs. States may charge the fee against the custodial parent, pay the fee out of State funds, or recover it from the noncustodial parent.

States also have the option of charging a late payment fee equal to between 3 and 6 percent of the amount of overdue support. Late payment fees may be charged to the noncustodial parents of AFDC and non-AFDC families and are to be collected only after the full amount of the support has been paid to the child. In addition, a State may at its option recover costs in excess of the application fee. Such recovery may be from either the custodial parent or the noncustodial parent. If a State chooses to make recovery from the custodial parent, it must have in effect a procedure whereby all persons in the State who have authority to order support are informed that such costs are to be collected from the custodial parent.

Finally, child support enforcement services must include the enforcement of spousal support, but only if a support obligation has been established with respect to the spouse; the child and spouse are living in the same household; and child support is being collected along with spousal support.

THE FEDERAL ROLE

The Federal statute provides that the child support program must be administered by a separate organizational unit under the control of a person designated by and reporting directly to the Secretary of Health and Human Services (HHS). Under the present organizational structure of the Department, this office is known as the Federal Office of Child Support Enforcement (OCSE). The Family Support Act of 1988 requires the appointment of an Assistant Secretary for Family Support within HHS to administer a number of programs, including the Child Support Enforcement program under title IV–D of the Act. Currently, this is the Assistant Secretary for the Administration for Children and Families.

A primary responsibility of the director is to establish such standards for State programs for locating absent parents, establishing paternity, and obtaining child support and support for the spouse (or former spouse) with whom the absent parent's child is living as he determines to be necessary to assure that the programs will be effective. In addition to this broad statutory mandate, the director is required to establish minimum organizational and staffing requirements for State child support agencies, and to review and approve State plans.

The statute also requires the director of the OCSE to provide technical assistance to the States to help them establish effective systems for collecting child and spousal support and establishing paternity. To fulfill this requirement, the OCSE operates a National Child Support Enforcement Reference Center as a central location for the collection and dissemination of information about State and local programs. OCSE also provides, under a contract with the American Bar Association Child Support Project, training and information dissemination on legal issues to persons working in the field of child support enforcement. Special initiatives, such as a recent effort to assist major urban areas in improving program performance, have also been undertaken by the OCSE.

The Child Support Enforcement Amendments of 1984 (Public Law 98–378) extend the research and demonstration authority in section 1115 of the Social Security Act to the child support enforcement program. This will make it possible for States to test innovative approaches to support enforcement so long as the modification does not disadvantage children in need of support nor result in an increase in Federal AFDC costs. Public Law 98–378 also authorizes special project grants to promote improvement in interstate enforcement. The authorization is $15 million for each fiscal year after 1986.

The director of the OCSE has full responsibility for program evaluation. Audits are required at least every 3 years to determine whether the standards and requirements prescribed by law and regulations have been met. Under the penalty provision, a State's AFDC matching funds must be reduced by an amount equal to at least 1 but no more than 2 percent for the first failure to comply substantially with the standards and requirements, at least 2 but no more than 3 percent for the second failure, and at least 3 but no more than 5 percent for the third and subsequent failures.

FEDERAL ENFORCEMENT TOOLS

The statute creates several Federal mechanisms to assist the States in performing their paternity and child support enforcement functions. These include use of the Internal Revenue Service, the Federal courts, and the Federal Parent Locator Service (FPLS).

The statute requires the Secretary of HHS, upon the request of a State, to certify to the Secretary of Treasury for collection by the IRS any amounts identified by the State as representing delinquent child support payments. The Secretary may certify only the amounts delinquent under a court or administrative order, and only upon a showing by the State that it has made diligent and reasonable efforts to collect amounts due using its own collection mechanisms. States must reimburse the Federal Government for any costs involved in making the collections. Collections may be made on behalf of both AFDC and non-AFDC families. Use by the States of this regular IRS collection mechanism (which may include seizure by the IRS of property, freezing of accounts, and other procedures) has been relatively infrequent. Using IRS collection methods, in fiscal year 1993, collections were made in only 329 cases nationwide, for a total collection of $155,677.

The availability of the IRS collection mechanism for child support was amplified in amendments enacted as part of the Omnibus Budget Reconciliation Act of 1981 (Public Law 97–35) to allow the collection of past due support from Federal tax refunds upon a simple showing by the State agency that an individual owes at least $150 in past-due support which has been assigned to the State as a condition of AFDC eligibility. Upon receiving this showing, the Secretary of Treasury is required to withhold from any tax refunds due that individual an amount equal to any past-due support. The withheld amount is sent to the State agency, together with notice of the taxpayer's current address.

Public Law 98–378 created a similar IRS offset program for non-AFDC families owed child support. States must submit to the IRS for withholding, the names of absent parents who have arrearages of at least $500 and who, on the basis of current payment patterns and the enforcement efforts that have been made, are unlikely to pay the arrearage before the IRS offset can occur. The law establishes specific notice requirements and mandates that the absent parent and any spouse be informed of the procedures which may be taken to protect the unobligated spouse's portion of the refund. The 1988 provision applied to refunds payable after December 31, 1985, and before January 1, 1991. Public Law 101–508 makes permanent the IRS offset program for non-AFDC families.

In fiscal year 1993, a total of 925,264 cases were offset, which resulted in child support collections of $609 million.

States also may have access to the Federal courts to enforce court orders for support. The director of the Office of Child Support Enforcement must approve a State's application for permission to use the courts of the United States to enforce court orders for support upon a finding that: (1) another State has not undertaken to enforce the court order of the originating State against an absent parent within a reasonable time; and (2) that use of the Federal courts is the only reasonable method of enforcing such order. This mechanism, designed to assist the States in enforcing interstate cases, has gone unused, apparently because the States view it as costly and complex.

Finally, the statute also requires the establishment of a Federal Parent Locator Service to be used to find absent parents in order to secure and enforce child support obligations. Upon request, the Secretary of HHS must provide to an authorized person the most recent address and place of employment of any absent parent if the information is contained in the records of the Department of Health and Human Services, or can be obtained from any other department or agency of the United States or of any State. The Secretary must also make available the services of the FPLS to any State that wishes to locate an absent parent or child for the purpose of enforcing any Federal or State law with respect to the unlawful taking or restraint of a child, or making or enforcing a child custody determination.

THE STATE ROLE

Each State is required to designate a single and separate organizational unit of State government to administer the program. Earlier child support legislation, enacted in 1967, had required that the program be administered by the welfare agency. The 1975 act deleted this requirement in order to give each State the opportunity to select the most effective administrative mechanism. Most States have placed the child support agency within the social or human services umbrella agency which also administers the AFDC program. However, two States have placed the agency in the department of revenue and two States have placed the agency in the office of the attorney general. The law allows the programs to be administered either on the State or local level. Ten programs are locally administered. A few programs are State administered in some counties and locally administered in others.

States must have plans, approved by the director of the OCSE, which set forth their functions and responsibilities. Both AFDC and non-AFDC families must be served. States must also enter into cooperative arrangements with appropriate courts and law enforcement officials to assist the child support agency in administering the program. These agreements may include provision for reimbursing courts and law enforcement officials for their assistance. States must operate a parent locator service to locate absent parents, and they must maintain full records of collections and disbursements, and otherwise maintain an adequate reporting system.

In order to facilitate the collection of support in interstate cases, a State must cooperate with other States in establishing paternity, locating absent parents, and in securing compliance with an order issued by another State.

The law requires the States to use several enforcement tools. They must use the IRS tax refund offset procedure for AFDC and non-AFDC families, and they must also determine periodically whether any individuals receiving unemployment compensation owe child support obligations. The State employment security agency is required to withhold unemployment benefits, and to pay the child support agency any outstanding child support obligations established by an agreement with the individual or through legal processes.

Public Law 98–378 mandated that States use a number of other enforcement techniques. These include: (1) imposing liens against real and personal property for amounts of overdue support; (2) withholding of State tax refunds payable to a parent who is delinquent in support payments; (3) making available information regarding the amount of overdue support owed to a consumer credit bureau upon a request; (4) requiring individuals who have demonstrated a pattern of delinquent payments to post a bond or give some other guarantee to secure payment of overdue support; (5) establishing expedited processes within the State judicial system or under administrative processes for obtaining and enforcing child support orders, and, at the option of the State, determining paternity; (6) notifying each AFDC recipient at least once each year of the amount of child support collected on behalf of that recipient; (7) permitting the establishment of paternity until a child's 18th birthday; and (8) at the option of the State, providing for cases not enforced by the State CSE agency, that child support payments must be made through the agency that administers the State's income withholding system if either the custodial or noncustodial parent requests that they be made in this manner.

State child support agencies are required to undertake child support collections on behalf of children receiving foster care maintenance payments under title IV–E of the Social Security Act, if an assignment of rights to support has been secured by the foster care agency. In addition, foster care agencies are required to take steps, where appropriate, to secure an assignment to the State of any rights to support on behalf of a child receiving foster care maintenance payments.

State agencies are also required, as a result of Public Law 98–378, to petition to include medical support as part of any child support order whenever health care coverage is available to the noncustodial parent at a reasonable cost. And, if a family loses AFDC eligibility as the result of increased collection of support payments, the State must continue to provide Medicaid benefits for 4 calendar months beginning with the month of ineligibility. States also must provide services to medically needy (Medicaid only) families referred to the State IV–D agency from the State Medicaid agency.

Finally, the statute requires each State to comply with any other requirements and standards that the Secretary determines to be necessary to the establishment of an effective child support program.

PATERNITY ESTABLISHMENT

Paternity establishment is a prerequisite for obtaining a child support order. In 1990, 28 percent of children born in the U.S. were born to unmarried women. According to the OCSE, paternity is established in less than one-third of these cases. Without paternity established, these children have no legal claim on their fathers' income. A major weakness of the CSE program is its poor performance in securing paternity for such children. In addition to financial benefits, establishing paternity can provide social, psychological, and emotional benefits and in some cases the father's medical history may be needed to give a child proper care.

In 1991, 35 percent of the 14.6 million children living solely with their mothers had a mother who had never married. Inasmuch as the percentage of children born to parents that are not married has been increasing during the last two decades, paternity establishment has become one of the more crucial elements of the CSE program.

In the 1980s legislation was enacted that contained provisions aimed at increasing the number of paternities established. P.L. 98–378, the Child Support Enforcement Amendments of 1984, required States to implement laws that permitted paternity to be established until a child's 18th birthday. P.L. 100–485, the Family Support Act of 1988 stipulated the following.

States are required to meet Federal standards for the establishment of paternity.

States are required to have all parties in a contested paternity case take a genetic test upon the request of any party, and are permitted to charge non-AFDC individuals for the costs of the paternity test.

States are encouraged to adopt simple civil processes for voluntarily acknowledging paternity and civil procedures for establishing paternity in contested cases.

States are reimbursed at a 90-percent Federal matching rate for laboratory testing to establish paternity.

Each State is required, in administering any law involving the issuance of birth certificates, to require each parent to furnish his or her SSN, unless the State finds good cause for not doing so.

Retroactive to 1984, any child for whom a paternity action was brought but whose suit was dismissed because of statute of limitations less than 18 years must be allowed to bring a new suit.

A 1992 OCSE report on paternity establishment says that paternity establishment has improved because of Federal requirements, improved genetic testing, and innovative State and local programs. Many States now have procedures through which a man may legally admit paternity (by signing a document that legally establishes paternity) without court involvement. Many States contend that voluntary acknowledgement of paternity procedures save money and require less time than paternity establishment procedures that involve the courts. While the number of paternities established through CSE reached a record high in 1991, huge disparities exist among States.

OBRA 93 required States to have in effect by October 1, 1993, the following paternity establishment procedures:

(1) for a simple civil process for voluntarily acknowledging paternity under which the State must explain the rights and responsibilities of acknowledging paternity and afford due process safeguards. Procedures must include a hospital-based program for the voluntary acknowledgment of paternity during the period immediately preceding or following the birth of a child;

(2) under which the voluntary acknowledgment of paternity creates a rebuttable, or at the option of the State, conclusive presumption of paternity, and under which such voluntary acknowledgments are admissible as evidence of paternity;

(3) under which the voluntary acknowledgment of paternity must be recognized as a basis for seeking a support order without first requiring any further proceedings to establish paternity;

(4) which provide that any objection to genetic testing results must be made in writing within a specified number of days prior to any hearing at which such results may be introduced in evidence, and if no objection is made the test results are ad-

missible as evidence of paternity without the need for foundation testimony or other proof of authenticity or accuracy;

(5) which create a rebuttable or, at the option of the State, conclusive presumption of paternity upon genetic testing results indicating a threshold probability of the alleged father being the father of the child;

(6) which require default orders in paternity cases upon a showing that process has been served on the defendant and whatever additional showing may be required by State law; and

(7) which require States to have expedited processes for paternity establishment in contested cases and to require that a State give full faith and credit to determinations of paternity made by other States.

A 1993 Urban Institute report[1] analyzes national survey data that was obtained to provide a better understanding of how paternity establishment is handled by CSE agencies in counties throughout the U.S. The study found:

At the local level paternity establishment is usually located in one of three settings: a legal agency like a prosecuting attorney's office or court, a non-legal agency like the human services department responsible for welfare, or a shared situation in which cases with cooperative fathers are handled by the human service agency and contested cases are transferred to a legal agency [35 percent of the counties transferred contested cases from the non-legal agency to the legal agency].

Counties generally use one of four approaches to establish paternity:

A no-consent process wherein all paternity cases are handled through the court and there are no opportunities to consent voluntarily outside a court hearing; a one-time consent process: alleged fathers are given one opportunity to consent voluntarily, usually right after notification of the allegation; a multi-consent process: alleged fathers are given at least two opportunities to consent, usually after notification and also after genetic testing; and a court-as-last-resort process: alleged fathers have to respond to a notification by filing with the court their intention to consent to or contest the allegation. The court's role after the initial notification is generally limited to handing contested cases after genetic tests. Multiple opportunities for consent are available. [The most common approach, used by 37 percent of the counties, was the multi-consent approach].

The report found that counties with the highest rate of paternity determinations offer multiple opportunities for voluntary consent and have adopted an organizational approach in which cooperative fathers are handled by the welfare agency and contested cases are transferred to a legal agency. The 27 counties that used these combined approaches show an average paternity rate of 65 percent

[1] Washington, D.C. The Urban Institute. "Promising Approaches to Improving Paternity Establishment Rates at the Local Level," Sonenstein, Freya L., Pamela A. Holcomb and Kristen S. Seefeldt. Feb. 1993.

when other factors are held constant. Given that it is unrealistic that other factors can be held constant (compared to rates between 22 and 45 percent in counties where other approaches were used). The report cautions readers that the findings from the analysis are merely suggestive of possible avenues to follow in seeking improvements in paternity establishment.

ENFORCEMENT OF MEDICAL SUPPORT

Health care for children can be a major expense for the custodial parent, and can be a burden for the State if public assistance is being provided to the children. Public Law 95–142, the Medicare-Medicaid Anti-Fraud and Abuse Amendments of 1977 (Section 1912 of the Social Security Act), permits State Medicaid agencies to use the CSE agency to assist in the enforcement of medical support rights due from or through a noncustodial parent, since it was not intended that the Medicaid agency establish a separate system for the enforcement of medical support obligations. On February 11, 1980, the OCSE and the Health Care Financing Administration (HCFA) published joint regulations to implement section 1912 of the act through optional cooperative agreements between the State Medicaid agency and the State CSE agency. Under these agreements the Medicaid agency reimburses the CSE agency for medical support enforcement activities performed pursuant to the agreement. In 35 jurisdictions the Federal Medicaid reimbursement rate is lower than the 66 percent matching rate for CSE activities (based on fiscal year 1993 rates), and nationwide it averages about 56 percent.

Section 16 of Public Law 98–378 requires the Secretary of the Department of Health and Human Services (DHHS) to issue regulations to require that State CSE agencies petition for the inclusion of medical support as part of any child support order whenever health care coverage is available to the noncustodial parent at reasonable cost. According to the Federal regulations, any employment-related or other group coverage is considered reasonable, under the assumption that health insurance is inexpensive to the employee/noncustodial parent. A 1983 study by the National Center for Health Services Research of the Public Health Service indicated that, for low-wage employees with employer-provided insurance coverage, 72 percent of the premium was paid for by the employer.

On October 16, 1985, the OCSE published regulations amending previous regulations and implementing section 16 of Public Law 98–378. The regulations stated that the CSE agency must obtain basic medical support information and provide this information to the State Medicaid agency. Also, if the custodial parent does not have satisfactory health insurance coverage, the CSE agency must petition the court or administrative authority to include medical support in new or modified support orders and inform the State Medicaid agency of any new or modified support orders that include a medical support obligation. The 1985 regulations also required the CSE agency to take steps to enforce medical support that has been ordered by a court or administrative process under State law. In addition, these regulations permit the use of CSE matching funds at the 66 percent rate for required medical support activities. Before these regulations were issued, medical support activities were pursued by CSE agencies only under optional cooperative agreements with Medicaid agencies. Some of the functions that the CSE agency may perform under a cooperative agreement with the Medicaid agency include: receiving referrals from the Medicaid agency, locating absent parents, establishing paternity, determining whether the noncustodial parent has a health insurance policy or plan that covers the child, obtaining sufficient information about the health insurance policy or plan to permit the filing of a claim with the insurer, filing a claim with the insurer or transmitting the necessary information to the Medicaid agency, securing health insurance coverage through court or administrative order (when it will not reduce the noncustodial parent's ability to pay child support), and recovering amounts necessary to reimburse medical assistance payments.

A report by the Urban Institute stated that although the practice of including medical coverage provisions in child support orders had increased, the priority and emphasis given such provision was still quite low (as of September 1985). It reported that child support staff were reluctant to go to court just for medical support, and that many judges would not order medical support if it might cause a reduction in cash support payments. The report also said that enforcing medical coverage provisions once they are established is very difficult, and that it requires the agency to monitor continuation of coverage and to act to restore coverage when it lapses.[2]

The Urban Institute study reported that in 1983, 4.6 million children with an absent parent were without public (Medicaid) or private health insurance. This represented 34 percent of all children with an absent parent. Another 4.9 million children with an absent parent were covered solely by Medicaid. The study estimated that including medical coverage in child support orders in 1984 might have benefited 1,353,000 totally uninsured children (those without Medicaid or private insurance) and perhaps another 300,000 to 466,000 children covered only by Medicaid at that time.[3]

According to the Census Bureau data on child support and alimony, 40 percent of the 5.7 million women who had a child support award in 1989 received health insurance coverage in their awards. For white women, the figure was 43 percent; for black women, 28 percent; and for women of Hispanic origin, 21 percent. For divorced women, the figure was 44 percent and for women who had never married, the figure was 26 percent.

On September 16, 1988, the OCSE issued regulations amending the medical support enforcement provisions. These regulations require the CSE agency to develop criteria to identify existing child support cases that have a high potential for obtaining medical support, and to petition the court or administrative authority to modify support orders to include medical support for targeted cases even if no other modification is anticipated. In addition, the CSE agency

---

[2] Nightingale, Demetra Smith, and others. "The Inclusion of Medical Coverage in Child Support Cases: Current Status and Options for the Future." Draft. Washington, Urban Institute, May 1986. p. vi. [Hereafter cited as Urban Institute, "The Inclusion of Medical Coverage in Child Support Cases."]

[3] Ibid., p. 24–25.

is required to provide the custodial parent with information regarding the health insurance coverage obtained by the noncustodial parent for the dependent child or children. Moreover, the 1988 regulation deletes the condition that CSE agencies may secure health insurance coverage under a cooperative agreement only when it will not reduce the noncustodial parent's ability to pay child support. The purpose of the medical support provisions is to expand the number of children for whom private health insurance coverage is obtained by increasing the availability of third-party resources to pay for medical care and thereby result in Medicaid cost savings to the States and the Federal Government. The Urban Institute report, however, concluded that while there is no doubt that many children could benefit from inclusion of medical insurance, especially those who currently have no public or private health care coverage, Medicaid savings would be relatively modest compared to total annual Medicaid costs.[4]

According to OCSE data, 53 percent of support orders established in fiscal year 1993 included health insurance, whereas only 30 percent of support orders that were enforced or modified in fiscal year 1993 included health insurance.

OBRA 93 included the following health insurance support provisions:

(1) prohibit an insurer from denying enrollment of a child under the health insurance coverage of the child's parent on the grounds that the child was born out of wedlock, is not claimed as a dependent on the parent's Federal income tax return, or does not reside with the parent or in the insurer's service area;

(2) require an insurer and an employer doing business in the State, in any case in which a parent is required by court or administrative order to provide health coverage for a child and the child is otherwise eligible for family health coverage through the insurer, (a) to permit the parent, without regard to any enrollment season restrictions, to enroll such child under such family coverage; (b) if the parent fails to provide health insurance coverage for a child, to enroll the child upon application by the child's other parent or the State child support or Medicaid agency; and (c) with respect to employers, not to disenroll (or eliminate coverage of) the child unless there is satisfactory written evidence that the order is no longer in effect, or the child is or will be enrolled in comparable health coverage through another insurer that will take effect not later than the effective date of the disenrollment;

(3) require an employer doing business in the State, in the case of health insurance coverage offered through employment and providing coverage for a child pursuant to a court or administrative order, to withhold from the employee's compensation the employee's share of premiums for health insurance, and to pay that share to the insurer. The Secretary of Health and Human Services may provide by regulation for such exceptions to this requirement (and other requirements described above that apply to employers) as the Secretary determines necessary to ensure compliance with an order, or with the limits on withholding that are specified in section 303(b) of the Consumer Credit Protection Act;

---

[4] Urban Institute, "The Inclusion of Medical Coverage in Child Support Cases," p. vi.

(4) prohibit an insurer from imposing requirements upon a State agency, which is acting as an agent or assignee of an individual eligible for medical assistance and covered by the insurer, that are different from requirements applicable to an agent or assignee of any other individual;

(5) require an insurer, in the case of a child who has coverage through the insurer of a noncustodial parent, (a) to provide the custodial parent with the information necessary for the child to obtain benefits; (b) to permit the custodial parent (or provider, with the custodial parent's approval) to submit claims for covered services without the approval of the noncustodial parent; and (c) to make payment on claims directly to the custodial parent, the provider, or the State agency; and

(6) permit the State Medicaid agency to garnish the wages, salary, or other employment income of, and to withhold State tax refunds to, any person who: (a) is required by court or administrative order to provide health insurance coverage to an individual eligible for Medicaid; (b) has received payment from a third party for the costs of medical services to that individual; and (c) has not reimbursed either the individual or the provider. The amount subject to garnishment or withholding would be the amount required to reimburse the State agency for expenditures for costs of medical services provided under the Medicaid program. However, claims for current or past-due child support shall take priority over any claims for the costs of medical services.

These provisions are effective April 1, 1994, or, if the Secretary determines that State legislation is needed, the State plan shall not be regarded as failing to comply with the requirements of title IV–D because it has not met these additional requirements before the first day of the first calendar quarter beginning after the close of the first regular session of the State legislature that begins after August 10, 1993. In the case of a State that has a two-year legislative session, each year of such session shall be deemed to be a separate regular session of the State legislature.

TABLE 11–6.—CHILD SUPPORT AWARD STATUS AND INCLUSION OF HEALTH INSURANCE IN AWARD, BY SELECTED CHARACTERISTICS OF WOMEN

[Women 15 years and older with own children under 21 years of age present from absent fathers as of spring 1990]

Characteristic	Total (thousands)	Awarded child support payments		
		Total (thousands)	Health insurance included in child support award	
			Number (thousands)	Percent of total awarded
Total	9,955	5,748	2,307	40.1
Current Marital Status [1]				
Remarried [2]	2,531	1,999	755	37.8
Divorced	3,056	2,347	1,038	44.2
Separated	1,352	648	298	46.0
Never married	2,950	704	186	26.4
Race and Hispanic Origin				
White	6,905	4,661	1,992	42.7
Black	2,770	955	271	28.4
Hispanic [3]	1,112	452	96	21.2
Age				
15 to 17 years	128	23	....	....
18 to 29 years	3,086	1,408	572	40.6
30 to 39 years	4,175	2,685	1,097	40.9
40 years and over	2,566	1,632	638	39.1
Years of School Completed				
Less than 12 years	2,372	875	233	26.6
High school: 4 years	4,704	2,916	1,218	41.8
College:				
1 to 3 years	1,988	1,293	575	44.5
4 years or more	891	664	281	42.3
Number of Own Children Present from an Absent Father				
One child	5,721	3,274	1,316	40.2
Two children	2,873	1,812	739	40.8
Three children	1,030	537	220	41.0
Four children or more	331	125	33	26.4

[1] Excludes a small number of current widowed women whose previous marriage ended in divorce.
[2] Remarried women whose previous marriage ended in divorce.
[3] Persons of Hispanic origin may be of any race.

Source: U.S. Bureau of the Census. Current Population Reports. Child Support and Alimony: 1989 (Supplemental Report). Series P–60, No. 173, September 1991. Washington, U.S. Government Printing Office, 1991. p. 11.

WAGE WITHHOLDING

The Family Support Act required immediate income withholding to begin in November 1990 for all new or modified orders being enforced by the State's CSE agency. As of January 1, 1994, States were required to provide for immediate wage withholding for all support orders initially issued on or after that date, regardless of whether a parent has applied for CSE services. Immediate income withholding has been enacted by about half of the States.

Public Law 98–378 required that States have in effect two distinct procedures for withholding wages of noncustodial parents. First, for cases enforced through the CSE agency, States were required to use a procedure that imposed wage withholding in child support cases whenever an arrearage accrued that was equal to the amount of support payable for 1 month. Second, for all child support cases, all new or modified support orders issued in the State were required to include a provision for wage withholding when an arrearage occurs. The intent of the second procedure was to ensure that orders not enforced through the CSE agency contain the authority necessary to permit wage withholding to be initiated by someone other than the CSE agency. The Family Support Act of 1988 (P.L. 100–485) extended the use of mandatory wage withholding to nondelinquent support. In fiscal year 1993, 53 percent of total collections or about $4.7 billion were made through wage withholding.

According to the Federal statute, State due-process requirements govern the scope of notice to provide to an obligor (i.e., noncustodial parent) when withholding is triggered. As a general rule, the noncustodial parent is entitled to advance notice of the withholding procedure. This notice, where required, must inform the noncustodial parent of the following: the amount that will be withheld; the application of withholding to any current or subsequent period of employment; the procedures available for contesting the withholding and the sole basis for objection (i.e., mistake of fact); the period allotted the noncustodial parent to contact the State to contest the withholding and the result of failure to contact the State within this timeframe (i.e., issuance of notification to the employer to begin withholding); the steps the State will take if the noncustodial parent contests the withholding including the procedure to resolve such contests.

If the noncustodial parent contests the income withholding notice, the State must conduct a hearing, determine if the withholding is valid, notify the noncustodial parent of the decision, and notify the employer to commence the deductions if withholding is upheld. All of this must occur within 45 days of the initial notice of withholding. Whether a State uses a judicial or an administrative process, the only basis for a hearing is a factual mistake about the amount owed (current and/or arrearage) or the identity of the noncustodial parent.

When withholding is uncontested or when a contested case is resolved in favor of the withholding, the administering agency must serve a withholding notice on the employer. The employer is required to withhold as much of the noncustodial parent's wages as is necessary to comply with the order. This will include the current support amount plus an amount to be applied toward liquidation of any arrearage. In addition, the employer may retain a fee to offset the administrative cost of implementing withholding.

The Federal Consumer Credit Protection Act (FCCPA) determines the maximum portion of an individual's total disposable earnings that is subject to garnishment. The FCCPA limits apply when enforcing an order for support. These limits are 50 percent of disposable earnings for a noncustodial parent who is the head of a household, and 60 percent for a noncustodial parent who is not supporting a second family. These percentages increase by 5 percentage points, to 55 and 65 percent, respectively, when the arrearages represent support that was due more than 12 weeks before the current pay period.

Upon receiving the notice, the employer must begin withholding the appropriate amount of the obligor's wages no later than the first pay period that occurs after 14 days following the date the notice was mailed. The 1984 amendments regulate the language in State statutes on the other rights and liabilities of the employer. For instance, the employer is subject to a fine for discharging a noncustodial parent or taking other forms of retaliation as a result of a withholding order. In addition, the employer is held liable for amounts not withheld as directed.

In addition to being able to charge the noncustodial parent a fee for the administrative costs associated with wage withholding, the employer can combine all support payments required to be withheld for multiple obligors into a single payment and forward it to the CSE agency or court with a list of the cases to which the payments apply. The employer need not vary from his normal pay and disbursement cycle to comply with withholding orders; however, support payments must be forwarded to the State or other designated agency within 10 days of the date on which the noncustodial parent is paid.

When the noncustodial parent changes jobs, the previous employer must notify the court or agency that entered the withholding order and provide specified information. The State must notify the new employer or income source to begin withholding from the obligor's wages.

In addition, States must develop procedures to terminate income withholding orders, for example, when all of the children are emancipated and no arrearage exists.

PROPERTY LIENS

The use of liens for child support enforcement was characterized during congressional debate on Public Law 98–378 as "simple to execute and cost effective and a catalyst for an absent parent to pay past due support in order to clear title to the property in question." (H. Rept. 527, 98th Cong., 1st sess., 1983) The report said that liens would complement the income withholding provisions of the 1984 law and be particularly helpful in enforcing support payments owed by noncustodial parents with substantial assets or income but who are not salaried employees.

Public Law 98–378 required States to enact laws and implement "procedures under which liens are imposed against real property for amount of overdue support owed by an absent parent who resides or owns property in the State." This can apply to such things as land, vehicles, houses, antique furniture, livestock, etc. The law provides, however, that States need not use liens in cases where, on the basis of guidelines that generally are available to the public, it determines that lien procedures would be inappropriate. This provision implicitly requires States to develop guidelines about use of liens.

Generally, a lien for delinquent child support is a statutorily created mechanism by which an obligee (i.e., custodial parent) obtains a nonpossessory interest in property belonging to the noncustodial parent. The interest of the custodial parent is a slumbering interest that allows the noncustodial parent to retain possession of the property, but affects the noncustodial parent's ability to transfer ownership of the property to anyone else. A child support lien converts the custodial parent from an unsecured to a secured creditor. As such, it gives the custodial parent priority over unsecured creditors and subsequent secured creditors. In some States a lien is established automatically upon entry of a support order and the first incidence of noncompliance by the obligor. Frequently, the mere imposition of a lien will motivate the delinquent parent to do whatever is necessary to remove the lien (i.e., pay past due support). When this is not the case, it may become necessary to enforce the lien. Liens are not self-executory. They merely impede the debtor's ability to transfer property. If a lien exists, a debtor must satisfy the judgment before the property may be sold or transferred. However, it is not necessary for the obligee to wait until the obligor tries to transfer the property before taking action. The obligee may enforce his judgment by execution and levy against the property if he believes that the amount of equity in the property justifies execution.

Several States have increased their use of liens by identifying individuals who possess appropriate assets through use of information obtained from Project 1099. Project 1099 is a cooperative effort involving State CSE agencies, the OCSE, and the IRS. It is named after the IRS form on which both earned and unearned income is reported. (Examples of reported earned and unearned incomes include: interest paid on savings accounts, stocks and bonds, and distribution of dividends and capital gains; rent or royalty payments; prizes, awards, or winnings; fees paid directors or subcontractors; and unemployment compensation.) Project 1099 was initiated in 1984 to assist in location efforts. Since fall 1988, Project 1099 routinely provides wage and employer information as well as location and asset information on noncustodial parents.

CREDIT BUREAU REPORTING

Public Law 98–378 requires that States establish procedures for reporting overdue child support obligations exceeding $1,000 to consumer reporting agencies (generally referred to as credit bureaus), if such information is requested by the credit bureau. States have the option of using such procedures in cases where the noncustodial parent is less than $1,000 in arrears. (Moreover, as in the case of liens, this collection procedure need not be used in cases found inappropriate under State guidelines.) The 1984 law requires States to provide the noncustodial parent an advance notice of its intent to release information regarding his child support arrearage and an opportunity for him to contest the accuracy of the information. The CSE agency may charge the credit bureau a fee for the information.

Although some States and counties had agreements in place with credit bureaus to obtain information about the location of absent parents, the 1984 provision authorizes the routine transfer of information concerning overdue child support to credit bureaus on a much broader basis. Moreover, it is in the interest of credit bureaus to request such information because overdue child support adversely affects an obligated parent's ability to pay other debts.

Public Law 102–537, the Ted Weiss Child Support Enforcement Act of 1992, amends the Fair Credit Reporting Act to require consumer credit reporting agencies to include in any consumer report information on child support delinquencies provided by or verified by State or local CSE agencies, which antedates the report by 7 years.

FEDERAL GARNISHMENT

The 1975 CSE legislation included a provision allowing garnishment of wages and other payments by the Federal Government for enforcement of child support and alimony obligations. The 1975 law provides that moneys (the entitlement to which is based upon remuneration for employment) payable by the United States to any individual are subject to legal proceedings brought for the enforcement against such individual of his legal obligation to provide child support or make alimony payments. The law sets forth in detail the procedures that must be followed for service of legal process and specifies that the term "based upon remuneration for employment" includes wages, periodic benefits for the payment of pensions, retirement or retired pay (included social security and other retirement benefits), and other kinds of Federal payments. The following Federal income sources may not be garnished: any payment as compensation for death under any Federal program, Federal black lung benefits, veterans' pensions or compensation benefits for a service-related disability or death, and amounts paid to defray employment-related expenses.

MILITARY ALLOTMENTS

Public Law 97–248, the Tax Equity and Fiscal Responsibility Act of 1982, requires allotments from the pay and allowances of any member of the uniformed service (on active duty) when he fails to make child (or child and spousal) support payments. The requirement arises when the service member fails to make support payments in an amount at least equal to the value of 2 months' worth of support. Provisions of the Federal Consumer Credit Protection Act apply, limiting the percentage of the member's pay that is subject to allotment. The amount of the allotment is the amount of the support payment, as established under a legally enforceable administrative or judicial order.

INTERSTATE ENFORCEMENT

State laws require parents to be responsible for the financial support of their children. During the 1930's and 1940's, such laws were used to establish and enforce support obligations when the noncustodial parent, custodial parent, and child lived in the same State. But when noncustodial parents lived out of State, enforcing child support was cumbersome and ineffective. Often the only option in these cases was to seek to extradite the noncustodial parent and, when successful, to jail the person for nonsupport. Extradition is the process used to bring an obligor charged with or convicted of a crime (in this case, criminal nonsupport) from an asylum State back to the State where the children are located. This procedure, rarely used, generally punished the irresponsible parent, but left the abandoned family without financial support.

A University of Michigan study of separated parents nationwide found that 12 percent lived in different States 1 year after divorce or separation. That proportion increased to 25 percent 3 years after, and to 40 percent 8 years after. Estimates based on the Federal income tax refund offset program and other sources suggest that approximately 30 percent of child support cases involve interstate residency of the custodial and noncustodial parents.[5]

Uniform Reciprocal Enforcement of Support Act (URESA)

Since 1950, interstate cooperation has been promoted through the adoption by the States of URESA. This act, which was first proposed by the National Conference of Commissioners on Uniform State Laws in 1950, has been enacted, in substance, in all 50 States, the District of Columbia, Guam, Puerto Rico, and the Virgin Islands. The act was amended in 1952 and 1958 and revised in 1968.

It is generally maintained that the increasing number of children who received AFDC benefits because of the absence of their father, together with the more frequent instances in which the father lived in another State, led many States to quickly adopt URESA. In 1940, 30.3 percent of AFDC children had an able-bodied father who was living away from the home. By 1950, the figure had reached 49.3 percent. About 32 States had enacted the original version of URESA within 5 years of its promulgation by the National Conference.

The purpose of URESA was to provide a system for the interstate enforcement of support orders without requiring the person seeking support to go (or have her legal representative go) to the State in which the noncustodial parent resided. Where the URESA provisions between the two States are compatible, the law can be used to establish paternity, locate an absent parent, and establish, modify, or enforce a support order. However, some observers note that the use of URESA procedures often result in lower orders for both current support and arrearages. They also contend that few CSE agencies attempt to use URESA procedures to establish paternity or to obtain a modification in a support order.

Long-arm statutes

Unlike URESA, interstate cases established or enforced by long-arm statutes use the court system in the State of the custodial parent rather than that of the noncustodial parent. When a person commits certain acts within a State, that person may be subjecting himself to the jurisdiction of that State, even if he does not live in that State. The long-arm of the law of the State where the event happens may reach out to grab the out-of-State person so that is-

[5] Weaver, Ray L., and Robert G. Williams. "Problems With URESA: Interstate Child Support Enforcement Isn't Working But Could." Paper prepared for ABA Third National Child Support Conference, May 10–12, 1989. Washington, American Bar Association 1989, p. 510 [Hereafter cited as Weaver and Williams, "Problems With URESA"]

sues relating to the event may be resolved where it happened. Under the long-arm procedure, the State must authorize by statute that the acts allegedly committed by the defendant are those that subject the defendant to the State's jurisdiction. An example is a paternity statute stating that if conception takes place in the State and the child lives in the State, the State may exercise personal jurisdiction over the alleged father. Long-arm statute language usually speaks of extending the State's jurisdiction over an out-of-State defendant to the maximum extent permitted by the U.S. Constitution under the Fourteenth Amendment's Due Process Clause. Long-arm statutes may be used to establish paternity, establish support awards, and enforce support orders.

Federal courts

The 1975 CSE law mandated that the State plan for CSE require States to cooperate with other States in establishing paternity, locating absent parents, and securing compliance with court orders and authorized the use of Federal courts as a last resort to enforce an existing order in another State if that State were uncooperative.

Federal law allows the U.S. district courts to be used for the enforcement of child support orders in interstate cases. If another State fails to undertake to enforce a child support order on behalf of the requesting State within a reasonable time, the requesting State may ask the OCSE to certify the case for use of the Federal courts. If the application meets certain procedural requirements and it is determined that use of the Federal courts is the only reasonable method of enforcing an order, the case is to be certified for action by the U.S. district court. (OCSE officials say that Federal courts also can establish support orders.)

Section 460 of the Social Security Act says that the district courts of the United States shall have jurisdiction, without regard to any amount in controversy, to hear and determine any civil action certified by the Secretary of DHHS under section 452(a)(8) of the act. A civil action under section 460 may be brought in any judicial district in which the claim arose, the plaintiff resides, or the defendant resides. Section 452(a)(8) says that the Secretary of DHHS shall receive applications from States for permission to use the courts of the United States to enforce court orders for support against noncustodial parents and, upon a finding that (A) another State has not undertaken to enforce a court order of the originating State against the noncustodial parent within a reasonable time, and (B) that using the Federal courts is the only reasonable method of enforcing such order, approve such applications.

As a condition to obtaining the certification from the Federal OCSE, the CSE agency of the initiating State must give the CSE agency of the responding State at least 60 days after first seeking assistance in enforcing the order, a 30-day warning of its intent to seek enforcement in Federal court. If the initiating State receives no response within the 30-day limit, or if the response is unsatisfactory, the initiating State may apply to the OCSE Regional Office for certification. The application must attest that the above requirements have been satisfied. Upon certification of the case, a civil action may be filed in the U.S. District Court. Although this interstate enforcement procedure has been available since enactment of the CSE program, there has only been one reported case of its use by a State (the initiating State was California, and the responding State was Texas).

Interstate income withholding

Interstate income withholding is a process in which the State of the custodial parent seeks the help of the State in which the noncustodial parent's income is derived to enforce a support order using the income withholding mechanism. Pursuant to Public Law 98–378, income withholding availability has been universal for all valid in-State or out-of-State orders issued or modified after October 1, 1985, and for all orders in CSE cases regardless of the date the order was issued. Although Federal law requires a State to enforce another State's valid orders through interstate income withholding, there is no Federal mandate that interstate income withholding procedures be uniform. Approaches vary from the Model Interstate Income Withholding Act to URESA registration. The preferred way to handle an interstate income withholding request is to use the interstate action transmittal form from one CSE agency to another. In CSE cases, Federal regulations required that by August 22, 1988, all interstate income withholding requests be sent to the enforcing State's central registry for referral to the appropriate State or local official. The actual wage withholding procedure used by the State in which the noncustodial parent lives is the same as that used in intrastate cases.

States decide whether or not to make interstate income withholding available in non-CSE cases. Some States do not allow non-CSE interstate income withholding, insisting that all such requests be channeled through the CSE agency. In those States, it is necessary for a private attorney to refer his client to the local CSE office.

1988 law

Public Law 100–485 includes some provisions affecting interstate child support enforcement. The law requires States to establish automated statewide, comprehensive case tracking and monitoring systems, which would improve each State's ability to manage interstate cases. The law also required the establishment of a 15-member commission to study interstate child support establishment and enforcement.

The U.S. Commission on Interstate Child Support's report to Congress includes 120 recommendations for improving the CSE program. The report highlights the following recommendations:

Establishment of an integrated, automated network linking all the States to provide quick access to locate and income information (which would include new hire information based on W–4 forms);

Establishment of income withholding across State lines from the person seeking enforcement directly to the income source in the other State;

Identical enactment by States of the Uniform Interstate Family Support Act (which would replace URESA);

State use of early, voluntary parentage determination for child born outside of marriage and uniform evidentiary rules for contested paternity cases;

Universal access to health care insurance for children of separated parents;

More emphasis on staff training and increased resources to ensure that all cases can be processed on a more timely basis; and

Revision of CSE funding to ensure that action is taken on cases most in need of attention.[6]

1992 law

Public Law 102–521, the Child Support Recovery Act of 1992, imposes a Federal criminal penalty for the willful failure to pay a past-due child support obligation with respect to a child who resides in another State that has remained unpaid for longer than a year or is greater than $5,000. For the first conviction the penalty would be a fine of not more than $5,000 and/or imprisonment for not more than 6 months; for a second conviction, a fine of up to $250,000 and/or imprisonment for up to 2 years.

Other procedures that aid interstate enforcement

In 1948, the National Conference of Commissioners on Uniform State Laws and the American Bar Association approved the Uniform Enforcement of Foreign Judgments Act (UEFJA), which simplifies the collection of child support arrearages in interstate cases. Revised in 1964 and adopted in only 30 States, UEFJA provides that upon the filing of an authenticated foreign (i.e., out-of-State) judgment and notice to the obligor, the judgment is to be treated in the same manner as a local one. A judgment is the official decision or finding of a court on the respective rights of the involved parties. UEFJA applies only to final judgments. As a general rule, child support arrearages that have been reduced to judgment are considered final judgments and thus can be filed under UEFJA.

SUMMARY INFORMATION ON COLLECTION TECHNIQUES

Table 11–7 shows the percentage of child support collections obtained through the use of selected enforcement techniques. According to the OCSE, most CSE collections come from noncustodial parents who are complying with their support orders. However, the information is not provided in the OCSE annual report, which identifies only collection techniques that are concentrated on delinquent payments. The report for fiscal year 1993 shows that 64 percent of the $8.9 billion in child support payments collected that year was obtained through the more publicized enforcement techniques: wage withholding, Federal income tax refund offset, State income tax refund offset, and unemployment compensation intercept. The remaining 36 percent is listed as collected by other means. Officials said most of these other collections come from noncustodial parents who were complying with their support orders by sending their

---

[6] U.S. Commission on Interstate Child Support. "Supporting Our Children: A Blueprint for Reform." 1992. p. xiii.

payments to the CSE agency. The other category also included collections from noncustodial parents who voluntarily sent money for their children even though a support order had never been established for them (less than one percent of all collections), and other enforcement techniques, such as liens against property, by posting of bonds or securities, and use of the full IRS collection procedure.

TABLE 11–7.—CHILD SUPPORT COLLECTIONS MADE BY VARIOUS ENFORCEMENT TECHNIQUES, FISCAL YEAR 1989–93

[Dollars in millions]

Enforcement techniques	Child support collections					Percent of total collections				
	1989	1990	1991	1992	1993	1989	1990	1991	1992	1993
Wage withholding	$2,144	$2,636	$3,266	$3,971	4,743	40.9	43.9	47.4	49.9	53.2
Federal income tax offset	411	444	476	585	570	7.9	7.4	6.9	7.3	6.4
State income tax offset	62	70	72	80	78	1.2	1.2	1.0	1.0	.9
Unemployment compensation intercept	54	80	143	269	286	1.0	1.3	2.1	3.4	3.2
Other [1]	2,570	2,780	2,929	3,060	3,232	49.0	46.2	42.6	38.4	36.3
Total collections	5,241	6,010	6,886	7,965	8,909	100.0	100.0	100.0	100.0	100.0

[1] The OCSE does not designate the source of most of these collections. According to the OCSE, the majority of collections in the other category came from noncustodial parents who were complying with their support orders by sending their payments to the CSE agency. Moreover, the OCSE officials maintain that reliability of collection data lessen when specified by techniques of collection.

Source: U.S. Department of Health and Human Services. Office of Child Support Enforcement. "Child Support Enforcement Statistics, Fiscal Year 1993."

BANKRUPTCY AND CHILD SUPPORT ENFORCEMENT

The 1975 child support legislation included a provision that stated that an assigned child support obligation was not discharged in bankruptcy (i.e., a person filing bankruptcy was not relieved of his child support obligation). In 1978 this provision was repealed and incorporated into the 1978 uniform law on bankruptcy. The bankruptcy law also listed exceptions to discharge including alimony, maintenance or support due a spouse, former spouse, or child of the debtor in connection with a separation agreement, divorce decree, or property settlement. In 1981, the provision stating that a child support obligation assigned to the State as a condition of AFDC eligibility is not dischargeable in bankruptcy was reinstated. In 1984, a provision was enacted that provided that child support obligations that have been assigned to the State as part of the CSE program may not be discharged in bankruptcy, regardless of whether they are on behalf of an AFDC family or a non-AFDC family and regardless of whether the debtor was married to the child's other parent.

LINKAGE BETWEEN AFDC AND CHILD SUPPORT ENFORCEMENT

The Social Security Act requires every State operating an AFDC program to run a CSE program. Federal law requires applicants for, and recipients of, AFDC to assign their support rights to the State in order to receive AFDC. In addition, each applicant or recipient must cooperate with the State if necessary to (1) establish the paternity of a child born outside of marriage, and (2) obtain child support payments, unless it is found not to be in the best interest of the child to do so.

Under the law, AFDC recipients or applicants may be excused from the requirement of cooperation if the AFDC agency determines that good cause for noncooperation exists, taking into consideration the best interests of the child on whose behalf aid is claimed. The determination is made according to standards in Federal regulations, the so-called good cause regulations. If good cause is found not to exist and if the relative with whom a child is living still refuses to cooperate, the relative is to be disqualified from AFDC and the child's benefits are to be sent in the form of a protective payment to a person other than the caretaker relative. (The same is true of refusal to assign to the State support rights: the child will not be disqualified from AFDC, but will receive AFDC benefits only in the form of protective payments.) Circumstances under which cooperation may be found to be against the best interests of the child are defined to include: situations in which cooperation is reasonably anticipated to result in physical or emotional harm to the child, or physical or emotional harm to the caretaker relative, of such nature that it reduces the capacity to care for the child adequately; situations in which the child was conceived as a result of incest or rape; and situations in which legal procedures are underway for the child's adoption. Families who do not receive AFDC assistance also are eligible for CSE and paternity determination services if they apply for services.

FUNDING

The Federal Government currently reimburses each State 66 percent of the cost of administering its CSE program. When the program began in 1975, the Federal match was 75 percent. In 1982, Public Law 97–248 reduced the Federal match to 70 percent (fiscal years 1983–87). In 1984 Public Law 98–378 reduced the Federal match to 68 percent in fiscal year 1988 and fiscal year 1989, and to 66 percent in fiscal year 1990 and years thereafter. These costs include moneys for locate services, paternity establishment, establishment of child support orders, and enforcement services.

The Federal Government also pays 90 percent of State costs of developing and improving management information systems, including expenditures on the hardware (i.e., computers) and 90 percent of laboratory costs incurred in determining paternity.

The Federal Government pays most of the costs of State CSE programs. States receive Federal funds to pay a majority share of the costs of operating CSE programs plus Federal incentive payments based on total collections and cost-effectiveness of their programs. State programs receive additional funding from the State government. Although the actual dollars contributed by the Federal Government are greater, the level of funding allocated by the State or local government determines the amount of resources available to the CSE agency.

INCENTIVE PAYMENTS TO STATES

In most States, the State share of CSE collections made on behalf of AFDC families can be calculated by subtracting the Federal medical assistance percentage from 100 percent (in some States, local governments also are entitled to part of the State's share of collections). In addition, States and localities receive Federal CSE incentive payments that come entirely from the Federal share of child support collections. The revised incentive formula, effective October 1, 1985, was designed to encourage States to develop CSE programs that emphasize collections on behalf of both AFDC and non-AFDC families, and to improve the program's cost effectiveness.

Under the incentive formula, each State receives an incentive payment equal to at least 6 percent of the State's total amount of AFDC support collections for the year, plus at least 6 percent of the State's total amount of non-AFDC collections for the year. The amount of the State's incentive payment could reach a high of 10 percent of the AFDC collections plus 10 percent of the non-AFDC collections, depending on the State's ratio of child support collections to administrative costs. (See table 11–8.)

There is a limit, however, on the incentive payment for non-AFDC collections. The incentive payments for such collections may not exceed 115 percent of incentive payments for AFDC collections. (This percentage was 100 percent in fiscal year 1986 and fiscal year 1987, 105 percent in fiscal year 1988, 110 percent in fiscal year 1989, and 115 percent in fiscal year 1990 and each year thereafter.)

TABLE 11–8.—INCENTIVE PAYMENT STRUCTURE

	Incentive payment received (percent)
Collection-to-cost ratio:	
Less than 1.4 to 1	6.0
At least 1.4 to 1	6.5
At least 1.6 to 1	7.0
At least 1.8 to 1	7.5
At least 2.0 to 1	8.0
At least 2.2 to 1	8.5
At least 2.4 to 1	9.0
At least 2.6 to 1	9.5
At least 2.8 to 1	10.0

The incentive formula seeks to assure that States provide equitable treatment for both AFDC and non-AFDC families. Under the old system, a State that incurred administrative costs to collect support for a non-AFDC family did not receive an incentive payment since incentives were paid only for AFDC collections. This practice generally resulted in the neglect of non-AFDC cases. The new incentive formula aims to remedy that by making payments for non-AFDC collections. At the same time it has placed a limit on non-AFDC incentive payments so as to lessen the possibility that States would merely transfer to the CSE program child support activities which were previously financed out of State and/or local moneys, with no increase in the level of child support services.

At State option, laboratory costs (for blood testing, etc.) to establish paternity may be excluded from the State's administrative costs in calculating the State's collection-to-cost ratios for purposes of determining the incentive payment. In addition, for purposes of calculating these ratios, interstate collections are credited to both the initiating and responding States. Incentives are paid according to the collection-to-cost ratios (ratio of AFDC collections to total administrative costs and ratio of non-AFDC collections to total administrative costs) shown in table 11–8.

Before 1984, a State that initiated a successful action to collect child support from another State generally did not receive an incentive payment. Rather, the jurisdiction that made the collection received the incentive payment. Public Law 98–378 provides that both States involved in an interstate collection be credited with the collection for purposes of computing incentive payments. This double-counting is intended to encourage States to pursue interstate cases as energetically as they pursue intrastate cases. States now will pay incentive for interstate cases to themselves out of the Federal share of collections they distribute.

In addition to substantial Federal reimbursement, States may use fees and cost recovery to help finance the CSE program (discussed later). Such fees and costs recovered from non-AFDC cases must be subtracted from the State's total administrative cost before calculating the Federal reimbursement amount; however, the lower administrative cost figure may result in greater Federal incentive payments by improving the State's collection-to-cost ratio.

PAYMENTS TO AFDC FAMILIES

Families receiving AFDC benefits automatically qualify (free of charge) for CSE services. Their cases are referred to the CSE agency. Federal law requires AFDC families (and applicants), as a condition of eligibility for aid, to assign their support rights to the State, to cooperate with the State in establishing the paternity of a child born outside of marriage, and to cooperate with the State in obtaining support payments. The provision requiring the AFDC applicant or recipient to assign to the State her rights to support covers both current support and any arrears which have accrued, and lasts as long as the family receives AFDC. When the family no longer receives AFDC, the mother or caretaker relative regains her right to collect current support, but if there are arrears, the State may claim those arrears up to the amount paid out as AFDC benefits.

Child support payments made on behalf of a child receiving AFDC are supposed to be paid to the CSE agency rather than directly to the family. If the child support collection is insufficient to disqualify the family from receiving AFDC payments, the family receives its full monthly AFDC grant plus the first $50 of the child support payment made in the child's behalf for that month. The remainder of that monthly child support payment is distributed to reimburse the State and Federal Governments in proportion to their assistance to the family. If the family's income, including the child support payment, is sufficient to make the family ineligible for AFDC payments, the family's AFDC benefits are ended, and future child support payments are paid directly from the noncustodial parent to the family.

Supplemental payments in "fill-the-gap" States

Notwithstanding the above procedures, some States are required to provide monthly supplemental payments to AFDC recipients who have less disposable income now than they would have had in July 1975 because child support is paid to the CSE agency instead of directly to the family. States required to pay supplemental payment are often referred to as "fill-the-gap" States. These States pay less assistance than their full need standard, and allow recipients to use child support income to make up all or part of the difference between the payment made by the State and the State's need standard.

Section 402(a)(28) of the Social Security Act requires States that had a fill-the-gap policy in 1975 and currently have such a policy, to add to the AFDC benefit all or part of the child support collection (the amount which would have caused no reduction in the AFDC benefit if it had been paid directly to the family).

Information obtained from the Office of Child Support Enforcement (June 1990) indicates that seven States that had fill-the-gap policies in July 1975 also have them now and thus must follow the benefit calculation rules of section 402(a)(28) when taking account of child support collections for AFDC families. They are: Georgia, Maine, Mississippi, South Carolina, Tennessee, Virginia, and Wyoming. Another 13 jurisdictions, which had fill-the-gap policies in July 1975, no longer have them. Were they to resume a fill-the-gap practice, they also would be required to treat child support collections as though they were paid directly to the family. These jurisdictions are: Alabama, Alaska, Arizona, Arkansas, Delaware, Indiana, Missouri, New Mexico, Puerto Rico, Texas, Virgin Islands, Washington, and West Virginia.

PAYMENTS TO NON-AFDC FAMILIES

Families who do not receive AFDC assistance also are eligible if they apply for services, unless they have left the AFDC rolls and are automatically provided continued CSE services.

The entire amount of child support payments collected on behalf of a non-AFDC child is paid directly to the family. Even so, the State still receives the Federal reimbursement (currently 66 percent) for the costs of establishing and enforcing child support obligations for these non-AFDC cases. In some States, parents may be ordered by the court to make and receive support payments directly or through a court registry or State child support clearinghouse without any formal application to the CSE agency. When this occurs, the money collected, since it is outside the CSE system, cannot be counted in determining the amount of Federal reimbursement to the State.

Non-AFDC families participate in the CSE program on a voluntary basis, except for Medicaid-only cases. Federal funding for services to non-AFDC families was made a permanent part of the program in 1980 by Public Law 96–272. Federal law requires the State to charge an application fee of up to $25 for CSE services for non-AFDC families. Some States charge the full $25, some less, and others use State funds to pay the fee or seek collection from the noncustodial parent.

In addition, CSE agencies are allowed to recover the actual costs of their services to non-AFDC families from either the custodial parent or the noncustodial parent, once current support has been covered. In practice, this means that costs are deducted from arrears that otherwise would be paid directly to the non-AFDC client. Recovery of these costs is contingent on payment of the arrears. However, it is the practice of most States not to recover the cost of their services. The amount of fees collected by the States for purposes of processing non-AFDC cases plus the amount of processing costs recovered by the States in excess of the fees charged decreases the amount of States' expenditures eligible for Federal CSE funding. Moreover, any interest earned on money from fees or recovered costs is considered CSE program income and must be used by the States to offset program expenditures. In fiscal year 1992, fees received and costs recovered for non-AFDC cases amounted to $29.2 million.

Several States try to recoup costs in non-AFDC cases by deducting their costs from the actual child support payment before sending it to the custodial parent. Because some of these custodial parents are only dollars away from qualifying for AFDC and because it generally is easier to get on welfare than to earn one's way off, some policymakers argue that this practice can result in welfare dependency; others maintain that it is unfair to the children.

ARREARAGES

To receive AFDC benefits, a custodial parent must assign to the State her right to collect child support payments. This assignment covers current support and any arrears, and lasts as long as the family receives AFDC. When the family stops receiving AFDC, the assignment ends. The mother regains her right to collect current support. However, if there are arrears, the State may claim those arrears up to the amount paid out in AFDC. As described earlier, when a mother receives AFDC and the CSE agency makes a collection on her behalf, it must distribute the collection in accordance with Federal law. First, up to the first $50 collected is given to the family (a disregard that does not affect the family's AFDC benefit or eligibility status). Second, the Federal and State Governments are reimbursed for the AFDC benefits paid to the family in that month. Third, if there is money left, the family receives it up to the amount of the current month's child support obligation. Fourth, if there is still money left, the State keeps it to reimburse itself for any arrears owed to it under the AFDC assignment. If no arrears are owed the State, the money is used to pay arrears owed to the family. Such moneys are considered income under the AFDC program and would reduce the family's AFDC benefit.

In the case of non-AFDC families, the sequence is different. First, if the family never received AFDC, all child support collections made on the family's behalf are sent to the family. Second, if the family had received AFDC before, collections go toward payment on the current month's support obligation. If any money is left, and it is considered an arrearage, the State decides whether the arrears will be paid to the family or State first. If the arrears are paid to the State, they are distributed between the Federal and State Governments as reimbursement for past AFDC benefits. Third, if there are no arrears, the collection is forwarded to the family and is credited toward future CSE payments.

According to the OCSE 17th annual report, in fiscal year 1992, the amount of total prior year support due, i.e., arrearages, amounted to $23.9 billion; $1.8 billion (8 percent) was paid in fiscal year 1992 on prior years' arrears.

DISTRIBUTION OF COLLECTIONS

Collections made on behalf of families receiving AFDC directly offset AFDC benefit costs and (except for the first $50 of current monthly support payments, which go directly to the family, and are disregarded as income for AFDC purposes) are shared between the Federal Government and the States in accordance with the matching formula used for the individual State's AFDC program.

In general, the initial determination of the Federal share of CSE collections is based on the rate of Federal financial participation in AFDC benefit costs. The Federal share of AFDC benefit costs generally is determined by the Federal medical assistance percentage. The Federal share of AFDC benefit costs (and, therefore, the Federal share of CSE/AFDC collections) is inversely related to State per capita income; within limits, the lower the State per capita income, the greater the Federal share. Nationally, this figure is about 55 percent. It ranges from a minimum of 50 percent to a statutory maximum of 83 percent. In fiscal year 1993, the highest matching rate was 79.01 percent (the Federal match for AFDC benefit costs in Mississippi). In fiscal year 1994, Mississippi's Federal AFDC matching rate dropped to 78.85 percent.

Even though the national average (gross) Federal share of AFDC collections is about 56 percent, Federal funds reimburse States for 66 percent of their CSE administrative costs. This lowers the net Federal share of support collections.

USE OF SUPPORT COLLECTIONS

The Federal share of child support collections paid by noncustodial parents of children receiving AFDC benefits is used first to pay incentives to States on their AFDC and non-AFDC collections. The remainder is used to offset Federal AFDC benefit costs. In fiscal year 1993, incentive payments amounted to $339 million, 44 percent of the Federal share of CSE collections. Payments made on behalf of non-AFDC families go to the family.

Neither Federal law nor regulations dictate the use of the State's share of child support savings; there are no Federal strings attached. However, child support collections in and of themselves can (1) prevent families from qualifying for welfare programs, (2) remove families from welfare rolls when the amount collected is sufficient, (3) partially offset State AFDC payments to families whose monthly child support is insufficient to remove them from welfare rolls, (4) recover or prevent the need for Medicaid payments through reimbursement from private health insurers in cases where the noncustodial parent has coverage, or where coverage is available, and (5) offset AFDC foster care costs. In addition, many States have chosen to reinvest child support savings back into the CSE program to increase the quality and effectiveness of the program. Some States use child support savings in other children and family programs. Others use child support savings wherever the State budget indicates the need.

EXTENT TO WHICH FEDERAL GOVERNMENT BEARS COST OF THE CHILD SUPPORT ENFORCEMENT PROGRAM

One of the purposes of the CSE program is to reduce public expenditures on welfare by obtaining support from noncustodial parents on an ongoing basis. The CSE program also provides services to nonwelfare parents who apply for services. One purpose of the non-AFDC component of the program is welfare cost avoidance, that is, preventing families from going on AFDC (or other welfare programs) by collecting child support from noncustodial parents.

Even with the reduced Federal matching rate (from 75 percent in 1975 to 66 percent in 1991), the Federal Government has never recovered its costs from the CSE program. Under the current financing arrangement, States can run inefficient programs and still make a profit from the CSE program. The cost of the CSE program to the Federal Government, however, has continued, since 1984, to increase steadily.

To illustrate, assume that an inefficient State spends $200 to collect a $300 child support payment from a noncustodial parent whose children are receiving AFDC benefits. Such a State (with a collection-to-cost ratio of 1.5) would qualify for an incentive payment of $19.50 (6.5 percent of AFDC collections, see table 11–9). Since the State pays 34 percent of administrative costs, the collection would cost the State $68, but the State's share of the collection would total $144.50. This means that the State would pay 34 percent of the cost and get 48 percent of the collection. Thus, the net gain to the State would be $76.50.[7] On the other hand, the collection would cost the Federal Government $132, and its share of the collection would amount to $105.50. Thus, the collection would cost the Federal Government $26.50. In other words, the Federal Government would pay 66 percent of the cost and get 35 percent of the collection. The recipient would get nearly 17 percent of the collection (the $50 passthrough). Table 11–11 shows that although the CSE program is a net gain for the States, it is a significant net cost to the Federal Government.

TABLE 11–9.—STATE AND FEDERAL SHARE OF CHILD SUPPORT COLLECTIONS

[AFDC Family]

	Collections	Cost of collections	Net gain
State share	$125+$19.50=$144.50	$68	+$76.50
Federal share	125 − 19.50= 105.50	132	− 26.50
Payment to recipient	50.00	0	+ 50.00
Total	300.00	200	+100.00

The point at which a State breaks even (exactly recovers collection costs) in child support payments on behalf of AFDC recipients primarily depends on the share of AFDC benefit costs that it pays, and this, in turn, is related inversely to State per capita income. This can be shown by calculating the approximate breakeven ratios (collections needed per dollar of administrative cost) for States with different Federal AFDC matching rates, but the same collection cost per case. In the following examples, it is assumed that the cost of making a collection is $100 per month per AFDC case. (This figure was the national average cost for fiscal year 1988; it was obtained by dividing total CSE administrative costs of AFDC cases by the average number of AFDC cases in which a collection was made).

Example 1.—State that pays 50 percent of AFDC benefit costs—maximum State share. (In fiscal year 1990, 11 States and the District of Columbia were in this position.)

Under the existing system, the breakeven collection amount for a State spending $100 per AFDC case to collect child support payments, retaining the maximum State share (50 percent) of AFDC/CSE collections, paying the standard 34 percent of CSE administrative costs, and receiving the minimum incentive payment of 6

---

[7] This is a simplified example. Actually, the State's share of savings is determined by adding the State's share of AFDC collections to the State's AFDC and non-AFDC incentive payments. Its share of total administrative costs is subtracted from these revenues. The calculations assume a 50–50 matching rate for AFDC benefits.

percent, is $105.[8] That is, the State need collect only $1.05 per $1 of total administrative cost in order to recover its share of costs. Conversely, the Federal breakeven ratio for this State's collections is approximately 2.17. That is, the State must collect about $217 in order for the Federal Government to break even.[9] (See table 11–10 and chart 11–1.)

Example 2.—State that pays the minimum share (less than 20 percent) of AFDC benefit costs.

This situation is illustrated by the case of Mississippi, which had a Federal matching rate of 80.18 percent (and, thus, a State matching rate of 19.82 percent) for AFDC benefit costs. The breakeven collection amount for Mississippi, assuming it also spent $100 per AFDC case to collect child support payments, would be $164. This is a breakeven ratio of 1.64. Conversely, the Federal breakeven ratio for Mississippi's CSE program is approximately 1.44. (See table 11–10 and chart 11–1.)

These illustrations show that the States that are entitled to a relatively small proportion of child support collections (because of paying a small share of AFDC benefit costs) have to collect more child support payments per administrative dollar than other States to recover their costs (other things being equal). (See table 11–10.)

TABLE 11–10.—STATE AND FEDERAL BREAKEVEN POINTS PER DOLLAR OF COLLECTION COSTS[1] FOR SELECTED FEDERAL AFDC MATCHING RATES

	State break-even	Federal break-even
Federal AFDC matching rate:		
50 percent	$1.05	$2.17
60 percent	1.17	1.83
70 percent	1.36	1.60
80 percent	1.64	1.44

[1] The breakeven point is the amount of collections at which the jurisdiction exactly recovers its share of the collection costs. In this table collection costs are assumed to be $100 per month, the fiscal year 1988 national average cost of AFDC collections. This average was obtained by dividing fiscal year 1988 AFDC expenditures by the average number of AFDC cases in which a collection was made that year.

---

[8] State share of collections = State share of costs at breakeven

$.5(C - \$50) + .06[(C - \$50) + \$50] = .34Y$

$.56C = .34Y + \$25$

Assume State receives 50–50 matching rate for AFDC benefit costs and assume Y = $100 (national average in fiscal year 1988). C = total collections, Y = cost of collections, and (C − $50) = X, which is the public share of collections. The incentive payment equals 6 percent of total collections.

[9] Federal share of collections = Federal share of costs at breakeven

$.5(C - \$50) - .08[(C - \$50) + \$50] = .66Y$

$.42C = .66Y + \$25$

Assume State receives 50–50 matching rate for AFDC benefit costs and assume Y = $100 (national average in fiscal year 1988). C = total collections, Y = cost of collections, and (C − $50) = X, which is the public share of collections. The incentive payment, a function of the collection-to-cost ratio, equals 8 percent of total collections in this example where the collection-to-cost ratio is 2.17 (see table 8).

CHART 11–1. STATE/FEDERAL PROFIT/LOSS AT VARIOUS SUPPORT COLLECTION AMOUNTS, AND AFDC MATCHING RATES

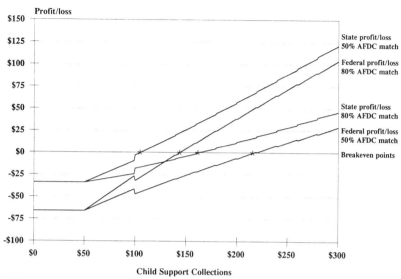

Child Support Collections

Note: When a family's income, including child support payments, makes the family ineligible for AFDC benefits, future support payments are paid to the family, and the Federal/State distribution of collections no longer applies.
Source: Congressional Research Service.

Table 11–11 shows that during the period 1979–93, the CSE program has produced new revenue for the States but incurred cost to the Federal Government. The States' share of collections has exceeded their share of administrative costs in each year, but the Federal share of collections has fallen increasingly short of their share of administrative costs. Net Federal costs have risen sharply from $43 million in fiscal year 1979 to $740 million in fiscal year 1993, a real increase of 745 percent (constant fiscal year 1993 dollars). Although net State savings increased in current dollars, from $244 million in fiscal year 1979 to $462 million in fiscal year 1993, there was a 7 percent decrease in constant fiscal year 1993 dollars.

In fiscal year 1992, 11 jurisdictions (Alabama, Arizona, Guam, Louisiana, Mississippi, Nebraska, New Mexico, Puerto Rico, Texas, the Virgin Islands, and West Virginia) did not achieve a savings from their CSE program. Moreover, in that same year, in only five States (Indiana, Iowa, North Dakota, South Dakota, and Wyoming) was the Federal share of child support savings positive. Despite the discussion above about breakeven points, it is not clear why these 11 jurisdictions did not recover their costs from the CSE program, nor why the Federal Government recovered its costs in the five other States (mentioned above).

TABLE 11–11.—FEDERAL AND STATE SHARE OF CHILD SUPPORT "SAVINGS," FISCAL YEARS 1979–93

[In millions]

	Federal share of child support savings [1]	State share of child support savings	Net public savings
Fiscal year:			
1979	− $43	$244	$201
1980	− 103	230	127
1981	− 128	261	133
1982	− 148	307	159
1983	− 138	312	174
1984	− 105	366	260
1985	− 231	317	86
1986	− 264	274	9
1987	− 337	342	5
1988	− 355	381	26
1989	− 480	403	− 77
1990	− 528	338	− 190
1991	− 586	385	− 201
1992	− 605	434	− 171
1993	− 740	462	− 278

[1] Negative "savings" are costs.

Source: U.S. Department of Health and Human Services. Office of Child Support Enforcement. Annual Reports to Congress, various years.

Table 11–11 also shows that the CSE program no longer produces a net public savings ($201 million savings in fiscal year 1979). Instead, in fiscal year 1993, the net cost of the program to the taxpayer was estimated at $278 million, up $107 million from fiscal year 1992. In addition, table 11–11 shows public savings dropping 67 percent from fiscal year 1984 to fiscal year 1985. This sudden decrease in public savings primarily was caused by the provision in 1984 law, first effective in fiscal year 1985, requiring that up to the first $50 received by the CSE agency on behalf of an AFDC family be passed through to the family without affecting their eligibility for AFDC or AFDC benefit payments. In fiscal year 1985, about 3.5 percent of CSE collections, $93.8 million went to AFDC families (pursuant to the $50 passthrough rule). In fiscal year 1993, $364.2 million (about 4.1 percent of CSE collections) was passed through to AFDC families. If these funds had not been spent to increase the incomes of poor children and their parents on AFDC, the net public savings from child support enforcement would have been a positive $86.2 million in fiscal year 1993.

Some question whether States have sufficient incentive to minimize costs, most of which are paid by the Federal Government. However, others argue that the intangible benefits of the CSE program make it worthwhile, despite considerations of cost-effectiveness. It is a fact that a large segment of the program, namely the non-AFDC component, by definition, provides no direct savings to the States or the Federal Government. Nevertheless, the non-AFDC component of the CSE program can achieve welfare cost avoidance in the following ways: by providing non-AFDC families with additional income sufficient to make them decide not to apply for public assistance (AFDC, food stamp, or Medicaid), even though eligible; by making non-AFDC families ineligible for public assistance and by continuing to make these families ineligible by reason of income; and by reducing the benefit levels of non-AFDC families who do receive public assistance benefits.

A recent study indicated that there was $1 in indirect savings, or welfare cost avoidance, for every $4 in child support collections made on behalf of non-AFDC families. If this were true in fiscal year 1992, the public avoided over $1.6 billion in additional welfare costs, more than paying for the program.

It also should be noted that once the CSE system matures (i.e., once the majority of existing cases have child support orders), the cost-effectiveness of the system probably will improve. However, because the benefits of establishing paternity or a child support award occur in future years as well as the current year, a static, point-in-time, analysis of costs and collections fails to account for the complexity and dynamic nature of the CSE system. It is an unfortunate irony that the more effective the program becomes at cost-avoidance, the less effective it will appear in such static calculations of "savings."

ROLE OF AUTOMATED SYSTEMS

In 1980, Congress authorized 90 percent Federal matching funds on an open-ended basis for CSE automated data systems, instead of the regular program rate (75 percent in 1980, 66 percent in fiscal year 1990 and years thereafter). Funds go to States that elect to establish an automated data processing and information retrieval system designed to assist management in the administration of the State plan, so as to control, account for, and monitor all factors in the support enforcement, collection, and paternity determination process. Funds may be used to plan, design, develop, and install or enhance the system. The Secretary of DHHS must approve the system as meeting specified conditions before matching is available.

In 1984, Congress made the 90 percent rate available to pay for the acquisition of computer hardware and necessary software. The 1984 legislation also specified that if a State met the Federal requirement for 90 percent matching, it could use its 90 percent matching funds to pay for the development and improvement of income withholding and other procedures required by the 1984 law.

In May 1986, the OCSE established a transfer policy requiring States seeking the 90 percent Federal matching rate to transfer existing automated systems from other States rather than to develop new ones, unless there were a compelling reason not to.

In 1988, Congress required States without comprehensive statewide automated systems to submit an advance planning document to the OCSE by October 1, 1991, for the development of such systems. All State systems must be approved as fully operating by October 1, 1995, at which time the 90 percent matching rate is to end. The new law allows many requirements for automated systems to be waived under certain circumstances. For instance, the DHHS

Secretary may waive a requirement if (1) a State demonstrates that it has an alternative system enabling it to substantially comply with program requirements or (2) a State provides assurance that additional steps will be taken to improve its program.

All States and territories submitted advance planning documents for automated child support systems as required by the Family Support Act of 1988. As of July 1, 1992, OCSE had approved plans for all States and territories. According to an August 1992 GAO report (IMTEC–92–46), the Federal Government had spent $258 million at the end of fiscal year 1991 in enhanced 90 percent matching funds for child support automtion. It is estimated that another $863 million in 90 percent matching funds will be spent by October 1, 1995.

According to a February 1989 GAO report entitled, "Child Support: State Progress in Developing Automated Enforcement Systems," States that develop automated systems with regular program funds also must obtain advance approval by the OCSE for expenditures that exceed $200,000. The GAO reported that oversight of system acquisition and operation under the regular program funding is less stringent than that of systems with enhanced funding.

Impact of Child Support Enforcement on AFDC and Poverty Status

For the 5.0 million women due child support payments in 1989 (including the nearly 1.2 million women who did not receive any payment), the average annual amount of child support owed was $2,252. The average annual amount of child support for the 3.7 million women who received child support payments was $2,995. If the full amount of payment due had been made to all women owed child support, the average annual amount would have been $3,292. (The average AFDC benefit per family in 1989 was about $4,600.) In 1989, 1.2 million (37 percent) of the 3.2 million women rearing children alone with incomes below the poverty level were supposed to receive child support payments. If full payment had been made to those 1.2 million women, 140,000 (4.4 percent of the 3.2 million and 11.8 percent of the 1.2 million) of them would have received enough income from child support payments to put them above the poverty level. This assumes that none of those poor women was a recipient of AFDC. For those receiving AFDC, the maximum they usually receive in the form of child support payments (via the CSE agency) is $50 monthly.

It is clear from the above illustration that the low level of child support awards due in 1989 limited the CSE program's antipoverty impact. The antipoverty effectiveness of the CSE program might be marginal for some families, given that Census Bureau data indicate that even being a member of a two-parent family is no guarantee against poverty. In 1991, 7.7 percent of white two-parent families with children under age 18 had incomes below the poverty level and 12.4 percent of black two-parent families were poor. This means that being in a two-parent family is not as much of a protection against poverty for blacks as it is for whites. Since the costs of achieving a moderate standard of living are sometimes higher for two households than for one, when a family breaks up, the father may have less money available to contribute to the support of his children. Thus, because the poverty rate of black children is relatively high even in two-parent families, the potential of child support for reducing the poverty rate of black children may be especially limited.

In 1989, $16.3 billion in child support payments were due, but actual payments totaled $11.2 billion. In 1985, $10.9 billion in child support payments were due, but actual payments totaled $7.2 billion. This meant that $3.7 billion or 33 percent of collections owed in 1985 went unpaid. While the almost $11 billion owed in child support in 1985 is a substantial amount, two basic studies indicate that fathers have the ability to pay from $24 to $30 billion annually in child support.

One study points out that the size of the estimate of the total amount that noncustodial fathers can afford to contribute to their children's maintenance ($26.6 billion annually) says nothing about the distribution of this money by income group. The study indicates that children whose fathers are in the highest income quintile would receive 46 percent of the $26.6 billion and that those whose fathers are in the lowest quintile would receive 3 percent of the $26.6 billion.

Another study based on data from the Panel Study of Income Dynamics, which covers divorces and separations during the period 1968–1981, indicates that poor children have not necessarily had poor fathers, and that increased child support payments from the absent fathers could substantially reduce their years of poverty. The study states that "the largest portion of the times when the custodial mother's family is poor are times when the absent father has enough income to keep himself and any new family he has formed out of poverty." This report concludes that if increased child support payments merely replace welfare support, many childhood years would remain in poverty. Some of the reasons for this finding are: (1) the absence of support awards in a large number of cases, (2) nonpayment or underpayment of existing awards, and (3) low award levels relative to the income of noncustodial parents.

Although the antipoverty potential of the CSE program is limited and difficult to estimate, it is clear that child support payments could have a large impact on AFDC costs. In fiscal year 1992, the sum collected by the CSE agency from AFDC parents equalled 11.4 percent of AFDC benefits. Researchers say that this overstates the impact of the CSE program, inasmuch as AFDC mothers would have collected some support if there were no CSE program and they were not required to give their child support rights to the welfare agency. One researcher estimates that only about 25 percent of the gain can be attributed directly to the CSE program. (This figure, applied to fiscal year 1992, leads to the estimate that if there had been no CSE program that year, mothers would have collected 8.5 percent of AFDC benefits, compared to the actual sum of 11.4 percent collected by the CSE agency.) The researcher said that if a successful system of mandatory wage withholding were adopted and greater efforts made to establish obligations, the CSE program might recover between 15 percent and 20 percent of total AFDC benefit expenditures. The OCSE annual fiscal year 1992 data show 10 States recovering at least 20 percent of total AFDC benefit payments through the efforts of the CSE program (on average, these are relatively smaller States with low AFDC benefit levels).

In addition, there is much research that indicates that child support payments could help reduce the severity of poverty for many non-AFDC children even if it did not end their poverty.

TABLE 11–12.—ESTIMATED TOTAL NUMBER AND PERCENT OF AFDC FAMILIES AFFECTED BY $50 PASSTHROUGH: 1985, 1990, 1992,[1] AND 1993

State	AFDC families 1993	Estimated families affected 1993	Percent of families affected			
			1985	1990	1992	1993
Alabama	50,994	18,510	11.7	19.1	33.4	36.3
Alaska	10,048	1,889	11.9	20.7	18.8	18.8
Arizona	68,725	2,695	4.8	4.9	7.3	3.9
Arkansas	26,098	7,697	15.9	19.7	27.7	29.5
California	717,181	82,517	13.8	12.7	11.3	11.5
Colorado	41,152	8,510	14.1	15.1	18.5	20.7
Connecticut	55,072	11,162	25.6	19.3	18.3	20.3
Delaware	11,256	2,511	21.7	18.0	21.6	22.3
District of Co- lumbia	24,589	1,872	5.8	7.5	7.9	7.6
Florida	247,505	37,925	11.4	24.0	15.9	15.3
Georgia	139,903	26,813	5.3	19.6	17.8	19.2
Guam	1,363	489	10.5	19.9	34.6	35.9
Hawaii	17,452	3,039	20.5	13.2	19.6	17.4
Idaho	7,436	3,922	46.7	46.6	49.6	52.7
Illinois	220,972	17,782	5.5	7.9	7.4	8.1
Indiana	68,904	23,807	25.9	27.8	43.4	34.6
Iowa	34,443	9,150	22.7	22.8	23.9	26.6
Kansas	27,729	9,664	15.2	24.0	31.5	34.9
Kentucky	73,601	12,534	7.6	13.4	15.5	17.0
Louisiana	88,712	8,238	6.9	8.5	9.3	9.3
Maine	21,161	7,339	25.6	39.3	23.0	34.7
Maryland	79,222	14,347	15.0	10.9	18.6	18.1
Massachusetts	106,962	12,252	20.2	16.3	11.2	11.5
Michigan	197,796	53,494	17.2	25.3	23.9	27.1
Minnesota	57,147	20,076	22.5	28.0	29.8	35.1
Mississippi	59,509	7,931	4.8	9.2	12.4	13.3
Missouri	84,700	14,833	8.2	18.5	17.9	17.5
Montana	10,535	1,906	13.9	15.2	18.3	18.1
Nebraska	15,452	4,512	11.3	20.6	27.5	29.2
Nevada	12,614	4,201	33.6	29.8	32.4	33.3
New Hampshire	10,462	3,589	12.6	13.5	27.1	34.1
New Jersey	121,685	25,361	15.4	15.8	19.9	20.8
New Mexico	29,500	2,927	7.6	11.8	9.5	9.9
New York	415,885	48,495	9.2	11.8	13.0	11.7
North Carolina .	127,390	24,211	15.0	19.5	18.9	19.0
North Dakota ...	5,974	2,340	25.1	36.7	38.5	39.2
Ohio	233,965	35,119	11.6	19.9	14.1	15.0
Oklahoma	47,696	4,626	8.4	13.4	7.5	9.7
Oregon	38,662	9,980	16.0	17.6	22.5	25.8

TABLE 11–12.—ESTIMATED TOTAL NUMBER AND PERCENT OF AFDC FAMILIES AFFECTED BY $50 PASSTHROUGH: 1985, 1990, 1992, [1] AND 1993—Continued

State	AFDC families 1993	Estimated families affected 1993	Percent of families affected			
			1985	1990	1992	1993
Pennsylvania ...	194,826	50,941	16.3	20.8	24.9	26.2
Puerto Rico	60,709	1,874	4.7	4.2	3.3	3.1
Rhode Island ...	21,434	2,728	13.9	17.9	11.1	12.7
South Carolina	52,110	13,173	8.9	26.3	23.8	25.3
South Dakota ..	7,167	1,897	17.6	21.4	24.2	26.5
Tennessee	102,909	10,988	9.8	15.2	11.4	10.7
Texas	270,257	18,049	3.1	5.8	6.1	6.7
Utah	18,229	4,721	26.9	23.7	25.7	25.9
Vermont	8,570	3,439	21.9	36.5	35.9	40.1
Virgin Islands ..	1,083	139	10.2	11.6	11.7	12.8
Virginia	72,824	17,424	14.9	24.9	24.5	23.9
Washington	85,259	27,243	18.0	24.8	28.7	32.0
West Virginia ...	33,042	3,641	6.6	7.1	9.0	11.0
Wisconsin	71,994	29,193	37.8	38.9	38.7	40.6
Wyoming	6,324	1,535	8.0	21.7	26.2	24.3
Nationwide total	4,616,169	775,230	13.2	16.3	16.3	16.8

NA=Not available.

[1] These estimates are based on the number of "paying" child support cases and are a low estimate of the number of families affected.

Note: These estimates are based on the number of "paying" child support cases adjusted for comparability with AFDC families.

Source: Office of Child Support Enforcement.

TABLE 11–13.—STATE PROFILE OF COLLECTIONS AND EXPENDITURES, FISCAL YEAR 1993 [1]

[In millions of dollars]

State	Total collections	AFDC collections	Non-AFDC collections	Total expenditures	Child support collections per dollar of total administrative expenditures			Incentive payments (estimate)
					Total	AFDC/FC total	Non-AFDC total	
Alabama	$113.2	$22.5	$90.7	$34.6	3.27	0.65	2.62	$3.8
Alaska	39.1	11.7	27.4	10.6	3.71	1.11	2.60	2.2
Arizona	66.6	18.6	48.0	37.1	1.79	0.50	1.29	2.2
Arkansas	49.1	16.2	32.9	15.3	3.20	1.06	2.15	2.1
California	736.9	335.2	401.6	290.6	2.54	1.15	1.38	48.4
Colorado	67.7	26.2	41.5	27.4	2.47	0.95	1.51	4.1
Connecticut	93.5	41.3	52.2	29.3	3.19	1.41	1.78	5.1
Delaware	26.7	7.8	18.9	11.1	2.39	0.70	1.69	1.1
District of Columbia	21.8	5.2	16.6	8.7	2.51	0.60	1.91	1.0
Florida	290.0	78.1	211.9	76.7	3.78	1.02	2.76	10.7
Georgia	205.6	84.6	120.9	46.0	4.47	1.84	2.63	13.9
Guam	5.0	2.3	2.7	2.7	1.89	0.88	1.00	0.4
Hawaii	37.3	9.1	28.3	9.8	3.79	0.92	2.87	1.2
Idaho	32.1	8.7	23.4	9.4	3.43	0.93	2.50	1.5
Illinois	183.9	55.7	128.1	77.8	2.36	0.72	1.65	8.1
Indiana	141.2	52.0	89.1	21.9	6.45	2.38	4.07	10.9
Iowa	109.3	36.8	72.5	21.2	5.14	1.73	3.41	5.3
Kansas	59.6	22.4	37.2	23.2	2.57	0.97	1.61	3.1
Kentucky	103.6	36.6	67.0	34.0	3.05	1.08	1.97	5.7
Louisiana	103.1	26.8	76.2	32.3	3.19	0.83	2.36	3.6
Maine	45.0	25.7	19.3	13.3	3.39	1.93	1.45	3.0
Maryland	219.1	51.3	167.8	48.0	4.56	1.07	3.49	5.5
Massachusetts	195.4	77.3	118.1	45.4	4.30	1.70	2.60	11.6
Michigan	874.5	169.6	704.9	103.7	8.43	1.64	6.80	24.9
Minnesota	214.5	56.0	158.5	51.1	4.20	1.10	3.10	6.8
Mississippi	53.5	21.6	31.9	24.3	2.20	0.89	1.31	3.0
Missouri	189.1	51.2	138.0	43.9	4.30	1.16	3.14	7.9
Montana	20.1	6.5	13.7	7.3	2.76	0.88	1.87	1.1
Nebraska	71.7	9.8	61.9	17.2	4.17	0.57	3.60	1.3
Nevada	37.6	7.0	30.6	15.8	2.39	0.45	1.94	1.7
New Hampshire	31.5	7.6	23.9	11.0	2.87	0.70	2.17	0.8
New Jersey	407.8	84.0	323.8	101.4	4.02	0.83	3.19	10.6
New Mexico	27.1	12.9	14.2	8.8	3.08	1.47	1.61	1.1
New York	536.4	184.6	351.8	172.9	3.10	1.07	2.03	22.2
North Carolina	197.3	70.3	127.0	61.7	3.20	1.14	2.06	9.2
North Dakota	18.7	6.1	12.6	4.6	4.05	1.32	2.73	1.0
Ohio	714.1	105.7	608.4	130.4	5.48	0.81	4.67	12.7
Oklahoma	52.2	18.8	33.4	16.7	3.13	1.13	2.00	2.9
Oregon	124.9	28.4	96.6	25.2	4.95	1.12	3.83	5.0
Pennsylvania	814.5	124.5	690.0	89.6	9.09	1.39	7.70	15.5
Puerto Rico	97.4	1.3	96.0	8.3	11.73	0.16	11.57	0.5
Rhode Island	26.7	15.0	11.7	6.1	4.35	2.44	1.91	1.8
South Carolina	79.3	24.6	54.7	20.4	3.88	1.20	2.68	2.8
South Dakota	18.1	5.1	13.1	3.7	4.90	1.37	3.53	0.8
Tennessee	116.2	33.4	82.7	21.4	5.42	1.56	3.86	4.5
Texas	309.5	66.2	243.3	134.1	2.31	0.49	1.81	9.8
Utah	56.2	19.5	36.7	19.6	2.86	0.99	1.87	2.4
Vermont	15.8	7.6	8.2	5.2	3.06	1.48	1.59	1.3
Virgin Islands	5.0	0.3	4.6	1.1	4.50	0.31	4.19	0.0
Virginia	151.9	39.6	112.3	49.2	3.09	0.80	2.28	6.0
Washington	307.3	100.3	206.9	89.8	3.42	1.12	2.30	15.6
West Virginia	49.0	16.9	32.1	17.7	2.77	0.95	1.82	1.5
Wisconsin	332.8	65.4	267.4	46.6	7.15	1.41	5.74	9.2
Wyoming	13.8	4.3	9.5	5.9	2.34	0.74	1.61	0.8
U.S. Totals	$8,909.3	$2,416.2	$6,492.7	$2,241.1	3.98	1.08	2.90	$339.2

[1] Totals may not add because of rounding.

Source: Office of Child Support Enforcement.

TABLE 11–14.—TOTAL CHILD SUPPORT COLLECTIONS, SELECTED FISCAL YEARS 1979–93

[In thousands of dollars]

State	1979	1983	1987	1990	1991	1992	1993
Alabama	6,854	8,643	39,976	66,174	80,952	98,141	113,273
Alaska	3,844	9,704	17,139	26,788	30,721	35,613	39,148
Arizona	6,411	10,563	20,114	27,837	33,277	46,447	66,580
Arkansas	3,921	7,401	16,267	26,010	32,783	42,065	49,147
California	199,945	254,586	394,882	522,646	591,243	653,681	736,855
Colorado	4,020	17,178	22,376	39,601	46,997	58,030	67,723
Connecticut	23,033	39,227	57,182	66,724	75,778	84,190	93,454
Delaware	5,814	8,097	13,871	20,161	22,692	25,926	26,663
District of Columbia	1,086	3,521	5,690	13,598	16,578	19,733	21,798
Florida	10,524	19,080	81,759	176,603	214,153	252,473	289,976
Georgia	5,554	13,439	48,082	113,095	143,014	174,467	205,566
Guam	160	391	627	1,440	3,162	4,697	5,003
Hawaii	5,150	10,087	15,985	27,638	30,096	34,404	37,327
Idaho	2,501	4,690	13,490	22,909	23,442	27,846	32,127
Illinois	10,740	32,025	89,622	136,019	150,134	183,308	183,889
Indiana	9,073	20,789	60,613	96,145	110,117	124,614	141,164
Iowa	13,017	29,185	48,516	70,982	80,693	96,046	109,278
Kansas	3,975	9,921	22,199	44,958	54,832	66,053	59,601
Kentucky	4,881	19,702	32,456	59,998	73,928	93,902	103,587
Louisiana	12,678	26,754	40,047	60,527	67,988	84,373	103,054
Maine	4,574	10,235	22,421	35,741	36,554	38,005	44,963
Maryland	20,856	77,129	97,889	151,352	163,626	194,009	219,085
Massachusetts	36,338	72,319	128,809	176,915	169,545	185,086	195,374
Michigan	248,414	273,799	531,137	644,734	697,634	782,804	874,483
Minnesota	21,370	44,893	79,467	139,345	160,363	189,495	214,480
Mississippi	1,662	4,887	15,444	30,532	40,277	48,289	53,505
Missouri	5,829	18,118	71,905	129,851	141,372	166,339	189,161
Montana	1,213	2,415	5,328	8,822	12,968	17,436	20,150
Nebraska	2,468	20,044	37,667	52,378	57,055	66,177	71,708
Nevada	3,487	5,556	9,844	16,210	23,346	32,080	37,641
New Hampshire	2,089	11,621	17,542	20,604	22,659	27,360	31,497
New Jersey	94,005	143,225	245,697	281,923	326,879	372,506	407,849
New Mexico	1,680	4,614	8,672	14,416	16,792	19,088	27,117
New York	136,361	174,454	269,218	373,718	437,371	487,738	536,374
North Carolina	9,168	30,830	69,768	120,344	140,222	167,894	197,254
North Dakota	1,723	2,723	5,483	10,414	12,309	15,599	18,693
Ohio	22,832	34,862	180,696	489,515	552,649	665,999	714,132
Oklahoma	1,826	5,233	16,365	32,169	39,922	46,540	52,170
Oregon	88,502	38,052	53,470	78,374	91,252	107,435	124,929
Pennsylvania	186,718	285,829	459,950	614,222	699,676	775,782	814,480
Puerto Rico	1,916	31,985	66,164	74,535	77,252	84,329	97,357
Rhode Island	3,575	7,196	11,823	20,044	21,609	24,880	26,671
South Carolina	3,545	7,461	33,581	52,320	58,857	68,798	79,280
South Dakota	1,407	2,847	6,275	11,024	13,119	15,881	18,112
Tennessee	8,976	19,077	38,406	71,502	77,032	84,818	116,152
Texas	8,207	17,941	61,184	132,318	192,797	251,157	309,502
Utah	6,624	13,594	24,766	38,071	43,895	52,610	56,199
Vermont	1,449	2,828	5,682	9,353	11,023	13,518	15,831
Virgin Islands	260	684	3,018	3,131	3,338	4,049	4,992
Virginia	9,197	13,617	58,859	110,560	129,919	145,114	151,919
Washington	27,018	41,643	72,320	175,750	222,409	267,455	307,251
West Virginia	1,592	3,434	9,724	21,658	23,527	35,561	49,016
Wisconsin	34,267	56,041	154,701	241,272	276,712	293,460	332,814
Wyoming	520	1,017	3,229	7,155	9,079	11,220	13,810
Nationwide total	1,332,847	2,024,184	3,917,399	6,010,125	6,885,619	7,964,522	8,909,166

Source: Office of Child Support Enforcement.

TABLE 11–15.—TOTAL AFDC COLLECTIONS, SELECTED FISCAL YEARS 1979–93

[In thousands of dollars]

State	1979	1983	1987	1990	1991	1992	1993
Alabama	6,830	7,789	15,050	19,484	22,788	23,001	22,539
Alaska	334	1,780	4,242	8,160	9,940	11,145	11,722
Arizona	642	1,459	4,805	6,102	7,401	12,693	18,616
Arkansas	2,428	4,593	8,771	11,799	13,800	15,766	16,249
California	117,532	136,963	198,152	248,440	286,261	314,232	335,235
Colorado	3,525	9,330	11,155	16,765	19,281	23,287	26,197
Connecticut	11,416	20,628	26,403	27,405	33,816	37,744	41,292
Delaware	1,386	2,276	4,150	5,826	6,661	7,306	7,798
District of Columbia .	907	2,421	2,912	4,118	4,407	4,927	5,197
Florida	8,598	10,408	33,511	48,364	57,071	69,765	78,081
Georgia	4,772	11,355	25,244	45,937	57,765	74,546	84,627
Guam	159	259	299	520	1,635	2,524	2,344
Hawaii	2,544	4,482	5,698	8,343	7,699	8,161	9,058
Idaho	2,047	3,806	5,034	6,952	7,482	8,543	8,746
Illinois	9,916	18,971	38,705	44,149	48,968	58,842	55,749
Indiana	8,116	17,646	31,466	38,124	45,030	49,247	52,040
Iowa	10,654	19,978	27,834	28,552	30,585	35,401	36,775
Kansas	3,454	7,807	12,155	15,209	17,454	20,869	22,402
Kentucky	4,615	6,316	11,676	22,286	27,502	34,702	36,565
Louisiana	5,244	9,641	15,798	20,861	23,089	25,975	26,827
Maine	4,133	8,402	15,557	21,089	21,063	21,477	25,683
Maryland	10,929	27,773	27,417	42,318	37,162	46,348	51,313
Massachusetts	29,145	40,476	53,962	68,968	66,969	71,784	77,292
Michigan	76,375	97,694	127,508	145,251	153,690	168,317	169,581
Minnesota	14,510	25,708	35,822	43,950	47,802	53,305	55,961
Mississippi	1,556	4,544	7,596	14,530	19,494	21,523	21,641
Missouri	4,165	11,500	23,525	38,056	37,021	49,653	51,153
Montana	685	1,834	3,365	4,394	5,251	6,413	6,464
Nebraska	2,083	3,675	6,160	6,990	7,431	9,195	9,797
Nevada	517	1,824	2,673	3,311	4,465	6,807	7,021
New Hampshire	2,089	2,649	2,744	3,606	4,385	6,337	7,638
New Jersey	28,622	41,103	58,890	61,473	76,644	83,509	84,020
New Mexico	1,160	2,891	4,120	5,573	6,421	7,850	12,922
New York	56,588	68,622	102,115	134,040	157,582	174,587	184,583
North Carolina	7,714	18,795	33,249	46,176	54,712	64,004	70,304
North Dakota	1,379	2,011	3,517	5,103	5,600	6,016	6,098
Ohio	21,974	33,403	66,866	76,888	84,304	100,833	105,719
Oklahoma	1,260	3,648	7,143	11,875	14,894	17,682	18,784
Oregon	12,977	12,645	14,744	18,877	21,989	25,637	28,357
Pennsylvania	33,190	47,135	77,932	96,328	113,735	123,784	124,490
Puerto Rico	439	917	1,803	1,707	1,600	1,428	1,344
Rhode Island	3,438	4,217	6,064	10,168	10,550	13,486	14,954
South Carolina	3,065	6,015	13,218	15,933	17,779	21,066	24,588
South Dakota	1,137	2,175	3,058	3,717	4,213	4,888	5,056
Tennessee	3,871	5,567	12,086	22,926	27,865	22,777	33,422
Texas	6,370	10,879	19,703	39,659	47,255	59,165	66,199
Utah	5,442	11,643	11,733	14,999	16,261	18,939	19,488
Vermont	1,201	2,626	4,079	5,578	6,380	6,649	7,638
Virgin Islands	143	140	241	210	233	282	343
Virginia	9,081	11,758	15,536	27,770	33,910	38,281	39,610
Washington	18,319	26,495	38,429	65,291	77,402	91,083	100,337
West Virginia	1,430	3,311	5,647	4,085	6,859	9,500	16,867
Wisconsin	26,044	39,582	57,468	59,303	61,179	63,813	65,439
Wyoming	379	790	1,489	2,584	3,226	3,749	4,345
Nationwide total	596,532	879,862	1,348,520	1,750,125	1,983,962	2,258,844	2,416,511

Source: Office of Child Support Enforcement.

TABLE 11-16.—TOTAL NON-AFDC COLLECTIONS, SELECTED FISCAL YEARS 1979-93

[In thousands of dollars]

State	1979	1983	1987	1990	1991	1992	1993
Alabama	16	854	24,926	46,691	58,165	75,140	$90,733
Alaska	3,510	7,924	12,897	18,628	20,781	24,468	27,426
Arizona	5,769	9,104	15,309	21,735	25,875	33,754	47,963
Arkansas	1,494	2,808	7,496	14,211	18,984	26,299	32,899
California	82,412	117,623	196,730	274,205	304,982	339,449	401,620
Colorado	496	7,848	11,221	22,836	27,715	34,743	41,527
Connecticut	11,617	18,599	30,779	39,319	41,960	46,445	52,161
Delaware	4,428	5,821	9,721	14,335	16,032	18,620	18,865
District of Columbia	179	1,100	2,778	9,481	12,171	14,806	16,601
Florida	1,926	8,672	48,248	128,239	157,081	182,707	211,896
Georgia	783	2,084	22,838	67,158	85,249	99,921	120,939
Guam	(¹)	131	327	920	1,527	2,172	2,659
Hawaii	2,606	5,605	10,287	19,295	22,397	26,243	28,269
Idaho	454	884	8,457	15,957	15,960	19,302	23,381
Illinois	823	13,054	50,917	91,870	101,167	124,467	128,140
Indiana	957	3,142	29,147	58,021	65,087	75,368	89,125
Iowa	2,363	9,701	20,682	42,430	50,109	60,645	72,503
Kansas	520	2,114	10,044	29,749	37,379	45,183	37,199
Kentucky	266	13,387	20,780	37,711	46,426	59,200	67,022
Louisiana	7,434	16,113	24,250	39,665	44,898	58,398	76,227
Maine	441	1,833	6,864	14,652	15,490	16,528	19,280
Maryland	9,927	49,356	70,473	109,034	126,464	147,660	167,771
Massachusetts	7,193	31,844	74,846	107,948	102,576	113,302	118,082
Michigan	172,039	176,105	403,629	499,483	543,944	614,488	704,903
Minnesota	6,861	19,184	43,645	95,395	112,561	136,190	158,519
Mississippi	106	343	7,848	16,002	20,783	26,766	31,864
Missouri	1,664	6,618	48,380	91,795	104,351	116,686	138,008
Montana	528	582	1,963	4,427	7,718	11,024	13,686
Nebraska	385	16,369	31,507	45,387	49,624	56,983	61,911
Nevada	2,970	3,731	7,172	12,899	18,881	25,273	30,620
New Hampshire	0	8,972	14,798	16,999	18,274	21,023	23,859
New Jersey	65,383	102,122	186,808	220,450	250,235	288,997	323,829
New Mexico	520	1,722	4,552	8,843	10,371	11,239	14,195
New York	79,773	105,831	167,103	239,678	279,289	313,151	351,791
North Carolina	1,454	12,035	36,519	74,167	85,510	103,890	126,951
North Dakota	344	712	1,966	5,312	6,708	9,583	12,595
Ohio	858	1,459	113,830	412,627	468,346	565,166	608,413
Oklahoma	566	1,585	9,222	20,293	25,028	28,858	33,386
Oregon	75,525	25,406	38,726	59,497	69,263	81,798	96,572
Pennsylvania	153,528	238,694	382,018	517,893	517,893	651,998	689,990
Puerto Rico	1,477	31,068	64,360	72,828	75,652	82,901	96,014
Rhode Island	137	2,979	5,759	9,876	11,059	11,394	11,717
South Carolina	480	1,446	20,363	36,387	41,078	47,732	54,692
South Dakota	270	672	3,217	7,307	8,906	10,993	13,056
Tennessee	5,105	13,510	26,321	48,575	49,167	62,041	82,730
Texas	1,837	7,062	41,481	92,659	145,543	191,993	243,303
Utah	1,183	1,952	13,032	23,073	27,634	33,671	36,712
Vermont	249	202	1,603	3,775	4,643	6,869	8,193
Virgin Islands	116	544	2,777	2,920	3,105	3,767	4,649
Virginia	116	1,858	43,323	82,789	96,008	106,833	112,309
Washington	8,699	15,148	33,891	110,459	145,006	176,372	206,914
West Virginia	162	123	4,076	17,574	16,668	26,061	32,149
Wisconsin	8,224	16,459	97,233	181,969	215,533	229,647	267,374
Wyoming	141	227	1,739	4,571	5,853	7,471	9,465
Nationwide total	736,315	1,144,322	2,568,880	4,260,000	4,901,657	5,705,678	6,492,655

¹ Less than $500.

Source: Office of Child Support Enforcement.

TABLE 11–17.—AVERAGE NUMBER OF AFDC CHILD SUPPORT ENFORCEMENT CASES IN WHICH A COLLECTION WAS MADE, SELECTED FISCAL YEARS 1978–93

State	1978	1983	1985	1987	1989	1990	1991	1992	1993
Total	458,439	594,679	684,114	608,986	657,585	700,803	755,328	831,172	872,579
Alabama	7,966	16,301	9,133	11,572	12,316	10,860	8,347	9,209	9,077
Alaska	246	1,154	1,120	1,038	1,213	1,387	1,718	1,949	2,168
Arizona	819	1,164	1,851	1,470	2,545	3,128	1,930	2,822	3,343
Arkansas	2,509	3,683	5,207	5,506	6,278	6,372	7,071	8,188	8,301
California	92,325	86,277	103,742	74,081	84,367	89,304	104,903	116,118	123,776
Colorado	3,177	4,129	5,687	4,092	4,771	4,437	4,581	5,126	5,210
Connecticut	8,002	13,591	15,565	13,337	7,470	6,578	7,128	8,445	9,437
Delaware	1,156	2,254	2,891	2,858	2,111	2,223	2,495	2,663	2,913
District of Columbia	708	1,508	1,925	2,138	2,553	1,758	1,940	2,281	2,437
Florida	7,376	11,856	16,468	30,114	34,883	38,500	40,687	40,135	44,727
Georgia	6,350	7,826	6,657	10,710	14,833	19,310	23,280	24,729	26,676
Guam	(1)	186	206	197	182	339	573	616	683
Hawaii	1,757	2,718	4,622	3,175	3,831	2,658	2,773	4,651	4,551
Idaho	1,346	936	4,343	1,245	1,522	1,752	1,992	2,356	2,719
Illinois	9,624	15,551	18,299	14,352	14,986	16,968	23,511	23,639	26,028
Indiana	9,488	19,514	22,058	16,188	17,716	20,444	26,344	30,823	31,159
Iowa	8,396	10,135	11,871	7,015	7,241	7,289	7,153	7,681	7,365
Kansas	2,859	4,205	4,769	3,798	3,565	4,595	5,268	6,120	6,857
Kentucky	3,083	4,601	6,729	6,853	8,699	10,741	12,513	13,516	15,217
Louisiana	5,204	6,944	7,836	9,916	11,582	11,842	12,198	12,510	12,164
Maine	2,368	6,141	7,178	4,734	5,200	5,515	5,767	5,287	7,013
Maryland	14,002	15,576	15,861	9,073	5,250	9,237	18,330	19,366	18,684
Massachusetts	17,782	22,655	25,350	17,211	16,610	16,029	16,106	17,961	18,378
Michigan	61,985	73,442	59,049	58,364	47,388	51,747	46,647	45,112	45,211
Minnesota	9,818	12,891	14,872	12,442	13,822	14,192	12,658	14,563	16,440
Mississippi	1,846	3,216	3,742	4,544	6,410	7,237	8,808	9,604	10,157
Missouri	(2)	2,465	7,716	6,483	9,894	11,178	11,241	13,430	14,135
Montana	748	1,178	1,600	849	1,086	1,140	1,298	1,551	1,816
Nebraska	1,509	1,841	2,362	2,555	2,666	2,811	3,255	4,802	4,811
Nevada	494	2,261	2,370	1,645	1,917	2,269	2,404	3,096	3,506
New Hampshire	1,530	1,512	1,021	981	988	1,091	1,454	2,240	2,703
New Jersey	16,243	24,712	27,686	25,182	18,415	17,591	19,728	24,376	26,241
New Mexico	1,429	2,027	2,034	2,175	3,147	3,766	4,383	3,865	4,385
New York	36,287	44,168	48,979	30,993	36,695	40,219	46,382	51,290	51,407
North Carolina	11,232	12,089	14,216	17,089	19,157	20,381	24,699	28,028	29,649
North Dakota	759	1,193	1,656	1,130	1,338	1,647	1,665	1,597	1,579
Ohio	24,419	28,064	32,582	35,273	40,308	35,973	34,446	38,445	39,857
Oklahoma	1,101	2,487	3,543	1,468	6,605	7,787	3,895	4,794	5,294
Oregon	6,761	4,020	6,687	5,935	5,829	6,437	7,437	8,321	9,495
Pennsylvania	15,172	35,405	42,088	49,100	45,772	47,039	52,269	59,514	61,998
Puerto Rico	413	2,281	3,736	3,588	3,991	3,696	3,103	3,026	2,811
Rhode Island	2,419	2,441	3,233	3,092	4,141	4,295	3,100	3,346	4,070
South Carolina	3,343	4,182	5,785	10,495	13,954	14,614	15,349	16,764	19,026
South Dakota	1,087	1,223	1,532	1,887	1,744	1,234	1,262	1,526	1,642
Tennessee	4,705	6,642	8,336	9,430	13,114	16,659	11,625	12,179	11,391
Texas	5,446	4,099	5,652	9,167	13,509	15,447	18,229	20,387	23,075
Utah	3,784	5,346	5,209	3,627	3,652	3,333	3,669	3,973	4,033
Vermont	953	2,223	2,329	1,984	2,462	2,596	2,826	3,556	4,114
Virgin Islands	232	82	199	220	184	133	135	165	193
Virginia	4,729	13,554	13,054	10,813	11,854	14,138	16,761	18,679	19,399
Washington	14,860	14,160	15,895	18,110	22,921	27,063	23,263	28,618	27,020
West Virginia	1,430	2,044	2,331	2,107	2,426	2,484	2,622	3,347	4,108
Wisconsin	16,868	26,106	44,799	26,847	31,438	30,143	30,426	32,693	31,984
Wyoming	294	420	453	738	1,034	1,197	1,681	2,094	2,146

[1] Data not reported for this item or insufficient data reported to perform indicated computation.
[2] Less than $500.

Source: Office of Child Support Enforcement.

TABLE 11–18.—AVERAGE NUMBER OF NON-AFDC CHILD SUPPORT ENFORCEMENT CASES IN WHICH A COLLECTION WAS MADE, SELECTED FISCAL YEARS 1978–93

State	1978	1983	1985	1987	1989	1990	1991	1992	1993
Total	248,590	507,031	653,803	934,177	1,247,228	1,362,821	1,554,740	1,749,427	1,953,580
Alabama	110	221	5,023	11,583	16,602	19,971	28,512	33,741	39,586
Alaska	2,309	3,035	3,205	3,184	3,637	3,947	4,211	4,598	4,997
Arizona	(1)	5,525	4,770	4,668	6,740	7,333	9,144	11,107	10,283
Arkansas	764	2,803	3,613	5,074	7,241	8,473	11,232	15,088	18,449
California	69,696	66,164	64,686	77,448	91,029	96,101	101,913	97,597	104,864
Colorado	1,017	3,647	3,976	4,537	6,054	7,281	9,008	10,492	11,360
Connecticut	(1)	7,826	9,392	9,884	10,606	11,289	13,289	14,441	15,721
Delaware	3,210	3,611	4,395	5,073	6,380	6,770	8,058	8,303	9,191
District of Columbia	93	478	1,007	1,264	2,653	4,252	4,964	5,704	6,278
Florida	1,200	8,002	7,593	25,573	50,995	56,329	66,748	67,948	77,734
Georgia	1,207	4,091	5,487	14,883	24,992	30,217	34,545	35,419	40,698
Guam	(1)	63	65	114	207	378	495	616	803
Hawaii	(1)	308	352	2,804	6,682	8,103	10,398	15,305	16,299
Idaho	455	591	1,047	2,529	5,540	6,493	7,403	8,689	9,889
Illinois	196	6,433	10,030	14,479	21,781	26,184	36,363	36,246	40,744
Indiana	450	1,784	2,881	12,759	17,990	25,586	27,111	34,855	36,865
Iowa	671	4,192	4,913	3,441	10,807	12,400	14,103	16,352	19,266
Kansas	210	1,449	758	5,260	9,308	11,520	13,855	16,003	18,846
Kentucky	255	3,657	3,647	15,549	13,686	17,473	20,489	23,531	28,950
Louisiana	6,866	9,517	10,636	11,695	14,883	16,739	20,001	24,194	28,146
Maine	638	296	1,496	3,862	5,774	6,425	6,510	5,479	7,630
Maryland	130	27,384	26,154	12,685	15,969	27,339	49,380	52,024	54,989
Massachusetts	(1)	0	0	26,549	27,950	22,921	14,264	24,605	25,899
Michigan	(1)	51,304	88,675	126,187	120,969	115,081	129,461	133,652	141,489
Minnesota	2,766	10,263	12,615	16,137	23,502	26,712	27,174	35,791	43,272
Mississippi	81	320	1,319	4,348	6,937	7,917	10,077	12,997	16,007
Missouri	(1)	1,631	5,362	14,676	22,802	26,994	32,317	38,492	41,022
Montana	444	348	344	800	1,012	1,448	2,208	2,748	3,750
Nebraska	176	4,942	7,874	10,540	13,464	14,748	14,883	15,185	17,771
Nevada	4,026	4,084	5,360	3,212	4,085	4,451	5,327	6,676	7,819
New Hampshire	(1)	5,433	4,939	5,474	5,809	5,260	5,875	7,077	7,870
New Jersey	20,000	38,557	45,868	51,706	65,947	66,885	68,753	78,789	84,267
New Mexico	286	1,806	2,249	2,462	4,490	5,360	5,758	5,947	5,849
New York	39,623	54,296	63,829	67,460	78,638	83,651	94,031	103,924	108,419
North Carolina	1,715	5,910	10,137	15,323	22,584	27,632	31,810	37,172	43,884
North Dakota	154	171	266	865	1,427	1,911	2,357	3,320	4,026
Ohio	1,430	4,594	10,853	39,114	100,069	101,553	107,806	135,535	149,104
Oklahoma	(1)	1,269	1,968	4,867	8,635	10,509	8,558	8,479	10,707
Oregon	17,957	16,262	19,331	20,620	23,747	25,657	19,754	21,810	25,063
Pennsylvania	49,621	92,084	108,498	123,248	140,750	147,885	171,525	182,098	190,671
Puerto Rico	710	17,908	26,873	30,490	35,346	35,295	36,731	33,075	41,130
Rhode Island	57	1,407	1,969	2,750	3,559	3,705	3,017	3,060	3,291
South Carolina	203	1,198	2,777	3,165	4,671	4,896	10,393	25,764	27,771
South Dakota	297	512	502	2,175	3,154	2,739	3,262	3,881	4,607
Tennessee	6,360	10,271	12,156	14,957	21,649	28,174	31,554	35,358	40,003
Texas	2,861	4,224	8,833	15,079	26,643	37,741	51,039	65,152	79,037
Utah	400	698	1,068	4,008	5,437	6,738	8,605	9,704	10,573
Vermont	181	194	393	967	1,459	1,659	1,870	2,433	3,154
Virgin Islands	1	262	1,288	1,252	1,499	1,247	1,301	1,348	1,538
Virginia	38	1,554	876	19,273	26,638	31,492	34,242	38,267	46,760
Washington	4,822	7,422	9,802	13,656	24,331	34,791	46,930	55,788	64,929
West Virginia	130	186	288	1,953	5,246	8,045	7,555	9,513	11,971
Wisconsin	4,685	6,719	20,288	41,953	63,554	56,769	65,718	70,780	88,601
Wyoming	89	125	77	563	1,669	2,352	2,853	3,275	1,738

[1] Data not reported for this item or insufficient data reported to perform indicated computation.

Source: Office of Child Support Enforcement.

TABLE 11-19.—SUPPORT ORDERS ESTABLISHED, ENFORCED, AND MODIFIED TO INCLUDE HEALTH INSURANCE, FISCAL YEAR 1993

State	Total number of orders established	Total number with health insurance	Percent with health insurance	Total number of orders enforced or modified	Total number enforced or modified with health insurance	Percent with health insurance
Alabama	13,671	3,127	22.87	296,358	5,351	1.81
Alaska	1,259	1,217	96.66	1,207	870	72.08
Arizona	3,898	3,405	87.35	156,764	10,789	6.88
Arkansas	6,954	5,811	83.56	4,702	3,990	84.86
California	104,092	80,317	77.16	594,850	363,218	61.06
Colorado	7,355	5,735	77.97	29,463	14,497	49.20
Connecticut	20,448	10,001	48.91	104,204	37,691	36.17
Delaware	1,634	1,632	99.88	3,693	3,682	99.70
District of Columbia	1,428	660	46.22	4,510	NA	0
Florida	11,892	NA	0	46,388	NA	0
Georgia	33,303	33,303	100.00	474,018	9,581	2.02
Guam	380	358	94.21	578	499	86.33
Hawaii	2,553	2,553	100.00	1,060	1,060	100.00
Idaho	2,630	2,630	100.00	69,399	6,246	9.00
Illinois	21,479	7,548	35.14	7,770	2,124	27.34
Indiana	34,882	NA	0	NA	NA	0
Iowa	10,345	8,903	86.06	228,412	77,990	34.14
Kansas	6,627	6,053	91.34	117,887	32,802	27.82
Kentucky	36,589	3,564	9.74	43,530	128	0.29
Louisiana	17,345	16,649	95.99	103,682	59,051	56.95
Maine	4,243	2,528	59.58	10,080	1,096	10.87
Maryland	17,139	13,416	78.28	69,111	10,715	15.50
Massachusetts	12,106	6,077	50.20	13,102	6,349	48.46
Michigan	36,121	36,121	100.00	925,860	39,269	4.24
Minnesota	15,966	11,948	74.83	32,975	23,533	71.37
Mississippi	8,726	NA	0	7,779	NA	0
Missouri	24,647	16,926	68.67	86,297	38,578	44.70
Montana	20,438	288	1.41	6,187	3,601	58.20
Nebraska	3,728	836	22.42	855	150	17.54
Nevada	4,189	2,259	53.93	36,363	1,393	3.83
New Hampshire	2,759	4,024	145.85	14,420	1,238	8.59
New Jersey	28,064	14,425	51.40	194,291	23,189	11.94
New Mexico	4,377	3,025	69.11	1,294	843	65.16
New York	34,433	13,770	39.99	42,884	17,151	39.99
North Carolina	33,313	21,730	66.23	9,200	1,868	20.30
North Dakota	1,608	1,483	92.23	2,186	108	4.94
Ohio	38,166	19,329	50.64	232,759	47,212	20.28
Oklahoma	7,541	4,195	55.63	7,333	1,403	19.13
Oregon	13,049	10,659	81.68	51,173	19,086	37.30
Pennsylvania	105,333	59,590	56.57	369,348	165,558	44.82
Puerto Rico	13,716	NA	0	1,941	91	4.69
Rhode Island	2,820	1,604	56.88	9,910	4,080	41.17
South Carolina	10,439	7,837	75.07	22,068	14,900	67.52
South Dakota	1,533	1,449	94.52	10,764	8,876	82.48
Tennessee	98,464	3,296	3.35	32,843	11,183	34.05
Texas	34,463	34,483	100.00	64,537	18,258	28.29
Utah	7,080	5,376	75.93	204,877	128,339	62.64
Vermont	1,124	1,124	100.00	3,969	3,969	100.00
Virgin Islands	412	157	38.11	1,049	329	31.35
Virginia	41.496	17,887	43.11	68,550	15,321	22.36
Washington	35,897	26,374	73.47	467,001	306,612	65.66
West Virginia	2,568	2,428	94.55	4,561	1,442	31.62
Wisconsin	28,378	9,095	32.05	88,485	49,526	55.97
Wyoming	4,583	3,178	69.34	4,333	322	7.43
Nationwide totals	1,037,683	550,363	53.04	5,386,860	1,595,157	29.61

Source: Office of Child Support Enforcement.

512

TABLE 11–20.—PERCENTAGE OF AFDC ASSISTANCE PAYMENTS RECOVERED THROUGH CHILD SUPPORT COLLECTIONS, SELECTED FISCAL YEARS 1979–93

State	1979	1985	1987	1989	1990	1991	1992	1993
Total	5.8	7.3	9.1	10.0	10.3	10.7	11.4	12.0
Alabama	8.5	21.0	23.2	30.8	31.7	33.7	27.0	23.8
Alaska	1.5	4.6	8.3	12.6	13.7	14.6	12.7	11.9
Arizona	2.0	2.5	5.1	3.8	4.4	4.2	5.4	7.1
Arkansas	4.8	15.2	17.6	21.0	20.7	23.6	26.5	28.0
California	6.5	4.5	6.1	6.0	5.9	6.3	6.5	7.1
Colorado	4.8	9.3	9.5	11.4	12.3	13.0	15.0	16.7
Connecticut	6.5	10.1	12.2	12.7	9.5	10.2	10.5	11.2
Delaware	4.4	14.6	17.3	21.2	20.3	20.6	19.7	19.8
District of Columbia	1.0	3.3	3.8	4.7	4.9	4.5	4.7	4.6
Florida	5.5	10.0	11.5	11.9	11.6	11.1	9.9	9.6
Georgia	4.3	9.8	10.4	12.4	14.3	15.4	18.2	20.1
Guam	5.3	6.4	9.1	11.9	10.8	32.7	34.6	28.7
Hawaii	2.9	6.6	8.9	7.3	8.8	7.4	6.9	6.7
Idaho	8.9	22.6	25.0	33.2	35.7	34.7	36.5	35.3
Illinois	1.5	3.2	4.8	5.0	5.6	5.7	7.0	6.6
Indiana	7.2	16.1	21.5	23.0	22.4	23.8	24.0	24.5
Iowa	9.0	15.0	19.3	19.2	20.1	20.6	23.2	24.3
Kansas	5.0	11.6	14.1	13.4	15.9	17.8	19.4	19.7
Kentucky	3.8	6.8	8.5	12.0	12.4	15.0	18.8	20.0
Louisiana	5.2	8.4	9.1	10.5	11.1	12.4	14.2	15.3
Maine	7.3	13.4	20.6	26.1	22.9	21.5	18.8	24.5
Maryland	6.1	11.6	11.2	13.0	14.5	11.4	14.2	16.9
Massachusetts	6.6	11.3	10.7	12.0	11.8	10.4	10.5	11.4
Michigan	9.0	9.7	12.5	13.0	13.9	15.1	15.7	16.6
Minnesota	7.8	10.5	12.7	14.2	14.4	14.6	16.3	17.3
Mississippi	2.9	7.9	9.4	13.7	16.8	22.3	24.2	24.9
Missouri	2.8	9.6	12.0	15.0	17.8	15.6	19.0	18.9
Montana	4.4	10.7	8.6	9.9	11.1	12.9	16.0	15.0
Nebraska	5.4	10.0	11.5	12.9	13.0	13.2	16.0	16.9
Nevada	6.3	14.9	16.4	12.4	12.2	14.1	17.1	16.6
New Hampshire	9.4	12.4	15.2	12.4	11.3	10.1	12.3	14.4
New Jersey	5.9	9.7	12.5	14.4	14.0	16.4	16.5	16.4
New Mexico	3.4	7.3	7.4	9.4	9.2	7.8	8.0	11.6
New York	3.5	4.0	5.0	5.6	6.4	6.7	7.2	7.0
North Carolina	5.6	15.0	17.4	18.9	18.8	18.4	19.6	20.5
North Dakota	9.6	14.7	16.8	17.4	21.0	23.4	24.0	24.1
Ohio	4.8	6.2	10.1	9.9	10.0	10.3	11.7	12.2
Oklahoma	1.6	7.5	6.4	8.0	9.0	9.9	10.7	11.1
Oregon	9.0	13.3	13.0	13.0	13.5	13.5	12.5	13.4
Pennsylvania	4.6	8.4	11.0	13.2	12.6	13.7	14.0	13.7
Puerto Rico	.7	2.4	2.7	2.3	2.4	2.1	1.8	1.7
Rhode Island	6.1	7.0	7.6	8.9	10.4	9.2	10.8	11.6
South Carolina	5.4	8.6	13.1	15.9	16.8	16.8	17.9	21.1
South Dakota	6.5	12.9	14.4	17.9	17.1	18.1	18.8	19.5
Tennessee	5.0	6.5	10.3	14.1	13.7	14.3	11.2	15.7
Texas	5.4	6.9	6.2	9.4	9.5	10.2	11.8	12.9
Utah	13.7	22.7	19.6	22.1	23.4	23.2	25.6	26.2
Vermont	4.1	8.4	11.1	13.4	12.7	13.0	12.7	14.7
Virgin Islands	8.5	7.6	8.3	7.9	7.3	7.1	8.5	10.2
Virginia	6.3	8.3	9.0	13.5	15.7	17.2	17.3	17.3
Washington	12.5	9.8	10.9	14.4	17.1	18.1	20.0	20.8
West Virginia	2.6	5.1	7.8	6.1	5.1	8.1	10.6	18.2
Wisconsin	9.5	8.8	12.4	15.4	15.5	15.7	16.2	17.0
Wyoming	5.6	5.5	8.2	10.0	13.5	13.3	14.3	17.0

Note: Payments to AFDC Unemployed Parent (UP) families have been excluded from the maintenance assistance payments totals in those States having AFDC–UP programs.

Source: Office of Child Support Enforcement.

TABLE 11–21.—FEDERAL INCOME TAX REFUND OFFSET PROGRAM COLLECTIONS, FISCAL YEARS 1983–93

[In thousands of dollars]

State	1983	1985	1987	1989	1990	1991	1992	1993
Alabama	1,555	3,208	5,135	7,450	8,009	8,827	20,586	17,321
Alaska	212	364	891	995	1,208	1,387	1,711	1,357
Arizona	385	1,062	2,049	2,592	2,605	2,876	4,007	8,049
Arkansas	1,104	1,886	3,770	4,490	4,669	5,575	7,106	6,631
California	35,034	34,926	46,287	50,472	57,624	57,098	67,569	60,173
Colorado	3,016	2,393	3,020	4,947	5,604	6,179	7,614	7,430
Connecticut	4,455	4,224	6,140	12,132	9,907	9,250	10,190	8,863
Delaware	166	1,284	1,319	1,812	1,966	2,467	2,683	2,223
District of Columbia	567	747	779	1,202	1,942	1,606	1,788	1,646
Florida	1,980	3,938	7,318	21,294	21,038	24,880	31,569	29,354
Georgia	1,526	3,711	7,258	11,566	13,032	15,693	22,016	21,778
Guam	13	14	44	26	13	11	51	42
Hawaii	817	846	1,122	1,511	1,573	1,976	2,328	3,496
Idaho	1,183	1,204	1,594	1,959	2,173	2,270	2,690	2,473
Illinois	4,525	9,019	15,415	13,887	19,307	18,876	26,631	19,924
Indiana	4,940	8,975	11,390	15,642	15,860	16,853	21,169	18,882
Iowa	5,526	6,784	7,798	8,990	8,828	9,439	11,240	9,941
Kansas	2,525	2,905	3,704	4,947	5,300	6,101	7,525	6,782
Kentucky	1,165	2,299	3,262	6,812	6,680	7,891	12,919	11,390
Louisiana	1,536	2,487	4,722	5,797	6,582	6,519	8,438	9,182
Maine	1,844	2,126	3,377	4,866	5,383	4,925	5,477	4,611
Maryland	5,688	6,118	9,646	17,039	14,343	14,182	15,542	14,867
Massachusetts	3,325	4,225	5,269	10,101	11,899	10,936	13,077	10,841
Michigan	18,250	20,013	25,893	30,246	29,854	32,776	44,968	42,748
Minnesota	5,576	5,904	6,762	7,936	8,096	8,831	9,904	8,734
Mississippi	1,019	1,976	2,252	4,147	4,958	6,392	8,270	8,389
Missouri	4,289	4,849	8,482	12,438	14,205	10,189	17,711	15,498
Montana	431	858	1,209	1,366	1,301	1,374	1,636	1,597
Nebraska	502	1,205	1,395	2,598	2,485	2,548	3,121	3,068
Nevada	354	389	433	630	768	1,363	2,449	2,184
New Hampshire	757	662	1,284	1,137	1,177	1,350	2,028	1,906
New Jersey	9,458	11,449	14,268	16,201	16,171	18,266	20,132	17,253
New Mexico	533	1,315	2,278	2,279	2,585	2,863	3,259	2,905
New York	9,945	11,996	27,991	23,472	24,763	31,307	33,734	29,445
North Carolina	4,235	4,291	7,229	11,359	11,270	12,718	16,410	16,971
North Dakota	352	534	848	773	1,302	1,501	1,767	1,586
Ohio	2,886	7,229	11,186	14,346	16,514	21,027	27,476	27,305
Oklahoma	703	2,179	2,218	4,197	4,647	5,803	7,575	6,752
Oregon	3,782	3,567	4,863	5,113	5,381	5,622	6,259	5,364
Pennsylvania	6,112	13,550	17,123	21,332	24,354	27,946	32,560	27,636
Puerto Rico	2	13	13	47	6	63	231	208
Rhode Island	838	775	880	1,401	1,548	1,522	1,799	1,359
South Carolina	368	832	1,789	2,788	3,233	3,449	4,678	5,091
South Dakota	374	623	998	1,465	1,498	1,648	2,110	1,925
Tennessee	642	1,592	3,025	7,110	7,539	8,341	16,033	12,126
Texas	3,906	5,928	11,316	17,934	19,926	24,133	34,346	35,816
Utah	2,540	2,765	2,991	3,730	4,066	4,297	5,604	5,184
Vermont	611	748	887	1,154	1,017	1,074	1,294	1,031
Virgin Islands	....	....	37	34	7	25	44	62
Virginia	1,674	3,532	6,840	8,913	9,761	10,298	12,594	12,108
Washington	4,278	6,201	10,510	12,537	13,732	13,957	17,417	16,447
West Virginia	1,038	1,823	2,013	2,944	3,066	3,265	3,705	3,378
Wisconsin	6,266	7,973	10,029	12,902	13,290	14,384	17,486	17,117
Wyoming	222	280	503	534	684	1,131	1,190	888
Nationwide total	175,021	229,798	338,853	443,594	474,748	515,279	661,711	609,336

Source: Office of Child Support Enforcement.

TABLE 11–22.—ADMINISTRATIVE EXPENDITURES FOR THE CHILD SUPPORT ENFORCEMENT PROGRAM, SELECTED FISCAL YEARS 1979–93

[In thousands of dollars]

State	1979	1987	1988	1989	1990	1991	1992	1993
Alabama	4,633	14,878	17,839	23,101	23,802	30,212	31,572	34,594
Alaska	2,137	5,625	5,751	5,699	6,464	8,450	9,084	10,559
Arizona	2,014	9,096	10,052	13,212	18,744	21,675	29,555	37,121
Arkansas	2,385	5,532	6,870	6,724	9,284	10,931	13,341	15,336
California	75,579	156,472	160,416	176,209	201,823	225,008	252,868	290,648
Colorado	3,861	11,806	13,746	15,160	14,043	14,590	21,494	27,450
Connecticut	5,463	19,682	22,097	24,412	27,135	28,465	28,363	29,288
Delaware	852	4,519	5,924	6,006	6,448	7,988	9,007	11,133
District of Columbia	1,652	5,876	5,745	7,116	7,630	8,825	8,455	8,697
Florida	7,047	41,385	46,094	55,167	66,445	74,947	83,228	76,721
Georgia	3,238	15,200	22,588	29,030	36,927	39,586	40,954	45,968
Guam	108	411	465	641	1,163	1,808	2,509	2,652
Hawaii	1,408	5,157	4,170	5,417	7,598	7,419	8,739	9,837
Idaho	1,063	3,321	4,320	4,822	5,697	7,309	7,691	9,360
Illinois	6,930	35,746	39,467	40,719	52,073	57,029	63,146	77,820
Indiana	4,269	11,601	13,119	14,458	15,643	15,626	19,006	21,897
Iowa	4,239	7,925	8,733	11,043	14,227	16,063	16,591	21,241
Kansas	1,819	8,609	11,037	16,256	16,290	15,970	17,708	23,166
Kentucky	4,027	12,533	15,621	19,460	23,519	31,727	31,637	33,985
Louisiana	7,079	17,587	17,108	17,970	19,408	27,101	30,756	32,263
Maine	1,229	5,986	6,306	7,917	9,351	11,729	12,838	13,274
Maryland	8,177	32,384	33,791	38,281	39,805	43,013	43,254	48,042
Massachusetts	6,710	37,266	37,083	51,432	46,587	50,618	44,298	45,445
Michigan	24,614	55,775	65,825	71,196	82,380	86,420	94,058	103,693
Minnesota	9,273	22,656	27,480	33,242	38,947	42,877	44,399	51,081
Mississippi	1,574	4,590	6,230	10,883	19,551	22,943	21,717	24,272
Missouri	5,355	15,811	20,797	22,814	27,577	29,766	34,096	43,941
Montana	943	1,685	1,865	1,669	3,223	4,659	7,327	7,306
Nebraska	1,378	7,242	8,559	10,312	11,698	14,125	18,683	17,201
Nevada	1,891	4,285	5,537	5,912	7,654	9,247	10,493	15,759
New Hampshire	847	3,292	3,825	5,042	5,558	7,912	8,401	10,971
New Jersey	21,677	54,968	65,428	69,957	77,113	93,525	92,697	101,411
New Mexico	1,437	4,347	5,608	6,258	7,213	8,376	8,307	8,808
New York	61,665	136,254	126,133	119,132	146,468	153,007	151,589	172,888
North Carolina	5,721	18,234	25,951	32,113	37,868	44,495	52,514	61,668
North Dakota	702	2,071	2,256	2,541	2,879	3,432	3,971	4,619
Ohio	11,581	32,001	28,784	64,637	67,891	92,006	124,551	130,380
Oklahoma	2,771	7,384	8,651	11,450	14,073	16,532	17,284	16,682
Oregon	7,475	13,267	13,985	15,164	17,457	20,364	21,078	25,229
Pennsylvania	19,639	60,842	60,040	62,328	70,542	87,180	83,729	89,583
Puerto Rico	862	3,495	4,156	5,789	10,795	5,476	8,084	8,302
Rhode Island	1,079	3,570	4,052	4,413	7,945	7,507	10,750	6,124
South Carolina	1,777	11,150	12,522	15,379	20,127	19,539	19,148	20,437
South Dakota	1,060	2,118	2,358	2,588	2,785	2,963	3,292	3,700
Tennessee	3,046	12,507	12,389	16,482	16,709	18,050	21,904	21,430
Texas	11,733	23,522	29,733	45,563	68,709	77,055	99,077	134,053
Utah	3,094	10,379	10,453	11,307	12,317	15,689	17,072	19,626
Vermont	649	1,956	2,116	2,897	2,588	3,229	4,794	5,168
Virgin Islands	483	730	824	990	749	1,613	969	1,109
Virginia	4,787	24,399	31,738	31,573	47,061	41,482	49,972	49,212
Washington	10,733	28,293	35,926	47,853	56,189	65,314	81,400	89,812
West Virginia	1,676	4,870	6,740	6,201	7,869	9,238	11,952	17,677
Wisconsin	7,562	24,959	31,512	35,719	41,906	41,404	42,982	46,552
Wyoming	160	696	901	1,552	2,121	2,592	2,306	5,897
Nationwide total	383,163	1,065,942	1,170,714	1,363,209	1,606,065	1,804,106	1,994,690	2,241,094

Source: Office of Child Support Enforcement.

TABLE 11–23.—TOTAL CHILD SUPPORT COLLECTIONS PER DOLLAR OF TOTAL ADMINISTRATIVE EXPENDITURES, SELECTED FISCAL YEARS 1978–93

State	1978	1985	1986	1987	1988	1989	1990	1991	1992	1993
U.S. ratio	3.35	3.31	3.45	3.68	3.94	3.85	3.75	3.82	3.99	3.98
Alabama	.75	2.00	2.45	2.69	2.50	2.46	2.78	2.68	3.11	3.27
Alaska	3.19	2.26	2.61	3.05	3.46	4.06	4.14	3.64	3.92	3.71
Arizona	.88	2.15	1.46	2.21	2.11	1.84	1.49	1.54	1.57	1.79
Arkansas	1.00	1.90	2.62	2.94	2.94	3.38	2.80	3.00	3.15	3.20
California	2.15	2.32	2.37	2.52	2.75	2.66	2.59	2.63	2.59	2.54
Colorado	1.78	2.08	1.89	1.90	1.99	2.21	2.82	3.22	2.70	2.47
Connecticut	4.20	3.38	3.49	2.91	2.73	2.76	2.46	2.73	2.97	3.19
Delaware	7.14	5.62	2.46	3.07	2.62	3.01	3.13	2.87	2.88	2.39
District of Columbia	.73	1.06	.92	.97	1.21	1.33	1.78	1.88	2.33	2.51
Florida	1.20	2.10	2.12	1.98	2.28	2.58	2.66	2.86	3.03	3.78
Georgia	2.22	2.23	2.59	3.16	2.88	3.06	3.06	3.61	4.26	4.47
Guam	....	1.46	1.39	1.53	1.62	1.28	1.24	1.98	1.87	1.89
Hawaii	1.71	2.38	2.26	3.10	3.62	3.62	3.64	4.06	3.94	3.79
Idaho	2.10	1.93	3.58	4.06	3.79	3.95	4.02	3.21	3.62	3.43
Illinois	2.10	2.14	2.40	2.51	2.68	2.77	2.61	2.63	2.90	2.36
Indiana	2.42	3.79	4.82	5.22	5.49	5.34	6.15	7.27	6.56	6.45
Iowa	3.49	5.92	6.77	6.12	6.36	5.66	4.99	5.02	5.79	5.14
Kansas	3.01	2.05	2.15	2.58	2.51	2.00	2.76	3.43	3.73	2.57
Kentucky	1.14	2.68	2.52	2.59	2.44	2.63	2.55	2.33	2.97	3.05
Louisiana	1.82	2.13	1.99	2.28	2.60	2.85	3.12	2.51	2.74	3.19
Maine	3.40	3.98	3.74	3.75	4.01	4.14	3.82	3.06	2.84	3.39
Maryland	2.14	3.86	3.77	3.02	3.31	3.36	3.80	3.80	4.49	4.56
Massachusetts	5.12	3.57	3.50	3.46	4.09	3.24	3.80	3.41	4.18	4.30
Michigan	9.50	7.62	8.33	9.52	8.80	8.58	7.83	8.07	8.20	8.43
Minnesota	2.15	2.91	3.02	3.51	3.59	3.65	3.58	3.74	4.27	4.20
Mississippi	.87	2.02	2.29	3.36	3.06	2.23	1.56	1.76	2.22	2.20
Missouri	.89	3.24	3.89	4.55	4.22	4.45	4.71	4.75	4.88	4.30
Montana	1.58	2.46	2.59	3.16	2.97	4.21	2.74	2.78	2.38	2.76
Nebraska	2.10	6.32	5.44	5.20	5.02	4.69	4.48	3.83	3.54	4.17
Nevada	1.83	2.04	2.10	2.30	1.95	2.22	2.12	2.52	3.06	2.39
New Hampshire	4.05	4.96	4.39	5.33	4.93	3.18	3.71	2.86	3.26	2.87
New Jersey	4.16	4.67	4.64	4.47	4.12	3.85	3.66	3.49	4.02	4.02
New Mexico	1.17	1.90	2.27	1.99	1.76	1.96	2.00	2.00	2.30	3.08
New York	1.75	1.96	1.83	1.98	2.36	2.74	2.55	2.81	3.22	3.10
North Carolina	1.50	2.94	3.26	3.83	3.32	3.20	3.18	3.15	3.20	3.20
North Dakota	1.83	2.29	2.46	2.65	3.14	3.31	3.62	3.59	3.93	4.05
Ohio	2.50	3.38	4.41	5.65	10.83	6.07	7.21	6.01	5.35	5.48
Oklahoma	.76	1.46	1.78	2.22	2.48	2.28	2.29	2.41	2.69	3.13
Oregon	9.48	4.05	4.47	4.03	4.27	4.45	4.49	4.48	5.10	4.95
Pennsylvania	9.14	6.68	7.78	7.56	8.52	8.97	8.71	8.03	9.27	9.09
Puerto Rico	.92	11.95	14.02	18.93	17.60	13.61	7.84	15.68	10.43	11.73
Rhode Island	3.51	3.52	3.90	3.31	3.65	3.67	2.52	2.22	2.31	4.35
South Carolina	2.38	1.70	2.37	3.01	3.23	3.01	2.60	3.01	3.59	3.88
South Dakota	.99	2.36	2.74	2.96	3.50	3.99	3.96	4.43	4.82	4.90
Tennessee	2.49	2.88	3.31	3.07	4.09	3.57	4.28	4.27	3.87	5.42
Texas	.74	2.17	2.01	2.60	2.81	2.41	1.93	2.50	2.53	2.31
Utah	1.99	1.95	2.21	2.39	2.86	2.92	3.09	2.80	3.08	2.86
Vermont	2.24	2.58	2.34	2.95	3.31	2.93	3.61	3.77	2.82	3.06
Virgin Islands	.40	3.27	2.14	4.13	4.16	3.11	4.18	2.07	4.10	4.50
Virginia	.72	1.85	1.57	2.41	2.39	3.03	2.35	3.13	2.91	3.09
Washington	2.96	2.48	2.42	2.56	2.48	2.66	3.13	3.41	3.29	3.42
West Virginia	.74	1.66	1.98	2.00	2.16	2.95	2.75	2.55	2.98	2.77
Wisconsin	3.80	3.73	4.78	6.20	6.01	6.18	5.76	6.68	6.83	7.15
Wyoming	3.18	1.64	3.27	4.64	4.91	3.50	3.37	3.50	4.87	2.34

Source: Office of Child Support Enforcement.

TABLE 11–24.—AFDC CHILD SUPPORT COLLECTIONS PER DOLLAR OF TOTAL ADMINISTRATIVE EXPENDITURES, FISCAL YEARS 1980–93

State	1980	1983	1985	1987	1989	1990	1991	1992	993
Alabama	1.22	0.85	1.16	1.01	0.81	0.82	.75	.73	.65
Alaska	.26	.44	.43	.75	1.21	1.26	1.18	1.23	1.11
Arizona	.27	.25	.27	.53	.34	.33	.34	.43	.50
Arkansas	.75	1.01	1.20	1.59	1.73	1.27	1.26	1.18	1.06
California	1.05	1.08	1.17	1.27	1.29	1.23	1.27	1.24	1.15
Colorado	.68	1.17	1.06	.94	.98	1.19	1.32	1.08	.95
Connecticut	2.05	1.73	1.66	1.34	1.24	1.01	1.26	1.33	1.41
Delaware	1.68	.69	2.02	.92	.88	.90	.83	.81	.70
District of Columbia	.48	.49	.59	.50	.51	.54	.50	.58	.60
Florida	1.11	.66	1.21	.81	.76	.73	.76	.84	1.02
Georgia	1.38	1.38	1.63	1.66	1.23	1.24	1.46	1.82	1.84
Guam	.79	.82	.95	.73	.55	.45	.92	1.01	.88
Hawaii	1.41	1.21	1.05	1.10	1.14	1.10	1.04	.93	.92
Idaho	1.99	1.77	1.43	1.52	1.27	1.22	1.02	1.11	.93
Illinois	1.07	1.16	1.09	1.08	.92	.85	.86	.93	.72
Indiana	1.66	2.61	2.77	2.71	2.58	2.44	2.93	2.59	2.38
Iowa	2.69	3.29	4.11	3.51	2.41	2.01	1.90	2.13	1.73
Kansas	1.35	1.50	1.75	1.41	.79	.93	1.09	1.18	.97
Kentucky	.82	.82	1.01	.93	.96	.95	.87	1.10	1.08
Louisiana	.86	.75	.81	.90	1.08	1.07	.85	.84	.83
Maine	2.78	2.86	2.97	2.60	2.63	2.26	1.74	1.53	1.93
Maryland	1.27	1.70	1.30	.85	.88	1.06	.86	1.07	1.07
Massachusetts	3.12	2.04	1.68	1.45	1.35	1.57	1.32	1.62	1.70
Michigan	2.91	2.36	2.50	2.29	1.94	1.76	1.78	1.74	1.64
Minnesota	1.36	1.48	1.52	1.58	1.27	1.13	1.11	1.20	1.10
Mississippi	1.14	1.55	1.41	1.65	1.07	.74	.85	.99	.89
Missouri	.78	1.27	1.69	1.49	1.35	1.38	1.24	1.46	1.16
Montana	.83	1.63	2.01	2.00	2.35	1.36	1.13	.88	.88
Nebraska	1.56	1.04	1.24	.85	.65	.60	.53	.49	.57
Nevada	.28	.53	.48	.62	.51	.43	.48	.65	.45
New Hampshire	2.09	1.21	.98	.83	.60	.65	.55	.75	.70
New Jersey	1.24	1.14	1.19	1.07	.88	.80	.77	.90	.83
New Mexico	.76	.90	1.13	.95	.82	.77	.77	.94	1.47
New York	.75	.79	.78	.75	.99	.91	1.02	1.15	1.07
North Carolina	1.29	1.53	1.54	1.82	1.29	1.22	1.23	1.22	1.14
North Dakota	1.68	1.61	1.67	1.70	1.65	1.77	1.63	1.51	1.32
Ohio	1.65	1.68	1.94	2.09	1.09	1.13	.92	.81	.81
Oklahoma	.40	.60	1.04	.97	.87	.84	.90	1.02	1.13
Oregon	1.40	1.15	1.44	1.11	1.11	1.08	1.08	1.22	1.12
Pennsylvania	1.35	1.10	1.13	1.28	1.49	1.37	1.30	1.48	1.39
Puerto Rico	.62	.27	.34	.52	.28	.16	.30	.18	.16
Rhode Island	2.52	1.97	2.09	1.70	1.72	1.28	1.08	1.25	2.44
South Carolina	2.04	2.08	1.19	1.19	.93	.79	.91	1.10	1.20
South Dakota	1.29	1.81	1.73	1.44	1.49	1.33	1.42	1.48	1.37
Tennessee	.92	.79	.72	.97	1.21	1.37	1.54	1.04	1.56
Texas	.49	.72	1.14	.84	.76	.58	.61	.60	.49
Utah	1.45	1.71	1.33	1.13	1.24	1.22	1.04	1.11	.99
Vermont	1.87	2.74	2.21	2.14	1.78	2.16	2.33	1.39	1.48
Virgin Islands	.28	.44	.29	.33	.23	.28	.14	.28	.31
Virginia	1.33	1.53	1.58	.64	.72	.59	.82	.77	.80
Washington	1.51	1.56	1.40	1.36	1.11	1.16	1.19	1.12	1.12
West Virginia	.96	1.30	1.61	1.16	.77	.52	74	.79	.95
Wisconsin	2.34	1.92	2.21	2.30	1.68	1.42	1.48	1.48	1.41
Wyoming	2.29	2.12	1.06	2.14	1.19	1.22	1.24	1.63	.74
Nationwide total	1.30	1.27	1.34	1.27	1.17	1.09	1.10	1.13	1.08

Source: Office of Child Support Enforcement.

517

TABLE 11–25.—NON–AFDC CHILD SUPPORT COLLECTIONS PER DOLLAR OF TOTAL ADMINISTRATIVE EXPENDITURES, FISCAL YEARS 1980–93

State	1980	1983	1985	1987	1989	1990	1991	1992	1993
Alabama	0.00	0.09	0.83	1.68	1.65	1.96	1.93	2.38	2.62
Alaska	1.82	1.97	1.83	2.29	2.86	2.88	2.46	2.69	2.60
Arizona	1.81	1.55	1.87	1.68	1.50	1.16	1.19	1.14	1.29
Arkansas	.68	.62	.70	1.35	1.65	1.53	1.74	1.97	2.15
California	1.10	.92	1.15	1.26	1.38	1.36	1.36	1.34	1.38
Colorado	.40	.98	1.01	.95	1.23	1.63	1.90	1.62	1.51
Connecticut	1.99	1.56	1.73	1.56	1.52	1.45	1.47	1.64	1.78
Delaware	4.71	1.76	3.60	2.15	2.12	2.22	2.04	2.07	1.69
District of Columbia	.14	.22	.47	.47	.82	1.24	1.38	1.75	1.91
Florida	.16	.55	.90	1.17	1.82	1.93	2.10	2.20	2.76
Georgia	.18	.25	.59	1.50	1.83	1.82	2.15	2.44	2.63
Guam	.01	.42	.51	.80	.74	.79	1.06	.87	1.00
Hawaii	2.02	1.51	1.32	1.99	2.48	2.54	3.02	3.00	2.87
Idaho	.52	.41	.49	2.55	2.68	2.80	2.18	2.51	2.50
Illinois	.11	.80	1.04	1.42	1.85	1.76	1.77	1.97	1.65
Indiana	.26	.46	1.02	2.51	2.77	3.71	4.34	3.97	4.07
Iowa	.69	1.64	1.81	2.61	3.25	2.98	3.12	3.66	3.41
Kansas	.31	.41	.30	1.17	1.21	1.83	2.34	2.55	1.61
Kentucky	2.26	1.74	1.67	1.66	1.67	1.60	1.46	1.87	1.97
Louisiana	1.07	1.25	1.32	1.38	1.76	2.04	1.66	1.90	2.36
Maine	.38	.62	1.01	1.15	1.51	1.57	1.32	1.31	1.45
Maryland	1.28	3.02	2.56	2.18	2.48	2.74	2.94	3.41	3.49
Massachusetts	1.16	1.61	1.89	2.01	1.89	2.32	2.09	2.56	2.60
Michigan	7.96	4.26	5.12	7.24	6.64	6.06	6.29	6.45	6.80
Minnesota	.72	1.11	1.39	1.93	2.38	2.45	2.63	3.07	3.10
Mississippi	.10	.12	.61	1.71	1.16	.82	.91	1.23	1.31
Missouri	.74	.73	1.55	3.06	3.11	3.33	3.51	3.42	3.14
Montana	.69	.52	.45	1.17	1.86	1.37	1.66	1.50	1.87
Nebraska	.30	4.62	5.08	4.35	4.04	3.88	3.30	3.05	3.60
Nevada	.98	1.09	1.55	1.67	1.71	1.69	2.04	2.41	1.94
New Hampshire	.08	4.08	3.98	4.50	2.58	3.06	2.31	2.50	2.17
New Jersey	2.90	2.83	3.47	3.40	2.97	2.86	2.73	3.12	3.19
New Mexico	.34	.54	.77	1.05	1.14	1.23	1.24	1.35	1.61
New York	1.47	1.22	1.18	1.23	1.75	1.64	1.79	2.07	2.03
North Carolina	.28	.98	1.40	2.00	1.91	1.96	1.92	1.98	2.06
North Dakota	.43	.57	.62	.95	1.66	1.84	1.95	2.41	2.73
Ohio	.06	.07	1.43	3.56	4.98	6.08	5.09	4.54	4.67
Oklahoma	.19	.26	.42	1.25	1.41	1.44	1.51	1.67	2.00
Oregon	8.15	2.30	2.61	2.92	3.34	3.41	3.40	3.88	3.83
Pennsylvania	6.70	5.56	5.55	6.28	7.48	7.34	6.72	7.79	7.70
Puerto Rico	1.56	9.21	11.61	18.42	13.32	6.75	15.38	10.25	11.57
Rhode Island	.10	1.39	1.43	1.61	1.95	1.24	1.14	1.06	1.91
South Carolina	.39	.50	.51	1.83	2.08	1.81	2.10	2.49	2.68
South Dakota	.38	.56	.64	1.52	2.50	2.62	3.01	3.34	3.53
Tennessee	1.55	1.92	2.16	2.10	2.36	2.91	2.72	2.83	3.86
Texas	.19	.47	1.03	1.76	1.65	1.35	1.89	1.94	1.81
Utah	.31	.29	.62	1.26	1.68	1.87	1.76	1.97	1.87
Vermont	.35	.21	.37	.82	1.15	1.46	1.44	1.43	1.59
Virgin Islands	.46	1.70	2.97	3.80	2.88	3.90	1.92	3.81	4.19
Virginia	.08	.24	.27	1.78	2.31	1.76	2.31	2.14	2.28
Washington	.85	.89	1.08	1.20	1.55	1.97	2.22	2.17	2.30
West Virginia	.07	.05	.05	.84	2.18	2.23	1.80	2.18	1.82
Wisconsin	.65	.80	1.52	3.90	4.50	4.34	5.21	5.34	5.74
Wyoming	.96	.61	.58	2.50	2.31	2.16	2.26	3.24	1.61
Nationwide total	1.88	1.66	1.97	2.41	2.68	2.65	2.72	2.86	2.90

Source: Office of Child Support Enforcement.

TABLE 11–26.—TOTAL NUMBER OF PATERNITIES ESTABLISHED, SELECTED FISCAL YEARS 1979–93

State	1979	1983	1987	1989	1990	1991	1992	1993
Total	137,645	208,270	269,161	339,243	393,304	472,105	515,857	553,135
Alabama	6,161	4,833	6,998	7,839	6,517	6,612	7,942	10,779
Alaska	3	105	364	797	767	673	906	1,070
Arizona	154	595	1,009	1,327	1,237	2,674	3,056	5,007
Arkansas	2,586	1,489	5,326	4,453	3,191	4,703	5,175	6,580
California	19,364	21,714	28,570	35,193	41,065	56,912	65,062	77,324
Colorado	1,046	1,033	1,291	1,939	1,864	2,887	4,135	5,258
Connecticut	3,029	4,563	3,908	3,888	4,499	5,309	6,196	5,368
Delaware	205	1,346	1,867	1,641	801	728	1,573	1,395
District of Columbia	386	811	1,021	2,079	2,791	3,895	2,792	2,884
Florida	7,078	10,679	12,136	13,399	19,534	17,907	16,119	10,879
Georgia	3,642	6,102	14,112	18,198	24,615	28,015	30,181	29,329
Guam	NA	173	122	109	563	884	642	440
Hawaii	854	1,181	1,061	1,295	1,843	1,672	1,419	1,746
Idaho	287	84	384	1,100	1,310	1,551	1,722	1,509
Illinois	3,025	7,339	20,848	29,926	25,496	21,157	18,900	19,017
Indiana	1,644	3,036	3,570	4,943	5,309	6,291	5,631	4,950
Iowa	575	922	1,664	1,980	3,045	1,904	4,416	4,952
Kansas	696	682	1,119	2,101	3,644	3,125	3,198	4,445
Kentucky	784	2,986	3,881	4,498	6,092	6,816	7,951	7,979
Louisiana	1,304	3,195	2,926	4,451	5,525	11,098	11,764	13,272
Maine	382	604	951	1,609	1,381	1,376	3,189	1,370
Maryland	13,307	8,211	6,671	9,995	7,538	12,081	11,259	9,993
Massachusetts	2,096	3,766	7,025	6,194	6,339	5,742	8,195	6,234
Michigan	7,529	17,374	18,274	23,142	25,574	27,955	29,087	28,076
Minnesota	1,786	2,994	3,856	6,098	5,661	7,695	5,348	3,749
Mississippi	932	1,797	1,824	7,929	10,740	11,950	8,978	8,588
Missouri	NA	17,522	14,308	11,146	16,242	21,976	23,982	24,292
Montana	92	37	179	388	429	677	1,155	413
Nebraska	NA	410	710	759	885	1,280	1,628	2,019
Nevada	233	409	531	664	1,033	1,655	1,702	1,602
New Hampshire	35	30	195	518	614	645	580	604
New Jersey	8,242	10,616	13,938	13,182	12,243	10,595	10,314	7,453
New Mexico	322	1,141	412	1,571	1,992	1,601	1,591	2,491
New York	17,503	15,884	18,239	18,056	20,492	30,197	34,434	42,748
North Carolina	6,592	7,368	9,916	11,663	14,504	18,186	19,308	21,371
North Dakota	293	440	1,134	820	784	935	1,446	1,386
Ohio	4,808	7,767	9,133	11,637	15,823	20,857	23,672	28,151
Oklahoma	43	1,811	512	1,361	2,710	4,939	2,721	2,764
Oregon	1,521	2,173	1,902	3,131	4,081	3,836	4,942	5,830
Pennsylvania	4,450	11,906	15,277	18,921	20,231	23,063	24,239	23,246
Puerto Rico	22	19	6	144	216	264	198	206
Rhode Island	347	451	601	673	868	764	1,425	2,001
South Carolina	1,378	2,552	3,994	5,243	5,273	6,066	6,996	8,331
South Dakota	60	172	552	504	509	687	916	1,333
Tennessee	5,003	6,592	7,666	9,647	8,976	10,309	10,902	11,463
Texas	202	1,085	684	6,465	12,623	19,627	24,890	30,002
Utah	487	1,546	1,292	1,801	2,087	2,484	2,957	3,496
Vermont	44	349	1,091	468	533	438	800	1,065
Virgin Islands	4	104	235	270	160	215	344	492
Virginia	1,452	2,351	2,667	8,471	13,647	15,971	18,038	21,506
Washington	656	1,700	4,066	5,762	6,985	8,601	10,540	12,539
West Virginia	156	467	288	820	997	1,324	2,373	2,790
Wisconsin	4,803	5,688	8,750	8,695	10,808	12,931	15,435	17,678
Wyoming	44	66	105	340	618	370	3,493	3,670

NA=Not available.

Source: Office of Child Support Enforcement.

TABLE 11–27.—OUT-OF-WEDLOCK BIRTHS AND IV–D PATERNITIES: 1987–91

State	Births to unmarried women					Paternities/births (percent)				
	1987	1988	1989	1990	1991	1987	1988	1989	1990	1991
Alabama	15,955	16,934	18,640	19,131	20,000	43.9	44.5	42.1	34.1	33.05
Alaska	2,564	2,627	2,869	3,113	3,148	14.2	22.9	27.8	24.6	21.38
Arizona	17,227	18,815	20,708	22,532	23,899	5.9	3.8	6.4	5.5	11.19
Arkansas	8,498	9,273	9,944	10,713	10,601	62.7	63.7	44.8	29.8	44.36
California	136,785	152,607	171,189	193,559	204,229	20.9	23.6	20.6	21.2	27.87
Colorado	10,171	10,431	10,787	11,374	12,684	12.7	14.8	18.0	16.4	22.76
Connecticut	11,045	11,460	13,005	13,330	13,581	35.4	30.4	29.9	33.8	39.09
Delaware	2,742	2,819	3,125	3,222	3,559	68.1	56.2	52.5	24.9	20.46
District of Columbia	6,094	6,507	7,580	7,692	7,806	16.8	16.2	27.4	36.3	49.90
Florida	48,200	52,867	58,305	63,169	64,101	25.2	28.1	23.0	30.9	27.94
Georgia	28,647	31,348	34,926	36,979	38,116	49.3	68.0	52.1	66.6	73.50
Hawaii	3,968	4,222	4,609	5,088	5,195	26.7	34.2	28.1	36.2	32.18
Idaho	2,073	2,216	2,561	2,738	2,924	18.5	26.6	43.0	47.8	53.04
Illinois	50,677	54,436	58,867	62,148	63,225	41.1	49.3	50.8	41.0	33.46
Indiana	17,260	18,543	19,898	22,562	24,294	20.7	27.7	24.8	23.5	25.90
Iowa	6,147	6,736	7,575	8,282	8,657	27.1	28.1	26.1	36.8	21.99
Kansas	6,633	7,025	7,577	8,397	8,746	16.9	21.4	27.7	43.4	35.73
Kentucky	10,658	11,206	12,048	12,829	13,796	36.4	38.4	37.3	47.5	49.41
Louisiana	23,594	24,752	25,692	26,601	27,694	12.4	14.0	17.3	20.8	40.07
Maine	3,338	3,489	3,806	3,931	4,180	28.5	50.9	42.3	35.1	32.92
Maryland	22,866	24,716	22,607	23,789	24,292	29.2	37.4	44.2	31.7	49.73
Massachusetts	17,616	19,559	21,798	22,886	22,873	39.9	41.4	28.4	27.7	25.10
Michigan	28,724	30,195	36,441	40,289	40,941	63.6	66.9	63.5	63.5	68.28
Minnesota	11,114	12,235	13,142	14,192	14,984	34.7	35.0	46.4	39.9	51.35
Mississippi	14,499	15,824	16,958	17,627	18,317	12.6	18.5	46.8	60.9	65.24
Missouri	17,823	19,124	21,123	22,643	23,736	80.3	40.9	52.8	71.7	92.59
Montana	2,379	2,430	2,539	2,757	2,898	7.5	13.0	15.3	15.6	23.36
Nebraska	4,006	4,333	4,662	5,056	5,181	17.7	17.7	16.3	17.5	24.71
Nevada	2,740	3,432	4,607	5,480	7,016	19.4	18.4	14.4	18.9	23.59
New Hampshire	2,511	2,503	2,797	2,967	2,996	7.8	13.8	18.5	20.7	21.53
New Jersey	26,647	28,580	29,364	29,756	31,972	52.3	45.6	44.9	41.1	33.14
New Mexico	8,067	8,711	9,447	9,704	10,445	5.1	11.2	16.6	20.5	15.33
New York	80,939	84,381	92,996	98,110	99,738	22.5	20.3	19.4	20.9	30.28
North Carolina	23,262	25,622	28,315	30,718	32,340	42.6	43.8	41.2	47.2	56.23
North Dakota	1,429	1,578	1,615	1,699	1,952	79.4	64.8	50.8	46.1	47.90
Ohio	39,237	42,448	45,921	48,289	50,826	23.3	19.7	25.3	32.8	41.04
Oklahoma	9,892	10,600	11,258	11,998	12,973	5.2	9.9	12.1	22.6	38.07
Oregon	8,672	9,435	10,436	11,041	11,324	21.9	18.9	30.0	37.0	33.87
Pennsylvania	41,143	43,919	47,093	49,258	51,360	37.1	36.7	40.2	41.1	44.90
Rhode Island	3,064	3,262	3,684	3,997	4,073	19.6	24.6	18.3	21.7	18.76
South Carolina	15,333	16,722	18,116	19,148	20,000	26.1	34.0	28.9	27.5	30.33
South Dakota	2,225	2,334	2,415	2,515	2,720	24.8	24.6	20.9	20.2	25.26
Tennessee	17,897	19,511	21,281	22,662	24,026	42.8	43.1	45.3	39.6	42.91
Texas	57,464	59,820	60,303	55,435	56,528	1.2	1.7	10.7	22.8	34.72
Utah	3,929	4,221	4,504	4,910	5,196	32.9	35.0	40.0	42.5	47.81
Vermont	1,459	1,510	1,685	1,666	1,811	74.8	115.0	27.8	32.0	24.19
Virginia	20,562	22,126	24,410	25,874	27,125	1.3	26.0	34.7	52.7	58.88
Washington	14,629	16,150	17,638	18,746	19,861	27.8	28.8	32.7	37.3	43.31
West Virginia	4,722	4,948	5,212	5,743	6,040	6.1	16.0	15.7	17.4	21.92
Wisconsin	14,698	15,528	16,815	17,656	18,235	59.5	55.8	51.7	61.2	70.91
Wyoming	1,189	1,229	1,276	1,383	1,546	8.8	6.4	26.7	44.7	23.93
U.S. total	933,013	1,005,299	1,094,169	1,165,384	1,213,769	28.8	30.5	31.0	33.7	38.78

Sources: National Center for Health Statistics. Monthly Vital Statistics Report, vol. 41, no. 9, Supplement, Feb. 25, 1993, page 36, U.S. Department of Health and Human Services, Office of Child Support Enforcement.

TABLE 11–28.—STATE SHARE OF SAVINGS FOR FIVE CONSECUTIVE FISCAL YEARS

[In thousands of dollars]

State	1989	1990	1991	1992	1993
Alabama	380	−518	−1,982	−3,053	−2,529
Alaska	2,264	2,469	2,982	3,431	3,797
Arizona	−1,219	−2,899	−3,125	−3,320	−4,242
Arkansas	1,574	1,013	1,830	1,009	530
California	79,779	76,552	88,584	98,465	101,406
Colorado	4,552	4,991	5,954	5,661	6,064
Connecticut	11,330	7,310	10,332	11,711	13,396
Delaware	797	812	923	902	455
District of Columbia	−3,145	−89	−574	144	757
Florida	5,601	2,932	7,179	11,482	14,368
Georgia	2,861	1,299	3,930	7,937	12,856
Guam	−87	−227	−293	−450	−305
Hawaii	1,648	1,622	1,502	1,655	1,873
Idaho	1,029	895	751	955	922
Illinois	10,935	5,159	5,785	9,767	3,716
Indiana	14,027	11,731	16,134	20,359	20,257
Iowa	11,767	11,631	10,840	11,765	11,000
Kansas	1,170	2,229	3,694	4,041	3,711
Kentucky	207	207	−475	1,958	3,467
Louisiana	696	150	−1,049	−1,845	−1,241
Maine	5,236	4,229	3,852	3,890	5,877
Maryland	6,860	8,631	6,120	10,366	12,037
Massachusetts	23,373	23,391	21,789	25,917	29,957
Michigan	57,413	54,088	58,032	53,107	52,078
Minnesota	13,969	12,083	11,468	12,377	12,274
Mississippi	−232	−2,987	−2,549	−1,243	−1,065
Missouri	8,046	9,002	7,846	11,772	10,303
Montana	1,093	769	454	532	618
Nebraska	−252	−572	−582	−2,093	−1,054
Nevada	−32	−417	−334	608	−172
New Hampshire	362	185	271	826	443
New Jersey	15,081	6,836	9,100	13,551	11,876
New Mexico	305	−148	−361	−224	1,278
New York	24,201	22,865	30,313	41,091	41,790
North Carolina	5,857	3,598	4,257	6,343	6,962
North Dakota	955	1,074	1,231	973	989
Ohio	21,558	12,040	6,054	445	3,453
Oklahoma	705	69	380	1,110	2,457
Oregon	3,703	2,658	3,358	4,863	5,935
Pennsylvania	22,018	19,846	21,226	27,102	29,234
Puerto Rico	−1,075	−3,121	−2,165	−2,008	−2,171
Rhode Island	2,999	3,439	3,940	4,375	5,427
South Carolina	490	−1,639	91	437	1,309
South Dakota	969	1,254	820	672	1,048
Tennessee	1,278	3,432	5,989	1,578	5,915
Texas	2,163	−4,832	−4,774	−6,111	13,969
Utah	1,362	1,111	892	980	343
Vermont	1,440	1,957	1,918	1,621	2,066
Virgin Islands	−223	−184	−459	−227	−256
Virginia	2,567	−1,113	4,292	4,324	6,347
Washington	15,386	14,053	22,038	19,695	24,875
West Virginia	−59	−1,214	−722	−1,047	16
Wisconsin	21,306	18,451	16,740	15,553	15,386
Wyoming	574	363	340	589	226
Nationwide total	403,400	338,469	384,691	433,317	462,092

Note.—Numbers may not sum to total due to rounding.

Source: Office of Child Support Enforcement.

Legislative Changes in the 103d Congress

1. State Paternity Establishment Programs

Public Law 103–66, the Omnibus Budget Reconciliation Act of 1993, increases the percentage of children for whom the State must establish paternity and requires States to adopt laws requiring civil procedures to voluntarily acknowledge paternity (including hospital-based programs).

2. Enforcement of Health Insurance Support

Public Law 103–66, the Omnibus Budget Reconciliation Act of 1993, requires States to adopt laws to ensure the compliance of health insurers and employers in carrying out court or administrative orders for medical child support and includes a provision that forbids health insurers to deny coverage to children who are not living with the covered individual or who were born outside of marriage.

TABLE 11–29.—CBO FEDERAL BUDGET COST ESTIMATES FOR CHILD SUPPORT ENFORCEMENT AMENDMENTS IN THE OMNIBUS BUDGET RECONCILIATION ACT OF 1993 (PUBLIC LAW 103–66)

[In millions of dollars]

	Fiscal years					Total
	1994	1995	1996	1997	1998	
Paternity establishment programs	0	0	−30	−70	−110	−210
Medical child support	0	−15	−20	−20	−25	−80
Total	0	−15	−50	−90	−135	−290

Source: Congressional Budget Office.

Legislative Changes in the 102d Congress

1. Criminal Penalties for Willful Failure to Pay Child Support in Interstate Cases

Public Law 102–521, the Child Support Recovery Act of 1992, imposes a Federal criminal penalty for the willful failure to pay a past-due child support obligation with respect to a child who resides in another State that has remained unpaid for longer than a year or is greater than $5,000. For the first conviction the penalty would be a fine of up to $5,000 and/or imprisonment for not more than 6 months; for a second conviction, a fine of not more than $250,000 and/or imprisonment for up to 2 years.

2. Inclusion of Child Support Debt Information By Consumer Credit Reporting Agencies

Public Law 102–537, the Ted Weiss Child Support Enforcement Act of 1992, amends the Fair Credit Reporting Act to require consumer credit reporting agencies to include in any consumer report information on child support delinquencies provided by or verified by State or local CSE agencies, which antedates the report by 7 years.

LEGISLATIVE CHANGES IN THE 101ST CONGRESS

1. Extension of IRS Intercept for non-AFDC Families

The Omnibus Budget Reconciliation Act of 1990 (P.L. 101–508) permanently extends the Federal provision that allows States to ask the IRS to collect child support arrearages of at least $500 out of income tax refunds otherwise due to noncustodial parents. The minor child restriction is to be eliminated for adults with a current support order who are disabled, as defined under OASDI or SSI. In addition, the offset can be used for spousal support when spousal and child support are included in the same support order.

2. Extension of Interstate Child Support Commission

The Omnibus Budget Reconciliation Act of 1990 (P.L. 101–508) extends the life of the Interstate Child Support Commission from July 1, 1991, to July 1, 1992, and requires it to submit its report no later than May 1, 1992. Also, the provision authorizes the Commission to hire its own staff.

3. Medicaid Transition in Child Support Cases

The Omnibus Budget Reconciliation Act of 1989 (P.L. 101–239) made permanent the requirement that Medicaid benefits continue for 4 months after a family loses AFDC eligibility as a result of collection of child support payments.

LEGISLATIVE CHANGES IN THE 100TH CONGRESS

During the second session of the 100th Congress, The Family Support Act of 1988 (P.L. 100–485) was enacted. It emphasized the duties of parents to work and support their children. The Act emphasized child support enforcement as the first line of defense against welfare dependence. It contained these provisions:

1. Guidelines for Child Support Award Amounts

Judges and other officials are required to use State guidelines for child support unless they are rebutted by a written finding that applying the guidelines would be unjust or inappropriate in a particular case. States must review guidelines for awards every 4 years. Beginning 5 years after enactment, States generally must review and adjust individual case awards every 3 years for AFDC cases. The same applies to other IV–D cases, except review and adjustment must be at the request of a parent.

2. Establishment of Paternity

States are required to meet Federal standards for the establishment of paternity. The standard relates to the percentage obtained by dividing the number of children in the State who are born out of wedlock, are receiving cash benefits or IV–D child support services, and for whom paternity has been established by the number of children who are born out of wedlock and are receiving cash benefits or IV–D child support services. To meet Federal requirements, this percentage in a State must: (1) be at least 50 percent; (2) be at least equal to the average for all States; or (3) have increased by 3 percentage points from fiscal years 1988 to 1991 and by 3 percentage points each year thereafter.

States are mandated to require all parties in a contested paternity case to take a genetic test upon request of any party.

The Federal matching rate for laboratory testing to establish paternity is set at 90 percent.

3. Disregard of Child Support

The child support enforcement disregard authorized under the Deficit Reduction Act of 1984 is clarified so that it applies to a payment made by the noncustodial parent in the month it was due even though it was received in a subsequent month.

4. Requirement for Prompt State Response

The Secretary of Health and Human Services is required to set time limits within which States must accept and respond to requests for assistance in establishing and enforcing support orders as well as time limits within which child support payments collected by the State IV-D agency must be distributed to the families to whom they are owed.

5. Requirement for Automated Tracking and Monitoring System

Every State that does not have a Statewide automated tracking and monitoring system in effect must submit an advance planning document that meets Federal requirements by October 1, 1991. The Secretary must approve each document within 9 months after submission. By October 1, 1995, every State must have an approved system in effect. Federal matching rates of 90 percent for this activity will expire after September 30, 1995.

6. Interstate Enforcement

A Commission on Interstate Child Support is established to hold one or more national conferences on interstate child support enforcement reform, and to report to Congress no later than October 1, 1990 on recommendations for improvements in the system and revisions in the Uniform Reciprocal Enforcement of Support Act.

7. Exclude Interstate Demonstration Grants in Computing Incentive Payments

Amounts spent by States for interstate demonstration projects are excluded from calculating the amount of the States' incentive payments.

8. Use of INTERNET System

The Secretaries of Labor and HHS are required to enter into an agreement to give the Federal Parent Locator Service prompt access to wage and unemployment compensation claims information useful in locating absent parents.

9. Wage Withholding

With respect to IV-D cases, each State must provide for immediate wage withholding in the case of orders that are issued or modified on or after the first day of the 25th month beginning after the date of enactment unless: (1) one of the parties demonstrates, and the court finds, that there is good cause not to require such withholding; or (2) there is a written agreement between both parties providing for an alternative arrangement. Present law requirements for mandatory wage withholding in cases where payments are in arrears apply to orders that are not subject to immediate wage withholding.

States are required to provide for immediate wage withholding for all support orders initially issued on or after January 1, 1994, regardless of whether a parent has applied for IV–D services.

10. Work and Training Demonstration Programs for Noncustodial Parents

The Secretary of HHS is required to grant waivers to up to 5 States to allow them to provide services to noncustodial parents under the JOBS program. No new power is granted to the States to require participation by noncustodial parents.

11. Data Collection and Reporting

The Secretary of HHS is required to collect and maintain State-by-State statistics on paternity determination, location of absent parent for the purpose of establishing a support obligation, enforcement of a child support obligation, and location of absent parent for the purpose of enforcing or modifying an established obligation.

12. Use of Social Security Number

Each State must, in the administration of any law involving the issuance of a birth certificate, require each parent to furnish his or her social security number (SSN), unless the State finds good cause for not requiring the parent to furnish it. The SSN shall not appear on the birth certificate, and the use of the SSN obtained through the birth record is restricted to child support enforcement purposes except under certain circumstances.

13. Notification of Support Collected

Each State is required to inform families receiving AFDC of the amount of support collected on their behalf on a monthly basis, rather than annually as provided under present law. States may provide quarterly notification if the Secretary of HHS determines that monthly reporting imposes an unreasonable administrative burden. This provision is effective 4 years after the date of enactment.

TABLE 11–30.—CBO FEDERAL BUDGET COST ESTIMATES FOR CHILD SUPPORT EN-FORCEMENT AMENDMENTS IN THE FAMILY SUPPORT ACT OF 1988 (PUBLIC LAW 100–485)

[In millions of dollars]

	Fiscal years—				
	1990	1991	1992	1993	Total
Mandate income withholding	....	− 25	− 55	− 90	− 170
Mandate child support guidelines	− 25	− 70	− 115	− 160	− 370
Mandate increases in paternity establishment	....	40	25	15	80
Mandate ADP for most States	2	7	7	7	23
Other	10	9	6	8	33
Total	− 13	− 39	− 132	− 220	− 404

Source: Congressional Budget Office.

The Omnibus Budget Reconciliation Act of 1987 (P.L. 100–203) required States to provide child support enforcement services to all families with an absent parent who receives Medicaid and have assigned their support rights to the State, regardless of whether they are receiving AFDC.

LEGISLATIVE CHANGES IN THE 99TH CONGRESS

During the second session of the 99th Congress, Public Law 99–509 was enacted. Titled the Omnibus Budget Reconciliation Act of 1986, the new law included one child support enforcement amendment prohibiting the retroactive modification of child support awards. Under this new requirement, State laws must provide for either parent to apply for modification of an existing order with notice provided to the other parent. No modification is permitted before the date of this notification.

LEGISLATIVE CHANGES IN THE 98TH CONGRESS

In November 1983, the House of Representatives adopted H.R. 4325, the Child Support Enforcement Amendments, which had been developed by the Subcommittee on Public Assistance and Unemployment Compensation and approved by the Committee on Ways and Means. In August 1984, the amendments were signed into law. The new law strengthens the child support enforcement and paternity establishment program. It requires States to implement effective enforcement tools and provides incentives to the States to make available services to both AFDC and non-AFDC families. The main provisions of the Child Support Enforcement Amendments of 1984 (P.L. 98–378) are summarized below:

1. Improved child support enforcement through requiring State laws and procedures.—States are required to enact laws establishing the following procedures with respect to their IV–D cases:

A. Mandatory wage withholding for all families (AFDC and non-AFDC) if support payments are delinquent in an amount equal to

1 month's support. States must also allow absent parents to request withholding at an earlier date.

B. Imposing liens against real and personal property for amounts of overdue support.

C. Withholding of State tax refunds payable to a parent of a child receiving IV–D services, if the parent is delinquent in support payments.

D. Making available information regarding the amount of overdue support owed by an absent parent, to any consumer credit bureau, upon request of such organization.

E. Requiring individuals who have demonstrated a pattern of delinquent payments to post a bond, or give some other guarantee to secure payment of overdue support.

F. Establishing expedited processes within the State judicial system or under administrative procedures for obtaining and enforcing child support orders and, at the option of the State, for determining paternity.

G. Notifying each AFDC recipient at least once each year of the amount of child support collected on behalf of that recipient.

H. Permitting the establishment of paternity until a child's 18th birthday.

I. At the option of the State, providing that child support payments must be made through the agency that administers the State's income withholding system if either the custodial or noncustodial parent requests that they be made in this manner.

2. *Federal matching of administrative costs.*—The Federal matching share is gradually reduced from 70 percent as follows: 68 percent in fiscal years 1988 and 1989, and 66 percent in fiscal year 1990 and each year thereafter.

3. *Federal incentive payments.*—The prior incentive formula which gave States 12 percent of their AFDC collections (paid for out of the Federal share of the collections) is replaced with a new formula that is designed to encourage States to develop programs that emphasize collections on behalf of both AFDC and non-AFDC families, and to improve program cost effectiveness. The basic incentive payment will be equal to 6 percent of the State's AFDC collections, and 6 percent of its non-AFDC collections. States may qualify for higher incentive payments, up to a maximum of 10 percent of collections, if their AFDC or non-AFDC collections exceed combined administrative costs for both AFDC and non-AFDC components of the program.

The total dollar amount of incentives paid for non-AFDC families may not exceed the amount of the State's incentive payment for AFDC collections for fiscal years 1986 and 1987. However, thereafter the incentive paid for non-AFDC collections will be capped at an amount equal to 105 percent of the incentive for AFDC collections in fiscal year 1988, 110 percent in fiscal year 1989, and 115 percent in fiscal year 1990 and any fiscal year thereafter.

4. *Matching for automated management systems used in income withholding and other procedures.*—The Act specifies that the 90 percent Federal matching rate that is currently available to States that elect to establish an automatic data processing and information retrieval system may be used, at the option of the State, for the development and improvement of the income withholding and

other procedures required in the new law through the monitoring of child support payments, the maintenance of accurate records regarding the payment of child support, and the provision of prompt notice to appropriate officials with respect to any arrearages that occur. Also, the Act specifies that the 90 percent matching is available to pay for the acquisition of computer hardware.

5. *Fees for services to non-AFDC families.*—States will be required to charge an application fee for non-AFDC cases not to exceed $25. The amount of the maximum allowable fee may be adjusted periodically by the Secretary to reflect changes in administrative costs. The State may charge the fee against the custodial parent, pay the fee out of State funds, or recover the fee from the noncustodial parent.

In addition, at the option of the State, a late payment fee equal to between 3 and 6 percent of the amount of overdue support may be charged to the noncustodial parents of AFDC and non-AFDC families. The State may not take any action which would have the effect of reducing the amount of support paid to the child and will collect the fee only after the full amount of the support has been paid to the child. The late payment fee provision is effective upon enactment.

6. *Continuation of support enforcement for AFDC recipients whose benefits are being terminated.*—States must provide that families whose eligibility for AFDC is terminated due to the receipt of (or an increase in) child support payments will be automatically transferred from AFDC to non-AFDC status under the IV–D program, without requiring application for IV–D services or payment of a fee.

7. *Special project grants to promote improvement in interstate enforcement.*—The Secretary is authorized to make demonstration grants to States which propose to undertake new or innovative methods of support collection in interstate cases. The authorization is $7 million in FY 1985, $12 million in FY 1986, and $15 million in FY 1987 and years thereafter.

8. *Periodic review of State programs; modification of penalty.*—The Director of the Federal Office of Child Support Enforcement is required to conduct audits at least every 3 years to determine whether the standards and requirements prescribed by law and regulations have been met. Under the penalty provision, a State's AFDC matching funds must be reduced by an amount equal to at least 1 but no more than 2 percent for the first failure to comply substantially with the standards and requirements, at least 2 but no more than 3 percent for the second failure, and at least 3 but no more than 5 percent for the third and any subsequent consecutive failures.

9. *Extension of sec. 1115 demonstration authority to the child support program.*—The sec. 1115 demonstration authority is expanded to include the child support enforcement program under specified conditions.

10. *Child support enforcement for certain children in foster care.*—State child support agencies are required to undertake child support collections on behalf of children receiving foster care maintenance payments under title IV–E, if an assignment of rights to support to the State has been secured by the foster care agency. In addition, foster care agencies are required to take steps, where ap-

propriate, to secure an assignment to the State of any rights to support on behalf of a child receiving foster care maintenance payments under the title IV–E foster care program.

11. Collection of spousal support.—Child support enforcement services must include the enforcement of spousal support, but only if a support obligation has been established with respect to the spouse, the child and spouse are living in the same household, and child support is being collected along with spousal support.

12. Modification in content of annual report by the Secretary.— The present annual report information requirements are expanded to include data needed to evaluate State programs.

13. Requirement to publicize the availability of child support services.—States must frequently publicize, through public service announcements, the availability of child support enforcement services, together with information as to the application fee for such services and a telephone number or postal address to be used to obtain additional information.

14. State commissions on child support.—The Governor of each State is required to appoint a State Commission on Child Support. The Commission must include representation from all aspects of the child support system including custodial and non-custodial parents, the IV–D agency, the judiciary, the Governor, the legislature, child welfare and social services agencies, and others.

Each State commission is to examine the functioning of the State child support system with regard to securing support and parental involvement for both AFDC and non-AFDC children, including but not limited to such specific problems as: (1) visitation; (2) establishment of appropriate objective standards for support; (3) enforcement of interstate obligations; and (4) additional Federal and State legislation needed to obtain support for all children.

15. Requirement to include medical support as part of any child support order.—The Secretary of Health and Human Services is required to issue regulations to require State agencies to petition to include medical support as part of any child support order whenever health care coverage is available to the absent parent at a reasonable cost. The regulations must also provide for improved information exchange between the State IV–D agencies and the medicaid agencies with respect to the availability of health insurance coverage.

16. Increased availability of Federal parent locator services to State agencies.—The prior law requirement that the States exhaust all State child support locator resources before they request the assistance of the Federal Parent Locator Service is repealed.

17. Extension of medicaid eligibility when support collection results in termination of AFDC eligibility.—If a family loses AFDC eligibility as the result (wholly or partly) of increased collection of support payments under the IV–D program, the State must continue to provide medicaid benefits for 4 calendar months beginning with the month of ineligibility. (The family must have received AFDC in at least 3 of the 6 months immediately preceding the month of ineligibility.)

18. Guidelines for determining support obligations.—Each State must develop guidelines to be used at the discretion of the court or administrative entity in determining support obligations.

19. Availability of social security numbers for purposes of child support enforcement.—The absent parent's social security number may be disclosed to child support agencies both through the Federal Parent Locator Service and by the IRS.

20. Collection of overdue support from Federal tax refunds.—Prior law requires the Secretary of the Treasury, upon receiving notice from a State child support agency that an individual owes past due support which has been assigned to the State as a condition of AFDC eligibility, to withhold from any tax refunds due that individual an amount equal to any past due support. The act extends this requirement to provide for withholding of refunds on behalf of non-AFDC families, under specified conditions.

21. Wisconsin child support initiative.—The Secretary of HHS is required to grant waivers to the State of Wisconsin to allow it to implement its proposed child support initiative in all or parts of the State as a replacement for the AFDC and child support programs. The State must meet specified conditions and give specific guarantees with respect to the financial well-being of the children involved.

22. Sense of the Congress that State and local governments should focus on the problems of child custody, child support, and related domestic issues.—The act incorporates the language of S. Con. Res. 84 urging State and local governments to focus on the vital issues of child support, child custody, visitation rights, and other related domestic issues that are within the jurisdictions of such governments.

Cost estimates for the major provisions of Public Law 98–378 appear below:

TABLE 11–31.—CBO FEDERAL BUDGET ESTIMATES FOR CHILD SUPPORT ENFORCEMENT AMENDMENTS OF 1984 (PUBLIC LAW 98–378)

[In millions of dollars]

	Fiscal year—				
	1984	1985	1986	1987	Total
Alter incentive payments to States	....	....	15	15	30
Reduce Federal matching to 68 percent in fiscal year 1988; 66 percent in fiscal year 1990	....	....	....	....	0
Require application fees; optional late payment fees	.	....	−5	−10	−10	−25
Mandate State enforcement techniques	....	−15	−25	−25	−65
Require IRS tax intercept for non-AFDC families thru fiscal year 1989	....	25	20	10	55
Authorize funds for interstate projects	....	7	12	15	34
Provide Medicaid for 4 months for families losing AFDC due to child support collection through fiscal year 1988	5	25	25	30	85
Other provisions	....	15	20	10	45
Impact of H.R. 4325 on CSE case levels:					
CSE expenditures	....	10	30	55	95
Offsetting effects on public assistance	....	−5	−20	−30	−55
Total	5	57	67	70	199

Note: The cost of disregarding the first $50 of child support payments is shown in the AFDC section.

Source: Congressional Budget Office.

The Tax Reform Act of 1984 (Public Law 98–369) was also enacted during the 98th Congress and included two tax provisions pertaining to alimony and child support.

Under prior law, alimony was deductible by the payor and includible in the income of the payee. The 1984 law revises the rules relating to the definition of alimony. Generally, only cash payments that will terminate on the death of the payee spouse will qualify as alimony. Alimony payments, if in excess of $10,000 per year, generally must be payable for at least 6 years and must not decline by more than $10,000. The prior law requirement that the payment be based on a legal support obligation has been repealed and payors are now required to furnish to the IRS the social security number of the payee spouse. A $50 penalty for failure to do so will be imposed. The provision is effective for divorce or separation agreements or orders executed after 1984.

The 1984 law also provides that the $1,000 dependency exemption for a child of divorced or separated parents generally will be allocated to the custodial parent unless the custodial parent signs a written declaration that he or she will not claim the exemption for the year. Each parent may claim the medical expenses that he or she pays for the child, for purposes of computing the medical expense deduction. The provision is effective for taxable years beginning after 1984.

Section 12. Child Care

INTRODUCTION

Child care has been the focus of heightened attention in recent years. The most significant factor influencing this trend has been the dramatic increase in the labor force participation of mothers. Currently, in a majority of American families with children—even those with very young children—the mother is in the labor force. Increased interest in child care also derives from concerns that some mothers are kept out of the labor force because of child care problems. Poor single mothers in pursuit of greater self-sufficiency for their families may be especially vulnerable. Though child care is viewed primarily as a support for families that enables mothers to work outside of the home, it is also often regarded as a potential source of enrichment services for children aimed at enhancing their development. The demand for preschool services with an early childhood development focus has increased among mothers working both within and outside of the home. Improving the availability of these services to poor children through programs such as Head Start is of particular concern since research has found that these children may especially benefit from early intervention.

Concerns that child care may be in short supply, not of good enough quality, or too expensive for many families escalated during the late 1980s into a national debate over the nature and extent of the Nation's child care problems and what, if any, Federal interventions would be appropriate. The debate culminated in the enactment of legislation in 1990 that expanded Federal support for child care by establishing two new State child care grant programs. The programs—the Child Care and Development Block Grant and the At-Risk Child Care program—were enacted as part of the Omnibus Budget Reconciliation Act of 1990 (P.L. 101–508). These new programs were preceded by enactment of a major welfare reform initiative, the Family Support Act of 1988 (P.L. 100–485), which authorized expanded child care assistance for welfare families and families leaving welfare. These new Federal child care initiatives reflect a significant shift in the emphasis of the child care policy debate, from discussions about whether the Federal Government should have an expanded role in child care to questions about what that role should be. Issues currently receiving attention include questions about how the new programs are being implemented at the Federal and State levels, what effect the programs will have on improving the availability and quality of child care, and how Federal child care programs will be integrated and/or coordinated with each other and State and local programs. In addition, the emerging debate on welfare reform has focused interest on the child care needs of families transitioning off of welfare, and of other low-income working families.

This chapter provides background information on the major indicators of the demand for and supply of child care, and the current Federal role in child care including a summary description of the major Federal programs that currently fund child care services.

LABOR FORCE PARTICIPATION OF MOTHERS

The dramatic increase in the labor force participation of mothers is commonly regarded as the most significant factor fueling the increased demand for child care services. A person is defined as participating in the labor force if he or she is working or seeking work. As shown in table 12–1, in 1947, just following World War II, slighty over one-fourth of all mothers with children between the ages of 6 and 17 were in the labor force. In 1993 three-quarters of such mothers were labor force participants. The increased labor force participation of mothers with younger children has also been dramatic. In 1947, it was unusual to find mothers with a preschoolage child in the labor force (only about 12 percent of all mothers with children under the age of 6 were in the labor force at that time). In 1993, nearly 60 percent of mothers with preschool-age children were in the labor force, a rate nearly 5 times higher than in 1947. Women with infant children have become increasingly engaged in the labor market as well. Today, over half of all mothers whose youngest child is under age 2 are in the labor market, while in 1975 less than one-third of all such mothers were labor force participants.

The rise in the number of single parent families has also contributed to increased demand for child care services. Single mothers with children represent a greater share of all families with children today than in the past; they also represent a larger share of the labor force today than ever before. Compared to married mothers with children, the labor force participation of single mothers (especially divorced mothers) has always been high. In recent years, however, married mothers with young children have especially increased their labor involvement, with rates of labor force participation approaching, and in some cases exceeding, those of single mothers (see table 12–2).

Mothers' attachment to the labor force differs depending upon the age of their youngest child and marital status, as tables 12–2 and 12–3 show. Table 12–3 provides a detailed breakdown of the labor force participation of women for March 1993, by marital status and the age of the youngest child. Among those with children under 18, divorced women have the highest labor force participation rates, followed by married and separated women. Widowed and never-married women have lower labor force participation rates.

As this table illustrates, no matter what the marital status of the woman, labor force participation rates tend to increase as the age of the youngest child increases. This is most pronounced for never-married women, whose participation rates exceed those of all but divorced women when their youngest child is between 14 and 17 years of age. Among all women with children under 18, 54 percent of those with a child under 3 participate, 64 percent of those whose youngest child is between 3 and 5 participate, and 75 percent of those whose youngest child is between 6 and 17 participate.

TABLE 12–1.—LABOR FORCE PARTICIPATION RATES OF WOMEN, BY PRESENCE AND
AGE OF YOUNGEST CHILD, SELECTED YEARS, 1947–93

	No chil-dren under 18	With children under age 18				
		Total	Age 6 to 17 only	Under age 6		
				Total	Under 3	Under 2
April 1947	29.8	18.6	27.3	12.0	N/A	N/A
April 1950	31.4	21.6	32.8	13.6	N/A	N/A
April 1955	33.9	27.0	38.4	18.2	N/A	N/A
March 1960	35.0	30.4	42.5	20.2	N/A	N/A
March 1965	36.5	35.0	45.7	25.3	21.4	N/A
March 1970	42.8	42.4	51.6	32.2	27.3	N/A
March 1975	45.1	47.3	54.8	38.8	34.1	31.5
March 1980	48.1	56.6	64.3	46.8	41.9	39.2
March 1981	48.7	58.1	65.5	48.9	44.3	42.0
March 1982	48.6	58.5	65.8	49.9	45.6	43.3
March 1983	48.7	58.9	66.3	50.5	46.0	44.5
March 1984	49.3	60.5	68.1	52.1	47.6	46.4
March 1985	50.4	62.1	69.9	53.5	49.5	48.0
March 1986	50.5	62.8	70.4	54.4	50.8	49.2
March 1987	50.5	64.7	72.0	56.7	52.9	51.9
March 1988	51.2	65.0	73.3	56.1	52.5	50.8
March 1989	51.9	65.7	74.2	56.7	52.4	51.7
March 1990	52.3	66.7	74.7	58.2	53.6	52.1
March 1991	52.0	66.6	74.4	58.4	54.5	53.8
March 1992	52.3	67.2	75.9	58.0	54.5	54.3
March 1993	52.1	66.9	75.4	57.9	53.9	54.2

Source: Department of Labor, Bureau of Labor Statistics.

TABLE 12–2.—LABOR FORCE PARTICIPATION RATES OF WOMEN WITH CHILDREN, BY MARITAL STATUS AND AGE OF YOUNGEST CHILD, MARCH OF SELECTED YEARS

[In percent]

	1960	1970	1980	1986	1987	1988	1989	1990	1991	1992	1993	Percent increase, 1970–93
All women with children	[1]30.4	[1]52.9	56.6	62.8	64.7	65.0	65.7	66.7	66.6	67.2	66.9	26.5
Married women:												
Youngest under 6	18.6	30.3	45.0	53.8	56.8	57.1	57.4	58.9	59.9	59.9	59.6	96.7
Youngest 6 or over	39.0	49.2	61.8	68.4	70.6	72.5	73.4	73.6	73.6	75.4	74.9	52.2
Separated women:												
Youngest under 6	NA	45.4	52.2	57.4	55.1	53.0	54.9	59.3	52.2	55.7	52.1	14.8
Youngest 6 or over	NA	60.6	66.6	70.6	72.6	69.3	68.0	75.0	74.7	71.6	71.6	18.2
Divorced women:												
Youngest under 6	NA	63.3	68.3	73.8	70.5	70.1	66.3	69.8	68.5	65.9	68.1	7.6
Youngest 6 or over	NA	82.4	82.3	84.7	84.5	83.9	85.7	85.9	84.6	85.9	83.6	1.5
Never-married women:												
Youngest under 6	NA	NA	44.1	47.5	49.9	44.7	48.9	48.7	48.8	45.8	47.4	NA
Youngest 6 or over	NA	NA	67.6	65.9	64.1	67.1	69.0	69.7	64.8	67.2	70.2	NA

[1] Excludes never-married women.

Source: Department of Labor, Bureau of Labor Statistics.

TABLE 12–3.—LABOR FORCE PARTICIPATION RATES OF WOMEN WITH CHILDREN UNDER 18, MARCH 1993, BY MARITAL STATUS AND AGE OF YOUNGEST CHILD

	Age of youngest child						
	Under 3	Under 6	Under 18	3 to 5	6 to 13	6 to 17	14 to 17
All women with child under 18 ...	53.9	57.9	66.9	63.7	75.0	75.4	76.5
Married, spouse present	57.5	59.6	67.5	63.1	74.7	74.9	75.6
Divorced	62.9	62.1	79.1	71.7	83.7	83.6	83.2
Separated	44.5	52.1	62.5	60.7	72.1	71.6	70.2
Widowed	47.2	50.4	58.4	50.4	49.4	60.5	71.6
Never-married	39.2	47.4	54.4	64.2	68.0	70.2	79.8

Source: Department of Labor, Bureau of Labor Statistics.

While there has been a substantial increase in the proportion of mothers in the labor force, the data can be misleading. Although 67 percent of mothers participated in the labor force in 1993, table 12–4 shows 46 percent worked full time and 16 percent worked part time. Another 4 percent were actively seeking a job. (Full time work is defined as 35 or more hours per week; part time work is defined as 34 hours or less.) Thirty-seven percent of mothers with children under age 6 worked full time, and 16 percent worked part time. As the table demonstrates, how much mothers work differs according to their marital status and the age of their children. Forty-six percent of married women with children worked full time; thus, over 50 percent either didn't work at all or worked part-time. Some 64 percent of all divorced mothers worked full time; 51 percent of divorced mothers with children under 6 worked full time. Only 33 percent of never-married mothers worked full time, and 11 percent worked part time.

CHILD CARE ARRANGEMENTS USED BY WORKING MOTHERS

Data are collected periodically by the Census Bureau on the types of child care arrangements used by families with working mothers. In using the data, note that they are derived from a survey in which mothers are asked about child care arrangements used by the family while the mother works. Because the survey asks about substitute *maternal* care (both paid and unpaid), it provides information on categories of care that generally are not considered child care (such as care provided by the father, even in cases where the father does not work at all, and school attendance). Further, the survey does not gather information on the child care arrangements used by the family while the father works. Though information is collected on the arrangements of families in which there is only a father present, it is considered too negligible to report.

TABLE 12–4.—LABOR FORCE PARTICIPATION RATES OF MOTHERS BY FULL OR PART-TIME EMPLOYMENT STATUS, MARCH 1993 [1]

[In percent]

	With children under 18	With children under 6
All mothers:		
Employed full time	46	37
Employed part time	16	16
Married, spouse present:		
Employed full time	46	38
Employed part time	18	17
Divorced:		
Employed full time	64	51
Employed part time	10	11
Never married:		
Employed full time	33	26
Employed part time	11	11

[1] Full-time workers work 35 hours or more per week, part-time workers work 1 to 34 hours a week.

Source: U.S. Department of Labor, Bureau of Labor Statistics.

The most recent Census Bureau statistics on child care arrangements in the United States are based on data collected for the period September to December 1991 (Fall 1991).[1] These data indicate that the types of child care arrangements used by families while the mother works vary depending on the age of the child, as well as the mother's work schedule, marital status and family income level. Table 12–5 shows the distribution of primary child care arrangements provided for preschoolers (children under age 5) and school-age children (children ages 5 to 14 years), by marital status and mother's work schedule. "Primary" child care arrangement refers to the arrangement used most frequently during a typical work week.

Families of preschoolers with working mothers rely more on care provided in an organized child care facility (25 percent), than on family day care (18 percent). Relative care is used for 24 percent of preschool children. Many families with young children do not rely on others for help with child care arrangements while the mother works, using parental care (29 percent), especially care by fathers (20 percent). Only 5 percent of families rely on care provided in the child's home by a nonrelative.

Preschool children of part-time employed mothers are much less likely to be cared for at an organized child care facility or by a family day care provider, and more likely to be cared for by a parent, than children of full-time employed mothers. Children of employed single mothers are much more likely to be cared for by a relative than children of married mothers.

---

[1] "Who's Minding the Kids? Child Care Arrangements, Fall 1991", U.S. Dept. of Commerce, Bureau of the Census, Series P 70–36, 1994. Data on child care arrangements of working mothers are based on the Survey of Income and Program Participation (SIPP).

TABLE 12–5.—PRIMARY CHILD CARE ARRANGEMENTS OF CHILDREN UNDER 15 WITH AN EMPLOYED MOTHER, BY MARITAL AND EMPLOYMENT STATUS OF THE MOTHER, FALL 1991

[In percent]

Age of child and type of arrangement	Mothers with children under 5 years			Mothers with children 5 to 14 years		
	Total	Employed full time	Employed part time	Total	Employed full time	Employed part time
ALL MARITAL STATUSES						
Children of employed mothers (in thousands)	9,854	6,188	3,666	21,220	14,646	6,574
Percent	100.0	100.0	100.0	100.0	100.0	100.0
Care in child's home	15.7	15.2	16.6	4.0	4.4	3.1
By grandparent	7.2	6.5	8.3	1.2	1.7	0.3
By other relative	3.2	2.8	3.8	1.9	1.6	2.5
By nonrelative	5.3	5.9	4.5	0.9	1.2	0.3
Care in another home	31.0	35.0	24.2	3.6	3.7	3.3
By grandparent	8.6	9.0	7.9	1.2	1.3	0.9
By other relative	4.5	5.4	2.9	1.0	0.9	1.1
By nonrelative [1]	17.9	20.6	13.3	1.4	1.5	1.3
Organized child care facilities	24.6	29.9	15.7	81.1	83.9	75.1
Day/group care center ...	15.8	19.3	9.7	1.4	1.8	0.6
Nursery school/preschool	7.3	8.5	5.2	0.5	0.5	0.5
Kindergarten/grade school	1.1	1.4	0.5	76.2	78.4	71.4
School-based activity	0.5	0.6	0.3	3.0	3.2	2.6
Parental care	28.7	19.9	43.5	8.6	5.3	15.9
By father	20.0	14.8	28.9	6.6	4.1	12.2
By mother at work [2]	8.7	5.2	14.6	2.0	1.2	3.7
Child cares for self	....	....	....	2.7	2.7	2.5
MARRIED, HUSBAND PRESENT						
Children of employed mothers (in thousands)	8,048	4,917	3,131	16,625	10,975	5,650
Percent	100.0	100.0	100.0	100.0	100.0	100.0
Care in child's home	13.7	12.6	15.4	2.9	3.3	3.5
By grandparent	5.6	5.2	6.4	0.9	1.4	....
By other relative	2.5	1.5	4.1	1.4	1.2	1.9
By nonrelative	5.5	5.9	4.9	0.5	0.7	0.1
Care in another home	29.5	34.7	21.4	2.5	2.7	2.0
By grandparent	8.1	9.1	6.6	0.9	1.1	0.5
By other relative	4.2	5.6	2.2	0.6	0.6	0.5
By nonrelative [1]	17.1	20.0	12.6	1.0	1.0	1.0
Organized child care facilities	24.1	29.7	15.3	81.8	84.6	76.2
Day/group care center ...	15.6	19.8	9.1	1.5	2.1	0.3
Nursery school/preschool	7.1	8.0	5.7	0.5	0.5	0.5

TABLE 12–5.—PRIMARY CHILD CARE ARRANGEMENTS OF CHILDREN UNDER 15 WITH AN EMPLOYED MOTHER, BY MARITAL AND EMPLOYMENT STATUS OF THE MOTHER, FALL 1991—Continued

[In percent]

Age of child and type of arrangement	Mothers with children under 5 years			Mothers with children 5 to 14 years		
	Total	Employed full time	Employed part time	Total	Employed full time	Employed part time
Kindergarten/grade school	0.8	1.1	0.4	76.5	78.4	72.9
School-based activity	0.6	0.8	0.2	3.3	3.7	2.4
Parental care	32.8	23.1	48.0	10.9	7.1	18.3
By father	22.9	17.0	32.4	8.4	5.5	14.0
By mother at work[2]	9.8	6.1	15.6	2.5	1.6	4.3
Child cares for self	....	....	....	2.0	2.2	1.5

ALL OTHER MARITAL STATUSES[3]

Age of child and type of arrangement	Total	Employed full time	Employed part time	Total	Employed full time	Employed part time
Children of employed mothers (in thousands)	1,806	1,270	536	4,595	3,671	924
Percent	100.0	100.0	100.0	100.0	100.0	100.0
Care in child's home	24.6	25.0	23.9	8.2	7.8	11.7
By grandparent	14.1	11.8	19.4	2.3	2.4	2.2
By other relative	6.0	7.7	2.2	3.5	2.8	6.3
By nonrelative	4.5	5.5	2.2	2.4	2.6	1.5
Care in another home	37.6	36.4	40.5	7.4	6.5	11.3
By grandparent	10.7	8.6	15.7	2.1	1.8	3.6
By other relative	5.6	5.0	6.9	2.3	1.7	4.7
By nonrelative[1]	21.3	22.8	17.7	3.0	3.0	3.1
Organized child care facilities	27.0	30.8	18.1	78.9	81.5	68.4
Day/group care center	16.3	17.6	13.4	1.2	0.9	2.3
Nursery school/preschool	8.1	10.6	2.4	0.5	0.5	0.6
Kindergarten/grade school	2.2	2.6	1.1	75.1	78.5	61.8
School-based activity	0.3	....	1.1	2.0	1.6	3.7
Parental care	10.7	7.9	17.5	0.3	....	1.6
By father	7.0	6.3	9.0	0.3	....	1.6
By mother at work[2]	3.7	1.6	8.6	....	....	....
Child cares for self	....	....	....	5.1	4.2	8.7

[1] Care in another's home by a nonrelative is known as "family day care."
[2] Includes women working at home or away from home.
[3] Includes married, husband absent (including separated), widowed, divorced, and never married women.

Source: Derived from "Who's Minding the Kids? Child Care Arrangements: Fall 1991," U.S. Department of Commerce, Bureau of the Census, Series P 70–36, 1994.

TABLE 12–6.—AFTER-SCHOOL CHILD CARE ARRANGEMENTS USED BY EMPLOYED
MOTHERS FOR CHILDREN 5–14, FALL 1991

Type of arrangement	Number (in thousands)	Percent
Total children	21,220	100.0
Care in child's home	2,359	11.2
By grandparent	616	2.9
By other relative	1,222	5.8
By nonrelative	521	2.5
Care in another home	2,647	12.5
By grandparent	961	4.5
By other relative	543	2.6
By nonrelative [1]	1,143	5.4
Organized child care facilities	2,105	9.9
Day/group care center	906	4.3
Nursery school/preschool	117	0.5
School-based activity	1,082	5.1
Parental care	3,225	15.2
By father	2,607	12.3
By mother at work [2]	618	2.9
Child cares for self	1,562	7.4
No care mentioned	9,322	43.9

[1] Care in another home by a nonrelative is known as a "family day care."
[2] Includes women working at home or away from home.

Source: Derived from "Who's Minding the Kids? Child Care Arrangements: Fall 1991," Bureau of the Census, 1994.

Table 12–5 also illustrates that 76 percent of school-age children are in grade school or kindergarten during most of the hours their mothers work. Though not generally regarded as a form of child care, school is reflected in this table because it is the "primary" occupation of these children during their mothers' working hours. The Census Bureau notes that the remaining 24 percent of school-age children are in school, but not during the majority of hours their mothers work.

Table 12–6 shows the types of *after school* arrangements used for school-age children by working mothers, as well as cases where there were no arrangements used at all. A total of 1.6 million school-age children (7.4 percent of children age 5–14) were reported to be in "self-care" or to be unsupervised by an adult for some time while their mothers were working. The Census Bureau study found that 3.7 percent of 5–11 year olds and 16.8 percent of 12–14 year olds were "latch-key" children. It is not known if the children in the "no care mentioned" category were unsupervised, or if other factors may account for their not being reported in a child care arrangement, such as travel time from school.

Table 12–7 shows that the type of child care arrangements used for children under 5 varies by the economic well-being of the family. Children in poor families are more likely to be cared for by rel-

TABLE 12–7.—PRIMARY CHILD CARE ARRANGEMENTS USED BY EMPLOYED MOTHERS FOR CHILDREN UNDER 5, BY POVERTY STATUS OF THE MOTHERS, FALL 1991

All marital statuses	Total	Poor [1]	Not poor
Total children of employed mothers (in thousands)	9,854	977	8,811
Percent	100.0	100.0	100.0
Care in child's home	15.7	19.0	15.4
By grandparent	7.2	8.1	7.1
By other relative	3.2	6.7	2.8
By nonrelative	5.3	4.2	5.5
Care in another home	31.0	23.7	31.7
By grandparent	8.6	8.2	8.5
By other relative	4.5	4.7	4.5
By nonrelative [2]	17.9	10.8	18.7
Organized child care facilities	24.6	21.0	25.1
Day/group care center	15.8	14.8	16.0
Nursery school/preschool	7.3	3.6	7.6
Kindergarten/grade school	1.1	0.6	1.0
School-based activity	0.5	2.0	0.5
Parental care	28.7	36.2	27.9
By father	20.0	26.7	19.4
By mother at work [3]	8.7	9.5	8.5
Child cares for self	....	....	....

[1] Below the poverty threshold, which was $13,924 annually or $1,160 monthly during the 1991 interview period for a family of 4.
[2] Care in another home by a nonrelative is known as "family day care."
[3] Includes women working at home or away from home.

Source: Derived from "Who's Minding the Kids? Child Care Arrangements: Fall 1991," Bureau of the Census, 1994.

atives or their father while their mother works than children in nonpoor families. In addition, children in nonpoor families use organized child care facilities slightly more than children in poor families (25 percent versus 21 percent). Children in nonpoor families rely more on family day care than do children living in poverty (19 percent versus 11 percent).

CHILD CARE COSTS

Research studies have found that the majority of families with working mothers with preschool-age children purchase child care services. The tendency to purchase care and the amount spent on care, both in absolute terms and as a percent of family income, generally varies by the type of child care used, family type (married or single mothers), and the family's economic situation.

The most recent survey of national parental child care expenditures [2,3] found that 57 percent of families with employed mothers

[2] National Child Care Survey, 1990. Hofferth, Sandra L., Brayfield, Sharon Deich, and Holcomb, Pamela. Conducted by the Urban Institute. Sponsored by the Administration for Children and Families, U.S. DHHS and the National Association for the Education of Young Children. Washington, D.C. 1991.
[3] Child care is defined as care provided while the mother is at work, and includes care provided by fathers, mothers, and children themselves.

paid for child care for their youngest child under age 5 during November 1989 to May 1990. Families with mothers employed full-time were more likely to purchase care than those with mothers employed part-time. Among mothers working full-time, 66 percent paid for care for their young children. In addition, as illustrated in table 12–8, families with lower incomes were less likely to purchase care than families with higher incomes. Among families with employed mothers with a preschool-age child, the study found that 68 percent of those with annual incomes at or above $50,000 paid for child care, compared to only 42 percent of those with annual incomes below $15,000.

Of those purchasing care, the average weekly payment for the care of all children in a family with a youngest child under age 5 was $63 during the survey period. Families with employed mothers who paid for relatives to care for their children paid the least for care (average weekly cost of $44 for a relative). In-home care by a nonrelative cost the most, at $94 on average. Average weekly expenditures for center care and family child care were $76 and $64, respectively.

TABLE 12–8.—MEAN WEEKLY CHILD CARE EXPENDITURES FOR ALL CHILDREN IN THE FAMILY AND PERCENTAGE OF INCOME SPENT ON CARE, BY POVERTY STATUS AND FAMILY INCOME, EMPLOYED MOTHERS WITH YOUNGEST CHILD UNDER 5 PAYING FOR CARE

	Percent paying for care	Average weekly cost of care	Percent of income spent on care
Total	57	$63.2	10.4
Poverty status:			
Below poverty	NA	37.3	23.2
Above poverty	NA	65.5	8.7
Annual family income:			
Under $15,000	42	37.9	24.8
$15,000 to $24,999	48	50.7	13.2
$25,000 to $34,999	52	50.7	8.8
$35,000 to $48,999	54	64.5	10.2
$50,000 or above	68	85.1	6.2

Source: Published and unpublished data from the National Child Care Survey, 1991.

Families with higher incomes tend to spend more on child care than families with lower incomes. However, lower income families that pay for care spend significantly higher proportions of their incomes on such services. The survey found that poor families spend 23 percent of their incomes on child care, compared to only 9 percent of incomes spent by nonpoor families. Families earning more than $50,000 spent 6 percent of their incomes on child care (table 12–8).

SUPPLY OF CHILD CARE PROVIDERS

The profile of child care settings (PCS) study, recently released by the U.S. Department of Education, is regarded as the most comprehensive national study of regulated child care/early education services since the 1970s.[4] It provides information on the supply and characteristics of State licensed child care centers and early education programs, center-based programs exempt from State or local licensing (such as programs sponsored by religious organizations or schools) and licensed family day care providers.

According to the study's findings, approximately 80,000 center-based early education and care programs were providing services in the United States at the beginning of 1990. The study estimates that about 12 percent of centers on State licensing lists were not operating during the time of the survey. It is estimated that operating centers had about 5.3 million spaces (defined as the sum of enrollment and vacancies), of which approximately 4.2 million were for preschool-age children and 1.1 million were for school-age children. With regard to utilization, the study found that an average of 88 percent of the available spaces in centers were filled. It concluded that this high overall utilization rate indicates that "the market seems to be working to increase supply as demand expands." As shown in table 12–9, centers are distributed across regions and urban/rural areas approximately in proportion to the population of children under age 5.

The study found that there were approximately 118,000 licensed family day care providers with a capacity to care for 860,000 children (defined as the number of children for whom the provider is licensed to provide care) operating in the United States at the beginning of 1990. It is estimated that this number is significantly less than counts of family day care providers obtained directly from licensing lists—by some 30 percent—because such lists are not generally up to date. About 82 percent of all family day care spaces were filled at the beginning of 1990. In contrast to centers, the study found that the distribution of family day care homes across regions of the United States is not proportional to the number of young children in those regions (table 12–9). The authors of the study postulate that this may be due to regional differences in State family day care licensing requirements.

When providers were asked how many vacancies were actually available, the study found that the average child care center has 4 full-time vacancies and that the average regulated family day care home has 1 full-time vacancy. For centers, the study reports that vacancies are concentrated in fewer than half of all centers and that two-thirds to three-fourths of all centers reported having no vacancies. Vacancies are also concentrated in less than half of all family day care homes. According to the study, more than half of all regulated homes reported being "unable or unwilling" to accept more children on a full-time basis.

It is assumed by child care researchers that the number of unregulated family day care providers far exceeds the number of reg-

[4] "A Profile of Child Care Settings: Early Education and Care in 1990." Kisker, Ellen Eliason, Hofferth, Sandra L., Phillips, Deborah A., and Farquhar, Elizabeth. Prepared under contract of the U.S. Department of Education by Mathematica Policy Research, Inc., 1991.

ulated family providers, though it is difficult to determine by how much. Based on an estimate that 4 million children are in family day care and that the average number of children per home ranges from 3 to 6, the PCS study estimates that there are from 550,000 to 1.1 million unlicensed providers. Based on this estimate, the estimated number of regulated family day care homes (118,000) represents 10 to 18 percent of the total number of family day care providers.[5]

TABLE 12–9.—DISTRIBUTION OF PRESCHOOL CHILDREN, EARLY CHILDHOOD PROGRAMS, AND PROGRAM SPACES BY REGION AND URBANICITY

[In percent]

	Children younger than 5[1]	Centers	Spaces in centers	Regulated home-based programs	Spaces in regulated home-base programs
Region:					
Northeast	19	18	16	14	11
South	35	41	42	21	20
Midwest	24	23	23	29	32
West	23	18	19	36	37
Urbanicity:					
Metropolitan	75	76	83	77	77
Nonmetropolitan	25	24	17	23	23

[1] The distribution of children younger than age 5 by region is estimated from projections of 1980 census data to 1988 (U.S. Bureau of the Census, 1989). The distribution of children younger than age 5 by urbanicity is estimated as the distribution of the population by urbanicity in 1980 (U.S. Bureau of the Census, 1983).

Source: Profile of Child Care Settings Study (Mathematica Policy Research, Inc., 1990).

WORK DISRUPTIONS CAUSED BY FAILED CHILD CARE ARRANGEMENTS

The Census Bureau also surveys working mothers about time they or their husbands lost from work because of a failed child care arrangement, such as could result from a provider being sick or having an emergency. Among all mothers of children under age 15, 14 percent reported they lost work time due to such a failure during December 1988. Interestingly, the incidence of time lost did not change by marital status. It is postulated that this may be because child care is the primary responsibility of mothers, even when both parents are present. Among married couple families, only .7 percent of fathers lost time from work because of a fallen-through child care arrangement. There is a higher incidence of work disruptions because of child care problems for mothers with children under 5. Nearly 8 percent of mothers with a youngest child 1 or 2 years of age lost work time from a failed child care arrangement during the one month survey period, and 6 percent of mothers of infants lost work time for this reason.

[5] See methodology discussed in "The Demand and Supply of Child Care in 1990, Joint Findings From the National Child Care Survey, 1990 and the Profile of Child Care Settings," National Association for the Education of Young Children, 1991.

THE FEDERAL ROLE

This section focuses on Federal programs aimed specifically at providing child care services or related services to working families or programs that are generally used for this purpose. The late 1980s were marked by increased child care activity at the Federal level. New child care programs for AFDC families and families leaving AFDC were enacted in 1988 as part of a major welfare reform initiative. The newest Federal child care programs, the Child Care and Development Block Grant and the At-Risk Child Care program, were enacted in 1990 as part of the Omnibus Budget Reconciliation Act of 1990 (P.L. 101–508). The establishment of these latter programs was the culmination of a lengthy, and often politically and philosophically contentious debate about what role the Federal Government should play in the area of child care. Lasting nearly 4 years, the debate centered on questions about the type of Federal subsidies that should be made available and for whom, whether or not the Federal Government should set national child care standards, conditions under which religious child care providers could receive Federal funds, and how best to assure optimal choice for parents in selecting child care arrangements for their children, including options that allow a mother to stay home. Differences stemming from philosophical and partisan views, as well as jurisdictional concerns, were reflected throughout the debate.

Though the new programs represent a significant expansion of Federal support for child care, the largest Federal source of child care assistance is still provided indirectly through the Tax Code, in the form of a nonrefundable tax credit for taxpayers who work or are seeking work. Other major sources of Federal child care assistance include the Social Services Block Grant, under title XX of the Social Security Act. The Child Care Food program, which subsidizes meals for children in child care, is the largest source of direct Federal assistance for child care. Head Start, the early childhood development program targeted to poor preschool children, is often characterized as a child care program. Head Start, which primarily operates on a part-day basis and does not operate during the summer, is not currently designed to meet the needs of parents working full-time.

Numerous other Federal programs provide assistance for child care services, training for child care providers, and related activities. Most of these programs are not child care programs per se, but support child care as a component of programs supporting other activities, such as job training, housing assistance, education, food stamps, nutrition assistance, and other kinds of services.

For example, under various Federal student financial aid programs, students can count a certain portion of child care expenses as part of the total cost of postsecondary education and thereby receive Federal student aid to cover these costs. Another example is the Job Training Partnership Act, under which funds are designated for supportive services that can include child care services for program participants. Reports cataloging so-called Federal child care programs include counts ranging from 28 to 46 programs, depending on how child care is defined.[6] Again, most of these programs are not child care programs but include some type of child care or related assistance. Federal funding for child care services provided under many of these programs is unknown or estimated. The *total* number of children receiving federally supported child care assistance is also unknown.

During congressional consideration of child care legislation in the late 1980's, concerns were often raised that the Federal role in this area lacked coordination and focus. Some argue that the new child care programs—with their different eligibility rules, standards requirements, and different Federal and State administering agencies—have continued the trend, and that there is still need for a unified, comprehensive Federal policy in the area of child care.

Though Congress requires the States and DHHS to collect and compile information on the child care services funded and families served by the major Federal child care programs, little information is actually available to make assessments about the impact of the recent expansions in Federal child care assistance. For example, there is virtually no information readily available on the types of child care providers serving subsidized families with respect to their level of quality or regulation. There is also little information about the total number of families served, the degree of choice they have in selecting care, and whether choice is inhibited by payment rates or other factors. For some programs, the lack of information can be attributed to reporting requirements that have never been implemented by DHHS (such as for title XX and the dependent care planning and development State grant program). In other cases, information collected is inadequate to make determinations about a program's impact (such as with the transitional child care program and the AFDC child care program).

Below is a brief description of major Federal programs that support child care and related activities. Table 10 presents a summary of the funding environment and eligibility under these programs.

---

[6] See "Child Care: Government Funding Sources, Coordination, and Service Availability." United States General Accounting Office, No. GAO/HRD-90-26BR. October 1989; Child Day Care: Funding Under Selected Programs. Congressional Research Service. U.S. Library of Congress. November 1, 1988. No. 88-686; Child Care: A Workforce Issue. U.S. Department of Labor. April 1988.

TABLE 12–10.—SUMMARY OF FUNDING ENVIRONMENT AND ELIGIBILITY UNDER THE MAJOR FEDERAL PROGRAMS THAT SUPPORT CHILD CARE AND RELATED ACTIVITIES

[In million of dollars]

Program	Budgetary classification	Statutory authority	Federal administration	Federal funding support	Fiscal year 1993 outlays [1]
Dependent care credit	Nonrefundable tax credit	Internal Revenue Code	U.S. Department of Treasury, Internal Revenue Service.	NA	$2,450 [2]
Child care for AFDC recipients.	Authorized entitlement	Social Security Act	DHHS, ACF [3]	Open-ended, Federal match at Medicaid rate.	([4])
Transitional child care assistance (TCC).	Authorized entitlement	Social Security Act	DHHS, ACF [3]	Open-ended, Federal match at Medicaid rate.	588 [4]
At-risk child care	Authorized entitlement	Social Security Act	DHHS, ACF [3]	Funding ceiling, Federal match at Medicaid rate.	308
Child care and development block grant.	Discretionary authorization.	Omnibus Budget Reconciliation Act of 1990.	DHHS, ACF [3]	Funding ceiling, 100 percent Federal funding.	732
Child and adult care food program.	Authorized entitlement	National School Lunch Act of 1946.	U.S. Department of Agriculture, Food and Nutrition Service.	Open-ended, 100 percent Federal funding.	1,200 [5]
Title XX social services block grant.	Authorized entitlement	Social Security Act	HHS, ACF [3]	Funding ceiling, 100 percent Federal funding.	NA—some portion of 2,800.

Program	Target population	Eligible children	Provider requirements	Reimbursement rates to providers
Dependent care credit	Taxpayers who need dependent care in order to accept or maintain employment.	Children under age 13	Centers only must meet applicable State and local standards.	NA

Program	Who is eligible	Children eligible	Provider standards	Cost/limit
Child care for AFDC recipients .	AFDC recipients who need dependent care to accept or maintain employment, or to participate in State-approved education/training.	Children under age 13 (unless incapable of self-care or under court supervision).	Must meet applicable State and local standards.	Cost up to $200 per month (under age 2), and $175 per month (2 or older). Not more than the 75th percentile of the local market rate.
Transitional child care assistance (TCC).	Families that lose AFDC eligibility due to employment (increase in income or hours worked).	Children under age 13	Must meet applicable State and local standards.	Same as AFDC.
At-risk child care	Low-income families not receiving AFDC who need child care in order to work, and are at risk of welfare eligibility if care not provided.	Children under age 13	Must meet applicable State and local standards or, if not regulated and with the exception of relatives, be registered.	Same as AFDC.
Child care and development block grant.	Families with incomes at or below 75 percent of State median income, with parents engaged in work or education/training.	Children under age 13 (unless incapable of self-care or under court supervision).	Must meet applicable State and local standards or, if not regulated, be registered (including relatives). With the exception of relatives, must also meet certain health and safety standards.	No limit.
Child and adult care food program.	NA	Children under age 13; migrant children under age 16.	Must meet applicable State and local standards.	Meal rates are indexed to inflation, and some rates vary by family income.
Title XX social services block grant.	State discretion	State discretion	Must meet applicable State and local standards.	No limit.

1 Source: Congressional Budget Office for programs, Joint Committee on Taxation for tax expenditures.   2 Projection for 1993.   3 Department of Health and Human Services, Administration for Children and Families.   4 Fiscal year 1993 outlays for AFDC and transitional child care assistance combined.   5 Obligations.

NA—Not applicable.

DEPENDENT CARE TAX CREDIT

Under section 21 of the Internal Revenue Code, a nonrefundable credit against income tax liability is available for up to 30 percent of a limited amount of employment-related dependent care expenses. Eligible employment-related expenses are limited to $2,400, if there is one qualifying individual, or $4,800, if there are two or more qualifying individuals. The credit may be claimed by an individual who maintains a household that includes one or more qualifying individuals. Generally, a qualifying individual is a dependent under the age of 13, a physically or mentally incapacitated dependent, or a physically or mentally incapacitated spouse. The costs of care must be incurred to enable a taxpayer (or taxpayer's spouse, if married) to work or look for work. Qualified expenses include the costs of household services.

The percentage used to calculate the credit depends on a taxpayer's adjusted gross income (AGI). A taxpayer whose AGI is $10,000 or less is allowed a credit equal to 30 percent of qualified work-related expenses. The credit percentage is reduced by 1 percentage point for each additional $2,000 in AGI above $10,000. For taxpayers whose AGI is greater than $28,000, the credit is equal to 20 percent of qualified expenses. The maximum amount of the credit is $720 for one qualifying individual and $1,440 for two or more qualifying individuals.

More detailed information on the dependent care tax credit is provided in section 16.

CHILD CARE PROGRAMS UNDER TITLE IV–A OF THE SOCIAL SECURITY ACT

Title IV–A of the Social Security Act, under which the Aid to Families with Dependent Children (AFDC) program is established, contains authorities for four different child care programs. Three of the programs fund child care services for low-income families, though each target a different low-income population. One program funds child care services for AFDC families who are working or participating in an approved work, education, or training program. A second program funds care for families for a limited period of time after they leave AFDC. A third program funds care for families who are "at risk" of becoming eligible for AFDC. The fourth program authorized under title IV–A is aimed at improving State child care licensing standards, enforcement of standards, and the training of child care providers. Each of the title IV–A child care programs is described briefly below.

Child care for AFDC recipients

Under the AFDC program, the Federal Government requires States to "guarantee" child care to recipients of AFDC if the care is needed for individuals to accept employment or remain employed. Child care also must be guaranteed to AFDC recipients who are participating in a State-approved education and training activity, including an AFDC job opportunities and basic skills (JOBS) training program.[7] The AFDC child care program is funded by an open-ended entitlement. The Federal share of a State's child care payments is based on the Medicaid matching rate, which varies by State and is inversely related to a State's per capita income. The program is administered on the Federal level by the Administration for Children and Families (ACF) of the U.S. Department of Health and Human Services, as part of the AFDC program.

State welfare agencies are responsible for administering the program at the State level and must inform AFDC applicants and recipients of the availability of child care assistance and the types and locations of child care services. The State agencies can provide child care directly, arrange for care with providers through contracts or vouchers, provide cash or vouchers in advance to families, reimburse families, or use other arrangements. States can also choose to disregard certain child care expenses—up to $175 per month per child age 2 and over and up to $200 per month per child under age 2—from the earned income of a family in determining the family's eligibility for AFDC benefits.

Reimbursement for child care costs must be at least equal to the lower of the actual cost of care or a statewide limit (which could be the child care disregard amount or a higher amount). Reimbursement cannot be more than the 75th percentile of the local market rate for the type of care being provided, as determined by each State.[8] The child care must meet applicable standards of State and local law. In addition, the law authorizing the program requires States to ensure that center-based child care is subject to State and local health and safety requirements, including fire safety protections. States must also endeavor to develop guidelines for family day care services.

Transitional child care (TCC) assistance

Under the AFDC program, the Federal Government requires States to "guarantee" child care to a family who loses AFDC eligibility due to increased hours of, or increased income from employment or loss of the income disregard due to the time limitations, if the care is necessary for an individual to accept or retain employment. To be eligible for transitional child care (TCC), families must have received AFDC in at least 3 of the 6 months immediately before the month in which they became ineligible for AFDC. The child care assistance under this program is limited to a period of 12 months after the last month for which the family received AFDC benefits. The program is operated under the same rules as those that apply to the child care program for eligible AFDC recipients, except that families must contribute to the cost of the care

---

[7] Under the Family Support Act of 1988 (P.L. 100–485), all States were required to have a JOBS program in place by October 1, 1990. The centerpiece of a major welfare reform initiative, JOBS is intended to prevent long-term welfare dependency by providing needy families with education, training, and employment. All AFDC recipients not otherwise exempt by law are required to participate in JOBS. The parent of a child under age 6 may be required to participate only if child care is guaranteed and if participation is limited to no more than 20 hours per week. A parent of a child under age 3 is exempt from participation, unless required to participate at State option. More detailed information on the AFDC JOBS program is provided in section 7.

[8] The 75th percentile does not mean 75 percent of the cost of care. To determine the 75th percentile, child care rates are ranked from lowest to highest. Starting from the bottom of the list, the amount separating the 75 percent of the providers with the lowest rates from the 25 percent with highest rates is the 75th percentile.

in accordance with a State-established sliding fee scale. It is also administered by ACF at the Federal level.

Concerns have been raised that families leaving AFDC because of increased earnings are not receiving transitional child care assistance, even though they may be eligible for assistance and need it. A General Accounting Office report addressing this issue concluded that data are not readily available to determine the extent to which eligible families receive and retain transitional child care benefits.[9] GAO found that data are not available from the States or DHHS on the number of families that meet all the TCC eligibility criteria. And many States did not have data on the number of families receiving TCC each month. Based on limited data from 20 States, GAO reported that the percentage of eligible families receiving TCC assistance ranged from 2 to 66 percent. According to the GAO report, no clear relationships were identified between utilization rates and State administrative policies.

At-Risk Child Care program

The At-Risk Child Care program authorized by the Omnibus Budget Reconciliation Act of 1990 (P.L. 101–508) entitles States to Federal matching funds for child care services for low-income families who are *not* receiving AFDC, need child care in order to work, and are "at risk" of becoming eligible for welfare if child care were not provided. The program is permanently authorized as a "capped entitlement" at $300 million annually. It is administered by ACF. States are entitled to matching funds for child care expenditures up to State allocation limits determined by a formula in the law. State allocations are based on the number of children under age 13 in a State compared to the total number of such children in the United States. If a State's grant award is less than its full allocation limit in one year, the difference can be applied to the State's allocation limit in the next year. Like the AFDC child care programs, the Federal share of a State's child care payments is based on the Medicaid matching rate, which varies by State.

The At-Risk program is similar to the AFDC child care programs with regard to the flexibility States are afforded in providing care. The requirements for reimbursement rates also are similar. Like the TCC program, families are required to make some contribution to the cost of care, based on a State-designed sliding fee scale. At-Risk child care must meet applicable standards of State and local law. In contrast to the other title IV–A child care programs, At-Risk child care providers not required to meet such standards (with the exception of those providing care solely to family members) must be registered by the State.

The At-Risk program is administered on the State level by the State welfare agency. Beginning in fiscal year 1993, States were required to report annually to the Federal Government on how they used program funds. Reports are to include information on the number of children served, the average cost of care, eligibility rules, child care licensing and regulatory requirements, and enforcement policies. The Secretary of the Department of Health and

---

[9] "Welfare to Work: Implementation and Evaluation of Transitional Benefits Need HHS Action," by the General Accounting Office GAO/HRD–92–118 September 1992.

Human Services is required to report to Congress annually on the State reports.

As of fiscal year 1993, all States, except Louisiana, had been approved by HHS to operate At-Risk programs. One state—Mississippi—did not operate a program in that year.

Table 12–11 provides data on Federal payments to States for AFDC child care and TCC for fiscal years 1991 through 1995. Table 12–12 provides State-specific information on child care options under the AFDC and TCC programs, based on State "supportive services" plans for the fiscal year 1993–1994 biennium. Table 12–13 provides data on Federal payments to States for At-Risk child care for fiscal years 1991 through 1995. Table 12–14 provides State-specific information on child care options under the At-Risk child care program, based on State "supportive services" plans for the fiscal year 1993–1994 biennium.

The most current State-by-State data on the number of JOBS participants who receive title IV–A child care subsidies are shown in table 12–15. The types of child care arrangements used by the JOBS participants' children is provided in table 12–16. The number of families not in JOBS who receive title IV–A child care assistance is shown in table 12–17. The type of care used by AFDC families not in JOBS who receive title IV–A child care assistance is shown in table 12–18. Current data on the number of children receiving TCC subsidies and the type of care arrangements used by their families are found in tables 12–19 and 12–20.

TABLE 12–11.—FEDERAL PAYMENTS TO STATES FOR AFDC CHILD CARE AND
TRANSITIONAL CHILD CARE, FISCAL YEARS 1991–95

[Fiscal year in thousands]

States	1991	1992	1993 [1]	1994 (est.) [1]	1995 (est.)
Alabama	$2,820	$5,981	$9,050	$10,150	$10,804
Alaska	445	1,329	1,262	1,416	1,507
Arizona	2,354	5,998	8,462	9,491	10,102
Arkansas	4,348	1,940	1,268	1,422	1,513
California	11,331	16,655	34,401	38,585	41,069
Colorado	3,649	4,082	5,315	5,961	6,345
Connecticut	5,301	6,563	7,061	7,920	8,430
Delaware	1,300	1,787	3,016	3,383	3,600
District of Colum- bia	2,799	4,284	1,855	2,081	2,215
Florida	20,678	17,506	20,136	22,585	24,039
Georgia	13,231	16,060	25,247	28,318	30,140
Guam	9	22	4	4	5
Hawaii	249	70	273	306	325
Idaho	756	775	1,069	1,199	1,276
Illinois	8,468	4,455	11,949	13,403	14,265
Indiana	12,828	4,640	7,101	7,965	8,477
Iowa	2,204	1,730	2,409	2,702	2,876
Kansas	3,233	5,388	6,677	7,489	7,972
Kentucky	5,027	9,188	10,450	11,721	12,475
Louisiana	12,741	10,955	15,512	17,399	18,519
Maine	1,354	361	1,083	1,215	1,293
Maryland	9,509	10,027	13,912	15,604	16,609
Massachusetts	24,889	24,933	23,991	26,909	28,641
Michigan	14,467	15,727	13,597	15,251	16,233
Minnesota	11,342	9,918	12,415	13,925	14,822
Mississippi	574	2,577	3,230	3,623	3,857
Missouri	1,196	8,624	14,348	16,093	17,129
Montana	1,144	2,943	1,988	2,230	2,373
Nebraska	5,152	5,630	7,455	8,362	8,900
Nevada	1,057	435	1,032	1,158	1,232
New Hampshire	1,621	2,013	2,495	2,799	2,979
New Jersey	2,195	6,653	9,309	10,442	11,114
New Mexico	2,026	1,745	3,994	4,479	4,768
New York	29,289	36,303	57,988	65,041	69,227
North Carolina	7,306	24,423	35,163	39,439	41,978
North Dakota	1,554	1,725	1,709	1,917	2,040
Ohio	9,394	18,407	34,071	38,214	40,674
Oklahoma	7,983	18,925	22,950	25,742	27,399
Oregon	6,260	5,392	8,768	9,835	10,468
Pennsylvania	(100)	28,647	31,105	34,888	37,134

TABLE 12–11.—FEDERAL PAYMENTS TO STATES FOR AFDC CHILD CARE AND
TRANSITIONAL CHILD CARE, FISCAL YEARS 1991–95—Continued

[Fiscal year in thousands]

States	1991	1992	1993 [1]	1994 (est.) [1]	1995 (est.)
Puerto Rico	223	2,901	0	0	0
Rhode Island	1,821	2,154	4,310	4,834	5,145
South Carolina	541	1,040	4,294	4,816	5,126
South Dakota	983	13,457	1,759	1,973	2,100
Tennessee	4,492	25,090	18,675	20,946	22,294
Texas	20,803	6,544	33,737	37,840	40,275
Utah	6,275	1,605	9,236	10,360	11,027
Vermont	1,626	3	2,023	2,269	2,416
Virgin Islands	11	11,164	11	13	14
Virginia	4,320	15,439	8,328	9,341	9,942
Washington	8,355	3,205	21,057	23,618	25,139
West Virginia	2,169	16,742	4,548	5,101	5,430
Wisconsin	8,242	2,300	12,390	13,897	14,791
Wyoming	957	....	2,076	2,329	2,479
Total	320,744	415,000	595,568	668,000	711,000

[1] Preliminary data.

Sources: DHHS, Administration for Children and Families; Office of Financial Management, Administration for Children and Families.

TABLE 12–12.—AFDC CHILD CARE AND TRANSITIONAL CHILD CARE (TCC)—SUMMARY OF STATE CHILD CARE OPTIONS

State	Method of providing AFDC child care [1]	Supplements dependent care disregard	Method of providing TCC [1]	Statewide limit; Special needs care (if different) [2]	Child care provided during gaps [3]
Alabama	2, 5, 6	No	5, 6	$303	1 month.
Alaska	2, 6	No	5, 6	$812	1 month.
Arizona	2, 6	No	5, 6	$455.40/$391.00	2 weeks/1 month.
Arkansas	2, 5, 6	Yes	5, 6	$300/$250	1 month.
California	1, 2, 3, 4, 5, 6, 7	No	3, 4, 5, 6, 7	$1,071.68/$876.83; $1,404.87/ $1,149.62.	2 weeks/1 month.
Colorado	2, 6, 7	Yes	5, 6, 7	$525; $1,050	2 weeks/1 month.
Connecticut	2, 3, 5, 7	No	3, 7	$325; $435	2 weeks/1 month.
Delaware	2, 4, 5, 6, 7	No	4, 5, 6, 7	$312.00/$297.60; $327.60/ $312.48.	Up to one month.
District of Columbia	2, 3, 4, 5, 6	No	3, 4, 5, 6	$635.50/$558.00	1 month.
Florida	2, 4, 5, 6	Yes	4, 5, 6	$364.50	2 weeks/ 1 month.
Georgia	2, 5, 6	No	5, 6	$324.75/$281.45	2 weeks.
Guam	2, 5, 6	Yes	5	$250/$230	1 month.
Hawaii	6	No	5, 7	$325	2 weeks/1month.
Idaho	2, 5, 6	No	5	$407/$330; $440	1 month.
Illinois	1, 2, 3, 5	Yes	6, 7	$900.55	2 weeks/1 month.
Indiana	2, 5, 6	No	5, 6	$200/$175	1 month.
Iowa	2, 7	NA	7	$1,635/$1,480; $1,790/$1,635	1 month.
Kansas	2, 5, 6	No	5, 6	$609/$452; $984/863	2 weeks/1 month.
Kentucky	2, 5, 6, 7	No	5, 6, 7	$496	2 weeks/1 month.
Louisiana	2, 3, 5, 6	No	3, 5	$238.30/$216.50	2 weeks/1 month.
Maine	2, 5, 6	No	5, 6	$551	2 weeks/1 month.
Maryland	2, 4, 5, 6	Yes	4, 6, 7	$662.42/$347.98; $387	2 weeks/1 month.
Massachusetts	2, 4, 6, 7	No	4, 6, 7	$1,294.92	2 weeks/1 month.
Michigan	2, 3, 4, 5	No	3	$1,050	1 month.
Minnesota	2, 5, 6	Yes	5, 6	$630/$464; $4,300	No.
Mississippi	4, 5, 6	No	4, 5, 6	$253/$230; $253	No.
Missouri	2, 5, 6	No	5, 6	$310.00/$271.25	2 weeks/1 month.
Montana	2, 6	No	6	$299.00/$258.75; $279.45	2 weeks.
Nebraska	2, 5, 6	Yes	5, 6	$1,150/$970; $3,000	1 month.
Nevada	2, 5	No	5	$420/$398	No.
New Hampshire	2, 3, 5, 6	No	3, 5, 6	$462	2 weeks.
New Jersey	2, 4	Yes	4	$707/$583	2 weeks/1 month.

State	Code[1]		Code[1]	Amount[2]	Time limit[3]
New Mexico	5	No	5	$330	2 weeks/1 month.
New York	1, 2, 3, 4, 5, 6	No	1, 3, 5, 6	$883.32	2 weeks/1 month.
North Carolina	1, 2, 3, 5, 6	No	1, 3, 4, 5, 6	$411; $1,754	2 weeks/1 month.
North Dakota	1, 2, 3, 5, 6	No	1, 5, 6	$200/$175	2 weeks/1month.
Ohio	2, 6	No	6	$894.40	2 weeks/1month.
Oklahoma	2, 4, 6	No	6	$372/$341; $775	2 weeks/1month.
Oregon	2, 4, 6	No	4	$450	1 month.
Pennsylvania	2, 3, 5, 6, 7	No	5, 7	$813	2 weeks/1 month.
Puerto Rico	1, 2, 3, 4, 5, 6	Yes	4, 6	$200/$175; $250	2 weeks/1 month.
Rhode Island	2, 6	No	6	$415.97/$285.98	No.
South Carolina	2, 6	No	6	$425	No.
South Dakota	2, 3	No	3, 5	$200/$175	2 weeks/1 month.
Tennessee	2, 4	No	4, 5	$358.80/$312.00	1 month.
Texas	2, 5, 6	No	5, 6	$482; $916	2 weeks/1 month.
Utah	2, 6	No	5, 6	$410.70/$296.70	No.
Vermont	2, 5, 6	No	5, 6	$603.75	2 weeks/1 month.
Virgin Islands	1, 2, 4	Yes	1, 5	$200; $300	1 month.
Virginia	2, 5, 6	No	5, 6	$667/$628	No.
Washington	2, 7	No	7	$516.35; $1,206.15	2 weeks/1 month.
West Virginia	2, 7	No	7	$300/$253; $300	2 weeks/1 month.
Wisconsin	1, 2, 3, 4, 5, 6, 7	Yes	4	$600/$500	2 weeks/1 month.
Wyoming	2, 6	Yes	6	$350	Up to 1 week.

[1] Key to the code: 1=Direct; 2=Dependent care disregard; 3=Cash in advance; 4=Voucher in advance; 5=Cash reimbursement; 6=Purchase of service; 7=Other.

[2] When 2 amounts are shown separated by a slash (/), the 1st amount is the statewide limit for children under 2. The 2nd amount is the statewide limit for children over 2. Statewide limits for handicapped/special needs children follow a semicolon (;) when different limits apply.

[3] At State option, child care provided: for up to two (2) weeks while participant is waiting to enter either approved education, training, or JOBS; OR for up to one (1) month if JOBS component activity is scheduled to begin within that period or to reserve child care arrangements which would otherwise be lost.

Source: Child Care Policy Branch, Division of JOBS Program. Based on biennial Supportive Services Plans filed in ACF Central Office as of 11/01/93.

TABLE 12–13.—FEDERAL PAYMENTS TO STATES FOR AT-RISK CHILD CARE, FISCAL YEARS 1991–95

[In thousands]

State	1991 actual	1992 actual	1993 actual [1]	1994 estimates [1]	1995 estimates
Alabama	$4,935	$4,934	$4,692	$4,625	$4,626
Alaska	808	1,211	825	903	854
American Samoa	0	....	0	145	72
Arizona	1,151	9,210	4,624	4,709	4,709
Arkansas	0	4,519	2,657	3,627	2,701
California	36,592	73,183	25,170	56,449	38,533
Colorado	0	8,103	4,320	4,062	4,062
Connecticut	3,455	3,455	3,485	4,574	4,574
Delaware	777	776	770	772	771
District of Columbia	677	677	648	537	537
Florida	13,231	13,230	13,632	13,904	13,904
Georgia	8,110	8,110	7,986	10,960	7,941
Guam	0	....	0	399	198
Hawaii	0	1,361	929	1,705	1,318
Idaho	1,392	2,088	879	1,439	1,383
Illinois	6,833	13,666	16,007	13,426	13,426
Indiana	6,538	6,537	6,538	9,800	6,332
Iowa	3,226	3,225	3,226	3,177	3,177
Kansas	3,070	3,070	3,052	2,999	2,999
Kentucky	4,294	4,294	4,551	4,109	4,109
Louisiana	0	5,903	0	10,927	5,408
Maine	1,367	1,367	809	1,335	1,335
Maryland	5,363	5,363	5,539	5,562	5,562
Massachusetts	6,122	6,121	6,287	6,240	6,240
Michigan	0	....	7,500	14,728	11,037
Minnesota	5,245	5,245	5,427	5,359	5,359
Mississippi	0	....	0	6,504	3,209
Missouri	5,966	5,966	6,022	5,926	5,926
Montana	0	843	568	1,825	973
Nebraska	1,951	1,951	1,958	1,929	1,929
Nevada	0	3,262	1,589	1,534	1,534
New Hampshire	1,280	1,280	1,290	1,261	1,261
New Jersey	8,290	8,290	8,000	8,272	8,272
New Mexico	0	3,401	2,580	2,072	2,072
New York	19,931	19,930	19,699	21,047	19,647
North Carolina	7,333	7,333	9,681	7,274	7,274
North Dakota	839	838	1,007	748	748
Ohio	12,734	12,733	12,598	12,334	12,334
Oklahoma	3,909	3,656	3,762	3,734	3,734
Oregon	3,194	5,029	3,354	3,352	3,352

TABLE 12–13.—FEDERAL PAYMENTS TO STATES FOR AT-RISK CHILD CARE, FISCAL YEARS 1991–95—Continued

[In thousands]

State	1991 actual	1992 actual	1993 actual [1]	1994 estimates [1]	1995 estimates
Pennsylvania	0	25,616	12,681	12,502	12,502
Puerto Rico	0	....	0	10,495	5,201
Rhode Island	1,057	1,056	1,046	1,041	1,041
South Carolina	4,294	4,294	4,174	4,797	4,124
South Dakota	914	913	431	1,419	891
Tennessee	0	....	575	10,786	5,401
Texas	8,923	37,103	26,480	22,556	22,556
Utah	2,995	2,995	2,732	2,826	2,826
Vermont	646	646	650	637	637
Virgin Islands	0	....	0	362	180
Virginia	6,768	6,767	6,963	7,128	6,950
Washington	5,649	8,941	5,997	6,038	6,038
West Virginia	0	2,001	1,762	1,802	1,802
Wisconsin	5,755	5,754	5,892	5,829	5,829
Wyoming	634	1,267	770	719	593
Total	216,248	357,535	271,816	352,338	300,000

[1] Preliminary data. Numbers for 1994 assume States receive payment for full entitlement amount (1994 entitlement plus carry-over from 1993 entitlement).

Source: DHHS, Administration for Children and Families, Office of Financial Management.

TABLE 12–14.—AT-RISK CHILD CARE—SUMMARY OF STATE CHILD CARE OPTIONS

State	Method of providing at-risk child care [1]	Statewide limit; Special needs care (if different) [2]	Rules for counting income for sliding fee scale	Child care provided during gaps [3]	Registration required for unlicensed providers
Alabama	1, 3, 4, 5	$303	TCC rules	2 weeks/1 month	Yes.
Alaska	2, 4	$812	Different	No	Yes.
Arizona	5	$455.40/$391.00	Different	2 weeks/1 month	Yes.
Arkansas	5	$300/$250	Different	2 weeks/1 month	Yes.
California	2, 3, 4, 5	$1,071.68/$876.83; $1,404.87/$1,149.62	TCC rules	2 weeks/1 month	Yes.
Colorado	4	$525; $1,050	AFDC rules	2 weeks/1 month	Yes.
Connecticut	5	$325; $435	Different	No	Yes.
Delaware	3, 4, 5	$312.00/$297.60; $531/$483	AFDC rules	1 month	Yes.
District of Columbia	5	$635.50/$558.00; $50/day	TCC rules	1 month	Yes.
Florida	3, 4, 5	$364.50	TCC rules	1 month	Yes.
Georgia	5	$324.75/$281.45; $350.73/$303.10	TCC rules	No	Yes.
Hawaii	2, 3, 5	$325	Different	2 weeks/1 month	Yes.
Idaho	3	$407/$330; $440	Different	2 weeks/1 month	Yes.
Illinois	4	$900.55	TCC rules	2 weeks/1 month	Yes.
Indiana	2, 3, 5	$625	Different	1 month	Yes.
Iowa	5	$1,635/$1,480; $5/day over LMR	TCC rules	No	Yes.
Kansas	3, 5	$609/$452; $690.90/$664.65	Different	2 weeks/1 month	Yes.
Kentucky	5	$496	TCC rules	2 weeks/1 month	AFDC-defined relatives are exempt.
Louisiana	No At-Risk Program.				
Maine	3, 4, 5	No statewide limit	Different	2 weeks/1 month	Yes.
Maryland	4, 5	$662.42/$347.98; $387	TCC rules	No	Yes.
Massachusetts	4, 5	$1,294.92	TCC rules	1 month	Yes.
Michigan	5	$1,050	TCC rules	No	Yes.
Minnesota	5	$630/$464; $4,300	TCC rules	No	Yes.
Mississippi	No At-Risk Program.				

State					AFDC-defined relatives are exempt.
Missouri	3, 4, 5	$542.50/$474.30	TCC rules	2 weeks/1 month	
Montana	3, 4	$299.00/$258.75; $279.45	AFDC rules	2 weeks	Yes.
Nebraska	3, 4, 5, 6	$1,150/$970; $3,000	Different	1 month	Yes.
Nevada	3, 4, 5	No statewide limit	Different	2 weeks/1 month	Yes.
New Hampshire	2, 3, 4	$462	TCC rules	1 month	Yes.
New Jersey	1, 3, 4, 5	$707/$583	TCC rules	2 weeks/1 month	Yes.
New Mexico	5	$330	TCC rules	1 month	Yes.
New York	1, 2, 3, 4, 5, 6	$883.32	TCC rules	2 weeks/1 month	Yes.
North Carolina	5	$411; $1,754	TCC rules	2 weeks/1 month	Yes.
North Dakota	3, 4	$345/$240	TCC rules	2 weeks/1 month	Grandparents, aunts/uncles are exempt.
Ohio	4, 5	$894.40	TCC rules	2 weeks/1 month	Yes.
Oklahoma	5	$372/$341; $775	TCC rules	No	Yes.
Oregon	5	$450	TCC rules	Up to 5 days in a one month period.	Yes.
Pennsylvania	4, 5	No statewide limit	Different	1 month	Yes.
Rhode Island	5	$415.97/$285.98	TCC rules	No	Yes.
South Carolina	4	$425	TCC rules	2 weeks/1 month	Yes.
South Dakota	5	$250; $400	Different	No	Yes.
Tennessee	2, 3, 4, 5	$358.80/$312.00	TCC rules	1 month	Yes.
Texas	3, 4, 5, 6	$482; $916	TCC rules	2 weeks/1 month	Yes.
Utah	2, 3, 4, 5	$410.70/$296.70	TCC rules	2 weeks/1 month	Yes.
Vermont	5	$603.75	TCC rules	No	Yes.

TABLE 12–14.—AT-RISK CHILD CARE—SUMMARY OF STATE CHILD CARE OPTIONS—Continued

State	Method of providing at-risk child care [1]	Statewide limit; Special needs care (if different) [2]	Rules for counting income for sliding fee scale	Child care provided during gaps [3]	Registration required for unlicensed providers
Virginia	3, 4, 5	$667/$628	TCC rules	2 weeks/1 month	Yes.
Washington	5	$516.35/$342.93; $1,206.15	Different	No	Yes.
West Virginia	5	$300/$253; $300	TCC rules	2 weeks/1 month	Yes.
Wisconsin	2, 3, 5	$600/$500	Different	2 weeks/1 month	Yes.
Wyoming	5	$350	TCC rules	Up to one week	Yes.

[1] Key to the code: 1=Direct; 2=Cash/voucher in advance; 3=Cash reimbursement; 4=Purchase of service; 5=Certificate; 6=Other.

[2] When 2 amounts are shown separated by a slash (/), the first amount is the statewide limit for children under 2. The second amount is the statewide limit for children over 2. Statewide limits for handicapped/special needs children are followed by a semicolon (;) when different limits apply.

[3] At State option, child care provided: for up to two (2) weeks while participant is waiting to enter either approved education, training, or JOBS; OR for up to one (1) month if JOBS component activity is scheduled to begin within that period or to reserve child care arrangements which would otherwise be lost.

Source: Child Care Policy Branch, Division of JOBS Program. Based on biennial Supportive Services Plans filed in ACF Central Office as of 11/01/93.

TABLE 12–15.—JOBS PARTICIPANTS RECEIVING TITLE IV–A PAID CHILD CARE, BY AFDC PROGRAM STATUS AND BY STATE—FISCAL YEAR 1992

State	JOBS participants by AFDC Program (case) status, average monthly number					
	Total participants	Receiving AFDC-basic	Receiving AFDC–UP	Eligible for AFDC–UP	Not receiving AFDC	AFDC applicant
Alabama	40	40	0	0	0	0
Alaska	330	291	39	0	0	0
Arizona	676	268	404	2	2	0
Arkansas	[1]	[1]	[1]	[1]	[1]	[1]
California	11,287	10,679	441	0	0	167
Colorado	1,110	1,033	6	1	69	1
Connecticut	8	8	0	0	0	0
Delaware	121	0	0	0	0	121
District of Columbia	486	483	3	0	0	0
Florida	3,670	3,317	8	7	237	101
Georgia	2,753	2,475	6	5	173	94
Guam	[1]	[1]	[1]	[1]	[1]	[1]
Hawaii	84	81	3	0	0	0
Idaho	316	311	3	0	2	0
Illinois	2,837	2,761	1	75	0	0
Indiana	2,061	1,949	46	0	9	57
Iowa	[1]	[1]	[1]	[1]	[1]	[1]
Kansas	1,126	886	57	0	128	55
Kentucky	3,650	0	102	1	29	3,518
Louisiana	1,491	1,483	1	0	7	0
Maine	540	508	28	0	6	0
Maryland	1,806	1,516	34	5	50	201
Massachusetts	3,517	3,319	19	0	158	21
Michigan	9,500	8,701	217	0	109	473
Minnesota	884	0	0	0	884	0
Mississippi	546	525	3	0	0	18
Missouri	1,812	1,778	34	0	0	0
Montana	[1]	[1]	[1]	[1]	[1]	[1]
Nebraska	[1]	[1]	[1]	[1]	[1]	[1]
Nevada	343	332	0	0	11	0
New Hampshire	117	112	5	0	0	0
New Jersey	4,518	4,350	45	0	123	0

TABLE 12-15.—JOBS PARTICIPANTS RECEIVING TITLE IV-A PAID CHILD CARE, BY AFDC PROGRAM STATUS AND BY STATE—FISCAL YEAR 1992—Continued

State	JOBS participants by AFDC Program (case) status, average monthly number					
	Total participants	Receiving AFDC-basic	Receiving AFDC-UP	Eligible for AFDC-UP	Not receiving AFDC	AFDC applicant
New Mexico	1,142	1,090	31	0	21	0
New York	13,594	13,316	278	0	0	0
North Carolina	3,515	3,400	77	0	38	0
North Dakota	1,022	948	74	0	0	0
Ohio	[1]	[1]	[1]	[1]	[1]	[1]
Oklahoma	4,088	4,075	13	0	0	0
Oregon	1,822	1,704	103	0	0	15
Pennsylvania	7,209	7,180	29	0	0	0
Puerto Rico	573	566	0	0	7	0
Rhode Island	1,810	1,778	0	0	7	25
South Carolina	[1]	[1]	[1]	[1]	[1]	[1]
South Dakota	363	352	0	0	11	0
Tennessee	1,639	1,503	47	0	89	0
Texas	2,134	2,057	32	0	45	0
Utah	2,467	2,442	8	0	0	17
Vermont	447	436	9	0	2	0
Virgin Islands	28	26	0	0	0	2
Virginia	[1]	[1]	[1]	[1]	[1]	[1]
Washington	2,423	2,141	271	0	0	11
West Virginia	[1]	[1]	[1]	[1]	[1]	[1]
Wisconsin	2,613	2,149	403	0	61	0
Wyoming	35	35	0	0	0	0
U.S. total	102,513	92,362	2,880	96	2,278	4,897

[1] Data not reported by the State.

Source: DHHS, Administration for Children and Families.

TABLE 12-16.—AFDC CHILDREN IN THE JOBS PROGRAM RECEIVING TITLE IV-A PAID CHILD CARE, BY PRIMARY TYPE OF CARE ARRANGEMENT AND STATE—FISCAL YEAR 1992

State	Total children	Children by type of care arrangement (avg. monthly no.)							Unknown	Percent children in center care	Percent provided by a relative
		Care provided by a nonrelative in				Care provided by a relative in					
		Center care	Group family day care	Family day care	In child's home	Group family day care	Family day care	In child's home			
Alabama	40	26	0	0	0	14	0	0	0	65.0	35.0
Alaska	543	341	44	51	30	6	60	10	1	62.8	14.0
Arizona	1,159	814	8	66	2	0	194	75	0	70.2	23.2
Arkansas	(1)	(1)	(1)	(1)	(1)	(1)	(1)	(1)	(1)	(1)	(1)
California	18,284	4,220	1,460	8,217	897	353	1,405	1,519	213	23.1	17.8
Colorado	1,761	1,126	239	54	41	0	190	111	0	63.9	17.1
Connecticut	8	0	0	0	0	0	4	0	4	0.0	50.0
Delaware	194	131	1	61	1	0	0	0	0	67.5	0.0
District of Columbia	687	483	0	29	0	0	113	62	0	70.3	25.5
Florida	5,998	5,448	0	274	85	0	66	65	60	90.8	2.2
Georgia	4,328	2,571	(1)	280	234	0	(1)	1,243	0	59.4	28.7
Guam	(1)	(1)	(1)	(1)	(1)	(1)	(1)	(1)	(1)	(1)	(1)
Hawaii	109	33	0	22	0	3	49	2	0	30.3	49.5
Idaho	509	220	43	129	0	1	91	0	25	43.2	18.1
Illinois	4,565	949	28	1,085	964	0	1,021	518	0	20.8	33.7
Indiana	3,508	860	197	739	188	11	992	494	27	24.5	42.7
Iowa	(1)	(1)	(1)	(1)	(1)	(1)	(1)	(1)	(1)	(1)	(1)
Kansas	1,865	993	333	218	135	37	94	55	0	53.2	10.0
Kentucky	5,720	1,928	0	1,108	1,006	0	0	645	1,033	33.7	11.3
Louisiana	2,386	1,672	0	34	117	0	45	423	95	70.1	19.6
Maine	831	149	151	230	93	4	126	64	14	17.9	23.3
Maryland	3,085	976	131	470	298	0	639	567	4	31.6	39.1
Massachusetts	4,851	2,364	397	1,755	0	0	19	316	0	48.7	6.9
Michigan	15,029	2,476	919	5,042	2,800	575	1,868	1,077	272	16.5	23.4
Minnesota	1,422	727	294	174	0	72	50	105	0	51.1	16.0

TABLE 12–16.—AFDC CHILDREN IN THE JOBS PROGRAM RECEIVING TITLE IV–A PAID CHILD CARE, BY PRIMARY TYPE OF CARE ARRANGEMENT AND STATE—FISCAL YEAR 1992—Continued

State	Total children	Children by type of care arrangement (avg. monthly no.)							Unknown	Percent children in center care	Percent provided by a relative
		Care provided by a nonrelative in				Care provided by a relative in					
		Center care	Group family day care	Family day care	In child's home	Group family day care	Family day care	In child's home			
Mississippi	969	470	38	59	17	32	223	128	2	48.5	39.5
Missouri	2,984	1,260	0	935	77	0	581	131	0	42.2	23.9
Montana	(1)	(1)	(1)	(1)	(1)	(1)	(1)	(1)	(1)	(1)	(1)
Nebraska	(1)	(1)	(1)	(1)	(1)	(1)	(1)	(1)	(1)	(1)	(1)
Nevada	586	148	1	15	132	0	50	240	0	25.3	49.5
New Hampshire	175	85	33	0	23	8	0	16	10	48.6	13.7
New Jersey	7,034	2,836	29	3,657	489	12	11	0	0	40.3	0.3
New Mexico	1,950	493	313	0	619	0	359	166	0	25.3	26.9
New York	20,777	4,314	476	10,380	1,647	0	2,857	1,036	67	20.8	18.7
North Carolina	5,299	3,253	4	594	149	0	701	510	88	61.4	22.9
North Dakota	1,466	241	136	696	85	0	236	72	0	16.4	21.0
Ohio	(1)	(1)	(1)	(1)	(1)	(1)	(1)	(1)	(1)	(1)	(1)
Oklahoma	7,079	6,337	0	710	15	0	17	0	0	89.5	0.2
Oregon	2,810	0	495	1,597	1,004	19	685	0	14	0.0	25.1
Pennsylvania	11,201	5,204	3,415	14	6	938	119	423	203	46.5	12.2
Puerto Rico	831	22	223	95	243	259	466	101	6	2.6	57.6
Rhode Island	2,711	1,392	173	114	243	150	466	149	24	51.3	28.2
South Carolina	(1)	(1)	(1)	(1)	(1)	(1)	(1)	(1)	(1)	(1)	(1)
South Dakota	535	213	0	236	33	0	28	22	3	39.8	9.3
Tennessee	2,629	1,573	284	91	77	273	95	222	14	59.8	22.4
Texas	3,628	2,699	0	37	0	0	0	8	884	74.4	0.2
Utah	4,108	2,580	415	1,051	62	173	0	0	0	62.8	0.0
Vermont	725	141	233	0	45	0	5	133	0	19.4	42.2
Virgin Islands	62	2	0	19	0	0	5	36	0	3.2	66.1
Virginia	(1)	(1)	(1)	(1)	(1)	(1)	(1)	(1)	(1)	(1)	(1)

Washington	3,554	1,566	705	0	510	109	250	414	0	44.1	21.8
West Virginia	(¹)	(¹)	(¹)	(¹)	(¹)	(¹)	(¹)	(¹)	(¹)	(¹)	(¹)
Wisconsin	4,138	2,134	0	861	248	0	366	264	265	51.6	15.2
Wyoming	35	13	0	0	0	0	0	0	22	37.1	0.0
U.S. total	162,128	65,457	11,218	41,199	12,372	3,035	14,075	11,422	3,350	40.4	17.6

¹ Data not reported by the State.

Source: DHHS, Administration for Children and Families.

TABLE 12–17.—NON-JOBS FAMILIES [5] RECEIVING IV–A PAID CHILD CARE, WITH AND WITHOUT EARNED INCOME, BY AFDC PROGRAM STATUS AND BY STATE—FISCAL YEAR 1992

[Average monthly number]

State	Total [1] families	Families with earnings and				Families without earnings and		
		Receiving AFDC-basic	Receiving AFDC-UP	Applying for AFDC	In transition	Receiving AFDC-basic	Receiving AFDC-UP	Applying for AFDC
Alabama [2]	1,072	0	0	(3)	1,072	0	0	(3)
Alaska	115	8	2	(3)	73	32	2	(3)
Arizona	2,253	1,257	(4)	(4)	940	56	(4)	(4)
Arkansas	2,519	1,945	3	(3)	345	227	(3)	(3)
California	1,595	(4)	(4)	(4)	1,595	(3)	(3)	(3)
Colorado	314	(4)	(4)	(4)	314	(3)	(3)	(3)
Connecticut	1,167	(4)	(4)	(3)	680	(4)	(4)	(3)
Delaware	375	250	0	0	126	(3)	(3)	(3)
District of Columbia	147	71	0	(3)	76	0	0	0
Florida	4,391	1,932	12	(3)	2,447	0	0	(3)
Georgia	4,794	2,235	2	(3)	801	1,745	13	(3)
Guam	5	0	0	0	5	0	0	0
Hawaii	232	187	3	0	42	0	0	0
Idaho	437	262	1	(3)	142	32	13	(3)
Illinois	1,552	42	1	(3)	1,353	143	22	(3)
Indiana	1,896	53	1	(3)	607	1,213	(3)	(3)
Iowa	826	587	7	0	232	0	0	0
Kansas	(4)	(4)	(4)	(4)	(4)	(3)	(3)	(3)
Kentucky	680	10	0	(3)	623	45	2	(3)
Louisiana	1,185	7	(3)	(3)	1,175	3	(3)	(3)
Maine	130	(4)	(4)	(4)	130	(4)	(4)	(4)
Maryland	3,193	924	(4)	(3)	357	1,912	(4)	(3)
Massachusetts	2,620	901	46	65	1,608	(4)	(4)	(4)

State								
Michigan	8,070	(4)	(4)	(4)	632	7,060	378	(4)
Minnesota	1,172	(4)	(4)	(3)	1,017	145	10	(3)
Mississippi	134	0	0	(3)	133	1	6	(3)
Missouri	2,191	132	2	(3)	1,078	972	0	(3)
Montana	160	(4)	(4)	(3)	160	0	57	(3)
Nebraska	2,825	710	42	1	522	1,492	0	1
Nevada	161	(4)	(4)	(3)	161	0	14	(3)
New Hampshire	780	122	33	(3)	215	395	(4)	(3)
New Jersey	4,396	(4)	(4)	(4)	(4)	(4)	4	(4)
New Mexico	555	(4)	(4)	(3)	261	290	(3)	(3)
New York	4,669	3,355	29	(3)	1,285	(3)	(3)	(3)
North Carolina	6,428	5,028	13	7	1,386	0	0	0
North Dakota	398	170	2	7	214	12	56	0
Ohio	3,026	553	54	(3)	1,353	1,010	38	(3)
Oklahoma	1,886	581	0	(3)	555	561	0	(3)
Oregon	2,730	1,197	19	0	1,450	8	(3)	143
Pennsylvania	5,488	2,888	548	7	3,762	(3)	(3)	50
Puerto Rico	(3)	(3)	(3)	(3)	(3)	(3)	0	(3)
Rhode Island	346	233	0	(3)	113	0	0	(3)
South Carolina	1,009	853	2	0	154	0	2	0
South Dakota	788	254	0	(3)	312	223	1	(3)
Tennessee	3,574	1,369	4	(3)	1,608	591	(4)	(3)
Texas	5,848	1,808	11	(3)	3,988	40	24	(3)
Utah	1,056	116	24	11	906	(4)	0	(3)
Vermont	990	349	6	0	65	539	4	(4)
Virgin Islands	23	18	0	0	6	0	0	6
Virginia	2,484	346	1	(3)	995	1,139	16	0
Washington	2,442	2,171	81	0	189	258	113	0
West Virginia	732	266	17	(3)	175	965	5	(3)
Wisconsin	5,863	3,349	400	0	1,037	965		0
Wyoming	1,180	802	84	(3)	64	230		(3)

TABLE 12–17.—NON-JOBS FAMILIES [5] RECEIVING IV–A PAID CHILD CARE, WITH AND WITHOUT EARNED INCOME, BY AFDC PROGRAM STATUS AND BY STATE—FISCAL YEAR 1992—Continued

[Average monthly number]

State	Total [1] families	Families with earnings and				Families without earnings and		
		Receiving AFDC-basic	Receiving AFDC–UP	Applying for AFDC	In transition	Receiving AFDC-basic	Receiving AFDC–UP	Applying for AFDC
U.S. totals	102,908	37,341	1,450	91	38,539	21,339	780	200

[1] "Total Families" may not equal the sum of the categories due to incomplete, inconsistent, or duplicated State reporting.
[2] Children-level data are used as a proxy for one or more categories or for "Total Families."
[3] The State indicates that the data are not applicable.
[4] Data are applicable to the State, but not reported.
[5] Data are reported for AFDC recipients who are employed or participating in a non-JOBS education and training program, Tribal JOBS participants, and families receiving transitional child care.

Source: DHHS/Administration for Children and Families.

TABLE 12–18.—NON-JOBS AFDC FAMILIES[5] RECEIVING IV–A PAID CHILD CARE, BY TYPE OF CARE ARRANGEMENT AND BY STATE—FISCAL YEAR 1992

[Preliminary data]

| State | Total[1] families | Families by type of care arrangement (average monthly number) | | | | |
| | | Care provided by a relative | | Care provided by a nonrelative in | | |
		In child's home	Outside child's home	Child's home	Family day care home	Center care
Alabama	(4)	(4)	(4)	(4)	(4)	(4)
Alaska	42	6	5	3	11	19
Arizona	1,301	14	85	4	134	1,063
Arkansas	2,175	14	23	13	168	1,956
California	(4)	(4)	(4)	(4)	(4)	(4)
Colorado	(4)	(4)	(4)	(4)	(4)	(4)
Connecticut	487	(4)	(4)	(4)	(4)	(4)
Delaware	250	1	1	1	72	186
District of Columbia	71	(4)	(4)	(4)	(4)	(4)
Florida	1,944	10	16	16	76	1,826
Georgia	3,994	270	462	280	211	2,771
Guam	0	0	0	0	0	0
Hawaii	190	(4)	(4)	(4)	(4)	(4)
Idaho	295	9	37	16	106	134
Illinois	199	7	14	21	50	107
Indiana	1,289	152	307	68	372	466
Iowa	1,426	(4)	(4)	(4)	(4)	(4)
Kansas	(4)	(4)	(4)	(4)	(4)	(4)
Kentucky	57	5	14	14	22	22
Louisiana	10	1	2	(3)	5	2
Maine	(4)	(4)	(4)	(4)	(4)	(4)
Maryland	2,836	0	0	0	1,370	1,467
Massachusetts	1,012	81	104	388	441	0
Michigan	7,438	(4)	(4)	(4)	(4)	(4)
Minnesota	164	10	22	16	77	39
Mississippi	1	0	1	0	0	0
Missouri	1,113	26	85	55	405	603
Montana	(4)	(4)	(4)	(4)	(4)	(4)
Nebraska	2,303	85	41	101	1,094	1,089
Nevada	(4)	(4)	(4)	(4)	(4)	(4)
New Hampshire	565	30	61	48	110	198
New Jersey	3,254	(4)	(4)	(4)	(4)	(4)
New Mexico	306	15	65	78	43	106
New York	3,384	72	282	168	2,155	708
North Carolina	5,041	322	734	175	627	3,184
North Dakota	184	39	91	21	38	7
Ohio	1,673	0	125	0	799	750
Oklahoma	1,330	1	4	8	142	1,177
Oregon	1,280	213	251	156	636	333
Pennsylvania	3,436	(4)	(4)	(4)	(4)	(4)
Puerto Rico	(3)	(3)	(3)	(3)	(3)	(3)
Rhode Island	233	(4)	(4)	(4)	(4)	(4)
South Carolina	933	(4)	(4)	(4)	(4)	(4)
South Dakota	476	39	67	39	222	132
Tennessee	1,966	50	120	32	241	1,522
Texas	44	1	5	(3)	1	38

TABLE 12–18.—NON-JOBS AFDC FAMILIES [5] RECEIVING IV–A PAID CHILD CARE, BY TYPE OF CARE ARRANGEMENT AND BY STATE—FISCAL YEAR 1992—Continued

[Preliminary data]

| State | Total [1] families | Families by type of care arrangement (average monthly number) | | | | |
| | | Care provided by a relative | | Care provided by a nonrelative in | | |
		In child's home	Outside child's home	Child's home	Family day care home	Center care
Utah	151	(2)	(2)	1	45	103
Vermont	925	91	121	100	364	247
Virgin Islands	18	0	1	0	4	13
Virginia	1,490	71	60	62	576	720
Washington	2,378	354	249	430	524	822
West Virginia	557	28	150	0	145	235
Wisconsin	4,827	196	533	150	1,973	1,975
Wyoming	1,121	43	151	27	423	476
U.S. totals	64,169	2,256	4,289	2,491	13,682	24,496

[1] "Total Families" may not equal the sum of the categories due to incomplete, inconsistent, or duplicative State reporting.

[2] The State does not define "Type of Care Arrangements" according to Federal reporting requirements.

[3] The State indicates that the data are not applicable.

[4] Data are applicable to the State, but not reported.

[5] Data are reported for AFDC recipients who are employed or participating in a non-JOBS education and training program, and Tribal JOBS participants.

Source: DHHS, Administration for Children and Families.

TABLE 12–19.—CHILDREN RECEIVING TRANSITIONAL CHILD CARE, BY QUARTER AND BY STATE—FISCAL YEAR 1992, PRELIMINARY DATA

[Average monthly number]

State	October 1991 to December 1991	January 1992 to March 1992	April 1992 to June 1992	July 1992 to September 1992	Fiscal year 1992
Alabama	1,020	950	1,073	1,245	1,072
Alaska	115	107	104	82	102
Arizona	1,427	1,505	1,743	1,887	1,641
Arkansas	329	342	610	471	438
California	2,053	2,130	2,204	2,442	2,207
Colorado	586	586	586	586	586
Connecticut	792	772	803	900	817
Delaware	162	201	226	227	204
District of Columbia [1]	82	68	65	88	76
Florida	4,367	3,930	3,626	3,884	3,952
Georgia	1,160	1,283	1,346	1,606	1,349
Guam	9	8	8	3	7
Hawaii	65	52	41	47	51
Idaho	195	197	230	256	220
Illinois	1,771	2,172	2,504	2,785	2,308
Indiana	673	884	1,194	1,235	997
Iowa	344	339	364	362	352
Kansas	1,572	1,610	1,707	1,096	1,496
Kentucky	860	919	951	920	913
Louisiana	1,688	1,763	1,814	2,129	1,849
Maine	145	173	221	273	203
Maryland	[1] 302	579	633	704	[2] 656
Massachusetts	1,627	2,107	3,744	2,267	2,436
Michigan [1]	654	711	748	415	632
Minnesota	1,488	1,477	1,567	1,815	1,587
Mississippi	219	213	226	215	218
Missouri	1,429	1,581	1,876	2,215	1,776
Montana	305	305	334	348	323
Nebraska [1]	525	530	518	515	522
Nevada	316	414	335	303	342
New Hampshire	287	302	337	407	333
New Jersey	1,704	1,768	2,972	1,811	2,064
New Mexico	[1] 220	439	455	747	[2] 547
New York	1,513	1,731	1,869	2,128	1,808
North Carolina	2,123	2,538	2,914	3,242	2,704
North Dakota	277	276	268	275	274
Ohio	1,827	1,961	2,305	2,707	2,200
Oklahoma	840	872	978	998	922
Oregon	2,309	2,372	2,560	2,993	2,559
Pennsylvania	([4])	([4])	6,041	6,496	6,269
Puerto Rico	([3])	([3])	([3])	([3])	([3])
Rhode Island	177	170	162	([4])	170
South Carolina	195	200	233	221	212
South Dakota	487	486	498	513	496
Tennessee	2,187	2,229	2,896	2,639	2,488

TABLE 12–19.—CHILDREN RECEIVING TRANSITIONAL CHILD CARE, BY QUARTER AND BY STATE—FISCAL YEAR 1992, PRELIMINARY DATA—Continued

[Average monthly number]

State	October 1991 to December 1991	January 1992 to March 1992	April 1992 to June 1992	July 1992 to September 1992	Fiscal year 1992
Texas	5,617	6,258	6,568	7,212	6,414
Utah	788	856	957	1,049	913
Vermont	33	40	55	66	48
Virgin Islands	7	6	6	3	6
Virginia	1,445	1,486	1,486	1,883	1,575
Washington	94	199	409	528	307
West Virginia	296	293	341	342	318
Wisconsin	1,469	1,422	1,722	1,960	1,643
Wyoming [2]	53	65	71	69	65
U.S. totals	50,228	53,877	67,494	69,610	63,667

[1] Family-level data are used as a proxy.
[2] The fiscal year average consists of January 1992 through September 1992.
[3] The State indicates that the data are not applicable.
[4] Data are applicable, but not reported.

Source: DHHS/Administration for Children and Families.

TABLE 12–20.—FAMILIES RECEIVING TRANSITIONAL CHILD CARE BY TYPE OF CARE ARRANGEMENT AND BY STATE—FISCAL YEAR 1992

State	Families by type of care arrangement (average monthly number)					
	Total [1] families	Care provided by a relative		Care provided by a nonrelative in		
		In child's home	Outside child's home	Child's home	Family day care home	Center care
Alabama [2]	1,072	76	105	46	236	609
Alaska	73	1	2	0	21	49
Arizona	940	12	36	2	99	791
Arkansas	345	43	14	3	23	262
California	1,589	128	190	147	701	446
Colorado	314	(4)	(4)	(4)	(4)	(4)
Connecticut	680	(4)	(4)	(4)	(4)	(4)
Delaware	126	0	1	0	34	97
District of Columbia	76	(4)	(4)	(4)	(4)	(4)
Florida	2,447	29	25	40	159	2,195
Georgia	801	84	132	72	50	463
Guam	5	2	3	0	0	1
Hawaii	42	0	5	0	31	6
Idaho	142	4	34	7	65	38
Illinois	1,353	104	388	194	311	357
Indiana	607	81	182	40	212	118
Iowa	232	0	0	0	34	199
Kansas	(4)	(4)	(4)	(4)	(4)	(4)
Kentucky	623	68	116	130	15	295
Louisiana	1,175	128	285	35	550	177

TABLE 12–20.—FAMILIES RECEIVING TRANSITIONAL CHILD CARE BY TYPE OF CARE ARRANGEMENT AND BY STATE—FISCAL YEAR 1992—Continued

State	Families by type of care arrangement (average monthly number)					
	Total [1] families	Care provided by a relative		Care provided by a nonrelative in		
		In child's home	Outside child's home	Child's home	Family day care home	Center care
Maine	130	5	9	12	92	12
Maryland	357	37	24	22	139	136
Massachusetts	1,608	0	0	120	133	1,356
Michigan	632	([4])	([4])	([4])	([4])	([4])
Minnesota	992	29	79	32	514	338
Mississippi	133	15	27	4	17	69
Missouri	1,078	41	118	91	402	488
Montana	160	([4])	40	([4])	81	41
Nebraska	522	27	15	31	291	192
Nevada	161	10	3	13	6	130
New Hampshire	215	11	23	22	43	83
New Jersey	1,352	([4])	([4])	([4])	([4])	([4])
New Mexico	261	20	45	64	38	95
New York	1,285	4	73	5	441	762
North Carolina	1,386	104	292	96	242	652
North Dakota	212	15	54	19	119	27
Ohio	1,353	0	62	0	703	588
Oklahoma	555	1	5	1	64	484
Oregon	1,450	14	348	21	903	194
Pennsylvania	3,762	([4])	([4])	([4])	([4])	([4])
Puerto Rico	([3])	([3])	([3])	([3])	([3])	([3])
Rhode Island	113	5	7	1	16	85
South Carolina	154	([4])	([4])	([4])	([4])	([4])
South Dakota	312	29	37	34	163	63
Tennessee	1,608	110	203	52	273	970
Texas	3,388	46	197	9	105	3,658
Utah [5]	906	([4])	([4])	8	298	600
Vermont	65	11	9	21	17	4
Virgin Islands	6	0	0	0	0	6
Virginia	995	87	82	24	325	477
Washington	200	26	21	33	48	72
West Virginia	175	11	75	([3])	58	67
Wisconsin	1,037	42	115	32	424	424
Wyoming	65	2	9	1	32	21
U.S. totals	39,870	1,462	3,490	1,484	8,528	18,197

[1] "Total Families" may not equal the sum of the categories due to incomplete, inconsistent, or duplicated State reporting.
[2] Children-level data are used as a proxy for one or more categories or for "Total Families."
[3] The State indicates that the data are not applicable.
[4] Data are applicable to the State, but not reported.
[5] The State does not define "Type of Care Arrangements" according to Federal reporting requirements.

Source: DHHS/Administration for Children and Families.

CHILD CARE LICENSING AND IMPROVEMENT GRANTS

The Family Support Act of 1988 (P.L. 100–485) amended title IV–A of the Social Security Act to authorize $13 million for each of fiscal years 1990 and 1991 for Federal matching grants to States for improvement of State licensing and registration requirements and to monitor child care for children receiving AFDC care. The Omnibus Budget Reconciliation Act of 1990 (P.L. 101–508) modified the purposes of the grant program so that, beginning with fiscal year 1991, grants are used for enforcing standards with respect to all title IV–A child care instead of for monitoring AFDC care. The law also required States to spend at least 50 percent of their grants for the training of child care providers. Public Law 101–508 authorized $50 million for the program for each of fiscal years 1992, 1993, and 1994. State allocations are based on the number of AFDC children in a State compared to the total in the United States. States must provide matching funds equal to not less than 10 percent of the amount of the grant. Congress did not appropriate funds for the program for fiscal years 1992 through 1994.

CHILD CARE AND DEVELOPMENT BLOCK GRANT

The Child Care and Development Block Grant program was authorized as an amendment to the Omnibus Budget Reconciliation Act of 1990, and is targeted to child care services for low-income families, as well as for activities to improve the overall quality and supply of child care for families in general. Appropriated funds are distributed to States, territories, and tribes (grantees) based on a formula in law, and no match is required. The formula reserves up to 0.5 percent for the territories and up to 3 percent for Indian tribes and tribal organizations. Remaining funds are allocated to the States based on the States' proportion of children under age 5 and the number of children receiving free or reduced-priced school lunches, as well as the States' per capita income.

The program is authorized for 5 years, through fiscal year 1995, at the following levels: $750 million for fiscal year 1991, $825 million for fiscal year 1992, $925 million for fiscal year 1993, and "such sums as necessary" for fiscal years 1994 and 1995. For fiscal year 1991, $732 million was appropriated for the program and was available for obligation on September 7, 1991. For fiscal year 1993, $893 million was appropriated and is available for obligation on September 30, 1993. Table 12–21 provides State allocations for fiscal years 1992 and 1993.

The law requires States to use 25 percent of their allotments for activities to improve the quality of child care and to increase the availability of early childhood development and before- and after-school child care services. The remaining 75 percent is for child care services *and* for activities to improve the quality and availability of child care. States must use at least 75 percent of the 25 percent share (18.5 percent of a State's total allotment) to establish, expand, or operate, through grants or contracts, early childhood development or before- and after-school child care programs or both. Twenty percent (5 percent of total funds) must be used for at least one or more of the following quality improvement activities: providing assistance to resource and referral programs; providing grants or loans to assist providers in meeting applicable State and local child care standards; monitoring the compliance and enforcement of State and local regulatory requirements; providing training and technical assistance in relevant child care areas, such as health and safety, nutrition, first aid, child abuse detection and prevention; and improving salaries of child care workers. States can use the remaining 5 percent (1.25 percent) for any of the activities allowed under the 25 percent share. With regard to the 75 percent of funds, regulations provide that 90 percent must be used for services, and up to 10 percent can be used for activities to improve child care quality and availability *and* administrative costs. Grantees can spend more on administrative costs associated with setting up voucher programs if granted permission of DHHS.

Children under age 13 who come from families with incomes at or below 75 percent of the grantee median income and reside with parents (or a parent) who are working, attending school, or in a job training program are eligible for services. Children also are eligible if they are receiving or need to receive protective services. Priority is to be given to serving children in very low-income families and children with special needs.

Child care providers receiving block grant assistance must meet all licensing or regulatory requirements, including registration requirements, applicable under State or local law. Providers who are 18 years of age or older who care only for grandchildren, nieces, or nephews must be registered and comply only with any State requirements that govern relative care. Providers that are *not* required by State or local law to be licensed or regulated must be registered with the State as a condition of funding. Registration procedures must be designed to facilitate payment and permit the State to inform providers of the availability of health and safety training, technical assistance, and other information. Providers (except grandparents, aunts, and uncles) must also meet certain health and safety standards if they are not already doing so. The standards must cover: prevention and control of infectious diseases (including immunization); building and physical premises safety; and minimum health and safety training appropriate to the provider setting (i.e., center, family home, etc.).

States have the option of imposing more stringent standards and requirements on child care providers funded under the program than those imposed on other providers in the State. Any reductions that are made in child care standards must be reported and explained to DHHS in the State's annual report on the program. In addition, States are required to conduct a one-time review of their child care licensing and regulatory requirements and policies. The requirement is to be waived if such a review was conducted in the last 3 years.

States are required to give eligible families the option of (1) enrolling their children with an eligible provider that has a grant from or contract with the State's block grant program or (2) receiving a child care certificate with which they can purchase child care. This option only applies to funding for child care services from the 75 percent portion of the State's allocation. Certificates are not an option in providing early childhood development and before- and after-school care under the 25 percent set-aside.

Child care certificates can be used only to pay for child care services from eligible providers, including sectarian child care providers. Certificates must be issued directly to the parent and must be worth amounts that are commensurate with contract/grant values. States have until October 1, 1992, to have a certificate program in place. States are directed by the regulations to make the certificate option available to all families offered services under the program. Certificates can be checks or other disbursements at the discretion of the State.

Payment rates for child care funded by the block grant must be sufficient to ensure equal access for eligible children to comparable child care in the State or substate area that is provided to children not eligible for Federal or State child care subsidies. In addition, the payment rates must take into account variations in the cost of child care due to setting, age of children, and special needs of children.

The block grant program contains specific requirements with regard to the use of funds for religious activities. Under the program, a provider that receives operating assistance as a result of a direct grant from, or contract with, a Government agency may not use the assistance for any sectarian purpose or activity, including religious worship and instruction. However, a sectarian provider that receives a child care certificate from an eligible parent is not so restricted in the use of funds.

States are required to report annually to the Secretary of DHHS on how they used their funds. Reports are to include information on the number of children served, types and number of providers assisted, child care staff salaries and compensation, improvements made in child care quality and availability, and descriptions of health and safety standards. States must also conduct program audits and submit reports to the State legislature and the Secretary of DHHS. The Secretary of DHHS must report to Congress annually on the State reports.

At the Federal level, the program is administered by the Administration for Children and Families, DHHS. DHHS is required to coordinate all child care activities within the agency and with similar activities in other Federal agencies. DHHS is also required to publish a list of State child care standards at least once every 3 years, give technical assistance to the States in operating their block grant programs, and monitor State compliance with program requirements.

TABLE 12–21.—STATE ALLOCATIONS UNDER THE CHILD CARE AND DEVELOPMENT BLOCK GRANT, 1991–94

[By fiscal years; in thousands of dollars]

State	1991 actual	1992 actual	1993 actual	1994 estimate
Alabama	$16,692	18,408	19,085	19,082
Alaska	1,344	1,535	1,767	1,766
Arizona	12,195	14,064	15,790	15,788
Arkansas	9,043	9,966	10,550	10,548
California	76,561	90,062	100,638	100,622
Colorado	8,074	8,981	9,731	9,730
Connecticut	5,252	5,994	6,475	6,474
Delaware	1,369	1,547	1,702	1,702
District of Columbia	1,420	1,644	1,698	1,697
Florida	32,788	38,408	43,179	43,172
Georgia	21,973	25,037	27,447	27,443
Hawaii	2,642	2,902	3,025	3,025
Idaho	3,628	4,072	4,374	4,373
Illinois	27,217	30,716	33,117	33,112
Indiana	13,731	15,372	16,604	16,601
Iowa	7,191	7,755	8,470	8,468
Kansas	6,853	7,366	7,866	7,865
Kentucky	13,646	15,256	16,298	16,296
Louisiana	21,669	23,624	24,156	24,152
Maine	2,997	3,379	3,657	3,657
Maryland	9,185	10,339	11,444	11,442
Massachusetts	9,858	11,130	12,377	12,375
Michigan	22,120	24,658	26,717	26,712
Minnesota	10,465	11,581	12,366	12,364
Mississippi	14,631	15,845	16,376	16,373
Missouri	13,768	15,270	16,304	16,301
Montana	2,532	2,780	2,944	2,943
Nebraska	4,359	4,809	5,074	5,073
Nevada	2,441	2,874	3,293	3,292
New Hampshire	1,832	2,058	2,241	2,240
New Jersey	12,858	14,805	16,182	16,180
New Mexico	6,994	7,597	8,260	8,258
New York	41,373	46,605	50,536	50,528
North Carolina	20,624	23,390	24,883	24,879
North Dakota	2,092	2,236	2,289	2,288
Ohio	26,424	29,531	32,042	32,037
Oklahoma	11,292	12,524	13,373	13,370
Oregon	7,115	8,139	8,875	8,873
Pennsylvania	25,038	27,797	29,687	29,683
Puerto Rico	22,509	23,545	24,724	24,721

TABLE 12–21.—STATE ALLOCATIONS UNDER THE CHILD CARE AND DEVELOPMENT
BLOCK GRANT, 1991–94—Continued

[By fiscal years; in thousands of dollars]

State	1991 actual	1992 actual	1993 actual	1994 estimate
Rhode Island	1,984	2,252	2,478	2,477
South Carolina	13,644	15,351	16,443	16,440
South Dakota	2,747	2,956	3,085	3,084
Tennessee	15,751	17,521	18,585	18,582
Texas	66,622	74,989	80,706	80,694
Utah	6,625	7,137	8,340	8,339
Vermont	1,260	1,432	1,539	1,539
Virginia	13,151	14,844	16,426	16,423
Washington	11,354	12,974	14,029	14,027
West Virginia	6,065	6,479	6,671	6,670
Wisconsin	11,914	13,080	13,937	13,935
Wyoming	1,386	1,517	1,593	1,593
Subtotal	706,298	794,133	859,448	859,308
Territories	3,660	4,115	4,453	4,452
Indian tribe set aside	21,957	24,688	26,719	26,714
Discretionary funds	....	2,062	2,092	2,232
Total budget authority	731,915	825,000	892,711	892,711

Totals may differ from sum of individual amounts because of rounding.

Source: Administration for Children and Families, DHHS.

TITLE XX—SOCIAL SERVICES BLOCK GRANT

Title XX of the Social Security Act authorizes grants to States for providing social services that are determined appropriate by the State. The program operates as a "capped entitlement", under which States are allocated funds based on their relative population size up to a nationwide ceiling. No matching funds are required. In addition, there are no Federal eligibility requirements for participants. The program is administered at the Federal level by ACF, DHHS. The Omnibus Budget Reconciliation Act of 1989 (P.L. 101–239) permanently authorized $2.8 billion annually for the program, beginning in fiscal year 1990.

Available information on use of title XX funds indicates that a majority of States typically spend some portion of their grants on child care services. According to State reports on the intended use of title XX funds (known as preexpenditure reports), 45 States funded child care services in fiscal year 1990. Another source of data on title XX is the Voluntary Cooperative Information System (VCIS) of the American Public Welfare Association funded by DHHS. VCIS is a national data base comprised of aggregate State program statistics. The VCIS found that, based on data from 23 States, child care services accounted for 16 percent of fiscal year 1990 title XX expenditures. In addition, expenditures for child care services accounted for 22 percent of expenditures for services for children among 14 States. VCIS data from 25 States provide information on eligibility rules States use for title XX services in fiscal year 1990. Twenty of those States determine eligibility for child care services based on income standards. AFDC recipients are eligible for title XX child care in 16 States. Individuals can be eligible for title XX child care in 15 States without regard to income.

More information on title XX, including State allocations, is provided in section 13.

STATE DEPENDENT CARE PLANNING AND DEVELOPMENT GRANTS

The State dependent care grant program provides Federal matching funds to States to plan, develop, establish, expand, improve, or operate before- and after-school child care programs for school-age children and resource and referral systems that provide information on dependent care services. Funds are allotted to States based on State total population compared to the United States' total population, except that no State can receive less than $50,000 in each fiscal year. The program is administered at the Federal level by ACF, DHHS. The program is authorized through fiscal year 1994 by the Augustus F. Hawkins Human Services Reauthorization Act of 1990 (P.L. 101–501). The law authorized $20 million for each of fiscal years 1990 and 1991 and such sums as may be necessary for fiscal years 1992 through 1994. For fiscal year 1993, the dependent care program received $12.9 million in appropriations.

States are required to use 40 percent of their grants on resource and referral systems for services for children and/or the elderly and 60 percent on school-age child care programs and services. These percentage requirements may be waived if States request it. Resource and referral information services funded by the program cannot include dependent care services that are out of compliance with State and local laws. Funds for school-age child care services must be targeted to low-income families. Such services must meet State and local child care licensing laws and regulations. States cannot use funds to make cash payments to intended program recipients of dependent care services, including child care services.

Public Law 101–501 required States to collect information on the number of children who participate in program-funded school-age child care, characteristics of these children, salary levels of child care program employees, and the number of clients served by resource and referral programs funded by the program. DHHS has never compiled this information.

CHILD AND ADULT CARE FOOD PROGRAM

The Child and Adult Care Food program is permanently authorized under the National School Lunch Act of 1946. The program provides Federal financial assistance for breakfasts, lunches, suppers, and snacks as well as commodity assistance for lunches (and when commodities are available, breakfasts) served to children in licensed child care centers and family or group day care homes. Children under age 12, migrant children under age 15, and handicapped children (no age limit) are eligible to participate, although the vast majority of children served are between 3 and 5 years old. Funded at $1.3 billion in fiscal year 1993, the child care food program is the single largest source of direct financial assistance child care. The program is administered at the Federal level by the Food and Nutrition Service of the U.S. Department of Agriculture.

Program sponsorship is restricted to public and private nonprofit sponsors, and generally, to for-profit sponsors if at least 25 percent of the children in their care receive support under the Social Services Block Grant (title XX of the Social Security Act).

The child care food program has three components: a child day care center component, a family and group home care component, and an adult care component. Although *all* children participating in child care centers, as in the school lunch and breakfast programs, are eligible to receive subsidized meals or snacks regardless of their family income, the Federal reimbursement for each meal or snack varies according to need, and the same family income cutoff levels apply. Child care centers may receive subsidies for up to two meals and two snacks, or three meals and one snack for each child in care more than 8 hours a day. Otherwise, subsidies are provided for up to two meals and one snack, or one meal and two snacks per day. The reimbursement rates for meals served in child care centers are the same as those provided for school lunches and breakfasts; there also are snack reimbursement rates set for this program, and these are annually adjusted for inflation.

The family and group home care components of the child care food program operates differently. There is no income test for meals or snacks served,[12] and all breakfasts, lunches, suppers, and snacks are subsidized at the same rates, with variation only by the type of meal being served. Reimbursement is provided for no more than two meals and one snack, or one meal and two snacks per child per day, regardless of the length of time a child is in care, except in Minnesota where a pilot project allows one additional meal or snack reimbursement per child per day. Administrative payments also are provided for sponsors of family and group day care homes, at a set rate per month.

The child care food program is also eligible to receive a guaranteed level of commodity support for each lunch served, and when appropriate commodities are available, for breakfasts. The guaranteed level of commodity assistance may be provided in the form of the actual commodities or in their cash equivalents.

As noted above, for-profit child care centers generally may not participate in the child care food program unless they receive title XX block grant funds for 25 percent or more of the children in their care. Thus, for-profit facilities that serve low-income children without the benefit of title XX block grant funds are not able to participate in the child care food program regardless of how many low-income children are served.

---

[12] An exception exists for children of individuals operating family and group day care homes, who may not receive federally subsidized meals unless their family income is below 185 percent of poverty.

Section 13. Title XX Social Services Block Grant Program

THE EVOLUTION OF THE SOCIAL SERVICES BLOCK GRANT PROGRAM [1]

Social services for recipients of public aid were not funded under the original Social Security legislation, the Social Security Act of 1935, although it was later argued that cash alone would not address the needs of the poor. State social services expenditures for welfare recipients became eligible for 50 percent Federal funding in 1956, but many States chose not to particpate. The Social Security Act was amended in 1962, with emphasis on the importance of preventive and rehabilitative services, and a higher Federal matching rate for services of 75 percent. The 1962 amendments also expanded eligibility for social services to both former and potential welfare recipients. No limit was placed on the Federal expenditure level.

In 1967, the Social Security Act again was amended to authorize funding for so-called "hard" social services, such as job training and child care, in a more aggressive effort to move people from welfare to work. The new legislation also required States to establish a single organizational unit in the State agency responsible for administering social services, and provided an enhanced match (85 percent) for social services provided during the first year after the law took effect.

Administration of the Federal social services program was formally separated from administration of the Federal cash assistance program in 1967, as part of a reorganization within the Department of Health, Education, and Welfare, and States were required by regulation to separate the administration of cash assistance and social services in 1972.

Federal spending for social services increased from $281.6 million for fiscal year 1967 to $1,688.4 million for fiscal year 1972, prompting legislation (P.L. 92–512) which placed a ceiling on Federal expenditures for social services of $2.5 billion and directed that funds be divided among States according to their relative populations. The law also limited to 10 percent the amount of funds that could be spent on services to former or potential welfare recipients.

Legislation signed into law on January 4, 1975, established title XX of the Social Security Act. Under the legislation, the $2.5 billion ceiling on Federal social services expenditures was retained, along with the population-based allocation formula. The legislation was designed to give maximum flexibility to the States in designing their social services programs, but included public participation planning requirements, limitations on the use of funds for certain activities, and certain eligibility requirements.

---

[1] History of the program is from "Title XX of the Social Security Act: Program Description, Current Issues," by Karen Spar, Congressional Research Service, February 27, 1981.

By fiscal year 1981 the entitlement ceiling for the title XX social services program was $2.9 billion. An additional $16.1 million was available apart from title XX for social services expenditures of the territories, and $75 million was available to the States for staff training costs related to title XX activities, for a total of $2.991 billion for all Federal social services expenditures. Under Public Law 96–272, enacted in 1980, the title XX entitlement ceiling was scheduled to increase to $3 billion for fiscal year 1982, and by $100 million a year until it reached $3.3 billion for fiscal year 1985.

The Omnibus Budget Reconciliation Act of 1981 (P.L. 97–35) amended title XX to establish a block grant, under which funding for social services to the States and territories, and social services staff training, were combined. The legislation also reduced the title XX entitlement ceiling to $2.4 billion for fiscal year 1982 and provided for increases to $2.45 billion for fiscal year 1983, $2.5 billion for fiscal year 1984, $2.6 billion for fiscal year 1985 and $2.7 billion for fiscal year 1986 and years thereafter. The law also eliminated Federal mandates regarding priority recipients, and eliminated provisions relating to the targeting of services to low-income individuals and families.

The emergency jobs bill (P.L. 98–8), enacted in March 1983, appropriated an additional $225 million for fiscal year 1983 that also was available for carryover to fiscal year 1984. These additional funds were allocated to the States on the basis of a formula intended to respond to the needs of the unemployed served by the jobs bill. One-half of the funds was allocated on the basis of population; one-third based on the number of unemployed individuals in the State; and one-sixth among those States whose average unadjusted unemployment rate from June 1982 through November 1982 was 9.4 percent or higher. In October 1983, as part of legislation to extend the Federal supplemental compensation program (P.L. 98–135), the title XX ceiling was increased by $200 million for fiscal 1984 to $2.7 billion and by $100 million for fiscal year 1985 to $2.7 billion.

Because of the concern by Congress of reports of child sexual abuse in day care centers, a $25 million increase in title XX funding for fiscal year 1985 was appropriated for use by the States in providing training of child day care staff, State licensing and enforcement officials, and the parents of children in child day care. The earmarked funds were included in the continuing resolution for fiscal year 1985 (P.L. 98–473). States were required to have in effect by September 30, 1985, procedures for screening and conducting background and criminal history checks of child care staff, or one-half of the day care training allotment was to be deducted from the regular State title XX allocation in fiscal year 1986 or 1987. According to HHS, only six States enacted such procedures by the required date. As required by Public Law 98–473, in January 1985, the Secretary of HHS distributed to States a Model Child Care Standards Act with particular attention to staff training and supervision, employment history checks, and parent visitation.

The 1987 Budget Reconciliation Act (P.L. 100–203) included a $50 million increase in the title XX entitlement ceiling for fiscal year 1988. These funds were not appropriated.

The Medicare and Medicaid Patient Program Act of 1987 (P.L. 100–93) amended title XX to exclude individuals and entities who have committed acts of fraud or abuse under the Medicaid, Medicare, Maternal and Child Health, or the title XX programs from receiving title XX funds.

The Omnibus Reconciliation Act of 1989 (P.L. 101–239) included a permanent $100 million increase in the title XX entitlement ceiling to $2.8 billion, beginning for fiscal year 1990.

The Omnibus Budget Reconciliation Act of 1993 (P.L. 103–66) made $1 billion available to states under title XX for those places designated as qualified empowerment zones or enterprise communities. This temporary program is described in more detail at the end of this section.

TITLE XX ALLOCATION FORMULA AND HISTORICAL FUNDING LEVELS

Title XX social services block grant funds are allocated to the States on the basis of population. The allotments for Puerto Rico, Guam, the Virgin Islands and the Northern Marianas from the national total are based on their allocation for fiscal year 1981 adjusted to reflect the new total funding level. The 1987 Budget Reconciliation Act (P.L. 100–203) extended eligibility for title XX funds to American Samoa. The Federal funds are available to States without a State matching requirement, compared to the 25-percent State matching required for most title XX funds under prior title XX law.

Table 13–1 shows the title XX funding levels, in both nominal dollars and real 1994 dollars, from fiscal year 1977 through fiscal year 1994 and future years. Over the 17-year period (1977 to 1994), title XX funding has declined in real terms by $3,826 million, a reduction of 58 percent. Table 2 shows the total funds available to each State and territory under title XX in selected fiscal years from 1989 to 1995.

TABLE 13–1.—TITLE XX SOCIAL SERVICES BLOCK GRANT FUNDING LEVELS

[In millions of dollars]

Fiscal year	Entitlement ceiling	
	Nominal dollars	1994 dollars
1977	[1] 2,796	6,626
1978	[1] 2,791	6,214
1979	[1] 2,991	6,115
1980	[2] 2,791	5,130
1981	[2] 2,991	4,999
1982	[3] 2,400	3,747
1983	[4] 2,675	3,995
1984	2,700	3,868
1985	[5] 2,725	3,764
1986	[6] 2,584	3,485
1987	2,700	3,538
1988	2,700	3,399
1989	2,700	3,244
1990	[7] 2,762	3,161
1991	2,800	3,050
1992	2,800	2,961
1993	2,800	2,874
1994 and future years	2,800	2,800
Change between 1977 and 1994:		
Dollar amount	4	−3,826
Percentage change	0	−57.7

[1] Included $16 million for Puerto Rico, Guam and the Virgin Islands and $59 million in fiscal year 1976, $80 million in fiscal year 1977 and $75 million in fiscal years 1978 and 1979 for title XX staff training.

[2] Included $16.1 million for Puerto Rico, Guam, the Virgin Islands and the Northern Marianas and $75 million for title XX staff training.

[3] Public Law 97–35 eliminated separate funding for title XX staff training.

[4] Includes $225 million appropriated in the emergency jobs bill (Public Law 98–8).

[5] Includes $25 million earmarked for training of day care providers, licensing officials and parents including training in the prevention of child abuse in child care settings.

[6] The entitlement ceiling for fiscal year 1986 was $2.7 billion. However, the Gramm-Rudman-Hollings legislation sequestration of funds for fiscal year 1986 reduced the funding by $116 million to $2.584 billion.

[7] The entitlement ceiling for fiscal year 1990 was $2.8 billion. However, the Gramm-Rudman-Hollings legislation sequestration of funds for fiscal year 1990 reduced the funding by $37.8 million to $2.762 billion.

Note.—Nominal dollars converted to constant 1994 dollars using the CPI–X1 price index, CBO forecast for 1994.

TABLE 13–2.—TITLE XX SOCIAL SERVICES BLOCK GRANT ALLOCATIONS BY STATE AND TERRITORY

[In millions, by fiscal year]

	1989	1991	1993	1994	1995 esti-mate
Total	$2,700.0	$2,800.0	$2,800.0	$2,800.0	$2,800.0
Alabama	45.1	46.5	46.2	45.1	45.1
Alaska	5.9	5.9	6.2	6.3	6.4
American Samoa .	.2	.2	.1	.1	.1
Arizona	36.5	39.9	41.0	41.4	41.8
Arkansas	26.4	27.1	28.3	26.2	26.2
California	300.5	320.7	333.2	335.4	336.9
Colorado	36.4	37.4	38.9	37.3	37.9
Connecticut	35.5	36.6	38.8	36.3	35.8
Delaware	7.1	7.5	7.5	7.5	7.5
District of Colum-bia	7.0	7.0	6.8	6.6	6.4
Florida	130.0	139.7	144.8	146.6	147.2
Georgia	68.0	71.8	72.5	73.1	73.7
Guam	.5	.5	.5	.5	.5
Hawaii	11.8	12.4	12.4	12.5	12.7
Idaho	11.2	11.4	11.3	11.5	11.6
Illinois	128.7	131.6	128.0	127.4	127.0
Indiana	61.3	62.9	62.1	61.9	61.8
Iowa	31.8	32.1	31.1	30.9	30.7
Kansas	27.4	28.3	27.7	27.5	27.5
Kentucky	41.5	42.2	41.3	41.0	41.0
Louisiana	50.1	49.9	47.2	46.9	46.8
Maine	13.1	13.7	13.7	13.6	13.5
Maryland	49.7	52.4	53.5	53.7	53.6
Massachusetts	65.0	66.7	67.4	66.2	65.5
Michigan	101.9	104.7	104.1	103.4	103.0
Minnesota	46.9	48.8	49.0	48.9	48.9
Mississippi	29.2	29.7	28.8	26.6	28.5
Missouri	56.4	58.2	57.3	57.0	56.7
Montana	9.1	9.1	8.9	8.9	9.0
Nebraska	17.8	18.1	17.7	17.6	17.5
Nevada	10.7	11.9	13.5	14.2	14.5
New Hampshire ...	11.4	12.3	12.4	12.2	12.1
New Jersey	84.9	87.5	86.5	85.7	85.0
New Mexico	16.5	17.1	17.0	17.1	17.3
New York	198.0	202.9	201.4	199.4	197.8
North Carolina	70.5	73.5	74.2	74.4	74.7

TABLE 13-2.—TITLE XX SOCIAL SERVICES BLOCK GRANT ALLOCATIONS BY STATE AND TERRITORY—Continued

[In millions, by fiscal year]

	1989	1991	1993	1994	1995 estimate
North Dakota	7.6	7.6	7.2	7.0	6.9
Northern Mariana Islands	.1	.1	.1	.1	.1
Ohio	119.8	123.0	121.4	120.8	120.2
Oklahoma	36.8	36.7	35.2	35.1	35.1
Oregon	30.1	31.3	31.8	32.3	32.5
Pennsylvania	132.4	135.9	133.0	132.1	131.1
Puerto Rico	14.0	14.5	14.5	14.5	14.5
Rhode Island	10.9	11.2	11.2	11.1	11.0
South Carolina	37.6	39.3	39.0	39.3	39.3
South Dakota	7.9	8.1	7.8	7.8	7.8
Tennessee	53.5	55.4	54.6	54.7	54.8
Texas	185.8	190.7	190.2	191.5	192.7
Utah	18.5	19.1	19.3	19.5	19.8
Vermont	6.0	6.3	6.3	6.3	6.2
Virgin Islands	.5	.5	.5	.5	.5
Virginia	64.5	68.1	69.3	69.4	69.6
Washington	49.7	52.6	54.5	55.4	56.1
West Virginia	21.4	21.3	20.1	19.9	19.8
Wisconsin	53.3	55.0	54.8	54.7	54.7
Wyoming	5.6	5.4	5.1	5.1	5.1

Source: Department of Health and Human Services.

TITLE XX PROGRAM GOALS

The purpose of the title XX social services block grant program is to provide assistance to States to enable them to furnish services directed at the five goals of the statute:

—Achieving or maintaining economic self-support to prevent, reduce, or eliminate dependency;

—Achieving or maintaining self-sufficiency, including reduction or prevention of dependency;

—Preventing or remedying neglect, abuse, or exploitation of children and adults unable to protect their own interests, or preserving, rehabilitating or reuniting families;

—Preventing or reducing inappropriate institutional care by providing for community-based care, home-based care, or other forms of less intensive care; and

—Securing referral or admission for institutional care when other forms of care are not appropriate, or providing services to individuals in institutions.

States are given wide discretion to determine the services to be provided and the groups who may be eligible for services, usually low income families and individuals. In addition to supporting social services, the law allows States to use their allotment for staff training, administration, planning, evaluation, and purchasing technical assistance in developing, implementing, or administering the State social service program. States decide what amount of the Federal allotment to spend on services, training, and administration.

Some restrictions are placed on the use of title XX funds. Funds cannot be used for the following: most medical care except family planning; rehabilitation and certain detoxification services; purchase of land, construction, or major capital improvements; most room and board except emergency short-term services; educational services generally provided by public schools; most social services provided in and by employees of hospitals, nursing homes, and prisons; cash payments for subsistence; child day care services that do not meet State and local standards; and wages to individuals as a social service except wages of welfare recipients employed in child day care.

DATA ON SERVICES, RECIPIENTS AND EXPENDITURES UNDER TITLE XX

To date, limited information has been available on the use of title XX funds by the States. Under the title XX social services block grant program each State must submit a report to the Secretary of Health and Human Services on the intended use of its funds. These pre-expenditure reports are only required to include information about the types of activities to be funded and the characteristics of the individuals to be served.

The Family Support Act of 1988, Public Law 100–485, will strengthen reporting requirements. The new legislation requires States to submit annual reports containing detailed information on the services actually funded and the individuals served through title XX funds. The Department of Health and Human Services published a final rule on November 15, 1993 implementing the reporting requirements and providing uniform definitions of services.

Table 13–3 is a comparison of the primary services offered by the States taken from a Departmental summary of the pre-expenditure reports for fiscal years 1983 through 1993. Based on these reports, at least 35 States use title XX funds for each of the following services: protective services for children; child day care; home-based services; case management services; services for the disabled; foster care for children; adoption services; prevention/intervention services; adult protective services; and social support services.

In addition to the pre-expenditure reports, another source of data on title XX is from the Voluntary Cooperative Information System (VCIS) of the American Public Welfare Association funded by HHS.[2] The VCIS is a national data base comprised of aggregate State program statistics. A total of 33 State or territorial agencies participated in the data gathering activity for fiscal year 1990. The annual VCIS report cautions that the VCIS data base is incomplete even for these States since a number of States were able to provide only partial data or their data could not be used due to lack of con-

---

[2] This discussion of the VCIS summary is drawn directly from: "A Statistical Summary of the VCIS Social Services Block Grant (SSBG) Data for FY 86," American Public Welfare Association, February 1990.

formity with the reporting guidelines. Furthermore, the VCIS data base is comprised of both estimated and actual service and expenditure data. In the absence of more complete data, however, the data can be used to describe the characteristics of recipients, services and expenditures under the social services block grant in fiscal year 1990 for the States supplying information. However, without the application of an appropriate sampling technology, it is not possible to determine the extent to which the data can be generalized to the nation as a whole.

VCIS data from 31 States show that the Federal title XX social services block grant dollars combined with other Federal dollars (e.g., title IV–B, WIN, etc.) accounted for 46 percent of total social services expenditures in the 31 States during fiscal year 1990, while State dollars accounted for 41 percent of the total. Local dollars and private contributions accounted for 13 percent of the total.

VCIS data from 28 States show that 10 services accounted for almost three-quarters of all services provided under the title XX social services block grant, measured in terms of recipient counts. These services are: protective services for children (18 percent); information and referral services (12 percent); child day care services (8 percent); homemaker/home management/chore services (7 percent); counseling services (6 percent); preventive services for children and their families (5 percent); family planning services (5 percent); substitute care and placement services for children (5 percent); protective services for adults/elderly (4 percent); and services to status offenders and juvenile delinquents (3 percent).

Data from 23 States show that five services accounted for over two-thirds of the expenditures under the block grant in fiscal year 1990. These services include homemaker/home management/chore services (25 percent); child day care services (16 percent); protective services for children (12 percent); substitute care and placement services for children (12 percent); and services for disabled/handicapped persons (6 percent).

TABLE 13–3.—COMPARISON OF THE NUMBER OF STATES [1] OFFERING SELECTED SERVICES FOR FISCAL YEARS 1983–93

Services	1983	1986	1988	1990	1992	1993
Adoption	36	39	29	35	34	36
Case management [2]	......	......	26	26	33	38
Counseling	30	38	22	21	24	23
Day care—adults	37	31	23	26	28	27
Day care—children	50	52	51	45	47	49
Education/training	28	43	19	17	17	19
Emergency [3]	......	......	15	16	17	21
Employment [3]	......	......	21	23	22	23
Family planning	35	30	26	26	26	23
Foster care—adults	25	19	12	10	11	16
Foster care—children	34	31	29	30	31	37
Health-related	26	36	22	23	30	34
Home based [4]	51	55	45	46	46	45
Home delivered/congregate meals	23	28	20	20	22	20
Housing improvement	14	18	10	16	14	14
Information and referral	36	34	23	25	27	26
Legal	17	17	17	13	16	19
Placement	18	20	17	16	17	16
Prevention/intervention [5]	11	35	33	27	31	36
Protective—adults	44	46	34	30	32	36
Protective—children	52	54	38	42	46	50
Residential care/treatment	19	29	21	25	29	27
Social support [6]	2	25	27	45	37	35
Special services—children	19	28	27	19	18	22
Special services for the disabled	36	41	39	34	38	38
Special services for juvenile delinquents [2]	......	......	16	14	18	17
Substance abuse services	7	13	10	11	15	12
Services for unmarried parents	10	10	13	13	14	20
Transportation	25	33	30	25	27	30
Other [7]	5	36	20	19	19	13

[1] Includes 50 States, the District of Columbia, and the 5 eligible Insular areas.

[2] Identified as separate service for the first time in 1987. This is not meant to imply that the service was first available in 1987.

[3] Identified as a separate service for the first time in 1988. This is not meant to imply that the service was first available in 1988.

[4] Home based services include: homemaker, chore, home health, companionship, and home maintenance.

[5] Prevention/Intervention Services include: Investigation/assessment, family centered early intervention, home evaluation and supervision, preventive and restorative.

[6] Social Support Services include: socialization, recreation, camping, physical activity, living skills (money management), day treatment, family development, social adjustment, community living services, family management, life skills education, personal and financial management.

[7] Other Services include: social services in correctional facilities, services to Hispanics, homeless services, and Indian reservation services.

Source: U.S. Department of Health and Human Services—Fiscal Year Preexpenditure Reports.

TRANSFER OF FUNDS AMONG BLOCK GRANTS

Public Law 97–35, which created the title XX block grant, gave States the authority to transfer up to 10 percent of their annual allotment to one or any combination of the three health care block grants and/or the low-income home energy assistance block grant. (The three health care block grants are: the preventive health and health services block grant; the maternal and child health services block grant; and the alcohol, drug abuse, and mental health services block grant.) In turn, most other block grant statutes allow States to transfer funds to the title XX program.

According to the fiscal year 1993 pre-expenditure reports submitted to HHS by States, two States planned to transfer title XX funds to other programs. Florida planned to transfer funds to the Substance Abuse and Mental Health Services Administration Block Grant Program, and North Carolina planned to transfer funds to the Maternal and Child Health Services Block Grant and the Preventive Health and Health Services Block Grant Programs. Sixteen States planned to transfer funds from the Low-Income Home Energy Assistance Block Grant to supplement title XX funds (the Augustus F. Hawkins Human Services Reauthorization Act of 1990 eliminated the authority to transfer LIHEAP funds to other block grants, beginning for fiscal year 1994).

SOCIAL SERVICES IN EMPOWERMENT ZONES AND ENTERPRISE COMMUNITIES

The Omnibus Budget Reconciliation Act of 1993 will make $1 billion available on an entitlement basis under title XX for the Secretary of HHS to make grants to States for social services for qualified empowerment zones and enterprise communities (the legislation also provides certain tax incentives for zones and communities). Nine empowerment zones and 95 enterprise communities will be designated (subject to the availability of eligible areas) during 1994 and 1995. Six empowerment zones and 65 enterprise communities will be located in eligible urban areas and three empowerment zones and 30 enterprise communities will be located in rural areas.

An empowerment zone or enterprise community is qualified for purposes of the title XX grant if it has been designated a zone or community under part I of subchapter U of chapter I of the Internal Revenue Code of 1986 and if its strategic plan (required in an application for designation under the Internal Revenue Code) is qualified.

A qualified plan is a plan that: (1) includes a detailed description of the activities proposed for the area that are to be funded with the grant; (2) contains a commitment that the amounts provided will not be used to supplant Federal or non-Federal funds for services and activities which promote the purposes of the grant; (3) to the extent a State does not use the funds on certain program options, explains the reasons why not; and (4) was developed in cooperation with the local government or governments with jurisdiction over the zone or community.

With respect to each empowerment zone, the Secretary will make one grant ($50 million if urban, $20 million if rural) to each State in which the zone lies on the date of its designation, and a second grant of the same amount on the first day of the following fiscal year. With respect to each enterprise community, the Secretary will make one grant (equal to $\frac{1}{95}$ of $280 million) to each State in which the community lies on the date of its designation. States are required to remit to the Secretary any amount paid to the State this is not obligated by the end of the 2-year period beginning with the date of payment.

States (in conjunction with the local governments with jurisdiction over the zone or community) will have broad discretion in the use of the grant funds. States are required to use the funds for social services directed at three goals that are goals of the basic title XX grant program: achieving or maintaining economic self-support to prevent, reduce or eliminate dependency; achieving or maintaining self-sufficiency, including reduction or prevention of dependency; or preventing or remedying neglect, abuse, or exploitation of children and adults unable to protect their own interests, or preserving, rehabilitating or reuniting families. The funds also must be used in accordance with the strategic plan and on activities that benefit residents of the zone or community.

Despite the similar purposes for which funds may be used, the range of allowable services is narrower in some respects, and broader in others, under the title XX empowerment zone provisions relative to the basic title XX program. For example, the basic title XX program includes a broader range of purposes than those outlined above for the empowerment zone program. On the other hand, certain restrictions of the basic title XX program (e.g., restrictions that limit drug treatment services to initial detoxification, and restrictions on the use of funds for the payment of wages) are waived under the empowerment zone program, in order to carry out certain specified program options.

Section 14. Child Welfare, Foster Care, Adoption Assistance

BACKGROUND

Child welfare services focus on improving the conditions of children and their families and on improving or providing substitutes for functions the parents have difficulty in performing. Many private, nonprofit and government entities work to provide a range of child welfare services to families in need. The primary responsibility for child welfare services in the government, however, rests with the States. Each State has its own legal and administrative structures and programs that address the needs of children and there are many differences among the States. The Federal Government has also been involved in efforts to improve the welfare of children in specific areas of national concern since the early 1900's. Numerous Federal programs provide support for such services today, including several programs under titles IV–B and IV–E of the Social Security Act. In addition, services relating to child welfare may be provided at State discretion under the social services block grant program (title XX of the Social Security Act).[1]

Child welfare services encompass a broad range of activities, including child protection, care of the homeless and neglected, child social and nutritional development, and children in out-of-home care. The services provided may be supportive (e.g., help the family cope with problems or provide protection for children while the family learns to perform appropriate parenting roles); supplementary (e.g., provide financial assistance); or substitutive (e.g., foster care).[2]

It is generally agreed that it is in the best interests of children to live with their families. To this end, experts emphasize the value of preventive and rehabilitative services intended to help families stay together whenever possible, and emphasize the need to limit the duration of foster care placements by returning children to their homes whenever appropriate and finding permanent living arrangements for children who cannot be returned home.

This philosophy is reflected in the Federal programs authorized under titles IV–B and IV–E which support services to promote the welfare of children. Title IV–B authorizes funds to States for a broad range of child welfare services, including family preservation and family support services, and title IV–E authorizes the foster care, independent living, and adoption assistance programs. The child welfare and foster care programs are intended to operate in consort to help prevent the need for out-of-home placement of chil-

---

[1] At the Federal level, programs that fund child welfare services (in addition to those under titles IV–B, IV–E and XX) include Head Start, and several programs that provide funding directed at specific problems, such as child abuse, homelessness, runaways, and teenage pregnancy.

[2] This typology is adapted from Kadushin, Alfred, and Judith A. Martin. Child Welfare Services. Macmillan Publishing Co., New York, 1988. pp. 26–28.

dren and, in cases where such placement is necessary, to provide protections and permanent placement for the children involved. In addition, funding is provided under the foster care program to assist States with the maintenance costs of low-income (AFDC-eligible) children in foster care. The independent living program is intended to help States facilitate the transition of older children from foster care to independent living; and the adoption assistance program is primarily to help States support the adoption of AFDC- or SSI-eligible children with "special needs" such as ethnic background, age, membership in a sibling group, or a mental or physical handicap.

THE ADOPTION ASSISTANCE AND CHILD WELFARE ACT OF 1980 (P.L. 96–272) AND SUBSEQUENT AMENDMENTS

Federal assistance to enable States to make maintenance payments for children who were not living with a parent and had been placed elsewhere by a child welfare agency—that is, who were living in foster care—first became available under what was then called the Aid to Dependent Children (ADC) program (title IV–A of the Social Security Act) in 1961.

Foster care under title IV–A of the Social Security Act was amended in 1980 by Public Law 96–272. This legislation continued AFDC foster care as a required Federal matching grant program, but transferred it to a newly created title IV–E. It also changed the funding mechanism for this program and the child welfare services program under title IV–B, providing linkages between the two to encourage less reliance on foster care placement and greater use of services aimed at preventing placement and encouraging family rehabilitation. The entitlement nature of AFDC foster care was retained, but under title IV–E its open-endedness was potentially limited by a provision that was contingent on the funding level of title IV–B. The legislation specified a number of protections to help prevent inappropriate placements or long-term stays in foster care, and a number of programs were established to provide services to specialized foster care populations. Under title IV–E, a new Federal matching grant program for payments to parents who adopt a child with special needs was also established and permanently authorized. Funding for adoption assistance is on an open-ended entitlement basis.

The foster care and adoption assistance programs were amended in the 99th Congress, under the Consolidated Omnibus Budget Reconciliation Act of 1985 (COBRA, P.L. 99–272). This legislation also established a new entitlement program under title IV–E to help States facilitate the transition of children age 16 and over from AFDC foster care to independent living. The program is called the independent living program.

During the 99th Congress, legislation was also enacted as part of the Tax Reform Act of 1986 (P.L. 99–514) that amended the adoption assistance program under title IV–E to provide for Federal matching funds for the one-time adoption expenses of children with special needs, whether or not the children are eligible for AFDC or SSI payments.

During the 100th Congress, legislation was enacted to expand the independent living program to include children ages 16 or over who are in any foster care situation and to provide services for specified children for 6 months after foster care payments or foster care ends (P.L. 100–647).

During the first session of the 101st Congress, legislation was enacted as part of the Omnibus Reconciliation Act of 1989 (P.L. 101–239) to increase the authorization level of the IV–B program from $266 million to $325 million; and to extend the independent living program through 1992, increase the entitlement ceiling from $45 million to $50 million for fiscal year 1990, $60 million for fiscal year 1991, and $70 million for fiscal year 1992, and establish a State match beginning for fiscal year 1991.

During the second session of the 101st Congress, the Omnibus Budget Reconciliation Act of 1990 (P.L. 101–508) made several minor amendments to the child welfare, foster care and adoption assistance programs. Among other things, these amendments now require States to distinguish between traditional administrative costs and child placement costs which previously had been classified as administrative costs, and give States the option of providing independent living services to foster children up to age 21.

The 103rd Congress enacted significant child welfare amendments, contained in the Omnibus Budget Reconciliation Act of 1993 (P.L. 103–66), which are designed to buttress the goals of Federal child welfare programs of strengthening family life for children and ensuring more children in the child welfare system a stable, permanent home on a timely basis. This legislation created a new capped entitlement under title IV–B for a broad range of services to families (including foster, adoptive and extended families), termed "family preservation" and "family support" services. The legislation also includes a set-aside for grants to State courts for assessments and improvements of judicial child welfare proceedings. Public Law 103–66 authorizes a 3-year enhanced match to States for planning, designing, developing or installing child welfare data collection systems. The legislation permanently authorizes the independent living program, and also permanently authorizes a 75 percent matching rate for certain State training expenses.

FEDERAL CHILD WELFARE PROGRAMS TODAY

The Social Security Act contains the primary sources of Federal funds available to States for child welfare, foster care, and adoption activities. These funds include both nonentitlement authorizations (under which specific appropriations are made for a program, effective for 1 year, a fixed number of years, or permanently) and authorized entitlements (under which the Federal government has a binding obligation to make payments to any person or unit of government that meets the eligibility criteria established by law). The programs include the title IV–B child welfare services program, the title IV–E foster care program, the title IV–E adoption assistance program, and the title XX social services block grant program. Table 14–1 lists these programs, as well as the independent living program, and their funding environments.

Table 14–2 provides data on the level of Federal funds which have been used by or allocated to States under titles IV–B, IV–E and XX for fiscal years 1983 through 1993, and DHHS projections for fiscal years 1994 through 1999. Under the title XX social services block grant program, States have discretion over what portion of their allocation they will spend on child welfare, foster care and adoption activities, as well as a range of other activities not directly focused on children. As this table shows, detailed data on child welfare services spending by States under the title XX program are not available.

In addition to the funds allocated to the States or available on an entitlement basis, approximately $10.9 million was appropriated for fiscal year 1994 for research and demonstration activities and for direct Federal grants to public and private entities for child welfare staff training, authorized under section 426 of title IV–B.

Funds available to States from the title IV–B child welfare program and title XX social services program may be used for services to families and children without regard to their eligibility for AFDC. Federal matching funds for foster care maintenance payments under title IV–E are only provided in those cases where the child would have been eligible for AFDC if still in the home. All children determined to have "special needs" related to their being adopted, as defined under title IV–E, are eligible for reimbursement of certain nonrecurring costs of adoption under the title IV–E adoption assistance program. However, only AFDC- or SSI-eligible "special needs" children are eligible for federally matched adoption assistance payments available under title IV–E. Funds available to States for the title IV–E independent living program may be used for services which facilitate the transition of children from foster care to independent living, regardless of whether or not they receive AFDC foster care assistance.

Table 14–3 provides data on participation under the title IV–B, IV–E and XX programs. As this table demonstrates, only limited data are available on participation in these programs. Table 14–4 shows the Congressional Budget Office projections for Federal foster care and adoption assistance for 1994 through 1999 under current law. Between 1994 and 1999, the federally funded foster care caseload is projected to increase from 245,000 to 298,000 (22 percent). Total IV–E foster care costs are expected to increase 56 percent, from $2,670,000 in 1994 to $4,176,000 in 1999. Over the same time period, the adoption assistance caseload is projected to increase from 91,000 to 143,000 (57 percent), while total adoption assistance costs are estimated to increase from $308 million to $530 million (72 percent).

TABLE 14–1.—FUNDING ENVIRONMENT OF THE FEDERAL PROGRAMS WHICH SUPPORT FOSTER CARE, CHILD WELFARE, AND ADOPTION SERVICES

Program	Budgetary classification	Federal support of total
Title IV–E Foster Care Program:		
Foster care assistance payments.	Authorized entitlement ..	Open-ended Federal match at Medicaid rate.
Placement services and administrative costs.	Authorized entitlement ..	Open-ended Federal match of 50 percent.[1]
Training expenses	Authorized entitlement ..	Open-ended Federal match of 75 percent.
Title IV–E Adoption Assistance Program:		
Adoption assistance payments.	Authorized entitlement ..	Open-ended Federal match at Medicaid rate.
Nonrecurring adoption expenses.	Authorized entitlement ..	Open-ended Federal match of 50 percent.[2]
Placement services and administrative costs.	Authorized entitlement ..	Open-ended Federal match of 50 percent.
Training expenses	Authorized entitlement ..	Open-ended Federal match of 75 percent.
Title IV–E Independent Living Program.	Authorized entitlement ..	100 percent Federal funding, with a funding ceiling.[3]
Title IV–B Child Welfare Services Program:		
Child welfare services (subpart 1).	Nonentitlement authorization.	Federal match of 75 percent, total capped at State allotment.
Family preservation and family support (subpart 2).	Authorized entitlement ..	Federal match of 75 percent, with a funding ceiling.[4]
Title XX Social Services Block Grant Program.	Authorized entitlement ..	100 percent Federal funding, with a funding ceiling.

[1] 75 percent matching is available from fiscal year 1994 through fiscal year 1996 for certain costs related to data collection.

[2] The Federal Government reimburses 50 percent of up to $2,000 of expenditures for any one placement.

[3] Beginning for fiscal year 1991, States are required to provide 50 percent matching for any Federal funding claimed that exceeds $45 million.

[4] Program authorized through fiscal year 1998.

TABLE 14–2.—FEDERAL FUNDING FOR CHILD WELFARE, FOSTER CARE, AND ADOPTION ACTIVITIES UNDER TITLES IV–B AND IV–E OF THE SOCIAL SECURITY ACT, 1983–99, UNDER CURRENT LAW[1]

[In millions of dollars]

Fiscal year	Title IV–B child welfare services	Title IV–E foster care State claims			State use of FC funds for IV–B, CWS (transfers)	Title IV–E adoption assistance State claims			Title XX SSBG program (CWS portion)
		Total[2]	Maintenance payments	Administration, training		Total[3]	Assistance payments	Administration, training	
1983	156.3	394.8	276.9	117.9	32.6	12.6	11.3	1.3	N/A
1984	165.0	445.2	297.8	147.4	32.2	25.7	20.2	5.5	N/A
1985	200.0	546.2	355.3	190.9	19.6	41.8	31.6	10.2	N/A
1986	198.1	605.4	391.6	213.8	14.9	55.0	40.6	14.4	N/A
1987	222.5	792.6	479.7	312.9	11.3	73.7	53.9	19.8	N/A
1988	239.4	891.1	548.3	342.8	5.1	97.1	74.1	23.0	N/A
1989	246.7	1,153.1	646.0	507.1	1.6	110.5	86.2	24.3	N/A
1990	252.6	1,473.2	835.0	638.2	5.3	135.7	104.9	30.8	N/A
1991	273.9	1,819.2	1,030.4	788.8	0.9	175.3	130.3	45.0	N/A
1992	273.9	2,232.8	1,203.8	1,029.0	0.0	219.6	161.4	58.2	N/A
1993	294.6	2,547.0	1,365.0	1,182.0	N/A	272.4	197.3	75.1	N/A
1994 (estimate)	294.6	2,606.5	1,447.0	1,159.5	N/A	325.0	235.0	90.0	N/A
1995 (estimate)	294.6	2,914.0	1,413.0	1,501.0	N/A	378.0	274.0	104.0	N/A
1996 (estimate)	294.6	3,384.0	1,684.0	1,700.0	N/A	420.0	304.0	116.0	N/A
1997 (estimate)	294.6	3,647.0	1,866.0	1,781.0	N/A	457.0	331.0	126.0	N/A
1998 (estimate)	294.6	3,997.0	2,049.0	1,948.0	N/A	492.0	357.0	135.0	N/A
1999 (estimate)	294.6	4,378.0	2,252.0	2,126.0	N/A	528.0	383.0	145.0	N/A

[1] Funding for family preservation and family support services under subpart 2 of title IV–B is not included in this table.
[2] Total includes administration and training expenditures, as well as maintenance payments, but does not include transfers to the title IV–B child welfare services program. Differences in total due to rounding.
[3] Total includes administration and training expenditures, maintenance payments, and nonrecurring payments. Differences in total due to rounding.

Source: Department of Health and Human Services.

TABLE 14–3.—PARTICIPATION IN CHILD WELFARE, FOSTER CARE, AND ADOPTION ACTIVITIES UNDER TITLES IV–B, IV–E, AND XX OF THE SOCIAL SECURITY ACT, 1983–99, UNDER CURRENT LAW [1]

Fiscal year	Title IV–B child welfare services	Title IV–E foster care assistance payments [2]	State use of FC funds for IV–B, CWS (transfers)	Title IV–E independent living program [3]	Title IV–E adoption assistance payments [2]	Title XX SSBG program (CWS portion)
1983	NA	97,370	NA	....	5,309	NA
1984	NA	102,051	NA	....	11,581	NA
1985	NA	109,122	NA	....	16,009	NA
1986	NA	110,586	NA	....	21,989	NA
1987	NA	118,549	NA	20,182	27,588	NA
1988	NA	132,757	NA	18,931	34,698	NA
1989	NA	156,871	NA	44,191	40,666	NA
1990	NA	167,981	NA	44,365	44,024	NA
1991	NA	202,687	NA	45,284	54,818	NA
1992	NA	222,315	NA	57,360	66,197	NA
1993	NA	232,668	NA	57,918	78,044	NA
1994 [3]	NA	245,800	NA	NA	90,800	NA
1995 [3]	NA	256,400	NA	NA	102,500	NA
1996 [3]	NA	267,200	NA	NA	110,200	NA
1997 [3]	NA	278,200	NA	NA	116,300	NA
1998 [3]	NA	289,300	NA	NA	121,000	NA
1999 [3]	NA	300,900	NA	NA	125,800	NA

[1] Participation data on family preservation and family support activities under subpart 2 of title IV–B are not included in this table.
[2] Average monthly number of recipients.
[3] Estimate.

Source: Department of Health and Human Services.

TABLE 14–4.—CBO BASELINE PROJECTIONS FOR THE FEDERAL FOSTER CARE AND ADOPTION ASSISTANCE PROGRAMS

[By fiscal year, In millions of dollars]

	1994	1995	1996	1997	1998	1999
Foster care:						
Title IV–E caseload (thousands)	245	257	268	278	288	298
Average monthly maint. payment (Federal share)	$502	$527	$554	$582	$612	$644
Federal costs (millions):						
Maintenance payments	1,438	1,552	1,763	1,943	2,116	2,299
Administrative and child placement services	1,135	1,354	1,491	1,518	1,626	1,727
Training	97	104	118	131	142	150
Total claims	2,670	3,010	3,372	3,593	3,884	4,176
Adoption assistance:						
Title IV–E caseload (thousands)	91	103	113	123	133	143
Average monthly payment	$211	$217	$223	$230	$237	$245
Federal costs (millions):						
Maintenance payments	230	267	302	339	378	419
Administrative and child placement services	70	75	80	86	91	96
Training	9	10	11	12	14	15
Total claims	308	351	393	437	482	530
Independent living: Federal costs	70	70	70	70	70	70
Total costs	3,025	3,355	3,757	4,049	4,371	4,710

Note.—Numbers may not add to totals due to rounding.
Source: Congressional Budget Office, March 1994 baseline.

THE TITLE IV–B CHILD WELFARE SERVICES PROGRAM

Subpart 1: Grants to States for child welfare services

The child welfare services program under subpart 1 of title IV–B permanently authorizes 75 percent Federal matching grants to States for services that protect the welfare of children. These services are to address problems that may result in neglect, abuse, exploitation or delinquency of children; prevent the unnecessary separation of children from their families and restore children to their families, when possible; place children in adoptive homes if restoration is not possible; and assure adequate foster care when children cannot return home or be placed for adoption. There are no Federal income eligibility requirements for the receipt of the child welfare services.

TABLE 14–5.—TITLE IV–B CHILD WELFARE SERVICES: STATE-BY-STATE ALLOCATIONS

[In thousands of dollars]

	Fiscal years			
	1987 actual	1992 actual	1993 actual	1994 appropriation
Alabama	4,783	5,432	5,798	5,798
Alaska	417	614	675	675
Arizona	3,344	4,418	4,781	4,781
Arkansas	2,838	3,273	3,496	3,496
California	20,445	27,289	30,049	30,049
Colorado	2,772	3,558	3,845	3,845
Connecticut	2,081	1,942	2,066	2,066
Delaware	570	717	764	764
District of Columbia	386	431	448	448
Florida	9,105	11,773	12,946	12,946
Georgia	6,622	7,737	8,386	8,386
Hawaii	656	1,180	1,281	1,281
Idaho	1,304	1,581	1,734	1,734
Illinois	9,932	11,338	12,157	12,157
Indiana	5,572	6,709	7,115	7,115
Iowa	2,861	3,364	3,566	3,566
Kansas	2,150	2,885	3,083	3,083
Kentucky	4,154	4,883	5,192	5,192
Louisiana	5,106	6,350	6,750	6,750
Maine	1,313	1,443	1,533	1,533
Maryland	3,440	3,924	4,256	4,256
Massachusetts	2,714	4,336	4,567	4,567
Michigan	8,888	10,196	10,860	10,860
Minnesota	3,937	4,753	5,093	5,093
Mississippi	3,519	4,177	4,438	4,438
Missouri	4,958	5,798	6,218	6,218

TABLE 14–5.—TITLE IV–B CHILD WELFARE SERVICES: STATE-BY-STATE ALLOCATIONS—
Continued

[In thousands of dollars]

	Fiscal years			
	1987 actual	1992 actual	1993 actual	1994 appropriation
Montana	978	1,136	1,212	1,212
Nebraska	1,641	1,996	2,137	2,137
Nevada	775	1,170	1,326	1,326
New Hampshire	950	1,028	1,078	1,078
New Jersey	5,424	4,936	5,308	5,308
New Mexico	1,642	2,291	2,493	2,493
New York	13,529	14,490	15,530	15,530
North Carolina	6,432	7,771	8,326	8,326
North Dakota	750	942	983	983
Ohio	10,402	12,283	13,053	13,053
Oklahoma	3,332	4,144	4,428	4,428
Oregon	2,586	3,283	3,576	3,576
Pennsylvania	10,038	11,905	12,650	12,650
Rhode Island	888	1,025	1,070	1,070
South Carolina	4,015	4,747	5,101	5,101
South Dakota	853	1,038	1,107	1,107
Tennessee	5,001	5,933	6,329	6,329
Texas	16,243	21,845	23,688	23,688
Utah	2,555	3,196	3,478	3,478
Vermont	632	713	750	750
Virginia	4,907	5,891	6,322	6,322
Washington	3,774	5,169	5,668	5,668
West Virginia	2,226	2,454	2,565	2,565
Wisconsin	4,672	5,639	6,033	6,033
Wyoming	101	703	751	751
American Samoa	N/A	175	183	183
Guam	304	376	395	395
Northern Marianas	110	124	127	127
Puerto Rico	3,671	7,094	7,532	7,532
Virgin Islands	202	311	328	328
Total	222,500	273,911	294,624	294,624

NA: Not applicable; jurisdiction not eligible under statute.
Totals may differ from sum of State amounts because of rounding.

Source: Department of Health and Human Services.

Requirements in Public Law 96–272 limited the use of title IV–B funds for child day care, foster care maintenance payments and adoption assistance payments to the 1979 title IV–B appropriation of $56.6 million. In addition, States are required to implement certain foster care protections for all children in foster care in order to be eligible for child welfare services funding over specified levels. (The foster care protections are described later in this section.)

The authorization level for the child welfare services program was $266 million annually since fiscal year 1977. The authorization level has been increased to $325 million under Public Law 101–239 beginning for fiscal year 1990. Appropriations for the program increased from $163.6 million in fiscal year 1981 to $294.6 million in fiscal year 1994 (see table 14–2).

Child welfare services funds are distributed to States on the basis of their under-21 population and per capita income. Because of minimal reporting requirements under the program, there are no reliable national or State-by-State data on the exact number of children served, their characteristics, or the services provided. Table 14–5 details the State-by-State distribution of child welfare services funds for selected fiscal years.

Subpart 2: Grants to States for family preservation and community-based family support services

Grants to States for family preservation and family support services are authorized as a capped entitlement under subpart 2 of title IV–B. States currently have the flexibility to expend their child welfare services grant funds available under subpart 1 of title IV–B for family support and preservation services, but few States use a significant share of such funds for these two categories of services. Entitlement funding is authorized for 5 years, at the following ceiling levels: $60 million in fiscal year 1994; $150 million in fiscal year 1995; $225 million in fiscal year 1996; $240 million in fiscal year 1997; and either $255 million in fiscal year 1998, or the fiscal year 1997 level adjusted for inflation, whichever is greater.

From these ceiling amounts, $2 million in fiscal year 1994 and $6 million in each of fiscal years 1995–1998 are reserved for use by the Secretary of HHS in funding research, training, technical assistance and evaluation of family preservation and support activities. In addition, $5 million in fiscal year 1995 and $10 million in each of the subsequent 3 fiscal years are reserved for a grant program for State courts (described below). Finally, 1 percent of the family preservation and family support entitlement is reserved for allotment to Indian tribes. Table 14–6 shows State allotments of family preservation and family support entitlement funds in fiscal year 1994, and estimated State allotments for fiscal years 1995–1998.

After these set-asides are made, remaining entitlement funds are allocated among States according to their relative shares of children receiving food stamps, subject to a 25 percent nonfederal match. States must submit a State plan to HHS, and must use at least 90 percent of their funds for two categories of services: family preservation services; and community-based family support services, with no more than 10 percent of funds used for administrative costs. States must devote "significant" portions of their allotments to each of the two categories of services. The Federal statute does not specify a percentage or minimum amount of funds that must be used for either family preservation or family support. However, in its program guidance to States issued on January 18, 1994, HHS stated that allocations of less than 25 percent to either type of service will require a strong rationale. (Final regulations will be published by HHS in summer or fall, 1994.)

Family preservation services are intended for children and families (including extended and adoptive families) that are at risk or in crisis. Services include programs to help reunite children with their biological families, if appropriate, or to place them for adoption or another permanent arrangement; programs to prevent placement of children in foster care, including intensive family preservation services; programs to provide follow-up services to families after a child has been returned from foster care; respite care to provide temporary relief for parents and other caregivers (including foster parents); and services to improve parenting skills.

Family support services are intended to reach families which are not yet in crisis and to prevent crises, such as child abuse or neglect, from occurring. Family support services are generally community-based activities to promote the well-being of children and families, to increase the strength and stability of families (including adoptive, foster and extended families), to increase parents' confidence and competence, to provide children with a stable and supportive family environment, and to enhance child development. Examples include parenting skills training, respite care to relieve parents and other caregivers, structured activities involving parents and children to strengthen their relationships, drop-in centers for families, information and referral services, and early developmental screening for children.

States must submit a fiscal year 1994 application to HHS no later than June 30, 1994, and a 5-year plan covering fiscal years 1995–98 by June 30, 1995. States may spend up to $1 million of their fiscal year 1994 allotment for planning and development of their 5-year plan, with no required non-Federal match.

The Secretary of HHS is required to evaluate family preservation and family support programs and to submit interim evaluation findings to Congress by December 31, 1996, and final evaluation findings by December 31, 1998.

As stated above, a portion of the entitlement funds is reserved for a grant program to the highest State courts to assess and improve certain child welfare proceedings. The court set-aside equals $5 million in fiscal year 1995 and $10 million in each of fiscal years 1996–1998. A 25 percent nonfederal match is required in each of the last 3 fiscal years.

Courts will use grant funds to assess their procedures and effectiveness in determinations regarding foster care placement, termination of parental rights, and recognition of adoptions. Courts also will use these grant funds to implement changes found necessary as a result of these assessments.

TABLE 14–6.—TITLE IV–B FAMILY PRESERVATION AND FAMILY SUPPORT SERVICES

[Fiscal year 1994 State allotments] [1]

[Estimated State allotments fiscal years 1995–98] [2]

State	Fiscal year 1994 allotment	Fiscal year 1995 allotment	Fiscal year 1996 allotment	Fiscal year 1997 allotment	Fiscal year 1998 allotment
Alabama	$1,199,639	$2,880,911	$4,344,445	$4,646,141	$4,957,838
Alaska	77,754	186,726	280,936	301,139	321,341
Arizona	1,005,253	2,414,096	3,632,104	3,893,294	4,154,484
Arkansas	577,604	1,387,105	2,086,955	2,237,031	2,387,107
California	6,925,694	16,631,924	25,023,389	26,822,863	28,622,330
Colorado	616,481	1,480,468	2,227,423	2,387,600	2,547,778
Connecticut	444,311	1,067,004	1,605,350	1,720,793	1,836,236
Delaware	105,524	253,413	381,271	408,688	436,106
District of Columbia	194,386	466,814	702,341	752,847	803,353
Florida	2,615,879	6,281,986	9,451,497	10,131,169	10,810,840
Georgia	1,555,088	3,734,514	5,618,724	6,022,775	6,426,826
Hawaii	194,386	466,814	702,341	752,847	803,353
Idaho	155,509	373,451	561,872	602,278	642,683
Ilinois	2,504,802	6,015,235	9,050,160	9,700,970	10,351,781
Indiana	938,606	2,254,046	3,391,302	3,635,175	3,879,049
Iowa	427,649	1,026,991	1,545,149	1,656,263	1,767,377
Kansas	372,110	893,616	1,344,481	1,441,164	1,537,848
Kentucky	1,083,007	2,600,822	3,913,040	4,194,433	4,475,826
Louisiana	1,888,321	4,534,767	6,822,737	7,313,370	7,804,003
Maine	244,371	586,852	882,942	946,436	1,009,930
Maryland	760,882	1,827,244	2,749,162	2,946,858	3,144,554
Massachusetts	960,822	2,307,396	3,471,569	3,721,215	3,970,861
Michigan	2,304,862	5,535,083	8,327,752	8,926,614	9,525,475
Minnesota	655,358	1,573,831	2,367,891	2,538,170	2,708,448
Mississippi	1,155,208	2,774,210	4,173,910	4,474,062	4,774,214
Missouri	1,149,654	2,760,873	4,153,843	4,452,552	4,751,261
Montana	133,293	320,101	481,605	516,238	550,871
Nebraska	233,263	560,177	842,809	903,416	964,024
Nevada	161,063	386,789	581,939	623,787	665,636
New Hampshire	94,416	226,738	341,137	365,669	390,200
New Jersey	1,132,992	2,720,860	4,093,642	4,388,022	4,682,402
New Mexico	455,419	1,093,679	1,645,484	1,763,813	1,882,142
New York	4,043,228	9,709,736	14,608,684	15,659,216	16,709,749
North Carolina	1,160,762	2,787,548	4,193,976	4,495,572	4,797,167
North Dakota	99,970	240,076	361,204	387,178	413,153
Ohio	2,782,496	6,682,112	10,053,503	10,776,466	11,499,429
Oklahoma	694,236	1,667,194	2,508,359	2,688,739	2,869,119
Oregon	510,957	1,227,055	1,846,152	1,978,912	2,111,672
Pennsylvania	2,360,401	5,668,459	8,528,421	9,141,713	9,755,004
Rhode Island	188,832	453,477	682,274	731,337	780,400

TABLE 14–6.—TITLE IV–B FAMILY PRESERVATION AND FAMILY SUPPORT SERVICES—
Continued

[Fiscal year 1994 State allotments] [1]
[Estimated State allotments fiscal years 1995–98] [2]

State	Fiscal year 1994 allotment	Fiscal year 1995 allotment	Fiscal year 1996 allotment	Fiscal year 1997 allotment	Fiscal year 1998 allotment
South Carolina	805,313	1,933,945	2,909,697	3,118,937	3,328,178
South Dakota	127,739	306,764	461,538	494,728	527,918
Tennessee	1,327,378	3,187,674	4,795,983	5,140,869	5,485,755
Texas	5,376,160	12,910,748	19,424,733	20,821,595	22,218,457
Utah	294,356	706,890	1,063,544	1,140,025	1,216,506
Vermont	105,524	253,413	381,271	408,688	436,106
Virginia	927,499	2,227,371	3,351,168	3,592,155	3,833,143
Washington	938,606	2,254,046	3,391,302	3,635,175	3,879,049
West Virginia	572,050	1,373,768	2,066,888	2,215,521	2,364,154
Wisconsin	821,975	1,973,957	2,969,897,	3,183,467	3,397,037
Wyoming	77,754	186,726	280,936	301,139	321,341
American Samoa .	90,857	122,095	149,102	154,893	160,684
Guam	129,726	219,181	296,518	313,102	329,687
Northern Mariana	80,428	96,047	109,551	112,446	115,342
Puerto Rico	1,442,746	3,498,785	5,276,321	5,657,497	6,038,672
Virgin Islands	117,401	188,397	249,776	262,938	276,101
Totals:	57,400,000	137,500,000	206,750,000	221,600,000	236,450,000
Set Asides: Indians (1%)	600,000	1,500,000	2,250,000	2,400,000	2,550,000
T, TA & Eval	2,000,000	6,000,000	6,000,000	6,000,000	6,000,000
Courts	0	5,000,000	10,000,000	10,000,000	10,000,000
Subtotal .	2,600,000	12,500,000	18,250,000	18,400,000	18,550,000
Total for fiscal year	$60,000,000	$150,000,000	$225,000,000	$240,000,000	$255,000,000

[1] Fiscal year 1994. State allotments are based on the statutory formula using Food Stamp data (section 433(c)). Allotments for the territories and insular areas are based on the title IV–B formula (section 433(b)). The table also includes the set-asides for grants to Indian Tribes and State courts, and grants for research, evaluation, and training and technical assistance (section 403(d)).
[2] Fiscal years 1995–98. State allotments for these years should be used only for planning purposes. They are based on current information and will need to be revised when future Food Stamp data and appropriations are known.

Source: Department of Health and Human Services.

THE TITLE IV–E AFDC FOSTER CARE PROGRAM

The AFDC foster care program under title IV–E is a permanently authorized entitlement program that provides open-ended matching funds to States for the maintenance payments made for AFDC-eligible children in foster care family homes, private nonprofit child care facilities, or public child care institutions housing up to 25 people. The program is required of States participating in the AFDC program (all States participate). The Federal matching rate of total expenditures for a given State is that State's Medicaid matching rate, which averages about 57 percent nationally. States may claim open-ended Federal matching at a rate of 50 percent for their child placement services and administrative costs for this program. States also may claim open-ended Federal matching at a rate of 75 percent for State training expenditures (for training of personnel employed or preparing for employment by the State or local agency administering the program, and training of foster and adoptive parents).

States are *required* to provide foster care maintenance payments to AFDC-eligible children removed from the home of a relative if the child received or would have been eligible for AFDC prior to removal from the home and if the following apply: (1) the removal and foster care placement were based on a voluntary placement agreement [3] or a judicial determination that remaining in the home would be contrary to the child's welfare and reasonable efforts were made to eliminate the need for removal or to return the child to his home; and (2) care and placement of the child are the responsibility of specified public agencies. Children in the AFDC foster care program are eligible for Medicaid; the State in which the child resides is responsible for providing the Medicaid coverage.

The maintenance payments under the title IV–E foster care program are for the costs of food, shelter, clothing, daily supervision, school supplies, general incidentals, liability insurance for the child, and reasonable travel to the child's home for visits.

Foster care expenditures and participation rates

The average estimated monthly number of children in AFDC foster care has more than doubled between 1983 and 1993, from 97,370 in fiscal year 1983 to 232,668 in fiscal year 1993 (see table 14–3). Table 14–7 provides a State-by-State breakdown of estimated fiscal year 1993 foster care expenditures. Note that California and New York account for almost half of the estimated fiscal year 1993 expenditures. More detailed data on foster children and their characteristics are described later in this section.

State claims for child placement services and administrative costs for the title IV–E foster care program have increased considerably since 1981. Current HHS regulations give the following examples of allowable child placement services and administrative

---

[3] "Voluntary placement" is defined as "out-of-home placement of minor, by or with participation of a State agency, after the parents or guardian of the minor have requested the assistance of the agency and signed a voluntary placement agreement." "Voluntary placement agreement" is defined as "a written agreement, binding on the parties of the agreement, between the State agency, any other agency acting on its behalf, and the parents or guardians of a minor child which specifies, at a minimum, the legal status of the child and rights and obligations of the parents or guardians, the child, and the agency while the child is in placement" (sec. 472(f)).

costs for the foster care program: referral to services, preparation for and participation in judicial determinations, placement of the child, development of the case plan, case reviews, case management and supervision, recruitment and licensing of foster homes and institutions, rate setting, and a proportionate share of agency overhead. As discussed later, many of these activities are required of States (i.e., they are foster care "protections"). Table 14–7 provides a State breakdown of foster care expenditures in fiscal year 1993 between maintenance payments and administration and training expenditures. A more detailed discussion of growth in child placement services and administrative costs is contained later in this section.

TABLE 14–7.—FEDERAL FOSTER CARE EXPENDITURES UNDER TITLE IV–E, FISCAL YEAR 1993 [1]

[In millions of dollars]

State	Maintenance payments	Child placement services and administration	Training	Total	Child placement services and administration as percent of total
Alabama	$1.51	$3.06	$0.11	$4.68	65.38
Alaska	1.99	2.42	0.00	4.41	54.88
Arizona	7.81	9.42	0.74	17.97	52.42
Arkansas	2.29	4.90	2.56	9.75	50.26
California	232.18	227.57	18.31	478.06	47.60
Colorado	4.90	14.42	0.95	20.27	71.14
Connecticut	4.90	10.35	0.65	15.90	65.09
Delaware	0.35	0.92	0.07	1.34	68.66
District of Columbia	4.40	6.80	0.00	11.20	60.71
Florida	14.63	28.90	2.35	45.88	62.99
Georgia	8.48	14.28	1.74	24.50	58.29
Hawaii	0.78	2.13	0.00	2.91	73.20
Idaho	0.72	1.39	0.04	2.15	64.65
Illinois	73.88	40.37	3.34	117.59	34.33
Indiana	22.92	14.73	0.00	37.65	39.12
Iowa	7.40	5.83	0.43	13.66	42.68
Kansas	7.44	10.61	1.32	19.37	54.78
Kentucky	12.73	16.98	4.35	34.06	49.85
Louisiana	16.56	10.90	1.10	28.56	38.17
Maine	7.20	1.32	0.92	9.44	13.98
Maryland	23.82	17.38	3.40	44.60	38.97
Massachusetts	26.49	30.56	0.35	57.40	53.24
Michigan	47.41	54.36	1.50	103.27	52.64
Minnesota	18.71	12.40	1.89	33.00	37.58
Mississippi	1.56	2.22	0.31	4.09	54.28
Missouri	12.71	14.68	1.68	29.07	50.50
Montana	3.26	1.31	0.01	4.58	28.60
Nebraska	5.38	3.19	1.59	10.16	31.40
Nevada	1.61	1.20	0.07	2.88	41.67
New Hampshire	3.67	3.61	0.09	7.37	48.98
New Jersey	11.88	13.27	0.15	25.30	52.45
New Mexico	3.56	1.21	0.69	5.46	22.16
New York	416.04	345.53	17.66	779.23	44.34
North Carolina	14.25	3.24	0.14	17.63	18.38
North Dakota	2.49	2.44	0.48	5.41	45.10

TABLE 14–7.—FEDERAL FOSTER CARE EXPENDITURES UNDER TITLE IV–E, FISCAL YEAR 1993 [1]—Continued

[In millions of dollars]

State	Mainte-nance pay-ments	Child place-ment serv-ices and administra-tion	Training	Total	Child place-ment serv-ices and administra-tion as per-cent of total
Ohio	44.82	43.24	3.92	91.98	47.01
Oklahoma	5.09	2.63	0.47	8.19	32.11
Oregon	7.27	6.79	0.02	14.08	48.22
Pennsylvania	125.88	48.26	6.32	180.46	26.74
Rhode Island	3.19	4.77	0.12	8.08	59.03
South Carolina	4.72	3.45	0.65	8.82	39.12
South Dakota	1.27	1.26	0.04	2.57	49.03
Tennessee	9.14	5.34	1.29	15.77	33.86
Texas	38.48	32.09	1.61	72.18	44.46
Utah	3.03	2.80	0.13	5.96	46.98
Vermont	4.18	2.37	0.10	6.65	35.64
Virginia	4.46	6.57	2.36	13.39	49.07
Washington	8.07	11.59	0.23	19.89	58.27
West Virginia	2.24	1.59	0.44	4.27	37.24
Wisconsin	18.90	23.68	0.00	42.58	55.61
Wyoming	0.75	0.30	0.00	1.05	28.57
Total	1,307.40	1,130.63	86.69	2,524.72	44.78

[1] Does not include $22 million in disputes and reconciliations.
Totals may differ from sum of State amounts because of rounding.

Source: Department of Health and Human Services.

Foster care payment rates

Table 14–8 shows each State's basic family foster care maintenance rates that are paid out on a monthly basis, as determined in an annual survey conducted by the American Public Welfare Association (APWA). States are allowed to set them at any level; thus, the rates vary widely. For instance, in 1993 the minimum basic monthly rate for a 16-year-old foster child in the State of Ohio was $203 compared with $593 in the State of Connecticut and $621 in the State of Alaska. New York City had a monthly payment rate of $547. The nationwide average for this age group was $393 per month compared with $318 for 2-year-olds and $336 for foster children that were 9 years of age.

The 1980 legislation stipulated that title IV–E foster care payments may be made for children in public institutions, whereas previously under title IV–A payments were limited to children in private nonprofit institutions or foster family homes. These public institutions may accommodate up to 25 children. Facilities operated primarily for the detention of delinquents, including forestry camps and training schools, are noneligible institutions. It is generally agreed that the costs associated with institutional care are substantially higher than the cost of family foster care. The North

American Council on **Adoptable** Children (NACAC) estimates that for 1990, the daily **costs** associated with basic family foster care were between $8 and $15 (up to $30 for a child with special needs). Comparatively, residential foster care was estimated on average to cost $100 a day per child.

TABLE 14–8.—FOSTER CARE BASIC MONTHLY MAINTENANCE RATES FOR CHILDREN AGES 2, 9, AND 16

State	Age 2				Age 9				Age 16			
	1987	1991	1992	1993	1987	1991	1992	1993	1987	1991	1992	1993
Alabama	168	181	199	205	188	202	222	229	198	213	234	241
Alaska	428	561	588	588	478	499	523	523	565	592	621	621
Arizona	223	247	295	295	223	247	284	284	282	305	362	362
Arkansas	175	195	300	300	190	210	325	325	220	240	375	375
California	294	345	345	345	340	400	400	400	412	484	484	484
Colorado	235	296	302	313	266	296	302	313	318	352	359	372
Connecticut	268	386	497	515	302	424	506	524	350	478	572	593
Delaware	264	301	301	301	266	304	304	304	342	391	391	391
District of Columbia	304	304	304	437	304	304	304	437	317	317	361	526
Florida	233	296	296	296	233	296	296	296	293	372	372	372
Georgia	300	300	300	300	300	300	300	300	300	300	300	300
Hawaii	194	529	529	529	233	529	529	529	301	529	529	529
Idaho	138	198	198	198	165	205	205	205	204	278	278	278
Illinois	233	268	295	311	259	299	329	326	282	325	358	377
Indiana	226	281	405	405	245	330	462	462	280	398	518	518
Iowa	159	198	258	308	201	243	289	322	285	300	356	382
Kansas	187	304	305	304	245	304	305	304	280	386	386	386
Kentucky	248	265	263	263	263	288	285	285	300	333	330	330
Louisiana	199	283	283	298	232	316	316	331	265	349	349	364
Maine	244	296	296	......	250	304	304	......	291	353	353	......
Maryland	285	535	535	535	285	535	535	535	303	550	560	550
Massachusetts	362	410	410	415	362	410	410	415	433	486	486	492
Michigan	315	332	354	354	315	332	354	354	395	416	442	442
Minnesota	285	341	358	377	285	341	358	377	375	442	464	487
Mississippi	130	145	175	175	150	165	205	205	160	175	250	250
Missouri	174	209	212	212	212	255	259	259	232	281	286	286
Montana	283	307	318	322	283	307	318	322	354	384	402	406

TABLE 14-8.—FOSTER CARE BASIC MONTHLY MAINTENANCE RATES FOR CHILDREN AGES 2, 9, AND 16—Continued

State	Age 2				Age 9				Age 16			
	1987	1991	1992	1993	1987	1991	1992	1993	1987	1991	1992	1993
Nebraska	210	222	326	326	210	291	393	394	210	351	463	461
Nevada	275	281	281	281	275	281	281	281	330	337	337	337
New Hampshire	200	200	200	324	251	251	251	354	354	354	354	418
New Jersey	203	244	256	264	215	259	272	280	253	305	320	320
New Mexico	236	258	258	258	247	270	270	270	259	281	281	281
New York	312	353	353	367	375	424	424	441	434	490	490	510
New York City	342	386	386	401	403	455	455	473	465	526	526	547
North Carolina	215	265	265	265	215	265	265	265	215	265	265	265
North Dakota	240	260	260	265	287	312	312	318	345	416	416	424
Ohio	240	289	297	203	270	328	342	203	300	366	381	203
Oklahoma	300	300	300	300	360	360	360	360	420	420	420	420
Oregon	200	285	295	305	234	295	306	317	316	363	378	391
Pennsylvania	558	303	330	306	558	319	392	357	558	377	450	459
Rhode Island	223	274	270	273	223	274	270	273	275	335	330	334
South Carolina	138	182	182	182	158	209	209	209	208	275	275	275
South Dakota	188	237	237	251	230	291	291	308	276	349	349	370
Tennessee	139	255	225	336	190	226	226	262	224	267	267	385
Texas	243	420	554	476	243	420	554	476	274	420	554	476
Utah	198	300	300	310	198	300	300	310	225	300	300	310
Vermont	210	371	321	321	249	371	321	321	268	447	397	386
Virginia	193	246	246	251	244	288	288	294	309	365	365	372
Washington	184	270	278	278	227	332	342	342	268	392	405	405
West Virginia	161	161	161	161	202	202	202	202	242	242	242	242
Wisconsin	163	231	231	240	224	257	257	267	284	324	324	337
Wyoming	300	400	400	400	300	400	400	400	330	400	400	400
Average monthly rates	239	294.35	310.25	318.53	263	313.94	331.00	336.14	307	365.31	385.90	392.98

Note: Most States and/or counties supplement these basic rates with additional payments.

Source: American Public Welfare Association, March 1994.

Exclusion of foster children from AFDC assistance units

The Deficit Reduction Act of 1984 (P.L. 98–369) required that certain blood-related, adoptive parents or siblings must be included in the family unit if the family applies for income assistance under the AFDC program. Because there was no statutory exclusion for foster care recipients, AFDC operating policy required that their income be included with the family's when the family's eligibility was determined. Enacted in 1986 by Public Law 99–514, section 478 of title IV–E stated that a foster child who is receiving maintenance payments funded under title IV–E may not be considered a family member during the time the family receives AFDC, and that the child's income in the form of maintenance payments, and other income and resources, must be excluded from the family's as well.

The Omnibus Budget Reconciliation Act of 1990 (P.L. 101–508) repealed section 478 and added a new section 408 to title IV–A stipulating that foster children receiving maintenance payments under title IV–E or under State or local programs are not considered family members for purposes of AFDC. Similarly, the law now specifies that children receiving adoption assistance payments under either title IV–E or State or local law are not considered family members for AFDC purposes, unless the family would lose benefits as a result.

THE TITLE IV–E INDEPENDENT LIVING PROGRAM

In 1986, title IV–E was amended by Public Law 99–272 (Consolidated Omnibus Budget Reconciliation Act of 1985) to include section 477, which established the independent living program to assist youth who would eventually be emancipated from the foster care system. Several surveys conducted during the mid-1980s showed that a significant number of homeless shelter users had been recently discharged from foster care. The program's services were designed to assist adolescent youth who are not provided the benefits believed to come from reunification with their original family, or placement in an adoptive home.

An annual entitlement amount of $45 million was established for 1987 and 1988 to provide States with the resources to establish and implement services to assist AFDC-eligible children age 16 and over make a successful transition from foster care to independent adult living when they become ineligible for foster care maintenance payments at age 18. The same amount was made available the following year and the program was expanded under Public Law 100–647. States could now provide independent living services to all youth in foster care aged 16 to 18 (not just title IV–E-eligible youth) and States could claim followup services provided to youth up to 6 months after their emancipation from substitute care. Under Public Law 101–508, States have the option of serving individuals up to age 21 in the independent living program. Funds are allocated on the basis of each State's relative share of children receiving IV–E foster care in 1984.

Public Law 101–239 increased the amount of Federal entitlement funds available to the States for the independent living program to $50 million for fiscal year 1990, $60 million for fiscal year 1991, and $70 million for fiscal year 1992. Beginning in fiscal year 1991,

States are required to provide 50 percent matching for any Federal funding claimed that exceeds the original $45 million funding level. In 1993, Congress permanently extended the authority for independent living, under Public Law 103–66.

Section 477 of title IV–E instructed HHS to carry out a study of the program's effectiveness. Under contract with HHS, Westat, Inc. completed the first phase of the study in 1989 and the second phase in 1992. The first phase is a purely descriptive assessment of the needs of youth emancipated from foster care between January 1, 1987 and July 31, 1988; States' development of independent living programs to serve these youth; and the proportion of youth served.

The first report found that independent living services offered by the States generally fall into the following categories: basic skills training (including health promotion, housekeeping, money management, decisionmaking, and food and nutrition management); education initiatives (including private tutoring, and GED and college preparation); and employment initiatives (including job training and placement, and personal presentation and social skills). In addition, 14 States held teen conferences designed to bring these foster care youth together for workshops to provide them with supportive contacts, teach them independent living skills, focus on self-esteem building, and help prepare them for their impending emancipation from foster care.

The report concluded that emancipated youth were a troubled population. In the study population, two-thirds of 18-year-olds did not complete high school or a GED and 61 percent had no job experience. In addition, 38 percent had been diagnosed as emotionally disturbed, 17 percent had a drug abuse problem, 9 percent had a health problem, and 17 percent of the females were pregnant. The group also lacked placement stability. During the time they were in foster care 58 percent experienced at least three living arrangements and approximately 30 percent of the youth had been in substitute care for an average of 9 years. The report found evidence that Public Law 99–272 has influenced States to develop policies for services that adolescents should receive before their emancipation from foster care. Of the 49 States that responded, 22 had such a written policy before the law was enacted. By 1988, when the study was concluded, an additional 18 States had initiated the process of developing similar policies. (By 1990, all States had an independent living program plan.)

Of the total 34,600 youth emancipated from foster care during the study period, 31 percent received services through their State's formalized independent living program, 29 percent received nonformalized (but related) services, and 40 percent received no independent living services at all.

The second phase of the Westat report was released in 1992, and follows up on youths who had been emancipated from foster care during the period from January 1987 and July 1988. Interviews were conducted with these youths between November 1990 and March 1991 about their experiences after leaving foster care. The second phase report suggests six major findings.

First, the type of skills encouraged by the independent living program was positively related to outcomes, particularly when combined training was provided in money management, credit, consumer education and employment. To achieve the best results, Westat said, skill training should be closely targeted to the outcome it is intended to improve (e.g., maintaining a job, becoming a high school graduate, avoiding young parenthood, having access to medical care when needed, etc.), and should be provided in combination with other skill areas.

Second, Westat found that young people were better off according to several measures if they completed high school before leaving foster care, rather than after discharge, regardless of whether they received skill training.

Third, Westat found that the status of older foster care youth 2½ to 4 years after discharge is "adequate at best" and services are needed for this population to improve their outcomes. For example, Westat reported that only 54 percent of the study population had completed high school, 49 percent were employed at the time of the interview, 38 percent maintained a job for at least 1 year, 40 percent were a cost to the community in some way at the time of the interview (receiving public assistance, incarcerated, etc.), 60 percent of the young women had given birth to a child, 25 percent had been homeless for at least one night, their median weekly salary was $205, and only 17 percent were completely self-supporting.

Fourth, Westat reported that extended family members were an important resource to former foster care youth. The majority had continuing contact with either parents or extended family members and 54 percent had gone to live with extended family members after discharge.

Fifth, Westat found that becoming a young mother, which had happened to 60 percent of the women in the study group, was associated with poorer outcomes. For example, only 47 percent of young mothers had completed high school while 67 percent of those women in the study group who had not had children completed high school. Of mothers, 21 percent completed further schooling after foster care discharge, compared with 50 percent of nonmothers. At the time of the interviews, 34 percent of mothers were employed, compared with 55 percent of nonmothers, and 23 percent of mothers had held a job for more than a year, compared with 33 percent of nonmothers.

Finally, 61 percent of the women in the study group who had given birth to children were a cost to the community, compared with 22 percent of those who had not had children.

Westat's last finding was that 30 percent of the study group had faced barriers to obtaining health care when needed, primarily as a result of lack of money or health insurance.

TABLE 14–9.—TITLE IV–E—INDEPENDENT LIVING FEDERAL AWARDS—FISCAL YEAR 1993

[In thousands of dollars]

State	Total awards
Alabama	1,038
Alaska	13
Arizona	359
Arkansas	280
California	12,879
Colorado	826
Connecticut	778
Delaware	209
District of Columbia	702
Florida	1,018
Georgia	1,134
Hawaii	18
Idaho	110
Illinois	2,906
Indiana	1,020
Iowa	464
Kansas	737
Kentucky	792
Louisiana	1,073
Maine	584
Maryland	1,238
Massachusetts	656
Michigan	4,082
Minnesota	1,178
Mississippi	514
Missouri	1,336
Montana	244
Nebraska	449
Nevada	159
New Hampshire	330
New Jersey	2,371
New Mexico	214
New York	11,953
North Carolina	972
North Dakota	198
Ohio	2,952
Oklahoma	640
Oregon	960
Pennsylvania	4,785
Rhode Island	325

TABLE 14–9.—TITLE IV–E—INDEPENDENT LIVING FEDERAL AWARDS—FISCAL YEAR 1993—Continued

[In thousands of dollars]

State	Total awards
South Carolina	598
South Dakota	193
Tennessee	650
Texas	1,842
Utah	209
Vermont	305
Virginia	875
Washington	848
West Virginia	335
Wisconsin	1,603
Wyoming	46
Total	70,000

Source: Department of Health and Human Services.

THE TITLE IV–E ADOPTION ASSISTANCE PROGRAM

The title IV–E adoption assistance program is an open-ended entitlement program required of States that participate in AFDC (all States participate). The program is permanently authorized under title IV–E and allows States to develop adoption assistance agreements with parents who adopt eligible children with special needs. Federal matching funds are provided to States that, under these agreements, provide adoption assistance payments to parents who adopt AFDC- or SSI-eligible children with special needs. In addition, the program authorizes Federal matching funds for States that reimburse the nonrecurring adoption expenses of adoptive parents of special needs children (regardless of AFDC or SSI eligibility).

Definition of special needs

A special needs child is defined in the statute as a child with respect to whom the State determines there is a specific condition or situation, such as age, membership in a minority or sibling group, or a mental, emotional, or physical handicap, which prevents placement without special assistance. Before a child can be considered to be a child with special needs, the State must determine that the child cannot or should not be returned to the biological family, and that reasonable efforts have been made to place the child without providing adoption assistance. States have considerable latitude in defining special needs eligibility criteria and individually determining whether a child is eligible. For example, some States add religion or not being able to place the child without subsidy to the definition of special needs.

Adoption assistance agreements and payments

An adoption assistance agreement is a written agreement between the adoptive parents, the State IV–E agency, and other relevant agencies (such as a private adoption agency) specifying the nature and amount of assistance to be given. Under the adoption assistance agreement, States may make monthly adoption assistance payments for AFDC- and SSI-eligible children with special needs who are adopted.

Adoption assistance payments are based on the circumstances of the adopting parents and the needs of the child. No means test can be used to determine eligibility of parents for the program; however, States do use means tests to determine the amount of the payment. Payments may be adjusted periodically if circumstances change, with the concurrence of the adopting parents. However, the payments may not exceed the amount the family might have received on behalf of the child under AFDC foster care for foster family care. Adoption assistance payments may continue until the child is age 18, or, at State option, age 21 if the child is mentally or physically handicapped. In addition, payments are discontinued if the State determines that the parents are no longer legally responsible for the support of the child. Federally subsidized payments may start as soon as an agreement is signed and the child has been placed in an adoptive home. Parents who have been receiving adoption assistance payments must keep the State or local agency informed of circumstances that would make them ineligible for payments, or eligible for payments in a different amount.

The Federal matching rate for the adoption assistance payments is based on each State's Medicaid matching rate (which ranges from 50 to 83 percent depending on State per capita income, and averages about 57 percent nationally). States may also claim openended Federal matching for the costs of administering the program (50 percent) and for training both staff and adoptive parents (75 percent).

Not all families of adopted IV–E eligible children with special needs actually receive adoption assistance payments. (The adoptive parents' circumstances may be such that an adoption subsidy is not needed or wanted.) Adopted AFDC or SSI eligible children with special needs are also eligible for Medicaid if an adoption assistance agreement is in effect, whether or not adoption assistance payments are being made. Therefore, there are some IV–E eligible children with special needs for whom adoption assistance payments are not made but who are eligible for Medicaid.[4]

The structure of adoption subsidy programs varies across States. Some States offer basic maintenance payments and also allow additional payments for certain activities (such as family counseling) or for certain groups of children (such as children with severe handicaps). Other States offer one level of payment to everyone with no special allowances. Some States allow parents to request changes

---

[4] States also have the option under the Medicaid program to provide Medicaid coverage for other special needs children (those not eligible for AFDC or SSI) who are adopted if they have been identified as a special category of medically needy children under a State's Medicaid program. Pursuant to the 1985 budget reconciliation legislation, effective October 1, 1986, a child for whom an adoption assistance agreement is in effect is eligible for Medicaid from the State in which the child resides regardless of whether the State is the one with which the adoptive parents have an adoption assistance agreement.

in payment levels on a regular basis if circumstances change for a child, and others allow very little change once the adoption agreement is signed. Some States start payments as soon as placement is made, and others not until the adoption is finalized. Also, payments may not start immediately upon adoption finalization but may be written into agreements to start at a later date if it is thought that the child's circumstances will warrant payments as the child gets older.

Not all children who receive adoption subsidies from States are eligible for Federal IV–E funds. The American Public Welfare Association (APWA) estimates that at the end of 1990 (the latest year for which data are available), approximately 52 percent of the estimated 99,000 children nationwide whose families received adoption subsidies were IV–E eligible. The non-IV–E children's adoption subsidies are paid solely by the State in which their adoption agreement was signed. States differ in whether comparable IV–E children and non-IV–E children receive similar adoption subsidy amounts.

More detailed data on adoptive children and their characteristics are presented later in this section.

Nonrecurring adoption costs

The adoption assistance program also authorizes Federal matching funds for States to pay the one-time adoption expenses of parents of special needs children (regardless of AFDC or SSI eligibility). To qualify, the children must be covered by an adoption assistance agreement. Effective January 1, 1987, parents may receive reimbursement of up to $2,000 for these nonrecurring adoption expenses under the adoption assistance program, and States may claim 50 percent Federal matching for these payments. Qualified adoption expenses are defined as reasonable and necessary adoption fees, court costs, attorney fees, and other expenses which are directly related to the legal adoption of a child with special needs. States vary in the maximum amount they allow parents to receive under this provision. (See table 14–10 for State-by-State data on maximum reimbursement rates.) Regulations for the program were not published until 1988. Prior to January 1987, up to $1,500 of nonrecurring costs of adopting a child with special needs could be claimed as a tax deduction. The 1986 tax reform legislation repealed the adoption expense deduction.

By May 1991, the majority of States had implemented programs to reimburse parents for nonrecurring adoption expenses. However, average reimbursements have not equaled the $2,000 Federal cap, with the average payment being $664 in 1992. According to the American Public Welfare Association, most States report that actual repayment of nonrecurring adoption expenses has not created the degree of financial or administrative burden initially feared by most States. One reason is that a lower number of applicants and eligible children have been served than initially expected. This is partially due to lower numbers of requests being processed by nonpublic agency adoption sources, which do not process special needs adoptions at the same volume as public agencies. A second reason is that the expenses claimed have not been excessively costly to reimburse because many items are already covered under the States' adoption programs.

TABLE 14–10.—STATE REIMBURSEMENT OF NONRECURRING ADOPTION COSTS, 1992

State	Has your State implemented the reimbursement program?	Maximum payment	Estimated average payment as of May 1991	Estimated average payment as of April 1992	Major reimbursement cost(s)
Alabama	Yes	$1,000	$350	$412	Attorney fees.
Alaska	Yes	2,000	1,200	829	Attorney fees.
Arizona	Yes	2,000	2,000	1,596	Agency fees.
Arkansas	Yes	1,500	100	500	Legal fees.
California	Yes	400	400	400	Agency fees.
Colorado	Yes	800	250	250	Legal fees especially filing.
Connecticut	Yes	750	90	90	Probate court fees.
Delaware	Yes	2,000	300	300	Legal fees.
District of Columbia	No [1]	2,000	....	....	
Florida	Yes	1,000	400	400	Attorney fees, hotel cost for intrastate placement.
Georgia	Yes	700	400	400	Legal fees.
Hawaii	Yes	2,000	N/A	N/A	
Idaho	Yes	2,000	N/A	350	Attorney fees.
Illinois	Yes	1,500	N/A	N/A	
Indiana	Yes	1,500	635	....	
Iowa	Yes	(2)	700	700	Legal fees.
Kansas	Yes	2,000	N/A	N/A	
Kentucky	Yes	1,000	378	378	Attorney fees.
Louisiana	Yes	1,000	400	600	Legal costs.
Maine	No [3]	....	....	....	
Maryland	Yes	2,000	N/A	2,000	Home study by private agency.
Massachusetts	Yes	2,000	400	....	
Michigan	No [4]	2,000	....	....	
Minnesota	Yes	2,000	2,000	2,000	Agency fees, esp. for interstate adoptions, transportation.
Mississippi	Yes	1,000	500	500	Attorney fees.
Missouri	Yes	2,000	N/A	[5]45	Legal fees.
Montana	Yes	2,000	1,000	1,000	Attorney fees, home study by private agency.
Nebraska	Yes	1,500	N/A	....	
Nevada	Yes	250	250	250	Legal fees.
New Hampshire	Yes	2,000	2,000	2,000	Home study.
New Jersey	Yes	2,000	N/A	850	Home study, legal fees.
New Mexico	Yes	2,000	500	500	Legal fees.
New York	Yes	2,000	500	500	Legal fees.
North Carolina	Yes	[6]2,000	N/A	176	Legal fees.

TABLE 14–10.—STATE REIMBURSEMENT OF NONRECURRING ADOPTION COSTS, 1992— Continued

State	Has your State implemented the reimbursement program?	Maximum payment	Estimated average payment as of May 1991	Estimated average payment as of April 1992	Major reimbursement cost(s)
North Dakota	Yes	2,000	350	540	Legal fees, home study by private agency.
Ohio	Yes	2,000	761	672	Legal fees.
Oklahoma	Yes	2,000	2,000	350	Attorney fees.
Oregon	Yes	2,000	300	[7] 450	Legal fees.
Pennsylvania	Yes	2,000	N/A	[8] 700	
Rhode Island	Yes	1,000	N/A	902	Home study by private agency.
South Carolina	Yes	1,500	750	750	Legal fees.
South Dakota	Yes	1,500	650	650	Legal fees and travel.
Tennessee	Yes	2,000	700	700	Legal fees.
Texas	Yes	1,500	N/A	N/A	
Utah	Yes	2,000	327	327	Attorney fees.
Vermont	Yes	2,000	1,500	1,500	Home study by private agency.
Virginia	Yes	2,000	280	[9] 396	
Washington	Yes	1,500	655	780	Legal fees.
West Virginia	No [10]	2,000	....	....	
Wisconsin	Yes	2,000	486	468	Agency fees or home study by private agency.
Wyoming	Yes	2,000	350	350	Legal fees.
Average	....	1,651	682	664	

[1] District of Columbia: Legislation is necessary to authorize reimbursement for costs; amount indicated is the proposed amount.

[2] Iowa: Any expenses over $500 that fall under special services category, e.g., supplies, equipment, counseling, must be submitted to department for approval. The department has not set a ceiling on the amount available under the reimbursement program.

[3] Maine: Legislation recently enacted for summer 1992 implementation.

[4] Michigan: Legislation has been enacted. Implementation scheduled for the near future.

[5] Missouri: Low cost of legal fees is due to successful efforts to secure pro bono legal representation.

[6] North Carolina: Program effective date was 7/1/91.

[7] Oregon: Private agencies have raised their fees to $2,000.

[8] Pennsylvania: The average payment amount indicated is for the first quarter of fiscal year 1992, October 1, 1991, through December 31, 1991.

[9] Virginia: The estimated average payment is for the period 6/91 through 3/92.

[10] West Virginia: Implementation target date is September 1992.

Note: Legal fees include attorney fees, court costs, and birth certificate; Agency fees include training, home study, attorney and court costs, and post placement supervision.

Source: American Public Welfare Association, Administrators of the Interstate Compact on Adoption and Medical Assistance.

Adoption assistance expenditures

The number of children on whose behalf monthly adoption assistance payments are made and the Federal expenditures for these payments have increased significantly since the program began. In fiscal year 1981, only 6 States participated in the program, with payments being made for an average of 165 children per month. In fiscal year 1993, 50 States plus the District of Columbia participated, and served an average monthly number of 78,044 children (see table 14–11).

TABLE 14–11.—ADOPTION ASSISTANCE STATE CLAIMS, FISCAL YEARS 1990–93, AND AVERAGE NUMBER OF CHILDREN RECEIVING ADOPTION ASSISTANCE, FISCAL YEAR 1993

[In thousands of dollars]

Name of State	Fiscal year				
	1990 Claims	1991 Claims	1992 Claims	1993 Claims	1993 Average monthly number of children
Alabama	$384	$1,054	$1,064	$1,195	229
Alaska	170	360	590	839	185
Arizona	1,182	1,338	1,661	3,117	552
Arkansas	507	582	676	1,241	241
California	19,742	27,747	30,228	36,623	10,860
Colorado	774	1,177	1,120	1,961	554
Connecticut	1,137	1,529	2,634	3,652	865
Delaware	251	330	374	413	171
District of Columbia	772	(191)	820	1,269	226
Florida	5,354	5,357	7,974	8,257	2,890
Georgia	1,076	1,341	2,064	3,146	849
Hawaii	81	47	160	243	60
Idaho	294	330	364	570	143
Illinois	4,643	4,376	5,691	7,558	3,637
Indiana	1,636	2,540	4,021	5,711	1,390
Iowa	996	2,878	2,745	2,923	1,134
Kansas	539	725	878	1,576	968
Kentucky	2,206	2,692	2,927	3,052	694
Louisiana	1,481	2,746	5,829	7,656	1,026
Maine	984	1,229	2,294	2,646	427
Maryland	1,005	1,219	1,679	2,385	358
Massachusetts	3,618	5,010	6,232	7,134	1,379
Michigan	11,881	14,202	17,538	21,868	6,299
Minnesota	1,101	1,462	1,707	4,003	816
Mississippi	351	398	416	410	236
Missouri	1,695	2,470	5,452	4,674	2,447
Montana	192	603	530	631	173
Nebraska	665	767	992	1,179	481
Nevada	162	204	249	333	79
New Hampshire	295	438	623	600	349
New Jersey	2,844	4,157	5,031	6,009	2,047
New Mexico	1,178	1,609	1,817	1,798	575

TABLE 14–11.—ADOPTION ASSISTANCE STATE CLAIMS, FISCAL YEARS 1990–93, AND AVERAGE NUMBER OF CHILDREN RECEIVING ADOPTION ASSISTANCE, FISCAL YEAR 1993—Continued

[In thousands of dollars]

Name of State	Fiscal year				
	1990 Claims	1991 Claims	1992 Claims	1993 Claims	1993 Average monthly number of children
New York	33,336	39,200	44,422	57,520	14,934
North Carolina	739	836	1,092	1,748	912
North Dakota	172	250	353	466	94
Ohio	9,608	14,167	18,850	22,964	5,901
Oklahoma	1,069	1,161	1,632	1,960	401
Oregon	969	1,547	2,371	2,804	1,481
Pennsylvania	2,960	4,263	5,437	6,820	2,730
Rhode Island	3,069	3,353	3,612	4,399	500
South Carolina	1,568	1,766	2,063	2,235	549
South Dakota	50	492	544	555	230
Tennessee	1,345	2,010	2,098	3,573	617
Texas	4,546	5,233	6,744	9,142	2,634
Utah	376	447	668	748	205
Vermont	1,147	1,248	1,749	2,009	313
Virginia	1,014	1,655	1,961	2,291	1,104
Washington	620	2,055	4,007	1,987	1,652
West Virginia	197	230	257	285	67
Wisconsin	3,714	4,565	5,290	6,171	1,365
Wyoming	45	79	112	60	15
Total	135,740	175,283	219,642	272,409	78,044

Totals may differ from sum of State amounts because of rounding.

Source: Department of Health and Human Services.

Federal expenditures for the assistance payments portion have increased from less than $400,000 in fiscal year 1981 to an estimated $235 million in fiscal year 1994, and are expected to be $274 million in fiscal year 1995.

U.S. Department of Health and Human Services (HHS) data indicate that expenditures for child placement services and administration for the adoption assistance program have increased significantly in recent years, as with the title IV–E foster care program. In fiscal year 1981, claims totaled $100,000; in fiscal year 1994 they will total an estimated $90 million and are expected to be $104 million in fiscal year 1995. States may claim matching funds for the following placement service and administrative activities: recruitment of adoptive homes, placement of the child in the adoptive home, home studies of the prospective adoptive home, case planning, case management, and case review activities during the preadoptive period.

PROTECTIONS FOR CHILDREN IN FOSTER CARE

PROTECTIONS LINKED TO TITLE IV–B CHILD WELFARE SERVICES FUNDING

To encourage States to use their title IV–B allocations to fund services to help keep families together and prevent the placement of children in substitute care, the 1980 legislation requires that if the title IV–B appropriation exceeds the Federal appropriation in 1979 ($56.5 million) States may not use any of these funds in excess of their allocation of $56.5 million for foster care maintenance payments, adoption assistance, or work-related child care. Appropriations for title IV–B have consistently exceeded this amount.

Further, if the appropriation for the title IV–B program exceeds $141 million in any year, States are not eligible for any of their allotment above this amount unless certain protections have been implemented: (1) a one-time inventory of children in foster care more than 6 months, to determine the appropriateness of (and necessity for) the current foster care placement, whether the child should be returned to his parents or freed for adoption, and the services necessary to achieve this placement goal; (2) a statewide information system from which the status, demographic location, and placement goals of every child in care for the preceding 12 months can be determined; (3) a case review system to assure procedural safeguards for each child in foster care, including a 6-month court or administrative review and an 18-month dispositional hearing to assure placement in a setting that is the least restrictive (most family-like) setting available, in close proximity to the original home, and in the best interest of the child; (4) a reunification program to return children to their original homes. These provisions are contained in section 427 of the act.

In addition to the procedures specified above, States must implement a preplacement preventive service program if the title IV–B appropriation amount is $325 million for 2 consecutive years. If all these procedures and programs are not implemented by a State, its allotted amount of title IV–B funds is reduced to its share of the $56 million it received in fiscal year 1979. Through fiscal year 1994, the amount appropriated to title IV–B has never been sufficient to trigger this provision.

The review process for enforcing compliance with these provisions is discussed later in this section.

MANDATORY PROTECTIONS FOR FOSTER CHILDREN FUNDED UNDER TITLE IV–E

The 1980 legislation also strengthened the State plan requirements for title IV–E foster care or adoption assistance payments to emphasize protections for foster children originating from families eligible for AFDC at the time of placement. By law, for children receiving payments under the title IV–E State plan, States must establish: (1) by fiscal year 1984, specific goals as to the maximum number of children in care more than 24 months, and a description of the steps they will take to meet these goals; (2) a case plan review system to be conducted every 6 months on each child in foster care including:

—a written document describing the child's placement and its appropriateness;

—a plan, if necessary, for compliance with requirements made by judicial determination;

—a plan of services to be provided to improve family conditions and facilitate the reunification of the child with his or her family, or—if this is not possible—to provide for a permanent placement and/or otherwise serve the needs of the child during the time it is placed in foster care; and

(3) beginning in fiscal year 1984, that case plans must show that reasonable efforts have been made prior to placement to prevent the need for placement or to return the child home if removed. As of the same date, eligibility for Federal matching funds for cases involving a judicial placement requires a determination by the court that these efforts have been met.

As a result of legislation passed in the 101st Congress, a foster child's case record must now include his or her health and education records. Beginning in fiscal year 1990, the names and addresses of the child's health and educational providers must be recorded as well as the child's grade level performance, school record, and assurances that the child's placement takes into account the proximity of the school in which the child was enrolled at the time of placement. In addition, a record of the child's immunizations, known medical problems, required medications, and other relevant information must be included.

The 1980 law also provided sanctions for noncompliance with these State plan requirements and mandated an independent audit of States' title IV–E programs (including adoption assistance) in an administrative review. The review process is described later.

"REASONABLE EFFORTS REQUIREMENT"

Public Law 96–272 includes the requirement that reasonable efforts must be made to prevent the placement of a child in foster care, and to reunify a foster child with his or her parents. The Social Security Act specifies the requirement in two separate provisions. First, in order for a State to be eligible for title IV–E funding, its State plan must specify that reasonable efforts will be made prior to the placement of a child in foster care to prevent the need for foster care and make it possible for the child to eventually return home (sec. 471 (a)(15)). Second, for each child entering foster care after October 1, 1983, a judicial determination must be made that there were reasonable efforts to prevent placement in substitute care (sec. 472(a)(1)).

A 1984 policy announcement issued by ACYF (ACYF–PA–84–1) and a subsequent Federal regulation issued by the Department in 1986 (45 CFR 1356–7), do not define the term "reasonable efforts"; instead this definition has been left to States. State compliance with Federal reasonable efforts provisions are audited in title IV–E reviews by HHS.

According to a 1987 American Bar Association (ABA) publication by Debra Ratterman, G. Diane Dodson, and Mark A. Hardin, a total of 21 States had statutes addressing the judicial determination of reasonable efforts as of 1986. The ABA reports that States have continued to develop statutory guidelines since 1986. The

ABA report found that State agencies also play a role in defining reasonable efforts through their interpretation of State court requirements to provide preplacement preventive services.

In addition to placement, adherence to reasonable effort is a requirement for the termination of parental rights in many States. For example, New York's statute specifies "diligent efforts," which require that prior to the termination of parental rights an authorized agency must: consult and cooperate with the parents of a child in developing a plan for the provision of appropriate services, make suitable arrangements for the parents to visit the child, provide services and other assistance to the parents, inform the parents at appropriate intervals of the child's health, and make suitable arrangements with a correctional facility if one of the parents is incarcerated and visiting with the child would be in the best interest of the child.

The interpretation of reasonable efforts varies substantially from State to State. According to the 1987 ABA report, the State of Florida defines reasonable efforts as "the exercise of ordinary diligence and care by the division." Definitions which go further also differ in fundamental ways. For example, Arkansas statutes state that "reasonable efforts means the exercise of reasonable diligence and care by the responsible State agency to utilize available services related to meeting the needs of the juvenile and the family," but the definition of reasonable effort in the State of Missouri "assumes the availability of a reasonable program of services to children and their families."

However, there is anecdotal evidence that at least some jurisdictions are not interpreting the requirement in the best interest of the families and children it is designed to protect. Representatives of the ABA report that in some cities the placement of children in foster care and the termination of parental rights is routinely ordered by court judges without reviewing (or in some cases requiring) documentation that reasonable efforts were adhered to by the placement agency. Because in these cases there is no review of agency practices, families that could benefit from preplacement prevention services may not receive them and children may be unnecessarily placed in foster care.

An assessment of the New York City Child Welfare Administration conducted by the New York State Department of Social Services and published in May 1989, found that in a review of 46 cases in which placement occurred, seven did not document that reasonable efforts were followed. Of the remaining cases, 24 contained adequate documentation, and in 15 cases, reasonable efforts were deemed unnecessary because the child was determined to be in immediate danger, and emergency placement was granted.

As a result of the lack of definition of the term "reasonable efforts" in either the Federal statute or the Federal regulations, Federal courts are more and more becoming a source of direction for defining reasonable efforts in individual cases. Nationwide, foster children, parents, and advocacy groups have brought suits against State and local child welfare systems challenging their failure, in whole or in part, to make reasonable efforts to preserve or reunify families. Litigation efforts have been designed to force reform of inadequate child welfare systems. Federal courts are also becoming increasingly involved in the child welfare system, although this has traditionally been an area that has been within exclusive State jurisdiction. Many of the child welfare suits brought against government officials address significant issues that affect the constitutional and statutory rights of children. The result of much of this litigation has been the imposition of governmental liability for action as well as inaction in the administration of child welfare agencies, and increased Federal judicial intervention in the operation of child welfare agencies.

Federal courts are becoming increasingly involved in interpreting the reasonable efforts requirement, and in the administration of the child welfare system. On March 25, 1992, the U.S. Supreme Court decided in *Suter* v. *Artist M.,* an Illinois case, that the reasonable efforts requirement of the Adoption Assistance and Child Welfare Act does not confer a private right, on the child beneficiaries of the act, to enforce its provisions under 42 U.S.C. 1983, which is a general law creating a right to sue a State official or agency for "deprivation of any rights, privileges, or immunities secured by the Constitution and laws." Moreover, the Court also decided that the beneficiaries of the act—abused and neglected foster children—could not enforce its provisions through an implied right of action under the act itself.

The plaintiffs, abused and neglected children in State custody, brought suit under the Adoption Act and under 42 U.S.C. 1983 alleging that the State social services agency failed to (1) make "reasonable efforts" to prevent the removal of children from their homes, (2) make "reasonable efforts" to reunify children who have been removed from their homes with their families, (3) notify appropriate agencies when a child is mistreated while placed in another home, and (4) develop case plans to assure proper services are provided to children while in placement. The defendants in the case, State officials, questioned the appropriateness of involvement by the Federal judiciary in the resolution of child welfare disputes, and in the operation of child welfare systems.

Both the district court and the seventh circuit court of appeals held that "reasonable efforts" requirements of the Adoption Act conferred enforceable rights on the child beneficiaries which were sufficiently specific to be enforceable in an implied cause of action directly under the Adoption Act or in an action brought under 42 U.S.C. 1983. The Supreme Court reversed, and construed the "reasonable efforts" requirement to impose only a generalized duty on the State, to be enforced not by the child beneficiaries, but by the Secretary of Health and Human Services either through the reduction or elimination of payments or the denial of reimbursements for lack of compliance. The Court found that the Adoption Act does not create any rights, privileges, or immunities within the meaning of section 1983, and fails to provide the "unambiguous notice" that is necessary before States receiving Federal grants can be subjected to suit.

DETERMINING STATE COMPLIANCE WITH FEDERAL REVIEW REQUIREMENTS

As described earlier, section 427 of title IV–B specifies the child protections that must be in place in order for a State to receive its allotment of appropriated title IV–B funds in excess of $141 million. Over time, these "incentive funds" have grown in importance, rising from just 10 percent ($15.3 million) of the total amount appropriated for title IV–B in 1982, to 52 percent ($153.6 million) of the appropriation for 1994.

REQUIRED CHILD PROTECTIONS

In 1980, following the enactment of Public Law 96–272, HHS identified a total of 18 child protections required by section 427 of title IV–B. In what came to be known as "427 reviews," the caseload of each State receiving incentive funds is examined to determine compliance with these child protections. States are not required to initiate this review process, but all States have elected to undergo reviews in order to receive the substantial incentive funds. The HHS reviews require the following:

—that the case plan for each child include a:

(1) description of the type of home or institution in which the child is to be placed;

(2) discussion of the appropriateness of the placement;

(3) plan to achieve placement in the least restrictive (most family-like) setting;

(4) plan for placement in close proximity to the parents' home, consistent with the best interest and special needs of the child;

(5) statement of how the responsible agency plans to carry out the voluntary placement agreement or judicial determination;

(6) plan for ensuring that the child will receive proper care;

(7) plan for providing services to the parents, child, and foster parents to improve conditions in the parents' home and facilitate the return of the child to the home, or into a permanent placement;

(8) plan for services to address the needs of the child while in foster care;

(9) discussion of the appropriateness of services provided;

—that the status of each child in foster care be reviewed periodically but no less frequently than once every 6 months by a court or administrative review (see protections 14 and 15) to determine the:

(10) continuing necessity for and appropriateness of placement;

(11) extent of compliance with the case plan;

(12) extent of progress made toward alleviating or "mitigating" the causes of foster placement;

(13) likely date the child may be returned home or placed for adoption or provided legal guardianship;

—that all administrative reviews must:

(14) be open to the participation of the parents;

(15) be conducted by a panel of appropriate persons, at least one of whom is not responsible for the case management of, or the delivery of services to, the child or parents;

—that procedural safeguards that pertain to parental rights are followed when:

(16) the child is removed from the parents' home;

(17) a change is made in the child's placement;
(18) any determination of the parents' visitation privileges is made.

TABLE 14–12.—REQUIREMENTS OF SECTIONS 427 AND 475 AND HHS'S COMPLIANCE REVIEW COMPONENTS

Requirement	Description	Review component
Inventory, sec. 427(a)(1)	Includes all children in foster care under State responsibility for 6 months preceding the inventory. State determines appropriateness of and necessity for current foster placement. Whether a child can or should be returned to parents or be freed for adoption. Services necessary to facilitate either the return of a child or the child's placement for adoption or legal guardianship.	Administrative review.
Statewide information system, sec. 427(a)(2)(A).	Includes status, demographic characteristics, location, and placement goals of foster children in care the preceding 12 months.	Administrative review.
Service program, sec. 427(a)(2)(C).	To help children where appropriate, return to families or be placed for adoption or legal guardianship.	Administrative review.
Case plan, sec. 427(a)(2)(B).	A written document that includes:	Major requirement of case record review.
	a plan to achieve placement in the least restrictive (most family-like) setting available.	Protection 3.
	a plan for placement in close proximity to the parents home consistent with the best interest and special needs of the child (sec. 475(5)(A)).	Protection 4.
	a description of type of home or institution in which a child is to be placed.	Protection 1.
	a discussion of appropriateness of placement	Protection 2.
	a statement of how the responsible agency plans to carry out the voluntary placement agreement or judicial determination made in accordance with sec. 472(a)(1).	Protection 5.
	a plan for ensuring that the child will receive proper care.	Protection 6.
	a plan for providing services to the parents, child, and foster parents to improve conditions in the parents home and facilitate the return of the child home or permanent placement.	Protection 7.
	a plan for services to address the needs of a child while in foster care.	Protection 8.
	a discussion of appropriateness of services provided.	Protection 9.
	where appropriate for a child 16 or over, a description of programs and services to prepare for transition to independent living.	Not part of 427 review.
Case reviews, sec. 427(a)(2)(B).	Status of each child is reviewed periodically but not less frequently than once every 6 months by a court or administrative review to determine:	Major requirement of case record review.

TABLE 14–12.—REQUIREMENTS OF SECTIONS 427 AND 475 AND HHS'S COMPLIANCE REVIEW COMPONENTS—Continued

Requirement	Description	Review component
	continuing necessity for and appropriateness of placement.	Protection 10.
	extent of compliance with case plan.	Protection 11.
	extent of progress made toward alleviating or "mitigating" causes of foster placement.	Protection 12.
	likely date child may be returned home or placed for adoption or provided legal guardianship.	Protection 13.
	Administrative review means:	
	open to participation of the parents	Protection 14.
	conducted by panel or appropriate persons, at least one of whom is not responsible for the case management of, or the delivery of services to, the child or parents.	Protection 15.
Dispositional hearing, sec. 427(a)(2)(B) and sec. 475(5).	To be held:	
	in family or juvenile court or other court of competent jurisdiction or by administrative body approved by the court	Major requirement of case record review.
	no later than 18 months after the original placement (and periodically thereafter during care).	Major requirement of case record review.
	to determine future status of the child (return to parent, continue foster care for special period on permanent or long-term basis, placement for adoption).	Major requirement of case record review.
	to determine transition services needed for a child 16 or older (added effective October 1, 1988).	Effective Oct. 1, 1988.
Procedural safeguards, sec. 427(a)(2)(B) and sec. 475(5).	Applied to:	
	parental rights pertaining to removal of child from parent's home	Protection 16.
	a change in child's placement	Protection 17.
	any determination of parents' visitation privileges.	Protection 18.

Source: GAO/PEMD–89–17 "Implementation and Effects of Foster Care Reforms," and HHS.

HHS SECTION 427 REVIEW PROCEDURES

As outlined in pertinent ACYF Policy Information Questions (PIQs), and in the "Section 427 Review Handbook" published by the Department in August 1988, the 427 review process of a State's foster care system (administered by the Administration for Children, Youth, and Families (ACYF), consists of two phases: (1) the administrative review, and (2) the survey of case records. The process is initiated when a State "self-certifies" after determining that it is in compliance with the 18 protections on the basis of the State's understanding of the statute. An administrative review is then conducted to determine if all policy and procedural systems necessary to implement the child protections are in place at a Statewide level. Specifically the administrative review verifies that the State has:

—conducted an inventory of the children in foster care;

—implemented a statewide information system;
—established a service program designed to assist foster children return home, or be placed for adoption or legal guardianship;
—instituted a case review system.

If the State has fully implemented these administrative components, the review process proceeds to the case record survey stage.

Three separate case record surveys are conducted in each State (an initial, subsequent, and triennial review) by a team composed of Federal and State personnel. Each of these reviews demands a higher level of compliance, and a State must have successfully passed the preceding review before proceeding to the next one. If a State does not meet the standards established for any review, the review is conducted each succeeding year until the State passes.

The initial review is conducted for the fiscal year in which the State certifies its eligibility. If a State meets the requirements of the initial review, a subsequent review is conducted the following fiscal year. Three years after successful passage of the subsequent review, a triennial review is conducted. Every 3 years following successful passage of this highest level of compliance, it is Departmental policy to re-review State practices. However, a State which has passed two successive section 427 triennial reviews will now be on a 5-year review cycle (quinquennial review). States that fall into this category will be reviewed every fifth fiscal year following the fiscal year of the last successfully completed review.

For a case to successfully pass an initial, subsequent, or triennial review, the case record must include:
—a written case plan;
—an official record documenting that timely periodic reviews were held at least once every 6 months by a court or by an administrative review; and that
—a timely dispositional hearing was held by a court or court-appointed body no later than 18 months after the placement of the child, and periodically thereafter (time period determined by State) to determine the future status of the child;

Initial reviews require evidence that 13 of the 18 child protections (listed earlier) be present in 66 percent of the case records sampled, and subsequent reviews require this in 80 percent of the cases sampled in a State. Triennial reviews require evidence of 15 of the 18 child protections in 90 percent of the cases sampled.

If a State is found out of compliance, ACYF issues a disallowance against the State's allotment of incentive funds for the coming fiscal year. States may appeal the disallowance to the HHS Departmental Appeals Board (DAB). There is a moratorium on the collection of funds disallowed under section 427 and certain funds disallowed under title IV–E resulting from on-site Federal financial reviews. Both moratorium provisions expire on September 30, 1994.

According to HHS, virtually all funding disallowances (resulting from sampled cases found not in compliance during periodic reviews) occur as a result of States not holding periodic reviews and dispositional hearings within the time frame specified in the statute. Table 14–13 summarizes the outcomes of section 427 reviews since 1981. As of March 1994, 46 States or jurisdictions were in compliance as of their most recent reviews, 4 States had decisions pending, and 2 States had been denied.

TABLE 14–13.—CHILDREN'S BUREAU, CHILD WELFARE DIVISION, 427 REVIEW STATUS REPORT

[In fiscal years]

State	1981	1982	1983	1984	1985	1986	1987	1988	1989	1990	1991	1992
Alabama			AI				AT			AT		
Alaska				AS			AI			W	D	AS
Arizona	AI	AS			AT							
Arkansas	AI	DS	AS			AT		DS	DS			
California			AI	AS		AT	AT	Nd		D	P	
Colorado	AI	AS			AT		DT		AT	DT		
Connecticut	AI	AS	AS		DT	DT	AT	AT	AT	AT	DT	
Delaware		AI	DI				AT	DT	DT	P	DT	
District of Columbia		AI	DS	AS	AI	AS	AT		AT	AT		
Florida		AI	AS			AT	AT	AI	AT	AT		
Georgia		AI				AT						AT
Hawaii								AI	AT			
Idaho	AI	AS	AS			AT			AS		P	
Illinois				DT	P							
Indiana	AI	AI	AI	AS			AT			AT		
Iowa	AI	AS			AT			AT	AT			
Kansas	AI	AS			AT			AT	AS			
Kentucky	AI	AS		AI	AT			AT	AT			
Louisiana		AS		AS	AS			AT			AT	
Maine	W	W	AI	P	P		AT			AT		
Maryland	AI	DS	DS			AS						
Massachusetts	W				P	AS		A				
Michigan	AI	AS			AT			AT				
Minnesota	W	AI	AS			AT		AT	AT	AT		
Mississippi	W	AI	AS		AT	AT		AT	AT	AT		
Missouri	AI	AS			AT			AT	AT			
Montana	AI	AS			AT			AT				
Nebraska	W	AI	AS			AT		AT	AT			
Nevada	W	AI	AS			AT		AT	AT			

TABLE 14-13.—CHILDREN'S BUREAU, CHILD WELFARE DIVISION, 427 REVIEW STATUS REPORT—Continued

[In fiscal years]

State	1981	1982	1983	1984	1985	1986	1987	1988	1989	1990	1991	1992
New Hampshire		DI	AI	DS	W	DS	DS	AS				
New Jersey	AI	AS	AS		AT			AT			AT	
New Mexico		AI	AS			AT			AT			
New York	AI	AS	AS		AT	AT		AT	AT			
North Carolina		AI										
North Dakota	AI	AS			AT			AT	AT			
Ohio	DI	DI		DI	AI	AS						
Oklahoma	AI	AS			AT			AT				
Oregon	AI	AS			AT			AT		AT	AT	
Pennsylvania			AI	AS			AT			AT		
Puerto Rico	DI	W	DS								AI	SP
Rhode Island	DI	AI	DS	AS			AT			D	AT	
South Carolina	AI	AS			AT			AT				
South Dakota	AI	AS			AT			AT				
Tennessee	AI	AS	AS		AT	AT		AT	AT			
Texas		AI	AS			AT			AT			
Utah	AI	AS	DS		AT			AT	AT			
Vermont	DI	AI	DS	W	W	AS						
Virginia	AI	DS		AS			AT			AT		
Washington	AI	AS			AT			AT			AT	
West Virginia		AI			DT	DT		DT	P	PT		
Wisconsin		AI	AS			AT		AT	AT			
Wyoming	AI	DS	DS	De						AS		

Note: A—Approved, D—Denied, I—Initial review, S—Subsequent review, T—Triennial review, W—Withdrew, C—Certified, P—Decision pending, De—Decertified, Nd—No decision.

Source: Department of Health and Human Services.

FEDERAL REVIEW PROCEDURES UNDER TITLE IV–E

In addition to the review procedures described above to assure compliance with section 427(b), HHS reviews expenditures made under the title IV–E foster care and adoption assistance programs. Section 471(a)(13) of title IV–E requires, as a component of State plans under title IV–E, that States arrange for periodic and independent audits of their activities under both titles IV–B and IV–E, to be conducted at least once every 3 years. In addition, section 471(b) allows the Secretary of HHS to withhold or reduce payments to States upon finding that a State plan no longer complies with State plan requirements, or, in the State's administration of the plan, there is substantial failure to comply with its provisions. The Secretary must first provide reasonable notice and opportunity for a hearing.

In practice, the Secretary may disallow expenditures for Federal reimbursement under title IV–E as a result of several review procedures, including audits conducted pursuant to section 471(a)(13). Disallowances may result from audits conducted by the HHS inspector general, regional office reviews of quarterly expenditure reports submitted by States as part of the claims reimbursement process, or Federal financial reviews.

Financial reviews consist of two stages and are based on a statistically valid sample of between 200 and 300 payment units in the State. In stage I, 50 payment units of the total sample are reviewed. If the stage I review indicates that the State's systems are operating accurately and proper payments are being made, a stage II review is not conducted. However, disallowances of ineligible claims may be made during a stage I review, based only on the individual payments reviewed. If State systems do not appear to be operating properly or if the stage I review indicates errors in excess of established error rates, a stage II review is conducted. A minimum of 150 payment units, in addition to the 50 reviewed during stage I, will be reviewed. Disallowances will be made based on extrapolation from the sample to the universe of claims submitted for payment during the period reviewed.

Title IV–E reviews are conducted retrospectively, after conclusion of the fiscal year. However, States are not generally reviewed annually, and States may be reviewed for more than one fiscal year at a time. States may appeal disallowances to the departmental appeals board.

RECENT TRENDS AFFECTING CHILD WELFARE POPULATIONS AND PROGRAMS

Data on social problems that are a common focus of child welfare services—such as incidence and causes of child abuse and neglect, and trends in foster care caseloads—are sometimes used to show the need for both child protection and preventive services for families. Although these data do not represent the absolute number of children or families in need of services, they are often used to suggest trends in the need for services.

CHILD ABUSE AND NEGLECT

The number of reported cases of child abuse and neglect has more than quadrupled since 1976, according to available data. Between 1976 and 1987, the American Association for Protecting Children (AAPC), a division of the American Humane Association (AHA), was funded by HHS to collect data and provide analyses on reports of child abuse and neglect. In 1987, HHS ceased funding this activity. Since 1982, the National Committee for the Prevention of Child Abuse (NCPCA) has conducted an annual 50-State survey to monitor trends on child abuse and neglect reports. These surveys, however, are limited in scope compared with the data formerly collected by the AAPC.

According to the AAPC, reports of child abuse and neglect grew dramatically from 670,000 in 1976 to 2.9 million in 1992. Reports of child sexual abuse also grew from 6,000 in 1976 to 132,000 in 1986 (the last year for which AAPC sexual abuse data are available). Further, the NCPCA estimates that in 1992, more than 3 children per day (1,261 in total) died as a result of child abuse or neglect.

It is not clear whether the actual incidence of child abuse has increased over the years or whether there is only more reporting. Depending on the source, approximately 40–55 percent of reported cases of child abuse and neglect are eventually substantiated. However, it is generally believed that the above numbers do not represent the total amount of abuse and neglect that occurs, since many incidents are believed not to be reported.

SUBSTANCE ABUSE

There is widespread speculation that a significant portion of the increase in child abuse and neglect and foster care caseloads resulted from the introduction of crack cocaine into the country during the mid-1980s. The availability of crack has been linked to the abuse of children of all ages. According to a 1990 publication by the House Subcommittee on Human Resources, Ways and Means, New York City officials blame the introduction of crack for the threefold increase in that city's child abuse and neglect cases involving parental substance abuse between 1986 and 1988. However, the biggest impact that crack has had on the child welfare system is the large increases in very young infants entering the foster care system at birth as a result of prenatal drug usage, drug toxicity at birth, and abandonment at the time of birth in the hospital (boarder babies). Drug-exposed infants also often enter substitute care shortly after they are born as a result of a diagnosed failure to thrive, or parental abuse and neglect.

The National Association for Perinatal Addiction Research and Education (NAPARE) estimated in 1988 that 11 percent of all pregnant women use illegal drugs. A 1990 General Accounting Office (GAO) study conducted for the Senate Finance Committee reported that the actual number of drug-exposed infants born each year is unknown, although the study noted that the two most widely cited estimates are 100,000 and 375,000. An HHS office of the Inspector General (OIG) 1989 survey of 12 cities found that 30 to 50 percent of drug-exposed infants enter foster care. New York City has reported a 268 percent increase in referrals of drug-exposed infants to the child welfare system, from 1986 to 1989.

Data from a five-State foster care archive show how increasing numbers of drug-exposed infants are stretching State child welfare systems to their limits.[5] Data for California, Illinois, Michigan, New York, and Texas indicate that the most striking change in the characteristics of children entering foster care in the mid-to-late 1980s is the increase in the number of infants who were admitted into care.

Researchers have divided the period from 1983–92 into 3 discrete periods: 1983–86 (the period before admissions began to surge); 1987–89 (the period of most rapid growth); and 1990–92 (when caseloads in several States began to decline). Between 1983 and 1986, about 16 percent of first admissions into foster care in these 5 States were of children younger than 1 year of age. However, children under the age of 1 represented almost 23 percent of first admissions during the period 1987–89, and 24 percent of first admissions from 1990–92.

Looking at individual States included in the data archive, researchers found that the proportion of infants entering foster care nearly doubled in New York, from 16 percent of first admissions in 1983–86 to 28 percent in 1990–92. Infants entering foster care in Illinois increased as a percentage of first admissions from 16 percent in 1983–86 to 28 percent in 1990–92, and in Michigan, from 17 percent to 20 percent during the same time periods.

This rise in infant admissions is likely to result in larger foster care caseloads in the future, regardless of whether overall admissions begin to decline. Researchers in the five-State data archive found that infants who are placed in foster care tend to remain in care longer than children placed at older ages. Data for each of the five States indicated that duration of care generally decreased with age of placement.

Not only do younger children spend the longest length of time in foster care, but historically many children that are admitted and discharged from foster care eventually reenter care. During 1989, 15 percent of New York's admissions into foster care was comprised of children reentering care. A 1988 Illinois study by researchers Dr. Mark Testa and Dr. Robert George found that nearly 40 percent of the earliest cohorts of foster children that are reunified with their parents eventually reenter substitute care.

TRENDS IN FOSTER CARE CASELOADS

The incidence of all children in the United States who are in foster care has ranged from 3.9 per 1,000 in 1962 to 5.9 per 1,000 in 1990. Especially between 1987 and 1988, the incidence of children in foster care grew very substantially, increasing from 4.2 to 4.8 per 1,000 in 1988. The incidence has continued to grow sharply, rising to 5.2 per 1,000 in 1989 and to 5.9 per 1,000 in 1990.

The number of children in Federally assisted AFDC/title IV–E foster care has grown significantly in the years since the program was created. The number grew from 1962 to 1976, then decreased

---

[5] "The Multi-State Foster Care Data Archive: Year One Results," Chapin Hall Center for Children, data presented at a conference in Washington, D.C., Nov. 5, 1993.

slightly from 1976 to 1983. Since 1983, the number of foster children funded under title IV–E has increased steadily. In 1972, approximately 22 percent of the total foster care population was funded under title IV–E. By 1992, this proportion increased to 50 percent (See table 14–14).

More detailed information is available on these trends from a number of State data systems. Currently, some of the most interesting data are from a multi-State data archive, in which California, Illinois, Michigan, New York and Texas are participating. According to a first-year report from the archive presented at a conference in Washington in November 1993, a total of 204,157 children were in foster care in these 5 States as of Dec. 31, 1992 (of which California and New York accounted for 70 percent). The 5-State figure represented almost half of the nation's total number of foster children, as estimated by the American Public Welfare Association's voluntary data collection system.

All five States have seen tremendous growth in their foster care populations during the period from 1988–92. In fact, in every State expect Michigan, the number of children in care had doubled during the time period. Specific growth rates were as follows: California, 143 percent; Illinois, 135 percent; Michigan, 67 percent; New York, 125 percent; and Texas, 124 percent. The most intense growth in all five States was between the years 1987–89, when the caseload grew by almost 40 percent. Specifically in New York, the foster care population increased by 66 percent between 1987 and 1989. However, since then, growth in foster care caseloads has returned to the levels observed prior to 1987, except in Illinois and Texas. In fact, in Illinois, the foster care population grew by an additional 42 percent during the period from 1990–92.

When researchers separated the primary urban area in each of the five States from the balance of the State, they determined that 75 percent of the caseload growth during the decade from 1983–92 occurred in these urban areas. In fact, New York City and Cook County were responsible for virtually all of the foster care caseload growth in New York State and Illinois, respectively. Both of these urban areas experienced a tripling of their foster care populations during the time period. Since 1990, the growth rate in New York City has slowed, but there has not been a similar decline in the growth rate in Cook County.

Total caseload size is a function of both the number of children entering care (admissions) and the number of children leaving care (discharges). When looking at admissions and discharges, researchers in the five-State data archive found somewhat different patterns in each of the States. For example, the number of Illinois' admissions had been stable during the period from 1983–86, but increased by 34 percent from 1987–92. Throughout this entire period, the number of children discharged in Illinois stayed constant; therefore, the number of discharges did not offset the increase in admissions, resulting in overall growth in the total caseload.

In New York, both admissions and discharges grew from 1983–85, but discharges outnumbered admissions so that overall caseload size declined during that period. However, from 1985–87, discharges decreased by almost 8 percent while admissions grew by 34 percent, resulting in significant caseload growth. Admissions grew by an additional 28 percent from 1987–89. During this period, discharges also grew but only by 16 percent so that the overall caseload continued to increase. Since 1989, the number of admissions in New York has declined and discharges have grown, so that by 1992, the total size of the foster care population declined.

Texas and Michigan have been growth in both their numbers of admissions and discharges during the decade from 1983–92. However, admissions have exceeded discharges in both States during the period, resulting in overall growth. In California, admissions grew until 1989, and have since declined each year, along with a rapid increase in the number of discharges from 1988–90, resulting in a drop in the growth rate.

Researchers in the five-State data archive also looked at the length of time children stayed in foster care, and found that, for children placed between 1988 and 1992, the median duration was about a year and a half in California, Illinois and New York. The median duration was about 1 year in Michigan and less than 9 months in Texas. However, certain groups are more likely to stay in care longer. Specifically, the researchers found that children from urban areas in each of the States had significantly longer durations, and that black children in four of the five States stayed longer than all other racial or ethnic groups. Further, children placed as infants stayed in care longer than older children.

TABLE 14–14.—U.S. FOSTER CARE AND AFDC/IV–E FOSTER CARE POPULATION, TOTAL AFDC CHILDREN, AND U.S. POPULATION AGES 0 TO 18, 1962–93

Year	U.S. foster care population (end of fiscal year) [1]	AFDC/IV–E foster care children (average monthly number) [2]	Total AFDC children (average monthly number) [3]	U.S. population ages 0–18 (calendar year) [4]
1962	272,000	989	2,781,000	69,864,000
1963	276,000	2,308	2,921,000	71,164,000
1964	287,000	4,081	3,075,000	72,406,000
1965	300,000	5,623	3,243,000	73,520,000
1966	309,400	7,385	3,369,000	73,179,000
1967	309,600	8,030	3,558,000	73,429,000
1968	316,200	8,500	4,013,000	73,396,000
1969	320,000	16,750	4,591,000	74,000,000
1970	326,000	34,450	5,494,000	73,516,000
1971	330,400	57,075	6,963,000	73,665,000
1972	319,800	71,118	7,698,000	72,369,000
1973	NA	84,097	7,965,000	72,243,000
1974	NA	90,000	7,824,000	72,070,000
1975	NA	106,869	7,928,000	71,402,000
1976	NA	114,962	8,156,000	70,500,000
1977	NA	110,494	7,818,000	69,699,000
1978	NA	106,504	7,475,000	67,003,000
1979	NA	103,771	7,193,000	68,307,000
1980	[5] 302,000	100,272	7,320,000	67,913,000
1981	[5] 274,000	104,851	7,615,000	67,571,000
1982	[6] 262,000	97,309	6,975,000	67,118,000
1983	[6] 269,000	93,360	7,051,000	66,768,000

TABLE 14–14.—U.S. FOSTER CARE AND AFDC/IV–E FOSTER CARE POPULATION, TOTAL AFDC CHILDREN, AND U.S. POPULATION AGES 0 TO 18, 1962–93—Continued

Year	U.S. foster care population (end of fiscal year) [1]	AFDC/IV–E foster care children (average monthly number) [2]	Total AFDC children (average monthly number) [3]	U.S. population ages 0–18 (calendar year) [4]
1984	[6] 276,000	102,051	7,153,000	66,863,000
1985	[6] 276,000	109,122	7,165,000	66,797,000
1986	[6] 280,000	110,749	7,294,000	66,932,000
1987	[6] 300,000	118,549	7,381,000	67,221,000
1988	[6] 340,000	132,757	7,326,000	67,709,000
1989	[6] 383,000	156,658	7,370,000	67,877,000
1990	[6] 407,000	167,981	7,744,000	67,246,000
1991	[6] 429,000	202,687	8,498,000	NA
1992	[6] 442,000	222,315	9,199,000	NA
1993	NA	232,668	9,548,000	NA
1994 (estimate)	NA	245,800	9,690,000	NA

[1] Data from Child Welfare Research Notes #8 (July 1984), published by Administration for Children, Youth, and Families, HDS, HHS. This note cites as sources of data for the foster care population: annual reports from 1962–72 of the Children's Bureau and the National Center for Social Statistics, Social and Rehabilitation Services; National Study of Social Services to Children and their Families, published by ACYF in 1978, for 1977 data; and the Office of Civil Rights, HHS, report, "1980 Children and Youth Referral Survey: Public Welfare and Social Service Agencies" for 1980 data.

[2] Incomplete data based on voluntary reporting prior to 1975.

[3] Includes foster children 1971–1981.

[4] U.S. Census Bureau, Population Division, unpublished data (1962–1980); U.S. Department of Commerce, Bureau of the Census, Statistical Abstract of the United States 1985, 1990.

[5] Data were collected using a variety of methodologies and may not be comparable with each other or with other years.

[6] VCIS data supplied by the American Public Welfare Association.

INCREASE IN "KINSHIP" CARE

In recent years, States appear to have increased their use of "kinship" foster care, in which foster children are placed with their own relatives. Little reliable national data are available to document this trend, but some State reporting systems and national surveys support the conclusion that kinship care is growing as a form of foster care.

In its annual survey of State foster care reimbursement rates, the American Public Welfare Association (APWA) asked a series of questions about kinship care in late 1992. While many States could not distinguish relative placements from other foster care placements, at least 26 States indicated that they had experienced an increase in their use of kinship care during the last 3 years.

Children placed for foster care with relatives grew from 18 percent to 31 percent of the total foster care caseload during the period from 1986 through 1990 in 25 States that supplied information to the Inspector General of HHS. Kinship care is growing most rapidly in urban areas; for example, almost half of New York City's foster care population are children in kinship care. It appears that most of the recent growth in foster care in some parts of the country may actually have been growth in kinship care.

Kinship care providers most often are grandparents, and frequently are single grandmothers. As their numbers have increased in recent years, grandparent caregivers in many States and cities have organized into support groups, and are beginning to press for financial support and services at the State and Federal level. These groups often also include grandparents and relatives of children who are not necessarily under State custody, but who would be at risk of needing foster care in the absence of their relatives.

Many of the children who live in kinship homes receive federally subsidized public assistance, either through Aid to Families with Dependent Children (AFDC) or the Federal foster care program under title IV–E of the Social Security Act. At the end of 1992, an estimated 442,000 children were in foster care nationwide, and almost half participated in title IV–E, at a Federal cost in fiscal year 1993 of $2.6 billion. However, it is not known how many foster children are in kinship care, or how many kinship care children receive AFDC instead of foster care subsidies. Further, there is no explicit Federal policy regarding which program is more appropriate for kinship children and their caretakers.

State policies and practices governing the implementation of Federal programs vary widely. Particularly with regard to kinship families, these differences in State policies have a direct impact on family income and Federal costs. For example, eligibility for federally subsidized foster care payments is limited to licensed foster care providers. However, some States routinely license relatives as foster care providers, making them eligible for Federal foster care subsidies, while other States do not usually license relatives, leaving them eligible only for AFDC.

Under both AFDC and the Federal foster care program, States establish their own payment levels, and, in almost all States, foster care subsidies are significantly higher than AFDC payments. On average, foster care benefits for one child, payable in 1992, were 50 percent higher than the maximum AFDC benefit for one person, available as of January 1993.

Both title IV–E and AFDC are open-ended entitlements, with costs shared by the Federal and State governments. The Federal Government reimburses States for at least half of eligible spending under both programs; thus, Federal costs would increase if kinship families currently receiving AFDC were made eligible for the higher foster care subsidies under title IV–E. At the same time, some kinship families already are receiving Federal title IV–E subsidies, which raises the issue of equity for kinship families nationwide, or alternatively, the appropriateness of any families receiving it.

Additional Federal issues include the effect of Federal policies on child protection and permanency planning for children in kinship care, the adequacy of information about kinship care, and the relative roles of the Federal and State governments in establishing kinship care policy.

Little national information is available about kinship providers or the children in their care, although some research has been conducted on kinship care in certain States and cities. For example, several studies have produced information about the demographic characteristics of kinship providers. While the results of these studies vary, collectively they generate a picture of kinship providers as predominantly female, disproportionately minority, generally low-income, and with low educational attainment.

Two recent studies on the children in kinship care suggest that children placed with relatives are similar in many respects to children in traditional foster care. One difference found in both studies was racial composition; children in kinship care were more likely to be black than foster children living with non-relatives. Limited research available also has found that children placed with relatives tend to remain in care longer than children placed in non-relative foster care.

NATIONAL DATA ON FOSTER CARE AND ADOPTION ASSISTANCE

The primary source of national data on foster care is the Voluntary Cooperative Information System (VCIS) conducted by the American Public Welfare Association (APWA). This voluntary survey was begun by APWA with support from the U.S. Department of Health and Human Services (HHS) in 1982. VCIS data are available covering foster care activities in fiscal year 1982 through fiscal year 1990. In addition, some preliminary data are available from the VCIS on the total numbers of children in care through fiscal year 1992.

For fiscal year 1990, 41 States and Puerto Rico responded to the voluntary survey. However, not all States and jurisdictions were able to respond to every question in the survey; therefore, the data are incomplete for many items, and, according to APWA, should be considered "rough" national estimates. It also should be noted that definitions of some terms varied among States and that reporting periods were not identical among States. Although all data are reported as applicable to fiscal year 1990, States were able to use either the Federal fiscal year or their own annual reporting period or fiscal year, which fell between July 1989 and December 1990.

The VCIS data report on all children in substitute care under the management and responsibility of the State child welfare agency, including: foster family care (relative and nonrelative), group homes, child care facilities, emergency shelter care, supervised independent living, nonfinalized adoptive placements, and any other arrangement considered 24-hour substitute care by the State agency. No distinctions are made among these different forms of substitute care. Finalized adoptions are not included in the VCIS data; however, nonfinalized adoptions are reflected in the data.

Federal legislation in 1986 set in motion a process that will result in a mandatory Federal data collection system for foster care and adoption assistance. Once operational, the new data collection system will replace the VCIS. Development of this data collection system is discussed later in this section.

The VCIS data currently provide the most complete, albeit limited, picture of foster care children and their circumstances. At least one other study is useful in identifying major trends and in supplementing the VCIS findings.

The National Black Child Development Institute (NBCDI) reported in 1989 on the results of a 2½-year study of black children in foster care in five major cities (Detroit, Houston, Miami, New

York, and Seattle).[6] This study attempted to develop more detailed information than obtained through the VCIS system, such as information on children's education and health status, characteristics of their biological families, and specific reasons for placement. Readers should keep in mind that the NBCDI study focused only on black children, and took place only in five cities. Further, NBCDI identified several methodological limitations in its study. Data were collected primarily by volunteers and thus were subject to varying interpretations. Reporting periods varied among cities, and the definition of foster care used in the NBCDI survey, as in the VCIS reports, was the broadest possible and included all forms of 24-hour substitute care. Nonetheless, the NBCDI report is useful in supplementing other data and in drawing a general picture of the circumstances of a significant portion of the children in foster care.

NUMBER OF CHILDREN IN SUBSTITUTE CARE

No precise figure is currently available on the number of children in foster (or substitute) care at a given point in time. However, there are estimates of the number of children in substitute care. As mentioned above, readers should keep in mind that not all children described as being in substitute care are living in foster family homes, but may be in other forms of substitute care such as group homes or residential institutions, emergency shelters, or, if older teens, living alone with supervision.

Although the most recent complete VCIS data are for fiscal year 1990, VCIS data are also available on the total estimates of children in foster care through 1992. These numbers indicate dramatic increases in the second half of the 1980's, from 273,000 children at the beginning of 1986 to an estimated 442,000 children by the end of 1992 (see table 14–15).

In addition to the number of children reported as being in care on the first and last days of the fiscal year, the numbers of children who entered and left care during the year and a cumulative total number of children served throughout the year also were estimated by APWA, as shown below. As with all VCIS data, these numbers should be read carefully because not all States responded to all data questions; national figures are estimates based on State reports.

---

[6] Who Will Care When Parents Can't? A Study of Black Children in Foster Care. National Black Child Development Institute, Washington, DC, 1989.

TABLE 14–15.—NUMBER AND MOVEMENT OF SUBSTITUTE CARE CHILDREN, 1982–92

Year	Start of year	Entered care	Total served	Left care	End of year
1982	273,000	161,000	434,000	172,000	262,000
1983	263,000	184,000	447,000	178,000	269,000
1984	272,000	184,000	456,000	180,000	276,000
1985	270,000	190,000	460,000	184,000	276,000
1986	273,000	183,000	456,000	176,000	280,000
1987	280,000	222,000	502,000	202,000	300,000
1988	312,000	199,000	511,000	171,000	340,000
1989	347,000	222,000	565,000	182,000	383,000
1990	379,000	238,000	617,000	210,000	407,000
1991	412,000	224,000	636,000	207,000	429,000
1992	421,000	238,000	659,000	217,000	442,000

Source: APWA.

The following table shows the number of children in substitute care, by State, based on VCIS data collected by APWA.

TABLE 14–16.—STATE SUBSTITUTE CARE POPULATIONS FOR FISCAL YEARS 1990, 1991, AND 1992, BASED ON VCIS DATA [1]

State	Fiscal years		
	1990	1991	1992
Alabama	4,420	4,383	4,133
Alaska	3,852	1,942	1,496
Arizona	3,379	3,618	3,909
Arkansas	1,351	1,326	1,981
California	79,482	80,880	83,849
Colorado	3,892	5,519	4,390
Connecticut	4,121	4,202	4,252
Delaware	NA	655	638
District of Columbia	2,313	NA	2,152
Florida	10,664	10,235	9,928
Georgia	15,179	15,500	16,999
Guam	NA	NA	89
Hawaii	1,659	1,600	1,214
Idaho	548	877	1,235
Illinois	20,753	23,776	29,542
Indiana	7,492	8,126	8,455
Iowa	3,425	4,609	3,606
Kansas	3,976	7,112	7,838
Kentucky	3,810	6,422	6,966
Louisiana	5,379	5,799	5,722
Maine	1,745	1,814	1,944
Maryland	6,473	4,859	5,816
Massachusetts	11,856	13,232	13,147
Michigan	9,000	11,282	11,121
Minnesota	7,310	7,898	7,895

TABLE 14–16.—STATE SUBSTITUTE CARE POPULATIONS FOR FISCAL YEARS 1990, 1991, AND 1992, BASED ON VCIS DATA [1]—Continued

State	Fiscal years		
	1990	1991	1992
Mississippi	2,832	2,830	3,169
Missouri	8,241	7,143	8,171
Montana	1,224	1,494	1,691
Nebraska	1,543	2,660	2,985
Nevada	2,566	1,563	1,664
New Hampshire	1,505	2,095	2,630
New Jersey	8,879	8,451	8,024
New Mexico	2,042	2,304	2,118
New York	63,371	65,171	62,705
North Carolina	7,170	9,619	10,275
North Dakota	393	695	759
Ohio	18,062	17,298	17,099
Oklahoma	3,435	3,803	2,892
Oregon	4,261	3,996	4,031
Pennsylvania	16,665	17,508	18,491
Puerto Rico	1,961	3,194	2,796
Rhode Island	2,680	3,311	2,755
South Carolina	3,286	3,698	5.066
South Dakota	567	613	674
Tennessee	4,971	5,217	5,312
Texas	6,698	7,200	9,965
Utah	1,174	1,405	895
Vermont	1,063	1,088	1,162
Virginia	6,217	6,590	6,305
Virgin Islands	183	NA	NA
Washington	13,302	13,956	11,327
West Virginia	1,997	1,997	2,315
Wisconsin	6,037	6,403	6,812
Wyoming	484	605	907

[1] Numbers of children in substitute care at the end of State fiscal year.

Source: APWA/VCIS.

Table 14–17 lists the average monthly number of children in foster care who received Federal funding under title IV–E for the years 1986, 1990, 1992, and 1993. These figures are lower than VCIS estimates because they do not include the substantial number of children who were not determined eligible for Federal funding (i.e., they were not from AFDC-eligible homes). In 1993, there were 110 percent more children in foster care than in 1986 and nearly 39 percent more children in foster care in 1993 than in 1990.

TABLE 14–17.—TITLE IV–E FOSTER CARE AVERAGE MONTHLY NUMBER OF CHILDREN, 1986–93

[In thousands]

State	Fiscal years				Percent change	
	1986	1990	1992	1993	1986–93	1990–93
Alabama	1,450	965	887	810	−44	−16
Alaska	8	347	347	303	3,573	−13
Arizona	481	866	1,541	1,771	268	105
Arkansas	434	323	573	715	65	122
California	23,901	40,286	45,542	48,526	103	21
Colorado	1,440	2,011	2,632	2,521	75	25
Connecticut	1,104	2,006	1,658	1,482	34	−26
Delaware	289	125	248	183	−37	47
Dist of Col	928	593	318	657	−29	11
Florida	1,374	3,454	4,180	4,191	205	21
Georgia	1,893	2,647	3,226	3,254	72	23
Hawaii	46	41	148	368	700	792
Idaho	435	138	185	225	−48	63
Illinois	4,378	9,340	10,977	11,349	159	22
Indiana	1,310	1,822	2,214	2,541	94	40
Iowa	940	1,189	1,368	1,502	60	26
Kansas	1,076	1,113	1,344	1,371	27	23
Kentucky	1,613	1,536	1,724	1,797	11	17
Louisiana	2,274	2,618	2,705	2,784	22	6
Maine	655	774	952	1,000	53	29
Maryland	1,511	803	2,656	3,073	103	283
Massachusetts	1,018	3,695	5,713	7,904	676	114
Michigan	6,823	8,218	9,001	8,672	27	6
Minnesota	1,574	2,100	2,660	3,607	129	72
Mississippi	627	723	871	868	38	20
Missouri	2,114	2,410	4,608	4,555	115	89
Montana	281	364	501	557	98	53
Nebraska	799	1,036	1,238	1,291	62	25
Nevada	222	462	508	621	179	34
New Hampshire	249	414	505	526	111	27
New Jersey	3,840	2,816	3,202	4,115	7	46
New Mexico	601	729	756	875	46	20
New York	17,188	31,036	55,361	53,475	211	72
North Carolina	1,411	3,561	2,763	2,985	112	−16
North Dakota	256	308	442	402	57	31
Ohio	4,166	5,164	6,201	6,546	57	27
Oklahoma	885	894	1,465	1,379	56	54
Oregon	1,313	2,218	1,882	1,882	43	−15
Pennsylvania	7,058	8,823	15,478	15,020	113	70

TABLE 14–17.—TITLE IV–E FOSTER·CARE AVERAGE MONTHLY NUMBER OF CHILDREN,
1986–93—Continued

[In thousands]

State	Fiscal years				Percent change	
	1986	1990	1992	1993	1986–93	1990–93
Rhode Island	434	433	676	673	55	55
South Carolina	946	1,209	1,572	1,652	75	37
South Dakota	302	219	191	225	− 26	3
Tennessee	1,031	1,876	3,850	6,533	534	248
Texas	2,917	3,595	4,602	4,920	69	37
Utah	283	385	469	454	61	18
Vermont	500	860	798	1,145	129	33
Virginia	1,795	1,878	2,175	1,778	− 1	− 5
Washington	983	2,751	2,632	2,484	153	− 10
West Virginia	759	1,166	873	1,017	34	− 13
Wisconsin	2,620	5,562	5,795	5,987	129	8
Wyoming	53	85	102	97	83	14
Totals	110,586	167,981	222,315	232,668	110	39

CHARACTERISTICS OF CHILDREN IN SUBSTITUTE CARE

Much of the demographic data collected on children in substitute care through the VCIS reflect three different groupings: children entering care during the study period, all children remaining in care at the end of the period, and children who left care during the period. The following sections will summarize these data. Again, readers should keep in mind that different numbers of States provided information for each data element; therefore, comparisons should be made cautiously.

Age.—The following table shows the age breakdown of children entering care, in care, and leaving care during fiscal year 1990. APWA's analysis of these data with comparable information from previous years shows gradual increases in the percentages of younger children entering foster care from fiscal year 1982 through fiscal year 1990.

TABLE 14–18.—AGES OF CHILDREN ENTERING, IN, AND LEAVING SUBSTITUTE CARE, FISCAL YEAR 1990

[In percent]

Age range	Entering	In care	Leaving
All ages	100	100	100
Under 1 year	16.1	4.9	5.2
1 to 5 years	26.1	31.1	26.5
6 to 12 years	26.2	32.3	25.6
13 to 18 years	31.1	29.7	39.3
19 years and older	.4	1.7	3.2
Age unknown	.1	.3	.2
Median age (years)	7.8	8.6	10.3
Number of States reporting	22	23	23

Source: APWA.

Gender.—Children of both genders are placed at roughly equal rates. The VCIS data report that 51 percent of children in substitute care in fiscal year 1990 were male. A comparison of this finding with data from previous years found no significant change since the study was begun in fiscal year 1982.

Race/Ethnicity.—Although a significant portion of the children in foster care are white, black children are overrepresented in the foster care population. The following table indicates the racial composition of children who entered substitute care during fiscal year 1990, who were in care at the end of fiscal year 1990, and who left substitute care during fiscal year 1990. APWA's comparison of these data with comparable information from previous years indicates a decrease in the percentage of white children in foster care since fiscal year 1982, and increases in the percentages of black children and hispanic children.

TABLE 14–19.—RACE/ETHNICITY OF CHILDREN ENTERING, IN, AND LEAVING CARE, FISCAL YEAR 1990

[In percent]

Race/ethnicity	Entering	In care	Leaving
White	47.2	39.3	49.9
Black	30.8	40.4	29.4
Hispanic	13.7	11.8	12.8
Other	4.6	4.3	4.7
Unknown	3.7	4.2	3.2
Number of States reporting	23	31	25

Source: APWA.

Disability/Health Status.—Based on reports from 16 States, APWA found that 13 percent of children in substitute care at the end of fiscal year 1990 had one or more disabling conditions.

The National Black Child Development Institute did not specifically address the issue of disability but did determine that 75 percent of the black children in its five-city study were reported as "healthy" or "having no health problems." The NBCDI also attempted to gather information on the children's mental health but determined that for 80 percent of the children under age 6, mental health assessments were either not conducted or were not included in the child's record. Mental health assessments were conducted and included in the records for 41 percent of the 6- to 12-year-olds, and for 56 percent of the children between 13 and 18 years of age. The NBCDI did not report the results of these assessments, however.

School assessments of children in the NBCDI study, to the extent that they were available, indicated that 7 percent of the total population (including children not yet of school age) were found to have an educational disability and 1 percent were mentally retarded. Of the total population of foster children included in the study, school assessments were not applicable for 41 percent (this group included children not yet of school age), and were not included in the child's record for another 16 percent of the total. Of the remainder of children, 20 percent were assessed by schools as average, 3 percent were assessed as above average, and 12 percent were considered below average.

Family Characteristics.—The NBCDI study attempted to gather information on the characteristics of biological families of the children who were placed in foster care. These data must be read cautiously because they are based on a small sample and information on each factor was not necessarily included in all records examined by NBCDI. Thus, while these data cannot necessarily be used to generalize about the families of all black children in foster care, the information is nonetheless interesting and is among the only recent national information on biological families of foster children.

The NBCDI study found that mothers of black foster children in the five-city survey were, on average, 23 years old when their children were born and 29 years old when their children were placed in substitute care. Fathers of foster children had an average age of 28 when their children were born and an average age of 34 when their children were placed in care.

Information on the educational level of mothers of foster children was not available in 45 percent of cases. Of those for whom information was available, about 47 percent of mothers had attended some high school, and another 31 percent had high school or equivalency diplomas. About 10 percent of mothers had gone through 8th grade or less, and another 10 percent had attended some college or technical school. College graduates comprised 2 percent of the mothers.

A large number of parents or primary caregivers were reported as having health problems, according to the NBCDI research. Information was not available for 15 percent of the parents or primary caregivers. Moderate or major health problems were reported for 48 percent of parents or primary caregivers, another 6 percent had minor health problems, and 46 percent were reported as healthy. Of particular significance was the type of health problem or illness experienced by parents. Among primary caregivers with a health problem, substance abuse was reported as the problem in 78 percent of cases. Again, it should be remembered that this finding is based on a small sample in five cities.

Almost half—46 percent—of black foster children in the NBCDI study came from single-parent families. Another 12 percent came from families with both parents present. About 9 percent of children came from extended families with a parent present and other relatives, and an equal number lived in extended families with relatives but without a parent present. Ten percent of children came from "augmented" families with a parent present and other adults who were not relatives, and 2 percent were from augmented families with no parent present. About 5 percent of children were from blended or stepfamilies, and 6 percent of children in the NBCDI study group had been living in hospitals before placement in foster care.

Mothers were the head of household for 62 percent of the study children before they had been placed in foster care. In 13 percent of cases, fathers were the head of household, and grandparents were household heads in another 10 percent of cases. For the remainder, the head of household was another relative, a family friend, or a stepparent.

The majority of foster children in the NBCDI study came from households receiving public assistance. AFDC was the primary source of income for 65 percent of the cases, and earnings were the primary source of income for 28 percent. Another 6 percent of households received their primary income from Social Security or Supplemental Security Income.

Finally, the NBCDI collected information on the average number of siblings of children in foster care. The children in the study group in the 5 cities had an average of 2.2 siblings, although these brothers and sisters did not necessarily live with the child or family at the time of placement.

REASONS FOR PLACEMENT IN SUBSTITUTE CARE

For fiscal year 1990, the VCIS data report the reasons children were placed in substitute care in 19 States. The majority of children—71.1 percent—were placed in substitute care either for their protection or because their parent was unable or unavailable to care for them.

TABLE 14–20.—REASONS CHILDREN ENTERED SUBSTITUTE CARE, FISCAL YEAR 1990

	Percent
Protective service	50.2
Parent condition or absence	20.9
Status offense/delinquent	11.3
Relinquishment of parental rights	.8
Handicap of child	1.9
Other	12.5
Unknown	2.4

Source: APWA.

The National Black Child Development Institute categorized reasons for placement differently in its study, but its overall finding was similar to that of APWA; the majority of children were placed in out-of-home care primarily for their own protection. Neglect was the cause in 41 percent of cases, and abuse was the cause in 26 percent of the cases. Another 8 percent of children had been abandoned, and "inability of parent" was cited in 5 percent of cases. In 17 percent of the cases, children were placed through a voluntary agreement between the parents and the placement agency.

The NBCDI attempted to obtain more detailed reasons for children entering substitute care. Parent-related or environmental reasons were reported in almost all cases studied by NBCDI, although these were not necessarily the primary cause of placement. Multiple causes were often reported for each case; therefore, the following percentages total to more than 100 percent.

The most frequently reported parent-related factor was drug abuse in the family, reported in 36 percent of cases, followed by alcoholism, reported in 20 percent of cases. These figures cannot necessarily be added to achieve a total for substance abuse, since drug abuse and alcoholism may both have been reported for the same case. Other parental factors included mental illness (reported in 14 percent of cases) and incarceration (reported in 11 percent of cases).

Environmental factors included inadequate housing (reported in 30 percent of cases), and homelessness or living in a shelter (reported in 11 percent). Again, these numbers should not be added because both factors may have been reported for the same case. Poverty was reported as an environmental factor contributing to a child's placement in 25 percent of the cases.

Child-related factors contributing to foster care placement were reported in roughly a third of the cases looked at by NBCDI in the five cities. Again, it should be remembered that these factors, like the parental and environmental factors described above, were not necessarily the primary cause for placement, but more likely were one of several factors resulting in the child's removal from home. When child-related causes were reported, the most frequently reported factor was emotional or behavioral problems of the child, cited in 62 percent of cases. The next most common factor was the child running away, reported in 24 percent of cases. In 12 percent of cases with child-related factors as categorized by NBCDI, the children were boarder babies in hospitals. Antisocial behavior on the part of the child was cited in 11 percent of cases with reported child-related factors.

PERMANENCY GOALS

The following table indicates the permanency planning goals for substitute care children in fiscal year 1990, according to reports from 26 States. As the table shows, family reunification was the permanency goal for more than half the children in care.

TABLE 14–21.—PERMANENCY PLANNING GOALS FOR CHILDREN IN CARE, FISCAL YEAR
1990

	Percent
Family reunification	60.1
Long-term foster care	12.0
Adoption	15.1
Independent living	5.2
Guardianship	3.1
Care and protection in substitute care	2.2
Unknown	2.3

Source: APWA.

Comparing the data in table 14–21 with earlier years shows a significant increase in family reunification as a permanency goal. Family reunification was the goal for 39.2 percent of children in fiscal year 1982, according to VCIS data, compared with 60.1 percent of substitute care children in fiscal year 1990, as indicated in the above table.

The NBCDI study also looked at permanency plans for black children in its study group and found that reunification with parents (usually the mother) was the most prevalent permanency goal (42 percent of the children in substitute care), followed by other relative placement (17 percent). Adoption was the permanency goal for another 17 percent of children in care in the NBCDI study; long-term foster care was the goal for 8 percent; and independent living was the permanency goal for 9 percent of children.

For those children still in care for whom family reunification was a goal, the NBCDI study attempted to determine what barriers to reunification existed. Multiple barriers were identified; therefore, the following percentages total to over 100 percent because more than one barrier was identified in many cases. The leading reported barrier to reunification was lack of cooperation from the parent (46 percent), followed by inadequate housing (34 percent). Drug addiction of the parent was identified in 30 percent of cases, and a lack of parenting skills was identified in 26 percent of cases. Lack of finances was cited in 22 percent of cases, and parents' whereabouts were unknown in 20 percent. Mental instability of parents was reported in 15 percent of cases; legal barriers were cited in 11 percent; and alcoholism of parents was reported in 10 percent of cases.

LIVING ARRANGEMENTS OF CHILDREN IN SUBSTITUTE CARE

The VCIS data for fiscal year 1990 contain information on the living arrangements of substitute care children in 28 States. The following table shows that the majority of substitute care children were living in foster family homes, although a significant percentage were living in either group homes, residential treatment centers, or emergency shelters.

TABLE 14–22.—LIVING ARRANGEMENTS OF CHILDREN IN CARE, FISCAL YEAR 1990

	Percent
Foster family homes	74.5
Nonfinalized adoptions	2.7
Group homes/residential treatment/emergency shelters	16.4
Independent living	.5
Other	5.6
Unknown	.3

Source: APWA.

While the NBCDI study did not collect data on the living arrangements of black children in substitute care, the issue of relative caretakers was explored. Relatives were considered as possible placements for children in 73 percent of cases reviewed by NBCDI in the 5 cities. Of those relatives considered as resources, 57 percent actually provided some assistance, and of these, 68 percent provided foster homes for related children.

When viewed as a percentage of all substitute care children in the NBCDI study, relatives served as foster parents for somewhat less than 30 percent of children. In 13 percent of cases where relatives provided assistance, they served as legal guardians but not necessarily as foster parents. Relatives most commonly providing assistance to substitute care children were grandparents, who accounted for 53 percent of the relatives providing aid.

The VCIS data for fiscal year 1990 included some limited information on children placed in unlicensed/unpaid relatives' homes. Only 7 States could provide actual data on such children, but a total of 9 States said that such children were included in their counts of children placed in substitute care. In the 7 States that reported data, 19.3 percent of their caseload lived in unlicensed/unpaid relatives' homes, ranging from 7.4 percent in one State to 32.6 percent in another.

NUMBER AND DURATION OF PLACEMENTS WHILE IN FOSTER CARE

The VCIS collected data on the number of placements experienced by children in care at the end of fiscal year 1990, during the preceding 3 years. As the table below shows, more than half the children in care at the end of fiscal year 1990 had experienced more than one placement, according to data from 15 States.

TABLE 14–23.—NUMBER OF PLACEMENTS DURING PREVIOUS THREE YEARS, FOR CHILDREN IN CARE AT END OF FISCAL YEAR 1990 [1]

	Percent
1 placement	42.6
2 placements	27.5
3 to 5 placements	23.6
6 or more placements	6.1
Unknown	.2

[1] Includes current placement.

Source: APWA.

A comparison of these data with previous years, while not strictly comparable due to differences in the number of States reporting, suggests a trend toward more multiple placements between fiscal year 1982 and fiscal year 1990. Specifically, a total of 43.1 percent of children in care at the end of fiscal year 1982 had been in more than one placement, compared with 57.2 percent at the end of fiscal year 1990.

The NBCDI study calculated the average number of placements experienced by black children in its study group, including both children still in care at the end of the study period and children who had been discharged from substitute care during the study period. The average number of placements reported by NBCDI was 2.2 per child. However, in two of the study cities—Miami and Seattle—children are usually placed in a temporary setting before being transferred to a more permanent foster home, potentially inflating the average number of placements reported.

The following table indicates the length of time in continuous care experienced by children who remained in care at the end of 1990.

TABLE 14–24.—LENGTH OF TIME IN CONTINUOUS CARE, FISCAL YEAR 1990

[In percent]

	Children in care
0 to 6 months	17.8
6 to 12 months	14.8
1 to 2 years	23.9
2 to 3 years	15.8
3 to 5 years	16.9
5 years or more	10.2
Unknown	.6
Median (years)	1.7
Number of States	22

Source: APWA.

A comparison with fiscal year 1982 data on length of stay for children remaining in care at the end of the year indicates that the percentage of children in care for 5 or more years has decreased from 18.2 percent to 10.2 percent, and the percentage of children in care 6 months or less is somewhat less in 1990 as it was in 1982 (21.7 percent), although it had increased slightly in the interim years. Fiscal year 1982 data were reported for 26 States.

The NBCDI study also examined the length of time black children spent in substitute care and found that children in its study group spent an average of 13 months in care, although this average fluctuated widely from 7 months in Houston to 26 months in Miami. This variation may be due to the manner in which the information was collected. The NBCDI study also explored the issue of caseworker turnover, and found that children in its study group had an average of 2.5 caseworkers during their tenure in foster care.

OUTCOMES FOR CHILDREN LEAVING CARE

Data are available from the VCIS from 24 States on the outcomes for children who left care during fiscal year 1990. The following table indicates that two-thirds of children were reunified with their families.

TABLE 14-25.—OUTCOMES FOR CHILDREN WHO LEFT CARE, FISCAL YEAR 1990

	Percent
Reunified	66.6
Adopted	7.7
Reached age of majority/emancipated	6.5
Other [1]	15.7
Unknown	3.5

[1] "Other" includes such reasons as running away, marriage, incarceration, death, discharge to another agency, or legal guardianship established.

Source: APWA.

A comparison of these data with earlier years indicates that family reunification significantly increased from 49.7 percent in fiscal year 1982 to 66.6 percent in fiscal year 1990.

When evaluating these data on outcomes for children leaving care, it should be remembered that a portion of these children will likely return to substitute care at some point. For example, 15 percent of children entering care in fiscal year 1990 were reentrants.

Of those black children in the NBCDI study who were discharged during the study period, 55 percent were reunified with their families and another 23 percent were placed with relatives. Legal guardianship was established for 8 percent of the children, and 7 percent were adopted. Independent living for older children was established for 4 percent, and in 2 percent of cases, children left without authorization.

CHARACTERISTICS OF CHILDREN IN ADOPTIVE CARE [7]

National data on the characteristics of children for whom adoption assistance payments are made are not available. However, APWA's Voluntary Cooperative Information System (VCIS) is the primary source of data on the national child welfare system, and publishes the only comprehensive data estimates on the adoption of special needs children who at some time have been part of the substitute care system.[8] Not all of the children described in VCIS data are the beneficiaries of adoption subsidies. VCIS collects information from States and compiles it in an annual report, with data available from fiscal years 1982 through 1990. APWA notes that the data in its reports should be treated as rough estimates given

[7] Children in adoptive care have had a finalized adoption, are in a nonfinalized adoptive home, or are awaiting adoptive placement.

[8] Substitute care is defined as a living arrangement in which children are residing outside of their own homes under the case management and planning responsibility of the primary State child welfare agency or of child placing agencies under contract to the primary agency. Living arrangements can include foster family or adoptive foster homes (both relative and nonrelative), group homes, child care facilities, emergency shelter, supervised independent living, nonfinalized adoptive home placements, and all other arrangements regarded as 24-hour substitute care by the State agency.

the voluntary nature of the information, and the fact that not all States report data on all questions, or conform to the same data definitions.

VCIS collects information on adoptions related to substitute care children only. VCIS divides children in adoptive care into those with finalized adoptions, awaiting adoptive placement, or residing in nonfinalized adoptive homes. Children in the latter two categories are included in VCIS's definition of substitute care. VCIS collects data on the age, race/ethnicity, special needs status, and relation to adoptive parents of these children. The numbers below represent national estimates that APWA calculated based on data received from reporting States. Not all of the children described below were adopted with subsidies.

TABLE 14–26.—FINALIZED ADOPTIONS AND CHILDREN AWAITING ADOPTIVE PLACEMENT, FISCAL YEAR 1990

[In percentages]

	Finalized adoptions [1]	Children awaiting adoptive placement [2]
Age:		
0 to 1 year	[3] 4.5	[3] 4.0
1 to 5 years	49.7	36.2
6 to 12 years	37.4	43.2
13 to 18 years	7.7	15.8
19 years and older	.2	.7
Unknown	.5	.1
Race/ethnicity:		
White	[4] 50.8	[6] 44.3
Black	29.2	42.8
Hispanic	13.3	7.0
Other	4.5	3.7
Unknown	2.2	2.2
Special needs status:		
1 or more special needs	[5] 66.7	[7] 71.7
No special needs	33.3	27.9
Unknown	0	.4
Time awaiting adoptive placement: [8]		
0 to 6 months	....	19.4
6 to 12 months	....	12.4
1 to 2 years	....	21.4
2 years or more	....	46.3
Unknown	....	.5

[1] Data reported on the number of finalized adoptions which took place during fiscal year 1990.
[2] Data reported on the number of children awaiting placement at the end of fiscal year 1990.
[3] Data provided by 20 States.
[4] Data provided by 27 States.
[5] Data provided by 19 States.
[6] Data provided by 25 States.
[7] Data provided by 18 States.
[8] Data provided by 16 States.

Source: American Public Welfare Association.

VCIS reported that 17,000 children had a finalized adoption in fiscal year 1990, and 18,000 were placed in a nonfinalized adoptive home. Another 20,000 were still in substitute care and awaiting adoptive placement at the end of fiscal year 1990. Of the adoptions that were finalized in fiscal year 1990, the 2 largest age groups of children were between 1 and 5 years of age (49.7 percent) and between 6 and 12 years of age (37.4 percent). About half of these children (50.8 percent) were white, while 29.2 percent were black. Two-thirds of these children had one or more special needs that could pose barriers to adoption.

Less than half (41.5 percent) of the children whose adoptions were finalized in fiscal year 1990 were adopted by people completely unrelated to them. Another 47.2 percent of the children were adopted by nonrelative foster parents. Seven percent were adopted by relatives.

The composition of children awaiting adoptive placement is somewhat different from children whose adoptions were finalized. These children are generally older and include a greater percentage of black children (42.8 percent versus 29.2 percent of finalized children). In addition, of the children awaiting adoptive placement, 46.3 percent had been waiting for 2 or more years.

TABLE 14–27.—PROPORTION OF SPECIAL NEEDS CHILDREN IN FOSTER CARE, AWAITING ADOPTION, AND ADOPTED, 1984 TO 1990

Status	1984	1985	1988	1990
Number of children in foster care	276,000	276,000	340,000	406,000
(Percent with special needs)	22	18	22	13
Number of foster children awaiting adoption	17,000	16,000	18,000	20,000
(Percent with special needs)	43	51	64	72
Number of foster children adopted	20,000	16,000	19,000	17,000
(Percent with special needs)	57	62	59	67

Source: "State Child Welfare Abstracts 1980–1985," Maximus Inc. prepared for Office of Social Services Policy, Assistant Secretary for Planning and Evaluation, HHS, December 1987; VCIS data.

TRENDS IN CHILD WELFARE AND FOSTER CARE COSTS

Given the trends in foster care caseloads and the Federal requirements of Public Law 96–272, it is not surprising that funding for the title IV–E foster care program has increased significantly from 1981 to 1994. Based on administration estimates for fiscal year 1994, Federal title IV–E expenditures increased 744 percent (from $308.8 million to $2,606 million). Although the program has not been fully funded since 1981, funding for the title IV–B child welfare services program increased by 80 percent from 1981 to 1994 ($163.6 million to $294.6 million). Funding for the title XX social services block grant, which States may use for child welfare services, has actually fallen in nominal terms.

According to a 1990 analysis of 31 State child welfare plans by the American Public Welfare Association, it appears that the Federal Government contributes more than 40 percent (42.6 percent in 1990) of child welfare costs, including the costs of foster care. State plans indicate that the remaining child welfare costs are paid by State, local and private sources. As stated above, Federal child welfare funding sources primarily include the title IV–B child welfare services program; title IV–E foster care, adoption assistance and independent living programs; and title XX social services. State and other nonfederal spending is used to meet title IV–B and title IV–E matching requirements, plus other child welfare costs such as 100 percent of the expense of maintaining non-AFDC-eligible children in foster care.

TITLE IV–E PLACEMENT, ADMINISTRATIVE AND TRAINING COSTS

In recent years an increasing proportion of title IV–E costs has been expended on child placement services, administration, and training. Table 14–28 shows HHS and CBO estimates of title IV–E expenditures through fiscal year 1999. It should be noted that expenditures for services and administration include expenditures on behalf of children who are "candidates" for foster care, as well as children who are actual recipients of foster care maintenance benefits. In other words, funds are expended on behalf of certain children before and during the time a title IV–E eligibility determination is made; as a result, Federal reimbursement is provided for administration and services for some children who, ultimately, are determined not eligible for title IV–E maintenance payments.

Table 14–29 shows Federal foster care expenditures by State in 1982, 1986, 1991, and 1993. Between 1982 and 1993, total foster care expenditures increased from $374 million to $2,525 million (575 percent). Over this time period, foster care maintenance costs increased from $301 million to $1,307 million (334 percent). Because of the large increase in placement costs relative to maintenance costs, the share of total cost represented by maintenance costs decreased between 1986 and 1993. Over this time period, the total cost of foster care increased an average of 317 percent.

TABLE 14–28.—PROPORTION OF TITLE IV–E FOSTER CARE EXPENDITURES SPENT ON CHILD PLACEMENT, ADMINISTRATION AND TRAINING, FISCAL YEARS 1983–99[1]

Fiscal year	Total Federal title IV–E expenditure (in millions)	Placement, administration and training expenditures (in millions)	Placement, administration and training proportion of total
Actual:			
1983	$394.8	$117.9	0.30
1984	445.2	147.4	0.33
1985	546.2	190.9	0.35
1986	605.4	213.8	0.35
1987	792.6	312.9	0.39
1988	891.1	342.8	0.38
1989	1,153.1	507.1	0.44
1990	1,473.2	638.2	0.43
1991	1,819.2	788.8	0.43
1992	2,232.8	1,029.0	0.46
1993	2,547.0	1,182.0	0.46
HHS Estimate:			
1994	2,606.5	1,159.5	0.44
1995	2,914.0	1,501.0	0.52
1996	3,384.0	1,700.0	0.50
1997	3,647.0	1,781.0	0.49
1998	3,997.0	1,948.0	0.49
1999	4,378.0	2,126.0	0.49
CBO Estimate:			
1994	2.670.0	1,232.0	0.46
1995	3,010.0	1,458.0	0.48
1996	3,372.0	1,609.0	0.48
1997	3,593.0	1,649.0	0.46
1998	3,884.0	1,768.0	0.46
1999	4,176.0	1,877.0	0.45

[1] Does not include transfers to title IV–B.

Sources: Based on data from HHS and CBO.

TABLE 14–29.—FEDERAL FOSTER CARE EXPENDITURES, 1982–93

State	Total expenditures (dollars in millions)				Maintenance costs (dollars in millions)				Maintenance cost as a percentage of total		Percentage growth in total expenditures, 1986–93
	1982	1986	1991	1993[1]	1982	1986	1991	1993[1]	1986	1993	
Alabama	2.19	2.09	5.16	4.68	2.12	1.83	1.43	1.51	87.6	32.3	124
Alaska	0.48	(0.03)	3.50	4.41	0.48	(0.04)	1.43	1.99	133.3	45.1	NA
Arizona	1.29	2.80	11.43	17.98	1.24	1.24	3.72	7.81	44.3	43.4	542
Arkansas	0.45	0.68	4.85	9.75	0.42	0.50	1.76	2.29	73.5	23.5	1,334
California	59.00	136.68	354.69	478.06	52.02	81.75	185.50	232.18	59.8	48.6	250
Colorado	1.06	2.32	7.45	20.28	1.03	2.29	4.48	4.90	98.7	24.2	774
Connecticut	1.51	3.55	25.59	15.90	1.51	2.32	8.13	4.90	65.4	30.8	348
Delaware	0.34	0.29	1.35	1.35	0.32	0.39	0.57	0.35	134.5	25.9	366
District of Columbia	7.88	5.65	4.70	11.20	6.24	3.82	2.69	4.40	67.6	39.3	98
Florida	1.93	3.90	25.36	45.88	1.80	2.88	10.98	14.63	73.8	31.9	1,076
Georgia	5.01	8.26	24.13	24.51	2.04	4.69	7.39	8.48	56.8	34.6	197
Hawaii	0.03	0.08	1.24	2.91	0.03	0.06	0.09	0.78	75.0	26.8	3,538
Idaho	0.26	0.26	1.20	2.15	0.24	0.24	0.28	0.72	92.3	33.5	727
Illinois	7.29	14.24	67.45	117.59	6.26	14.24	40.36	73.88	100.0	62.8	726
Indiana	0.88	1.08	7.13	37.65	0.86	0.84	2.49	22.92	77.8	60.9	3,386
Iowa	1.43	2.66	9.26	13.66	0.91	1.74	3.56	7.40	65.4	54.2	414
Kansas	3.24	3.79	12.95	19.37	2.85	2.98	6.36	7.44	78.6	38.4	411
Kentucky	1.30	5.93	30.69	34.06	1.26	4.97	11.98	12.73	83.8	37.4	474
Louisiana	5.59	11.93	26.12	28.55	4.83	6.11	14.67	16.56	51.2	58.0	139
Maine	2.20	3.48	12.26	9.44	2.14	2.05	4.79	7.20	58.9	76.3	171
Maryland	2.96	9.72	28.95	44.61	2.78	4.03	14.23	23.82	41.5	53.4	359
Massachusetts	2.91	5.32	29.47	57.40	2.83	2.87	17.01	26.49	53.9	46.2	979
Michigan	25.34	46.16	128.27	103.28	18.72	35.17	52.49	47.41	76.2	45.9	124
Minnesota	4.42	8.37	24.87	33.00	3.93	5.22	12.60	18.71	62.4	56.7	294

TABLE 14-29.—FEDERAL FOSTER CARE EXPENDITURES, 1982-93—Continued

State	Total expenditures (dollars in millions)				Maintenance costs (dollars in millions)				Maintenance cost as a percentage of total		Percentage growth in total expenditures, 1986-93
	1982	1986	1991	1993[1]	1982	1986	1991	1993[1]	1986	1993	
Mississippi	0.89	0.83	2.16	4.08	0.82	0.76	1.07	1.56	91.6	38.2	392
Missouri	2.07	13.49	29.30	29.08	1.94	5.45	14.29	12.71	40.4	43.7	116
Montana	1.26	1.40	5.87	4.58	0.83	0.97	2.47	3.26	69.3	71.2	227
Nebraska	1.77	3.11	7.16	10.17	1.36	1.87	3.73	5.38	60.1	52.9	227
Nevada	0.37	0.39	2.54	2.88	0.35	0.36	0.92	1.61	92.3	55.9	638
New Hampshire	0.82	1.27	5.05	7.37	0.58	0.79	1.97	3.67	62.2	49.8	480
New Jersey	2.04	16.89	16.30	25.30	1.95	8.49	8.07	11.88	50.3	47.0	50
New Mexico	0.21	2.67	6.28	5.46	0.21	1.44	3.04	3.56	53.9	65.2	104
New York	149.80	162.91	515.79	779.23	109.86	113.95	366.10	416.04	69.9	53.4	378
North Carolina	1.89	2.34	8.65	17.64	1.79	2.18	6.55	14.25	93.2	80.8	654
North Dakota	0.81	0.99	3.82	5.42	0.77	0.79	1.90	2.49	79.8	45.9	447
Ohio	3.70	24.78	52.52	91.97	3.27	8.10	26.40	44.82	32.7	48.7	271
Oklahoma	1.91	3.63	11.64	8.20	1.81	2.07	8.21	5.09	57.0	62.1	126
Oregon	4.98	7.35	14.01	14.07	3.41	4.39	6.91	7.27	59.7	51.7	91
Pennsylvania	33.57	34.13	118.45	180.45	31.27	26.02	82.02	125.88	76.2	69.8	429
Rhode Island	0.99	2.30	5.74	8.08	0.99	1.48	2.54	3.19	64.3	39.5	251
South Carolina	0.53	2.49	9.70	8.82	0.48	1.71	4.74	4.72	68.7	53.5	254
South Dakota	0.77	0.60	2.01	2.57	0.73	0.58	1.07	1.27	96.7	49.4	328
Tennessee	1.74	1.86	19.63	15.77	1.66	1.82	11.23	9.14	97.8	58.0	748
Texas	5.62	11.37	54.76	72.18	5.33	7.21	28.54	38.48	63.4	53.3	535
Utah	0.45	1.01	3.85	5.96	0.38	0.49	2.05	3.03	48.5	50.8	490
Vermont	1.10	2.35	6.59	6.65	0.69	1.25	4.32	4.18	53.2	62.9	183
Virginia	2.93	3.23	12.48	13.39	2.55	2.76	5.09	4.46	85.4	33.3	315
Washington	3.15	3.84	16.14	19.89	1.62	1.48	6.10	8.07	38.5	40.6	418
West Virginia	1.45	8.62	7.61	4.27	1.45	4.57	5.69	2.24	53.0	52.5	(50)

Wisconsin	9.94	12.14	32.20	42.59	8.20	8.23	15.81	18.90	67.8	44.4	251
Wyoming	0.08	0.16	0.92	1.06	0.08	0.16	0.60	0.75	100.0	70.8	563
Total	373.83	605.36	1,819.24	2,524.80	301.24	391.56	1,030.42	1,307.40	64.7	51.8	317

[1] Does not include disputes and reconciliations.
Totals may differ from sum of State amounts because of rounding.

Source: Department of Health and Human Services.

EXPLAINING GROWTH IN FEDERAL FOSTER CARE EXPENDITURES

Some have argued that programs funded under title IV–E are becoming more expensive for the Federal Government because a growing number of States are transferring costs they had traditionally paid for themselves to the Federal Government as administrative expenses. During an April 1987 hearing of the House Select Committee of Children, Youth, and Families, Sydney Olsen, the Assistant Secretary for Human Development Services (HDS) testified "it appears that States are finding ways to refinance existing services through these entitlements and that the growth in administrative cost does not reflect increases in services or improved management." Then-Assistant Secretary Olsen also expressed concern that the open-ended entitlement of title IV–E was being exploited by States which were hiring consultants to help them "capture" more available Federal funds. As evidence, the Assistant Secretary pointed to the high variability of title IV–E administrative and cost claims among States.

In October of 1987, the HHS Office of Inspector General published a report on the high absolute levels of title IV–E administrative and training costs and the wide variation of claims among States. The report found that the administrative costs associated with the foster care program are much higher than those associated with similar programs such as AFDC, and the Medicaid and Food Stamp programs. However, this was attributed to the fact that regulations implementing Public Law 96–272 expressly defined many activities as allowable administrative costs that were not reimbursed by the Federal Government when foster care was part of AFDC. By regulation, claimable title IV–E administrative costs include:

— referral to services at time of intake;
— preparation for, and participation in, judicial determinations;
— placement in foster care;
— development of a case plan;
— case reviews;
— case management and supervision;
— recruitment and licensing of foster homes and institutions; and
— foster care rate setting.

The 1987 report also found that much of the variation of States' administrative cost claims was linked to the degree of sophistication of each State's accounting practices. Not all States had sophisticated systems capable of documenting all allowable costs. Some other States chose to deliberately underclaim these expenses so that they could transfer unutilized funds to title IV–B child welfare services. The report concluded that some of the measures by which HHS documented the rapidly rising administrative costs associated with title IV–E were inappropriate:

> * * * some measures of relative State performance such as administrative cost per child and the ratio of administrative to maintenance costs better reflect charges to the Federal Government rather than the costs of running the program. Similarly, the use of percentage change in administrative cost to measure relative growth over time is complicated. Many States had an artificially low base in

the early years (shortly after Public Law 96–272 was enacted) due both to their inability to claim all appropriate costs and the absence of required program components (page ii).

The 1987 report also stated that in seven separate studies HDS had failed to document that States were systematically transferring ineligible title IV–E administrative costs to the Federal Government. The report concluded that although HDS did uncover some random accounting errors "there was no evidence found to demonstrate patterns of abuse." In fact, OIG did an audit of the State of Missouri, in which claimed administrative costs had risen "precipitously" and found no serious State violations of Federal guidelines or regulations. The report also noted that HDS had presented no information to document how the consultant accounting and cost claim recommendations to States violated the regulations.

In addition, the report noted that the decision by the HHS Departmental Appeals Board (DAB) concerning the State of Missouri's title IV–E allowable administrative cost claims, which was issued shortly before the report's publication, would further expand the allowable expenses that could be charged as administration and training. It has been generally accepted that this has been the case, further strengthening the claim that administrative expenses include more than program "overhead." The Inspector General's office issued another report dated August 1990. The report presents the following specific findings, which generally tend to be consistent with the findings made in the 1987 report.

(1) The term "administrative costs" is a misnomer. Most of the activities being funded are not traditional administrative costs, but are "important child placement services". According to the IG report, administrative costs grew from $143 million in fiscal year 1985 to $400 million in fiscal year 1988. However, only 20 percent of the cost increase is attributable to administration of the program. Nearly 80 percent relates to direct service activities that the IG classified as "child placement services".

(2) The current procedure used to account for costs does not allow for examining any correlation between increased administrative costs and increased services to foster children.

(3) Cost increases occurred for two primary reasons: the expanded definition of allowable administrative activities provided in Public Law 96–272, and a broad interpretation of that definition by the Departmental Appeals Board. Other factors contributing to the increases were the States' use of consultants, a 19-percent increase in the number of title IV–E children, increases in the number of case workers, and cost-of-living increases for State employees.

(4) Variations in costs among States resulted from using nonhomogeneous cost indicators, a lack of uniformity in defining and allocating allowable costs, a gradual trend by States to use consultants for identifying opportunities to maximize Federal funding sources, and States' revision of cost allocation plans to capture costs for children who are "candidates" for IV–E foster care (but who may not ultimately receive foster care maintenance payments).

The report concludes that legislative and administrative measures are necessary for containing escalating administrative costs, and outlines various options.

During the second session of the 101st Congress, legislation was enacted as part of the Omnibus Budget Reconciliation Act of 1990 (P.L. 101–508) designed to provide better information on State reimbursement for administrative costs. Under the provisions of Public Law 101–508, "child placement services" is added as a separate category for which States may claim reimbursement, in addition to administrative costs. Prior to this provision, States claimed reimbursement for child placement services as administrative costs. The effect of the amendment, while not changing the type of services for which States may claim reimbursement, is designed to provide more specific information on how Federal matching funds are used.

Foster Care and Adoption Data and Information Collection System

LACK OF ADEQUATE DATA

Historically, there has been a lack of reliable data in the area of foster care and adoption. In fact, all 50 States did not even report their average monthly foster care caseload under the federally assisted program until 1975. Moreover, States have never been required to collect data on non-federally-assisted foster care. This lack of data was one of several concerns that Congress hoped to address with enactment of the Adoption Assistance and Child Welfare Act of 1980 (P.L. 96–272).

The 1980 law imposed several requirements on States in order for them to receive incentive funds under the title IV–B child welfare services program, including a one-time inventory of children in foster care and a statewide information system for tracking children in foster care. Shortly after enactment of Public Law 96–272, HHS wrote detailed guidelines for the implementation of these requirements, which were published as an interim final rule on December 31, 1980. However, HHS withdrew these regulations the following March, stating that the Office of Management and Budget (OMB) had not reviewed and approved certain sections. In 1982, the Department issued a policy information question (ACYF–PIQ–82–06) which restated the law's requirement that States have an information system, but did not specify the system's content. The 1980 regulations were never re-issued.

Since 1982, HHS has funded the American Public Welfare Association (APWA) to conduct a voluntary annual survey of States, known as the Voluntary Cooperative Information System (VCIS). The VCIS has been the only source of nationally aggregated data on the number and characteristics of children in foster and adoptive care. However, the VCIS is of limited use for various reasons. For example, not all States participate fully in the survey, reporting periods are not consistent among States, and there is a serious time lag between when data are collected and subsequently published. Further, data are available only in an aggregated, State-specific format, preventing the type of analysis that could be conducted with case-specific data.

ENACTMENT OF 1986 REPORTING REQUIREMENT AND HHS RESPONSE

In response to the need for better data collection, Congress in 1986 approved an amendment to title IV–E (section 479) requiring that an advisory committee be established and submit a report to Congress and HHS with recommendations for establishing, administering and financing a system for collecting data on adoption and foster care in the United States. This amendment (contained in the Omnibus Budget Reconciliation Act, P.L. 99–509) required that the Secretary of HHS issue final regulations for the system by December 31, 1988, and that mandatory data collection be fully implemented no later than October 1, 1991.

The advisory committee submitted its final report in 1987, with detailed recommendations for a mandatory system that would collect data on all children covered by the protections of section 427. The advisory committee recommended that the Federal Government cover all expenses associated with system start-up and development through September 30, 1991, including costs of hardware acquisition, and that ongoing operational costs be funded at the 50 percent Federal matching rate available for administrative costs.

In May 1989, HHS responded to the advisory committee's report by submitting an implementation plan to Congress. This plan would have required States to collect information only on children under the responsibility of a State public child welfare agency (excluding foster and adoptive children placed privately by private licensed facilities), and would have required States to finance their data collection systems by using existing title IV–B funds and claiming 50 percent Federal matching to the extent allowed as title IV–E administrative costs.

On September 27, 1990, HHS published proposed regulations, based largely on the 1989 report, to implement the data collection system, which has become known as the Adoption and Foster Care Analysis and Reporting System (AFCARS). The population to be covered would have been children under the responsibility of the State child welfare agency, and financing would have come from the title IV–E administrative cost match. States would have been able to claim only that portion of their costs that related to children eligible for title IV–E, although the system would have required States to collect data on non-IV–E children as well.

OBRA OF 1993 AND FINAL RULES FOR AFCARS AND SACWIS

In 1993, Congress enacted the Omnibus Budget Reconciliation Act (P.L. 103–66) which added a new capped entitlement for family preservation and family support services to the child welfare programs authorized under title IV–B. As part of this legislation, Congress also amended section 479, the title IV–E provision added in 1986 that required establishment of a foster care and adoption data collection system.

The 1993 amendment authorizes an enhanced Federal matching rate to States for certain costs related to data collection for fiscal years 1994–1996. The statute specifies that this enhanced match of 75 percent is available for costs of planning, design, development and installation of statewide mechanized data collection and information retrieval systems, including costs of hardware, as long as the systems do the following: comply with HHS regulations; to the extent practicable, be able to interface with State child abuse and neglect data collection systems and with AFDC data collection systems; and be determined by HHS to provide more efficient, economical and effective administration of State child welfare programs.

The 1993 law provides that ongoing operational costs of State data collection and information retrieval systems will be matched at the 50 percent Federal rate available for administrative expenses under title IV–E. After fiscal year 1996, the enhanced match will expire and all data collection costs will be matched at the 50 percent rate. Further, the amendment specifies that States may claim reimbursement for data collection systems without regard to whether they are used for foster and adoptive children who are not eligible for title IV–E assistance.

On December 22, 1993, HHS published two sets of rules in the Federal Register: interim final rules for Statewide Automated Child Welfare Information Systems (SACWIS), issued in response to enactment of Public Law 103–66; and final rules implementing AFCARS. Under the interim final rules for SACWIS, States must develop "comprehensive" child welfare data collection systems, of which AFCARS will be a component, in order to qualify for Federal funding, including the 75 percent enhanced match. According to HHS, "comprehensive" means that a State SACWIS system must include child welfare services, foster care and adoption assistance, family preservation and support services, and independent living.

Under the interim final rules, State SACWIS systems must do the following, at a minimum:

Meet the AFCARS requirements;

Provide for electronic data exchange, within the State, with data collection systems operated under AFDC, Medicaid, child support enforcement and the National Child Abuse and Neglect Data System (unless not practicable for certain reasons);

Provide for automated data collection on all children in foster care under the responsibility of the State child welfare agency, to support implementation of section 427 protections and requirements;

Collect and manage information necessary to facilitate delivery of child welfare services, family preservation and family support services, family reunification services, and permanent placement;

Collect and manage information necessary to determine eligibility for the foster care, adoption assistance and independent living programs;

Support necessary case management requirements;

Monitor case plan development, payment authorization and issuance, review and management including eligibility determinations and redeterminations; and

Ensure confidentiality and security of information in the system.

In addition, optional SACWIS functions could include (if cost-beneficial) resource management, tracking and maintenance of legal and court information, administration and management of staff and workloads, licensing verification, risk analysis, and interfacing with other automated information systems.

Under the final AFCARS rules, States will be required to collect case-specific data on all children in foster care for whom the State child welfare agency has responsibility for placement, care or supervision, regardless of their eligibility for title IV–E. Further, States will be required to collect data on all adopted children who were placed by the State child welfare agency, and on all adopted children for whom the State provides adoption assistance (ongoing payments or for nonrecurring expenses), care or services either directly or by contract with other private or public agencies. States will report data to HHS twice a year, with the first reporting period being October 1, 1994–March 31, 1995, and the first transmission of data due no later than May 15, 1995. Penalties for noncompliance with AFCARS requirements will not be imposed during the first 6 reporting periods (Oct. 1, 1994–Sept. 30, 1997). Half-penalties will be imposed during the following 2 reporting periods, and full penalties will be imposed on States out of compliance for the reporting period beginning October 1, 1998.

Section 15. Federal Social Welfare Programs in Outlying Areas

The following table shows the outlying areas in which the major Federal social welfare programs are in effect and those areas in which they are not in effect.

The word "yes" in the column headed "covered" under each outlying area designates that Federal law permits the program to operate in that area. The column headed "special rules" notes whether the program operates in that area according to the same rules that apply in the States or according to different rules. The notes to the table explain the nature of any special rules.

The programs included in the table are:
—Aid to families with dependent children (AFDC)
—Aid to the aged, blind, or disabled (AABD)
—Supplemental security income (SSI)
—Food stamps
—Medicaid
—Medicare
—Old-age, survivors, and disability insurance (OASDI)
—Unemployment compensation
—Earned income tax credit (EITC)
—Maternal and child health (MCH) block grant
—Title IV–B child welfare services
—Title IV–E foster care and adoption assistance
—Title XX social services
—School lunch and school breakfast
—Special supplemental food program for women, infants, and children (WIC)
—Summer food service
—Child care food

In general, extension of these programs to jurisdictions other than States requires that the law authorizing the program specify the area as eligible to participate. Thus, where the table indicates that the area is not covered ("no" under the column headed "covered"), the program cannot be implemented without a change in Federal law.

In some cases, a program is available to outlying areas by law, but the jurisdiction has not implemented it (these programs are noted by footnotes "2", "3" or "14"). In addition, all programs administered by the U.S. Department of Agriculture may be extended to outlying areas at the discretion of the Secretary of Agriculture, even though the area is not specifically mentioned in the authorizing legislation. (These programs are noted by footnote "7".) Where such programs have not been implemented, they could be if the Secretary were to authorize operation.

TABLE 15-1.—FEDERAL SOCIAL WELFARE PROGRAMS IN THE OUTLYING AREAS

Program	Puerto Rico		Virgin Islands		Guam		Northern Marianas		American Samoa		Marshall Islands and Micronesia		Palau	
	Covered	Special rules	Covered	Special rules	Covered	Special rules	Covered	Special rules	Covered	Special rules	Covered	Special rules	Covered	Special rules
AFDC	Yes	Yes[1]	Yes	Yes[1]	Yes	Yes[1]	Yes[2]	Yes[2]	Yes[3]	Yes[3]	No		No	
AABD	Yes	No	Yes	No	Yes	No	No[2]	No[2]	No		No		No	
SSI	No[4]		No		No		Yes		No		No		No	
Food stamps	Yes[4]	Yes[5]	Yes	Yes[5]	Yes	Yes[5]	Yes	Yes[6]	No[7]		No		No	
Medicaid	Yes	Yes[8]	Yes	Yes[8]	Yes	Yes[8]	Yes	Yes[8]	Yes	Yes[8]	No		No	
Medicare	Yes	Yes[9]	Yes	Yes[10]	Yes	Yes[10]	Yes	Yes[10]	Yes	Yes[10]	No		No	
OASDI	Yes	No	Yes	No	Yes	No	Yes	No[11]	Yes	No	No		No	
Unemployment compensation	Yes	No	Yes	No	No		No		No		No		No	
EITC	No[12]		No[12]		No[12]		No[12]		No[12]		No[12]		No[12]	
Maternal/child health	Yes	No	Yes	No	Yes	No	Yes	No	Yes	No	Yes	No	Yes	No
Child welfare	Yes	Yes[13]	Yes	Yes[13]	Yes	Yes[13]	Yes[14]	Yes[13]	Yes[3]	Yes[13]	No		No	
Foster care/adoption	Yes[14]	Yes[13]	Yes[14]	Yes[13]	Yes[14]	Yes[13]	Yes[14]	Yes[13]	Yes	Yes[3]	No		No	
Social services	Yes	Yes[13]	Yes	Yes[13]	Yes	Yes[13]	Yes[14]	Yes[13]	Yes	Yes[13]	No		No	
School lunch/breakfast	Yes[15]	Yes[17]	Yes	Yes[17]	Yes	Yes[17]	Yes[14]	Yes[17]	Yes[14]	Yes[16]	No		Yes[14]	Yes[18]
WIC	Yes	No	Yes	No	Yes	No	Yes[14]	No	Yes[14]	No	No		Yes[14]	No
Summer food service	Yes	No	Yes	No	Yes[14]	No	Yes[14]	No	Yes[14]	No	No		Yes[14]	Yes
Child care food	Yes	No	Yes	No	Yes	No	Yes[14]	No	Yes[14]	No	No		Yes[14]	Yes

[1] The Federal matching rate is 75 percent rather than a rate based on per capita income. However, the Social Security Act sets a dollar maximum on Federal payments for AFDC, Emergency Assistance, AABD, and Foster Care and Adoption Assistance, combined.

[2] The Northern Mariana Islands do not operate an AFDC or an AABD program. However, section 502 of P.L. 94-241 specifies that all Federal services and financial assistance programs applicable to Guam shall be applicable to the Northern Marianas. Nevertheless, this provision is irrelevant with respect to the AABD program because the Northern Marianas operate the SSI program which replaces AABD.

[3] Since October 1, 1988, jurisdiction has been eligible to participate, but has not implemented this program. If the program were implemented, the Federal matching rate would be 75 percent. However, the Social Security Act sets a dollar maximum on Federal payments for both AFDC and Foster Care and Adoption Assistance, combined.

[4] Puerto Rico receives a block grant of Federal funds with which it operates a cash Nutrition Assistance program for needy households under rules similar to food stamps.

[5] The regular Food Stamp program operates in the Virgin Islands and Guam, except that benefit levels differ from those for the 48 contiguous States (recognizing substantially higher food prices), and the degree to which recipients' income is "disregarded" for excessively high nonfood living expenses differs from the 48 States (recognizing significant differences in these costs of living). Similar adjustments also are made for Alaska and Hawaii.

[6] Under the terms of the 1976 covenant with the Commonwealth and P.L. 96-597 a variant of the regular Food Stamp program operates in the Northern Mariana Islands. The four basic differences from the regular Food Stamp program are: (1) Federal funding is limited to $3.7 million; (2) benefit levels are significantly higher than in the 48 contiguous States; (3) income eligibility limits are substantially lower than in the 48 States; and (4) a portion of each recipient's food stamp allotment (25 percent) must be used to purchase locally produced food (coupons for local food are differentiated by color).

[7] P.L. 96-597 (Sec. 601(c)) authorizes the Secretary of Agriculture to extend, at his discretion, the Food Stamp program (and other Agriculture Department programs) to American Samoa. If the Secretary chooses to extend the programs to Samoa, he may specify special rules for the program.

[8] The Federal matching rate is 50 percent rather than a rate based on per capita income, and Sec. 1108(c) of the Social Security Act sets a dollar maximum on Federal Medicaid payments to the territories.

[9] Hospital reimbursement rates under the prospective payment system in Puerto Rico are lower than in the States.

[10] Hospital prospective payment system in not applicable.

[11] Currently operating under transitional rules until coverage is complete.

[12] Some U.S. Government employees who are subject to the U.S. income tax while assigned to work in a U.S. territory might be eligible for EITC, but the general population would not be eligible.

[13] Special rules govern how funding allocations are made to these jurisdictions (or would govern if the jurisdiction elected to implement the program), as distinct from the way allocations are made to States.

[14] Jurisdiction is eligible to participate, but has chosen not to implement this program.

[15] Definition of "school" includes nonprofit child care centers in Puerto Rico.

[16] American Samoa receives an annual grant to operate its school food service programs.

[17] Different payment rates for meals served apply to Puerto Rico, the Virgin Islands, Guam, and the Northern Marianas.

[18] Palau receives an annual grant to operate its school food service programs.

Source: Congressional Research Service.

Table 15–2 shows the benefit expenditures for the territories for the programs of old-age assistance, aid to the blind, aid to the permanently and totally disabled, aid to families with dependent children (AFDC), supplemental security income (SSI), food stamps, child nutrition, and special supplemental food program for women, infants, and children (WIC) for fiscal years 1970 through 1990. As can be seen in the table, total expenditures for the nutrition programs, including food stamps and programs such as school lunch and school breakfast, overwhelm the amount of money spent on programs such as AFDC. This variation exists because AFDC and other cash assistance programs are capped at significantly lower levels than the nutrition programs.

TABLE 15–2.—TOTAL BENEFIT EXPENDITURES ON ADULT PROGRAMS, AFDC, SSI, FOOD STAMPS, CHILD NUTRITION, AND WIC, SELECTED YEARS, FISCAL YEAR 1970–92

[In thousands of dollars]

	Fiscal year—					
	1970	1975	1980	1985	1990	1992
Guam:						
OAA [1]	$191	$432	$645	$757	$1,425	$1,455
AB [2]	5	5	13	7	6	3
APTD [3]	37	113	213	308	323	222
AFDC	708	1,728	3,324	2,683	5,047	7,800
SSI	NA	NA	NA	NA	NA	NA
Food stamps	NA	3,540	14,581	18,316	14,522	28,230
Child nutrition [4]	[6] 380	[6] 1,250	2,670	3,680	3,060	3,166
WIC [5]	NA	NA	NA	1,270	2,490	3,068
Puerto Rico:						
OAA [1]	3,390	4,000	4,309	6,676	6,446	6,317
AB [2]	116	73	58	118	135	128
APTD [3]	2,342	2,738	3,930	9,909	11,399	12,781
AFDC	25,261	26,434	59,105	62,953	73,162	76,900
SSI	NA	NA	NA	NA	NA	NA
Food stamps	NA	261,006	825,126	789,400	895,474	972,561
Child nutrition [4]	[6] 13,340	[6] 44,140	84,200	131,350	137,860	149,609
WIC [5]	NA	[6] 2,210	17,140	57,970	87,780	105,903
Virgin Islands:						
OAA [1]	163	186	191	224	303	329
AB [2]	4	5	4	3	13	6
APTD [3]	32	73	152	200	434	431
AFDC	633	1,928	1,397	2,795	2,958	3,500
SSI	NA	NA	NA	NA	NA	NA
Food stamps	NA	5,916	18,951	23,061	18,355	18,517
Child nutrition [4]	[6] 380	[6] 1,960	3,560	5,330	4,250	4,416
WIC [5]	NA	[6] 610	1,120	3,980	4,780	5,223
Northern Marianas:						
SSI	NA	NA	1,379	1,784	1,926	2,045
Food stamps	NA	NA	NA	2,000	1,585	1,858
Child nutrition [4]	NA	NA	270	2,000	2,540	2,746

[1] Old-age assistance.
[2] Aid to the blind.
[3] Aid to the permanently and totally disabled.
[4] Child nutrition includes school lunch, school breakfast, child care food, summer service, nutrition education and training, state administrative expenses, and special milk programs. Also includes the value of commodities provided for meal service programs, except where otherwise noted.
[5] WIC-Special Supplemental Food Program for Women, Infants, and Children—amounts reflect the value of monthly food packages and costs for nutrition services and administration.
[6] Cash assistance only. Data not available on commodity donations for those years.

Source: Congressional Research Service.

Section 16. Tax Expenditures and Other Tax Provisions Related to Retirement, Health, Poverty, Employment, and Disability

INTRODUCTION

The preceding sections of this publication discuss direct payments to individuals for retirement, health, public assistance, employment, and disability benefits provided through entitlement programs within the jurisdiction of the Committee on Ways and Means. The Federal Government also provides indirect payments to individuals by means of special income tax provisions that yield preferential tax treatment. These provisions, called tax expenditures, are entirely within the jurisdiction of the committee. Those relating to the above-mentioned policy objectives are described in this section.

CONCEPT OF TAX EXPENDITURES

The term "tax expenditure" suggests that the goals of these favorable tax provisions in many cases could alternatively be accomplished by direct expenditure programs. They can be viewed as Federal spending through the tax system. Tax expenditures are similar in nature to entitlement programs—they are not subject to the annual appropriations process and are available as entitlements to eligible individuals and corporations. They are administered by the Internal Revenue Service.

Estimates of tax expenditures measure the decreases in individual and corporate income tax receipts that result from the preferential provisions in income tax laws and regulations.[1] These are intended to provide economic incentives or tax relief for particular activities to particular kinds of taxpayers. As defined in the Congressional Budget Act, the concept of tax expenditures refers to the corporate and individual income taxes. Federal excise, employment, and estate and gift taxes also have preferential provisions, but these are not included in this section.

TYPES OF TAX EXPENDITURES

Several different types of income tax provisions can deliver preferential treatment. Exclusions, exemptions, and deductions reduce taxable income. Special, lower tax rates may apply to certain types of income. Tax credits are subtracted, dollar for dollar, from tax liability. Tax deferrals occur when recognition of income is delayed or when deductions more properly allocated to a future year are allowed in the current year.

---

[1] Estimates of tax expenditures are provided in annual publications of the Joint Committee on Taxation and in the President's budget.

MEASUREMENT OF TAX EXPENDITURES

Estimates of tax expenditures as revenue losses are subject to important limitations. Each tax expenditure is measured in isolation. The difference between the estimate of tax receipts under present law including a tax preference and the higher level of tax receipts if the provision did not exist is the amount of the tax expenditure. For this computation, it is assumed that nothing else changes. Specifically, the availability of tax expenditures may cause taxpayers to behave differently. These behavioral changes are not taken into account when measuring tax expenditures.

If two or more items were to be eliminated simultaneously, the result of the combined changes might produce a different revenue effect than the sum of the separate amounts for each item. Therefore, adding the amounts of various tax expenditure items can be misleading.

USE OF DISTRIBUTIONAL ANALYSIS

Analyzing the effectiveness of tax provisions at achieving their policy goals often involves examining the distribution of benefits from the provisions, i.e. the forgone revenue allocated by the income class of those who take advantage of the provisions. The income concept used to show the distribution of tax expenditures by income class is adjusted gross income plus (1) tax-exempt interest, (2) employer contributions for health plans and life insurance, (3) employer share of FICA taxes, (4) workers' compensation, (5) nontaxable Social Security benefits, (6) insurance value of Medicare benefits, (7) corporate income tax liability attributed to shareholders, (8) minimum tax preferences, and (9) excluded income of U.S. citizens living abroad.

This definition of income includes items that clearly increase the ability to pay taxes, but that are not included in the definition of adjusted gross income. However, it omits certain items that clearly affect ability to consume goods and services, including accrual of pension benefits, other fringe benefits (such as military benefits, veterans benefits, and parsonage allowances), means-tested transfer payments (such as Aid to Families with Dependent Children, Supplemental Security Income, food stamps, housing subsidies, and general assistance), and imputed rent on owner-occupied homes.

The tax return is the unit of analysis. Table 16–1 shows the distribution of all tax returns for 1994 by income class.

Unless specifically indicated, all distributional tables exclude returns filed by dependents. All projections of income and deduction items and tax parameters are based on economic assumptions consistent with the January 1994 forecast of the Congressional Budget Office.

TABLE 16–1.—DISTRIBUTION OF TAX RETURNS BY INCOME CLASS, 1994

[Money amounts in millions of dollars, returns in thousands]

Income class (thousands)	All returns [1]	Taxable returns	Itemized returns		Tax liability
			Total	Taxable	
Below $10	24,145	2,467	178	16	− $4,469
$10 to $20	25,012	10,308	957	413	756
$20 to $30	20,784	14,456	2,254	1,617	20,671
$30 to $40	16,698	14,578	3,579	3,237	37,145
$40 to $50	11,941	11,465	4,163	3,992	41,337
$50 to $75	18,006	17,848	10,232	10,133	101,078
$75 to $100	7,486	7,446	5,864	5,851	75,339
$100 to $200	5,377	5,351	4,763	4,747	105,129
$200 and over	1,417	1,414	1,309	1,306	164,438
Total	130,866	85,333	33,299	31,312	541,424

[1] Includes filing and nonfiling units. Filing units include all taxable and nontaxable returns. Nonfiling units include individuals with income that is exempt from Federal income taxation (e.g., transfer payments, interest from tax-exempt bonds, etc.).

Note.—Detail may not add to total due to rounding.

Source: Joint Committee on Taxation.

TAX EXPENDITURE ESTIMATES

Table 16–2 provides estimates of the 25 tax expenditures related to retirement, health, poverty, employment, disability and housing. The largest ones are the exclusion of employer-paid pension contributions ($69.5 billion in 1995), the exclusion of employer-paid health insurance premiums ($53.5 billion), and the deduction for interest on home mortgages ($45.8 billion). It is interesting to compare the size of these tax expenditures to the size of spending programs in these areas. The Congressional Budget Office estimates [2] that the Federal government will directly spend $273 billion in 1995 on the two major health programs (Medicare and Medicaid) and $412 billion on retirement programs (Social Security and federal retirement programs). Direct federal subsidies for housing are of two general types: funds to build and maintain low-cost housing available only to low-income Americans, and below-market mortgage interest rates for certain owner-occupied housing. These are funded through discretionary appropriations, not through entitlements. In total, these are considerably smaller than the mortgage interest tax deduction.

---

[2] CBO, "The Economic and Budget Outlook: Fiscal Years 1995–1999" (January 1994).

TABLE 16–2.—TAX EXPENDITURE ESTIMATES: FISCAL YEARS 1995–99

[Billions of dollars]

Item	1995	1996	1997	1998	1999
Tax expenditures related to retirement:					
Net exclusion of pension contributions and earnings	69.5	73.5	78.0	82.8	87.9
Keogh plans	3.2	3.3	3.5	3.7	4.0
Individual retirement plans	8.4	8.8	9.3	9.8	10.3
Exclusion of Social Security and railroad retirement benefits [1]	23.1	24.1	25.1	26.1	27.1
Tax expenditures related to health:					
Exclusions of employer contributions for medical insurance premiums and medical care [2]	45.8	49.9	53.8	57.9	62.3
Exclusion of Medicare benefits:					
Medicare Part A	8.0	9.2	10.8	12.6	14.8
Medicare Part B	5.1	6.1	7.3	8.7	10.4
Deductibility of medical expenses	4.1	4.5	5.0	5.5	6.0
Tax expenditures related to poverty:					
Earned income tax credit:					
Nonrefundable portion	3.4	3.7	4.1	4.6	5.1
Refundable portion	17.7	19.4	21.3	23.3	25.5
Exclusion of public assistance and SSI cash benefits ...	0.5	0.5	0.6	0.6	0.7
Tax expenditures related to employment:					
Dependent care credit	2.7	2.8	2.8	2.9	3.0
Exclusion of employer-provided dependent care [3]	0.6	0.7	0.8	0.9	1.0
Employee stock ownership plans (ESOPs)	0.9	1.0	1.1	.?	1.2
Exclusion for benefits provided under cafeteria plans [4] .	3.8	4.4	5.0	5./	6.5

Tax expenditures related to elderly and disabled:
Exclusion of workers' compensation and special benefits for disabled coal miners:

Workers' compensation	3.9	4.0	4.2	4.4	4.6
Special benefits for disabled coal miners	0.1	0.1	0.1	0.1	0.1
Additional standard deduction for elderly and blind	1.9	2.0	2.1	2.2	2.4
Tax credit for elderly and disabled	(5)	(5)	(5)	(5)	(5)
Tax expenditures related to housing:					
Deductibility of mortgage interest	53.5	56.8	60.2	63.9	67.8
Deductibility of property tax on owner-occupied housing	13.7	14.5	15.3	16.2	17.1
Deferral of capital gain on sale of principal residence	14.8	15.3	15.9	16.4	17.0
Exclusion of capital gain on sale of residence of persons 55 and over	4.9	5.1	5.3	5.5	5.7
Exclusion of interest on State and local government bonds for owner-occupied housing	1.7	1.8	1.8	1.7	1.7
Depreciation of rental housing in excess of alternative depreciation system	1.7	1.6	1.5	1.3	1.2
Exclusion of interest on State and local government bonds for rental housing	0.9	0.9	0.8	0.8	0.7
Low-income housing tax credit	2.2	2.6	3.0	3.3	3.7

[1] In addition to OASDI benefits for retired workers, these figures also include disability insurance benefits and benefits for dependents and survivors.
[2] Estimate includes employer-provided health insurance purchased through cafeteria plans.
[3] Estimate includes employer-provided child care purchased through dependent care flexible spending accounts.
[4] Estimate includes amounts of employer-provided health insurance purchased through cafeteria plans and employer-provided child care purchased through flexible spending accounts. These amounts are also included in other line items in this table.
[5] Less than $50 million.

Source: Joint Committee on Taxation.

The remainder of this chapter will discuss specific tax expenditures related to retirement, health, poverty, employment, disability, and housing. The discussion includes legislative history, an explanation of current law, and a brief assessment of the effects of each tax expenditure.

NET EXCLUSION OF PENSION CONTRIBUTIONS AND EARNINGS

Legislative history

Prior to 1921, no special tax treatment applied to employee retirement trusts. Retirement payments to employees and contributions to pension trusts were deductible by the employer as an ordinary and necessary business expense. Employees were taxed on amounts actually received as well as on employer contributions to a trust if there was a reasonable expectation of benefits accruing from the trust. The 1921 Code provided an exemption for a trust forming part of a qualified profit-sharing or stock bonus plan.

The rules relating to qualified plans were substantially revised by the Employee Retirement Income Security Act of 1974 (ERISA), which added overall limitations on contributions and benefits and other requirements on minimum participation, coverage, vesting, benefit accrual, and funding. Further revisions of these rules have been made in every major tax bill since then.

Since ERISA, Congress has also acted to broaden the range of qualified plans. In the Revenue Act of 1978, Congress provided special rules for qualified cash or deferred arrangements under section 401(k). Under these arrangements, known popularly as 401(k) plans, employees can elect to receive cash or have their employers contribute a portion of their earnings to a qualified profit sharing, stock bonus, or pre-ERISA money purchase pension plan.

An employee stock ownership plan (ESOP) is a special type of qualified plan that is designed to invest primarily in securities of the employer maintaining the plan. Certain qualification rules and tax benefits apply to ESOPs that do not apply to other types of qualified plans.

Explanation of provision

In general.—Under a plan of deferred compensation that meets the qualification standards of the Internal Revenue Code, an employer is allowed a deduction for contributions to a tax-exempt trust to provide employee benefits. Similar rules apply to plans funded with annuity contracts. An employer that makes contributions to a qualified plan in excess of the deduction limits is subject to a 10-percent excise tax on such excess (sec. 4972).

The qualification rules limit the amount of benefits that can be provided through a qualified plan and require that benefits be provided on a basis that does not discriminate in favor of highly compensated employees. In addition, qualified plans are required to meet minimum standards relating to participation (the restrictions that may be imposed on participation in the plan), coverage (the number of employees participating in the plan), vesting (the time at which an employee's benefit becomes nonforfeitable), and benefit accrual (the rate at which an employee earns a benefit). Also, minimum funding standards apply to the rate at which employer contributions are required to be made to the plan to ensure the solvency of pension plans.

If a defined benefit pension plan is terminated, any assets remaining after satisfaction of the plan's liabilities may revert to the employer. Such reversions are included in the gross income of the employer and are subject to income tax plus an additional excise tax payable by the employer. The excise tax is 20 percent if the employer establishes a qualified replacement plan or provides certain benefit increases. Otherwise, the excise tax is 50 percent.

Minimum participation rules.—A qualified plan generally may not require as a condition of participation that an employee complete more than one year of service or be older than age 21 (sec. 410(a)).

Vesting rules.—A plan is not a qualified plan unless a participant's employer-provided benefit vests at least as rapidly as under one of two alternative minimum vesting schedules.

Benefit accrual rules.—The protection afforded employees under the minimum vesting rules depends not only on the minimum vesting schedules, but also on the accrued benefits to which these schedules are applied. In the case of a defined contribution plan, the accrued benefit is the participant's account balance. In the case of a defined benefit plan, a participant's accrued benefit is determined under the plan benefit formula, subject to certain restrictions. In general, the accrued benefit is defined in terms of the benefit payable at normal retirement age and does not include certain ancillary nonretirement benefits.

Each defined benefit plan is required to satisfy one of three accrued benefit tests. The primary purpose of these tests is to prevent undue backloading of benefit accruals (i.e., by providing low rates of benefit accrual in the employee's early years of service when the employee is most likely to leave and by concentrating the accrual of benefits in the employee's later years of service when he or she is most likely to remain with the employer until retirement).

Coverage rules.—A plan is not qualified unless the plan satisfies at least one of the following coverage requirements: (1) the plan benefits at least 70 percent of all nonhighly compensated employees, (2) the plan benefits a percentage of nonhighly compensated employees that is at least 70 percent of the percentage of highly compensated employees benefiting under the plan, or (3) the plan meets an average benefits test. In addition, a plan is not a qualified plan unless it benefits the lesser of (1) 50 employees or (2) 40 percent of the employees of the employer (sec. 401(a)(26)).

General nondiscrimination rule.—In general, a plan is not a qualified plan if the contributions or benefits under the plan discriminate in favor of highly compensated employees.

Limitations on contributions and benefits.—The maximum annual benefit that may be provided by a defined benefit pension plan (payable at the Social Security retirement age) is the lesser of (1) 100 percent of average compensation, or (2) $118,800 for 1994 (sec. 415(b)). The dollar limit is adjusted annually for inflation. The dollar limit is reduced if payments of benefits begin before the Social Security retirement age and increased if benefits begin after the Social Security retirement age.

Funding rules.—Pension plans are required to meet a minimum funding standard for each plan year (sec. 412). In the case of a defined benefit pension plan, an employer must contribute an annual amount sufficient to fund a portion of participants' projected benefits determined in accordance with one of several prescribed funding methods, using reasonable actuarial assumptions. Plans with asset values of less than 100 percent of current liabilities are subject to additional, faster funding rules.

Taxation of distributions.—An employee who participates in a qualified plan is taxed when the employee receives a distribution from the plan to the extent the distribution is not attributable to employee contributions. With certain exceptions, a 10-percent additional income tax is imposed on early distributions from a qualified plan. A 15-percent excise tax is imposed on distributions that exceed a certain amount in any year.

Failure to satisfy qualification requirements.—If a plan fails to satisfy the qualification requirements, the trust that holds the plan's assets is not tax-exempt, an employer's deduction for plan contributions is only allowed when the employee includes the contributions or benefits in income, and benefits generally are includible in an employee's income when they are no longer subject to a substantial risk of forfeiture.

Effect of provision

The tax treatment of pension contributions and earnings has encouraged employers to establish qualified retirement plans and to compensate employees in the form of pension contributions to such plans. The tax advantage of being compensated through pension contributions consists of two parts. One advantage is the ability to earn tax-free returns to savings. When saving is done through a pension plan, the employee earns a higher rate of return than on fully-taxed savings.[3] The second advantage is that an employee's tax rate may be lower during retirement than during the working years.

These tax provisions directly benefit only persons who work for employers with qualified plans and who work for a sufficient period of time before their benefits vest in such plans. The current extent of this coverage and recent trends in coverage are described below.

Coverage

The term covered, as used here, means that an employee is accruing benefits in an employer pension or other retirement plan. The best current comprehensive evidence on pension coverage comes from the 1988 Survey of Employee Benefits, a supplement to the May 1988 Current Population Survey. The data referred to below come from that survey unless otherwise noted.

As of May 1988, 48 percent of full-time wage and salary workers employed in the private sector reported that they were covered by an employer-sponsored pension. Most of these workers were covered by basic defined benefit or defined contribution plans (31 per-

---

[3] This applies to pension contributions made by employers. Employees may also be able to contribute to qualified plans. Employee contributions may be made with after-tax dollars. If so, the tax advantage given to these contributions is smaller than the tax advantage given to employer contributions, and consists of the deferral of tax on accumulated earnings.

cent), and another 8 percent had both a basic plan and a 401(k) type contributory plan (see table 16–3).[4] For another 9 percent, the 401(k) type plan was their only retirement plan. Most employers contributed to their 401(k) type plan. While 48 percent of full-time workers in private employment had employer-sponsored plans, 46 percent had employer-financed plans.

TABLE 16–3.—COVERAGE UNDER EMPLOYER-SPONSORED PENSION OR RETIREMENT PLANS: DISTRIBUTION BY TYPE OF FULL-TIME PRIVATE WAGE AND SALARY WORKERS AGED 16 OR OLDER (PERCENT COVERED)

Coverage status	Total	Men	Women
Number of private wage and salary workers aged 16 or older (in thousands)	71,485	43,188	28,296
Employer-sponsored plan	48	51	44
Basic pension only	31	33	29
Basic and 401(k) type	8	9	8
401(k) type only	9	9	8
Employer contributes	7	7	7
Employer does not contribute	1	2	1
Not covered	51	48	55
Don't know	1	1	1

Source: John R. Woods, "Pension Coverage Among Private Wage and Salary Workers: Preliminary Findings From the 1988 Survey of Employee Benefits," Social Security Bulletin, 52:10 (October 1989), p. 8.

Pension coverage varies substantially among full-time, privately employed workers. Differences depend on the age of the worker, job earnings, the industry of employment, the size of the firm, and whether the worker is represented by a union.

Younger workers are much less likely to be covered by a pension than middle-aged and older workers. Coverage rates rise steadily from 12 percent for those under age 21 to 50–60 percent for those aged 40 or over. This pattern holds for both men and women. However, the jump in coverage for middle-aged men is about 10 percentage points larger than the increase for middle-aged women (see table 16–4).

Higher-paying jobs are more likely to offer pensions. Just 13 percent of workers earning less than $10,000 per year in 1988 were covered compared to 72 percent for those earning $30,000 or more (see table 16–5). Coverage may be higher for higher-paying jobs because of the greater value of the pension tax benefits to workers in higher tax brackets and because of the declining replacement rate of Social Security at higher earnings levels. Lower-paying jobs may also be filled more often by part-time workers who are not covered by their employer's plan. The similarity in coverage between men and women with the same earnings, shown in table 16–5, suggests that the higher overall coverage rate among men is due to their greater representation in higher-paying jobs.

[4] Some private-sector employees contribute to 403(b) tax-sheltered annuities instead of 401(k) plans.

TABLE 16–4.—DISTRIBUTION BY AGE AND GENDER, COVERAGE UNDER EMPLOYER-FI-NANCED PENSION OR RETIREMENT PLAN, FULL-TIME PRIVATE WAGE AND SALARY WORKERS AGED 16 OR OLDER (PERCENT COVERED)

Age (in years)	Total	Men	Women
Total	46	49	43
Under 21	12	12	11
21 to 25	25	24	26
25 to 29	42	41	42
30 to 34	48	48	48
35 to 39	54	57	49
40 to 44	57	61	51
45 to 49	56	61	49
50 to 54	58	63	49
55 to 59	56	60	49
60 or older	47	51	40

Source: John R. Woods, "Pension Coverage Among Private Wage and Salary Workers: Preliminary Findings From the 1988 Survey of Employee Benefits," Social Security Bulletin, 52:10 (October 1989), p. 10.

TABLE 16–5.—DISTRIBUTION BY WORKERS' EARNINGS, COVERAGE UNDER EMPLOYER-FINANCED PENSION OR RETIREMENT PLAN, FULL-TIME PRIVATE WAGE AND SALARY EMPLOYEES AGE 16 OR OLDER (PERCENT COVERED) [1]

Earnings	Total	Men	Women
Total [2]	46	49	43
Under $10,000	13	12	13
$10,000 to $14,999	33	27	39
$15,000 to $19,999	47	43	51
$20,000 to $24,999	58	57	60
$25,000 to $29,999	66	65	68
$30,000 to $39,999	72	71	73
$40,000 and over	72	72	73

[1] Based on 1988 earnings.
[2] Total includes workers not responding on earnings, not shown separately.

Source: Social Security Administration tabulations from 1988 Survey of Employee Benefits, supplement to May 1988 Current Population Survey.

Industries with high pension coverage include manufacturing, mining, financial services, and transportation and public utilities. Coverage rates are nearly 60 percent in each of these industries.[5] In contrast, coverage rates are under 30 percent in agriculture, retail trade, and services other than financial and professional. Part of the difference among industries appears to be due to differences in firm size. Coverage is much lower for smaller firms. Smaller firms are less likely to offer comprehensive fringe benefit packages as part of total compensation. Only 11 percent of full-time workers in firms with fewer than 10 employees are covered. The rate rises

[5] John R. Woods, "Pension Coverage Among Private Wage and Salary Workers: Preliminary Findings From the 1988 Survey of Employee Benefits," Social Security Bulletin, 52:10 (October 1989), p. 13.

with employer size but does not reach the 46 percent average rate until firms have 250 or more employees (table 16–6). Workers represented by a union are also more likely to be covered under a pension than are other workers. Seventy-five percent of those represented by a union are covered compared to 43 percent of those without a union. Union representation is particularly important in coverage among small employers.

TABLE 16–6.—DISTRIBUTION BY SIZE OF FIRM, COVERAGE UNDER EMPLOYER-FI-NANCED PENSION OR RETIREMENT PLANS, FULL-TIME PRIVATE WAGE AND SALARY WORKERS AGED 16 AND OLDER (PERCENT COVERED)

Firm size (number of workers)	Total	Men	Women
Total [1]	46	49	43
Fewer than 10	11	12	9
10 to 24	22	22	20
25 to 49	29	33	23
50 to 99	40	43	35
100 to 249	45	49	39
250 or more	67	71	63

[1] Total includes workers for whom firm size is unknown, not shown separately.

Source: John R. Woods, "Pension Coverage Among Private Wage and Salary Workers: Preliminary Findings From the 1988 Survey of Employee Benefits," Social Security Bulletin, 52:10 (October 1989), p. 15.

Significant differences in coverage also are apparent between full-time private wage and salary workers and other wage and salary workers. Coverage is much lower among part-time workers and much higher among public employees.

Trends in coverage

At the outset of World War II, private employer pensions were offered by about 12,000 firms. Pensions spread rapidly during and after the war, encouraged by high marginal tax rates and war-time wage controls that exempted pension benefits. By 1972, when the first comprehensive survey was undertaken, 48 percent of full-time private employees were covered. Subsequent surveys found that coverage reached 50 percent in 1979, but by 1983 had fallen back to 48 percent. The decline continued in the 1980's, reaching 46 percent in 1988.[6]

The decline in coverage in the 1980s was concentrated among younger men. The coverage rate among older men has fallen less dramatically, and among women it has risen at some ages and fallen at others. Explanations for the decline in coverage among young men include the shifting of employment shares from manufacturing to services and the declining share of employees represented by a union contract. Both factors affect men more than women and new job entrants more than long-tenured workers.

The decline in pension coverage has occurred at the same time that employers have been shifting from defined benefit plans. De-

---

[6] John R. Woods, "Pension Coverage Among Private Wage and Salary Workers: Preliminary Findings From the 1988 Survey of Employee Benefits," Social Security Bulletin, 52:10 (October 1989), p. 17.

fined benefit plans provided basic plan coverage for 87 percent of private wage and salary workers in 1975.[7] This proportion dropped to 83 percent by 1980 and to 71 percent by 1985. This shifting composition has largely been the result of rapid growth in primary defined contribution plans. Employee stock ownership plans and 401(k) plans have been among the most rapidly growing defined contribution plans.

INDIVIDUAL RETIREMENT PLANS

Legislative history

The Employee Retirement Income Security Act of 1974 added section 219 of the Internal Revenue Code, providing a tax deduction for certain contributions to individual retirement arrangements (IRAs) and permitting the deferral of tax on amounts held in such arrangements until withdrawal. Active participants in employer plans were not permitted to make deductible IRA contributions.

The Economic Recovery Tax Act of 1981 expanded eligibility to individuals who were active participants and increased the amount of the permitted deduction. The Tax Reform Act of 1986 limited the full IRA deduction to individuals with income below certain levels and to individuals who are not active participants in employer plans. Individuals who are not entitled to the full IRA deduction may make nondeductible contributions to an IRA.

Explanation of provision

An individual who is an active participant in an employer plan may deduct IRA contributions up to the lesser of $2,000 ($2,250 for an individual with a nonworking spouse) or 100 percent of compensation if the individual's adjusted gross income (AGI) does not exceed $25,000 for an unmarried individual, $40,000 for a married couple filing a joint return, and $0 for a married individual filing separately. A couple is not treated as married if the spouses file separate returns and do not live together at any time during the year. The deduction is phased out over the following AGI ranges: (1) $25,000–$35,000 for unmarried individuals, (2) $40,000–$50,000 for married individuals filing a joint return, and (3) 0–$10,000 for married individuals filing separate returns. An individual is entitled to make nondeductible contributions to the extent deductible contributions are disallowed as a result of the phaseout.

An individual who is not an active participant in an employer plan may deduct IRA contributions up to the limits described above without limitation based on income.

The investment income of IRA accounts is not taxed until withdrawn. Withdrawn amounts attributable to deductible contributions and all earnings are includible in income. A 10-percent additional income tax is levied unless the withdrawal (1) is made after the IRA owner attains age 59½ or dies, (2) is made on account of the disability of the IRA owner, or (3) is one of a series of substantially equal periodic payments made not less frequently than annu-

---

[7] John A. Turner and Daniel Beller, eds., "Trends in Pensions," Department of Labor, 1989, pp. 65, 357.

ally over the life or life expectancy of the IRA owner (or the IRA owner and his or her beneficiary).

Effect of provision

Use of IRAs expanded significantly when eligibility was expanded in 1982 to all persons with earnings and contracted correspondingly in 1987 when deductibility was restricted for higher-income taxpayers who were covered by an employer-provided pension. The number of taxpayers claiming a deductible IRA contribution jumped from 3.4 million in 1981 to 12.0 million in 1982 and to 15.5 million in 1986. In 1987, only 7.3 million taxpayers reported deductible contributions. Since then, the number has continued to fall (see table 16–7).

TABLE 16–7.—USE OF DEDUCTIBLE IRAs FROM 1980 TO 1992

Year	Number of tax returns deducting IRA contributions (millions)	Total IRA deductions (billions)
1980	2.6	$3.4
1981	3.4	4.8
1982	12.0	28.3
1983	13.6	32.1
1984	15.2	35.4
1985	16.2	38.2
1986	15.5	37.8
1987	7.3	14.1
1988	6.4	11.9
1989	5.8	10.8
1990	5.2	9.9
1991	4.7	9.0
1992 *p*	4.3	8.2

p=Preliminary.

Source: Internal Revenue Service, Statistics of Income, 1981 to 1992.

Upper-income taxpayers facing higher marginal tax rates receive more benefit per dollar of IRA deduction than do lower-income taxpayers facing lower marginal tax rates. When IRAs were available to all workers the percentage of taxpayers contributing to an IRA was substantially higher among taxpayers with higher income. For example, in 1985, 13.6 percent of taxpayers with AGI between $10,000 and $30,000 contributed to an IRA compared with 74.1 percent of taxpayers with AGI between $75,000 and $100,000.

The decline in IRA use between 1985 and 1990 among those with AGI between $10,000 and $30,000 appears to be larger than the reduction required by the change in law, since the restrictions on deductible contributions apply only to a small fraction of taxpayers with AGI below $30,000.

Eligibility percentages and the real value of the IRA contribution limits decrease over time because present law does not index the contribution limits or the income eligibility limits for inflation. For example, the real value of a $2,000 contribution has declined more than 30 percent since 1986 because of inflation.

Congress established IRAs to allow workers not covered by employer pension plans to have tax-advantaged retirement saving. Nonetheless, since 1981 IRA participation rates have been higher among those covered by an employer-provided pension plan than those without one, and many of those who are not covered by a pension plan do not contribute to an IRA. For example, in 1987, 10 percent of full-time private-sector earners without pension coverage contributed to an IRA, while 15 percent of those with coverage contributed.[8]

EXCLUSION OF SOCIAL SECURITY AND RAILROAD RETIREMENT BENEFITS

Legislative history

Social Security benefits.—The exclusion from gross income for Social Security benefits was not initially established by statute. Prior to the Social Security Amendments of 1983, the exclusion was based on a series of administrative rulings issued by the Internal Revenue Service in 1938 and 1941.[9]

Under the Social Security Amendments of 1983, a portion of the Social Security benefits paid to higher income taxpayers is included in gross income. The Congress stated that Social Security benefits are in the nature of benefits received under other retirement systems, which are subject to taxation to the extent they exceed a worker's nondeductible contributions, and that taxing a portion of Social Security benefits improves tax equity by treating more equally all forms of retirement income and other income that is designed to replace wages. In 1993, the Omnibus Budget Reconciliation Act increased the amount of benefits subject to tax for some benefit recipients but did not increase the number of beneficiaries who pay tax on benefits.

Railroad retirement benefits.—The exclusion from gross income of benefits paid under the railroad retirement system was enacted in the Railroad Retirement Act of 1935. A portion of the benefits payable under the railroad retirement system (generally, tier 1 benefits) is equivalent to Social Security benefits. The tax treatment of tier 1 railroad retirement benefits was modified in the Social Security Amendments of 1983 to conform to the tax treatment of Social Security benefits. Other railroad retirement benefits are taxable in the same manner as employer-provided retirement benefits. The Consolidated Omnibus Budget Reconciliation Act of 1985 provided that tier 1 benefits are taxable in the same manner as Social Security benefits only to the extent that Social Security benefits otherwise would be payable. Other tier 1 benefits are taxable in the same manner as all other railroad retirement benefits.

---

[8] John R. Woods, "Pension Coverage Among Private Wage and Salary Workers: Preliminary Findings From the 1988 Survey of Employee Benefits," Social Security Bulletin, 52:10 (October 1989), p. 9.

[9] See I.T. 3194, 1938–1 C.B. 114, I.T. 3229, 1938–2 C.B. 136, and I.T. 3447, 1941–1 C.B. 191.

Explanation of provision

For taxpayers whose "modified adjusted gross income" exceeds certain limits, a portion of Social Security and tier 1 railroad retirement benefits is included in taxable income. "Modified adjusted gross income" is adjusted gross income plus interest on tax-exempt bonds plus 50 percent of Social Security and tier 1 railroad retirement benefits. A two-tier structure applies. The base tier is $25,000 for unmarried individuals and $32,000 for married couples filing joint returns, and zero for married persons filing separate returns who do not live apart at all times during the taxable year. The amount of benefits includible in income is the lesser of (1) 50 percent of the Social Security and tier 1 railroad retirement benefits, or (2) 50 percent of the excess of the taxpayer's combined income over the base amount.

The second tier applies to taxpayers with "modified adjusted gross income" of at least $34,000 (unmarried taxpayers) or $44,000 (married taxpayers filing joint returns). For these taxpayers, the amount of benefits includible in gross income is the lesser of (1) 85 percent of Social Security benefits, or (2) the sum of 85 percent of the amount by which modified adjusted gross income exceeds the second-tier thresholds, and the smaller of the amount included under prior law or $4,500 (unmarried taxpayers) or $6,000 (married taxpayers filing jointly). The portion of tier 1 railroad retirement benefits potentially includible in taxable income under the above formula is the amount of benefits the taxpayer would have received if covered under Social Security. Pursuant to section 72(r) of the Internal Revenue Code of 1986, all other benefits payable under the railroad retirement system are includible in income when received to the extent they exceed employee contributions.

Effect of provision

About 15 percent of all Social Security recipients pay taxes on their benefits. A large percentage of any current Social Security recipient's benefit does not constitute a return of the recipient's contributions (which were originally made with after-tax dollars).

The tax expenditure per tax return from the exclusion is generally greater for those with incomes above $40,000 than for those with incomes below $40,000. This is related to the likelihood that higher income retirees were generally higher income individuals during their working years who were more likely to be eligible for the maximum benefit. The tendency for the tax expenditure per return to rise with income would be greater in the absence of the partial taxation of Social Security benefits.

EXCLUSION OF EMPLOYER CONTRIBUTION FOR MEDICAL INSURANCE PREMIUMS AND MEDICAL CARE

Legislative history

In 1943, the Internal Revenue Service (IRS) ruled that employer contributions to group health insurance policies were not taxable to the employee. Employer contributions to individual health insurance policies, however, were declared to be taxable income in an IRS revenue ruling in 1953.

Section 106 of the Internal Revenue Code, enacted in 1954, reversed the 1953 IRS ruling. As a result, employer contributions to all accident or health plans generally are excluded from taxable income. Under section 105 of the Internal Revenue Code, benefits received under an employer's accident or health plan generally are not included in the employee's income.

In the Revenue Act of 1978, Congress added section 105(h) to tax the benefits payable to highly compensated employees under a self-insured medical reimbursement plan if the plan discriminated in favor of highly compensated employees.

Explanation of provision

Gross income of an employee generally excludes employer-provided coverage under an accident or health plan. The exclusion applies to coverage provided to former employees, their spouses, or dependents. Amounts excluded include those received by an employee for personal injuries or sickness if the amounts are paid directly or indirectly to reimburse the employee for expenses incurred for medical care. However, this exclusion does not apply in the case of amounts paid to a highly compensated individual under a self-insured medical reimbursement plan if the plan violates the non-discrimination rules of section 105(h).

Present law permits employers to prefund medical benefits for retirees. Postretirement medical benefits may be prefunded by the employer in two basic ways: (1) through a separate account in a tax-qualified pension plan (sec. 401(h)); or (2) through a welfare benefit fund (secs. 419 and 419A). Generally, the amounts contributed are excluded from the income of the plan or participants. Although amounts held in a section 401(h) account are accorded tax-favored treatment similar to assets held in a pension trust, the benefits provided under a section 401(h) account are required to be incidental to the retirement benefits provided by the plan. Amounts contributed to welfare benefit funds are subject to certain deduction limitations (secs. 419 and 419A). Additionally, the fund is subject to income tax relating to any set-aside to provide postretirement medical benefits.

Effect of provision

The exclusion for employer-provided health coverage provides an incentive for compensation to be furnished to the employee in the form of health coverage, rather than in cash subject to current taxation.

For example, an employer designing a compensation package for an employee would be indifferent between paying the employee one dollar in cash and purchasing one dollar's worth of health insurance for the employee.[10] Because the employee is likely to pay federal and state income taxes and payroll taxes on cash compensation and no tax on health insurance contributions made on his behalf, the employee would likely prefer that some compensation be in the form of health insurance. Employees subject to tax at the

---

[10] To the extent the employer bears a portion of the payroll tax, the employer may actually prefer to provide compensation through health insurance (which is not subject to payroll tax).

highest marginal tax rates have the greatest incentive to receive compensation in nontaxable forms.

The tax preference that the exclusion provides is substantial and has resulted in widespread access to health care. A majority of the population now receives health insurance as a consequence of their own employment or of a family member's employment. In 1993, for 59 percent of the population employment-based health insurance was the primary source of health coverage, while 6 percent purchased insurance privately, 13 percent received Medicare benefits, and 8 percent received Medicaid benefits. Fifteen percent of the population had no health insurance.[11]

Health coverage through employer-based plans tends to be more prevalent in the manufacturing sector of the economy, among medium and large firms, and for more highly paid workers, especially those over the age of 30. (See Table 16–8).

Despite the widespread use of employer-provided health plans, the problem of access has worsened over the last 1½ decades. In 1980, 11 percent of the population had no health insurance. This has risen steadily to the 15 percent of the population without insurance in 1993.

---

[11] The Congressional Budget Office. *The Tax Treatment of Employment-Based Health Insurance.* (Washington, D.C.) March 1994. p. 7.

TABLE 16–8.—PRIMARY SOURCE OF HEALTH INSURANCE FOR WORKERS UNDER AGE 65, BY DEMOGRAPHIC CATEGORY, 1992

Category	Number of workers (millions)	Percentage distribution by source of insurance				
		Own employer	Other employer	Individual policy	Public insurance [1]	No insurance
All workers	107.3	60.2	14.8	7.6	2.3	15.2
Industry:						
Agriculture	2.6	24.2	14.2	25.2	3.4	33.0
Construction	6.3	45.5	14.2	9.7	2.4	28.2
Finance	7.3	65.7	15.9	7.9	1.1	9.5
Government	5.3	83.8	8.3	1.9	1.5	4.5
Manufacturing	19.1	76.9	8.0	3.2	1.2	10.7
Mining	0.6	81.1	6.0	3.0	1.1	8.7
Retail trade	16.1	42.4	18.4	10.6	3.8	24.9
Services:						
Professional	26.2	62.1	19.6	7.0	2.3	8.9
Other	11.4	39.0	18.7	12.1	3.9	26.2
Transportation	7.9	77.1	7.5	4.7	1.0	9.6
Wholesale trade	4.5	67.2	13.4	6.3	1.5	11.6
Wage rate [2]:						
Below $5.00	9.0	21.6	18.3	12.0	9.9	38.2
$5.00 to $9.99	36.9	53.7	17.5	6.2	2.8	19.8
$10.00 to $14.99	24.2	76.0	11.5	3.9	0.8	7.7
$15.00 or more	23.7	84.9	8.2	2.9	0.3	3.7
Family income as percentage of poverty level:						
Under 100	6.5	16.4	2.8	12.8	15.7	52.3
100 to 199	15.4	43.4	9.3	9.2	4.9	33.2
200 to 299	19.7	58.2	14.9	7.9	1.5	17.5
300 and over	65.7	69.1	17.2	6.6	0.5	6.6
Firm size (number of employees):						
Fewer than 10	21.2	24.6	24.6	19.9	3.2	27.7
10 to 24	9.3	46.4	18.4	9.5	3.3	22.4
25 to 99	13.7	57.5	14.6	5.9	2.6	19.4
100 to 499	15.2	69.4	12.6	4.1	2.2	11.7
500 to 999	6.0	74.8	11.7	3.6	1.6	8.4
1,000 or more	41.7	76.9	10.2	3.3	1.6	8.0
Age (years):						
Under 30	26.7	51.9	11.4	8.6	3.4	24.6
30 to 39	33.5	61.4	15.9	5.9	2.3	14.5
40 to 49	26.8	64.1	17.2	6.8	1.5	10.3
50 to 64	20.2	64.2	14.1	10.0	1.5	10.2

[1] Public insurance includes Medicaid, Medicare, and coverage provided by the Department of Veterans Affairs.

[2] "Wage" is the hourly wage for hourly employees and earnings per week divided by hours worked for nonhourly employees. The figures exclude individuals for whom an hourly wage could not be determined.

Note. These estimates are CBO estimates based on the March 1992 Current Population Survey.

Source: The Congressional Budget Office. "The Tax Treatment of Employer-Based Health Insurance." (Washington, D.C.) March 1994. p. 9.

CAFETERIA PLANS

Legislative history

Under present law, compensation generally is includible in gross income when received. An exception applies if an employee may choose between cash and certain employer-provided nontaxable benefits under a cafeteria plan.

Prior to 1978 the Employee Retirement Income Security Act of 1974 provided that an employer contribution made before January 1, 1977, to a cafeteria plan in existence on June 27, 1974, was required to be included in an employee's gross income only to the extent that the employee actually elected taxable benefits. If a plan did not exist on June 27, 1974, the employer contribution was to be included in income to the extent the employee could have elected taxable benefits. The Revenue Act of 1978 set up permanent rules for plans that offer an election between taxable and nontaxable benefits.

The Deficit Reduction Act of 1984 (P.L. 98–369) clarified the types of employer-provided benefits that could be provided through a cafeteria plan, added a 25-percent concentration test, and required annual reporting to the IRS by employers.

The Tax Reform Act of 1986 also modified the rules relating to cafeteria plans in several respects.

Explanation of provision

A participant in a cafeteria plan (section 125) is not treated as having received taxable income solely because the participant had the opportunity to elect to receive cash or certain nontaxable benefits. In order to meet the requirements of section 125, the plan must be in writing, must include only employees (including former employees) as participants, and must satisfy certain nondiscrimination requirements.

In general, a nontaxable benefit may be provided through a cafeteria plan if the benefit is excludable from the participant's gross income by reason of a specific provision of the Code. These include employer-provided health coverage, group-term life insurance coverage, and benefits under dependent care assistance programs. A cafeteria plan may not provide qualified scholarships or tuition reduction, educational assistance, miscellaneous employer-provided fringe benefits, or deferred compensation except through a qualified cash or deferred arrangement.

If the plan discriminates in favor of highly compensated individuals regarding eligibility to participate, to make contributions or to receive benefits under the plan, then the exclusion does not apply. For purposes of these nondiscrimination requirements, a highly compensated individual is an officer, a shareholder owning more than 5 percent of the employing firm, a highly compensated individual determined under the facts and circumstances of the case, or a spouse or dependent of the above individuals.

Effects of provision

The optimal compensation of employees (in a tax planning sense) would require that employers and employees arrive at the compensation package that provides the largest after-tax benefit to the employee at minimum after-tax cost to the employer.[12] Both the potential taxation of compensation provided to employees and the deductibility of compensation provided by the employer would be considered. If only income taxes were considered, employers would be indifferent between the payment of $1 in salary or wages and the payment of $1 in fringe benefits to an employee, because both types of compensation are fully deductible. When the employer payments for FICA and FUTA taxes are considered, the employer might actually find it less costly to compensate an employee with a dollar's worth of fringe benefit not subject to FICA and FUTA taxes rather a dollar of wage or salary payments that have these taxes assessed on them.

The employee, however, would prefer to be compensated in the form that provides the highest after-tax value. An additional dollar of salary or wage paid to the employee will be subject to tax. If a fringe benefit is excludable from the employee's income, the employee pays no tax on receipt of the benefit. Consequently, the employee receives greater compensation via this fringe benefit. This differential treatment of salary or wage payments and excludable fringe benefits implies that compensation packages designed to minimize the joint tax liability of employers and employees could include substantial amounts of excludable fringe benefits.

Employees may have different preferences about the allocation of their compensation. For example, an employee with no dependents may place little value on employer-provided life insurance. Cafeteria plans permit employees some discretion as to the provided benefits, and will tend to be preferred to benefit plans where all employees of the firm receive the identical benefit package.

Cafeteria plans are a growing part of compensation plans, particularly for larger employers. The Bureau of Labor Statistics estimated that in 1991, 36 percent of employees at large and medium sized firms were eligible for flexible benefits and/or reimbursement accounts. This figure has grown from an estimated 5 percent in 1986.[13] Smaller firms generally do not offer cafeteria plans to their workers. For example, in 1992, only 14 percent of the workers in small, private establishments (non-farm establishments with fewer than 100 employees) were eligible to participate in a cafeteria plan. The lower figure for smaller firms reflects in part the less generous fringe benefit packages provided by smaller firms.

Like any income exclusion, the exclusion from gross income for cafeteria plan benefits can lead to inequities in the tax system. Employees with the same total compensation can have taxable incomes that are substantially different because of the form in which compensation is received. The exclusion for cafeteria plan benefits also may be used in some cases to avoid the 7.5 percent of AGI floor on deductible medical expenses. The use of cafeteria plans reduces the after-tax cost of health care to employees using these plans, which could cause these employees to purchase an unnecessarily large amount of health care services. Overutilization in-

[12] This analysis follows that contained in Myron Scholes and Mark Wolfson, "Taxes and Business Strategy: A Planning Approach," Prentice-Hall, 1992; see especially chapter 10.

[13] The source for these data is "Employee Benefits in Medium and Large Firms, 1991", Bureau of Labor Statistics, Department of Labor, (May, 1993) and "Employee Benefits in Small Private Establishments, 1992", Bureau of Labor Statistics, Department of Labor, (forthcoming).

creases health care costs.[14] On the other hand, cafeteria plans could encourage employers to increase the share of premiums, copayments, and deductibles paid by employees, resulting in increased employee awareness of the costs of their health plans. This incentive could result in reduced health care costs.

HEALTH CARE CONTINUATION RULES

Legislative history

The Consolidated Omnibus Budget Reconciliation Act of 1985 added sections 106(b), 162(i)(2), and 162(k) to the Internal Revenue Code under which certain group health plans are required to offer health coverage to certain employees and former employees, as well as to their spouses and dependents. Parallel requirements were added to title I of the Employee Retirement Income Security Act of 1974 and the Public Health Services Act. If an employer failed to satisfy the health care continuation rules, the employer was denied a deduction for contributions to its group health plans and highly compensated employees were required to include in taxable income the employer-provided value of the coverage received under such plans.

The Technical and Miscellaneous Revenue Act of 1988 made several changes to the health care continuation rules. Sections 106(b), 162(i)(2), and 162(k) were repealed and replaced by section 4980B. Section 4980B imposes an excise tax on the employer or other responsible party who fails to satisfy the rules instead of denying deductions and the exclusion.

Explanation of provision

The health care continuation rules in section 4980B require that an employer provide qualified beneficiaries with the opportunity to participate for a specified period in the employer's health plan after that participation otherwise would have terminated.

The qualifying events that may trigger rights to continuation coverage are: (1) the death of the employee, (2) the voluntary or involuntary termination of the employee's employment (other than by reason of gross misconduct), (3) a reduction of the employee's hours, (4) the divorce or legal separation of the employee, (5) the employee becoming entitled to benefits under Medicare, and (6) a dependent child of the employee ceasing to be a dependent under the employer's plan. The maximum period of continuation coverage is 36 months, except in the case of termination of employment or reduction of hours for which the maximum period is 18 months. The 18-month period is extended to 29 months in certain cases involving the disability of the qualified beneficiary. Certain events, such as the failure by the qualified beneficiary to pay the required premium, may trigger an earlier cessation of the continuation coverage.

A beneficiary has a prescribed period of time during which to elect continuation coverage after the employee receives notice from the plan administrator of the right to continuation coverage.

---

[14] See, for instance, "A Study of Cafeteria Plans and Flexible Spending Accounts," U.S. Department of Health and Human Services, July 1985.

EXCLUSION OF MEDICARE BENEFITS

Legislative history

The exclusion from income of Medicare benefits has never been expressly established by statute. A 1970 IRS ruling, Rev. Rul. 70–341, 1970–2 C.B. 31, provided that the benefits under Part A of Medicare are not includible in gross income because they are disbursements made to further the social welfare objectives of the Federal Government. The Internal Revenue Service relied on a similar ruling, Rev. Rul. 70–217, 1970–1 C.B. 13, with respect to the excludability of Social Security disability insurance benefits in reaching this conclusion. (For background on the exclusion of Social Security benefits, see above.) Rev. Rul. 70–341 also held that benefits under Part B of Medicare are excludable as amounts received through accident and health insurance (though the subsidized portion of Part B also may be excluded under the same theory applicable to the exclusion of Part A benefits).

Explanation of provision

Benefits under Part A and Part B of Medicare are excludable from the gross income of the recipient. In general, Part A pays for certain in-patient hospital care, skilled nursing facility care, home health care, and hospice care for eligible individuals (generally the elderly and the disabled). Part B covers certain services of a physician and other medical services for elderly or disabled individuals who elect to pay the required premium.

DEDUCTIBILITY OF MEDICAL EXPENSES

Legislative history

An itemized deduction for unreimbursed medical expenses above a specified floor has been allowed since 1942. From 1954 through 1982, the floor under the medical expense deduction was 3 percent of the taxpayer's adjusted gross income ("AGI"); a separate floor of 1 percent of AGI applied to expenditures for medicine and drugs.

In the Tax Equity and Fiscal Responsibility Act of 1982 (TEFRA), the floor was increased to 5 percent of AGI (effective for 1983 and thereafter) and was applied to the total of all eligible medical expenses, including prescription drugs and insulin. TEFRA made nonprescription drugs ineligible for the deduction and eliminated the separate floor for drug costs.

The Tax Reform Act of 1986 increased the floor under the medical expense deduction to 7.5 percent of AGI, beginning in 1987.

Explanation of provision

Individuals who itemize deductions may deduct amounts they pay during the taxable year, if not reimbursed by insurance or otherwise, for medical care of the taxpayer and of the taxpayer's spouse and dependents, to the extent that the total of such expenses exceeds 7.5 percent of AGI (sec. 213).

Medical care expenses eligible include (1) health insurance (including after-tax employee contributions to employer health plans); (2) diagnosis, treatment, or prevention of disease, or for the purpose of affecting any structure or function of the body; (3) transportation primarily for and essential to medical care; (4) lodging away from home primarily for and essential to medical care, up to $50 per night; and (5) prescription drugs and insulin.

Expenses paid for the general improvement of health, such as fees for exercise programs, are not eligible for the deduction unless prescribed by a physician to treat a specific illness. A deduction is not allowed for cosmetic surgery or similar procedures that do not meaningfully promote the proper function of the body or treat disease. However, such expenses are deductible if the cosmetic procedure is necessary to correct a deformity arising from a congenital abnormality, an injury resulting from an accident, or disfiguring disease.

Medical expenses are not subject to the general limitation on itemized deductions applicable to taxpayers with adjusted gross incomes above a certain limit ($111,800 for 1994 and adjusted annually for inflation).

Effect of provision

The Code allows taxpayers to claim an itemized deduction if unreimbursed medical expenses absorb a substantial portion of income and thus adversely affect the taxpayer's ability to pay taxes. In order to limit the deduction to extraordinary medical expenses, medical expenses are deductible only to the extent that they exceed 7.5 percent of the taxpayer's AGI.

Table 16–9 shows the effect on medical expense deductions of the increases in the floor on medical deductions. In the absence of those increases, one would have expected the number of taxpayers claiming the deduction and the average deduction claimed to have increased because of inflation of medical costs. However, increasing the floor should reduce the number of taxpayers claiming the deduction and should increase the average deduction claimed because many taxpayers with relatively modest expenses no longer qualify while taxpayers with large expenses continue to qualify. The average deduction claimed has increased substantially, from $769 in 1980 to $4,420 in 1992. Both increases in the floor (to 5 percent in 1983 and to 7.5 percent in 1987) substantially reduced the number of taxpayers claiming deductions.

TABLE 16–9.—TAX RETURNS CLAIMING DEDUCTIBLE MEDICAL AND DENTAL EXPENSES, 1980–92

Year	Total number of returns filed (in millions)	Returns claiming medical and dental expenses	
		Number of returns (in millions)	Deductible expenses (in billions)
1980	93.2	19.5	$15.0
1981	95.4	21.4	17.9
1982	95.3	22.0	21.7
1983	96.3	9.7	18.1
1984	99.4	10.7	21.5
1985	101.7	10.8	22.9
1986	103.0	10.5	25.1
1987	107.0	5.4	17.2

TABLE 16–9.—TAX RETURNS CLAIMING DEDUCTIBLE MEDICAL AND DENTAL EXPENSES, 1980–92—Continued

Year	Total number of returns filed (in millions)	Returns claiming medical and dental expenses	
		Number of returns (in millions)	Deductible expenses (in billions)
1988	109.7	4.8	18.0
1989	112.1	5.1	20.9
1990	113.7	5.1	21.5
1991	114.7	5.3	23.7
1992	p 106.3	p 5.0	p 22.1

p=Preliminary.

Source: Internal Revenue Service, "Statistics of Income," various years.

Taxpayers in higher tax-rate brackets receive more of a benefit from each dollar of deductible medical expense than do taxpayers in lower tax-rate brackets. However, because the floor automatically rises with a taxpayer's income, higher-income taxpayers are able to deduct a smaller amount (if any) of medical expenses above their floor than are lower-income taxpayers incurring the same aggregate amount of medical expenses.

In 1994, 4,877,000 taxpayers are expected to claim the itemized deduction for medical expenses. Of that number, 60 percent have incomes of $50,000 or less. (See Table 16–10.)

TABLE 16–10.—DISTRIBUTION OF ITEMIZED DEDUCTIONS FOR MEDICAL EXPENSES, 1994

Income class (thousands)	Returns (thousands)	Amount (millions)	Average
0 to $10	15	$3	$191
$10 to $20	247	82	333
$20 to $30	742	293	395
$30 to $40	1,021	470	460
$40 to $50	896	502	561
$50 to $75	1,312	1,038	791
$75 to $100	413	638	1,545
$100 to $200	206	502	2,444
$200 and over	26	265	10,173
Total	4,877	3,793	778

Source: Joint Committee on Taxation.

EARNED INCOME TAX CREDIT

Legislative history

The earned income tax credit (Code sec. 32) was enacted in 1975.

Generally, the credit equals a specified percentage of wages up to a maximum dollar amount. The maximum amount applies over a certain income range and then diminishes to zero over a specified phaseout range. The income ranges and percentages have been revised several times since original enactment, expanding the credit. (See Table 16–11.)

In 1987, the credit was indexed for inflation. In 1990 and 1993, the expansions of the credit were quite large. In 1990, auxiliary credits were added for very young children and for health insurance premiums paid on behalf of a qualifying child. These were repealed in 1993. Also in 1993, the group eligible for the credit was expanded to include childless workers.

TABLE 16–11.—EARNED INCOME TAX CREDIT PARAMETERS, 1975–96

Calendar year	Credit rate (per-cent) [2]	Minimum income for maximum credit	Maximum credit	Phaseout rate (per-cent)	Phaseout range	
					Beginning income	Ending income
1975–78	10	$4,000	$400	10.00	$4,000	$8,000
1979–80	10	5,000	500	12.50	6,000	10,000
1981–84	10	5,000	500	12.50	6,000	10,000
1985–86	11	5,000	550	12.22	6,500	11,000
1987	14	6,080	851	10.00	6,920	15,432
1988	14	6,240	874	10.00	9,840	18,576
1989	14	6,500	910	10.00	10,240	19,340
1990	14	6,810	953	10.00	10,730	20,264
1991:						
One child	16.7	7,140	1,192	11.93	11,250	21,250
Two children .	17.3	7,140	1,235	12.36	11,250	21,250
1992:						
One child	17.6	7,520	1,324	12.57	11,840	22,370
Two children .	18.4	7,520	1,384	13.14	11,840	22,370
1993:						
One child	18.5	7,750	1,434	13.21	12,200	23,050
Two children .	19.5	7,750	1,511	13.93	12,200	23,050
1994:						
One child	26.3	7,750	2,038	15.98	11,000	23,750
Two children .	30.0	8,425	2,528	17.86	11,000	25,300
1996: [1] [2]						
One child	34.0	6,160	2,094	15.98	11,290	24,395
Two children .	40.0	8,900	3,560	21.06	11,620	28,524

[1] Projection.
[2] Credit rates and phaseout rates remain the same for all years after 1996. Income amounts are indexed for inflation.

Source: Joint Committee on Taxation.

Explanation of provision

Eligibility.—The EITC is available to low-income working taxpayers. Three separate schedules apply.

Taxpayers with one qualifying child may claim a credit in 1994 of 26.3 percent of their earnings up to $7,750, resulting in a maximum credit of $2,038. The maximum credit is available for those with earnings between $7,750 and $11,000. At $11,000 of earnings the credit begins to phase down at a rate of 15.98 percent of the amount of earnings above that amount. The credit is phased down to $0 at $23,753 of earnings. In 1995, the credit rate for a one-child family is 34.0 percent; the maximum credit begins at $6,160 of earnings and applies up to $11,290; the phase down rate continues to be 15.98 percent, resulting in a $0 credit at $24,395.

Taxpayers with more than one qualifying child may claim a credit in 1994 of 30.0 percent of earnings up to $8,425, resulting in a maximum credit of $2,528. The maximum credit is available for those with earnings between $8,425 and $11,000. At $11,000 of earnings the credit begins to phase down at a rate of 17.68 percent of earnings above that amount. The credit is phased down to $0 at

$25,300 of earnings. In 1995, the credit rate for a family with more than one qualifying child is 36.0 percent; the maximum credit begins at $8,650; the phase-down rate is 20.22 percent of earnings above $11,290, resulting in a $0 credit at $26,690. In 1996, the credit rate is 40.0 percent; the maximum credit begins at $8,900 and applies up to $11,620; the phase-down rate is 21.06, resulting in a $0 credit at $28,525.

Taxpayers with no qualifying children may claim a credit if they are over age 25 and below age 65. The credit is 7.65 percent of earnings up to $4,000, resulting in a maximum credit of $306. The maximum is available for those with incomes between $4,000 and $5,000. At $5,000 of earnings, the credit begins to phase down at rate of 7.65 percent of earnings above that amount, resulting in a $0 credit at $9,000.

All income thresholds are indexed for inflation annually.

In order to be a qualifying child, an individual must satisfy a relationship test, a residency test, and an age test. The relationship test requires that the individual be a child, stepchild, a descendent of a child, or a foster or adopted child of the taxpayer. The residency test requires that the individual have the same place of abode as the taxpayer for more than half the taxable year. This household must be located in the United States. The age test requires that the individual be under 19 (24 for a full-time student) or be permanently and totally disabled.

Refundability and advance payment.—The EITC is the only refundable tax credit; i.e., if the amount of the credit exceeds the taxpayer's Federal income tax liability, the excess is payable to the taxpayer as a direct transfer payment.

Under an advance payment system (available since 1979), eligible taxpayers may elect to receive the benefit of the credit in their periodic paychecks, rather than waiting to claim a refund on their return filed by April 15 of the following year. In 1993, Congress required that the IRS begin to notify eligible taxpayers of the advance payment option. After two years, the Secretary of Treasury is required to report on the effect of notification on participation.

Interaction with means-tested programs.—The treatment of the EITC for purposes of AFDC and food stamp benefit computations has varied since inception of the credit. When enacted in 1975, the credit was not considered income in determining AFDC and food stamp benefits, and the credit could not be received on an advance basis. From January 1979 through September 1981, the credit was treated as earned income when actually received.

From October 1981 to September 1984, the amount of the credit was treated as earned income and was imputed to the family even though it may not have been received as an advance payment. Pursuant to the Deficit Reduction Act of 1984, the credit was treated as earned income only when received, either as an advance payment or as a refund after conclusion of the year.

Under the Family Support Act of 1988, States generally were required to disregard any advance payment or refund of the EITC when calculating AFDC eligibility or benefits. However, the credit was counted against the gross income eligibility standard (185 percent of the State need standard) for both applicants and recipients.

OBRA 1990 specified that, effective January 1, 1991, the EITC was not to be taken into account as income (for the month in which the payment is received or any following month) or as a resource (for the month in which the payment is received or the following month) for determining the eligibility or amount of benefit for AFDC, Medicaid, SSI, food stamps, or low-income housing programs.

Effect of provision

Eighteen million taxpayers are expected to take advantage of the EITC in 1994 (see Table 16–12). Their claims are expected to total $19.6 billion, 84 percent of which will be refunded as direct payments to these families. When the credit is fully phased in in 1996, 18.7 million families are expected to take advantage of the credit. Their claims are expected to total $25.1 billion. As table 16–12 also shows, two-thirds of the tax relief or direct spending from the EITC accrues to single parents who file as heads of households.

Table 16–13 shows the total amount of earned income credit received for each of the calendar years since the inception of the program, the number of recipient families, the amount of the credit received as refunded payments, and the average amount of credit received per family.

TABLE 16–12.—DISTRIBUTION OF TAX EXPENDITURES: EARNED INCOME TAX CREDIT

[Number in thousands; amount in millions]

Income class (thousands)	Joint returns		Head of household and single returns		All returns	
	Number	Amount	Number	Amount	Number	Amount
1994						
$0 to $10	1,044	1,029	5,040	4,124	6,084	5,153
$10 to $20	2,003	3,291	4,233	6,473	6,236	9,764
$20 to $30	2,330	2,002	2,620	2,193	4,950	4,194
$30 to $40	443	296	264	182	707	478
$40 to $50	53	32	6	6	59	39
$50 to $75	21	16	2	4	23	20
$75 to $100	(1)	(2)	(1)	(2)	(1)	(2)
$100 to $200	....	....	....	....	....	....
$200 and over	....	....	....	....	....	....
Total	5,893	6,665	12,166	12,982	18,059	19,647
Percent distribution by type of return	32.6	30.8	67.4	69.2	100.0	100.0
1996						
$0 to $10	970	1,164	4,480	4,259	5,450	5,423
$10 to $20	1,780	3,796	4,237	7,824	6,017	11,620
$20 to $30	2,438	3,162	2,950	3,398	5,388	6,560
$30 to $40	970	727	700	584	1,670	1,312
$40 to $50	114	92	16	13	129	105
$50 to $75	33	31	3	6	36	37
$75 to $100	3	2	(1)	(2)	3	2
$100 to $200	(1)	(2)	....	....	(1)	(2)
$200 and over	....	....	....	....	....	....
Total	6,305	8,974	12,387	16,084	18,692	25,058
Percent distribution by type of return	33.7	35.8	66.3	64.2	100	100

[1] Less than 500 returns.
[2] Less than $500,000.

Source: Joint Committee on Taxation.

TABLE 16–13.—EARNED INCOME TAX CREDIT 1975–96

Calendar year to which credit applies	Number of families who received credit (thousands)	Total amount of credit (millions)	"Refunded" portion of credit [1] (millions)	Average credit per family
1975	6,215	$1,250	$900	$201
1976	6,473	1,295	890	200
1977	5,627	1,127	880	200
1978	5,192	1,048	801	202
1979	7,135	2,052	1,395	288
1980	6,954	1,986	1,370	286
1981	6,717	1,912	1,278	285
1982	6,395	1,775	1,222	278
1983	7,368	1,795	1,289	224
1984	6,376	1,638	1,162	257
1985	7,432	2,088	1,499	281
1986	7,156	2,009	1,479	281
1987	8,738	3,931	2,930	450
1988	11,148	5,896	4,257	529
1989	11,696	6,595	4,636	564
1990	12,612	6,928	5,303	549
1991 [2]	13,105	10,589	7,849	808
1992 [3]	13,433	12,434	9,625	926
1993 [3]	14,004	13,239	10,883	945
1994 [3]	18,059	19,647	16,549	1,088
1995 [3]	18,411	22,806	19,220	1,239
1996 [3]	18,692	25,058	21,026	1,341

[1] This is the portion of the credit that exceeds tax liability. It is treated as a budget outlay because it is a direct payment to the beneficiary.
[2] Preliminary.
[3] Projection.

Source: Joint Committee on Taxation.

EXCLUSION OF PUBLIC ASSISTANCE AND SSI BENEFITS

Legislative history

While there is no specific statutory authorization, a number of revenue rulings under Code section 61 have held specific types of public assistance payments are excludable from gross income. Revenue rulings generally exclude Government transfer payments from income because they are considered to be general welfare payments. Taxing benefits provided in kind, rather than in cash, would require valuation of these benefits, which could create administrative difficulties.

Explanation of provision

The Federal Government provides tax-free public assistance benefits to individuals either by cash payments or by provision of certain goods and services at reduced cost or free of charge. Cash payments come mainly from the Aid to Families with Dependent Children (AFDC) and Supplemental Security Income (SSI) programs. In-kind payments include food stamps, Medicaid, and housing assistance. None of these payments are subject to income tax.

DEPENDENT CARE TAX CREDIT

Legislative history

Under section 21 of the Internal Revenue Code, taxpayers are allowed an income tax credit for certain employment-related expenses for dependent care. The Internal Revenue Code of 1954 provided a deduction to gainfully employed women, widowers, and legally separated or divorced men for certain employment-related dependent care expenses. The deduction was limited to $600 per year and phased out for families with incomes between $4,500 and $5,100.

The Revenue Act of 1964 made husbands with incapacitated wives eligible for the dependent care deduction and raised the threshold for the income phaseout from $4,500 to $6,000.

The Revenue Act of 1971 (1) made any individual who maintained a household and was gainfully employed eligible for the deduction, (2) modified the definition of a dependent, (3) raised the deduction limit to $4,800 per year, (4) increased from $6,000 to $18,000 the income level at which the deduction began to phase out, (5) allowed the deduction for household services in addition to direct dependent care, and (6) limited the deduction with respect to services outside the taxpayer's household.

The Tax Reduction Act of 1975 increased from $18,000 to $35,000 the income level at which the deduction began to be phased out.

The Tax Reform Act of 1976 replaced the deduction with a non-refundable credit. This change broadened eligibility to those who do not itemize deductions and provided relatively greater benefit to lower-income taxpayers. In addition, the Act eased the rules related to family status and simplified the computation.

In the Economic Recovery Tax Act of 1981, Congress provided a higher ceiling on creditable expenses, a larger credit for lower-income individuals, and modified rules relating to care provided outside the home.

The Family Support Act of 1988 reduced to 13 the age of a child for whom the dependent care credit may be claimed, reduced the amount of eligible expenses by the amount of expenses excludible from that taxpayer's income under the dependent care exclusion, and disallowed the credit unless the taxpayer reports on his or her tax return the correct name, address, and taxpayer identification number (generally, an employer identification number or a Social Security number) of the dependent care provider.

Explanation of provision

A taxpayer may claim a nonrefundable credit against income tax liability for up to 30 percent of a limited amount of employment-related dependent care expenses. Eligible employment-related expenses are limited to $2,400 if there is one qualifying dependent or $4,800 if there are two or more qualifying dependents. Generally, a qualifying individual is a dependent under the age of 13 or a physically or mentally incapacitated dependent or spouse.

Employment-related dependent care expenses are expenses for the care of a qualifying individual incurred to enable the taxpayer to be gainfully employed, other than expenses incurred for an overnight camp. For example, amounts paid for the services of a housekeeper generally qualify if such services are performed at least partly for the benefit of a qualifying individual; amounts paid for a chauffeur or gardener do not qualify.

Expenses that may be taken into account in computing the credit generally may not exceed an individual's earned income or, in the case of married taxpayers, the earned income of the spouse with the lesser earnings. Thus, if one spouse is not working, no credit generally is allowed. Also, the amount of expenses eligible for the dependent care credit is reduced, dollar for dollar, by the amount of expenses excludible from that taxpayer's income under the dependent care exclusion (discussed below).

The 30-percent credit rate is reduced, but not below 20 percent, by 1 percentage point for each $2,000 (or fraction thereof) of adjusted gross income (AGI) above $10,000. Because married couples are required to file a joint return to claim the credit, a married couple's combined AGI is used for purposes of this computation.

Effect of provision

From 1976 to 1992, the number of families who claimed the dependent care credit increased from 2.7 to 5.5 million, the aggregate amount of credits claimed increased from $0.5 billion to $2.3 billion, and the average amount of credit claimed per family increased from $206 to $423 (see table 16–14). In 1994, 6.1 million families are expected to claim an average credit of $435, for a total of $2.7 billion.

Changes made in the Family Support Act of 1988 generally reduced the attractiveness of the dependent care credit, resulting in the dramatic drop in utilization of the credit that occurred in 1989. The number of families who claimed the credit dropped by about one-third and the amount of credit claimed declined by over $1.373

billion. The average credit claimed, though, remained relatively constant.

Most of the dependent care credit is claimed by families filing joint returns.

Preliminary data for 1992 from the Internal Revenue Service show that about 15 percent of the benefit from the credit accrues to families with AGI of less than $20,000; about 48 percent to families with AGI between $20,000 and $50,000; and about 36 percent to families with AGI above $50,000.[15]

TABLE 16–14.—DEPENDENT CARE TAX CREDIT, 1976–94

Calendar year	Number of returns claiming dependent credit (thousands)	Aggregate amount of credit claimed (millions)	Average credit claimed per return
1976	2,660	$548	206
1977	2,910	521	179
1978	3,431	654	191
1979	3,833	793	207
1980	4,231	956	226
1981	4,578	1,148	251
1982	5,004	1,501	300
1983	6,367	2,051	322
1984	7,456	2,649	351
1985	8,417	3,127	372
1986	8,950	3,398	380
1987	8,520	3,438	404
1988	9,023	3,813	423
1989	6,028	2,440	405
1990	6,144	2,549	415
1991 [1]	5,380	2,285	425
1992 [1]	5,498	2,324	423
1993 [2]	5,717	2,450	428
1994 [2]	6,121	2,662	435

[1] Preliminary.
[2] Projection.

Source: Joint Committee on Taxation.

EXCLUSION FOR EMPLOYER-PROVIDED DEPENDENT CARE

Legislative history

The value of certain employer-provided dependent care is excluded from the employee's gross income. The Economic Recovery Tax Act of 1981 added this exclusion (section 129) and amended Code sections 3121(a)(18) and 3306(b)(13) to exclude such employer-provided dependent care from wages for purposes of the Federal Insurance Contributions Act (FICA) and the Federal Unemployment Tax Act (FUTA). The Tax Reform Act of 1986 modified the nondiscrimination rules and limited the exclusion to $5,000 a

[15] The Internal Revenue Service. *SOI Bulletin*. Volume 13, number 2. Fall 1993. p. 30.

year ($2,500 in the case of a separate return by a married individual). The Family Support Act of 1988 required the amount of employer-provided dependent care excluded from the taxpayer's income to reduce, dollar for dollar, the amount of expenses eligible for the dependent care credit.

Explanation of provision

Amounts paid or incurred by an employer for dependent care assistance provided to an employee generally are excluded from the employee's gross income if the assistance is furnished under a program meeting certain requirements. These requirements include that the program be described in writing, satisfy certain nondiscrimination rules, and, provide for notification to all eligible employees. The type of dependent care eligible for the exclusion is the same as the type of expenses eligible for the dependent care credit.

The dependent care exclusion is limited to $5,000 per year except that a married taxpayer filing a separate return may exclude only $2,500. Amounts excluded from gross income generally are excludible from wages for employment tax purposes.

Effect of provision

The exclusion provides an incentive to taxpayers with expenses for dependent care to seek compensation in the form of dependent care assistance rather than in cash subject to taxation. This incentive is of greater value to employees in higher tax brackets.

Many employees covered by the exclusion for employer-provided dependent care also are eligible to use the dependent care tax credit. While the limitations on the exclusion and the credit differ, the credit generally is less valuable than the exclusion for taxpayers who are above the 15-percent tax bracket.

According to a survey of private firms with 100 or more workers conducted by the Department of Labor, nearly one-tenth of full-time workers at these firms were eligible for child care benefits provided by the employer in the form of on-site or near-site child care facilities or through direct reimbursement of employee expenses.[16] A more prevalent form of providing dependent care benefits is through reimbursement accounts, which may cover other nontaxable fringe benefits, such as out-of-pocket health care expenses, in addition to dependent care. Slightly over one-third of full-time employees at large and medium sized firms were eligible for such accounts in 1991.

TARGETED JOBS TAX CREDIT

Legislative history

Congress enacted the targeted jobs tax credit (Code sec. 51) in the Revenue Act of 1978. A taxpayer is eligible to claim the credit if the taxpayer employs individuals who receive payments under means-tested transfer programs, economically disadvantaged (as measured by family income), or are disabled.

---

[16] The source of these data is "Employee Benefits in Medium and Large Firms, 1991," Bureau of Labor Statistics, Department of Labor, May 1993.

The targeted jobs credit was subsequently extended with certain modifications several times. The credit is scheduled to expire for individuals hired after December 31, 1994.

Explanation of provision

The targeted jobs tax credit is available to employers on an elective basis for hiring individuals from nine targeted groups. The targeted groups are: (1) vocational rehabilitation referrals, (2) economically disadvantaged youths aged 18 through 22, (3) economically disadvantaged Vietnam-era veterans, (4) Supplemental Security Income (SSI) recipients, (5) general assistance recipients, (6) economically disadvantaged cooperative education students aged 16 through 19, (7) economically disadvantaged former convicts, (8) Aid to Families with Dependent Children (AFDC) recipients and Work Incentive (WIN) registrants, and (9) economically disadvantaged summer youth employees aged 16 or 17. Targeted group membership must be certified.

An individual is a member of an economically disadvantaged family if the designated local agency determines that the family had an income during the previous 6-month period that, when annualized, would be 70 percent or less of the Bureau of Labor Statistics lower living standard income level. These income levels vary by geographic region, with the highest levels generally applying to metropolitan areas in the Northeast and the lowest levels generally applying to nonmetropolitan areas in the Southeast.

The credit generally is equal to 40 percent of the first $6,000 of qualified first-year wages paid to a member of a targeted group. Thus, the maximum credit generally is $2,400 per individual. With respect to economically disadvantaged summer youth employees, however, the credit is equal to 40 percent of up to $3,000 of wages, for a maximum credit of $1,200.

The credit is not available for wages paid to a targeted group member unless the individual either (1) is employed by the employer for at least 90 days (14 days in the case of economically disadvantaged summer youth employees) or (2) has completed at least 120 hours of work performed for the employer (20 hours in the case of economically disadvantaged summer youth employees). Also, the employer's deduction for wages must be reduced by the amount of the credit. A taxpayer may not claim the credit for wages paid to a targeted-group individual who performs the same or substantially similar services as an employee participating in or affected by a strike or lockout.

Effect of provision

The targeted jobs tax credit serves as a subsidy to the employer for hiring targeted group members. For example, the targeted jobs credit would provide an effective subsidy of about 18 percent of the first-year wages of a full-time employee hired at the minimum wage ($4.25 per hour) by a corporate employer.[17] In 1991, almost

---

[17] Assume a corporation hired a member of a targeted group full-time at the minimum wage of $4.25 an hour. Wage payments to the employee would be $8,500 and the credit to the employer would be $2,400. The employer's actual subsidy is smaller however, because he must reduce his deduction for wages paid by the amount of the credit. At a 35 percent tax rate, this

Continued

three-quarters of all certifications were for economically disadvantaged youths age 18 to 22 (52.4 percent) or AFDC recipients and WIN registrants (21.0 percent).

EXCLUSION OF WORKERS' COMPENSATION AND SPECIAL BENEFITS FOR DISABLED COAL MINERS

Legislative history

Workers' compensation.—Workers' compensation benefits generally are not taxable under section 104(a)(1) of the Internal Revenue Code of 1986. Workers' compensation benefits are treated as Social Security benefits to the extent that they reduce Social Security benefits received (see above). This exclusion from gross income was first codified in the Revenue Act of 1918. The Ways and Means Committee report for that Act suggests that such payments were not subject to tax even prior to the 1918 Act.

Benefits for disabled coal miners.—Payments made to coal miners or their survivors for death or disability resulting from pneumoconiosis (black lung disease) under the Federal Coal Mine Health and Safety Act of 1969 (as amended) are excluded from gross income. Payments made as a result of claims filed before December 31, 1972, originally were excluded from Federal income tax by the Federal Coal Mine Health and Safety Act of 1969. Later payments are excluded from gross income because they are considered to be in the nature of workers' compensation (Rev. Rul. 72–400, 1972–2 C.B. 75).

Explanation of provision

Workers' compensation.—Gross income does not include amounts received as workers' compensation for personal injuries or sickness. This exclusion also applies to benefits paid under a workers' compensation act to a survivor of a deceased employee.

Benefits for disabled coal miners.—Benefits for disabled coal miners (black lung benefits) are not includible in gross income.

There are two types of black lung programs. The first involves Federal payments to coal miners and their survivors due to death or disability, payable for claims filed before July 1, 1973 (December 31, 1973, in the case of survivors). This program provided total annual payments of around $850 million to approximately 200,000 beneficiaries in 1991.[18]

The second program requires coal mine operators to insure payment of black lung benefits for claims filed on or after July 1, 1973 (December 31, 1973, in the case of survivors) in a federally mandated workers' compensation program. Benefits include medical treatment as well as cash payments. These benefits are paid from a trust fund financed by an excise tax on coal production if there is no responsible operator (an operator for whom the miner worked for at least one year) or if the responsible operator is in default.

---

results in $840 of additional tax. Thus, the net subsidy would be $1,560. This is 18 percent of the $8,500 wage cost.

[18] Social Security Bulletin, various issues.

This program provided total annual payments of around $610 million to approximately 156,550 claimants in 1986.[19]

ADDITIONAL STANDARD DEDUCTION FOR THE ELDERLY AND BLIND

Legislative history

From 1954 through 1986, an additional personal exemption was allowed for a taxpayer or a spouse who was 65 years or older at the close of the year. An additional personal exemption also was allowed for a taxpayer or a spouse who was blind.

The Tax Reform Act of 1986 repealed the additional personal exemption for the elderly and blind and replaced it with an additional standard deduction amount. These additional standard deduction amounts are adjusted for inflation.

Explanation of provision

The additional standard deduction amount for the elderly or the blind is $750 in 1994 for an elderly or a blind individual who is married (whether filing jointly or separately) or is a surviving spouse, and $1,500 for such an individual who is both elderly and blind. The additional amount is $950 for a head of household who is elderly or blind ($1,900, if both), and for a single individual (i.e., an unmarried individual other than a surviving spouse or head of household) who is elderly or blind.

The definitions of elderly and blind status have not been changed since 1954. An elderly person is an individual who is at least 65 years of age. Blindness is defined in terms of the ability to correct a deficiency in distance vision or the breadth of the area of vision. An individual is blind only if central vision acuity is not better than 20/200 in the better eye with correcting lenses, or if visual acuity is better than 20/200 but is accompanied by a limitation in the fields of vision such that the widest diameter of the visual field subtends an angle no greater than 20 degrees.

Effect of provision

The additional standard deduction increases the tax threshold for elderly and blind taxpayers. For example, the additional amount is $1,500 for two elderly individuals filing a joint return, raising the tax threshold in 1994 from $11,250 to $12,750.

In 1994, about 11.9 million taxpayers are expected to claim the extra standard deduction. Of those, 9.4 million are expected to benefit from the additional deductions. (The others are expected to itemize their deductions.) About 70 percent of the 9.4 million beneficiaries have incomes of less than $40,000.

TAX CREDIT FOR THE ELDERLY AND CERTAIN DISABLED INDIVIDUALS

Legislative history

The present tax credit for individuals who are age 65 or over, or who have retired on permanent and total disability, was enacted in the Social Security Amendments of 1983 (Code sec. 22). This credit

---

[19] Department of Labor, Employment Standards Administration, "Annual Report on Administration of Black Lung Benefits Act During Calendar Year 1986," January 1989, tables 3 and 6.

replaced the previous credit for the elderly, which had been enacted in the Tax Reform Act of 1976. Prior to that provision, the tax law provided a retirement income credit, which initially was enacted in the Internal Revenue Code of 1954.

Explanation of provision

Individuals who are age 65 or older may claim a nonrefundable income tax credit equal to 15 percent of a base amount. The credit also is available to an individual, regardless of age, who is retired on disability and who was permanently and totally disabled at retirement. For this purpose, an individual is considered permanently and totally disabled if he or she is unable to engage in any substantial gainful activity by reason of any medically determinable physical or mental impairment that can be expected to result in death, or that has lasted or can be expected to last for a continuous period of not less than 12 months. The individual must furnish proof of disability to the IRS.

The maximum base amount is $5,000 for unmarried elderly or disabled individuals and for married couples filing a joint return if only one spouse is eligible; $7,500 for married couples filing a joint return with both spouses eligible; or $3,750 for married couples filing separate returns. For a nonelderly, disabled individual the initial base amount is the lesser of the applicable specified amount or the individual's disability income for the year. Consequently, the maximum credit available is $750 (15 percent of $5,000), $1,125 (15 percent of $7,500), or $562.50 (15 percent of $3,750).

The maximum base amount is reduced by the amount of certain nontaxable income of the taxpayer, such as nontaxable pension and annuity income or nontaxable Social Security, railroad retirement, or veterans' nonservice-related disability benefits. In addition, the base amount is reduced by one-half of the taxpayer's AGI in excess of certain limits: $7,500 for a single individual, $10,000 for married taxpayers filing a joint return, or $5,000 for married taxpayers filing separate returns. These computational rules reflect that the credit is designed to provide tax benefits to individuals who receive only taxable retirement or disability income, or who receive a combination of taxable retirement or disability income plus Social Security benefits that generally are comparable to the tax benefits provided to individuals who receive only Social Security benefits (including Social Security disability benefits).

Effect of provision

In 1991, $57 million in elderly and disabled credit was claimed. The utilization rate and average credit granted has been relatively stable since the credit was modified by the Social Security Amendments of 1983, as shown in table 16–15.

TABLE 16–15.—CREDIT FOR THE ELDERLY AND DISABLED, 1976–94 [1]

	Number of families who received credit (thousands)	Total amount of credit (millions)	Average credit per return
Calendar year:			
1976	1,011	$206	$204
1977	569	93	163
1978	689	145	210
1979	607	132	217
1980	562	135	240
1981	474	124	262
1982	483	131	271
1983	423	116	275
1984	475	107	225
1985	460	106	230
1986	430	86	200
1987	354	67	189
1988	357	69	193
1989	320	65	202
1990	342	63	183
1991 [1]	280	54	193
1992 [1]	281	67	238
1993 [2]	208	[2] 62	298
1994 [2]	158	[2] 32	203

[1] Preliminary.
[2] Projection.

Source: Joint Committee on Taxation.

TAX EXPENDITURES RELATED TO HOUSING

OWNER-OCCUPIED HOUSING

Legislative history

Deductibility of mortgage interest.—Prior to the Tax Reform Act of 1986, all interest payments on indebtedness incurred for personal use (e.g., to purchase consumption goods) were deductible in computing taxable income. The 1986 Act amended section 163(h) of the Internal Revenue Code to disallow deductions for all personal interest except for interest on indebtedness secured by a first or second home.

In the Omnibus Budget Reconciliation Act of 1987, Congress further restricted the deductibility of mortgage interest. Only two classes of interest were distinguished as deductible: interest on acquisition indebtedness and interest on home equity indebtedness. Acquisition indebtedness, defined as indebtedness secured by a residence and used to acquire or improve the residence by which it is secured, was limited to $1,000,000 ($500,000 in the case of a married individual filing a separate return). Home equity indebtedness, defined as any nonacquisition indebtedness secured by a residence (for example, a home equity loan), was limited to the lesser of (1) $100,000 ($50,000 for married taxpayers filing separately) or (2) the excess of the fair market value of the residence over the acquisition indebtedness.

Deferral of capital gains from sale of principal residence.—Prior to 1951, capital gains on housing were taxed when realized. This treatment was consistent with the tax treatment of other capital assets. In 1951, Congress added section 112(n) to the Internal Revenue Code of 1939, permitting capital gains from the sale of a principal residence to be deferred (rolled over) as long as a new principal residence was purchased within the 24-month period beginning 12 months before the date of sale of the old residence and ending 12 months after the sale of the old residence. When capital gains are rolled over, the basis of the newly purchased house must be reduced by the amount of deferred gains. This rollover period had been extended twice and now is 24 months before and 24 months after the sale of the old residence.

Exclusion of capital gains for certain taxpayers.—In the Revenue Act of 1964, Congress introduced section 121 of the Internal Revenue Code of 1954, which permitted a one-time exclusion of all or part of the gain on the sale of a principal residence by older individuals. This exclusion was limited to homeowners who had lived in the property as a principal residence for 5 out of the last 8 years before the property's sale or exchange. Furthermore, full exclusion was permitted only for houses that sold for $20,000 or less.

The parameters of this exclusion have been modified and expanded a number of times. Currently, the one-time exclusion is allowed to taxpayers 55 or older for capital gain up to $125,000 if they have lived in the property as a principal residence for 3 of the past 5 years.

Explanation of provisions

Homeowners may deduct a number of expenses related to housing as itemized deductions in computing taxable income. These include payments of interest on qualified residence debt, certain interest on home equity loans, certain payments of points (i.e., upfront interest payments) on the purchase of a house, and payments of real property taxes. Interest on acquisition debt of $1,000,000 or less is fully deductible, as is any interest on debt secured by a residence that was incurred on or before October 13, 1987. Interest on home equity indebtedness of $100,000 is fully deductible for regular tax purposes, as long as the total amount of debt (acquisition plus home equity indebtedness) does not exceed the fair market value of the house. Interest on home equity indebtedness exceeding $100,000 (and incurred after October 13, 1987) or exceeding the difference between the fair market value of the home and the acquisition indebtedness is not deductible. Interest paid on home equity loans is generally not deductible in computing the alternative minimum tax.

Capital gains from the sale of residences generally are subject to tax when realized, unless one of two conditions is met. First, capital gains are not taxed if a new residence of equal or greater value is purchased or constructed within a period 24 months before to 24 months after the first residence is sold. If the price of the new residence is less than the selling price of the old residence (less any selling expenses) then the difference between the two prices must be recognized as a gain. The basis of the new residence must be reduced by the amount of the excluded gain.

Second, taxpayers age 55 or older may exclude once in their lifetime up to $125,000 ($62,500 for married taxpayers filing separately) of capital gain on the sale of a principal residence.

Effects of provision

The Tax Code has provided favorable treatment for housing consumption in a number of ways. Two of the largest subsidies are that the imputed rental value of owner-occupied housing is not taxed and that capital gains generated by investment in housing are given favorable tax treatment. The annual economic net return to an investment in owner-occupied housing consists of the rental value of the home plus any capital gains (or losses) on the house (whether realized or not), less the interest paid on mortgage debt outstanding and costs of repairs and maintenance. Because the tax system does not include the imputed value of homeowners' rent in gross income, this part of the return is untaxed.

However, because the rental value of homes is difficult to measure, the tax expenditures estimated are only for deductibility of mortgage interest and property taxes, the deferral of capital gains, and the exclusion of capital gains for taxpayers older than 55.

In the President's budget submission for fiscal year 1995, the Administration estimates forgone revenue from tax expenditures.[20] The fiscal year 1995 revenue loss from the deductibility of mortgage interest on owner-occupied housing is projected to be $54.8 billion; from the deferral of capital gains on homes sales, $14.6 billion; and the one-time exclusion of capital gains on home sales for people age 55 and older, $5.0 billion. Preliminary tax return information for 1992 indicates that 27 million taxpayers claimed the deduction for mortgage interest. Data are not yet available on how many claimed the one-time exclusion. (It is not possible to identify how many taxpayers deferred tax on home sales because homeowners do not have to report gain to the IRS until it is realized.)

This favorable treatment of owner-occupied housing may affect both the home ownership rate and the share of total investment in housing in the United States.

Homeownership.—The traditional view has been that the tax system encourages homeownership. Consider an investor who buys a house for $100,000 that could be rented for $10,000 per year. Excluding tax considerations, that investor would be equally well off purchasing a $100,000 bond that paid $10,000 per year in interest, and renting a similar house for $10,000. However, the investor who purchases the house pays no tax on the return to the investment (the $10,000 per year in imputed rent), whereas the investor who rents and purchases a bond pays tax on the $10,000 of interest.

Such preferential treatment may benefit neighborhoods because it encourages homeownership and home improvement. The United States has maintained a high rate of homeownership—64 percent of all American households own the homes they live in. Some feel that the tax preferences may be larger than necessary to maintain high rates of home ownership.

---

[20] *Analytical Perspectives, Budget of the United States Government, Fiscal Year 1995.* p. 77.

Investment in housing.—The tax advantages for owner-occupied housing encourage people to invest in homes instead of taxable business investments. This shift may lead to a relatively low rate of investment in business assets in the United States. One study suggested that housing capital is 25 percent higher and other capital is 12 percent lower than it would be if tax policy provided equal treatment for all forms of capital.[21] Currently, about one-third of net private investment goes into owner-occupied housing, so even a modest shift of investment to other assets could have sizable effects.

LOW-INCOME HOUSING CREDIT

Legislative history

The low-income rental housing tax credit was first enacted in the Tax Reform Act of 1986. The Omnibus Budget Reconciliation Act of 1989 substantially modified the credit. The Omnibus Budget Reconciliation Act of 1993 modified the credit and made it permanent.

Explanation of provision

A tax credit may be claimed by owners of residential rental property used for low-income rental housing. The credit is claimed annually, generally for a period of 10 years. New construction and rehabilitation expenditures for low-income housing projects are eligible for a maximum 70 percent present value credit, claimed annually for 10 years. The acquisition cost of existing projects that meet the substantial rehabilitation requirements and the cost of newly constructed projects receiving other Federal subsidies are eligible for a maximum 30 percent present value credit, also claimed annually for 10 years. These credit percentages are adjusted monthly based on an Applicable Federal Rate.

The credit amount is based on the qualified basis of the housing units serving the low-income tenants. A residential rental project will qualify for the credit only if (1) 20 percent or more of the aggregate residential rental units in the project are occupied by individuals with 50 percent or less of area median income, or (2) 40 percent or more of the aggregate residential rental units in the project are occupied by individuals with 60 percent or less of area median income. These income figures are adjusted for family size. Maximum rents that may be charged families in units on which a credit is claimed depend on the number of bedrooms in the unit. The rent limitation is 30 percent of the qualifying income of a family deemed to have a size of 1.5 persons per bedroom (e.g., a two-bedroom unit has a rent limitation based on the qualifying income for a family of three).

Credit eligibility also depends on the existence of a 30-year extended low-income use agreement for the property. If property on which a low-income housing credit is claimed ceases to qualify as low-income rental housing or is disposed of before the end of a 15-year credit compliance period, a portion of the credit may be recaptured. The 30-year extended use agreement creates a State law

---

[21] See Edwin S. Mills, "Dividing up the Investment Pie: Have We Overinvested in Housing?", Philadelphia Business Review, March-April 1987, 13–23.

right to enforce low-income use for an additional 15 years after the initial 15-year recapture period.

In order for a building to be a qualified low-income building, the building owner generally must receive a credit allocation from the appropriate credit authority. An exception is provided for property that is substantially financed with the proceeds of tax-exempt bonds subject to the State's private-activity bond volume limitation. The low-income housing credit is allocated by State or local government authorities subject to an annual limitation for each State based on State population. The annual credit allocation per State is $1.25 per resident.

Effect of provision

Comprehensive data from tax returns concerning the low income housing tax credit currently are unavailable. However, table 16–16 presents data from a survey of State credit allocating agencies. These data indicate that allocation of the available credit rose from approximately 20 percent in 1987, the initial year of credit availability, to nearly complete allocation in 1989, but allocation subsequently fell to 65 percent in 1990. There are several reasons why the 1990 experience may not be indicative of the long-term use of the credit. First, 1990 was the first year following substantial modification to the credit, including the requirement of an additional low-income commitment beyond the credit compliance period. The substantial modification may be expected to delay some use of the credit. Moreover, the initial allocative authority for 1990 was limited to $0.9375 per capita per State rather than the $1.25 per capita per State for 1987–89. While the Omnibus Budget Reconciliation Act of 1990 restored 1990 credit authority to $1.25 per capita per State, the restoration occurred late in the calendar year and the reaction of allocation agencies and investors may have been delayed. In addition, 1990 was marked by a general economic slowdown in the real estate industry. On the other hand, the 1991 and 1992 data on credit authority reflect credits unallocated or returned from prior years carried over to 1991 and 1992.

TABLE 16–16.—ALLOCATION OF THE LOW INCOME HOUSING CREDIT, 1987–92

Years	Authority (millions)	Allocated (millions)	Percentage allocated (percent)
1987	$313.1	$62.9	20.1
1988	311.5	209.8	67.4
1989	314.2	307.2	97.8
1990	317.7	213.1	67.0
1991 [1]	497.3	400.6	80.6
1992 [1]	476.8	332.7	70.0

[1] Increased authority includes credits unallocated from prior years carried over to the current year.

Source: Survey of State allocating agencies.

THE EFFECT OF TAX EXPENDITURES ON THE INCOME AND TAXES OF
THE ELDERLY AND THE POOR

Table 16–17 presents values of the personal exemptions, standard deductions, additional standard deductions for the elderly and
the blind, and taxable income brackets for 1990 to 2000. The figures for 1995 to 2000 are based on Congressional Budget Office
projections.

TABLE 16–17.—PERSONAL EXEMPTIONS, STANDARD DEDUCTIONS, AND TAXABLE INCOME BRACKETS

	1990	1991	1992	1993	1994	1995	Projected				
							1996	1997	1998	1999	2000
Personal exemptions	$2,050	$2,150	$2,300	$2,350	2,450	2,500	2,550	2,650	2,750	2,800	2,900
Standard deductions:											
Joint	5,450	5,700	6,000	6,200	6,350	6,550	6,750	6,950	7,150	7,350	7,600
Single	3,250	3,400	3,600	3,700	3,800	3,900	4,050	4,150	4,300	4,400	4,550
Head of household	4,750	5,000	5,250	5,450	5,600	5,750	5,900	6,100	6,300	6,500	6,700
Additional standard deductions for elderly/blind:											
Joint (each individual)	650	650	700	700	750	750	800	800	850	850	900
Single/head of household	800	850	900	900	950	950	1,000	1,000	1,050	1,100	1,100
Taxable Income Brackets											
Joint returns:											
15 percent rate ends at	32,450	34,000	35,800	36,900	38,000	39,000	40,150	41,350	42,650	44,000	45,350
28 percent rate ends at	78,400	82,150	86,500	89,150	91,850	94,300	97,050	100,000	103,100	106,300	109,600
31 percent rate ends at	....	....	....	140,000	140,000	143,700	147,900	152,350	157,100	161,950	167,000
36 percent rate ends at	....	....	....	250,000	250,000	256,600	264,100	272,100	280,550	289,250	298,200
Single returns:											
15 percent rate ends at	19,450	20,350	21,450	22,100	22,750	23,350	24,050	24,750	25,550	26,350	27,150
28 percent rate ends at	47,050	49,300	51,900	53,500	55,100	56,550	58,250	60,000	61,850	63,750	67,750
31 percent rate ends at	....	....	....	115,000	115,000	118,000	121,500	125,150	129,050	133,050	137,150
36 percent rate ends at	....	....	....	250,000	250,000	256,600	264,100	272,100	280,550	289,250	298,200
Heads of households:											
15 percent rate ends at	26,050	27,300	28,750	29,600	30,500	31,300	32,200	33,200	34,200	35,250	36,350
28 percent rate ends at	67,200	70,450	74,150	76,400	78,700	80,800	83,150	85,700	88,350	91,100	93,900
31 percent rate ends at	....	....	....	127,500	127,500	130,850	134,700	138,750	143,050	147,500	152,050
36 percent rate ends at	....	....	....	250,000	250,000	256,600	264,100	272,100	280,550	289,250	298,200

Note.—The 39.6 percent rate begins at $250,000 (for 1993 and 1994), regardless of filing status. This income threshold is indexed for inflation beginning in 1995. The amounts shown in the table as the end points for the 36 percent bracket are also the beginning points for the 39.6 percent bracket.

Source: Congressional Budget Office.

HYPOTHETICAL TAX CALCULATIONS FOR SELECTED FAMILIES

Table 16–18 presents examples of tax liabilities for hypothetical taxpayers. The table presents 1994 Federal income and payroll tax burdens. The worker is assumed to bear both the employer and employee shares of FICA tax (7.65 percent for each). Taxpayers claim the earned income tax credit, if eligible, and they claim the standard deduction. They do not itemize. Income sources are listed in the table's footnotes for each example.

TABLE 16–18.—EXAMPLES OF FEDERAL INCOME AND PAYROLL TAX LIABILITIES OF HYPOTHETICAL TAXPAYERS, 1994

Income	Income tax liability	FICA tax liability	Total tax liability	Overall average tax rate [1] (percent)	Overall marginal tax rate [1] (percent)
Joint filer—3 exemptions: [2]					
$10,000	−$2,038	$1,530	−$508	−4.7	14.2
$30,000	2,445	4,590	7,035	21.8	28.1
$50,000 [12]	4,898	7,650	12,548	23.3	40.2
$100,000 [13]	15,402	10,042	25,444	24.2	30.5
Head of household—2 personal exemptions: [2]					
$10,000	−2,038	1,530	−508	−4.7	14.2
$30,000	2,865	4,590	7,455	23.1	28.1
$50,000 [12]	5,863	7,650	13,513	25.1	40.2
$100,000 [13]	17,063	10,042	27,105	25.8	33.4
Elderly couple filing joint return:					
$10,000 [3]	0	0	0	0.0	[6] 0.0
$30,000 [4]	788	0	788	2.6	[7] 15.0
$50,000 [5]	4,688	1,530	6,218	12.2	40.0
Elderly single filer:					
$10,000 [8]	0	0	0	0.0	[6] 0.0
$30,000 [9]	2,389	0	2,389	8.0	[11] 22.5
$50,000 [10]	8,712	3,060	11,772	22.8	40.2

[1] The average tax rate is total tax liability divided by income plus the employer share of FICA. The marginal rate computations also count the employer share of FICA tax as income to the employee (for both payroll and income tax purposes). Unless otherwise noted, all calculations assume the taxpayer takes the standard deduction rather than itemized deductions.

[2] Assumes one child, one earner, and all income is wage income.

[3] All income is Social Security.

[4] $12,000 is Social Security, $12,000 is a taxable pension and $6,000 is taxable interest.

[5] Same as above plus additional $10,000 of taxable interest and $10,000 of wages.

[6] If the marginal dollar of income is assumed to consist of wage income, the marginal tax rate would be 14.2 percent. This represents the FICA tax liability on this income.

[7] If the marginal dollar of income is assumed to consist of wage income, the marginal tax rate would be 28.1 percent, representing both the income tax liability and the FICA tax liability on this income.

[8] $7,500 is Social Security, $2,500 is taxable pension.

[9] $7,500 is Social Security, $7,500 is taxable pension, $15,000 is taxable interest.

[10] Same as above plus $20,000 of wages.

[11] If the marginal dollar of income is assumed to consist of wage income, the marginal tax rate would be 35.1 percent, representing both the income tax liability (22.5 percent marginal rate reflects the inclusion of 50 cents of Social Security benefits as taxable for each additional dollar of AGI) and the FICA tax liability on this income.

[12] Assumes taxpayer claims itemized deductions of $10,000.

[13] Assumes taxpayer claims itemized deductions of $20,000.

Source: Joint Committee on Taxation.

TAX TREATMENT OF THE ELDERLY

Present law contains several provisions that reduce, or in some cases eliminate, the burden of Federal income tax on senior citizens. These provisions are: the exemption from income taxation of some or all of an individual's Social Security benefits; a tax credit for certain taxpayers who do not receive substantial Social Security income; and an additional standard deduction for taxpayers age 65 and older. These are described in detail in preceding portions of this section.

As a result of these favorable tax provisions, the tax threshold (the level of income, excluding Social Security, at which tax liability is incurred) for elderly taxpayers is well above the poverty level. For example, in 1994, a single elderly individual with $5,000 in Social Security benefits can have up to $7,200 in other income without incurring tax liability (or total income of $12,200). An elderly married couple filing jointly with $5,000 in excluded Social Security benefits has a tax threshold of $13,500 (or total income of $18,500). Table 16–19 displays similar information for other years and for varying amounts of Social Security benefits.

The combination of these tax provisions ensures that an estimated 43 percent of elderly individuals will have no tax liability for 1994 (see table 16–20).

TABLE 16–19.—INCOME TAX THRESHOLDS FOR ELDERLY INDIVIDUALS,[1] SELECTED YEARS, 1988–2000

Year and filing status	Amount of Social Security income			
	Zero	$2,500	$5,000	$7,500
1988:				
Single	9,633	7,967	5,700	5,700
Joint	15,067	13,400	11,733	10,100
1990:				
Single	9,900	8,233	6,100	6,100
Joint	15,567	13,900	12,233	10,850
1991:				
Single	10,100	8,433	6,400	6,400
Joint	15,867	14,200	12,533	11,300
1992:				
Single	10,367	8,700	6,800	6,800
Joint	16,333	14,667	13,000	12,000
1993:				
Single	10,467	8,800	6,950	6,950
Joint	16,533	14,867	13,200	12,300
1994:[2]				
Single	10,633	8,967	7,200	7,200
Joint	16,833	15,167	13,500	12,750
1995:[2]				
Single	10,733	9,067	7,350	7,350
Joint	17,033	15,367	13,700	13,050
1996:[2]				
Single	10,900	9,233	7,600	7,600
Joint	17,300	15,633	13,967	13,450
1997[2]:				
Single	11,033	9,367	7,800	7,800
Joint	17,587	15,900	14,233	13,850
1998[2]:				
Single	11,233	9,567	8,100	8,100
Joint	17,900	16,233	14,567	14,350
1999[2]:				
Single	11,367	9,700	8,300	8,300
Joint	18,100	16,433	14,767	14,650
2000[2]:				
Single	11,533	9,867	8,550	8,550
Joint	18,467	16,800	15,133	15,200

[1] The tax threshold is the amount of adjusted gross income (excluding Social Security) at which tax liability begins. Table assumes taxpayers are 65 or older, are not blind, and receive no tax-exempt disability benefit, annuity, or pension income other than Social Security income.

[2] Estimated.

Source: Congressional Budget Office.

DISTRIBUTION OF FAMILY INCOME AND TAXES

Table 16–20 presents estimates of the distribution of families and individuals by the Federal individual income tax rate brackets for calendar year 1995. This allows for comparison of data about the elderly to data about other types of families and about the total population. As shown in the bottom panel, slightly over 28 million families pay no Federal income taxes. There are slightly over 54 million families with 134 million individuals who are in the 15 percent bracket. These families on average had income of approximately $35,000 and paid Federal taxes of $2,315 per family. There are approximately 4 million families who face marginal income tax rates of 31 percent or above.

Table 16–21 is a more complicated version of table 6. It illustrates for various types of wage-earners the additional (marginal) Federal tax these wage-earners will pay if they earn one more dollar of wages. For purposes of this table, marginal tax rates include both Federal income and payroll taxes. The majority of single wage earners have income between $20,000 and $30,000 per year and face marginal tax rates of 20.0 to 24.9 percent.

TABLE 16–20.—DISTRIBUTION OF FAMILIES AND PERSONS BY MARGINAL FEDERAL INCOME TAX RATE, 1995

[Number of families and persons in thousands]

Marginal tax rate (percent)	Families		Persons		Families	
	Number	Percent	Number	Percent	Average pre-tax income ($) [1]	Average Federal income tax ($)
Families with children:						
0	8,944	24.0	34,161	23.4	9,830	−1,152
15	20,023	53.6	78,719	53.9	41,785	2,445
28	7,214	19.3	28,405	19.5	89,984	9,979
31	639	1.7	2,551	1.8	165,775	26,437
36	262	0.7	1,018	0.7	238,058	44,553
39.6	265	0.7	1,099	0.8	703,165	198,206
Total	37,346	100.0	145,952	100.0	51,626	5,132
Families with aged head:						
0	10,831	48.6	15,564	43.4	14,099	−1
15	8,193	36.7	14,273	39.8	35,260	1,757
28	2,564	11.5	4,786	13.3	77,171	9,814
31	421	1.9	709	2.0	138,572	22,574
36	184	0.8	359	1.0	245,045	50,011
39.6	106	0.5	203	0.6	975,682	221,219
Total	22,298	100.0	35,895	100.0	37,932	3,659
Other families:						
0	8,248	16.4	10,871	13.4	5,937	−88
15	25,593	51.0	41,371	51.1	30,261	2,391
28	14,163	28.2	24,789	30.6	69,274	8,690
31	1,403	2.8	2,388	3.0	130,708	21,393
36	470	0.9	977	1.2	241,126	52,271
39.6	295	0.60	631	0.8	861,466	212,503
Total	50,173	100.0	81,026	100.0	46,952	5,997
All families:						
0	28,023	25.5	60,595	23.1	10,334	−394
15	53,809	49.0	134,363	51.1	35,310	2,315
28	23,941	21.8	57,980	22.1	76,360	9,199
31	2,463	2.2	5,648	2.2	141,150	22,903
36	916	0.8	2,354	0.9	241,034	49,609
39.6	665	0.6	1,933	0.7	816,659	208,203
Total	109,817	100.0	262,873	100.0	46,710	5,228

[1] Excluding corporate income taxes and employer paid Social Security and U.I. taxes.

Source: Congressional Budget Office.

TABLE 16–21.—DISTRIBUTION OF EARNERS BY INCOME AND MARGINAL TAX RATES ON WAGES,[1] 1995

[In thousands of earners, tax rates in percent]

Marginal tax rate	Income in thousands of 1995 dollars									All incomes
	<10	10–20	20–30	30–40	40–50	50–75	75–100	100–200	200+	
	All earners ages 21–64 without Social Security benefits									
Less than 0	2,842	341	43	6	3	0	0	0	0	3,236
0 to 4.9	1,414	46	14	0	0	0	0	0	0	1,474
5.0 to 9.9	4,822	1,155	184	31	8	4	2	0	0	6,206
10.0 to 14.9	0	0	0	0	0	0	0	0	0	0
15.0 to 19.9	755	102	13	2	12	135	2	0	0	1,022
20.0 to 24.9	2,705	12,079	14,124	12,001	10,825	8,097	46	0	0	59,877
25.0 to 29.9	0	1,844	354	7	38	1,103	1,686	819	0	5,850
30.0 to 34.9	1,600	55	7	129	152	146	317	1,767	9	4,183
35.0 to 39.9	0	2,081	1,603	3,720	2,463	13,404	7,176	3,316	255	34,018
40.0 to 44.9	0	1,209	2,683	49	6	8	0	177	882	5,014
45.0 to 49.9	0	0	1	0	0	10	0	94	508	613
Total	14,139	18,912	19,026	15,947	13,507	22,907	9,229	6,173	1,654	121,493
Mean marginal tax rate	5.6	24.4	26.6	25.8	25.1	30.6	34.4	34.9	43.3	25.6
Mean marginal income tax rate	-2.0	16.8	19.0	18.1	17.5	23.4	28.0	30.2	39.9	18.3
Mean marginal Social Security tax rate	7.6	7.6	7.6	7.6	7.6	7.3	6.3	4.8	3.4	7.3

TABLE 16–21.—DISTRIBUTION OF EARNERS BY INCOME AND MARGINAL TAX RATES ON WAGES,[1] 1995—Continued

[In thousands of earners, tax rates in percent]

Marginal tax rate	Income in thousands of 1995 dollars									All incomes
	<10	10–20	20–30	30–40	40–50	50–75	75–100	100–200	200+	
				Single earners						
Less than 0	2,005	129	10	4	1	0	0	0	0	2,150
0 to 4.9	1,235	19	6	0	0	0	0	0	0	1,260
5.0 to 9.9	3,723	380	1	2	0	0	0	0	0	4,107
10.0 to 14.9	0	0	0	0	0	0	0	0	0	0
15.0 to 19.9	563	15	4	1	1	1	0	0	0	583
20.0 to 24.9	2,705	10,466	8,399	1,712	312	42	4	0	0	23,639
25.0 to 29.9	0	328	4	5	27	464	78	14	0	921
30.0 to 34.9	1,600	42	4	0	2	131	314	206	0	2,299
35.0 to 39.9	0	1,291	797	3,689	2,437	1,927	76	80	54	10,351
40.0 to 44.9	0	742	629	3	2	0	0	9	94	1,478
45.0 to 49.9	0	0	0	0	0	0	0	2	0	2
Total	11,831	13,411	9,854	5,415	2,784	2,565	471	311	147	46,789
Mean marginal tax rate	7.8	24.5	25.1	31.5	34.1	34.2	32.8	34.9	41.1	22.5
Mean marginal income tax rate	0.1	16.9	17.5	23.8	26.5	28.0	30.3	32.8	39.6	15.1
Mean marginal Social Security rate	7.6	7.6	7.6	7.6	7.6	6.2	2.5	2.1	1.4	7.5

Married earners

										Total
Less than 0	837	212	33	3	1	0	0	0	0	1,086
0 to 4.9	180	27	8	0	0	0	0	0	0	214
5.0 to 9.9	1,099	775	183	29	8	4	2	0	0	2,100
10.0 to 14.9	0	0	0	0	0	0	0	0	0	0
15.0 to 19.9	192	87	10	2	11	135	2	0	0	438
20.0 to 24.9	0	1,613	5,725	10,290	10,512	8,055	42	0	0	36,237
25.0 to 29.9	0	1,516	350	2	11	639	1,608	805	0	4,930
30.0 to 34.9	0	14	3	129	150	15	3	1,561	9	1,884
35.0 to 39.9	0	790	806	31	26	11,477	7,100	3,236	201	23,667
40.0 to 44.9	0	468	2,054	46	4	8	0	169	788	3,537
45.0 to 49.9	0	0	1	0	0	10	0	92	508	611
Total	2,308	5,500	9,172	10,532	10,724	20,342	8,757	5,862	1,506	74,705
Mean marginal tax rate	−5.2	24.1	28.3	22.8	22.8	30.2	34.4	34.9	43.5	27.5
Mean marginal income tax rate	−12.9	16.5	20.6	15.2	15.1	22.8	27.9	30.0	39.9	20.3
Mean marginal Social Security rate	7.6	7.6	7.6	7.6	7.6	7.4	6.5	4.9	3.6	7.2

TABLE 16-21.—DISTRIBUTION OF EARNERS BY INCOME AND MARGINAL TAX RATES ON WAGES,[1] 1995—Continued

[In thousands of earners, tax rates in percent]

Marginal tax rate	Income in thousands of 1995 dollars									All incomes
	<10	10–20	20–30	30–40	40–50	50–75	75–100	100–200	200+	
	Earners with children									
Less than 0	2,591	321	35	6	3	0	0	0	0	2,956
0 to 4.9	0	3	2	0	0	0	0	0	0	5
5.0 to 9.9	1,165	738	97	26	1	0	0	0	0	2,026
10.0 to 14.9	0	0	0	0	0	0	0	0	0	0
15.0 to 19.9	0	0	0	2	3	133	2	0	0	141
20.0 to 24.9	0	394	3,020	6,914	6,653	6,099	21	0	0	23,101
25.0 to 29.9	0	1,813	351	2	11	487	1,055	474	0	4,193
30.0 to 34.9	0	0	0	24	21	4	4	734	0	788
35.0 to 39.9	0	1,690	1,104	32	141	5,095	3,541	1,480	21	13,104
40.0 to 44.9	0	1,096	2,569	47	6	6	0	102	455	4,282
45.0 to 49.9	0	0	0	0	0	0	0	50	211	260
Total	3,756	6,055	7,178	7,053	6,839	11,825	4,623	2,839	688	50,856
Mean marginal tax rate	−16.8	28.1	32.2	22.8	22.9	28.5	34.2	34.7	43.7	25.1
Mean marginal income tax rate	−24.4	20.4	24.5	15.1	15.3	21.1	27.9	30.0	40.2	17.9
Mean marginal Social Security rate	7.6	7.6	7.6	7.6	7.6	7.3	6.2	4.7	3.4	7.2

[1] Marginal tax rates are the combined tax rates on an additional dollar of earnings of the Federal individual income tax and the employee share of the Social Security payroll tax (FICA).

Source: Congressional Budget Office tax simulation model.

FEDERAL TAX TREATMENT OF FAMILIES IN POVERTY

During the 1970s and early 1980s, inflation gradually increased the tax burdens of the poor and lowered the real income level at which a poor family became liable for income tax. Legislation passed by Congress reversed or slowed this trend, but in the absence of indexing, inflation during this period gradually offset these legislative efforts. This trend can be measured in two ways. One measure is the degree to which the income at which a poor family begins to pay income taxes (termed the tax threshold, or alternatively, the tax entry point) exceeds or falls below the poverty threshold. A second measure is the actual amount of tax liability incurred by a family with income at the poverty line.

Table 16–22 shows the income tax threshold, the poverty level, and the tax threshold as a percent of the poverty level for a married couple with two children in selected years since 1959. These figures demonstrate that before 1975 a family of four was generally liable for Federal income tax if the family's income was significantly below the poverty line. In 1975, following the enactment of the earned income tax credit (EITC), a family of four incurred no tax liability until its income exceeded the poverty threshold by 22 percent. Over the next decade this margin eroded; by 1984, a poor family of four incurred income tax liability when its income was 17 percent below the poverty line.

Table 16–23 shows the income tax burden and payroll tax burden of households with incomes at the poverty line for families of different sizes. This table shows that a family of four in 1978 had an income tax refund (through the earned income tax credit) of $134; the refund offset 33 percent of the family's payroll tax burden of $403. By 1986, a family in the same situation incurred a positive tax liability of $363. Combined income and payroll taxes represented 4 percent of income for a family with income equal to the poverty level in 1978; by 1986, combined income and payroll taxes consumed 10.4 percent of family income.

The Tax Reform Act of 1986 significantly increased the income tax entry point for poor families with children from $9,575 in 1986 to $15,110 in 1988. Because the system was indexed for inflation, future increases in the Consumer Price Index will not increase the tax burden for poor families.

TABLE 16–22.—RELATIONSHIP BETWEEN INCOME TAX THRESHOLD AND POVERTY LEVEL FOR A FAMILY OF FOUR, ASSUMING FULL USE OF THE EARNED INCOME TAX CREDIT, 1959–2000

Year	Income tax threshold	Poverty level	Tax threshold as a percent of poverty level
1959	$2,667	$2,973	89.7
1960	2,667	3,022	88.3
1965	3,000	3,223	93.1
1969	3,000	3,743	80.2
1970	3,600	3,968	90.7
1971	3,750	4,137	90.6
1972	4,300	4,275	100.6
1974	4,300	5,038	85.4
1975	6,692	5,500	121.7
1976	6,892	5,815	118.5
1977	7,520	6,191	121.7
1978	7,533	6,662	113.1
1979	8,626	7,412	116.4
1980	8,626	8,414	102.5
1981	8,634	9,287	93.0
1982	8,727	9,862	88.5
1983	8,783	10,178	86.3
1984 [2]	8,783	10,610	82.8
1986	9,575	11,203	85.5
1987	13,288	11,611	114.4
1988	15,110	12,092	125.0
1989	15,656	12,675	123.5
1990	16,296	13,359	122.0
1991	17,437	13,924	125.2
1992	18,548	14,335	129.4
1993	19,187	14,774	129.9
1994 [1]	21,098	15,173	139.1
1995 [1]	22,372	15,612	143.3
1996 [1]	23,710	16,092	147.3
1997 [1]	24,463	16,593	147.4
1998 [1]	25,239	17,104	147.6
1999 [1]	25,966	17,635	147.2
2000 [1]	26,797	18,187	147.3

[1] Estimated.

[2] Effective payroll tax calculated as 6.7 percent for 1984 because in this year employees were allowed a payroll tax credit equal to 0.3 percent of taxable wages.

Note.—Poverty levels used are the Bureau of the Census poverty thresholds. These differ from the poverty guidelines used by the Office of Management and Budget to determine eligibility for many government transfer programs. The poverty levels are for all families, not just those with heads under age 65. Tax thresholds represent the income level at which a family of 4 making full use of the earned income tax credit owes positive income tax. They are based on the schedule for a married nonelderly couple filing jointly.

Source: Congressional Budget Office.

TABLE 16–23.—TAX THRESHOLDS, POVERTY LEVELS, AND FEDERAL TAX AMOUNTS FOR DIFFERENT FAMILY SIZES WITH EARNINGS EQUAL TO THE POVERTY LEVEL, ASSUMING FULL USE OF THE EARNED INCOME TAX CREDIT, 1978–2000 [1]

	Family size					
	1	2	3	4	5	6
Poverty levels:						
1978	$3,311	$4,249	$5,201	$6,662	$7,880	$8,891
1982	4,900	6,280	7,690	9,862	11,680	13,210
1984	5,277	6,759	8,276	10,610	12,562	14,211
1986	5,572	7,138	8,737	11,203	13,259	14,986
1988	6,024	7,704	9,435	12,092	14,305	16,149
1990	6,652	8,509	10,419	13,359	15,792	17,839
1991	6,932	8,865	10,860	13,924	16,456	18,587
1992	7,143	9,137	11,186	14,335	16,592	19,137
1993 [3]	7,362	9,417	11,529	14,774	17,101	19,724
1994 [4]	7,560	9,671	11,840	15,173	17,562	20,255
1995 [4]	7,779	9,951	12,183	15,612	18,070	20,842
1996 [4]	8,019	10,257	12,557	16,092	18,626	21,483
1997 [4]	8,268	10,576	12,948	16,593	19,206	22,151
1998 [4]	8,523	10,902	13,347	17,104	19,797	22,833
1999 [4]	8,787	11,241	13,761	17,635	20,412	23,543
2000 [4]	9,062	11,592	14,192	18,187	21,050	24,279
Income tax thresh-old: [1]						
1978	3,200	5,200	6,930	7,520	8,183	9,167
1982	3,300	5,400	8,237	8,727	9,216	9,706
1984	3,300	5,400	8,315	8,783	9,251	9,719
1986	3,560	5,830	9,063	9,575	10,086	10,598
1988	4,950	8,900	13,940	15,110	16,280	17,450
1990	5,300	9,550	15,066	16,296	17,526	18,756
1991	5,550	10,000	16,179	17,437	18,616	19,794
1992	5,900	10,600	17,217	18,548	19,774	21,000
1993	6,050	10,900	17,841	19,187	20,405	21,624
1994	7,179	11,250	18,887	21,098	22,222	23,347
1995 [4]	7,359	11,550	19,387	22,372	23,437	24,501
1996 [4]	7,583	11,850	19,924	23,710	24,770	25,831
1997 [4]	7,810	12,250	20,555	24,463	25,565	26,668
1998 [4]	8,080	12,650	21,208	25,239	26,383	27,527
1999 [4]	8,288	12,950	21,809	25,966	27,131	28,296
2000 [4]	8,558	13,400	22,518	26,797	28,004	29,210
Income tax at pov-erty level: [1]						
1978	16	0	−280	−134	−12	0
1982	202	106	−134	285	417	491
1984	226	149	−9	364	478	569
1986	230	144	−76	363	480	564
1988	161	0	−874	−648	−427	−243
1990	203	0	−953	−691	−433	−229
1991	207	0	−1,192	−905	−591	−328
1992	187	0	−1,324	−1,053	−711	−422
1993 [3]	197	0	−1,434	−1,153	−829	−463
1994 [4]	86	0	−1,904	−1,790	−1,367	−891

TABLE 16–23.—TAX THRESHOLDS, POVERTY LEVELS, AND FEDERAL TAX AMOUNTS FOR DIFFERENT FAMILY SIZES WITH EARNINGS EQUAL TO THE POVERTY LEVEL, ASSUMING FULL USE OF THE EARNED INCOME TAX CREDIT, 1978–2000 [1]—Continued

	Family size					
	1	2	3	4	5	6
1995 [4]	95	0	−1,952	−2.240	−1,743	−1,183
1996 [4]	99	0	−2,006	−2,618	−2,085	−1,483
1997 [4]	104	0	−2,064	−2,694	−2,144	−1,524
1998 [4]	100	0	−2,127	−2,777	−2,210	−1,570
1999 [4]	113	0	−2,195	−2,867	−2,282	−1,623
2000 [4]	114	0	−2,263	−2,953	−2,350	−1,670
Payroll tax at poverty level:						
1978	200	257	315	403	477	538
1982	328	421	515	661	783	885
1984 [2]	354	453	555	711	842	953
1986	398	510	625	801	948	1,071
1988	452	579	709	908	1,074	1,213
1990	509	651	797	1,022	1,208	1,365
1991	530	678	831	1,065	1,259	1,422
1992	547	699	856	1,098	1,298	1,466
1993 [3]	563	720	882	1,130	1,308	1,509
1994 [4]	578	740	906	1,161	1,343	1,550
1995 [4]	595	761	932	1,194	1,382	1,594
1996 [4]	613	785	961	1,231	1,425	1,643
1997 [4]	633	809	991	1,269	1,469	1,695
1998 [4]	652	834	1,021	1,308	1,514	1,747
1999 [4]	672	860	1,053	1,349	1,562	1.801
2000 [4]	693	887	1,086	1,391	1,610	1,857
Combined income and payroll tax at poverty level:						
1978	216	257	35	269	465	538
1982	530	527	381	946	1,200	1,376
1984	580	602	546	1,075	1,320	1,521
1986	628	654	549	1,164	1,428	1,635
1988	614	579	−165	256	647	970
1990	712	651	−156	331	775	1,136
1991	738	678	−362	160	668	1,094
1992	734	699	−467	45	587	1,044
1993 [3]	760	720	−552	−22	480	1,046
1994 [4]	665	740	−998	−629	−24	658
1995 [4]	690	761	−1,020	−1,046	−361	412
1996 [4]	712	785	−1,045	−1,387	−660	161
1997 [4]	736	809	−1,073	−1,425	−675	171
1998 [4]	752	834	−1,106	−1,468	−695	177
1999 [4]	785	860	−1,142	−1,518	−721	178
2000 [4]	808	887	−1,177	−1,562	−739	188

TABLE 16–23.—TAX THRESHOLDS, POVERTY LEVELS, AND FEDERAL TAX AMOUNTS FOR DIFFERENT FAMILY SIZES WITH EARNINGS EQUAL TO THE POVERTY LEVEL, ASSUMING FULL USE OF THE EARNED INCOME TAX CREDIT, 1978–2000 [1]—Continued

	Family size					
	1	2	3	4	5	6
Combined tax as percent of income at poverty level:						
1978	6.5	6.1	0.7	4.0	5.9	6.1
1982	10.8	8.4	5.0	9.6	10.3	10.4
1984	11.0	8.9	6.5	10.1	10.5	10.7
1986	11.3	9.2	6.3	10.4	10.8	10.9
1988	10.2	7.5	−1.7	2.1	4.5	6.0
1990	10.7	7.6	−1.5	2.5	4.9	6.4
1991	10.6	7.6	−3.3	1.1	4.1	5.9
1992	10.3	7.7	−4.2	0.3	3.5	5.5
1993 [3]	10.3	7.7	−4.8	−0.2	2.8	5.3
1994 [4]	8.8	7.7	−8.4	−4.1	−0.1	3.3
1995 [4]	8.9	7.7	−8.4	−6.7	−2.0	2.0
1996 [4]	8.9	7.7	−8.3	−8.6	−3.5	0.7
1997 [4]	8.9	7.7	−8.3	−8.6	−3.5	0.8
1998 [4]	8.8	7.7	−8.3	−8.6	−3.5	−0.8
1999 [4]	8.9	7.7	−8.3	−8.6	−3.5	0.8
2000 [4]	8.9	7.7	−8.3	−8.6	−3.5	0.8

[1] The table reflects assumptions that all family income consists of wages or salaries, that families of two or more include a married couple (rather than an unmarried head of household with one or more dependents), that all family members are under age 65, and that families of three or more persons are eligible for the earned income tax credit. For families of three or more, the effect of the earned income tax credit is included. Negative figures in the table reflect refundability of the earned income tax credit. The poverty level figures are for all families, not just those with heads under age 65.

[2] Effective payroll tax is calculated as 6.7 percent for 1984 because in this year employees were allowed a payroll tax credit equal to 0.3 percent of taxable wages.

[3] Estimated.

[4] Projected.

Source: Congressional Budget Office.

Section 17. The Pension Benefit Guaranty Corporation [1]

The Pension Benefit Guaranty Corporation (PBGC) was established under title IV of the Employee Retirement Income Security Act of 1974 (ERISA) (88 Stat. 829, Public Law 93–406) to insure private pension beneficiaries against the complete loss of promised benefits if their defined benefit pension plan is terminated without adequate funding.

EXPLANATION OF THE CORPORATION AND ITS FUNCTIONS

ADMINISTRATION

The PBGC is a Government-owned corporation. A three-member board of directors, chaired by the Secretary of Labor, administers the Corporation. The Secretary of Commerce and the Secretary of the Treasury are the other directors. ERISA provides for a seven-member Advisory Committee, appointed by the President, for staggered 3-year terms. The Advisory Committee advises the PBGC on issues such as the appointment of trustees in termination proceedings, investment of funds, plan liquidations, and other matters as requested by the PBGC.

PLAN TERMINATION INSURANCE

Defined benefit and defined contribution plans

There are two basic kinds of pension plans: "defined benefit" and "defined contribution" plans. Under a defined benefit plan, employees receive a fixed benefit at retirement prescribed by a formula set forth in the plan. The employer makes annual contributions to the plan based on actuarial calculations designed to ensure that the plan has sufficient funds to pay the benefit prescribed by the formula. Under a defined contribution plan, no particular benefit is promised. Instead, benefits are based on the balance of an individual account maintained for the benefit of the employee. The benefit received by an employee at retirement is generally dependent on two factors: total contributions made to the plan on the employee's behalf during the employee's participation in the plan, and the investment experience of the amounts contributed on the employee's behalf. Under either type of pension plan, employees may also be permitted to make contributions.

Under a defined contribution plan, the employee bears all the risk of poor investment performance of the assets invested in a plan. Whether the funds are invested well or poorly, the employee

---

[1] This section draws from: a CBO report entitled "Federal Insurance of Private Pension Benefits," October 1987; the PBGC Annual Report to Congress Fiscal Year 1992; a Joint Committee on Taxation print entitled "Current Issues Relating to PBGC Premiums and Single-Employer Defined Benefit Pension Plans," May 15, 1987; and a Joint Committee on Taxation print entitled "Present Law and Issues Relating to Pension Benefit Guaranty Corporation Guarantees of Retirement Annuities Paid By Insurance Companies," April 4, 1990.

gets at retirement only what was contributed plus the amount actually earned.

Under a defined benefit plan, the employer bears more of the risk of loss. The Internal Revenue Code and ERISA contain minimum funding standards that require the employer to make contributions to a defined benefit plan to fund promised benefits. Thus, for example, if the plan experiences poor investment performance, actuarial miscalculations, or low benefit estimates, the employer will be required to make additional contributions to the plan. However, the minimum funding rules provide for funding over a period of time, and do not require that the plan have assets to pay all the benefits earned under the plan at any particular time. Thus, it is possible for a defined benefit plan to terminate without having sufficient assets to pay promised benefits. The PBGC insures defined benefit plan benefits up to certain limits to protect plan participants in the event of such a termination. However, the PBGC does not protect all benefits promised under a plan so that even under a defined benefit plan, the employees bear some risk of loss.

Defined benefit plans are fewer in number than defined contribution plans, but cover more participants and account for a greater volume of assets. In 1990, defined benefit pension plans accounted for 16 percent of all pension plans, but were the primary form of coverage for 62 [2] percent of all pension participants and accounted for 57 percent of pension assets.

The PBGC insures benefits only under certain defined benefit plans and only up to certain monthly amounts. Private defined benefit pension plans insured by the PBGC continue to be well funded in general, with more than $1 trillion in assets, exceeding liability by several hundred billion dollars. However, the PBGC faces substantial direct exposure from a relatively small number of single-employer plans, concentrated in the steel, airline, tire and automobile industries, with unfunded liabilities of $53 billion, as of December 31, 1992. Underfunding in multiemployer plans, as of January 1, 1991 (the most recent information available) totaled $10.6 billion. The operations of the insurance program, and insurance limits, are described below. Defined contribution plans are not insured by the PBGC.

Single-employer and multiemployer plans

Defined benefit plans insured by the PBGC fall into two categories: single-employer plans and multiemployer plans. Multiemployer plans are collectively bargained arrangements maintained by more than one employer. Single-employer plans, whether or not collectively bargained, are each maintained by one employer.

The risk to the PBGC posed by single-employer plans is different from that posed by multiemployer plans. Generally, single-employer plans are more vulnerable to the risk of underfunding due to financial weakness of the sponsoring employer; the PBGC is more vulnerable to the risk that a single employer will be unable to make up the difference between funded and promised benefits.

---

[2] Figure of 62 percent primary coverage is for 1991.
Source: EBRI, December 1993 Issue Brief on pension coverage and participation.

Issues concerning insurance of multiemployer plans are more likely to concern the allocation of liabilities as firms enter and leave the participating group.

The PBGC insures the benefits of 41 million pension plan participants, including active workers and retirees. Of these, 78 percent, or about 32 million, are covered by approximately 64,000 single-employer pension plans, and 22 percent, or about 8.9 million, are covered by approximately 2,000 multiemployer plans.

Other requirements for PBGC coverage

The PBGC covers only those defined benefit plans which meet the qualification requirements of Section 401 of the Internal Revenue Code. These are also the requirements that plans must meet in order to receive the significant tax benefits available to pension plans.

Generally, to be qualified under the Internal Revenue Code, a pension plan must be established with the intent of being a permanent and continuing arrangement; must provide definitely determinable benefits; may not discriminate in favor of highly compensated employees with respect to coverage, contributions or benefits; and must cover a minimum number of participants.

Pension plans specifically excluded from insurance by the PBGC include government and church plans, defined contribution plans, plans of fraternal societies financed entirely by member contributions and plans maintained by certain professionals with 25 or fewer participants.

PLAN TERMINATION

Single-employer plans

An employer can voluntarily terminate a single-employer plan only in a standard or distress termination. The participants and the PBGC must be notified of the termination. The PBGC may involuntarily terminate a plan.

a. Standard terminations

A standard termination is permitted only if plan assets are sufficient to cover benefit liabilities. Generally, benefit liabilities equal all benefits earned to date by plan participants, including vested and nonvested benefits (which automatically become vested at the time of termination), and including certain early retirement supplements and subsidies. Benefit liabilities may also include certain contingent benefits (for example, plant shutdown benefits). If assets are sufficient to cover benefit liabilities (and other termination requirements, such as notice to employees, have not been violated), the plan distributes benefits to participants. The plan provides for the benefit payments it owes by purchasing annuity contracts from an insurance company, or otherwise providing for the payment of benefits, for example, by providing the benefits in lump sum distributions.

Assets in excess of the amounts necessary to cover benefit liabilities may be recovered by the employer in an asset reversion. The asset reversion is included in the gross income of the employer and is also subject to a nondeductible excise tax. The excise tax is 20

percent of the amount of the reversion if the employer establishes
a qualified replacement plan, or provides certain benefit increases
in connection with the termination. Otherwise, the excise tax is 50
percent of the reversion amount.

b. Distress terminations

If assets in the plan are not sufficient to cover benefit liabilities,
the employer may not terminate the plan unless the employer
meets one of four criteria necessary for a "distress" termination:
—The contributing sponsor, and every member of the controlled
  group of which the sponsor is a member, is being liquidated in
  bankruptcy or other similar State insolvency proceedings;
—The contributing sponsor and every member of the sponsor's
  controlled group is being reorganized in bankruptcy or similar
  State proceeding;
—The PBGC determines that termination is necessary to allow
  the employer to pay its debts when due;
—The PBGC determines that termination is necessary to avoid
  unreasonably burdensome pension costs caused solely by a decline in the employer's work force.
These requirements, added by the Single Employer Pension Plan
Amendments Act of 1986 (SEPPAA) and modified by the Pension
Protection Act of 1987 (PPA), are designed to ensure that the liabilities of an underfunded plan remain the responsibility of the employer, rather than the PBGC, unless the employer meets strict
standards of financial need indicating genuine inability to continue
funding the plan.

c. Involuntary terminations

In order to terminate a plan involuntarily, the PBGC must obtain a court order. The PBGC may institute court proceedings only
if the plan in question has not met the minimum funding standards, will be unable to pay benefits when due, a substantial owner
has received a distribution greater than $10,000 (other than by rea-
son of death), or the liability of the PBGC may reasonably be expected to increase if the plan is not terminated. The PBGC must
terminate a plan if the plan is unable to pay benefits that are currently due. A court may order termination of the plan in order to
protect the interests of participants, to avoid unreasonable deterio-
ration of the plan's financial condition, or to avoid an unreasonable
increase in the PBGC liability under the plan.

d. PBGC trusteeship

When an underfunded plan terminates in a distress or involuntary termination, the plan effectively goes into PBGC receivership.
The PBGC becomes the trustee of the plan, takes control of any
plan assets, and assumes responsibility for liabilities under the
plan. The PBGC makes payments for benefit liabilities promised
under the plan with assets received from two sources: assets in the
plan before termination, and assets recovered from the employer
(see below). The balance, if any, of guaranteed benefits owed to
beneficiaries is paid from the PBGC's revolving funds (see below)

e. Employer liability to the PBGC

Following a distress or involuntary termination, the plan's contributing sponsor and every member of that sponsor's controlled group is liable to the PBGC for the excess of the value of the plan's liabilities as of the date of plan termination over the fair market value of the plan's assets on the date of termination. The liability is joint and several, meaning that each member of the controlled group can be held responsible for the entire liability. Generally, the obligation is payable in cash or negotiable securities to the PBGC on the date of termination. Failure to pay this amount upon demand by the PBGC may trigger a lien on the property of the contributing employer's controlled group for up to 30 percent of its net worth. Obligations in excess of this amount are to be paid on commercially reasonable terms acceptable to the PBGC.

f. Benefit payments

When an underfunded plan terminates, the benefits that the PBGC will pay depend on the statutory guaranty, asset allocation, and recovery on the PBGC's employer liability claim.

Guaranteed benefits.—Within certain limits, the PBGC guarantees any retirement benefit that was nonforfeitable (vested) on the date of plan termination other than benefits that vest solely on account of the termination, and any death, survivor or disability benefit that was owed or was in payment status at the date of plan termination. Generally only that part of the retirement benefit that is payable in monthly installments (rather, than for example, lump sum benefits payable to encourage early retirement) is guaranteed. Retirement benefits that commence before the normal age of retirement are guaranteed, provided they meet the other conditions of guarantee. Contingent benefits (for example, early retirement benefits provided only if a plant shuts down) are guaranteed only if the triggering event occurs before plan termination.

There is a statutory ceiling on the amount of monthly benefits payable to any individual that may be guaranteed. This ceiling is indexed according to changes in the Social Security wage base, and is $2,556.82 in 1994 for a single life annuity payable at age 65. This limit is actuarially reduced for benefits payable before age 65, or payable in a different form.

The reduction in the maximum guarantee for benefits paid before age 65 is 7 percent for each of the first 65 years under age 65, 4 percent for each of the next 5 years, and 2 percent for each of the next 10 years. The reduction in the maximum guarantee for benefits paid in a form other than a single life annuity depends on the type of benefit, and if there is a survivor's benefit, the percentage of the benefit continuing to surviving spouse and the age difference between the participant and spouse.

For example, consider a retiree who, at plan termination in 1994, is age 60 and whose spouse is 2 years younger. The participant is receiving a joint and 50 percent survivor's benefit (a benefit that continues to a surviving spouse upon the death of the participant at a reduced level of 50 percent). In this case, the maximum guarantee applicable to the participant is $1,465.82 per month

[$2,556.82 × .90 joint and survivor benefit form × .65 (participant age) × .98 (spouse 2 year younger)]

The guarantee for any new benefit, including benefits under new plans and benefits provided by amendment to already existing plans, is phased in over 5 years following creation of the benefit.

Asset allocation.—Assets of a terminated plan are allocated to pay benefits according to a priority schedule established by statute. Under this schedule, some nonguaranteed benefits are payable from plan assets before certain guaranteed benefits. For example, certain benefits that have been in pay status for more than 3 years have priority over guaranteed benefits not in pay status.

Section 4022(c) benefits.—The PBGC is also required to pay participants a portion of their unfunded, nonguaranteed benefits based on a ratio of recovery on the employer liability claim to the amount of that claim.

As a result of the asset allocation and section 4022(c) benefits, reimbursement to the PBGC for its payment of guaranteed benefits may be less than the total value of assets recovered from the terminated plan.

Multiemployer plans

In the case of multiemployer plans, the PBGC insures plan insolvency, rather than plan termination. Accordingly, a multiemployer plan need not be terminated to qualify for PBGC financial assistance, but must be found to be insolvent. A plan is insolvent when its available resources are not sufficient to pay the plan benefits for the plan year in question, or when the sponsor of a plan in reorganization reasonably determines, taking into account the plan's recent and anticipated financial experience, that the plan's available resources will not be sufficient to pay benefits that come due in the next plan year.

If it appears that available resources will not support the payment of benefits at the guaranteed level, the PBGC will provide the additional resources needed as a loan. The PBGC may provide loans to the plan year after year. If the plan recovers from insolvency, it must begin repaying loans on reasonable terms in accordance with regulations.

The PBGC guarantees benefits under a multiemployer plan of the same type as those guaranteed under a single employer plan, but a different guarantee ceiling applies. As a result of the Multiemployer Pension Plan Amendments Act of 1980 (Public Law 96–364, referred to as MPPAA), the limit for multiemployer plans is the sum of 100 percent of the first $5 of monthly benefits per year of credited service, and 75 percent of the next $15 of monthly benefits. (The 75 percent is reduced to 65 percent for plans that do not meet certain pre-ERISA minimum funding standards.)

MPPAA requires that PBGC conduct a study every 5 years to determine whether changes are needed in the multiemployer premium rate or guarantee. PBGC completed the second such study in 1990, confirming the program's financial solvency, but also finding that inflation had devalued the existing guarantee limits.

FINANCIAL CONDITION OF THE PBGC

OVERVIEW

According to its most recent annual report, the PBGC's multiemployer plan insurance program is in sound financial condition. Assets exceeded liabilities by $276 million at the end of the fiscal year 1993.

However, by the end of fiscal year 1993, the larger single-employer program was showing an accumulated deficit of $2.9 billion. That is, the assets in PBGC's single-employer program were $2.8 billion less than the value of PBGC's liability for future benefit payments. PBGC's assets are comprised of premiums collected, assets recovered from terminated plans and recoveries from employers, and accumulated investment income. PBGC's liability for future benefit payments is the (discounted) present value of the stream of future benefit payments PBGC is obligated to pay participants and beneficiaries of terminated plans and plans booked as probable terminations.

MAJOR CASES

Major Single-Employer Cases

The past year saw the conclusion of several of PBGC's largest cases, as The LTV Corporation, Continental Airlines, and Trans World Airlines all began to consummate their agreements with PBGC and emerged from bankruptcy reorganizations. Negotiations and litigation continued in a number of other major cases.

The LTV Corporation

LTV emerged from bankruptcy on June 28, 1993. The company's plan of reorganization included an agreement finalized earlier in the year with PBGC under which LTV immediately contributed $787 million in cash to three underfunded LTV Steel pension plans as part of a nearly $2 billion initial infusion to the plans. That payment began the process of eliminating the plans' underfunding of $3 billion based on a 28-year payment schedule.

Also as part of the agreement, the district court approved a request by PBGC, LTV, and LTV's creditors to vacate prior court decisions on the amount and priority of PBGC's bankruptcy claims.

As a result of the settlement, LTV's pension plans remain ongoing and approximately 100,000 participants, including nearly 60,000 retirees, are receiving full benefits. PBGC will monitor the plans closely as LTV goes forward and continues the necessary funding of the plans.

Eastern Air Lines / Continental Airlines

As part of Continental's bankruptcy reorganization in April 1993, the airline and PBGC finalized an agreement that settled Continental's joint-and-several liability for unpaid contributions of approximately $58 million due the terminated Eastern Air Lines pension plans and approximately $700 million in unfunded pension liabilities. The agreement also provided additional protection for Continental's ongoing pension plans. Continental and its subsidiaries had been part of Eastern's group of commonly controlled companies. PBGC received more than $21 million in cash, an airplane trust worth $70–75 million, and approximately 5 percent of the new Continental common stock. Continental's pensions plans also received an extra contribution of $10 million of new Continental stock to protect the pensions of Continental's employees.

Trans World Airlines (TWA)

TWA's emergence from bankruptcy in November 1993 followed the settlement reached in early January between PBGC, TWA, the airline's creditors and unions, and Carl Icahn, the former owner of TWA. That agreement, negotiated in 1992 and signed in early January 1993, resolved Mr. Icahn's and TWA's liabilities for TWA's two defined benefit pension plans, which were underfunded by about $1 billion as of December 1992.

Under the agreement, Mr. Icahn provided TWA with $200 million in financing and relinquished control of the airline to its employees and creditors. TWA's pension plans, which are ongoing but with no future benefit accruals, were assumed by Pichin Corporation, an Icahn company that will be responsible for minimum funding payments to the plans. The annual funding will be provided in part by TWA through payments on secured 15-year notes totalling $300 million. The balance of the required payments, up to a total of $200 million, will be made by another Icahn company. If the plans terminate in the future, PBGC will receive the balance of the TWA notes, as well as annual payments totalling $240 million from Mr. Icahn's group of companies. All of TWA's and Mr. Icahn's commitments under the agreement are secured.

Astrum International (formerly E–II Holdings, Inc.)

In a case demonstrating the value of PBGC's early warning program, Astrum responded to early PBGC action with measures that protect the pensions of 19,000 workers and retirees from two affiliated companies. Astrum had planned a reorganization in bankruptcy that would have relieved it of liability for the pension plans of two related companies, which were underfunded by as much as $40 million. PBGC successfully intervened to negotiate protection for the plans prior to conclusion of the bankruptcy proceeding. The resulting agreement assures continued funding of, and Astrum's continued secondary liability for, the plans which will remain in operation.

Lone Star Industries, Inc.

PBGC reached an agreement with the bankrupt Lone Star regarding the company's 10 pension plans, which are underfunded by a total of about $73 million. Under the agreement, which still needs bankruptcy court approval, Lone Star would contribute up to $13 million to the plans over and above its minimum required contribution. In addition, PBGC will receive security valued at a minimum of $30 million to protect against future termination of the plans.

Collins v. PBGC; Page v. PBGC

In these consolidated class-action suits, the plaintiffs—participants in plans that terminated before September 26, 1980, without having been amended to adopt ERISA's minimum vesting standards—sought a court ruling requiring PBGC to guarantee their benefits as if their plans had been amended. PBGC had determined at the time their plans terminated that only those benefits vested under the express terms of their plans were guaranteeable. PBGC and the plaintiffs were discussing a settlement as the year ended.

CF&I Steel Corporation

PBGC has been seeking recovery on its claims for a CF&I plan that was underfunded by about $220 million when terminated in March 1992. Under CF&I's consensual plan of reorganization confirmed early in the year, PBGC will receive a share of liquidation proceeds that will include a limited partnership interest in the business that was transferred to new owners by an asset sale, and may include cash and other consideration. PBGC's preliminary estimate of the total value of the potential recovery is about $33 million. PBGC may recover additional amounts depending on the outcome of its appeal of bankruptcy court rulings on its claims.

White Consolidated Industries, Inc.

PBGC has been seeking to establish White's liability for the estimated $120 million underfunding in several pension plans transferred in a 1985 transaction with Blaw Knox Corporation. PBGC alleged that a principal purpose of White in entering into the transaction was to evade the pension liabilities. PBGC terminated two of the plans, with total underfunding of about $97 million, when they ran out of money. Although a district court denied White's liability for the plans, an appellate court reinstated PBGC's lawsuit against White. The U.S. Supreme Court denied White's petition for review and the case continues in district court.

New Valley Corporation (Formerly Western Union Corporation)

New Valley, which sponsors one pension plan that is underfunded by about $470 million, has been in bankruptcy since November 1991. Both New Valley and its unsecured creditors have proposed separate reorganization plans. PBGC is actively negotiating to ensure that the pension plan will be adequately protected under any reorganization proposals.

Pan Am Corporation

By yearend, PBGC's bankruptcy claims against Pan Am for $914 million of unfunded benefits and $350 million in contributions owed to three terminated Pan Am pensions plans were still unresolved. Court hearings on PBGC's claims and related issues were postponed until April 1994.

Wean, Inc.

PBGC pressed bankruptcy claims totalling about $121 million against Wean that included $13 million for Wean's underfunded pension plans and $108 million for a now-terminated underfunded plan that Wean had transferred to United Engineering and Foundry, Inc. PBGC asserts that one of Wean's principal purposes of the transaction was to evade liability to PBGC for the United Engineering plan. PBGC settled its claims against United Engineering and continues to pursue an agreement with Wean.

LOSSES

Through the end of fiscal year 1993, the PGBC's single-employer program had incurred net losses of $6 billion (see table 17–1). PBGC's net losses equal the portion of guaranteed benefit liabilities not covered by plan assets or recoverable employer liability. These losses will eventually have to be covered through higher premiums, earnings on PBGC assets, or other sources of revenues.

TABLE 17–1.—LOSS EXPERIENCE FROM SINGLE-EMPLOYER PLANS [1]

[Dollars in millions]

Year of termination	Number of plans	Benefit liability	Trust plan assets	Recoveries from employers	Net losses	Average net loss per terminated plan
1975–1981	824	$741	$295	$129	$317	$0.4
1982–1987	689	2,694	848	184	1,661	2.4
1988–1993	335	4,579	1,871	312	2,396	7.2
Total	1,848	8,014	3,014	626	4,374	....
Probable future terminations	46	3,645	1,403	616	1,627	....
Total	1,894	$11,659	$4,417	1,242	$6,001	....

[1] Stated amounts are subject to change until PBGC finalizes values for liabilities, assets, and recoveries of terminated plans. Amounts in this table are valued as of the date of each plan's termination and differ from amounts reported in PBGC's Financial Statements which are valued as of the end of the stated fiscal year.

Note: Numbers may not add up to totals due to rounding.

Source: PBGC Fiscal Year 1993 Annual Report.

PBGC's losses have increased considerably over time. Within that trend, there has been substantial annual variability due to the sporadic terminations of very large underfunded plans. Fewer underfunded plans terminated in 1993 than the previous year, and losses from underfunded plans declined slightly because of fewer new major terminations.

Table 17–1 demonstrates the growth in net losses over the Corporation's history. In the 6 years from 1988 to 1993, net losses, not including probable terminations, exceeded the losses of the prior 6 years by 44 percent and were more than 7 times greater than the losses from the first 7 years of PBGC's operation. PBGC also faces probable losses of $1,627 million for 46 plans that are expected to terminate after fiscal 1993 year end. Those probable terminations represent 27 percent of PBGC's total net losses since inception.

As shown by table 17–2, the number of single-employer plan terminations that result in claims against the PBGC is a tiny fraction of all plan terminations. In fiscal year 1993, PBGC permitted completion of about 6,700 standard terminations and 88 distress or involuntary terminations of underfunded plans. While terminations of underfunded plans made up less than 2 percent of all terminations, PBGC's deficit in the single-employer program grew slightly to $2.9 billion, reflecting PBGC's vulnerability to termination of large underfunded plans.

TABLE 17–2.—TOTAL NUMBER OF TERMINATED SINGLE-EMPLOYER PLANS, NUMBER OF PLANS WITH CLAIMS AGAINST PBGC, AND ACCUMULATED DEFICIT

	Number of terminated plans	Number of claims against PBGC	Accumulated deficit end of year (millions of dollars)
Fiscal year:			
1975	2,568	100	− 15.7
1976	9,104	171	− 41.0
1977	7,331	130	− 95.3
1978	5,260	102	− 137.8
1979	4,888	81	− 146.4
1980	4,033	103	− 94.6
1981	5,084	137	− 188.8
1982	6,131	131	− 332.8
1983	6,870	146	− 523.3
1984	7,711	96	− 462.0
1985	8,723	107	− 1,325.3
1986	6,915	118	− 3,826.4
1987	10,924	91	− 1,548.5
1988	10,836	79	− 1,543.3
1989	11,433	58	− 1,123.6
1990	11,462	60	− 1,912.8
1991	7,586	72	− 2,510.0
1992	8,018	47	− 2,737.1
1993	6,788	[1]65	− 2,771.8
Total	141,665	1,894	− 2,896.8

[1] Includes 46 plans with claims of $1 million or more that were probable terminations as of the end of fiscal year 1993.

Source: Pension Benefit Guaranty Corporation.

FINANCING

The sources of financing for PBGC are per-participant premiums collected from insured plans, assets in terminated underfunded plans for which the PBGC has become trustee, investment earnings, and amounts owed to the PBGC by employers who have terminated underfunded plans. In addition, PBGC has the authority to borrow up to $100 million from the Treasury.

Single-employer premiums.—An employer who maintains a covered single-employer defined benefit pension plan must pay an annual premium for each participant under the plan. Initially set at $1 per participant, the per-participant premium was raised to $2.60 beginning in 1979, and then raised again by the Single Employer Pension Plan Amendments Act (SEPPAA) to $8.50 beginning in 1986. The Pension Protection Act of 1987, contained in the

Omnibus Budget Reconciliation Act of 1987, raised the basic premium to $16, and imposed an additional variable rate, or risk-related, premium on underfunded plans. The variable rate premium was initially set at $6 per each $1,000 of the plan's unfunded vested benefits, up to a maximum of $34 per participant. Accordingly, the maximum premium was $50 per participant.

The Omnibus Budget Reconciliation Act of 1990 (OBRA 90) increased the basic premium to $19, the variable rate premium to $9 per each $1,000 of the plan's unfunded vested benefits, up to a maximum of $53 per participant. Thus, beginning in 1991, the maximum premium is $72 per participant. OBRA 90 did not change the ratio of revenue raised by the basic and variable rate portions of the premium. Single-employer premium income equaled $890 million in 1993.

Multiemployer plan premiums.—The premium for multiemployer plans was initially $0.50 per participant. The Multiemployer Pension Plan Amendments Act raised the premium to $1.40 for years after 1980. This was set to increase gradually to its current level, $2.60. Multiemployer premium income equaled $23 million in 1993.

Assets from terminated plans.—When the PBGC becomes trustee of a terminated plan, it receives control of any assets in the plan. These assets are placed in one of two trust funds (one for multiemployer plans, one for single-employer plans).

Employer liability.—An employer which terminates an underfunded defined benefit plan is liable to the PBGC for certain amounts. Before the changes made by SEPPAA, an employer's liability was generally capped at 30 percent of the employer's net worth. SEPPAA removed this limit, leaving employers whose liability would have been capped liable for an additional share of unfunded benefit commitments above 30 percent of net worth. The Pension Protection Act of 1987 further increased employer liability, leaving employers liable for all amounts up to 100 percent of unfunded benefit liabilities.

Investment income.—The PBGC maintains two separate financial programs, each consisting of a revolving fund and a trust fund, to sustain its single-employer and multiemployer plan insurance programs. Its revolving funds consist of collected premiums and income resulting from investment of the premiums. They had a value of $5 billion as of September 30, 1993.

The trust funds consist of assets received from all terminated plans of which the PBGC is or will be a trustee, and employer liability payments. These assets are invested in a diversified portfolio of investments including equities, fixed income securities, and real estate. The net market value of the trust funds was $3.3 billion as of September 30, 1993.

Chart 17–1 diagrams the relationship between the PBGC's financing and its payment of guaranteed benefits to plan participants.

CHART 17–1. FINANCIAL STRUCTURE OF THE PENSION BENEFIT GUARANTY CORPORATION

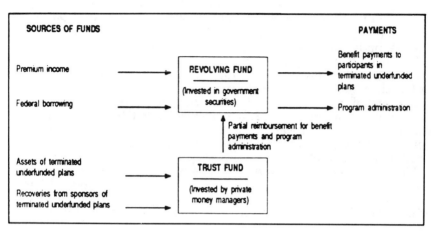

SOURCE: Congressional Budget Office.

LEGISLATIVE HISTORY

SINGLE EMPLOYER PLANS

The PBGC was established under the Employee Retirement Income Security Act of 1974 (ERISA) for the purpose of insuring benefits under defined benefit pension plans. As originally structured, in the case of a single-employer plan, termination of a plan triggered the PBGC insurance mechanism. The contributing employer was liable to the PBGC for unfunded insured benefits up to 30 percent of the net worth of the employer. If unfunded insured liability exceeded this amount, the PBGC had to absorb the excess and spread the loss over insured plans. Employers generally faced no restrictions on their ability to terminate an underfunded plan.

The Single Employer Pension Plan Amendments Act of 1986 (SEPPAA)

By September 30, 1985, the PBGC reported that the deficit in its single-employer insurance program was $1.3 billion, and growing rapidly. Congress responded by enacting SEPPAA. Major reforms under SEPPAA, which was included as title XI of the Consolidated Omnibus Budget Reconciliation Act of 1985 (P.L. 99–272), included:

1. Raising the per-participant premium to $8.50, from $2.60.

2. Providing that an underfunded plan may be terminated only if the contributing employer, and every member of the employer's controlled group, meets certain criteria of "financial distress". As a result, employers could not place the liability for underfunded plans on the PBGC without demonstrating real financial inability to maintain and fund the plan.

3. Providing that, in addition to the liability to the PBGC under prior law for the lesser of the unfunded guaranteed benefits or 30 percent of the collective net worth of the controlled group, employer liability also included the amount by which 75 percent of unfunded guaranteed benefits exceeded 30 percent of net worth.

4. Providing that unpaid and waived contributions were due and payable in full as of the date of termination.

5. Creating a new liability to plan participants for certain nonguaranteed benefits.

Pension Protection Act of 1987

By the beginning of 1987, it became increasingly apparent that the reforms implemented under SEPPAA were inadequate to ensure the long-term solvency of the PBGC. Accordingly, Congress enacted the Pension Protection Act of 1987 as part of the Omnibus Budget Reconciliation Act of 1987 (P.L. 100–203), which included a number of significant reforms:

1. *Variable rate premium.*—Increasing the basic premium to $16, and instituting an additional premium that rises with the degree of underfunding in the plan and, thus, the risk posed by the plan to the PBGC.

2. *Minimum funding standards.*—Requiring faster funding of unfunded benefits, to reduce the PBGC's exposure in the event of plan termination.

3. *Employer liability to the PBGC.*—Making the controlled group liable for minimum funding contributions to ongoing plans.

4. *Unpaid employer contributions.*—Improving the status of a claim for unpaid employer contributions in bankruptcy by giving such a claim the same status as a tax claim.

5. *Distress criteria.*—The use of Chapter 11 (bankruptcy reorganization) as a criterion for termination was tightened. The employer was now required to show that liquidation would necessarily follow if the plan were not terminated.

6. *Additional payments to participants.*—Section 4049 of ERISA was repealed. The full employer liability now runs solely to the PBGC. The PBGC will pay participants and beneficiaries a portion of their outstanding benefit liabilities (i.e., unfunded benefit liabilities that are not guaranteed benefits) from the PBGC's employer liability recovery.

The Act included additional significant reforms, including revised minimum funding rules, a quarterly pension funding requirement, a strengthening of the PBGC's lien authority, a reduction of the number of times an employer may "waive," or decline to make, otherwise required plan contributions, and other modifications.

MULTIEMPLOYER PLAN INSURANCE PROGRAM

Coverage for multiemployer plans under ERISA was structured similarly to that of single-employer plans. However, the PBGC was not required to insure benefits of multiemployer plans that terminated before July 1, 1978. Congress extended the deadline for mandatory pension coverage several times, until enactment of the Multiemployer Pension Plan Amendments Act of 1980, or MPPAA (P.L.

96–364). MPPAA required more complete funding for multiemployer plans, especially those in financial distress. It also improved the ability of plans to collect contributions from employers. MPPAA changed the insurable event that triggers PBGC protection to plan insolvency, rather than plan termination. Thus, if a multiemployer plan becomes financially unable to pay benefits at the guaranteed level when due, the PBGC will provide financial assistance to the plan, in the form of a loan. Finally, MPPAA imposed withdrawal liability on employers who ceased to contribute to a multiemployer plan.

BUDGETARY TREATMENT

Since 1981, administrative expenses of the PBGC and the benefit payments to participants in plans under the PBGC's trusteeship have been counted as Federal outlays. Certain receipts of the agency—including premium payments, interest on balances in the revolving fund, and transfers to the revolving fund from the trust fund—offset PBGC expenses in the Federal budget. Liabilities for future benefit payments and other accruals are not taken into account. In each year since 1981 (when the program was first included in the Federal budget) the effect of the PBGC has been to reduce overall Federal outlays (see table 17–3). During this period, the PBGC reported receipts in excess of benefit payments and administrative costs by a cumulative total of more than $4.4 billion. In years before 1981, Federal accounts for the PBGC would also have shown annual inflows exceeding expenses in each year of program operation. Under the present method of cash budgeting, the annual surpluses may obscure the impact of PBGC's growing future liabilities.

TABLE 17–3.—FEDERAL BUDGETARY TREATMENT OF THE PBGC, 1975–93

[In millions of dollars]

	Expenses [1]	Offsetting collec- tions [2]	Outlays appearing in the Federal budget [3]
Not included in the Federal budget [4]			
Fiscal year:			
1975	3.2	35.5	NA
1976	12.8	28.5	NA
1977	21.0	41.0	NA
1978	47.6	61.9	NA
1979	52.3	91.5	NA
1980	59.1	90.1	NA
Total	196.0	348.5	NA
Included in the Federal budget [4]			
Fiscal year:			
1981	79.4	123.1	− 29.0
1982	104.3	157.0	− 66.9
1983	161.2	182.4	− 9.5
1984	180.0	189.8	− 9.9
1985	195.3	210.4	− 19.1
1986	272.1	343.9	− 105.9
1987	508.6	636.8	− 71.9
1988	489.4	560.3	− 277.7
1989	779.8	1,190.1	− 149.1
1990	744.6	1,175.3	− 679.9
1991	598.7	1,339.4	− 787.3
1992	766.4	1,491.3	− 654.5
1993	833.3	2,323.2	− 1,508.2
Total	5,713.1	9,914.0	− 4,368.9

[1] Includes primarily administrative costs and benefit payments.

[2] Includes primarily premium income, interest income, and transfers from the pension insurance trust fund to the revolving fund.

[3] Outlays do not equal the difference between expenses and offsetting collections because of changes in obligated program balances between the beginning and the end of the fiscal year.

[4] The PBGC was first included in the Federal budget in 1981, in accordance with Public Law 96–364.

Note: This table includes both the single-employer and multiemployer pension insurance programs. (NA=not applicable.)

Source: Congressional Budget Office using data from the appendix to the Federal budget, various years.

FUTURE FINANCIAL STATUS OF THE PBGC

In its fiscal year 1993 annual report, PBGC estimated $53 billion of unfunded liabilities in single-employer defined benefit pension plans as of December 31, 1992, an increase from the $38 billion reported in 1992. Multiemployer plans represent $10.6 billion in underfunding as of January 1, 1991. The reasons for this growth include benefit increases in certain plans and falling interest rates.

Not all pension underfunding represents likely claims upon PBGC's insurance. PBGC's most recent analyses disclose reasonable possible losses of about $13 billion, compared to last year's $12 billion. This exposure is concentrated in a relatively small number of companies, primarily in the automobile, steel, tire, and airline industries.

PBGC annually publishes a list of 50 companies with the largest pension underfunding. PBGC's most recent listing showed unfunded vested benefits among the 50 companies as of December 31, 1992 of $38.0 billion, an increase of 30 percent from the prior year. The data was verified with the companies named on the list and is based on publicly available information. Experience has indicated, however, that PBGC's losses after a plan terminates often exceed estimated amounts because of lower contributions prior to plan termination and more early retirements than anticipated.

Historically, most of the claims made against PBGC have come from flat-benefit plans that cover hourly workers in unionized companies. Because benefits are often increased at regular intervals as part of contract negotiations, new liabilities are added before old ones are funded, leaving the plans chronically underfunded. The current-law funding rules, which require funding based on current legal obligations, do not allow flat-benefit plans to anticipate yet-to-be bargained future benefit increases.

In contrast, final-pay or final-salary plans are almost always overfunded relative to insured termination liabilities because their funding schedules anticipate ever-increasing salaries, and therefore, future benefit levels. Consequently, typical final-pay plans have funding ratios of 120 percent, while flat-benefit plans typically are 77 percent funded. Therefore, the average final-pay plan can absorb considerable changes in interest rates, actuarial assumptions, and investment performance without posing exposure to PBGC. Flat-benefit plans cannot.

The future financial condition of the pension insurance program is highly uncertain because it will depend largely on how many private pension plans terminate and on the amount of underfunding in those plans. Both factors are hard to forecast accurately. Moreover, as was discussed above, a few pension plans with extremely large unfunded liabilities have dominated PBGC's past claims, and its future may likewise depend significantly on the fate of a few large plans, making liabilities even more difficult to predict. Future terminations will probably be influenced by overall economic conditions, by the prosperity of particular industries, by competition from abroad, and by a variety of factors that are specific to particular firms—such as their competitive position in the industry, their agreements with labor groups, and the assessments of their financial prospects that are necessary to obtain credit. In addition, PBGC's losses with respect to future terminations will depend on how well companies fund their plans, and on the PBGC's position in bankruptcy proceedings. Finally, pending litigation could have a material impact on the financial condition of the PBGC.

The PBGC in its fiscal year 1993 annual report presented three different forecasts of future claims and resulting deficits and surpluses to indicate the potential variability of its financial condition.

Forecast A is based on the average annual net claim over the entire PBGC history ($505 million per year) and projects a deficit of $1.9 billion by the end of fiscal year 2003. Forecast B is based on the average annual net claim for the most recent 12 fiscal years ($695 million per year). Under Forecast B, PBGC's projected deficit would grow to $5 billion by the end of fiscal year 2003. Forecast C assumes $1.2 billion of net claims each year and assumes that termination of the plans with approximately $13 billion of underfunding that represent reasonably possible losses will occur over the next 10 years. Under Forecast C, PBGC's deficit is projected to reach $13.8 billion by the end of fiscal year 2003.

TABLE 17–4.—YEAR-BY-YEAR PROJECTIONS OF PBGC DEFICITS UNDER VARIOUS FORECASTS, SINGLE-EMPLOYER PROGRAM [1]

[Amounts as of September 30; in billions of dollars]

	Forecast A	Forecast B	Forecast C
1993	2.9	2.9	2.9
1994	2.7	2.9	3.5
1995	2.5	2.9	4.1
1996	2.3	3.0	4.9
1997	2.2	3.1	5.8
1998	2.0	3.3	6.8
1999	1.9	3.5	7.9
2000	1.8	3.8	9.1
2001	1.8	4.1	10.5
2002	1.8	4.5	12.1
2003	1.9	5.0	13.8

[1] PBGC's fiscal year-end deficit equals the amount by which PBGC's liabilities exceed PBGC's assets. The largest component of PBGC's total liabilities is the present value of future benefit payments, including amounts owed to participants in terminated plans and plans with a high probability of termination.

Source: PBGC.

PBGC's current method of forecasting future claims is based on PBGC's experience over the last decade. This method fails to take into account the uncertainty facing PBGC regarding future economic conditions. Because of the limitations of the current method, PBGC is building a simulation model to improve understanding of the uncertainty of its future claims forecasts. The model is being designed to simulate bankruptcy rates and pension funding over a 30-year period and will forecast PBGC's financial conditions over a broad set of possible economic scenarios. PBGC anticipates its model will measure the uncertainty surrounding forecasts of future claims, and also will have the capacity to measure the impact of various proposals to change PBGC's program.

RECENT CONGRESSIONAL AGENCY OVERSIGHT REPORTS

In response to growing concerns about the financial stability of the PBGC, the agency has been the subject of oversight investigation by the Congressional Budget Office (CBO), the General Accounting Office (GAO), and by the Congressional Research Service (CRS).

On February 4, 1993, CBO released its report, "Controlling Losses of the Pension Benefit Guaranty Corporation." The report examines the causes of PBGC's losses and offers options for reforming the program. The report concludes that the PBGC currently has $2.5 billion more in liabilities than it has in assets, and that, without reform, this deficit can be expected to increase by tens of billions of dollars. CBO notes that there is no serious possibility that the Federal Government will allow the PBGC to default on its obligations to plan participants, but that the prospect of a taxpayer-financed bailout is increasingly likely.

CBO offers three major reasons for the persistent and increasing PBGC losses. First, the PBGC premiums are too low to cover the administrative costs and underfunding associated with terminated, insured plans. Second, the Employee Retirement Income Security Act of 1974 (ERISA) permits companies to underfund their defined benefit pension plans. Third, neither the PBGC nor the Congress have established a system to properly assess and manage the losses that inevitably result from permitting companies to underfund their plans.

Finally, CBO offers several suggestions to help ensure fiscal balance in the PBGC insurance system. CBO notes that over the short-term Congress must make adjustments to ensure that PBGC has sufficient assets with which to meet its pension liabilities. Over the long-term Congress must improve the structural capacity of the Federal Government to operate the pension insurance program by gathering better information about risks, giving immediate budget recognition to these liabilities as they accrue, allowing PBGC to adjust premiums more quickly to reflect changes in risks of loss in the system, and by requiring that private capital be at least partially at risk to increase the incentive of companies to monitor and control losses under the pension insurance program.

On December 30, 1992, GAO released its report, "Hidden Liabilities Increase Claims Against Government Insurance Program" (GAO/HRD 93–7). The report reviews the factors that cause hidden liabilities, assesses the impact of these factors on recent claims against the pension insurance program, and analyzes PBGC's ability to control these factors.

The report concludes that the Federal Government's exposure to unfunded liabilities in private pension plans is much larger than plans have indicated on their annual reports to the Internal Revenue Service (IRS). In a survey of 44 terminated pension plans trusteed by the PBGC, underfunding was $1 billion (58 percent) higher at the time of termination than most recently reported to the IRS. Therefore, when a pension plan terminates with insufficient assets, PBGC is likely to absorb unfunded liabilities considerably greater than the plan previously reported.

GAO found that 80 percent of this discrepancy was due to differences in actuarial assumptions used to value plan liabilities, the payment of special shutdown and early retirement benefits, and earlier-than-anticipated retirements of plan participants. The remaining 20 percent of the hidden liabilities were due to PBGC's receipt of fewer assets than reported by the plan primarily as the result of benefit payments from the plan and missed contributions to the plan.

GAO found that PBGC has little ability to control its exposure from these hidden liabilities. Further, GAO found that financially troubled plan sponsors sometimes take actions that increase the burden on PBGC, such as raising benefits in lieu of increasing wages or failing to make contributions to their plans. In subsequent congressional testimony, GAO reported that in a separate review of the underfunded pension plans sponsored by eight companies with significantly underfunded pension plans during the 1990–91 time period, it found that aggregate underfunding increased by over $5 billion, of which nearly $2.2 billion was attributable to benefit increases in these plans.

On February 1, 1993, CRS released its report "Are Pension Guarantees Another Savings and Loan Collapse in the Making?" (93–121 EPW). In this report, CRS examines the similarities and differences between PBGC today and the Federal Savings and Loan Insurance Corporation (FSLIC) in the years before the S&L collapse. The report concludes that while not strictly analogous, there are similarities. CRS notes that just as deposit insurance weakened the incentive of depositors to remove funds from risky thrifts, pension insurance creates a similar "moral hazard" incentive for pension plan sponsors and participants to allow plans to become underfunded. In addition, just as FSLIC was reluctant to act promptly to shut down insolvent thrifts, the PBGC is reluctant to cut its losses by terminating pension plans. Finally, the primary financial information presented to Congress in the Federal budget for the ill-fated FSLIC was, and for PBGC is, short-term cash flows that do not reflect the long-term liabilities that are accruing and can fail to give an indication of a deteriorating long-term situation.

The CRS report concludes by noting that the PBGC has only limited power to act on information about its own financial health since Congress has set in statute PBGC premiums and rules governing pension insurance and plan funding standards. The PBGC has limited control over its financial condition, and ultimately the solvency of the PBGC depends on how Congress responds to information about the financial status of the pension program. Unless significant changes are made in the way pension insurance is priced and benefits funded, it may be necessary to curtail the pension promises that the Government guarantees. Otherwise, taxpayer revenue ultimately may be needed.

Section 18. Description of Other Major Federal Assistance Programs Not Within the Jurisdiction of the Committee on Ways and Means

Several Federal programs outside of the jurisdiction of the Committee on Ways and Means provide benefits to some share of those people who also benefit from assistance programs that are within the jurisdiction of the committee. This appendix describes several such programs: food stamps; Medicaid; housing assistance; school lunch and breakfast programs; the supplemental food program for Women, Infants, and Children (WIC); assistance provided under the Job Training Partnership Act; Head Start; the Low-Income Home Energy Assistance Program (LIHEAP); Veterans' Benefits and Services Programs; and Workers' Compensation programs.

Most families receiving AFDC would have incomes low enough to qualify them—or particular members of their families—for assistance under these programs. Unlike the principal assistance programs under the jurisdiction of the Committee on Ways and Means, participation in Head Start, LIHEAP, and other programs are limited either by appropriations, or, in the case of the school feeding programs, by the willingness of schools to participate. Income received from AFDC is counted in determining eligibility for these programs—as well as benefit levels, in some cases. However, because these programs provide in-kind rather than cash assistance, benefits received under these programs are not counted in determining eligibility for AFDC.

Tables 18–1 and 18–2 describe the overlap in recipients between programs within the jurisdiction of the Committee on Ways and Means and other major Federal assistance programs. Table 18–1 illustrates that 86.2 percent of AFDC recipient households received food stamps some time during the first quarter of 1992; 21.5 percent received WIC; 96.2 percent received Medicaid, 55.5 percent received free or reduced-price school meals; and 29.5 percent received housing assistance of some form.

Table 18–2 illustrates the reverse. For example, 47.5 percent of food stamp households received AFDC benefits at some time during the first quarter of 1992; 24.8 percent of food stamp households received SSI; and 6.4 percent of food stamp households received unemployment compensation benefits.

TABLE 18–1.—PERCENT OF RECIPIENTS IN PROGRAMS WITHIN THE JURISDICTION OF THE COMMITTEE ON WAYS AND MEANS RECEIVING ASSISTANCE FROM OTHER MAJOR FEDERAL ASSISTANCE PROGRAMS

[Households, first quarter of 1992]

	AFDC	SSI	Social Security	Unemployment compensation	Medicare
Number of households receiving benefits (in thousands)	4,057	3,957	26,688	4,502	24,084
Percent receiving:					
Food stamps	86.2	46.2	7.3	10.4	6.6
WIC	21.5	4.3	0.8	4.0	0.7
Free or reduced-price school meals	55.5	18.2	3.7	12.7	2.4
Public or subsidized rental housing	29.5	23.8	7.5	3.9	7.8
Medicaid	96.2	99.8	13.8	14.2	14.0
VA compensation or pensions	1.9	4.0	6.5	2.2	6.9

Note: Table reads that 86.2 percent of AFDC households, also receive food stamps. The 994,000 SSI recepients living in California receive a higher SSI payment in lieu of food stamps, and thus are not included in the food stamp percentages.

Source: U.S. Bureau of the Census, Survey of Income and Program Participation.

TABLE 18–2.—PERCENT OF RECIPIENTS IN OTHER MAJOR FEDERAL ASSISTANCE PROGRAMS RECEIVING ASSISTANCE UNDER PROGRAMS WITHIN THE JURISDICTION OF THE COMMITTEE ON WAYS AND MEANS

[Households, first quarter of 1992]

	Food stamps	WIC	Free or reduced school meals	Public or subsidized rental housing	Medicaid	VA compensation or pensions
Number of households receiving benefits (in thousands)	7,358	2,500	7,982	4,871	10,533	2,699
Percent receiving:						
AFDC	47.5	34.8	28.2	24.6	37.0	2.8
SSI	24.8	6.8	9.0	19.3	37.5	5.9
Social Security	26.4	8.8	12.5	40.9	34.9	64.6
Unemployment compensation	6.4	7.2	7.2	3.6	6.1	3.7
Medicare	21.5	6.3	7.1	38.7	32	61.8

Note: Table reads that 47.5 percent of food stamp recipient households receive AFDC. The 994,000 SSI recepients living in California receive a higher SSI payment in lieu of food stamps, and thus are not included in the food stamp percentages.

Source: U.S. Bureau of the Census, Survey of Income and Program Participation.

Table 18–3 illustrates the percentage of households receiving AFDC or SSI and also receiving assistance from other programs for selected time periods. This table is constructed from table 18–1 in previous editions of this document. As shown in table 18–3, the number of households receiving AFDC and SSI benefits in the first quarter of 1991 has increased significantly in comparison to earlier years. In the first quarter of 1992, the number of households receiving SSI benefits had another significant increase, while the number of AFDC households stayed relatively constant.

The percentage of households receiving other benefits has fluctuated over the period. For most types of benefits, there is no discernible pattern, and the percentage has remained consistently the same. The one exception to this general rule is the percentage of AFDC households also receiving public or subsidized rental housing. Between the second quarter of 1987 and the first quarter of 1990, the percentage of AFDC households receiving housing benefits increased from 19.4 percent to 34.7 percent. The percentage had dropped down again slightly by the first quarter of 1992.

TABLE 18–3.—PERCENT OF HOUSEHOLDS RECEIVING AFDC OR SSI AND ALSO RECEIVING ASSISTANCE FROM OTHER PROGRAMS FOR SELECTED TIME PERIODS

	1984	1986	1987	1988	1990	1991	1992
Quarter	4	1	2	4	1	1	1
AFDC:							
Number of households receiving benefits (in thousands)	3,585	3,617	3,527	3,329	3,434	4,051	4,057
Percent receiving:							
Food Stamps	81.4	80.3	81.7	84.6	82.7	84.6	86.2
WIC	15.3	15.1	18.6	19.1	18.7	16.3	21.5
Free or reduced-price school meals	49.2	50.5	55.6	52.5	52.7	52.2	55.5
Public or subsidized rental housing	23.0	24.8	19.4	31.3	34.7	31.5	29.5
Medicaid	93.2	95.2	95.5	95.6	97.6	96.9	96.2
VA compensation or pensions	2.8	1.7	1.9	.9	1.3	2.4	1.9
SSI:							
Number of households receiving benefits (in thousands)	3,008	3,110	3,341	3,186	3,037	3,593	3,957
Percent receiving:							
Food Stamps	46.5	44.7	39.7	42.2	41.3	44.3	46.2
WIC	2.5	2.7	2.5	2.5	3.0	2.2	4.3
Free or reduced-price school meals	12.7	14.7	11.9	15.5	15.3	17.5	18.2
Public or subsidized rental housing	21.6	20.7	20.0	22.2	21.4	24.9	23.8
Medicaid	100.0	100.0	99.6	99.6	99.7	99.6	99.8
VA compensation or pensions	4.7	5.2	7.7	6.1	5.7	3.1	4.0

Note: The 994,000 SSI recepients living in California receive a higher SSI payment in lieu of food stamps, and thus are not included in the food stamp percentages.

FOOD STAMP PROGRAM

Food stamps are designed primarily to increase the food purchasing power of eligible low-income households to a point where they can buy a nutritionally adequate low-cost diet. Participating households are expected to be able to devote 30 percent of their counted monthly cash income to food purchases.[1] Food stamp benefits then make up the difference between the household's expected contribution to its food costs and an amount judged to be sufficient to buy an adequate low-cost diet. This amount, the maximum food stamp benefit level, is derived from the U.S. Department of Agriculture's lowest-cost food plan (the Thrifty Food Plan), varied by household size, and adjusted annually for inflation. Thus, a participating household with no counted cash income receives the maximum monthly allotment for its household size, intended to enable it to purchase an adequate low-cost diet with its food stamps alone, while one with some counted income receives a lesser allotment, normally reduced from the maximum at the rate of 30 cents for each dollar of counted income and intended to enable it to purchase an adequate low-cost diet with a combination of food stamps and its own cash.

Benefits are available to nearly all households that meet Federal eligibility tests for limited monthly income and liquid assets, as long as certain household members fulfill work registration and employment and training program requirements. In addition, recipients in the two primary Federal/State cash welfare programs, the AFDC and SSI programs, generally are automatically eligible for food stamps, as are recipients of State general assistance payments, if the household is composed entirely of AFDC, SSI, or general assistance beneficiaries.[2]

ADMINISTRATION, PROGRAM VARIATIONS, AND FUNDING

The regular Food Stamp program operates in all 50 States, the District of Columbia, Guam, and the Virgin Islands. The Federal Government is responsible for virtually all of the rules that govern the program and, with limited variations for Alaska, Hawaii, and the territories, these rules are nationally uniform. States, the District of Columbia, and the territories may choose to offer the program or not. However, if they do offer food stamp assistance, it must be made available throughout the jurisdiction and comply with Federal rules. Sales taxes on food stamp purchases may not be charged, and food stamp benefits do not affect other assistance available to low-income households, nor are they taxed as income.

Alternative programs are offered in Puerto Rico and the Northern Mariana Islands, and program variations occur in a number of demonstration projects and in those jurisdictions that have elected to exercise the limited number of program options allowed.

Funding is overwhelmingly Federal, although the States and other jurisdictions have financial responsibility for significant ad-

---

[1] Because not all of a household's income is actually counted when determining its food stamp benefits, the program, in effect, assumes that most participants are able to spend about 20 percent of their total cash monthly income on food.

[2] Except for SSI recipients in California, where a State-financed adjustment to SSI benefits has replaced food stamp assistance, and general assistance programs that do not meet certain Federal standards.

ministrative costs, as well as liability for erroneous benefit determinations (as assessed under the food stamp "quality control" system).

Federal administrative responsibilities

At the Federal level, the program is administered by the Agriculture Department's Food and Nutrition Service (FNS). The FNS gives direction to welfare agencies through Federal regulations that define eligibility requirements, benefit levels, and administrative rules. It is also responsible for (1) printing food stamp coupons and distributing them to welfare agencies and (2) approving, and overseeing participation by retail food stores and other outlets that may accept food stamps. Other Federal agencies that have administrative roles to play include: the Federal Reserve System (through which food stamps are redeemed for cash, and which has some jurisdiction over "electronic benefit transfer" methods for issuing food stamp benefits), the Social Security Administration (responsible for the social security numbers recipients must have, provision of limited application "intake" services, and providing information to verify recipients' income), the Internal Revenue Service (providing assistance in verifying recipients' income and assets), and the Immigration and Naturalization Service (helping welfare offices confirm alien applicants' status).

State and local administrative responsibilities

States, the District of Columbia, Guam, and the Virgin Islands, through their local welfare offices, have primary responsibility for the day-to-day administration of the Food Stamp program. They determine eligibility, calculate benefits, and issue food stamp allotments following Federal rules. They also have a significant say about carrying out employment and training programs and some administrative features of the program (e.g., the extent to which verification of household circumstances is pursued, the method by which food stamps are issued). Most often, the Food Stamp program is operated through the same welfare agency and staff that runs the Federal/State AFDC and Medicaid programs.

Puerto Rico and the Northern Mariana Islands

In addition to the regular Food Stamp program, the Food Stamp Act directs funding for a nutrition assistance program in the Commonwealth of Puerto Rico. Separate legislation authorizes a variant of the Food Stamp program in the Commonwealth of the Northern Mariana Islands.

Since July 1982, Puerto Rico has operated a nutrition assistance program of its own design, funded by an annual Federal "block grant." [3] The Commonwealth's nutrition assistance program differs from the regular Food Stamp program primarily in that: (1) funding is limited to an annual amount specified by law; [4] (2) the Food Stamp Act allows the Commonwealth a great deal of flexibility in

---

[3] Prior to July 1982, the regular Food Stamp program operated in Puerto Rico, although with slightly different eligibility and benefit rules.

[4] For fiscal year 1993, $1.051 billion was earmarked; approximately $30 million of this amount was used to fund 2 special projects—a cattle tick eradication program and a wage-subsidy program. The block grant funds the full cost of benefits and half the cost of administration.

program design, as opposed to the regular program's extensive Federal rules; (3) benefits are paid in cash (checks) rather than food stamp coupons; (4) income and liquid assets eligibility limits are about half those used in the regular Food Stamp program; (5) maximum benefit levels are about one-quarter less than in the 48 contiguous States and the District of Columbia; and (6) different rules are used in counting income for eligibility and benefit purposes. In fiscal year 1993, Puerto Rico's nutrition assistance program aided approximately 1.44 million persons each month with monthly benefits averaging $58 a person.

Under the terms of the 1976 Covenant with the Commonwealth of the Northern Mariana Islands and implementing legislation (P.L. 96–597), a variant of the Food Stamp program was negotiated with the Commonwealth and began operations in July 1982. The program in the Northern Marianas differs primarily in that: (1) it is funded entirely by Federal money, up to a maximum grant of $3.7 million a year; (2) a portion of each household's food stamp benefit must be used to purchase locally produced food; (3) maximum allotments are about 20 percent higher than in the 48 contiguous States and the District of Columbia; and (4) income eligibility limits are about half those in the regular program. In fiscal year 1993, the Northern Marianas' program assisted some 2,900 people each month with monthly benefits averaging $72 a person.

Program options

The Food Stamp Act authorizes demonstration projects to test program variations that might improve operations.[5] In addition, States are allowed to implement a few optional aspects of the Food Stamp program. States may require "monthly reporting" and "retrospective budgeting" for parts of their food stamp caseload. They may disregard the first $50 a month in child support payments, if they pay the benefit cost of doing so. States or localities may choose to run "workfare" programs, and State welfare agencies exercise primary responsibility in the design of food stamp employment and training programs. And States can operate "outreach" programs, with Federal cost-sharing, to inform low-income persons about food stamps.

Funding

The Food Stamp Act provides 100 percent Federal funding of food stamp benefits. The Federal Government is also responsible for its own administrative costs: overseeing program operations (including oversight of participating food establishments), printing and distributing food stamp coupons to welfare agencies, redeeming

---

[5] At present, eight types of demonstration projects are underway: (1) "cashout" projects for the elderly and SSI recipients, (2) "electronic benefit transfer" projects testing alternative methods of benefit delivery, (3) projects providing cash benefits to very poor households who are eligible for expedited service, (4) projects testing simplified AFDC/FS application and benefit determination procedures, (5) "welfare reform" demonstrations testing various combinations of standardized AFDC/FS rules, cashing out food stamp benefits, and merging AFDC/FS rules and benefits, (6) a project granting quarterly (instead of monthly) benefit payments to SSI recipients eligible for very small benefits, (7) demonstrations conforming the operations of the AFDC JOBS program and the food stamp program's employment and training activities, and (8) awards to nonprofit organizations to test ways to improve program responsiveness to specific target groups in the low-income population.

food stamp coupons through the Federal Reserve, and payments to the Social Security Administration for certain intake services.

In most instances, the Federal Government provides half the cost of State welfare agency administration, including the cost of optional outreach activities.[6] The 50-percent Federal share can be increased to as much as 60 percent where the State has a very low rate of erroneous benefit determinations. And, the cost of carrying out employment and training programs for food stamp recipients is shared in two ways: (1) each State receives a Federal grant for basic operating costs (a formula share of $75 million a year) and (2) additional operating costs, as well as expenses for support services to participants (e.g., transportation, child care) are eligible for a 50-percent Federal match.[7] Finally, States are allowed to retain a portion of improperly issued benefits that they recover (other than those caused by welfare agency error): 25 percent of recoveries in fraud cases and 10 percent in other circumstances.

---

[6] Until April 1994, the cost of certain activities was matched at more than the 50-percent rate: costs associated with the development of computer capability and fraud control activities were eligible for 63 and 75 percent Federal sharing, respectively; costs for implementing the Systematic Alien Verification for Entitlements (SAVE) program were fully reimbursed by the Federal Government.

[7] The Federal 50-percent share for support services is limited. Coverage extends to (1) dependent care costs up to $160 per dependent per month and (2) other expenses (e.g., transportation) up to $25 per participant per month. Beginning in September 1994, States will be allowed to set their own limits on dependent care costs eligible for Federal matching, so long as they are not higher than local market rates.

TABLE 18-4.—RECENT FOOD STAMP ACT EXPENDITURES

[In millions of dollars]

Fiscal year	Benefits [2] (Federal)	Administration [1]		Total
		Federal	State and local	
1979	6,480	515	388	7,383
1980	8,685	503	375	9,563
1981	10,630	678	504	11,812
1982	10,408	709	557	11,674
1983	11,955	778	612	13,345
1984	11,499	971	805	13,275
1985	11,556	1,043	871	13,470
1986	11,415	1,113	935	13,463
1987	11,344	1,195	996	13,535
1988	11,999	1,290	1,080	14,369
1989	12,483	1,332	1,101	14,916
1990	15,090	1,422	1,174	17,686
1991	18,249	1,516	1,247	21,012
1992	21,883	1,656	1,375	24,914
1993	23,032	1,774	1,498	26,304

[1] All Federal administrative costs associated with the Food Stamp program and Puerto Rico's block grant are included: Federal matching for the various administrative and employment and training expenses of States and other jurisdictions, and direct Federal administrative costs. Figures for Federal administrative costs beginning with fiscal year 1989 include only those paid out of food stamp appropriation and the food stamp portion of the general appropriation for food program administration. Figures for earlier years include estimates of food stamp related Federal administrative expenses paid out of other Agriculture Department accounts.

State and local costs are estimated based on the known Federal shares and represent an estimate of all administrative expenses of participating States and other jurisdictions (including Puerto Rico).

[2] All benefit costs associated with the Food Stamp program and Puerto Rico's block grant are included. The benefit amounts shown in the table reflect small downward adjustments for overpayments collected from recipients and, beginning in 1989, issued but unredeemed benefits. Over time, the figures reflect both changes in benefit levels and numbers of recipients.

Source: Budget documents prepared by the FNS. Compiled by the Congressional Research Service.

ELIGIBILITY

The Food Stamp program has financial, employment/training-related, and "categorical" tests for eligibility. Its financial tests require that most of those eligible have monthly income and liquid assets below limits set by food stamp law. Under the employment/training-related tests, certain household members must register for work, accept suitable job offers, and fulfill work or training requirements (such as looking or training for a job) established by State welfare agencies. The limited number of categorical eligibility rules make some automatically eligible for food stamps (most AFDC, SSI, and general assistance recipients), and categorically deny eligibility to others (e.g., strikers, illegal and temporarily resident aliens, those living in institutional settings). Applications cannot be denied because of the length of a household's residence in a welfare agency's jurisdiction or because it has no fixed mailing address or does not reside in a permanent dwelling.

The food stamp household

The basic food stamp beneficiary unit is the "household." A food stamp household can be either a person living alone or a group of individuals living together; there is no requirement for cooking facilities. It is unrelated to recipient units in other welfare programs (e.g., AFDC families with dependent children, elderly or disabled individuals and couples in the SSI program).

Generally speaking, individuals living together constitute a single food stamp household, if they customarily purchase food and prepare meals in common. Members of the same household must apply together, and their income, expenses, and assets normally are aggregated in determining food stamp eligibility and benefits. However, persons who live together can sometimes be considered *separate* households for food stamp purposes, some related co-residents are required to apply *together,* and special rules apply to those living together in *institutional* settings. Most often, persons living together receive larger aggregate benefits if they are treated as more than one food stamp household. In determining whether co-residents are treated as separate households, the following rules are applied.

Unrelated co-residents may apply and be treated as separate households if they purchase food and prepare meals separately (this includes roomers and live-in attendants).

As with unrelated persons, *elderly or disabled adults* (together with their spouses)[8] and *parents of minor children* (together with their children) may apply and be treated separately from any other related co-residents, if they purchase food and prepare meals separately. Moreover, elderly persons who live with others and *cannot* purchase food and prepare meals separately because of a substantial disability may apply and be treated separately from their co-residents, as long as their co-residents' income is below prescribed limits.

On the other hand, separate household treatment is *barred* for certain related co-residents, regardless of how food is purchased and meals are prepared:

— Co-resident spouses may not apply and be treated separately;
— Children under 18 and their co-resident parent(s) or caretaker(s) may not apply and be treated separately, although persons caring for foster children may opt to exclude the child(ren) from their household unit, and categorically ineligible parents (e.g., certain aliens) may apply on behalf of their otherwise eligible children;
— Except for the elderly, disabled, and parents with minor children, closely related adult co-residents (i.e., parents and their adult children, brothers and sisters) may not apply and be treated separately.

Effective September 1994, the definition of a food stamp household is revised to provide that persons who live together, but purchase food and prepare meals separately, may apply separately, except for: (1) spouses, (2) parents and their children (21 years or

---

[8] In the Food Stamp program, "elderly" persons are those age 60 or older. The "disabled" generally are beneficiaries of governmental disability-based assistance (e.g., social security or SSI disability recipients, disabled veterans, certain disability retirement annuitants, recipients of disability-based Medicaid or general assistance).

younger), other than children who themselves have a spouse or children, and (3) minors 18 years or younger (excluding foster children) who live under the parental control of a caretaker.

Finally, although those living in institutional settings generally are barred from food stamps, individuals in certain types of group living arrangements may be eligible and are automatically treated as separate households, regardless of how food is purchased and meals are prepared. These arrangements must be approved by State or local agencies and include: residential drug addict or alcoholic treatment programs, small group homes for the disabled, shelters for battered women and children, and shelters for the homeless.

Thus, different food stamp households can live together, food stamp recipients can reside with nonrecipients, and food stamp households themselves may be "mixed" (include recipients and nonrecipients of other welfare benefits).

Income eligibility

Except for households composed entirely of AFDC, SSI, or general assistance recipients (who generally are automatically eligible for food stamps), *monthly cash income* is the primary food stamp eligibility determinant.[9]

In establishing eligibility for households *without an elderly or disabled member,* the Food Stamp program uses both the household's *basic* (or "gross") monthly income and its *counted* (or "net") monthly income.

When judging eligibility for households *with elderly or disabled members,* only the household's *counted* monthly income is considered; in effect, this applies a more liberal income test to elderly and disabled households.

Basic (or gross) monthly income includes all of a household's *cash* income, only excepting the following "exclusions" (disregards): (1) most payments made to third parties (rather than directly to the household);[10] (2) unanticipated, irregular, or infrequent income, up to $30 a quarter; (3) loans (deferred repayment student loans are treated as student aid, see below); (4) income received for the care of someone outside the household; (5) nonrecurring lump-sum payments such as income tax refunds and retroactive lump-sum social security payments (these are instead counted as liquid assets); (6) energy assistance; (7) expense reimbursements that are not a "gain or benefit" to the household; (8) income earned by schoolchildren; (9) the cost of producing self-employment income; (10) Federal postsecondary student aid (e.g., Pell grants, student loans)[11] (11) advance payments of Federal earned income tax credits; (12) "on-the-job" training earnings of dependent children under 19 in Job Training Partnership Act (JTPA) programs, as well as JTPA monthly "allowances;" (13) income set aside by disabled SSI recipients under an approved "plan to achieve self-sufficiency" (PASS); and

---

[9] Although they do not have to meet food stamp income and assets tests, AFDC, SSI, and general assistance households must still have their income calculated under food stamp rules to determine their food stamp *benefits.*

[10] Some third-party ("vendor") payments for normal living expenses are *not* disregarded.

[11] Postsecondary student aid other than Federal aid is disregarded to the extent that it is used or earmarked for tuition, mandatory school fees or expenses, loan origination fees, and miscellaneous education-related expenses.

(14) payments required to be disregarded by provisions of Federal law outside the Food Stamp Act (e.g., various payments under laws relating to Indians, payments under the Older Americans Act employment program for the elderly).

Counted (or net) monthly income is computed by subtracting certain "deductions" from a household's basic (or gross) monthly income. It recognizes that not all of a household's income is equally available for food purchases by disregarding a standard portion of income, plus amounts representing work expenses or excessively high non-food living expenses.

For households *without an elderly or disabled member,* counted monthly income equals their basic (gross) monthly income less the following deductions:

—an inflation-indexed (each October) "standard deduction" set at $131 a month in fiscal year 1994, regardless of household size; [12]

—20 percent of any earned income, in recognition of taxes and work expenses;

—out-of-pocket dependent care expenses, when related to work or training, up to $160 a month per dependent, rising to $200 a month for children under age 2 and $175 a month for other dependents in September 1994; and

—any shelter expenses, to the extent they *exceed* 50 percent of counted income after all other deductions, up to a periodically adjusted ceiling standing at $207 a month from October 1993 through June 1994, and rising to $231 in July 1994. [13]

For households *with an elderly or disabled member,* counted monthly income equals their basic (gross) monthly income less the following deductions:

—the same standard, earned income, and dependent care deductions noted above;

—any shelter expenses, to the extent they exceed 50 percent of counted income after all other deductions, *with no limit;* and

—any out-of-pocket medical expenses (other than those for special diets) that are incurred by an elderly or disabled household member, to the extent they exceed a "threshold" of $35 a month.

Finally, during fiscal year 1995, States will implement a newly enacted additional deduction: households will be allowed to deduct any amounts paid as legally obligated child support.

Except for those households comprised entirely of AFDC, SSI, or general assistance recipients, in which case food stamp eligibility generally is automatic, all households must have counted (net) monthly income that does not exceed the Federal poverty guidelines, as adjusted for inflation each October. Households without an elderly or disabled member also must have basic (gross) monthly income that does not exceed 130 percent of the inflation-adjusted Federal poverty guidelines. Both these income eligibility limits are uniform for the 48 contiguous States, the District of Columbia,

---

[12] Different standard deductions are used for Alaska ($223), Hawaii ($185), Guam ($262), and the Virgin Islands ($115).

[13] Different ceilings prevail in Alaska, Hawaii, Guam, and the Virgin Islands. Through June 1994, they are $359, $295, $251, and $152; in July 1994, they will rise to $402, $330, $280, and $171.

Guam, and the Virgin Islands; somewhat higher limits (based on higher poverty guidelines) are applied in Alaska and Hawaii.

TABLE 18–5.—COUNTED (NET) AND BASIC (GROSS) MONTHLY INCOME ELIGIBILITY LIMITS

[Effective October 1993 through September 1994]

Household size	48 States, D.C., and the territories	Alaska	Hawaii
COUNTED (NET) MONTHLY INCOME ELIGIBILITY LIMITS [1]			
1 person	$581	$725	$670
2 persons	786	982	905
3 persons	991	1,239	1,140
4 persons	1,196	1,495	1,375
5 persons	1,401	1,752	1,610
6 persons	1,606	2,009	1,845
7 persons	1,811	2,265	2,080
8 persons	2,016	2,522	2,315
Each additional person	+205	+257	+235
BASIC (GROSS) MONTHLY INCOME ELIGIBILITY LIMITS [2]			
1 person	$756	$943	$871
2 persons	1,022	1,277	1,177
3 persons	1,289	1,610	1,482
4 persons	1,555	1,944	1,788
5 persons	1,822	2,278	2,093
6 persons	2,088	2,611	2,399
7 persons	2,355	2,945	2,704
8 persons	2,621	3,279	3,010
Each additional person	+267	+334	+306

[1] Set at the applicable Federal poverty guidelines, updated for inflation through calendar 1992.
[2] Set at 130 percent of the applicable Federal poverty guidelines, updated for inflation through calendar 1992.

Allowable assets

Except for those households who are automatically eligible for food stamps because they are composed entirely of AFDC, SSI, or general assistance recipients, eligible households must have *counted "liquid" assets* that do not exceed federally prescribed limits. Households without an elderly member cannot have counted liquid assets above $2,000. Households with an elderly member cannot have counted liquid assets above $3,000.

Counted liquid assets include cash on hand, checking and savings accounts, savings certificates, stocks and bonds, individual retirement accounts (IRAs) and "Keogh" plans (less any early withdrawal penalties), and nonrecurring lump-sum payments such as insurance settlements. Certain "less liquid" assets are also counted: a portion of the value of vehicles (generally, the "fair market value" in excess of $4,500) and the equity value of property not producing income consistent with its value (e.g., recreational property).

Counted assets *do not include* the value of the household's residence (home and surrounding property), business assets, personal property (household goods and personal effects), lump-sum earned income tax credit payments, burial plots, the cash value of life insurance policies and pension plans (other than Keogh plans and IRAs), and certain other resources whose value is not accessible to the household or are required to be disregarded by other Federal laws.

Work registration and employment and training program requirements

Unless exempt, adult applicants for food stamps must register for work, typically with the welfare agency or a State employment service office. To maintain eligibility, they must accept a suitable job if offered one and fulfill any work, "job search," or training requirements established by administering welfare agencies. If the household head fails to fulfill any of these requirements, the entire household is disqualified, typically for 2 months; in other cases, failure to comply disqualifies the noncomplying household member only.

Those who are *exempt by law* from work registration, having to accept a suitable job offer, and employment and training program requirements (work, job search, training) include: persons physically or mentally unfit for work, those under age 16 or age 60 or older, and individuals between 16 and 18 (if they are not head of household or are attending school or a training program); persons working at least 30 hours a week or earning the minimum wage equivalent; persons caring for dependents who are disabled or under age 6, and those caring for children between ages 6 and 12 if adequate child care is not available (this second exemption is limited to allowing these persons to refuse a job offer if care is not available); individuals already subject to and complying with another assistance program's work, training, or job search requirements (i.e., those in AFDC work, training, or job search programs or fulfilling unemployment compensation job search requirements); otherwise eligible postsecondary students; and residents of drug addiction and alcoholic treatment programs.

Those not exempted by one of the above-listed rules must, at least, register for work and accept suitable job offers. However, the main thrust of the food stamp employment and training program is to ensure that nonexempt recipients ("mandatory" work registrants) also fulfill some type of work, job search, or training obligation. To carry this out, welfare agencies are required to operate an employment and training program of their own design for work registrants whom they designate. Welfare agencies may require all work registrants to participate in one or more components of their program, or limit participation (with the Agriculture Department's approval) by *further exempting* additional categories and individuals for whom participation is judged "impracticable" or not "cost-effective." But they must allow otherwise exempt recipients to participate as volunteers and may set up special programs for them.

Once the "pool" of work registrants who will be required to participate in an employment or training program is identified, welfare agencies must place at least 15 percent of them in one or more program components. Program components can include any or all of the following activities, at the welfare agency's option: supervised job search or training for job search, workfare, work experience or training programs, education programs to improve basic skills, or any other employment or training activity approved by the Agriculture Department.

Recipients who take part in an employment or training activity beyond work registration cannot be required to *work* more than the minimum wage equivalent of their household's benefit, and *total hours of participation* (including both work and any other required activity) cannot exceed 120 hours a month. Welfare agencies also must provide participants support for costs directly related to participation (e.g., transportation and child care). Agencies may limit this support to $25 per participant per month for all support costs other than dependent care, and to local market rates for necessary dependent care.

Categorical eligibility rules and other limitations

A few food stamp rules deny food stamp eligibility for reasons other than financial need (limited income or liquid assets) or compliance with work registration or employment and training program requirements: (1) Where the head of household has voluntarily quit a job without good cause, the household's eligibility is barred for 90 days; (2) Households containing members on strike are ineligible, unless eligible prior to the strike; (3) Postsecondary students (in school half-time or more) who are physically and mentally fit for work and between ages 18 and 50 are ineligible unless they are assigned to school by a JTPA or other employment and training program, are employed at least 20 hours a week or participating in a federally financed work-study program, are a parent with responsibility for the care of a dependent child under age 6, an AFDC recipient, responsible for a child between 6 and 12 and do not have access to child care adequate to allow both work and school, or are a full-time single parent student responsible for a child under age 12; (4) Eligibility is barred to illegal or temporarily resident aliens; [14] (5) Eligibility is denied persons living in institutional settings, except for those in special SSI-approved small group homes for the disabled, persons living in drug addiction or alcoholic treatment programs, and persons in shelters for battered women and children or shelters for the homeless; (6) Boarders are ineligible unless they apply together with the household they are boarding with; (7) Eligibility is denied those who transfer assets for the purpose of qualifying for food stamps; (8) Those who intentionally violate food stamp rules are disqualified for specific time periods ranging from 6 months (on first violation) to permanently (on a third violation); (9) Those failing to provide social security numbers, or to cooperate in providing information needed to verify eligibility or benefit determinations, are ineligible.

---

[14] In addition, a legal alien's sponsor's income and assets may deny the alien eligibility.

BENEFITS

Food stamp benefits are a function of a household's size, its *counted (net)* monthly income, and maximum monthly benefit levels (in some cases, adjusted for geographic location). An eligible household's counted income is determined (as for eligibility), its maximum benefit level is established (depending on its size and location), and a benefit is calculated by subtracting its expected contribution (30 percent of its counted income) from its maximum allotment; maximum allotments are available only to those with no counted monthly income. Allotments are not taxable and food stamp purchases may not be charged sales taxes. Receipt of food stamps does not affect eligibility for or benefits provided by other welfare programs, although some programs use food stamp participation as a "trigger" for eligibility and others take into account the general availability of food stamps in deciding what level of benefits to provide. In fiscal year 1993, monthly benefits averaged $68 a person and about $170 a household.

Maximum monthly allotments

Maximum monthly food stamp allotments are tied to the cost of purchasing a nutritionally adequate low-cost diet, as measured by the Agriculture Department's Thrifty Food Plan (TFP).[15] Maximum allotments are set at: the monthly cost of the TFP for a 4-person family consisting of a couple between ages 20 and 50 and 2 school-age children, adjusted for family size (using a formula reflecting economies of scale developed by the HNIS), increased by 3 percent, and rounded down to the nearest whole dollar. They are adjusted for food price inflation annually, each October, to reflect the cost of the TFP in the immediately previous June.

Maximum allotments are standard in the 48 contiguous States and the District of Columbia; they are higher, reflecting substantially different food costs, in Alaska, Hawaii, Guam, and the Virgin Islands.

---

[15] The TFP is the cheapest of four food plans designed by the Agriculture Department's Human Nutrition Information Service (HNIS) and is priced monthly (using data from price surveys done for the CPI–U).

TABLE 18–6.—MAXIMUM MONTHLY FOOD STAMP ALLOTMENTS

[Effective October 1993 through September 1994]

Household size	48 States and D.C.	Alaska [1]	Hawaii	Guam	Virgin Islands
1 person	$112	$147	$187	$166	$144
2 persons	206	271	343	304	265
3 persons	295	388	492	436	380
4 persons	375	492	625	553	483
5 persons	446	585	742	657	573
6 persons	535	702	890	789	688
7 persons	591	776	984	872	760
8 persons	676	887	1125	997	869
Each additional person	+85	+111	+141	+125	+109

[1] Maximum monthly allotments for designated urban areas of Alaska. Two separate higher allotment levels are applied in remote rural areas of Alaska. They are 29 and 56 percent higher than the urban allotments shown here.

Minimum and prorated benefits

Eligible one- and two-person households are guaranteed a minimum monthly food stamp allotment of $10. Minimum monthly benefits for other household sizes vary from year to year, depending on the relationship between changes in the income eligibility limits and the adjustments to the cost of the TFP, and in a few cases, benefits can be reduced to zero before income eligibility limits are exceeded (making some households eligible for no benefit). At present, minimum monthly allotments for households of three or more persons range from $2 to slightly over $80.

In addition, a household's calculated monthly allotment can be prorated (reduced) for one month. On application, a household's first month's benefit is reduced to reflect the date of application. If a previously participating household does not meet eligibility recertification requirements in a timely fashion, but does become certified for eligibility subsequently, benefits for the first month of its new certification period normally are prorated to reflect the date when recertification requirements were met.

Application processing and issuing food stamps

Food stamp benefits are normally issued monthly. The local welfare agency must either deny eligibility or make food stamps available within 30 days of initial application and must provide food stamps without interruption if an eligible household reapplies and fulfills recertification requirements in a timely manner. Households in immediate need because of little or no income and very limited cash assets, as well as the homeless and those with extraordinarily high shelter expenses, must be given expedited service (provision of benefits within 5 days of initial application).

Food stamp issuance is a welfare agency responsibility and issuance practices differ among welfare agencies. Most food stamp coupons are issued by: (1) providing (usually mailing) recipients an authorization-to-participate (ATP) card that is then turned in at a local issuance point (e.g., a bank or post office) when picking up their monthly allotment, or (2) mailing food stamp coupon allotments directly to recipients. However, several pilot projects issue cash benefits, and in a small but growing number of areas, electronic benefit transfer (EBT) systems are used. EBT systems replace coupons with an ATM-like card used to make food purchases at the point of sale by deducting the purchase amount from the recipient's food stamp benefit account.

Using food stamps

Food stamp benefits are issued in the form of booklets of coupons. The smallest coupon denomination is $1; if change of less than $1 is due on a food stamp purchase, it is returned in cash. Typically, participating households use their food stamps in approved grocery stores to buy food items for home preparation and consumption. However, the actual list of approved uses for food stamps is more extensive, and includes: (1) food for home preparation and consumption, not including alcohol, tobacco, or hot foods intended for immediate consumption; (2) seeds and plants for use in gardens to produce food for personal consumption; (3) in the case of the elderly and SSI recipients (and their spouses), meals prepared and served through approved communal dining programs for the elderly and disabled; (4) in the case of the elderly and those who are disabled to an extent that they cannot prepare all of their meals, home-delivered meals provided by programs for the homebound; (5) meals prepared and served to residents of drug addiction and alcoholic treatment programs, small group homes for the disabled, shelters for battered women and children, and shelters or other establishments serving the homeless; and (6) where the household lives in certain remote areas of Alaska, equipment for procuring food by hunting and fishing (e.g., nets, hooks, fishing rods, and knives). As noted earlier, sales taxes may not be charged on food stamp purchases.

Quality control

Since the early 1970s, the Food Stamp program, like other welfare programs, has had a "quality control" system to monitor the degree to which erroneous eligibility and benefit determinations are made by welfare agencies. The system was established by regulation in the1970s as an administrative tool to enable welfare officials to identify problems and needed corrective actions. Today, by legislative directive, it is also used to calculate and impose fiscal liabilities ("sanctions") on States that have very high rates of erroneous benefit payments (very high dollar "error rates").

Under the quality control system, welfare agencies, with Federal oversight, continuously sample their active food stamp caseloads, as well as the correctness of decisions to deny or end benefits, and perform in-depth investigations of the eligibility and benefit status of randomly chosen cases in the samples looking for errors in applying Federal rules and otherwise erroneous benefit and eligibility outcomes. Over 90,000 cases are reviewed each year, and each State's sample is designed to provide a statistically valid picture of erroneous decisions and, in most instances, their dollar value in benefits. The resulting error rate information is used by program managers to chart needed changes in administrative practices, and, by the Federal Government, to assess fiscal sanctions on States with error rates above certain "tolerance levels," to reward States with error rates below a separate lower tolerance level, and to review welfare agency plans for action to correct procedures to control errors. Both error rate findings and any assessed sanctions are subject to appeal through administrative law judges and the Federal courts. Sanctions may be reduced or waived if the State shows "good cause" or if it is determined that the sanction amounts should be "invested" in improved State administration. Interest may be charged on outstanding sanction liabilities if the administrative appeals process takes more than 1 year.

Quality control reviews generate annual estimates of caseload and dollar error rates: the proportion of cases in which an error is found and the dollar value of the errors as a proportion of total benefit dollars. Caseload and dollar error rates are calculated for overpayments (including incorrect payments to eligible and ineligible households) and underpayments. The accuracy of welfare agency decisions denying or terminating assistance also is measured, with an error rate reflecting the proportion of denials and terminations that were improper; no dollar value is calculated. The total national weighted average dollar error rate for overpayments was estimated at 8.2 percent in fiscal year 1992; this was up from 7 percent in 1991 (the all-time low) and was the highest rate recorded since 1985. The fiscal year 1992 caseload error rate for overpayments was estimated at 17.6 percent. Error rates for underpayments have been relatively unchanged over time. In fiscal year 1992, the national weighted average underpayment dollar error rate was estimated at 2.5 percent, and the underpayment caseload error rate was 9.9 percent. Finally, the rate of denials and terminations found improper was 5.1 percent in 1992.

The dollar error rates reported through the food stamp quality control system are used as the basis for assessing the financial liability of States for overpaid and underpaid benefits. Although well over $500 million in sanctions have been assessed since the early 1980s, only approximately $5 million has been collected. The appeals process has delayed collection, and sanctions have been forgiven or waived both by Congress and the administration. In amending the rules governing sanctions in 1988 and 1990, Congress forgave accumulated sanctions, and, in late 1992, the administration waived sanctions by allowing States to invest the amounts in improved administration.

Rules governing fiscal sanctions have changed a number of times. Under the most recent revision (1993), sanctions are assessed States with combined (overpayment and underpayment) dollar error rates above the national weighted average combined error rate for the year in question (10.7 percent in 1992). Each State's sanction amount is determined by using a "sliding scale" so that its penalty assessment equals an amount reflecting the degree to which the State's combined error rate exceeds the national average (the "tolerance level"). For example, if the tolerance level is 10 percent and a State's error rate is 12 percent, the State would be assessed a sanction of 0.4 percent of benefits paid in the State that year: i.e., the State's error rate is 2 percentage points, or 20 percent, above the tolerance level, and it is assessed a sanction representing 20 percent of the amount by which it exceeds the tolerance level (2 percentage points × 0.2 = 0.4). A State with a combined error rate of 14 percent would owe a penalty of 1.6 percent of benefits, or 40 percent of the amount by which it exceeds the 10-percent tolerance level (4 percentage points × 0.4 = 1.6). Thus, the degree to which a State is assessed sanctions increases as its error rate rises, rather than having sanctions assessed equally on each dollar above the tolerance level. In fiscal year 1992, 12 States had combined error rates above the 10.7 percent tolerance level.

States also can receive increased Federal funding for administration if their error rates are below a second, much lower threshold. States with a combined error rate below 6 percent are entitled to a larger-than-normal Federal share of their administrative costs. The regular 50-percent Federal match is, depending on the degree to which the State's error rate is below 6 percent, raised to a maximum of 60 percent, as long as the State's rate of improper denials and terminations is below the national average. This "enhanced" administrative funding has typically totaled $5–10 million a year; in fiscal year 1992, six States had combined error rates below 6 percent.

Finally, the quality control system also identifies the various sources of error and requires that the majority of States develop and carry out corrective action plans to improve payment accuracy using the information gathered through quality control reviews. These reviews generally show that the primary "responsibility" for overpayment errors is almost evenly split between welfare agencies and clients, and the most common errors are related to establishing food stamp expense "deductions" and households' income.

TABLE 18–7.—FOOD STAMP QUALITY CONTROL ERROR RATES: FISCAL YEAR 1992

[Percent of benefits paid or not paid in error]

State	Underpayment error rate	Overpayment error rate	Combined error rate
Alabama	1.76	6.47	8.23
Alaska	1.20	7.12	8.32
Arizona	3.19	10.16	13.35
Arkansas	2.23	5.25	7.47
California	3.71	7.00	10.71
Colorado	1.80	5.81	7.61
Connecticut	2.47	5.65	8.12
Delaware	1.51	6.87	8.38
D.C.	3.10	7.46	10.56
Florida	3.96	15.71	19.68
Georgia	2.65	8.30	10.96
Guam	2.16	6.84	8.99
Hawaii	.99	2.86	3.85
Idaho	2.45	4.73	7.18
Illinois	2.42	7.55	9.97
Indiana	3.23	10.33	13.56
Iowa	3.08	7.68	10.76
Kansas	1.27	5.62	6.89
Kentucky	1.79	3.06	4.85
Louisiana	1.82	7.33	9.15
Maine	2.31	6.12	8.43
Maryland	2.00	6.99	8.99
Massachusetts	1.22	6.16	7.38
Michigan	1.97	7.08	9.05
Minnesota	2.23	8.25	10.48
Mississippi	1.80	8.28	10.08
Missouri	2.64	7.13	9.77
Montana	1.99	6.68	8.75
Nebraska	2.52	6.69	9.21
Nevada	1.35	5.49	6.83
New Hampshire	2.43	9.63	12.06
New Jersey	3.13	5.04	8.17
New Mexico	2.85	5.70	8.55
New York	2.97	8.23	11.20
North Carolina	2.34	6.55	8.89
North Dakota	1.58	4.30	5.89
Ohio	1.88	11.31	13.19
Oklahoma	2.64	6.28	8.92
Oregon	1.74	7.47	9.21
Pennsylvania	1.95	6.18	8.13
Rhode Island	1.30	3.10	4.40
South Carolina	1.99	7.01	9.00
South Dakota	.92	3.60	4.52
Tennessee	2.53	10.59	13.12
Texas	2.22	9.61	11.83
Utah	1.41	5.71	7.12
Vermont	1.59	4.74	6.33
Virginia	2.65	6.26	8.91

TABLE 18–7.—FOOD STAMP QUALITY CONTROL ERROR RATES: FISCAL YEAR 1992— Continued

[Percent of benefits paid or not paid in error]

State	Underpayment error rate	Overpayment error rate	Combined error rate
Virgin Islands	2.33	3.32	5.64
Washington	2.12	9.61	11.73
West Virginia	1.83	8.82	10.64
Wisconsin	2.57	6.74	9.32
Wyoming	2.73	5.92	8.65
U.S. average	2.50	8.19	10.69

Note: Underpayment and overpayment rates may not add to combined rates due to rounding.

Source: Food Stamp Quality Control Annual Report, Fiscal Year 1992.

INTERACTION WITH CASH ASSISTANCE PROGRAMS

The Food Stamp program is intertwined with cash assistance in two ways: it is administratively linked to cash welfare aid at the State and local levels, and its recipient population is made up largely of recipients of other government benefits.

At the State and local levels, the Food Stamp program is administered by the same welfare offices and personnel that administer cash assistance such as AFDC and general assistance. And joint food stamp/cash welfare application and interview procedures are the general rule. This coadministration does not apply for most elderly or disabled persons, whose SSI cash assistance is typically administered through Social Security Administration offices, although these offices do provide limited intake services for the Food Stamp program.

For most persons participating in the Food Stamp program, food stamp aid represents a second or third form of government payment. Fewer than 20 percent of food stamp households rely solely on nongovernmental sources for their cash income, although over 25 percent have some income from these sources (e.g., earnings, private retirement income). According to quality control data, the AFDC program contributes to the income of about 41 percent of food stamp households, and for almost all of them AFDC is their only cash income. SSI benefits go to some 19 percent of food stamp households, and almost one-third have no other income. About 20 percent of food stamp households receive social security or veterans benefits. And nearly 15 percent are paid general assistance, unemployment insurance, or workers' compensation benefits.

TABLE 18–8.—CHARACTERISTICS OF FOOD STAMP HOUSEHOLDS: 1980–91

[In percent]

Food stamp recipient households	Year and month survey was conducted											
	1980 (Aug.)	1981 (Aug.)	1982 (Aug.)	1983 (Feb.)	1984 (Aug.)	1985 (Summer)	1986 (Summer)	1987 (Summer)	1988 (Summer)	1989 (Summer)	1990 (Summer)	1991 (Summer)
With gross monthly income:												
Below the Federal poverty levels	87	90	95	93	93	94	93	94	92	92	92	91
Between the poverty levels and 130 percent of the poverty levels	10	9	5	7	6	6	6	6	8	8	8	9
Above 130 percent of the poverty levels	2	1	*	*	1	*	*	*	*	*	*	*
With earnings	19	20	18	20	19	20	21	21	20	20	19	20
With public assistance income[1]	65	69	69	75	71	68	69	74	72	73	73	70
With AFDC income	NA	40	42	50	42	39	38	41	42	42	43	41
With SSI income	18	19	18	18	18	19	18	21	20	21	19	19
With children	60	56	58	68	61	59	61	61	61	60	61	61
And female heads of household	NA	43	45	52	47	46	48	50	50	50	51	51
With elderly members[2]	23	21	20	18	22	21	20	21	19	20	18	17
With elderly female heads of household[2]	NA	14	14	12	16	16	15	15	14	14	11	10
Average household size	2.8	2.7	2.8	2.9	2.8	2.7	2.7	2.7	2.6	2.6	2.6	2.6

[1] Public assistance income includes AFDC, SSI, and general assistance.
[2] Elderly members and heads of household include those age 60 or older.
* Less than 0.5 percent.

Source: U.S. Department of Agriculture (Food and Nutrition Service) surveys of the characteristics of food stamp households.

Compiled by the Congressional Research Service.

Food Stamp Recipiency Rates

Table 18–9 shows gross food stamp participation or recipiency rates using three different measures for the United States from 1975 to 1993. The actual number of food stamp participants has fluctuated widely over the last 18 years, reaching its highest average monthly level of 27 million (not including Puerto Rico) in 1993. As a percentage of the total U.S. resident population, food stamp participation rose significantly from a rate of 8.1 participants per 100 persons in 1975 to 10.4 percent in 1993. In the poor and pretransfer poor populations, the food stamp participation rates in 1991 were 63.3 and 59.3 percent respectively. "Pretransfer poor" is defined as income including Social Security and other social insurance benefits but not including means-tested benefits in relationship to the poverty thresholds.

A recent report by the U.S. Department of Agriculture, entitled "Food Stamp Program Participation Rates: January 1989," provides a more refined analysis of Food Stamp program participation rates and the extent to which the program is serving its target population. The report estimates that 59 percent of individuals eligible for food stamps participated, and that 56 percent of eligible households participated. Those households received 66 percent of benefits payable if all eligible households had been enrolled. In addition, particular subgroups of the eligible population participated at different rates. Among groups defined by monthly income levels, participation rates were highest for those with the lowest income and declined as income levels rose. Participation rates were 81 percent for those with income below half the Federal poverty guidelines, 68 percent for those with income between half the guidelines and the guidelines themselves, and 17 percent for those with incomes above the poverty thresholds. Demographic groups also showed different participation rates. Eligible elderly households participated at a rate of 29 percent, while households composed of single adult females with children were enrolled the at rate of 78 percent and 90 percent of eligible disabled nonelderly adult households participated.

TABLE 18–9.—FOOD STAMP PARTICIPATION RATES IN THE UNITED STATES, 1975–93

Year	Number of food stamp participants (in millions)	Food stamp participation as percent of—		
		Total population [1]	Poor population [2]	Pre-transfer poor population [3]
1975	16.3	7.6	63.0	NA
1976	17.0	7.9	68.1	NA
1977	15.6	7.2	63.1	NA
1978	14.4	6.5	58.8	NA
1979	15.9	7.1	61.0	57.1
1980	19.2	8.4	65.6	60.7
1981	20.6	9.0	64.7	60.8
1982	20.4	8.8	59.3	56.3
1983	21.6	9.2	61.2	58.5
1984	20.9	8.8	62.0	58.5
1985	19.9	8.3	60.2	56.6
1986	19.4	8.0	59.9	56.2
1987	19.1	7.8	59.1	55.6
1988	18.7	7.6	58.9	55.2
1989	18.8	7.6	59.6	55.6
1990	20.0	8.0	59.6	55.7
1991	22.6	9.0	63.3	59.3
1992	25.4	10.0	68.9	64.0
1993	27.0	10.4	NA	NA

[1] Total U.S. resident population was 258.4 million at the end of fiscal year 1993.
[2] Data on the U.S. poor population can be found in appendix J, table 3.
[3] Data on the U.S. pretransfer poor population can be found in appendix J, table 15, and previous editions of the Green Book. "Pretransfer" is defined as after social insurance income (including Social Security) but before receipt of any means-tested transfers.
NA—not available.
Note: Puerto Rico not included in table.

Table 18–10 shows the number of people (in thousands) who received food stamp benefits in each State, including the District of Columbia, Puerto Rico, and the territories, for selected fiscal years between 1975 and 1993. The number of recipients varies greatly by State; in 1993, the number of beneficiaries ranged from 13,000 to 18,000 in the territories and 34,000 in Wyoming to 2.9 million in California. In nearly all States, there was a significant increase between 1975 and 1993. This is reflected in the total number of enrollees, which increased from 17.4 million persons (plus 1.8 million in Puerto Rico) in 1975, to 27 million people (plus 1.4 million in Puerto Rico) in 1993.[16]

---

[16] The 17.4 million person enrollment for food stamps in 1975 differs from the 16.3 million person participation level noted in table 9 because it represents year-end enrollment as opposed to annual average participation. The same is true for 1979, for which table 10 shows enrollment of 17.1 million persons (excluding Puerto Rico), and table 9 shows 15.9 million persons. State-by-State participation for 1975 and 1979 is not available on an annual average basis.

TABLE 18-10.—FOOD STAMP RECIPIENTS, BY STATE: SELECTED YEARS, 1975-93

[Thousands of persons]

State	Fiscal years							
	1975[1]	1979[2]	1985[3]	1989[3]	1990[3]	1991[3]	1992[3]	1993[3]
Alabama	393	525	588	436	449	504	550	560
Alaska	12	25	22	26	25	30	38	43
Arizona	166	129	206	264	317	388	457	489
Arkansas	268	277	253	227	235	258	277	285
California	1,517	1,334	1,615	1,773	1,936	2,212	2,558	2,866
Colorado	162	145	170	211	221	241	260	273
Connecticut	189	155	145	114	133	171	202	215
Delaware	39	45	40	30	33	41	51	58
District of Columbia	112	100	72	58	62	72	82	87
Florida	767	828	630	668	781	1,021	1,404	1,500
Georgia	569	559	567	485	536	648	751	807
Hawaii	84	96	99	78	77	83	94	103
Idaho	39	47	59	61	59	65	72	79
Illinois	948	837	1,110	990	1,013	1,096	1,156	1,178
Indiana	255	275	406	285	311	375	448	497
Iowa	118	117	203	168	170	180	192	196
Kansas	63	73	119	128	142	156	175	188
Kentucky	449	405	560	447	458	496	529	530
Louisiana	502	523	644	725	727	742	779	779
Maine	151	121	114	84	94	116	133	138
Maryland	273	299	291	249	254	304	343	375
Massachusetts	560	429	337	314	347	397	429	443
Michigan	685	706	985	874	917	978	994	1,022
Minnesota	191	143	228	245	263	286	309	317
Mississippi	390	452	495	493	499	520	536	537
Missouri	299	280	362	404	431	490	549	591
Montana	38	33	58	56	57	61	66	70
Nebraska	50	55	94	92	95	99	107	113
Nevada	34	27	32	41	50	63	80	93
New Hampshire	66	44	28	22	31	47	58	60
New Jersey	565	524	464	353	381	441	495	531

New Mexico	154	159	157	151	157	188	221	244
New York	1,398	1,704	1,834	1,463	1,546	1,717	1,885	2,045
North Carolina	537	517	474	390	419	517	597	627
North Dakota	19	20	33	39	39	41	46	48
Ohio	924	760	1,133	1,068	1,078	1,171	1,251	1,269
Oklahoma	184	184	263	261	267	296	346	370
Oregon	208	160	228	213	216	240	265	283
Pennsylvania	893	923	1,032	916	954	1,052	1,137	1,186
Rhode Island	104	80	69	57	64	78	87	92
South Carolina	421	369	373	272	299	329	369	394
South Dakota	31	37	48	50	50	52	55	56
Tennessee	435	531	518	500	527	608	702	774
Texas	1,085	1,027	1,263	1,636	1,880	2,155	2,454	2,659
Utah	50	44	75	95	99	110	123	133
Vermont	46	40	44	34	38	47	54	58
Virginia	293	320	360	333	346	414	495	535
Washington	239	205	281	283	337	385	432	462
West Virginia	204	182	278	259	262	281	310	322
Wisconsin	163	171	363	291	286	294	334	337
Wyoming	11	11	27	27	28	31	33	34
Guam	21	18	20	13	12	11	20	13
Northern Marianas	NA	NA	4	4	4	2	2	3
Puerto Rico	1,800	1,822	1,480	1,460	1,480	1,490	1,480	1,440
Virgin Islands	25	34	32	16	18	15	16	18
Total	19,199	18,926	21,385	20,232	21,510	24,105	26,888	28,426

[1] Yearend participation, July 1975. Total does not match totals in other tables, which are annual average participation.

[2] Yearend participation, September 1979. Total does not match totals in other tables, which are annual average participation. During fiscal year 1979, and into 1980, participation increases were largely due to the elimination of the food stamp purchase requirement. Figures for Alabama and Mississippi are estimates.

[3] Annual average participation.

Source: U.S. Department of Agriculture, Food and Nutrition Service.

LEGISLATION

In the early 1980s, Congress enacted major revisions to the food stamp program to hold down costs and tighten administrative rules. The Omnibus Budget Reconciliation Act of 1981, the Agriculture and Food Act of 1981, and the Omnibus Budget Reconciliation Act of 1982 all contained amendments that the Congressional Budget Office has estimated held food stamp spending for fiscal years 1982 through 1985 nearly $7 billion (13 percent) below what would have been spent under pre-1981 law. These laws delayed various inflation indexing adjustments, reduced the maximum benefit guarantee by 1 percent (restored in 1984), established income eligibility ceilings at 130 percent of the Federal poverty levels, initiated prorating of first-month benefits, replaced the food stamp program in Puerto Rico with a nutrition assistance block grant, reduced benefits for those with earnings and high shelter expenses, ended eligibility for most postsecondary students and strikers, and raised fiscal penalties for States with high rates of erroneous benefit and eligibility determinations.

In 1985, the Food Security Act (P.L. 99–198) reauthorized food stamp appropriations through fiscal year 1990 and reversed the earlier trend, significantly liberalizing food stamp rules. Major new initiatives included: a requirement for States to implement employment and training programs for food stamp recipients, automatic food stamp eligibility for AFDC and SSI recipients, and a prohibition on collection of sales taxes on food stamp purchases. Benefits were raised for some disabled and those with earnings, high shelter costs, and dependent care costs. Puerto Rico's nutrition assistance block grant was increased. Eligibility standards were liberalized, primarily by increasing and easing limits on assets. This was followed by several laws in 1986 and 1987 that opened up access to and increased benefits for the homeless, liberalized treatment of student aid, energy assistance, and income received from employment programs for the elderly and charitable organizations, further added to benefits for those with high shelter costs, and allowed Washington State to operate a special AFDC/food stamp demonstration project (followed by similar authorization for Minnesota in 1989).

Legislation expanding eligibility and benefits continued into 1988 and 1989. The Hunger Prevention Act of 1988 (P.L. 100–435) increased food stamp benefits across the board, liberalized several eligibility and benefit rules, eased program access and administrative rules, and restructured the employment and training program and quality control system. The across-the-board benefit increase in maximum benefits (above normal inflation adjustments) called for by the act was 0.65 percent in fiscal year 1989, 2.05 percent in fiscal year 1990, and 3 percent in later years. Eligibility and benefit liberalizations included higher benefits for those with dependent care expenses, extension of liberal treatment for disabled applicants and recipients to new categories of disability, addition of a new income disregard for earned income tax credits, and liberalized treatment for farm households. Major provisions pertaining to program access and administration authorized 50-percent Federal cost sharing for State-option outreach activities, required coordination with cash welfare program application procedures, loosened rules governing monthly reporting and retrospective budgeting, allowed training of community volunteers to help screen applicants, and required, in some instances, issuance of the first 2 months' worth of benefits in a single allotment. Employment and training rules were revised by allowing some expansion in the types of activities supported (e.g., basic skills education), requiring increased support for participants' dependent care expenses, and mandating new performance standards for States. Finally, the food stamp quality control system was completely revamped to substantially reduce fiscal sanctions on States for erroneous benefit determinations, retroactively to fiscal year 1986.

The 1990 Food, Agriculture, Conservation, and Trade Act (P.L. 101–624) reauthorized food stamp appropriations through fiscal year 1995. Although early versions of this act would have significantly liberalized food stamp eligibility and benefit rules, budget constraints dictated minimal expansions: limited revisions for postsecondary students, forgiveness of most pre-1986 quality control fiscal sanctions on States, a few changes in administrative rules to open up program access and strengthen penalties for trafficking, and new pilot projects and study commissions for welfare program coordination. In addition, other laws eliminated a special requirement for single food stamp/SSI applications for those about to be discharged from institutions and barred the food stamp program from counting (as a liquid asset) lump-sum earned income tax credit payments.

Most recently, the Mickey Leland Childhood Hunger Relief Act (incorporated in the 1993 Omnibus Budget Reconciliation Act, P.L. 103–66) increased food stamp benefits and eased eligibility rules by: increasing and then removing the limit on special benefit adjustments (deductions) for households with very high shelter expenses, ending a practice of reducing benefits when there are short "procedural" breaks in enrollment, disregarding child support payments as income to the payor, increasing the degree to which vehicles are disregarded as assets in judging eligibility, revising the definition of a food stamp household to allow more persons who live together to apply separately, increasing the degree to which dependent care expense deductions can be claimed, expanding the degree to which Earned Income Tax Credits are disregarded as assets and State/local general assistance is disregarded as income, and boosting Puerto Rico's block grant. The Act also lowered the Federal share of some State administrative expenses (to 50 percent), reduced quality control fiscal penalties on States with high rates of erroneous benefit and eligibility determinations, and liberalized the appeals process for those penalties. Finally, it expanded support for employment and training programs for food stamp recipients, added a new method for collecting claims against recipients, and increased penalties related to trafficking in food stamps. The net cost of the 1993 amendments was estimated at $2.5 billion over fiscal years 1994–98.

TABLE 18–11.—HISTORICAL FOOD STAMP STATISTICS

| Fiscal year | Total Federal spending (in millions) [1] | | Average monthly participation (in millions of persons) | Average monthly benefits (per person) | | 4-person maximum monthly allotment [2] |
	Current dollars	Constant (1993) dollars [3]		Current dollars	Constant (1993) dollars [3]	
1972 [4]	$1,871	$6,242	11.1	$13.50	$45.00	$108
1973	2,211	6,865	12.2	14.60	45.00	112
1974	2,843	7,370	12.9	17.60	45.20	116
1975 [5]	4,624	10,922	17.1	21.40	50.10	150
1976	5,692	12,718	18.5	23.90	52.80	162
Transition quarter [6]	1,367	3,000	17.3	24.40	52.90	166
1977	5,469	11,707	17.1	24.70	52.40	166
1978	5,573	10,947	16.0	26.80	52.00	170
1979 [7]	6,995	12,326	17.7	30.60	53.20	182
1980	9,188	14,883	21.1	34.40	55.40	204
1981	11,308	16,824	22.4	39.50	58.50	209
1982 [8]	11,117	15,947	22.0	39.20	56.10	233
1983 [8]	12,733	17,985	23.2	43.00	60.60	253
1984 [8]	12,470	16,989	22.4	42.70	58.10	253
1985 [8]	12,599	16,893	21.4	45.00	60.30	264
1986 [8]	12,528	16,412	20.9	45.50	59.60	268
1987 [8]	12,539	15,710	20.6	45.80	57.30	271
1988 [8]	13,289	16,106	20.1	49.80	60.30	290
1989 [8]	13,815	15,664	20.2	51.90	58.60	300
1990 [8]	16,512	17,739	21.5	59.00	63.10	331
1991 [8]	19,765	20,589	24.1	63.90	65.80	352
1992 [8]	23,539	24,027	26.9	68.50	69.90	370
1993 [8]	24,806	24,806	28.4	68.00	68.00	375

[1] Spending for benefits and administration, including Puerto Rico.

[2] For the 48 contiguous States and the District of Columbia, as in effect at the beginning of the fiscal year in current dollars.

[3] Constant dollar adjustments were made using the overall Consumer Price Index for All Urban Consumers (CPI–U) for administrative costs and the CPI–U "food at home" component for benefits.

[4] The first fiscal year in which benefit and eligibility rules were, by law, nationally uniform and indexed for inflation.

[5] The first fiscal year in which food stamps were available nationwide.

[6] July through September 1976.

[7] The fiscal year in which the food stamp purchase requirement was eliminated, on a phased in basis.

[8] Includes funding for Puerto Rico's nutrition assistance grant; earlier years include funding for Puerto Rico under the regular food stamp program. Participation figures include enrollment in Puerto Rico (averaging 1.4 to 1.5 million persons a month under the nutrition assistance grant and higher figures in earlier years). Average benefit figures do not reflect somewhat lower benefits in Puerto Rico under its nutrition assistance grant.

Note: Figures in this table have been revised from similar tables presented in earlier versions of this print to reflect more recent spending information and more precise inflation adjustments for constant dollar amounts.

Source: Compiled by the Congressional Research Service.

MEDICAID [17]

Medicaid, authorized under title XIX of the Social Security Act, is a Federal-State matching entitlement program providing medical assistance for low-income persons who are aged, blind, disabled, members of families with dependent children and certain other pregnant women and children. Within Federal guidelines, each State designs and administers its own program. Thus there is substantial variation among the States in terms of persons covered, types and scope of benefits offered, and amounts of payments for services.

Medicaid eligibility is generally linked to eligibility under programs within the jurisdiction of the Committee on Ways and Means, namely AFDC and SSI. Further, some poor aged persons are covered under both the Medicare and Medicaid programs.

Eligibility

Eligibility for Medicaid has traditionally been linked to actual or potential receipt of cash assistance under the Aid to Families with Dependent Children (AFDC) or Supplemental Security Income (SSI) programs. Legislation in the last decade has gradually extended coverage to low-income pregnant women and children who have no ties to the welfare system, and has provided partial coverage for new groups of low-income Medicare beneficiaries.

Medicaid is available to two broad classes of eligible persons: the "categorically needy" and the "medically needy." The two terms once distinguished between welfare-related beneficiaries and those qualifying only under special Medicaid rules. However, nonwelfare groups have been added to the "categorically needy" list over the years. As a result, the terms are no longer especially helpful in sorting out the various populations for whom mandatory or optional Medicaid coverage has been made available, and some analysts believe they should be abandoned. However, the distinction between the categorically and medically needy is still an important one, because the scope of covered services that States must provide to the categorically needy is much broader than the minimum scope of services for the medically needy.

All States must cover certain mandatory groups of categorically needy individuals.[18] Coverage of additional categorically needy groups is optional, as is coverage of the medically needy. The following discussion describes the mandatory and optional categorically eligible groups within each of the two basic populations served by Medicaid: families with children and the aged, blind, and disabled. The medically needy are discussed separately at the end of this section.

---

[17] For further information on the Medicaid program see: U.S. Congress, House Committee on Energy and Commerce, Medicaid Source Book: Background Data and Analysis (A 1993 Update), Energy and Commerce Committee Print 103–A. U.S. Govt. Print. Off. January 1993.

[18] Arizona does not operate a traditional Medicaid program. Since 1982 it has operated a federally assisted medical assistance program for low-income persons under a demonstration waiver.

FAMILIES AND CHILDREN

AFDC-related groups

Mandatory.—States must provide Medicaid to all persons receiving cash assistance under AFDC, as well as to additional AFDC-related groups who are not actually receiving cash payments. These groups include: persons who do not receive a payment because the amount would be less than $10; persons whose payments are reduced to zero because of recovery of previous overpayments; certain work supplementation participants; certain children for whom adoption assistance agreements are in effect or for whom foster care payments are being made under title IV–E of the Social Security Act; and persons ineligible for AFDC because of a requirement that may not be imposed under Medicaid.

States are required to continue Medicaid for specified periods for certain families losing AFDC benefits after receiving them in at least 3 of the preceding 6 months. If the family loses AFDC benefits because of increased income from earnings or hours of employment, Medicaid coverage must be extended for 12 months. (During the second 6 months a premium may be imposed, the scope of benefits may be limited, or alternate delivery systems may be used.) If the family loses AFDC because of increased child or spousal support, coverage must be extended for 4 months. States are also required to furnish Medicaid to certain two-parent families whose principal earner is unemployed and who are not receiving cash assistance because the State is one of those permitted (under the Family Support Act of 1988) to set a time limit on AFDC coverage for such families.

Optional.—States are permitted, but not required, to provide coverage to additional AFDC-related groups. The most important of these are the "Ribicoff children," whose income and resources are within AFDC standards but who do not meet the definition of "dependent child." States may cover these children up to a maximum age of 18, 19, 20, or 21, at the State's option, and may limit coverage to reasonable subgroups, such as children in privately subsidized foster care, or those who live in certain institutional settings. States may also furnish Medicaid to persons who would receive AFDC if the State's AFDC program were as broad as permitted under Federal law.

Non-AFDC pregnant women and children

Beginning in 1986, Congress has extended Medicaid to groups of pregnant women and children who are defined in terms of family income and resources, rather than in terms of their ties to the AFDC program.

Mandatory.—States are required to cover pregnant women and children under age 6 with family incomes below 133 percent of the Federal poverty income guidelines. (The State may impose a resource standard that is no more restrictive than that for SSI, in the case of pregnant women, or AFDC, in the case of children.) Coverage for pregnant women is limited to services related to the pregnancy or complications of the pregnancy; children receive full Medicaid coverage.

Since July 1, 1991, States have been required to cover all children who are under age 19, who were born after September 30, 1983, and whose family income is below 100 percent of the Federal poverty level. (Coverage of such children through age 7 has been optional since OBRA 1987.) The 1983 start date means that coverage of 18-year-olds will take effect during fiscal year 2002.

Optional.—States are permitted, but not required, to cover pregnant women and infants under one year old with incomes below a State-established maximum that is above 133 percent of the poverty level but no more than 185 percent. As of July 1993, 34 States had made use of this option; 25 had set their income limits at the maximum of 185 percent.

AGED AND DISABLED PERSONS

SSI-related groups

Mandatory.—States are generally required to cover recipients of SSI. However, States may use more restrictive eligibility standards for Medicaid than those for SSI if they were using those standards on January 1, 1972 (before the implementation of SSI). States that have chosen to apply at least one more restrictive standard are known as "section 209(b)" States, after the section of the Social Security Amendments of 1972 (Public Law 92–603) that established the option. These States may vary in their definition of disability, or in their standards related to income or resources. There are 12 section 209(b) States:

Connecticut	Minnesota	North Dakota
Hawaii	Missouri	Ohio
Illinois	New Hampshire	Oklahoma
Indiana	North Carolina	Virginia

States using more restrictive income standards must allow applicants to deduct medical expenses from income (not including SSI or State supplemental payments, SSP) in determining eligibility. This process is known as "spenddown." For example, if an applicant has a monthly income of $400 (not including any SSI or SSP) and the State's maximum allowable income is $350, the applicant would be required to incur $50 in medical expenses before qualifying for Medicaid. As will be discussed below, the spenddown process is also used in establishing medically needy eligibility.

States must continue Medicaid coverage for several defined groups of individuals who have lost SSI or SSP eligibility. The "qualified severely impaired" are disabled persons who have returned to work and have lost eligibility as a result of employment earnings, but still have the condition that originally rendered them disabled and meet all non-disability criteria for SSI except income. Medicaid must be continued if such an individual needs continued medical assistance to continue employment and the individual's earnings are insufficient to provide the equivalent of SSI, Medicaid, and attendant care benefits the individual would qualify for in the absence of earnings. States must also continue Medicaid coverage for persons who were once eligible for both SSI and Social Security payments and who lose SSI because of a cost of living adjustment (COLA) in their Social Security benefits. Similar Medicaid continuations have been provided for certain other persons who lose SSI as a result of eligibility for or increases in Social Security or veterans' benefits. Finally, States must continue Medicaid for certain SSI-related groups who received benefits in 1973, including "essential persons" (persons who care for a disabled individual).

Optional.—States are permitted to provide Medicaid to individuals who are not receiving SSI but are receiving State-only supplementary cash payments.

Qualified Medicare beneficiaries and related groups

Mandatory.—Effective January 1, 1991, States must provide limited Medicaid coverage for "qualified Medicare beneficiaries" (QMBs). These are aged and disabled persons who are receiving Medicare, whose income is below 100 percent of the Federal poverty level, and whose resources do not exceed twice the allowable amount under SSI. States must pay Medicare part B premiums (and, if applicable, part A premiums) for QMBs, along with required Medicare coinsurance and deductible amounts.

Effective January 1, 1993, all States must pay part B premiums (but not part A premiums or part A or B coinsurance and deductibles) for beneficiaries who would be QMBs except that their incomes are between 100 percent and 110 percent of the poverty level; the upper limit rises to 120 percent on January 1, 1995.

States are also required to pay part A premiums, but no other expenses, for "qualified disabled and working individuals." These are persons who formerly received Social Security disability benefits and hence Medicare, have lost eligibility for both programs, but are permitted under Medicare law to continue to receive Medicare in return for payment of the part A premium. Medicaid must pay this premium on behalf of such individuals who have incomes below 200 percent of poverty and resources no greater than twice the SSI standard.

Optional.—States are permitted to provide full Medicaid benefits, rather than just Medicare premiums and cost-sharing, to QMBs who meet a State-established income standard that is no higher than 100 percent of the Federal poverty level.

Institutionalized persons and related groups (all optional)

States may provide Medicaid to certain otherwise ineligible groups of persons who are in nursing facilities or other institutions, or who would require institutional care if they were not receiving alternative services at home or in the community.

States may establish a special income standard for institutionalized persons, not to exceed 300 percent of the maximum SSI benefits payable to a person who is living at home and has no other resources. States may also provide Medicaid to persons who would qualify for SSI but for the fact that they are in an institution.

A State may obtain a waiver under section 2176 of OBRA 1981 to provide home and community-based services to a defined group of individuals who would otherwise require institutional care. Persons served under such a waiver may receive Medicaid coverage if they would be eligible if in an institution. Such individuals may also be covered in a State that terminates its waiver program in order to take advantage of a new, no-waiver home and community-based services option created by OBRA 1990.

A State may also provide Medicaid to several other classes of persons who need the level of care provided by an institution and would be eligible if they were in an institution. These include children who are being cared for at home, persons of any age who are ventilator-dependent, and persons receiving hospice benefits in lieu of institutional services.

THE MEDICALLY NEEDY (ALL OPTIONAL)

Forty-one States and other jurisdictions provide Medicaid to at least some groups of "medically needy" persons. These are persons who meet the nonfinancial standards for inclusion in one of the groups covered under Medicaid, but who do not meet the applicable income or resource requirements for categorically needy eligibility. The State may establish higher income or resource standards for the medically needy. In addition, individuals may spend down to the medically needy standard by incurring medical expenses, in the same way that SSI recipients in section 209(b) States may spend down to Medicaid eligibility. For the medically needy, spenddown may involve the reduction of assets, as well as of income.

The State may set its separate medically needy income standard for a family of a given size at any level up to 133⅓ percent of the maximum payment for a similar family under the State's AFDC program. States may limit the groups of individuals who may receive medically needy coverage. If the State provides any medically needy program, however, it must include all children under 18 who would qualify under one of the mandatory categorically needy groups, and all pregnant women who would qualify under either a mandatory or optional group, if their income or resources were lower.

As of October 1, 1993, the following States covered some groups of the medically needy:

American Samoa	Maryland	Pennsylvania
Arkansas	Massachusetts	Puerto Rico
California	Michigan	Rhode Island
Connecticut	Minnesota	Tennessee
District of Columbia	Montana	Texas
Florida	Nebraska	Utah
Georgia	New Hampshire	Vermont
Hawaii	New Jersey	Virgin Islands
Illinois	New York	Virginia
Iowa	North Carolina	Washington
Kansas	North Dakota	West Virginia
Kentucky	Northern Mariana Islands	Wisconsin
Louisiana	Oklahoma	
Maine	Oregon	

MEDICAID AND THE POOR

In 1992, Medicaid covered 11.2 percent of the total U.S. population (excluding institutionalized persons) and 47 percent of those with incomes below the Federal poverty level. Because categorical eligibility requirements for children are less restrictive than those for adults, poor children are much more likely to receive coverage. Table 18–12 shows Medicaid eligibility by age and income status in 1992, as reported in the March 1993 Current Population Survey (CPS) conducted by the Census Bureau. Note that persons shown as receiving Medicaid may have had other health coverage as well. Nearly all the elderly, for example, have Medicare and/or private coverage.

Children under age 6 with family incomes below poverty are most likely to be covered. Coverage rates drop steadily with age and income until age 65.

TABLE 18–12.—MEDICAID COVERAGE BY AGE AND INCOME STATUS, 1992

[All numbers are in thousands]

Age	Medicaid	Total	Percent with Medicaid
Poor:			
0 to 5	4,458	6,046	73.7
6 to 18	5,419	9,220	58.8
19 to 44	4,988	13,201	37.8
45 to 64	1,349	4,431	30.4
65 and over	1,205	3,983	30.2
Total	17,419	36,880	47.2
Family income between 100 and 133 percent of poverty:			
0 to 5	726	1,693	42.9
6 to 18	865	3,246	26.6
19 to 44	968	5,708	17.0
45 to 64	412	2,176	18.9
65 and over	564	3,004	18.8
Total	3,534	15,827	22.3
Family income between 133 percent and 185 percent of poverty:			
0 to 5	737	2,690	27.4
6 to 18	706	5,251	13.4
19 to 44	891	9,847	9.0
45 to 64	293	3,619	8.1
65 and over	426	4,644	9.2
Total	3,053	26,051	11.7
Family income greater than 185 percent of poverty:			
0 to 5	888	13,079	6.8
6 to 18	966	28,879	3.3
19 to 44	1,363	74,489	1.8
45 to 64	468	39,524	1.2
65 and over	720	19,240	3.7
Total	4,405	175,211	2.5
All individuals:			
0 to 5	6,809	23,508	29.0
6 to 18	7,956	46,596	17.1
19 to 44	8,210	103,245	8.0
45 to 64	2,522	49,750	5.1
65 and over	2,914	30,870	9.4
Total	28,411	253,969	11.2

Source: Current Population Survey (CPS), Annual March Income Supplement. Table prepared by CRS. The table excludes persons in institutions and approximately 300,000 children under age 15 whose income was not reported. The Medicaid counts are lower than those reported by HCFA, because some beneficiaries fail to report their coverage on the CPS. Some may also underreport their income. In addition, the income used to determine poverty status in this table includes cash welfare, while Medicaid eligibility is based on income prior to the receipt of welfare benefits.

Services

States are required to offer the following services to categorically needy recipients under their Medicaid programs: inpatient and outpatient hospital services; laboratory and X-ray services; nursing facility (NF) services for those over age 21; home health services for those entitled to NF care; early and periodic screening, diagnosis, and treatment (EPSDT) for those under age 21; family planning services and supplies; physicians' services, and nurse-midwife services. OBRA 1989 required States to provide ambulatory services offered by federally qualified health centers, effective April 1, 1990, and services furnished by certified family or pediatric nurse practitioners, effective July 1, 1990. States may also provide additional medical services such as drugs, eyeglasses, inpatient psychiatric care for individuals under age 21 or over 65 (see table 25). OBRA 1990 added two new optional services: home and community-based services for the functionally disabled elderly and community supported living arrangement services for the developmentally disabled. Total expenditures under these services are capped. States are permitted to establish limitations on the amount of care provided under a service category (such as limiting the number of days of covered hospital care or number of physicians' visits). Certain services to children may not be limited.

Federal law establishes the following requirements for coverage of the medically needy: (1) if a State provides medically needy coverage to any group it must provide ambulatory services to children and prenatal and delivery services for pregnant women; (2) if a State provides institutional services for any medically needy group it must also provide ambulatory services for this population group; and (3) if the State provides medically needy coverage for persons in intermediate care facilities for the mentally retarded (ICF/MRs) or institutions for mental diseases, it must offer to all groups covered in its medically needy program the same mix of institutional and noninstitutional services as required under prior law (that is, either all of the mandatory services or alternatively the care and services listed in 7 of the 25 paragraphs in the law defining covered services).

Financing

The Federal Government helps States share in the cost of Medicaid services by means of a variable matching formula which is adjusted annually. The matching rate, which is inversely related to a State's per capita income, can range from 50 percent to 83 percent though currently the highest rate is 78.85 percent. Federal matching for the territories is set at 50 percent with a maximum dollar limit placed on the amount each territory can receive. The Federal share of administrative costs is 50 percent for all States except for certain items where the authorized rate is higher.

Reimbursement Policy

States establish their own service reimbursement policies within general Federal guidelines. OBRA 1989 codified the regulatory requirement that payments must be sufficient to enlist enough providers so that covered services will be available to Medicaid beneficiaries at least to the extent they are available to the general population in a geographic area. Beginning April 1, 1990, States are required to submit to the Secretary their payment rates for pediatric and obstetrical services along with additional data that will assist the Secretary in evaluating the State's compliance with this requirement.

Until 1980, States were required to follow Medicare rules in paying for institutional services. The Boren amendment, enacted with respect to nursing homes in 1980 and extended to hospitals in 1981, authorized States to establish their own payment systems, as long as rates were reasonable and adequate to meet the costs of efficiently and economically operated facilities. Rates for hospitals must also be sufficient to assure reasonable access to inpatient services of adequate quality. A Supreme Court ruling in 1990, *Wilder* v. *Virginia Hospital Association,* affirmed that hospitals have the right under this rule to seek Federal court review of State reimbursement levels. Suits alleging inadequate hospital and nursing home payment have been filed in a number of States.

In addition to meeting general adequacy tests, State hospital reimbursement systems must provide for additional payments to facilities serving a disproportionate share of low-income patients. Unlike the comparable Medicare payments, Medicaid payments must follow a formula that considers a hospital's charity patients as well as its Medicaid caseload.

OBRA 1990 established new rules for Medicaid reimbursement of prescription drugs. The law denies Federal matching funds for drugs manufactured by a firm that has not agreed to provide rebates. Under amendments made by the Veterans Health Care Act of 1992, a manufacturer is not deemed to have a rebate agreement unless the manufacturer has entered into a master agreement with the Secretary of Veterans Affairs. Rebate amounts vary depending on the nature of the drug. The minimum rebate is 11 percent of the average price. OBRA 1990 established a 4-year moratorium on reductions in most payment rates for pharmacists.

Practitioners and providers are required to accept payments under the program as payment in full for covered services except where nominal cost-sharing charges may be required. States may generally impose such charges with certain exceptions. They are precluded from imposing such charges on services for children under 18, services related to pregnancy, family planning or emergency services, HMO services for the categorically needy, and services provided to NF inpatients who are required to spend all of their income for medical care except for a personal needs allowance.

ADMINISTRATION

Medicaid is a State-administered program. At the Federal level, the Health Care Financing Administration (HCFA) of the Department of Health and Human Services is responsible for overseeing State operations.

Federal law requires that a single State agency be charged with administration of the Medicaid program. Generally, that agency is either the State welfare agency, the State health agency, or the umbrella human resources agency. The single State agency may contract with other State entities to conduct some program functions. Further, States may process claims for reimbursement themselves or contract with fiscal agents or health insuring agencies to process these claims.

RECENT LEGISLATIVE CHANGES

The following is a summary of the major Medicaid changes enacted as part of the Omnibus Budget Reconciliation Act of 1990 (OBRA 1990), Public Law 101–508:

1. *Reimbursement for prescribed drugs.*—The law requires manufacturers of prescription drugs to provide rebates to State Medicaid programs. States will be required to cover all the drugs manufactured by a firm entering into a rebate agreement. The minimum rebate is 10 percent of the average manufacturer price for the product. Beginning in 1993, States are required to have prospective (i.e., point-of-sale) and retrospective drug utilization review (DUR) programs, to assure that prescriptions are appropriate and medically necessary. Until the end of 1993, enhanced Federal matching payments are provided for State administrative costs related to the rebate and DUR programs. The law establishes a 4-year moratorium on reductions in most payment rates for pharmacists.

2. *Required payment of premiums and cost-sharing for enrollment under group health plans where cost-effective.*—Effective January 1, 1991, the law requires States to pay premiums for group health plans for which Medicaid beneficiaries are eligible, when it is cost-effective to do so. Guidelines for determining cost-effectiveness are to be issued by the Secretary. States will pay any cost-sharing required by a plan and continue to furnish any Medicaid benefits not covered under the plan. Providers under group health plans will be required to accept plan payment as payment in full for Medicaid enrollees.

3. *Protection of low-income Medicare beneficiaries.*—The law accelerates phase-in of the requirement that States pay Medicare premiums and cost-sharing for QMBs, Medicare beneficiaries with incomes below 100 percent of the Federal poverty level; for all but 5 States, the requirement was effective January 1, 1991. All States must pay part B premiums (but not part A premiums or cost-sharing) for beneficiaries with incomes below 110 percent of the poverty level in 1993 and below 120 percent in 1995.

4. *Child health provisions.*—Effective July 1, 1991, all States are required to cover children under age 19 who were born after September 30, 1983, and whose family income is below 100 percent of the Federal poverty level. States are required to accept Medicaid applications for mothers and children at locations other than welfare offices, and are required to continue benefits for pregnant women until 2 months after the end of the pregnancy, and for infants through the first year of life. States are required to make additional payments for outlier cases and are prohibited from imposing durational limits on coverage for patients who are under age 1 in any hospital or under age 6 in a disproportionate share hospital.

5. *Home and community-based care as optional service.*—The law permits States to provide home and community-based services to functionally disabled Medicaid beneficiaries aged 65 or over, effec-

tive the later of July 1, 1991, or 30 days after the publication of interim rules. States will be permitted to limit eligibility for the services without waivers and thus to provide the services without meeting cost-effectiveness tests. Federal matching payments cannot exceed 50 percent of what it would have cost to provide Medicare nursing facility care to the same group of beneficiaries. Total Federal expenditures will be limited to $580 million over the period fiscal years 1991 to 1995.

6. *Community supported living arrangements.*—The law permits between two and eight States to provide community supported living arrangement services to developmentally disabled individuals who live with their families or in small community residential settings, effective the later of July 1, 1991, or 30 days after the publication of interim rules. Services will include personal assistance, training and habilitation, and other services needed to help with activities of daily living. Total Federal expenditures will be limited to $100 million over the period fiscal years 1991 to 1995.

7. *Payments for COBRA continuation coverage.*—The Consolidated Omnibus Budget Reconciliation Act of 1985 (COBRA, Public Law 99–272) provides that employees or dependents leaving an employee health insurance group in a firm with 20 or more employees must be offered an opportunity to continue buying insurance through the group for 18 to 36 months (depending on the reason for leaving the group). OBRA 1990 permits State Medicaid programs to pay for COBRA continuation coverage, when it is cost effective to do so, effective January 1, 1991. States may pay premiums for individuals with incomes below 100 percent of poverty and resources less than twice the SSI limit who are eligible for continuation coverage under a group health plan offered by an employer with 75 or more employees.

8. *Miscellaneous.*—The law establishes demonstration projects in three to four States to test the effect of providing Medicaid to families with incomes below 150 percent of the Federal poverty level that do not meet categorical eligibility requirements, and projects in two States to provide Medicaid coverage for early intervention services for HIV-infected individuals who do not meet disability criteria. The law also includes new measures to ensure the quality of physician services under Medicaid, technical corrections in nursing home reform provisions, and numerous other technical and miscellaneous amendments.

The following is a summary of the major changes enacted in the Medicaid Voluntary Contribution and Provider-Specific Tax Amendments of 1991, Public Law 102–234.

1. *Voluntary contributions and provider-specific taxes.*—The law caps Federal matching payments for State Medicaid spending that is financed with revenues from provider donations or taxes. Generally effective January 1, 1992, before the Federal share is computed, a State's expenditures for Medicaid are reduced by revenues received by a State or local government from provider-related donations, and health care related taxes that are not broad based. Broad based taxes are those that are uniformly imposed on all providers in a class, or all business in a class furnished by the providers. States with non-broad based taxes in effect or approved as of November 22, 1991, are permitted to continue them temporarily,

but the taxes may not be increased. States with voluntary contribution programs in effect or reported as of September 30, 1991, for States' fiscal year 1992, may continue them temporarily but may not increase them. During fiscal year 1993–95, Federal matching funds for revenue from voluntary contributions, provider specific taxes, and broad based taxes will be limited to the greater of 25 percent of the State share of Medicaid expenditures or the amount of donations and taxes collected in the State in fiscal year 1992.

Federal matching funds are allowable for certain donations. These are bona fide provider donations that are not related to Medicaid payments to the provider, and donations in the form of payment for outstationing Medicaid eligibility workers. Beginning in fiscal year 1993, the latter type of donations will be limited to 10 percent of a State's Medicaid administrative costs.

2. *Payments for disproportionate share hospitals.*—The law places an aggregate national cap of 12 percent of Medicaid expenditures on payment adjustments for disproportionate share hospitals (DSH). Beginning with fiscal year 1993, a national DSH payment limit is projected, and each State receives a DSH allotment for the fiscal year; Federal matching payments will be denied for DSH payments that exceed a State's annual allotment. For the part of fiscal year 1992 beginning on or after January 1, 1992, Federal matching payments will be made only for DSH adjustments paid in accordance with a State plan in effect or submitted by September 30, 1991, or November 26, 1991, if the State has used specific criteria to designate a hospital as DSH. Higher payments are permitted if necessary to meet the minimum adjustments required by Medicaid law.

Two 1991 acts concern enrollment in two health maintenance organizations. The law specifies that no more than 75 percent of the enrollees of an HMO may be Medicaid or Medicare beneficiaries. Public Law 102–276 authorized a waiver of this requirement for the Dayton Area Health Plan. Public Law 102–317 authorized a similar waiver for the Tennessee Primary Care Network.

The following is a summary of major Medicaid changes enacted in the Veterans Health Care Act of 1992, Public Law 102–585, pertaining to Medicaid reimbursement policies for prescription drugs.

1. *Calculation of best price.*—The law excludes certain prices from calculation of best price (the lowest price available from a manufacturer) for Medicaid drug rebates. The law excludes the prices charged to the Indian Health Service, the Department of Veterans Affairs, veterans' State homes, the Department of Defense, the Public Health Service and certain private and nonprofit hospitals, as well as any prices charged under the Federal Supply Schedule of the General Services Administration or under State pharmaceutical assistance programs.

2. *Rebate amounts.*—The law changes the minimum basic rebates for brand name drugs to 15.7 percent of the average manufacturer price (AMP) in calendar year 1993, 15.4 percent of the AMP in 1994, 15.2 percent of the AMP in 1995, and 15.1 percent of the AMP thereafter. In each calendar year, the basic rebate is the greater of the percentage stated, or the difference between the AMP and the best price.

The following is a summary of major Medicaid changes enacted in the Omnibus Budget Reconciliation Act of 1993 (OBRA 93), Public Law 103–66.

1. *Medicaid Fraud Control Units.*—The law changed the State option to a requirement that each State operate a Medicaid fraud and abuse control unit unless the State demonstrates that effective operation of a unit would not be cost-effective and that, in the absence of a unit, beneficiaries will be protected from abuse and neglect.

2. *Prescription drug formularies.*—States have been prohibited from using drug formularies (lists of covered and excluded drug products) and from imposing restrictions on new drug products for 6 months after a drug is approved by the Food and Drug Administration. Effective October 1, 1993, OBRA 93 allows States to use formularies to cover only the State's designated drug(s) in a class of therapeutic alternatives and impose certain requirements on prescriptions for new drugs.

3. *Asset and trust provisions.*—Some individuals must spend their assets down to a State-established level before Medicaid pays for nursing facility and other medical care. To try to ensure that these persons apply their assets to the cost of their care and do not give them away in order to gain Medicaid eligibility sooner than they otherwise would, Medicaid prohibits persons from transferring assets for less than fair market value.

OBRA 93 amends Medicaid law to close "loopholes" that allow individuals to shelter or divest assets in order to become eligible for Medicaid-covered long-term care. States are required to provide for a delay in Medicaid eligibility for institutionalized persons or their spouses who dispose of assets for less than fair market value. A transfer that occurred during the 36-month period prior to an application for coverage would trigger a period of ineligibility beginning with the month the assets were transferred. Under the OBRA 93 amendments, the period of ineligibility is determined by comparing the cost of care and the fair market value of the assets transferred.

The law requires that States seek recovery of Medicaid expenditures from the estate of a deceased beneficiary who received certain Medicaid benefits. Amounts paid by Medicaid for nursing facility services, home and community-based care, and related hospital and prescription drug services must be recovered from the estates of individuals who were over age 55 when such services were received.

OBRA 93 provides for exemptions to these asset transfer and recovery provisions if application of the law would result in "undue hardship" according to criteria established by the Secretary.

4. *Child support enforcement.*—A child who is covered by Medicaid may also be covered by private health insurance that is carried by a noncustodial parent. To improve medical support for children, Medicaid law is amended to mandate that States have laws in effect to require the cooperation of employers and insurers in obtaining parental coverage.

5. *Disproportionate share hospitals (DSH).*—OBRA 93 law prohibits States from designating a hospital as a DSH unless Medicaid beneficiaries account for at least 1 percent of the hospital's impatient days. In addition, the law requires that DSII payments to a

State or locally owned or operated facility cannot exceed the costs the facility incurs in furnishing inpatient or outpatient service to Medicaid beneficiaries or uninsured patients. For this purpose, a facility's cost is net of payments received from Medicaid (other than DSH payments) and from uninsured individuals.

6. *Physician referral.*—OBRA 93 limits Medicaid payments for designated health services (including clinical laboratory, physical and occupational therapy, radiology, or other diagnostic services, home health and other services) if such services are furnished upon referral from a physician who has a specified financial relationship with the provider furnishing the service.

7. *Childhood immunization.*—OBRA 93 established a new entitlement program under which States are entitled to receive vaccines purchased by the Federal government for federally eligible children up to age 18. Providers registered in a State's immunization program are entitled to receive free vaccines for children covered under the new law. Children eligible to receive federally-purchased vaccines are Medicaid-eligible, American Indian or Alaska Native, children whose health insurance does not cover the cost of vaccines, and children who receive immunization at federally qualified health centers or rural health clinics.

8. *Tuberculosis-related services.*—OBRA 93 permits States to provide Medicaid coverage for outpatient tuberculosis-related services to tuberculosis-infected individuals who meet the income and resource limits that apply to disabled persons.

PROGRAM DATA

Under current law, Federal Medicaid outlays are projected to reach $96.2 billion in fiscal year 1995, a 12 percent increase over the $85.8 billion projected for fiscal year 1994. Medicaid program data are presented in the following tables 18–13 to 18–24.

TABLE 18–13.—HISTORY OF MEDICAID PROGRAM COSTS

Fiscal year	Total		Federal		State	
	Dollars (in millions)	Percent increase	Dollars (in millions)	Percent increase	Dollars (in millions)	Percent increase
1966[1]	1,658	....	789	....	869	....
1967[1]	2,368	42.8	1,209	53.2	1,159	33.4
1968[1]	3,686	55.7	1,837	51.9	1,849	59.5
1969[1]	4,166	13.0	2,276	23.9	1,890	2.2
1970[1]	4,852	16.5	2,617	15.0	2,235	18.3
1971	6,176	27.3	3,374	28.9	2,802	25.4
1972[2]	8,434	36.6	4,361	29.3	4,074	45.4
1973	9,111	8.0	4,998	14.6	4,113	1.0
1974	10,229	12.3	5,833	16.7	4,396	6.9
1975	12,637	23.5	7,060	21.0	5,578	26.9
1976	14,644	15.9	8,312	17.7	6,332	13.5
TQ[3]	4,106	NA	2,354	NA	1,752	NA
1977	17,103	[4]16.8	9,713	[4]16.9	7,389	[4]16.7
1978	18,949	10.8	10,680	10.0	8,269	11.9
1979	21,755	14.8	12,267	14.9	9,489	14.8
1980	25,781	18.5	14,550	18.6	11,231	18.4
1981	30,377	17.8	17,074	17.3	13,303	18.4
1982	32,446	6.8	17,514	2.6	14,931	12.2
1983	34,956	7.7	18,985	8.4	15,971	7.0
1984	37,569	7.5	20,061	5.7	17,508	9.6
1985[5]	40,917	8.9	[6]22,655	12.9	[6]18,262	4.3

Year						
1986	44,851	9.6	24,995	10.3	19,856	8.7
1987	49,344	10.0	27,435	9.8	21,909	10.3
1988	54,116	9.7	30,462	11.0	23,654	8.0
1989	61,246	13.2	34,604	13.6	26,642	12.6
1990	72,492	18.4	41,103	18.8	31,389	17.8
1991	91,519	26.2	52,532	27.8	38,987	24.2
1992	118,166	29.1	67,827	29.1	50,339	29.1
1993	132,010	11.7	75,774	11.7	56,236	11.7
1994 (current law estimate)	152,371	15.4	87,156	15.0	65,215	16.0
1995 (current law estimate)	168,806	10.8	96,388	10.6	72,418	11.0

[1] Includes related programs which are not separately identified, though for each successive year a larger portion of the total represents Medicaid expenditures. As of Jan. 1, 1970, Federal matching was only available under Medicaid.

[2] Intermediate care facilities (ICFs) transferred from the cash assistance programs to Medicaid effective January 1, 1972. Data for prior periods do not include these costs.

[3] Transitional quarter (beginning of Federal fiscal year moved from July 1 to Oct. 1).

[4] Represents increase over fiscal year 1976, i.e., five calendar quarters.

[5] Includes transfer of function of State fraud control units to Medicaid from Office of Inspector General.

[6] Temporary reductions in Federal payments authorized for fiscal years 1982–84 were discontinued in fiscal year 1985.

Note: Totals may not add due to rounding.

Source: "Budget of the U.S. Government" fiscal years 1969–95, and Health Care Financing Administration, Division of Budget.

TABLE 18-14.—UNDUPLICATED NUMBER OF MEDICAID RECIPIENTS BY ELIGIBILITY CATEGORY, FISCAL YEARS 1972–92

[Number in thousands]

Fiscal year	Total	Aged 65 or over	Blindness	Permanent and total disability	Dependent children under age 21	Adults in families with dependent children	Other Title XIX
1972	17,606	3,318	108	1,625	7,841	3,137	1,576
1973	19,622	3,496	101	1,804	8,659	4,066	1,495
1974	21,462	3,732	135	2,222	9,478	4,392	1,502
1975	22,007	3,615	109	2,355	9,598	4,529	1,800
1976	22,815	3,612	97	2,572	9,924	4,774	1,836
1977 [1]	22,832	3,636	92	2,710	9,651	4,785	1,959
1978	21,965	3,376	82	2,636	9,376	4,643	1,852
1979	21,520	3,364	79	2,674	9,106	4,570	1,727
1980 [2]	21,605	3,440	92	2,819	9,333	4,877	1,499
1981 [2]	21,980	3,367	86	2,993	9,581	5,187	1,364
1982 [2]	21,603	3,240	84	2,806	9,563	5,356	1,434
1983 [2]	21,554	3,371	77	2,844	9,535	5,592	1,129
1984 [2]	21,607	3,238	79	2,834	9,684	5,600	1,187
1985 [2]	21,814	3,061	80	2,937	9,757	5,518	1,214
1986 [2]	22,515	3,140	82	3,100	10,029	5,647	1,362
1987 [2]	23,109	3,224	85	3,296	10,168	5,599	1,418
1988 [2]	22,907	3,159	86	3,401	10,037	5,503	1,343
1989 [2]	23,511	3,132	95	3,496	10,318	5,717	1,175
1990	25,255	3,202	83	3,635	11,220	6,010	1,105
1991	28,280	3,359	85	3,983	13,415	6,778	658
1992	30,926	3,742	84	4,378	15,104	6,954	664

[1] Fiscal Year 1977 began in October 1976 and was the first year of the new Federal fiscal cycle. Before 1977, the fiscal year began in July.

[2] Beginning in fiscal year 1980, recipients' categories do not add to the unduplicated total due to the small number of recipients that are in more than one category during the year.

Source: HCFA, BDMS, OPS, Division of Medicaid Statistics, Fiscal Years 1972–91, Office of the Actuary, Fiscal years 1993 and beyond. December 22, 1993.

TABLE 18–15.—MEDICAID RECIPIENTS BY BASIS OF ELIGIBILITY BY STATE: FISCAL YEAR 1992

State	Total recipients [1]	Aged	Blind	Disabled	AFDC children	AFDC adults	Other Title XIX
Alabama	466,918	69,882	1,586	100,187	198,418	91,022	4,574
Alaska	57,540	3,388	81	4,633	32,479	16,959	0
Arizona	402,212	23,258	693	43,696	236,155	98,410	0
Arkansas	320,875	51,489	1,289	67,511	97,549	70,969	32,068
California	4,485,743	491,686	24,306	609,612	2,008,346	1,256,752	60,350
Colorado	258,690	30,621	157	34,254	125,026	65,065	3,567
Connecticut	316,278	55,102	281	37,836	146,719	76,340	0
Delaware	60,696	5,358	105	8,461	31,687	13,558	1,325
District of Columbia	108,514	11,541	5	16,731	55,304	24,812	121
Florida	1,537,926	186,180	3,403	204,373	811,973	294,157	37,840
Georgia	863,670	99,625	4,722	139,095	412,087	198,838	1,112
Hawaii	99,666	13,817	15	10,239	47,368	26,111	0
Idaho	86,924	8,783	52	12,480	44,224	20,758	627
Illinois	1,313,140	105,955	1,359	213,951	669,474	303,931	18,470
Indiana	506,829	52,433	1,172	70,558	252,765	127,264	0
Iowa	278,828	38,333	619	39,000	116,983	68,277	14,868
Kansas	226,991	25,268	115	27,057	108,272	53,397	0
Kentucky	583,089	61,052	1,924	113,316	257,105	136,641	1,882
Louisiana	702,264	96,403	1,797	111,025	345,662	147,377	0
Maine	162,441	22,332	207	27,281	69,082	37,367	5,567
Maryland	377,075	49,749	306	61,045	182,487	77,702	5,786
Massachusetts	686,235	105,314	10,362	122,202	295,507	152,849	0
Michigan	1,129,023	84,998	2,212	167,448	565,350	309,015	0
Minnesota	406,491	57,801	461	41,697	195,047	99,891	11,594
Mississippi	486,861	65,989	1,634	92,784	321,010	3,973	1,471
Missouri	554,477	78,916	1,127	76,338	258,573	137,413	2
Montana	60,186	8,115	76	12,618	20,690	3,434	13,740
Nebraska	150,791	19,939	223	17,612	67,553	31,793	13,671
Nevada	77,525	9,091	415	9,998	36,551	18,840	1,584
New Hampshire	71,179	13,882	486	9,442	33,815	13,224	0

TABLE 18–15.—MEDICAID RECIPIENTS BY BASIS OF ELIGIBILITY BY STATE: FISCAL YEAR 1992—Continued

State	Total recipients [1]	Aged	Blind	Disabled	AFDC children	AFDC adults	Other Title XIX
New Jersey	697,083	78,663	1,200	107,949	327,381	175,240	0
New Mexico	211,805	14,106	560	25,446	128,312	43,381	0
New York	2,557,701	339,784	3,732	370,858	1,141,711	516,124	185,492
North Carolina	785,043	120,599	1,047	91,385	368,882	203,130	0
North Dakota	57,068	10,713	28	7,067	24,213	12,488	2,189
Ohio	1,442,289	152,083	957	162,159	777,458	345,594	4,038
Oklahoma	360,039	55,955	670	42,863	178,902	80,951	698
Oregon	295,320	29,138	1,190	34,906	150,943	79,143	0
Pennsylvania	1,174,779	136,293	942	195,284	562,049	237,670	41,807
Rhode Island	213,388	39,660	521	40,936	87,193	43,452	1,629
South Carolina	431,083	72,339	1,812	67,685	198,972	90,212	63
South Dakota	64,230	9,751	149	10,045	31,097	13,188	0
Tennessee	785,231	93,455	2,574	156,723	367,193	153,950	11,336
Texas	2,024,554	265,254	3,921	189,471	1,100,136	465,772	0
Utah	137,264	8,814	117	14,305	72,860	39,726	24
Vermont	77,502	10,643	94	10,546	34,342	21,058	455
Virginia	515,064	78,411	1,146	76,752	244,340	114,415	0
Washington	568,673	50,639	365	81,049	232,246	156,546	46,259
West Virginia	308,034	31,609	272	49,168	131,024	93,117	2,844
Wisconsin	440,136	66,845	1,189	87,560	161,587	78,107	40,657
Wyoming	42,401	3,086	8	3,890	23,523	11,023	570
Puerto Rico	885,405	127,011	469	48,779	709,146	0	0
Virgin Islands	13,221	1,143	6	889	7,265	3,403	515
United States	30,027,764	3,614,140	83,684	4,328,527	14,387,625	6,950,426	568,280
All jurisdictions	30,926,390	3,742,294	84,159	4,378,195	15,104,036	6,953,829	568,795

[1] Total recipients include unknowns which are not reflected in this table.

Source: HCFA, BDMS, Office of Programs Systems, data from Division of Medicaid Statistics December 22, 1993.

TABLE 18–16.—MEDICAID EXPENDITURES BY BASIS OF ELIGIBILITY BY STATE: FISCAL YEAR 1992

[In millions of dollars]

State	Total expenditures [2]	Aged	Blind	Disabled	AFDC children	AFDC adults	Other title XIX	Aged, blind and disabled as a percent of total exp.	AFDC children as a percent of total exp.
Alabama	1,056	352	4	392	148	149	9	70.9	14.0
Alaska	187	37	(1)	48	53	48	0	46.0	28.5
Arizona	209	13	1	63	96	35	0	37.3	45.8
Arkansas	885	266	6	367	87	85	74	72.2	9.9
California	8,692	2,251	96	2,983	1,309	1,860	129	61.3	15.1
Colorado	814	233	4	303	129	128	17	66.4	15.9
Connecticut	1,663	797	4	570	163	129	0	82.4	9.8
Delaware	219	62	1	96	32	25	3	72.3	14.7
District of Columbia	499	140	(1)	212	92	54	(1)	70.7	18.4
Florida	3,518	1,074	14	1,160	756	457	57	63.9	21.5
Georgia	2,149	538	28	735	356	471	1	60.6	16.6
Hawaii	270	112	(1)	64	44	48	0	65.4	16.3
Idaho	275	72	(1)	118	42	41	1	69.3	15.4
Illinois	4,070	872	9	1,995	651	486	56	70.7	16.0
Indiana	2,225	557	9	930	401	322	9	67.2	18.0
Iowa	855	238	2	332	119	133	29	67.0	13.9
Kansas	620	187	(1)	225	100	86	0	66.6	16.2
Kentucky	1,543	361	8	609	279	279	1	63.3	18.1
Louisiana	2,479	532	10	972	533	433	0	61.0	21.5
Maine	642	240	1	235	76	76	13	74.1	11.8
Maryland	1,612	445	2	644	276	193	52	67.7	17.1
Massachusetts	3,248	1,256	88	1,224	372	308	0	79.1	11.5
Michigan	2,802	652	10	1,232	459	449	0	67.6	16.4
Minnesota	1,750	713	6	631	196	183	21	77.1	11.2
Mississippi	881	264	5	317	289	2	4	66.5	32.8
Missouri	1,350	472	5	461	234	175	(1)	69.4	17.3
Montana	217	77	(1)	95	17	5	15	79.6	7.9
Nebraska	468	168	2	153	63	50	33	69.0	13.4
Nevada	282	64	3	100	49	52	7	59.4	17.4
New Hampshire	340	167	7	112	33	20	0	84.2	9.8
New Jersey	2,802	912	8	1,163	311	400	0	74.3	11.1

TABLE 18–16.—MEDICAID EXPENDITURES BY BASIS OF ELIGIBILITY BY STATE: FISCAL YEAR 1992—Continued

[In millions of dollars]

State	Total expenditures [2]	Aged	Blind	Disabled	AFDC children	AFDC adults	Other title XIX	Aged, blind and disabled as a percent of total exp.	AFDC children as a percent of total exp.
New Mexico	478	93	4	160	148	73	0	53.8	30.9
New York	15,281	6,214	102	5,710	1,766	1,207	283	78.7	11.6
North Carolina	2,083	647	9	673	414	341	0	63.8	19.9
North Dakota	253	99	(¹)	98	30	22	2	78.2	11.9
Ohio	4,308	1,535	4	1,374	853	541	1	67.6	19.8
Oklahoma	1,004	288	2	299	272	141	1	58.7	27.1
Oregon	748	201	20	288	137	103	0	68.0	18.3
Pennsylvania	3,547	1,368	3	1,265	513	345	54	74.3	14.5
Rhode Island	774	283	3	346	72	64	6	81.6	9.3
South Carolina	1,151	329	6	414	218	184	(¹)	65.0	19.0
South Dakota	231	85	1	90	34	20	0	76.3	14.9
Tennessee	1,735	441	7	646	354	255	32	63.1	20.4
Texas	4,407	1,402	16	1,228	976	785	0	60.0	22.1
Utah	365	64	1	139	72	88	(¹)	55.8	19.6
Vermont	222	75	(¹)	93	22	30	1	75.6	10.1
Virginia	1,511	486	6	525	273	222	0	67.3	18.0
Washington	1,347	420	2	423	184	286	32	62.7	13.6
West Virginia	795	200	1	276	111	175	32	60.0	13.9
Wisconsin	1,677	663	8	693	124	102	62	81.4	7.4
Wyoming	114	34	(¹)	33	26	21	1	58.1	22.6
Puerto Rico	158	23	(¹)	33	127	0	0	19.9	80.1
Virgin Islands	5	1	(¹)	9	2	1	(¹)	35.2	34.6
United States	90,651	29,054	530	33,316	14,363	12,184	1,032	69.4	15.8
All jurisdictions	90,814	29,078	530	33,326	14,491	12,185	1,032	69.3	16.0

¹ Denotes expenditures of less than $500,000.

² Total expenditures include unknowns which are not reflected in this table.

Source: HCFA, BDMS, Office of Programs Systems, data from Division of Medicaid Statistics, December 22, 1993.

TABLE 18–17.—TOTAL AND PER CAPITA MEDICAID PAYMENTS FOR CATEGORICALLY NEEDY AND MEDICALLY NEEDY, PRELIMINARY ESTIMATES, FISCAL YEARS 1975, 1981 AND 1992

	1975			1981			1992			Percent change 1975–92	
	Total amount (millions)	Percent of total	Per capita	Total amount (millions)	Percent of total	Per capita	Total amount (millions)	Percent of total	Per capita	Total spending	Per capita
Categorically needy:											
Receiving cash payments	$7,188	58.7	$431	$14,534	53.4	$861	$41,742	46.0	$2,238	$480.7	$419.3
Aged	1,341	11.0	555	2,480	9.1	1,270	5,795	6.4	3,778	332.1	580.7
Blind	61	.5	717	109	.4	1,527	334	0.4	4,669	447.5	551.2
Disabled	2,042	16.7	1,094	5,616	20.6	2,490	19,863	21.9	6,097	872.7	457.3
AFDC children	1,850	15.1	222	3,002	11.0	361	8,376	9.2	891	352.8	301.4
Adults in AFDC families	1,895	15.5	478	3,328	12.2	769	7,374	8.1	1,682	289.1	251.9
Not receiving cash payments	1,753	14.3	1,261	4,736	17.4	2,641	16,064	17.7	4,243	816.4	236.5
Aged	1,275	10.4	2,331	3,143	11.6	5,273	7,085	7.8	11,658	455.7	400.1
Blind	12	.1	1,094	19	.1	2,785	80	0.1	15,310	566.7	1,299.5
Disabled	353	2.9	1,854	1,214	4.5	5,146	5,065	5.6	11,913	1,334.8	542.6
AFDC children	61	.5	152	153	.6	302	1,764	1.9	1,156	791.8	660.5
Adults in AFDC families	27	.2	144	87	.3	298	1,428	1.6	1,606	5,188.9	1,015.3
Other title XIX	25	.2	463	120	.4	734	643	0.7	1,927	2,472.0	316.2
Total, categorically needy	8,941	73.0	495	19,270	70.8	1,032	57,807	63.7	2,577	546.5	420.6
Medically needy:											
Aged	1,742	14.2	2,672	4,303	15.8	5,260	8,927	9.8	11,724	412.5	338.8
Blind	20	.2	1,472	27	.1	3,132	71	0.1	21,865	255.0	940.0
Disabled	657	5.4	2,202	2,471	9.1	4,924	5,243	5.8	13,876	698.0	530.2
AFDC children	274	2.2	324	353	1.3	460	1,592	1.8	943	481.0	191.0
Adults in AFDC families	140	1.1	368	348	1.3	613	1,265	1.4	1,930	803.6	424.5
Other title XIX	467	3.8	267	433	1.6	360	268	0.3	1,844	–42.6	590.6
Total, medically needy	3,301	27.0	838	7,935	29.2	2,145	17,367	19.1	4,782	426.1	470.6
Grand total	12,242	100.0	556	27,205	100.0	1,216	90,814	100.0	2,936	641.8	428.1

Note: Totals may not add due to rounding. Fiscal year 1975 ends in June; fiscal years 1981 and 1988 end in September. Total includes other coverage groups and unknowns. Other categories not shown in the total for 1991 are: Other coverage pre-88, $6,799; coverage from 88, $4,070; and mass unknown, $220.

Source: HCFA, BDMS, OPS, Division of Medicaid Statistics, December 22, 1993.

TABLE 18–18.—MEDICAID RECIPIENTS AND PAYMENTS BY BASIS OF ELIGIBILITY, FISCAL YEAR 1992

	Amount (in millions)	Percent of total	Recipients (in thousands)	Percent of total	Per capita payments
Age 65 and over	29,077.6	32.0	3,742.3	12.1	7,770.0
Blind	530.0	0.6	84.2	0.3	6,297.7
Disabled	33,325.8	36.7	4,378.2	14.2	7,611.8
Dependent children under age 21	14,491.0	16.0	15,104.0	48.8	959.4
Adults in families with dependent children	12,185.2	13.4	6,953.8	22.5	1,752.3
Other title XIX	1,031.9	1.1	568.8	1.8	1,814.3
Total	90,813.5	100.0	30,926.4	100.0	2,936.4

Note: Recipients and payments totals include unknowns which are not shown in this table.

Source: HCFA, BDMS, Office of Programs Systems. Data from Division of Medicaid Statistics, December 22, 1993.

TABLE 18–19.—MEDICAID PAYMENTS AND PER CAPITA PAYMENTS BY BASIS OF ELIGIBILITY, FISCAL YEARS 1975, 1981, AND 1984–92

[Amounts in millions of dollars]

	1975	1981	1984	1985	1986	1987	1988	1989	1990	1991	1992	Percent change, 1975–92
					In Nominal Dollars							
Payments:												
Age 65 and over	4,358	9,926	12,815	14,096	15,097	16,037	17,135	18,558	21,508	25,453	29,078	567.3
Blind	93	154	219	249	277	309	344	409	434	475	530	47.6
Disabled	3,052	9,301	11,758	13,203	14,635	16,507	18,250	20,476	23,969	27,798	33,326	991.8
Dependent children under age 21	2,186	3,508	3,979	4,414	5,135	5,508	5,848	6,892	9,100	11,690	14,491	562.9
Adults in families with dependent children	2,062	3,763	4,420	4,746	4,880	5,592	5,883	6,897	8,590	10,439	12,185	491.0
Other title XIX	492	552	700	798	980	1,078	1,198	1,137	1,051	973	1,032	109.9
Total	12,242	27,204	33,891	37,508	41,005	45,050	48,710	54,500	64,859	77,048	90,814	641.8
Per capita payment:												
Age 65 and over	1,205	2,948	3,957	4,605	4,808	4,975	5,425	5,926	6,717	7,577	7,770	544.6
Blind	850	1,784	2,766	3,104	3,401	3,644	4,005	4,319	5,212	5,572	6,298	641.0
Disabled	1,296	3,108	4,149	4,496	4,721	5,008	5,366	5,858	6,595	6,979	7,612	487.3
Dependent children under age 21	228	366	411	452	512	542	583	668	811	871	959	321.2
Adults in families with dependent children	455	725	789	860	864	999	1,069	1,206	1,429	1,540	1,752	248.9
Other title XIX	273	405	590	658	719	761	891	967	1,062	1,732	1,814	564.2
Total, per capita payment	556	1,238	1,569	1,719	1,821	1,949	2,126	2,318	2,568	2,725	2,936	427.9

TABLE 18–19.—MEDICAID PAYMENTS AND PER CAPITA PAYMENTS BY BASIS OF ELIGIBILITY, FISCAL YEARS 1975, 1981, AND 1984–92—Continued

[Amounts in millions of dollars]

	1975	1981	1984	1985	1986	1987	1988	1989	1990	1991	1992	Percent change, 1975–92
					In Constant 1992 Dollars							
Payments:												
Age 65 and over	11,723	15,584	17,300	18,466	19,173	19,886	20,391	21,156	23,229	26,217	29,078	148.0
Blind	250	242	296	326	352	383	409	466	469	489	530	112.0
Disabled	8,210	14,603	15,873	17,296	18,586	20,469	21,718	23,343	25,887	28,632	33,326	305.9
Dependent children under age 21	5,880	5,508	5,372	5,782	6,521	6,830	6,959	7,857	9,828	12,041	14,491	146.4
Adults in families with dependent children	5,547	5,908	5,967	6,217	6,198	6,934	7,001	7,863	9,277	10,752	12,185	119.7
Other title XIX	1,323	867	945	1,045	1,245	1,337	1,426	1,296	1,135	1,002	1,032	–22.0
Total [1]	32,931	42,710	45,753	49,135	52,076	55,862	57,965	62,130	70,048	79,359	90,814	175.8
Per capita payment:												
Age 65 and over	3,241	4,628	5,342	6,033	6,106	6,169	6,456	6,756	7,254	7,804	7,770	139.7
Blind	2,287	2,801	3,734	4,066	4,319	4,519	4,766	4,924	5,629	5,739	6,298	173.4
Disabled	3,486	4,880	5,601	5,890	5,996	6,210	6,386	6,678	7,123	7,188	7,612	118.4
Dependent children under age 21	613	575	555	592	650	672	694	762	876	897	959	56.4
Adults in families with dependent children	1,224	1,338	1,065	1,127	1,097	1,239	1,272	1,375	1,543	1,586	1,752	43.1
Other title XIX	734	636	797	862	913	944	1,060	1,102	1,147	1,784	1,814	147.1
Total, per capita payment	1,496	1,944	2,118	2,252	2,313	2,417	2,530	2,643	2,773	2,807	2,936	96.3

[1] Data exclude unknowns.

Note: Total may not add due to rounding. Fiscal year 1975 ends in June; all other fiscal years end in September. Nominal dollars converted to constant dollars using CPI–U price index. Total expenditures includes other coverage groups and unknowns for fiscal year 1992.

Source: HCFA, BDMS, OPS, Division of Medicaid Statistics, December, 1993, and Congressional Research Service.

TABLE 18–20.—MEDICAID PAYMENTS BY SERVICE CATEGORY, FISCAL YEARS 1975, 1981, 1990–92

[Amounts in millions of constant 1990 dollars]

	1975		1981		1990		1992		Average annual percent change 1975–92
	Amount	Percent	Amount	Percent	Amount	Percent	Amount	Percent of total	
Inpatient hospital	$9,396	30.9	$11,693	29.7	$18,388	28.4	$23,743	28.3	5.6
General	8,389	27.6	10,423	26.4	16,674	25.7	21,715	25.9	5.8
Mental	1,007	3.3	1,271	3.2	1,714	2.6	2,029	2.4	4.2
Skilled nursing facilities	¹6,052	19.9	5,846	14.8	8,026	12.4	21,752	25.9	7.8
Intermediate care facilities	5,632	18.5	10,870	27.6	17,021	26.2	(¹)	(¹)	(¹)
Intermediate care facilities for the mentally retarded	945	3.1	4,341	11.0	7,354	11.3	7,853	9.4	2.0
Other	4,687	15.4	6,530	16.6	9,667	14.9	(¹)	(¹)	(¹)
Physician	3,046	10.0	3,044	7.7	4,018	6.2	5,638	6.7	3.7
Dental	843	2.8	787	2.0	593	0.9	786	0.9	−0.4
Other practitioner	316	1.0	330	0.8	372	0.6	497	0.6	2.7
Outpatient hospital	927	3.0	2,041	5.2	3,324	5.1	4,877	5.8	10.3
Clinic	967	3.2	540	1.4	1,688	2.6	2,604	3.1	6.0
Lab and X-ray	313	1.0	213	0.5	721	1.1	956	1.1	6.8
Home health	174	0.6	620	1.6	3,404	5.2	4,514	5.4	21.1
Prescribed drugs	2,026	6.7	2,224	5.6	4,420	6.8	6,250	7.4	6.9
Family planning	167	0.5	201	0.5	265	0.4	462	0.6	6.2
Early and periodic screening ²	(²)	0.0	97	0.2	198	0.3	478	0.6	(¹)
Rural health clinic ²	(²)	0.0	6	0.0	34	0.1	125	0.1	(¹)
Other	579	1.9	897	2.3	2,385	3.7	3,317	4.0	10.8
Total	30,440	100.0	39,414	100.0	64,859	100.0	83,904	100	6.1

¹ Prior to fiscal year 1991, there were two categories of Medicaid nursing home care: skilled nursing facilities or intermediate nursing facilities. ² 1975 data not available.

Note: Totals may not add due to rounding. Fiscal year 1975 ends in June; all other fiscal years end in September. Spending amounts put in constant dollars using the Consumer Price Index (CPI–U). Data exclude unknowns. Source: HCFA, BDMS, Office of Programs Systems. Data from Division of Medicaid Statistics. December 22, 1993.

TABLE 18–21.—MEDICAID RECIPIENTS BY SERVICE CATEGORY, FOR FISCAL YEARS 1975, 1981, 1989–92

[In thousands]

	Fiscal year—					
	1975	1981	1989	1990	1991	1992
Inpatient hospital:						
General	3,432	3,703	4,171	4,593	5,137	5,768
Mental	67	90	90	92	5,072	77
Nursing facilities [1]	1,312	1,385	1,452	1,461	1,499	1,573
Intermediate care facilities for the mentally retarded	69	151	148	147	146	151
Physician	15,198	14,403	15,686	17,078	19,321	21,627
Dental	3,944	5,173	4,214	4,552	5,209	5,700
Other practitioner	2,673	3,582	3,555	3,873	4,282	4,711
Outpatient hospital	7,437	10,018	11,344	12,370	14,137	15,120
Clinic	1,086	1,755	2,391	2,804	3,511	4,115
Laboratory & X ray	4,738	3,822	7,759	8,959	10,505	11,804
Home health	343	402	609	719	813	925
Prescribed drugs	14,155	14,256	15,916	17,294	19,602	22,030
Family planning	1,217	1,473	1,564	1,752	2,185	2,550
Early and periodic screening	(2)	1,969	2,524	2,952	3,957	4,982
Rural health clinics	(2)	81	166	224	405	743
Other	2,911	2,344	4,583	5,126	5,957	6,702
Unduplicated total	22,007	21,980	23,511	25,255	28,280	30,926

[1] Prior to fiscal year 1991, there were 2 categories of Medicaid nursing home care: skilled nursing facilities or intermediate nursing facilities.
[2] 1975 data not available.

Source: HCFA, BDMS, Office of Programs Systems, Division of Medicaid Statistics, December 1993.

TABLE 18–22.—MEDICAID MEDICAL VENDOR PAYMENTS BY BASIS OF ELIGIBILITY AND TYPE OF SERVICE: FISCAL YEAR 1992

[In millions of dollars]

Type of service	Aged	Blind	Disabled	AFDC Children	AFDC Adults	Other title XIX	Total
Inpatient hospital services	1,869.9	86.1	8,927.4	6,554.6	5,480.8	466.1	23,384.9
Mental hospital services for the aged	908.5	.4	57.2	2.5	1.9	2.5	973.0
SNF/ICF mental health services for the aged	114.4	.0	5.1	0	0	0	119.5
Inpatient psychiatric services, age <22	.3	.4	344.9	617.4	11.4	126.9	1,101.3
Intermediate care facility for the mentally retarded	519.6	130.9	7,837.9	37.6	14.2	4.7	8,545.0
Nursing facility services	19,596.5	107.5	3,762.0	15.1	45.7	8.3	23,535.0
Physician's services	399.6	24.1	1,485.0	1,946.9	2,138.9	94.1	6,088.5
Dental services	52.0	1.6	133.2	417.0	225.3	21.8	850.8
Other practitioners' services	66.1	2.6	199.3	136.7	126.0	7.1	537.8
Outpatient hospital services	310.8	19.4	1,600.9	1,736.1	1,521.3	84.4	5,272.8
Clinic services	174.1	18.0	1,555.6	572.5	414.8	79.0	2,814.0
Home health services	2,249.6	55.1	2,383.7	121.4	55.5	19.6	4,885.0
Family planning services	1.1	.5	25.8	57.3	408.5	6.6	499.7
Lab and x ray services	53.1	4.0	310.6	221.6	432.0	11.3	1,032.7
Prescribed drugs	2,190.9	48.9	2,873.7	806.3	805.2	37.0	6,762.0
Early and periodic screening	.1	.3	36.2	449.1	16.8	13.5	516.0
Rural health clinic services	4.4	.3	20.1	61.0	46.8	1.8	134.4
Other care	565.8	30.1	1,764.8	737.5	440.0	47.0	3,585.1
Unknown	.9	0	2.7	.4	.1	0	4.1
Total	29,077.6	530.0	33,325.8	14,491.0	12,185.2	1,031.9	90,641.6

TABLE 18–22.—MEDICAID MEDICAL VENDOR PAYMENTS BY BASIS OF ELIGIBILITY AND TYPE OF SERVICE: FISCAL YEAR 1992—Continued

[In percent]

Type of service	Aged	Blind	Disabled	AFDC		Other title XIX	Total
				Children	Adults		
Inpatient hospital services	6.4	16.2	26.8	45.2	45.0	45.2	25.8
Mental hospital services for the aged	3.1	.1	.2	0	0	.2	1.1
SNF/ICF mental health services for the aged	.4	0	0	0	0	0	.1
Inpatient psychiatric services, age <22	0	.1	1.0	4.3	.1	12.3	1.2
Intermediate care facility for the mentally retarded	1.8	24.7	23.5	.3	.1	.5	9.4
Nursing facility services	67.4	20.3	11.3	.1	.4	.8	26.0
Physician's services	1.4	4.5	4.5	13.4	17.6	9.1	6.7
Dental services	.2	.3	.4	2.9	1.8	2.1	.9
Other practitioners' services	.2	.5	.6	.9	1.0	.7	.6
Outpatient hospital services	1.1	3.7	4.8	12.0	12.5	8.2	5.8
Clinic services	.6	3.4	4.7	4.0	3.4	7.7	3.1
Home health services	7.7	10.4	7.2	.8	.5	1.9	5.4
Family planning services	0	.1	.1	.4	3.4	.6	.6
Lab and x ray services	.2	.8	.9	1.5	3.5	1.1	1.1
Prescribed drugs	7.5	9.2	8.6	5.6	6.6	3.6	7.5
Early and periodic screening	0	.1	.1	3.1	.1	1.3	.6
Rural health clinic services	0	.1	.1	.4	.4	.2	.1
Other care	1.9	5.7	5.3	5.1	3.6	4.6	4.0
Unknown	0	0	0	0	0	0	0
Total	100.0	100.0	100.0	100.0	100.0	100.0	100.0

Source: HCFA, BDMS, Office of Programs Systems. Data from Division of Medicaid Statistics, December 22, 1993.

TABLE 18–23.—AVERAGE EXPENDITURE PER RECIPIENT BY BASIS OF ELIGIBILITY BY STATE: FISCAL YEAR 1992

State	Total	Aged	Blind	Disabled	AFDC Children	AFDC Adults	Other title XIX
United States	$3,019	$8,039	$6,332	$7,697	$998	$1,753	$1,816
All jurisdictions	2,936	7,770	6,298	7,612	959	1,752	1,814
Alabama	2,262	5,042	2,785	3,915	746	1,636	1,966
Alaska	3,248	10,934	6,068	10,467	1,640	2,806	0
Arizona	520	579	1,870	1,446	406	359	0
Arkansas	2,758	5,163	4,653	5,430	896	1,192	2,320
California	1,938	4,579	3,959	4,894	652	1,480	2,137
Colorado	3,145	7,618	25,435	8,845	1,033	1,961	4,691
Connecticut	5,258	14,458	14,836	15,070	1,111	1,691	0
Delaware	3,611	11,515	5,914	11,369	1,014	1,842	2,170
District of Columbia	4,595	12,171	5,493	12,658	1,658	2,187	2,603
Florida	2,288	5,770	4,133	5,676	932	1,553	1,495
Georgia	2,488	5,405	6,019	5,283	865	2,369	1,106
Hawaii	2,706	8,115	2,701	6,282	929	1,831	0
Idaho	3,159	8,154	6,587	9,481	955	1,979	1,534
Illinois	3,099	8,233	6,983	9,327	972	1,599	3,045
Indiana	4,390	10,627	7,635	13,181	1,585	2,531	0
Iowa	3,065	6,206	3,972	8,522	1,015	1,952	1,981
Kansas	2,730	7,410	4,076	8,322	928	1,619	0
Kentucky	2,647	5,908	4,139	5,374	1,085	2,039	582
Louisiana	3,530	5,514	5,470	8,755	1,541	2,937	0
Maine	3,950	10,751	3,918	8,604	1,094	2,044	2,420
Maryland	4,276	8,942	7,577	10,553	1,512	2,484	9,015
Massachusetts	4,733	11,925	8,495	10,015	1,259	2,015	0
Michigan	2,482	7,674	4,345	7,359	811	1,454	0
Minnesota	4,306	12,339	12,384	15,130	1,007	1,829	1,839
Mississippi	1,809	4,005	2,870	3,416	899	575	2,754
Missouri	2,435	5,975	4,149	6,043	906	1,276	333
Montana	3,599	9,500	3,507	7,543	832	1,564	1,118
Nebraska	3,103	8,421	7,586	8,710	926	1,560	2,397
Nevada	3,635	7,035	7,971	10,018	1,343	2,753	4,447
New Hampshire	4,779	12,040	14,507	11,883	986	1,501	0
New Jersey	4,019	11,592	6,471	10,776	950	2,281	0
New Mexico	2,259	6,622	6,847	6,301	1,153	1,682	0
New York	5,975	18,288	27,316	15,396	1,547	2,338	1,525
North Carolina	2,654	5,368	8,314	7,359	1,121	1,679	0
North Dakota	4,430	9,275	6,169	13,891	1,238	1,765	1,095
Ohio	2,987	10,090	3,815	8,474	1,098	1,564	340
Oklahoma	2,788	5,156	3,095	6,976	1,521	1,747	1,022
Oregon	2,532	6,906	16,468	8,237	905	1,298	0
Pennsylvania	3,019	10,038	3,435	6,477	912	1,451	1,295
Rhode Island	3,628	7,128	5,864	8,458	825	1,480	3,572
South Carolina	2,670	4,549	3,235	6,112	1,097	2,039	2,419
South Dakota	3,597	8,755	3,517	9,006	1,109	1,530	0
Tennessee	2,210	4,723	2,831	4,121	964	1,655	2,818

TABLE 18–23.—AVERAGE EXPENDITURE PER RECIPIENT BY BASIS OF ELIGIBILITY BY STATE: FISCAL YEAR 1992—Continued

State	Total	Aged	Blind	Disabled	AFDC Children	AFDC Adults	Other title XIX
Texas	2,177	5,284	4,193	6,481	887	1,685	0
Utah	2,662	7,318	7,532	9,694	985	2,206	4,962
Vermont	2,863	7,013	4,580	8,792	653	1,428	2,420
Virginia	2,934	6,204	4,869	6,841	1,116	1,936	0
Washington	2,368	8,301	4,784	5,214	791	1,825	689
West Virginia	2,580	6,312	4,433	5,618	844	1,880	11,274
Wisconsin	3,811	9,922	7,143	7,915	768	1,301	1,533
Wyoming	2,685	10,894	2,418	8,357	1,093	1,875	1,512
Puerto Rico	178	178	177	178	178	0	0
Virgin Islands	372	611	86	1,161	234	388	314

Source: HCFA, BDMS, Office Program Systems, Data from Division of Medicaid Statistics, December 22, 1993.

TABLE 18–24.—OPTIONAL MEDICAID SERVICES AND NUMBER OF STATES [1] OFFERING EACH SERVICE AS OF OCTOBER, 1993

Service	States offering service to categorically needy only	States offering service to both categorically and medically needy	Total
Podiatrists' services	14	33	47
Optometrists' services	16	35	51
Chiropractors' services	7	20	27
Psychologists' services	8	23	31
Medical social workers' services	2	5	7
Nurse Anesthetists' services	11	16	27
Private duty nursing	7	20	27
Clinic services	17	37	54
Dental services	16	34	50
Physical therapy	15	30	45
Occupational therapy	12	25	37
Speech, hearing and language disorder	16	27	43
Prescribed drugs	17	39	56
Dentures	11	30	41
Prosthetic devices	18	37	55
Eyeglasses	16	33	49
Diagnostic services	9	24	33
Screening services	8	23	31
Preventive services	7	23	30
Rehabilitative services	14	37	51
Services for age 65 or older in mental institution:			
A. Inpatient hospital services	16	24	40
B. SNF services	13	20	33
C. ICF/MR services	22	28	50
Inpatient psychiatric services for under age 21	13	28	41
Christian Science nurses	3	2	5
Christian Science sanitoria	6	9	15
SNF for under age 21	23	29	52
Emergency hospital services	14	30	44
Personal care services	10	22	32
Transportation services	16	39	55
Case management services	12	33	45
Hospice services	10	25	35
Respiratory care services	5	11	16

[1] Includes the territories. Thus the maximum number is 53.

Source: Health Care Financing Administration, Office of Prepaid Health Care, Medicaid Bureau, Office of Intergovernmental Affairs.

FEDERAL HOUSING ASSISTANCE [19]

A number of Federal programs administered by the Department of Housing and Urban Development (HUD) and the Farmers Home Administration (FmHA) address the housing needs of lower-income households. Housing assistance has never been provided as an entitlement to all households that qualify for aid. Instead, each year the Congress has appropriated funds for a number of new commitments. Because these commitments generally run from 5 to 50 years, the appropriation is actually spent gradually, over many years. These additional commitments have expanded the pool of available aid, thus increasing the total number of households that can be served. They have also contributed to growth in Federal outlays in the past and have committed the Government to continuing expenditures for many years to come.

This section describes recent trends in the number and mix of new commitments, as well as trends in expenditures.

TRENDS IN FEDERAL HOUSING ASSISTANCE

The Federal Government has traditionally provided housing aid directly to lower-income households in the form of rental subsidies and mortgage-interest subsidies. Recent legislation, the 1990 Cranston-Gonzalez National Affordable Housing Act (hereafter referred to as the 1990 Housing Act), authorized a new, indirect approach in the form of housing block grants to State and local governments, which may use these funds for various housing assistance activities specified in the law. Over the past decade, both the number of households receiving aid and total federal expenditures have increased each year, but the growth in assisted households has slowed during the 1980s.

Types of housing assistance

A number of different housing assistance programs have evolved in response to changing housing policy objectives. The primary purpose of housing assistance has always been to improve housing quality and to reduce housing cos*   * lower-income households. Other goals have included promot   *ial construction, expanding housing opportunities   groups and groups with special housing need   od preservation and revitalization, increas   d, most recently, empowering the poor to b

New housing programs have   e because of shifting priorities among these   related problems changed—and because o   eral costs associated with some approache   become inactive in that the Congress st   ds for new assistance commitments thro   ising programs traditionally have involved   bligations, however, these so-called inactive   o play an important role today by serving a large   useholds through commitments for which funds were approp   some time ago.

[19] This discussion draws directly from a CBO Study entitled "Current Housing Problems and Possible Federal Responses," December 1988. For this report, CBO has updated all figures with 5 additional years of data.

Traditional rental assistance.—Most Federal housing aid is now targeted to very-low-income renters through the rental assistance programs administered by HUD and the FmHA.[20] Rental assistance is provided through two basic approaches: (1) project-based aid, which is typically tied to projects specifically produced for lower-income households through new construction or substantial rehabilitation; and (2) household-based subsidies, which permit renters to choose standard housing units in the existing private housing stock. Some funding is also provided each year to modernize units built with federal aid.

Rental assistance programs generally reduce tenants' rent payments to a fixed percentage—currently 30 percent—of their income after certain deductions, with the Government paying the remaining portion of the contract rents.

Almost all project-based aid is provided through production-oriented programs, which include the public housing program, the section 8 new construction and substantial rehabilitation program, and the section 236 mortgage-interest-subsidy program—all administered by HUD—and the section 515 mortgage-interest-subsidy program administered by the FmHA.[21] New commitments are being funded through three of the four—the public housing program, a modified version of the section 8 new construction program for elderly and disabled families only, and the section 515 program. Some assistance has also been funded annually under two small HUD programs authorized in 1983—the rental housing development grants (HoDAG) and the rental rehabilitation block grant programs.[22] These programs distributed funds through a national competition and by formula, respectively, to units of local government that meet eligibility criteria established by statute.

Some project-based aid is also provided through several components of HUD's section 8 existing-housing program, which tie subsidies to specific units in the existing-housing stock, many of which have received other forms of aid or mortgage insurance through HUD. These components—all of which are currently active—include the section 8 loan management set-aside (LMSA) and property disposition (PD) components, which are designed to improve cash flows in selected financially troubled projects that are or were insured by the Federal Housing Administration (FHA); the section 8 conversion assistance component, which subsidizes units that were previously aided through other programs; and the section 8 moderate rehabilitation program, which provides subsidies tied to units that are brought up to standard by the owner.[23]

Household-based subsidies are provided through two other components of the section 8 existing-housing program—section 8 rental certificates and vouchers. These programs, both of which are cur-

---

[20] For more detailed description of the various types of programs, see Congressional Research Service, HUD Housing Assistance Programs: Their Current Status, 93–222E (February, 1993); and Congressional Research Service, Housing Assistance in the United States, 91–872E (December 1991).

[21] A small number of renters continue to receive project-based subsidies through the now inactive section 221(d)(3) below-market interest rate (BMIR) and rent supplement programs.

[22] The Housing and Community Development Act of 1987 terminated the HoDAG program at the end of fiscal year 1989, and the 1990 Housing Act repealed the rental rehabilitation block grant program at the end of fiscal year 1991.

[23] The 1990 Housing Act repealed the section 8 moderate rehabilitation program at the end of fiscal year 1991, except for single-room occupancy units for the homeless.

rently active, tie aid to households, who choose standard units in the private housing stock. Certificate holders generally must occupy units whose rents at initial occupancy are within guidelines—the so-called fair market rents (FMRs)—established by HUD. Voucher recipients, however, are allowed to occupy units with rents above the HUD guidelines, provided that they pay the difference.

Traditional homeowners' assistance.—Each year, the Federal Government also assists some lower- and moderate-income households in becoming homeowners by making long-term commitments to reduce their mortgage interest.[24] Most of this aid has been provided through the section 502 program administered by the FmHA, which supplies direct mortgage loans at low interest rates roughly equal to the long-term Government borrowing rates or provides guarantees for private loans whose interest rates may not exceed those set by the Department of Veterans Affairs. Many homebuyers, however, receive much deeper subsidies through the interest-credit component of this program, which reduces their effective interest rate to as low as 1 percent. A number of homebuyers have received aid through the section 235 program administered by HUD, which provides interest subsidies for mortgages financed by private lenders. New commitments are now being made only through the section 502 program, but a small number of homeowners continue to receive aid from prior commitments made under the section 235 program.[25] Both programs generally reduce mortgage payments, property taxes, and insurance costs to a fixed percentage of income, ranging from 20 percent for the FmHA program to 28 percent for the latest commitments made under the HUD program. Households with relatively low incomes generally would have to pay larger shares, however, since mortgage payments must cover a minimum interest rate—currently 1 percent and 4 percent for the FmHA and HUD programs, respectively. Starting in 1991, however, the FmHA may allow some very-low-income households, to defer up to 25 percent of their monthly payments, subject to later repayment.

New directions in housing assistance.—The 1990 Housing Act, enacted in November 1990, authorizes several new housing assistance approaches. The major initiatives of the 1990 act are: the HOME investment partnerships block grant program, the homeownership and opportunity for people everywhere (HOPE) program, and the national homeownership trust demonstration. For 1994, funds were appropriated for both the HOME and HOPE programs but not for the homeownership trust demonstration.

The HOME investment partnerships program is designed to increase the supply of housing affordable to low-income families through the provision of Federal grants to State and local governments. Funds may be used for tenant-based rental assistance or for acquisition, rehabilitation or, in limited circumstances, construction of both rental and ownership housing. Participating jurisdiction must provide matching contributions for HOME funds—25 percent for funds used for rental assistance or rehabilitation, including sub-

---

[24] In addition, a small number of very-low-income homeowners receive grants or loans each year from the FmHA for housing repairs.

[25] The Housing and Community Development Act of 1987 terminated the section 235 program at the end of fiscal year 1989.

stantial rehabilitation; and 30 percent for funds used for new construction.

The multifaceted homeownership and opportunity for people everywhere (HOPE) program is designed to increase homeownership opportunities among low-income households, to combine traditional housing assistance programs for certain homeless people with supportive services, and to preserve certain federally assisted rental housing units for low-income use. To increase ownership opportunities, HOPE grants are provided to private nonprofits, cooperatives, public agencies, and instrumentalities to enable low-income households to become owners of units in public and Indian housing and other multifamily or single-family properties that are owned or whose mortgages are held by various Federal agencies, State or local governments, or by the Resolution Trust Corporation. To address the needs of homeless individuals with mental illness, substance abuse problems, or AIDS, the shelter plus care component of HOPE provides funds for section 8-like rental assistance, to be combined with supportive services funded at the State or local level. Finally, to address the potential loss of low-income rental housing projects whose owners are eligible to terminate the low-income use through prepaying their mortgages, HOPE provides funds for incentives to owners not to prepay; to assist residents or other qualified organizations in purchasing the projects; and for vouchers to assist tenants adversely affected by prepayment.

The national homeownership trust demonstration is designed to lower the cost of ownership for moderate-income, first-time homebuyers by establishing a trust fund to help buy down the maximum mortgage interest rate on eligible properties to 6 percent. An eligible property would be a single-family residence or cooperative unit for which the mortgage amount does not exceed the limits established for FHA insurance.

Trends in commitments for housing assistance

Although the Federal Government has been subsidizing the shelter costs of lower-income households since 1937, more than half of all currently outstanding commitments were funded over the past 18 years. Between 1977 and 1994, about 2.7 million net new commitments were funded to aid lower-income renters. Another 1.0 million new commitments were provided in the form of mortgage assistance to lower- and moderate-income homebuyers. Between 1977 and 1983, the number of net new rental commitments funded each year declined steadily, however, from 375,000 to 78,000. Trends have been somewhat erratic since 1983. Over the 18-year period, commitments for new homebuyers generally decreased, ranging from a high of 140,000 in 1980 to a low of less than 24,000 in 1991 (see table 18–25).

TABLE 18–25.—NET NEW COMMITMENTS FOR RENTERS AND NEW COMMITMENTS FOR HOMEBUYERS, 1977–94

Fiscal year	Net new commitments for renters			New commitments for homebuyers
	Existing housing	New construction	Total	
1977	127,581	247,667	375,248	112,234
1978	126,472	214,503	340,975	112,214
1979	102,669	231,156	333,825	107,871
1980	58,402	155,001	213,403	140,564
1981	83,520	94,914	178,434	74,636
1982	37,818	48,157	85,975	66,711
1983	54,071	23,861	77,932	54,550
1984	78,648	36,719	115,367	44,409
1985	85,741	42,667	128,408	45,387
1986	85,476	34,375	119,851	25,479
1987	72,788	37,247	110,035	24,132
1988	65,295	36,456	101,751	26,200
1989	68,858	30,049	98,907	25,264
1990	61,309	23,491	84,800	24,968
1991	55,900	28,478	84,378	23,879
1992 [1]	62,595	38,324	100,919	25,690
1993 [1]	50,593	34,065	84,658	30,982
1994 (estimate) [1]	64,791	35,861	100,652	42,230

[1] Figures are not adjusted for units for which funds were deobligated because data were unavailable.

Note: Net new commitments for renters represent net additions to the available pool of rental aid and are defined as the total number of commitments for which new funds are appropriated in any year. To avoid double-counting, these numbers are adjusted for the number of commitments for which such funds are deobligated or canceled that year (except where noted otherwise); the number of commitments for units converted from one type of assistance to another; in the FmHA Section 515 program, the number of units that receive more than one subsidy; starting in 1985, the number of commitments specifically designed to replace those lost because private owners of assisted housing opt out of the programs or because public housing units are demolished; and, starting in 1989, the number of commitments for units whose section 8 contracts expire.

New commitments for homebuyers are defined as the total number of new loans that the FmHA or HUD makes or subsidizes each year. This measure of program activity is meant to indicate how many new homebuyers can be helped each year and is therefore not adjusted to account for homeowners who leave the programs in any year because of mortgage repayments, prepayments, or foreclosures. Thus, it does not represent net additions to the total number of assisted homeowners and therefore cannot be added to net new commitments for renters.

Source: Congressional Budget Office based on data provided by the Department of Housing and Urban Development and the Farmers Home Administration.

The production-oriented approach in rental programs has been sharply curtailed in recent years in favor of the less costly section 8 existing-housing and voucher programs. Between 1977 and 1982, commitments through programs for new construction and substantial rehabilitation ranged annually from 53 percent to 73 percent of the total; since then, however, they have ranged between 28 percent and 40 percent of all additional rental commitments.

The total number of households receiving assistance has increased substantially, from 3.2 million at the beginning of fiscal year 1977 to an estimated 5.8 million at the beginning of fiscal year 1994—an increase of more than 80 percent (see table 27). This increase results largely from net new commitments over the past 18 years, but also from commitments made before 1977 that have been processed during this period. The number of households receiving rental subsidies increased from 2.1 million to 5.0 million. The number of homeowners receiving assistance in a given year rose from less than 1.1 million in 1977 to over 1.2 million in 1983, but then declined steadily to less than 0.8 million by 1994. The latter pattern reflects commitments for newly assisted households being more than offset by loan repayments, prepayments, and foreclosures among previously assisted households, and by sales of 141,000 loans by the FmHA to provide investors. (Although these 141,000 families continued to benefit from these loans, even after the transfer to the private sector, data are not readily available on the attrition of these loans between 1988 and 1994). Thus, the proportion of all assisted households that receives homeownership assistance has declined from 34 percent at the beginning of 1977 to 13 percent at the beginning of 1994. Among rental assistance programs, the shift away from production-oriented programs toward existing housing is reflected in the increasing proportion of renters receiving aid through the latter approach, from 13 percent at the beginning of fiscal year 1977 to 40 percent at the beginning of 1994, with the proportion of renters receiving household-based subsidies increasing from 8 percent to 28 percent.

TABLE 18–26.—TOTAL HOUSEHOLDS RECEIVING ASSISTANCE BY TYPE OF SUBSIDY, 1977–94

[Households in thousands]

	Assisted renters					Total assisted homeowners [1]	Total assisted homeowners and renters [1]
	Existing housing			New construction	Total assisted renters		
	Household based	Project based	Subtotal				
Beginning of fiscal year:							
1977	162	105	268	1,825	2,092	1,071	3,164
1978	297	126	423	1,977	2,400	1,082	3,482
1979	427	175	602	2,052	2,654	1,095	3,749
1980	521	185	707	2,189	2,895	1,112	4,007
1981	599	221	820	2,379	3,012	1,127	4,139
1982	651	194	844	2,559	3,210	1,201	4,411
1983	691	265	955	2,702	3,443	1,226	4,668
1984	728	357	1,086	2,836	3,700	1,219	4,920
1985	749	431	1,180	2,931	3,887	1,193	5,080
1986	797	456	1,253	2,986	3,998	1,176	5,174
1987	893	473	1,366	3,047	4,175	1,126	5,301
1988	956	490	1,446	3,085	4,296	918	5,213
1989	1,025	509	1,534	3,117	4,402	892	5,295
1990	1,090	527	1,616	3,141	4,515	875	5,390
1991	1,137	540	1,678	3,180	4,613	853	5,465
1992	1,166	554	1,721	3,204	4,680	826	5,506
1993	1,326	574	1,900	3,196	4,851	774	5,625
1994	1,392	593	1,985	3,213	5,008	751	5,759

[1] Starting 1988, figures reflect a one-time decrease of 141,000 in the number of assisted homeowners because of asset sales by the FmHA to private investors.

Note: Figures for total assisted renters have been adjusted since 1980 to avoid double-counting households receiving more than one subsidy.

Source: Congressional Budget Office based on data provided by the Department of Housing and Urban Development and the Farmers Home Administration.

BUDGET AUTHORITY AND OUTLAYS FOR HOUSING ASSISTANCE

Funding for most additional commitments for housing assistance is provided each year through appropriations of long-term budget authority for subsidies to households and through appropriations of budget authority for grants, direct loans and loan guarantees to public housing agencies, homebuyers, and developers of rental housing.

Annual appropriations of new budget authority for housing assistance have been cut dramatically during the 1980s. These cuts reflect four underlying factors: the previously mentioned reduction in the number of newly assisted households; the shift toward cheaper existing-housing assistance; a systematic reduction in the average term of new commitments from more than 24 years in 1977 to about 8 years in 1994; and the changes in the method for financing the construction and modernization of public housing (since 1987) and the construction of housing for the elderly and the disabled (since 1991).[26] For HUD's programs alone, appropriations of budget authority declined (in 1994 dollars) from a high of $71.5 billion in 1978 to a low of $10.7 billion in 1989 (see table 18–27). The increased levels of budget authority since 1990 reflect for a large part the cost of renewing expiring section 8 contracts. Similarly, new lending authority for FmHA's direct loan and loan guarantee programs decreased (in 1994 dollars) from a high of $7.7 billion in 1979 to a low of $2.1 billion in 1991, increasing somewhat to $3.2 billion in 1994.

TABLE 18–27.—NET BUDGET AUTHORITY APPROPRIATED FOR HOUSING AID ADMINISTERED BY HUD, 1977–94

[In millions of current and 1994 dollars]

Fiscal year	Net budget authority	
	Current dollars	1994 dollars
1977	28,579	67,622
1978	32,169	71,496
1979	25,123	51,274
1980	27,435	50,385
1981	26,022	43,429
1982	14,766	23,028
1983	10,001	14,934
1984	11,425	16,369
1985	11,071	15,298
1986	10,032	13,526
1987	8,979	11,768
1988	8,592	10,815
1989	[1] 8,879	10,668
1990	[1] 10,557	12,084
1991	[1] 19,239	20,962
1992	[1] 18,855	19,944
1993	[1] 20,236	20,773
1994 (estimate)	[1] 19,371	19,371

[1] Includes $99 million, $1,164 million, $8,814 million, $7,585 million, $6,926 million, and $5,278 million for renewing expiring section 8 contracts in 1989, 1990, 1991, 1992, 1993, and 1994 respectively.

Note: All figures are net of funding rescissions, exclude reappropriations of funds, but include supplemental appropriations. Totals include funds appropriated for public housing operating subsidies, and, starting in 1992, for HOME and HOPE grants. Excludes budget authority for HUD's section 202 loan fund and for programs administered by the Farmers Home Administration.

Source: Congressional Budget Office, based on data provided by the Department of Housing and Urban Development.

[26] Before 1987, new commitments for the construction and modernization of public housing were financed over periods ranging from 20 to 40 years, with the appropriations for budget authority reflecting both the principal and interest payments for this debt. Starting in 1987, these activities are financed with up-front grants, which reduces their budget authority requirements by between 51 percent and 67 percent. Similarly, prior to 1991, housing for the elderly and the disabled was financed by direct federal loans for the construction, coupled with 20-year-section 8 rental assistance, which helped repay the direct loan. Starting in 1991, the loans have been replaced by grants, which has reduced the amount of budget authority required for annual rental assistance.

TABLE 18–28.—OUTLAYS FOR HOUSING AID ADMINISTERED BY HUD, 1977–94

[In millions of current and 1994 dollars]

Fiscal year	Outlays	
	Current dollars	1994 dollars
1977	2,928	6,924
1978	3,592	7,981
1979	4,189	8,550
1980	5,364	9,852
1981	6,733	11,233
1982	7,846	12,238
1983	9,419	14.065
1984	11,000	15,750
1985	25,064	34,630
1986	12,179	16,420
1987	12,509	16,390
1988	13,684	17,223
1989	14,466	17,381
1990	15,690	17,960
1991	16,897	18,411
1992	18,242	19,200
1993	20,487	21,030
1994 (estimate)	21,816	21,810

Note: The bulge in outlays in 1985 is caused by a change in the method of financing public housing, which generated close to $14 billion in one-time expenditures. This amount paid off—all at once—the capital cost of public housing construction and modernization activities undertaken between 1974 and 1985, which otherwise would have been paid off over periods of up to 40 years. Because of this one-time expenditure, however, future outlays for public housing will be lower than they would have been otherwise.

Source: Congressional Budget Office based on data provided by the Department of Housing and Urban Development.

On the other hand, with the continuing increase in the number of households served, total outlays (expenditures on behalf of all households actually receiving aid in a given year) for all of HUD's housing assistance programs combined have risen steadily (in 1994 dollars), from $6.9 billion in fiscal year 1977 to an estimated $21.8 billion in fiscal year 1994, an increase of 215 percent (see table 18–28). Moreover, despite measures to contain costs, and the increase in household contributions from 25 percent to 30 percent of adjusted income, average Federal outlays per unit for all programs combined have generally continued to rise in real terms, from around $2,750 in 1977 to an estimated $4,540 in 1994—an increase of 65 percent (see table 18–29).[27]

Several factors have contributed to this growth. First, rents in assisted housing have probably risen faster than the income of assisted households, causing subsidies to rise faster than the inflation index used here—the revised Consumer Price Index, for all urban

[27] The change in the method for financing the construction and modernization of public housing caused a large one-time expenditure in 1985, when most of the outstanding debt incurred since 1974 for construction and modernization was paid off (see table 29). Without that bulge in expenditures, average outlays per unit in 1985 would have been about $3,950 in 1994 dollars.

consumers (CPI–U–X1).[28] Second, the number of households that occupy units completed under the section 8 new construction program has risen. These recently constructed units require larger subsidies compared with the older units that were built some time ago under the mortgage-interest subsidy programs and the public housing program. Third, the share of households receiving less costly homeownership assistance has decreased. Fourth, housing aid is being targeted toward a poorer segment of the population, requiring larger subsidies per assisted household.

TABLE 18–29.—PER UNIT OUTLAYS FOR HOUSING AID ADMINISTERED BY HUD, 1977–94

[In current and 1994 dollars]

Fiscal year	Per unit outlays	
	Current dollars	1994 dollars
1977	1,160	2,750
1978	1,310	2,910
1979	1,430	2,910
1980	1,750	3,210
1981	2,100	3,510
1982	2,310	3,600
1983	2,600	3,890
1984	2,900	4,150
1985	6,420	8,870
1986	3,040	4,090
1987	3,040	3,980
1988	3,270	4,110
1989	3,390	4,070
1990	3,610	4,130
1991	3,830	4,180
1992	4,060	4,300
1993	4,450	4,570
1994 (estimate)	4,540	4,540

Note: The peak in outlays per unit in 1985 of $8,870 is attributable to the bulge in 1985 expenditures associated with the change in the method for financing public housing. Without this change, outlays per unit would have amounted to around $3,950 in 1994 dollars.

Source: Congressional Budget Office based on data provided by the Department of Housing and Urban Development.

[28] For example, between 1980 and 1990, the CPI–U–X1 increased 59 percent. Over the same period, median household income of renters and the Consumer Price Index for residential rents increased by 70 percent and 71 percent, respectively, but the maximum rents allowed for section 8 existing-housing rental certificates—the so-called fair market rents—rose 85 percent.

SCHOOL LUNCH AND BREAKFAST PROGRAMS

The National School Lunch Program (NSLP) and the School Breakfast Program (SBP) provide Federal cash and commodity support to participating public and private schools and nonprofit residential institutions that serve meals to children. Each program has a three-tiered reimbursement system that allows children from households with incomes at or below 130 percent of the poverty line to receive free meals, permits children with incomes between 130 percent and 185 percent of poverty to receive meals at a reduced price, and provides a small subsidy for the meals of children who do not apply for, or whose family income does not qualify them for free or reduced price meals.[29] Children in AFDC or food stamp families are automatically eligible to receive free breakfast and lunch. An estimated 56 percent of households receiving AFDC also receive free or reduced-price meals.[30]

The NSLP provides subsidized lunches to children in most schools. During fiscal year 1993, the average daily participation was 24.8 million students. More than 4.1 billion meals were served at a total Federal program cost of $4.7 billion (see table 18–30). In fiscal year 1993, 93,000 elementary and secondary schools participated in the NSLP. Nearly 44 million children were enrolled in these schools, and 58 percent of these students participated in the program. Just over half of the meals subsidized by the NSLP go to children from lower income families although nearly 90 percent of Federal funding is used for these children's lunches. In fiscal year 1993, 47 percent of the children receiving NSLP lunches received free lunches, 7 percent received reduced-price lunches, and the remaining 46 percent paid full price for their meals.

The SBP serves far fewer students than does the NSLP. In fiscal year 1993, the program had an average daily participation of 5.4 million students, with total Federal program costs of $868 million (see table 18–31). The program operated in 55,000 schools, or just over half of the schools participating in the school lunch program. Nearly 27 million children were enrolled in these schools, of whom 20 percent participated in the program. The SBP also differs from the NSLP in that most of the schools that offer the program are in low-income areas, and the children who participate in the program are predominantly from low- and moderate-income families. In fiscal year 1993, 88 percent of the SBP participants received free or reduced-price breakfasts.

---

[29] For example, in the 1993–94 school year, the NSLP schools receive Federal cash subsidies of $1.73, $1.33, and $0.17, respectively, for each free, reduced-price, or "full-price" lunch served to children from these three income categories. An additional 14 cents worth of commodity assistance is mandated for all lunches. The corresponding levels of Federal subsidies in the SBP are $0.96, $0.66, and $0.19. Additional subsidies are available for "severe need" schools, and "bonus" commodity assistance is also offered if Federal commodity stocks are available.

[30] Other programs that provide nutritional assistance to children include the Child Care Food Program, the Summer Food Service Program, and the Special Milk Program.

TABLE 18–30.—THE NATIONAL SCHOOL LUNCH PROGRAM: PARTICIPATION AND FEDERAL COSTS, FISCAL YEARS 1977–93

[Dollars in millions]

Fiscal year	Participation 9 month average (in millions) [1]				Federal costs [4]	Federal costs in constant 1993 dollars
	Free meals	Reduced-price meals	Full-price meals [2]	Total [3]		
1977	10.5	1.3	14.5	26.3	$2,111.1	$5,066.6
1978	10.3	1.5	14.9	26.7	2,293.6	5,160.6
1979	10.0	1.7	15.3	27.0	2,659.0	5,424.4
1980	10.0	1.9	14.7	26.6	3,044.9	5,450.4
1981	10.6	1.9	13.3	25.8	2,959.5	4,764.8
1982	9.8	1.6	11.5	22.9	2,611.5	3,917.3
1983	10.3	1.5	11.2	23.0	2,828.6	3,101.5
1984	10.3	1.5	11.5	23.3	2,948.2	4,098.0
1985	9.9	1.6	12.1	23.6	3,034.4	4,096.4
1986	10.0	1.6	12.2	23.8	3,160.2	4,139.9
1987	10.0	1.6	12.4	24.0	3,245.6	4,154.4
1988	9.8	1.6	12.8	24.2	3,383.7	4,162.0
1989	9.7	1.6	12.7	24.2	3,479.4	4,070.0
1990	9.9	1.6	12.8	24.1	3,676.4	4,117.6
1991	10.3	1.8	12.1	24.2	4,072.9	4,317.3
1992	11.1	1.7	11.7	24.5	4,474.5	4,608.7
1993	11.8	1.7	11.3	24.8	4,663.8	4,663.8

[1] In order to reflect participation for the actual school year (September through May), these estimates are based on 9 month averages of October through May, plus September, rather than averages of the 12 months of the fiscal year (October through September).
[2] The Federal Government provides a small subsidy for these meals.
[3] Details may not sum to total because of rounding.
[4] Includes cash payments and entitlement commodities and cash in lieu of commodities; does not include value of bonus commodities.

Note: Constant dollars were calculated using the fiscal year CPI–U.

Sources: U.S. Department of Agriculture, Food and Nutrition Service, "Annual Historical Review of FNS Programs: Fiscal Year 1988, "Food Program Update fiscal year 1990 (January 1991), and "Review of FNS Food Assistance Program Activity, fiscal year 1991 (December 1991), and fiscal year 1992 (December 1992).
For fiscal year 1993, "Program Information Report" (January 1994).

TABLE 18–31.—THE SCHOOL BREAKFAST PROGRAM: PARTICIPATION AND FEDERAL COSTS, FISCAL YEARS 1977–93

[Dollars in millions]

| Fiscal year | Participation 9 month average (in millions) [1] | | | | Federal costs [4] | Federal costs in constant 1993 dollars |
	Free meals	Reduced-price meals	Full-price meals [2]	Total [3]		
1977	2.0	0.1	0.4	2.5	$148.6	$356.6
1978	2.2	.2	.4	2.8	181.2	407.7
1979	2.6	.2	.5	3.3	231.0	471.2
1980	2.8	.2	.6	3.6	287.8	515.2
1981	3.0	.2	.5	3.8	331.7	534.0
1982	2.8	.2	.4	3.3	317.3	476.0
1983	2.9	.1	.3	3.4	343.8	498.5
1984	2.9	.1	.4	3.4	364.0	506.0
1985	2.9	.2	.4	3.4	379.3	512.1
1986	2.9	.2	.4	3.5	406.3	532.3
1987	3.0	.2	.4	3.7	446.8	571.9
1988	3.0	.2	.5	3.7	482.0	592.9
1989	3.1	.2	.5	3.8	507.0	593.2
1990	3.3	.2	.5	4.0	589.1	659.8
1991	3.6	.2	.6	4.4	677.2	717.8
1992	4.0	.3	.6	4.9	782.6	806.1
1993	4.4	.3	.7	5.4	868.4	868.4

[1] In order to reflect participation for the actual school year (September through May), these estimates are based on 9 month averages of October through May, plus September, rather than averages of the 12 months of the fiscal year (October through September).
[2] The Federal Government provides a small subsidy for these meals.
[3] Details may not sum to totals due to rounding.
[4] Does not include the value of any USDA bonus commodities donated to the program for no charge.

Note: Constant dollars were calculated using the fiscal year CPI–U.

Sources: U.S. Department of Agriculture, Food and Nutrition Service: "Annual Historical Review of FNS Programs, Fiscal Year 1988," "Food Program Update, fiscal year 1990" (January 1991), and "Review of FNS Food Assistance Program Activity, fiscal year 1991" (December 1991) and fiscal year 1992 (December 1992). For fiscal year 1993, "Program Information Report" (January 1994).

THE SPECIAL SUPPLEMENTAL FOOD PROGRAM FOR WOMEN, INFANTS, AND CHILDREN (WIC)

The Special Supplemental Food Program for Women, Infants, and Children (WIC) provides food assistance and nutritional screening to low-income pregnant and postpartum women and their infants, as well as to low-income children up to age 5. Participants in the program must have incomes at or below 185 percent of poverty, and must be nutritionally at risk. Under the Child Nutrition Act of 1966, nutritional risk is defined as detectable abnormal nutritional conditions; documented nutritionally-related medical conditions; health-impairing dietary deficiencies; or conditions that predispose people to inadequate nutrition or nutritionally related medical problems.

Beneficiaries of the special supplemental food program for women, infants, and children (WIC) receive supplemental foods each month in the form of actual food items or, more commonly, vouchers for purchases of specific items in retail stores. The law requires that the WIC program provide foods containing protein, iron, calcium, vitamin A, and vitamin C. Among the items that may be included in a food package are milk, cheese, eggs, infant formula, cereals, and fruit or vegetable juices. U.S. Department of Agriculture (USDA) regulations require tailored food packages that provide specified types and amounts of food appropriate for six categories of participants: (1) infants from birth to 3 months, (2) infants from 4–12 months, (3) women and children with special dietary needs, (4) children from 1–5 years of age, (5) pregnant and nursing mothers, and (6) postpartum nonnursing mothers. In addition to food benefits, recipients also must receive nutrition education.

The cost of providing WIC benefits varies widely depending on the recipient category, type of package and foods contained in it, as well as by regional differences in food and administrative costs. The USDA estimated that in fiscal year 1993 the national average monthly cost of a WIC food package was $29.82 per participant, and the average monthly per participant administrative cost was $9.77. Thus, the total average cost of serving each WIC participant in fiscal year 1993 was estimated at $39.59 per month or $475 annually.

The WIC program has categorical, income, and nutritional risk requirements for eligibility. Only pregnant and postpartum women, infants, and children under age 5 may participate. Income eligibility is set by each State. Regulations permit States to use either the income cutoff level set for the reduced-price school lunch program (185 percent of the poverty income guideline, currently $26,548 for a family of four), or the income level that is used for free and reduced-price health care, as long as this is not higher than 185 percent of the poverty level. States are prohibited by regulation from using income criteria that are lower than 100 percent of the poverty level. Most States use 185 percent as the cut-off level for WIC income eligibility. South Dakota uses 175 percent statewide. WIC applicants also must show evidence of health or nutrition risk, medically verified by a health professional, in order to qualify for the program.

WIC participants receive benefits for a specified period of time, and in some cases must be recertified during this time period to show continued need. Pregnant women may continue benefits throughout their pregnancy and for up to 6 months after childbirth without recertification. Nursing mothers are certified at 6-month intervals ending with their infant's first birthday.

WIC, which is federally funded, but administered by State and local agencies, does not serve all who are eligible. In fiscal year 1993, Federal costs totaled $2.8 billion and the program served over 5.9 million women, infants, and children (see table 18–32). In July of 1987, the USDA released a report of the WIC eligibility study ("Estimation of Eligibility for the WIC Program") which found that in 1984, an estimated 9.6 million persons were income-eligible for the WIC program, and 7.5 million of those were estimated to be at nutritional risk and, thus, fully eligible for the WIC program.

In 1991, the Congressional Budget Office (CBO) updated and revised USDA reestimates to reflect more recent Census data on income and population growth. Using slightly higher assumptions of nutritional risk than the USDA, CBO estimated that a total of 8.5 million persons were eligible for WIC in fiscal year 1991. In that year, the program served some 4.8 million recipients, or 56 percent of those estimated to be eligible by CBO. Another USDA study released in February 1992 "Study of WIC Participant and Program Characteristics, 1990," indicated that in 1990 nearly three-quarters (73 percent) of WIC participants had incomes at or below the poverty level. The CBO has projected that in fiscal year 1994 some 9.6 million mothers and children will be eligible for WIC, and that 7.6 million of them would apply for the program and receive benefits if sufficient funds were available to fully fund the program.

TABLE 18–32.—THE SUPPLEMENTAL FOOD PROGRAM FOR WOMEN, INFANTS, AND CHILDREN (WIC): PARTICIPATION AND FEDERAL COSTS, FISCAL YEARS 1977–93

[Dollars in millions]

Fiscal year	Participation (in thousands)				Federal costs [2]	Federal costs in constant 1992 dollars
	Women	Infants	Children	Total [1]		
1977	165.0	213.0	471.0	848.0	$255.9	$597.1
1978	240.0	308.0	633.0	1,181.0	379.6	827.5
1979	312.0	389.0	782.0	1,483.0	525.4	1,039.6
1980	411.0	507.0	995.0	1,913.0	724.7	1,261.9
1981	446.0	585.0	1,088.0	2,119.0	874.4	1,370.1
1982	478.0	623.0	1,088.0	2,189.0	948.2	1,384.5
1983	542.0	730.0	1,265.0	2,537.0	1,123.1	1,583.5
1984	657.0	825.0	1,563.0	3,045.0	1,386.3	1,876.7
1985	665.0	874.0	1,600.0	3,138.0	1,488.9	1,945.6
1986	712.0	945.0	1,655.0	3,312.0	1,580.5	2,014.3
1987	751.0	1,019.0	1,660.0	3,429.0	1,663.6	2,061.7
1988	815.0	1,095.0	1,683.0	3,593.0	1,802.4	2,145.9
1989	951.8	1,259.6	1,907.0	4,118.4	1,929.4	2,192.2
1990	1,035.0	1,412.5	2,069.4	4,516.9	2,125.9	2,301.0
1991	1,120.1	1,558.8	2,213.8	4,892.6	2,301.1	2,370.9
1992	1,221.5	1,684.1	2,505.2	5,410.8	2,566.5	2,566.5
1993	1,364.9	1,741.9	2,813.4	5,920.3	2819.5	2,737.0

[1] Details may not sum to totals due to rounding.
[2] Includes funding for WIC studies, surveys, and pilot projects.

Note: Constant dollars were calculated using the fiscal year CPI–U.

Sources: U.S. Department of Agriculture, Food and Nutrition Service, "Annual Historical Review of FNS Programs: Fiscal Year 1986," and U.S. Department of Agriculture, Food and Nutrition Service, "Food Program Updates for Fiscal Year 1990" (January 1991), and "Food Program Update. A Review of FNS Food Assistance Program Activity. Fiscal Year 1993" (December 1993).

JOB TRAINING PARTNERSHIP ACT

Title II of the Job Training Partnership Act of 1982 (JTPA) provides block grants to States to fund training and related services for economically disadvantaged youths and adults.

Title II consists of three programs: the II–A adult training program, the II–B summer youth employment and training program, and the II–C youth training program. Prior to the 1992 amendments to JTPA, which became effective July 1, 1993—the beginning of program year 1993—Title II–A provided services to both adults and youth. (Since data for program year 1993 will not be available until sometime after June 30, 1994, the end of the program year, the title II–A data presented here are for both adults and youth.)

The title II JTPA programs are administered by States and localities, which select participants and design projects within Federal guidelines.

The programs are intended to increase participants' future employment and earnings and reduce their dependence on welfare. Services authorized under title II–A include institutional and on-the-job training, work experience, job search assistance, counseling, and other work-related assistance. In general, participants must be economically disadvantaged, which is defined as being a member of a family whose total income for the 6-month period prior to application (exclusive of unemployment compensation, child support payments, and welfare payments) does not exceed the higher of the poverty line or 70 percent of the Bureau of Labor Statistics' lower living standard. Members of families receiving Aid to Families With Dependent Children (AFDC) or other cash welfare payments and those eligible for food stamps are also defined as economically disadvantaged.

As shown in table 18–33, of title II–A participants who terminated during program year 1992, 46 percent were white, 33 percent were black and 18 percent were Hispanic. Fifty percent were younger than 22. Of participants who terminated, 52 percent entered employment, and the average hourly wage for terminees who entered employment was $5.79.

Since the program was implemented in 1983, about one-fifth of the participants terminating activities authorized by title II–A were AFDC recipients at the time that they enrolled—27 percent in program year 1991 (July 1991–June 1992).

Among title II–A terminees who were AFDC recipients at the time of enrollment in program year 1991, women comprised 79 percent of the total, as compared with 47 percent of title II–A participants who did not receive AFDC. Among AFDC recipients, 34 percent were school dropouts, compared with 26 percent of those JTPA participants who were not AFDC recipients. AFDC recipients were more likely to be placed in classroom training (57 percent) than non-AFDC recipients (39 percent), and were less likely to participate in on-job-training (9 percent) than non-AFDC recipients (17 percent). The average entered employment rate in program year 1991 for AFDC recipients in JTPA was 39 percent, compared with an average entered employment rate of 54 percent for those JTPA participants who did not receive AFDC. The average hourly starting wage for AFDC recipients entering employment was $5.64, compared with $5.81 for non-AFDC recipients.

TABLE 18–33.—CHARACTERISTICS OF JTPA TITLE II–A TERMINEES, SELECTED PROGRAM YEARS, 1988–92

Selected Characteristics	Program Years				
	1988	1989	990	1991	1992
Total terminees	734,600	692,300	565,200	549,700	510,652
Sex:					
Male	47	45	43	44	44
Female	53	55	57	56	56
Minority status:					
White (excluding Hispanic)	53	53	52	50	46
Black (excluding Hispanic)	31	32	33	34	33
Hispanic	12	12	12	12	18
Other	3	3	4	4	4
Age at enrollment:					
Younger than 19	25	25	25	28	(2)
19–21	16	15	16	15	(2)
Adults, age 22–54	54	55	54	52	49
55 and older	5	5	5	5	1
Economically disadvantaged	95	93	93	93	NA
Receiving AFDC	21	22	24	27	27
Receiving public assistance (including AFDC)	42	43	46	50	30
U.C. claimant	4	4	5	6	7
Education status:					
School dropout	29	29	28	28	24
Student (HS or less)	17	18	19	21	27
High school graduate (or more)	53	53	53	51	49
Program activity:					
Classroom training, basic	11	11	14	[1] 44	NA
Classroom training, other	23	24	26	[1] 44	NA
On-the-job training	22	22	18	15	NA
Job search assistance	15	17	16	15	NA
Work experience	8	7	7	6	NA
Other services	21	18	19	20	NA
Median length of stay (in days)	103.7	110.3	128.8	138.0	[3] 27
Average entered employment rate	67	61	55	50	52
Average hourly wage at termination	$5.01	$5.29	$5.54	$5.78	$5.79

[1] Basic and other classroom training combined.

[2] The Job Training Annual Status Report, used for 1992, differs in its methodology from the Job Training Quarterly Survey used for 1988 through 1991. In 1992, 50 percent of the terminees were age 21 or younger.

[3] The 1992 data are in weeks rather than days. In 1992, the median length of stay was 27 weeks.

Source: JTQS Special Paper No. 10, "Review of JTPA Participant Characteristics and Program Outcomes Program Years 1984 through 1989." Department of Labor, October 1991; Job Training Quarterly Survey. "JTPA Title II A and III Enrollments and Terminations During Program Year 1990," Department of Labor, January 1992, Job Training Quarterly Survey. "JTPA Title II–A and III Enrollments and Terminations During Program Year 1991," Department of Labor, February 1993. Job Training Annual Status Report 1992, Department of Labor, February 1994.

In fiscal year 1993, an estimated $1.7 billion is expected to be spent for JTPA II–A and II–C grants, providing training and other services to about 566,000 new enrollees. Data on participation (new enrollees) and budget authority for recent fiscal years are provided in table 18–34 below. Fiscal Year 1994 figures are estimates based on assumptions of continued spending.

TABLE 18–34.—JOB TRAINING PROGRAMS [1] FOR THE DISADVANTAGED: NEW
ENROLLEES, FEDERAL APPROPRIATIONS AND OUTLAYS, FISCAL YEARS 1975–93

Fiscal year	New enrollees	Budget authority (millions)	Outlays (millions)	Budget authority in constant 1990 dollars	Outlays in constant 1990 dollars
1975	1,126,000	$1,580	$1,304	$3,755	$3,099
1976	1,250,000	1,580	1,697	3,515	3,775
1977	1,119,000	2,880	1,756	5,964	3,636
1978	965,000	1,880	2,378	3,658	4,627
1979	1,253,000	2,703	2,547	4,829	4,550
1980	1,208,000	3,205	3,236	5,154	5,203
1981	1,011,000	3,077	3,395	4,493	4,958
1982	(2)	1,594	2,277	2,175	3,107
1983	(2)	2,181	2,291	2,846	2,990
1984	716,200	1,886	1,333	2,361	1,669
1985	803,900	1,886	1,710	2,279	2,066
1986	1,003,900	1,783	1,911	2,101	2,252
1987	960,700	1,840	1,880	2,108	2,154
1988	873,600	1,810	1,902	1,991	2,092
1989	823,200	1,788	1,868	1,877	1,961
1990	630,000	1,745	1,803	1,745	1,803
1991	[3] 603,900	1,779	1,746	1,694	1,676
1992	[3] 602,300	1,774	1,767	1,637	1,632
1993 [3]	566,000	1,692	1,747	(2)	(2)
1994 [3]	556,400	1,647	1,616	(2)	(2)

[1] Figures shown in years 1975 through 1983 are for training activities under the Comprehensive Employment and Training Act (CETA); public service employment under CETA is not included. Figures shown in years 1984 through 1992 are for activities under title II–A of the Job Training Partnership Act. Fiscal year 1993 through 1994 reflect figures for titles II–A and of the amended Job Training Partnership Act.
[2] Comparable figures are not available for these years.
[3] Estimate.

Source: Employment and Training Administration, Department of Labor (DOL), Employment and Training Reports of the President, Job Training Quarterly Survey data, budget briefing documents, conversation with DOL officials.

Title II–B of JTPA authorizes a summer employment and training program for economically disadvantaged youngsters, aged 14–21. Services include a full range of remedial education, classroom and on-job-training, as well as work experience for which participants are paid minimum wage. The summer program is administered through the nationwide network of local service delivery areas.

Approximately $849 million was appropriated for the summer of 1993 with an estimated 614,600 participants served. For the summer of 1994, $876.7 has been appropriated to date to serve an estimated 623,300 individuals.

In the summer of 1993, 41 percent of title II–B enrollees were ages 14 and 15, and 59 percent were between the ages of 16 and 21. During that summer, 5 percent of enrollees were dropouts, while 86 percent were students and 8 percent were high school graduates. Black youth comprised 42 percent of summer enrollees, while 29 percent were white and 25 percent were Hispanic. Eight percent had limited English-speaking ability, and 15 percent of summer youth had disabilities.

Table 18–35 presents a funding and participation history of the summer program.

TABLE 18–35.—SUMMER YOUTH EMPLOYMENT PROGRAM: FEDERAL APPROPRIATIONS, OUTLAYS, AND PARTICIPATION LEVELS, FISCAL YEARS 1984–94 [1]

[Dollars in millions]

	Appropriations	Outlays	Outlays (1990 dollars)	Participants
1984	$824.5	$583.8	$730.7	767,600
1985	724.5	776.3	938.0	785,000
1986	636.0	746.1	879.2	634,400
1987	750.0	722.7	828.1	722,900
1988	718.1	707.1	777.7	604,500
1989	709.4	697.4	732.1	632,700
1990	699.8	699.5	699.5	538,000
1991	682.9	697.8	663.0	[2] 771,903
1992	[3] 995.2	957.8	649.6	[2] 614,600
1993	[4] 1,024.9	914.9	([5])	[2] 623,300
1994	[6] 888.3	990.8	([5])	[2] 623,200

[1] Because JTPA is an advance-funded program, appropriations for the summer youth program in a particular fiscal year are generally spent the following summer. For example, fiscal year 1984 appropriations were spent during the summer of 1985.

[2] Estimate.

[3] Includes $500 million supplemental appropriation for summer 1992. The remaining $495.2 million is for summer 1993.

[4] Includes $354.2 million for summer 1993 and $670.7 for summer 1994.

[5] Not available.

[6] Includes $206.0 million for summer 1994 and $682.3 million for summer 1995.

Source: Employment and Training Administration, Department of Labor (DOL), appropriations justifications documents, telephone conversation with DOL officials.

Job Corps, authorized by title IV–B of JTPA, serves economically disadvantaged youth, ages 14–24, who demonstrate both the need for, and the ability to benefit from, an intensive and wide range of services provided in a residential setting. The program is administered directly by the Federal Government through contractors and currently operates at 108 centers around the country. Services include basic education, vocational skill training, work experience, counseling, health care, and other supportive services.

Labor Department data for program year 1992 (July 1, 1992–June 30, 1993) indicate that about 61 percent of Job Corps enrollees are male, 50 percent are black, 31 percent are white, and 13 percent are Hispanic. Eighty percent are high school dropouts, and 72 percent have never worked full-time. Forty-two percent of Job Corps enrollees come from families on public assistance.

The average length of stay for Job Corps enrollees in program year 1991 was 7.8 months, and the Labor Department estimates that 54 percent of terminees entered employment after leaving the program, while another 11 percent either continued their education or entered another training program, for a total positive termination rate in 1991 of 65 percent.

Table 18–36 provides a funding and participation history of Job Corps since 1982. The program was first authorized in the mid-

1960's by the Economic Opportunity Act and has been authorized under JTPA since 1982.

TABLE 18-36.—JOB CORPS: FEDERAL APPROPRIATIONS, OUTLAYS, AND PARTICIPATION, FISCAL YEARS 1982-94

[Dollars in millions]

	Appropriations	Outlays	Outlays (1990 dollars)	New enrollees
1982	$589.6	$595.0	$811.8	53,581
1983	618.0	563.3	735.1	60,465
1984	599.2	580.6	726.7	57,386
1985	617.0	593.0	716.5	63,020
1986	612.5	594.5	700.6	64,964
1987	656.4	630.6	722.6	65,150
1988	716.1	688.5	757.3	68,068
1989	741.8	689.5	723.8	62,550
1990	802.6	739.6	739.6	61,453
1991	867.5	769.4	769.0	62,205
1992	919.5	834.1	789.1	[1] 64,917
1993	966.1	[1] 936.4	N.A.	[1] 60,419
1994	1,040.5	[1] 1,000.0	N.A.	[1] 60,472

[1] Estimate.

Source: Department of Labor (DOL) budget documents, telephone conversation with D.O.L. officials.

HEAD START

Head Start began operating in 1965 under the general authority of the Economic Opportunity Act of 1964. Head Start provides a wide range of services to primarily low-income children, ages 0 to 5, and their families. Its goals are to improve the social competence, learning skills, and health and nutrition status of low-income children so that they can begin school on an equal basis with their more advantaged peers. The services provided include cognitive and language development, medical, dental, and mental health services (including screening and immunizations); and nutritional and social services. Parental involvement is extensive, through both volunteer participation and employment of parents as Head Start staff. Formal training and certification as child care workers is provided to some parents through the Child Development Associate program.

Head Start's eligibility guidelines require that at least 90 percent of the children served come from families with incomes at or below the poverty line. At least 10 percent of the enrollment slots in each local program must be available for children with disabilities. In fiscal year 1993 713,903 children were served in Head Start programs, at a total Federal cost of $2.776 billion. Approximately 55 percent of Head Start children in families receiving AFDC benefits. Table 18-37 provides historical data on participation in and funding of the Head Start program, while table 18-38 provides characteristics of children enrolled in the program.

TABLE 18–37.—HEAD START: PARTICIPATION AND FEDERAL FUNDING, FISCAL YEARS
1965–94

[Dollars in millions]

Fiscal year	Enrollment	Appropriations
1965 (summer only)	561,000	$96.4
1966	733,000	198.9
1967	681,400	349.2
1968	693,900	316.2
1969	663,600	333.9
1970	477,400	325.7
1971	397,500	360.0
1972	379,000	376.3
1973	379,000	400.7
1974	352,800	403.9
1975	349,000	403.9
1976	349,000	441.0
1977	333,000	475.0
1978	391,400	625.0
1979	387,500	680.0
1980	376,300	735.0
1981	387,300	818.7
1982	395,800	911.7
1983	414,950	912.0
1984	442,140	995.8
1985	452,080	1,075.0
1986	451,732	1,040.0
1987	446,523	1,130.5
1988	448,464	1,206.3
1989	450,970	1,235.0
1990	548,470	[1] 1,552.0
1991	583,471	1,951.8
1992	621,078	2,201.8
1993	713,903	2,776.3
1994 (est.)	750,000	3,326.0

[1] After sequestration.
[2] Projected enrollment.

LOW-INCOME HOME ENERGY ASSISTANCE PROGRAM (LIHEAP)

The predecessor to the Low-Income Home Energy Assistance Program (LIHEAP) was created by title III of the Crude Oil Windfall Profit Tax Act of 1980 (P.L. 96–223). The purpose of LIHEAP is to help low-income households meet their energy-related expenses. In fiscal year 1981, $1.85 billion was appropriated for the program.

In 1981, title XXVI of the Omnibus Budget Reconciliation Act (OBRA) (Public Law 97–35), the Low-Income Home Energy Assistance Act of 1981, authorized the Secretary of Health and Human Services to make LIHEAP allotments to States for fiscal years 1982–84. The Act permitted States to provide three types of energy assistance. States can: (1) help eligible households pay their home heating or cooling bills, (2) use up to 15 percent of their LIHEAP allotment for low-cost weatherization, and (3) provide assistance to households during energy-related emergencies.

TABLE 18–38.—CHARACTERISTICS OF CHILDREN ENROLLED IN HEAD START

[In percent]

Fiscal year	Age of children enrolled					Enrollment by race				
	Disabled children	5 and older	4	3	Under 3	Native American	Hispanic	Black	White	Asian
1980	11.9	21	55	24	0	4	19	42	34	1
1982	12.0	17	55	26	2	4	20	42	33	1
1984	11.9	16	56	26	2	4	20	42	33	1
1986	12.2	15	58	25	2	4	21	40	32	3
1988	12.7	11	63	23	3	4	22	39	32	3
1990	13.5	8	64	25	3	4	22	38	33	3
1991	13.1	7	63	27	3	4	22	38	33	3
1992	13.4	7	63	27	3	4	23	37	33	3
1993	13.0	6	64	27	3	4	24	36	33	3

Source: Health and Human Services.

The Human Services Reauthorization Act of 1984 (Public Law 98–558) amended the Low-Income Home Energy Assistance Act of 1981 and authorized appropriations for fiscal years 1985 and 1986. Appropriations for fiscal years 1982, 1983, and 1984 were $1.875, $1.975, and $2.075 billion, respectively. Public Law 98–619 appropriated $2.1 billion for fiscal year 1985. Public Law 99–178 appropriated $2.1 billion for fiscal year 1986.[31]

The Human Services Reauthorization Act of 1986, Public Law 99–425, amended the Act and extended the appropriations authorization through fiscal year 1990. Authorized appropriations levels are: $2.050 billion for fiscal year 1987; $2.132 billion for fiscal year 1988; $2.218 billion for fiscal year 1989; and $2.307 billion for fiscal year 1990. The appropriations for fiscal years 1987, 1988, 1989 and 1990 were $1.825 billion, $1.532 billion, $1.383 billion, and $1.443 billion, respectively.[32]

The Augustus F. Hawkins Human Services Reauthorization Act of 1990, Public Law 101–501, amended the act and extended the appropriations authorization through fiscal year 1994. The National Institutes of Health Revitalization Act, Public Law 103–43, extended the appropriation authorization through fiscal year 1995. Major amendments in the 1990 Act included permission for grantees to request waivers to spend up to 25 percent of their allotment on weatherization activities, a reduction in the percentage of allotments that can be carried over from year to year, elimination of authority to transfer funds to other block grants (beginning in fiscal

[31] The Balanced and Emergency Deficit Control Act of 1985, as reaffirmed by Public Law 99–366, required the cancellation of $90.3 million of fiscal year 1986 budget authority.

[32] Funding for Federal administration is not included beginning with fiscal year 1988; these funds are now appropriated through a separate budget account. The fiscal year 1989 appropriation for allotments to States and territories (and training and technical assistance) was reduced from $1.4 billion to $1.383 billion (1.2 percent) under the terms of Public Law 100–436.

year 1994), provision for forward funding based on a July–June "program year," and establishment of a new "leveraging incentive" grant award program. Under the leveraging incentive program grantees are to be rewarded for adding their own or other funds to the LIHEAP or finding other ways to stretch Federal dollars (e.g., purchasing fuel in bulk at discount rates); the program was authorized at $25 million for fiscal year 1992 and $50 million a year for fiscal years 1993, 1994, and 1995. Overall authorized appropriations levels were: $2.150 billion for fiscal year 1991; $2.230 billion for fiscal year 1992, and such sums as are necessary for fiscal years 1993, 1994, and 1995. The fiscal year 1991 appropriation was $1.610 billion, including a $195 million energy emergency "contingency fund" that was distributed to States in late January 1991 in response to large increases in home heating oil prices. For fiscal year 1992, $1.5 billion was appropriated, including $406 million that was not made available to grantees until September 30, 1992. In fiscal year 1993, $1.346 billion was appropriated, $682 million of which was not made available to grantees until September 30, 1993. The fiscal year 1993 appropriation included $1.437 billion in "advance funding" for the first three quarters of fiscal year 1994, October 1993/June 1994 (this represented the first step in the process of converting the LIHEAP from a fiscal year funding cycle to a "program year" cycle, under which grantees know their allocations before the heating season begins. An additional $600 million "contingency fund" is available in 1994 if requested by the Administration because of emergency needs. In February 1994 $300 million of this fund was released to 23 States hit by unusually harsh winter weather. LIHEAP received $1.475 billion in advance funding for program year 1995 (October 1994/June 1995) as part of the fiscal year 1994 Labor/HHS/Education Appropriation.

The Human Services Reauthorization Act of 1994, Public Law 103–252, amended the act and extended appropriations authorization for LIHEAP and the leverage incentive program through fiscal year 1999. LIHEAP appropriations are authorized at $2.0 billion for fiscal years 1995 through 1999; authorized appropriation levels for the leveraging incentive program are $50 million for fiscal year 1996 and 1997 and such sums as may be necessary for fiscal years 1998 and 1999. Major amendments to the act include: a permanent authorization of $600 million in each of the fiscal years to meet additional home energy needs arising from a natural disaster or other emergency; allowing for the targeting of such emergency funds to individual States; permitting States to give priority to households with the highest home energy burden in relation to household income, emphasizing households with young children, elderly, or disabled members; and the establishment of the Residential Energy Assistance Challenge Option (R.E.A.Ch.), an incentive grant program designed to increase efficient energy use, minimize health and safety risks, and prevent hopelessness among low-income families with high energy burdens. Up to 25 percent of leveraging incentive monies may be used to fund R.E.A.Ch. demonstrations.

ALLOTMENTS TO STATES [33]

The maximum amount of LIHEAP funds that a State can carry over to the next fiscal year is 10 percent. This provision applies to a State's allotment after adjustments have been made for tribal set aside. States must explain why funds are held over until the next fiscal year and what types of assistance the funds will provide. The amount carried over does not affect the State's subsequent fiscal year allocation. Amounts above 10 percent that are not spent by the State must be reallocated by the Secretary of Health and Human Services. Special allotment and set-aside rules apply to grants for Indian tribes and the territories.

Table 18–39 shows State allotments for 1981 and selected recent fiscal years, and table 18–40 illustrates the number of households receiving benefits from the single largest program component, heating assistance, average heating benefits and total dollars spent on heating assistance.

ELIGIBILITY AND TYPES OF ASSISTANCE

States have considerable discretion to determine eligibility criteria for LIHEAP and the types of energy assistance to be provided. At State option, LIHEAP payments can be made to households, based on categorical eligibility, where one or more persons are receiving: Supplemental Security Income, Aid to Families with Dependent Children, food stamps, or needs-tested veterans' benefits. States can also elect to make payments to households with incomes that are up to 150 percent of the Federal poverty income guidelines or 60 percent of the State's median income, whichever is greater. Individuals who are denied benefits are entitled to an administrative hearing. The term "household" is defined as any individual or group of individuals who are living together as one economic unit and for whom residential energy is customarily purchased in common, or who make undesignated payments for energy in the form of rent. States cannot establish an income eligibility ceiling that is below 110 percent of the poverty level, but may give priority to those households with the highest energy costs in relation to household income, taking into consideration the presence of very young children, frail elderly, or persons with disabilities. States also are prohibited from treating categorically eligible and income eligible households differently with respect to LIHEAP. However, Public Law 103–185 permits States to reduce benefits to tenants of federally assisted housing if it is determined that such a reduction is reasonably related to any utility allowance they may receive. LIHEAP benefits cannot be used to calculate income or resources, or affect other benefits, under Federal or State law, including public assistance programs.

States are required to give assurances that the largest benefits go to those households that have the lowest income and highest energy costs relative to their income, taking into account family size. In addition, States are to conduct outreach activities aimed at mak-

---

[33] As the result of court settlements of oil price overcharges under the Emergency Petroleum Allocation Act of 1973, substantial additional funding has been made available to States to supplement Federal LIHEAP appropriations; in fiscal year 1991, an estimated $109 million of these supplemental funds were used for the LIHEAP.

ing households with elderly or handicapped individuals aware that energy assistance is available. These outreach services may include: toll-free information hotlines, special application periods, transportation to LIHEAP application offices, and home visits. Section 607(a) of Public Law 98–558 directs the Department of Health and Human Services to collect annual data, including information on the number of LIHEAP households in which at least one household member is 60 years old or handicapped.

States also have considerable discretion in the methods they have available to provide assistance to eligible households. Methods vary by State and program. A list of methods that are used includes cash payments, vendor payments, two-party checks, vouchers/coupons, and payments directly to landlords. When paying home energy suppliers directly, States are required to give assurances that suppliers will charge the eligible households the difference between the amount of the assistance and the actual cost of home energy. Also, States may use Federal funds to provide tax credits to energy suppliers who supply home energy to low-income households at reduced rates.

PLANNING AND ADMINISTRATION

States are required to submit an application for funds to the Secretary of Health and Human Services. As part of the annual application, the chief executive officer of the State is required to make several assurances related to eligibility requirements, anticipated use of funds, as well as to satisfy planning and administrative requirements. States are prohibited from using more than 10 percent of their total LIHEAP allotment for planning and administrative costs.

States must provide for public participation and public hearings in the development of the State plan, including making it, and any substantial revisions, available for public inspection and allowing public comment on the plan. Public Law 98–558 requires States to engage an independent person or organization to prepare an audit at least once every 2 years. However, the Single Audit Act of 1984 (P.L. 98–502) supersedes this requirement in most instances, and requires grantees to conduct an annual audit of all Federal financial assistance received. The law also contains two other related provisions. First, the Comptroller General is directed to evaluate, at least once every 3 years, whether a State's LIHEAP expenditures are consistent with law. Second, the Department of Health and Human Services is to develop regulations to prevent waste, fraud, and abuse in LIHEAP.

TABLE 18-39.—LOW-INCOME HOME ENERGY ASSISTANCE PROGRAM STATE ALLOTMENTS

[In thousands of dollars]

States	Fiscal year—						
	[1] 1981	1985	1990	1991	1992	1993	1994
Alabama	15,674	18,234	11,961	15,856	12,664	11,344	12,127
Alaska	7,505	7,247	7,635	9,594	8,034	7,241	7,741
Arizona	6,426	8,150	5,785	6,200	6,125	5,486	5,865
Arkansas	11,960	13,973	9,127	11,069	9,663	8,656	9,253
California	84,088	97,894	64,168	68,764	67,940	60,855	65,056
Colorado	29,319	33,299	22,373	23,419	23,688	21,218	22,683
Connecticut [2]	38,247	43,440	29,187	35,541	30,902	27,680	34,986
Delaware [2]	5,077	5,931	3,874	5,471	4,102	3,674	4,214
District of Columbia	5,940	6,940	4,533	5,269	4,799	4,299	4,595
Florida	25,921	28,970	18,926	21,731	20,039	17,950	19,188
Georgia	19,609	22,910	14,964	17,439	15,844	14,191	15,171
Hawaii	1,975	2,243	1,507	1,531	1,596	1,429	1,528
Idaho [2]	11,181	12,877	8,727	9,493	9,240	8,277	8,848
Illinois [2]	105,862	123,679	80,784	85,711	85,533	76,614	93,921
Indiana [2]	47,431	55,371	36,577	41,069	38,727	34,689	39,408
Iowa [2]	29,470	38,581	25,922	28,719	27,466	24,584	34,335
Kansas	15,515	18,211	11,905	12,901	12,605	11,290	12,069
Kentucky [2]	24,943	29,141	19,034	22,537	20,153	18,052	24,639
Louisiana	16,024	18,867	12,228	13,203	12,947	11,597	12,398
Maine [2]	27,513	27,914	18,908	23,550	20,020	17,932	27,275
Maryland [2]	29,285	34,214	22,348	29,361	23,662	21,194	29,288
Massachusetts [2]	82,707	86,878	58,383	69,364	61,815	55,369	73,071
Michigan [2]	111,598	113,951	76,697	86,099	81,206	72,738	126,605
Minnesota [2]	72,409	82,239	55,256	62,063	58,504	52,404	93,421
Mississippi	13,930	15,683	10,255	12,391	10,858	9,725	10,397
Missouri	37,885	48,026	32,268	35,779	34,165	30,603	32,715
Montana	11,350	12,298	10,236	10,938	10,838	9,708	10,378
Nebraska	13,799	19,032	12,820	13,851	13,573	12,158	12,997
Nevada	3,560	4,151	2,717	3,214	2,877	2,577	2,754
New Hampshire [2]	14,481	16,447	11,051	13,648	11,700	10,480	14,352

New Jersey[2]	71,025	82,849	54,200	66,929	57,386	51,402	61,894
New Mexico	8,867	9,973	7,242	8,123	7,668	6,868	7,342
New York[2]	231,907	263,291	176,970	214,983	187,373	167,835	240,880
North Carolina	34,561	40,378	26,374	35,612	27,924	25,013	26,739
North Dakota[2]	7,995	14,612	11,120	12,503	11,773	10,546	19,376
Ohio[2]	93,651	109,413	71,465	78,365	75,666	67,776	96,381
Oklahoma	15,998	16,004	10,995	12,250	11,641	10,427	11,147
Oregon	22,723	25,808	17,340	19,298	18,360	16,445	17,580
Pennsylvania[2]	124,568	141,479	95,059	107,475	100,647	90,152	116,857
Rhode Island[2]	12,594	14,220	9,610	11,572	10,175	9,114	11,471
South Carolina	13,822	14,544	9,500	12,451	10,058	9,009	9,631
South Dakota[2]	10,241	11,434	9,031	10,691	9,562	8,565	11,150
Tennessee	25,267	29,520	19,281	21,652	20,415	18,286	19,548
Texas	41,261	48,206	31,487	36,455	33,337	29,861	31,922
Utah	13,289	14,827	10,397	11,062	11,008	9,860	10,541
Vermont[2]	10,854	12,328	8,283	9,813	8,770	7,855	13,197
Virginia[2]	39,019	41,677	27,222	36,051	28,822	25,817	28,277
Washington	33,104	40,896	28,522	31,495	30,199	27,050	28,917
West Virginia[2]	16,507	19,285	12,596	13,676	13,337	11,946	16,503
Wisconsin[2]	61,679	74,027	49,738	56,987	52,662	47,171	65,147
Wyoming	3,561	6,195	4,163	4,605	4,407	3,948	4,220
U.S. total	1,813,177	2,077,577	1,390,749	1,607,819	1,472,503	1,318,961	1,709,998

[1] Includes reallocation of funds and crisis intervention funds. Source: Low Income Energy Assistance Program; Report to Congress for Fiscal Year 1981; U.S. Department of Health and Human Services.
[2] Includes $300 million in LIHEAP contingency funds released in February 1994 to states hit by unusually harsh winter weather under the 1994 Emergency Supplemental Appropriations Act, Public Law 103–211.

Note: Columns may not add due to rounding. The table includes payments to Indian tribal organizations and excludes funding for Federal Administrative costs, payments to commonwealths and territories, and "leveraging" incentive grants.

Source: U.S. Department of Health and Human Services.

TABLE 18–40.—HEATING ASSISTANCE BENEFITS, NUMBER OF HOUSEHOLDS ASSISTED, AND AVERAGE BENEFIT BY STATE

[Fiscal year 1993]

State	Heating assistance benefits [1]	Estimated number of households assisted	Estimated average benefit (in dollars)
Total	$954,484,219	5,403,664	NA
Alabama	4,480,459	36,132	124
Alaska	4,652,490	13,370	348
Arizona [2]	3,906,462	26,941	145
Arkansas	5,265,738	53,536	98
California [2]	35,189,243	380,460	92
Colorado	23,358,952	70,811	330
Connecticut	29,104,137	73,052	475
Delaware	3,288,026	14,141	233
District of Columbia	3,308,603	15,081	219
Florida [2]	10,403,596	111,867	93
Georgia	9,637,845	60,194	160
Hawaii [2]	1,002,076	6,300	200
Idaho	5,227,737	28,842	182
Illinois	54,888,350	234,512	245
Indiana	29,592,410	112,895	254
Iowa	15,610,411	66,320	235
Kansas	5,184,191	30,350	171
Kentucky	17,421,342	155,548	112
Louisiana	4,529,551	50,328	90
Maine	15,470,441	55,574	290
Maryland	21,662,246	89,461	242
Massachusetts	51,347,839	143,367	360
Michigan	67,600,000	362,000	187
Minnesota	39,362,933	109,367	360
Mississippi	5,992,297	40,220	149
Missouri	26,041,474	128,553	203
Montana	4,754,242	21,216	224
Nebraska	6,500,000	35,600	182
Nevada	1,791,182	9,794	183
New Hampshire	9,751,5900	24,740	394
New Jersey	49,908,052	165,000	283
New Mexico	5,445,385	69,000	117
New York	103,270,642	922,059	112
North Carolina	20,625,239	193,481	106
North Dakota	7,812,043	17,201	454
Ohio	35,173,467	328,994	107
Oklahoma	7,359,553	75,750	96

TABLE 18–40.—HEATING ASSISTANCE BENEFITS, NUMBER OF HOUSEHOLDS ASSISTED, AND AVERAGE BENEFIT BY STATE—Continued

[Fiscal year 1993]

State	Heating assist-ance benefits [1]	Estimated number of households as-sisted	Estimated aver-age benefit (in dollars)
Oregon	12,529,063	58,730	201
Pennsylvania	51,561,008	311,009	166
Rhode Island	9,770,578	25,604	381
South Carolina	7,428,422	83,311	90
South Dakota	6,935,609	19,016	319
Tennessee	12,778,314	63,829	200
Texas	6,927,484	75,000	92
Utah	7,948,771	36,969	215
Vermont	6,379,014	15,800	402
Virginia	24,317,772	124,763	195
Washington	14,335,672	64,330	216
West Virginia	6,217,484	53,599	116
Wisconsin	38,604,000	128,333	300
Wyoming	2,830,784	11,314	250

[1] State estimates of heating assistance obligations for fiscal year 1993 from the following available funds: fiscal year 1992 LIHEAP funds carried over for use in fiscal year 1993; "oil overcharge" funds made available by States for use in LIHEAP; Federal LIHEAP allotments (net of set-asides for Indian tribes); and any State or other funds made available for LIHEAP heating assistance.

[2] Benefits for heating and cooling assistance combined.

Source: U.S. Department of Health and Human Services, March 1994. Data compiled from telephone interviews with State offices conducted in September 1993.

VETERANS' BENEFITS AND SERVICES

The Department of Veterans Affairs (DVA) offers a wide range of benefits and services to eligible veterans, members of their families, and survivors of deceased veterans. The DVA programs include veterans compensation and veterans pensions—the main cash-assistance entitlement programs—readjustment and rehabilitation benefits, education and job training programs, medical care services, and the housing and loan guaranty programs. Also, the DVA provides life insurance, burial benefits, and special counseling and outreach programs. In fiscal year 1993, Federal outlays for veterans' benefits and services were $35.7 billion.

VETERANS' COMPENSATION AND VETERAN'S PENSIONS

Service-connected compensation is paid to veterans who have incurred injuries or illnesses while in service. The amounts of the monthly payments are determined by disability ratings that are based on presumed average reductions in earnings capacities caused by the disabilities. Disability ratings generally range from 10 percent to 100 percent in 10-percent intervals; multiple injuries may result in combined-degree ratings, however, and some injuries are compensable at a zero-percent rating. Death compensation or dependency and indemnity compensation is paid to survivors of veterans who died as a result of service-connected causes. In 1993, about 2.2 million disabled veterans and 311,748 survivors received $13.4 billion in compensation payments.

Veterans pensions are means-tested cash benefits paid to war veterans who have become permanently and totally disabled from non-service-connected causes, and to survivors of war veterans. Under the current or "improved law" program, benefits are based on family sizes, and the pensions provide a floor of income: for 1994, the basic benefit before subtracting other income sources is $10,240 for a veteran with one dependent ($7,818 for a veteran living alone). Somewhat less generous benefits are available to survivors; a surviving spouse with no children could receive two-thirds of the basic benefit amount given a single veteran. About 895,596 persons received $3.5 billion in veterans pension payments in 1993.

READJUSTMENT, EDUCATION, AND TRAINING BENEFITS

Several DVA programs support readjustment, education, and job training for veterans and military personnel who meet certain eligibility criteria. In 1992, the largest of these programs was the Montgomery GI bill (MGIB). The MGIB provides an entitlement to basic educational assistance to most persons who are, or have been, members of the Armed Forces or the Selected Reserve for specified periods of time after June 30, 1985. The purposes of the MGIB are to provide educational assistance to help in the readjustment to civilian life, to aid in recruitment and retention of qualified personnel in the Armed Forces, and to develop a more highly educated and productive work force.

Under the MGIB, contributions are required, and veterans can receive a basic educational benefit of up to $400 per month for 36 months while in an educational program.

There are also several employment and training programs for veterans, including transition assistance for service persons scheduled for separation from active duty and programs for veterans who have been unable to find employment following military service.

Net outlays from the DVA account in 1993 for all education and training programs came to $826 million.

MEDICAL PROGRAMS

The DVA provides inpatient and outpatient medical and health-related services, and operates 172 hospital centers, 128 nursing homes, 37 domiciliaries, and 353 outpatient clinics. The DVA extends free priority care to service-connected disabled veterans, to veterans in special categories, and to needy nonservice-connected veterans—in 1994, those with incomes $23,896 or less if married with one dependent, plus $1,330 for each additional dependent, or $19,912 or less if single. Veterans eligible under these criteria are called "mandatory care" veterans, and they are entitled to hospital care. As facilities and other resources permit, the DVA provides care to non-service-connected veterans with incomes that exceed the mandatory care income limits. Medical care for these veterans requires copayments. DVA-operated nursing home care is augmented by DVA-supported care under contract in private community nursing homes and with per diem payments for veterans in State-run homes for veterans.

The DVA operates a nationwide health system. In 1993, approximately 2.8 million different veterans were VA patients of which almost all received outpatient care and 500,000 received inpatient care. Construction and modernization of facilities, as well as medical research and training programs. are also funded through DVA appropriations. In 1993, DVA medical programs cost the Federal Government $14.8 billion (see table 43).

TABLE 18–41.—EXPENDITURES FOR VETERANS BENEFITS AND SERVICES, FOR SELECTED FISCAL YEARS

[In millions of dollars]

Fiscal year	Compensation and pensions [1]	Readjustment, education, job training	Medical programs [2]	Housing loans [3]	Other veterans benefits and services	Total
1975	7,860	4,593	3,665	24	458	16,599
1980	11,688	2,342	6,515	−23	665	21,185
1981	12,909	2,254	6,965	201	662	22,991
1982	13,710	1,947	7,517	102	682	23,958
1983	14,250	1,625	8,272	3	696	24,846
1984	14,400	1,359	8,861	244	751	25,614
1985	14,714	1,059	9,547	214	758	26,292
1986	15,031	526	9,872	114	813	26,356
1987	14,962	454	10,266	330	769	26,782
1988	15,963	454	10,842	1,292	877	29,428
1989	16,544	459	11,343	878	843	30,066
1990	15,241	278	12,134	517	943	29,112
1991	16,961	427	12,889	85	987	31,349
1992	17,296	783	14,091	901	1,067	34,138
1993	17,758	826	14,812	1,299	1,025	35,720

[1] Primarily compensation and pension benefits. Includes small amounts for insurance and burial benefits.

[2] Medical program expenditure data include outlays for direct medical services, medical research and training, and construction programs.

[3] Numbers provided for expenditures under housing loans are not comparable to program expenditures in the other columns because they are revolving funds with loan outlays and repayments.

Source: Department of Veterans Affairs.

TABLE 18–42.—NUMBER OF RECIPIENTS OF VETERANS BENEFITS AND SERVICES, FOR SELECTED FISCAL YEARS

[In thousands]

Fiscal year	Compensation and pensions	Readjustment, education, job training	Medical programs [1]	Housing loans
1975	4,855	2,804	1,985	290
1980	4,646	1,232	2,671	297
1981	4,535	1,074	2,765	188
1982	4,407	900	2,720	103
1983	4,286	755	2,933	245
1984	4,123	629	3,026	252
1985	4,005	491	2,963	179
1986	3,900	388	2,942	314
1987	3,850	312	2,900	479
1988	3,762	273	2,922	235
1989	3,686	330	3,344	130
1990	3,614	329	3,018	196
1991	3,546	275	2,963	181
1992	3,462	318	2,927	266
1993	3,397	362	2,800	383

[1] Reprints are the number of applicants during the year.

Source: Department of Veterans Affairs.

WORKERS' COMPENSATION [34]

Workers' compensation programs provide cash and medical benefits to persons with job-related disabilities and survivors' benefits to dependents of those whose death resulted from a work-related accident or illness. In 1991, workers' compensation laws protected approximately 93.6 million workers in 51 jurisdictions, including the District of Columbia. Although the laws vary from State to State, the underlying principle is that employers should assume the costs of occupational disabilities without regard to fault. Prior to the enactment of workers' compensation laws (the first of which was in 1908), a worker was only protected in cases where employer negligence could be proven as the cause of injury or death. By 1949, all States had enacted laws to cover workers and their dependents in *any* case of occupational disability or death.

Workers' compensation benefits are paid by insurance companies, special State insurance funds, or by employers acting as self-insurers. State programs are administered by industrial commissions or special units within State departments of labor. The Federal programs (except for a part of the Black Lung benefit program) are administered by the U.S. Department of Labor.

Three-fourths of all compensable claims for workers' compensation benefits and one-fourth of all such cash benefits paid involve a temporary total disability; i.e., an employee is unable to work at all while he or she is recovering from the injury, but is expected to recover fully. Most States will pay benefits for the duration of the disability as long as the condition continues to improve with medical treatment. If the temporary total disability becomes permanent, most State laws provide for weekly benefits either for life or as long as the disability lasts.

If a worker becomes permanently disabled (less than 1 percent of all claims), he or she may be eligible for cash benefits under both workers' compensation and the Social Security Disability Insurance (DI) program. The 1965 Amendments to the Social Security Act stipulate a reduction in Social Security payments so that total benefits under both programs do not exceed the higher of 80 percent of a workers' former earnings or the total family benefit under Social Security before the offset.

The remaining disability claims filed under workers' compensation involve permanent partial disabilities of either major or minor severity. Benefits are paid to cover the cost of the injury (including permanent loss of function and handicap) and to compensate for future reduction in earnings due to the disability.

Coverage

Coverage is compulsory for most private employers except in New Jersey, South Carolina and Texas. If employers reject coverage in these States, they lose the use of common-law defenses against suits by employees. Many State programs exempt employees of nonprofit, charitable, or religious institutions, as well as very

---

[34] Drawn from William J. Nelson, Jr., "Workers' Compensation: Coverage, Benefits, and Costs, 1989," Social Security Bulletin, Spring 1992/Vol. 55, No. 3, pp. 51–56, and "Workers' Compensation: Coverage, Benefits, and Costs, 1990–91," Social Security Bulletin, Fall 1993/Vol. 56, No. 3, pp. 68–74.

small employers, domestic and agricultural employment, and casual labor. The coverage of State and local public employees differs widely from one State program to another.

In 1991, the proportion of covered workers was 87 percent, the same as it was in 1990. Wages and salaries of covered workers (total covered payroll) totaled $2,300 billion, representing 84 percent of all civilian wage and salary payments in that year and a 2.2 percent increase over 1990.

Benefits

Benefit levels are established by State formulas and are usually calculated as a percentage of weekly earnings at the time of injury or death (generally 66⅔ percent). Each State (and Federal Government for Federal workers) sets a maximum benefit level, which is periodically adjusted. Most often, maximum benefits range between two-thirds and 100 percent of the State's average weekly wage. As of January 1993, the maximum weekly benefit varied from $236 in Mississippi, to $769 in Connecticut and $1,249 for Federal employees. Workers' compensation benefits are calculated as a proportion of gross pre-injury or death earnings (in most cases) and are not subject to income taxes.

Approximately $42.2 billion was provided in 1991 by workers' compensation programs in total benefit payments, including medical care and hospitalization benefits. This represents an increase of 10.3 percent over 1990. Increases in wages, medical costs, and the number of workers have all contributed the rise in payments, as well as rising maximum benefit levels. Benefit levels also are affected by changes in the incidence and severity of occupational injuries and diseases. Bureau of Labor Statistics' survey data indicate that the rate of on-the-job injuries and illnesses per 100 full-time workers was 8.4 in 1991, down from 8.8 in 1990. However, the number of workdays lost per case was 22.2, the highest in more than 50 years of collecting data (some of this may be due to improved record keeping and monitoring).

Although occupational disease claims currently account for only about 2 percent of workers' compensation claims, the amendment and interpretation of State laws that cover illnesses with long latency periods is expected to increase this ratio. In addition, medical advances and improved technology are leading to the identification of different types of disorders. For example, circulation trauma disorder, caused by constant repetitive motion, pressure or vibration, was deemed the cause of 48 percent of all occupational illnesses in 1987, nearly double the rate 5 years before.

Types of payments

Payments for medical and hospital care for work-related injuries and illnesses totalled more than $16.8 billion in 1991, about 40 percent of the $42.2 billion paid under all workers' compensation programs. Cash compensation payments accounted for the remaining 60 percent of total expenditures. Of the $25.3 billion in such payments, more than 92 percent was paid to disabled workers, with the remainder going to workers' survivors. Black Lung benefit payments totaled $1.4 billion in 1991, which is a 25 percent decrease from the peak year of 1980. As older beneficiaries of Black Lung payments die and fewer new claimants enter the program, the payment level will continue to decline.

Types of insurers

Generally, employers insure against their workers' compensation liability through commercial insurance companies. However, they also may self-insure by providing proof of financial ability to carry their own risk (normally, large employers), purchase their insurance through a State "fund" (essentially, a State-run insurance company), or buy insurance commercially through a State-established "high-risk" insurance pool. Nearly half the States have "competitive" State funds, and employers may buy private insurance, self-insure, or buy from the State fund. In 2 States, employers must insure through an "exclusive" State fund, and in 4 States employers must self-insure or buy insurance from their exclusive State fund. In 1991, about 58 percent of all benefits were paid by private insurers, 23 percent by State funds or federally supported funding (Federal workers and black lung benefits), and 19 percent by self-insurers.

Employer costs

The cost to employers to provide workers' compensation to employees was $55.2 billion in 1991, a 4 percent increase over the 1990 figure. These costs include the benefits paid, administration of the insurance operation, claims processing, rehabilitation costs, profits, taxes, and reserves for future benefits. The insurance premium paid by employers varies with the risk involved and the employer's industrial classification with regards to the hazards of a particular industry, which may at times be modified by experience rating. In 1991, the components of employer costs were as follows:
— $35.7 billion paid to private carriers;
— $10.8 billion paid to State funds and for Federal programs (the Federal employee program and that part of the Black Lung benefits program financed by employers); and
— $8.7 billion in the cost of self-insurance (benefits paid by self-insurers plus estimated administrative expenses).

Rising employer costs for workers' compensation now represent $590 for each worker protected by workers' compensation programs, compared with $296 in 1982. Employers' costs per $100 of covered payroll also have grown: in 1991, they averaged $2.40 per $100 of payroll, up from $1.75 in 1982.

Program data

Table 18–43 shows the estimated number of workers covered and the total annual payroll in covered employment for selected years between 1948 and 1991. Over that time period, the number of workers covered in an average month increased from 36.0 to 93.6 million, and the amount of total payroll in covered employment increased from $105 billion to $2,300 billion.

Table 18–44 illustrates the benefit payment amounts under workers' compensation by type of benefit for years 1987, 1988, 1989, 1990, and 1991. In 1991, total benefits paid equaled $42,169 million, of which $40,778 was paid in regular benefits and $1,391 for the Black Lung benefit program.

TABLE 18–43.—ESTIMATED NUMBER OF WORKERS COVERED IN AVERAGE MONTH AND
TOTAL ANNUAL PAYROLL IN COVERED EMPLOYMENT, BY SELECTED YEARS, 1948–91 [1]

Year	Workers covered in average month		Total payroll in covered employment	
	Number (in millions)	Percent of employed wage and salary workers [2]	Amount (in billions)	Percent of civilian wage and salary disbursements
1948	36.0	77.0	$105	79.9
1953	40.7	80.0	154	81.5
1958	42.5	80.2	192	83.1
1963	47.3	80.5	254	83.7
1968	56.8	83.8	376	83.0
1973	66.3	86.3	578	84.2
1978	75.6	86.7	922	84.3
1983	78.0	85.6	1,382	84.6
1988	91.3	87.0	2,000	84.2
1990	95.1	87.0	2,250	84.0
1991	93.6	87.0	2,300	84.0

[1] Before 1963, excludes Alaska and Hawaii.
[2] Beginning 1968, excludes those under age 16 and includes certain workers previously classified as self-employed.
Source: Social Security Bulletin, March 1991 and Fall 1993, Social Security Administration.

TABLE 18–44.—ESTIMATED WORKERS' COMPENSATION BENEFIT PAYMENT AMOUNTS, BY
TYPE OF BENEFIT, 1987–91

[In millions]

Type of benefit	1987	1988	1989	1990	1991
Regular Program	$25,773	$29,234	$32,837	$36,804	$40,778
Medical and hospitalization	9,794	11,401	13,299	15,067	16,715
Compensation	15,979	17,833	19,538	21,737	24,063
Disability	15,046	16,956	18,553	20,635	22,840
Survivor	933	877	985	1,102	1,223
Black Lung Program	1,545	1,499	1,479	1,434	1,391
Medical and hospitalization	118	117	125	120	117
Compensation	1,426	1,381	1,354	1,314	1,274
Disability	698	657	618	577	533
Survivor	729	725	736	737	741
Total (Regular and Black Lung)	27,318	30,733	34,316	38,238	42,169
Medical and hospitalization	9,912	11,518	13,424	15,187	16,832
Compensation	17,406	19,215	20,892	23,051	25,337
Disability	15,775	17,613	19,171	21,212	23,373
Survivor	1,631	1,602	1,721	1,839	1,964

Source: Social Security Bulletin, March 1991 and Fall 1993, Social Security Administration.

PART 2
APPENDICES

APPENDIX A. DATA ON THE ELDERLY

This appendix presents historical and current data on the demographic and economic characteristics of the elderly, including information on population, life expectancy, labor force participation, marital status, living arrangements, poverty rates, and income. Data sources are noted at the bottom of each table.

The following definitions may be useful for reading the tables:

(1) "Aged" and "elderly" each refer to any person 65 years old or older.

(2) "OASDI" and "Social Security" are used interchangeably.

(3) "Supplemental security income" is, at times, abbreviated "SSI."

(4) The concepts "unrelated individual" and "unit" are used many times throughout this appendix. "Unrelated individual" refers to any individual living alone. "Unit" refers to an individual living alone, a couple living alone or a family.

TABLE A–1.—ELDERLY AS A PERCENT OF TOTAL POPULATION AND DISTRIBUTION OF ELDERLY BY AGE AND SEX, 1940 TO 2025

	1940	1950	1960	1970	1980	1990	2000 [1]	2025 [1]
Population 65 years and older (in thousands)	9,556	12,807	17,268	20,892	26,125	31,995	35,170	60,599
Population age 65 and older as a percent of total population	6.8	8.0	9.1	9.7	11.1	12.3	12.4	18.2
Population age 75 and older as a percent of total population	2.0	2.5	3.1	3.7	4.4	5.2	5.9	7.5
Population age 85 and older as a percent of total population	0.3	0.4	0.5	0.7	1.0	1.3	1.5	1.9
Certain age and sex groupings as a percent of the population 65 years and older:								
Total 65 years and older	100.0	100.0	100.0	100.0	100.0	100.0	100.0	100.0
Men 65 and older	48.4	46.8	44.5	41.6	40.3	40.8	41.1	43.9
Men 65 to 74	34.8	32.6	30.2	26.9	26.3	25.9	23.9	27.8
Men 75 to 84	11.9	12.2	12.2	12.4	11.3	12.1	13.8	13.0
Men 85 and older	1.7	2.0	2.2	2.4	2.8	2.9	3.5	3.2
Women 65 and older	51.6	53.2	55.5	58.4	59.7	59.2	58.9	56.1
Women 65 to 74	35.8	35.7	35.7	34.7	33.9	31.8	28.5	31.0
Women 75 to 84	13.4	14.7	16.3	19.2	19.3	19.8	21.4	17.8
Women 85 and older	2.3	2.8	3.5	4.6	6.5	7.5	9.0	7.3

[1] Projection.

Note: Population data include total U.S. plus the outlying areas covered under the Social Security program and an adjustment for population undercount.

Source: 1993 Annual Report of the Board of Trustees of the Federal Old-Age and Survivors Insurance and Disability Insurance Trust Funds, and unpublished estimates from the Office of the Actuary, Social Security Administration. Population figures are as of July 1 of the year.

TABLE A-2.—LIFE EXPECTANCY [1] FOR MEN AND WOMEN, 1900-2070

Year	Life expectancy at birth		Life expectancy at age 65	
	Male	Female	Male	Female
Actual:				
1900	46.4	49.0	11.4	11.7
1910	50.1	53.6	11.4	12.1
1920	54.5	56.3	11.8	12.3
1930	58.0	61.3	11.8	12.9
1940	61.4	65.7	11.9	13.4
1950	65.6	71.1	12.8	15.1
1960	66.7	73.2	12.9	15.9
1970	67.1	74.9	13.1	17.1
1980	69.9	77.5	14.0	18.4
1990 [2]	71.1	78.8	14.9	18.9
Projected [3]:				
2000	72.6	79.7	15.4	19.4
2010	74.0	80.5	15.8	19.7
2020	74.7	81.2	16.3	20.2
2030	75.3	81.8	16.7	20.6
2040	75.9	82.4	17.1	21.1
2050	76.5	82.9	17.5	21.5
2060	77.0	83.5	17.9	22.0
2070	77.5	84.0	18.3	22.4

[1] The life expectancy for any year is the average number of years of life remaining for a person if that person were to experience the death rates by age observed in, or assumed for, the selected years.
[2] Estimated.
[3] Based on the intermediate mortality assumptions of the 1993 Annual Report of the Board of Trustees of the Federal Old-Age and Survivors Insurance and Disability Insurance Trust Funds.

Source: Office of the Actuary, Social Security Administration.

TABLE A–3.—LABOR FORCE PARTICIPATION RATES [1], 1950–93

Sex	1950	1955	1960	1965	1970	1975	1980	1985	1990	1993
Men:										
55 to 64	86.9	87.9	86.8	84.6	83.0	75.8	72.3	67.9	67.7	66.5
55 to 59	(2)	92.5	91.6	90.2	89.5	84.4	81.9	79.6	79.8	78.2
60 to 64	(2)	82.5	81.1	78.0	75.0	65.7	61.0	55.6	55.5	54.1
60 to 61	(2)	(2)	(2)	84.8	82.6	75.2	71.8	68.9	68.8	66.1
62 to 64	(2)	(2)	(2)	73.2	69.4	58.8	52.8	46.1	46.4	46.1
65 and over	45.8	39.6	33.1	27.9	26.8	21.7	19.1	15.8	16.4	15.6
Women:										
55 to 64	27.0	32.5	37.2	41.4	43.0	41.0	41.5	42.0	45.3	47.3
55 to 59	(2)	35.6	42.2	47.1	50.4	47.9	48.6	50.3	55.3	57.1
60 to 64	(2)	29.0	31.4	34.0	36.1	33.3	33.3	33.4	35.5	37.1
60 to 61	(2)	(2)	(2)	40.4	41.4	39.5	39.8	40.3	42.9	45.2
62 to 64	(2)	(2)	(2)	29.5	32.3	29.0	28.6	28.7	30.7	31.8
65 and over	9.7	10.6	10.8	10.0	9.7	8.3	8.1	7.3	8.7	8.2

[1] Civilian labor force as percent of civilian noninstitutional population aged 16 or older.
[2] Data not available.

Source: Bureau of Labor Statistics.

TABLE A-4.—MARITAL STATUS OF AGED INDIVIDUALS[1], 1960-92

	1960		1970[2]		1980[3]		1990		1992	
	65 to 74	75 and over	65 to 74	75 and over	65 to 74	75 and over	65 to 74	75 and over	65 to 74	75 and over
Men:										
Number (in thousands)	4,778	2,280	5,333	3,031	6,459	3,234	8,013	4,320	8,266	4,533
Percent	100.0	100.0	100.0	100.0	100.0	100.0	100.0	100.0	100.0	100.0
Married	78.9	59.1	77.6	79.7	81.6	69.4	80.2	69.9	79.1	70.2
Widowed	12.7	31.6	11.0	30.4	8.5	24.0	9.2	23.7	10.2	23.7
Divorced	1.7	1.5	2.9	1.5	4.4	2.2	6.0	3.1	6.1	2.6
Never married	6.7	7.8	8.5	6.6	5.4	4.4	4.7	3.4	4.6	3.5
Women:										
Number (in thousands)	5,529	3,054	6,741	4,608	8,549	5,411	9,966	7,267	10,174	7,616
Percent	100.0	100.0	100.0	100.0	100.0	100.0	100.0	100.0	100.0	100.0
Married	45.6	21.8	45.4	20.8	50.1	23.3	53.2	25.4	53.0	25.6
Widowed	44.4	68.3	43.7	70.5	40.3	68.0	36.1	65.6	35.9	65.0
Divorced	1.7	1.2	3.0	1.3	4.0	2.3	6.2	3.6	6.7	4.0
Never married[4]	8.4	8.6	7.9	7.4	5.6	6.4	4.6	5.4	4.4	5.4

[1] Civilian noninstitutional population only.
[2] Estimates based on weights derived from the 1960 decennial census.
[3] Estimates based on weights derived from the 1970 decennial census.
[4] Never married was reported as "single" for 1960.

Note: Details may not add to totals due to rounding.

Source: U.S. Bureau of the Census, Current Population Reports, series P-20, Nos. 135, 212, 365, 423, 445, 450, and 461.

TABLE A–5.—LIVING ARRANGEMENTS OF THE ELDERLY, 1970–92

[Civilian noninstitutionalized population, number in thousands]

Living arrangement	Total 65 and over		Widowed men		Widowed women	
	Number	Percent	Number	Percent	Number	Percent
Total:						
1970[2]	19,061	100.0	1,333	100.0	5,946	100.0
1980[3]	24,194	100.0	1,342	100.0	7,295	100.0
1990	29,566	100.0	1,755	100.0	8,367	100.0
1992	30,590	100.0	1,917	100.0	8,601	100.0
In families:						
1970[2]	13,347	70.0	499	37.4	2,386	40.1
1980[3]	16,355	67.6	385	28.7	2,194	30.1
1990	19,737	66.8	525	29.9	2,202	26.3
1992	20,351	66.5	53.6	28.0	2,305	26.8
Living alone:						
1970[2]	5,071	26.6	708	53.1	3,309	55.7
1980[3]	7,328	30.3	893	66.5	4,916	67.4
1990	9,176	31.0	1,117	63.6	5,946	71.1
1992	9,523	31.1	1,241	64.7	6,070	70.6
Other:						
1970[2]	645	3.4	124	9.3	251	4.2
1980[3]	511	2.1	65	4.8	186	2.5
1990	653	2.2	113	6.4	220	2.6
1992	716	2.3	142	7.4	227	2.6

[1] Excludes persons in institutions (nursing homes, etc.). The number of such persons age 65 years and over was estimated to be 0.8 million in 1970, and 1.6 million in 1989.

[2] Estimates based on weights derived from the 1970 decennial census.

[3] Estimates based on weights derived from the 1980 decennial census.

Source: Bureau of the Census, Current Population Reports, P–20, Nos. 445, 450, 461 and unpublished data.

TABLE A–6.—POVERTY STATUS OF ALL PERSONS, AND THE ELDERLY BY SEX, RACE/ETHNICITY AND LIVING ARRANGEMENT, 1959–92

[Percent below the poverty level]

	1959	1966	1970	1973[1]	1980	1990	1992
All persons	22.4	14.7	12.6	11.1	13.0	13.5	14.5
Persons 65 years old and over	35.2	28.5	24.5	16.3	15.7	12.2	12.9
Both sexes:							
Living arrangement:							
Living in families	NA	NA	14.7	9.4	8.5	5.8	7.1
Unrelated individuals	NA	NA	47.1	32.0	30.6	24.7	24.9
Race/ethnicity:							
Black	NA	NA	48.0	37.1	38.1	21.9	22.0
Hispanic[2]	NA	NA	NA	24.9	30.8	14.6	14.2
White	NA	NA	22.5	14.4	13.6	4.3	5.7
Men	NA	NA	19.0	12.4	10.9	7.6	8.9
Living arrangement:							
Living in families	NA	NA	14.9	9.4	8.2	5.4	6.7
Unrelated individuals	NA	NA	38.9	27.1	24.4	17.3	18.6
Race/ethnicity:							
Black	NA	NA	41.3	32.4	31.4	27.8	26.9
Hispanic[2]	NA	NA	NA	22.0	27.0	18.6	17.4
White	NA	NA	17.0	10.4	9.0	5.6	7.1
Women	NA	NA	28.5	19.0	19.0	15.4	15.7
Living arrangement:							
Living in families	NA	NA	14.5	9.3	8.8	6.3	7.5
Unrelated individuals	NA	NA	49.7	33.5	32.3	26.9	26.8
Race/ethnicity:							
Black	NA	NA	53.2	40.5	42.6	37.9	37.7
Hispanic[2]	NA	NA	NA	24.7	34.3	25.3	25.3
White	NA	NA	26.5	17.2	16.8	13.2	13.6

[1] First year in which Hispanic data are available.   [2] Hispanics may be of any race.   NA—Not available.

Source: U.S. Bureau of the Census, Current Population Reports series P–60.

TABLE A–7.—POVERTY RATES OF THE ELDERLY BY AGE, SEX, AND MARITAL STATUS:
1992

	65 and over	65 to 74	75 to 84	85 and over
Male total	8.9	8.1	9.7	13.2
Married	6.6	6.0	7.5	10.5
Widowed	15.0	13.7	15.7	16.7
Divorced/separated/never married	17.6	18.1	16.5	NA
Female total	15.7	12.7	18.9	22.7
Married	6.4	5.6	8.0	NA
Widowed	21.5	18.9	23.2	23.8
Divorced/separated/never married	26.0	25.6	27.0	NA
Total	12.9	10.7	15.3	19.8

NA—Not available due to unreliability of estimate. Percentage base represents fewer than 250,000 persons.

Source: March 1993 Current Population Survey (CPS). Table prepared by CRS.

861

TABLE A–8.—TOTAL MONEY INCOME OF ELDERLY UNITS, 1992

Amount of income	All units			Married couples			Nonmarried persons		
	Age 65 and over	Age 65–69	Age 85 and over	Age 65 and over	Age 65–69	Age 85 and over	Age 65 and over	Age 65–69	Age 85 and over
Number (in thousands)	23,579	6,746	2,409	9,595	3,395	427	13,983	3,351	1,982
Total percent	100.0	100.0	100.0	100.0	100.0	100.0	100.0	100.0	100.0
0–$4,999	8.2	7.0	13.6	2.4	2.4	4.3	12.2	11.5	15.9
$5,000–$9,999	26.8	19.3	41.0	7.5	6.4	10.3	40.2	32.4	47.5
$10,000–$14,999	17.9	15.9	19.1	14.2	12.3	20.7	20.6	19.4	18.9
$15,000–$19,999	12.4	12.2	9.9	15.3	11.6	21.2	10.4	12.7	7.5
$20,000–$29,999	15.8	18.8	8.0	24.8	24.3	17.9	9.5	13.3	5.9
$30,000–$39,999	8.0	10.6	3.9	14.9	16.9	10.4	3.4	4.2	2.4
$40,000–$49,999	4.1	5.6	2.2	7.5	8.4	7.5	1.7	2.7	1.1
$50,000–$74,999	3.7	5.6	1.0	7.2	9.2	3.0	1.4	2.1	0.4
$75,000–$99,999	1.1	2.1	0.4	2.8	3.5	1.7	0.4	0.7	0.2
$100,000–$149,999	0.3	2.1	0.3	2.2	3.4	1.7	0.3	0.7	0.0
$150,000–$199,999	0.3	0.7	0.2	0.7	1.3	1.3	0.1	0.1	0.0
$200,000 or more	0.2	0.3	0.2	0.4	0.5	0.3	0.1	0.1	0.2
Median	$13,959	$18,087	$9,299	$23,817	$26,873	$18,347	$9,554	$11,302	$8,108

Source: 1993 Current Population Survey, tabulated by the Office of Research and Statistics, Social Security Administration.

862

TABLE A–9.—AMOUNT OF INCOME FROM SOURCES OTHER THAN SOCIAL SECURITY, AMONG SOCIAL SECURITY BENEFICIARIES AGE 65 AND OVER, 1992

Unit income other than Social Security	All units	Married couples	Nonmarried persons
Number (in thousands)	21,719	8,958	12,762
Total percent	100.0	100.0	100.0
None	14.2	6.4	19.7
Loss or $1–$1,999	20.7	12.0	17.8
$2,000–$3,999	10.8	7.7	12.9
$4,000–$5,999	8.1	6.8	9.0
$6,000–$7,999	7.1	7.9	6.5
$8,000–$9,999	5.7	6.4	5.3
$10,000–$14,999	9.9	13.3	1.8
$15,000–$19,999	6.2	9.4	3.9
$20,000–$29,999	7.5	12.5	4.0
$30,000–$39,999	3.9	6.9	1.8
$40,000–$74,999	3.8	6.9	1.7
$75,000–$99,999	0.9	1.7	0.3
$100,000–$199,999	0.9	2.0	0.1
$200,000 or more	0.1	0.2	0.1
Median income other than Social Security	$4,918	$10,937	$2,357
Median Social Security income	$8,044	$11,656	$6,748

Source: 1993 Current Population Survey, tabulated by the Office of Research and Statistics, Social Security Administration.

TABLE A–10.—INCOME SOURCES OF ELDERLY UNITS [1] AND RELATIVE IMPORTANCE OF SOURCES, 1992

	Percent of units with income from each source			Percent of aggregate unit income from each source		
	Total	Poor [2]	Nonpoor	Total	Poor [2]	Nonpoor
Number of units (in thousands)	23,187	3,514	19,673	NA	NA	NA
Number of aged individuals (in thousands)	30,870	3,983	26,887	NA	NA	NA
Percent of units	100.0	15.2	84.8	NA	NA	NA
Earnings [3]	32.3	9.3	36.4	30.0	5.0	30.9
OASDI, railroad retirement	93.6	89.8	94.2	32.6	67.7	31.3
Pensions	45.6	8.6	52.2	16.0	2.6	16.4
Unemployment compensation, workers compensation, veterans payments	8.8	4.8	9.5	1.5	1.6	1.5
AFDC, SSI, general assistance	8.7	25.3	5.7	1.0	10.0	0.7
Child support, alimony	5.3	2.7	5.7	0.9	0.6	0.9
Interest, dividends [3]	70.1	33.7	76.6	17.5	3.5	18.0
Food stamps [4]	5.7	23.6	2.5	0.2	3.1	0.1
Housing assistance [4]	5.9	16.9	3.9	0.4	5.8	0.2

[1] Families and unrelated individuals with any member age 65 or older.
[2] Based on census ("Orshansky") poverty levels.
[3] Negative income (i.e., losses) set to zero.
[4] The cash values of food stamps and housing assistance were estimated using their market values. Their cash values are excluded from total income for purposes of determining poverty status. Cash values of food stamps and housing assistance are included in total income for calculating the percentage share of total income.
NA—Not applicable.

Note: Details may not sum to totals due to rounding.

Source: March 1993 Current Population Survey (CPS). Table prepared by CRS.

TABLE A–11.—INCOME SOURCES OF ELDERLY MARRIED COUPLES AND RELATIVE IMPORTANCE OF SOURCES, 1992

	Percent of couples with income from each source			Percent of aggregate total income from each source		
	Total	Poor [2]	Nonpoor	Total	Poor [2]	Nonpoor
Number of married couples (in thousands)	6,076	347	5,729	NA	NA	NA
Percent of married couples	100.0	5.7	94.3	NA	NA	NA
Earnings [3]	20.8	5.5	21.8	12.8	2.5	12.9
OASDI, railroad retirement	97.2	86.5	97.8	40.7	73.1	40.3
Pensions	60.9	14.6	63.7	22.0	4.8	22.2
Veterans, UC, and other compensation	8.4	3.7	8.7	1.3	2.0	1.3
AFDC, SSI, general assistance	2.4	14.4	1.7	0.3	7.9	0.2
Child support, alimony	3.0	0.4	3.2	0.5	0.0	0.5
Interest, dividends [3]	82.4	45.4	84.6	22.5	5.2	22.7
Food stamps [4]	1.6	17.8	0.6	0.0	2.9	0.0
Housing assistance [4]	1.3	4.4	1.1	0.1	1.6	0.0

[1] Both members age 65 or over.
[2] Based on Orshansky poverty levels.
[3] Negative incomes (i.e., losses) set to zero.
[4] The cash values of food stamps and housing assistance were estimated using their market values. Their cash values are excluded from total income for purposes of determining poverty status. Cash values of food stamps and housing assistance are included in total income for calculating the percentage share of total income.

NA—Not applicable.

Source: March 1993 Current Population Survey (CPS). Table prepared by CRS.

TABLE A–12. INCOME SOURCES OF ELDERLY UNRELATED INDIVIDUALS [1] AND RELATIVE IMPORTANCE OF SOURCES, 1992

	Percent of units with income from each source			Percent of aggregate total income from each source		
	Total	Poor [2]	Nonpoor	Total	Poor [2]	Nonpoor
Number of individuals (in thousands)	10,041	2,498	7,543	NA	NA	NA
Percent of individuals	100.0	24.9	75.1	NA	NA	NA
Earnings [3]	12.4	2.9	15.5	10.0	0.7	11.0
OASDI, Railroad retirement	94.9	92.5	95.7	45.2	74.6	42.2
Pensions	37.8	7.3	47.9	17.4	2.1	18.9
Veterans, UC, and other compensation	5.0	3.8	5.5	1.5	0.9	1.6
AFDC, SSI, general assistance	8.3	23.7	3.2	1.2	8.2	0.4
Child support, alimony	3.5	1.6	4.2	0.8	0.4	0.9
Interest, dividends [3]	63.9	33.9	73.8	22.3	3.3	24.3
Food stamps [4]	7.0	22.2	1.9	0.2	2.0	0.0
Housing assistance [4]	11.2	20.9	8.0	1.4	7.9	0.7

[1] Age 65 and over living alone.
[2] Based on ("Orshansky") poverty levels.
[3] Negative incomes (i.e., losses) set to zero.
[4] The cash values of food stamps and housing assistance were estimated using their market values. Their cash values are excluded from total income for purposes of determining poverty status. Cash values of food stamps and housing assistance are included in total income for calculating the percentage share of total income.

NA—Not applicable.

Source: March 1993 Current Population Survey (CPS). Table prepared by CRS.

TABLE A–13.—RECEIPT OF SOCIAL SECURITY, SUPPLEMENTAL SECURITY INCOME AND FOOD STAMPS, AMONG POOR AND NEAR-POOR ELDERLY UNITS,[1] 1992

Type of benefit received	Units with income below 100 percent of poverty threshold		Units with income of 100 to 149.9 percent of poverty threshold	
	Number (in thousands)	Percent	Number (in thousands)	Percent
Total	3,377	100.0	3,578	100.0
Social Security [2]	3,057	90.5	3,483	97.3
SSI	761	22.5	393	11.0
Food stamps	779	23.1	237	6.6
Social Security only [3]	2,131	63.1	2,993	83.7
SSI only [3]	51	1.5	25	0.7
Food stamps only [3]	19	0.6	0	0.0
Social Security and food stamps [4]	308	9.1	133	3.7
Social Security and SSI [4]	258	7.6	263	7.4
SSI and food stamps [4]	92	2.7	11	0.3
All three income sources	360	10.7	93	2.6
No Social Security, SSI, or food stamps	158	4.7	59	1.6

[1] Includes couples with an elderly head and unrelated individuals.

[2] Includes railroad retirement.

[3] This row, which is labeled "social security only", means the family receives only Social Security and does not receive SSI or food stamps. The family could be receiving other types of income. The same is true of the following 2 rows.

[4] Family receives only the two types of income specified but not the third. The family could be receiving other sources of income than the three mentioned.

Source: March 1993 Current Population Survey (CPS). Table prepared by CRS.

APPENDIX B. HEALTH STATUS, INSURANCE, AND EXPENDITURES OF THE ELDERLY, AND BACKGROUND DATA ON LONG-TERM CARE

Although the health status of the elderly appears to have been improving in recent decades, many elderly persons have conditions that require medical and long-term health care, sometimes in substantial amounts. Nearly all elderly persons have some insurance that protects them, at least partially, from the expenses arising from health care use. Many are well insured for their acute care needs—that is, for hospital and physician services. Others face greater risk of high out-of-pocket expenditures. This appendix reports on the health status, health insurance, and health care expenditures of the elderly.

HEALTH STATUS

By various measures, the health status of the elderly population has been improving over the years. For example, life expectancy at age 65 has increased from 13.9 years in 1950 to 17.2 years in 1989 (see table B–1). The improvements in life expectancy—or, alternatively, the declines in mortality rates—have been greater for females than for males. Morbidity indicators—such as the incidence of high blood pressure—also improved among those aged 65 to 74 years between the early 1960's and the late 1970's (see table B–2).

TABLE B–1.—LIFE EXPECTANCY AT BIRTH AND AT 65 YEARS OF AGE, BY SEX, BY RACE, UNITED STATES, SELECTED YEARS 1900–90

[Remaining life expectancy in years]

Year	At birth			At 65 years			At birth	
	Both sexes	Male	Female	Both sexes	Male	Female	White	Black
1900 [1][2]	47.3	46.3	48.3	11.9	11.5	12.2	47.6	[3] 33.0
1950 [2]	68.2	65.6	71.1	13.9	12.8	15.0	69.1	60.7
1960 [2]	69.7	66.6	73.1	14.3	12.8	15.8	70.6	63.2
1970	70.9	67.1	74.8	15.2	13.1	17.0	71.7	64.1
1980	73.7	70.0	77.4	16.4	14.1	18.3	74.4	68.1
1984	74.7	71.2	78.2	16.8	14.6	18.6	75.3	69.7
1985	74.7	71.2	78.2	16.7	14.6	18.6	75.3	69.5
1986	74.8	71.3	78.3	16.8	14.7	18.6	75.4	69.4
1987	75.0	71.5	78.4	16.9	14.8	18.7	75.6	69.4
1988	74.9	71.5	78.3	16.9	14.9	18.6	75.6	69.2
1989	75.3	71.8	78.6	17.2	15.2	18.8	76.0	69.2
Provisional data:								
1988 [2]	74.9	71.4	78.3	16.9	14.8	18.6	75.5	69.5
1989 [2]	75.2	71.8	78.5	17.2	15.2	18.8	75.9	69.7
1990 [2]	75.4	72.0	78.8	17.3	15.3	19.0	76.0	70.3

[1] Death registration area only; includes 10 States and the District of Columbia.
[2] Includes deaths of nonresidents of the United States.
[3] Figure is for the all other population.

Source: National Center for Health Statistics, Health, United States, 1989, Hyattsville, Maryland: Public Health Service, 1990.

TABLE B–2.—SELECTED HEALTH STATUS INDICATORS FOR PERSONS 65–74 YEARS OF AGE, BY SEX, 1960–62, 1971–74, AND 1976–80

[Percent of population]

Health status indicator	Both sexes			Male			Female		
	1960–62	1971–74	1976–80	1960–62	1971–74	1976–80	1960–62	1971–74	1976–80
Borderline or definite elevated blood pressure [1]	73.8	70.3	63.1	65.9	65.4	62.0	80.3	74.1	63.9
Definite elevated blood pressure [2]	48.7	40.9	34.5	40.5	36.4	33.3	55.4	44.4	35.5
High-risk serum cholesterol levels [3]	37.3	31.3	27.2	20.8	19.9	18.1	50.8	40.0	34.3
Overweight [4]	34.6	31.5	32.7	23.8	23.0	25.2	43.3	38.0	38.5

[1] Borderline or definite elevated blood pressure is defined as either systolic pressure of at least 140 mmHg or diastolic pressure of at least 90 mmHg or both based on a single measurement.

[2] Definite elevated blood pressure is defined as either systolic pressure of at least 160 mmHg or diastolic pressure of at least 95 mmHg or both based on a single measurement.

[3] High-risk serum cholesterol levels are defined by age-specific cut points of the cholesterol distribution. For 40 years of age and over, high risk is greater than 260 milligrams/deciliter. Risk levels defined by NIH Consensus Development conference statement on lowering blood cholesterol, December 10, 1984.

[4] Overweight is defined for men as body mass index greater than or equal to 27.8 kilograms/meter^2, and for women as body mass index greater than or equal to 27.3 milograms/meter^2. These cut points were used because they represent the sex-specific 85th percentiles for persons 20–29 years of age in the 1976–80 National Health and Nutrition Examination Survey.

Source: National Center for Health Statistics, Health, United States, 1985, DHHS Pub. No. (PHS) 86–1232, pp. 76–79. Data are based on physical examinations of a sample of the civilian, noninstitutionalized population.

Despite the trend toward improved health status of the elderly, their needs for medical and long-term care services remain substantial. First, greater life expectancy postpones the probable need for terminal illness care. (About two-thirds of the deaths in the United States are of the elderly. A recent study found that the 6 percent of Medicare beneficiaries who died in 1978 accounted for 28 percent of Medicare expenditures.[1]) Second, many of the elderly have one or more chronic conditions, many of which give rise to the need for continuing health care. Table 3 shows the incidence of several common chronic conditions among the elderly. Nearly half report having arthritis, about 40 percent report high blood pressure, and almost 30 percent report heart disease. The incidence of many chronic conditions is directly related to age and inversely related to family income.

Self-assessed health is a common method used to measure health status, with responses ranging from "excellent" to "poor." Nearly 71 percent of elderly people living in the community describe their health as excellent, very good, or good, compared with others their age; only 29 percent report that their health is fair or good (see table B–4).

Income is directly related to one's perception of his or her health. About 26 percent of older people with incomes over $35,000 described their health as excellent compared to others their age, while only 10 percent of those with low incomes (less than $10,000) reported excellent health.

TABLE B–3.—SELECTED CHRONIC CONDITIONS PER 1,000 ELDERLY PERSONS, BY AGE AND FAMILY INCOME, 1988

Chronic condition	All elderly	Age		Family income			
		65–74	75 and over	Less than $10,000	$10,000 to $19,999	$20,000 to $34,999	$35,000 and over
Arthritis	486	445	550	608	452	471	397
Cataracts	168	118	246	183	174	131	150
Hearing impairment .	315	274	381	308	364	259	314
Deformity or ortho-pedic impairment	161	151	177	182	179	136	140
Hernia of abdominal cavity	58	54	64	72	67	46	51
Diabetes	92	95	88	98	101	76	71
Heart disease	296	272	334	346	324	269	257
High blood pressure .	373	373	374	472	396	345	321
Emphysema	38	36	41	52	48	34	(1)

[1] Sample size is too small for reliable estimate.

Source: U.S. Department of Health and Human Services, National Center for Health Statistics, Vital and Health Statistics: Current estimates from the National Health Interview Survey, 1988, Series 10, No. 173, October 1989.

---

[1] J. Lubitz and R. Prihoda, "The Use and Costs of Medicare Services in the Last Two Years of Life," Health Care Financing Review, Volume 5, 1984, pp. 117–131.

TABLE B–4.—SELF-ASSESSED HEALTH STATUS OF THE ELDERLY, BY FAMILY INCOME, 1989

[In percent]

Characteristic	All persons [1] (thousands)	All health status [3]	Self-assessed health status [2]				
			Excellent	Very good	Good	Fair	Poor
All persons 65 [4]	29,219	100.0	16.4	23.1	31.9	19.3	9.2
Sex:							
Men	12,143	100.0	16.9	23.2	30.8	18.4	10.7
Women	17,076	100.0	16.1	23.0	32.8	20.0	8.1
Family income:							
Under $10,000	5,612	100.0	10.3	19.4	29.7	25.0	15.6
$10,000 to $19,999	8,002	100.0	14.8	21.7	33.9	21.1	8.5
$20,000 to $34,999	5,242	100.0	20.2	25.7	32.5	15.7	5.9
$35,000 and over	3,484	100.0	26.0	26.8	30.3	11.7	5.1

[1] Includes unknown health status.

[2] Excludes unknown health status.

[3] The categories related to this concept result from asking the respondent, "Would you say—health is excellent, very good, good, fair, or poor?" As such, it is based on the respondent's opinion and not directly on any clinical evidence.

[4] Includes unknown family income.

Note.—Percentages may not add to 100 percent due to rounding.

Source: National Center for Health Statistics. "Current Estimates from the National Health Interview Survey, 1989." Vital and Health Statistics Series 10, No. 176 (October 1990). Data are based on household interviews of the civilian, noninstitutionalized population.

CAUSES OF DEATH FOR THE ELDERLY [2]

In the United States, about 7 out of every 10 elderly persons die from heart disease, cancer, or stroke. Heart disease was the major cause of death in 1950, and remains so today even though there have been rapid declines in death rates from heart disease since 1968, especially among females. Death rates from cancer continue to rise in comparison to heart disease, especially deaths caused by lung cancer (chart B–1). In 1988, however, heart disease accounted for 40 percent of all deaths among persons 65+, while cancer accounted for 21 percent of all deaths in this age group.[3] Even if cancer were eliminated as a cause of death, the average life span would be extended by less than 2 years because of the prevalence of heart disease. Eliminating deaths due to heart disease, on the other hand, would add an average of 5 years to life expectancy at age 65, and would lead to a sharp increase in the proportion of older persons in the total population.[4]

---

[2] This entire section is from Aging America: Trends and Projections, 1987–88 edition.

[3] National Center for Health Statistics. "Annual Summary of Births, Marriages, Divorces, and Deaths: United States, 1985." Monthly Vital Statistics Report Vol. 34, No. 13 (September 1986).

[4] National Center for Health Statistics. "United States Life Tables Eliminating Certain Causes of Death." U.S. Decennial Life Tables for 1979–81 Vol. 1, No. 2 (forthcoming).

CHART B–1. DEATH RATES FOR LEADING CAUSES OF DEATH FOR PEOPLE AGE 75–84: 1950–89

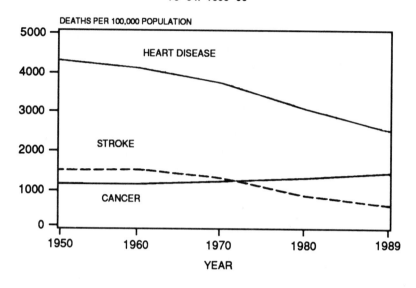

SOURCES: National Center for Health Statistics, *Health, United States, 1989.* DHHS Pub. No. (PHS)90-1232, Washington: Department of Health and Human Services (March 1990).

National Center for Health Statistics, "Annual Summary of Births, Marriages, Divorces, and Deaths: United States, 1989." *Monthly Vital Statistics Report* Vol. 38, No. 13 (August 30, 1990).

National Center for Health Statistics, "Advance Report of Final Mortality Statistics, 1988." *Monthly Vital Statistics Report* Vol. 39, No. 7, Supplement (November 28, 1990).

The third leading cause of death among the elderly—stroke (cerebrovascular disease)—has been decreasing over the past 30 years. Reasons for this dramatic decline are not fully understood. Part of the decline may be attributable to better control of hypertension. Better diagnosis and improved management and rehabilitation of stroke victims may also be related factors.[5] In 1988, cerebrovascular disease accounted for only 8 percent of all deaths in the 65+ age group.

Table B–5 shows the 10 leading causes of death for three subgroups of the older population.

The factors which have led to reductions in mortality may or may not also lead to overall improvements in health status. If Americans continue to live only to about age 85, control of life-threatening disease could produce a healthier older population. But, if the life-span is increased dramatically in future years beyond age 85, the onset of illness may only be delayed, without an actual shortening of the period of illness.

---

[5] National Center for Health Statistics. Health, United States, 1985. DHHS Pub. No. (PHS) 86–1232, Washington: Department of Health and Human Services, December 1985.

TABLE B–5.—DEATH RATES FOR TEN LEADING CAUSES OF DEATH AMONG OLDER
PEOPLE, BY AGE: 1988

[Rates per 100,000 population in age group]

Cause of death	65+	65–74	75–84	85+
All causes	5,105	2,730	6,321	15,594
Diseases of the heart	2,066	984	2,543	7,098
Malignant neoplasms	1,068	843	1,313	1,639
Cerebrovascular diseases	431	155	554	1,707
Chronic obstructive pulmonary diseases ...	226	152	313	394
Pneumonia and influenza	225	60	257	1,125
Diabetes	97	62	125	222
Accidents	89	50	107	267
Atherosclerosis	69	15	70	396
Nephritis, nephrotic syndrome, nephrosis .	61	26	78	217
Septicemia	56	24	71	199
All other causes	717	359	890	2,330

Source: National Center for Health Statistics. "Advanced Report of Final Mortality Statistics, 1988."
Monthly Vital Statistics Report Vol. 39, No. 7, Supplement (November 28, 1990).

MEDICARE REIMBURSEMENT AND OUT-OF-POCKET LIABILITIES OF
THE ELDERLY

Tables B–6 through B–8 illustrate for 6 selected years how Medicare reimbursement, acute health care costs, and out-of-pocket liabilities of Medicare enrollees have changed. The years chosen are 1975, 1980, 1985, 1990, 1995, and 2000 (projected values). Constant 1990 dollar values were obtained using the CPI–U.

The fastest-growing component of Medicare reimbursement is for benefits under the Supplementary Medical Insurance (SMI) program. For SMI, reimbursements increase at an annual rate of 13.3 percent, while the growth in total costs (including enrollees' share of costs) is 11.3 percent (see table B–6). As a result, the share of SMI costs reimbursed by Medicare increases significantly over the period—from about 64 percent in 1975 to about 74 percent by 1990. Through 1985, the growth in Medicare's share is due to the declining significance of the SMI deductible, so that more enrollees' costs were eligible for reimbursement.

In the Hospital Insurance (HI) program, by contrast, the rate of growth in reimbursement is slower than the growth in enrollee's copayment costs. Consequently, the share of HI costs reimbursed by Medicare has decreased from 93 percent in 1975 to 91 percent in 1990.

Overall, the share of costs reimbursed by Medicare has increased slightly. The percentage of costs paid by Medicare for services covered under Medicare was 82.2 percent in 1975 and 83.4 percent in 1990 (see table B–6). The other side of this—the share of costs paid directly by enrollees—is shown in the third panel of table B–7. Total direct costs plus Medicare reimbursement equals the total or 100 percent.

TABLE B–6.—REIMBURSEMENTS AND OUT-OF-POCKET COSTS UNDER MEDICARE, SELECTED CALENDAR YEARS

[Incurred costs per HI or SMI enrollee]

	1975	1980	1985	1990	1995	2000	Annual growth 1975–2000 (percent)
				In current dollars			
Hospital insurance:							
Reimbursement	$458	$906	$1,539	$1,959	$3,027	$4,385	9.5
Copayments	34	66	117	188	246	329	9.5
Total	492	972	1,656	2,146	3,273	4,714	9.5
Supplementary medical insurance:							
Reimbursement	184	402	763	1,298	1,951	3,309	12.2
Copayments	83	138	246	394	544	864	9.8
Balance-billing	22	56	87	68	42	67	4.6
Total	289	597	1,096	1,760	2,537	4,240	11.3
Total Medicare reimbursement	642	1,308	2,302	3,257	4,978	7,694	10.4
Total costs under Medicare	781	1,569	2,752	3,906	5,810	8,954	10.2

	In constant 1990 dollars						
Hospital insurance:							
Reimbursement	1,065	1,439	1,870	1,959	2,589	3,221	4.5
Copayments	79	104	143	188	210	242	4.6
Total	1,144	1,543	2,012	2,146	2,800	3,463	4.5
Supplementary medical insurance:							
Reimbursement	428	639	927	1,298	1,669	2,431	7.2
Copayments	193	220	299	394	465	635	4.9
Balance-billing	51	89	106	68	36	49	-0.2
Total	672	947	1,332	1,760	2,170	3,115	6.3
Total Medicare reimbursement	1,493	2,077	2,797	3,257	4,258	5,752	5.5
Total costs under Medicare	1,816	2,490	3,344	3,906	4,970	6,578	5.3
Percent of costs paid by Medicare	82.2	83.4	83.6	83.4	85.7	85.9	0.2

Note.—1995 values are projected. The CPI–U was used to obtain constant dollars.

Source: Congressional Budget Office (February 1993 baseline).

TABLE B–7.—ENROLLEE COSTS UNDER MEDICARE, SELECTED CALENDAR YEARS

[Incurred costs per HI or SMI enrollee]

	1975	1980	1985	1990	1995	2000	Annual growth 1975–2000 (percent)
			In current dollars				
HI copayments	$34	$66	$117	$188	$246	$329	9.5
SMI copayments	83	138	246	394	544	864	9.8
Balance-billing	22	56	87	68	42	67	4.6
Total direct costs	139	260	451	649	832	1,260	9.2
Premium costs	80	110	186	343	553	728	9.2
Total enrollee costs	219	371	637	993	1,385	1,988	9.2
Enrollee per capita income [1]	5,158	8,431	12,767	15,454	19,141	23,074	6.2
			In constant 1990 dollars				
HI copayments	79	104	143	188	210	242	4.6
SMI copayments	193	220	299	394	465	635	4.9
Balance-billing	51	89	106	68	36	49	−0.2
Total direct costs	323	413	547	649	712	926	4.3
Premium costs	187	175	226	343	473	535	4.3

877

Total enrollee costs	510	588	773	993	1,185	1,461	4.3
Enrollee per capita income [1]	11,998	13,386	15,513	15,454	16,374	16,951	1.4

Percent of costs under Medicare paid by enrollees, by source of payment

HI copayments	4.3	4.2	4.3	4.8	4.2	3.7	−0.7
SMI copayments	10.6	8.8	8.9	10.1	9.4	9.6	−0.4
Balance-billing	2.8	3.6	3.2	1.7	0.7	0.7	−5.2
Total direct costs	17.8	16.6	16.4	16.6	14.3	14.1	−0.9
Premium costs	10.3	7.0	6.8	8.8	9.5	8.1	−0.9
Total	28.1	23.6	23.1	25.4	23.8	22.2	−0.9
Enrollee-paid costs as a percent of enrollee per capita income [1]	4.3	4.4	5.0	6.4	7.2	8.6	2.9

[1] From Current Population Survey, adjusted for underreporting.

Note.—1995 values are projected. The CPI–U was used to obtain constant dollars.

Source: Congressional Budget Office (February 1994 baseline).

In constant dollars, HI copayments have increased the most rapidly between 1975 and 1995. However, between 1990 and 1995, premium costs are expected to rise the most rapidly due equally to copayments and premiums. In contrast, the cost to the enrollee from balance-billing has decreased significantly since 1985—a direct policy result of the participating physician program and the imposition of lower limits on balance billing. See table B–8 for deductible amounts and monthly premium amounts under Medicare.

Enrollees are spending an increasing share of their income for health care. In 1975, about 4.3 percent of enrollees' per capita income went to cover their share of acute health care costs under Medicare. By 2000, enrollees will have to pay an estimated 8.6 percent of their per capita income to cover their share of costs under Medicare.

Although direct household spending for health care by elderly households, that is households headed by a person 65 or older, as a share of household income has increased since the early 1970's, it has remained relatively stable in recent years. Chart B–2 illustrates direct household spending for health care as a percentage of household income before taxes for elderly and nonelderly households for years 1984 through 1992. In 1992, direct household spending for health care as a percentage of household income for elderly households was 11.9 percent, on average, up slightly from 10.6 percent in 1984. Over the same period, nonelderly households spent around 3.5 percent of their household income for health care.

TABLE B–8.—COPAYMENT AND PREMIUM VALUES UNDER MEDICARE, SELECTED CALENDAR YEARS

	1975	1980	1985	1990	1995	2000	Annual growth 1975–2000 (in percent)
	In current dollars						
Hospital insurance:							
Hospital deductible	$92	$180	$400	$592	$720	$916	9.6
Supplementary medical insurance:							
Annual deductible	60	60	75	75	100	100	2.1
Monthly premium [1]	6.70	9.20	15.50	28.60	46.10	60.70	9.2
	In constant 1990 dollars						
Hospital insurance:							
Hospital deductible	214	286	486	592	616	673	4.7
Supplementary medical insurance:							
Annual deductible	139	95	91	75	86	73	−2.5
Monthly premium [1]	15.57	14.61	18.83	28.60	39.43	44.59	4.3

[1] The 1980 SMI monthly premium amount is the average of values for the first and second halves of the year.

Note.—Values after 1990 are projected. The CPI–U was used to get constant dollars.

Source: Congressional Budget Office (February 1994 baseline).

CHART B-2. DIRECT HOUSEHOLD SPENDING FOR HEALTH CARE AS A PERCENTAGE OF HOUSEHOLD INCOME BY TYPE OF HOUSEHOLD, 1984-92

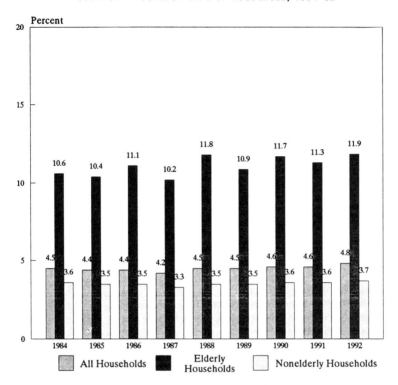

All Households   Elderly Households   Nonelderly Households

SOURCE: Congressional Budget Office calculations based on data from the Consumer Expenditure Surveys (CES) of the Bureau of Labor Statistics, 1984-1992.

NOTES: Direct household spending for health care consists of the amount directly paid for health insurance premiums by a household, as well as out-of-pocket spending for health care services, including deductibles and copayments.

Elderly households are those in which the primary home owner or renter in the household is 65 or older. Such households may include individuals younger than 65. Nonelderly households are those in which the primary home owner or renter in the household is younger than 65. Such households may include individuals age 65 or older.

Although expenditures for health care by the institutionalized population are not collected by the CES, if a member residing in the household contributes to health-related expenses of an institutionalized person, then those expenditures are counted as direct household spending for health care.

Household income refers to income before taxes.

Analyzing Trends in Medicare Spending, 1967–98 [6]

Between 1980 and 1985, total Medicare spending for hospital inpatient services grew at an annual rate of 14.6 percent. The estimated growth rate for 1985 to 1992 is 6.8 percent. The difference in these rates is due to changes in four separate trends: Medicare enrollment, admissions per enrollee, real expenditures per admission, and the general rate of inflation.

Reduced inflation contributes to the lower rate of growth in total Medicare inpatient spending. General inflation is estimated at 3.9 percent per year from 1985 to 1992, compared with 5.6 percent for 1980 to 1985. The growth rate for 1985 to 1992 would thus be about 1.7 percentage points higher at the previous rate of inflation.

Real Medicare inpatient spending per enrollee removes the effects of changes in Medicare enrollment and general inflation from total Medicare inpatient spending (see table B–9). Since both enrollment and prices are almost always increasing, the growth of real per enrollee spending is slower than the growth of total spending. Real inpatient spending per enrollee grew at an annual rate of 6.4 percent between 1980 and 1985, and the estimate for 1985 to 1992 is 0.1 percent. The difference in these rates is due to changes in admissions per enrollee and real expenditures per admission.

The number of Medicare enrollees grew at an annual rate of 1.7 percent between 1980 and 1985, and the estimate for 1985 to 1991 is about the same. Medicare enrollment thus makes no contribution to the observed difference in spending growth between the early and late 1980's.

The trend in admissions per enrollee did change, however. In 1984, Medicare's peer review organizations were set up to monitor inpatient cases for appropriateness of treatment and site of care. Simultaneously, admission rates among the Medicare population—which had been increasing through 1983—began to decline. Although admission rates inched up again after 1987, rates in 1989 for people age 65 or more (a proxy for the Medicare population) were still only 85 percent of rates in 1983. Perhaps Medicare's preadmission approval requirements for certain procedures, coupled with retrospective payment denials for care deemed inappropriate, encouraged physicians either to forgo some elective procedures for their Medicare patients or to move them to the outpatient sector. It should be noted that admissions for the non-Medicare population decreased for each year since 1981. Given this trend, some credit for lower admissions rates must go to changes in practice patterns and other factors not associated with Medicare policy.

A reduction in real expenditures per admission makes the greatest contribution to decreased spending growth. This decline is primarily due to smaller increases in payment rates under PPS since the very large increases in the first 2 years (1984 and 1985). At the previous rate of increase in Medicare expenditures per admission, the estimated growth in total inpatient spending between 1985 and 1991 would be 12.0 percent per year, rather than 5.1 percent. The

[6] The following section borrows heavily from a memorandum prepared by Sandra Christensen, of the Congressional Budget Office, February 4, 1991. Updated April 1992.

estimated real growth in spending per enrollee would have been 6.4 percent per year, rather than -0.3 percent.

Costs in hospital outpatient departments have dropped relative to the previous trend, indicating that hospital inpatient costs have not simply been shifted to the outpatient sector. Savings relative to trend for hospital outpatient and home health services may in large part reflect unsustainably large rates of growth during the trend period from 1975 through 1980. Introduction of a new payment methodology (a blend of a fixed rate and the hospital's costs) for certain surgical procedures performed in outpatient departments tended to reduce costs somewhat, but this effect was partially offset by the shift of services from the inpatient sector. During the 1980s, Medicare's administrative agents implemented stricter standards for determining coverage of home health services (tending to reduce costs), but increased demand for services from patients discharged earlier from hospitals than they would have been prior to the prospective payment system would have worked to increase Medicare's spending for home health.

Growth in spending for physicians' services has not slowed as much as hospital spending relative to previous trends despite the disproportionate impact on physicians of budget reconciliation bills. Apparently, growth in the volume of physicians' services has accelerated by enough to offset some of the enacted reductions in payment rates. Although not all of this growth was in response to fee cuts, growth in the volume of services was enough to completely offset the fee freeze in place from 1984 through 1986, but was insufficient to offset entirely the effects of subsequent fee cuts for "overvalued" procedures.

Spending for skilled nursing facilities (SNFs) increased significantly. During the period from 1975 through 1980, real spending per enrollee for SNFs was falling. This trend was reversed during the 1980s. In 1988, growth in SNF spending accelerated sharply because of a revision in the manual used by administrative agents to determine Medicare coverage that greatly relaxed the definition of covered care to make it conform with legislative language. Growth in SNF spending further accelerated in 1989 under provisions of the Medicare Catastrophic Coverage Act, which briefly eliminated the requirement for a hospital stay prior to a covered SNF stay and which reduced the copayments required of enrollees for SNF stays.

Table B–9 shows Medicare spending per enrollee in constant 1990 dollars where the CPI–U has been used to obtain constant dollars. The first column includes both Medicare benefits and administration. All other columns include spending on benefits only.

TABLE B–9.—REAL SPENDING PER ENROLLEE

[Fiscal years, in constant 1990 dollars]

ESTIMATES BY THE HEALTH CARE FINANCING ADMINISTRATION

Fiscal years	Medicare Bft+Adm	HI Bft	SMI Bft	Hospital inpatient	SNF	HH & Hospice	OPD	Physician & Lab	Hospital Inp+OPD
1967	648	470	134	449	18	4	3	130	451
1968	974	669	264	599	62	10	8	254	608
1969	1,138	792	293	721	62	12	13	276	735
1970	1,155	768	327	712	48	13	17	306	728
1971	1,194	818	315	779	32	12	21	289	800
1972	1,269	872	331	841	25	12	26	300	867
1973	1,244	861	324	831	23	12	25	294	856
1974	1,292	878	337	845	24	17	36	292	881
1975	1,479	1,030	382	989	27	21	54	321	1,043
1976	1,615	1,108	431	1,061	28	30	67	353	1,128
1977	1,756	1,208	484	1,156	28	35	80	393	1,236
1978	1,877	1,289	516	1,237	26	39	90	413	1,327
1979	1,941	1,317	557	1,264	25	42	98	445	1,362
1980	2,051	1,386	600	1,333	23	44	107	480	1,439
1981	2,216	1,501	650	1,447	21	46	117	521	1,563
1982	2,414	1,637	715	1,563	22	56	138	574	1,702
1983	2,565	1,710	795	1,620	24	66	152	642	1,772
1984	2,654	1,755	835	1,659	23	74	151	682	1,810
1985	2,876	1,921	885	1,821	22	80	159	725	1,980
1986	2,924	1,880	978	1,781	22	78	192	785	1,973
1987	3,002	1,829	1,110	1,735	23	72	215	894	1,950
1988	3,036	1,787	1,180	1,688	25	75	227	952	1,915
1989	3,133	1,845	1,215	1,691	75	81	241	972	1,932

Year									
1990	3,328	1,976	1,282	1,780	85	112	258	1,021	2,039
1991	3,303	1,918	1,315	1,695	70	155	267	1,047	1,962
1992	3,561	2,147	1,337	1,840	98	212	293	1,041	2,133

ESTIMATES BY THE CONGRESSIONAL BUDGET OFFICE

Year									
1993	3,734	2,286	1,371	1,889	134	264	319	1,050	2,208
1994	3,993	2,439	1,477	1,971	160	311	351	1,124	2,322
1995	4,216	2,546	1,593	2,032	171	345	387	1,204	2,419
1996	4,421	2,624	1,720	2,078	178	371	430	1,287	2,507
1997	4,865	2,926	1,860	2,307	198	424	476	1,381	2,782
1998	5,117	3,036	2,002	2,392	203	444	527	1,472	2,919
1999	5,410	3,176	2,154	2,510	207	463	588	1,562	3,098
2000	5,729	3,327	2,323	2,638	211	483	660	1,659	3,298

AVERAGE ANNUAL GROWTH RATES (In percents)

Period									
1975–80	6.8	6.1	9.5	6.1	−3.4	16.3	14.7	8.4	6.7
1980–85	7.0	6.7	8.1	6.4	−0.7	12.5	8.3	8.6	6.6
1985–90	3.0	0.6	7.7	−0.4	31.0	7.1	10.2	7.1	0.6
1990–95	4.8	5.2	4.4	2.7	15.0	25.2	8.4	3.3	3.5
1995–2000	6.3	5.5	7.8	5.4	4.2	6.9	11.3	6.6	6.4

Notes.—Column 1 includes both benefits and administrative costs. All other columns include only benefits. The CPI–U was used to obtain constant dollars.

Source: Congressional Budget Office (February 1994).

From 1975 to 1985, total real spending per enrollee grew at an annual rate of 7.0 percent. From 1985 to 1990, there was a dramatic decline in the real growth rate in HI expenditures per capita due mostly to a drop in the inpatient hospital growth rate. This growth rate fell from 6.4 percent to −0.3 percent between the first 5 years of the 1980's and the subsequent years. While the outpatient growth rate increased slightly, the total real hospital spending growth rate declined from 6.5 percent annually to 0.7 percent between 1980 to 1985 as compared with 1985 to 1990. This decline in the hospital spending growth rate results in a 3.9 percentage point reduction in the total Medicare spending growth rate—a decline of 56 percent.

If the total growth rate in Medicare spending continued between 1985 and 1990 at the same 7.0 percent rate exhibited between 1980 and 1985, total Medicare costs per enrollee would be $4,282 in 1991, or almost $1,000 per enrollee more than the actual estimate. This would imply additional Medicare spending of about $34 billion in that year.

TOTAL HEALTH CARE EXPENDITURES FOR THE ELDERLY

Expenditures for personal health care services for the elderly nearly quadrupled between 1977 and 1987, rising from $43 billion to an estimated $162 billion (see table B–10).

Government programs (Federal and State) account for two-thirds of estimated 1987 spending for the aged (see table B–10). The most significant of these programs is Medicare which pays for nearly half of the aged's health bill. Medicaid funds about 12 percent of the expenditures.

Health insurance coverage of the elderly

Table B–11 shows the sources of health insurance coverage for the noninstitutionalized population aged 65 and over in 1992. Over 95 percent of the aged population was enrolled in Medicare, and more than three-quarters of the Medicare enrollees had some form of supplemental coverage. Beneficiaries with incomes below the Federal poverty level were least likely to have supplemental coverage; those who had such coverage were more likely to rely on Medicaid. Higher income groups were more likely to obtain supplemental coverage through individually purchased medigap policies or through employer-based plans. Of those with incomes greater than 200 percent of the poverty level, 41.3 percent had employer coverage, compared to just 5.4 percent of those below poverty. (It should be noted that the Current Population Survey (CPS), on which table 11 is based, does not distinguish between primary and secondary sources of coverage. Some of the individuals reporting both Medicare and employer-based plans relied on the employer plan as their primary insurer, with Medicare functioning as a secondary payer.) About 3.6 percent of the elderly had more than one

TABLE B–10.—PERSONAL HEALTH CARE EXPENDITURES FOR PEOPLE 65 YEARS OF AGE OR OVER, BY SOURCE OF FUNDS AND TYPE OF SERVICE, 1977, 1984, AND 1987

[In millions of dollars]

Year and source of funds	Type of service				
	Total care	Hospital	Physician	Nursing home	Other care
1977					
Total	43,425	18,906	7,782	10,696	6,041
Private	15,669	2,319	3,323	5,424	4,603
Consumer	15,499	2,263	3,320	5,352	4,564
Out-of-pocket	12,706	927	2,147	5,264	4,368
Insurance	2,793	1,336	1,173	88	195
Other private	170	56	3	72	39
Government	27,756	16,587	4,458	5,272	1,438
Medicare	19,171	14,087	4,158	348	578
Medicaid	6,049	733	232	4,453	631
Other government	2,536	1,767	68	470	230
1984					
Total	119,872	54,200	24,770	25,105	15,798
Private	39,341	6,160	9,827	13,038	10,316
Consumer	38,875	5,964	9,818	12,856	10,237
Out-of-pocket	30,198	1,694	6,468	12,569	9,467
Insurance	8,677	4,270	3,350	287	770
Other private	466	196	9	182	79
Government	80,531	48,040	14,943	12,067	5,482
Medicare	58,519	40,524	14,314	539	3,142
Medicaid	15,288	2,595	467	10,418	1,808
Other government	6,724	4,920	162	1,110	532
1987					
Total	162,000	67,900	33,500	32,800	27,800
Private	60,600	10,100	11,900	19,200	19,500
Government	101,500	57,900	21,600	13,600	8,300
Medicare	72,200	47,300	20,300	600	4,100
Medicaid	19,500	3,300	500	11,900	3,700

Source: Office of Financial and Actuarial Analysis, Health Care Financing Administration as reported in Waldo, Daniel R., and Helen C. Lazenby. "Demographic characteristics and health care use and expenditures by the aged in the United States: 1977–84." Health Care Financing Review, Fall 1984 No. 1, p. 1; and Waldo, Daniel R. et al. "Health Expenditures by Age Group, 1977 and 1987." Health Care Financing Review, Summer 1989, Vol. 10, No. 4 and errata reprint Fall 1989, Vol. 11, No. 1, p. 167.

TABLE B-11.—SOURCES OF HEALTH INSURANCE COVERAGE FOR THE NON-INSTITUTIONALIZED ELDERLY, BY RATIO OF INCOME TO POVERTY, 1992

[Population in thousands]

	Individuals with family income—						Total	
	Under 100 percent of poverty		100–199 percent of poverty		200 percent of poverty or more			
	Number	Percent	Number	Percent	Number	Percent	Number	Percent
Total Medicare	3,819	95.9	8,647	98.0	17,238	95.4	29,704	96.2
Medicare only	1,381	34.7	2,597	29.5	2,700	15.0	6,678	21.6
Medicare plus:								
Private supplement	961	24.1	3,395	38.5	5,739	31.7	10,095	32.7
Employer coverage	214	5.4	1,323	15.0	7,459	41.3	8,996	29.1
Medicaid	1,099	27.6	855	9.7	413	2.3	2,367	7.6
CHAMPUS	45	1.1	179	2.0	228	1.3	452	1.5
2 or more supplements	120	3.0	298	3.4	698	3.9	1,116	3.6
Insured through non-Medicare plan only	42	1.0	89	1.0	678	3.8	809	2.6
Uninsured	122	3.0	85	1.0	150	1.0	356	1.2
Total	3,983	100.0	8,822	100.0	18,065	100.0	30,870	100.0
Percent of all elderly		12.9		28.5		58.5		100.0

[1] Sample size too small for reliable estimates.

Source: CRS analysis of data from the March 1993 Current Population Survey.

source of supplemental coverage, such as both employer and individual medigap coverage, or both medigap and Medicaid. This figure does not include individuals who obtained multiple policies from a single basic coverage source, such as those who purchased more than one private medigap policy.

About 1.2 million elderly persons did not report Medicare coverage in 1992. Of these, 809,000 had coverage from some other source. An estimated 25 percent of these are Federal annuitants who are covered through the Federal Employees Health Benefits Program (this estimate is based on unpublished data from the Office of Personnel Management). Approximately 356,000 persons aged 65 or over were without health insurance coverage in 1992.

BACKGROUND DATA ON LONG-TERM CARE

The phrase "long-term care" refers to a broad range of medical, social, personal, supportive, and specialized housing services needed by individuals who have lost some capacity for self-care because of a chronic illness or condition. Chronic illnesses or conditions often result in both functional impairment and physical dependence on others for an extended period of time. Major subgroups of persons needing long-term care include the elderly and nonelderly disabled, persons with developmental disabilities (primarily persons with mental retardation), and persons with mental illness. This section of appendix B focuses on the elderly long-term care population.

The range of chronic illnesses and conditions resulting in the need for supportive long-term care services is extensive. Unlike acute medical illnesses, which occur suddenly and may be resolved in a relatively short period of time, chronic conditions last for an extended period of time and are not typically curable. Although chronic conditions occur in individuals of all ages, their incidence, especially as they result in disability, increases with age. These conditions may include heart disease, strokes, arthritis, osteoporosis, and vision and hearing impairments. Dementia, the chronic, often progressive loss of intellectual function, is also a major cause of disability in the elderly.

The presence of a chronic illness or condition alone does not necessarily result in a need for long-term care. For many individuals, their illness or condition does not result in a functional impairment or dependence and they are able to go about their daily routines without needing assistance. It is when the illness or condition results in a functional or activity limitation that long-term care services may be required.

The need for long-term care by the elderly is often measured by assessing limitations in a person's capacity to manage certain functions or activities. For example, a chronic condition may result in dependence in certain functions that are basic and essential for self-care, such as bathing, dressing, eating, toileting, and/or moving from one place to another. These are referred to as limitations in "activities of daily living," or ADLs. Another set of limitations, which reflect lower levels of disability, are used to describe difficulties in performing household chores and social tasks. These are referred to as limitations in "instrumental activities of daily living," or IADLs, and include such functions as meal preparation, cleaning, grocery shopping, managing money, and taking medicine. Limitations can vary in severity and prevalence, so that persons can have limitations in any number of ADLs or IADLs, or both.

Long-term care services are often differentiated by the settings in which they are provided. In general, services are provided either in nursing homes or in home and community-based care settings. Nursing home care includes a wide variety of services that range from skilled nursing and therapy services to assistance with such personal care functions as bathing, dressing, and eating. Nursing home services also include room and board. All of these services are considered to be formally provided services, in that they require persons to pay the facility for care that is provided.

Home and community-based care also includes a broad range of skilled and personal care services, as well as a variety of home management activities, such as chore services, meal preparation, and shopping. Home care services can be provided formally by home care agencies, visiting nurse associations, and day care centers. Home care is also provided informally by family and friends who are not paid for the services they provide. In contrast to nursing home care, which by necessity is formally provided care, most home and community-based care is provided informally by family and friends. Research has shown that more than 70 percent of those elderly persons living in the community and needing long-term care assistance rely exclusively on nonpaid sources of assistance for their care.

The long-term care population

Chart B–3 shows that an estimated 10.6 million persons of all ages require assistance with one or more ADLs or IADLs. About two-thirds of this total, or 7.1 million persons, are elderly. This is about one-quarter of the nation's elderly population.

Another 3.5 million persons under the age of 65 are limited in ADLs and/or IADLs. Some of these persons have congenital or developmental conditions such as cerebral palsy or mental retardation. Others are disabled from traumatic accidents or the onset of chronic conditions such as multiple sclerosis.[7] It should be noted that these estimates do not adequately measure the need for long-term care among young children, since ADL and IADL limitations are not appropriate measures of their disabilities.

Chart B–3 also indicates that the great majority of persons with ADL and/or IADL limitations live in the community. Of the total disabled population, 84 percent live in the community. The nursing home population amounts to only 16 percent of the total, with the elderly by far the greatest share of this group.

Based on the projected growth of the elderly population in the future, major increases can be anticipated in the number of persons needing assistance with ADL and/or IADL limitations. Currently 32 million persons are 65 years of age and older. That number is expected to double to about 66 million by the year 2030. The 85+ population, the group at greatest risk of needing and using long-term care services, is expected to increase from 3.3 million persons

---

[7] A Call for Action, p. 91.

in 1990 to 8.1 million in 2030.[8] One study has estimated that the number of elderly needing assistance with ADLs and/or IADLs will grow from 7.1 million to 13.8 million by 2030, and the number requiring nursing home care will grow from 1.5 million to 5.3 million by that year.[9]

CHART B–3. PERSONS WITH ADL AND/OR IADL LIMITATIONS, 1990

Total 10.6 million

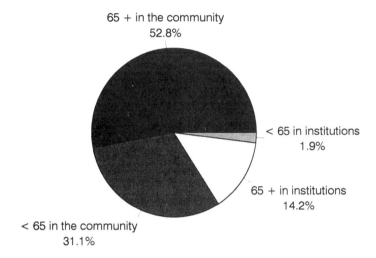

65 + in the community
52.8%

< 65 in institutions
1.9%

65 + in institutions
14.2%

< 65 in the community
31.1%

Source: A Call for Action, The Pepper Commission, Final Report, September 1990. Based on Lewin/ICF Estimates Prepared for the Commission.

THE NURSING HOME POPULATION [10]

Demographic characteristics

Analysis of the 1985 National Nursing Home Survey (NNHS) shows that the great majority of nursing home residents are 65 years of age and older. In 1985, 88 percent of residents were 65 years of age and older, and 12 percent were under the age of 65. As the top half of table 12 indicates, less than 5 percent of the total elderly population in the country were residents of nursing homes on any given day in 1985, and 0.1 percent of the under 65 population were residents in that year.

Although in the aggregate less than 5 percent of the total elderly population was in a nursing home on any given day in 1985,

---

[8] U.S. Senate, Special Committee on Aging. "Aging America: Trends and Projections." November 1989. Sen. Prt. 101–59, p. 4.
[9] A Call for Action, p. 108.
[10] This material is drawn largely from "Characteristics of Nursing Home Residents and Proposals for Reforming Coverage of Nursing Home Care," by Richard Price, Richard Rimkunas, and Carol O'Shaughnessy, CRS Report for Congress, No. 90–471 EPW, September 24, 1990.

younger and older age groups of the elderly show very different rates of utilization. Table B–12 and chart 4 show that about 1 percent of the 65–74 age group and about 6 percent of the 75–84 age group resided in nursing homes in 1985. For the very old, those 85 and older, however, the incidence rate increases dramatically. In 1985, 22 percent of the 85 and older group resided in nursing homes. This group accounted for 40 percent of total nursing home residents, and 45 percent of the elderly nursing home population.

TABLE B–12.—NURSING HOME RESIDENTS AS A PROPORTION OF TOTAL POPULATION, BY AGE AND SEX, 1985

[All nursing home and U.S. population estimates in thousands]

Age	All residents		
	Nursing home pop.	U.S. pop.	Percent
Under 65	173	210,197	0.1
65 to 74	212	17,009	1.2
75 to 84	508	8,836	5.7
85 and older	597	2,695	22.1
65 and older	1,317	28,540	4.6
Total	1,490	238,737	0.6

Age	Males			Females		
	Nursing home pop.	U.S. pop.	Percent	Nursing home pop.	U.S. pop.	Percent
Under 65	89	104,623	0.1	84	105,574	0.1
65 to 74	81	7,475	1.1	132	9,534	1.4
75 to 84	141	3,293	4.3	367	5,543	6.6
85 and older	112	769	14.6	485	1,926	25.2
65 and older	334	11,537	2.9	984	17,003	5.8
Total	423	116,160	0.4	1,068	122,577	0.9

Note.—Figures are based on the number of current nursing home residents and U.S. Census Bureau estimates of the resident population. Figures do not reflect the likelihood of any individual being in a nursing home; rather these estimates indicate the percent of the total population that resided in nursing homes at a given point in time in 1985.

Source: Estimates prepared by CRS using the 1985 National Nursing Home Survey, Current Resident File, and U.S. Bureau of the Census, Current Population Report, United States Population Estimates, by Age, Sex and Race: 1980 to 1987, series P–25, No. 1022, March 1988. These estimates are subject to limitations of the data and methods employed.

Chart B–4 also illustrates that, among each of the age groups of the elderly, women were more likely to reside in nursing homes than men. For the elderly as a whole, women were twice as likely to be residing in nursing homes in 1985 as men (6 percent of women as opposed to 3 percent for men). The difference for men and women is particularly striking in the 75–84 and 85 and older age groups. Higher incidence rates for women, largely the result of longer life expectancies for women, mean a nursing home population that is predominately female. Chart B–5 indicates that 72 percent of nursing home residents were female in 1985.

CHART B–4. SHARE OF RESIDENT POPULATION IN NURSING HOMES, 1985

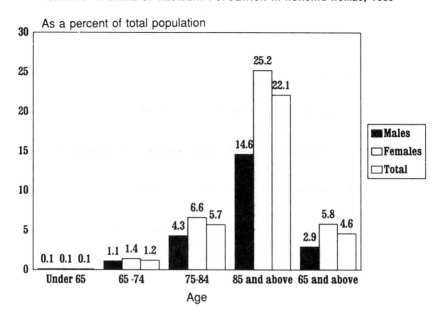

CHART B–5. DISTRIBUTION OF CURRENT RESIDENTS, BY SEX, 1985

(In Thousands)

Female 1,066
71.6%

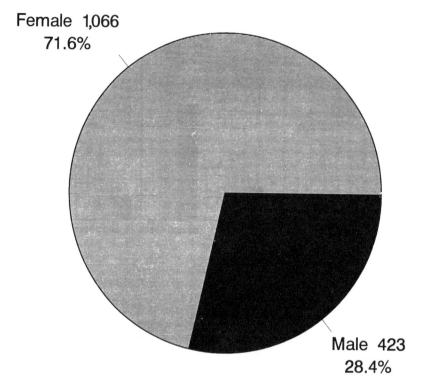

Male 423
28.4%

Studies have shown that persons without spouses are more likely to enter nursing homes than persons with spouses.[11] Because many disabled persons often require a great deal of assistance, spouses are often the only person outside of nursing homes able to provide such intensive care. Chart B–6 indicates that, at admission, only 16 percent of nursing home residents were married. Of the remaining, 56 percent were widowed, 18 percent had never been married, and about 8 percent were either divorced or separated.

Chart B–7 shows that, among the elderly, the proportion of residents who were married at admission decreases with age, and the proportion who were widowed increases.

[11] "Financing of Long-Term Care." Submitted to the Assistant Secretary of Planning and Evaluation, U.S. Department of Health and Human Services. Contract No. HHS–100–86–051, September 30, 1988. p. I–9.

CHART B–6. DISTRIBUTION OF CURRENT RESIDENTS, BY MARITAL STATUS AT ADMISSION, 1985

(In Thousands)

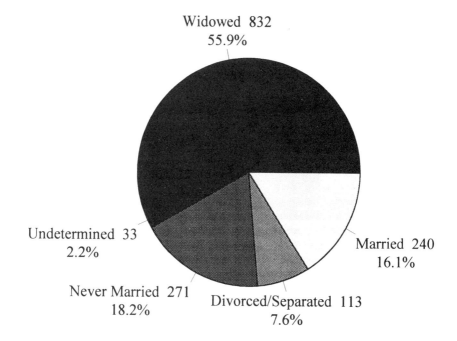

Widowed 832
55.9%

Undetermined 33
2.2%

Married 240
16.1%

Never Married 271
18.2%

Divorced/Separated 113
7.6%

Total Residents = 1.5 million

CHART B–7. PERCENT OF CURRENT RESIDENTS, MARRIED AND WIDOWED, BY AGE, 1985

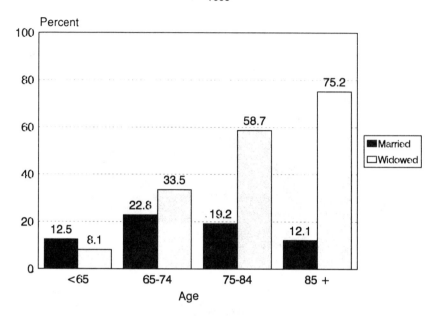

Number and type of ADL limitations of nursing home residents

Chart B–8 presents data on the number of limitations in ADLs exhibited by nursing home residents of all ages in 1985. This figure shows that nursing home residents have substantial functional limitations. Seventy-eight percent of residents needed the assistance of others in two or more ADLs. Almost 55 percent of the nursing home population was severely impaired with four or more ADLs.

Chart B–8 also shows that slightly more than 20 percent of nursing home residents were judged to have no, or only one, activity limitation. A review of the diagnosis classifications of residents by their number of ADLs shows that residents whose primary diagnosis was a mental disorder were disproportionately represented among the total number of residents who had no activity limitation. About 35 percent of those with no ADLs had a mental disorder as their primary diagnosis. Mental disorders include a wide range of disabilities, including dementias, psychoses, and mental retardation. Persons with mental disorders but without limitations in ADLs may be residents of nursing homes because they require supervision or because of the unavailability of other housing and social service arrangements in the community.

CHART B–8. DISTRIBUTION OF CURRENT RESIDENTS BY NUMBER OF ADL LIMITATIONS, 1985

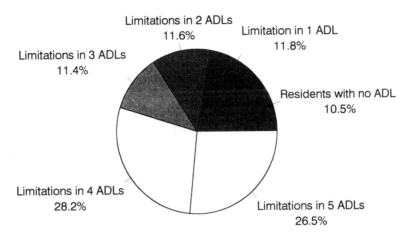

Limitations in 2 ADLs
11.6%

Limitation in 1 ADL
11.8%

Limitations in 3 ADLs
11.4%

Residents with no ADL
10.5%

Limitations in 4 ADLs
28.2%

Limitations in 5 ADLs
26.5%

total residents = 1.5 million

Chart B–9 presents data on the extent to which nursing home residents have various kinds of limitations in ADLs. The most frequently found limitation among residents was bathing, with 88 percent of residents needing the assistance of another person. The least prevalent ADL was in eating, with slightly more than one-third of residents needing assistance with this ADL. About three-quarters of residents needed assistance to dress and two-thirds needed assistance in getting out of a bed or chair (transferring). About half of all residents needed the assistance of others in getting to the toilet or in caring for an ostomy bag or catheter.

In developing measures of functional limitations, researchers have found an ordered regression in functional abilities as part of the natural aging process. Loss of functioning begins with activities which are most complex and least basic, such as bathing or dressing. Functions which are least complex and most basic, such as feeding oneself, are retained longer. That is, persons are most able to retain their ability to feed themselves, but are less likely to retain their ability to bathe or dress without the assistance of others.[12] In addition, persons who are the most severely impaired are least likely to be able to eat independently, and therefore are more likely to have limitations in all the other ADLs. This ordered regression in stages of functioning is reflected in the nursing home population. As shown in chart B–9, higher proportions of residents needed assistance in bathing or dressing than those who needed assistance in eating.

---

[12] Katz, Sidney and Amechi Akpom. "A Measure of Primary Sociobiological Functions." International Journal of Health Services, Vol. 6, No. 3, 1976.

CHART B–9. PERCENT OF RESIDENTS REQUIRING ASSISTANCE OF ANOTHER PERSON IN PERFORMING ACTIVITY, 1985

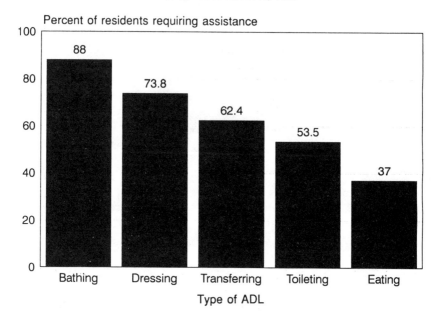

Percent of residents requiring assistance

Nursing home length of stay

The profile of nursing home residents presented above suggests a fairly homogeneous population: largely very elderly, female, widowed, and very disabled. However, an examination of length-of-stay patterns among the nursing home population suggests a more diverse group of persons using care than might be suggested by demographic data alone.

Analysis of discharge data from the NNHS shows at least two major users of nursing home care, as illustrated in charts B–10 and B–11. Chart B–10 portrays the distribution of persons discharged from nursing homes in 1984–85, according to their length of stay. Chart B–11 shows the distribution of days of care used by all discharged residents. It should be noted that the discharge file of the NNHS does not provide a comprehensive picture of the use of nursing home care by a single group of persons over time. As a result, estimates based on discharge survey data must be considered very general orders of magnitude of lengths of stay in a nursing home.

Chart B–10 shows that most nursing home stays are relatively short. About 52 percent of persons discharged from nursing homes had stays of less than 90 days and about 63 percent of persons discharged had stays of less than 6 months. In contrast, 27 percent of persons discharged had long stays of 1 year or longer, and 17 percent had stays of 2 years or longer.

The distribution of total days of care used by discharged residents is strikingly different. Chart B–11 shows that persons with stays of less than 3 months accounted for only 4 percent of days of care. Those with stays of less than 6 months accounted for 8 percent of all days. On the other hand, persons with stays of 2 or more years accounted for about 73 percent of all discharge days. In other words, persons with short stays accounted for the majority of persons discharged from nursing homes, but very few of the days of care used. Those with long stays accounted for relatively few of those persons discharged from nursing homes, but the bulk of days used.

CHART B–10. DISTRIBUTION OF DISCHARGED RESIDENTS BY LENGTH OF STAY, 1984–85

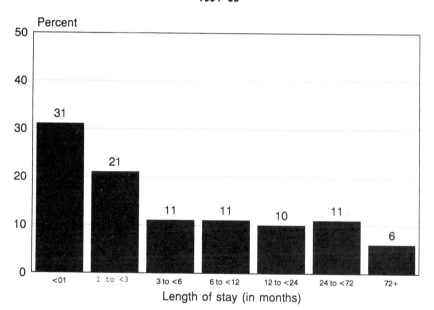

CHART B–11. DISTRIBUTION OF TOTAL DAYS USED BY DISCHARGED RESIDENTS, BY LENGTH OF STAY, 1984–85

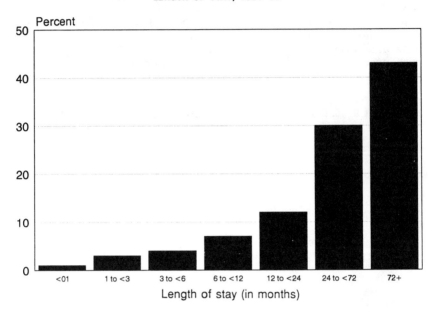

Length of stay (in months)

Status of nursing home residents following discharge

Chart B–12 shows the distribution of residents by their status following discharge. In 1984–85, the largest share of persons— about 50 percent—were discharged from the nursing home to a hospital or other health care facility, including nursing homes (about 7 percent were discharged to another long-term care facility). About 28 percent of discharges were due to death in the nursing home. About 22 percent of the residents were discharged to the community. This mortality rate and the rate of return to the community may be conservative estimates. For example, 10 percent of those discharged from nursing homes to other health facilities died in these other facilities. Others are likely to have returned to the community.

CHART B–12. DISTRIBUTION OF DISCHARGED RESIDENTS BY LIVING ARRANGEMENT AFTER DISCHARGE, 1984–85

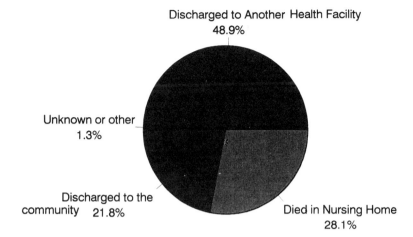

Total Residents = 1.2 Million

The community-based long-term care population

Chart B–13 below showed that the great majority of persons with ADL and/or IADL limitations live in the community. Almost 9 million persons of all ages, or 84 percent of the total population with ADL and/or IADL limitations, live in the community. The elderly represented almost 63 percent of this total.

Chart B–13 shows the number and percent of elderly persons living in the community with ADL limitations by type of limitation, as of 1984.[13] A total of 3.7 million elderly persons living in the community, or 14 percent of the total elderly population, reported some limitation in their ability to bathe, transfer, dress, toilet, or eat. The prevalence of these ADLs forms a hierarchy similar to that shown above in chart B–8 for the nursing home population. The most prevalent limitation was in bathing, with 10 percent of the elderly reporting difficulty with this ADL. The least common was in eating, with 2 percent of elderly persons reporting difficulty.

---

[13] Rowland, Diane. "Measuring the Elderly's Need for Home Care," Health Affairs, winter 1989, vol. 8, p. 42.

CHART B–13. PERCENT OF ELDERLY IN THE COMMUNITY WITH ADL LIMITATIONS, BY TYPE OF LIMITATION, 1984

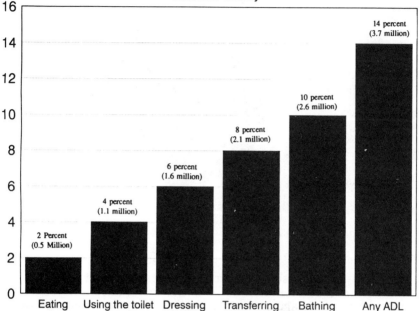

Percent based on 26.4 million persons 65 years or older.

Source: Roland, Diane. Health Affairs, v.8, p. 42 Measuring the Elderly's Need for Home Care.

Chart B–14 indicates that 54 percent of the elderly population with any kind of ADL limitation in 1984 had two or more ADLs. This was about 2 million persons. Almost 22 percent has 4 or 5 limitations. The severity of impairment is not uniform in the disabled population. Among the 2 million persons with two or more ADLs, 1.1 million reported some difficulty and 0.9 million reported a lot of difficulty or inability to perform at least two ADLs.[14]

---

[14] Rowland, p. 43.

CHART B–14. DISTRIBUTION OF ADL'S AMONG NONINSTITUTIONALIZED ELDERLY POPULATION HAVING ONE OR MORE ADL LIMITATIONS, 1984

Estimates based on 1984 Supplement on Aging. National Health Interview Survey

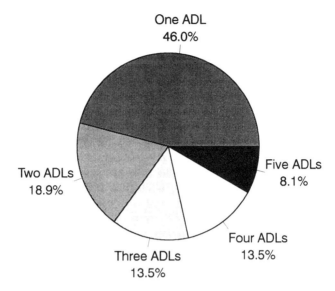

One ADL
46.0%

Two ADLs
18.9%

Five ADLs
8.1%

Three ADLs
13.5%

Four ADLs
13.5%

Total = 3.7 million impaired persons 65 years or older

Studies have shown that the great bulk of care provided to persons living in the community with ADL and/or IADL limitations is provided informally by family and friends who are not paid for the care they provide. Chart B–15 indicates that 70 percent of severely disabled elderly persons receiving long-term care in the community relied solely on informally provided care. Only 3 percent relied only on formal or paid care.

More than 7 million spouses, adult children, other relatives, friends, and neighbors provided unpaid assistance to disabled elderly persons in 1984.[15] Seven out of ten informal caregivers bear the major responsibility for care provided, and one of three is a sole provider. Three-quarters of all caregivers are female—wives and daughters of persons needing care. Research has shown that caregivers often reduce their work hours, take time off without pay, or quit jobs because of elder caregiving responsibilities. In addition, many caregivers are themselves elderly—one-quarter are between the ages of 65 to 74 and another 10 percent are 75 or older.

---

[15] A Call for Action, p. 93–95. This discussion draws heavily on this report and research published by Robyn Stone, et al., "Caregivers of the Frail Elderly: A National Profile," The Gerontologist, vol. 27, 1987.

Use of formal, paid services by elderly persons living in the community is related to various characteristics of this group.[16] Differences in functional status have been found to be strongly related to use of formal home and community-based care, with the likelihood of using any formal service increasing as levels of impairment increase. Age is also linked to the use of formal services, largely explained by the fact that age is associated with decreasing functional status. In general and in each age group of the elderly, more women use formal home and community-based care services than men. This is related to the longer life expectancies of women. Persons living alone are more than twice as likely to use formal services as compared to those living with other persons. In addition, the amount of money spent on home care services has been found to be directly related to income; that is, out-of-pocket expenses for home care increase substantially as median family income increases.[17]

CHART B–15. SOURCE OF HOME CARE SERVICES FOR THE SEVERELY DISABLED ELDERLY POPULATION, 1989

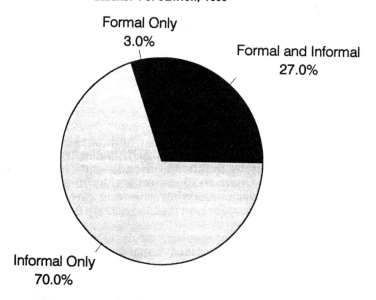

Formal Only
3.0%

Formal and Informal
27.0%

Informal Only
70.0%

Note: Severely disabled refers to those persons with three or more ADL limitations.

Source: Lewin/ICF and the Brookings Institution, 1989 estimates based on National Long-Term Care Survey, 1982.

---

[16] This material is drawn largely from Short, Pamela and Joel Leon, "Use of Home and Community Services by Persons Ages 65 and Older with Functional Difficulties," National Medical Expenditure Survey, Research Findings 5, Department of Health and Human Services, Agency for Health Care Policy and Research, September 1990, p. 7–9.
[17] Liu, Korbin, Kenneth Manton, and Barbara Liu, "Home Care Expenses for the Disabled Elderly," Health Care Financing Review. Winter 1985, vol. 7, No. 2, p. 55.

Public and private spending for long-term care

Table B–13 indicates that sizable public and private funds are being spent on long-term care services. For two major categories of long-term care services, nursing home and home care, total national spending amounted to almost $107.8 billion in 1993. This total is for all age groups using long-term care. By far the greatest portion of spending is for nursing home care. About $75 billion, or 70 percent of the total, was spent for nursing home care in 1993.

Public programs paid about 60 percent of the Nation's total nursing home bill. Medicaid payments accounted for almost all of this amount. Medicaid is the Federal-State health program for the poor and for those who have become poor as the result of incurring large medical care expenses. In 1993, Medicaid spending for nursing home care amounted to 48 percent of total national nursing home spending.

Table B–13 shows that private spending accounted for about $30 billion, or the remaining 40 percent of national spending. Nearly all private spending for nursing home care was paid directly by consumers out-of-pocket with income and/or accumulated resources. Private insurance coverage for long-term nursing home care is very limited, with private insurance payments amounting to 0.1 percent of total spending for nursing home care in 1993.

Spending for home health care services amounted to $33 billion, or 30 percent of the total. Public programs accounted for about 72 percent of total home health care spending. Out-of-pocket payments accounted for almost all of private spending, private insurance again being very limited for this care. Most home and community-based care, as discussed above, is provided by family and friends who are not paid for the services they provide.

Major Federal programs supporting long-term care

Five programs represent the major source of Federal financial support available for nursing home and community-based long-term care—Medicaid, Medicare, the Social Services Block Grant (SSBG), the Older Americans Act, and the Supplemental Security Income (SSI) program. None of these programs supports the full range of long-term care services. Certain programs provide health services but exclude social services. Others provide strictly social services. Some have income eligibility requirements, others do not.

Medicaid is the Nation's major program of financial support for long-term care, principally because of its coverage of nursing home care. Medicaid payments for nursing home care (excluding nursing homes for the mentally retarded) amounted to about 27 percent of total Medicaid spending in fiscal year 1991. Comparatively little funding is devoted to home and community-based care. Coverage of both nursing home and home and community-based services is restricted to those persons who have limited income and assets. In general, Medicaid rules limit eligibility to those persons who qualify for cash welfare assistance or who incur large health care expenses that deplete their income and assets.[18]

TABLE B–13.—ESTIMATED LONG-TERM CARE SPENDING FOR ALL AGE GROUPS, BY SOURCE, 1993

[Dollars in billions]

Source of spending	Amount
Nursing home care:	
Medicaid	$36.3
Medicare	5.7
Other Federal	1.0
Other State	2.5
Out-of-pocket payments and other	29.6
Private insurance	0.1
Total	75.2
Home health care:	
Medicaid	7.4
Medicare	10.1
Other Federal programs	1.6
Other State	4.5
Out-of-pocket payments and other	8.9
Private insurance	0.1
Total	32.6
Total long-term care expenditures	107.8

Source: Office of the Assistant Secretary for Planning and Evaluation, Office of Disability, Aging, and Long-Term Care Policy, Department of Health and Human Services.

Medicare, the Federal health insurance program for the elderly and disabled, is focused primarily on coverage for acute health care costs and was never envisioned to provide protection for long-term care. Coverage of nursing home care, for instance, is limited to short-term stays in certain kinds of nursing homes, referred to as skilled nursing facilities, and only for those persons who demonstrate a need for daily skilled nursing care following a hospitalization. Many persons who require long-term nursing home care do not need daily skilled nursing care, and therefore, do not qualify for Medicare's benefit. As a result of this restriction, Medicare paid for about 7.6 percent of the Nation's expenditures for nursing home care in 1993.

For similar reasons, Medicare pays for only limited amounts of community-based long-term care services, primarily through the program's home health benefit. To qualify for home health services, the person must be in need of skilled nursing care on an intermittent basis, or physical or speech therapy. Most chronically impaired persons do not need skilled care to remain in their homes, but

[18] Most States extend Medicaid eligibility to persons who qualify for welfare benefits under the Supplemental Security Income (SSI) program. SSI requires that persons have assets that do not exceed $2,000 and income that does not exceed $446 per month in 1994.

rather nonmedical supportive care and assistance with basic self-care functions and daily routines that do not require skilled personnel.

Three other Federal programs—SSBG, the Older Americans Act, and the SSI program—provide support for community-based long-term care services for impaired elderly persons. The SSBG provides block grants to the States for a variety of home-based services for the elderly as well as the disabled and children. The Older Americans Act also funds a broad range of in-home services for the elderly. Under the SSI program, the federally administered income assistance program for aged, blind, and disabled persons, many States provide supplemental payments to the basic SSI payment to support selected community-based long-term care services for certain eligible persons, including the frail elderly. However, since funding available for these three programs is limited, their ability to address the financing problems in long-term care is also very limited.

Spending down for Medicaid coverage of nursing home care

As discussed above, the Medicaid program is the major public source of support for the cost of nursing home care. Its spending for nursing home care is driven largely by its coverage of persons who are not initially poor but who become poor by depleting their assets on the cost of care. At an average cost of $35,000 a year, nursing home costs can quickly deplete the resources of an elderly individual, especially after prolonged stays, and these costs also exceed the monthly income of most persons. The depletion of financial resources on the cost of care and the movement from private payment for care to Medicaid coverage is referred to as the "spend-down" process. In 1991, Medicaid nursing home payments for elderly persons who spent down amounted to 60 percent of total Medicaid payments for all services for all elderly beneficiaries.[19]

Numerous studies have looked at Medicaid spend-down in the last 5 years. A recent review of these studies, "A Synthesis and Critique of Studies on Medicaid Asset Spenddown" by Adams, Meiners and Burwell, found that they generally use two different measures of Medicaid asset spenddown.[20] One method measures the percentage of persons originally admitted to nursing homes as private payers who eventually convert to Medicaid prior to final discharge.

---

[19] Spending down under Medicaid is a two-step process. First persons must meet the resources or assets test. The term "resources" generally refers to liquid assets such as cash on hand, savings and checking accounts, stocks and bonds, etc. In order to become eligible for Medicaid, the value of the individual's available resources must be less than a State-determined dollar standard, usually $2,000 for an individual without a spouse, the level used for the SSI program. Certain items, such as the house, are excluded as countable resources under SSI and Medicaid rules. Second, after an individual has depleted virtually all accumulated resources on the cost of nursing home care, or has transferred resources (for less than fair market value) prior to the time when eligibility could be denied because of the transfer, income standards are then considered. Most States have no absolute upper limit on income for applicants residing in nursing homes. These States have what are known as medically needy programs. As long as the applicant's current monthly income is insufficient to cover medical expenses, including the cost of care in the nursing home, the applicant can become eligible for Medicaid. Other States use a special income level to determine eligibility for persons residing in nursing homes. Like the medically needy, these persons have income in excess of cash welfare program standards. By Federal law, the special income level used by States can be no more than three times the basic SSI payment level, or $1,302 in 1993. This rule is known as the "300 percent rule."

[20] This material draws heavily on Adams, E. Kathleen, Mark Meiners, and Brian Burwell, "A Synthesis and Critique of Studies on Medicaid Asset Spenddown," Office of the Assistant Secretary for Planning and Evaluation, Department of Health and Human Services, January 1992.

This method is a measure of the risk to individuals of spending down to Medicaid over the course of their lifetimes, given the probability they enter a nursing home as private payers.

A second method of measuring Medicaid spenddown examines the percentage of Medicaid residents of nursing homes who were not eligible for Medicaid when they were originally admitted. This method can be useful in capturing the proportion of State Medicaid expenditures for nursing home care that is accounted for by those who spend down.

The review of spenddown studies, which use several different national and State-level data bases, found widely varying estimates of spenddown as measured by these two methods. According to the review, the critical factor explaining differences among these studies is the length of time that persons are studied. The proportion of persons spending down during a single stay is much lower than the proportion of persons who spend down over their entire lifetime, since half or more of persons using nursing home care have multiple stays. In general, studies using national data tend to show lower estimates of spenddown than do State studies that tend to observe people over longer time intervals.

The review of spenddown studies found that between 20 and 25 percent of persons who originally enter nursing homes as private payers convert to Medicaid before final discharge. For this method of measuring spenddown, not enough State studies exist to determine the extent to which spenddown rates vary from State to State.

On the other hand, estimates of spenddown as measured by the percentage of Medicaid residents of nursing homes who were not eligible for Medicaid when they were originally admitted vary considerably across States, reflecting variations in Medicaid eligibility policies across the States as well as other factors. Studies measuring spenddown according to this method have found spenddown rates of 27 percent for Michigan, 31 percent for Wisconsin, and 39 to 45 percent for Connecticut.

Spenddown studies have also examined the length of time it takes for persons to spend down after nursing home admission. The results of these studies reveal that of those people who spend down, the majority spend down within a year of nursing home admission. This finding suggests that most people who spend down have limited assets when they first enter a nursing home.

Certain State studies also show that people who spend down to Medicaid spend more time on Medicaid after converting to Medicaid coverage than they spend as private payers prior to conversion. The studies show that Medicaid-paid days account for at least 65 to 75 percent of all nursing home days used by those who spend down. However, the research also shows that, once eligible for Medicaid, people who spend down pay a greater proportion of total nursing home costs, through contributions of their income they are required to make before Medicaid makes its payment, than persons who are eligible for Medicaid at initial admission. As a result, people who spend down account for a somewhat lower percentage of total Medicaid expenditures than their percentage of Medicaid-covered nursing home days.

Private long-term care insurance

Private long-term care insurance is generally considered to be the most promising private sector option for providing the elderly additional protection for long-term care expenses. Long-term care insurance is a relatively new, but rapidly growing, market. In 1986, approximately 30 insurers were selling long-term care insurance policies of some type and an estimated 200,000 persons were covered by these policies. By 1987, a Department of Health and Human Services Task Force on Long-Term Care Insurance found 73 companies writing long-term care insurance policies covering 423,000 persons. As of December 1992, the Health Insurance Association of America found that more than 2.9 million policies had been sold, with 135 insurers offering coverage. (Note that this is a cumulative total of policies sold; fewer persons would be covered, due to failure to pay premiums because of death, a change in income, a decision not to continue coverage, etc.)

Although growth has been considerable in a short period of time, the private insurance industry has approached this potential market with caution. Insurers are concerned about the potential for adverse selection in long-term care insurance, where only those persons likely to need care actually buy insurance. In addition, they point to the problem of induced demand for services that can be expected to be generated by the availability of new long-term care insurance. With induced demand, sometimes also referred to as moral hazard, individuals decide to use more services than they otherwise would because they have insurance and/or will shift from nonpaid to paid providers for their care. In addition, insurers are concerned that, given the nature of many chronic conditions, persons who need long-term care will need it for the remainder of their lives, resulting in an open-ended liability for the insurance company.

As a result of these risks, insurers have designed policies that limit their liability for paying claims. Policies have been medically underwritten to exclude persons with certain conditions or illnesses. They have contained benefit restrictions that limit access to covered care. Policies also limit the period of coverage they offer, typically to a maximum of 4 or 5 years. In addition, most plans provide indemnity benefits that pay only a fixed amount for each day of coverage service. If these amounts are not updated for inflation, the protection offered by the policy can be significantly eroded by the time a person actually needs care. Today payment amounts can generally be updated for inflation, but only with significant increases in premium costs.

These design features of long-term care insurance raise issues about the quality of coverage offered purchasers of policies. The insurance industry has responded to some of these concerns by offering new products that provide broadened coverage and fewer restrictions. One of the key issues outstanding in the debate on the role private insurance can play in financing long-term care is the affordability of coverage. The Health Insurance Association of America has reported that policies paying $80 a day for nursing home care and $40 a day for home health care with inflation protection and a 20-day deductible period and a 4-year maximum coverage period had an average annual premium in December 1992 of

$1,597 when purchased at the age of 65 and $5,334 when purchased at the age of 79. Many elderly persons cannot afford these premiums.

The insurance industry believes that affordability of premiums can be greatly enhanced if the pool of persons to whom policies are sold is expanded. The industry has argued that the greatest potential for expanding the pool of persons buying coverage and reducing premiums lies with employer-based group coverage. Premiums should be lower in employer-based group coverage because younger age groups with lower levels of risk of needing long-term care would be included, allowing insurance companies to build up reserves to cover future payments of benefits. In addition, group coverage has lower administrative expenses.

As of December 1992, 506 employers offered a long-term care insurance plan to their employees. These employer-based plans covered over 350,000 employees, their spouses, retirees, parents, and parents-in-law.

But just how broadly based employer interest is in a new long-term care benefit is unclear at the present. Many employers currently face large unfunded liabilities for retiree pension and health benefits. Also, many employers have recently experienced substantial increases in premiums for their current health benefits plans. Very few employers contribute to the cost of a long-term care plan. Most employers require that the employee pay the full premium cost of coverage. In contrast, the majority of medium and large sized employers pay the full premium cost of regular health care benefits for their employees.

APPENDIX C. NATIONAL AND INTERNATIONAL HEALTH CARE EXPENDITURES AND HEALTH INSURANCE COVERAGE

NATIONAL HEALTH EXPENDITURES

During 1965 (the year prior to the beginning of the Medicare and Medicaid programs) national health expenditures were $41.6 billion; by 1993 annual expenditures were $898 billion, over 21 times that amount (see table 1). Hospital care expenditures are the largest component of national health expenditures, representing 38 percent of total national health spending in 1993. In terms of per capita spending, $1,101 was spent for hospital care in 1991, compared to $681 in 1985, an increase of 62 percent over 6 years (see table 3).

Adjusting for inflation, health care expenditures have still increased substantially, rising from $179.9 billion in 1965 (in constant 1991 dollars) to $751.8 billion in 1991, an increase of about 318 percent (see table 2). The largest increases occurred between 1965 and 1970 (45 percent) and 1985 to 1991 (41 percent). The annual rate of increase in inflation-adjusted per capita expenditures from 1980 to 1985 was 4.3 percent. For the years 1986 to 1991, the comparable rate was 5.4 percent.

Of the various sources of payment for personal health care expenditures in 1993, private health insurance was the largest (see table 5). In 1993, private health insurance payments (including premiums paid for both employers and employees) were $289 billion and accounted for 32 percent of all payments for personal health care. The Federal Government accounted for 31 percent ($280 billion) of personal health spending (including payments for both Medicare and Medicaid), 14.5 percent ($130 billion) was paid by State and local sources, and 18 percent ($162 billion) was paid by direct (out-of-pocket) payments by individuals. Philanthropy and in-plant health services accounted for 4.1 percent.[1]

---

[1] Personal health expenditures accounted for 88 percent of national health expenditures in 1991. The remaining 12 percent was expended on program administration; administrative costs of private health insurance and profits earned by private health insurance; noncommercial health research; new construction; and government public health activities.

TABLE C–1.—NATIONAL HEALTH EXPENDITURES: AGGREGATE AMOUNTS FOR SELECTED CALENDAR YEARS 1960–93

[Dollar amounts in billions]

	1960	1965	1970	1975	1980	1985	1990	1991	1993	2000 [1]
Total	$27.1	$41.6	$74.4	$132.9	$250.1	$422.6	$675.0	$751.8	$898	$1,613
Percent of GNP	5.3	5.9	7.4	8.4	9.2	10.5	12.2	13.2	(1)	(1)
Health services and supplies	$25.4	$38.2	$69.1	$124.7	$238.9	$407.2	$652.4	$728.6	(1)	(1)
Personal health care	23.9	35.6	64.9	116.6	219.4	369.7	591.5	660.2	(1)	(1)
Hospital care	9.3	14.0	27.9	52.4	102.4	168.3	258.1	288.6	340	604
Physicians' services	5.3	8.2	13.6	23.3	41.9	74.0	128.8	142.0	168	315
Dentists' services	2.0	2.8	4.7	8.2	14.4	23.3	34.1	37.1	43	69
Other professional services	.6	.9	1.5	3.5	8.7	16.6	30.7	35.8	47	110
Home health care	.0	.1	.1	.4	1.3	3.8	7.6	9.8	18	47
Drugs and other medical nondurables	4.2	5.9	8.8	13.0	21.6	36.2	55.6	60.7	70	112
Vision products and other medical durables	.8	1.2	2.0	3.1	4.6	7.1	11.7	12.4	14	23
Nursing home care	1.0	1.7	4.9	9.9	20.0	34.1	53.3	59.9	74	138
Other personal health care	.7	.8	1.4	2.7	4.6	6.4	11.5	14.0	18	34
Program administration and net cost of private health insurance	1.2	1.9	2.8	5.1	12.2	25.2	38.9	43.9	(1)	(1)
Government public health activities	.4	.6	1.4	3.0	7.2	12.3	22.0	24.5	(1)	(1)
Research, and construction of medical facilities	1.7	3.5	5.3	8.3	11.3	15.4	22.7	23.1	(1)	(1)

[1] Estimates prepared by the Congressional Budget office.

Note: Numbers may not add to totals due to rounding.

Source: Health Care Financing Administration, Office of the Actuary: Data from the Office of National Health Statistics.

TABLE C-2.—NATIONAL HEALTH EXPENDITURES: IN CONSTANT 1991 DOLLARS, FOR SELECTED CALENDAR YEARS 1960–91

[Dollar amounts in billions]

	1960	1965	1970	1975	1980	1985	1986	1987	1988	1989	1990	1991
Total	$125.0	$179.9	$261.1	$336.6	$413.4	$534.9	$565.3	$592.5	$628.7	$663.8	$703.4	$751.8
Health services and supplies	117.2	165.0	242.4	315.6	394.8	515.4	545.5	571.8	605.9	641.1	679.8	728.6
Personal health care	110.1	154.0	227.8	295.1	362.6	468.0	498.1	526.7	555.8	583.2	616.3	660.2
Hospital care	42.7	60.7	98.0	132.6	169.3	213.0	223.4	232.9	244.1	255.2	268.9	288.6
Physicians' services	24.3	35.4	47.7	58.9	69.2	93.6	102.0	111.5	121.0	127.5	134.3	142.0
Dentists' services	9.0	12.1	16.4	20.9	23.7	29.4	30.7	32.5	33.9	34.8	35.5	37.1
Other professional services	2.8	3.7	5.3	8.9	14.4	21.0	23.1	25.4	27.4	29.7	32.0	35.8
Home health care	.2	.3	.5	1.0	2.2	4.9	5.0	4.9	5.2	6.2	7.9	9.8
Drugs and other medical nondurables	19.6	25.5	30.9	33.0	35.7	45.8	49.4	51.7	53.3	55.4	58.0	60.7
Vision products and other medical durables	3.7	5.4	7.1	7.8	7.5	9.0	10.0	10.9	11.7	11.4	12.2	12.4
Nursing home care	4.5	7.3	17.1	25.2	33.0	43.2	45.6	47.6	49.3	52.2	55.6	59.9
Other personal health care	3.2	3.6	4.8	6.9	7.5	8.1	8.8	9.3	10.1	10.7	12.0	14.0
Program administration and net cost of private health insurance	5.4	8.3	9.7	12.8	20.2	31.9	30.6	27.6	30.9	37.1	40.6	43.9
Government public health activities	1.7	2.7	4.9	7.7	11.9	15.6	16.8	17.5	19.1	20.8	22.9	24.5
Research, and construction of medical facilities	7.8	14.9	18.7	21.0	18.6	19.5	19.8	20.7	22.8	22.7	23.6	23.1

Note: Constant dollar expenditures are calculated using the consumer price index for all urban consumers (CPI–U).

Source: Health Care Financing Administration, Office of the Actuary: Data from the Office of National Health Statistics.

TABLE C–3.—NATIONAL HEALTH EXPENDITURES: PER CAPITA AMOUNTS FOR SELECTED CALENDAR YEARS 1960–91

[Dollar amounts per capita]

	1960	1965	1970	1975	1980	1985	1986	1987	1988	1989	1990	1991
Total	$143	$204	$346	$592	$1,064	$1,711	$1,824	$1,962	$2,146	$2,352	$2,601	$2,868
Health services and supplies	134	187	322	555	1,016	1,648	1,760	1,893	2,068	2,271	2,513	2,779
Personal health care	126	175	302	519	933	1,497	1,607	1,744	1,898	2,066	2,279	2,518
Hospital care	49	69	130	233	436	681	721	771	833	904	994	1,101
Physicians' services	28	40	63	104	178	299	329	369	413	452	496	542
Dentists' services	10	14	22	37	61	94	99	108	116	123	131	141
Other professional services	3	4	7	16	37	67	75	84	93	105	118	137
Home health care	0	0	1	2	6	16	16	16	18	22	29	37
Drugs and other medical nondurables	22	29	41	58	92	146	159	171	182	196	214	231
Vision products and other medical durables	4	6	9	14	19	29	32	36	40	41	45	47
Nursing home care	5	8	23	44	85	138	147	157	168	185	205	229
Other personal health care	4	4	6	12	19	26	28	31	34	38	44	53
Program administration and net cost of private health insurance	6	9	13	23	52	102	99	91	106	131	150	167
Government public health activities	2	3	6	14	31	50	54	58	65	74	85	94
Research, and construction of medical facilities	9	17	25	37	48	62	64	69	78	80	87	88

Note: Numbers may not add to totals due to rounding.

Source: Health Care Financing Administration, Office of the Actuary: Data from the Office of National Health Statistics.

TABLE C–4.—NATIONAL HEALTH EXPENDITURES: PER CAPITA AMOUNTS, IN CONSTANT 1991 DOLLARS, FOR SELECTED CALENDAR YEARS 1960–91

[Dollar amount per capita]

	1960	1965	1970	1975	1980	1985	1986	1987	1988	1989	1990	1991
Total	$658	$882	$1,216	$1,499	$1,758	$2,165	$2,266	$2,352	$2,471	$2,583	$2,710	$2,868
Health services and supplies	616	809	1,129	1,406	1,679	2,086	2,187	2,270	2,381	2,495	2,619	2,779
Personal health care	579	755	1,061	1,314	1,542	1,894	1,997	2,091	2,185	2,269	2,374	2,518
Hospital care	225	298	457	591	720	862	896	924	959	993	1,036	1,101
Physicians' services	128	174	222	262	294	379	409	443	476	496	517	542
Dentists' services	48	59	76	93	101	119	123	129	133	135	137	141
Other professional services	15	18	25	40	61	85	93	101	108	116	123	137
Home health care	1	1	2	5	9	20	20	20	20	24	30	37
Drugs and other medical nondurables	103	125	144	147	152	185	198	205	209	216	223	231
Vision products and other medical durables	20	26	33	35	32	37	40	43	46	45	47	47
Nursing home care	24	36	80	112	141	175	183	184	194	203	214	229
Other personal health care	17	17	22	31	32	33	35	37	40	42	46	53
Program administration and net cost of private health insurance	28	41	45	57	86	129	123	109	122	144	156	167
Government public health activities	9	13	23	34	51	63	67	69	75	81	88	94
Research, and construction of medical facilities	41	73	87	93	79	79	80	82	90	88	91	88

Average annual [percentage increase]	60–65	65–70	70–75	75–80	80–85	85–90	89–90	90–91
Total	6.0	6.6	4.3	3.2	4.3	4.8	4.9	5.8
Health services and supplies	5.6	6.9	4.5	3.6	4.4	4.7	5.0	6.1
Personal health care	5.4	7.1	4.4	3.3	4.2	4.8	4.6	6.1
Hospital care	5.8	8.9	5.3	4.0	3.7	3.7	4.3	6.3
Physicians' services	6.3	5.0	3.4	2.3	5.2	6.4	4.3	4.7

Note: Constant dollar expenditures are calculated using the consumer price indices for all urban consumers (CPI–U). Average annual amounts are calculated on unrounded numbers.

Source: Health Care Financing Administration, Office of the Actuary: Data from the Office of National Health Statistics.

TABLE C–5.—PERSONAL HEALTH CARE EXPENDITURES: AGGREGATE AMOUNTS AND PERCENTAGE DISTRIBUTION FOR SELECTED CALENDAR YEARS 1960–93

	1960	1965	1970	1975	1980	1985	1990	1991	1993 [1]	2000 [1]
	Amount in billions of dollars									
Total	$23.9	$35.6	$64.9	$116.6	$219.4	$369.7	$591.5	$660.2	$898	$1,069
Private	18.8	28.4	42.5	71.3	132.3	221.5	349.2	377.0	411	789
Private health insurance	5.0	8.7	15.2	29.9	65.3	114.2	191.2	209.3	⋯	519
Out of pocket	13.3	19.0	25.6	38.5	59.5	94.4	136.5	144.3	162	246
Other private sources of funds	.4	.7	1.7	2.9	7.6	12.9	21.5	23.4	37	59
Public	5.1	7.3	22.4	45.3	87.1	148.2	242.3	283.3	411	789
Federal	2.1	3.0	14.6	31.0	63.5	111.7	177.0	204.1	280	555
State and local	3.0	4.3	7.8	14.4	23.6	36.6	65.3	79.1	130	234
	Percentage distribution									
Total	100.0	100.0	100.0	100.0	100.0	100.0	100.0	100.0	100.0	100.0
Private	78.6	79.6	65.4	61.1	60.3	59.9	59.0	57.1	54.3	51.1
Private health insurance	21.0	24.3	23.4	25.6	29.7	30.9	32.3	31.7	32.2	32.1
Out of pocket	55.9	53.4	39.5	33.1	27.1	25.5	23.1	21.9	18.0	15.2
Other private sources of funds	1.7	1.9	2.6	2.5	3.5	3.5	3.6	3.6	4.1	3.7
Public	21.4	20.4	34.6	38.9	39.7	40.1	41.0	42.9	45.7	48.9
Federal	8.9	8.3	22.6	26.6	28.9	30.2	29.9	30.9	31.2	34.4
State and local	12.5	12.0	12.0	12.3	10.8	9.9	11.0	12.0	14.5	14.5

[1] Estimates prepared by the Congressional Budget Office.

Note: Numbers may not add to totals due to rounding. Percentage amounts are calculated on unrounded numbers.

Source: Health Care Financing Administration, Office of the Actuary: Data from the Office of National Health Statistics.

EXPENDITURES FOR HOSPITAL CARE

In 1991, hospital expenses accounted for 38.4 percent, or $289 billion, of total national health expenditures, down from 41 percent in 1980.

Table C–6 displays historical trends on increases in hospital costs from 1965 to the present, focusing specifically on community hospital expenditures. Community hospitals are defined as all non-Federal short-term general hospitals (excluding, after 1971, hospital units of institutions) and account for 85 percent of hospital spending. Four measures are presented (total expenses, adjusted expenses per inpatient day, adjusted expenses per admission, and inpatient expenses). Total expenses have been growing slightly faster than inpatient expenses over time, reflecting tremendous growth in outpatient services and decreasing admissions and length of stay.

The total expenses of community hospitals, including inpatient and outpatient expenses, were $278.9 billion in 1993, an increase of 6.9 percent over the preceding year. The average cost of a day of hospital care (adjusted to include outpatient care) increased by 8.1 percent to $1,002 in 1993. The average cost per hospital admission (also adjusted to include outpatient care), or "cost per case," rose to $6,226 in 1993, an increase of 5.4 percent. These were the lowest rates of growth in almost a decade for all of these measures.

Figure 1 presents the annual percentage increases in expenses per adjusted admission, removing the effects of inflation. As of October 1993, the real rate of growth in expenses per adjusted admission was the slowest since 1980.

TABLE C–6.—SELECTED COMMUNITY HOSPITAL EXPENSES DATA, TOTALS AND
PERCENTAGE INCREASES, 1965–93

Year	Total expenses		Adjusted expenses per inpatient day [1]		Adjusted expenses per admission		Inpatient expenses [2]	
	Amount (billions)	Percent change	Amount	Percent change	Amount	Percent change	Amount (billions)	Percent change
1965	$9.220	8.6	$41	7.5	$315	8.1	$8.414	8.7
1966	10.497	13.8	46	12.2	356	13.0	9.611	14.2
1967	12.624	20.3	53	15.2	425	19.4	11.551	20.2
1968	14.720	16.6	59	11.3	482	13.4	13.371	15.8
1969	17.247	17.2	68	15.2	551	14.3	15.635	16.9
1970	20.261	17.5	78	14.7	608	10.3	18.328	17.2
1971	22.496	11.0	87	11.5	670	10.2	20.269	10.6
1972	25.223	12.1	96	10.3	729	8.8	22.622	11.6
1973	28.248	12.0	105	9.4	784	7.5	25.173	11.3
1974	32.759	16.0	118	12.4	873	11.4	29.077	15.5
1975	38.492	17.5	138	16.9	1,017	16.5	33.971	16.8
1976	45.842	19.1	158	14.5	1,168	14.8	40.321	18.7
1977	53.006	15.6	181	14.5	1,312	12.3	46.437	15.2
1978	59.802	12.8	203	12.2	1,466	11.7	52.131	12.3
1979	67.833	13.4	226	11.3	1,618	10.4	59.060	13.3
1980	79.340	17.0	256	13.3	1,836	13.5	68.962	16.8
1981	94.187	18.7	299	16.8	2,155	17.4	81.651	18.4
1982	109.091	15.8	348	16.4	2,489	15.5	94.346	15.5
1983	120.220	10.2	391	12.5	2,742	10.2	103.403	9.5
1984	126.028	4.6	443	13.3	2,947	7.5	107.000	3.2
1985	134.043	6.6	493	11.2	3,226	9.4	111.402	4.4
1986	146.032	8.9	535	8.6	3,527	9.3	119.281	7.1
1987	161.322	10.5	581	8.6	3,860	9.5	129.300	8.4
1988	177.770	10.2	632	8.8	4,194	8.6	140.482	8.2
1989	195.377	9.9	690	9.3	4,586	9.3	152.147	8.3
1990	217.113	11.1	765	10.7	5,021	9.5	165.792	9.0
1991	238.633	9.9	844	10.3	5,460	8.8	178.401	7.6
1992	260.994	9.4	927	9.8	5,905	8.1	191.401	7.3
1993 [3]	278.928	6.9	1,002	8.1	6,226	5.4	202.179	5.6

[1] Adjusted to account for the volume of outpatient visits.
[2] Based on ratio of inpatient to total patient revenues applied to total expenses.
[3] Estimate based on January through October 1993 compared with January through October 1992.

Source: American Hospital Association, National Hospital Panel Survey.

A variety of factors other than overall inflation contribute to aggregate changes in hospital expenses, including: population growth, aging of the population, inflation over and above general inflation in the prices of goods and services purchased by the hospitals (input factor prices), and changes in the type and mix (intensity) of services rendered (due to such factors as changes in the use of technology or treatment patterns). While more than half of the overall growth in inpatient hospital expenditures between 1980 and 1990 was due to overall inflation, more than 10 percent was attributable to population growth, and one-fifth to excess inflation in hospital prices (see Figure C–2). The remainder was due to changes in utilization and intensity.

Expenditures for hospital care are financed primarily by third parties (see Table C–7). In 1991, private health insurers paid 35.2

percent of the total, Medicare and Medicaid paid 33.7 percent, and other government programs paid 15.9 percent. The amount financed out-of-pocket by consumers was an estimated 3.4 percent.

Table C-7 also shows that the Medicare share of spending dropped steadily from 1985 to 1989, the first such decreases since the early 1970s. HCFA attributed this decline to the relatively slow growth in Medicare payments per hospital admission.

TRENDS IN HOSPITAL UTILIZATION

Admissions

From 1978 to 1983, total admissions increased at an annual rate of 1.1 percent, and admissions for persons age 65 and over increased an average of 4.8 percent per year (see Table C-8). With the introduction of Medicare's prospective payment system (PPS), admissions of patients 65 and older declined sharply, contrary to most expectations. Admissions of younger patients, however, had been decreasing for several years before that. Between 1987 and 1992, total admissions continued to decrease, but at a slower rate, due to an increase among the older population. 1993 was the first time in 12 years that overall admissions increased due to a slower rate of decline among the under 65 population and an increase for the over 65 population. Even for the older group, however, admission rates have not returned to pre-PPS levels.

Average length of stay

Before the implementation of PPS, average length of stay (LOS) for all adults was relatively constant at between 7.0 and 7.2 days (see Table C-9). With the introduction of PPS, there was a significant drop in LOS. From 1982 to 1984, LOS dropped by 6.9 percent, to 6.6 days, for all adults and 10.9 percent, to 8.8 days, for adults age 65 and over in 1985. LOS stabilized at these levels throughout the rest of the 1980s. LOS began to decline again in 1990, and, as of 1993, had declined by 6 percent for all adults and 8 percent for adults aged 65 and over, to 6.2 and 8.0 days respectively.

Hospital occupancy

With slight increases in admissions and stable LOS, occupancy rates averaged around 75 percent in the early 1980s (see Table C-11). The number of hospital beds was increasing, exceeding 1 million by 1983. During the early years of PPS, however, occupancy rates decreased dramatically. From 1983 to 1986, the average occupancy rate fell from 72.2 percent to 63.4 percent. There was a slight increase in occupancy rates in the late 1980s, but by 1993 the average occupancy rate had fallen to 61.5 percent, despite a decline in the number of beds to just over 900,000.

Hospital employment

Hospitals experienced a significant downturn in total employment levels at the time PPS was introduced (see Table C-10). During 1984 and 1985, total hospital FTEs declined 2.3 percent. Between 1986 and 1992, however, total hospital employment consistently increased. Much of this growth may be attributed to increased employment in the outpatient area. During the late 1980s, growth in the number of part-time personnel exceeded growth in the number of full-time personnel in every year. In 1992, the number of full-time personnel grew faster than the number of part-time personnel for the first time in at lease 15 years. This trend continued in 1993, but the rate of increase in both types of personnel slowed dramatically, from 1.7 percent to 1.0 percent for full-time personnel and .9 percent to .4 percent for part-time personnel.

FIGURE C–1.—REAL ANNUAL INCREASES IN EXPENSES PER ADJUSTED ADMISSION (IN PERCENT), 1965–93

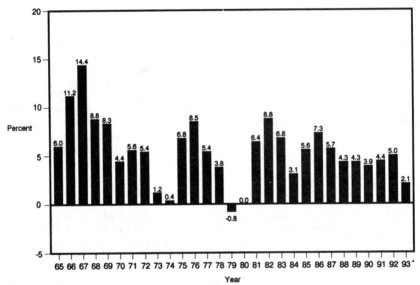

* Estimate based on January through October 1993 compared with January through October 1992.

SOURCE: ProPAC analysis of AHA National Hospital Panel Survey data.

FIGURE C–2.—FACTORS ACCOUNTING FOR GROWTH IN NATIONAL INPATIENT HOSPITAL EXPENDITURES, 1980–90

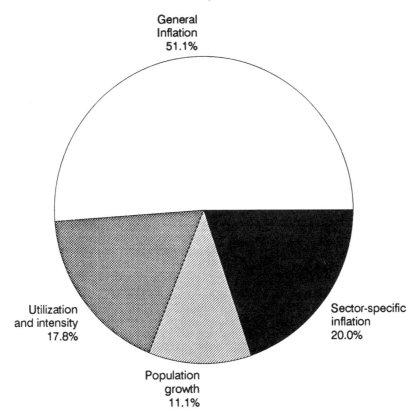

General
Inflation
51.1%

Utilization
and intensity
17.8%

Sector-specific
inflation
20.0%

Population
growth
11.1%

SOURCE: Health Care Financing Administration Office of the Actuary.

TABLE C–7.—EXPENDITURES FOR HOSPITAL CARE, BY SOURCE OF FUNDS, 1980, 1985, AND 1988–91

[Amounts in billions]

Source of payment	1980		1985		1988		1989		1990		1991	
	Amount	Percent	Amount	Percent	Amount	Percent	Amount	Percent	Amount	Percent	Amount	Percent
Total	$102.4	100.0	$168.3	100.0	$212.0	100.0	$232.4	100.0	$258.1	100.0	$288.6	100.0
Out of pocket	5.3	5.2	8.8	5.2	10.4	4.9	10.8	4.7	10.3	4.0	9.9	3.4
Third-party payments	97.1	94.8	159.5	94.8	201.6	95.1	221.6	95.3	247.7	96.0	278.7	96.6
Private health insurance	37.5	36.6	59.6	35.4	76.2	36.0	84.3	36.3	94.3	36.6	101.5	35.2
Other private funds	5.0	4.9	8.3	4.9	11.1	5.3	12.6	5.4	13.9	5.4	14.7	5.1
Government	54.6	53.3	91.6	54.4	114.3	53.9	124.7	53.7	139.5	54.0	162.6	56.3
Federal	41.3	40.4	71.8	42.7	86.2	40.6	94.0	40.4	104.0	40.3	119.1	41.3
Medicare	26.4	25.8	48.6	28.9	57.5	27.1	62.5	26.9	67.4	26.1	73.3	25.4
Medicaid[1]	5.3	5.2	8.4	5.0	11.2	5.3	13.0	5.6	16.3	6.3	23.9	8.3
Other Federal programs	9.7	9.4	14.8	8.8	17.5	8.3	18.5	8.0	20.3	7.8	21.9	7.6
State and local	13.3	12.9	19.7	11.7	28.1	13.2	30.7	13.2	35.5	13.7	43.5	15.1
Medicaid[2]	4.4	4.3	7.1	4.2	8.8	4.2	9.9	4.3	12.6	4.9	19.4	6.7
Other State and local programs	8.9	8.7	12.7	7.5	19.3	9.1	20.8	8.9	22.9	8.9	24.0	8.3

[1] Federal share only.
[2] State and local share only.

Note.—Numbers may not add to totals because of rounding.

Source: Health Care Financing Administration, Office of the Actuary: Data from the Office of National Health Statistics.

TABLE C–8.—PERCENT CHANGE IN HOSPITAL ADMISSIONS, 1978–93

Year	Admissions		
	All	Under age 65	Age 65 and over
1978	0.4	− 1.0	4.9
1979	2.7	1.7	5.3
1980	2.9	1.5	6.7
1981	.9	0.0	3.0
1982	0.0	− 1.6	4.1
1983	− .5	− 2.8	4.7
1984	− 3.7	− 4.2	− 2.6
1985	− 4.9	− 4.7	− 5.2
1986	− 2.1	− 2.5	− 1.0
1987	− .6	− 1.0	.4
1988	− .4	− 1.6	2.0
1989	− 1.1	− 2.0	1.2
1990	− .5	− 1.6	1.7
1991	− 1.1	− 2.9	2.5
1992	− 0.8	− 2.2	1.7
1993 [1]	0.2	− 1.0	2.2
Average annual change:			
1978–83	1.1	− .4	4.8
1984–93	− 1.5	− 2.4	0.3

[1] Estimate based on January through October 1993 compared with January through October 1992.

Source: American Hospital Association National Hospital Panel Survey.

TABLE C–9.—CHANGE IN AVERAGE LENGTH OF STAY, ALL ADULTS AND ADULTS AGE 65 AND OVER, 1978–93

Year	All adults length of stay (days)	Percent change	Age 65 and over (days)	Percent change
1978	7.2	− 0.3	10.6	− 1.2
1979	7.1	− 1.1	10.4	− 1.9
1980	7.2	.6	10.4	− .1
1981	7.2	.4	10.4	− .1
1982	7.2	− .7	10.1	− 2.3
1983	7.0	− 2.0	9.7	− 4.4
1984	6.7	− 5.1	9.0	− 7.5
1985	6.6	− 1.7	8.8	− 2.1
1986	6.6	.6	8.8	.4
1987	6.6	.8	8.9	1.0
1988	6.6	0.0	8.8	− .7
1989	6.6	0.0	8.8	0.0
1990	6.6	0.0	8.7	− 1.1
1991	6.5	− 1.5	8.5	− 2.3
1992	6.4	− 1.5	8.3	− 2.4
1993 [1]	6.2	− 3.1	8.0	− 3.6
Average annual change:				
1978–83	....	− .5	....	− 1.7
1984–93	....	− 1.2	....	− 1.9

[1] Estimate based on January through October 1993 compared with January through October 1992.

Source: American Hospital Association National Hospital Panel Survey.

TABLE C–10.—PERCENT CHANGE IN HOSPITAL EMPLOYMENT, 1978–93

Year	Total hospital FTE's	Personnel		
		Total	Full-time	Part-time
1978	3.7	4.1	3.3	6.8
1979	3.5	3.9	3.0	6.7
1980	4.7	5.2	4.0	9.1
1981	5.4	6.0	4.8	9.4
1982	3.7	3.7	3.6	4.1
1983	1.4	1.5	1.2	2.3
1984	− 2.3	− 2.1	− 2.6	− .8
1985	− 2.3	− 1.8	− 2.7	− .1
1986	.3	.4	.3	.7
1987	.7	.9	.4	2.3
1988	1.1	1.4	.7	3.3
1989	1.6	1.9	1.2	3.6
1990	2.1	2.3	1.8	3.6
1991	.6	.7	.6	1.0
1992	1.6	1.5	1.7	.9
1993 [1]	.9	.8	1.0	.4
Average annual change:				
1978–83	3.7	4.1	3.3	6.4
1984–93	.4	.6	.2	1.5

[1] Estimate based on January through October 1993 compared with January through October 1992.

Source: American Hospital Association National Hospital Panel Survey.

TABLE C–11.—CHANGE IN INPATIENT HOSPITAL OCCUPANCY RATES AND NUMBER OF BEDS, 1978–93

Year	Percent		Number of beds	Percent change
	Occupancy rates	Change		
1978	73.8	− 0.8	954,001	0.9
1979	74.5	.9	959,269	.6
1980	75.9	1.9	970,456	1.2
1981	75.8	−.1	986,917	1.7
1982	74.6	− 1.6	997,720	1.1
1983	72.2	− 3.2	1,003,658	.6
1984	66.6	− 7.8	992,616	− 1.1
1985	63.6	− 4.5	974,559	− 1.8
1986	63.4	− .3	963,133	− 1.2
1987	64.1	1.1	954,458	− .9
1988	64.5	.6	942,306	− 1.3
1989	65.2	1.1	930,994	− 1.2
1990	64.5	− 1.1	921,447	− 1.0
1991	63.5	− 1.6	911,781	− 1.0
1992	62.4	− 1.7	907,661	− .5
1993[1]	61.5	− 1.4	901,985	− .6
Annual average:				
1978–83		− .5		1.0
1984–92		− 1.6		− 1.0

[1] Estimate based on January through October 1993.

Source: American Hospital Association National Hospital Panel Survey.

EXPENDITURES FOR PHYSICIANS' SERVICES

Personal health care expenditures for physicians' services were $142.0 billion in 1991, an increase of 10.2 percent from the previous year (see table 12). In 1991, 18.9 percent of national health expenditures and 21.5 percent of personal health expenditures were for physicians' services (see table C–1). Physicians, however, affect personal health care expenditures more than this might indicate. Physicians have considerable discretion in determining the volume of all medical services. It is estimated that physicians' decisions (such as ordering hospitalizations, drugs, laboratory tests) directly influence over 70 percent of all health care spending.

Third-party (public expenditures and private insurance) payments financed a large majority of physicians' services. In 1991, private health insurance paid $66.8 billion (47 percent) for such services. The remainder was split between direct patient payments and public expenditures. Patients or their families paid $25.7 billion (18 percent) for physicians' services. Public programs paid $49.4 billion (35 percent) for such services, of which $32.8 billion was Federal Medicare payments (see table C–12).

Inflation was a major cause of growth in spending for physicians' services. Physicians' fees have risen more rapidly (5.6 percent in 1993) than prices in the economy as a whole (3.0 percent) as measured by the Consumer Price Index (CPI) (see table C–13).

An analysis done by the Health Care Financing Administration found that expenditures for physicians' services over a 10-year span increased from $41.9 billion in 1980 to $142.0 billion in 1991, an average annual growth rate of 11.7 percent.

The average physician net income in 1991, after expenses but before taxes, was $170,600, a 6.3 percent increase over the previous year (see table C–14). Surgeons had the highest average net incomes in 1991 ($233,800) and general and family practitioners the lowest ($111,500). In 1991, the average net income of pediatricians increased faster than any other specialty (12.0 percent).

By region, average net income growth varied greatly, ranging from − 9.3 percent in Mountain region to 9.5 percent in the Middle Atlantic region. Physicians in the East South Central and West South Central regions had the highest average net incomes ($179,400 and $193,300 respectively). Physicians in the New England region had the lowest average net incomes ($143,800). The growth rates differed rather significantly between metropolitan and nonmetropolitan areas, as shown in table C–14. The average net incomes of self-employed physicians ($191,000) continued to be higher than those of employee physicians ($134,000).

Table C–15 shows average physician net incomes in nominal and real (or constant) dollars. Real income is expressed in 1991 dollars. Physicians' average net income increased about 182 percent between 1977 and 1991. However, average real incomes increased about 26 percent during this period, at an average annual rate of 1.8 percent.

Table C–16 shows physicians' median net incomes by specialty. Between 1981 and 1991, real net income increased in all specialties. Table C–17 shows the distribution of physicians' net incomes in 1991 for all physicians and selected specialties. While the average net income of all physicians was $170,600, half of all physicians earned less than $139,000. One-fourth of all physicians earned less than $95,000, while one-fourth earned more than $210,000. Anesthesiologists, radiologists, obstetricians/gynecologists and surgeons had the highest median incomes, with half earning $200,000 or more.

The continuing survey of physicians' incomes conducted by the magazine Medical Economics showed that, on average, physicians received 83 percent of their 1992 gross practice incomes from third parties (see table C–18). On average, 17 percent came from commercial insurers, 14 percent from Blue Shield, 26 percent from Medicare, 10 percent from health maintenance organizations (HMOs) and independent practice associations (IPAs), and 6 percent from preferred provider organizations (PPOs). As table C–18 indicates, the importance of each source of payment varied by specialty. Cardio/thoracic surgeons received the highest percentage of gross pay from Medicare (50 percent), while pediatricians, on average, received only 1 percent of their gross income from Medicare.

TABLE C-12.—EXPENDITURES FOR PHYSICIAN SERVICES [1] BY SOURCE OF FUNDS, 1980, 1985, AND 1987-91

	1980		1985		1987		1988		1989		1990		1991	
	Amount	Percent	Amount	Percent	Amount	Percent	Amount	Percent	Amount	Percent	Amount	Percent	Amount	Percent
Total	$41.9	100.0	$74.0	100.0	$93.0	100	$105.1	100.0	$116.1	100.0	$128.8	100.0	$142.0	100.0
Out-of-pocket payments	11.3	26.9	16.1	21.8	19.0	20.4	20.9	19.9	22.5	19.4	24.1	18.7	25.7	18.1
Third-party payments	30.6	73.1	57.8	78.2	74.0	79.6	84.3	80.1	93.6	80.6	104.8	81.3	116.3	81.9
Private health insurance	18.0	42.9	33.7	45.6	42.6	45.8	49.1	46.7	53.9	46.4	60.7	47.1	66.8	47.0
Other private funds	(²)	(²)	(²)	(²)	(²)	(²)	(²)	(²)	(²)	(²)	(²)	(²)	(²)	(²)
Government	12.6	30.2	24.1	32.6	31.4	33.8	35.1	33.4	39.6	34.1	44.0	34.2	49.4	34.8
Federal	9.7	23.1	19.2	26.0	25.1	27.0	28.1	26.7	31.7	27.3	34.9	27.1	39.0	27.5
Medicare	7.9	19.0	16.7	22.5	21.7	23.3	24.2	23.0	27.4	23.6	29.7	23.1	32.8	23.1
Medicaid	1.2	2.8	1.6	2.2	2.0	2.2	2.2	2.1	2.5	2.2	3.1	2.4	4.0	2.8
Other Federal programs	.5	1.3	1.0	1.3	1.4	1.5	1.7	1.6	1.8	1.5	2.0	1.6	2.2	1.6
State and local	3.0	7.1	4.9	6.6	6.3	6.8	7.0	6.7	7.9	6.8	9.1	7.1	10.4	7.3
Medicaid	1.0	2.3	1.2	1.7	1.5	1.7	1.5	1.5	1.7	1.5	2.1	1.7	2.9	2.0
Other State and local programs	2.0	4.8	3.6	4.9	4.8	5.1	5.5	5.2	6.2	5.3	7.0	5.4	7.5	5.3

[1] Encompasses the cost of all services and supplies provided in physicians' offices, the cost for services of private practitioners in hospitals and other institutions, and the cost of diagnostic work performed in independent clinical laboratories. The salaries of staff physicians are counted with expenditures for the services of the employing institution.

[2] Less than $50 million.

Source: Health Care Financing Administration: Office of the Actuary: Data from the Office of National Health Statistics.

Note: Numbers may not add to totals due to rounding.

TABLE C–13.—ANNUAL RATES OF CHANGE IN THE CONSUMER PRICE INDEX (CPI–U),[1]
1965–93

	CPI all items	CPI, all items less medical care	Medical care total	Physicians' services
1965	1.6	1.6	2.4	3.6
1966	2.9	3.1	4.4	5.6
1967	3.1	2.1	7.2	7.2
1968	4.2	4.2	6.0	5.6
1969	5.5	5.4	6.7	7.0
1970	5.7	5.9	6.6	7.5
1971	4.4	4.1	6.2	7.0
1972	3.2	3.2	3.3	3.0
1973	6.2	6.4	4.0	3.4
1974	11.0	11.2	9.3	9.2
1975	9.1	9.0	12.0	12.1
1976	5.8	5.3	9.5	11.4
1977	6.5	6.3	9.6	9.1
1978	7.6	7.6	8.4	8.4
1979	11.3	11.5	9.2	9.1
1980	13.5	13.6	11.0	10.5
1981	10.3	10.4	10.7	11.0
1982	6.2	5.9	11.6	9.4
1983	3.2	2.9	8.8	7.8
1984	4.3	4.1	6.2	6.9
1985	3.6	3.4	6.3	5.9
1986	1.9	1.5	7.5	7.2
1987	3.6	3.5	6.6	7.3
1988	4.1	3.9	6.5	7.2
1989	4.8	4.6	7.7	7.4
1990	5.4	5.2	9.0	7.1
1991	4.2	3.9	8.7	6.0
1992	3.0	2.8	7.4	6.3
1993	3.0	2.7	5.9	5.6

[1] CPI index for all urban consumers.

Source: U.S. Department of Labor, Bureau of Labor Statistics, Consumer Price Index.

TABLE C-14.—PHYSICIANS' AVERAGE NET INCOME AFTER EXPENSES BUT BEFORE TAXES, SURVEY RESULTS, 1983–91

	Average net income [1] (in thousands of dollars)									Percent change 1990–91
	1983	1984	1985	1986	1987	1988	1989	1990	1991	
All physicians [2]	104.1	108.4	112.2	119.5	132.3	144.7	155.8	164.3	170.6	6.3
Specialty:										
General/family practice	68.5	71.1	77.9	80.3	91.5	94.6	95.9	102.7	111.5	8.6
Internal medicine	93.3	103.2	101.0	109.4	121.8	130.9	146.5	152.5	149.6	−1.9
Surgery	145.5	151.8	155.4	162.4	187.9	207.5	220.5	236.4	233.8	−1.1
Pediatrics	70.7	74.5	77.1	81.8	85.3	94.9	104.7	106.5	119.3	12.0
Obstetrics/gynecology	119.9	116.2	122.7	135.9	163.2	180.7	194.3	207.3	221.8	7.0
Radiology	148.0	139.8	150.8	168.8	180.7	188.5	210.5	219.4	229.8	4.7
Psychiatry	80.0	85.5	88.6	91.5	102.7	111.4	111.7	116.5	127.6	9.5
Anesthesiology	144.7	145.4	140.2	150.2	163.1	194.5	185.8	207.4	221.1	6.6
Census Division:										
New England	84.5	87.3	108.3	107.1	110.6	132.9	128.3	142.5	143.8	.9
Middle Atlantic	98.6	98.4	107.9	114.6	126.1	135.0	152.5	156.1	171.0	9.5
East North Central	114.3	109.4	118.9	126.6	137.6	147.0	155.6	172.4	174.1	1.0
West North Central	110.5	110.7	113.7	120.7	133.9	138.0	159.2	151.4	164.2	8.4
South Atlantic	106.7	114.5	112.6	119.6	133.8	156.0	165.6	169.0	168.8	−.1
East South Central	114.9	122.2	115.0	122.6	141.2	164.8	173.0	169.0	179.4	6.1
West South Central	124.4	119.1	123.3	129.0	140.4	160.7	170.5	178.8	193.3	8.1
Mountain	91.4	102.3	97.5	108.5	125.5	132.1	142.6	170.9	155.0	−9.3
Pacific	103.1	109.4	113.6	119.0	135.4	136.0	148.1	162.5	172.4	6.1

Location:										
Nonmetropolitan	87.2	90.9	94.2	107.7	117.9	120.9	129.4	130.5	150.4	15.2
Metropolitan:										
Less than 1,000,000	111.0	115.1	118.1	124.5	140.4	154.1	164.1	172.7	174.8	1.2
1,000,000 and over	106.3	106.4	112.8	117.5	127.9	140.7	153.4	163.3	170.4	4.3
Employment Status:										
Self-employed	115.9	118.6	124.5	131.1	146.2	160.0	175.3	185.6	191.0	2.9
Employee	77.6	80.4	83.8	91.7	99.6	113.0	119.2	119.8	134.0	11.8

[1] Average net income after expenses but before taxes. These figures include contributions made into pension, profit-sharing, and deferred compensation plans.
[2] Includes physicians in specialties not reported separately.

Source: Socioeconomic Characteristics of Medical Practice, 1993, American Medical Association.

TABLE C–15.—AVERAGE PHYSICIAN NET INCOME AFTER EXPENSES, BEFORE TAXES, 1977–91

[Dollars in thousands]

	Nominal	Real (1991)
1977	$60.4	$135.8
1978	64.6	134.5
1979	77.4	145.2
1980	NA	NA
1981	89.9	134.7
1982	97.7	137.9
1983	104.1	142.4
1984	108.4	142.1
1985	112.2	142.0
1986	119.5	148.5
1987	132.3	158.6
1988	144.7	166.6
1989	155.8	171.1
1990	164.3	171.2
1991	170.6	170.6

NA: Not available.

Note.—No data for 1980. Real (1991 dollars) incomes are calculated using the consumer price index for all urban consumers.

Source: CRS analysis of data from: Gonzales, Martin L., and David W. Emmons, eds., "Socioeconomic Characteristics of Medical Practice, 1993," American Medical Association.

TABLE C–16.—MEDIAN PHYSICIAN NET INCOME AFTER EXPENSES, BEFORE TAXES, 1981 AND 1991

[Dollars in thousands]

	Median net income			Average annual percent change	
	1981	1991 nominal	1991 real [1]	Nominal	Real
All physicians [2]	$75	$139	$93	6.9	3.3
Specialty:					
General/family practice ..	60	98	65	5.4	0
Internal medicine	72	125	83	4.2	0
Surgery	100	200	133	0	−4.3
Pediatrics	55	105	70	5.0	0
Obstetrics/gynecology	96	200	133	8.7	3.9
Radiology	105	223	149	1.2	7.2
Psychiatry	64	110	73	2.8	−1.4
Anesthesiology	105	210	140	5.0	.7
Pathology	75	153	102	2.0	−1.9
Census Division:					
New England	65	124	83	3.3	0
Middle Atlantic	70	136	91	8.8	4.6
East North Central	80	133	89	−5.0	−8.3
West North Central	80	141	94	8.5	4.4
South Atlantic	77	130	87	−2.0	−5.4
East South Central	80	150	100	7.1	3.1
West South Central	80	150	100	0	−3.9
Mountain	74	137	91	1.5	−3.2
Pacific	77	150	100	11.1	6.4

[1] In 1981 dollars.
[2] Includes physicians in specialties not listed separately.

Source: Gonzalez, Martin L., and David W. Emmons, eds. "Socioeconomic Characteristics of Medical Practice, 1993," American Medical Association.

TABLE C–17.—DISTRIBUTION OF PHYSICIAN NET INCOME AFTER EXPENSES, BEFORE TAXES, BY SPECIALTY AND CENSUS DIVISION, 1991

[In thousands of dollars]

	125th Per-centile	150th Per-centile	175th Per-centile	Mean
All physicians [1]	95	139	210	170.6
Specialty:				
General/family practice	74	98	128	111.5
Internal medicine	90	125	177	149.6
Surgery	133	200	287	223.8
Pediatrics	80	105	145	119.3
Obstetrics/gynecology	124	200	300	221.8
Radiology	150	223	300	229.8
Psychiatry	88	110	159	127.6
Anesthesiology	157	210	275	221.1
Pathology	110	153	230	197.7
Census division:				
New England	90	124	180	143.8
Middle Atlantic	95	136	210	171.0
East North Central	90	133	208	174.1
West North Central	100	141	200	164.2
South Atlantic	90	130	200	168.8
East South Central	98	150	230	179.4
West South Central	100	150	250	193.3
Mountain	97	137	200	155.0
Pacific	93	150	220	172.4

[1] Includes physicians in specialties not listed separately.

Source: Gonzalez, Martin L., and David W. Emmons, eds. "Socioeconomic Characteristics of Medical Practice, 1993." American Medical Association.

TABLE C-18.—THIRD PARTY SOURCES OF PHYSICIAN PAYMENT FOR SELECTED SPECIALTIES, 1992

Specialty	Commercial plans		Blue Shield		Medicare		Medicaid		HMOs/IPAs		PPOs	
	Average annual payment	As percent of gross practice income	Average annual payment	As percent of gross practice income	Average annual payment	As percent of gross practice income	Average annual payment	As percent of gross practice income	Average annual payment	As percent of gross practice income	Average annual payment	As percent of gross practice income
Cardiologists	$61,400	15	$56,100	14	$177,490	46	$18,220	5	$27,530	6	$16,730	4
Cardio/thoracic surgeons	61,200	12	70,670	14	241,890	50	31,410	6	44,000	10	17,980	4
Family practice	33,420	14	30,290	12	54,170	22	25,320	11	27,720	12	18,140	7
Gastroenterologists	58,600	14	57,500	15	151,640	40	21,620	6	32,140	10	19,810	5
General practice	30,870	14	23,940	12	45,230	24	20,210	12	23,300	10	15,250	5
General surgeons	62,430	19	53,810	17	103,590	33	26,100	9	31,890	10	20,510	6
Pediatricians	36,860	15	33,350	14	810	1	53,800	24	31,890	15	22,830	9
Plastic surgeons	84,410	20	61,030	14	54,450	13	13,910	4	25,960	6	30,810	7
Psychiatrists	38,910	20	23,610	13	22,780	11	10,870	6	10,000	5	13,190	6
Internists	31,060	12	33,700	12	101,320	39	12,380	5	22,230	10	16,290	6
Neurosurgeons	154,920	26	77,130	14	118,990	22	35,290	7	55,620	10	39,880	7
OBG specialists	96,590	24	80,930	20	24,290	7	47,860	11	58,280	15	48,860	11
Orthopedists	122,860	24	78,430	17	95,950	21	28,810	6	43,510	9	38,570	7
All surgical specialists	83,980	20	66,010	16	105,590	26	32,030	8	41,800	10	30,930	7
All non-surgical specialists	46,460	15	39,730	14	87,000	28	24,080	10	28,480	10	18,370	6
All M.D.s	55,600	17	45,710	14	86,070	26	26,390	10	32,150	10	22,030	6

Source: Terry, Ken, "Where more of your income is coming from," Medical Economics, Nov. 22, 1993.

SUPPLY OF HOSPITAL BEDS

The national supply of community hospital beds per 1,000 population steadily increased from the 1940's, reaching a peak of 4.6 beds per 1,000 population in 1975. By 1989, the number of beds had dropped to 3.8 per 1,000 population, and remained at that level in 1990. Similar trends can be seen in the nine census regions, except for New England, which has seen a reduction since 1940 from 4.4 beds to 3.4 beds per 1,000 population in 1990, and the Pacific region, where the reduction has been from 4.1 beds in 1940 to 2.7 beds in 1990. The area experiencing the largest increase has been the East South Central, where beds increased from 1.7 per 1,000 population in 1940 to 5.1 in 1980, falling back to 4.8 in 1990. (see table C–19).

TABLE C–19.—COMMUNITY HOSPITAL BEDS PER 1,000 POPULATION AND AVERAGE ANNUAL PERCENT CHANGE, ACCORDING TO GEOGRAPHIC DIVISION AND STATE: UNITED STATES, SELECTED YEARS 1940–90

[Data are based on reporting by facilities]

Geographic division and State	Beds per 1,000 civilian population									Average annual percent change			
	1940 [1]	1950 [1]	1960 [2]	1970	1980	1985	1988	1989	1990	1940–60 [1][2]	1960–70 [2]	1970–80	1980–90
United States	3.2	3.3	3.6	4.3	4.5	4.2	3.9	3.8	3.8	0.6	1.8	0.5	−1.7
New England	4.4	4.2	3.9	4.1	4.1	4.0	3.6	3.5	3.4	−0.6	0.5	0.0	−1.9
Maine	3.0	3.2	3.4	4.7	4.7	4.2	3.9	3.8	3.8	0.6	3.3	0.0	−2.1
New Hampshire	4.2	4.2	4.4	4.0	3.9	3.4	3.2	3.1	3.1	0.2	−0.9	−0.3	−2.3
Vermont	3.3	4.0	4.5	4.5	4.4	3.8	3.1	3.1	3.1	1.6	0.0	−0.2	−3.4
Massachusetts	5.1	4.8	4.2	4.4	4.4	4.4	4.0	3.8	3.6	−1.0	0.5	0.0	−2.0
Rhode Island	3.9	3.8	3.7	4.0	3.8	3.6	3.3	3.2	3.2	−0.3	0.8	−0.5	−1.7
Connecticut	3.7	3.6	3.4	3.4	3.5	3.3	3.0	3.0	2.9	−0.4	0.0	0.3	−1.9
Middle Atlantic	3.9	3.8	4.0	4.4	4.6	4.4	4.1	4.1	4.2	0.1	1.0	0.4	−0.9
New York	4.3	4.1	4.3	4.6	4.5	4.4	4.2	4.2	4.2	0.0	0.7	−0.2	−0.7
New Jersey	3.5	3.2	3.1	3.6	4.2	3.9	3.7	3.7	3.7	−0.6	1.5	1.6	−1.3
Pennsylvania	3.5	3.8	4.1	4.7	4.8	4.7	4.4	4.3	4.4	0.8	1.4	0.2	−0.9
East North Central	3.2	3.2	3.6	4.4	4.7	4.5	4.1	4.0	3.9	0.6	2.0	0.7	−1.8
Ohio	2.7	2.9	3.4	4.2	4.7	4.6	4.2	4.0	4.0	1.2	2.1	1.1	−1.6
Indiana	2.3	2.6	3.1	4.0	4.5	4.2	4.1	3.9	3.9	1.5	2.6	1.2	−1.4
Illinois	3.4	3.6	4.0	4.7	5.1	4.7	4.3	4.1	4.0	0.8	1.6	0.8	−2.4
Michigan	4.0	3.3	3.3	4.3	4.4	4.1	3.8	3.7	3.7	−1.0	2.7	0.2	−1.7
Wisconsin	3.4	3.7	4.3	5.2	4.9	4.6	4.0	3.9	3.8	1.2	1.9	−0.6	−2.5
West North Central	3.1	3.7	4.3	5.7	5.8	5.4	5.1	4.9	4.9	1.6	2.9	0.2	−1.7
Minnesota	3.9	4.4	4.8	6.1	5.7	5.2	4.8	4.5	4.4	1.0	2.4	−0.7	−2.6
Iowa	2.7	3.2	3.9	5.6	5.7	5.2	5.2	5.0	5.1	1.9	3.7	0.2	−1.1
Missouri	2.9	3.3	3.9	5.1	5.7	5.2	4.9	4.8	4.8	1.5	2.7	1.1	−1.7
North Dakota	3.5	4.3	5.2	6.8	7.4	7.4	7.0	7.0	7.0	2.0	2.7	0.8	−0.6
South Dakota	2.8	4.4	4.5	5.6	5.5	6.6	5.6	5.8	6.1	2.4	2.2	−0.2	1.0
Nebraska	3.4	4.2	4.4	6.2	6.0	6.0	5.8	5.5	5.4	1.3	3.5	−0.3	−1.0
Kansas	2.8	3.4	4.2	5.4	5.8	5.2	4.7	4.8	4.8	2.0	2.5	0.7	−1.9
South Atlantic	2.5	2.8	3.3	4.0	4.5	4.1	3.8	3.7	3.7	1.4	1.9	1.2	−1.9
Delaware	4.4	3.9	3.7	3.7	3.6	3.5	3.1	3.0	3.0	−0.9	0.0	−0.3	−1.8
Maryland	3.9	3.6	3.3	3.1	3.6	3.4	2.9	2.9	2.9	−0.8	−0.6	1.5	−2.1
District of Columbia	5.5	5.5	5.9	7.4	7.3	7.8	7.8	7.9	7.5	0.4	2.3	−0.1	0.3
Virginia	2.2	2.5	3.0	3.7	4.1	3.8	3.5	3.4	3.3	1.6	2.1	1.0	−2.1
West Virginia	2.7	3.1	4.1	5.4	5.5	5.1	4.7	4.7	4.7	2.1	2.8	0.2	−1.6
North Carolina	2.2	2.6	3.4	3.8	4.2	3.7	3.4	3.4	3.4	2.2	1.1	1.0	−2.1
South Carolina	1.8	2.4	2.9	3.7	3.9	3.6	3.3	3.2	3.3	2.4	2.5	0.5	−1.7

TABLE C–19.—COMMUNITY HOSPITAL BEDS PER 1,000 POPULATION AND AVERAGE ANNUAL PERCENT CHANGE, ACCORDING TO GEOGRAPHIC DIVISION AND STATE: UNITED STATES, SELECTED YEARS 1940–90—Continued

[Data are based on reporting by facilities]

Geographic division and State	Beds per 1,000 civilian population									Average annual percent change			
	1940[1]	1950[1]	1960[2]	1970	1980	1985	1988	1989	1990	1940–60[1][2]	1960–70[1][2]	1970–80	1980–90
Georgia	1.7	2.0	2.8	3.8	4.6	4.3	4.1	4.1	4.0	2.5	3.1	1.9	-1.4
Florida	2.8	2.9	3.1	4.4	5.1	4.6	4.2	4.0	4.0	0.5	3.6	1.5	-2.4
East South Central	1.7	2.1	3.0	4.4	5.1	5.0	4.7	4.7	4.8	2.9	3.9	1.5	-0.6
Kentucky	1.8	2.2	3.0	4.0	4.5	4.4	4.3	4.3	4.4	2.6	2.9	1.2	-0.2
Tennessee	1.9	2.3	3.4	4.7	5.5	5.3	4.8	4.8	4.9	3.0	3.3	1.6	-1.1
Alabama	1.5	2.0	2.8	4.3	5.1	5.0	4.6	4.6	4.6	3.2	4.4	1.7	-1.0
Mississippi	1.4	1.7	3.3	4.4	5.3	5.2	5.4	5.2	5.3	3.7	4.3	1.9	0.0
West South Central	2.1	2.7	2.9	4.3	4.7	4.2	3.9	3.8	3.9	2.3	2.7	0.9	-1.8
Arkansas	1.4	1.6	3.9	4.2	5.0	4.8	4.5	4.5	4.7	3.7	3.8	1.8	-0.6
Louisiana	3.1	3.8	3.2	4.2	4.8	4.6	4.4	4.4	4.6	1.2	0.7	1.3	-0.4
Oklahoma	1.9	2.5	3.3	4.5	4.6	4.1	4.0	3.9	4.0	2.6	3.5	0.2	-1.4
Texas	2.0	2.7	3.5	4.3	4.7	4.1	3.7	3.6	3.5	2.5	2.7	0.9	-2.9
Mountain	3.6	3.8	3.5	4.3	3.8	3.5	3.3	3.1	3.1	-0.1	2.1	-1.2	-2.0
Montana	4.9	5.3	5.1	5.8	5.9	5.5	5.6	5.7	5.8	0.2	1.3	0.2	-0.2
Idaho	2.6	3.4	3.2	4.0	3.7	3.5	3.2	3.2	3.2	1.0	2.3	-0.8	-1.4
Wyoming	3.5	3.9	4.6	5.5	3.6	4.3	4.8	4.7	4.9	1.4	1.8	-4.1	3.1
Colorado	3.9	4.2	3.8	4.6	4.2	3.6	3.3	3.0	3.2	-0.1	1.9	-0.9	-2.7
New Mexico	2.7	2.2	2.9	3.5	3.1	2.9	2.8	2.9	2.9	0.4	1.9	-1.2	-0.7
Arizona	3.4	4.0	3.0	4.1	3.6	3.2	2.9	2.8	2.7	-0.6	3.2	-1.3	-2.8
Utah	3.2	2.9	2.8	3.6	3.1	2.7	2.7	2.6	2.6	0.7	2.5	-1.5	-1.7
Nevada	5.0	4.4	3.9	4.2	4.2	3.7	3.2	3.0	2.9	-1.2	0.7	0.0	-3.6
Pacific	4.1	3.2	3.1	3.7	3.5	3.2	2.9	2.8	2.7	-1.4	1.8	-0.6	-2.6
Washington	3.4	3.6	3.3	3.5	3.1	3.0	2.7	2.6	2.5	-0.1	0.6	-1.2	-2.1
Oregon	3.5	3.1	3.5	4.0	3.5	3.2	2.9	2.9	2.9	0.0	1.3	-1.3	-1.9
California	4.4	3.3	3.0	3.8	3.6	3.2	2.9	2.9	2.7	-1.9	2.4	-0.5	-2.8
Alaska			2.4	2.3	2.7	2.2	2.4	2.5	2.3		-0.4	1.6	-1.6
Hawaii			3.7	3.4	3.1	2.8	2.7	2.7	2.8		-0.8	-0.9	-1.0

[1] 1940 and 1950 data are estimated based on published figures.
[2] 1960 includes hospital units of institutions.

Sources: American Medical Association: Hospital service in the United States. JAMA 116(11):1055–1144, 1941, and 146(2):109–184, 1951. (Copyright 1941 and 1951. Used with the Permission of the American Medical Association); American Hospital Association: Hospitals. JAHA 35(15):383–430, Aug. 1, 1961. (Copyright 1961: Used with the permission of the American Hospital Association.); Data computed by the Centers for Disease Control and Prevention, National Center for Health Statistics. Division of Analysis from data compiled by the Division of Health Care Statistics, National Master Facility Inventory and the American Hospital Association 1990 annual survey; U.S. Bureau of the Census; Current Population Reports. Series P–25, Nos. 72, 304, 460, 640, 970, 1010, 1044, and 1058. Washington. U.S. Government Printing Office. 1953, 1965, 1971, 1976, 1980, 1985, 1989, and 1990; Health, United States, 1991; DHHS Pub. No. (PHS) 93–1232.

SUPPLY OF PHYSICIANS

Physician supply has grown rapidly over the past three decades. The number of active physicians in the country has increased from 334,028 in 1970 to 653,062 in 1992. This growth rate exceeded the rate at which the population of the Nation grew during the decade.

Table C–20 indicates that between 1965 and 1992, the number of physicians per 100,000 civilians grew from 161 to 255. As table C–21 below indicates, the ratio of nonfederal physicians-to-population increased from 148 physicians per 100,000 population in 1970 to 248 physicians per 100,000 population in 1992. This table also indicates variations in the supply of physicians relative to population by State. In 1992, the District of Columbia had the highest ratio (705 physicians per 100,000 population) while Alaska had the lowest ratio (146 physicians per 100,000 population).

TABLE C–20.—PHYSICIAN SUPPLY BY MAJOR CATEGORIES, 1970–92

Category	1970		1980		1990		1992	
	Number	Percent	Number	Percent	Number	Percent	Number	Percent
Total Physicians	334,028	....	467,679	....	615,421	....	653,062	....
Federal	29,501	9	17,787	4	20,475	3	19,216	3
Nonfederal	301,323	91	443,502	96	592,166	97	631,137	97
Patient Care	278,535	83	376,512	80	503,870	82	535,220	82
Nonpatient Care	32,310	10	38,404	9	43,440	8	42,888	7
Male	308,627	92	413,395	88	511,227	83	534,543	82
Female	25,401	8	54,284	12	104,194	17	118,519	18
International medical graduates	57,217	17	97,726	21	131,764	21	144,399	22
Metropolitan (nonfederal only)	258,265	86	385,365	87	521,668	88	557,900	88
Nonmetropolitan (nonfederal only)	43,058	14	58,137	13	70,498	12	73,237	12
Total physician-population ratio (per 100,000 persons)	161	....	202	....	244	....	255	....

Source: American Medical Association, 1993.

TABLE C–21.—NON-FEDERAL PHYSICIAN/POPULATION RATIOS AND RANK BY STATE

[Ratios: Non-Federal physicians (M.D.'s) per 100,000 civilian population]

State	1970	1975	1985	1990	1992	1992 rank
United States [1]	148	169	220	237	248	
Alabama	90	103	152	170	183	40
Alaska	74	95	137	155	146	51
Arizona	144	185	220	233	233	20
Arkansas	92	103	150	165	179	33
California	194	219	266	272	273	11
Colorado	178	186	216	232	245	16
Connecticut	192	224	302	332	346	5
Delaware	134	155	203	217	228	21
District of Columbia	390	467	607	658	705	1
Florida	155	185	236	251	257	12
Georgia	108	126	172	187	196	35
Hawaii	160	185	239	266	283	9
Idaho	94	104	133	142	150	49
Illinois	138	164	217	229	247	15
Indiana	102	116	156	171	181	41
Iowa	103	113	149	167	175	44
Kansas	118	137	179	195	203	32
Kentucky	102	122	162	181	195	37
Louisiana	120	131	187	200	215	29
Maine	111	133	193	208	218	26
Maryland	183	217	334	360	374	3
Massachusetts	207	237	331	364	380	2
Michigan	125	145	190	201	212	30
Minnesota	151	172	223	240	255	13
Mississippi	84	94	126	144	149	50
Missouri	129	148	195	209	223	24
Montana	104	116	155	181	192	39
Nebraska	116	134	170	185	202	33
Nevada	114	129	173	175	166	47
New Hampshire	140	162	207	227	238	18
New Jersey	146	174	243	267	284	8
New Mexico	113	130	184	206	218	26
New York	236	258	318	339	360	4
North Carolina	111	132	185	209	221	25
North Dakota	96	106	168	184	202	33
Ohio	133	147	199	213	226	23
Oklahoma	103	113	149	160	168	46
Oregon	144	171	215	233	243	17
Pennsylvania	152	169	234	256	275	10
Rhode Island	160	194	248	277	294	7

TABLE C–21.—NON-FEDERAL PHYSICIAN/POPULATION RATIOS AND RANK BY STATE—
Continued

[Ratios: Non-Federal physicians (M.D.'s) per 100,000 civilian population]

State	1970	1975	1985	1990	1992	1992 rank
South Carolina	93	114	161	177	181	41
South Dakota	81	90	143	154	170	45
Tennessee	119	139	189	210	227	22
Texas	117	135	174	188	196	35
Utah	138	155	185	200	208	31
Vermont	187	207	268	288	301	6
Virginia	125	149	214	233	238	18
Washington	149	168	223	241	251	14
West Virginia	104	124	171	183	195	37
Wisconsin	120	137	188	207	216	28
Wyoming	101	108	140	156	158	48

[1] Excludes counts of physicians in U.S. possessions and with unknown addresses.

Source: American Medical Association, Physician Characteristics and Distribution in the U.S. 1993 edition. Table A–20.

The number of physicians in the United States is expected to continue to grow at a faster rate than the general population. According to the American Medical Association, there were 248 non-federal physicians per 100,000 population in 1992. The Department of Health and Human Services projects ratios of 271 in 2000 and 298 in 2020.

In 1992, about 35 percent of physicians were in primary care specialties, defined as general and family practice, internal medicine, and pediatrics.

Currently, there are approximately 88,620 residents in training. Growth in the number of residencies over the past twenty years reflects both steep increases in the number of first-year positions during the late 1970s and the increased length of training in many specialties. The number of U.S. medical school graduates, which rose rapidly in the late 1960s and early 1970s, has been relatively stable over the past decade (see table C–23).

Since the late 1970s, efforts to restrict the flow of international medical graduates (IMGs) have included stricter immigration laws and more rigorous competency requirements. As a result, table C–24 shows that IMGs dropped from over 40 percent of all residents in 1971 to about 17 percent in 1985. Since then, the percentage of IMGs has risen to 22 percent.

TABLE C–22.—PHYSICIAN SUPPLY FOR SELECTED SPECIALTIES, 1980–92

Specialty	Federal and non-federal physicians					
	1980		1985		1992	
	Total	Office based	Total	Office based	Total	Office based
Total physicians	467,679	272,000	552,716	330,197	653,062	389,364
Anesthesiology	15,958	11,338	22,021	15,300	28,148	19,998
Cardiovascular diseases	9,823	6,729	13,224	9,063	16,478	11,460
Dermatology	5,660	4,378	6,582	5,333	7,912	6,318
Diagnostic radiology	7,048	4,191	12,887	7,749	17,253	10,900
Emergency medicine	....	....	11,283	7,295	15,470	9,373
Family practice	27,530	18,378	40,021	29,694	50,969	40,479
Gastroenterology	4,046	2,737	5,917	4,136	7,946	5,724
General practice	32,519	29,642	27,030	24,579	20,719	18,575
General surgery	34,034	22,426	38,169	24,762	39,211	24,956
Internal medicine	71,531	40,617	90,417	52,891	109,017	65,312
Neurology	5,685	3,253	7,776	4,700	9,742	6,330
Neurological Surgery	3,341	2,468	4,019	2,880	4,501	3,310
Obstetrics/gynecology	26,305	19,513	30,867	23,543	35,273	27,115
Ophthalmology	12,974	10,603	14,881	12,221	16,433	13,742
Orthopedic surgery	13,996	10.728	17,166	13,045	20,640	15,832
Otolaryngology	6,553	5,266	7,267	5,755	8,373	6,646
Pathology [1]	13,642	6,081	15,767	7,054	17,428	8,155
Pediatrics [2]	29,462	18,210	36,839	23,211	45,921	29,668
Plastic Surgery	2,980	2,438	3,951	3,301	4,688	4,044
Psychiatry [3]	30,752	17,965	36,038	20,887	41,023	24,811
Pulmonary diseases	3,715	2,048	5,083	3,038	6,337	4,009
Radiology	11,653	7,802	10,109	7,363	7,848	5,854
Urological surgery	7,743	6,228	8,836	7,089	9,452	7,688
Other surgical specialties [4]	2,852	2,261	3,000	2,434	2,989	2,394
Other remaining specialties [5]	22,825	11,741	19,740	9,498	26,228	13,805
Unspecified	12,289	4,959	8,250	3,376	8,109	2,866
Other categories [6]	52,763	....	55,576	....	74,954	....

Note: Data for 1992 are as of January 1. Data for 1985 and before are as of December 31.

[1] Includes pathology and forensic pathology.
[2] Includes pediatrics and pediatric cardiology.
[3] Includes psychiatry and child psychiatry.
[4] Includes colon and rectal surgery and thoracic surgery.
[5] Includes aerospace medicine, allergy/immunology, general preventive medicine, nuclear medicine, occupational medicine, physical medicine and rehabilitation, public health, radiation oncology, and other.
[6] Includes not classified, inactive, and address unknown: these categories are included in total physicians only, not in office-based physicians.

Source: AMA Physician Masterfile for 1980, 1985, and 1992.

TABLE C–23.—MEDICAL SCHOOL GRADUATES, FIRST-YEAR RESIDENTS AND TOTAL RESIDENTS, 1965–92

Year	Medical school graduates	First-year residents	Total residents
1965	7,409	9,670	31,898
1966	7,574	10,316	31,898
1967	7,743	10,419	33,743
1968	7,973	10,464	35,047
1969	8,059	10,808	37,139
1970	8,367	11,552	39,463
1971	8,974	12,066	42,512
1972	9,551	11,500	45,081
1973	10,391	11,031	49,082
1974	11,613	11,628	52,685
1975	12,714	13,200	54,500
1976	(1)	14,258	56,872
1977	13,607	15,900	59,000
1978	14,393	16,800	63,163
1979	14,966	17,600	64,615
1980	15,135	18,702	61,465
1981	15,667	18,389	69,738
1982	15,985	18,976	69,142
1983	15,824	18,794	73,000
1984	16,327	19,539	75,125
1985	16,319	19,168	75,514
1986	16,125	18,183	76,815
1987	15,836	18,067	81,410
1988	15,887	17,941	81,093
1989	15,620	18,131	82,000
1990	15,336	18,322	82,902
1991	15,481	19,497	86,217
1992	15,386	19,794	88,620

[1] Not available.

Source: JAMA Medical Education issues.

TABLE C–24.—INTERNATIONAL GRADUATE MEDICAL RESIDENTS BY LOCATION OF EDUCATION AND CITIZENSHIP, 1971–92

	Total	Percent of all residents	U.S. citizens	Foreign nationals
1971	17,515	41	1,063	16,452
1976	16,634	29	1,783	14,851
1981	11,596	17	2,908	8,688
1983	14,084	19	4,961	9,123
1985	12,509	17	6,868	5,609
1991	17,017	20	5,107	11,910
1992	19,084	22	5,015	[1] 14,069

[1] Includes 6,192 permanent resident aliens.

Source: American Medical Association 1986 and JAMA Medical Education issues.

HEALTH INSURANCE COVERAGE

HEALTH INSURANCE STATUS IN 1992

Most people have some form of health insurance. In 1992, an estimated 85.4 percent of the total noninstitutionalized population had public or private coverage during at least part of the year. However, an estimated 37.3 million Americans, or 14.7 percent of the population, were without health insurance in 1992. All but 0.35 million of the uninsured were under age 65; consequently 16.6 percent of the nonelderly population were uninsured.

These estimates are based on an analysis of the March 1993 Current Population Survey (CPS), a household survey conducted by the Census Bureau of the Department of Commerce. Each year's March CPS asks whether individuals had coverage from selected sources of health insurance at any time during the preceding calendar year. Thus the March 1993 CPS reflects respondents' recollections of coverage during all of 1992.[2]

The questionnaires used in March 1988–93 differed from those used in previous years. In addition to the standard series of questions about sources of health insurance coverage, a separate part of the survey included further health insurance questions. Some respondents reported that they had no health insurance in one part of the questionnaire and reported that they had coverage in another part. Different analyses of the CPS data have used different assumptions in reconciling these discrepancies and other potential sources of error in the survey responses. Also, the March 1988–93 surveys included responses from population groups not surveyed in earlier surveys, including retirees and other nonworking individuals.

CHARACTERISTICS OF THE UNINSURED

Some segments of the population are more likely to have health insurance coverage than others, and different groups rely to a different extent on private insurance coverage and on public programs such as Medicare and Medicaid. Tables C–25 to C–27 divide the population according to age and income and show the sources of coverage for each group.[3] (The total noninstitutionalized population in 1992 was 253.9 million.)

---

[2] Some analysts have suggested that respondents may actually be reporting their coverage status at the time of the survey, rather than for the previous year.

[3] About 13 percent of the population reported more than one source of coverage during the year. The dual coverages many have been either at different points during the year or simultaneous. For the purpose of these tables, CRS has assigned each individual to one primary source of coverage according to the "coordination of benefits" rules typically used by private sector insurance companies.

TABLE C–25.—PERCENT OF U.S. NONINSTITUTIONALIZED POPULATION OBTAINING
HEALTH INSURANCE COVERAGE FROM SPECIFIED SOURCES, BY AGE, 1992

	Own job	Family member's job	Medicare	Medicaid	Other [1]	Uninsured
Age:						
Under 18	0.1	60.9	0.1	17.4	9.3	12.37
18 to 24	20.9	23.4	0.6	8.7	17.3	28.9
25 to 34	48.2	15.4	1.2	7.1	7.2	20.9
35 to 44	50.5	20.2	1.5	4.2	8.2	15.5
45 to 54	50.8	20.0	2.1	3.3	9.9	14.0
55 to 64	45.2	18.9	5.6	3.4	14.0	12.9
65 and over	4.4	9.0	84.8	0.1	0.5	1.2
Total	28.0	29.0	11.5	8.0	8.9	14.7

[1] "Other" includes, for example, privately purchased health insurance and Department of Veterans Affairs health care services.

Source: CRS analysis of data from the March 1993 Current Population Survey.

As table C–25 shows, the rate of insurance coverage is lowest among young adults; 28.9 percent of persons aged 18 to 24 were without coverage in 1992. Over the next several age groups, coverage rates increase, chiefly because older workers are more likely to obtain insurance through their own employment. Finally, the availability of Medicare to most individuals aged 65 and over meant that about 1 percent of this group was uninsured.

Table C–26 shows the percentage of the total uninsured population of each age group. Of the 37.3 million uninsured, 22.1 percent are children. Young adults (ages 18 to 24) total 18.8 percent and persons 25 to 34 total 23.4 percent of the uninsured.

TABLE C–26.—PERCENT OF U.S. NONINSTITUTIONALIZED POPULATION WITHOUT
HEALTH INSURANCE, BY AGE, 1992

Age	Percent of the uninsured
Under 18	22.1
18 to 24	18.8
25 to 34	23.4
35 to 44	16.7
45 to 54	10.7
55 to 64	7.3
65 and over	.95
Total	100.0

Note.—Items do not sum to 100.0 due to rounding.

Source: CRS analysis of data from the March 1993 Current Population Survey.

Table C–27 shows coverage rates by family income, expressed as a percentage of the Federal poverty income level. Those in the lowest income groups are least likely to have coverage. If they have coverage, the source is most likely to be Medicaid. As family income rises, both overall coverage rates and the degree of reliance on employer coverage increase.

TABLE C–27.—PERCENT OF U.S. NONINSTITUTIONALIZED POPULATION OBTAINING HEALTH INSURANCE COVERAGE FROM SPECIFIED SOURCES, BY FAMILY INCOME, 1992

Income as percent of poverty	Own job	Family member's job	Medicare	Medicaid	Other [1]	Uninsured
Under 50	2.3	4.0	6.1	49.2	8.7	29.6
50 to 99	5.3	8.6	17.7	32.2	8.4	27.8
100 to 133	10.5	17.1	21.3	13.8	9.5	27.8
134 to 185	16.7	24.5	18.6	6.7	9.3	24.3
185 to 249	24.0	33.1	14.8	2.5	9.0	16.7
250 and over	39.2	34.0	8.0	0.7	8.8	7.4
Total	28.0	28.9	11.5	7.9	8.9	14.7

[1] "Other" includes for example, privately purchased health insurance and Department of Veterans Affairs health care services.

Note.—Rows may not sum to 100.0 due to rounding.

Source: CRS analysis of data from the March 1993 Current Population Survey.

Table C–28 combines age and income and shows the percent of persons in each age/income group without health insurance. Overall, the trends shown in this table are similar to those in the previous tables: the rate of those without insurance drops with increasing age and income.

TABLE C–28.—PERCENT OF THE U.S. NONINSTITUTIONALIZED POPULATION WITHOUT HEALTH INSURANCE, BY AGE AND INCOME, 1992

Income as a percent of poverty level	Under 18	18 to 24	25 to 34	35 to 44	45 to 54	55 to 64	65 and over
Under 50	17.8	41.1	41.8	46.1	42.0	43.7	8.9
50 to 99	22.1	42.9	38.4	41.2	42.6	30.4	1.8
100 to 133	24.7	42.8	42.7	38.5	41.6	27.4	1.2
134 to 185	20.2	41.1	33.5	33.4	35.0	26.3	0.9
185 to 249	13.0	34.5	23.4	18.7	22.5	14.7	1.0
250 and over	4.5	18.1	11.7	6.9	6.5	6.3	0.7

Source: CRS analysis of data from the March 1993 Current Population Survey.

FACTORS IN EMPLOYMENT-BASED COVERAGE

In the United States, health insurance offered on a job is the single most important source of coverage. Employer plans covered 150.5 million Americans in 1992, or approximately 59.3 percent of the population. If only the nonaged are considered, this figure rises to over two-thirds. Persons covered under employer plans are almost equally divided between those obtaining coverage through their own work (77.0 million) and those obtaining coverage as dependents on another family member's policy (73.6 million).

One important factor in employment-based coverage is the degree of attachment to the labor force. Employers who provide coverage to their full-time workers may not offer that coverage to part-time employees. Workers in seasonal industries, who are employed only part of the year, are also less likely to be covered. Table C–29 shows the workforce attachment of the population without health insurance coverage in 1992. Over one-third of the uninsured, 14.0 million, worked only part time or part of the year, or were dependents of part time or part year workers, while another 16.1 percent had no work force attachment. However, 46.4 percent of the uninsured, approximately 17.3 million persons, were full year, full time workers or the dependents of such workers. All told, 31.4 million uninsured persons had at least some ties to the workforce.

The likelihood that workers will obtain coverage through their jobs is largely tied to two characteristics of employers: the size of the firm and the type of industry. Tables C–30 and C–32 show insurance coverage in 1992 for workers classed according to these two characteristics of their employers. As table C–30 indicates, workers in the smallest firms were least likely to obtain employer-based coverage and most likely to be uninsured.

TABLE C–29.—PERSONS WITHOUT HEALTH INSURANCE COVERAGE, BY ATTACHMENT TO THE WORKFORCE, 1992

[Thousands]

	Workers	Dependents	Total	Percent of un-insured
Nonworker	0	6,003	6,003	16.1
Full year/full time worker ..	9,633	7,708	17,342	46.4
Full year/part time worker .	1,892	813	2,706	7.2
Part year/full time worker ..	5,811	2,403	8,215	22.0
Part year/part time worker	2,529	560	3,090	8.3
Total	19,866	17,489	37,355	100.0

[1] Includes both heads of household and dependents with no workforce attachment.

Note.—Items may not sum to total due to rounding. Full year workers were employed 50 or more weeks during the year. Full time workers worked an average of 35 or more hours per week during the weeks they were employed.

Source: CRS analysis of data from the March 1993 Current Population Survey.

TABLE C–30.—PERCENT OF WORKERS OBTAINING HEALTH INSURANCE COVERAGE FROM SPECIFIED SOURCES, BY SIZE OF EMPLOYER, 1992

Firm size [1]	Own job	Family member's job	Medicare	Medicaid	Other [2]	Uninsured
1 to 9	14.0	25.6	5.1	6.2	21.9	27.2
10 to 24	25.0	29.0	2.3	7.1	11.3	25.3
25 to 99	33.3	31.7	2.1	5.7	8.1	19.2
100 to 499	39.3	35.7	1.6	4.8	5.5	12.9
500 to 999	41.3	39.4	1.1	3.3	5.5	9.3
1,000 and over	42.4	39.8	1.2	3.1	5.6	7.8
Unemployed or not in labor force	5.0	6.8	48.9	21.1	6.2	11.9
Total	28.0	29.9	11.5	7.9	8.9	14.7

[1] Firm size is that of the firm employing the worker for the longest period during the year.
[2] "Other" includes, for example, privately purchased health insurance and Department of Veterans Affairs health care services.
[3] Persons reporting coverage through their own current or past employment and also reporting that they did not work during the year. These include retirees, as well as some persons who responded inaccurately to one of the questions.

Source: CRS analysis of data from the March 1993 Current Population Survey.

TABLE C–31.—NUMBER OF WORKERS WITH HEALTH INSURANCE COVERAGE FROM SPECIFIED SOURCES, BY FIRM SIZE, 1992

[Thousands]

Firm size [1]	Own job	Family member's job	Medicare	Medicaid	Other [2]	Uninsured	Total
1 to 9	5,478.9	7,207.1	1,507.4	816.2	5,649.4	7,628.4	28,287.0
10 to 24	4,345.6	2,695.5	293.8	421.2	1,428.1	3,017.4	12,202.0
25 to 99	9,073.1	3,103.2	399.5	504.2	1,490.9	3,538.6	18,110.0
100 to 499	11,642.0	2,846.5	357.0	430.9	1,146.8	2,676.3	19,100.0
500 to 999	4,818.1	1,136.4	90.5	123.4	450.8	802.9	7,422.3
1,000 plus	33,262.0	6,749.7	693.2	923.7	3,006.6	4,760.5	49,396.0
Total	68,619.3	23,738.3	3,341.4	3,219.7	13,172.6	22,424.6	134,516.0

[1] Firm size is that of the firm employing the worker for the longest period during the year.
[2] "Other" includes, for example, privately purchased health insurance and Department of Veterans Affairs health care services.

Source: CRS analysis of data from the March 1993 Current Population Survey.

Table C–32 shows insurance coverage for workers by industry class. The industries showing the lowest rates of job-based coverage are those where employment is seasonal (as in agriculture or construction) and those that tend to use low-wage workers and/or part time workers (as in personal services, entertainment, and retail trade). Employer-provided health insurance is most common in industries with a stable work force, such as government, and those whose workers are generally in collective bargaining arrangements, such as manufacturing, transportation, and mining.

TABLE C–32.—PERCENT OF WORKERS OBTAINING HEALTH INSURANCE COVERAGE FROM SPECIFIED SOURCES, BY MAJOR INDUSTRY CLASS, 1992

Industry class [1]	Own job	Family member's job	Medicare	Medicaid	Other [2]	Uninsured
Agriculture, forestry and fisheries	10.6	19.1	5.8	8.2	26.6	29.4
Mining	37.0	46.3	1.1	2.8	5.0	7.7
Construction	22.2	31.0	1.7	5.9	12.4	26.6
Manufacturing, durable goods	39.2	42.9	1.1	2.6	4.2	9.9
Manufacturing, nondurable goods	40.0	37.9	1.5	4.1	4.9	13.5
Transportation, communications, and utilities	38.9	41.1	0.8	2.3	5.6	11.1
Wholesale trade	35.4	40.5	1.2	2.2	8.9	11.7
Retail trade	25.3	26.8	2.8	8.1	12.3	24.6
Finance, insurance, and real estate .	40.6	35.9	2.1	2.3	10.1	9.0
Business and repair services	24.6	29.0	2.7	7.4	12.3	23.9
Personal services, including household	17.2	21.6	6.1	10.5	13.7	30.9
Entertainment and recreation services	27.5	24.6	4.3	7.5	13.7	22.3
Professional and related services	40.5	33.5	2.6	3.8	9.7	9.8
Public administration	41.9	44.3	1.4	1.6	6.5	4.2

[1] Industry is that in which the worker was employed the longest during the year.
[2] "Other" includes, for example, privately purchased health insurance and Department of Veterans Affairs health care services.

Source: CRS analysis of data from the March 1993 Current Population Survey.

One major trend in employer health benefit plans in recent years is a shift towards self-insurance, under which an employer directly assumes the financial risk for health care costs incurred by their employees. A self-insured firm may use an insurance company only to perform administative tasks, such as claims processing, or it may carry out these functions in-house. Some firms are "partially insured"; they retain responsibility for most health care costs but buy protection for extraordinary expenses. Because of the financial risks involved, smaller firms are more likely to buy full coverage from a health insurance company.

TABLE C–33.—INSURANCE FUNDING ARRANGEMENTS BY FIRM SIZE, 1992

[Percent of conventional plans using arrangement]

Number of employees	1 to 24	25 to 99	100 to 999	1000 or more
Fully insured	91	90	67	46
Self-insured	9	10	33	54

Source: Health Insurance Association of America, Employer Sponsored Health Insurance in Private Sector Firms, 1992.

TRENDS IN HEALTH INSURANCE COVERAGE

An examination of the trends in health insurance coverage using the Current Population Survey is problematic because the health insurance questions asked by this survey and the types of individuals surveyed were changed beginning with the March 1988 survey. These changes result in a drop in the number of uninsured from 1986 to 1987 (and later years) that is unrelated to actual changes in insurance coverage. Thus, the data for 1986 and prior years are not comparable to data for 1987 and later years.

Between 1979 and 1986, the percent of the nonaged population who were uninsured increased from 14.6 percent to 17.5 percent. The number of uninsured would have been expected to grow from 28.4 to 30.8 million simply because the overall nonaged population grew. However, the number of nonaged uninsured actually grew from 28.4 million to 36.8 million. That is, the number of uninsured increased by 8.4 million people, yet only 2.4 million or 29 percent of the growth was due to an expanding nonaged population.

Table C–34 shows trends in the nonaged uninsured for selected years from 1979 to 1992. Most of the change in health insurance coverage occurred between 1979 and 1984; from 1984 to 1986, coverage rates remained fairly constant. The number and percent of the nonaged uninsured increased each year over the 1987–92 period, with the nonaged uninsured increasing to 37.0 million persons and 16.6 percent of the population in 1992.

To examine why the uninsured increased since 1979, table C–35 displays insurance coverage by source and year.

951

TABLE C–34.—NUMBER AND PERCENT OF THE NONAGED POPULATION WITHOUT HEALTH INSURANCE, 1979 AND 1983–92

	1979	1983	1984	1985	1986	1987[1]	1988[1]	1989[1]	1990[1]	1991[1]	1992[1]
Number uninsured (millions)	28.4	34.8	36.8	36.7	36.8	30.7	32.4	33.0	34.4	35.2	37.0
Percent uninsured (percent)	14.6	16.9	17.7	17.6	17.5	14.4	15.1	15.3	15.7	15.9	16.6

[1] Data for years after 1986 are not comparable to that for 1986 and prior years because of changes in the questions asked and the population groups surveyed.

Source: Table prepared by CRS based on data from the March 1980, and the March 1984 through the March 1993 CPS. Information from 1980 to 1982 is not presented due to errors on the CPS computer tapes for those years.

TABLE C–35.—SOURCES OF HEALTH INSURANCE COVERAGE BY YEAR FOR NONAGED POPULATION, 1979 AND 1983–92

	Percentage of nonelderly population										
	1979	1983	1984	1985	1986	1987[1]	1988[1]	1989[1]	1990[1]	1991[1]	1992[1]
Employment-based plans:											
Covered on own job	33.1	32.5	32.6	33.1	33.4	32.9	33.0	33.4	32.6	32.3	31.3
Covered through someone else	34.3	32.1	31.4	31.2	31.4	33.4	33.1	33.5	32.6	32.3	31.7
Total employment-based	67.4	64.6	64.0	64.3	64.8	66.3	66.1	66.9	65.2	64.6	63.0
Other plans[2]	17.9	18.5	18.3	18.1	17.7	19.3	18.8	17.8	19.0	19.5	20.4
Uninsured	14.6	16.9	17.7	17.6	17.5	14.4	15.1	15.3	15.7	15.9	16.6
Total	100.0	100.0	100.0	100.0	100.0	100.0	100.0	100.0	100.0	100.0	100.0

[1] Data for years after 1986 are not comparable to that for 1986 and prior years because of changes in the questions asked and the population groups surveyed.
[2] Excludes persons covered by employment-based plans.

Note.—Percentages may not add to 100.0 due to rounding.

Source: Table prepared by CRS based on data from the March 1980, and the March 1984 through the March 1993 CPS. Information from 1980 to 1982 is not presented due to errors on the CPS computer tapes for those years.

The most dramatic trend shown in table C–35 is the decline from 1979 to 1986 in the percent of the non-aged population covered by employment-based plans through another family member, from 34.3 percent to 31.4 percent. This proportion declined consistently between 1979 and 1984, and then leveled off. On the other hand, the percent of the nonelderly population covered by health insurance from their own work actually increased between 1979 and 1986 from 33.1 to 33.4 percent. This coverage declined during the early 1980s but increased by nearly a full percentage point between 1983 and 1986.

Coverage through one's own job increased slightly in 1988 and 1989 and has been declining since then to 31.3 percent in 1992. Coverage from someone else's job declined slightly in 1988, rose slightly in 1989, and has declined to 31.7 percent in 1992 below the 1987 level of 33.4 percent. Coverage from plans not employment-based declined from 1987 to 1989, then increased in 1991 exceeding the 1987 level.

Uncompensated Care Costs in PPS Hospitals, 1980–92

Uncompensated care is a term used to describe inpatient and outpatient care given to patients who are unable or unwilling to pay. It includes charity care and bad debts. Charity care is care given for which no payment is expected. Bad debt consists of charges that are not paid by uninsured individuals or partial charges, such as copayments, that are not paid by insured individuals. For this analysis, these charges have been adjusted to reflect the cost of care that was provided but not paid for.

Public hospitals and some private institutions receive government operating subsidies that at least partially offset their uncompensated care losses. These subsidies are not always directed specifically towards charity care, but they nonetheless serve to lessen the burden of a high charity care load. This analysis thus examines uncompensated care both before and net of government subsidies.

The information for this analysis was provided by the American Hospital Association from their Annual Survey of Hospitals. It describes the trend and distribution of uncompensated care in hospitals from 1980 to 1992.

The financial burden of uncompensated care increased substantially through the 1980s and continues to grow. Before offsetting operating subsidies from State and local governments, total uncompensated care costs in community hospitals increased 11.7 percent per year, reaching $14.9 billion by 1992 (see table C–36). Over the 12-year period, this is about 1 percent faster than the growth in total hospital costs. However, this masks the slowdown that occurred in more recent years. From 1980 to 1986, uncompensated care costs grew almost 3 percent faster than total hospital costs, but from 1986 to 1992, they grew almost 1 percent slower.

The portion of uncompensated care costs that was not covered by government operating subsidies grew even faster: 13 percent per year. This is because government subsidies have not increased as fast as total hospital cost inflation, with the lag being most pronounced starting in 1988 (see chart C–1). Between 1980 and 1992, the proportion of uncompensated care costs covered by government subsidies dropped from 28 percent to 19 percent.

The burden of uncompensated care is widespread. Uncompensated care has traditionally been associated with large, urban public hospitals; over the last decade, however, the problem increasingly affected the entire industry. In 1992, uncompensated care accounted for 6 percent of hospital costs before government subsidies and 5 percent net of government subsidies (see table C–37). Urban government and major public teaching hospitals carried the largest uncompensated care burden as a percentage of total expenses both before and after government subsidies; however, they also received the most relief from government subsidies. Geographically, rural hospitals receive proportionally less support than urban hospitals. Voluntary and proprietary hospitals, on average, receive almost no relief from uncompensated care through government subsidies, although they provide an amount of uncompensated care equal to 5 percent and 4 percent of total costs, respectively.

While a hospital's uncompensated care load is an important determinant of its overall financial condition, it is not the predominant factor in predicting financial performance. Perhaps the most important factor in this regard is the degree to which hospitals are able to generate revenue from other payers and non-patient care sources to cover their uncompensated care costs and Medicaid shortfalls.

TABLE C–36.—HOSPITAL UNCOMPENSATED CARE COSTS AND GOVERNMENT OPERATING SUBSIDIES, 1980–92

Measure	Amount (in billions)				Average annual percent change		
	1980	1986	1991	1992	1980–86	1986–92	1980–92
Uncompensated care costs before government subsidies	$3.6	$8.9	$13.4	$14.9	14.7	8.9	11.7
Government operating subsidies	1.1	2.0	2.6	2.8	10.6	6.0	8.2
Uncompensated care costs net of government subsidies	2.8	6.9	10.8	12.1	16.1	9.7	12.8
Proportion of uncompensated care costs covered by government subsidies (percent)	27.7	22.3	19.6	18.9	....	....	....

Note.—Includes all community hospitals.

Source: ProPAC analysis of American Hospital Association Annual Survey data.

CHART C–1. CUMULATIVE GROWTH IN UNCOMPENSATED CARE COSTS AND GOVERNMENT SUBSIDIES, 1980–92

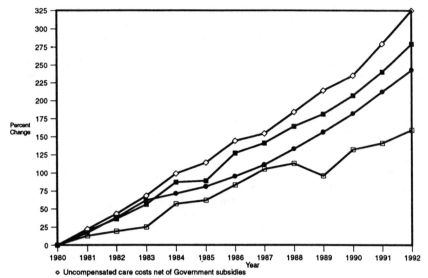

◇ Uncompensated care costs net of Government subsidies
■ Uncompensated care costs before Government subsidies
● Total hospital costs
□ Government operating subsidies

SOURCE: ProPAC analysis of AHA Annual Survey data.

TABLE C–37.—HOSPITAL UNCOMPENSATED CARE COSTS AS A PERCENT OF TOTAL COSTS, BY HOSPITAL GROUP, 1992

[In percent]

Hospital group	Uncompensated care costs before government subsidies	Uncompensated care costs net of government subsidies
All hospitals	6.0	4.9
Large urban	6.4	4.9
Other urban	5.6	4.9
Rural	5.3	4.8
Voluntary	4.8	4.6
Proprietary	3.9	3.9
Urban government	14.4	6.9
Rural government	6.5	5.0
Major teaching:		
Public	17.9	7.3
Non-public	5.3	4.8
Other teaching	4.9	4.9
Non-teaching	4.6	4.6
Disproportionate share:		
Large urban	8.3	5.7
Other urban	6.8	5.6
Rural	6.5	6.2
Non-disproportionate share	4.2	4.1

Note: Includes data for all community hospitals, except teaching and DSH hospitals which are PPS hospitals only.

Source: ProPAC analysis of American Hospital Association Annual Survey data.

INTERNATIONAL HEALTH SPENDING [4]

This section analyzes trends in health expenditures for 24 Organization for Economic Cooperation and Development (OECD) countries from 1970 to 1991. Table C–38 illustrates total health expenditures as a percentage of gross domestic product (GDP). In 1970, the mean percent of GDP was 5.1 percent, with the United States being 45 percent higher than the average with 7.4 percent of GDP. By 1991, the overall mean percent of GDP comprised of health expenditures had increased to 7.9 percent while the United States health spending as a share of GDP had increased to 13.4 percent, some 70 percent greater than the overall average.

The second to the last column in table C–38 presents per capita health expenditures denominated in U.S. dollars. The last column illustrates public health expenditures as a percent of total health

[4] The data and analysis in this section are from Health Affairs, "Health Care Systems in Twenty-four Countries," by George J. Schieber, Jean-Pierre Poullier, and Leslie M. Greenwald, Fall 1991. Also, OECD press release, March 5, 1993.

spending. This ranged from 61 percent in the United States to over 90 percent in Luxembourg, Norway, Sweden, Germany, Iceland, Ireland, Spain, Switzerland, and the U.K. with an OECD average of 84.2 percent.

TABLE C–38.—TOTAL HEALTH EXPENDITURE AS A PERCENTAGE OF GROSS DOMESTIC PRODUCT [GDP], PER CAPITA HEALTH SPENDING AND PERCENT OF MEDICAL EXPEND-ITURES COVERED BY PUBLIC INSURANCE SCHEME, FOR SELECTED CALENDAR YEARS 1960–91

[In percent except per capita]

Country	1960	1970	1980	1985	1990	1991	Per capita	Percent [1]
Australia	4.9	5.7	7.3	7.7	8.2	8.6	$1,407	70.0
Austria	4.4	5.4	7.9	8.1	8.3	8.4	1,448	84.0
Belgium	3.4	4.1	6.6	7.4	7.6	7.9	1,377	86.0
Canada	5.5	7.1	7.4	8.5	9.5	10.0	1,915	84.0
Denmark	3.6	6.1	6.8	6.3	6.3	6.5	1,151	85.0
Finland	3.9	5.7	6.5	7.2	7.8	8.9	1,426	82.0
France	4.2	5.8	7.6	8.5	8.8	9.1	1,650	74.5
Germany	4.8	5.9	8.4	8.7	8.3	8.5	1,659	92.0
Greece	2.9	4.0	4.3	4.9	5.4	5.2	404	85.0
Iceland	3.5	5.2	6.4	7.1	8.3	8.4	1,447	93.0
Ireland	4.0	5.6	9.2	8.2	7.0	7.3	840	90.0
Italy	3.6	5.2	6.9	7.0	8.1	8.3	1,408	75.0
Japan	3.0	4.6	6.6	6.6	6.6	6.6	1,267	87.0
Luxembourg	N/A	4.1	6.8	6.8	7.2	7.2	1,494	91.0
Netherlands	3.9	6.0	8.0	8.0	8.2	8.3	1,360	71.0
Norway	3.3	5.0	6.6	6.4	7.4	7.6	1,305	90.0
New Zealand	4.3	5.2	7.2	6.5	7.2	7.6	1,050	N/A
Portugal	N/A	3.1	5.9	7.0	6.7	6.8	624	N/A
Spain	1.5	3.7	5.6	5.7	6.6	6.7	848	90.0
Sweden	4.7	7.2	9.4	8.8	8.6	8.6	1,443	94.0
Switzerland	3.3	5.2	7.3	7.6	7.8	7.9	1,713	91.0
Turkey	N/A	N/A	4.0	2.8	4.0	4.0	142	N/A
United Kingdom	3.9	4.5	5.8	6.0	6.2	6.6	1,035	93.0
United States	5.3	7.4	9.2	10.5	12.4	13.4	2,867	61.0
OECD Average	3.9	5.1	7.0	7.2	7.6	7.9	1,262	84.2

[1] Percent of medical expenditures covered by public insurance scheme.

Source: Schieber, George J. and Jean-Pierre Poullier. "International Health Spending: Issues and Trends." Health Affairs, Spring 1991 p. 109; Schieber, George J., Jean-Pierre Poullier, and Leslie M. Greenwald, "Health Care Systems in Twenty-four Countries." Health Affairs, Fall 1991, p. 24. Also, OECD press release, March 5, 1993.

APPENDIX D. MEDICARE REIMBURSEMENT TO HOSPITALS

Medicare part A provides reimbursement for inpatient hospital care through a payment system based on prospectively set rates, the prospective payment system (PPS), for hospital cost reporting periods beginning on or after October 1, 1983.

Before the passage of the Social Security Amendments of 1983 (P.L. 98–21) the Medicare program reimbursed hospitals according to the reasonable costs they incurred in providing services to Medicare beneficiaries. Because the actual reasonable costs could not be determined until after the hospital had provided the services and reported its costs to the Medicare program, this method of reimbursement was known as retrospective cost-based reimbursement.

Under authority provided by the Social Security Amendments of 1972 (P.L. 92–603), the Department of Health and Human Services (HHS) placed certain limits on inpatient routine operating costs recognized as reasonable (referred to as section 223 limits for the specific section in the law). The Tax Equity and Fiscal Responsibility Act of 1982 (P.L. 97–248, commonly referred to as TEFRA) expanded previously existing limits to include all other inpatient hospital operating costs. Further, it established a new 3-year Medicare ceiling (or target rate) on the allowable annual rate of increase in operating costs per case for inpatient hospital services. TEFRA also required that HHS develop proposals for the prospective payment of hospitals under Medicare. The proposal from HHS was presented to the Congress at the end of 1982.

Legislation based on this prospective payment proposal was enacted in Public Law 98–21, which established a new method of Medicare reimbursement for hospital inpatient care—the prospective payment system (PPS). This appendix describes the major reimbursement provisions of PPS.

GENERAL SUMMARY

Medicare payment for hospital inpatient services is made according to a prospective payment system, rather than a retrospective cost-based system. Medicare payments are made at predetermined, specific rates which represent the average cost, nationwide, of treating a Medicare patient according to his or her medical condition. The classification system used to group hospital inpatients according to their diagnoses is known as diagnosis-related groups (DRGs). Separate DRG rates apply depending on whether a hospital is located in a large urban area (greater than 1 million population, or 970,000 in New England), other urban area, or rural area of the country, as determined by the Office of Management and Budget (OMB) Metropolitan Statistical Area (MSA) system.

During a 4-year transition period, a declining portion of the total prospective payment was based on a hospital's historical reasonable costs and an increasing portion was based on a combination of regional and national Federal DRG rates. In the fifth year of the program (fiscal year 1988) and thereafter, Medicare payments are generally determined under a national DRG payment methodology. Special transition provisions apply to hospitals located in certain geographic regions.

If a hospital can treat a patient for less than the payment amount, it can keep the savings. If the treatment costs more, the hospital must absorb the loss. A hospital is prohibited from charging Medicare beneficiaries any amounts (except for deductibles, copayment amounts, and for services not covered by Medicare) which represent any difference between the hospital's cost of providing covered care and the Medicare DRG payment amount.

Certain hospital costs are excluded from the prospective payment system and are paid on a reasonable cost basis. In addition, certain hospitals are excluded from the new system and continue to be reimbursed on a reasonable cost basis, subject to rate of increase limits. Authority is provided for States to establish their own all-payer hospital payment systems if they meet certain Federal requirements.

BASIC PAYMENT SYSTEM

Unless excluded from the prospective payment system, each Medicare participating hospital is paid a predetermined payment rate per discharge for each type of patient treated. Types of patients are defined by the diagnosis related groups patient classification system which assigns each hospital inpatient to one of 487 patient categories (DRGs) based on the diagnosis and the type of treatment received (medical or surgical).

The payment rate for each DRG is the product of two components: a base payment amount which applies for all DRGs, and a relative weighting factor for the particular DRG. The base payment amount is intended to represent the cost of a typical (average) Medicare inpatient case. The relative weighting factor represents the relative costliness of an average case in the particular DRG compared to the cost of the overall average Medicare case (i.e., relative to the base payment amount). When the DRG relative weights are each multiplied by the base payment amount, the result is a complete set of prices for all DRGs. Separate DRG rates apply to hospitals located in large urban, other urban, or rural areas (separate base payment amounts apply in these areas, but the DRG relative weighting factors are the same). In addition, the base payment amount (and, therefore, each DRG rate) is adjusted for area differences in hospital wage levels compared to the national average hospital wage level.

Transition period

Although the transition to prospective payment rates was completed in fiscal year 1988, special transition provisions apply to hospitals located in certain geographic regions.

In a few regions with historically higher costs, Public Law 100–203 provided for the continued use of Federal amounts based in part on regional rates until September 30, 1990. Under this transition provision, known as the "regional floor," the DRG payment rate is determined as the higher of 100 percent of the national amount, or 85 percent of the national amount plus 15 percent of the regional amount.

Public Law 101–403, the Continuing Resolution of October 1, 1990, extended the regional floor provision on a budget neutral basis through October 20, 1990. Public Law 101–508 (OBRA 1990) extended the regional floor provision for discharges occurring before October 1, 1993, not subject to budget neutrality. Public Law 103–66 (OBRA 1993) extended the provision until October 1, 1996.

Update factors

PPS payment rates are updated each year using an "update factor." The annual update factor applied to increase the Federal base payment amounts is determined, in part, by the projected increase in the hospital market basket index. The market basket index measures the cost of goods and services purchased by hospitals, yielding one price inflator for all hospitals in a given year. Table 1 shows the categories of expense used in developing the index. The update factor also includes adjustments for increases in hospital productivity, technological change, and other factors that affect the level of operating cost per discharge. The annual update factor is also adjusted to include increases in average payments per case attributable to increases in case mix due to changes in coding and reporting accuracy.

Before fiscal year 1988, the same factor was used for all hospitals; however, in subsequent years separate factors have been applied to hospitals according to their locations. Separate update factors were set for hospitals located in large urban, other urban, and rural areas. Beginning October 1, 1994, the other urban and rural standardized amounts will be equalized. Table D–2 compares the hospital market basket increases to actual updates for the past 11 years and shows the increases in PPS payments per case that resulted from the updates and other policy changes.

From October 1, 1990, through October 20, 1990, the PPS hospital update factors were set equal to the full market basket increase. Public Law 101–508 provided for a freeze in hospital payments at fiscal year 1990 levels for the period from October 21, 1990, through December 31, 1990. For this period, the market basket percentage increase applicable to PPS and PPS-exempt hospitals was deemed to be equal to zero (0) percent.

OBRA 1990 (Public Law 101–508) set separate update factors for hospitals located in large and other urban areas, and for hospitals located in rural areas. The factors were designed to eliminate the payment differential between other urban and rural hospitals by fiscal year 1995. For large and other urban hospitals, the following update factors are: for fiscal year 1991, for discharges occurring on or after January 1, 1991, the market basket increase (MBI) minus 2.0 percentage points; for fiscal year 1992, the MBI minus 1.6 percentage points; for fiscal year 1993, the MBI minus 1.55 percentage points; and for fiscal year 1994–95, the full MBI.

TABLE D–1.—HOSPITAL PROSPECTIVE PAYMENT INPUT PRICE INDEX (THE "MARKET BASKET"), EXPENSE CATEGORIES AND RATES OF PRICE CHANGE FOR SELECTED FEDERAL FISCAL YEARS.

Expense categories	Base year FFY 1987 weights[1]	FFY percentage rates of price change					
		1990(H)	1991(H)	1992(H)	1993(H)	1994(P)	1995(P)
Total	100.00	4.8	4.3	3.0	3.0	3.4	3.7
1. Wages and Salaries(L)	52.22	5.0	4.6	3.7	3.1	3.1	3.2
2. Employee Benefits(L)	9.50	7.8	7.0	6.2	5.9	5.7	6.0
3. Professional Fees(L)	1.65	4.8	4.5	4.0	3.4	3.3	3.3
4. Energy and Utilities	2.37	8.2	7.5	-5.0	1.0	4.7	3.7
A. Fuel Oil, Coal, and Other Petroleum	0.62	21.9	11.4	-14.4	-2.2	12.0	5.9
B. Electricity	1.14	2.7	7.1	1.8	1.2	0.3	1.7
C. Natural Gas	0.34	-1.2	-0.9	-1.9	10.2	4.7	2.5
D. Motor Gasoline	0.23	11.1	8.4	-11.2	-2.8	5.9	7.6
E. Water and Sewerage	0.04	6.6	6.9	7.1	5.9	5.7	5.6
5. Professional Liability Insurance	1.43	-0.6	-2.5	4.8	4.3	6.1	8.6
6. All Other	32.84	3.7	3.2	1.5	1.9	2.7	3.5
A. All Other Products	21.79	3.3	2.8	1.1	1.9	2.2	3.2
1. Pharmaceuticals	3.87	9.2	8.3	7.2	5.0	4.4	4.9
2. Food	3.30	4.1	1.8	0.9	1.3	2.6	2.8
a. Direct Purchase	2.11	3.7	0.7	0.0	1.1	2.6	2.4
b. Contract Service	1.19	4.7	3.8	2.4	1.7	2.6	3.6
3. Chemicals	3.13	-3.1	2.3	-4.4	1.5	1.2	3.7
4. Medical Instruments	2.67	3.0	1.7	1.9	2.5	2.3	2.9
5. Photographic Supplies	2.62	5.1	-0.3	-0.7	-0.8	0.7	1.7
6. Rubber and Plastics	2.32	0.7	1.9	-0.3	0.9	0.5	0.8
7. Paper Products	1.40	1.7	-0.4	-2.1	-0.4	2.1	5.2
8. Apparel	1.14	3.0	2.1	1.6	1.9	1.9	2.1
9. Machinery and Equipment	0.50	3.1	2.3	0.5	0.5	1.3	2.3

961

	Weight[1]						
10. Miscellaneous Products	0.83	4.6	3.8	0.8	1.6	1.5	2.9
B. All Other Services	11.05	4.3	3.8	2.4	1.9	3.7	4.1
1. Business Services(L)	3.85	4.9	3.2	2.4	1.4	3.0	4.1
2. Computer Services(L)	1.99	6.9	4.1	1.3	3.1	3.5	3.6
3. Transportation and Shipping	1.23	4.1	5.7	1.0	3.1	4.4	5.0
4. Telephone	0.99	0.4	1.3	1.2	0.2	2.0	2.4
5. Blood Services(L)	0.59	0.3	-0.1	6.5	-0.2	1.4	2.6
6. Postage(L)	0.37	0.0	10.8	4.9	0.0	20.0	13.2
7. All Other Labor Intensive Services(L)	1.23	3.9	4.1	3.4	2.1	2.9	3.4
8. All Other Non-Labor Intensive Services	0.80	5.0	5.0	3.0	3.0	2.9	3.2

[1] Weights may not sum to 100.00 due to rounding.
L=Considered labor-related.
H=Historical data subject to change only upon revision of underlying series.
P=Projected data subject to change in future forecasts.
FFY=Federal Fiscal Year.

Source: Health Care Financing Administration, OACT, release of the DRI/McGraw-Hill Fourth Quarter Forecast, December, 1993.

The update factors for rural hospitals are: for fiscal year 1991, for discharges occurring on or after January 1, 1991, the MBI minus 0.7 percentage points; for fiscal year 1992, the MBI minus 0.6 percentage points; for fiscal year 1993, the MBI minus 0.55 percentage points; for fiscal year 1994, the MBI plus 1.5 percentage points; and for fiscal year 1995, the amount necessary to provide rural hospitals with an average standardized amount equal to that of other urban hospitals.

OBRA 1993 (Public Law 103–66) reestablished the update factors for fiscal years 1994 and 1995; however, it still completed the transition to eliminate the payment differential between urban and rural hospitals by fiscal year 1995. The legislated update factors are as follows: for fiscal year 1994, MBI–2.5 percent for large and other urban hospitals and MBI–1.0 percent for rural hospitals; for fiscal year 1995, MBI–2.5 percent for large and other urban hospitals and "an amount necessary to equalize the rural and urban standardized amounts" for rural hospitals; in fiscal year 1996, all hospitals will receive an update of MBI–2.0 percent; in fiscal year 1997, the update for all hospitals is MBI–0.5 percent; for fiscal year 1998 and thereafter, hospitals receive the full MBI.

For fiscal year 1994, the market basket increase is estimated to be 4.3 percent, providing the following net fiscal year update factors: for large and other urban hospitals, 1.8 percent; for rural hospitals, 3.3 percent.

DRG weighting factors

Public Law 98–21 required the HHS Secretary to adjust the DRG definitions and weighting factors in fiscal year 1986 and at least every 4 years thereafter to reflect changes in treatment patterns, technology, and other factors which may change the relative use of hospital resources. Public Law 99–509, however, required the Secretary to adjust the DRG definitions and weighting factors each year, beginning in fiscal year 1988.

OBRA 1989 required the Secretary to reduce the weighting factor for each DRG by 1.22 percent for discharges in fiscal year 1990. In addition, the Secretary is prohibited from adjusting DRG weighting factors on other than a budget neutral basis beginning in fiscal year 1991.

Table D–3 shows the 20 DRGs accounting for the largest numbers of Medicare inpatient discharges during fiscal year 1992. DRG relative weights appear in table D–21 at the end of this appendix.

Source and calculation of the hospital wage index

The hospital wage index is used to adjust a hospital's base payment amount for the wage level of the hospital's area. This is accomplished by multiplying the labor-related component of the Federal portion of the payment amount by a wage index. The wage index is intended to measure the average wage level for hospital workers in each urban area (metropolitan statistical area or MSA) or rural area (non-MSA parts of States) relative to the national average wage level.

TABLE D–2.—COMPARISON OF INCREASES IN HOSPITAL MARKET BASKET, PPS
UPDATES, AND PPS PAYMENTS PER CASE, FISCAL YEARS 1984–94

(In percent)

Fiscal year	Increases in hospital market basket [1]	Actual update	Increase in PPS payments per case [2]
1984	4.9	4.7	18.5
1985	4.0	4.5	10.5
1986	4.3	.5	3.1
1987	3.7	1.2	5.3
1988	4.7	1.5	5.8
Large urban [3]		1.5	
Other urban [4]		1.0	
Rural		3.0	
1989	5.4	3.3	6.5
Large urban		3.4	
Other urban		2.9	
Rural		3.9	
1990	5.5	[5] 4.7	5.3
Large urban		[5] 4.4	
Other urban		[5] 3.7	
Rural		[5] 8.4	
1991	5.2	3.4	5.5
Large urban		3.2	
Other urban		3.2	
Rural		4.5	
1992	4.4	3.0	4.9
Large urban		2.8	
Other urban		2.8	
Rural		3.8	
1993	4.1	2.7	3.7
Large urban		2.6	
Other urban		2.6	
Rural		3.6	
1994	4.3	2.0	2.9
Large urban		1.8	
Other urban		1.8	
Rural		3.3	

[1] Based on data available when final PPS rule was issued.

[2] Increases for 1984 through 1991 based on data from Medicare Cost Reports, which correspond to hospital cost reporting periods, rather than Federal fiscal years. Increases for 1992 through 1994 based on PPS update and estimated case-mix index increase.

[3] Large urban = metropolitan areas with populations of one million or more.

[4] Other urban = metropolitan areas with populations of less than one million.

[5] Actual updates for fiscal year 1990 adjusted to reflect 1.22 percent across-the-board reduction in DRG weights.

Source: ProPAC.

TABLE D–3.—SHORT STAY HOSPITAL DISCHARGES, TWENTY DIAGNOSIS-RELATED GROUPS WITH THE MOST DISCHARGES IN FISCAL YEAR 1992

DRG description	Discharges	Percent total	Average length of stay (days)
Total, all DRGs	10,992,430	100.0	8.4
20 Leading DRGs	4,801,419	43.7	8.7
127 Heart failure and shock	662,105	6.0	7.4
89 Simple pneumonia and pleurisy [1]	393,665	3.6	8.4
14 Specific cerebrovascular disorders except transient ischemic attack	353,510	3.2	9.4
140 Angina pectoris	332,895	3.0	4.3
209 Major joint and limb reattachment procedures	300,260	2.7	9.5
88 Chronic obstructive pulmonary disease	291,325	2.7	7.2
182 Esophagitis, gastroenteritis, and miscellaneous digestive disorders	231,640	2.1	6.0
296 Nutritional and miscellaneous metabolic disorders [1]	223,210	2.0	7.9
430 Psychoses	223,175	2.0	16.9
174 G.I. Hemmorrhage [2]	221,200	2.0	6.6
138 Cardiac arrhythmia and conduction disorders [2]	196,638	1.8	6.8
320 Kidney and urinary tract infections [1]	168,770	1.5	7.9
79 Respiratory infections and inflammations [1]	161,240	1.5	11.2
112 Vascular procedures except major reconstruction without pump	159,995	1.5	6.8
121 Circulatory disorders with acute myocardial infarction and cerebrovascular complications, discharged alive	158,276	1.4	9.1
416 Septicemia [2]	154,045	1.4	10.0
462 Rehabilitation	149,510	1.4	19.0
148 Major small and large bowel procedures [2]	146,625	1.3	16.8
124 Circulatory disorders except acute myocardial infarction, with cardiac catheterization and complex diagnosis	138,315	1.3	6.7
16 Transient ischemic attack & precerebral occlusions	135,020	1.2	6.2

[1] Age greater than 17, with complications.
[2] With complications.

Source: Health Care Financing Administration, Bureau of Data Management and Stragtegy, data from the Medicare Decision Support System; data development by the Office of Research and Demonstrations.

Until May 1, 1986, the index was based on compensation and employment data for hospital workers, for calendar year 1981, as reported to the Bureau of Labor Statistics in the U.S. Department of Labor. The wage index reflected average hospital wages in each urban and rural area as a percentage of the national average hospital wage. However, because many hospitals relied on varying proportions of part-time employment, there was a concern that the wage index tended to understate actual levels of hospital hourly wage rates in facilities that relied heavily on part-time workers.

In final regulations published on September 1, 1987 (52 FR 33039, Sept. 1, 1987), the Secretary changed the method of calculating the national average wage level, and updated the wage index data. The national average wage level was calculated by dividing national aggregate wages and salaries by the national aggregate number of paid hours of hospital employment. Under this method, the index as a whole was not likely to be sensitive to minor changes in the data for individual labor market areas.

Public Law 100–203 (OBRA 1987) required the Secretary to update the wage index by October 1, 1990, and at least every 3 years thereafter. Updates are to be based on a periodic survey of the wages and wage related costs of PPS hospitals. To the extent feasible, the survey must be designed to measure earnings and hours of paid employment by occupational category, and to permit exclusion of the wages and wage related costs hospitals incur in providing skilled nursing facility services.

OBRA 1989, required the Secretary to update the area wage index annually, beginning in fiscal year 1993, in a budget neutral manner.

For discharges occurring on or after January 1, 1991, and before October 1, 1993, OBRA 1990 requires the use of a wage index based solely on a 1988 wage survey. OBRA 1990 requires the Secretary to apply the wage index without regard to previous surveys of wages and wage-related costs. Tables D–18, D–19, and D–20, at the end of this appendix, give the current wage index values for each metropolitan area, for all rural areas in a state, and a special index for hospitals that are reclassified as urban areas.

The calculation of the index begins with the area average hospital hourly wage. For each MSA or non-MSA area (i.e., all non-MSA counties in a State) total county compensation and total paid hours data are summed separately over all counties included in the area. Then aggregate hospital compensation for the area is divided by aggregate paid hours of hospital employment in the area to produce the area average hourly wage. The hospital wage index is calculated by dividing the average hourly wage for each area by the national average hourly wage (determined by dividing national aggregate compensation by national aggregate paid hours of employment).

This procedure results in an index number, such as 0.9175 (Asheville, North Carolina) or 1.2165 (Sacramento, California), for each MSA or non-MSA area in the United States. Since the national average wage level is represented by an index value of 1.000, the wage index value for any area has a direct and simple interpretation. The value of 1.2165 for Sacramento means that the hourly wage rate for hospital workers is 21.65 percent higher in the Sacramento MSA than nationwide.

Thus, in computing the Federal portion of the hospital payment rates applicable for hospitals in the Sacramento MSA, the labor-related component of the national large urban adjusted standardized payment amount ($2,646.19) is multiplied by 1.2165 in order to adjust for the higher level of hourly wage rates in this area. Similarly, the calculation of the labor portion of the rates for hospitals in Asheville would involve a reduction in the published labor-related component of the national adjusted standardized payment amount, to reflect the fact that hourly wage levels in this MSA are 8.25 percent lower than the national average (as indicated by the wage index value of 0.9175).

SAMPLE PAYMENT CALCULATION

The Federal large urban, other urban, and rural base payment amounts per discharge for fiscal year 1994 were published in the Federal Register on September 1, 1993 (see table D-4). The payment rates for most hospitals are computed using the national adjusted operating standardized amounts. However, hospitals located in regions where the regional rate (sum of labor and non-labor portions) is higher than the national rate may use a blended rate equal to 85 percent of the national rate plus 15 percent of the regional rate. Puerto Rico has its own adjusted operating standardized amounts for DRG payment purposes, which are based on a blend of the Puerto Rico-specific large urban, other urban, or rural amount and a special national amount.

Each payment amount is divided into a labor-related component and a nonlabor related component. The sum of these components represents the base payment amount that would apply for a hospital located in an area with a wage index of 1.0 (i.e., average wage rates for hospital workers in the area match the national average of hospital wage rates across all areas).

The basic payment to a hospital for a case in a particular DRG is the applicable national (or blend of national and regional, if appropriate) payment amount, adjusted by the local wage index value and multiplied by the weighting factor for the DRG.

For an example of a payment calculation, assume a hospital is located in Washington, DC. Such a hospital would be in a large urban area in the South Atlantic census region. As this is not one of the regions affected by the regional floor, payment is based on the large urban national standardized amount. First, the labor-related portion of this amount ($2,646.19 in fiscal year 1994) is multiplied by the appropriate wage index (1.0828 for Washington, DC):

$$\$2,646.19 \times 1.0828 = \$2,865.29$$

To this total is added the nonlabor-related portion of the standardized amount:

$$\$2,865.29 + \$1,090.21 = \$3,955.50$$

For each discharge, this new total is then multiplied by the relative weight factor for the DRG to which the case has been assigned. These weights range from a low of 0.1240 for DRG 382 (false labor) to a high of 19.4679 for DRG 480 (liver transplant). The payment rates for the sample hospital in fiscal year 1994 would therefore vary from a low of \$490.48 (\$3,955.50×0.1240) to a high of \$77,005.27 (\$3,955.50×19.4679).

In addition to the basic payment amount for each case, additional payments may be made to teaching hospitals and hospitals that serve a disproportionate share of low-income patients. Any hospital may receive additional payments for outliers (cases with extraordinarily high costs or a very long stay, relative to other cases in the DRG) and for treatment of beneficiaries with end stage renal disease. Finally, certain hospital costs are excluded from PPS and reimbursed separately. The next sections of this appendix discuss additional PPS payments and the separate reimbursement of excluded costs.

TABLE D-4.—NATIONAL AND REGIONAL ADJUSTED STANDARDIZED AMOUNTS, LABOR/NONLABOR, FISCAL YEAR 1994

	Large urban		Other urban		Rural	
	Labor related	Nonlabor related	Labor related	Nonlabor related	Labor related	Nonlabor related
National average	$2,646.19	$1,090.21	$2,604.30	$1,072.95	$2,698.19	$869.31
Regional:						
New England (CT, ME, MA, NH, RI, VT)	2,778.92	1,138.39	2,734.93	1,120.37	2,991.46	1,031.69
Middle Atlantic (PA, NJ, NY)	2,496.61	1,078.50	2,457.09	1,061.43	2,864.92	975.30
South Atlantic (DE, DC, FL, GA, MD, NC, SC, VA, WV)	2,665.05	995.33	2,622.86	979.58	2,738.74	845.71
East North Central (IL, IN, MI, OH, WI)	2,810.97	1,177.65	2,766.47	1,159.00	2,773.33	939.95
East South Central (AL, KY, MS, TN)	2,557.71	901.26	2,517.22	886.99	2,714.37	788.64
West North Central (IA, KS, MN, MO, NB, ND, SD)	2,665.81	1,073.03	2,623.60	1,056.05	2,638.17	842.55
West South Central (AR, LA, OK, TX)	2,650.47	988.59	2,608.51	972.95	2,530.11	774.85
Mountain (AZ, CO, ID, MT, NV, NM, UT, WY)	2,556.76	1,058.92	2,516.28	1,042.16	2,558.62	891.18
Pacific (AK, CA, HI, OR, WA)	2,487.02	1,209.59	2,447.65	1,190.44	2,488.47	1,003.96
Puerto Rico:						
Regional	2,379.97	494.98	2,342.29	487.14	1,839.16	396.47
National	2,644.11	1,028.04				

Source: Federal Register, September 1, 1993.

ADDITIONAL PAYMENT AMOUNTS

In addition to the DRG prospective payment rates, Medicare payments are made to hospitals for the following items or services:

Graduate medical education

Financing of graduate medical education, the period of training following medical school, is provided predominantly through inpatient revenues (both hospital payments and faculty physician fees) and a complex mix of Federal and State government funds. The federal government is the largest single explicit financing source for graduate medical education through the Medicare program and through its support of residencies in Veterans Administration hospitals. Medicare recognizes the costs of graduate medical education under two mechanisms: direct medical education payments and an indirect medical education adjustment. In fiscal year 1993, Medicare paid approximately $1.7 billion in direct medical education payments and $3.7 billion in indirect adjustments.

Direct medical education costs

The direct costs of approved medical education programs (such as the salaries of residents and teachers and other education costs for residents, and for nurses, and allied health professionals trained in provider-operated programs) are excluded from the prospective payment system. The direct medical education costs for the training of nurses and allied health professionals in provider-operated programs are paid for on a reasonable cost basis.

Public Law 99–272 (COBRA), replaced reasonable cost reimbursement for graduate medical education through residency training programs for physicians, with formula payments based on each hospital's per resident costs. Medicare's payment to each hospital equals the hospital's cost per full-time equivalent (FTE) resident, times the weighted average number of FTE residents, times the percentage of inpatient days attributable to Medicare Part A beneficiaries. Each hospital's per FTE resident amount is calculated using data from the hospital's cost reporting period that began in fiscal year 1984, increased by 1 percent for hospital cost reporting periods beginning July 1, 1985, and updated in subsequent cost reporting periods by the change in the CPI. The number of FTE residents is calculated at 100 percent after July 1, 1986, only for residents in their initial residency period (i.e., within the minimum number of years of formal training necessary to satisfy specialty requirements for board eligibility plus 1 year, but not to exceed 5 years). For residents not in their initial residency period, the weighing factor is 75 percent before July 1, 1987, and 50 percent after that date. On or after July 1, 1986, residents who are foreign medical graduates are not to be counted as FTE residents unless they have passed certain designated examinations.

HHS issued final regulations implementing the COBRA payment changes for graduate medical education costs on September 29, 1989. The changes are effective retroactively to 1985. OBRA 1990 prohibited the Secretary from recouping overpayments to hospitals resulting from the COBRA payment changes for graduate medical education until October 1, 1991. In addition, the act limits the amount of the recoupment to 25 percent of the total overpayment in each of four years beginning in fiscal year 1992.

In addition, Public Law 101–508 provided for a freeze in the update applicable for graduate medical education per-resident payment amounts for portions of cost reporting periods occurring from October 21, 1990, through December 31, 1990.

Hospital-based nursing and allied health professionals education programs operated at a hospital but controlled by another institution were included in PPS payment rates until an exception was enacted in TAMRA, allowing hospitals paid under a demonstration waiver to receive reasonable cost reimbursement for the costs of the nursing school. Public Law 101–239 allowed such hospitals to continue to be reimbursed on a reasonable cost basis if, before June 15, 1989, and thereafter, the hospital incurred substantial costs in training students and operating the school, the nursing school and hospital share some common board members, and all instruction is provided at the hospital or in the immediate proximity of the hospital. In addition, hospitals paid under the TAMRA exception are allowed to be reimbursed for reasonable costs of training nursing students retroactively for hospital cost reporting periods beginning in fiscal year 1986.

OBRA 1990 provides for payment on a passthrough basis (exempt from PPS) to hospitals for the clinical training of nurses or allied health education programs that are hospital-supported, as distinct from hospital-operated. The act requires hospitals to meet specific requirements to qualify for such payments, including the requirement that hospitals must have claimed and been paid for such costs prior to October 1, 1989. The Secretary is prohibited from recouping overpayments made to such hospitals and is required to refund any overpayments already recouped.

OBRA 93 provided that the amounts paid per resident for the direct costs of graduate medical education would not be updated by the CPI for cost reporting periods beginning during fiscal years 1994 and 1995, except for primary care residents and residents in obstetrics and gynecology. Primary care residents are defined to include family medicine, general internal medicine, general pediatrics, preventive medicine, geriatric medicine, and osteopathic general practice.

The allowable initial residency period will be defined to include only the period until the resident is first eligible for board certification, excluding the current-law allowance for one additional year. In addition, up to 2 years of a residency in preventive medicine will not count toward the limitation on the initial residency period.

The Secretary of HHS was directed to adjust the base-year payment amounts for certain grant-supported residency programs in family and community medicine, to the extent that the program is no longer supported by such grants. The base-year amounts also are adjusted for hospitals not required to pay FICA taxes or make a contribution to certain pension plans prior to enactment of the Omnibus Budget Reconciliation Act of 1990.

Indirect medical education costs

Additional payments are made to hospitals under the prospective system for the indirect costs attributable to approved medical education programs. These indirect costs may be due to a variety of factors, including the extra demands placed on the hospital staff as a result of the teaching activity or additional tests and procedures that may be ordered by residents. Congressional reports on the PPS authorizing legislation indicate that the indirect medical education payments are also to account for factors not necessarily related to medical education which may increase costs in teaching hospitals, such as more severely ill patients, increased use of diagnostic testing, and higher staff-to-patient ratios.

The additional payment to a hospital is based on a formula that provides an increase of approximately 7.7 percent in the Federal portion of the DRG payment, for each 0.1 increase in the hospital's intern and resident to bed ratio on a curvilinear basis (i.e., the increase in the payment is less than proportional to the increase in the ratio of interns and residents to bed size).

Public Law 100–647 extended the 7.7 percent indirect medical education adjustment until October 1, 1995. Public Law 101–508 makes the indirect medical education adjustment of 7.7 percent permanent.

Disproportionate share hospitals

Public Law 99–272 (COBRA) provided that additional payments would be made to hospitals that serve a disproportionate share of low-income patients; the adjustment was extended until October 1, 1990, by OBRA 1987 (Public Law 100–203) and to October 1, 1995 by Public Law 100–647, the Technical and Miscellaneous Revenue Act (TAMRA) of 1988. A hospital's disproportionate patient percentage is defined as the hospital's total number of inpatient days attributable to Federal Supplemental Security Income Medicare beneficiaries divided by the total number of Medicare patient days, plus the number of Medicaid patient days divided by the total patient days.

Public Law 101–508 (OBRA 1990), revised the formulas for computing the disproportionate share adjustment, effective January 1, 1991. Table D–5 shows the minimum disproportionate patient percentages required to qualify for the adjustment and the formulas for computing the adjustment effective October 1, 1993.

TABLE D–5.—CRITERIA TO QUALIFY FOR DISPROPORTIONATE SHARE ADJUSTMENT AND FORMULAS FOR COMPUTING ADDITIONAL PAYMENT, EFFECTIVE OCTOBER 1, 1993

Type of hospital	Qualifying disproportionate patient percentage (P)	Formula or fixed percentage adjustment
Urban, 100 or more beds .	15 percent	(P–15)(.6) .65 + 2.5
Urban, 100 or more beds .	20.2 percent	(P–20.2) .8 + 5.88
Urban, 100 or more beds .	30 percent of inpatient revenue from State or local indigent care funds.	35 percent
Urban, under 100 beds	40 percent	5 percent
Rural, over 500 beds	Not specified in law; regulations set threshold at 15 percent.	Same as urban, 100 or more beds
Rural, over 100 beds	30 percent	4 percent
Rural, under 100 beds	45 percent	4 percent
Rural, sole community hospital.	30 percent	10 percent
Rural, rural referral center and—		
(a) not a sole community hospital, 100 or more beds.	30 percent	(P–30)(.6) + 4.0
(b) not a sole community hospital, under 100 beds.	45 percent	(P–30)(.6) + 4.0
(c) also a sole community hospital.	30 percent	Greater of 10 percent or (P–30)(.6) + 4.0

Note.—The disproportionate patient percentage (P) is equal to the sum of (a) the number of Medicare inpatient days provided to Supplemental Security Income recipients divided by total Medicare patient days, and (b) the number of inpatient days provided to Medicaid beneficiaries divided by total inpatient days.

Source: ProPAC.

ESRD beneficiary discharges

Effective with cost reporting periods beginning on or after October 1, 1984, additional payments are made to hospitals for inpatient dialysis provided to end-stage renal disease (ESRD) beneficiaries if total discharges of such beneficiaries from non-ESRD related DRGs account for 10 percent or more of the hospital's total Medicare discharges. A hospital meeting the criteria is paid an additional payment for each ESRD beneficiary discharge based on the estimated weekly cost of dialysis and the average length of stay of its ESRD beneficiaries.

Outliers

Additional amounts are paid to hospitals for atypical cases (known as "outliers") which have either extremely long length of stay (day outliers) or extraordinarily high costs (cost outliers) compared to most discharges classified in the same DRG. The law requires that total outlier payments to all hospitals covered by the system represents no less than 5 percent and no more than 6 percent of the total estimated PPS payments for the fiscal year. Effective with discharges occurring on or after October 1, 1984, a transferring hospital may qualify for an additional payment for extraordinarily high-cost cases meeting the criteria for cost outliers. Outlier payments are financed by an offsetting overall reduction in the Federal portion of the base payment amount per discharge. Effective October 1, 1986, Public Law 99–509 established separate urban and rural set-aside factors for financing outlier payments. The separate set-aside factors for rural and urban hospitals for financing outlier payments will end when the other urban/rural payment differential is phased out in fiscal year 1995, as enacted in OBRA 1990.

Public Law 100–203 increased payments for outlier cases classified in DRGs relating to patients with burns from April 1, 1988, through September 30, 1989. This legislation also prohibited the Secretary from issuing any final regulations before September 1, 1988, which changed the method of payment for outlier cases (other than burn cases).

The Secretary published new outlier rules on September 30, 1988, effective for discharges on or after October 1, 1988. The new rules modified the thresholds used in determining whether a case is an outlier and increased the allowable payment amounts for cost outliers. The effect of the changes increased the proportion of all outlier payments going to cost outliers. Previously, about 85 percent of outlier payments were made for length of stay outliers and 15 percent for cost outliers. Under the new rules, 60 percent of payments are made for cost outliers and 40 percent for length of stay outliers. (Cases that meet both length of stay and cost outlier criteria are paid under the policy that produces the higher payment.)

To determine the amount of additional payments for outlier cases, the length of stay (LOS) for each case in a DRG is first compared against the applicable LOS threshold for the category. If the LOS for a case exceeds the threshold, then the case qualifies as a day outlier. In this instance, the hospital is paid its regular payment rate per discharge (for this DRG), plus the Federal portion of a per diem amount (55 percent of the hospital's Federal per diem rate for the DRG) for each Medicare covered day above the LOS threshold.

If the case does *not* qualify as a day outlier, then it may qualify as a cost outlier. The case will qualify for extra payments on this basis if the hospital's Medicare covered charges for the case, adjusted to operating costs (and reduced by its indirect teaching and disproportionate share adjustments, if applicable), exceed its cost outlier threshold for the DRG. In this instance, the hospital is paid its regular payment rate per discharge for the DRG, plus the Federal portion of 75 percent of the difference between its adjusted (and reduced) charges for the case and the cost outlier threshold.

In October 1991, Medicare began a transition from cost-based to prospective payment for hospital capital expenses (see below). In the August 30, 1991, final rule implementing this change, the Secretary established a unified outlier payment system for capital and operating costs. For day outliers, payments for covered days were set equal to 60 percent of the combined per diem operating and capital payment rates for the DRG. For cost outliers, payments are made only if the combined operating and capital cost for the case exceed the cost outlier threshold for the DRG. As in the case of operating cost payments, standard Federal capital payment amounts are reduced to establish a pool for outlier payments.

OBRA 1993 legislated two changes in outlier policy that will become effective in fiscal year 1995. First, day outliers will be phased out over a period of four years. By fiscal year 1999, all outlier payments will be based solely on cost. Second, cost-outlier thresholds will be based on a fixed amount beyond the payment rate for each case so that hospitals will incur the same loss on every case before outlier payments are applied.

Table D–6 shows the changes in outlier policy that have occurred since 1988.

TABLE D–6.—OUTLIER POLICY PARAMETERS, FISCAL YEARS 1988–94

	1988	1989 [1]	1990	1991	1992	1993	1994
Pool target	5.6% (urban), 2.5% (rural)	5.6% (urban), 2.2% (rural)	5.6% (urban), 2.2% (rural)	5.5% (urban), 2.3% (rural)	5.6% (urban), 2.1% (rural), 5.0% (capital)	5.5% (urban), 2.2% (rural), 5.0% (capital)	5.4% (urban), 2.3% (rural), 5.5% (capital)
Length of stay thresholds [2]	Lesser of 18 days or 2.0 x S.D.	Lesser of 24 days or 3.0 x S.D.	Lesser of 28 days or 3.0 x S.D.	Lesser of 29 days or 3.0 x S.D.	Lesser of 32 days or 3.0 x S.D.	Lesser of 23 days or 3.0 x S.D.	Lesser of 23 days or 3.0 x S.D.
Cost thresholds	Greater of 2.0 x DRG Federal rate or $14,000	Greater of 2.0 x DRG Federal rate or $28,000	Greater of 2.0 x DRG Federal rate or $34,000	Greater of 2.0 x DRG Federal rate or $35,000	Greater of 2.0 x DRG Federal rate or $44,000 [3]	Greater of 2.0 x DRG Federal rate or $35,500 [3]	Greater of 2.0 x DRG Federal rate or $36,000. [3]
Cost-to-charge ratio used for cost outliers.	66.0%	Hospital-specific	Hospital-specific	Hospital-specific	Hospital-specific	Hospital-specific	Hospital-specific
Marginal cost factor	60.0%	60.0% (LOS), 75.0% (cost)	60.0% (LOS), 75.0% (cost)	60.0% (LOS), 75.0%(cost)	60.0% (LOS), 75.0% (cost)	55.0% (LOS), 75.0% (cost)	55.0% (LOS), 75.0% (cost).

[1] Effective for discharges after October 31, 1988. For discharges between October 1 and October 31, 1988, transitional thresholds applied as follows: length of stay, lesser of 22 days or 2 standard deviations; cost, greater of 2 times Federal rate of $23,750.

[2] The LOS threshold for a DRG is set at the lesser of the national average LOS for all cases in the DRG plus a fixed number of days (e.g., 18 days in fiscal year 1988) or the national average LOS for the DRG plus a fixed number of standard deviations (e.g., 2.0 SD in fiscal year 1988). The number of days represented by a fixed number of standard deviations varies among the DRG categories.

[3] Combined operating/capital cost threshold.

Source: Annual Federal Register notices.

Payment For Capital

Until fiscal year 1992, Medicare paid its proportionate share of hospitals' reasonable capital-related costs, based on services used by beneficiaries as a proportion of total services furnished by the hospital. (Payments in recent years have been subject to fixed percentage reductions to be described below.) Four basic types of costs are allowable for Medicare reimbursement:

(1) Interest on mortgages, bonds, or other borrowing used to finance capital investments or current operations. Interest costs are generally offset by any interest income earned by the hospital on investments.

(2) Depreciation, figured on a straight line basis, for plant and equipment, but not for land.

(3) Rental payments for plant and equipment.

(4) Property taxes and insurance premiums related to capital assets.

One other type of capital cost was formerly recognized under Medicare, but has not been reimbursable for hospital services since fiscal year 1989: return on equity for investor-owned hospitals. Return on equity payments provided a return to investors equivalent to what they would have earned if they had used their money for some other purpose.

When the new PPS system was enacted in 1983, Congress excluded capital costs. However, the Secretary was instructed to report to Congress on methods for including capital in PPS and was authorized (but not required) to implement prospective payment for capital on or after October 1, 1986.

The Secretary's authority to include capital in PPS was postponed twice. The Supplemental Appropriations Act of 1986 (Public Law 99–349) delayed prospective capital payment until October 1, 1987. The Omnibus Budget Reconciliation Act of 1987 (Public Law 100–203) delayed prospective payment until October 1, 1991. However, the Secretary was required, not merely authorized, to implement a prospective system by that date. The system was required to provide for capital payments to be made on a per-discharge basis, with adjustments based on each discharge's classification under the DRGs or some similar system. At the Secretary's discretion, the system could include adjustments to reflect variations in costs of construction or borrowing, exceptions (including exceptions for hospitals with existing obligations), and adjustments to reflect hospital occupancy rates.

While prospective payment for capital has been delayed, Congress has included in budget reconciliation legislation fixed percentage reductions in amounts otherwise payable by Medicare for capital costs. These cuts began in fiscal year 1987, with a 3.5 percent reduction. Medicare would compute its share of total costs for each hospital and then reduce that computed share by 3.5 percent. The percentage reduction increased to 7 percent for the first quarter of fiscal year 1988, 12 percent for the rest of that fiscal year, and 15 percent for fiscal year 1989 through fiscal year 1991. (Delays in completing budget legislation have meant that there were brief intervals in 1987 and 1989 when no reduction was taken). The reductions originally applied only to capital costs related to inpatient care. Beginning in fiscal year 1990, capital payments for outpatient hospital services were also reduced. (The reductions did not apply to certain types of rural hospitals defined in Medicare law, including sole community hospitals, essential access community hospitals, and rural primary care hospitals.)

The Omnibus Budget Reconciliation Act of 1990 (Public Law 101–508) continued capital payment reductions through fiscal year 1995, with the reduction percentage lowered to 10 percent for fiscal year 1992 through 1995. Because prospective payment began in fiscal year 1992, the reductions are not applied directly to each hospital's computed capital costs. Instead, the Secretary is required to set payments under the new system (or under the new system and PPS combined) in such a way as to achieve an aggregate inpatient hospital capital spending reduction of 10 percent, as compared to what would have been spent under the reasonable cost system. The Omnibus Budget Reconciliation Act of 1993 (Public Law 103–66) extended the 10 percent reduction in outpatient capital payment through fiscal year 1998.

The administration's proposed rules for prospective payment for capital costs were published in the Federal Register on February 28, 1991. After a period for public comment, final rules were published on Aug. 30, 1991. The final rule provides for a 10-year transition to fully prospective payment beginning October 1, 1991.

Under the rule, the Secretary establishes a standard per case capital payment rate, based on average capital costs per case in fiscal year 1989 and updated for inflation and other factors. The base rate is adjusted in order to meet the requirement that capital payment rates be set in such a way as to achieve an aggregate saving of 10 percent relative to what would have been paid under a full cost system. For fiscal year 1993 the standard Federal payment rate for capital is $417.29 ($320.99 in Puerto Rico). Rates are adjusted using the DRG weights and a geographic factor based on area wage indices.

Hospitals in large urban areas receive a 3 percent increase and hospitals in Alaska and Hawaii receive a cost of living adjustment. A disproportionate share adjustment is provided for urban hospitals with more than 100 beds. A hospital receives approximately a 2.1 percent point increase in capital payments for each 10 percent increment in its disproportionate share percentage.

An adjustment is also made for the indirect costs of medical education. This adjustment is based on the ratio of residents to average daily inpatient census. Capital payments increase approximately 2.8 percentage points for each 10 percent increment in the residents to average daily census ratio. Additional capital payments are issued for outlier cases.

During a transition period that ends September 30, 2000, each individual hospital's capital payment rate is a blended rate based partly on its own historic capital costs and partly on the Federal rate. In fiscal year 1993, rates are 80 percent hospital-specific and 20 percent Federal. The hospital-specific portion will drop by 10 percent a year, until fully Federal rates take effect in fiscal year 2001.

The Omnibus Budget Reconciliation Act of 1993 (Public Law 103–66) reduced the Federal rate for inpatient capital expenses by 7.4 percent to correct for inflation forecast errors.

The transition rules include two provisions to assist hospitals most disadvantaged by the shift to prospective payment: a "hold harmless" payment system and exception payments for certain facilities. Hospitals with base year capital costs above average continue to be paid on a cost basis for the portion of their costs related to "old" capital investments (generally assets put in use or obligated by the end of 1990). The rest of the hospital's capital payments are based on the prospective rates. For example, if 75 percent of a hospital's costs are for depreciation and interest on a pre-1990 building, the hospital is paid Medicare's share of those costs (subject to the current 10 percent reduction). For "new" capital, it receives a portion of the prospective rate based on the hospital's own ratio of new to total capital. In this case, because old capital accounts for 75 percent of costs, the hospital's new capital payment is 25 percent of the prospective rate for each case treated. This hold harmless payment system will continue until the end of the 10-year transition, or until a hospital's old capital costs drop to the point at which it is more advantageous for the hospital to shift to fully prospective payment.

Exception payments are made to hospitals whose capital payments under the new system fall significantly short of their actual capital costs. Most hospitals are assured of receiving a minimum of 70 percent of costs. Specified urban hospitals with a disproportionate share of low-income patients receive at least 80 percent of costs, and rural sole community hospitals at least 90 percent. Computation of exception payments is cumulative. If a hospital received more than the minimum in one year but a shortfall the next, the surplus from the first year would be applied before any additional payment would be made in the second year.

Table D–7 shows the distribution of estimated total capital payments to PPS hospitals by geographic location and type of hospital for fiscal year 1994.

Table D–8 shows two sets of projections of the level and the rate of increase of aggregate payments and payments per case for capital-related costs in fiscal years 1984 through 1999.

Both sets of projections for capital reflect recently enacted provisions which phase out payments for a return on equity capital for proprietary providers. The second set also includes the anticipated effects of statutory reductions in reimbursements for capital-related costs (i.e., 3.5 percent for portions of cost-reporting periods in fiscal year 1987, 12 percent for fiscal year 1988, 15 percent for fiscal year 1989 and the last three quarters of fiscal year 1990, 15 percent in fiscal year 1991, and 10 percent for fiscal years 1992–95) enacted in the Omnibus Budget Reconciliation Act of 1986 (Public Law 99–509), in the Omnibus Budget Reconciliation Act of 1987 (Public Law 100–203), in the Omnibus Budget Reconciliation Act of 1989 (Public Law 101–239), and in the Omnibus Budget Reconciliation Act of 1990 (Public Law 101–508). The second set of estimates in table 7 also include the effect of regulations implementing prospective payment for inpatient capital-related costs (effective in fiscal year 1992), including the budget neutrality requirement through fiscal year 1995 enacted in OBRA 1990.

TABLE D–7.—CAPITAL-RELATED PAYMENTS TO PPS HOSPITALS (INCURRED AMOUNTS FOR FISCAL YEAR 1994)

Hospital group	Number of hospitals [1]	Medicare discharges (in thousands)	Capital payments (in millions of dollars)	PPS and capital payments (in millions of dollars)	Capital payments as a percentage of PPS and capital payments
All hospitals	5,350	10,397	$8,030	$74,780	10.7
Large MSA [2]	1,637	4,730	4,130	39,620	10.4
Other urban	1,352	3,635	2,850	25,490	11.2
Rural	2,361	2,032	1,040	9,680	10.8
Urban, 99 or fewer beds	757	480	300	2,600	11.6
Urban, 100 to 199 beds	901	1,654	1,300	11,010	11.8
Urban, 200 to 299 beds	611	2,121	1,680	15,290	11.0
Urban, 300 to 499 beds	529	2,643	2,260	21,550	10.5
Urban, 500 or more beds	191	1,467	1,450	14,660	9.9
Rural, 49 or fewer beds	1,208	376	140	1,470	9.7
Rural, 50 to 99 beds	718	630	300	2,780	10.8
Rural, 100 to 149 beds .	223	379	210	1,890	11.2
Rural, 150 to 199 beds .	106	257	140	1,300	10.8
Rural, 200 or more beds	106	389	240	2,240	10.9
By Payment Classification:					
Large MSA	1,816	5,236	4,530	43,110	10.5
Other urban	1,430	3,435	2,630	23,540	11.2
Rural referral	205	557	340	3,210	10.7
Rural sole community [3]	563	325	150	1,560	9.8
Other rural	1,336	824	350	3,340	10.5
Teaching, 100 or more residents	225	1,253	1,350	14,680	9.2
Teaching, fewer than 100 residents	816	3,065	2,510	23,570	10.6
Nonteaching	4,309	6,078	4,170	36,540	11.4
Disproportionate share [4]	1,832	4,713	4,010	38,190	10.5
Nondisproportionate share	3,518	5,684	4,020	36,590	11.0
Urban, by Region:					
New England	172	535	440	4,330	10.2
Middle Atlantic	447	1,620	1,370	13,920	9.9
South Atlantic	453	1,380	1,160	10,280	11.3
East North Central	498	1,488	1,140	11,080	10.2
East South Central	170	530	440	3,650	11.9
West North Central	188	532	430	3,990	10.8
West South Central	382	818	750	5,940	12.6
Mountain	126	326	280	2,470	11.1
Pacific	503	1,043	950	9,160	10.3
Puerto Rico	50	95	30	290	11.3

TABLE D–7.—CAPITAL-RELATED PAYMENTS TO PPS HOSPITALS (INCURRED AMOUNTS FOR FISCAL YEAR 1994)—Continued

Hospital group	Number of hospitals [1]	Medicare discharges (in thousands)	Capital payments (in millions of dollars)	PPS and capital payments (in millions of dollars)	Capital payments as a percentage of PPS and capital payments
Rural, by Region:					
New England	53	58	30	330	9.8
Middle Atlantic	85	150	80	800	9.6
South Atlantic	303	392	220	1,920	11.3
East North Central	313	330	170	1,570	10.6
East South Central	290	325	160	1,420	11.0
West North Central	552	298	140	1,320	10.6
West South Central	365	260	130	1,140	11.2
Mountain	244	115	70	590	11.6
Pacific	151	99	50	560	9.6
Puerto Rico	5	5	NA	NA	NA
Voluntary [5]	3,028	7,673	5,990	56,430	10.6
Proprietary	779	1,230	1,070	8,330	12.9
Government	1,514	1,480	950	9,920	9.6

[1] Number of hospitals for which data were available.

[2] "Large MSA" indicates Metropolitan Statistical Areas with more than 1 million people or New England County Metropolitan Areas with more than 970,000 people.

[3] Sole community hospitals that are also rural referral centers are included in the rural referral category.

[4] Hospitals that receive a disproportionate share adjustment for treating a relatively high proportion of low-income patients.

[5] Ownership type was not available for 29 hospitals.

NA—not available.

Note.—PPS payments are the payments to PPS hospitals for the operating costs of providing inpatient services to Medicare enrollees, including enrollees' copayments. Capital payments are Medicare's payments for the capital-related expenses of providing inpatient care. Unless otherwise indicated "urban" and "rural" categories are based on hospitals' geographic locations. Numbers may not add to totals because of rounding.

Source: Congressional Budget Office estimates based on data from the Health Care Financing Administration and the Prospective Payment Assessment Commission.

PAYMENTS ON A REASONABLE COST BASIS

Costs for certain items are excluded from the prospective payment system and thus are not included in the prospective payment rates. Medicare pays for its share of the following costs according to the former reasonable cost-based system:

Physicians in teaching hospitals

If a teaching hospital so elects, the direct medical and surgical services of physicians in such hospitals will be excluded from the prospective payment system and paid for on the basis of reasonable costs.

TABLE D-8.—ESTIMATED OUTLAYS FOR INPATIENT CAPITAL-RELATED COSTS UNDER MEDICARE'S HOSPITAL INSURANCE PROGRAM, FISCAL YEARS 1984-99 [1]

	Without OBRA 1986, 1987, 1989, 1993 percentage reductions and without Aug. 30, 1991 regulation			With OBRA 1986, 1987, 1989, 1990, 1993 percentage reductions and with Aug. 30, 1991 regulation [2]		
	Aggregate payments (billions)	Year to year per- cent in- crease	Payments per case	Aggregate payments (billions)	Year to year per- cent in- crease	Payments per case
Fiscal year:						
1984	$3.5	NA	$310	$3.5	NA	$310
1985	4.0	15.8	380	4.0	15.8	380
1986	4.4	8.9	425	4.4	8.9	425
1987	4.7	6.8	460	4.5	1.4	440
1988	5.0	7.0	490	4.4	-1.0	430
1989	5.2	3.8	505	4.2	-4.2	410
1990	5.7	9.2	545	5.2	21.8	495
1991	6.4	11.7	605	6.0	15.3	570
1992	7.6	18.6	685	6.9	14.1	620
1993	8.6	13.3	760	7.7	11.7	680
1994	9.5	11.3	820	8.4	9.4	720
1995	10.6	11.3	885	9.3	10.9	775
1996	11.7	10.6	950	10.2	9.5	825
1997	12.9	9.9	1,015	11.1	9.2	875
1998	14.1	9.3	1,080	12.1	9.1	930
1999	15.3	8.8	1,160	13.2	9.0	990

[1] Both projections for capital-related payments reflect current law provisions which phased out payments for return-on-equity capital for proprietary providers during fiscal year 1987 through fiscal year 1989. Estimates are CBO's February 1991, projections.

[2] Includes freeze at fiscal year 1987 payment levels from Oct. 1, 1987, through Nov. 20, 1987; percentage reductions were 3.5 percent in fiscal year 1987, 12 percent in fiscal year 1988, 15 percent in fiscal year 1989, 15 percent in the last three quarters of fiscal year 1990, 15 percent in fiscal year 1991, and 10 percent for fiscal years 1992-95. Under current law, regulations implementing (effective fiscal year 1992) prospective payment for inpatient capital-related costs will primarily affect the distribution of payments with aggregate levels not to exceed those projected above, for fiscal year 1992 through fiscal year 1995. Final regulation on prospective payment of capital issued on Aug. 30, 1991, implements budget neutrality requirements of OBRA 1990 through fiscal year 1995. Payment rates are updated thereafter by the 2-year moving average increase in Medicare capital costs per case, adjusted for case mix change, that occurred 3 and 4 years previous to the fiscal year in question.

Organic acquisition costs

Organ acquisition costs

The estimated net expenses associated with Medicare organ acquisition in certified transplantation centers are excluded from the prospective payment system and paid on a reasonable cost basis.

Passthrough payments for hemophilia inpatients

OBRA 1989 excluded the cost of administering blood clotting factors for hemophilia inpatients from PPS, for items furnished from June 19, 1990, through December 19, 1991. OBRA 1993 further extended this provision through fiscal year 1994. The price per unit for the blood clotting factors was set at a predetermined rate, in consultation with ProPAC, and the cost of administering the blood clotting factors was determined by multiplying a predetermined price per unit of blood clotting factor by the number of units provided to the individual.

Bad debts of Medicare beneficiaries

An additional payment is made to hospitals for bad debts attributable to unpaid deductible and copayment amounts related to covered services received by Medicare beneficiaries.

The Secretary is prohibited from making any change in the policy in effect on August 1, 1987, including changes in hospital documentation requirements. OBRA 1989 prohibits the Secretary from requiring hospitals to change their bad debt collection policy if a fiscal intermediary accepted the policy in accordance with the rules in effect as of August 1, 1987, for indigency determination procedures, for record keeping, and for determining whether to refer a claim to an external collection agency. For such facilities, the Secretary also may not collect from the hospital on the basis of an expectation of a change in the hospital's collection policy.

SPECIAL TREATMENT OF CERTAIN FACILITIES

Certain exceptions and adjustments to the prospective payment rates are provided as follows:

Sole community hospitals

Sole community hospitals (SCHs) are hospitals that (because of factors such as isolated location, weather conditions, travel conditions, or absence of other hospitals) are the sole source of inpatient services reasonably available in a geographic area. For cost reporting periods beginning before April 1, 1990, SCHs were paid on the same basis as all other hospitals were paid in the first year of the transition period: 25 percent of the payment is based on Federal regional DRG rates and 75 percent on each hospital's cost base.

Under the provisions of OBRA 89, the criteria for SCH designation was liberalized by allowing hospitals to be designated as such if they were located more than 35 road miles from another hospital. In addition, OBRA 89 provided the Secretary with the authority to designate a hospital as an SCH if, by reason of factors such as travel time to the nearest alternative source of appropriate inpatient care, location, weather conditions, travel conditions, or absence of other like hospitals, the Secretary determines that it is the sole source of inpatient hospital services reasonably available to individuals in a geographic area.

In addition, OBRA 1989 established new payment provisions that apply to all SCHs for cost reporting periods beginning after April 1, 1990. An SCH may receive the higher of the following rates as the basis of reimbursement: a target amount based on 100 percent hospital-specific prospective rates based on fiscal year 1982 costs updated to the present; a target amount based on hospital-specific prospective rates based on fiscal year 1987 costs updated to the present; or the Federal PPS rate. Current SCHs not meeting the new criteria are allowed to continue to qualify for payments as an SCH.

OBRA 1989 made permanent the provision by which an SCH may request additional payments if the hospital experiences a decrease of more than 5 percent in its total inpatient cases due to circumstances beyond its control. An SCH may receive such payments if it meets sole community hospital criteria but is not being paid as a sole community hospital. As of September 1992, 607 hospitals were classified as sole community providers.

Medicare dependent hospitals

OBRA 1989 created a new classification of hospitals termed Medicare dependent hospitals. Medicare dependent hospitals are hospitals that are located in a rural area, have 100 beds or less, are not classified as a sole community provider, and for which not less than 60 percent of inpatient days or discharges in the hospital cost reporting period that began during fiscal year 1987 were attributable to Medicare. These hospitals are reimbursed in the same fashion as sole community providers during cost reporting periods beginning on or after April 1, 1990, and ending on or before March 31, 1993. As of September 1992, there were 501 Medicare dependent hospitals. OBRA 1993 (Public Law 103–66) extended additional payments to Medicare dependent hospitals through September 30, 1994, on a phase-down basis.

Referral centers

The Secretary is authorized to provide exceptions and adjustments as appropriate for regional and national referral centers. These centers are defined as:

(1) rural hospitals having 275 or more beds;

(2) hospitals having at least 50 percent of their Medicare patients referred from other hospitals or from physicians not on the hospital's staff, at least 60 percent of their Medicare patients residing more than 25 miles from the hospital, and at least 60 percent of the services furnished to Medicare beneficiaries are furnished to those who live 25 miles or more from the hospital; or

(3) rural hospitals meeting the following criteria for hospital cost reporting periods beginning on or after October 1, 1985:

(a) a case mix index equal to or greater than the median case mix for all urban hospitals (the national standard), or the median case mix for urban hospitals located in the same census region, excluding hospitals with approved teaching programs. (The case mix index is a measure of the relative costliness of the hospital's mixture of cases among the DRGs compared to the national average mixture of medicare cases);

(b) a minimum of 5,000 discharges, the national discharge criterion (3,000 in the case of osteopathic hospitals), or the median number of discharges in urban hospitals for the region in which the hospital is located; and

(c) at least one of the following three criteria: more than 50 percent of the hospital's medical staff are specialists, at least 60 percent of discharges are for inpatients who reside more than 25 miles from the hospital, or at least 40 percent of inpatients treated at the hospital have been referred either from physicians not on the hospital's staff or from other hospitals.

Referral centers are paid prospective payments based on the applicable urban payment amount rather than the rural payment amount, as adjusted by the hospital's area wage index. The applicable amount is the "other urban" rate (i.e., the rate for urban areas with 1 million or fewer people) for all referral centers except those (if any) located in MSAs greater than 1 million.

Under the regulations, once a hospital has achieved referral center status, it is paid at the applicable urban rate for a 3-year period. Public Law 99–509 permitted hospitals designated as regional referral centers, as of the date of enactment, to continue their designation through cost reporting periods beginning before October 1, 1989. OBRA 89 extended the status of current referral centers for three additional years, including all hospitals classified as referral centers as of September 30, 1989. OBRA 93 extended the classification through fiscal year 1994 for those classified on September 30, 1992. As of September 1992, 180 hospitals were qualified as referral centers.

Hospitals in rural counties treated as urban counties

Hospitals in areas that are reclassified from urban to rural under OMB's MSA system are allowed a 2-year transition period during which they are paid a blend of the applicable urban and rural rates.

Public Law 100–203 provided for the reclassification of rural hospitals as urban if the county in which the hospital was located was adjacent to two or more MSAs and met criteria regarding commuting patterns of its residents to the central counties of the adjacent MSAs. For fiscal year 1993, 50 rural hospitals have been reclassified under this provision. If treating a hospital located in a rural county as being located in an urban area reduced the wage index for that urban area or for other rural areas in the State, Public Law 100–647 required an adjustment to ensure that, for discharges during fiscal year 1990 and 1991, no other area suffered a reduced wage index.

Public Law 101–239 (OBRA 1989) allows hospitals to apply for reclassification from rural to urban and allows counties to apply for reclassification from rural to urban. In addition, OBRA 1989 establishes a floor for area wage indices so that the reclassification of hospitals under the new procedures or the rules enacted in OBRA

1987 cannot result in the reduction of a county's wage index below the wage index for other rural areas within the same State.

Public Law 101–239 requires the Secretary to establish a Geographic Classification Review Board to consider appeals by hospitals for a change in classification from rural to urban, or from one urban area to another urban area. Reclassification may be for use of an adjacent area's standardized amount (large or other urban) or use of its wage index. The Secretary has provided by regulation that a hospital must be in a county adjacent to the area to which it seeks reclassification.

The Act also revises the rules for the adjustment of wage indices required as a result of the reclassification of hospitals under the OBRA 1987 provision or under the new procedures for reclassification. If reclassification of a county into an urban area reduces the wage index for that area by 1 percent or less, then the MSA wage index applies to hospitals in the reclassified county, but the reclassified county is to be excluded from the computation of the index. If the reclassification reduces the urban area's wage index by more than 1 percent, separate wage indices are to be computed for the original urban area and for the reclassified county. If the reclassification of a rural county results in a reduction in the wage index for the other rural counties in the State, the index is to be computed as if the reclassification had not occurred. Finally, no reclassification can reduce any area's wage index to a level below the index for rural areas in the State. The new rules are effective April 1, 1990.

OBRA 1990 provided that if including wages of all redesignated hospitals in the wage index of the MSA to which they are redesignated reduces the MSA's wage index by more than 1 percentage point, then the original wage index (calculated without the wages of the redesignated hospitals) is applied to hospitals in the MSA. Redesignated hospitals would receive a wage index combining their wages plus the wages of the MSA to which they were redesignated. OBRA 1990 also extended the due date for initial applications for reclassification submitted to the Geographic Classification Review Board until November 6, 1990, and clarifies the Secretary's ability to review decisions of the Board. For fiscal year 1993, 823 rural hospitals (34 percent) and 370 urban hospitals (13 percent have been reclassified by the Board.

In a final rule issued September 1, 1992, the Secretary provided that, beginning in fiscal year 1994, no hospital may be reclassified for wage index purposes unless its hourly wages equal 108 percent of the average for its current area and 84 percent (90 percent if weighted for occupational categories) of the average for the area to which it seeks reclassification.

Section 602k hospitals

Prior to Public Law 98–21, payments for nonphysician services (in such areas as radiology, laboratory, physical therapy, prosthetics) provided to Medicare beneficiaries who were hospital inpatients were made either (1) to the hospital under part A of Medicare on a reasonable cost basis or (2) to an outside supplier of the service under part B of Medicare on the basis of reasonable charges. The practice of billing under part B for services provided to hospital inpatients is known as the "unbundling" of part A services.

Public Law 98–21 provided that, effective October 1, 1983, for all hospitals participating in the Medicare program (including those under prospective payment, excluded hospitals, and those paid under State cost control systems), all nonphysician services provided to hospital inpatients will be paid only as hospital services under the part A program. The Secretary has authority to waive this requirement during the transition period to allow billing under part B for hospitals that had such extensive billings under part B prior to October 1, 1982, that compliance with the new requirement would threaten the stability of patient care (commonly referred to as 602k hospitals). As of December 1985, there were four 602k hospitals.

HOSPITALS EXCLUDED FROM THE PROSPECTIVE PAYMENT SYSTEM

The following hospitals are by law excluded from the prospective payment system and are paid on the basis of reasonable costs, subject to the TEFRA rate of increase limits: psychiatric hospitals, rehabilitation hospitals, psychiatric or rehabilitation units which are distinct parts of a hospital, alcohol and drug abuse hospitals and such distinct units of hospitals (for cost reporting periods beginning before October 1, 1987), children's hospitals (with patients averaging under 18 years of age), long-term hospitals (with an average inpatient length of stay greater than 25 days), and hospitals outside the 50 States and the District of Columbia. Public Law 99–509 provided that hospitals located in Puerto Rico will be included in PPS, specially adjusted for Puerto Rico, effective with discharges occurring on or after October 1, 1987. Public Law 101–239 exempts cancer hospitals (hospitals extensively involved in treatment for and research on cancer) classified as such before December 31, 1990, from PPS. In addition, the act provides an exemption for any hospital classified as a cancer hospital before December 31, 1991, that is located in a State that has a PPS waiver under section 1814(b) (i.e., Maryland). In addition, there are special cases where the prospective payment system is not applied, such as for emergency services provided to Medicare beneficiaries in hospitals not participating in Medicare and Veterans' Administration hospital services provided to Medicare beneficiaries.

OBRA 1990 increased the cost limits imposed on hospitals exempt from PPS. Under prior law, hospitals with costs in excess of the cost limits imposed by the Tax Equity and Fiscal Responsibility Act (TEFRA) would be reimbursed for their cost up to the TEFRA limit. Under OBRA 1990, hospitals with costs in excess of the cost limits imposed by TEFRA will receive 50 percent of the costs that are in excess of the limit, up to a maximum of 110 percent of the limit. In addition, the Secretary is directed to develop a new prospective payment methodology for exempt hospitals, or to substantially modify the current target-rate system.

OBRA 1993 provided for an update factor to the cost limits of market basket minus 1.0 percentage point for fiscal years 1994 through 1997. A hospital with operating costs in fiscal year 1990 that exceed the target amount by more than 10 percent are exempt from the update reduction, with partial reductions applied to hospitals near the threshold.

Hospitals reimbursed under approved State cost control systems are also excluded from the prospective rates.

Section 1886(c) of the Social Security Act (as added by TEFRA) gave the HHS Secretary discretion to reimburse hospitals in a State according to the State's hospital reimbursement control system rather than according to Medicare's reimbursement methods if the State requests this change and if HHS determines that the State system meets certain requirements. Currently one State has a waiver to operate its own system: Maryland. New York has a waiver convering four counties participating in the Finger Lakes Area Hospital Corporation (FLAHC) rural hospital payment demonstration.

Public Laws 98–21 and 98–369 added several more requirements for State systems. According to final regulations published by HHS on April 24, 1986 (51 F.R. 15481), implementing these legislative changes, HHS has the discretion to allow Medicare hospital reimbursement to be made in accordance with a State reimbursement control system if the chief executive officer of the State requests approval of the State system, and provided that the State system:

(a) Applies to substantially all non-federal acute care hospitals in the State.

(b) Applies to at least 75 percent of all inpatient revenues or expenses for the State.

(c) Provides assurances that payers, hospital employees and patients in the State will be treated equitably under its system.

(d) Provides assurances that its system will not result in greater Medicare expenditures over 36-month periods.

(e) Does not preclude health maintenance organizations (HMOs) or competitive medical plans (CMPs) from negotiating directly with hospitals concerning payment for inpatient services.

(f) Limits hospital charges to Medicare beneficiaries to deductibles, coinsurance, and services for which the beneficiary would not be entitled to have payment made under Medicare part A; and prohibits payment under part B of Medicare for nonphysician services provided to hospital inpatients unless this prohibition is waived.

Public Law 101–239 (OBRA 1989) requires the Secretary's test of effectiveness of a State cost containment system to be based on the aggregate rate of increase from October 1, 1984, to the most recent date for which annual data are available. This provision extends the waiver for the FLAHC rural hospital payment demonstration.

Special provisions apply to States that have existing demonstration projects approved by HCFA under section 402 of the Social Security Amendments of 1967 or section 222(a) of the Social Security Amendment of 1972 for the operation of State reimbursement control systems. HHS approval of a State's application to continue the operation of a system upon expiration of the demonstration project is mandatory if, and for so long as, the system meets the minimum requirements described in items (a) through (f) above.

Public Law 101–508 revises the Secretary's test of effectiveness of a State cost containment system to be based on the rate of increase in costs per hospital inpatient admission as compared to the rate of increase in such costs with respect to all hospitals between January 1, 1981, and the present. In addition, OBRA 1990 provides that a State no longer qualifying for a PPS waiver be provided with a reasonable period, not to exceed two years, for transition from the State system to the national payment system, and requires restoration of the waiver if the State returns to compliance during the transition period.

ADMINISTRATION

Prospective Payment Assessment Commission

Public Law 98–21 required the Director of the Congressional Office of Technology Assessment (OTA) to appoint by April 1, 1984, a commission of 15 independent experts, known as the Prospective Payment Assessment Commission (ProPAC). Public Law 99–272 added two members to ProPAC, bringing the total to 17 members.

The Commission must report to Congress by March 1 of each year its recommendation of an update factor for PPS payment rates and for other changes in reimbursement policy.[1]

The Secretary is required to submit to Congress recommendations that take into account ProPAC's recommendations, and include a written explanation of those recommendations that differ from those of the Commission.

By June 1 of each year, ProPAC also submits a report to Congress which provides background information on trends in health care delivery and financing, including the impact of the prospective payment system on providers and beneficiaries.[2]

Administrative and judicial review

Administrative and judicial appeals are allowed under procedures and authorities already established under the Medicare program. However, the law precludes administrative and judicial review of: (1) the "budget neutrality" adjustment (see above), and (2) the DRG payment amounts, including the establishment of DRGs, the methodology for classifying discharges within DRGs, and the DRG weighting factors.

Review activities

Public Law 97–248, the Tax Equity and Fiscal Responsibility Act of 1982 (known as TEFRA) replaced the existing Professional Standards Review Organization (PSRO) program with the utilization and quality control peer review program. The Secretary of the Department of Health and Human Services was required to enter into performance-based contracts with physician-sponsored or physician-access organizations known as Peer Review Organizations (PRO's) by November 15, 1984. As a condition of receiving payments under the prospective payment system, hospitals are re-

---

[1] See Prospective Payment Assessment Commission. Report and Recommendation to the Secretary, U.S. Department of Health and Human Services, March 1, 1994.

[2] See Prospective Payment Assessment Commission, Medicare Prospective Payment and the American Health Care System. Report to Congress, June 1993.

quired to enter into an agreement with a PRO under which the PRO will review the validity of diagnostic and procedural information provided by the hospitals; the completeness, adequacy and quality of care provided; and the appropriateness of admissions patterns, discharges, lengths of stay, transfers, and services furnished in outlier cases.

Since 1982, the statute governing the PRO program has been amended numerous times, and the PROs are now operating under the third "scope of work." In addition to reviewing inpatient care and some ambulatory care services, the PROs are now required to review hospital readmissions within 31 days of a previous hospital discharge to determine if the previous inpatient services and the posthospital services met professionally recognized standards of care. This provision was enacted as part of the Omnibus Budget Reconciliation Act of 1986 (P.L. 99–509), partly in response to congressional concerns that the prospective payment system was encouraging hospitals to discharge patients prematurely to inappropriate levels of care.

HISTORICAL TRENDS IN PPS PAYMENTS AND HOSPITAL MEDICARE COST, REVENUE, AND UTILIZATION

Aggregate PPS payments

Prospective payment system (PPS) payments for fiscal year 1992 are estimated at $58.5 billion (see table D–9). Of that amount, $6.1 billion is accounted for by beneficiary deductibles and copayments and payments made by other third-party payers, and $52.3 billion by payments from the Medicare program. Under current law, PPS payments are expected to exceed $91.6 billion by fiscal year 1998, with $81.8 billion coming from the Medicare trust fund and $9.8 billion from beneficiaries and other payers.

Trends in PPS costs, revenues, and margins

In the following tables, references to PPS1 through PPS8 indicate the first through the eighth years of operation of the Medicare prospective payment system. Hospitals were phased into PPS beginning October 1, 1983, depending on when the hospital's accounting or fiscal year began. Thus, PPS1 is the first year of prospective payment for each individual hospital and generally overlaps Federal fiscal years 1984 and 1985.

The increase in the PPS payment rates (DRG prices) has differed from the update factor each year. For example, in the first 2 years, the PPS payment rates were required to be adjusted so that aggregate payments to hospitals included in PPS would be equal to the aggregate payments they would have received if they had been paid under the provisions of prior law (the target rate of increase limits established in TEFRA, Public Law 97–248). As a result of this budget neutrality adjustment, the actual increases in the DRG prices were lower than the increases provided by the PPS update factors for those years. In the third year, the PPS rates were frozen by the Congress, and the update factor of 0.5 percent established in COBRA (Public Law 99–272) applied for only the last 5 months of the fiscal year. DRG rate increases in each year also have been affected by changes in policy that required recalculation or adjustment of the Federal base payment amounts or the DRG relative weights.

Actual annual increases in average payments per case, in turn, depend on a variety of factors in addition to the increase in the PPS rates, including the increase in reported case mix and other changes in payment policies.

Following an increase of only 1.9 percent in the first year of PPS, PPS operating costs per discharge rose about 10 percent per year during the second and third years, and about 9 percent in the fourth through sixth years. However, the rate of increase declined in the seventh and eighth years, to 8.3 percent and 7.3 percent, respectively (see table D–10). PPS payment per discharge increases were substantial during the first 2 years of PPS, but were dramatically lower in the next 6 years. In each year, per discharge payments have grown faster than the PPS market basket index. PPS payment increases have also been greater than the update factor, primarily because of the increased frequency of higher-weighted DRGs. The cumulative increases in costs and payments per discharge in the first 8 years of PPS are 86.9 percent and 77.9 percent, respectively (see chart D–1).

PPS margins are defined as PPS payments less PPS operating costs divided by PPS payments. The aggregate PPS margin was above 14 percent in each of the first 2 years of PPS, falling to 1.0 percent in the sixth year, − 1.5 percent by the seventh year, and − 3.4 percent in the eighth year (se table D–11). The seventh year of PPS was the first year in which aggregate PPS operating costs exceeded aggregate payments. Sixty-three percent of all hospitals incurred losses under PPS during the eighth year, compared with only 17 percent in the first year (see table D–12).

PPS margins do not represent the bottom line for the hospital industry. Total margins, which include expenses and revenues related to Medicare and other inpatient and outpatient care as well as other facility activities, increased steadily from the early 1970s to the early 1980s, peaking in 1984. After a slight decline, the total margin has been increasing slightly in the past few years, from 3.5 percent in PPS5 to 4.5 percent in PPS8. These margins are comparable to pre-PPS levels.

Margins by hospital type

PPS margins vary by hospital type. During the first 4 years of PPS, urban hospitals had substantially higher margins than rural hospitals. Within both categories, margins increased with bed size. The urban/rural margin differential decreased in the fifth year, because policy changes in recent years have increased payments to rural hospitals relative to urban hospitals. In the eighth year, both the urban and rural margins were negative, but the difference between the two margins was 1.3 percentage points, compared with 7.4 percentage points in the first year. Major teaching hospitals and large urban hospitals with disproportionate shares of poor patients had relatively high margins during the first 8 years of PPS.

Distribution of PPS hospitals, cases, and payments

Estimates for fiscal year 1993 show that PPS payments continue to vary substantially across hospital groups (see table D–13). For example, 53 percent of all PPS hospitals are located in urban areas; these hospitals account for 78 percent of all PPS discharges and receive 86 percent of all PPS payments. By contrast, rural hospitals account for 47 percent of PPS hospitals and 22 percent of PPS discharges and 14 percent of PPS payments.

The IME adjustment is intended to recognize hospitals' indirect costs of operating approved graduate medical education programs. The DSH adjustment is intended to compensate hospitals that treat large proportions of low-income patients. Almost all IME and DSH payments go to hospitals located in urban areas. In fiscal year 1993, urban hospitals received 98 percent of IME payments and 95 percent of DSH payments.

Outlier payments are intended to protect hospitals from the risk of financial losses due to cases with exceptionally long stays or high costs. Large, urban teaching hospitals and those located in the Middle Atlantic region received the highest proportion of outlier payments. Small urban hospitals, all rural hospitals, and hospitals located in the Mountain region received the lowest percentage of outlier payments.

For all PPS hospitals, the basic DRG payment was estimated to account for 86 percent of fiscal year 1993 PPS payments (see table D–14). Indirect medical education, disproportionate share, and outlier payments were expected to account for 14 percent of all PPS payments, or about $9.2 billion. The basic DRG payment comprised more than a 10 percent greater proportion of the payments to rural hospitals (96 percent) than to urban hospitals (85 percent), due the urgan hospitals' greater reliance on outlier, IME, and DSH payments. These additional payments accounted for 16 percent of payments to urban hospitals, but only 4 percent of payments to rural hospitals.

Effects of policy changes on PPS payments

Since the implementation of PPS, the distribution of Medicare payments to hospitals has changed. Some redistribution has resulted from changes in hospital behavior, but much of it is attributable to policy decisions. These include the transition to national average rates, reductions in teaching hospital payments, the addition of a disproportionate share adjustment and increases in the size of that adjustment for many hospitals, and large update factors for rural hospitals in recent years.

The update factor and other policy decisions implemented between fiscal years 1984 and 1993 increased per-case PPS payment rates by 28.4 percent (see table D–15). These policy decisions have redistributed PPS payments to rural hospitals, particularly to sole community hospitals. Small rural hospitals have been helped much more than large hospitals in any location, while urban hospitals with fewer than 100 beds have fared worse than most groups. Similarly, major teaching hospitals received relatively little benefit from payment policy changes. On a regional basis, the hospitals in the Northeast benefitted the most from these changes while those in the Mid-Atlantic region gained the least.

The Medicare case-mix index (CMI) reflects the mix of each hospital's cases across DRGs. Because hospitals are paid on this basis, an increase in the CMI results in a proportional increase in PPS payments. CMI changes have, in some instances, partially offset the intended effects of policy decisions. For example, case mix change has shifted payments toward urban hospitals, teaching hospitals, and large hospitals.

Over the last 10 years, the combined effects of update factors, policy decisions, and CMI growth increased per case PPS payments by 64 percent across all hospitals. Overall, rural hospitals, especially sole community hospitals, reaped gains from these changes while Mid-Atlantic and small urban hospitals received the smallest cumulative increases in their payments.

Additional hospital data

Table D–16 displays summary characteristics of hospitals participating in the Medicare prospective payment system. These data are derived from PPS payment simulations by the Congressional Budget Office.

TABLE D–9.—ESTIMATED INCURRED PPS PAYMENTS TO HOSPITALS, BY PAYMENT TYPE, FISCAL YEARS 1992–99

[In billions]

Payment type	1992	1993	1994	1995	1996	1997	1998	1999
Gross PPS payments ...	$58.5	$62.5	$66.8	$71.0	$75.4	$81.0	$87.2	$94.2
Indirect teaching	3.3	3.3	3.6	3.9	4.2	4.5	4.9	5.4
Disproportionate share	2.3	3.0	3.3	3.5	3.8	4.1	4.4	4.9
Outlier [1]	2.5	3.2	3.4	3.6	3.8	4.1	4.4	4.8
Less copayments	(6.1)	(6.1)	(6.5)	(6.9)	(7.3)	(7.8)	(8.3)	(8.8)
Net payment from Medicare	52.3	56.3	60.3	64.1	68.1	73.2	78.9	85.2

[1] Outlier payments due to the indirect medical education adjustment are included in the indirect teaching payments; outlier payments due to the disproportionate share adjustment are included in the disproportionate share payments.

Source: Congressional Budget Office.

TABLE D–10.—PERCENT CHANGE IN PPS OPERATING COSTS, PAYMENTS, AND DISCHARGES, FIRST 8 YEARS OF PPS

Year [1]	Operating costs	Payments	Discharges	Operating costs per discharge	Payments per discharge	Market basket	Update factor
PPS1	−4.6	11.0	−6.3	1.9	18.5	4.9	4.7
PPS2	4.3	4.2	−5.7	10.6	10.5	3.9	4.5
PPS3	5.7	−0.6	−3.6	9.7	3.1	3.9	0.5
PPS4	7.5	3.8	−1.4	9.0	5.3	3.7	1.2
PPS5	10.0	6.6	0.8	9.2	5.8	4.7	1.5
PPS6	10.5	7.7	1.1	9.3	6.5	5.4	3.3
PPS7	10.7	7.6	2.2	8.3	5.3	4.5	[2] 4.7
PPS8	9.7	7.8	2.2	7.3	5.5	4.3	3.4
Cumulative effect:							
PPS1	....	....	....	1.9	18.5	4.9	4.7
PPS2	....	....	....	12.7	30.9	9.0	9.4
PPS3	....	....	....	23.6	35.0	13.2	10.0
PPS4	....	....	....	34.8	42.2	17.4	11.2
PPS5	....	....	....	47.2	50.4	23.0	12.9
PPS6	....	....	....	60.8	60.2	29.6	16.6
PPS7	....	....	....	74.2	68.7	35.4	22.1
PPS8	....	....	....	86.9	77.9	36.9	22.9

[1] Data on costs, payments and cases are for hospital accounting years beginning during each Federal fiscal year. Data on the market basket and update factor are from the corresponding Federal fiscal year (1984 for PPS1, etc.).

[2] Adjusted for 1.22 percent across-the-board reduction in DRG weights for fiscal year 1990.

Note.—Hospitals in Maryland, Massachusetts, New Jersey, and New York excluded from PPS1 and PPS2. Hospitals in Maryland and New Jersey also excluded from PPS3 through PPS5. Data based on cohorts of hospitals with cost reports available in each 2 successive years.

Source: ProPAC analysis of Medicare Cost Report data from the Health Care Financing Administration.

CHART D–1.—CUMULATIVE INCREASES IN PPS MARKET BASKET, UPDATE, AND PAYMENTS AND COSTS, FIRST 10 YEARS OF PPS, IN PERCENT

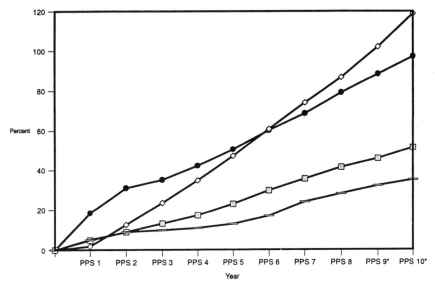

Percent

● Payments per discharge   ◇ Costs per discharge   □ Market basket   — PPS update factor

* Costs and payments are estimated for PPS 9 and PPS 10.
SOURCE: ProPAC analysis of Medicare Cost Report data from the Health Care Financing Administration.

TABLE D–11.—PPS OPERATING MARGINS, BY HOSPITAL GROUP, FIRST 8 YEARS OF PPS

[In percent]

Hospital group	PPS 1	PPS 2	PPS 3	PPS 4	PPS 5	PPS 6	PPS 7	PPS 8
All hospitals	14.5	14.4	9.8	6.9	3.6	1.0	−1.5	−3.4
Urban	15.8	15.5	10.9	7.8	4.3	1.6	−1.1	−3.2
Rural	8.4	8.8	3.3	1.1	−0.4	−2.2	−3.9	−4.5
Large urban	16.5	15.5	11.1	7.8	4.2	1.6	−0.3	−1.7
Other urban	14.9	15.4	10.7	8.0	4.5	1.5	−2.1	−5.0
Rural referral	10.1	13.6	8.7	6.0	4.1	1.6	−2.1	−3.4
Sole community	8.5	6.9	2.3	0.8	−1.9	−4.4	−2.5	−2.0
Other rural	7.5	6.5	0.1	−2.3	−3.1	−4.3	−5.6	−6.2
Major teaching	19.4	21.3	16.5	14.1	11.1	8.5	7.1	8.7
Other teaching	16.5	16.3	11.9	8.6	5.1	2.7	0.0	−1.8
Non-teaching	12.3	11.6	6.5	3.5	0.7	−2.1	−5.0	−7.3
Disproportionate share:								
Large urban	17.0	16.0	12.4	10.2	8.1	6.0	4.9	4.1
Other urban	14.9	16.1	11.9	9.6	6.8	4.3	1.4	−0.7
Rural	9.6	10.3	3.8	2.0	0.9	0.4	−0.4	−0.8
Non-disproportionate share	13.8	13.5	8.3	4.7	0.8	−2.1	−5.1	−7.2
Payment adjustments:								
IME and DSH	17.4	17.9	14.2	12.0	9.7	7.5	5.7	4.7
IME only	17.0	17.3	12.0	8.0	2.9	0.4	−2.3	−3.8
DSH only	12.9	12.3	7.4	5.1	3.0	0.9	−1.3	−3.2
No IME or DSH	12.0	11.2	6.1	2.7	−0.5	−3.6	−6.9	−9.4
Urban <100 beds	13.2	12.3	6.7	3.9	0.9	−1.2	−4.0	−8.3
Urban 100–199 beds	14.3	12.9	8.2	5.7	2.8	−0.4	−3.5	−5.3
Urban 200–299 beds	15.0	14.0	9.4	5.7	2.4	−0.5	−3.3	−5.4
Urban 300–399 beds	16.1	15.8	11.4	8.2	4.8	2.3	−0.6	−3.1
Urban 400–499 beds	15.6	17.5	13.6	10.0	6.1	3.5	1.1	−1.0
Urban 500+ beds	19.0	18.9	14.0	11.5	7.3	4.1	2.0	0.5
Rural <50 beds	6.3	5.7	−0.2	−1.0	−1.6	−1.6	−2.3	−4.1
Rural 50–99 beds	8.8	7.2	1.7	−0.3	−1.9	−3.0	−3.2	−3.3
Rural 100–149 beds	8.8	8.1	3.0	1.0	−0.3	−2.1	−3.4	−3.7
Rural 150–199 beds	7.9	9.9	4.5	2.3	1.5	−1.4	−5.2	−5.1
Rural 200+ beds	10.0	13.7	7.4	3.4	1.0	−2.4	−5.5	−6.6
Voluntary	15.0	15.1	10.5	7.5	4.0	1.5	−1.1	−3.3
Proprietary	14.7	13.0	8.1	4.9	1.4	−2.3	−5.0	−4.8
Urban government	15.2	15.1	10.3	7.8	5.7	3.1	0.7	−1.5
Rural government	7.2	6.3	0.6	−1.8	−2.1	−3.7	−4.4	−5.5
Rural government	7.2	6.3	0.6	−1.8	−2.1	−3.7	−4.4	−5.5

Notes.—Data for each PPS year (PPS 1, PPS 2, etc.) correspond to each hospital's cost reporting period beginning in that year. For instance, the PPS 1 year includes data from each hospital's cost report beginning during the first year of PPS (Federal fiscal year 1984). Excludes hospitals in Maryland; includes hospitals in Massachusetts and New York, beginning with PPS 3; and includes hospitals in New Jersey, beginning with PPS 6.

IME=Indirect medical education payments.
DSH=Disproportionate share payments.

Source: ProPAC analysis of Medicare Cost Report data from the Health Care Financing Administration.

TABLE D-12.—DISTRIBUTION OF PPS OPERATING MARGINS, AND PERCENTAGE OF HOSPITALS WITH NEGATIVE MARGINS, FIRST 8 YEARS OF PPS

Percentile	PPS 1	PPS 2	PPS 3	PPS 4	PPS 5	PPS 6	PPS 7	PPS 8
10th	-6.7	-8.4	-14.6	-18.1	-23.0	-24.9	-27.6	-29.9
25th	3.4	2.1	-3.4	-6.4	-9.3	-11.5	-13.9	-16.5
Median	11.2	10.7	5.7	3.8	1.5	-0.8	-3.0	-4.9
75th	17.7	17.8	13.4	11.9	10.6	8.9	7.2	5.8
90th	23.1	24.2	19.5	18.8	18.3	17.2	16.2	14.5
Percentage of hospitals with negative PPS operating margins	16.8	18.7	31.7	39.1	46.0	52.1	57.5	62.6

Note.—Data for each PPS year (PPS 1, PPS 2, etc.) correspond to each hospital's cost reporting period beginning in that year. For instance, the PPS 1 year includes data from each hospital's cost report beginning during the first year of PPS (Federal fiscal year 1984). Excludes hospitals in Maryland; includes hospitals in Massachusetts and New York, beginning with PPS 3; and New Jersey, beginning with PPS 6.

Source: ProPAC analysis of Medicare Cost Report data from the Health Care Financing Administration.

TABLE D–13.—DISTRIBUTION OF PPS HOSPITALS AND DISCHARGES AND ESTIMATED FISCAL YEAR 1993 PPS PAYMENTS, BY HOSPITAL GROUP

Hospital group	Number of hospitals	PPS hospitals (percent)	PPS discharges (percent)	PPS operating payments (percent)			
				Total	Outlier	IME	DSH
All hospitals	5,329	100	100	100	100	100	100
Urban	2,845	53	78	86	93	98	95
Rural	2,484	47	22	14	7	2	5
Large urban	1,447	27	41	48	54	69	58
Other urban	1,398	26	38	37	40	30	37
Rural referral	236	4	6	5	3	1	2
Sole community	583	11	4	2	1	(1)	1
Other rural	1,665	31	12	7	3	(1)	2
Major teaching	225	4	10	16	20	62	34
Other teaching	805	15	31	34	38	38	33
Non-teaching	4,299	81	59	49	42	0	33
Disproportionate share:							
Large urban	606	11	17	24	27	46	58
Other urban	592	11	18	19	19	20	37
Rural	438	8	5	3	2	1	5
Non-disproportionate share	3,693	69	60	54	52	33	0
Payment adjustments:							
IME and DSH	563	11	21	29	33	67	67
IME only	467	9	20	22	24	33	0
DSH only	1,073	20	19	17	14	0	33
No IME or DSH	3,226	61	40	32	28	0	0
Urban <100 beds	663	12	4	3	2	(1)	(1)
Urban 100–199 beds	857	16	15	14	12	4	17
Urban 200–299 beds	605	11	20	20	20	12	18
Urban 300–399 beds	343	6	15	17	18	16	20

TABLE D–13.—DISTRIBUTION OF PPS HOSPITALS AND DISCHARGES AND ESTIMATED FISCAL YEAR 1993 PPS PAYMENTS, BY HOSPITAL GROUP—Continued

Hospital group	Number of hospitals	PPS hospitals (percent)	PPS discharges (percent)	PPS operating payments (percent)			
				Total	Outlier	IME	DSH
Urban 400–499 beds	184	3	10	12	15	19	14
Urban 500+ beds	193	4	14	19	25	47	27
Rural <50 beds	1,230	23	4	2	(1)	(1)	(1)
Rural 50–99 beds	760	14	7	4	1	(1)	1
Rural 100–149 beds	258	5	4	3	1	(1)	1
Rural 150–199 beds	121	2	3	2	1	(1)	1
Rural 200+ beds	115	2	4	3	3	1	2
New England	228	4	6	6	7	11	3
Middle Atlantic	547	10	17	20	29	32	23
South Atlantic	761	14	17	16	17	11	19
East North Central	820	15	18	17	12	21	12
East South Central	466	9	8	7	7	3	8
West North Central	747	14	8	7	5	7	3
West South Central	753	14	11	9	9	5	12
Mountain	350	7	4	4	4	2	2
Pacific	657	12	11	13	11	9	18
Voluntary	3,036	57	74	75	77	79	65
Proprietary	773	15	12	11	12	2	10
Urban government	403	8	8	9	10	18	22
Rural government	1,087	20	7	4	1	(1)	2

[1] Less than 0.5 percent.

Note.—PPS payments estimated using PPS rules in effect as of January 1, 1993. Excludes hospitals in Maryland. Columns may not add to 100 due to rounding. IME = indirect medical education payments. DSH = disproportionate share payments.

Source: ProPAC estimates based on ProPAC PPS payment model and fiscal year 1991 MedPAR file data from the Health Care Financing Administration.

TABLE D–14.—DISTRIBUTION OF ESTIMATED FISCAL YEAR 1993 PPS PAYMENTS, BY
PAYMENT TYPE AND HOSPITAL GROUP

[In percent]

Hospital group	PPS operating payments			
	Basic DRG	Outlier	IME	DSH
All hospitals	85.9	4.3	5.6	4.1
Urban	84.2	4.7	6.5	4.6
Rural	95.9	2.0	0.6	1.5
Large urban	82.1	4.8	8.1	5.0
Other urban	86.9	4.6	4.4	4.1
Rural referral	94.2	2.6	1.4	1.7
Sole community	97.6	1.2	(1)	1.2
Other rural	96.6	1.8	0.2	1.4
Major teaching	64.8	5.2	21.4	8.6
Other teaching	85.1	4.8	6.2	3.9
Non-teaching	93.5	3.7	0.0	2.8
Disproportionate share:				
Large urban	73.9	4.9	11.1	10.1
Other urban	81.6	4.3	6.0	8.1
Rural	89.8	2.3	1.5	6.4
Non-disproportionate share	92.4	4.2	3.4	0.0
Payment adjustments:				
IME and DSH	72.4	4.9	13.1	9.5
IME only	86.7	4.8	8.5	0.0
DSH only	88.1	3.7	0.0	8.2
No IME or DSH	96.3	3.7	0.0	0.0
Urban <100 beds	96.0	3.0	0.6	0.3
Urban 100–199 beds	89.7	3.7	1.6	4.9
Urban 200–299 beds	88.5	4.4	3.4	3.7
Urban 300–399 beds	85.1	4.7	5.3	4.9
Urban 400–499 beds	80.8	5.4	9.1	4.7
Urban 500+ beds	75.0	5.5	13.7	5.7
Rural <50 beds	98.9	0.5	(1)	0.6
Rural 50–99 beds	98.1	1.2	(1)	0.7
Rural 100–149 beds	95.8	2.1	0.2	1.9
Rural 150–199 beds	95.8	2.6	0.3	1.3
Rural 200+ beds	91.7	3.4	2.3	2.6
New England	83.7	4.7	9.6	2.0
Middle Atlantic	79.6	6.3	9.2	4.9
South Atlantic	86.6	4.6	3.8	5.0
East North Central	87.3	3.1	6.8	2.8
East South Central	88.1	4.2	2.7	5.0
West North Central	90.1	2.9	5.3	1.7

TABLE D–14.—DISTRIBUTION OF ESTIMATED FISCAL YEAR 1993 PPS PAYMENTS, BY PAYMENT TYPE AND HOSPITAL GROUP—Continued

[In percent]

Hospital group	PPS operating payments			
	Basic DRG	Outlier	IME	DSH
West South Central	87.9	4.1	2.9	5.1
Mountain	91.2	3.8	3.3	1.8
Pacific	87.0	3.5	3.7	5.8
Voluntary	86.1	4.4	6.0	3.6
Proprietary	90.4	4.8	1.1	3.7
Urban government	74.9	4.4	10.8	9.9
Rural government	95.9	1.5	0.4	2.3

[1] Less than 0.5 percent.

Notes.—PPS payments estimated using PPS rules in effect as of January 1, 1993. Excludes hospitals in Maryland. Columns may not add to 100 due to rounding. DRG=diagnosis-related group. IME=indirect medical education payments. DSH=disproportionate share payments.

Source: ProPAC estimates based on ProPAC PPS payment model and fiscal year 1991 MedPAR file data from the Health Care Financing Administration.

TABLE D–15.—EFFECTS OF PPS UPDATE FACTORS AND OTHER PAYMENT POLICY CHANGES ON PER-CASE PPS PAYMENT RATE, BY HOSPITAL GROUP

[In percent]

Hospital group	Fiscal year					Fiscal years 1984–93		
	1984–89	1990	1991	1992	1993	Total PPS policy effect	Cumulative increase in case-mix index [1]	Total case mix and policy effect
All hospitals	10.3	5.2	4.5	2.3	3.6	28.4	28.0	64.4
Urban	7.8	4.4	4.2	1.2	4.0	23.4	30.2	60.7
Rural	16.7	9.2	5.1	7.7	2.1	47.2	17.9	73.6
Large urban	8.0	4.4	4.4	0.7	3.9	23.2	29.9	60.1
Other urban	7.9	4.5	4.0	1.8	4.0	24.2	30.4	62.0
Rural referral	7.2	7.3	3.1	8.4	2.8	32.0	23.9	63.6
Sole community	18.6	15.1	8.7	5.2	2.7	60.3	14.1	82.8
Other rural	20.3	8.5	5.1	8.0	1.5	50.3	14.7	72.4
Major teaching	−0.8	4.8	6.6	0.6	4.3	16.3	36.9	59.1
Other teaching	7.4	4.5	3.8	1.6	3.9	22.8	31.6	61.6
Non-teaching	13.4	5.5	4.3	3.1	3.3	33.0	24.0	64.9
Disproportionate share:								
Large urban	8.6	5.5	5.7	0.9	4.0	27.2	31.1	66.7
Other urban	8.8	5.1	4.5	2.7	3.8	27.3	30.6	66.3
Rural	14.5	9.9	5.8	10.4	2.7	51.0	19.1	79.8
Non-disproportionate share	10.9	4.9	3.9	2.1	3.5	27.7	26.9	62.1
Payment adjustments:								
IME and DSH	5.6	5.2	5.3	1.3	4.1	23.3	33.6	64.7
IME only	5.4	4.1	3.8	1.2	3.9	19.6	32.1	58.1
DSH only	13.8	5.9	5.1	4.1	3.5	36.3	24.8	70.0
No IME or DSH	13.1	5.3	3.9	2.7	3.2	31.2	23.7	62.3
Urban <100 beds	8.6	3.0	3.2	0.5	3.2	19.8	18.2	41.6
Urban 100–199 beds	10.3	4.1	4.2	1.6	3.8	26.1	23.5	55.8
Urban 200–299 beds	9.0	3.8	4.3	1.1	3.9	24.0	27.7	58.4
Urban 300–399 beds	8.3	4.9	3.9	1.3	4.0	24.4	31.4	63.4
Urban 400–499 beds	6.1	5.2	4.0	1.0	3.9	21.7	33.6	62.7
Urban 500+ beds	2.9	4.3	4.4	1.2	4.4	18.3	37.3	62.4

TABLE D-15.—EFFECTS OF PPS UPDATE FACTORS AND OTHER PAYMENT POLICY CHANGES ON PER-CASE PPS PAYMENT RATE, BY HOSPITAL GROUP—Continued

[In percent]

Hospital group	Fiscal year					Fiscal years 1984–93		
	1984–89	1990	1991	1992	1993	Total PPS policy effect	Cumulative increase in case-mix index [1]	Total case mix and policy effect
Rural <50 beds	20.9	12.4	5.8	5.1	0.8	52.1	7.4	63.3
Rural 50–99 beds	19.3	10.2	6.0	7.0	1.8	51.8	14.2	73.3
Rural 100–149 beds	15.8	8.5	5.0	8.6	2.4	46.7	19.9	76.0
Rural 150–199 beds	12.4	7.8	3.7	8.6	2.8	40.3	19.5	67.7
Rural 200 + beds	7.9	6.6	4.7	9.1	2.9	35.2	25.6	69.7
New England	13.0	4.5	8.0	1.8	4.0	34.9	21.1	63.4
Middle Atlantic	3.2	5.4	4.0	0.5	3.6	17.9	27.2	50.0
South Atlantic	8.8	5.3	7.0	3.2	4.0	31.6	30.5	71.8
East North Central	8.4	4.2	3.0	2.8	3.2	23.4	27.1	56.8
East South Central	9.2	6.5	4.5	3.5	3.9	30.7	27.8	67.0
West North Central	16.0	6.0	2.1	3.1	2.8	33.0	28.4	70.8
West South Central	10.6	6.8	3.5	2.9	4.0	30.8	31.1	71.4
Mountain	8.8	5.3	4.8	2.4	3.5	27.2	26.6	61.0
Pacific	14.6	4.0	4.5	1.6	3.6	31.1	26.9	66.4
Voluntary	9.6	4.9	4.2	2.1	3.6	26.7	27.8	61.9
Proprietary	9.0	5.0	5.1	2.4	4.3	28.4	33.9	71.9
Urban government	8.2	5.5	5.2	0.6	4.0	25.5	29.5	62.5
Rural government	17.8	10.1	5.5	7.3	1.9	49.6	14.4	71.2

[1] The estimated effect of the change in case mix for fiscal years 1992 and 1993 by group is based on the actual annual rate of change by group for fiscal years 1985 through 1991.

Note.—Figures are not estimates of actual changes in fiscal year PPS hospital payments. They are meant to isolate the effects of changes in PPS rules on PPS payment rates, holding all other factors constant. Payments for each year are estimated based on the PPS rules in effect on the last day of the fiscal year. The effect of change in case mix is reflected only in the last two columns. Excludes hospitals in Maryland; includes hospitals in Massachusetts and New York beginning with fiscal year 1987 and New Jersey beginning with fiscal year 1989. IME=indirect medical education payments. DSH=disproportionate share payments.

Source: ProPAC estimates based on ProPAC PPS payment model and fiscal year 1991 MedPAR file data from the Health Care Financing Administration.

TABLE D–16.—SUMMARY CHARACTERISTICS OF PPS HOSPITALS, BY HOSPITAL GROUP

Hospital group	Number of hospitals [1]	Estimated Medicare discharges (thousands, 1995)	Average number of beds (1992)	Estimated average case mix (1995)[2]	Average wage index (1994)[3]	Estimated PPS payment (dollars per case, 1995)[4]
All hospitals	5,350	10,661	151	1.50	0.99	$6,660
Urban	2,989	8,578	217	1.54	1.02	7,190
Rural	2,361	2,083	69	1.26	0.81	4,460
Large MSA [5]	1,637	4,850	234	1.55	1.09	7,770
Other urban	1,352	3,727	195	1.54	0.92	6,450
Rural referral	248	710	188	1.40	0.83	5,140
Rural sole community [6]	579	345	50	1.19	0.81	4,550
Other rural	1,534	1,028	57	1.18	0.79	3,960
Major teaching [7]	233	1,064	448	1.72	1.11	11,360
Other teaching	808	3,365	294	1.58	1.00	7,260
Nonteaching	4,309	6,233	109	1.39	0.94	5,530
Disproportionate share:[8]						
Large MSA	735	2,257	280	1.57	1.10	8,840
Other urban	630	2,015	243	1.56	0.91	6,850
Rural	467	561	97	1.27	0.79	4,620
Nondisproportionate share	3,518	5,828	116	1.46	0.98	5,940
Urban, 50 or fewer beds	322	111	34	1.16	1.00	4,650
Urban, 51 to 100 beds	463	419	76	1.28	0.99	5,090
Urban, 101 to 200 beds	888	1,694	146	1.39	1.01	6,110
Urban, 201 to 400 beds	954	3,837	284	1.53	1.01	6,900
Urban, 401 or more beds	362	2,517	557	1.70	1.04	8,830
Rural, 50 or fewer beds	1,252	409	32	1.10	0.79	3,750
Rural, 51 to 100 beds	684	634	72	1.21	0.80	4,160
Rural, 101 to 200 beds	320	644	138	1.30	0.82	4,660
Rural, 201 or more beds	105	396	273	1.43	0.83	5,320
New England	225	608	175	1.47	1.13	7,310
Middle Atlantic	532	1,815	254	1.48	1.12	7,760
South Atlantic	756	1,816	176	1.53	0.91	6,340

TABLE D–16.—SUMMARY CHARACTERISTICS OF PPS HOSPITALS, BY HOSPITAL GROUP—Continued

Hospital group	Number of hospitals [1]	Estimated Medicare discharges (thousands, 1995)	Average number of beds (1992)	Estimated average case mix (1995)[2]	Average wage index (1994)[3]	Estimated PPS payment (dollars per case, 1995)[4]
East North Central	811	1,864	172	1.49	0.96	6,470
East South Central	460	877	138	1.44	0.82	5,450
West North Central	740	851	91	1.51	0.89	5,930
West South Central	747	1,105	126	1.50	0.87	5,980
Mountain	370	452	95	1.52	0.97	6,400
Pacific	654	1,171	143	1.54	1.20	7,910
Puerto Rico	55	103	172	1.33	0.50	2,790
Government, Urban [9]	451	867	199	1.55	0.99	7,940
Government, Rural	1,063	650	55	1.19	0.78	4,120
Voluntary, Urban	1,940	6,652	241	1.55	1.03	7,210
Voluntary, Rural	1,088	1,216	81	1.29	0.83	4,630
Proprietary, Urban	576	1,045	154	1.51	0.98	6,460
Proprietary, Rural	203	217	78	1.28	0.82	4,500

[1] Number of hospitals for which data were available.
[2] Weighted by case-mix-adjusted PPS payments.
[3] Weighted by wage-index-adjusted PPS payments.
[4] Incurred payments (including copayments) divided by the number of Medicare discharges.
[5] Hospitals located in Metropolitan Statistical Areas with more than 1 million people or New England County Metropolitan Areas with more than 970,000 people.
[6] Scle community hospitals that are also rural referral centers are included in the rural referral category.
[7] Teaching hospitals for which the ratio of the number of full-time-equivalent interns and residents to the number of beds is .25 or larger.
[8] Hospitals that receive a disproportionate share adjustment for treating a relatively high proportion of low-income patients.
[9] Ownership type was not available for 29 hospitals.

Note.—Years refer to federal fiscal years. Urban and rural categories are based on hospitals' geographic locations.

Source: Congressional Budget Office estimates based on data from the Health Care Financing Administration and the Prospective Payment Assessment Commission.

TABLE D–17.—HISTORICAL TRENDS IN FACTORS AFFECTING PPS RATES AND AVERAGE PAYMENTS PER CASE

[Percentage change from previous year]

	Fiscal year—													
	1982	1983	1984	1985	1986	1987	1988	1989	1990	1991	1992	1993	1994	1995
Market basket index [1] ...	8.1	5.5	4.9	4.1	2.9	3.2	4.7	5.4	5.5	5.2	[2]4.4	[3]4.1	4.3	4.7
Annual update factor [4]	....	....	....	....	....	1.15	1.76	3.33	5.71	2.83	2.99	2.73	2.04	2.61
Case mix index [5]	....	....	8.4	3.1	2.5	2.1	3.2	2.5	0.84	2.5	1.4	1.3	2.0	2.0
Average payments per discharge [6]	13.8	10.2	10.8	15.0	8.0	3.6	2.8	13.0	8.4	4.9	7.3	4.7	5.0	4.8
Average payments per beneficiary [6]	15.2	11.4	7.8	6.6	1.5	-0.3	1.2	9.4	8.1	3.8	10.3	5.8	6.1	6.2

[1] Estimates as published in the Federal Register for fiscal years 1982–94; fiscal year 1995 President's Budget assumptions shown for fiscal year 1995.
[2] 4.7 for hospitals excluded from the prospective payment system.
[3] 4.2 for hospitals excluded from the prospective payment system.
[4] Estimates as published in the Federal Register for fiscal years 1987–94; fiscal year 1995 President's Budget assumptions used for fiscal year 1995.
[5] Estimates based on historical data for fiscal years 1982–93; fiscal year 1995 President's Budget assumptions shown for fiscal years 1994–95.
[6] Estimated based on historical data and fiscal year 1995 President's Budget assumptions; estimates for fiscal years 1989 and 1990 include the effect of provisions of the Medicare Catastrophic Coverage Act of 1988.
[7] Not available from this office.

Source: Health Care Financing Administration, Office of the Actuary, Office of Medicare and Medicaid Cost Estimates.

TABLE D–18.—WAGE INDEX FOR URBAN AREAS

Urban area (constituent counties or county equivalents)	Wage index
Abilene, TX (Taylor, TX)	.8830
Aguadilla, PR (Aguada, PR, Aguadilla, PR, Moca, PR)	.5525
Akron, OH (Portage, OH, Summit, OH)	.8122
Albany, GA (Dougherty, GA, Lee, GA)	.8493
Albany-Schenectady-Troy, NY (Albany, NY, Montgomery, NY, Rensselaer, NY, Saratoga, NY, Schenectady, NY, Schoharie, NY)	.9033
Albuquerque, NM (Bernalillo, NM, Sandoval, NM, Valencia, NM)	.9861
Alexandria, LA (Rapides, LA)	.9130
Allentown-Bethlehem-Easton, PA (Carbon, PA, Lehigh, PA, Northampton, PA)	.9973
Altoona, PA (Blair, PA)	.9342
Amarillo, TX (Potter, TX, Randall, TX)	.8667
Anchorage, AK (Anchorage, AK)	1.2201
Ann Arbor, MI (Lenawee, MI, Livingston, MI, Washtenaw, MI)	1.2539
Anniston, AL (Calhoun, AL)	.7998
Appleton-Oshkosh-Neenah, WI (Calumet, WI, Outagamie, WI, Winnebago, WI)	.8743
Arecibo, PR (Arecibo, PR, Camuy, PR, Hatillo, PR)	.3705
Asheville, NC (Buncombe, NC, Madison, NC)	.9175
Athens, GA (Clarke, GA, Madison, GA, Oconee, GA)	.8324
Atlanta, GA (Barrow, GA, Bartow, GA, Carroll, Ga, Cherokee, GA, Clayton, GA, Cobb, GA, Coweta, GA, De Kalb, GA, Douglas, GA, Fayette, GA, Forsyth, GA, Fulton, GA, Gwinnett, GA, Henry, GA, Newton, GA, Paulding, GA, Pickens, GA, Rockdale, GA, Spalding, GA, Walton, GA)	.9402
Atlantic City-Cape May, NJ (Atlantic City, NJ, Cape May, NJ)	1.0584
Augusta-Aiken, GA–SC (Columbia, GA, McDuffie, GA, Richmond, GA, Aiken, SC, Edgefield SC)	.8899
Austin-San Marcos, TX (Bastrop, TX, Caldwell, TX, Hays, TX, Travis, TX, Williamson, TX)	.9209
Bakersfield, CA (Kern, CA)	1.0857
Baltimore, MD (Anne Arundel, MD, Baltimore, MD, Baltimore City, MD, Carroll, MD, Harford, MD, Howard, MD, Queen Annes, MD)	1.0036
Bangor, ME (Penobscot, ME)	.9191
Barnstable-Yarmouth, MA (Barnstable, MA)	1.3351
Baton Rouge, LA (Ascension, LA, East Baton Rouge, LA, Livingston, LA, West Baton Rouge, LA)	.8659
Beaumont-Port Arthur, TX (Hardin, TX, Jefferson, TX, Orange, TX)	.8934
Bellingham, WA (Whatcom, WA)	1.1147
Benton Harbor, MI (Berrien, MI)	.7923
Bergen-Passaic, NJ (Bergen, NJ, Passaic, NJ)	1.1331
Billings, MT (Yellowstone, MT)	.8992
Biloxi-Gulfport-Pascagoula, MS (Hancock, MS, Harrison, MS, Jackson, MS)	.8056
Binghamton, NY (Broome, NY, Tioga, NY)	.9098
Birmingham, AL (Blount, AL, Jefferson, AL, Saint Clair, AL, Shelby, AL)	.9006
Bismarck, ND (Burleigh, ND, Morton, ND)	.8759
Bloomington, IN (Monroe, IN)	.8525
Bloomington-Normal, IL (McLean, IL)	.8566
Boise City, ID (Ada, ID, Canyon, ID)	.8883

TABLE D–18.—WAGE INDEX FOR URBAN AREAS—Continued

Urban area (constituent counties or county equivalents)	Wage index
Boston-Brockton-Nashua, MA–HN (Bristol, MA, Essex, MA, Middlesex, MA, Norfolk, MA, Plymouth, MA, Suffolk, MA, Worcester, MA, Hillsborough, NH, Merrimack, NH, Rockingham, NH, Strafford, NH)	1.1503
Boulder-Longmont, CO (Boulder, CO)	.8197
Brazoria, TX (Brazoria, TX)	.8655
Bremerton, WA (Kitsap, WA)	.9529
Brownsville-Harlingen-San Benito, TX (Cameron, TX)	.8479
Bryan-College Station, TX (Brazos, TX)	.9054
Buffalo-Niagara Falls, NY (Erie, NY, Niagara, NY)	.9117
Burlington, VT (Chittenden, VT, Franklkn, VT, Grand Isle, VT)	.9458
Caguas, PR (Caguas, PR, Cayey, PR, Cidra, PR, Gurabo, PR, San Lorenzo, PR)	.5039
Canton, OH (Carroll, OH, Stark, OH)	.8718
Casper, WY (Natrona, WY)	.8408
Cedar Rapids, IA (Linn, IA)	.8475
Champaign-Urbana, IL (Champaign, IL)	.8720
Charleston-North Charleston, SC (Berkeley, SC, Charleston, SC, Dorchester, SC)	.8947
Charleston, WV (Kanawha, WV, Putnam, WV)	.8786
Charlotte-Gastonia-Rock Hill, NC–SC (Cabarrus, NC, Gaston, NC, Lincoln, NC, Mecklengburg, NC, Rowan, NC, Union, NC, York, SC)	.9648
Charlottesville, VA (Albermale, VA, Charlottesville City, VA, Fluvanna, VA, Greene, VA)	.9477
Chattanooga, TN–GA (Catoosa, GA, Dade, GA, Walker, GA, Hamilton, TN, Marion, TN)	.9088
Cheyenne, WY (Laramie, WY)	.7538
Chicago, IL (Cook, IL, De Kalb, IL, Du Page, IL, Grundy, IL, Kane, IL, Kendall, IL, Lake, IL, McHenry, IL)	1.0593
Chico-Paradise, CA (Butte, CA)	1.0071
Cincinnati, OH–KY–IN (Dearborn, IN, Boone, KY, Campbell, KY, Gallatin, KY, Grant, KY, Kenton, KY, Pendleton, KY, Brown, OH, Clermont, OH, Hamilton, OH, Warren, OH)	.9548
Clarksville-Hopkinsville, TN–KY (Christian, KY, Montgomery, TN)	.6826
Cleveland-Lorain-Elyria, OH (Ashtabula, OH, Cuyahoga, OH, Geauga, OH, Lake, OH, Lorain, OH, Medina, OH)	.9817
Colorado Springs, CO (El Paso, CO)	.9464
Columbia, MO (Boone, MO)	.9312
Columbia, SC (Lexington, SC, Richland, SC)	.8851
Columbus, GA–AL (Russell, AL, Chattanoochee, GA, Muscogee, GA)	.7562
Columbus, OH (Delaware, OH, Fairfield, OH, Franklin, OH, Licking, OH, Madison, OH, Pickaway, OH, Union, OH)	.9902
Corpus Christi, TX (Nueces, TX, San Patricio, TX)	.8334
Cumberland, MD–WV (Allegeny, MD, Mineral, WV)	.8103
Dallas, TX (Collin, TX, Dallas, TX, Denton, TX, Ellis, TX, Henderson, TX, Hunt, TX, Kaufman, TX, Rockwall, TX)	.9649
Danville, VA (Danville City, VA, Pittsylvania, VA)	.7881
Davenport-Rock Island-Moline, IA–IL (Scott, IA, Henry, IL, Rock Island, IL)	.8300
Dayton-Springfield, OH (Clark, OH, Greene, OH, Miami, OH, Montgomery, OH)	.9424
Daytona Beach, FL (Volusia, FL)	.8826

TABLE D–18.—WAGE INDEX FOR URBAN AREAS—Continued

Urban area (constituent counties or county equivalents)	Wage index
Decatur, AL (Lawrence, AL, Morgan, AL)	.7995
Decatur, IL (Macon, IL)	.8011
Denver, CO (Adams, CO, Arapahoe, CO, Denver, CO, Douglas, CO, Jefferson, CO)	1.0935
Des Moines, IA (Dallas, IA, Polk, IA, Warren, IA)	.8676
Detroit, MI (Lapeer, MI, Macomb, MI, Monroe, MI, Oakland, MI, Saint Clair, MI, Wayne, MI)	1.0790
Dothan, AL (Dale, AL, Houston, AL)	.7793
Dover, DE (Kent, DE)	.8728
Dubuque, IA (Dubuque, IA)	.8324
Duluth-Superior, MN–WI (St. Louis, MN, Douglas, WI)	.9166
Dutchess County, NY (Dutchess, NY)	1.0623
Eau Claire, WI (Chippewa, WI, Eau Claire, WI)	.8481
El Paso, TX (El Paso, TX)	.9537
Elkhart-Goshen, IN (Elkhart, IN)	.8560
Elmira, NY (Chemung, NY)	.8558
Enid, OK (Garfield, OK)	.7985
Erie, PA (Erie, PA)	.9169
Eugene-Springfield, OR (Lane, OR)	.9480
Evansville, IN–KY (Posey, IN, Vanderburgh, IN, Warrick, IN, Henderson, KY)	.8904
Fargo-Moorhead, ND–MN (Clay, MN, Cass, ND)	.9557
Fayetteville, NC (Cumberland, NC)	.8519
Fayetteville-Springdale-Rogers, AR (Benton, AR, Washington, AR)	.7247
Flint, MI (Genessee, MI)	1.0689
Florence, AL (Colbert, AL, Lauderdale, AL)	.7707
Florence, SC (Florence, SC)	.8671
Fort Collins-Loveland, CO (Larimor, CO)	.9885
Fort Lauderdale, FL (Broward, FL)	1.0573
Fort Myers-Cape Coral, FL (Lee, FL)	.9279
Fort Pierce-Port St. Lucie, FL (Martin, FL, St. Lucie, FL)	1.0477
Fort Smith, AR–OK (Crawford, AR, Sebastian, AR, Sequoyah, OK)	.7611
Fort Walton Beach, FL (Okaloosa, FL)	.8825
Fort Wayne, IN (Adams, IN, Allen, IN, De Kalb, IN, Huntington, IN, Wells, IN, Whitley, IN)	.8893
Fort Worth-Arlington, TX (Johnson, TX, Parker, TX, Tarrant, TX)	.9550
Fresno, CA (Fresno, CA, Madera, CA)	1.0244
Gadsden, AL (Etowah, AL)	.7747
Gainesville, FL (Alachua, FL)	.8911
Galveston-Texas City, TX (Galveston, TX)	.9865
Gary, IN (Lake, IN, Porter, IN)	.8740
Glens Falls, NY (Warren, NY, Washington, NY)	.9393
Goldsboro, NC (Wayne, NC)	.8399
Grand Forks, ND–MN (Polk, MN, Grand Forks, ND)	.8795
Grand Rapids-Muskegon-Holland, MI (Allegan, MI, Kent, MI, Muskegon, MI, Ottawa, MI)	.9764
Great Falls, MT (Cascade, MT)	.8906
Greeley, CO (Weld, CO)	.8714
Green Bay, WI (Brown, WI)	.8852

TABLE D–18.—WAGE INDEX FOR URBAN AREAS—Continued

Urban area (constituent counties or county equivalents)	Wage index
Greensboro-Winston-Salem-High Point, NC (Alamance, NC, Davidson, NC, Davie, NC, Forsyth, NC, Guilford, NC, Randolph, NC, Stokes, NC, Yadkin, NC)	.9283
Greenville, NC (Pitt, NC)	.9331
Greenville-Spartanburg-Anderson, SC (Anderson, SC, Cherokee, SC, Greenville, SC, Pickens, SC, Spartanburg, SC)	.8715
Hagerstown, MD (Washington, MD)	.8830
Hamilton-Middletown, OH (Butler, OH)	.8122
Harrisburg-Lebanon-Carlisle, PA (Cumberland, PA, Dauphin, PA, Lebanon, PA, Perry, PA)	.9995
Hartford, CT (Hartford, CT, Litchfield, CT, Middlesex, CT, Tolland, CT)	1.2086
Hickory-Morganton, NC (Alexander, NC, Burke, NC, Caldwell, NC, Catawba, NC)	.8800
Honolulu, HI (Honolulu, HI)	1.0995
Houma, LA (Lafourche, LA, Terrebonne, LA)	.7765
Houston, TX (Chambers, TX, Fort Bend, TX, Harris, TX, Liberty, TX, Montgomery, TX, Waller, TX)	.9908
Huntington-Ashland, WV–KY–OH (Boyd, KY, Carter, KY, Greenup, KY, Lawrence, OH, Cabell, WV, Wayne, WV)	.8971
Huntsville, AL (Limestone, AL, Madison, AL)	.8158
Indianapolis, IN (Boone, IN, Hamilton, IN, Hancock, IN, Hendricks, IN, Johnson, IN, Marion, IN, Morgan, IN, Shelby, IN)	.9871
Iowa City, IA (Johnson, IA)	.9706
Jackson, MI (Jackson, MI)	.9277
Jackson, MS (Hinds, MS, Madison, MS, Rankin, MS)	.7519
Jackson, TN (Madison, TN)	.8007
Jacksonville, FL (Clay, FL, Duval, FL, Nassau, FL, St. Johns, FL)	.8968
Jacksonville, NC (Onslow, NC)	.7197
Jamestown, NY (Chautaqua, NY)	.7688
Janesville-Beloit, WI (Rock, WI)	.8415
Jersey City, NJ (Hudson, NJ)	1.0966
Johnson City-Kingsport-Bristol, TN–VA (Carter, TN, Hawkins, TN, Sullivan, TN, Unicoi, TN, Washington, TN, Bristol City, VA, Scott, VA, Washington, VA)	.8472
Johnstown, PA (Cambria, PA, Somerset, PA)	.8786
Joplin, MO (Jasper, MO, Newton, MO)	.7697
Kalamazoo-Battlecreek, MI (Calhoun, MI, Kalamazoo, MI, Van Buren, MI)	1.0945
Kankakee, IL (Kankakee, IL)	.8458
Kansas City, KS–MO (Johnson, KS, Leavenworth, KS, Miami, KS, Wyandotte, KS, Cass, MO, Clay, MO, Clinton, MO, Jackson, MO, Lafayette, MO, Platte, MO, Ray, MO)	.9538
Kenosha, WI (Kenosha, WI)	.8846
Killeen-Temple, TX (Bell, TX, Coryell, TX)	1.0169
Knoxville, TN (Anderson, TN, Blount, TN, Knox, TN, Loudon, TN, Sevier, TN, Union, TN)	.9247
Kokomo, IN (Howard, IN, Tipton, IN)	.8616
LaCrosse, WI-MN (Houston, MN, La Crosse, WI)	.8409
Lafayette, LA (Arcadia, LA, Lafayette, LA, St. Laundry, LA, St. Martin, LA)	.8144
Lafayette, IN (Clinton, IN, Tippecanoe, IN)	.8415
Lake Charles, LA (Calcasieu, LA)	.8134

TABLE D–18.—WAGE INDEX FOR URBAN AREAS—Continued

Urban area (constituent counties or county equivalents)	Wage index
Lakeland-Winter Haven, FL (Polk, FL)	.8335
Lancaster, PA (Lancaster, PA)	.9520
Lansing-East Lansing, MI (Clinton, MI, Eaton, MI, Ingham, MI)	.9633
Laredo, TX (Webb, TX)	.6953
Las Cruces, NM (Dona Ana, NM)	.8919
Las Vegas, NV-AZ (Mohave, AZ, Clark, NV, Nye, NV)	1.0714
Lawrence, KS (Douglas, KS)	.8793
Lawton, OK (Comanche, OK)	.8453
Lewiston-Auburn, ME (Androscoggin, ME)	.9644
Lexington, KY (Bourbon, KY, Clark, KY, Fayette, KY, Jessamine, KY, Madison, KY, Scott, KY, Woodford, KY)	.8291
Lima, OH (Allen, OH, Auglaize, OH)	.8441
Lincoln, NE (Lancaster, NE)	.8904
Little Rock-North Little Rock, AR (Faulkner, AR, Lonoke, AR, Pulaski, AR, Saline, AR)	.8306
Longview-Marshall, TX (Gregg, TX, Harrison, TX, Upshur, TX)	.8720
Los Angeles-Long Beach, CA (Los Angeles, CA)	1.2719
Louisville, KY–IN (Clark, IN, Floyd, IN, Harrison, IN, Scott, IN, Bullitt, KY, Jefferson, KY, Oldham, KY)	.9407
Lubbock, TX (Lubbock, TX)	.8678
Lynchburg, VA (Amherst, VA, Bedford City, VA, Bedford, VA, Campbell, VA, Lynchburg City, VA)	.8226
Macon, GA (Bibb, GA, Houston, GA, Jones, GA, Peach, GA, Twiggs, GA)	.9704
Madison, WI (Dane, WI)	.9977
Mansfield, OH (Crawford, OH, Richland, OH)	.8158
Mayaguez, PR (Anasco, PR, Cabo Rojo, PR, Hormigueros, PR, Mayaguez, PR, Sabana Grande, PR, San German, PR)	.5397
McAllen-Edinburg-Mission, TX (Hidalgo, TX)	.8497
Medford-Ashland, OR (Jackson, OR)	.9768
Melbourne-Titusville, FL (Brevard, FL)	.9356
Memphis, TN–AR–MS (Critteneden, AR, De Soto, MS, Fayette, TN, Shelby, TN, Tipton, TN)	.8546
Merced, CA (Merced, CA)	1.0021
Miami, FL (Dade, FL)	.8515
Middlesex-Somerset-Hunterdon, NJ (Hunterdon, NJ, Middlesex, NJ, Somerset, NJ)	1.0871
Milwaukee, WI (Milwaukee, WI, Ozaukee, WI, Washington, WI, Waukesha, WI)	.9240
Minneapolis-St. Paul, MN–WI (Anoka, MN, Carver, MN, Chisago, MN, Dakota, MN, Hennepin, MN, Isanti, MN, Ramsey, MN, Scott, MN, Sherburne, MN, Washington, MN, Wright, MN, Pierce, WI, St. Croix, WI)	1.0855
Mobile, AL (Baldwin, AL, Mobile, AL)	.7801
Modesto, CA (Stanislaus, CA)	1.1471
Monmouth-Ocean, NJ (Monmouth, NJ, Ocean, NJ)	1.0082
Monroe, LA (Ouachita, LA)	.7663
Montgomery, AL (Autauga, AL, Elmore, AL, Montgomery, AL)	.7564
Muncie, IN (Delaware, IN)	.8456
Myrtle Beach, SC (Horry, SC)	.7906
Naples, FL (Collier, FL)	.9646

TABLE D–18.—WAGE INDEX FOR URBAN AREAS—Continued

Urban area (constituent counties or county equivalents)	Wage index
Nashville, TN (Cheatham, TN, Davidson, TN, Dickson, TN, Robertson, TN, Rutherford, TN, Sumner, TN, Williamson, TN, Wilson, TN)	.9105
Nassau-Suffolk, NY (Nassau, NY, Suffolk, NY)	1.2855
New Haven-Bridgeport-Stamford-Danbury-Waterbury, CT (Fairfield, CT, New Haven, CT)	1.2289
New London-Norwich, CT (New London, CT)	1.1589
New Orleans, LA (Jefferson, LA, Orleans, LA, St. Bernard, LA, St. Charles, LA, St. James, LA, St. John The Baptist, LA, St. Tammany, LA)	.9443
New York, NY (Bronx, NY, Kings, NY, New York, NY, Putnam, NY, Queens, NY, Richmond, NY, Rockland, NY, Westchester, NY)	1.4020
Newark, NJ (Essex, NJ, Morris, NJ, Sussex, NJ, Union, NJ)	1.1145
Newburgh, NY–PA (Orange, NY, Pike, PA)	.8560
Norfolk-Virginia Beach-Newport News, VA–NC (Currituck, NC, Chesapeake City, VA, Gloucester, VA, Hampton City, VA, Isle of Wight, VA, James City, VA, Matthews, VA, Newport News City, VA, Norfolk City, VA, Poquoson City, VA, Portsmouth City, VA, Suffolk City, VA, Virginia Beach City, VA, Williamsburg City, VA, York, VA)	.8541
Oakland, CA (Alameda, CA, Contra Costa, CA)	1.4369
Ocala, FL (Marion, FL)	.8490
Odessa-Midland, TX (Ector, TX, Midland, TX)	.8735
Oklahoma City, OK (Canadian, OK, Cleveland, OK, Logan, OK, McClain, OK, Oklahoma, OK, Pottawatomie, OK)	.8455
Olympia, WA (Thurston, WA)	1.0326
Omaha, NE–IA (Pottawattamie, IA, Cass, NE, Douglas, NE, Sarpy, NE, Washington, NE)	.9900
Orange County, NY (Orange, NY)	1.3409
Orlando, FL (Lake, FL, Orange, FL, Osceola, FL, Seminole, FL)	.9782
Owensboro, KY (Daviess, KY)	.7654
Panama City, FL (Bay, FL)	.8359
Parkersburg-Marietta, WV–OH (Washington, OH, Wood, WV)	.7748
Pensacola, FL (Escambia, FL, Santa Rosa, FL)	.8429
Peoria-Pekin, IL (Peoria, IL, Tazewell, IL, Woodford, IL)	.8706
Philadelphia, PA–NJ (Burlington, NJ, Camden, NJ, Gloucester, NJ, Salem, NJ, Bucks, PA, Chester, PA, Delaware, PA, Montgomery, PA, Philadelphia, PA)	1.1254
Phoenix-Mesa, AZ (Maricopa, AZ, Pinal, AZ)	1.0223
Pine Bluff, AR (Jefferson, AR)	.8714
Pittsburgh, PA (Allegheny, PA, Fayette, PA, Washington, PA, Westmoreland, PA)	.9950
Pittsfield, MA (Berkshire, MA)	1.1001
Ponce, PR (Guayanilla, PR, Juana Diaz, PR, Penuelas, PR, Ponce, PR, Villalba, PR, Yauco, PR)	.5167
Portland, ME (Cumberland, ME, Sagadahoc, ME, York, ME)	.9381
Portland-Vancouver, OR–WA (Clackamas, OR, Columbia, OR, Multnomah, OR, Washington, OR, Yamhill, OR, Clark, WA)	1.1051
Providence-Warwick, RI (Bristol, RI, Kent, RI, Newport, RI, Providence, RI, Washington, RI)	1.0717
Provo-Orem, UT (Utah, UT)	.9960
Pueblo, CO (Pueblo, CO)	.8260
Punta Gorda, FL (Charlotte, FL)	.9133

TABLE D–18.—WAGE INDEX FOR URBAN AREAS—Continued

Urban area (constituent counties or county equivalents)	Wage index
Racine, WI (Racine, WI)	.8298
Raleigh-Durham-Chapel Hill, NC (Chatham, NC, Durham, NC, Franklin, NC, Johnston, NC, Orange, NC, Wake, NC)	.9521
Rapid City, SD (Pennington, SD)	.8220
Reading, PA (Berks, PA)	.9082
Redding, CA (Shasta, CA)	1.1622
Reno, NV (Washoe, NV)	1.2009
Richland-Kennewick-Pasco, WA (Benton, WA, Franklin, WA)	.9214
Richmond-Petersburg, VA (Charles City Co., VA, Chesterfield, VA, Colonial Heights City, VA, Dinwiddie, VA, Goochland, VA, Hanover, VA, Henrico, VA, Hopewell City, VA, New Kent, VA, Petersburg City, VA, Powhatan, VA, Prince George, VA, Richmond City, VA)	.8801
Riverside-San Bernardino, CA (Riverside, CA, San Bernardino, CA)	1.2021
Roanoke, VA (Botetourt, VA, Roanoke, VA, Roanoke City, VA, Salem City, VA)	.8358
Rochester, MN (Olmsted, MN)	1.0078
Rochester, NY (Genesse, NY, Livingston, NY, Monroe, NY, Ontario, NY, Orleans, NY, Wayne, NY)	.9761
Rockford, IL (Boone, IL, Winnebago, IL)	.8708
Rocky Mount, NC (Edgecombe, NC, Nash, NC)	.8743
Sacramento, CA (El Dorado, CA, Placer, CA, Sacramento, CA)	1.2165
Saginaw-Bay City-Midland, MI (Bay, MI, Midland, MI, Saginaw, MI)	.9549
St. Cloud, MN (Benton, MN, Stearns, MN)	.9825
St. Joseph, MO (Andrews, MO, Buchanan, MO)	.8811
St. Louis, MO–IL (Clinton, IL, Jersey, IL, Madison, IL, Monroe, IL, St. Clair, IL, Franklin, MO, Jefferson, MO, Lincoln, MO, St. Charles, MO, St. Louis, MO, St. Louis City, MO, Warren, MO)	.9182
Salem, OR (Marion, OR, Polk, OR)	.9443
Salinas, CA (Monterey, CA)	1.3187
Salt Lake City-Ogden, UT (Davis, UT, Salt Lake, UT, Weber, UT)	.9669
San Angelo, TX (Tom Green, TX)	.7887
San Antonio, TX (Bexar, TX, Comal, TX, Guadalupe, TX, Wilson, TX)	.8210
San Diego, CA (San Diego, CA)	1.2040
San Francisco, CA (Marin, CA, San Francisco, CA, San Mateo, CA)	1.4086
San Jose, CA (Santa Clara, CA)	1.4254
San Juan-Bayamon, PR (Aquas Buenas, PR, Barceloneta, PR, Bayamon, PR, Canovanas, PR, Carolina, PR, Catano, PR, Ceiba, PR, Comerio, PR, Corozal, PR, Dorado, PR, Fajardo, PR, Florida, PR, Guaynabo, PR, Humacao, PR, Juncos, PR, Los Piedras, PR, Loiza, PR, Luguillo, PR, Manati, PR, Naranjito, PR, Rio Grande, PR, San Juan, PR, Toa Alta, PR, Toa Baja, PR, Trujillo Alto, PR, Vega Alta, PR, Vega Baja, PR, Yabucoa, PR)	.4969
San Luis Obispo-Atascadero-Pasa Robles, CA (San Luis Obispo, CA)	1.2505
Santa Barbara-Santa Maria-Lompoc, CA, Santa Barbara, CA)	1.1637
Santa Cruz-Watsonville, CA (Santa Cruz, CA)	.9727
Santa Fe, NM (Los Alamos, NM, Santa Fe, NM)	.9985
Santa Rosa, CA (Sonoma, CA)	1.3084
Sarasota-Bradenton, FL (Manatee, FL, Sarasota, FL)	.9712
Savannah, GA (Bryan, GA, Chatham, GA, Effingham, GA)	.8675

TABLE D–18.—WAGE INDEX FOR URBAN AREAS—Continued

Urban area (constituent counties or county equivalents)	Wage index
Scranton-Wilkes Barre-Hazelton, PA (Columbia, PA, Lackawanna, PA, Luzerne, PA, Wyoming, PA)	.8605
Seattle-Bellevue-Everett, WA (Island, WA, King, WA, Snohomish, WA)	1.0985
Sharon, PA (Mercer, PA)	.8885
Sheboygan, WI (Sheboygan, WI)	.8229
Sherman-Denison, TX (Grayson, TX)	.8912
Shreveport-Bossier City, LA (Bossier, LA, Caddo, LA, Webster, LA)	.8967
Sioux City, IA–NE (Woodbury, IA, Dakota, NE)	.8537
Sioux Falls, SD (Lincoln, SD, Minnehaha, SD)	.8719
South Bend, IN (St. Joseph, IN)	.9486
Spokane, WA (Spokane, WA)	1.0170
Springfield, IL (Menard, IL, Sangamon, IL)	.8727
Springfield, MO (Christian, MO, Greene, MO, Webster, MO)	.7866
Springfield, MA (Hampden, MA, Hampshire, MA)	1.0320
State College, PA (Centre, PA)	.9446
Steubenville-Weirton, OH–WV (Jefferson, OH, Brooke, WV, Hancock, WV)	.8013
Stockton-Lodi, CA (San Joaquin, CA)	1.1147
Sumter, SC (Sumter, SC)	.7691
Syracuse, NY (Cayuga, NY, Madison, NY, Onondaga, NY, Oswego, NY)	.9869
Tacoma, WA (Pierce, WA)	1.0165
Tallahassee, FL (Gadsden, FL, Leon, FL)	.8339
Tampa-St. Petersburg-Clearwater, FL (Hernando, FL, Hillsborough, FL, Pasco, FL, Pinellas, FL)	.9351
Terre Haute, IN (Clay, IN, Vermillion, IN, Vigo, IN)	.8599
Texarkana, OK-Texarkana, TX (Miller, AR, Bowie, TX)	.8085
Toledo, OH (Fulton, OH, Lucas, OH, Wood, OH)	.9970
Topeka, KS (Shawnee, KS)	.9211
Trenton, NJ (Mercer, NJ)	1.0103
Tucson, AZ (Pima, AZ)	.9843
Tulsa, OK (Creek, OK, Osage, OK, Rogers, OK, Tulsa, OK, Wagoner, OK)	.8311
Tuscaloosa, AL (Tuscaloosa, AL)	.8511
Tyler, TX (Smith, TX)	.9119
Utica-Rome, NY (Herkimer, NY, Oneida, NY)	.8705
Vallejo-Fairfield-Napa, CA (Napa, CA, Solano, CA)	1.2013
Ventura, CA (Ventura, CA)	1.2161
Victoria, TX (Victoria, TX)	.8928
Vineland-Millville-Bridgeton, NJ (Cumberland, NJ)	1.0046
Visalia-Tulare-Porterville, CA (Tulare, CA)	1.0667
Waco, TX (McLennan, TX)	.7748
Washington, DC–MD–VA–WV (District of Columbia, DC, Calvert, MD, Charles, MD, Frederick, MD, Montgomery, MD, Prince Georges, MD, Alexandria City, VA, Arlington, VA, Clarke, VA, Culpepper, VA, Fairfax, VA, Fairfax City, VA, Falls Church City, VA, Fauquier, VA, Fredericksburg City, VA, King George, VA, Loudoun, VA, Manassas City, VA, Manassas Park City, VA, Prince William, VA, Spotsylvania, VA, Stafford, VA, Warren, VA, Berkeley, WV, Jefferson, WV)	1.0828
Waterloo-Cedar Falls, IA (Black Hawk, IA)	.8726
Wausau, WI (Marathon, WI)	.9774
West Palm Beach-Boca Raton, FL (Palm Beach, FL)	1.0254
Wheeling, OH–WV (Belmont, OH, Marshall, WV, Ohio, WV)	.7694

TABLE D–18.—WAGE INDEX FOR URBAN AREAS—Continued

Urban area (constituent counties or county equivalents)	Wage index
Wichita, KS (Butler, KS, Harvey, KS, Sedgwick, KS)	.9777
Wichita Falls, TX (Archer, TX, Wichita, TX)	.7951
Williamsport, PA (Lycoming, PA)	.8503
Wilmington-Newark, DE–MD (New Castle, DE, Cecil, MD)	1.0667
Wilmington, NC (New Hanover, NC, Brunswick, NC)	.9037
Yakima, WA (Yakima, WA)	.9421
Yolo, CA (Yolo, CA)	1.1391
York, PA (York, PA)	.9075
Youngstown-Warren, OH (Columbiana, OH, Mahoning, OH, Trumbull, OH)	.9327
Yuba City, CA (Sutter, CA, Yuba, CA)	1.0585
Yuma, AZ	.9617

Source: Federal Register, September 1, 1993.

TABLE D–19.—WAGE INDEX FOR RURAL AREAS

Nonurban area	Wage index	Nonurban area	Wage index
Alabama	0.6935	New Hampshire	0.9684
Alaska	1.2939	New Jersey	(N/A)
Arizona	0.8488	New Mexico	0.7480
Arkansas	0.6871	New York	0.8560
California	0.9727	North Carolina	0.7804
Colorado	0.8197	North Dakota	0.7204
Connecticut	1.2545	Ohio	0.8122
Delaware	0.8359	Oklahoma	0.6884
Florida	0.8515	Oregon	0.9176
Georgia	0.7573	Pennsylvania	0.8786
Hawaii	1.0841	Puerto Rico	0.5256
Idaho	0.8471	Rhode Island	(N/A)
Illinois	0.7316	South Carolina	0.7691
Indiana	0.7720	South Dakota	0.6960
Iowa	0.7327	Tennessee	0.7536
Kansas	0.7069	Texas	0.7522
Kentucky	0.7511	Utah	0.9025
Louisiana	0.7118	Vermont	0.8765
Maine	0.8493	Virgin Islands	(N/A)
Maryland	0.8618	Virginia	0.7658
Massachusetts	1.0741	Washington	0.9348
Michigan	0.8616	West Virginia	0.8484
Minnesota	0.8141	Wisconsin	0.8298
Mississippi	0.6657	Wyoming	0.7833
Missouri	0.7331		
Montana	0.8029		
Nebraska	0.7168		
Nevada	0.9324		

N/A = All counties within state are classified urban.

Source: Federal Register, September 1, 1933

TABLE D–20.—WAGE INDEX FOR HOSPITALS THAT ARE RECLASSIFIED

Area reclassified to—	Wage index	Area reclassified to—	Wage index
Albany, GA	0.8493	Houston, TX	0.9908
Albany-Schenectady-Troy, NY	0.9033	Huntington-Ashland, WV-KY-OH	0.8817
Albuquerque, NM	0.9861	Huntsville, AL	0.7954
Alexandria, LA	0.9130	Indianapolis, IN	0.9871
Anchorage, AK	1.2201	Jackson, MS	0.7519
Anchorage, AK (Rural Alaska Hospitals)	1.2939	Jackson, TN	0.8007
Atlanta, GA	0.9402	Johnson City-Kingsport-Bristol, TN-VA	0.8472
Augusta-Aiken, GA-SC	0.8899	Joplin, MO	0.7697
Baton Rouge, LA	0.8659	Kalamazoo-Battlecreek, MI	1.0749
Benton Harbor, MI	0.7923	Kansas City, KS-MO	0.9538
Benton Harbor, MI (Rural Michigan Hospitals)	0.8616	Kokomo, IN	0.8440
		Lafayette, LA	0.8144
Billings, MT	0.8992	Lafayette, IN	0.8415
Biloxi-Gulfport, MS	0.7807	Lansing-East Lansing, MI	0.9633
Binghamton, NY	0.8820	Lexington, KY	0.8291
Birmingham, AL	0.9006	Lima, OH	0.8441
Bismark, ND	0.8475	Lincoln, NE	0.8469
Boston-Brockton-Nashua, MA-NH	1.1503	Little Rock-North Little Rock, AK	0.8306
Brazoria, TX	0.8441	Los Angeles-Long Beach, CA	1.2719
Bryan-College Station, TX	0.8864	Macon, GA	0.9254
Caguas, PR	0.5039	Mansfield, OH	0.8158
Caguas, PR (Rural Puerto Rico Hospitals)	0.5256	Medford-Ashland, OR	0.9768
Charleston-North Charleston, SC	0.8947	Memphis, TN-AR-MS	0.8341
Charleston, WV	0.8786	Miami, FL	0.7704
Charlotte-Gastonia-Rock Hill, NC–SC	0.9648	Miami, FL (Rural Florida Only)	0.8515
Chattanooga, TN-GA	0.8929	Middlesex-Somerset-Hunterdon, NJ	1.0651
Chicago, IL	1.0593	Milwaukee, WI	0.9240
Chico-Paradise, CA	1.0071	Minneapolis-St. Paul, MN-WI	1.0855
Cincinnati, OH-KY-IN	0.9548	Modesto, CA	1.1471
Cleveland-Lorain-Elyria, OH	0.9688	Monroe, LA	0.7663
Columbia, MO	0.8967	Montgomery, AL	0.7564
Columbus, OH	0.9902	Myrtle Beach, SC	0.7906
Dallas, TX	0.9649	Nashville, TN	0.9105
Davenport-Rock Island-Moline, IA-IL	0.8300	New Haven-Bridgeport-Sramford-Danbury-Waterbury, CT	1.2289
Dayton-Springfield, OH	0.9424	New London-Norwich, CT	1.1589
Denver, CO	1.0821	New Orleans, LA	0.9443
Des Moines, IA	0.8676	New York, NY	1.4020
Detroit, MI	1.0790	Newark, NJ	1.1008
Dothan, AL	0.7793	Newburgh, NY–PA	0.9908
Dubuque, IA	0.8324	Oakland, CA	1.4369
Duluth, Superior, MN-WI	0.9166	Odessa-Midland, TX	0.8735
Dutchess County, NY	1.0623	Oklahoma, City, OK	0.8455
Elkhart-Goshen, IN	0.8390	Olympia, WA	1.0326
Eugene-Springfield, OR	0.9480	Omaha, NE-IA	0.9900
Fargo-Moorhead, ND-MN	0.9111	Orange County, NY	1.3409
Fayetteville, NC	0.8281	Owensboro, KY	0.7654
Flint, MI	1.0689	Peoria-Pekin, IL	0.8249
Florence, AL	0.7707	Philadelphia, PA-NJ	1.1151
Florence, SC	0.8671	Pittsburgh, PA	0.9786
Fort Lauderdale, FL	1.0573	Portland-Vancouver, OR-WA	1.1051
Fort Pierce-Port St. Lucia, FL	0.9876	Provo-Orem, UT	0.9609
Fort Smith, AR	0.7611	Pueblo, CO	0.8260
Fort Walton Beach, FL	0.8691	Raleigh-Durham-Chapel Hill, NC	0.9521
Fort Wayne, IN	0.8893	Reno, NV	1.2009
Fort Worth-Arlington, TX	0.9550	Roanoke, VA	0.8358
Fresno, CA	1.0244	Saginaw-Bay City-Midland, MI	0.9549
Gadsden, AL	0.7747	St. Cloud, MN	0.9711
Glens Falls, NY	0.9393	St. Louis, MO-IL	0.9182
Great Falls, MT	0.8906	Salinas, CA	1.3087
Green Bay, WI	0.8852	Salt Lake City-Ogden, UT	0.9669
Greenville-Spartanburg-Andersen, SC	0.8715	San Francisco, CA	1.4086
Harrisburg-Lebanon-Carlise, PA	0.9995	San Juan, PR	0.4969
Hartford, CT	1.1968	Santa Fe, NM	0.9503
Honolulu, HI	1.0995		

TABLE D–20.—WAGE INDEX FOR HOSPITALS THAT ARE RECLASSIFIED

Area reclassified to—	Wage index	Area reclassified to—	Wage index
Santa Rosa, CA	1.2827	Wichita, KS	0.9356
Seattle-Bellevue-Everett, WA	1.0985	Rural Alabama	0.6935
Sherman-Denison, TX	0.8912	Rural Georgia	0.7573
South Bend, IN	0.9305	Rural Kentucky	0.7511
Springfield, IL	0.8727	Rural Kentucky (Rural TN Hospitals)	0.7536
Syracuse, NY	0.9749	Rural Louisiana	0.7118
Tampa-St. Petersburg-Clearwater, FL	0.9351	Rural Michigan	0.8616
Texarkana, TX-Texarkana, AR	0.8085	Rural Minnesota	0.8141
Topeka, KS	0.9221	Rural North Carolina	0.7804
Tucson, AZ	0.9843	Rural South Dakota	0.6960
Tulsa, OK	0.8311	Rural South Dakota (Rural ND Hospitals)	0.7168
Tyler, TX	0.9012	Rural Utah	0.9025
Victoria, TX	0.8659	Rural Virginia	0.7656
Waterloo-Cedar Falls, IA	0.8726	Rural West Virginia	0.7969
Wausau, WI	0.9225		

Source: Federal Register, September 1, 1993

TABLE D–21.—DRG RELATIVE WEIGHTS FROM FISCAL YEAR 1993 TO FISCAL YEAR 1994

DRG	MDC	Type	Title	Fiscal year 1993 weight	Fiscal year 1994 weight	Percent change
1	1	SURG	Craniotomy age >17 except for trauma	3.2324	3.1556	−2.4
2	1	SURG	Craniotomy for trauma age >17	3.1311	3.1381	0.2
3	1	SURG	Craniotomy age 0–17	2.9627	3.0176	1.9
4	1	SURG	Spinal procedures	2.3612	2.3847	1.0
5	1	SURG	Extracranial vascular procedures	1.5504	1.5361	−0.9
6	1	SURG	Carpal tunnel release	0.5437	0.6271	15.3
7	1	SURG	Periph and cranial nerve and other nerv syst proc with CC	2.6363	2.5180	−4.5
8	1	SURG	Periph and cranial nerve and other nerv syst proc w/o CC	0.7944	0.8576	8.0
9	1	MED	Spinal disorders and injuries	1.2786	1.3397	4.8
10	1	MED	Nervous system neoplasms with CC	1.2884	1.2819	−0.5
11	1	MED	Nervous system neoplasms w/o CC	0.7649	0.7691	0.5
12	1	MED	Degenerative nervous system disorders	0.9550	0.9449	−1.1
13	1	MED	Multiple sclerosis and cerebellar ataxia	0.8336	0.8108	−2.7
14	1	MED	Specific cerebrovascular disorders except TIA	1.2160	1.2056	−0.9
15	1	MED	Transient ischemic attack and precerebral occlusions	0.8662	0.6766	−21.9
16	1	MED	Nonspecific cerebrovascular disorders with CC	1.1086	1.1141	0.5
17	1	MED	Nonspecific cerebrovascular disorders w/o CC	0.6424	0.6648	3.5
18	1	MED	Cranial and peripheral nerve disorders with CC	0.9170	0.9202	0.3
19	1	MED	Cranial and peripheral nerve disorders w/o CC	0.5958	0.5927	−0.5
20	1	MED	Nervous system infection except viral meningitis	2.0042	2.0613	2.8
21	1	MED	Viral meningitis	1.4505	1.4304	−1.4
22	1	MED	Hypertensive encephalopathy	0.7261	0.7286	0.3
23	1	MED	Nontraumatic stupor and coma	0.8202	0.8407	2.5
24	1	MED	Seizure and headache age >17 with CC	0.9714	0.9759	0.5
25	1	MED	Seizure and headache age >17 w/o CC	0.5282	0.5426	2.7
26	1	MED	Seizure and headache age 0–17	1.0516	0.9878	−6.1

27	MED	1	Traumatic stupor and coma, coma >1 HR	1.3744	1.3311	−3.2
28	MED	1	Traumatic stupor and coma, coma <1 HR age >17 with CC	1.2208	1.2078	−1.1
29	MED	1	Traumatic stupor and coma, coma <1 HR age >17 w/o CC	0.5885	0.5941	1.0
30	MED	1	Traumatic stupor and coma, coma <1 HR age 0–17	0.3593	0.3660	1.9
31	MED	1	Concussion age >17 with CC	0.7707	0.7335	−4.8
32	MED	1	Concussion age >17 w/o CC	0.4454	0.4494	0.9
33	MED	1	Concussion age 0–17	0.2494	0.2540	1.8
34	MED	1	Other disorders of nervous system with CC	1.1442	1.1103	−3.0
35	MED	1	Other disorders of nervous system w/o CC	0.5590	0.5656	1.2
36	SURG	2	Retinal procedures	0.6238	0.6087	−2.4
37	SURG	2	Orbital procedures	0.7883	0.7843	−0.5
38	SURG	2	Primary iris procedures	0.3584	0.3716	3.7
39	SURG	2	Lens procedures with or without vitrectomy	0.4858	0.4723	−2.8
40	SURG	2	Extraocular procedures except orbit age >17	0.5150	0.5586	8.5
41	SURG	2	Extraocular procedures except orbit age 0–17	0.3713	0.3782	1.9
42	SURG	2	Intraocular procedures retina, iris and lens	0.5968	0.5777	−3.2
43	MED	2	Hyphema	0.4026	0.3814	−5.3
44	MED	2	Acute major eye infections	0.5767	0.5949	3.2
45	MED	2	Neurological eye disorders	0.5989	0.6047	1.0
46	MED	2	Other disorders of the eye age >17 w CC	0.7217	0.7288	1.0
47	MED	2	Other disorders of the eye age >17 w/o CC	0.4156	0.4047	−2.6
48	MED	s	Other disorders of the eye age 0–17	0.4079	0.4155	1.9
49	MED	3	Major head and neck procedures	1.6029	1.7937	11.9
50	SURG	3	Sialoadenectomy	0.6594	0.6732	2.1
51	SURG	3	Salivary gland procedures except sialoadenectomy	0.6278	0.6515	3.8
52	SURG	3	Cleft lip and palate repair	0.7859	0.7697	−2.1
53	SURG	3	Sinus and mastoid procedures age >17	0.7237	0.7645	5.6
54	SURG	3	Sinus and mastoid procedures age 0–17	0.6994	0.7124	1.9
55	SURG	3	Miscellaneous ear, nose, mouth and throat procedures	0.5469	0.5761	5.3
56	SURG	3	Rhinoplasty	0.6168	0.6412	4.0
57	SURG	3	T and A proc, except tonsillectomy and/or adenoidectomy only, age >17.	0.8845	0.9116	3.1

TABLE D–21.—DRG RELATIVE WEIGHTS FROM FISCAL YEAR 1993 TO FISCAL YEAR 1994—Continued

DRG	MDC	Type	Title	Fiscal year		Percent change
				1993 weight	1994 weight	
58	3	SURG	T and A, except tonsillectomy and/or adenoidectomy only, age 0–17	0.3145	0.3203	1.8
59	3	SURG	Tonsillectomy and/or adenoidectomy only, age 17	0.4273	0.4158	–2.7
60	3	SURG	Tonsillectomy and/or adenoidectomy only, age 0–17	0.2655	0.2704	1.8
61	3	SURG	Myringotomy w tube insertion age –17	0.8613	1.10307	19.7
62	3	SURG	Myringotomy w tube insertion age 0–17	0.3136	0.3194	1.8
63	3	SURG	Other ear, nose, mouth and throat O.R. procedures	1.0429	1.0520	0.9
64	3	MED	Ear, nose, mouth and throat malignancy	1.1039	1.1571	4.8
65	3	MED	Dysequilibrium	0.4922	0.4952	0.6
66	3	MED	Epistaxis	0.4885	0.4909	0.5
67	3	MED	Epiglottitis	0.8424	0.8481	0.7
68	3	MED	Otitis media and Uri age >17 with CC	0.7216	0.7158	–0.8
69	3	MED	Otitis media and Uri age >17 w/o CC	0.5000	0.5126	2.5
70	3	MED	Otitis media and Uri age 0–17	0.6126	0.3978	–35.1
71	3	MED	Laryngotracheitis	0.7664	0.6838	–10.8
72	3	MED	Nasal trauma and deformity	0.5844	0.6079	4.0
73	3	MED	Other ear, nose, mouth and throat diagnoses age >17	0.7522	0.7591	0.9
74	3	MED	Other ear, nose, mouth and throat diagnoses age 0–17	0.3480	0.3545	1.9
75	4	SURG	Major chest procedures	3.0400	3.0397	–0.0
76	4	SURG	Other resp system O.R. procedures w CC	2.3973	2.4770	3.3
77	4	SURG	Other resp system O.R. procedures w/o CC	1.0208	1.0443	2.3
78	4	MED	Pulmonary embolism	1.4350	1.4292	–0.4
79	4	MED	Respiratory infections and inflammations age >17 with CC	1.7510	1.7332	–1.0
80	4	MED	Respiratory infections and inflammations age >17 w/o CC	0.9617	0.9278	–3.5
81	4	MED	Respiratory infections and inflammations age 0–17	1.1200	1.1403	1.9
82	4	MED	Respiratory neoplasms	1.2809	1.3105	2.3
83	4	MED	Major chest trauma with CC	0.9490	0.9403	–0.9

84	4	MED	Major chest trauma w/o CC	0.4783	0.4986	4.2
85	4	MED	Pleural effusion with CC	1.1969	1.1891	−0.7
86	4	MED	Pleural effusion w/o CC	0.6711	0.6691	−0.3
87	4	MED	Pulmonary edema and respiratory failure	1.3597	1.3495	−0.8
88	4	MED	Chronic obstructive pulmonary disease	0.9941	1.0067	1.3
89	4	MED	Simple pneumonia and pleurisy age >17 with CC	1.1581	1.1447	−1.2
90	4	MED	Simple pneumonia and pleurisy age >17 w/o CC	0.7090	0.6990	−1.4
91	4	MED	Simple pneumonia and pleurisy age 0–17	0.7985	0.7767	−2.7
92	4	MED	Interstitial lung disease with CC	1.1975	1.2039	0.5
93	4	MED	Interstitial lung disease w/o CC	0.7723	0.7550	−2.2
94	4	MED	Pneumothorax with CC	1.2774	1.2433	−2.7
95	4	MED	Pneumothroax w/o CC	0.5973	0.6067	1.6
96	4	MED	Bronchitis and asthma age >17 with CC	0.9369	0.8776	−6.3
97	4	MED	Bronchitis and asthma age >17 w/o OC	0.6191	0.6067	−2.0
98	4	MED	Bronchitis and asthma age 0–17	0.8924	0.6840	−23.4
99	4	MED	Respiratory signs and symptoms with CC	0.7623	0.7149	−6.2
100	4	MED	Respiratory signs and symptoms w/o CC	0.5049	0.5004	−0.9
101	4	MED	Other respiratory system diagnoses with CC	0.9135	0.9035	−1.1
102	4	MED	Other respiratory system diagnoses w/o CC	0.5426	0.5282	−2.7
103	5	SURG	Heart transplant	12.5568	14.0215	11.7
104	5	SURG	Cardiac valve procedure and with cardiac cath	7.7521	7.6559	−1.2
105	5	SURG	Cardiac valve procedure and w/o cardiac cath	5.8291	5.7990	−0.5
106	5	SURG	Coronary bypass with cardiac cath	5.6583	5.6791	0.4
107	5	SURG	Coronary bypass w/o cardiac cath	4.2348	4.2005	−0.8
108	5	SURG	Other cardiothoracic procedures	5.8725	5.8690	−0.1
109	......		No longer valid	NV	NV	NV
110	5	SURG	Major cardiovascular procedures with CC	4.0823	4.0494	−0.8
111	5	SURG	Major cardiovascular procedures w/o CC	2.2979	2.3214	1.0
112	5	SURG	Percutaneous cardiovascular procedures	1.9874	1.9736	−0.7
113	5	SURG	Amputation for circ system disorders except upper limb and toe	2.7789	2.7931	0.5
114	5	SURG	Upper limb and toe amputation for circ system disorder	1.5957	1.5631	−2.0

TABLE D-21.—DRG RELATIVE WEIGHTS FROM FISCAL YEAR 1993 TO FISCAL YEAR 1994—Continued

DRG	MDC	Type	Title	Fiscal year		Percent change
				1993 weight	1994 weight	
115	5	SURG	Perm cardiac pacemaker implant with AMI, heart failure or shock	3.6092	3.5886	-0.6
116	5	SURG	Other perm cardiac pacemaker implant or AICD lead or gen proc	2.4604	2.4248	-1.4
117	5	SURG	Cardiac pacemaker revision except device replacement	1.2264	1.1328	-7.6
118	5	SURG	Cardiac pacemaker device replacement	1.5858	1.5419	-2.8
119	5	SURG	Vein ligation and stripping	0.9650	0.9834	1.9
120	5	SURG	Other circulatory system O.R. procedures	1.9906	1.9626	-1.4
121	5	MED	Circulatory disorders with AMI and C.V. comp disch alive	1.6114	1.6017	-0.6
122	5	MED	Circulatory disorders with AMI w/o C.V. comp disch alive	1.1532	1.1325	-1.8
123	5	MED	Circulatory disorders with AMI, expired	1.4090	1.4116	0.2
124	5	MED	Circulatory disorders except AMI, with card cath and complex diag	1.2029	1.2307	2.3
125	5	MED	Circulatory disorders except AMI, with card cath w/o complex diag	0.7587	0.7960	4.9
126	5	MED	Acute and subacute endocarditis	2.8464	2.7299	-4.1
127	5	MED	Heart failure and shock	1.0150	1.0234	0.8
128	5	MED	Deep vein thrombophlebitis	0.7873	0.7825	-0.6
129	5	MED	Cardiac arrest, unexplained	1.2831	1.1959	-6.8
130	5	MED	Peripheral vascular disorders with CC	0.9106	0.9042	-0.7
131	5	MED	Peripheral vascular disorders w/o CC	0.5861	0.5831	-0.5
132	5	MED	Atherosclerosis with CC	0.7591	.07594	0.0
133	5	MED	Atherosclerosis w/o CC	0.5312	0.5257	-1.0
134	5	MED	Hypertension	0.5655	0.5614	-0.7
135	5	MED	Cardiac congenital and vascular disorders age >17 with CC	0.8625	0.8609	-0.2
136	5	MED	Cardiac congenital and vascular disorders age >17 w/o CC	0.5266	0.5489	4.2
137	5	MED	Cardiac congenital and vascular disorders age 0-17	0.6411	0.6530	1.9
138	5	MED	Cardiac arrhythmia and conduction disorders with CC	0.8110	0.8038	-0.9
139	5	MED	Cardiac arrhythmia and conduction disorders w/o CC	0.5020	0.4946	-1.5
140	5	MED	Angina pectoris	0.6219	0.6241	0.4
141	5	MED	Syncope and collapse with CC	0.6998	0.7053	0.8

142	MED	5	Syncope and collapse w/o CC	0.5048	0.5150	2.0
143	MED	5	Chest pain	0.5164	0.5189	0.5
144	MED	5	Other circulatory system diagnoses with CC	1.0650	1.0659	0.1
145	MED	5	Other circulatory system diagnoses w/o CC	0.6240	0.6122	−1.9
146	SURG	6	Rectal resection with CC	2.5394	2.4955	−1.7
147	SURG	6	Rectal resection w/o CC	1.5192	1.5328	0.9
148	SURG	6	Major small and large bowel procedures with CC	3.1353	3.1719	1.2
149	SURG	6	Major small and large bowel procedures w/o CC	1.4948	1.5127	1.2
150	SURG	6	Peritoneal adhesiolysis with CC	2.5484	2.5505	0.1
151	SURG	6	Peritoneal adhesiolysis w/o CC	1.1885	1.1738	−1.2
152	SURG	6	Minor small and large bowel procedures with CC	1.7736	1.7955	1.2
153	SURG	6	Minor small and large bowel procedures w/o CC	1.0426	1.0821	3.8
154	SURG	6	Stomach, esophageal and duodenal procedures age >17 with CC	4.0491	4.1338	2.1
155	SURG	6	Stomach, esophageal and duodenal procedures age >17 w/o CC	1.4617	1.3811	−5.5
156	SURG	6	Stomach, esophageal and duodenal procedures age 0–17	0.8510	0.8668	1.9
157	SURG	6	Anal and stomal procedures with CC	0.9575	1.0048	4.9
158	SURG	6	Anal and stomal procedures w/o CC	0.4975	0.5100	2.5
159	SURG	6	Hernia procedures except inguinal and femoral age >17 with CC	1.0747	1.0901	1.4
160	SURG	6	Hernia procedures except inguinal and femoral age >17 w/o CC	0.6168	0.6378	3.4
161	SURG	6	Inguinal and femoral hernia procedures age >17 with CC	0.7820	0.8260	5.6
162	SURG	6	Inguinal and femoral hernia procedures age >17 w/o CC	0.4651	0.4823	3.7
163	SURG	6	Hernia procedures age 0–17	0.4843	0.6795	40.3
164	SURG	6	Appendectomy with complicated principal diag with CC	2.1607	2.1679	0.3
165	SURG	6	Appendectomy with complicated principal diag w/o CC	1.2080	1.2055	−0.2
166	SURG	6	Appendectomy w/o complicated principal diag with CC	1.3251	1.3413	1.2
167	SURG	6	Appendectomy w/o complicated principal dial w/o CC	0.7495	0.7801	4.1
168	SURG	3	Mouth procedures with CC	0.9902	1.0321	4.2
169	SURG	3	Mouth procedures w/o CC	0.5788	0.5824	0.6
170	SURG	6	Other digestive system O.R. procedures with CC	2.7310	2.7524	0.8
171	SURG	6	Other digestive system O.R. procedures w/o CC	1.0898	1.0894	0.0
172	MED	6	Digestive malignancy with CC	1.2990	1.0894	0.0

TABLE D–21.—DRG RELATIVE WEIGHTS FROM FISCAL YEAR 1993 TO FISCAL YEAR 1994—Continued

DRG	MDC	Type	Title	Fiscal year 1993 weight	Fiscal year 1994 weight	Percent change
173	6	MED	Digestive malignancy w/o CC	0.6346	0.6318	−0.4
174	6	MED	G.I. hemorrhage with CC	0.9794	0.9657	−1.4
175	6	MED	G.I. hemorrhage w/o CC	0.5506	0.5354	−2.8
176	6	MED	Complicated peptic ulcer	1.0331	1.0453	1.2
177	6	MED	Uncomplicated peptic ulcer with CC	0.7931	0.7986	0.7
178	6	MED	Uncomplicated peptic ulcer w/o CC	0.5720	0.5804	1.5
179	6	MED	Inflammatory bowel disease	1.1044	1.1072	0.3
180	6	MED	G.I. obstruction with CC	0.9279	0.9180	−1.1
181	6	MED	G.I. obstruction w/o CC	0.5007	0.4969	−0.8
182	6	MED	Esophagitis, gastroent and misc disorders age >17 with CC	0.7721	0.7617	−1.3
183	6	MED	Esophagitis, gastroent and misc digest disorders age >17 w/o CC	0.5296	0.5291	−0.1
184	6	MED	Esophagitis, gastroent and misc digest disorders age 0–17	0.5625	0.4735	−15.8
185	3	MED	Dental and oral dis except extractions and restorations, age >17	0.7854	0.8248	5.0
186	3	MED	Dental and oral dis except extractions and restorationsm age 0–17	0.4174	0.4251	1.8
187	3	MED	Dental extractions and restorations	0.5650	0.5852	3.6
188	6	MED	Other digestive system diagnoses age >17 with CC	0.9971	1.0050	0.8
189	6	MED	Other digestive system diagnoses age >17 w/o CC	0.4804	0.4775	−0.6
190	6	MED	Other digestive system diagnoses age 0–17	0.6796	0.7577	11.5
191	7	SURG	Pancreas, liver and shunt procedures with CC	4.4652	4.3319	−3.0
192	7	MED	Pancreas, liver and shunt procedures w/o CC	1.7051	1.6460	−3.5
193	7	SURG	Biliary tract proc with CC except only cholecyst with or w/o C.D.E	3.0376	3.0940	1.9
194	7	SURG	Biliary tract proc w/o CC except only cholecyst with or w/o C.D.E	1.6333	1.5991	−2.1
195	7	SURG	Cholecystectomy with C.D.E. with CC	2.2744	2.4066	5.8
196	7	SURG	Cholecystectomy with C.D.E. w/o CC	1.4039	1.5073	7.4
197	7	SURG	Cholecystectomy except by Laparoscope, w/o C.D.E., with CC	1.6916	2.0082	18.7
198	7	SURG	Cholecystectomy except by Laparoscope, w/o C.D.E., w/o CC	0.8757	1.0432	19.1
199	7	SURG	Hepatobiliary diagnostic procedure for malignancy	2.3376	2.3557	0.8

DRG	MDC	Type	Description			
200	7	SURG	Hepatobiliary diagnostic procedure for non-malignancy	2.7205	2.8054	3.1
201	7	SURG	Other hepatobiliary or pancreas O.R. procedures	2.5221	3.1526	25.0
202	7	MED	Cirrhosis and alcoholic hepatitis	1.2996	1.3176	1.4
203	7	MED	Malignancy of hepatobiliary system or pancreas	1.2158	1.2180	0.2
204	7	MED	Disorders of pancreas except malignancy	1.1158	1.1302	1.3
205	7	MED	Disorders of liver except malig, cirr, ALC hepa with CC	1.2249	1.2470	1.8
206	7	MED	Disorders of liver except malig, cirr, ALC hepa w/o CC	0.6113	0.6181	1.1
207	7	MED	Disorders of the biliary tract with CC	0.9814	0.9896	0.8
208	7	MED	Disorders of the biliary tract w/o CC	0.5564	0.5521	−0.8
209	8	SURG	Major joint and limb reattachment procedures—lower extremity	2.3686	2.3491	−0.8
210	8	SURG	Hip and femur procedures except major joint age >17 with CC	1.9077	1.8702	−2.0
211	8	SURG	Hip and femur procedures except major joint age >17 w/o CC	1.3307	1.3031	−2.1
212	8	SURG	Hip and femur procedures except major joint age 0–17	1.0345	1.4486	40.0
213	8	SURG	Amputation for musculoskeletal system and conn tissue disorders	1.7686	1.7485	−1.1
214	8	SURG	Back and neck procedures with CC	1.8686	1.8857	0.9
215	8	SURG	Back and neck procedures w/o CC	1.0905	1.0926	0.2
216	8	SURG	Biopsies of musculoskeletal system and connective tissue	2.0429	2.0570	0.7
217	8	SURG	Wnd debrid and skin graft except hand, for muscskelet and conn tiss dis.	3.0601	3.0563	−0.1
218	8	SURG	Lower extrem and humer proc except hip, foot, femur age >17 with	1.4186	1.4195	0.1
219	8	SURG	Lower extrem and humer proc except hip, foot, femur age >17 w/o C	0.8956	0.9015	0.7
220	8	SURG	Lower extrem and humer proc except hip, foot, femur age 0–17	0.9392	0.9556	1.9
221	8	SURG	Knee procedures with CC	1.7828	1.7992	0.9
222	8	SURG	Knee procedures w/o CC	0.9544	0.9846	3.2
223	8	SURG	Major shoulder/elbow proc, or other upper extremity proc w CC	0.8087	0.8126	0.5
224	8	SURG	Shoulder, elbow or forearm proc, exc major joint proc w/o CC	0.6538	0.6698	2.4
225	8	SURG	Foot procedures	0.8212	0.8568	4.3
226	8	SURG	Soft tissue procedures with CC	1.3241	1.3096	−1.1
227	8	SURG	Soft tissue procedures w/o CC	0.6767	0.6886	1.5
228	8	SURG	Major thumb or joint proc, or oth hand or wrist proc w CC	0.7961	0.8225	3.3
229	8	SURG	Hand or wrist proc, except major joint proc, w/o CC	0.5539	0.5679	2.5

TABLE D–21.—DRG RELATIVE WEIGHTS FROM FISCAL YEAR 1993 TO FISCAL YEAR 1994—Continued

DRG	MDC	Type	Title	Fiscal year		Percent change
				1993 weight	1994 weight	
230	8	SURG	Local excision and removal of int fix devices of hip and femur	0.9179	0.9353	1.9
231	8	SURG	Local excision and removal of int fix devices except hip and femur	1.1044	1.1159	1.0
232	8	SURG	Arthroscopy	1.1792	1.1082	−6.0
233	8	SURG	Other musculoskelet sys and conn tiss O.R. proc with CC	1.8579	1.8454	−0.7
234	8	SURG	Other musculoskelet sys and conn tiss O.R. proc w/o CC	0.8957	0.9321	4.1
235	8	MED	Fractures of femur.	1.0209	0.9730	−4.7
236	8	MED	Fractures of hip and pelvis	0.8128	0.7922	−2.5
237	8	MED	Sprains, strains, and dislocations of hip, pelvis and thigh	0.5496	0.5536	0.7
238	8	MED	Osteomyelitis	1.5435	1.5082	−2.3
239	8	MED	Pathological fractures and musculoskeletal and conn tiss malignancy .	1.0415	1.0388	−0.3
240	8	MED	Connective tissue disorders with CC	1.1468	1.1488	0.2
241	8	MED	Connective tissue disorders w/o CC	0.5782	0.5682	−1.7
242	8	MED	Septic arthritis	1.1864	1.1356	−4.3
243	8	MED	Medical back problems	0.6834	0.7011	2.6
244	8	MED	Bone diseases and specific arthropathies with CC	0.7353	0.7437	1.1
245	8	MED	Bone diseases and specific arthropathies w/o CC	0.5043	0.4798	−4.9
246	8	MED	Non-specific arthropathies	0.5706	0.5962	4.5
247	8	MED	Signs and symptoms of musculoskeletal system and conn tissue	0.5682	0.5547	−2.4
248	8	MED	Tendonitis, myositis and bursitis	0.6750	0.6939	2.8
249	8	MED	Aftercare, musculoskeletal system and connective tissue	0.6965	0.6638	−4.7
250	8	MED	FX, sprn and disl of forearm, hand, foot age >17 with CC	0.7047	0.7174	1.8
251	8	MED	FX, sprn, strn and disl of forearm, hand, foot age >17 w/o CC	0.4395	0.4449	1.2
252	8	MED	FX, sprn, strn and disl of forearm, hand, foot age 0–17	0.3549	0.3615	1.9
253	8	MED	FX, sprn, strn and disl of uparm, lowleg ex foot age >17 with CC	0.7774	0.7706	−0.9
254	8	MED	FX, sprn, and disl of uparm, lowleg ex foot age >17 w/o CC	0.4231	0.4272	1.0
255	8	MED	FX, sprn, strn and disl of uparm, lowleg ex foot age 0–17	0.4709	0.4796	1.8
256	8	MED	Other musculoskeletal system and connective tissue diagnoses	0.8505	0.6366	−25.1

257	9	SURG	Total mastectomy for malignancy with CC	0.8950	0.8845	−1.2
258	9	SURG	Total mastectomy for malignancy w/o CC	0.7002	0.6959	−0.6
259	9	SURG	Subtotal mastectomy for malignancy with CC	0.8774	0.8372	−4.6
260	9	SURG	Subtotal mastectomy for malignancy w/o CC	0.5659	0.5743	1.5
261	9	SURG	Breast proc for non-malignancy except biopsy and local excision	0.7183	0.7272	1.2
262	9	SURG	Breast biopsy and local excision for non-malignancy	0.5345	0.6071	13.6
263	9	SURG	Skin graft and/or debrid for skin ulcer or cellulitis with CC	2.5403	2.4460	−3.7
264	9	SURG	Skin graft and/or debrid for skin ulcer or cellulitis w/o. CC	1.2662	1.2346	−2.5
265	9	SURG	Skin graft and/or debrid except for skin ulcer or cellulitis w CC	1.3939	1.4065	0.9
266	9	SURG	Skin graft and/or debrid except for skin ulcer or cellulitis w/o	0.6978	0.7108	1.9
267	9	SURG	Perianal and pilonidal procedures	0.6245	0.6592	5.6
268	9	SURG	Skin, subcutaneous tissue and breast plastic procedures	0.7519	0.8198	9.0
269	9	SURG	Other skin, subcut tiss and breast proc with CC	1.6958	1.7166	1.2
270	9	SURG	Other skin, subcut tiss and breast proc w/o CC	0.6343	0.6456	1.8
271	9	MED	Skin ulcers	1.1970	1.1783	−1.6
272	9	MED	Major skin disorders with CC	1.0477	1.0206	−2.6
273	9	MED	Major skin disorders w/o CC	0.6583	0.6514	−1.0
274	9	MED	Malignant breast disorders with CC	1.1572	1.1183	−3.4
275	9	MED	Malignant breast disorders w/o CC	0.5957	0.5050	−15.2
275	9	MED	Non-malignant breast disorders	0.6085	0.6351	4.4
277	9	MED	Cellulitis age >17 with CC	0.9036	0.8917	−1.3
278	9	MED	Cellulitis age >17 w/o CC	0.5941	0.5828	−1.9
279	9	MED	Cellulitis age 0–17	0.7479	0.7618	1.9
280	9	MED	Trauma to the skin, subcut tiss and breast age >17 with CC	0.6808	0.6755	−0.8
281	9	MED	Trauma to the skin subcut tiss and breast age >17 w/o CC	0.4270	0.4195	−1.8
282	9	MED	Trauma to the skin subcut tiss and breast age 0–17	0.3476	0.3540	1.8
283	9	MED	Minor skin disorders with CC	0.7558	.07253	−4.0
284	9	MED	Minor skin disorders w/o CC	0.4450	0.4469	0.4
285	10	SURG	Amputat of lower limb for endoc, nutrit, and metabol disorders	2.7519	2.5637	−6.8
286	10	SURG	Adrenal and pituitary procedures	2.3944	2.2821	−4.7
287	10	SURG	Skin grafts and wounds debrid for endoc, nutgrit, and metab disorder	2.1744	2.1927	0.8

TABLE D-21.—DRG RELATIVE WEIGHTS FROM FISCAL YEAR 1993 TO FISCAL YEAR 1994—Continued

DRG	MDC	Type	Title	Fiscal year		Percent change
				1993 weight	1994 weight	
288	10	SURG	O.R. procedures for obesity	2.0378	2.0725	1.7
289	10	SURG	Parathyroid procedures	1.0252	0.9920	−3.2
290	10	SURG	Thyroid procedures	0.7448	0.7637	2.5
291	10	SURG	Thyroglossal procedures	0.4896	0.5074	3.6
292	10	SURG	Other endocrine, nutri and metab O.R. proc with CC	2.8428	2.7658	−2.7
293	10	SURG	Other endocrine, nutri and metab O.R. proc w/o CC	1.1284	1.1010	−2.4
294	10	MED	Diabetes age >35	0.7491	0.7466	−0.3
295	10	MED	Diabetes age 0–35	0.7721	0.7562	−2.1
296	10	MED	Nutritional and misc metabolic disorders age >17 with CC	0.9410	0.9313	−1.0
297	10	MED	Nutritional and misc metabolic disorders age >17 w/o CC	0.5271	0.5244	−0.5
298	10	MED	Nutritional and misc metabolic disorders age 0–17	0.4777	0.5627	17.8
299	10	MED	Inborn errors of metabolism	0.8392	0.8271	−1.4
300	10	MED	Endocrine disorders with CC	1.1251	1.0982	−2.4
301	10	MED	Endocrine disorders w/o CC	0.5811	0.5777	−0.6
302	11	SURG	Kidney transplant	3.8885	3.8871	0.0
303	11	SURG	Kidney, ureter and major bladder procedures for neoplasm	2.6532	2.5929	−2.3
304	11	SURG	Kidney, ureter and major bladder proc for non-neopl with CC	2.4103	2.3897	−0.9
305	11	SURG	Kidney, ureter and major bladder proc for non-neopl w/o CC	1.1548	1.1127	−3.6
306	11	SURG	Prostatectomy with CC	1.2744	1.2474	−2.1
307	11	SURG	Prostatectomy w/o CC	0.6889	0.6620	−3.9
308	11	SURG	Minor bladder procedures with CC	1.4315	1.4452	1.0
309	11	SURG	Minor bladder procedures w/o CC	0.7287	0.7580	4.0
310	11	SURG	Transurethral procedures with CC	0.8880	0.9006	1.4
311	11	SURG	Transurethral procedures w/o CC	0.5153	0.5206	1.0
312	11	SURG	Urethral procedures age >17 with CC	0.8082	0.8334	3.1
313	11	SURG	Urethral procedures, age >17 w/o CC	0.4623	0.4551	−1.6
314	11	SURG	Urethral procedures, age 0–17	0.4389	0.4470	1.8

315	SURG	11	Other kidney and urinary tract O.R. procedures	2.0362	2.0341	−0.1
316	MED	11	Renal failure	1.2896	1.2903	0.1
317	MED	11	Admit for renal dialysis	0.5075	0.5194	2.3
318	MED	11	Kidney and urinary tract neoplasms with CC	1.1244	1.1215	−0.3
319	MED	11	Kidney and urinary tract neoplasms w/o CC	0.5069	0.5298	4.5
320	MED	11	Kidney and urinary tract infections age >17 with CC	0.9807	0.9677	−1.3
321	MED	11	Kidney and urinary tract infections age >17 w/o CC	0.6252	0.6112	−2.2
322	MED	11	Kidney and urinary tract infections age 0–17	0.6389	0.4952	−22.5
323	MED	11	Urinary stones with CC and/or ESW lithotripsy	0.7381	0.7290	−1.2
324	MED	11	Urinary stones w/o CC	0.3858	0.3864	0.2
325	MED	11	Kidney and urinary tract signs and symptoms age >17 with CC	0.6551	0.6607	0.9
326	MED	11	Kidney and urinary tract signs and symptoms age >17 w/o CC	0.4152	0.4024	−3.1
327	MED	11	Kidney and urinary tract signs and symptoms age 0–17	0.7038	0.7169	1.9
328	MED	11	Urethral stricture age >17 with CC	0.6363	0.6597	3.7
329	MED	11	Urethral stricture age >17 w/o CC	0.4113	0.3881	−5.6
330	MED	11	Urethral stricture age 0–17	0.2830	0.2882	1.8
331	MED	11	Other kidney and urinary tract diagnoses age >17 with CC	0.9765	0.9829	0.7
332	MED	11	Other kidney and urinary tract diagnoses age >17 w/o CC	0.5347	0.5430	1.6
333	MED	11	Other kidney and urinary tract diagnoses age 0–17	0.9590	0.9641	0.5
334	SURG	12	Major male pelvic procedures with CC	1.7728	1.7535	−1.1
335	SURG	12	Major male pelvic procedures w/o CC	1.3597	1.3630	0.2
336	SURG	12	Transurethral prostatectomy with CC	0.8704	0.8540	−1.9
337	SURG	12	Transurethral prostatectomy w/o CC	0.6066	0.6050	−0.3
338	SURG	12	Testes procedures, for malignancy	0.9386	0.9395	0.1
339	SURG	12	Testes procedures, non-malignancy age >17	0.7572	0.8093	6.9
340	SURG	12	Testes procedures, non-malignancy age 0–17	0.4401	0.4483	1.9
341	SURG	12	Penis procedures	0.9681	0.9646	−0.4
342	SURG	12	Circumcision age >17	0.5766	0.5848	1.4
343	SURG	12	Circumcision age 0–17	0.3845	0.3916	1.8
344	SURG	12	Other male reproductive system O.R. procedures for malignancy	1.0568	1.0183	−3.6
345	SURG	12	Other male reproductive system O.R. proc except for malignancy	0.7521	0.7344	−2.4

TABLE D–21.—DRG RELATIVE WEIGHTS FROM FISCAL YEAR 1993 TO FISCAL YEAR 1994—Continued

DRG	MDC	Type	Title	Fiscal year		Percent change
				1993 weight	1994 weight	
346	12	MED	Malignancy, male reproductive system, with CC	0.9906	0.9338	−5.7
347	12	MED	Malignancy, male reproductive system, w/o CC	0.5120	0.4928	−3.8
348	12	MED	Benign prostatic hypertrophy with CC	0.6815	0.6856	0.6
349	12	MED	Benign prostatic hypertrophy w/o CC	0.3952	0.3904	−1.2
350	12	MED	Inflammation of the male reproductive system	0.6707	0.6668	−0.6
351	12	MED	Sterilization, male	0.3384	0.3447	1.9
352	12	MED	Other male reproductive system diagnoses	0.5801	0.5326	−8.2
353	13	SURG	Pelvic evisceration, radical hysterectomy and radical vulvectomy	1.9031	1.9624	3.1
354	13	SURG	Uterine, adnexa proc for non-ovarian/adnexal malig with CC	1.3686	1.3794	0.8
355	13	SURG	Uterine, adnexa proc for non-ovarian/adnexal malig w/o CC	0.8493	0.8717	2.6
356	13	SURG	Female reproduction system reconstructive procedures	0.7030	0.7096	0.9
357	13	SURG	Uterine and adnexa proc for ovarian or adnexal malign	2.3097	2.3153	0.2
358	13	SURG	Uterine and adnexa proc for non-malignancy with CC	1.1066	1.1042	−0.2
359	13	SURG	Uterine and adnexa proc for non-malignancy w/o CC	0.7723	0.7834	1.4
360	13	SURG	Vagina, cervix and vulva procedures	0.8024	0.8126	1.3
361	13	SURG	Laparoscopy and incisional tubal interruption	0.9767	1.0037	2.8
362	13	SURG	Endoscopic tubal interruption	0.5057	0.5151	1.9
363	13	SURG	D&C, conization and radio-implant, for malignancy	0.6251	0.6340	1.4
364	13	SURG	D&C, conization except for malignancy	0.5659	0.5930	4.8
365	13	SURG	Other female reproductive system O.R. procedures	1.7093	1.7034	−0.3
366	13	MED	Malignancy, female reproductive system with CC	1.2158	1.1948	−1.7
367	13	MED	Malignancy, female reproductive system w/o CC	0.4808	0.4769	−0.8
368	13	MED	Infections, female reproductive system	0.8820	0.9489	7.6
369	13	MED	Menstrual and other female reproductive system disorders	0.5321	0.5201	−2.3
370	14	SURG	Cesarean section with CC	0.8916	0.8699	−2.4
371	14	SURG	Cesarean section w/o CC	0.6461	0.6289	−2.7
372	14	MED	Vaginal delivery with complicating diagnoses	0.4619	0.5174	12.0

373	MED	Vaginal delivery w/o complicating diagnosis	0.3182	0.3247	2.0
374	SURG	Vaginal delivery with sterilization and/or D&C	0.6297	0.5859	−7.0
375	SURG	Vaginal delivery with O.R. proc except steril and/or D&C	0.6921	0.7049	1.8
376	MED	Postpartum and post abortion diagnoses w/o O.R. procedure	0.3247	0.3894	19.9
377	SURG	Postpartum and post abortion diagnoses with O.R. procedure	0.8392	0.8600	2.5
378	MED	Ectopic pregnancy	0.7694	0.7580	−1.5
379	MED	Threatened abortion	0.2743	0.3346	22.0
380	MED	Abortion w/o D&C	0.3430	0.2958	−13.8
381	SURG	Abortion with D&C, aspiration curettage or hysterotomy	0.4326	0.3943	−8.9
382	MED	False labor	0.1486	0.1240	−16.6
383	MED	Other antepartum diagnoses with medical complications	0.3947	0.4059	2.8
384	MED	Other antepartum diagnoses w/o medical complications	0.2701	0.2620	−3.0
385	MED	Neonates, died or transferred to another acute care facility	1.2418	1.2648	1.9
386	MED	Extreme immaturity or respiratory distress syndrome, neonate	3.7035	3.7722	1.9
387	MED	Prematurity w major problems	1.8545	1.8889	1.9
388	MED	Prematurity w/o major problems	1.1747	1.1965	1.9
389	MED	Full term neonate w major problems	1.4229	1.5295	7.5
390	MED	Neonate w other significant problems	1.1340	0.9165	−19.2
391	MED	Normal newborn	0.2252	0.2294	1.9
392	SURG	Splenectomy age >17	3.1287	3.3043	5.6
393	SURG	Splenectomy age 0–17	1.5437	1.5723	1.9
394	SURG	Other O.R. procedures of the blood and blood forming organs	1.5966	1.6781	5.1
395	MED	Red blood cell disorders age >17	0.7881	0.8057	2.2
396	MED	Red blood cell disorders age 0–17	0.6802	0.3079	54.7
397	MED	Coagulation disorders	1.1905	1.2292	3.3
398	MED	Reticuloendothelial and immunity disorders with CC	1.2091	1.2431	2.8
399	MED	Reticuloendothelial and immunity disorders w/o CC	0.6735	0.6822	1.3
400	SURG	Lymphoma and leukemia w major O.R. procedure	2.5572	2.5309	−1.0
401	SURG	Lymphoma and non-acute leukemia w other O.R. proc w CC	2.3497	2.3778	1.2
402	SURG	Lymphoma and non-acute leukemia w other O.R. proc w/o CC	0.8536	0.8850	3.7
403	MED	Lymphoma and non-acute leukemia w CC	1.6827	1.6757	−0.4

TABLE D–21.—DRG RELATIVE WEIGHTS FROM FISCAL YEAR 1993 TO FISCAL YEAR 1994—Continued

DRG	MDC	Type	Title	Fiscal year		Percent change
				1993 weight	1994 weight	
404	17	MED	Lymphoma and non-acute leukemia w/o CC	0.7428	0.7377	-0.7
405	17	MED	Acute leukemia w/o major O.R. procedures age 0–17	1.0565	1.0761	1.9
406	17	SURG	Myeloprolif disord or poorly diff neopl w maj O.R. proc with CC	2.7669	2.6133	-5.6
407	17	SURG	Myeloprolif disord or poorly diff neopl w maj O.R. proc w/o CC	1.1999	1.1204	-6.6
408	17	SURG	Myeloprolif disord or poorly diff neopl w other O.R. proc	1.3279	1.4241	7.2
409	17	MED	Radiotherapy	0.9886	0.9922	0.4
410	17	MED	Chemotherapy without acute leukemia as secondary diagnosis	0.6095	0.6679	9.6
411	17	MED	History of malignancy w/o endoscopy	0.4256	0.4152	-2.4
412	17	MED	History of malignancy w endoscopy	0.4257	0.4758	11.8
413	17	MED	Other myeloprolif dis or poorly diff neopl diag with CC	1.3335	1.3849	3.9
414	17	MED	Other myeloprolif dis or poorly diff neopl diag w/o CC	0.6857	0.7091	3.4
415	18	SURG	O.R. procedure for infectious and parasitic diseases	3.5162	3.5723	1.6
416	18	MED	Septicemia age >17	1.5222	1.5141	-0.5
417	18	MED	Septicemia age 0–17	0.8974	0.7002	-22.0
418	18	MED	Postoperative and post-traumatic infections	0.9679	0.9665	-0.1
419	18	MED	Fever of unknown origin age > 17 with CC	0.9500	0.9511	0.1
420	18	MED	Fever of unknown origin age >17 w/o cc	0.6510	0.6365	-2.2
421	18	MED	Viral illness age >17	0.6882	0.6758	-1.8
422	18	MED	Viral illness and fever of unknown origin age 0–17	0.7629	0.5888	-22.8
423	18	MED	Other infectious and parasitic diseases diagnoses	1.5976	1.6246	1.7
424	19	SURG	O.R. procedure with principal diagnoses of mental illness	2.4058	2.4684	2.6
425	19	MED	Acute adjust react and disturbances of psychosocial dysfunction	0.7045	0.7127	1.2
426	19	MED	Depressive neuroses	0.6023	0.6128	1.7
427	19	MED	Neuroses except depressive	0.6322	0.6184	-2.2
428	19	MED	Disorders of personality and impulse control	0.7703	0.7084	-8.0
429	19	MED	Organic disturbances and mental retardation	0.9460	0.9379	-0.9
430	19	MED	Psychoses	0.9040	0.9153	1.2

				NV	NV	NV
431	19	MED	Childhood mental disorders	0.5980	0.6980	16.7
432	19	MED	Other mental disorder diagnoses	0.7113	0.7357	3.4
433	20	MED	Alcohol/drug abuse or dependence, left AMA	0.3545	0.3512	−0.9
434	20	MED	Alc/drug abuse or dependence, detox or other sympt trt with CC	0.7494	0.7321	−2.3
435	20	MED	Alc/drug abuse or dependence, detox or other sympt trt w/o CC	0.4818	0.4529	−6.0
436	20	MED	Alc/drug dependence with rehabilitation therapy	0.9869	0.9691	−1.8
437	20	MED	Alc/drug dependence, combined rehab and detox therapy	1.0888	0.9970	−8.4
438			No longer valid	NV	NV	NV
439	21	SURG	Skin grafts for injuries	1.2126	1.3853	14.2
440	21	SURG	Wound debridements for injuries	1.8359	1.7125	−6.7
441	21	SURG	Hand procedures for injuries	0.7321	0.7122	−2.7
442	21	SURG	Other O.R. procedures for injuries with CC	1.9106	1.9292	1.0
443	21	SURG	Other O.R. procedures for injuries w/o CC	0.7518	0.7398	−1.6
444	21	MED	Traumatic injury age >17 with CC	0.7643	0.7431	−2.8
445	21	MED	Traumatic injury age >17 w/o CC	0.4649	0.4635	−0.3
446	21	MED	Traumatic injury age 0–17	0.4869	0.4959	1.8
447	21	MED	Allergic reactions age >17	0.4919	0.4869	−1.0
448	21	MED	Allergic reactions age 0–17	0.3523	0.3588	1.8
449	21	MED	Poisoning and toxic effects of drugs age >17 with cc	0.7889	0.7929	0.5
450	21	MED	Poisoning and toxic effects of drugs age >17 w/o cc	0.4325	0.4224	−2.3
451	21	MED	Poisoning and toxic effects of drugs age 0–17	0.5268	1.0266	94.9
452	21	MED	Complications of treatment with CC	0.8550	0.82232	−3.7
453	21	MED	Complications of treatment w/o CC	0.4175	0.4177	0.0
454	21	MED	Other injury, poisoning and toxic eff diag with CC	0.8873	0.9107	2.6
455	21	MED	Other injury, poisoning and toxic eff diag w/o CC	0.4130	0.4166	0.9
456	22	MED	Burns, transferred to another acute care facility	1.7285	2.1688	25.5
457	22	MED	Extensive burns w/o O.R. procedure	2.0147	1.6312	−19.0
458	22	SURG	Non-extensive burns with graft	3.8787	3.7459	−3.4
459	22	SURG	Non-extensive burns with wound debridement or other O.R. proc	1.8906	2.1042	11.3
460	22	MED	Non-extensive burns w/o O.R. procedure	1.0032	1.0508	4.7

TABLE D–21.—DRG RELATIVE WEIGHTS FROM FISCAL YEAR 1993 TO FISCAL YEAR 1994—Continued

DRG	MDC	Type	Title	Fiscal year 1993 weight	Fiscal year 1994 weight	Percent change
461	23	SURG	O.R. proc with diagnoses of other contact with health services	0.8808	0.8656	−1.7
462	23	MED	Rehabilitation	1.7805	1.7205	−3.4
463	23	MED	Signs and symptoms with CC	0.7277	0.7249	−0.4
464	23	MED	Signs and symptoms w/o CC	0.4567	0.4591	0.5
465	23	MED	Aftercare with history of malignancy as secondary diagnosis	0.3531	0.3740	5.9
466	23	MED	Aftercare w/o history of malignancy as secondary diagnosis	0.5328	0.5516	3.5
467	23	MED	Other factors influencing health status	0.4469	0.4168	−6.7
468	(1)	SURG	Extensive O.R. procedure unrelated to principal diagnosis	3.4195	3.4842	1.9
469	(1)		Principal diagnosis invalid as discharge diagnosis	NV	NV	NV
470	(1)		Ungroupable	NV	NV	NV
471	(1)	SURG	Bilateral or multiple major joint procs of lower extremity	3.8976	3.8651	−0.8
472	22	SURG	Extensive burns with O.R. procedure	11.7093	11.633	−0.1
473	17	MED	Acute leukemia w/o major O.R. procedure age >17	3.4402	3.5702	3.8
474	(1)		No longer valid	NV	NV	NV
475	4	MED	Respiratory system diagnosis with ventilator support	3.5965	3.7175	3.4
476	(1)	SURG	Prostatic O.R. procedure unrelated to principal diagnosis	2.2014	2.2361	1.6
477	(1)	SURG	Non-extensive O.R. procedure unrelated to principal diagnosis	1.4337	1.4628	2.0
478	5	SURG	Other vascular procedures with CC	2.1645	2.1897	1.2
479	5	SURG	Other vascular procedures w/o CC	1.2718	1.3027	2.4
480		SURG	Liver transplant	20.1614	19.4679	−3.4
481	(1)	SURG	Bone marrow transplant	15.2244	14.3709	−5.6
482	(1)	SURG	Tracheostomy for face, mouth and neck diagnoses	3.4826	3.5756	2.7
483	(1)	SURG	Tracheostomy except for face, mouth and neck diagnoses	16.6590	16.9858	2.0
484	24	SURG	Craniotomy for multiple significant trauma	6.5706	5.6612	−13.8
485	24	SURG	Limb reattach, hip and femur procs for multi sign trauma	3.1669	3.2361	2.2
486	24	SURG	Other O.R. procedures for multiple significant trauma	4.8231	4.6756	−3.1
487	24	MED	Other multiple significant trauma	1.9406	1.9379	−0.1
488	25	SURG	HIV with extensive O.R. procedure	4.1539	4.3859	5.6

489	25	MED	HIV with major related condition	1.9151	1.8468	− 3.6
490	25	MED	HIV with or w/o other related condition	1.1285	1.1174	− 1.0
491	8	SURG	Major joint and limb reattachment procedurees-upper extremity	1.5676	1.6092	2.7
492	17	MED	Chemotherapy with acute leukemia as secondary diagnosis	2.7815	3.5861	28.9
493	7	SURG	Laparoscopic cholecystectomy with/out C.D.E. with CC	NC	1.5268	NC
494	7	SURG	Laparoscopic cholecystectomy with/out C.D.E. with/out CC	NC	0.8233	NC

[1] DRG definition substantially revised for discharges occurring on or after October 1, 1991.
NC Denotes a new DRG category defined for discharges occurring on or after October 1, 1991.
NV Denotes a DRG cartegory that is not valid for classification and payment under PPS.

Additional sources of information

Prospective Payment Assessment Commission. Report and recommendations to the Secretary, U.S. Department of Health and Human Services. [Washington] March 1, 1994, 138 p.
———. Medicare prospective payment and the American health care system: report to the Congress. [Washington] June 1993. 170 p.
U.S. Congress. House. Committee on Ways and Means. Subcommittee on Health. Budget Issues Relating to Payment Under Part A of the Medicare Program and Payment for Hospital Outpatient and End-Stage Renal Disease Services. Hearing, 103d Congress, 1st Session, March 18, 1993.
U.S. Congress. Office of Technology Assessment. Medicare's prospective payment system: strategies for evaluating cost, quality, and medical technology. [Washington] U.S. Government Printing Office, October 1985. 232 p. (OTA–H–262)
U.S. Department of Health and Human Services. Review of the impact of outlier and transfer payment policy upon rural hospitals. Report to Congress. [Washington] May 1988. 70 p.
———. Reimbursement of rural referral centers under the Medicare prospective payment system. Report to Congress. [Washington] Feb. 1988. 100 p.
———. Studies of urban-rural and related geographical adjustments in the Medicare prospective payment system. [Washington] Dec. 1987. 149 p.
———. Reimbursement of sole community hospitals under Medicare's prospective payment system. Report to Congress. [Washington] Dec. 1987. 85 p.
———. Impact of the Medicare Hospital Prospective Payment System 1986 Annual Report. Report to Congress. Washington, May 1989.
U.S. Department of Health and Human Services. Office of Inspector General. Office of Analysis and Inspections. Hospital closure: 1987. Washington, May 1989.
———. National DRG validation study: Special report on coding accuracy. [Washington] February 1988. 17 p. (Audit Control No. OAI–12–88–01010)
———. National DRG validation study: Special report on premature discharges. [Washington] February 1988. 27 p. (Audit Control No. OAI–05–88–00740)
U.S. General Accounting Office. Medicare: Improvements Needed in the Identification of Inappropriate Hospital Care; Report to the Chairman, Subcommittee on Health, House Committee on Ways and Means. [Washington] U.S. Government Printing Office, December 1989. 92 p. (GAO)/PEMD–90–7)
———. Medicare: Indirect medical education payments are too high; report to congressional committees. [Washington] U.S. Govt. Print. Off., 1989. 58 p. (GAO/HRD–89–33)
U.S. Congressional Budget Office. Setting Medicare's Indirect Teaching Adjustment for Hospitals. Washington, May 1989. 28 p.
———. Medicare's Disproportionate Share Adjustment for Hospitals. Washington, May 1990. 71 p.
———. Rural Hospitals and Medicare's Prospective Payment System. December 1991. 55 p.
U.S. Library of Congress. Congressional Research Service.
———. Medicare, Medicaid, and other health provisions of the Consolidated Budget Reconciliation Act of 1985 (P.L. 99–272 (known as COBRA)) [by] Jennifer O'Sullivan [Washington] 1986. 128 p. CRS Report 86–196 EPW.
———. Medicare, and Medicaid provisions of the Deficit Reduction Act of 1984 (P.L. 98–369) [by] Jennifer O'Sullivan. [Washington] 1985. 94 p. CRS Report 85–27 EPW.
———. Medicare: Prospective Payments for Inpatient Hospital Services [by] Celinda Franco. [Washington] 1987. (Archived) CRS Issue Brief 87180.
———. Rural hospitals, [by] Mark Merlis. Washington, 1989. 108 p. CRS Report 89–296 EPW.
———. Medicare: Payment for Hospital Capital Costs [by] Mark Merlis. [Washington] 1991. (Archived) CRS Issue Brief 91028.
———. Medicare: Description of Hospital Reimbursement of Inpatient Hospital Care Under the Prospective Payment System [by] Celinda Franco. [Washington] 1993. 6 p. CRS Report 93–230.
———. Medicare: FY 1994 Budget [by] Mark Merlis and Richard Price. [Washington] 1993. CRS Issue Brief 93051.

APPENDIX E. MEDICARE REIMBURSEMENT TO PHYSICIANS

PHYSICIAN PAYMENT REFORM

The Omnibus Budget Reconciliation Act of 1989 (OBRA 1989) provided for the implementation, beginning January 1, 1992, of a new payment system for physicians' services paid for by Medicare. A new fee schedule payment system replaces the previous reasonable charge payment system. The new system was enacted in response to two principal concerns. The first was the rapid escalation in program payments. Over the 1965–89 period, Medicare spending for physicians' services had increased at an average annual rate of 11.7 percent, outstripping both the increase in medical care inflation and the rate of growth in the number of Medicare enrollees. The second concern was that the use of the reasonable charge payment had led, in many cases, to payments which were not directly related to the resources used.

Under the new system, payments are made under a fee schedule which is based on a resource-based relative value scale (RBRVS). The new system is being phased in over the 1992–96 period. OBRA 1989 also created a volume performance standard to moderate the rate of growth in physician expenditures. Further, it increased protections for beneficiaries by placing more stringent limits on amounts that physicians can bill in excess of Medicare's approved payment amount. Taken together, these three elements are referred to as the three-part physician payment reform package. The legislation also authorized increased funding for research on patient outcomes for selected medical treatments and surgical procedures to assess their appropriateness, necessity, and effectiveness. The Omnibus Budget Reconciliation Act of 1990 (OBRA 1990) contained several modifications and clarifications to the OBRA 1989 provisions. Further changes were included in the Omnibus Budget Reconciliation Act of 1993 (OBRA 1993).

The Department of Health and Human Services (DHHS) issued final implementing regulations on November 25, 1991. Additional regulations were issued on November 25, 1992 and December 2, 1993.

MEDICARE FEE SCHEDULE

The Secretary of DHHS is required to establish a fee schedule before January 1 of each year that sets payment amounts for all physicians' services furnished in all fee schedule areas for the year. The fee schedule amount for a service is equal to the product of:

The *relative value for the service;*

The *geographic adjustment factor* (GAF) for the service for the fee schedule area; and

The national dollar *conversion factor* for the year.

Relative value unit. The relative value unit (RVU) for each service has three components.

The *physician work component* reflects physician time and intensity, including activities before and after patient contact.

The *practice expense or overhead component* includes all categories of practice expenses (exclusive of malpractice liability insurance costs). Included are office rents, employee wages, physician compensation, and physician fringe benefits.

The *malpractice expense component* reflects costs of obtaining malpractice insurance.

The proportion that each component represents of the total RVU varies by service.

Geographic adjustment factor. The second major factor used in calculation of the fee schedule is the geographic adjustment factor (GAF) for the fee schedule area. There are currently 217 fee schedule areas nationwide.

The GAF is designed to account for geographic variations in the costs of practicing medicine and obtaining malpractice insurance as well as a portion of the difference in physicians' incomes that is not attributable to these factors.

The GAF is the sum of three indices. Separate geographic practice cost indices (GPCIs) have been developed for each of the three components of the RVU, namely a work GPCI, a practice expense or overhead GPCI, and a malpractice GPCI. In effect, a separate geographic adjustment is made for each component. However, as required by law, only one-quarter of the geographic variation in physician work resource costs is taken into account in the formula. (Table E–25 at the end of this chapter shows the GAF values for each of the 217 fee schedule areas nationwide.)

The three GPCI-adjusted RVU values are summed to produce an indexed RVU for each locality.

Conversion factor. The conversion factor is a dollar multiplier which converts the geographically adjusted relative value for a service to an actual payment amount for the service. The law requires the establishment of an initial dollar conversion factor. The conversion factor is updated annually beginning in 1992.

The law required the calculation of an initial dollar conversion factor which was *budget neutral* relative to 1991 predicted expenditure levels. This means that if the initial conversion factor had applied in 1991, Medicare spending would equal what was projected to be spent under the reasonable charge payment system in that year. The law also contained provisions relating to payment calculations during the 1992–96 phase-in period; these are the transition provisions. The Department's final implementing regulations included an adjustment to reconcile the calculations required under both the budget neutrality and transition provisions. (This adjustment to the "adjusted historical payment basis" is discussed under "Transition rules" below.)

The initial dollar conversion factor was set at $30.42. The 1992 update was set at 1.9 percent. (See discussion of update calculation below.) Therefore the 1992 conversion factor was $31.001.

In 1993 two conversion factors applied—one for surgical services and one for nonsurgical services. The 1993 conversion factor for surgical services was $31.96, and the conversion factor for nonsurgical services was $31.25.

Beginning in 1994, a third conversion factor applies for primary care services. The 1994 conversion factor for surgical services is $35.15; the conversion factor for primary care services is $33.72; the conversion factor for other nonsurgical services is $32.91.

Payment formula. In simplified terms the payment for each service is calculated as follows:

PAYMENT=   CF× $[(RVU_{work} \times GPCI_{work}) +$
$(RVU_{practice\ expense} \times GPCI_{practice\ expense}) +$
$(RVU_{malpractice} \times GPCI_{malpractice})]$

Where:

CF=conversion factor

RVU_{work}=physician work relative value units for the service;

$GPCI_{work}$=geographic practice cost index value for physician work in the locality (the value reflects only one-quarter of the variation in physician work as required by law);

$RVU_{practice\ expense}$=practice expense or overhead relative value units for the service;

$GPCI_{practice\ expense}$=geographic practice cost index value for practice expense or overhead applicable in the locality;

$RVU_{malpractice}$=malpractice relative value units for the service;

$GPCI_{malpractice}$=geographic practice cost index value for malpractice applicable in the locality.

Transition rules. The law establishes specific payment rules for the 1992–1996 phase-in period. To determine payments in 1992, comparisons were made between the fee schedule amount and the "adjusted historical payment basis" (AHPB) in the payment locality. Generally, the AHPB was equal to the average Medicare allowance for the service in the locality in 1991, updated to 1992. Implementing regulations applied a 5.5 percent downward adjustment to this amount in order to maintain budget neutrality over the 5-year transition period.

If the reduced AHPB in a locality was less than 15 percent over or under the fee schedule amount, payments were made on the basis of the fee schedule beginning in 1992. A transition was provided in the case of differences larger than 15 percent. In 1992, the reduced AHPB amounts were increased or decreased by *15 percent of the fee schedule amount,* whichever was appropriate. Thus, for a service more than 15 percent *below* the fee schedule the payment equaled the reduced AHPB *plus* 15 percent fee schedule amount. For a service more than 15 percent *above* the fee schedule, the payment equaled the reduced AHPB *minus* 15 percent fee schedule amount.

For 1993–95, payment is based on a blend of the previous year's amount (updated to the current year) and the fee schedule amount; over the period, a gradually increasing portion is based on the fee schedule. In 1993, 75 percent was based on the previous year's amount adjusted by the update factor specified for the year and 25 percent was based on the fee schedule amount for the year. The percentage attributable to the previous year's fee is reduced to 67 percent in 1994 and 50 percent in 1995. All services are paid on the basis of the fee schedule beginning in 1996.

MEDICARE VOLUME PERFORMANCE STANDARDS; CONVERSION FACTOR UPDATE

A key element of the fee schedule is the conversion factor. One consideration in establishing the annual update in the conversion factor is whether efforts to stem the annual rate of growth in physician payments have succeeded. This is measured by the Medicare volume performance standard (MVPS).

Medicare volume performance standards. The law requires the calculation of annual MVPSs, which are standards for the rate of expenditure growth. The purpose of these standards is to provide an incentive for physicians to get involved in efforts to stem expenditure increases. The relationship of actual expenditures to the MVPS is one factor used in determining the annual update in the conversion factor.

Implementation of the MVPS provision began in fiscal year 1990. OBRA 1989 effectively set a performance standard rate of increase for fiscal year 1990 for all physicians' services and specified a process for determining the standard in future years. OBRA 1990 specified that the fiscal year 1991 MVPS rates of increase were to be set at the estimated baseline percentage increase in expenditures, minus 2 percentage points. The amount of this reduction is referred to as the "performance standard factor." OBRA 1993 increased the performance standard factor from 2.0 to 3.5 percentage points for 1994, and to 4 percent points for each succeeding year. OBRA 1990 also provided, beginning for fiscal year 1991, for the calculation of a standard for all physicians' services, and for two subcategories of physicians' services: surgical services and other services. Beginning in fiscal year 1994, OBRA 1993 required separate MVPS rates of increase for surgical, primary care, and other nonsurgical services.

Generally, the Congress is expected to specify the performance standard rates of increase. The Secretary of DHHS is required to make a recommendation to the Congress by April 15 each year. In making the recommendation, the Secretary is to consider inflation, changes in the number of part B enrollees, changes in technology, appropriateness of care, and access to care. The Physician Payment Review Commission (PhysPRC), a Congressional advisory body, is required to review the Secretary's recommendation and submit its own recommendation by May 15.

The Congress is then expected to establish the standard rates of increase. If the Congress does not specify the MVPS, however, the rates of increase are determined based on a default formula. The default standard is the product of the following four factors reduced by a performance standard factor:

> Secretary's estimate of the weighted average percentage increase in physicians' fees for services for the portions of the calendar years included in the fiscal year involved;
>
> Secretary's estimate of the percentage change from the previous year in the number of part B enrollees;
>
> Secretary's estimate of the average annual percentage growth in volume and intensity of physicians' services for the preceding 5 fiscal years; and

Secretary's estimate of the percentage change in physician expenditures in the fiscal year (not taken into account above) which will result from changes in law or regulations.

In fiscal year 1991, the performance standard factor was 1 percentage point; this increased to 1.5 percentage points in fiscal year 1992, to 2 percentage points in fiscal year 1993, to 3.5 percentage points in fiscal year 1994, and to 4.0 percentage points in subsequent years.

The MVPS for fiscal year 1994 is based on the default formula. It is set at 8.6 percent for surgical services, 10.5 percent for primary care services, 9.2 percent for other nonsurgical services, and 9.3 percent for all physicians' services (see table E–1).

TABLE E–1.—MEDICARE VOLUME PERFORMANCE STANDARDS

[In percent]

Fiscal year	Surgical	Nonsurgical	Primary Care	All
1990	(1)	(1)	(2)	9.1
1991	3.3	8.6	(2)	7.3
1992	6.5	11.2	(2)	10.0
1993	8.4	10.8	(2)	10.0
1994	8.6	9.2	10.5	9.3

[1] Separate performance standards for surgical and nonsurgical services not required for fiscal year 1990.

[2] Separate performance standards for primary care services not required for fiscal years 1990–93.

TABLE E–2.—CBO PROJECTIONS OF MEDICARE VOLUME PERFORMANCE STANDARDS[1]

[Fiscal years, in percent]

	1993	1994	1995	1996	1997	1998	1999
MVP standard overall[2]	10.0	9.3	10.0	4.8	5.0	4.0	4.1
Growth in overall expenditures	5.5	8.9	11.2	10.7	11.1	9.6	9.1
Difference	4.5	0.4	−1.3	−6.0	−6.1	−5.6	−5.1
Maximum allowable reduction	−2.0	−2.5	−5.0	−5.0	−5.0	−5.0	−5.0
MEI adjustment	−1.3	9.3	4.5	0.4	−1.3	−5.0	−5.0
Legislative adjustments[3]	0.0	−2.3	−2.2	0.0	0.0	0.0	0.0
Projected MEI (calendar year)	2.7	2.3	2.9	2.8	2.7	2.6	2.5
Adjusted overall MEI (calendar year)	1.4	9.3	5.2	3.2	1.4	−2.4	−2.5

[1] Because of uncertainty over the redistributive effects of the physician fee schedule on the categories of services, CBO projects only an overall default standard for 1995–99.

[2] The 1993 and 1994 Standards were announced by the Secretary of HHS. Standard values for 1995–99 are CBO projections.

[3] The increase in physician's fees in 1994 and 1995 were reduced by OBRA 1993 legislation. Surgical services were reduced by 3.6% in 1994 and 2.7% in 1995. Medical services (other than primary care) were reduced by 2.6% in 1994, 2.7% in 1995. The numbers shown in this table reflect a weighted reduction across all physician services that were used by CBO to calculate an overall update.

Source: Congressional Budget Office.

Table E–2 shows CBO projections of the MVPS and components of the MVPS through fiscal year 1999.

Conversion factor update. Annual updates in payments under the fee schedule are made by updating the dollar conversion factor. The

Congress is generally expected to specify the percentage increase in the conversion factor. In April of each year (beginning in 1991), the Secretary of DHHS is required to recommend to the Congress an update (or updates) in the conversion factor for the following year.

In making the update recommendation, the Secretary is required to consider a number of factors including the percentage change in actual expenditures in the preceding fiscal year compared to the MVPS for that year, changes in volume and intensity of services, beneficiary access to care, and the increase in the Medicare Economic Index (MEI). The MEI is a percentage figure which is revised annually; it has been used in the program to limit annual increases in recognized fees. The MEI is generally intended to reflect annual increases in the costs of operating a medical practice; however, for several years the MEI percentage was set by the Congress. (See table E–3 for a history of MEI updates.)

The PhysPRC is required to review the Secretary's update recommendation and submit its own recommendation to Congress by May 15 of each year.

For 1993, separate updates were required for surgical and nonsurgical services. Beginning with the 1994 update, OBRA 1993 required separate updates for surgical services, primary care services, and other nonsurgical services. OBRA 1993 also modified the MVPS by including anesthesia services in the MVPS for surgical services.

The Congress either specifies the update to the conversion factor or a default formula, specified in law, applies. The *default fee update* is equal to the Secretary's estimate of the MEI increased or decreased by the percentage difference between the increase in actual expenditures and the MVPS for the second preceding fiscal year. (Thus, the 1994 updates reflect actual fiscal year 1992 experience.) However, the law specifies a lower limit on the default update. Before the enactment of OBRA 1993, the maximum downward adjustment in the update was 2 percentage points in 1992 and 1993, 2.5 percentage points in calendar years 1994 and 1995, and 3 percentage points for any succeeding calendar year. However, OBRA 1993 changed for maximum downward adjustment for 1995 and any succeeding year to 5.0 percentage points. There is no restriction on upward adjustments to the MEI.

OBRA 1993 required the MEI for calendar year 1994 to be reduced by 3.6 percentage points for surgical services and 2.6 percentage points for nonsurgical services other than primary care services. OBRA 1993 also required the MEI to be reduced by 2.7 percentage points in 1995 for both surgical and nonprimary care nonsurgical services. Primary care services were exempt from the statutory reductions in the MEI in 1994 and 1995.

The default formula was used to calculate the update for calendar year 1994. The 1994 MEI is 2.3 percent. The conversion factor was increased to 10 percent for surgical services, 7.9 percent for primary care services, and 5.3 percent for other nonsurgical services. The fee updates were set above the MEI because the growth rates in spending for both surgical and nonsurgical services were less than the fiscal year 1992 volume performance standards. (See table E–3 for previous fee schedule updates.

TABLE E–3.—MEDICARE UPDATE FACTORS FROM 1973–1994

Medicare economic index	Index value	Annual increase (percent)
July 1, 1973	1.000	NA
July 1, 1975 to June 30, 1976	1.179	17.90
July 1, 1976 to June 30, 1977	1.276	8.23
July 1, 1977 to June 30, 1978	1.357	6.35
July 1, 1978 to June 30, 1979	1.426	5.08
July 1, 1979 to June 30, 1980	1.533	7.50
July 1, 1980 to June 30, 1981	1.658	8.15
July 1, 1981 to June 30, 1982	1.790	7.96
July 1, 1982 to June 30, 1983	1.949	8.88
July 1, 1983 to June 30, 1984	2.063	5.85
July 1, 1984 to Apr. 30, 1986	2.063	[1] 0
May 1, 1986 to Dec. 31, 1986	2.148	[2] 4.15
Jan. 1, 1987 to Mar. 31, 1988	2.217	[3] 3.20

	Primary care services	Other services	Anesthesiology, radiology, & overvalued procedures [8]
Apr. 1, 1988 to Dec. 31, 1988	[4] 3.60	[4] 1.00	1.00
Jan. 1, 1989 to Mar. 31, 1990	[5] 3.00	[5] 1.00	1.00
Apr. 1, 1990 to Dec. 31, 1990	[6] 4.20	[7] 2.00	0
Jan. 1, 1991 to Dec. 31, 1991	2.00	0	0

Physician fee schedule update	Primary care services	Surgical services	Other nonsurgical services
Jan. 1, 1992 to Dec. 31, 1992	1.90	1.90	1.90
Jan. 1, 1993 to Dec. 31, 1993	0.80	3.10	0.80
Jan. 1, 1994 to Dec. 31, 1994	7.90	10.00	5.30

[1] MEI was held constant during fee freeze.

[2] Percentage increase was mandated by Public Law 99–272 and applied only to participating physicians.

[3] Percentage increase was mandated by Public Law 99–509 and applied to both participating and nonparticipating physicians. Prevailing charges of nonparticipating physicians were 96 percent of the prevailing charges for participating physicians.

[4] Percentage increase was mandated by Public Law 100–203. Prevailing charges for services provided by nonparticipating physicians are 95.5 percent of the prevailing charges for participating physicians.

[5] Percentage increase was mandated by Public Law 100–203. Prevailing charges for services provided by nonparticipating physicians are 95 percent of the prevailing charges for participating physicians.

[6] Prevailing charges for services provided by nonparticipating physicians are 95 percent of the prevailing charges for participating physicians.

[7] Percentage increase was mandated by P.L. 100–239. Prevailing charges for services provided by nonparticipating physicians are 95 percent of the prevailing charges for participating physicians.

[8] Services considered overpriced are specified in table 2 in the "Joint Explanatory Statement of the Committee of Conference" submitted with the conference report to accompany P.L. 100–239.

NA—Not applicable.

Source: Health Care Financing Administration, Office of the Actuary, Office of Medicare and Medicaid Cost Estimates.

LIMITS ON BENEFICIARY LIABILITY

Medicare pays 80 percent of the fee schedule amount after the beneficiary has met the $100 deductible for the year. The beneficiary is responsible for the remaining 20 percent, known as coinsurance. If a physician does not accept *assignment* on a claim, the beneficiary may be liable for additional charges known as *balance billing charges*. However, the law places certain limits on these balance billing charges.

Assignment/participation. The new payment system retains the Medicare concepts of assignment and participation. As under the previous reasonable charge payment system, a physician is able to choose whether or not to accept assignment on a claim paid under the fee schedule. In the case of an assigned claim, the physician bills the program directly and is paid an amount equal to 80 percent of the fee schedule amount (less any unmet deductible). The physician may not charge the beneficiary more than the applicable deductible and coinsurance amounts. In the case of nonassigned claims, the physician still bills the program directly; however, Medicare payment is made to the beneficiary. In addition to the deductible and coinsurance amounts, the beneficiary is liable for the difference between the fee schedule amount and the physician's actual charge, subject to certain limits. This is known as the *balance billed* amount.

A physician may become a *participating physician*. A participating physician is one who voluntarily enters into an agreement with the Secretary of DHHS to accept assignment on all claims for the forthcoming year. Medicare patients of these physicians never face balance billing charges.

The law includes a number of incentives for physicians to become participating physicians, chief of which is higher recognized fee schedule amounts. The fee schedule amount for a nonparticipating physician is only 95 percent of the recognized amount for a participating physician.

The law specifies that physicians are required to accept assignment on all claims for persons who are dually eligible for Medicare and Medicaid. This includes "qualified Medicare beneficiaries" (QMBs); these are persons with incomes below poverty for whom Medicaid is required to pay Medicare premiums and cost-sharing charges.

Balance billing limits. For several years, the law has placed limits on balance billing charges. From 1987–90, the program placed a physician-specific limit on actual charges of physicians which was known as the maximum allowable actual charge or (MAAC). Beginning in 1991, new limits were phased in.

The new limiting charges are set at a maximum percentage above the recognized payment amount (the prevailing charge in 1991 or the Medicare fee schedule amount in subsequent years) for nonparticipating physicians. Recognized payment amounts for nonparticipating physicians are 95 percent of such amounts for participating physicians. The limiting charges are therefore a percentage of this reduced amount.

In 1991, a physician's limiting charge was the same percentage (not to exceed 25 percent) above the 1991 recognized payment amount as their 1990 MAAC was above the 1990 recognized payment amount. This was referred to as the 125-percent limit. In 1991 only, the limit for evaluation and management services was 140 percent.

In 1992, a physician's limiting charge was the same percentage (not to exceed 20 percent) above the 1992 payment amount as their 1991 limiting charge was above the 1991 recognized payment amount. This was referred to as the 120-percent limit. For 1993 and subsequent years, the limiting charge for nonparticipating physicians is 115 percent of the fee schedule amount.

Because certain items and services are excluded from the physician fee schedule, beneficiaries do not have limiting charge protection for them. OBRA 1993 expanded the scope of the limiting charge protection, however. Beginning in 1994, the limiting charge provision applies to drugs and biologicals that are furnished incident to physicians' services. In addition, the limiting charge provisions now apply to nonparticipating suppliers.

MEDICAL CARE OUTCOMES AND EFFECTIVENESS RESEARCH

In the fourth part of the physician payment reform package, Congress created a new agency, the Agency for Health Care Policy and Research, which replaced the then existing National Center for Health Services Research in the Public Health Service. The mission of the new agency is to enhance the quality, appropriateness and effectiveness of health care services and access to such services. These goals are to be accomplished by establishing a broad base of scientific research and promoting improvements in the clinical practice of medicine and the organization, financing and delivery of health care services.

Specifically, the agency is directed to conduct and support research, demonstration projects, evaluations, training, guideline development and the dissemination of information on health care services and delivery systems, including activities on: (1) the effectiveness, efficiency, and quality of health care services; (2) the outcomes of health care services and procedures; (3) clinical practice, including primary care and practice-oriented research; (4) health care technologies, facilities and equipment; (5) health care costs, productivity and market forces; (6) health promotion and disease prevention; (7) health statistics and epidemiology; and (8) medical liability.

IMPACT OF MEDICARE FEE SCHEDULE

The Medicare Fee Schedule was designed to remove many of the inequities of the previous payment system by shifting payment away from tests and procedures toward evaluation and management services. Because the fee schedule was intended to be implemented in a budget-neutral fashion, total outlays under the new system were expected to match the outlays that would have occurred under the previous payment system. In general, under the new payment system, primary care physicians were expected to receive higher payments per service, and specialty physicians were expected to receive lower payments per service.

The overall payment level under the Medicare Fee Schedule is established through the conversion factor. In effect, the conversion factor translates the relative value units for individual procedures into actual dollar payments. Increaes or decreases in the overall level of payments are accomplished by adjusting the level of the conversion factor. In moving from the former payment system to the fee schedule, DHHS was required to set the initial conversion factor in a budget-neutral manner. Inaccuracies in setting the conversion factor could result in either underpayment to physicians or in excess outlays by the Medicare program. This calculation of the conversion factor required DHHS to make a number of important assumptions regarding both the number and type of services that would be provided. Of particular importance was the projected increase in the volume and intensity of services in response to changes in payment rates. The Department contended that past experience suggested that implementation of the new payment system would be accompanied by increases in volume and intensity of services. To account for these increases, DHHS made a "baseline adjustment" in the conversion factor.

Using data from 1991, 1992, and 1993, PhysPRC has examined the initial impact of the Medicare Fee Schedule on physicians. Table E–4 shows the change in Medicare payment to physicians between 1991 and 1993, by specialty. Changes in payment measured from 1991 to 1993 reflect four aspects of payment reform: two years of transition to the Medicare Fee Schedule, the uniform upate for 1992, the differential update for surgical and nonsurgical services for 1993, and refinements to the relative values for 1993.

From 1991 to 1993, physicians' payments per service declined by 4 percent. Surgical specialties had about an 8 percent reduction in payment per service compared with the 2 percent increase for medical specialties. Specialties that predominantly provide evaluation and management services fared better. Payments to general and family practitioners increased by 17 percent over the two-year period, while those to internists rose by 2 percent. Pathologists and thoracic surgeons had the largest reduction of 16 percent, followed by gastroenterologists, radiologists, and cardiologists with reductions ranging from 10 percent to 12 percent.

The total Medicare payment a physician receives depends not only on the payment per service but also on changes in the number and intensity of services billed. Although physicians had about a 4 percent reduction in payment overall, a 6 percent increase in the number and intensity of services per physician led to about a 4 percent increase in total Medicare payment per physician over the 2-year period.

While payment rates to a majority of specialties fell, on average, most of these specialties provided more services. These increases, however, did not completely offset the reductions for most surgical specialties which had net reductions in Medicare payment. With restrictions on balance billing and higher participation rates, most surgical specialties had total reductions in Medicare revenue ranging from 6 percent to 12 percent over the 2-year period. Only urologists saw no change from 1991 to 1993. With increases in both payment per service and the number of services provided, family and general practitioners saw total Medicare payment increase by 23 percent from 1991 to 1993, while total Medicare revenue increased by 19 percent.

Using data from 1991 and 1993, PhysPRC also examined the initial impact of the Medicare Fee Schedule on physicians by state. Table E–5 shows the estimated change in Medicare payment rates by state and service category between 1991 and 1993. Overall, payment rates for all services declined by 3 percent from 1991 to 1993, while those for primary care services increased by 11 percent. Medicare payment rates for all services declined in all but 13 states. In contrast, payment rates for primary care services increased in all but 4 states. Changes in payment rates for all services ranged from a 5 percent increase in Colorado to a 9 percent decrease in Alaska and Nevada. Payment rates for primary care services increased substantially in many states, with 19 states experiencing increases of 20 percent or more. Payment rate changes for primary care services ranged from a 32 percent increase in Mississsippi to a 9 percent decrease in Alaska.

TABLE E–4.—CHANGE IN MEDICARE PAYMENT, BY SPECIALTY, 1991–93

[Percentage change]

Specialty	Medicare payment per service	Volume and intensity of services per physician	Medicare payment per physician	Medicare revenue per physician[1]
Medical	2	8	8	4
Cardiology	− 10	19	8	4
Family/general practice	17	6	23	19
Gastroenterology	− 12	21	8	6
Internal medicine	2	− 4	− 2	− 6
Other medical	0	19	16	12
Surgical	− 8	4	− 4	− 8
General surgery	− 6	4	− 2	− 6
Ophthalmology	− 8	2	− 8	− 10
Orthopedic surgery	− 8	4	− 4	− 10
Thoracic surgery	− 16	10	− 8	− 12
Urology	− 4	8	4	0
Other surgical	− 2	4	2	− 2
Radiology/Pathology	− 12	16	2	0
Radiology	− 12	15	0	0
Pathology	− 16	32	10	6
All Physicians	− 4	6	4	0

[1] Includes balance billing.

Note.—For these analyses, ER physicians were redesignated as general practitioners, which lead to substantial changes in estimates of payments per service for family and general practitioners and for internists. In addition, vascular surgeons were combined with general surgeons, while cardiac surgeons were combined with thoracic surgeons.

Source: Physician Payment Review Commission analysis of 1991 and 1993 Medicare claims, 5 percent sample of beneficiaries.

TABLE E–5.—ESTIMATED PERCENT CHANGE IN MEDICARE PAYMENT RATES, BY STATE
AND CATEGORY OF SERVICE, 1991–93

State	All services	Primary care services	Other services
Alabama	−1	14	−5
Alaska	−9	−9	−9
Arizona	−6	−3	−7
Arkansas	−3	21	−8
California	−6	0	−7
Colorado	5	21	2
Connecticut	−5	0	−6
Delaware	0	16	−4
District of Columbia	−3	6	−5
Florida	−7	1	−9
Georgia	−2	19	−6
Hawaii	−6	−3	−8
Idaho	2	21	−2
Illinois	−2	15	−6
Indiana	−1	19	−6
Iowa	3	28	−1
Kansas	−1	21	−5
Kentucky	1	23	−3
Louisiana	−3	23	−8
Maine	0	18	−5
Maryland	−5	7	−8
Massachusetts	−3	2	−4
Michigan	1	21	−3
Minnesota	1	24	−3
Mississippi	4	32	−1
Missouri	−1	17	−4
Montana	−1	17	−4
Nebraska	−1	21	−5
Nevada	−9	−6	−10
New Hampshire	4	27	−1
New Jersey	0	17	−3
New Mexico	−2	15	−7
New York	−2	8	−4
North Carolina	0	18	−4
North Dakota	−1	19	−5
Ohio	−3	11	−6
Oklahoma	−1	17	−4
Oregon	1	13	−2
Pennsylvania	−3	12	−6
Puerto Rico and Virgin Islands	−5	1	−7

TABLE E–5.—ESTIMATED PERCENT CHANGE IN MEDICARE PAYMENT RATES, BY STATE AND CATEGORY OF SERVICE, 1991–93—Continued

State	All services	Primary care services	Other services
Rhode Island	0	17	−4
South Carolina	2	28	−3
South Dakota	−1	19	−4
Tennessee	0	21	−4
Texas	−2	20	−6
Utah	4	28	−1
Vermont	2	22	−4
Virginia	1	20	−3
Washington	0	15	−3
West Virginia	−2	9	−5
Wisconsin	0	14	−3
Wyoming	4	21	0
All States	−3	11	−5

Note.—CPT codes for visit services were converted from 1991 to 1993 coding before calculating fee changes. Therapeutic radiology services and dialysis services were omitted due to difficulties calculating fees per unit of service.

Source: PPRC analysis of Medicare 1993 BMAD procedure file and 1993 5 percent beneficiary Standard Analytic File data. 1993 data are calculated from claims incurred in the first six months of 1993 only.

SELECTED FEE SCHEDULE ISSUES

Establishment of relative values. Relative value units (RVUs) for physician work were based primarily on work done by a Harvard University research team. DHHS used panels of carrier medical directors to review comments received on the values contained in the proposed regulations to fill gaps in the Harvard relative value scale (RVS), and to resolve identified anomalies.

In recognition of that fact that further refinements might be necessary, DHHS designated the relative work values implemented on January 1, 1992 as "initial" values. Final RVUs for existing procedure codes under the fee schedule and interim RVUs for new and revised codes were issued in November 1992 and again in December 1993.

Due to changes in RVUs for codes reviewed as part of the refinement process, the addition of new codes to the fee schedule, and the revisions in payment policies, DHHS determined that net increases would have added a projected $45 million in expenditures in calendar year 1994. Because certain revisions to the fee schedule are to be made in a budget-neutral manner, a uniform adjustment factor of − 1.3 percent was added to all RVUs for 1994. This budget-neutral adjustment factor is the sum of two different adjustment factors that were necessary. The $45 million that would have been added to Medicare payments required an adjustment to all RVUs of − 0.1 percent to ensure budget neutrality. Two additional OBRA

1993 changes, elimination of electrocardiogram (EKG) reductions and new physician reductions, required an adjustment to all RVUs of − 1.2 percent to ensure budget neutrality for these issues.

OBRA 1993 required that an adjustment be made to practice expense RVUs for services for which practice expense RVUs exceed 128 percent of the corresponding work RVUs (and whose services are performed less than 75 percent of the time in an office setting). For services meeting these criteria, the 1994 practice expense RVUs were reduced by 25 percent of the amount by which the practice expense RVUs exceed the 1994 work RVUs. In 1995 and 1996, the excess, as determined for 1994, will be reduced an additional 25 percent each year. Practice expense RVUs will not be reduced to an amount less than 128 percent of the 1994 work RVU for a service. Certain services that are provided in office settings at least 75 percent of the time are exempt from cuts in practice expense RVUs.

Visit codes. Approximately one-third of Medicare expenditures for physicians' services are made for medical visits and consultations; these are referred to as evaluation and management services. Physicians bill for these services based on current procedure and terminology (CPT) codes developed by the American Medical Association (AMA).

Historically, there were wide variations in the way physicians used visit codes. To a degree, these differences could be accommodated under the old reasonable charge payment system. However, uniform definitions were needed under the new fee schedule. This is because a single relative value is assigned to each code nationwide.

The CPT editorial panel adopted new definitions and new code numbers for all visit categories, effective January 1, 1992. The physician work relative value units are based on these new definitions. The new definitions rely primarily on the clinical content of the visit to differentiate among levels of care. Most codes also indicate the typical amount of time spent by a physician in performing the service; this is an ancillary factor in code selection.

PhysPRC's analysis of claims data for all of 1992 and the first half of 1993 reveals some important successes concerning the new coding system. Physicians appear to be using the new codes in a more discriminating fashion. For all classes of visits (for example, office visit with a new patient) fewer physicians used only one level of service in coding, and more physicians used all the levels of service. The most substantial improvements came in hospital visits. Tracking the average level of service within classes of visits over the first six quarters demonstrated stable patterns of coding over time.

Global surgery policy. Medicare carriers have typically bundled payment for services associated with a surgery into one code, which is referred to as a global surgical service. Historically, there have been differences among carriers in the scope and duration of services included in the global surgery payment.

A uniform global surgery policy has been in effect since January 1992. The services included in the package are all preoperative services provided on the day before the surgery, all intraoperative services that are a normal and necessary part of the surgical procedure, and all related services provided during a 90-day postoperative period (with the exception of services provided in connection with return trips to the operating room). The initial consultation with the surgeon is outside the global surgical package.

Specific rules also apply for minor surgeries and endoscopies. No payment will generally be made for a visit on the same day as the procedure unless a separately identifiable service is furnished. A zero or 10 day postoperative period applies for minor surgeries. (Those with a 10 day period are listed in an addendum to the final regulations.) There is no postoperative period for endoscopies performed through an existing body orifice. Other endoscopies are subject to either the major or minor surgical service policy, whichever is appropriate.

Anesthesia services. For several years, payments to anesthesiologists were made on the basis of a fee schedule which predated the RBRVS fee schedule. This anesthesia fee schedule used a separate set of relative values, known as the relative value guide, for anesthesia services which were developed by the American Society of Anesthesiology. Generally, the number of relative value units was the sum of base units and time units.

Generally, the allowable base units from the relative value guide were used when anesthesia services were integrated into the overall fee schedule. Unlike the policy for other services, DHHS temporarily retained the use of actual time in the final regulations; this was done pending further study of the issue. The retention of actual time requires that anesthesia services have a separate conversion factor. The anesthesia conversion factor in 1994, which reflects updates and budget neutrality adjusters, is $14.20.

Anesthesia services may be performed directly by the anesthesiologist, by a certified registered nurse anesthetist (CRNA) under the medical direction of an anesthesiologist or by a nonmedically directed CRNA. If a physician personally performs the anesthesia service, payment is based on the anesthesia-specific conversion factor and unreduced base units and time units with each time unit equivalent to 15 minutes. If a physician medically directs an anesthesia service on or after January 1, 1994, the allowance is 60 percent of the allowance for the same service personally performed by the anesthesiologist. This percentage is reduced each year so that beginning January 1, 1998, it is 50 percent.

The allowance for an anesthesia service furnished by a medically directed CRNA on or after January 1, 1994 is calculated at 60 percent of the allowance for the same service personally performed by the anesthesiologist. This percentage is reduced each year so that beginning January 1, 1998, it is 50 percent. Anesthesia services furnished by a nonmedically directed CRNA are calculated based on allowable base and time units, the same as for anesthesia services personally furnished by an anesthesiologist, and a statutorily mandated national conversion factor, that is geographically adjusted. The nonmedically directed conversion factor is limited by the physician anesthesia conversion factor for the same payment area.

Beginning in 1994, the allowance for the teaching anesthesiologist's involvement in a single anesthesia case with an anesthesia intern or resident is determined in the same manner as the allowance for the anesthesa service personally furnished by the nonteaching anesthesiologist.

Radiology services. Prior to 1992, radiology services performed by radiologists (or physicians for whom radiology services accounted for at least 50 percent of their Medicare billings) were paid under a radiology fee schedule. The relative values were based on values developed by the American College of Radiology. In 1992, as required by law, the radiologist fee schedule was integrated into the overall physician fee schedule. Prior relationships among radiology services were preserved, while appropriate modifications were made to develop consistent relationships between the physician work involved in radiology services and all other physician services. The work, practice expense, and malpractice RVUS were integrated separately.

Special payment rules apply to certain categories of radiology services. For portable x-ray services, national relative value units have been established which reflect equipment set-up costs per procedure. Associated transportation costs will continue to be priced locally.

The use of complete procedure codes has been discontinued for interventional radiological services; this is consistent with CPT changes. Payment of the full fee schedule amount is made for the radiological portion (supervision and interpretation code) of an interpretive radiologic service and for the primary nonradiologic service (the surgical code). For any other procedure codes, a reduction applies.

Payments for electrocardiograms (EKGs). For the 1994 fee schedule, separate payment for EKG interpretations performed in conjunction with visits and consultations is restored. (Separate payment had been barred since January 1, 1992.) The RVUs for visits and consultations will be reduced by the number of RVUs that were added to account for EKG interpretations. To ensure budget neutrality, a 0.3 percent reduction will be made to all RVUs including EKGs, visits, and consultations. (The 0.3 percent reduction corrects an error made in HCFA's original calculation in adding EKG RVUs to visit and consultation RVUs.) To ensure the provision is budget neutral throughout the remainder of the transition to the physician fee schedule, HCFA will reduce the 1994 transition payment amount by 0.7 percent.

New physicians. Prior to January 1, 1994, new physicians were paid at a reduced rate for the first four years of practice. This policy did not apply to primary care services or services furnished in health manpower shortage areas. This policy was first incorporated in OBRA 1987; it was subsequently expanded and modified by OBRA 1989 and OBRA 1990. The payment adjustment was rescinded by OBRA 1993, so Medicare payments for services furnished by new pysicians and practitioners are now the same as payments made for the same services furnished by established physicians. To maintain budget neutrality, a 0.9 percent reduction was applied to all fee schedule RVUs and transition amounts for physician services (but not anesthesia services), anesthesia conversion factors, and the prevailing charge or fee schedule amount for practitioner services.

Physician pathology services. A limited number of the services listed in the pathology section of the CPT are identified as physician pathology services. The remainder are generally clinical diagnostic laboratory services which are paid under a separate fee schedule.

The law requires an adjustment to reflect the technical component of furnishing physician pathology services through a laboratory that is independent of a hospital and separate from a physician's office. DHHS set the technical component at 15 percent of the professional component amount. DHHS also identified a new category of services—clinical laboratory interpretation services. Fifteen clinical laboratory codes have been identified for which a separate payment may be made if the interpretation is requested by the patient's attending physician, results in a written narrative report, and requires exercise of medical judgment by the pathologist.

Defining geographic payment localities. Under the reasonable charge system, Medicare used 240 payment localities nationwide. These payment localities have been retained under the fee schedule except in five States (Nebraska, North Carolina, Ohio, Oklahoma, and Minnesota) where physicians demonstrated overwhelming support for using statewide localities. There are currently 217 payment localities under the fee schedule.

OBRA 1989 required PhysPRC to conduct a study to determine the feasibility of using an alternative configuration, such as States or metropolitan statistical areas, for payment purposes under the fee schedule. PhysPRC recommended use of statewide fee schedule areas except in States with high intrastate price variation; in these States, up to five areas would be defined. DHHS is examining this and other recommendations. A change in the current locality structure would require a statutory change.

PAYMENT FOR CLINICAL LABORATORY SERVICES

Since 1984, payment for clinical laboratory services has been made on the basis of a fee schedule established on a regional, statewide or carrier service area basis. As a matter of practice, the Secretary has established fee schedules on a carrier service area basis. The law set the initial fee schedule payment amount for services performed in physicians' offices or independent laboratories at the 60th percentile of the prevailing charge level established for the fee screen year beginning July 1, 1984. Similarly, the initial fee schedule payment amount for services provided by hospital-based laboratories serving hospital outpatients was set at the 62nd percentile of the prevailing charge level. Subsequent amendments limited the percentage differential to "qualified hospitals." A qualified hospital is a sole community hospital (as that term is used for payment under Medicare's hospital prospective payment system) which provides some clinical diagnostic tests 24 hour a day in order to serve a hospital emergency room which is available to provide services 24 hours a day, 7 days a week.

The fee schedule payment amounts have been increased periodically since 1984 to account for inflation, though scheduled increases have in some instances been delayed and in one case did not occur. Allowable annual increases in 1991, 1992, and 1993 are limited to

2 percent. Allowable annual increases in 1994 and 1995 would be 0 percent.

Effective April 1, 1988, the law reduced the fee schedule amounts by 8.3 percent for certain automated tests and tests (except for cytopathology tests) that were subject to lowest charge level limits prior to implementation of the fee schedule. The reduced payment amounts serve as the basis for all future updates for these services.

Beginning in 1988, the law established *national ceilings* on payment amounts. Initially the ceiling was set at 115 percent of the median for all fee schedules established for that test. This percentage has been lowered several times. Beginning January 1, 1991, the level is set at 88 percent of the median of all fee schedules for that test. The national ceiling on payment amounts would be lowered to 84 percent beginning January 1, 1994, 80 percent beginning January 1, 1995 and 76 percent beginning January 1, 1995.

Payment for clinical laboratory services (except for those provided by a rural health clinic) may only be made on the basis of assignment. The law specifically applies the assignment requirement to clinical laboratory services provided in physicians offices. Payment for clincial laboratory services equals 100 percent of the fee schedule amount; no beneficiary cost-sharing is imposed.

Laboratories are required to meet the requirements of the Clinical Laboratory Improvement Act (CLIA). This legislation, which focuses on the quality and reliability of medical tests, was substantially revised in 1988 (CLIA 1988). CLIA 1988 strengthened Federal regulation of laboratories and expanded Federal oversight to virtually all laboratories in the country, including physicians office laboratories. Implementing regulations were issued February 28, 1992; technical and clarifying corrections were issued January 19, 1993.

HISTORICAL DATA

ASSIGNMENT RATE EXPERIENCE

The total number of assigned claims as a percentage of total claims received by medicare carriers for physicians and other medical services is known as the total assignment rate. Initially, the net assignment rate was computed in the same manner except that it omitted hospital-based physicians and group-practice prepayment plans which were considered assigned by definition (this distinction is no longer made). The net assignment rate declined until the mid-1970's when the rate leveled off at about 50 percent. Since 1985, the rate has increased significantly rising to 89.2 percent in 1993. This reflects both the impact of the participating physician program as well as the requirement that laboratory services must be paid on an assigned basis. Chart E–1 and table E–6 show the net assignment rates for fiscal years 1969–93.

CHART E-1. NET ASSIGNMENT RATES (1969-1993)

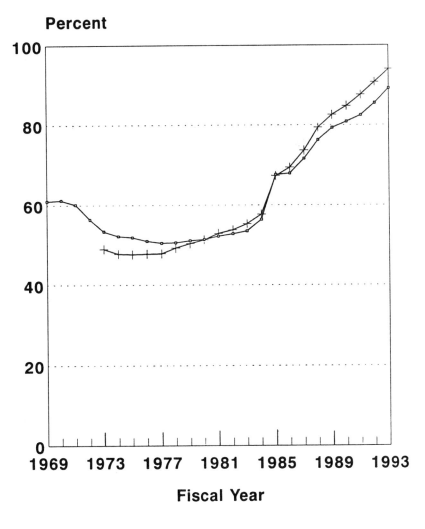

Percent

Fiscal Year

— Claims + Covered Charges

TABLE E-6.—NET ASSIGNMENT RATES,[1] BY YEAR, 1969–93

[In percent]

Fiscal year	Claims	Covered charges
1969	61.0	NA
1970	61.2	NA
1971	60.1	NA
1972	56.4	NA
1973	53.4	49.0
1974	52.2	47.8
1975	51.9	47.7
1976	51.0	47.8
1977	50.5	47.9
1978	50.6	49.3
1979	51.1	50.4
1980	51.4	51.3
1981	52.2	52.9
1982	52.8	53.8
1983	53.5	55.3
1984	56.4	57.7
1985	67.7	67.4
1986	68.0	69.5
1987	71.7	73.7
1988	76.3	79.4
1989	79.3	82.6
1990	80.9	84.8
1991	82.5	87.6
1992	85.5	90.8
1993	89.2	94.0

[1] Both measures of assignment exclude claims from hospital-based physicians and group-practice prepayment plans that are considered assigned by definition.

Source: Health Care Financing Administration, Bureau of Program Operations.

The statistics included in table E–6 are program-wide data. Assignment rates vary geographically. For example, the assignment rate (taken as a percent of dollars) for physician services in fiscal year 1993 ranged from a low of 50.2 percent in South Dakota to a high of 99.8 percent in Rhode Island. The national average assignment rate for physicians services during this period was 93.2 percent (see table E–7).

TABLE E–7.—PHYSICIAN ASSIGNMENT RATES AS PERCENT OF ALLOWED CHARGES, BY STATE, FOR SELECTED YEARS [1]

[In percent]

Census division/State	Fiscal year—						
	1985	1987 [2]	1989	1990	1991	1992	1993
National	65.5	70.8	80.6	83.0	86.1	89.4	93.2
New England:							
Maine	81.5	84.3	91.4	92.4	94.4	96.7	98.0
New Hampshire	56.5	58.3	67.8	69.9	80.8	89.4	93.9
Vermont	64.3	71.7	93.4	94.7	95.9	97.8	98.6
Massachusetts [3]	93.7	98.2	99.3	99.5	99.5	99.6	99.7
Rhode Island	94.0	95.1	97.1	98.7	99.7	99.7	99.8
Connecticut	57.6	62.8	80.4	84.7	87.7	91.7	94.7
Middle Atlantic:							
New York	70.3	73.9	81.1	81.9	84.4	87.7	90.7
New Jersey	62.3	63.8	70.4	73.0	76.3	80.5	85.4
Pennsylvania	88.1	91.0	94.9	95.7	98.5	99.1	99.4
East North Central:							
Ohio	50.8	58.8	77.8	82.6	87.3	92.5	97.7
Indiana	49.6	59.2	74.7	77.2	81.5	85.7	92.9
Illinois	51.7	59.9	72.4	75.9	78.8	83.2	89.2
Michigan	88.2	89.7	93.6	94.5	94.4	95.9	97.8
Wisconsin	51.7	54.6	65.6	68.2	71.7	78.2	86.8
West North Central:							
Minnesota	30.6	39.9	46.1	47.6	52.3	57.1	67.1
Iowa	46.9	53.2	67.5	69.8	73.4	78.8	85.6
Missouri [4]	50.1	61.2	72.3	74.9	78.5	83.7	91.6
North Dakota	30.5	36.3	50.3	55.0	67.1	72.1	74.9
South Dakota	18.7	26.7	38.7	39.2	40.2	43.3	50.2
Nebraska	47.3	43.4	59.6	64.9	70.3	76.8	83.8
Kansas [5]	72.7	78.7	87.2	88.8	91.9	94.5	96.2
South Atlantic:							
Delaware	81.8	81.9	88.1	90.5	92.9	95.2	96.8
Maryland [6]	81.6	84.6	91.6	91.4	92.8	94.3	96.7
District of Columbia [7]	78.1	80.5	86.5	87.5	89.4	92.1	94.1
Virginia [8]	66.4	73.4	85.1	87.3	89.6	92.5	95.7
West Virginia	66.7	76.9	90.3	93.2	95.5	97.2	98.4
North Carolina	60.3	66.2	79.2	80.8	83.9	88.8	93.7
South Carolina	64.9	75.4	85.8	87.1	88.9	91.6	94.4
Georgia	63.9	69.1	80.5	83.5	86.6	90.3	94.0
Florida	62.2	68.6	80.3	84.1	87.6	91.0	95.0
East South Central:							
Kentucky	50.3	63.5	80.8	84.8	88.8	91.9	95.5
Tennessee	55.6	65.5	80.9	84.0	89.5	93.1	96.3
Alabama	74.6	91.7	90.1	92.3	94.9	96.6	98.0
Mississippi	63.5	73.5	85.4	88.1	90.6	93.1	95.6
West South Central:							
Arkansas	72.6	81.1	90.3	92.0	93.7	95.4	96.6
Louisiana	51.0	67.8	84.8	88.0	91.0	93.8	95.2
Oklahoma	39.0	48.6	66.0	68.2	72.8	77.8	85.0
Texas	63.0	67.2	78.0	79.9	83.0	87.4	91.6

TABLE E–7.—PHYSICIAN ASSIGNMENT RATES AS PERCENT OF ALLOWED CHARGES, BY STATE, FOR SELECTED YEARS [1]—Continued

[In percent]

Census division/State	Fiscal year—						
	1985	1987 [2]	1989	1990	1991	1992	1993
Mountain:							
Montana	42.6	42.9	50.7	53.0	54.8	61.3	72.7
Idaho	25.2	26.4	33.7	36.1	40.2	40.1	54.1
Wyoming	33.8	30.4	40.2	43.9	48.9	57.5	69.0
Colorado	56.0	56.8	67.6	70.4	74.1	79.7	86.8
New Mexico	58.3	57.6	71.7	76.1	80.1	84.9	91.5
Arizona	52.8	57.1	72.0	76.2	80.3	84.4	89.6
Utah	63.1	69.4	79.9	80.4	83.1	88.4	92.8
Nevada	81.6	86.8	94.4	96.0	97.4	98.4	99.0
Pacific:							
Washington	45.5	46.6	50.8	54.8	60.8	69.2	74.3
Oregon	38.7	46.9	58.4	59.9	63.2	69.3	82.1
California	71.3	74.0	87.7	84.4	87.4	90.2	93.8
Alaska	54.4	64.3	78.5	79.6	83.2	89.1	93.9
Hawaii	61.2	72.0	80.7	82.9	85.8	93.1	96.1

[1] Rates reflect covered charges for physician claims processed during the period.

[2] The actual participation period was January 1987 through March 1988, and the participation agreements were in effect for that time.

[3] Massachusetts enacted a Medicare mandatory assignment provision, effective April 1986. The fact that the assignment rates shown here are not 100 percent may be explained by the inclusion in the data base of billings by practitioners other than allopathic and osteopathic physicians, which are included in the Medicare statutory definition of "physician".

[4] For fiscal year 1993, includes data for all counties in Missouri plus two counties on the State border located in Kansas.

[5] For fiscal year 1993, includes data for all counties in Kansas excluding two counties on the State border.

[6] For fiscal year 1993, includes data for all counties in Maryland excluding two counties on the State border.

[7] For fiscal year 1993, includes data for DC plus two counties in Maryland located on the State border plus a few counties and cities located in Virginia, near the State border.

[8] For fiscal year 1993, includes data for all counties in Virginia excluding a few counties and cities near the State border.

Source: Health Care Financing Administration, Bureau of Program Operations.

PARTICIPATING PHYSICIAN PROGRAM DATA

Physician participation rates have increased significantly since the inception of the program (see tables E–8 and E–9). For the calendar year 1993 participation period, the physician participation rate (including limited licensed practitioners) had risen to 59.8 percent accounting for 85.5 percent of allowed charges for physician services during the period.

1059

TABLE E–8.—MEDICARE PHYSICIAN PARTICIPATION RATES: PERCENT OF PHYSICIANS AND LIMITED LICENSED PRACTITIONERS WITH AGREEMENTS AND THEIR SHARE OF ALLOWED CHARGES, 1984–1993

Participation period	Percent of physicians signing agreements	Participating physicians' covered charges as a percent of total [1]
October 1984–September 1985	30.4	36.0
October 1985–April 1986	28.4	36.3
April 1986–December 1986 [2]	28.3	38.7
January 1987–March 1988	30.6	48.1
April 1988–December 1988	37.3	57.9
January 1989–March 1990	40.2	62.0
April 1990–December 1990	45.5	67.2
January 1991–December 1991	47.6	72.3
January 1992–December 1992	52.2	78.8
January 1993–December 1993	59.8	85.5

[1] Rates reflect covered charges for physician services processed during period.
[2] The actual participation period was May through December of 1986, and participation agreements were in effect for that time. However, charge data are generally collected by quarter; thus, the data for the last three quarters of 1986 are used as a proxy for the participation period.

Source: Health Care Financing Administration, Bureau of Program Operations.

Table E–10 shows the percentage of participating physicians and limited licensed practitioners as a percentage of total physicians and limited licensed practitioners for each State. The national average of participating physicians and limited licensed practitioners continues to increase. By the calendar year 1993 participation period, this percentage had risen to 59.8.

TABLE E–9.—PARTICIPATION RATES AS PERCENTAGE OF PHYSICIANS, BY SPECIALTY, FOR SELECTED PARTICIPATION PERIODS

Specialty	Oct. 1985–Apr. 1986	Jan. 1987–Mar. 1988	Jan. 1989–Mar. 1990	Apr. 1990–Dec. 1990	Jan. 1991–Dec. 1991	Jan. 1992–Dec. 1992	Jan. 1993–Dec. 1993
Physicians (M.D.s and D.O.s):							
General practice	27.3	25.6	35.8	39.7	44.0	48.0	55.1
General surgery	33.9	37.2	52.2	55.8	60.5	66.3	73.8
Otology, laryngology, rhinology	24.6	27.0	41.2	45.2	49.6	57.0	66.2
Anesthesiology	21.1	20.3	28.3	30.8	36.5	49.3	64.6
Cardiovascular disease	35.6	43.2	55.5	60.6	65.4	72.0	78.7
Dermatology	34.0	38.1	48.7	53.4	57.0	61.6	69.8
Family practice	25.5	27.1	39.7	47.2	50.8	57.7	66.1
Internal medicine	32.5	33.6	45.2	48.8	52.6	57.8	66.2
Neurology	34.8	39.2	49.2	53.1	56.1	63.8	71.8
Obstetrics-gynecology	29.1	31.5	44.2	48.8	52.6	58.0	65.7
Ophthalmology	27.3	35.1	50.5	55.6	60.0	66.1	73.2
Orthopedic surgery	29.0	32.6	49.2	53.7	58.4	65.5	74.9
Pathology	39.6	41.2	50.6	53.4	59.2	65.8	73.3
Psychiatry	30.0	28.6	37.8	41.6	44.1	48.8	53.5
Radiology	41.3	39.8	49.6	55.6	62.0	68.2	74.7
Urology	27.8	30.9	45.6	49.6	53.6	61.7	71.8
Nephrology	50.8	49.7	60.0	66.5	71.7	76.3	82.4
Clinic or other group practice—not GPPP	33.8	50.6	67.8	68.7	73.9	77.0	75.5
Other medical specialties	32.4	30.1					
Other surgical specialties	18.2	14.8					
Other physicians				29.2		35.9	50.5
Total physicians				45.5	49.6	55.3	63.5

Limited license practitioners (LLP):

Chiropractor	25.4	19.7	24.8	26.2	28.6	31.4	35.6
Podiatry-surgical chiropody	38.2	33.4	52.6	54.0	59.6	64.2	70.9
Optometrist	44.0	44.1	48.9	54.0	56.9	59.0	62.7
Other limited license practitioners (audiologist, psychologist, physical therapist)	36.8	30.9	35.3	38.4	36.4	35.8	43.9
Certified registered midwife	....	....	....	15.2	23.8	40.7	51.0
Certified registered nurse anesthetist	....	....	....	12.5	26.3	31.3	43.8
Total limited license practitioners	....	....	....	40.0	40.0	41.0	47.4
Suppliers:							
Independent laboratory	28.4	37.2	20.1	45.4	49.7	52.4	55.4
Durable medical equipment suppliers	22.7	16.6	30.1	21.7	23.1	24.2	30.8
Ambulance service suppliers	28.6	27.9	43.8	32.1	32.3	34.4	36.4
Miscellaneous suppliers (orthotists, prosthetists, portable x ray suppliers)	22.5	15.5	17.5	17.5	17.7	18.2	25.7
Total supplies	....	....	....	21.8	22.6	23.7	29.5

Source: Health Care Financing Administration, Bureau of Program Operations.

TABLE E-10.—PHYSICIAN AND LIMITED LICENSED PRACTITIONER PARTICIPATION RATES AS PERCENTAGE OF PHYSICIANS AND LIMITED LICENSED PRACTITIONERS, BY STATE, FOR SELECTED PARTICIPATION PERIODS

State	Oct. 1985–Apr. 1986	Jan. 1987–Mar. 1988	Jan. 1989–Mar. 1990	Apr. 1990–Dec. 1990	Jan. 1991–Dec. 1991	Jan. 1992–Dec. 1992	Jan. 1993–Dec. 1993
Alabama	58.2	68.8	75.9	74.6	82.7	83.4	85.1
Alaska	10.4	27.1	38.8	48.0	53.8	55.1	60.4
Arizona	15.4	28.1	41.2	53.5	61.3	64.5	76.2
Arkansas	45.2	42.0	53.1	53.9	59.9	57.8	62.1
California	30.0	38.9	54.0	57.7	60.8	62.6	65.9
Colorado	28.1	19.5	28.1	33.9	35.3	48.0	55.7
Connecticut	22.2	17.4	29.3	32.8	40.8	48.1	55.4
Delaware	23.9	31.2	37.5	42.5	43.9	51.9	57.4
District of Columbia	30.5	28.0	34.4	37.9	39.8	45.9	50.6
Florida	25.7	24.9	32.8	34.4	36.5	41.5	55.6
Georgia	33.1	25.8	49.7	49.5	53.6	57.2	74.9
Hawaii	20.6	47.8	53.7	56.8	57.3	64.1	75.9
Idaho	11.0	10.4	16.0	17.3	19.5	22.9	37.1
Illinois	23.1	26.7	40.0	42.3	46.9	50.8	57.6
Indiana	18.2	26.9	40.0	42.6	45.1	49.3	55.8
Iowa	29.7	25.1	45.3	48.1	51.9	58.8	61.8
Kansas	45.4	51.4	61.6	57.1	62.6	70.3	73.2
Kentucky	24.3	34.2	50.5	56.4	59.5	64.0	73.6
Louisiana	18.8	18.1	32.6	34.6	42.9	44.6	44.0
Maine	35.4	34.2	51.2	48.7	50.3	51.6	52.0
Maryland	30.4	30.1	42.8	45.9	45.3	58.7	72.5
Massachusetts	48.1	43.8	46.9	50.5	50.8	50.0	50.2
Michigan	44.0	32.7	41.7	44.7	53.7	51.7	58.1
Minnesota	18.5	22.4	25.4	27.5	29.3	34.4	44.4
Mississippi	19.1	23.6	33.4	38.0	42.7	47.9	53.6
Missouri	35.2	24.5	39.6	45.7	49.0	51.8	67.5
Montana	24.3	17.0	21.5	23.4	24.8	23.7	54.7
Nebraska	20.0	25.7	42.5	49.2	56.5	61.1	70.6
Nevada	21.7	33.5	57.0	69.8	72.9	75.4	84.9

New Hampshire	26.9	25.9	28.0	30.9	32.7	38.5	43.0
New Jersey	18.0	22.7	26.0	27.6	29.6	36.5	42.6
New Mexico	17.7	30.8	36.3	45.6	49.7	53.6	66.8
New York	20.8	24.1	29.8	30.4	34.6	36.9	40.7
North Carolina	39.1	31.4	54.2	52.9	58.1	68.2	72.8
North Dakota	10.9	20.5	31.7	42.2	43.9	45.8	55.0
Ohio	21.7	28.9	46.8	50.8	52.5	57.3	76.6
Oklahoma	13.8	20.8	31.6	36.4	39.0	44.4	53.9
Oregon	18.5	26.1	36.9	41.7	46.7	51.7	59.2
Pennsylvania	50.8	32.1	39.0	42.1	45.9	53.0	59.7
Rhode Island	46.7	50.8	58.8	67.0	67.8	70.3	80.9
South Carolina	17.9	25.3	42.1	55.5	57.9	63.0	67.3
South Dakota	8.0	12.7	20.0	19.6	20.6	23.7	31.6
Tennessee	21.1	43.4	57.6	58.4	63.7	67.6	70.5
Texas	19.7	19.4	28.9	36.4	38.9	52.9	61.3
Utah	29.3	42.2	54.7	65.1	65.6	69.5	80.3
Vermont	41.5	34.1	40.5	43.8	45.4	54.2	56.5
Virginia	29.6	33.6	40.9	46.0	48.1	49.7	52.2
Washington	23.6	26.9	31.4	34.7	46.1	53.1	64.7
West Virginia	22.9	37.5	59.1	63.2	66.3	68.4	75.9
Wisconsin	31.0	35.1	40.0	46.5	46.8	55.5	66.8
Wyoming	18.3	20.3	19.3	34.6	39.1	50.2	53.3
National	28.4	30.6	40.7	44.1	47.6	52.2	59.8

Source: Health Care Financing Administration, Bureau of Program Operations.

Table E-11 shows the allowed charges of participating physicans as a percent of total allowed charges, by State, for several participation periods. This percentage increased substantially, rising from 36 percent in the October 1984 to September 1985 period to 85.5 percent in the calendar 1993 participation period.

TABLE E–11.—ALLOWED CHARGES OF PARTICIPATING PHYSICIANS AS A PERCENT OF TOTAL ALLOWED CHARGES, BY STATE, FOR SELECTED PARTICIPATION PERIODS [1]

[In percent]

Census division/State	Oct. 1984–Sept. 1985	Jan. 1987–Mar. 1988 [2]	Jan. 1989–Mar. 1990	Apr. 1990–Dec. 1990	Jan. 1991–Dec. 1991	Jan. 1992–Dec. 1992	Jan. 1993–Dec. 1993
National	36.0	48.1	62.0	67.2	72.3	78.8	85.5
New England:							
Maine	50.9	64.8	79.4	80.5	84.2	89.9	92.4
New Hampshire	40.1	36.0	42.8	46.2	68.3	80.7	88.1
Vermont	37.3	46.8	81.4	85.9	90.2	93.4	94.8
Massachusetts	70.7	89.1	95.4	95.0	96.7	96.3	95.9
Rhode Island	68.7	85.8	88.8	95.2	97.6	98.5	98.9
Connecticut	30.7	45.3	65.9	67.9	76.2	82.4	87.9
Middle Atlantic:							
New York	31.5	40.8	51.7	58.0	63.7	72.2	77.7
New Jersey	21.5	32.8	42.3	49.6	55.2	61.8	72.6
Pennsylvania	71.4	75.1	81.6	87.9	92.3	95.4	98.0
East North Central:							
Ohio	24.9	41.5	61.9	70.9	79.1	86.3	94.6
Indiana	18.9	43.3	60.6	65.2	70.2	80.9	89.1
Illinois	29.4	42.0	58.1	61.8	66.1	72.2	82.2
Michigan	55.4	71.9	85.6	86.0	86.5	92.0	95.1
Wisconsin	31.3	31.7	42.7	48.9	45.6	61.5	76.9
West North Central:							
Minnesota	9.9	14.6	20.2	25.4	28.6	35.5	49.5
Iowa	28.5	41.0	54.2	57.8	61.9	71.0	80.8
Missouri [3]	26.7	37.5	41.8	40.1	40.4	45.3	67.7
North Dakota	6.9	16.0	32.3	45.5	53.2	61.2	65.8
South Dakota	3.2	10.4	19.5	21.2	21.1	24.6	36.0

1066

TABLE E–11.—ALLOWED CHARGES OF PARTICIPATING PHYSICIANS AS A PERCENT OF TOTAL ALLOWED CHARGES, BY STATE, FOR SELECTED PARTICIPATION PERIODS [1]—Continued

[In percent]

Census division/State	Oct. 1984–Sept. 1985	Jan. 1987–Mar. 1988 [2]	Jan. 1989–Mar. 1990	Apr. 1990–Dec. 1990	Jan. 1991–Dec. 1991	Jan. 1992–Dec. 1992	Jan. 1993–Dec. 1993
Nebraska	30.5	31.8	51.7	54.8	60.3	69.7	79.8
Kansas [4]	48.0	NA	82.5	82.3	86.8	91.3	94.6
South Atlantic:							
Delaware	57.0	58.5	70.8	76.6	81.7	87.2	93.5
Maryland [5]	57.8	67.4	80.4	83.3	85.6	86.4	87.1
District of Columbia [6]	60.3	66.6	73.9	76.8	80.8	85.4	90.1
Virginia [7]	31.0	53.0	69.5	71.2	78.4	84.1	90.9
West Virginia	34.5	59.3	77.5	80.6	85.2	90.0	93.4
North Carolina	34.4	44.9	55.2	63.9	68.3	82.4	87.1
South Carolina	29.9	55.2	68.5	67.6	71.6	79.3	86.6
Georgia	29.3	43.0	50.7	65.9	74.9	82.8	81.6
Florida	30.0	41.9	61.6	68.8	74.9	81.8	89.0
East South Central:							
Kentucky	22.3	44.7	64.3	72.6	76.9	84.3	90.7
Tennessee	25.1	41.3	57.4	68.5	76.8	86.8	91.8
Alabama	42.5	66.9	81.3	84.9	88.5	91.7	94.9
Mississippi	14.3	44.9	65.3	68.3	73.9	82.1	88.6
West South Central:							
Arkansas	47.9	68.3	81.0	84.5	86.5	90.0	93.4
Louisiana	16.2	48.2	71.0	76.7	81.2	86.6	89.4
Oklahoma	16.6	24.9	39.1	50.0	57.7	62.8	74.0
Texas	26.2	38.9	52.5	56.9	63.6	72.6	81.5
Mountain:							
Montana	25.6	23.8	29.9	29.7	34.1	42.7	58.9

Idaho	8.6	9.3	13.2	17.5	21.1	23.5	41.2
Wyoming	15.7	14.1	19.7	25.8	31.9	44.1	61.0
Colorado	23.5	34.0	47.7	50.5	55.9	63.5	76.4
New Mexico	34.1	28.1	39.5	51.1	57.8	64.9	78.2
Arizona	32.7	38.3	49.8	60.2	67.8	75.2	83.7
Utah	43.8	58.4	68.9	65.1	75.1	81.8	83.1
Nevada	41.5	63.4	69.9	82.1	87.5	92.3	96.0
Pacific:							
Washington	17.5	20.2	26.9	31.8	37.9	45.2	50.7
Oregon	17.3	25.5	34.8	43.3	50.7	59.8	73.6
California	42.2	50.2	67.2	71.2	75.6	80.0	86.6
Alaska	17.2	34.3	50.0	49.3	58.0	70.9	81.3
Hawaii	39.7	53.5	58.6	70.1	74.3	84.7	90.6

[1] Rates reflect covered charges for physician claims processed during the period.

[2] The actual participation period is January 1987 through March 1988, and the participation agreements were in effect for that time.

[3] For fiscal year 1993, includes data for all counties in Missouri plus two counties on the State border located in Kansas.

[4] For fiscal year 1993, includes data for all counties in Kansas excluding two counties on the State border.

[5] For fiscal year 1993, includes data for all counties in Maryland excluding two counties on the State border.

[6] For fiscal year 1993, includes data for DC plus two counties in Maryland located on the State border plus a few counties and cities located in Virginia, near the State border.

[7] For fiscal year 1993, includes data for all counties in Virginia excluding a few counties and cities near the State border.

Source: Health Care Financing Administration, Bureau of Program Operations.

PARTICIPATION, ASSIGNMENT, AND CHARGE REDUCTIONS

Historically the difference between the physician's billed charge and Medicare's approved or reasonable charge was referred to as the reasonable charge reduction. Beginning in 1992, with implementation of the fee schedule, the term reasonable charge reduction no longer applies. Instead, the term charge reduction refers to the difference between the physicians' billed charge and the fee schedule amount. Charge reductions were made on 85.5 percent of unassigned claims in fiscal year 1993. The average amount of the reduction was 16.9 percent of billed charges, or $17.26 per approved claim. Beneficiaries were liable for these reduction amounts, although it is not known how often physicians actually collected from beneficiaries. The total reduced on all unassigned claims was $797.5 million in fiscal year 1993.

Through 1984, approximately the same proportions of assigned and unassigned claims were reduced (see table E–12), and were reduced by similar proportions and amounts. From 1984 to 1993, the proportions of assigned and unassigned claims reduced remained about the same, but the percentage and amounts of the reductions diverged. The percent and dollar reductions on assigned claims continued to increase while the percent and dollar reductions of unassigned claims decreased. This pattern was due to the imposition of limits on the actual charges of nonparticipating physicians. That is, the MAAC limits, and the new balance billing limits beginning in 1991, limited the rate of increase in prices for unassigned services relative to the overall increase in reasonable charges. The substantial growth in the overall percentage of services billed on an assigned basis also may have contributed to this pattern.

As a result, total beneficiary liability for charge reductions on unassigned claims fell. Total liability peaked in 1985 at $2,812.7 million, and declined to $797.5 million by 1993.

TABLE E–12.—REASONABLE CHARGE REDUCTIONS FOR MEDICARE PART B (EXCLUDES CLAIMS FROM HOSPITAL-BASED PHYSICIANS AND GROUP-PRACTICE PREPAYMENT PLANS) FOR ASSIGNED AND NOT ASSIGNED CLAIMS, FISCAL YEARS 1975, 1980, AND 1985–1993

	1975	1980	1985	1986	1987	1988	1989	1990	1991	1992	1993
Percentage of claims reduced:											
Assigned	68.3	80.0	81.7	82.5	83.0	85.5	86.3	87.6	86.7	87.0	[1]88.2
Not assigned	75.6	83.7	84.6	84.9	82.5	85.7	89.2	89.2	90.7	85.4	[1]85.5
Percentage reduction in charges for covered services:											
Assigned	16.4	22.5	27.0	28.4	27.9	29.3	30.9	32.6	35.2	39.2	42.1
Not assigned	16.6	22.3	25.6	26.6	25.5	24.7	25.2	25.3	24.0	19.7	16.9
Amount reduced per approved claim:											
Assigned	$11.13	$21.81	$33.19	$36.43	$36.98	$39.97	$43.72	$48.22	$54.20	$63.60	$79.49
Not assigned	$13.45	$21.96	$33.12	$33.15	$31.44	$29.47	$29.67	$28.97	$24.84	$18.95	$17.26
Amount reduced on claims not assigned (in millions)	$450.1	$1,454.0	$2,571.9	$2,812.5	$2,677.8	$2,312.6	$2,213.7	$2,198.0	$1,948.5	$1,317.0	$797.5

[1] Figure may be slightly overstated due to the possibility of a claim being counted more than once because more than one type of reduction is applied.

Source: Health Care Financing Administration, Bureau of Program Operations.

The impact of charge reductions on unassigned claims was spread unevenly across the population. Calendar 1993 data show a 16.4 percent national average reduction on unassigned claims (see table E–13). Beneficiary liability for these charge reductions ranged from a high of $95.8 million in New York to a low of $0.1 million in Rhode Island.

TABLE E–13.—CHARGE REDUCTIONS FOR UNASSIGNED CLAIMS, BY STATE,[1] JANUARY–DECEMBER, 1993

[Dollar amounts in millions]

Census division/State	Covered charges [2]		Percent reduction in unassigned charges	Amount reduced, unassigned charges [2]
	Total	Unassigned		
National	$76,655.0	$4,155.2	16.4	$683.4
New England:				
Maine	333.0	6.3	15.3	1.0
New Hampshire	260.8	13.3	14.7	2.0
Vermont	120.7	1.9	15.9	0.3
Massachusetts [3]	2,356.7	10.2	14.2	1.4
Rhode Island	369.2	1.5	9.1	0.1
Connecticut	1,267.8	51.9	14.6	7.6
Middle Atlantic:				
New York	6,201.3	495.1	19.3	95.8
New Jersey	2,911.8	312.1	16.6	51.9
Pennsylvania	5,821.7	36.3	15.0	5.4
East North Central:				
Ohio	3,345.0	44.4	19.4	8.6
Indiana	1,436.7	92.6	17.0	15.7
Illinois	2,953.0	251.2	17.0	42.6
Michigan	3,261.4	62.1	18.2	11.3
Wisconsin	1,143.0	126.6	14.7	18.6
West North Central:				
Minnesota	704.6	205.1	16.1	33.1
Iowa	647.3	79.8	14.5	11.6
Missouri [4]	1,721.5	115.3	5.4	6.2
North Dakota	184.2	41.0	16.2	6.6
South Dakota	155.6	61.8	15.6	9.6
Nebraska	347.0	50.1	16.1	8.1
Kansas [5]	528.4	18.0	14.4	2.6
South Atlantic:				
Delaware	243.8	6.5	14.6	0.9
Maryland [6]	1,281.3	35.9	16.4	5.9
District of Columbia [7]	1,015.6	49.9	17.9	9.0
Virginia [8]	1,253.0	46.6	14.7	6.8
West Virginia	549.7	7.5	17.7	1.3
North Carolina	2,061.8	97.5	16.6	16.3
South Carolina	840.9	43.9	21.4	9.4
Georgia	1,794.9	79.7	20.5	16.4
Florida	7,204.7	272.2	18.6	50.5
East South Central:				
Kentucky	1,092.1	34.2	15.9	5.4

TABLE E–13.—CHARGE REDUCTIONS FOR UNASSIGNED CLAIMS, BY STATE,[1] JANUARY–
DECEMBER, 1993—Continued

[Dollar amounts in millions]

Census division/State	Covered charges [2]		Percent re-duction in unassigned charges	Amount re-duced, un-assigned charges [2]
	Total	Unassigned		
Tennessee	$1,622.7	$48.8	15.0	7.3
Alabama	1,398.5	22.7	17.0	3.9
Mississippi	660.8	23.0	16.5	3.8
West South Central:				
Arkansas	774.9	20.1	17.2	3.5
Louisiana	1,319.5	44.4	17.4	7.7
Oklahoma	723.2	81.9	16.9	13.9
Texas	4,181.9	270.8	17.1	46.4
Mountain:				
Montana	159.6	35.7	17.7	6.3
Idaho	140.6	53.6	16.1	8.7
Wyoming	50.2	11.2	15.1	1.7
Colorado	626.0	57.8	17.1	9.9
New Mexico	252.3	17.2	17.1	3.0
Arizona	1,018.4	87.7	16.3	14.2
Utah	256.9	15.9	17.0	2.7
Nevada	452.4	4.8	18.5	0.9
Pacific:				
Washington	769.6	144.1	4.5	6.4
Oregon	553.1	82.6	16.5	13.6
California	7,677.3	377.9	18.2	68.8
Alaska	46.7	2.4	17.6	0.4
Hawaii	219.4	7.6	20.0	1.5

[1] Rates reflect covered charges for physician claims processed during the period. National data exclude data for Puerto Rico, the Virgin Islands, the Railroad Retirement Board, and Parenteral and Enteral Claims. As a result of report changes effective April 1, 1992, charge reductions include: reasonable charge medical necessity and global fee/rebundling.
[2] Amounts in millions.
[3] Massachusetts enacted a Medicare mandatory assignment provision, effective April 1986. The fact that the assignment rates shown here are not 100 percent may be explained by the inclusion in the database of billings by practitioners other than allopathic and osteopathic physicians, which are included in the Medicare statutory definition of "physician".
[4] For fiscal year 1993, includes data for all counties in Missouri plus two counties on the State border located in Kansas.
[5] For fiscal year 1993, includes data for all counties in Kansas excluding two counties on the State border.
[6] For fiscal year 1993, includes data for all counties in Maryland excluding two counties on the State border.
[7] For fiscal year 1993, includes data for DC plus two counties in Maryland located on the State border plus a few counties and cities located in Virginia, near the State border.
[8] For fiscal year 1993, includes data for all counties in Virginia excluding a few counties and cities near the State border.

Source: Health Care Financing Administration, Bureau of Program Operations.

The changing pattern of charge reductions reflects, in part, over-all changes in participation and assignment rates. As shown in table E–14, participating physicians accounted for a growing share of total physician charges. During the first participation period (fiscal year 1985), participating physicians (30.4 percent of all physicians) accounted for 36.0 percent of all physician charges. In 1993, the proportion of physicians participating grew to 59.8 percent, and accounted for 85.5 percent of all physician charges. Total covered charges represented by unassigned claims declined from 34.5 percent to 6.0 percent over the same period. The proportion of charges billed by participation and assignment status varies by State; these data are shown in table E–15.

TABLE E–14.—DISTRIBUTION OF ALLOWED CHARGES FOR SERVICES BILLED, BY PARTICIPATION STATUS OF PHYSICIAN AND ASSIGNMENT STATUS OF CLAIM, 1984–1993 [1]

[In percent]

Time period	Total	Partici-pants	Nonparticipants	
			Assigned	Unas-signed
Oct. 1984–Sept. 1985	100.0	36.0	29.5	34.5
Oct. 1985–Mar. 1986	100.0	36.3	29.4	34.3
Apr. 1986–Dec. 1986 [2]	100.0	39.1	28.0	32.9
Jan. 1987–Mar. 1988 [3]	100.0	48.1	25.2	26.7
Apr. 1988–Dec. 1988	100.0	57.9	21.0	21.1
Jan. 1989–Mar. 1990	100.0	62.0	19.0	18.5
Apr. 1990–Dec. 1990	100.0	67.2	16.7	16.1
Jan. 1991–Dec. 1991	100.0	72.3	14.6	13.1
Jan. 1992–Dec. 1992	100.0	78.8	11.6	9.7
Jan. 1993–Dec. 1993	100.0	85.5	8.5	6.0

[1] Rates reflect covered charges for physician claims processed during the period. Data for up to seven carriers missing from various quarters.
[2] The actual participation period was May through December 1986, and the participation agreements were in effect for that time.
[3] The actual participation period is January 1987 through March 1988, and the participation agreements are in effect for that time.

Source: Health Care Financing Administration, Bureau of Program Operations.

TABLE E–15.—DISTRIBUTION OF ALLOWED CHARGES FOR SERVICES BILLED, BY PARTICIPATION STATUS OF PHYSICIAN AND ASSIGNMENT STATUS OF CLAIM, BY STATE, JANUARY–DECEMBER 1993 [1]

[In percent]

Census division/State	Total	Participating physician	Nonparticipating physician	
			Assigned	Unassigned
National	100.0	85.5	8.5	6.0
New England:				
Maine	100.0	92.4	5.8	1.8
New Hampshire	100.0	88.1	6.5	5.3
Vermont	100.0	94.8	4.0	1.2
Massachusetts	100.0	95.9	3.7	0.3
Rhode Island	100.0	98.9	0.9	0.2
Connecticut	100.0	87.9	7.4	4.7
Middle Atlantic:				
New York	100.0	77.7	13.7	8.7
New Jersey	100.0	72.6	14.0	13.4
Pennsylvania	100.0	98.0	1.5	0.5
East North Central:				
Ohio	100.0	94.6	4.4	1.1
Indiana	100.0	89.1	4.8	6.1
Illinois	100.0	82.2	8.6	9.2
Michigan	100.0	95.1	3.0	1.9
Wisconsin	100.0	76.9	11.8	11.3
West North Central:				
Minnesota	100.0	49.5	19.6	30.9
Iowa	100.0	80.8	6.4	12.8
Missouri [2]	100.0	67.7	25.3	7.1
North Dakota	100.0	65.8	9.9	24.3
South Dakota	100.0	36.0	16.5	47.5
Nebraska	100.0	79.8	5.8	14.5
Kansas [3]	100.0	94.6	2.0	3.4
South Atlantic:				
Delaware	100.0	93.5	3.5	3.0
Maryland [4]	100.0	87.1	9.9	3.1
District of Columbia [5]	100.0	90.1	4.4	5.6
Virginia [6]	100.0	90.9	5.4	3.7
West Virginia	100.0	93.4	5.2	1.4
North Carolina	100.0	87.1	7.1	5.9
South Carolina	100.0	86.6	8.3	5.1
Georgia	100.0	81.6	13.3	5.1
Florida	100.0	89.0	6.8	4.3
East South Central:				
Kentucky	100.0	90.7	5.5	3.7
Tennessee	100.0	91.8	4.9	3.3
Alabama	100.0	94.9	3.3	1.7
Mississippi	100.0	88.6	7.5	4.0
West South Central:				
Arkansas	100.0	93.4	3.6	3.0
Louisiana	100.0	89.4	6.3	4.3
Oklahoma	100.0	74.0	12.8	13.2

TABLE E–15.—DISTRIBUTION OF ALLOWED CHARGES FOR SERVICES BILLED, BY PAR-
TICIPATION STATUS OF PHYSICIAN AND ASSIGNMENT STATUS OF CLAIM, BY STATE,
JANUARY–DECEMBER 1993 [1]—Continued

[In percent]

Census division/State	Total	Participating physician	Nonparticipating physician	
			Assigned	Unassigned
Texas	100.0	81.5	11.0	7.5
Mountain:				
Montana	100.0	58.9	16.1	25.0
Idaho	100.0	41.2	16.1	42.7
Wyoming	100.0	61.0	10.7	28.3
Colorado	100.0	76.4	12.1	11.6
New Mexico	100.0	78.2	14.4	7.4
Arizona	100.0	83.7	7.0	9.4
Utah	100.0	83.1	10.9	6.0
Nevada	100.0	96.0	3.1	0.9
Pacific:				
Washington	100.0	50.7	25.2	24.0
Oregon	100.0	73.6	11.1	15.3
California	100.0	86.6	8.1	5.4
Alaska	100.0	81.3	13.1	5.6
Hawaii	100.0	90.6	6.0	3.3

[1] Rates reflect covered charges for physician claims processed during the period.
[2] For fiscal year 1993, includes data for all counties in Missouri plus two counties on the State border located in Kansas.
[3] For fiscal year 1993, includes data for all counties in Kansas excluding two counties on the State border.
[4] For fiscal year 1993, includes data for all counties in Maryland excluding two counties on the State border.
[5] For fiscal year 1993, includes data for DC plus two counties in Maryland located on the State border plus a few counties and cities located in Virginia, near the State border.
[6] For fiscal year 1993, includes data for all counties in Virginia excluding a few counties and cities near the State border.

Source: Health Care Financing Administration, Bureau of Program Operations.

DISTRIBUTION OF PHYSICIAN SERVICES

Tables E–16 to E–24 show the distribution of physicians' services for calendar year 1992. These tables provide data from the first year of the implementation of the Medicare Fee Schedule. As noted earlier, the fee schedule appears to be having its intended effect. The projected pattern of redistribution from the procedurally oriented specialties to the primary care specialties has begun taking place.

The 1992 data are tabulations from the 1992 National Claims History Procedure Summary, which is a summary of all claims filed with the Medicare carriers.

The totals shown will differ from total SMI outlay figures for 1992 shown in the budget for several reasons:

The amounts shown in these tables are allowed amounts, rather than reimbursements—that is, they include both Medicare's and the enrollee's share of approved changes.

The amounts shown are for services rendered during calendar year 1992; budget figures are for payments made during the fiscal year regardless of when the services were rendered.

The amounts shown are only for services reimbursed by carriers under the fee schedule; hence, they do not include Part B payments to hospital outpatient departments or to risk-based prepaid medical plans.

Further, the amounts shown underestimate what they are supposed to represent by a small amount because some claims for services rendered in 1992 had not been processed by carriers at the time the 1992 files were submitted to HCFA, and because some claims recorded had to be eliminated due to recording errors.

Table E–16 illustrates that in 1992, 77.2 percent of allowed amounts under the fee schedule were for physicians' services, and another 3.0 percent were for the services of limited license practitioners—psychologists, podiatrists, optometrists, audiologists, chiropractors, dentists, and physical therapists. About 4.7 percent went to independent laboratories in 1992, while 15.1 percent went to suppliers of medical equipment, prosthetics, and ambulance services.

TABLE E–16.—ALLOWED AMOUNTS FOR CLAIMS, BY TYPE OF PROVIDER, 1992

Type of provider	Allowed amounts (millions)	Percent of total	Percent inpatient
Physicians	$33,941.0	77.2	39.3
Limited license practitioners [1]	1,307.0	3.0	1.7
Laboratories	2,072.0	4.7	.2
Medical suppliers [2]	6,625.0	15.1	.8
All providers [3]	43,944.0	100.0	30.6

[1] Includes psychology, podiatry, optometry, audiology, chiropractice, dentistry, and physical therapy.
[2] Includes suppliers of medical equipment, prosthetics, and ambulance services.
[3] Total does not include charges for hospital outpatient department facility fees or for risk-based prepaid medical plans since these are not reimbursed under the CPR system.

Source: Health Care Financing Administration, Bureau of Data Management and Strategy, National Claims History Procedure Summary.

Almost 31 percent of all allowed amounts were for hospital inpatient services, and almost 40 percent of allowed amounts for physicians' services were inpatient. The share of physicians' services that are inpatient has dropped in recent years, from nearly 64 percent in 1981.

Table E–17 shows the distribution of spending for physicians' services by specialty. (It excludes limited license practitioners, labs, and suppliers.) In 1992, generalists accounted for 27.8 percent of spending, nonsurgical specialists for 24.1 percent, and surgical specialists for 31.7 percent. Radiologists, anesthesiologists, and pathologists together accounted for 13.6 percent of allowed amounts. Radiation oncologists, osteopathic manipulative therapists, intensivists, and emergency medicine physicians each accounted for less than 1 percent of total allowed amounts for physicians' services.

The major physician specialties treating the Medicare population, in descending order of importance as measured by total allowed amounts, were general internists (14.9 percent of allowed amounts), ophthalmologists (10.9 percent), radiologists (8.6 percent), cardiologists (8.4 percent) and family practitioners (6.0 percent).

The share of services provided on an inpatient basis varied by specialty, generally increasing with specialization. About 33 percent of the services of generalists were inpatient in 1992. The inpatient share for nonsurgical specialists was 46.6 percent and 39.3 percent for surgical specialists.

TABLE E–17.—ALLOWED AMOUNTS FOR PHYSICIANS' SERVICES, BY MEDICAL SPECIALTY, 1992

Specialty	Allowed amounts (millions)	Percent of total	Percent inpatient
Generalists:			
General practice	$1,114.0	3.3	18.6
Family practice	2,048.0	6.0	25.6
Internal medicine	5,054.0	14.9	38.6
Pediatrics	28.0	.1	25.6
Clinics	1,186.0	3.5	34.9
All generalists	9,430.0	27.8	32.9
Nonsurgical specialists:			
Allergy/Immunology	95.0	.3	10.6
Cardiology	2,860.0	8.4	58.2
Dermatology	682.0	2.0	1.4
Gastroenterology	950.0	2.8	45.2
Neurology	486.0	1.4	48.7
Psychiatry	664.0	2.0	41.2
Physical medicine and rehabilitation	217.0	.6	60.6
Pulmonary disease	639.0	1.9	68.3
Nuclear medicine	62.0	.2	27.1
Geriatric medicine	52.0	.2	34.3
Nephrology	539.0	1.6	52.8
Infectious disease	127.0	.4	74.6
Endocrinology	94.0	.3	37.4
Rheumatology	132.0	.4	16.2
Peripheral vascular disease	22.0	.1	61.8
Hematology/oncology	440.0	1.3	24.3
Medical oncology	117.0	.3	22.1
All nonsurgical specialists	8,176.0	24.1	46.6
Surgical specialists:			
General surgery	1,870.0	5.5	64.9
Otolaryngology	404.0	1.2	17.1
Neurosurgery	287.0	.8	84.3
Gynecology/Obstetrics	261.0	.8	41.7
Ophthalmology	3,689.0	10.9	3.6

TABLE E–17.—ALLOWED AMOUNTS FOR PHYSICIANS' SERVICES, BY MEDICAL
SPECIALTY, 1992—Continued

Specialty	Allowed amounts (millions)	Percent of total	Percent inpatient
Orthopedic surgery	1,611.0	4.7	61.1
Plastic and reconstructive surgery ...	164.0	.5	32.4
Colorectal surgery	69.0	.2	34.0
Thoracic surgery	718.0	2.1	89.3
Urology	1,362.0	4.0	35.9
Hand surgery	21.0	.1	21.4
Vascular surgery	141.0	.4	74.3
Cardiac surgery	164.0	.5	96.4
Surgical oncology	13.0	....	60.5
All surgical specialists	10,774.0	31.7	39.3
Radiology	2,912.0	8.6	29.9
Radiation oncology	268.0	.8	5.3
Anesthesiology	1,198.0	3.5	71.0
Pathology	519.0	1.5	46.0
Osteopathic manipulative therapy	30.0	.1	15.6
Critical care (Intensivists)	28.0	.1	76.5
Emergency medicine	215.0	.6	6.8
Other Physician specialties	389.0	1.1	49.3
Total—all physicians	33,941.0	100.0	39.3

Source: Health Care Financing Administration, Bureau of Data Management and Strategy, National Claims History Procedure Summary.

Table E–18 shows the distribution of spending for physicians' services by type of service. About 36.8 percent of spending was for medical care (nonsurgical) in 1992. About 35.5 percent of spending was for surgical procedures in total, adding together the amounts for surgeons, assistant surgeons, and anesthesiologists. About 10.6 percent was for diagnostic laboratory tests, which would include not only blood chemistry analysis and urinalysis, but also tests such as EKGs. About 10.3 percent of spending was for radiology, and 4.8 percent was for consultations.

TABLE E–18.—ALLOWED AMOUNTS FOR PHYSICIANS' SERVICES, BY TYPE OF SERVICE, 1992

Type of service	Allowed amounts (millions)	Percent of total	Percent inpatient
Medical care	$12,503.0	36.8	36.1
Surgery	10,490.0	30.9	49.9
Assistance at surgery	246.0	.7	89.2
Anesthesia	1,319.0	3.9	68.7
Diagnostic laboratory tests	3,597.0	10.6	18.7
Diagnostic radiology	2,775.0	8.2	26.8
Therapeutic radiology	698.0	2.1	5.0
Consultations [1]	1,641.0	4.8	62.0
Other [2]	672.0	2.0	1.5
All services	33,941.0	100.0	39.3

[1] Includes first and second opinions for surgery.
[2] Includes treatment for renal patients, pneumococcal vaccine, and medical supplies, among other things.

Source: Health Care Financing Administration, Bureau of Data Management and Strategy, National Claims History Procedure Summary.

Table E–19 lists the top 20 individual services, ranked by total allowed amounts on claims submitted by selected physicians for 1992. The most important exclusion is amounts for the services of anesthesiologists, since there would typically be a charge for anesthesiology for the surgical procedures. The amounts for surgical procedures include claims by both the primary surgeon and any assistant surgeons, but not the amounts for anesthesiologists.

The top 20 services (out of more than 7,000) accounted for 36.9 percent of all spending for all physicians' services in 1992. Cataract extraction with implantation of an intraocular lens was the highest-ranked surgical procedure, accounting by itself for 5.7 percent of total allowed amounts for physicians' services. Other surgical procedures in the top 20 included total knee replacement and heart catherization and coronary angiography. Most of the remaining services in the top 20 were evaluation and management services (that is, visits and consultations).

Table E–20 presents total allowed amounts for selected groups of generic services, and shows the percent of total allowed amounts for all physicians' services accounted for by each group. As in table E–19, certain physicians' services—most notably for anesthesiologists—are not included in the allowed amounts for each service group. No attempt was made to define and rank all possible service groups, so that there may be other important service groups that do not appear in the table. For example, diagnostic radiology accounts for 8.2 percent of allowed amounts for physicians' services (from table E–18), but radiological services do not appear in table E–20.

TABLE E–19.—THE TOP 20 SERVICES BILLED BY PHYSICIANS UNDER MEDICARE, 1992

Service code and description	Allowed amounts (millions) [1]	Percent of total
Top 20 services:		
99213—Office/outpatient visit, EST	$2,103	6.2
66984—Remove cataract, insert lens	1,947	5.7
99232—Subsequent hospital care	1,271	3.7
99214—Office/outpatient visit, EST	1,087	3.2
99231—Subsequent hospital care	1,027	3.0
99212—Office/outpatient visit, EST	675	2.0
99233—Subsequent hospital care comprehensive	514	1.5
93307—Echo exam of heart	419	1.2
99223—Initial hospital care	382	1.1
99215—Office/outpatient visit, EST	368	1.1
99254—Initial inpatient consult	357	1.1
66821—After cataract laser surgery	343	1.0
90844—Psychotherapy 45–50 Min	313	.9
99222—Initial hospital care	272	.8
92014—Eye exam & treatment	264	.8
27447—Total knee replacement	262	.8
99238—Hospital discharge day	250	.7
93547—Heart catheter & angiogram	245	.7
99244—Office consultation	224	.7
99255—Initial inpatient consult	212	.6
Total	12,536	36.9

[1] Amounts for surgical procedures include fees for primary and assistant surgeons, but not for anesthesiologists.

Source: Health Care Financing Administration, Bureau of Data Management and Strategy, National Claims History Procedure Summary.

The 21 service groups shown in table E–20 accounted for 44.1 percent of all allowed amounts for all physicians' services in 1992. The single most costly group was office visits (accounting for 14.4 percent of total allowed amounts for physicians' services), followed by hospital visits (11.1 percent). Cataract surgery of all types accounted for 5.8 percent of total allowed amounts for physicians' services. It should also be noted that the amount for hemodialysis includes only physician services and does not include the much larger amounts for the facility charges for hemodialysis that were not billed under the fee-for-service reimbursement system.

TABLE E–20.—ALLOWED AMOUNTS FOR SELECTED GROUPS OF PHYSICIANS' SERVICES, 1992

Service group	1991	
	Allowed amounts (millions) [1]	Percent of total
Hospital visits (99221–99238)	$3,764	11.1
Office visits (99201–99215)	4,896	14.4
Cataract surgery (66830–66985)	1,985	5.8
EKGs (93000–93018, 93015–26)	364	1.1
Transurethral surgery (52601)	159	.5
Coronary artery bypass (33510–33516)	495	1.5
Hip arthroplasty (27130–27132)	144	.4
Cardiac catheterization (93501–93553)	598	1.8
Colonoscopy (45378–45385, 44388–44393, 45355)	485	1.4
Hemodialysis/CAPD (90935–90947)	165	.5
Thromboendarterectomy (35301–35381)	100	.3
Knee arthroplasty (27446, 27447, 29881)	293	.9
Pacemaker implant/removal (33200–33210, 33232)	89	.3
Vein bypass (35501–35587)	71	.2
Emergency room visits (99281–99285)	610	1.8
SNF visits (99301–99313)	455	1.3
Nursing home visits (99321–99333)	36	.1
Home visits (99341–99353)	56	.2
Prostatectomy (55801–55845)	82	.2
EEGs (95816–95827, 95950, 95955)	33	.1
Pacemaker tests (93731–93736)	71	.2
Total	14,951	44.1

[1] Amounts for surgical procedures include fees for primary and assistant surgeons, but not for anesthesiologists.

Source: Health Care Financing Administration, Bureau of Data Management and Strategy, National Claims History Procedure Summary.

In recent years, there have been many changes in the delivery of health care services. Some of the more significant changes affecting Medicare services have been in the delivery of surgical services. First, there has been significant growth in the amount of surgical care provided by some specialties. Second, there has been a dramatic shift in the place of surgical care; that is, surgical care is now frequently provided in outpatient settings, whereas previously, most surgical care was provided in inpatient settings.

As shown in table E–21, the most significant shift in site of surgical care between 1980 and 1992 was out of inpatient settings and into other settings. Outpatient hospital settings benefited most from this shift, growing from only 3.3 percent of all surgical charges in 1980 to 25.5 percent in 1992. The proportions of surgery taking place in a physician's office and in other nonhospital settings also grew somewhat. In 1992 the proportion of all surgical care provided in inpatient settings had dropped to 47.9 percent.

TABLE E–21.—CHARGES SUBMITTED TO MEDICARE FOR ALL PHYSICIAN SURGICAL SERVICES, BY PLACE OF SERVICE, 1980, 1990–92

Place of service	Surgical charges [1]		
	Amount in millions	Percent of surgical charges	As percent of total settings charges
1980:			
Total	$3,828	100.0	31.8
Office	445	11.6	12.2
Outpatient hospital	129	3.3	29.5
Inpatient hospital	3,231	84.4	44.1
Other [2]	23	.6	3.7
1990:			
Total	11,048	100.0	33.3
Office	2,004	18.1	16.2
Outpatient hospital [1]	2,867	26.0	54.3
Inpatient hospital	5,563	50.4	40.6
Ambulatory surgical center	488	4.4	51.2
Other [2]	127	1.1	14.5
1991:			
Total	11,773	100.0	32.9
Office	2,230	18.9	16.1
Outpatient hospital [1]	2,993	25.4	52.5
Inpatient hospital	5,834	49.6	41.1
Ambulatory surgical center	514	4.4	54.2
Other [2]	201	1.7	18.9
1992:			
Total	10,958	100.0	31.3
Office	2,103	19.2	14.8
Outpatient hospital [1]	2,791	25.5	50.3
Inpatient hospital	5,249	47.9	39.2
Ambulatory surgical center	622	5.7	90.3
Other [2]	193	1.8	16.6

[1] May include some services rendered in an ambulatory surgical center.
[2] Includes homes, nursing homes, and other places of service.

Source: Health Care Financing Administration, Bureau of Data Management and Strategy, Part B Extract Summary System.

Table E–22 shows the percent of total surgical charges by specialty in 1980 and 1992. In 1980, three specialties (ophthalmology, general surgery, and orthopedic surgery) accounted for nearly half of all Medicare surgical care. These same three specialties accounted for close to the same proportion of total surgical care in 1992, but the shares among these specialties changed. While ophthalmologists accounted for only 13.6 percent in 1980, by 1991 their share had increased to 22.7 percent due primarily to the substantial growth in cataract surgery during the 1980s. For two specialties, gastroenterology and otology, laryngology and rhinology (or ENT), surgical care represented much larger proportions of their total Medicare practice in 1992 than in 1980. On the other hand, surgical charges for urologists represented much smaller proportions of their total Medicare practice in 1992 than in 1980.

TABLE E–22.—SUBMITTED SURGICAL CHARGES UNDER MEDICARE AS A SHARE OF TOTAL SURGICAL CHARGES AND AS A PERCENT OF TOTAL PRACTICE CHARGES, BY MEDICAL SPECIALTY, 1980 AND 1992

Specialty	Percent distribution of surgical charges		Surgical charges as a percent of total practice charges	
	1980	1992	1980	1992
All physicians	100.0	100.0	31.8	31.3
Ophthalmology	13.6	22.7	62.1	67.5
General surgery	22.1	11.9	71.6	70.0
Orthopedic surgery	13.0	10.6	73.6	71.9
Urology	10.7	6.5	75.6	52.6
Thoracic surgery	8.0	5.4	82.2	81.9
Clinic and other group practice	4.7	2.4	25.8	22.5
Internal medicine	4.2	3.3	6.9	7.1
Cardiovascular disease	2.7	7.3	22.4	28.0
Podiatry	3.0	4.0	53.5	61.4
Gastroenterology	1.7	5.6	45.9	65.2
Dermatology	2.4	4.3	60.9	69.3
Neurological surgery	2.9	2.0	70.2	78.2
Othology, laryngology, rhinology	1.9	.0	49.7	66.0
Plastic surgery	1.3	1.3	88.1	85.8
Other	8.4	12.6	....	9.9

Source: Health Care Financing Administration, Bureau of Data Management and Strategy, Part B Extract Summary System.

As shown in table E–23, many different medical specialties participated in the shift to outpatient surgery. In 1980, only two specialties (dermatology and podiatry) performed the majority of their surgical services in outpatient settings; in these cases, the care was generally provided in the physician's office. In 1992, seven specialties provided a majority of their surgical care in outpatient settings: ophthalmology, podiatry, gastroenterology, dermatology, ENT, internal medicine, and plastic surgery. Podiatrists and dermatologists continued primarily to work in their offices; internist split their non-inpatient work between office and outpatient settings, while the other specialties provided their surgical services in outpatient hospital and ambulatory surgical facilities. Most surgical specialties, such as general, orthopedic, cardiovascular, neurological and thoracic surgeons, remained closely tied to inpatient hospital settings.

TABLE E-23.—SUBMITTED SURGICAL CHARGES UNDER MEDICARE, BY MEDICAL SPECIALTY AND PLACE OF SERVICE, 1980 AND 1992

[In percent]

Specialty	1980					1992					
	All settings	Office	Inpatient hospital	Outpatient hospital	Other[1]	All settings	Office	Inpatient hospital	Outpatient hospital[2]	ASC[3]	Other[1]
All physicians	100.0	11.6	84.4	3.3	0.5	100.0	19.2	47.9	25.5	5.7	1.8
General surgery	100.0	4.4	92.6	2.9	.1	100.0	6.0	73.7	18.8	1.0	0.5
Cardiovascular disease	100.0	1.7	97.9	.4	(4)	100.0	2.6	86.4	10.3	0.1	0.6
Dermatology	100.0	94.6	4.0	.9	.6	100.0	97.5	0.5	1.3	0.4	0.3
Gastroenterology	100.0	12.0	75.6	12.3	.1	100.0	9.5	38.9	46.9	4.3	0.5
Internal medicine	100.0	17.5	76.6	5.7	.2	100.0	25.4	44.5	28.2	1.5	0.5
Neurological surgery	100.0	1.1	98.5	.5	(4)	100.0	1.6	94.8	3.2	0.1	0.3
Obstetrics/Gynecology	100.0					100.0	14.3	72.5	12.1	.8	0.3
Otology, Laryngology, Rhinology	100.0	12.6	83.7	3.7		100.0	14.0	4.0	55.2	25.4	1.4
Ophthalmology	100.0	7.9	87.1	5.0	.1	100.0	18.8	4.7	53.3	20.7	2.5
Orthopedic Surgery	100.0	6.3	90.2	3.4	.1	100.0	7.7	78.0	12.9	1.0	0.4
Plastic Surgery	100.0	13.0	67.2	19.7	.1	100.0	22.0	33.8	37.3	5.8	1.0
Thoracic surgery	100.0	.8	98.7	.5	(4)	100.0	1.3	95.8	2.6	0.1	0.2
Urology	100.0	8.0	90.6	1.4	.1	100.0	23.5	57.5	17.6	1.0	0.3
Podiatry	100.0	71.3	13.5	.9	14.3	100.0	70.4	1.6	5.3	1.3	21.4
Clinic and other group practice	100.0	10.1	85.3	4.5	.1	100.0	14.1	57.8	25.7	1.9	0.5
Other	100.0					100.0	21.0	54.7	22.2	1.5	0.6

[1] Includes homes, nursing homes, and other places of service.
[2] May include some services rendered in an ASC.
[3] Ambulatory surgical center.
[4] Less than .05.

Source: Health Care Financing Administration, Bureau of Data Management and Strategy, Part B Extract Summary System.

TABLE E–24.—PERCENT DISTRIBUTION OF ALLOWED SURGICAL CHARGES UNDER MEDICARE, BY MEDICAL SPECIALTY AND PLACE OF SERVICE, 1992

Place of service	Percent
Inpatient hospital:	
General surgery	18.4
Orthopedic surgery	17.2
Thoracic surgery	10.7
Urology	7.9
Cardiovascular disease	13.2
Clinic and other group practice	2.9
Gastroenterology	4.6
Internal medicine	3.0
Ophthalmology	2.2
Neurological surgery	4.1
Other medical and surgical specialties	15.8
Total	100.0
Office:	
Ophthalmology	22.2
Dermatology	21.9
Podiatry	14.7
Urology	8.0
Internal medicine	4.3
General surgery	3.7
Orthopedic surgery	4.3
Gastroenterology	2.8
Family practice	1.4
Clinic and other group practice	1.8
Other medical and surgical specialties	14.9
Total	100.0
Outpatient hospital:	
Ophthalmology	47.6
Gastroenterology	10.4
General surgery	8.8
Orthopedic surgery	5.4
Internal medicine	3.8
Urology	4.5
Clinic and other group practice	2.5
Otology, larynology, rhinology	0.9
Plastic surgery	1.9
Other medical and surgical specialties	14.3
Total	100.0

Source: Health Care Financing Administration, Bureau of Data Management and Strategy, Part B Extract Summary System.

In 1992, ophthalmologists provided most (47.6 percent) of the surgery done in outpatient hospital settings (see table E–24). The predominance of ophthalmologists in this setting is due to cataract surgery. Ophthalmologists also accounted for the largest proportion of office surgical charges, 22.2 percent. However, dermatologists and podiatrists also represented significant percentages of office surgical charges, 21.9 and 14.7 percent respectively. In inpatient settings, the traditional surgical specialties—general surgery, orthopedic surgery, cardiovascular surgery, thoracic surgery and urology accounted for 67.4 percent of all surgical charges.

TABLE E–25.—GEOGRAPHIC PRACTICE COST INDICES, BY MEDICARE CARRIER LOCALITY

Carrier number	Locality number	Locality name	Work	Practice expense	Mal-practice
510	5	Birmingham, AL	0.981	0.913	0.824
510	4	Mobile, AL	.964	.911	.824
510	2	North Central Alabama	.970	.867	.824
510	1	Northwest Alabama	.985	.869	.824
510	6	Rest of Alabama	.975	.851	.824
510	3	Southeast Alabama	.972	.869	.824
1020	1	Alaska	1.106	1.255	1.042
1030	5	Flagstaff (City), AZ	.983	.911	1.255
1030	1	Phoenix, AZ	1.003	1.016	1.255
1030	7	Prescott (City), AZ	.983	.911	1.255
1030	99	Rest of Arizona	.987	.943	1.255
1030	2	Tucson (City), AZ	.987	.989	1.255
1030	8	Yuma (City), AZ	.983	.911	1.255
520	13	Arkansas	.960	.856	.302
2050	26	Anaheim-Santa Ana, CA	1.046	1.220	1.370
542	14	Bakersfield, CA	1.028	1.050	1.370
542	11	Fresno/Madera, CA	1.006	1.009	1.370
542	13	Kings/Tulare, CA	.999	1.001	1.370
2050	18	Los Angeles, CA (1st of 8)	1.060	1.196	1.370
2050	19	Los Angeles, CA (2d of 8)	1.060	1.196	1.370
2050	20	Los Angeles, CA (3d of 8)	1.060	1.196	1.370
2050	21	Los Angeles, CA (4th of 8)	1.060	1.196	1.370
2050	22	Los Angeles, CA (5th of 8)	1.060	1.196	1.370
2050	23	Los Angeles, CA (6th of 8)	1.060	1.196	1.370
2050	24	Los Angeles, CA (7th of 8)	1.060	1.196	1.370
2050	25	Los Angeles, CA (8th of 8)	1.060	1.196	1.370
542	3	Marin/Napa/Solano, CA	1.012	1.198	1.370
542	10	Merced/Surrounding Counties, CA	1.018	1.009	1.370
542	12	Monterey/Santa Cruz, CA	1.023	1.108	1.370
542	1	North Coastal Counties, CA	1.003	1.072	1.370
542	2	Northeast Rural California	1.001	.990	1.370
542	7	Oakland-Berkeley, CA	1.028	1.258	1.370
542	27	Riverside, CA	1.026	1.080	1.370
542	4	Sacramento/Surrounding Counties, CA	1.026	1.088	1.370
542	15	San Bernardino/East Central, CA	1.025	1.077	1.370
2050	28	San Diego/Imperial, CA	1.026	1.090	1.370
542	5	San Francisco, CA	1.038	1.303	1.370
542	6	San Mateo, CA	1.038	1.303	1.370

TABLE E–25.—GEOGRAPHIC PRACTICE COST INDICES, BY MEDICARE CARRIER
LOCALITY—Continued

Carrier number	Locality number	Locality name	Work	Practice expense	Mal-practice
2050	16	Santa Barbara, CA	1.012	1.073	1.370
542	9	Santa Clara, CA	1.048	1.286	1.370
542	8	Stockton/Surrounding Counties, CA ..	1.019	1.027	1.370
2050	17	Ventura, CA	1.034	1.132	1.370
550	1	Colorado	.999	.988	.683
10230	4	Eastern Connecticut	.999	1.053	1.036
10230	1	Northwest and North Central Connecticut	1.002	1.071	1.025
10230	3	South Central Connecticut	1.018	1.103	1.188
10230	2	Southwest Connecticut	1.053	1.139	1.231
570	1	Delaware	1.026	1.018	.664
580	1	D.C.+MD/VA suburbs	1.059	1.168	.947
590	3	Fort Lauderdale, FL	.993	.981	1.376
590	4	Miami, FL	1.034	1.025	1.641
590	2	North/North central Florida cities	.975	.932	1.108
590	1	Rest of Florida	.966	.871	1.108
1040	1	Atlanta, GA	.975	1.022	.752
1040	4	Rest of Georgia	.956	.841	.752
1040	2	Small Georgia cities 02	.962	.895	.752
1040	3	Small Georgia cities 03	.961	.869	.752
1120	1	Hawaii	1.003	1.094	1.025
5130	12	North Idaho	.965	.917	.889
5130	11	South Idaho	.967	.936	.889
621	10	Champaign-Urbana, IL	.965	.920	1.137
621	16	Chicago, IL	1.044	1.114	1.773
621	3	De Kalb, IL	.978	.925	1.137
621	11	Decatur, IL	.981	.927	1.137
621	12	East St. Louis, IL	.989	.958	1.579
621	6	Kankakee, IL	.972	.925	1.137
621	8	Normal, IL	.997	.968	1.137
621	1	Northwest, IL	.974	.896	1.137
621	5	Peoria, IL	1.009	1.031	1.137
621	7	Quincy, IL	.974	.896	1.137
621	4	Rock Island, IL	.995	.958	1.137
621	2	Rockford, IL	1.010	1.018	1.137
621	13	Southeast Illinois	.974	.896	1.137
621	14	Southern Illinois	.974	.896	1.137
621	9	Springfield, IL	.996	.966	1.137
621	15	Suburban Chicago, IL	1.020	1.097	1.137
630	1	Metropolitan Indiana	.998	.963	.547
630	3	Rest of Indiana	.979	.896	.516
630	2	Urban Indiana	.980	.905	.516
640	5	Des Moines (Polk/Warren), IA	.997	.966	.666
640	3	North central Iowa	.971	.916	.666
640	2	Northeast Iowa	.972	.918	.666
640	6	Northwest Iowa	.969	.890	.666
640	4	South central Iowa (excludes Des Moines).	.962	.881	.666
640	1	Southeast Iowa (includes Iowa City)	.976	.933	.666

TABLE E–25.—GEOGRAPHIC PRACTICE COST INDICES, BY MEDICARE CARRIER LOCALITY—Continued

Carrier number	Locality number	Locality name	Work	Practice expense	Mal-practice
640	7	Southwest Iowa	.968	.900	.666
740	5	Kansas City, KS	.978	.964	1.134
650	1	Rest of Kansas	.953	.893	1.134
740	4	Suburban Kansas City, KS	.978	.964	1.134
660	1	Lexington and Louisville, KY	.984	.917	.667
660	3	Rest of Kentucky	.974	.875	.667
660	2	Small cities (city limits) KY	.976	.898	.667
528	7	Alexandria, LA	.985	.889	.808
528	3	Baton Rouge, LA	.991	.966	.808
528	6	Lafayette, LA	.982	.928	.808
528	4	Lake Charles, LA	.975	.907	.808
528	5	Monroe, LA	.979	.880	.808
528	1	New Orleans, LA	.994	1.003	1.185
528	50	Rest of Louisiana	.972	.880	.824
528	2	Shreveport, LA	1.003	.940	.808
21200	2	Central Maine	.942	.903	.716
21200	1	Northern Maine	.947	.912	.716
21200	3	Southern Maine	.956	.980	.716
690	1	Baltimore/Surrounding Counties, MD	1.027	1.040	.927
690	3	South+Eastern Shore, MD	1.011	1.010	.820
690	2	Western Maryland	1.006	1.013	.843
700	2	Massachusetts suburbs/rural (cities)	.997	1.072	.855
700	1	Massachusetts Urban	1.002	1.131	.855
710	1	Detroit, MI	1.059	1.091	1.736
710	2	Michigan, not Detroit	1.010	.971	1.196
720	00	Minnesota (Blue Shield)	.999	.971	.748
10240	00	Minnesota (Travelers)	.999	.971	.748
10250	1	Rest of Mississippi	.960	.838	.650
10250	2	Urban Mississippi (city limits)	.966	.902	.650
740	3	Kansas City (Jackson County), MO	.978	.964	1.179
740	2	North Kansas City (Clay/Platte), MO	.978	.964	1.179
11260	3	Rest of Missouri	.950	.847	1.179
740	6	Rural Northwest counties, Missouri	.953	.866	1.179
11260	2	Small Eastern Cities, MO	.954	.838	1.179
740	1	St. Joseph, MO	.950	.867	1.179
11260	1	St. Louis/Large Eastern Cities, MO	.988	.964	1.352
751	1	Montana	.967	.926	.718
655	00	Nebraska	.960	.883	.435
1290	3	Elko and Ely (Cities), NV	.984	1.026	1.144
1290	1	Las Vegas, et al (cities), NV	1.036	1.082	1.144
1290	2	Reno, et al (cities), NV	1.008	1.141	1.144
1290	99	Rest of Nevada	1.020	1.079	1.144
780	40	New Hampshire	.962	1.011	.602
860	2	Middle New Jersey	1.034	1.070	1.153
860	1	Northern New Jersey	1.040	1.131	1.153
860	3	Southern New Jersey	1.016	1.030	1.153
1360	5	New Mexico	.981	.925	.767
801	1	Buffalo/Surrounding Counties, NY	1.006	.942	.963
803	1	Manhattan, NY	1.059	1.255	1.647

TABLE E–25.—GEOGRAPHIC PRACTICE COST INDICES, BY MEDICARE CARRIER
LOCALITY—Continued

Carrier number	Locality number	Locality name	Work	Practice expense	Mal- practice
801	3	North central cities, New York	.997	.952	.963
803	2	New York City suburbs/Long Island, NY	1.060	1.229	1.929
803	3	Poughkpsie/N. New York City sub-urbs	1.004	1.018	1.325
14330	4	Queens, NY	1.059	1.255	1.861
801	2	Rochester/Surrounding Counties, NY	1.021	1.017	.963
801	4	Rest of New York	.988	.935	.963
5535	00	North Carolina	.968	.902	.378
820	1	North Dakota	.965	.895	.688
16360	00	Ohio	.993	.951	.920
1370	00	Oklahoma	.969	.911	.516
1380	2	Eugene, et al (cities), OR	.968	1.008	.951
1380	1	Portland, et al (cities), OR	.993	1.033	.951
1380	99	Rest of Oregon	.979	.997	.951
1380	3	Salem, et al (cities), OR	.974	.990	.951
1380	12	Southwest Oregon cities (city limits)	.974	.988	.951
865	2	Large Pennsylvania cities	1.008	1.001	1.440
865	1	Philly/Pitt Medium Schools/Hospitals	1.014	1.014	1.552
865	4	Rest of Pennsylvania	.975	.929	.986
865	3	Small Pennsylvania cities	.984	.945	.986
973	20	Puerto Rico	.882	.763	.466
870	1	Rhode Island	1.009	.998	.734
880	1	South Carolina	.971	.874	.448
820	2	South Dakota	.951	.857	.688
5440	35	Tennessee	.969	.896	.407
900	29	Abilene, TX	.971	.888	.504
900	26	Amarillo, TX	.972	.900	.504
900	31	Austin, TX	.969	.968	.504
900	20	Beaumont, TX	.998	.955	.504
900	9	Brazoria, TX	1.025	.955	.504
900	10	Brownsville, TX	.980	.888	.504
900	24	Corpus Christi, TX	.976	.944	.504
900	11	Dallas, TX	.996	.971	.504
900	12	Denton, TX	.996	.971	.504
900	14	El Paso, TX	.995	.894	.504
900	28	Fort Worth, TX	.973	.936	.504
900	15	Galveston, TX	.982	.968	.504
900	16	Grayson, TX	.964	.903	.504
900	18	Houston, TX	1.014	.982	.656
900	33	Laredo, TX	.968	.856	.504
900	17	Longview, TX	.968	.929	.504
900	21	Lubbock, TX	.950	.881	.504
900	19	Mc Allen, TX	.945	.873	.504
900	23	Midland, TX	1.023	.998	.504
900	2	Northeast rural Texas	.968	.883	.504
900	13	Odessa, TX	1.008	.971	.504
900	25	Orange, TX	.998	.955	.504
900	30	San Angelo, TX	.954	.902	.504

TABLE E–25.—GEOGRAPHIC PRACTICE COST INDICES, BY MEDICARE CARRIER
LOCALITY—Continued

Carrier number	Locality number	Locality name	Work	Practice expense	Mal-practice
900	7	San Antonio, TX	.973	.929	.504
900	3	Southeast rural Texas	.973	.895	.504
900	6	Temple, TX	.969	.886	.504
900	8	Texarkana, TX	.953	.883	.504
900	27	Tyler, TX	.984	.931	.504
900	32	Victoria, TX	.976	.973	.504
900	22	Waco, TX	.981	.871	.504
900	4	Western rural Texas	.961	.852	.504
900	34	Wichita Falls, TX	.969	.896	.504
910	9	Utah	.993	.952	.739
780	50	Vermont	.942	.941	.533
10490	1	Richmond+Charlottesville, VA	.975	.953	.462
10490	4	Rest of Virginia	.967	.888	.522
10490	3	Small town/Industrial Virginia	.971	.892	.531
10490	2	Tidewater+North Virginia Counties ...	.989	.994	.703
973	50	Virgin Islands	1.000	1.000	1.000
932	4	East central+Northeast Washington (excludes Spokane).	.991	.979	1.064
932	2	Seattle (King County), WA	1.019	1.049	1.064
932	3	Spokane+Richland (cities), WA	.996	.995	1.064
932	1	West+Southeast Washington (excludes Seattle).	1.008	.992	1.064
16510	16	Charleston, WV	.987	.962	.688
16510	18	Eastern Valley, WV	.962	.881	.688
16510	19	Ohio River Valley, WV	.962	.881	.688
16510	20	Southern Valley, WV	.960	.876	.688
16510	17	Wheeling, WV	.975	.900	.688
951	13	Central Wisconsin	.960	.888	.762
951	40	Green Bay, WI (Northeast)	.979	.913	.762
951	54	Janesville, WI (South-Central)	.970	.905	.762
951	19	La Crosse, WI (West-Central)	.976	.919	.762
951	15	Madison, WI (Dane County)	.977	.979	.762
951	46	Milwaukee suburbs, WI (SE)	1.010	1.008	.762
951	4	Milwaukee, WI	1.008	1.009	.762
951	12	Northwest Wisconsin	.966	.898	.762
951	60	Oshkosh, WI (East-Central)	.974	.911	.762
951	14	Southwest Wisconsin	.960	.888	.762
951	36	Wausau, WI (North-Central)	.971	.898	.762
825	21	Wyoming	.988	.938	.641

Note: Work GPCI is the ¼ work GPCI required by Pub. L. 101–239.
Source: Federal Register, Vol. 58, No. 230, December 2, 1993; 63848–63851.

APPENDIX F. DATA ON EMPLOYMENT, EARNINGS, AND UNEMPLOYMENT

The following tables and charts provide additional data on unemployment and the unemployment compensation program.

TABLE F-1.—CIVILIAN UNEMPLOYMENT RATE AND INSURED UNEMPLOYMENT RATE

Civilian Unemployment Rate—Total (Seasonally Adjusted)

Year	Jan.	Feb.	Mar.	Apr.	May	June	July	Aug.	Sept.	Oct.	Nov.	Dec.	Avg.
1970	3.9	4.2	4.4	4.6	4.8	4.9	5.0	5.1	5.4	5.5	5.9	6.1	4.9
1971	5.9	5.9	6.0	5.9	5.9	5.9	6.0	6.1	6.0	5.8	6.0	6.0	5.9
1972	5.8	5.7	5.8	5.7	5.7	5.7	5.6	5.6	5.5	5.6	5.3	5.2	5.6
1973	4.9	5.0	4.9	5.0	4.9	4.9	4.8	4.8	4.8	4.6	4.8	4.9	4.9
1974	5.1	5.2	5.1	5.1	5.1	5.4	5.5	5.5	5.9	6.0	6.6	7.2	5.6
1975	8.1	8.1	8.6	8.8	9.0	8.8	8.6	8.4	8.4	8.4	8.3	8.2	8.5
1976	7.9	7.7	7.6	7.7	7.4	7.6	7.8	7.8	7.6	7.7	7.8	7.8	7.7
1977	7.5	7.6	7.4	7.2	7.0	7.2	6.9	6.9	7.0	6.8	6.8	6.4	7.1
1978	6.4	6.3	6.3	6.1	6.0	5.9	6.2	5.9	6.0	5.8	5.9	6.0	6.1
1979	5.9	5.9	5.8	5.8	5.6	5.7	5.7	6.0	5.9	6.0	5.9	6.0	5.8
1980	6.3	6.3	6.3	6.9	7.5	7.6	7.8	7.7	7.5	7.5	7.5	7.2	7.1
1981	7.5	7.4	7.4	7.2	7.5	7.5	7.2	7.4	7.6	7.9	8.3	8.5	7.6
1982	8.6	8.9	9.0	9.3	9.4	9.6	9.8	9.8	10.1	10.4	10.7	10.7	9.7
1983	10.4	10.4	10.3	10.2	10.2	10.1	9.4	9.4	9.2	8.8	8.4	8.2	9.6
1984	8.0	7.8	7.8	7.8	7.5	7.2	7.5	7.5	7.4	7.3	7.1	7.2	7.5
1985	7.4	7.3	7.2	7.3	7.2	7.3	7.3	7.1	7.1	7.1	7.0	7.0	7.2
1986	6.8	7.2	7.2	7.1	7.2	7.1	7.0	6.8	7.0	6.9	6.9	6.7	7.0
1987	6.7	6.6	6.5	6.3	6.3	6.1	6.0	6.0	5.9	6.0	5.9	5.8	6.2
1988	5.8	5.7	5.6	5.4	5.6	5.3	5.4	5.6	5.4	5.3	5.4	5.3	5.5
1989	5.4	5.2	5.1	5.2	5.2	5.4	5.2	5.2	5.3	5.3	5.3	5.3	5.3
1990	5.3	5.3	5.3	5.4	5.3	5.3	5.5	5.6	5.7	5.7	5.9	6.1	5.5
1991	6.2	6.5	6.7	6.6	6.8	6.9	6.8	6.8	6.8	6.9	6.9	7.1	6.7
1992	7.1	7.3	7.3	7.2	7.5	7.8	7.7	7.6	7.5	7.4	7.3	7.3	7.4
1993	7.1	7.0	7.0	7.0	6.9	7.0	6.8	6.7	6.7	6.8	6.5	6.4	6.8

TABLE F-1.—CIVILIAN UNEMPLOYMENT RATE AND INSURED UNEMPLOYMENT RATE—Continued

Insured Unemployment Rate Under State Programs (Seasonally Adjusted)

Year	Jan.	Feb.	Mar.	Apr.	May	June	July	Aug.	Sept.	Oct.	Nov.	Dec.	Avg.
1970	2.5	2.7	2.8	3.2	3.5	3.6	3.6	3.7	4.0	4.4	4.4	4.0	3.4
1971	3.9	3.9	4.0	4.1	4.1	4.1	3.9	4.2	4.3	4.2	4.1	4.0	4.1
1972	3.7	3.7	3.6	3.6	3.6	3.5	3.7	3.4	3.4	3.2	3.2	3.2	3.5
1973	2.9	2.8	2.8	2.6	2.7	2.7	2.6	2.8	2.7	2.7	2.7	2.9	2.7
1974	3.1	3.2	3.3	3.2	3.2	3.3	3.3	3.4	3.5	3.7	4.4	5.0	3.5
1975	5.6	5.8	6.4	6.7	6.9	6.8	6.1	5.9	5.8	5.6	5.3	4.9	6.0
1976	4.6	4.3	4.3	4.4	4.5	4.5	4.6	4.6	4.7	4.7	4.7	4.4	4.6
1977	4.3	4.2	4.1	4.0	3.9	3.9	3.8	3.8	3.8	3.8	3.8	3.7	3.9
1978	3.5	3.7	3.6	3.3	3.2	3.2	3.3	3.4	3.2	3.1	2.9	3.2	3.3
1979	3.1	3.2	3.1	3.0	2.8	2.8	2.8	3.0	2.9	3.0	3.1	3.2	2.9
1980	3.3	3.3	3.4	3.7	4.2	4.4	4.4	4.3	4.2	4.0	3.8	3.6	3.9
1981	3.5	3.5	3.4	3.3	3.3	3.3	3.3	3.3	3.4	3.6	3.9	4.0	3.5
1982	4.2	4.0	4.3	4.6	4.5	4.7	4.7	4.7	5.0	5.2	5.3	4.8	4.6
1983	4.5	4.7	4.5	4.4	4.2	3.9	3.7	3.5	3.4	3.3	3.3	3.2	3.9
1984	2.9	2.8	2.9	2.8	2.8	2.7	2.7	2.7	2.7	2.8	2.7	3.0	2.8
1985	2.8	3.0	3.0	2.9	2.8	2.8	2.8	2.8	2.8	2.6	2.8	2.9	2.8
1986	2.7	2.8	2.9	2.8	2.8	2.9	2.8	2.9	2.8	2.8	2.8	2.7	2.8
1987	2.6	2.6	2.6	2.5	2.4	2.4	2.4	2.3	2.2	2.1	2.1	2.2	2.4
1988	2.3	2.3	2.2	2.1	2.1	2.1	2.1	2.1	2.0	2.0	2.0	2.0	2.1
1989	2.1	2.1	2.1	2.1	2.0	2.1	2.2	2.1	2.2	2.2	2.2	2.3	2.1
1990	2.3	2.3	2.3	2.3	2.3	2.3	2.4	2.4	2.4	2.6	2.8	2.8	2.4
1991	3.0	3.1	3.3	3.3	3.2	3.2	3.1	3.1	3.1	3.0	3.1	3.1	3.1
1992	3.2	3.1	3.1	3.2	3.1	3.1	3.1	3.1	3.1	3.0	2.8	2.6	3.0
1993	2.7	2.5	2.5	2.6	2.6	2.7	2.7	2.6	2.7	2.7	2.6	2.6	2.6

Source: U.S. Department of Labor, Bureau of Labor Statistics. Washington, D.C. 1994.

TABLE F-2.—STATE INSURED UNEMPLOYMENT RATES UNDER THE UNEMPLOYMENT COMPENSATION PROGRAM

[Calendar year]

	1985	1986	1987	1988	1989	1990	1991	1992	1993, by quarter			
									I	II	III	IV
Alabama	3.3	3.2	2.8	2.2	2.5	2.7	2.8	2.5	2.4	2.0	2.1	2.0
Alaska	7.1	8.0	6.6	5.6	6.3	6.2	6.2	6.3	6.9	5.5	4.0	5.6
Arizona	1.8	2.0	2.0	1.5	1.9	2.3	2.3	2.4	2.1	2.2	2.2	1.9
Arkansas	3.7	3.6	3.4	3.2	3.3	3.6	3.6	3.5	3.8	2.9	2.5	2.8
California	3.6	3.5	3.0	2.7	2.9	4.1	4.1	4.4	4.5	3.9	3.6	3.8
Colorado	2.3	2.5	2.4	2.0	2.2	1.8	1.8	1.8	2.0	1.6	1.3	1.5
Connecticut	1.8	1.6	1.4	1.3	1.3	3.9	3.9	3.8	3.8	3.5	3.4	3.0
Delaware	1.6	2.0	1.2	1.4	1.3	2.3	2.3	2.4	2.5	1.9	1.9	1.9
District of Columbia	2.1	2.1	2.0	1.8	1.9	2.6	2.6	2.5	2.4	2.2	2.4	2.2
Florida	1.4	1.6	1.2	1.1	1.1	2.3	2.3	2.4	1.9	2.2	2.9	2.3
Georgia	1.8	1.8	1.6	1.4	1.5	2.3	2.3	2.0	1.9	1.5	1.5	1.4
Hawaii	2.5	2.1	1.7	1.5	1.6	1.6	1.6	2.3	2.7	2.5	2.4	2.4
Idaho	4.5	4.8	4.2	3.6	3.9	3.0	3.8	3.7	5.1	3.3	2.4	2.6
Illinois	3.2	2.9	2.6	2.2	2.5	3.1	3.1	3.1	3.4	2.8	2.5	2.3
Indiana	2.3	2.1	1.7	1.4	1.6	1.9	1.9	1.7	1.8	1.3	1.2	1.2
Iowa	3.0	2.9	2.1	1.7	2.0	2.1	2.0	2.0	2.7	1.7	1.5	1.6
Kansas	2.4	2.7	2.4	2.1	2.2	2.2	2.2	2.2	2.3	1.8	1.7	1.8
Kentucky	3.3	3.2	2.4	2.3	2.4	2.9	3.0	2.4	2.7	2.0	1.8	1.8
Louisiana	4.4	5.3	4.1	3.0	3.7	2.3	2.4	2.6	2.5	2.1	2.0	1.9
Maine	3.5	2.9	2.3	1.9	2.1	5.0	5.0	3.9	4.0	3.0	2.1	2.5
Maryland	2.2	2.1	1.7	1.5	1.6	3.1	3.2	3.1	3.2	2.6	2.3	2.2
Massachusetts	2.4	2.5	1.8	2.0	1.9	4.3	4.4	3.6	3.6	3.0	2.6	2.5

TABLE F-2.—STATE INSURED UNEMPLOYMENT RATES UNDER THE UNEMPLOYMENT COMPENSATION PROGRAM—Continued

[Calendar year]

	1985	1986	1987	1988	1989	1990	1991	1992	1993, by quarter			
									I	II	III	IV
Michigan	3.2	3.4	3.5	3.3	3.4	4.0	4.0	3.5	3.6	2.7	2.7	2.4
Minnesota	2.6	2.5	2.1	2.0	2.0	2.4	2.3	2.2	2.8	1.8	1.4	1.6
Mississippi	3.7	4.0	3.2	2.7	3.0	3.2	3.2	3.0	2.8	2.2	2.1	1.9
Missouri	2.6	2.6	2.4	2.2	2.3	3.0	3.0	2.8	3.1	2.2	2.2	1.9
Montana	3.9	3.9	3.4	3.0	3.2	3.2	3.2	3.1	4.6	3.0	2.3	2.9
Nebraska	2.3	2.1	1.8	1.4	1.6	1.3	1.3	1.3	1.8	1.1	0.9	0.9
Nevada	2.8	2.8	2.4	2.0	2.2	3.4	3.4	3.2	3.4	2.9	2.5	2.6
New Hampshire	1.0	0.8	0.6	0.6	0.6	3.0	3.0	2.3	2.1	1.1	1.3	1.5
New Jersey	2.9	2.6	2.4	2.1	2.1	3.9	3.9	3.9	3.9	3.3	3.1	2.9
New Mexico	2.8	3.4	2.9	2.4	2.7	2.4	2.4	2.5	2.6	2.3	1.9	1.8
New York	2.8	2.5	2.2	2.1	2.2	3.7	3.6	3.6	3.5	2.9	2.8	2.8
North Carolina	2.3	1.9	1.6	1.4	1.5	2.6	2.6	2.0	1.7	1.3	1.2	1.3
North Dakota	3.1	2.9	2.6	2.3	2.5	2.0	1.9	1.9	2.8	1.5	1.1	1.3
Ohio	3.0	2.8	2.4	2.1	2.3	2.8	2.8	2.7	2.7	2.0	1.8	1.8
Oklahoma	2.4	3.3	2.3	1.8	2.1	1.8	1.8	2.0	1.8	1.6	1.5	1.4
Oregon	4.6	4.9	3.5	3.1	3.4	4.2	4.2	4.2	4.6	3.8	3.2	3.6
Pennsylvania	4.0	3.6	2.9	2.6	2.8	4.0	4.0	4.0	4.1	3.4	3.0	3.1
Puerto Rico	7.1	5.7	4.9	4.2	4.6	5.9	5.8	6.3	6.4	6.5	7.1	6.6
Rhode Island	3.6	3.1	2.7	2.7	2.7	5.4	5.4	4.9	4.9	3.9	3.6	3.7
South Carolina	2.9	2.1	1.7	1.6	1.7	2.8	2.8	2.6	2.5	1.9	1.9	2.0
South Dakota	1.6	1.4	1.3	1.2	1.2	0.9	0.9	0.9	1.5	0.8	0.6	0.6

Tennessee	2.7	2.4	2.1	2.1	2.1	3.0	3.0	2.5	2.6	1.8	1.9	1.8
Texas	1.6	2.5	2.2	1.8	2.1	2.0	2.0	2.2	2.2	1.9	1.9	1.9
Utah	2.4	2.5	2.2	1.7	2.0	1.6	1.6	1.6	2.0	1.4	1.1	1.0
Vermont	3.1	2.5	2.0	1.8	1.9	4.3	4.4	4.0	4.3	3.6	2.6	2.9
Virginia	2.7	3.2	1.1	1.2	1.2	1.3	2.2	1.6	1.5	1.2	1.0	1.0
Virgin Islands	1.2	1.0	0.9	0.9	0.9	1.7	1.9	1.8	1.4	1.4	1.8	3.0
Washington	4.4	4.1	3.7	3.6	3.6	4.0	4.0	4.0	4.7	3.7	3.4	3.9
West Virginia	4.6	4.2	3.6	3.1	3.4	4.0	3.9	3.6	3.8	3.1	3.0	3.0
Wisconsin	3.5	3.0	2.7	2.2	2.5	3.0	3.0	2.8	3.5	2.4	1.8	1.9
Wyoming	2.4	3.9	3.2	2.3	2.9	2.1	2.0	2.3	2.9	1.9	1.2	1.6
United States	2.8	2.8	2.4	2.1	2.1	2.4	3.1	3.1	3.2	2.6	2.4	2.4

Prepared by DOL/ETA/UIS. Division of Actuarial Services.

TABLE F–3.—SELECTED UNEMPLOYMENT RATES

Period	Unemployment rate (percent of civilian labor force in group, seasonally adjusted)											
	Total (all civilian workers)	By sex and age			By race			By selected groups				
		Men 20 years and over	Women 20 years and over	Both sexes 16–19 years	White	Black	Black and other [1]	Experienced wage and salary workers	Married men, spouse present	Women who maintain families	Full-time workers	Part-time workers
1976	7.7	5.9	7.4	19.0	7.0	14.0	13.1	7.3	4.2	10.1	7.3	10.1
1977	7.1	5.2	7.0	17.8	6.2	14.0	13.1	6.6	3.6	9.4	6.6	9.9
1978	6.1	4.3	6.0	16.4	5.2	12.8	11.9	5.6	2.8	8.5	5.6	9.0
1979	5.8	4.2	5.7	16.1	5.1	12.3	11.3	5.5	2.8	8.3	5.3	8.8
1980	7.1	5.9	6.4	17.8	6.3	14.3	13.1	6.9	4.2	9.2	6.9	8.8
1981	7.6	6.3	6.8	19.6	6.7	15.6	14.2	7.3	4.3	10.4	7.3	9.4
1982	9.7	8.8	8.3	23.2	8.6	18.9	17.3	9.3	6.5	11.7	9.6	10.5
1983	9.6	8.9	8.1	22.4	8.4	19.5	17.8	9.2	6.5	12.2	9.5	10.4
1984	7.5	6.6	6.8	18.9	6.5	15.9	14.4	7.1	4.6	10.3	7.2	9.3
1985	7.2	6.2	6.6	18.6	6.2	15.1	13.7	6.8	4.3	10.4	6.8	9.3
1986	7.0	6.1	6.2	18.3	6.0	14.5	13.1	6.6	4.4	9.8	6.6	9.1
1987	6.2	5.4	5.4	16.9	5.3	13.0	11.6	5.8	3.9	9.2	5.8	8.4
1988	5.5	4.8	4.9	15.3	4.7	11.7	10.4	5.2	3.3	8.1	5.2	7.6
1989	5.3	4.5	4.7	15.0	4.5	11.4	10.0	5.0	3.0	8.1	5.1	6.2
1990	5.5	4.9	4.8	15.5	4.7	11.3	10.1	5.3	3.4	8.2	5.2	7.4
1991	6.7	6.3	5.7	18.6	6.0	12.4	11.1	6.5	4.4	9.1	6.5	8.3
1992	7.4	7.0	6.3	20.0	6.5	14.1	12.7	7.1	5.0	9.9	7.1	9.2
1993	6.8	6.4	5.9	19.0	6.0	12.9	11.7	6.5	4.4	9.5	6.5	8.8

[1] Category includes: American Samoans, Native Americans, Asians, and Black Hispanics.

Source: Department of Labor, Bureau of Labor Statistics, and Economic Report of the President, Feb. 1994.

TABLE F–4.—SELECTED MEASURES OF UNEMPLOYMENT

Period	Unemployment (thousands)	Percent distribution of unemployment by duration [1]				Percent distribution of unemployment by reason [1]			
		Less than 5 weeks	5–14 weeks	15–26 weeks	27 weeks and over	Job losers	Job leavers	Reentrants	New entrants
1977	6,991	41.8	30.5	13.1	14.7	45.3	13.0	28.1	13.6
1978	6,202	46.2	31.0	12.4	10.4	41.7	14.1	29.9	14.3
1979	6,137	48.1	31.7	11.5	8.7	42.9	14.3	29.4	13.3
1980	7,637	43.1	32.3	13.8	10.7	51.7	11.7	25.2	11.4
1981	8,273	41.7	30.7	13.6	14.0	51.6	11.2	25.4	11.9
1982	10,678	36.4	31.0	16.0	16.6	58.7	7.9	22.3	11.1
1983	10,717	33.3	27.4	15.4	23.9	58.4	7.7	22.5	11.3
1984	8,539	39.2	28.7	12.9	19.1	51.8	9.6	25.6	13.0
1985	8,312	42.1	30.2	12.3	15.4	49.8	10.6	27.1	12.5
1986	8,237	41.0	32.0	12.4	14.5	47.9	13.0	25.7	13.4
1987	7,425	43.7	29.6	12.7	14.0	48.0	13.0	26.6	12.4
1988	6,701	46.0	30.0	12.0	12.1	46.1	14.7	27.0	12.2
1989	6,528	48.6	30.3	11.2	9.9	45.7	15.7	28.2	10.4
1990	6,874	46.1	32.0	11.8	10.1	48.3	14.8	27.4	9.5
1991	8,426	40.1	32.3	14.5	13.0	54.7	11.6	24.8	8.9
1992	9,384	34.8	29.4	15.2	20.6	56.4	10.4	23.7	9.5
1993	8,734	36.2	28.9	14.6	20.4	54.6	10.8	24.6	10.0

[1] Detail may not add to 100 percent because of rounding.

Source: Economic Report of the President, Feb. 1994.

TABLE F–5.—STATE UNEMPLOYMENT COMPENSATION PROGRAM EXHAUSTIONS—REGULAR BENEFITS

[In thousands]

	1973	1974	1975	1976	1977	1978	1979	1980	1981	1982	1983	1984	1985	1986	1987	1988	1989	1990	1991	1992	1993
January	152	147	229	332	261	211	184	215	309	258	421	269	238	290	230	176	168	203	265	359	291
February	127	129	230	295	251	184	160	201	275	267	394	245	207	208	220	170	150	169	228	303	264
March	143	146	278	326	290	201	193	220	291	341	470	251	228	231	245	198	176	191	261	343	303
April	138	167	369	305	265	192	185	259	289	362	431	245	253	256	244	183	166	197	306	364	288
May	141	178	406	273	242	193	195	251	246	338	398	243	235	233	206	174	174	208	314	324	248
June	119	159	438	282	254	176	162	246	244	378	383	198	194	214	204	172	162	184	277	333	268
July	119	190	487	263	215	151	169	298	247	360	336	213	235	245	212	161	161	208	350	356	268
August	124	174	413	254	234	158	166	256	215	365	341	212	205	212	179	169	173	202	316	311	267
September	100	145	370	239	198	138	140	254	207	351	264	163	182	210	170	142	148	169	276	294	251
October	111	155	350	212	183	133	161	292	200	347	244	197	208	223	160	138	152	198	303	276	235
November	110	152	291	231	192	144	159	259	201	384	249	183	180	183	183	148	156	190	260	255	243
December	112	186	336	251	192	149	162	319	265	424	248	188	214	241	184	148	154	205	314	304	260
Total	1,495	1,926	4,195	3,262	2,776	2,030	2,037	3,072	2,989	4,175	4,180	2,607	2,579	2,746	2,408	1,979	1,940	2,324	3,472	3,821	3,186

Source: U.S. Department of Labor, Employment and Training Administration, Unemployment Insurance Service, Division of Actuarial Services.

TABLE F-6.—STATE UNEMPLOYMENT COMPENSATION PROGRAM EXHAUSTIONS—EXTENDED BENEFITS

[In thousands]

	1975	1976	1977	1978	1979	1980	1981	1982	1983	1984	1985	1986	1987	1988	1989	1990	1991	1992	1993
January	52	366	177	126	11	24	169	9	91	7	4	5	9	0	(¹)	(¹)	2	(¹)	(¹)
February	50	215	166	66	10	15	128	14	95	6	4	6	0	(¹)	(¹)	(¹)	(¹)	(¹)	(¹)
March	100	244	187	50	13	18	134	38	128	7	(¹)	5	5	(¹)	2	2	(¹)	1	(¹)
April	161	253	177	45	15	28	117	114	153	6	7	5	1	1	3	3	3	1	(¹)
May	207	190	159	49	31	74	95	134	156	12	9	4	2	1	(¹)	(¹)	6	5	(¹)
June	228	197	170	49	19	66	90	193	120	3	5	3	2	1	1	1	25	4	(¹)
July	245	175	141	50	13	67	48	128	44	1	5	8	1	(¹)	(¹)	(¹)	16	4	(¹)
August	245	178	92	38	12	64	21	121	23	(¹)	6	14	1	0	0	(¹)	5	1	(¹)
September	271	180	94	23	11	139	23	126	11	(¹)	5	8	0	0	(¹)	(¹)	3	(¹)	(¹)
October	294	174	137	30	14	208	15	126	7	1	4	8	0	0	0	(¹)	4	(¹)	(¹)
November	258	187	136	12	12	147	14	93	6	3	3	7	0	0	0	(¹)	1	(¹)	(¹)
December	286	178	137	10	11	189	11	94	6	4	(¹)	13	0	0	0	2	(¹)	(¹)	(¹)
Year total	2,398	2,536	1,774	549	172	1,039	862	1,188	840	50	52	86	21	2	1	9	67	17	1

¹ Means less than 500.

Source: U.S. Department of Labor, Employment and Training Administration, Unemployment Insurance Service, Division of Actuarial Services.

TABLE F-7.—BENEFIT EXHAUSTIONS UNDER FEDERAL SUPPLEMENTAL BENEFITS (1975–78), FEDERAL SUPPLEMENTAL COMPENSATION (1982–85), AND EMERGENCY UNEMPLOYMENT COMPENSATION (1991–93)

[In thousands]

	Federal supplemental benefits				Federal supplemental compensation				Emergency unemployment compensation [1]		
	1975	1976	1977	1978	1982	1983	1984	1985	1991	1992	1993
January	......	169	91	49	......	226	225	98	......	23	244
February	7	164	80	6	......	419	168	80	......	28	188
March	33	181	96	1	......	315	145	89	......	26	211
April	33	169	97	......	......	68	113	83	......	56	186
May	73	136	112	......	......	113	115	75	......	174	183
June	105	129	63	......	......	730	95	33	......	120	200
July	185	108	49	......	......	352	96	......	......	336	183
August	150	103	58	......	......	291	94	......	......	142	193
September	149	74	51	......	......	300	79	......	......	146	185
October	157	81	119	......	18	215	90	......	......	146	160
November	145	92	48	......	350	130	81	......	(*)	170	202
December	174	93	35	......	314	424	81	......	1	245	322
Total	1,211	1,499	899	56	682	3,583	1,382	458	1	1,610	2,458

Notes:
*Less than 500.

(1) There was no program in 1979–81 and 1986–90.
(2) Data for August and September 1975 were not available. The $299,000 difference between the total for the year and the sum of available monthly data was prorated between August and September.
(3) FSC exhaustions are not additive because reachback provisions caused claimants to receive as many as 3 final payments.
(4) Reports were not received from all States for every month for EUC.

Source: U.S. Department of Labor, Employment and Training Administration, Unemployment Insurance Service, Division of Actuarial Services.

TABLE F–8.—UNEMPLOYMENT COMPENSATION PAID BY PROGRAM IN FISCAL YEAR 1993

[In millions of dollars]

State	Programs		Emergency	Total
	Regular	Extended		
Alabama	187	0	73	260
Alaska	104	(*)	63	166
Arizona	182	0	87	269
Arkansas	169	0	79	248
California	3,510	0	2,272	5,782
Colorado	168	0	81	249
Connecticut	535	0	347	882
Delaware	62	0	20	82
District of Columbia	115	0	48	163
Florida	712	0	466	1,178
Georgia	309	0	137	446
Hawaii	161	0	60	221
Idaho	80	0	39	119
Illinois	1,263	0	534	1,797
Indiana	195	0	84	279
Iowa	184	0	68	252
Kansas	176	0	79	255
Kentucky	209	0	91	300
Louisiana	169	0	86	255
Maine	105	0	89	194
Maryland	376	0	208	584
Massachusetts	835	0	499	1,335
Michigan	1,051	0	615	1,666
Minnesota	378	0	141	519
Mississippi	103	0	58	162
Missouri	333	0	182	515
Montana	49	0	19	67
Nebraska	50	0	14	64
Nevada	135	0	60	196
New Hampshire	41	0	27	68
New Jersey	1,239	0	896	2,135
New Mexico	66	0	28	94
New York	2,196	0	1,515	3,712
North Carolina	277	0	202	479
North Dakota	27	0	12	39
Ohio	757	0	433	1,190
Oklahoma	127	0	63	189
Oregon	357	0	212	569
Pennsylvania	1,548	0	1,038	2,586
Puerto Rico	198	(*)	107	306
Rhode Island	157	0	131	289
South Carolina	177	0	87	264
South Dakota	12	0	2	14
Tennessee	242	0	124	366
Texas	1,114	0	571	1,686
Utah	76	0	29	105
Vermont	57	0	25	82

TABLE F–8.—UNEMPLOYMENT COMPENSATION PAID BY PROGRAM IN FISCAL YEAR 1993—Continued

[In millions of dollars]

State	Programs		Emergency	Total
	Regular	Extended		
Virginia	227	0	137	364
Virgin Islands	4	0	NA	4
Washington	695	0	303	998
West Virginia	126	(*)	82	208
Wisconsin	427	0	134	561
Wyoming	25	0	11	36

NA—Not available.
*Less than $500,000.
Source: U.S. Department of Labor, Employment and Training Administration, Unemployment Insurance, Division of Actuarial Services. Data include State programs and programs for Federal employees and ex-service members.

TABLE F–9.—U.S. AVERAGE WAGE REPLACEMENT RATE: RATIO OF AVERAGE WEEKLY BENEFIT AMOUNT TO AVERAGE WEEKLY WAGE

Year	First quarter	Second quarter	Third quarter	Fourth quarter	Average
1971	NA	NA	NA	NA	.365
1972	NA	NA	NA	NA	.361
1973	NA	NA	NA	NA	.361
1974	NA	NA	NA	NA	.365
1975	.377	.375	.381	.368	.375
1976	.390	.374	.368	.359	.373
1977	.384	.361	.356	.361	.365
1978	.383	.360	.359	.359	.365
1979	.372	.357	.361	.362	.363
1980	.376	.376	.373	.350	.369
1981	.372	.359	.363	.358	.363
1982	.381	.378	.383	.373	.379
1983	.384	.378	.364	.360	.372
1984	.358	.355	.358	.352	.356
1985	.354	.352	.362	.352	.355
1986	.356	.361	.369	.353	.360
1987	.359	.362	.363	.342	.357
1988	.357	.357	.351	.333	.350
1989	.356	.361	.365	.343	.356
1990	.361	.370	.373	.346	.362
1991	.374	.374	.375	.343	.367
1992	.371	.372	.368	.369	.370
1993	.377	.367	.366	NA	NA

NA—Not available.
Prepared by DOL/ETA/UIS/DAS.

TABLE F–10.—NUMBER UNEMPLOYED 27 WEEKS OR LONGER AS A PERCENT OF ALL UNEMPLOYED (UNADJUSTED)

Year	First quarter	Second quarter	Third quarter	Fourth quarter
1971	8.7	11.1	11.0	10.8
1972	12.1	13.5	10.8	9.8
1973	8.6	8.5	7.0	7.4
1974	6.8	8.3	7.5	7.1
1975	8.7	14.8	18.7	19.1
1976	19.7	20.1	16.7	16.3
1977	15.5	16.5	13.6	12.9
1978	11.1	11.8	10.1	8.7
1979	9.0	9.5	8.1	8.3
1980	8.3	9.9	11.1	13.5
1981	15.3	15.0	13.7	12.3
1982	13.0	16.7	17.1	19.4
1983	23.2	26.3	23.8	21.9
1984	21.0	21.0	17.7	16.5
1985	15.8	16.4	14.7	14.7
1986	13.8	15.0	14.6	14.2
1987	14.0	15.1	13.9	12.9
1988	12.3	12.9	11.7	11.1
1989	10.4	10.5	9.0	9.6
1990	9.5	10.2	10.4	10.2
1991	10.8	12.9	13.6	14.9
1992	17.9	21.4	21.8	21.4
1993	20.4	20.2	20.3	20.6

Source: U.S. Department of Labor.

TABLE F–11.—RATIO OF INSURED UNEMPLOYMENT TO JOB LOSERS

Year	Job losers (thousands)	Insured unemployment		Ratio: Insured unemployment to job losers	
		All programs (thousands)	Regular programs (thousands)	All programs	Regular programs
1968	1,070	1,187	1,111	110.9	103.8
1969	1,017	1,177	1,101	115.7	108.3
1970	1,811	2,070	1,805	114.3	99.7
1971	2,323	2,608	2,150	112.3	92.6
1972	2,108	2,192	1,848	104.0	87.7
1973	1,694	1,793	1,632	105.8	96.3
1974	2,242	2,558	2,262	114.1	100.9
1975	4,386	4,937	3,986	112.6	90.9
1976	3,679	3,846	2,991	104.5	81.3
1977	3,166	3,308	2,655	104.5	83.9
1978	2,585	2,645	2,359	102.3	91.3
1979	2,635	2,592	2,434	98.4	92.4
1980	3,947	3,837	3,350	97.2	84.9
1981	4,267	3,410	3,047	79.9	71.4
1982	6,268	4,594	4,061	73.3	64.8
1983	6,258	3,775	3,396	60.3	54.3
1984	4,421	2,561	2,476	57.9	56.0
1985	4,139	2,693	2,611	65.1	63.1
1986	4,033	2,746	2,650	68.1	65.7
1987	3,566	2,401	2,332	67.3	65.4
1988	3,092	2,135	2,081	69.0	67.3
1989	2,983	2,205	2,158	73.9	72.3
1990	3,322	2,575	2,522	77.5	75.9
1991	4,608	3,406	3,342	73.9	72.5
1992	5,291	3,348	3,245	63.3	61.3
1993 (preliminary)	4,769	2,845	2,751	59.7	57.7

Source: Based on data from the Economic Report of the President, 1994.

TABLE F-12.—NET BALANCES IN STATE UNEMPLOYMENT INSURANCE ACCOUNTS

[In billions of dollars]

End of calendar year—	Actual	1993 dollars [1]
1960	6.4	30.6
1961	5.6	26.4
1962	6.0	27.7
1963	6.4	29.2
1964	7.1	31.8
1965	8.2	35.9
1966	9.7	41.0
1967	10.7	43.9
1968	11.7	45.7
1969	12.6	46.9
1970	11.9	42.0
1971	9.7	32.5
1972	9.4	30.0
1973	10.9	32.8
1974	10.5	29.0
1975	3.1	7.8
1976	0.9	2.1
1977	1.0	2.2
1978	4.6	9.5
1979	8.6	16.3
1980	6.6	11.4
1981	5.7	9.0
1982	-2.6	-3.9
1983	-5.8	-8.3
1984	2.2	3.0
1985	10.1	13.3
1986	15.4	19.7
1987	23.2	28.8
1988	31.1	37.2
1989	36.9	42.2
1990	37.9	41.5
1991	30.2	31.9
1992	25.8	26.5
1993	28.2	28.2

[1] Adjusted to 1993 dollars using the implicit price deflator for Gross Domestic Product.

Source: CBO based on data from the "Economic Report of the President"; DOL, "UI Financial Data" and "UI Data Summary."

TABLE F–13.—STATUS OF ADMINISTRATION ACCOUNT (ESAA), FISCAL YEAR 1995 BUDGET

[In billions of dollars]

Fiscal year	1993	1994	1995	1996	1997	1998	1999
FUTA income	....	4.35	4.43	4.50	4.57	4.63	3.78
Interest earnings	....	.10	.10	.09	.09	.10	.11
General revenue	....	.02	(¹)	.01	.01	.01	.01
State administration (outlays)	....	3.56	3.50	3.49	3.48	3.47	3.48
UI	....	2.47	2.40	2.38	2.37	2.36	2.37
ES, BLS, VETS	....	1.09	1.10	1.11	1.11	1.11	1.11
Federal administration	....	.06	.17	.17	.17	.17	.17
Balance (end of year)	2.22	3.27	2.32	2.40	2.47	2.54	1.65
Ceiling ²	1.42	1.47	1.46	1.45	1.45	1.44	1.44
Excess (shortfall)	.80	1.80	.86	.95	1.02	1.10	.21

[1] Less than $5 million.
[2] Statutory ceiling is 40 percent of current year's appropriation.

Source: U.S. Department of Labor, Employment and Training Administration, Unemployment Insurance Service, Division of Actuarial Services, "UI Outlook: FY 1995 President's Budget," Jan. 1994.

TABLE F–14.—STATUS OF EXTENDED BENEFIT ACCOUNT (EUCA), FISCAL YEAR 1995 BUDGET

[In billions of dollars]

Fiscal year	1993	1994	1995	1996	1997	1998	1999
FUTA income	....	1.09	1.11	1.13	1.14	1.16	0.94
Interest earnings	....	.11	.17	.29	0.41	.54	.68
General revenue advances	....	3.07	.36	....	....	....	....
Overflow from ESAA	....	.80	1.80	.86	.95	1.02	1.10
Advance from FUA	....	....	....	....	....	....	....
Repayment of FUA	....	1.55	....	....	....	....	....
EB outlays—Federal share	....	.05	.07	.15	.18	.18	.18
EUC	....	3.68	....	....	....	....	....
EUCA balance (end of year)	.88	.67	4.03	6.16	8.48	11.02	13.56
Ceiling ¹	8.36	11.64	12.29	12.93	13.53	14.10	14.20
Excess (shortfall)	(7.48)	(10.97)	(8.26)	(6.77)	(5.05)	(3.08)	(.64)

[1] Statutory ceiling is 0.375 percent of covered wages before October 1, 1993, and 0.5 percent after that date.

Source: U.S. Department of Labor, Employment and Training Administration, Unemployment Insurance Service, Division of Actuarial Services, "UI Outlook: FY 1995 President's Budget," Jan. 1994.

TABLE F–15.—STATUS OF LOAN ACCOUNT (FUA), FISCAL YEAR 1995 BUDGET

[In billions of dollars]

	Fiscal year						
	1993	1994	1995	1996	1997	1998	1999
Income:							
State repayments	....	0.50	0.23	0.16	0.20	0.30	0.44
State interest payments	....	.03	.02	.03	.04	.06	.07
Interest earnings	....	.32	.33	.33	.33	.34	.35
Overflow from ESAA	....	....	....	....	....	....	....
Repayment from EUCA	....	1.55	....	....	....	....	....
Outgo:							
State loans	....	0.52	0.38	0.39	0.38	0.43	0.77
Advance to EUCA	....	....	....	....	....	....	....
FUA balance (end of year)	4.22	6.82	6.02	6.15	6.35	6.62	6.71
Ceiling [1]	13.94	5.82	6.14	6.46	6.76	7.05	7.10
Excess (shortfall)	(9.72)	1.00	(.12)	(.31)	(.41)	(.43)	(.39)

[1] Statutory ceiling is 0.625 percent of covered wages before Oct. 1, 1993, and 0.25 percent after that date.

Source: U.S. Department of Labor, Employment and Training Administration, Unemployment Insurance Service, Division of Actuarial Services, "UI Outlook: FY 1995 President's Budget," Jan. 1994.

TABLE F–16.—STATUS OF STATE UNEMPLOYMENT INSURANCE ACCOUNTS—FISCAL YEAR 1995 BUDGET

[In billions of dollars]

	Fiscal year						
	1993	1994	1995	1996	1997	1998	1999
Income	....	23.81	23.89	24.58	25.16	26.03	27.23
Collections	....	21.56	22.01	22.56	23.11	23.63	24.23
Interest earnings	....	1.73	1.50	1.63	1.67	1.97	2.23
Loans	....	.52	.38	.39	.38	.43	.77
Excess reduced credits	....	....	....	....	....	....	....
Outgo	....	23.28	22.85	23.18	23.73	23.73	24.88
Benefits	....	22.78	22.62	22.96	23.35	23.46	24.55
Lump-sum repayments	....	.50	.23	.22	.18	.27	.33
Balance (end of year)	28.95	29.48	30.51	32.01	33.64	35.94	38.28
Outstanding loans	.22	.25	.40	.63	.81	.93	1.26
Net balance (excluding loans)	28.73	29.23	30.11	31.38	32.83	35.01	37.02

Source: U.S. Department of Labor, Employment and Training Administration, Unemployment Insurance Service, Division of Actuarial Services, "UI Outlook: FY 1995 President's Budget," Jan. 1994.

APPENDIX G. DATA ON FAMILIES

SELECTED INDICATORS OF THE STATUS OF CHILDREN

Teenage Pregnancy

	1973	1980	1985	1989	1990
Female population (ages 15 to 19)	10,193,000	10,381,000	9,174,000	8,840,000	8,645,000
Births	604,096	552,161	467,485	506,503	521,826
Induced abortions	231,900	444,780	399,200	370,900	350,970
Estimated miscarriages	144,010	154,910	133,420	136,390	139,460
Pregnancies	980,000	151,850	100,110	1,015,790	1,012,260

International Infant Mortality Rates (deaths per 1,000 live births)

	1950–52	1970–72	1980–82	1986–88
Japan	55.9	12.4	7.1	5.0
Sweden	20.9	11.0	6.9	6.0
Canada	39.4	17.8	9.7	7.5
United States (white)	26.0	17.1	10.5	8.7
England and Wales	29.1	17.7	11.3	9.3
United States (total)	28.7	19.2	12.0	10.1
Hungary	77.0	34.7	21.4	17.4
United States (black)	45.1	30.9	20.3	17.8

Out-of-Wedlock Births

	1980	1990	1991	Percent Change 1980–91
Under age 15	9,024	10,675	10,968	21.5
Ages 15 to 19	262,777	349,970	357,483	36.0
Ages 20 to 24	237,265	403,873	429,094	80.9
Ages 25 to 29	99,583	229,991	234,593	135.6
Ages 30 to 34	40,984	118,200	123,901	202.3
Ages 35 to 39	13,187	44,149	48,353	266.7
Age 40 and over	2,927	8,526	9,377	220.4
Total (ages 15–44)	665,747	1,165,384	1,213,769	82.3

Living Arrangements of Children Under Age 18 (in thousands)

	1960	1970	1980	1990	1992
Total in population	63,727	69,162	63,427	64,137	65,965
Living with 1 parent	5,829	8,199	12,466	15,867	17,578
Percent of all children	9.1	11.9	19.7	24.7	26.6
Living with never-married parent	243	557	1,820	4,853	6,258
Percent of all children	0.4	0.8	2.9	7.6	9.5

Children Below Poverty (number in thousands/rate per 1,000)

	1974	1979	1989	1990	1992
Total	10,156 (15.4)	10,377 (16.4)	12,590 (19.6)	13,431 (20.6)	14,617 (21.9)
Black	3,755 (39.8)	3,833 (41.2)	4,375 (43.7)	4,550 (44.8)	4,938 (46.6)
White	6,223 (11.2)	6,193 (11.8)	7,599 (14.8)	8,232 (15.9)	8,955 (16.9)
Hispanic	NA (NA)	1,535 (28.0)	2,603 (36.2)	2,865 (38.4)	3,116 (39.9)

Educational Achievement

	1970	1975	1985	1990	1991
High school dropouts (percentage of status dropouts, ages 18–24)					
Total	17.3	15.6	13.9	13.6	14.2
White	15.2	13.9	13.5	13.5	14.2
Black	33.3	27.3	17.6	15.1	15.6

	1970	1975	1985	1990	1993
Average SAT scores					
Verbal	460	434	431	424	424
Math	488	472	475	476	478

NA: not available

TABLE G–1.—TOTAL NUMBER AND RATES OF MARRIAGES AND DIVORCES FOR SELECTED YEARS, 1950–92

	Number (thousands)		Rate [1]	
	Marriages	Divorces	Marriages	Divorces
1950	1,667	385	11.1	2.6
1960	1,523	393	8.5	2.2
1970	2,159	708	10.6	3.5
1980	2,390	1,189	10.6	5.2
1985	2,413	1,190	10.1	5.0
1986	2,407	1,178	10.0	4.9
1987	2,421	1,157	9.9	4.8
1988	2,395	1,167	9.7	4.7
1989	2,404	1,163	9.7	4.7
1990	2,448	1,175	9.8	4.7
1991	2,371	1,187	9.4	4.7
1992 [2]	2,362	1,215	9.2	4.7

[1] Rate is per 1,000 of the population.
[2] Provisional data.

Source: National Center for Health Statistics, "Vital Statistics of the United States," annual and unpublished data.

TABLE G–2.—PERCENT NEVER MARRIED, BY AGE AND SEX, 1960–92

	1960	1970	1980	1990	1992
Women:					
Ages 20 to 24	28.4	35.8	50.2	62.8	65.7
Ages 25 to 29	10.5	10.5	20.9	31.1	33.2
Ages 30 to 34	6.9	6.2	9.5	16.4	18.8
Men:					
Ages 20 to 24	53.1	54.7	68.8	79.3	80.3
Ages 25 to 29	20.8	19.1	33.1	45.0	48.7
Ages 30 to 34	11.9	9.4	15.9	27.0	29.4

Source: U.S. Bureau of the Census, Current Population Reports, P20–468.

TABLE G–3.—NUMBER AND RATE OF BIRTHS TO UNMARRIED WOMEN, BY RACE[1] AND AGE OF MOTHER, 1980 AND 1991

Age	Out-of-wedlock births			Rate per 1,000 unmarried women		
	Total	White	Black	Total	White	Black
1980						
Under 15	9,024	3,144	5,707	NA	NA	NA
15 to 19	262,777	127,984	128,022	27.6	16.2	89.2
20 to 24	237,265	112,854	117,423	40.9	24.4	115.1
25 to 29	99,583	46,872	49,077	34.0	20.7	83.9
30 to 34	40,984	20,565	18,766	21.1	13.6	48.2
35 to 39	13,187	7,073	5,513	9.7	6.8	19.6
40 and over	2,927	1,571	1,229	2.6	1.8	5.6
Total (Ages 15–44) ...	665,747	320,063	325,737	29.4	17.6	82.9
1991						
Under 15	10,968	4,346	6,298	NA	NA	NA
15 to 19	357,483	207,035	139,325	44.8	32.8	108.5
20 to 24	429,094	251,228	163,532	68.0	51.5	147.5
25 to 29	234,593	136,727	89,198	56.5	44.6	100.9
30 to 34	123,901	72,484	46,370	38.1	31.1	60.1
35 to 39	48,353	29,607	16,357	18.0	15.2	25.6
40 and over	9,377	6,075	2,670	3.8	3.2	5.4
Total (Ages 15–44) ...	1,213,769	707,502	463,750	45.2	34.6	89.5

[1] Race is determined by race of the child for 1980 and by race of the mother for 1991.

NA: Not available.

Source: The National Center for Health Statistics, Advance Report of Final Natality Statistics, 1991, U.S. Monthly Vital Statistics Report, Vol. 41, No. 9, 1993 and 1980 data.

TABLE G-4.—TWO-PARENT AND ONE-PARENT FAMILIES AS PROPORTIONS OF ALL FAMILIES WITH CHILDREN PRESENT, BY RACE, FOR SELECTED YEARS

Subject	All races 1970	1980	1985	1988	1992	White 1970	1988	1992	Black 1970	1988	1992
					Number in thousands						
Total with children under 18	29,631	32,150	33,372	34,344	35,379	26,115	28,102	28,847	3,219	5,057	5,164
Two-parent family groups	25,823	25,231	24,573	24,977	24,880	23,477	22,012	21,909	2,071	2,055	1,948
One-parent family groups	3,808	6,920	8,779	9,367	10,499	2,638	6,090	6,938	1,148	3,002	3,216
Maintained by mother	3,415	6,230	7,737	8,146	9,028	2,330	5,100	5,753	1,063	2,812	2,994
Never married	248	1,063	2,208	2,707	3,284	73	1,050	1,391	173	1,605	1,799
Spouse absent	1,377	1,743	1,732	1,776	1,947	796	1,127	1,341	570	585	548
Separated	962	1,483	1,524	1,499	1,658	477	941	1,146	479	515	482
Divorced	1,109	2,721	3,228	3,121	3,349	930	2,568	2,692	172	471	550
Widowed	682	703	569	544	448	531	356	328	148	149	97
Maintained by father	393	692	1,042	1,221	1,472	307	989	1,186	85	191	222
					Percent distribution						
Total with children under 18	100.0	100.0	100.0	100.0	100.0	100.0	100.0	100.0	100.0	100.0	100.0
Two-parent family groups	87.1	78.5	73.6	72.7	70.3	89.9	78.3	75.9	64.3	40.6	37.7
One-parent family groups	12.9	21.5	26.3	27.3	29.7	10.1	21.7	24.1	35.7	59.4	62.3
Maintained by mother	11.5	19.4	23.2	23.7	25.5	8.9	18.1	19.9	33.0	55.6	58.0
Never married	.8	3.3	6.6	9.0	9.3	.3	7.0	4.8	5.4	31.7	34.8
Spouse absent	4.6	5.4	5.2	5.2	5.5	3.0	4.0	4.6	17.7	11.6	10.6
Separated	3.2	4.6	4.6	4.4	4.7	1.8	3.3	4.0	14.9	10.2	9.3
Divorced	3.7	8.5	9.7	9.1	9.5	3.6	9.1	9.3	5.3	9.3	9.3
Widowed	2.3	2.2	1.7	1.6	1.3	2.0	1.3	1.1	4.6	2.9	1.9
Maintained by father	1.3	2.2	3.1	3.6	4.2	1.2	3.5	4.1	2.6	3.8	4.3

Note.—Family groups consist of family households, related subfamilies, and unrelated subfamilies. Numbers may not sum to totals due to rounding.

Source: U.S. Bureau of the Census, Current Population Reports, Series P-20, Household and Family Characteristics: March of Each Year. Washington, U.S. Govt. Print. Off.

TABLE G-5.—LIVING ARRANGEMENTS OF CHILDREN UNDER 18 YEARS: FOR SELECTED YEARS, 1960–92

[Excludes persons under 18 years old who maintain households or family groups]

Living arrangements of children and marital status of parent	All races				
	1960	1970	1980	1990	1992
	Numbers in thousands				
Total number of children	63,727	69,162	63,427	64,137	65,965
Living with:					
Two parents	55,877	58,939	48,624	46,503	46,638
One parent	5,829	8,199	12,466	15,867	17,578
Mother only	5,105	7,452	11,406	13,874	15,396
Father only	724	748	1,060	1,993	2,182
Other relatives or nonrelatives only	2,021	2,024	2,337	1,768	1,749
	Percent distribution				
Percent	100.0	100.0	100.0	100.0	100.0
Living with:					
Two parents	87.7	85.2	76.7	72.5	70.7
One parent	9.1	11.9	19.7	24.7	26.6
Mother only	8.0	10.8	18.0	21.6	23.3
Father only	1.1	1.1	1.7	3.1	3.3
Other relatives or nonrelatives only	3.2	2.9	3.7	2.8	2.6

Note.—Numbers may not sum to totals due to rounding.

Source: U.S. Bureau of the Census. Current Population Reports, Series P–20. Marital Status and Living Arrangements: March of each year. Washington, U.S. Govt. Printing Off.

TABLE G–6.—LIVING ARRANGEMENTS OF CHILDREN UNDER 18 YEARS LIVING WITH ONE
PARENT FOR SELECTED YEARS, 1960–92

[Excludes persons under 18 years old who maintain households or family groups]

Living arrangements of children and marital status of parent	All races				
	1960	1970	1980	1990	1992
	Numbers in thousands				
Total children living with one parent	5,829	8,199	12,466	15,867	17,872
Never married	243	557	1,820	4,853	6,258
Married, spouse absent	2,700	3,521	3,898	3,767	4,214
Separated	1,608	2,484	3,327	3,222	3,605
Widowed	1,543	1,649	1,469	1,125	763
Divorced	1,343	2,473	5,281	6,122	6,637
	Percent distribution				
Percent	100.0	100.0	100.0	100.0	100.0
Never married	4.2	6.8	14.6	30.6	35.0
Married, spouse absent	46.3	42.9	31.3	23.7	23.6
Separated	27.6	30.3	26.7	20.3	20.2
Widowed	26.5	20.1	11.8	7.1	4.3
Divorced	23.0	30.2	42.4	38.6	37.1

Note.—Numbers may not sum to totals due to rounding.

Source: U.S. Bureau of the Census. Current Population Reports, Series P–20. Marital Status and Living Arrangements: March of each year. Washington, U.S. Govt. Printing Off.

TABLE G–7.—LIVING ARRANGEMENTS OF WHITE CHILDREN UNDER 18 YEARS

[Excludes persons under 18 years old who maintain households or family groups; numbers in thousands]

	1960	1970	1980	1990	1992
Total children	55,077	58,790	52,242	51,390	52,493
Living with:					
Two parents	50,082	52,624	43,200	40,593	46,735
One parent	3,932	5,109	7,901	9,870	10,971
Mother only	3,381	4,581	7,059	8,321	9,250
Father only	551	528	842	1,549	1,721
Other relatives or nonrelatives only	1,062	1,058	1,141	928	886
Percent	100.0	100.0	100.0	100.0	100.0
Living with:					
Two parents	90.9	89.5	82.7	79.0	77.4
One parent	7.1	8.7	15.1	19.2	20.9
Mother only	6.1	7.8	13.5	16.2	17.6
Father only	1.0	0.9	1.6	3.0	3.3
Other relatives or nonrelatives only	1.9	1.8	2.2	1.8	1.7
Total children living with one parent	3,932	5,110	7,901	9,869	10,971
Marital status of parent:					
Never married	61	131	552	1,894	2,449
Married, spouse absent	1,615	1,822	2,243	2,356	2,837
Separated	779	1,111	1,817	1,982	2,425
Widowed	1,139	1,160	1,000	774	624
Divorced	1,118	1,997	4,106	4,847	5,061
Percent	100.0	100.0	100.0	100.0	100.0
Marital status of parent:					
Never married	1.6	2.6	7.0	19.2	22.3
Married, spouse absent	41.1	35.7	28.4	23.9	25.9
Separated	19.8	21.7	23.0	20.1	22.1
Widowed	29.0	22.7	12.7	7.8	5.7
Divorced	28.4	39.1	52.0	49.1	46.1

NA Not available.

Source: U.S. Bureau of the Census. Current Population Reports, Series P–20. No. 410, 450, 461 and 468. Marital Status and Living Arrangements: March 1992, 1991, 1990, and 1985. Washington, U.S. Govt. Printing Off. Table prepared by Congressional Research Service.

TABLE G–8.—LIVING ARRANGEMENTS OF BLACK CHILDREN UNDER 18 YEARS

[Excludes persons under 18 years old who maintain households or family groups; numbers in thousands]

	1960	1970	1980	1990	1992
Total children	8,650	9,422	9,375	10,018	10,427
Living with:					
Two parents	5,795	5,508	3,956	3,781	3,714
One parent	1,897	2,996	4,297	5,485	5,934
Mother only	1,723	2,783	4,117	5,132	5,607
Father only	173	213	180	353	327
Other relatives or nonrelatives only	959	917	1,122	752	779
Percent	100.0	100.0	100.0	100.0	100.0
Living with:					
Two parents	67.0	58.5	42.2	37.7	35.6
One parent	21.9	31.8	45.8	54.8	56.9
Mother only	19.9	29.5	43.9	51.2	53.8
Father only	2.0	2.3	1.9	3.5	3.1
Other relatives or nonrelatives only	11.1	9.7	12.0	7.5	7.5
Total children living with one parent	1,897	2,995	4,297	5,484	5,934
Marital status of parent:					
Never married	182	423	1,235	2,839	3,314
Married spouse absent	1,085	1,651	1,573	1,251	1,290
Separated	829	1,343	1,463	1,125	1,156
Widowed	405	482	411	278	194
Divorced	225	438	1,078	1,117	1,136
Percent	100.0	100.0	100.0	100.0	100.0
Marital status of parent:					
Never married	9.6	14.1	28.7	51.8	55.9
Married spouse absent	57.2	55.1	36.6	22.8	21.7
Separated	43.7	44.8	34.0	20.5	19.5
Widowed	21.3	16.1	9.6	5.1	3.3
Divorced	11.9	14.6	25.1	20.4	19.1

NA Not available.

Note.—Black children include nonwhite in 1960.

Source: U.S. Bureau of the Census. Current Population Reports, Series P–20. No. 410, 450, 461 and 468. and Marital Status and Living Arrangements: March 1985, 1990, 1991, and 1992. Washington, U.S. Govt. Printing Off. Table prepared by Congressional Research Service.

TABLE G–9.—LIVING ARRANGEMENTS OF HISPANIC CHILDREN UNDER 18 YEARS

[Excludes persons under 18 years old who maintain households or family groups; numbers in thousands]

	1970	1980	1990	1992
Total children	4,006	5,459	7,174	7,619
Living with:				
Two parents	3,111	4,116	4,789	4,935
One parent	NA	1,152	2,154	2,447
Mother only	NA	1,069	1,943	2,168
Father only	NA	83	211	279
Other relatives or nonrelatives only	NA	191	231	237
Percent	100.0	100.0	100.0	100.0
Living with:				
Two parents	77.7	75.4	66.8	64.8
One parent	NA	21.1	30.0	32.1
Mother only	NA	19.6	27.1	28.5
Father only	NA	1.5	2.9	3.7
Other relatives or nonrelatives only	NA	3.5	3.2	3.1
Total children living with one parent	NA	1,152	2,154	2,447
Marital status of parent:				
Never married	NA	228	703	872
Married, spouse absent	NA	468	728	739
Separated	NA	400	577	600
Widowed	NA	103	149	137
Divorced	NA	353	574	699
Percent	NA	100.0	100.0	100.0
Marital status of parent:				
Never married	NA	19.8	32.6	35.6
Married, spouse absent	NA	40.6	33.8	30.2
Separated	NA	34.7	26.8	24.5
Widowed	NA	8.9	6.9	5.6
Divorced	NA	30.6	26.6	28.6

NA Not available.

Note.—Persons of Hispanic origin may be of any race.

Source: U.S. Bureau of the Census. Current Population Reports, Series P–20. No 410, 450, 461 and 468. Marital Status and Living Arrangements: March 1985, 1990, 1991, and 1992. Washington, U.S. Govt. Printing Off. Table prepared by Congressional Research Service.

TABLE G–10.—CHILDREN UNDER 18 YEARS OF AGE LIVING WITH BIOLOGICAL, STEP, AND ADOPTIVE MARRIED-COUPLE PARENTS, BY RACE OF MOTHER, 1980–90

[Numbers in thousands]

Category	1980		1990	
	Number	Percent	Number	Percent
All races:				
Total own children under 18 years	47,248	100.0	45,448	100.0
Biological mother and father	39,523	83.7	37,026	81.5
Biological mother-stepfather	5,355	11.3	6,643	14.6
Stepmother-biological father	727	1.5	608	1.3
Adoptive mother and father	1,350	2.9	974	2.1
Unknown mother or father	293	0.6	197	0.4
White:				
Total own children under 18 years	42,329	100.0	39,732	100.0
Biological mother and father	35,852	84.7	32,975	83.0
Biological mother-stepfather	4,362	10.3	5,258	13.2
Stepmother-biological father	664	1.6	549	1.4
Adoptive mother and father	1,209	2.9	815	2.1
Unknown mother or father	242	0.6	135	0.3
Black:				
Total own children under 18 years	3,775	100.0	3,671	100.0
Biological mother and father	2,698	71.5	2,336	63.6
Biological mother-stepfather	877	23.2	1,149	31.3
Stepmother-biological father	46	1.2	38	1.0
Adoptive mother and father	119	3.1	97	2.6
Unknown mother or father	35	0.9	51	1.4
Hispanic origin: [1]				
Total own children under 18 years	NA	NA	4,568	100.0
Biological mother and father	NA	NA	3,703	81.1
Biological mother-stepfather	NA	NA	699	15.3
Stepmother-biological father	NA	NA	38	0.8
Adoptive mother and father	NA	NA	101	2.2
Unknown mother or father	NA	NA	27	0.6

NA: Not available.

[1] Persons of Hispanic origin may be of any race.

Source: U.S. Bureau of the Census, Current Population Reports, P23–180, "Marriage, Divorce, and Remarriage in the 1990's," U.S. Government Printing Office, Washington, D.C., 1992.

TABLE G–11.—PERSONS LIVING IN MOTHER-ONLY FAMILIES BY MOTHER'S MARITAL STATUS, FAMILY LIVING ARRANGEMENT, AND FAMILY POVERTY STATUS, 1992[1]

[In thousands of persons]

Family type defined by mother's marital status	Total	Family living arrangement			
		Independent families	Extended families	Cohabiting [1]	Unrelated families
Number of persons:					
Total	26,609	18,455	4,379	2,240	1,535
Never-married	9,351	5,555	2,465	910	420
Separated/other	6,097	4,725	815	262	296
Divorced	9,912	7,226	945	1,006	734
Widowed	1,248	948	155	61	84
Number of poor persons:					
Total	13,001	9,524	1,463	1,281	733
Never-married	5,806	3,963	936	639	269
Separated/other	3,357	2,744	302	141	170
Divorced	3,472	2,554	182	475	261
Widowed	365	263	43	26	32
Poverty rate (percent poor):					
Total	48.9	51.6	33.4	57.2	47.7
Never-married	62.1	71.3	38.0	70.2	63.9
Separated/other	55.1	58.1	37.1	53.9	57.6
Divorced	35.0	35.3	19.2	47.2	35.6
Widowed	29.3	27.8	28.0	(3)	38.4
Number of families:					
Total	9,339	6,134	1,799	865	541
Never-married	3,448	1,879	1,063	354	152
Separated/other	1,974	1,465	303	102	104
Divorced	3,497	2,483	373	386	256
Widowed	420	308	60	23	29

[1] The CPS defines families on the basis of marital and blood relations, and treats families as a basic economic unit in its measures of family poverty and income. Under such definitions, an unmarried, cohabiting, couple would be viewed as two distinct economic units; either as two unrelated individuals, if no child dependents were involved, or as one or two single-parent families, if one or both members of the couple had children residing in the household. Cohabiting couples are identifiable on the CPS only by inference. The Census Bureau identifies such families as unmarried couple households—a household with only two adults who are unrelated and of the opposite sex (one of whom is the householder) with or without the presence of children under the age of 15. The CPS assigns a residing child to only one of the two adult members of the unmarried couple, even though the child may be the couple's offspring.

[2] Single female-headed families (either primary or unrelated subfamilies) with children, living in a household with either an unrelated single adult male, or with an unrelated family headed by a single adult male.   [3] Base of estimate less than 75,000. Estimate deemed to be unreliable.

Note.—Details may not sum to totals due to rounding. Numbers are estimates subject to sampling error. Caution should be exercised in interpreting differences based on small cell sizes. Percentages with a base of less than 75,000 are suppressed due to large sampling error. Marital status and family living arrangements are for the family head, as of March 1993. Poverty status is based on family income in the prior year (1992).

Source: Table prepared by Congressional Research Service (CRS), based on analysis of the March 1993 Current Population Survey (CPS) microdata files.

TABLE G-12.—PERSONS LIVING IN MOTHER-ONLY FAMILIES BY MOTHERS' MARITAL STATUS, FAMILY LIVING ARRANGEMENTS, AND FAMILY POVERTY STATUS—1987

[In thousands of persons]

Family type defined by mother's marital status	Total	Family living arrangement			Unrelated families
		Independent families	Extended families	Cohabiting[1]	
Number of persons:					
Total	23,497	16,655	4,279	1,502	1,061
Never-married	7,210	4,116	2,325	485	284
Separated/other	5,607	4,333	894	190	191
Divorced	8,808	6,699	840	747	521
Widowed	1,872	1,507	221	80	65
Number of poor persons:					
Total	11,360	8,437	1,600	813	510
Never-married	4,553	3,052	1,005	319	178
Separated/other	3,283	2,675	347	121	141
Divorced	2,913	2,232	167	341	173
Widowed	610	478	82	32	18
Poverty rate (percent poor):					
Total	48.3	50.7	37.4	54.1	48.1
Never-married	63.1	74.2	43.2	65.7	62.4
Separated/other	58.6	61.7	38.8	63.8	73.8
Divorced	33.1	33.3	19.8	45.7	33.3
Widowed	32.6	31.7	37.2	40.0	(2)
Number of families:					
Total	8,190	5,509	1,702	590	388
Never-married	2,689	1,391	979	203	116
Separated/other	1,786	1,334	320	69	64
Divorced	3,127	2,322	331	290	184
Widowed	588	462	73	29	24

[1] Single female-headed families (either primary or unrelated subfamilies) with children, living in a household with either an unrelated single adult male, or with an unrelated family headed by a single adult male.

[2] Base of estimate less than 75,000. Estimate deemed to be unreliable.

Note.—Details may not sum to totals due to rounding. Numbers are estimates subject to sampling error. Caution should be exercised in interpreting differences based on small cell sizes. Percentages with a base of less than 75,000 are suppressed due to large sampling error. Material status and family living arrangements are for the family head, as of March 1988. Poverty status is based on family income in the prior year (1987).

Source: Table prepared by CRS, based on analysis of the March 1988 CPS microdata files.

TABLE G–13.—CHANGE IN NUMBER OF PERSONS AND POOR PERSONS LIVING IN MOTH-ER-ONLY FAMILIES BY MOTHERS' MARITAL STATUS AND FAMILY LIVING ARRANGE-MENT, 1987 TO 1992

[In thousands of persons]

Family type defined by mother's marital status	Family living arrangement				
	Total	Inde-pendent families	Extended families	Cohabit-ing [1]	Unrelated families
Change in number of persons:					
Total	3,112	1,800	100	738	474
Never-married	2,141	1,439	141	425	136
Separated/other	490	392	−79	72	105
Divorced	1,104	527	104	260	213
Widowed	−624	−558	−66	−19	20
Change in number of poor persons:					
Total	1,641	1,087	−138	469	222
Never-married	1,253	911	−69	320	91
Separated/other	73	69	−45	20	29
Divorced	559	322	15	134	88
Widowed	−245	−215	−39	−6	14
Change in poverty rate (percent poor):					
Total	0.5	0.9	−4.0	3.1	−0.3
Never-married	−1.1	−2.8	−5.3	4.5	1.4
Separated/other	−3.5	−3.7	−1.7	−9.9	−16.2
Divorced	2.0	2.0	−0.6	−1.6	2.3
Widowed	−3.3	−3.9	−9.3	(2)	(2)

[1] Single female-headed families (either primary or unrelated subfamilies) with children, living in a household with either an unrelated single adult male, or with an unrelated family headed by a single adult male.

[2] Base of either estimate in difference is less than 75,000. Estimate deemed to be unreliable.

Note.—Details may not sum to totals due to rounding. Numbers are estimates subject to sampling error. Caution should be exercised in interpreting differences based on small cell sizes. Statistically signifi-cant changes at the 90 percent or better confidence interval are indicated by **bold** cells.

Source: Table prepared by CRS, based on analysis of the March 1993 and March 1988 (revised format) CPS microdata files.

TABLE G—14.—BIRTHS AND BIRTH RATES, BY RACE OF CHILD, AND BY RACE OF MOTHER,[1] SELECTED YEARS

Year	Total births				Birth rate[2]			
			All other				All other	
	All races	White	Total	Black	All races	White	Total	Black
1940	2,559,000	2,199,000	360,000	....	19.4	18.6	26.7	....
1950	3,632,000	3,108,000	524,000	....	24.1	23.0	33.3	....
1960	4,257,850	3,600,744	657,106	602,264	23.7	22.7	32.1	31.9
1970	3,731,386	3,091,264	640,122	572,362	18.4	17.4	25.1	25.3
1975	3,144,198	2,551,996	592,202	511,581	14.6	13.6	21.0	20.7
1980	3,612,258	2,898,732	713,526	589,616	15.9	14.9	22.5	22.1
1985	3,760,561	2,991,373	769,188	608,193	15.8	14.8	21.4	21.3
1986	3,756,547	2,970,439	786,108	621,221	15.6	14.6	21.4	21.5
1987	3,809,394	2,992,488	816,906	641,567	15.7	14.6	21.8	21.9
1988	3,909,510	3,046,162	863,348	671,976	16.0	14.8	22.5	22.6
1989	4,040,958	3,131,991	908,967	709,395	16.4	15.1	23.1	23.5
1990	4,158,212	3,290,273	867,939	684,336	16.7	15.8	21.7	22.4
1991	4,110,907	3,241,273	869,634	682,602	16.3	15.4	21.1	21.9

[1] Race is determined by race of the child for 1940 through 1989 and by raced the mother for 1990 and 1991.
[2] The birth rate is defined as the number of births per 1,000 of the population.

Source: National Center for Health Statistics. Advance report of final natality statistics, 1991. Monthly Vital Statistics Report, Vol. 42, No. 3 Suppl. DHHS, Hyattsville, MD, 1993.

TABLE G-15.—NUMBERS AND RATES OF BIRTHS, ABORTIONS, AND PREGNANCIES, BY AGE AT PREGNANCY OUTCOME,[1] ACCORDING TO YEAR, 1972–91

Year	Female population (thousands)	Total number				Rate (per 1,000 females)		
		Births	Induced abortions	Estimated miscarriages[2]	Pregnancies[3]	Birth	Abortion	Pregnancy
Women ages 15 to 19:								
1991	8,371	519,577	NA	NA	NA	62.1	NA	NA
1990	8,645	521,826	350,970	139,460	1,012,260	60.4	40.6	117.1
1989	8,840	506,503	370,900	136,390	1,015,790	57.3	42.0	114.9
1988	9,029	478,353	392,720	134,940	1,006,010	53.0	43.5	11.4
1987	9,139	462,312	381,640	130,630	974,580	50.6	41.8	106.6
1986	9,206	461,905	389,240	131,310	982,450	50.2	42.3	106.7
1985	9,174	467,485	399,200	133,420	100,110	51.0	43.5	109.0
1984	9,287	469,682	398,870	133,830	1,002,370	50.6	42.9	107.9
1983	9,515	489,286	411,330	138,990	1,039,600	51.4	43.2	109.3
1982	9,809	513,758	418,740	144,620	1,077,120	52.4	42.7	109.8
1981	10,096	527,392	433,330	148,810	1,109,540	52.2	42.9	109.9
1980	10,381	552,161	444,780	154,910	1,151,850	53.2	42.8	111.0
1979	10,497	549,472	444,600	154,350	1,146,430	52.3	42.4	109.4
1978	10,555	543,407	418,790	150,560	1,112,760	51.5	39.7	105.4
1977	10,581	559,154	396,630	151,500	1,107,290	52.8	37.5	104.6
1976	10,582	558,744	362,680	148,020	1,069,440	52.8	34.3	101.1
1975	10,466	582,238	326,780	149,130	1,058,160	55.6	31.2	101.1
1974	10,350	595,449	279,700	147,060	1,022,220	57.5	27.0	98.8
1973	10,193	604,096	231,900	144,010	980,000	59.3	22.8	96.1
1972	9,988	616,280	191,000	142,360	949,640	61.7	19.1	95.1
Women under age 15:[4]								
1991	1,661	12,014	NA	NA	NA	7.2	NA	NA
1990	1,593	11,657	12,580	3,590	27,830	7.3	7.9	17.5
1989	1,608	11,486	12,750	3,570	27,810	7.1	7.9	17.3
1988	1,573	10,588	13,650	3,480	27,720	6.7	8.7	17.6
1987	1,613	10,311	14,270	3,490	28,000	6.4	8.8	17.4
1986	1,706	10,176	15,690	3,600	29,470	6.0	9.2	17.3
1985	1,853	10,220	16,970	3,740	30,930	5.5	9.2	16.7
1984	1,819	9,965	16,920	3,690	30,570	5.5	9.3	16.8

1983	1,781	9,752	16,350	3,590	29,690	5.5	9.2	16.7
1982	1,748	9,773	14,590	3,410	27,770	5.6	8.3	15.9
1981	1,787	9,632	15,240	3,450	28,320	5.4	8.5	15.8
1980	1,850	10,169	15,340	3,570	29,080	5.5	8.4	15.9
1979	1,944	10,699	16,220	3,760	30,680	5.5	8.3	15.8
1978	2,020	10,772	15,110	3,670	29,550	5.3	7.5	14.6
1977	2,048	11,455	15,650	3,860	30,970	5.6	7.6	15.1
1976	2,080	11,928	15,820	3,960	31,710	5.7	7.6	15.2
1975	2,118	11,642	15,260	4,050	31,950	6.0	7.2	15.1
1974	2,086	12,642	15,420	3,850	29,800	6.0	6.4	14.3
1973	2,094	12,529	13,420	3,740	28,230	6.1	5.6	13.5
1972	2,093	12,861	11,630	NA	NA	5.8	NA	NA
1972		12,082						
Women ages 15 to 17:								
1991	4,860	188,225	NA	NA	NA	38.7	NA	NA
1990	4,881	183,327	129,820	49,650	362,800	37.6	26.6	74.3
1989	4,974	181,044	139,130	50,120	370,290	36.4	26.0	74.4
1988	5,251	176,624	158,330	51,160	386,110	33.6	30.2	73.5
1987	5,450	172,591	161,120	50,630	384,340	31.7	29.6	70.5
1986	5,520	168,572	165,240	50,240	384,050	30.5	29.9	69.6
1985	5,409	167,789	165,630	50,120	383,540	31.0	30.6	70.9
1984	5,373	166,744	160,900	49,440	377,080	31.0	29.9	70.2
1983	5,424	172,673	166,440	51,180	390,290	31.8	30.7	72.0
1982	5,618	181,162	168,410	53,070	402,640	31.8	30.0	71.7
1981	5,848	187,397	175,930	55,070	418,400	32.2	30.1	71.5
1980	6,063	198,222	183,350	57,980	439,550	32.0	30.2	72.5
1979	6,200	200,137	178,570	57,880	436,590	32.7	28.8	70.4
1978	6,286	202,661	169,270	57,460	429,390	32.3	26.9	68.3
1977	6,310	213,788	165,610	59,320	438,720	32.2	26.2	69.5
1976	6,319	215,493	152,700	58,370	426,560	33.9	24.2	67.5
1975	6,288	238,403	151,630	60,620	439,530	34.1	24.1	69.9
1974	6,276	234,177	139,850	60,820	434,860	36.1	22.3	69.3
1973	6,185	238,403	115,950	59,280	413,630	37.3	18.7	66.9
1972	6,071	236,641	95,500	56,880	389,020	38.5	15.7	64.1
						39.0		
Women ages 18 to 19:								
1991	3,510	331,351	NA	NA	NA	94.4	NA	NA
1990	3,762	338,499	221,150	89,810	649,460	90.0	58.8	172.6
1989	3,865	325,459	231,770	88,270	645,500	84.2	60.0	167.0
1988	3,778	301,729	234,390	83,780	619,900	79.9	62.0	164.1
1987	3,689	289,721	220,520	80,000	590,240	78.5	59.8	160.0
1986	3,686	293,333	224,000	81,070	598,400	79.6	60.8	162.3

TABLE G-15.—NUMBERS AND RATES OF BIRTHS, ABORTIONS, AND PREGNANCIES, BY AGE AT PREGNANCY OUTCOME,[1] ACCORDING TO YEAR, 1972-91

Year	Female population (thousands)	Total number				Rate (per 1,000 females)		
		Births	Induced abortions	Estimated miscarriages[2]	Pregnancies[3]	Birth	Abortion	Pregnancy
1985	3,765	299,696	233,570	83,300	616,570	79.6	62.0	163.8
1984	3,914	302,938	237,970	84,390	625,290	77.4	60.8	159.8
1983	4,092	316,613	244,890	87,810	649,310	77.4	59.8	158.7
1982	4,191	332,596	250,330	91,550	674,480	79.4	59.7	160.9
1981	4,248	339,995	257,400	93,740	691,140	80.0	60.6	162.7
1980	4,313	353,939	261,430	96,930	712,300	81.9	60.5	164.9
1979	4,297	349,335	266,030	96,470	711,840	81.3	61.9	165.7
1978	4,269	340,746	249,520	93,100	683,370	79.8	58.4	160.1
1977	4,271	345,366	231,020	92,180	668,570	80.9	54.1	156.5
1976	4,263	343,251	209,980	89,650	642,880	80.5	49.3	150.8
1975	4,178	354,968	175,150	88,510	618,630	85.0	41.9	148.1
1974	4,074	361,272	139,850	86,240	587,360	88.7	34.3	144.2
1973	4,008	365,693	115,950	84,730	566,370	91.2	28.9	141.3
1972	3,917	379,639	95,500	85,480	560,620	96.9	24.4	143.1

[1] Women's age is determined by the time the pregnancy ended. More pregnancies were experienced by teenagers than are reported here because most of the 19-year-olds who became pregnant had their births or abortions at age 20 and thus were not counted. [2] Calculated as 20 percent of births and 10 percent of abortions. [3] Sum of births, abortions and miscarriages. [4] Population is women aged 14.

NA: data not available.

Source: Stanley Henshaw, The Alan Guttmacher Institute, 120 Wall Street, New York, New York 10005, based on the following sources: Population: 1972–1979: U.S. Bureau of the Census, "Preliminary Estimates of the Population of the United States, by Age, Sex and Race: 1970–1981," Current Population Reports (CPR), P–25, No. 917, 1982, Table 2. 1980–1991: U.S. Bureau of the Census, "U.S. Population Estimates, by Age, Sex, Race and Hispanic Origin: 1980 to 1991," CPR, P–25, No. 1095, 1993, Table 1. Births: 1991: National Center for Health Statistics (NCHS), "Advance Report of Final Natality Statistics," Monthly Vital Statistics Report (MVSR), Table 2. Abortions: 1972: Centers for Disease Control, Abortion Surveillance 1972, Atlanta, 1974. 1973–1988: S.K. Henshaw and J. Van Vort Abortion Factbook, 1992 Edition; Readings, Trends, and State and Local Data to 1988, The Alan Guttmacher Institute, New York, 1992, Table 1, p. 172. 1989–1990: Unpublished data based on an estimate of 1,566,870 abortions in 1989 and 1,608,620 in 1990.

TABLE G–16.—NUMBER OF BIRTHS AND BIRTH RATES TO WOMEN AGES 15 TO 19, BY RACE OF CHILD AND BY RACE OF MOTHER,[1] 1960 TO 1991

Year	Number of births, all women under 20		Birth rate [2]					
	White	Black	All women 15 to 19		15 to 17		18 to 19	
			White	Black	White	Black	White	Black
1960	460,654	122,260	79.4	156.1	....	....	....	....
1961	474,514	....	79.2	155.2	....	....	....	....
1962	462,522	....	73.2	147.1	....	....	....	....
1963	445,892	....	68.2	142.6	....	....	....	....
1964	447,034	140,422	63.4	147.6	....	....	....	....
1965	446,198	146,268	60.6	144.6	....	....	....	....
1966	467,778	155,110	60.4	142.7	26.6	97.9	108.2	219.2
1967	438,000	160,285	58.9	141.8	25.7	99.5	104.0	213.4
1968	429,616	163,892	54.9	138.7	25.6	98.2	100.5	206.1
1969	437,958	168,588	54.7	137.0	26.4	96.9	99.2	202.5
1970	467,928	179,100	57.4	140.7	29.2	101.4	101.5	204.9
1971	450,856	178,948	53.6	134.5	28.5	99.4	92.3	192.6
1972	438,559	179,712	51.0	129.8	29.3	99.5	84.3	179.5
1973	429,740	176,551	49.0	123.1	29.2	96.0	79.3	166.6
1974	425,205	171,721	47.9	116.5	28.7	90.0	77.3	158.7
1975	415,202	168,359	46.4	111.8	28.0	85.6	74.0	152.4
1976	389,329	160,597	44.1	104.9	26.3	80.3	70.2	142.5
1977	396,854	161,772	44.1	104.7	26.1	79.6	70.5	142.9
1978	384,572	157,069	42.9	100.9	24.9	75.0	69.4	139.7
1979	388,209	158,944	43.7	101.7	24.7	75.7	71.0	140.4
1980	392,229	156,146	44.7	100.0	25.2	73.6	72.1	138.8
1981	373,983	148,703	44.3	96.5	25.1	70.4	70.4	134.4
1982	362,101	145,929	44.3	96.4	25.1	70.8	69.7	132.4
1983	342,183	142,105	43.3	95.8	24.7	70.6	67.7	130.2
1984	324,912	140,112	42.2	96.1	23.9	70.4	67.3	131.3
1985	322,826	140,130	42.5	97.9	24.0	70.7	69.2	136.4
1986	315,335	141,606	41.5	98.8	23.3	71.1	68.7	140.0
1987	312,108	144,853	41.5	101.1	24.0	74.2	67.3	141.4
1988	319,544	152,508	43.2	106.9	25.3	78.1	67.8	149.4
1989	335,731	163,609	46.6	116.2	27.4	84.4	70.9	159.4
1990	359,456	157,951	50.8	112.8	29.5	82.3	78.0	152.9
1991	357,548	157,375	52.8	115.5	30.7	84.1	83.5	158.6

[1] Race is determined by race of the child for 1960 through 1989 and by race of the mother for 1990 and 1991.
[2] Births per 1,000 women in the age group.

Sources: National Center for Health Statistics. Vital Statistics of the United States, 1989, Natality, 1993; previous issues of this annual report. National Center for Health Statistics, Advance Report of Final Natality Statistics, 1991 (Monthly Vital Statistics Report, Vol. 42, No. 3, Suppl., 1993).

TABLE G–17.—ESTIMATED BIRTH RATES FOR UNMARRIED WOMEN AGES 15–19, BY RACE OF CHILD AND BY RACE OF MOTHER [1]: 1966 TO 1991

[Births per 1,000 women]

Year	White		Black	
	15 to 17	18 to 19	15 to 17	18 to 19
1966	5.4	14.1	....	....
1970	7.5	17.6	77.9	136.4
1975	9.6	16.5	76.8	123.8
1980	11.8	23.6	69.6	120.2
1985	14.2	30.4	67.9	120.4
1986	14.5	32.7	68.4	124.3
1987	15.8	33.5	71.6	126.8
1988	17.1	35.7	75.6	135.1
1989	18.7	38.9	80.9	146.2
1990	20.4	44.9	78.8	143.7
1991	21.8	49.6	80.4	148.7

[1] Race is determined by race of the child for 1966 through 1989 and by race of the mother for 1990 and 1991.

Note.—For 1966–75, births to unmarried women are estimated for the United States from the data for registration areas in which marital status of mother was reported. Beginning 1980, data for states in which marital status was not reported have been inferred and included with data from the remaining states.

Source: National Center for Health Statistics. Vital Statistics of the United States, 1989, Volume I, Natality, 1993. National Center for Health Statistics. Advance Report of Final Natality Statistics, 1991 (Monthly Vital Statistics Report, Vol 42, No. 3, Suppl., 1993).

TABLE G–18.—ESTIMATED PREGNANCIES[1] PER 1,000 WOMEN AGED 15–19, BY RACE

	1980			1985			1988		
	Total	White	Black	Total	White	Nonwhite	Total	White	Nonwhite
Alabama	117	NA	NA	112	NA	NA	110	NA	NA
Alaska	124	NA	NA	144	NA	NA	111	NA	NA
Arizona	123	115	195	128	124	150	127	122	160
Arkansas	117	104	168	111	99	150	115	99	168
California	140	127	272	151	NA	NA	154	NA	NA
Colorado	114	105	192	112	107	187	102	98	148
Connecticut	81	NA	NA	96	NA	NA	107	NA	NA
Delaware	106	NA	NA	101	NA	NA	117	NA	NA
District of Columbia	200	NA	NA	211	NA	NA	209	NA	NA
Florida	131	NA	NA	126	NA	NA	133	NA	NA
Georgia	131	111	172	132	115	160	122	98	171
Hawaii	106	81	NA	125	97	137	134	96	149
Idaho	96	96	NA	78	77	NA	73	73	NA
Illinois	101	78	190	103	NA	NA	112	NA	NA
Indiana	102	92	193	87	77	170	89	54	134
Iowa	79	NA	NA	67	NA	NA	69	NA	NA
Kansas	101	93	199	84	78	150	88	79	178
Kentucky	111	NA	NA	92	NA	NA	96	NA	NA
Louisiana	118	93	163	109	88	142	107	79	153
Maine	87	86	NA	92	91	NA	82	81	NA
Maryland	123	103	174	121	94	184	129	92	204
Massachusetts	86	NA	NA	97	NA	NA	97	NA	NA
Michigan	102	NA	NA	107	NA	NA	111	NA	NA
Minnesota	77	73	240	62	55	222	69	60	195
Mississippi	125	97	162	113	90	138	106	77	142
Missouri	106	92	205	95	79	195	99	78	220
Montana	93	85	NA	82	74	NA	74	64	NA
Nebraska	81	NA	NA	75	NA	NA	75	NA	NA
Nevada	144	134	226	125	118	168	142	134	190
New Hampshire	81	NA	NA	89	NA	NA	87	NA	NA

TABLE G-18.—ESTIMATED PREGNANCIES [1] PER 1,000 WOMEN AGED 15–19, BY RACE—Continued

	1980			1985			1988		
	Total	White	Black	Total	White	Nonwhite	Total	White	Nonwhite
New Jersey	96	74	210	113	70	296	112	30	107
New Mexico	126	118	NA	116	115	126	124	122	140
New York	101	78	207	117	89	225	116	89	199
North Carolina	110	92	153	114	97	152	122	99	177
North Dakota	75	68	NA	60	53	NA	57	49	NA
Ohio	101	88	190	96	83	177	96	51	136
Oklahoma	120	107	187	113	NA	NA	105	62	123
Oregon	119	112	NA	95	94	119	105	103	128
Pennsylvania	90	NA	NA	87	NA	NA	87	NA	NA
Rhode Island	83	98	NA	89	NA	NA	86	NA	NA
South Carolina	114	98	140	102	92	117	114	93	148
South Dakota	86	74	NA	70	57	NA	69	55	NA
Tennessee	113	102	157	104	95	134	110	93	177
Texas	137	NA	NA	131	NA	NA	117	NA	NA
Utah	95	94	NA	75	73	NA	69	67	NA
Vermont	95	94	NA	82	83	NA	81	81	NA
Virginia	107	94	152	106	93	141	106	89	156
Washington	122	NA	NA	103	97	165	109	103	157
West Virginia	104	NA	NA	87	NA	NA	78	NA	NA
Wisconsin	85	NA	NA	73	NA	NA	74	NA	NA
Wyoming	127	NA	NA	98	NA	NA	82	NA	NA
Total	111	NA	NA	110	93	NA	NA	NA	NA

[1] Pregnancy Rates are calculated as the sum of 1.2×the birth rate and 1.1×the abortion rate.

NA: Data not available.

Source: Lotus Diskettes, Child Tends, Inc., Washington, D.C. March, 1994.

TABLE G–19.—ABORTIONS PER 1,000 WOMEN AGED 15–19, BY RACE, BASED ON STATE OF RESIDENCE

	1980			1985			1988		
	Total	White	Black	Total	White	Black	Total	White	Black
Alabama	32	NA	NA	32	NA	NA	32	NA	NA
Alaska	43	NA	NA	59	NA	NA	38	NA	NA
Arizona	41	39	41	43	46	27	40	42	25
Arkansas	25	26	23	23	23	21	27	27	30
California	69	60	150	79	NA	NA	76	NA	NA
Colorado	49	43	76	51	49	84	39	38	50
Connecticut	40	NA	NA	52	NA	NA	58	NA	NA
Delaware	40	NA	NA	37	NA	NA	49	NA	NA
District of Columbia	114	NA	NA	113	NA	NA	110	NA	NA
Florida	55	NA	NA	51	NA	NA	52	NA	NA
Georgia	41	42	36	44	42	46	37	32	45
Hawaii	41	40	NA	61	59	62	68	58	71
Idaho	23	23	NA	21	21	NA	17	18	8
Illinois	31	25	40	38	NA	NA	43	NA	NA
Indiana	30	27	53	24	21	47	25	NA	NA
Iowa	25	NA	NA	25	NA	NA	27	NA	NA
Kansas	30	29	44	23	23	28	27	25	38
Kentucky	22	NA	NA	16	NA	NA	22	20	46
Louisiana	24	22	28	22	21	24	23	21	26
Maine	27	27	NA	36	36	NA	30	29	63
Maryland	64	59	76	59	51	77	61	49	87
Massachusetts	47	NA	NA	45	NA	NA	53	NA	NA
Michigan	44	NA	NA	50	NA	NA	49	NA	NA
Minnesota	31	31	81	24	23	47	29	28	49

TABLE G-19.—ABORTIONS PER 1,000 WOMEN AGED 15–19, BY RACE, BASED ON STATE OF RESIDENCE—Continued

	1980			1985			1988		
	Total	White	Black	Total	White	Black	Total	White	Black
Mississippi	22	27	16	19	22	15	16	17	15
Missouri	34	29	61	29	25	55	30	23	72
Montana	32	32	NA	28	29	NA	24	25	16
Nebraska	24	NA	NA	27	NA	NA	27	NA	NA
Nevada	67	67	66	57	58	45	59	60	49
New Hampshire	37	NA	NA	46	NA	NA	43	NA	NA
New Jersey	49	41	85	63	38	170	60	NA	NA
New Mexico	36	35	NA	30	33	12	35	36	24
New York	54	42	107	64	49	120	61	47	107
North Carolina	38	35	43	41	38	48	45	40	57
North Dakota	23	22	NA	17	18	NA	18	19	13
Ohio	35	30	64	33	28	59	31	NA	NA
Oklahoma	27	27	32	29	NA	NA	27	NA	NA
Oregon	52	49	NA	41	41	37	43	43	47
Pennsylvania	38	NA	NA	35	NA	NA	34	NA	NA
Rhode Island	40	NA	NA	40	NA	NA	36	NA	NA
South Carolina	33	36	27	26	30	20	33	33	33
South Dakota	21	20	NA	18	18	NA	15	16	3
Tennessee	33	33	33	29	29	31	31	27	42
Texas	44	NA	NA	39	NA	NA	31	30	38

Utah	15	14	NA	15	14	NA	15	14	32
Vermont	43	43	NA	36	36	NA	37	37	26
Virginia	45	44	48	45	43	49	46	42	59
Washington	60	NA	NA	46	44	62	47	45	61
West Virginia	20	NA	NA	19	NA	NA	17	NA	NA
Wisconsin	34	NA	NA	25	NA	NA	26	NA	NA
Wyoming	29	NA	NA	30	NA	NA	23	NA	NA
Total	43	38	NA	44	38	71	NA	NA	NA

NA: Data not available.

Source: Lotus Diskettes, Child Trends, Inc., Washington, D.C., March 1994.

TABLE G-20.—BIRTH RATES PER 1,000 WOMEN AGED 15-19, BY RACE

	1980			1985			1990		
	Total	White	Black	Total	White	Black	Total	White	Black
Alabama	68	53	103	64	51	94	71	55	105
Alaska	64	48	123	56	42	82	65	54	91
Arizona	66	60	124	67	61	122	76	72	115
Arkansas	75	63	118	73	61	120	80	66	132
California	53	51	89	53	50	93	71	74	101
Colorado	50	48	91	48	46	88	55	52	106
Connecticut	31	24	90	31	24	93	39	31	103
Delaware	51	37	110	51	36	116	55	37	120
District of Columbia	62	16	74	72	17	89	93	12	121
Florida	59	43	126	58	43	121	69	53	135
Georgia	72	54	110	68	53	98	76	57	116
Hawaii	51	31	143	48	27	107	61	42	68
Idaho	60	59	NA	47	45	65	51	50	58
Illinois	56	41	122	51	35	119	63	44	144
Indiana	58	52	112	52	46	110	59	52	122
Iowa	43	41	126	35	33	101	41	39	119
Kansas	57	51	125	52	47	112	56	51	132
Kentucky	72	69	107	63	61	91	68	64	116
Louisiana	76	58	110	72	53	108	74	52	112
Maine	47	47	NA	42	42	54	43	43	91
Maryland	43	31	76	46	32	82	53	36	96
Massachusetts	28	26	74	29	26	76	35	31	90
Michigan	45	37	92	43	35	86	59	43	131
Minnesota	35	33	126	31	27	129	36	31	152
Mississippi	84	56	120	76	52	109	81	56	113
Missouri	58*	50	115	54	45	119	63	50	144
Montana	49	42	NA	44	35	114	48	40	72
Nebraska	45	41	117	40	34	129	42	37	135
Nevada	59	50	128	55	47	122	73	69	129
New Hampshire	34	33	NA	32	33	26	33	33	46

New Jersey	35	23	97	34	22	94	41	28	100
New Mexico	72	66	107	73	68	104	78	76	95
New York	35	26	74	36	28	74	44	37	76
North Carolina	58	45	88	57	45	85	68	52	107
North Dakota	42	36	NA	36	30	92	35	29	65
Ohio	53	46	100	50	42	104	58	48	129
Oklahoma	75	64	126	69	60	113	67	60	116
Oregon	51	49	114	43	42	95	55	54	108
Pennsylvania	41	35	91	40	32	106	45	35	125
Rhode Island	33	30	96	36	31	116	44	39	114
South Carolina	65	49	92	63	47	91	71	54	101
South Dakota	53	43	NA	46	34	156	47	35	75
Tennessee	64	55	100	61	52	100	72	60	121
Texas	74	68	112	72	68	104	75	71	114
Utah	65	65	97	50	49	110	49	48	110
Vermont	40	40	NA	36	36	11	34	34	33
Virginia	48	38	82	46	36	82	53	41	99
Washington	47	44	97	45	41	102	53	52	94
West Virginia	68	67	80	54	54	67	57	57	74
Wisconsin	40	35	128	39	31	148	43	31	175
Wyoming	79	77	NA	59	56	138	56	55	99
Total	53.0	45	100	51.0	NA	NA	59.9	NA	NA

NA: Data not available.

Source: Lotus Diskettes, Child Trends, Inc., Washington, D.C., March 1994.

TABLE G–21.—PERCENTAGE OF BABIES BORN TO WOMEN OBTAINING EARLY CARE, OR LATE OR NO CARE,[1] BY RACE OF CHILD AND BY RACE OF MOTHER,[2] SELECTED YEARS, 1970–91

Year	Percent born to women obtaining early care			Percent born to women obtaining late or no care		
	White	Black	Total	White	Black	Total
1970	72.4	44.4	68.0	6.2	16.6	7.9
1975	75.9	55.8	72.4	5.0	10.5	6.0
1980	79.3	62.7	76.3	4.3	8.8	5.1
1981	79.4	62.4	76.3	4.3	9.1	5.2
1982	79.3	61.5	76.1	4.5	9.6	5.5
1983	79.4	61.5	76.2	4.6	9.7	5.6
1984	79.6	62.2	76.5	4.7	9.6	5.6
1985	79.4	61.8	76.2	4.7	10.0	5.7
1986	79.2	61.6	75.9	5.0	10.6	6.0
1987	79.4	61.1	76.0	5.0	11.1	6.1
1988	79.4	61.1	75.9	5.0	10.9	6.1
1989	79.0	60.4	75.5	5.2	11.7	6.4
1990	79.2	60.6	75.8	4.9	11.3	6.1
1991	79.5	61.9	76.2	4.7	10.7	5.8

[1] Early care is defined as care received in the first through third month of pregnancy. Late or no care is received in the final trimester, or the seventh through ninth month, or no care received.

[2] Race is determined by race of the child for 1970 through 1989 and by race of the mother for 1990 and 1990.

Source: National Center for Health Statistics. Vital Statistics of the United States, Volume I, Natality (annual issues). National Center for Health Statistics. Advance Report of Final Natality Statistics, 1991 (Monthly Vital Statistics Report, Vol. 42, No. 3, Suppl., 1993).

TABLE G–22.—INFANT, NEONATAL AND POSTNEONATAL MORTALITY RATES BY RACE,[1] FOR SELECTED YEARS, 1940–91

Year	All races	White	All other	
			Total	Black
Infant Mortality Rate [2]				
1940	47.0	43.2	73.8	72.9
1950	29.2	26.8	44.5	43.9
1960	26.0	22.9	43.2	44.3
1970	20.0	17.8	30.9	32.6
1975	16.1	14.2	24.2	26.2
1980	12.6	11.0	19.1	21.4
1985	10.6	9.3	15.8	18.2
1986	10.4	8.9	15.7	18.0
1987	10.1	8.6	15.4	17.9
1988	10.0	8.5	15.0	17.6
1989	9.8	8.1	16.3	18.6
1990	9.2	7.6	15.5	18.0
1991	8.9	7.3	15.1	17.6
Neonatal Mortality Rate [3]				
1940	28.8	27.2	39.7	39.9
1950	20.5	19.4	27.5	27.8
1960	18.7	17.2	26.9	27.8
1970	15.1	13.8	21.4	22.8
1975	11.6	10.4	16.8	18.3
1980	8.5	7.5	12.5	14.1
1985	7.0	6.1	10.3	12.1
1986	6.7	5.8	10.1	11.7
1987	6.5	5.5	10.0	11.7
1988	6.3	5.4	9.7	11.5
1989	6.2	5.1	10.3	11.9
1990	5.8	4.8	9.9	11.6
1991	5.6	4.5	9.5	11.2
Postneonatal Mortality Rate [4]				
1940	18.3	16.0	34.1	33.0
1950	8.7	7.4	16.9	16.1
1960	7.3	5.7	16.4	16.5
1970	4.9	4.0	9.5	9.9
1975	4.5	3.8	7.5	7.9
1980	4.1	3.5	6.6	7.3
1985	3.7	3.2	5.5	6.1
1986	3.6	3.1	5.6	6.3
1987	3.6	3.1	5.4	6.1
1988	3.6	3.1	5.4	6.2
1989	3.6	2.9	6.0	6.7
1990	3.4	2.8	5.7	6.4
1991	3.4	2.8	5.6	6.3

[1] As of 1989, race for live births (the denominator of infant mortality rates) is tabulated according to race of mother. For all prior years, race is tabulated according to race of child.

[2] Deaths before the age of one.

[3] Deaths under 28 days.

[4] Deaths from 28 days to 11 months.

Source: National Center for Health Statistics. Advance report of final mortality statistics, 1991. Monthly Vital Statistics Report, Vol. 42, No. 2 Suppl. DHHS, Hyattsville, MD, 1993.

TABLE G-23.—ACQUIRED IMMUNODEFICIENCY SYNDROME (AIDS) CASES, ACCORDING TO AGE AT DIAGNOSIS, SEX, RACE AND HISPANIC ORIGIN 1985–92

[Data are based on reporting by State health departments]

Age at diagnosis, sex, race, and Hispanic origin	All years[1] Percent distribution	All years[1]	Number, by year of report							
			1985	1986	1987	1988	1989	1990	1991	1992
Total[2]	...	244,939	8,210	13,147	21,088	30,719	33,595	41,653	43,701	45,472
Male										
All males, 13 years and over[2]	100.0	214,981	7,555	12,002	19,082	27,108	29,625	36,378	37,656	38,789
White, not Hispanic	58.0	124,778	4,798	7,527	12,332	16,060	17,509	20,935	20,686	20,740
Black, not Hispanic	27.5	59,083	1,712	2,760	4,321	7,159	8,055	10,292	11,105	12,031
Hispanic	13.4	28,809	987	1,608	2,242	3,648	3,729	4,749	5,431	5,498
Female										
All females, 13 years and over[2]	100.0	25,928	526	962	1,684	3,040	3,374	4,552	5,378	5,940
White, not Hispanic	26.7	6,924	143	268	545	853	949	1,228	1,362	1,457
Black, not Hispanic	56.1	14,538	286	523	896	1,655	1,896	2,543	3,101	3,391
Hispanic	16.2	4,207	93	160	229	500	493	741	862	1,026
Children										
All children under 13 years[2]	100.0	4,030	129	183	322	571	596	723	667	743
White, not Hispanic	21.6	871	27	42	85	150	111	162	145	128
Black, not Hispanic	57.3	2,308	83	105	162	304	342	385	403	468
Hispanic	20.1	811	19	35	72	112	136	168	112	138
Under 1 year	39.7	1,601	54	78	141	193	239	284	248	305
1 to 12 years	60.3	2,429	75	105	181	378	357	439	419	438

[1] Includes cases prior to 1985.   [2] Includes all other races not shown separately.

Note: The AIDS case definition was changed in September 1987 to allow for the presumptive diagnosis of AIDS-associated diseases and conditions and to expand the spectrum of human immunodeficiency virus-associated diseases reportable as AIDS. Excludes residents of U.S. territories. Data are updated periodically because of reporting delays. Data for all years have been updated through December 31, 1992.

Source: National Center for Health Statistics: "Health, United States, 1992," DHHS Pub.No. (PHS) 93–1232. Washington, U.S. Government Printing Office, 1993. Data from Centers for Disease Control and Prevention. National Center for Infectious Diseases, AIDS Program.

TABLE G–24.—TOBACCO, ALCOHOL, AND DRUG USE AMONG HIGH SCHOOL SENIORS, BY SUBSTANCE AND FREQUENCY OF USE, 1975–92

Substance and frequency of use	Class of				
	1975	1980	1985	1989	1992
	Percentage reporting having ever used drugs				
Cigarettes	73.6	71.0	68.8	65.7	61.8
Alcohol	90.4	93.2	92.2	90.7	87.5
Any illicit drug	55.2	65.4	60.6	50.9	40.7
Marijuana only	19.0	26.7	20.9	19.5	15.6
Any illicit drug other than marijuana[1]	36.2	38.7	39.7	31.4	25.1
Selected illicit drugs:					
Cocaine	9.0	15.7	17.3	10.3	6.1
Heroin	2.2	1.1	1.2	1.3	1.2
LSD	11.3	9.3	7.5	8.3	8.6
Marijuana/hashish	47.3	60.3	54.2	43.7	32.6
PCP	NA	9.6	4.9	3.9	2.4
	Percentage reporting use of drugs in the previous 30 days				
Cigarettes	36.7	30.5	30.1	28.6	27.8
Alcohol	68.2	72.0	65.9	60.0	51.3
Any illicit drug	30.7	37.2	29.7	19.7	14.4
Marijuana only	15.3	18.8	14.8	10.6	8.1
Any illicit drug other than marijuana[1]	15.4	18.4	14.9	9.1	6.3
Selected illicit drugs:					
Cocaine	1.9	5.2	6.7	2.8	1.3
Heroin	0.4	0.2	0.3	0.3	0.3
LSD	2.3	2.3	1.6	1.8	2.0
Marijuana/hashish	27.1	33.7	25.7	16.7	11.9
PCP	NA	1.4	1.6	1.4	0.6

NA: Not available.

[1] Other illicit drugs include hallucinogens, cocaine, and heroin, or any other opiates, stimulants, sedatives, or tranquilizers nor prescribed by a doctor.

Note.—A revised questionnaire was used in 1982 and later years to reduce the inappropriate reporting of nonprescription stimulants. This slightly reduced the positive responses for some types of drug use.

Source: U.S. Department of Health and Human Services, Public Health Service, National Institutes of Health, National Survey Results on Drug Use from the Monitoring the Future Study, 1975–92, and University of Michigan, Institute for Social Research, Monitoring the Future, various years.

TABLE G–25.—DEATH RATES FOR ALL CAUSES, ACCORDING TO SEX, RACE, AND AGE: UNITED STATES, 1950 TO 1991

[Deaths per 100,000 resident population]

Sex, race and age	1950	1960	1970	1980	1990	1991
All races						
Under 1 year	3,299.2	2,696.4	2,142.4	1,288.3	971.9	916.6
1 to 4 years	139.4	109.1	84.5	63.9	46.8	47.4
5 to 14 years	60.1	46.6	41.3	30.6	24.0	23.6
15 to 24 years	128.1	106.3	127.7	115.4	99.2	100.1
White males						
Under 1 year	3,400.5	2,694.1	2,113.2	1,230.3	896.1	860.3
1 to 4 years	135.5	104.9	83.6	66.1	45.9	45.5
5 to 14 years	67.2	52.7	48.0	35.0	26.4	26.5
15 to 24 years	152.4	143.7	170.8	167.0	131.3	128.2
Black males						
Under 1 year	....	5,306.8	4,298.9	2,586.7	2,112.4	1,957.4
1 to 4 years	....	208.5	150.5	110.5	85.8	88.4
5 to 14 years	95.1	75.1	67.1	47.4	41.7	42.4
15 to 24 years	289.7	212.0	320.6	209.1	252.2	278.1
White females						
Under 1 year	2,566.8	2,007.7	1,614.6	962.5	690.0	659.2
1 to 4 years	112.2	85.2	66.1	49.3	36.1	37.6
5 to 14 years	45.1	34.7	29.9	22.9	17.9	17.2
15 to 24 years	71.5	54.9	61.6	55.5	45.9	46.6
Black females						
Under 1 year	....	4,162.2	3,368.8	2,123.7	1,735.5	1,580.8
1 to 4 years	....	173.3	129.4	84.4	67.6	70.8
5 to 14 years	72.2	53.8	43.8	30.5	27.5	25.8
15 to 24 years	213.1	107.5	111.9	70.5	68.7	72.6

Source: National Center for Health Statistics: National Vital Statistics System, Unpublished Tabulations. February, 1994.

Note: Death rates under 1 year (based on population estimates) differ from infant mortality rates (based on live births).

TABLE G–26.—DEATH RATES FOR MOTOR VEHICLE ACCIDENTS, ACCORDING TO SEX, RACE, AND AGE: UNITED STATES, 1950 TO 1991

[Deaths per 100,000 resident population]

Sex, race and age	1950	1960	1970	1980	1990	1991
All Races						
Under 1 year	8.4	8.1	9.8	7.0	4.9	4.3
1 to 4 years	11.5	10.0	11.5	9.2	6.3	5.9
5 to 14 years	8.8	7.9	10.2	7.9	5.9	5.6
15 to 24 years	34.4	38.0	47.2	44.8	34.1	32.0
15 to 24 years						
White male	58.3	62.7	75.2	73.8	52.5	48.3
Black male	41.6	46.4	58.1	34.9	36.1	35.0
White female	12.6	15.6	22.7	23.0	19.5	19.6
Black female	11.5	9.9	13.4	8.0	9.9	10.0

Source: National Center for Health Statistics: National Vital Statistics System, Unpublished Tabulations. February, 1994.

TABLE G–27.—DEATH RATES FOR HOMICIDE AND LEGAL INTERVENTION, ACCORDING TO SEX, RACE AND AGE: UNITED STATES 1950 TO 1991

[Deaths per 100,000 resident population]

Sex, race, and age	1950	1960	1970	1980	1990	1991
All races						
5 to 14 years	0.5	0.5	0.9	1.2	1.5	1.4
15 to 24 years	6.3	5.9	11.7	15.6	19.9	22.4
15 to 24 years						
White male	3.7	4.4	7.9	15.5	15.4	16.9
Black male	58.9	46.4	102.5	84.3	138.3	158.9
White female	1.3	1.5	2.7	4.7	4.0	4.4
Black female	16.5	11.9	17.7	18.4	18.9	21.6

Source: National Center for Health Statistics: National Vital Statistics System, Unpublished Tabulations. February, 1994.

TABLE G–28.—DEATH RATES FOR SUICIDE ACCORDING TO SEX, RACE, AND AGE: IN UNITED STATES, 1950 TO 1991

[Deaths per 100,000 resident population]

Sex, race and age	1950	1960	1970	1980	1990	1991
All races						
5 to 14 years	0.2	0.3	0.3	0.4	0.8	0.7
15 to 24 years	4.5	5.2	8.8	12.3	13.2	13.1
15 to 24 years						
White male	6.6	8.6	13.9	21.4	23.2	23.0
Black male	4.9	4.1	10.5	12.3	15.1	16.4
White female	2.7	2.3	4.2	4.6	4.2	4.2
Black female	1.8	1.3	3.8	2.3	2.3	1.6

Source: National Center for Health Statistics: National Vital Statistics System, Unpublished Tabulations. February, 1994.

TABLE G–29.—MEAN SAT SCORES FOR COLLEGE-BOUND SENIORS 1967–93

	Verbal			Math		
	Males	Females	Total	Males	Females	Total
1967 [1]	463	468	466	514	467	492
1968 [1]	464	466	466	512	470	492
1969 [1]	459	466	463	513	470	493
1970 [1]	459	461	460	509	465	488
1971 [1]	454	457	455	507	466	488
1972	454	452	453	505	461	484
1973	446	443	445	502	460	481
1974	447	442	444	501	459	480
1975	437	431	434	495	449	472
1976	433	430	431	497	446	472
1977	431	427	429	497	445	470
1978	433	425	429	494	444	468
1979	431	423	427	493	443	467
1980	428	420	424	491	443	466
1981	430	418	424	492	443	466
1982	431	421	426	493	443	467
1983	430	420	425	493	445	468
1984	433	420	426	495	449	471
1985	437	425	431	499	452	475
1986	437	426	431	501	451	475
1987	435	425	430	500	453	476
1988	435	422	428	498	455	476
1989	434	421	427	500	454	476
1990	429	419	424	499	455	476
1991	426	418	422	497	453	474
1992	428	419	423	499	456	476
1993	428	420	424	502	457	478

[1] The averages for 1967 through 1971 are estimates. College-Bound Seniors reports were not prepared in those years.

Source: The College Board, 1993.

TABLE G–30.—EVENT DROPOUT RATES FROM GRADES 10 TO 12, BY SEX AND RACE, 1973–92 [1]

[In percent]

	White		Black		Hispanic [2]	
	Male	Female	Male	Female	Male	Female
1973	6.1	5.3	12.0	8.4	7.9	12.0
1974	7.0	5.1	10.8	12.2	12.5	7.2
1975	5.0	5.8	8.3	9.0	10.1	11.6
1976	6.3	5.0	8.5	6.2	7.3	6.8
1977	6.9	5.6	8.3	9.0	10.3	5.2
1978	6.9	5.3	11.0	9.7	15.6	8.5
1979	6.6	5.8	7.5	11.5	10.2	9.1
1980	6.4	4.9	8.0	8.5	16.9	6.9
1981	5.6	4.9	9.4	10.2	10.6	10.9
1982	5.3	4.9	9.0	6.5	9.5	9.0
1983	5.4	4.2	7.0	6.8	13.7	6.2
1984	5.3	4.6	6.2	5.3	12.2	10.1
1985	4.9	4.7	8.3	7.2	9.3	9.8
1986 [3]	4.2	4.1	5.0	4.6	11.7	12.4
1987 [3]	4.1	3.4	6.2	6.4	5.0	6.2
1988 [3]	5.1	4.3	6.7	6.0	12.3	8.4
1989 [3]	4.1	3.8	6.9	8.6	7.6	7.7
1990 [3]	4.1	3.5	4.1	6.0	8.7	7.2
1991 [3]	3.6	3.8	5.5	7.0	10.4	4.8
1992 [3]	3.8	4.4	3.3	6.7	5.8	8.6

[1] Event dropout rates measure the percentage of students who leave high school in a single year, without having completed a high school diploma.

[2] Persons of Hispanic origin may be of any race.

[3] Numbers for these years reflect new editing procedures by the Bureau of the Census for cases with missing data on school enrollment items.

Source: U.S. Department of Commerce, Bureau of the Census, Current Population Reports, Series P–20, "School Enrollment—Social and Economic Characteristics of Students", October of each year, U.S. Government Printing Office, Washington, D.C.

TABLE G–31.—HIGH SCHOOL COMPLETION RATES FOR PERSONS 19 AND 20 YEARS OLD, BY RACE/ETHNICITY: OCTOBER 1973 THROUGH OCTOBER 1992

[In percent]

Year	Total	Race/Ethnicity [1]		Hispanic
		White non-Hispanic	Black non-Hispanic	
1973	82.2	85.9	68.2	54.7
1974	80.6	84.6	65.6	58.8
1975	81.0	84.7	66.0	62.6
1976	81.1	85.2	67.6	57.3
1977	81.4	84.9	69.1	60.0
1978	80.9	85.2	67.1	56.1
1979	80.4	83.8	68.5	59.8
1980	81.1	85.6	71.0	51.3
1981	80.8	84.8	71.8	56.8
1982	80.6	84.7	69.4	58.8
1983	81.2	85.2	73.2	57.9
1984	82.0	85.4	75.3	63.0
1985	83.1	87.0	73.8	64.8
1986	83.0	87.8	75.0	65.8
1987[2]	82.9	86.4	79.3	63.7
1988[2]	82.1	87.1	73.5	53.6
1989[2]	81.8	86.8	74.8	59.4
1990[2]	82.8	87.3	77.6	59.7
1991	81.4	89.8	83.5	56.3
1992	83.3	88.8	75.6	59.2

[1] Not shown separately are non-Hispanics who are neither black nor white, but who are included in the total.

[2] Numbers for these years reflect new editing procedures instituted by the Bureau of the Census for cases with missing data on school enrollment items.

Source: U.S. Department of Education, "Dropout Rates in the United States: 1992," September 1993, based on data from U.S. Bureau of the Census, Current Population Survey, October (various years).

TABLE G-32.—TRENDS IN DEMOGRAPHIC CHARACTERISTICS AND INCOME COMPOSITION OF FEMALE-HEADED FAMILIES WITH CHILDREN, 1979, 1989, AND 1992

	Poor[1]			Nonpoor[1]			Total		
	1979	1989	1992	1979	1989	1992	1979	1989	1992
Number of families (in thousands)	2,458	3,434	4,090	3,729	4,431	4,697	6,187	7,865	8,787
Family characteristics:									
Percent never-married	26.0	37.3	41.1	10.2	17.6	19.6	16.5	26.2	29.6
Percent with head age 15 to 19	3.9	2.9	3.5	0.4	0.3	0.5	1.8	1.5	1.9
Percent with head age 20 to 29	36.4	37.3	36.5	21.7	17.3	16.5	27.6	26.0	25.8
Percent with head 30 and over	59.6	59.8	59.9	77.8	82.3	83.0	70.6	72.5	72.3
Percent white non-Hispanic[2]	43.1	42.6	44.1	69.4	64.1	64.2	59.0	54.7	54.9
Percent black non-Hispanic	44.9	42.0	41.0	24.7	27.6	26.8	32.7	33.9	33.4
Percent Hispanic	12.0	15.4	14.8	5.9	8.4	9.0	8.3	11.4	11.7
Average family size	3.7	3.4	3.4	3.2	3.0	3.0	3.4	3.2	3.2
Percent with income from:									
Earnings[3]	49.7	49.0	49.9	94.8	96.2	95.8	76.9	75.6	74.4
OASDI, railroad retirement	12.6	10.8	8.9	21.5	16.3	16.2	18.0	13.9	12.8
Pensions	1.1	1.7	1.2	4.4	5.8	5.4	3.0	4.0	3.4
UC and other compensation	6.3	4.7	6.6	14.9	11.3	11.5	11.5	8.4	9.2
AFDC, SSI, general assistance	65.0	60.9	63.2	18.2	11.0	12.8	36.8	32.8	36.3
Child support, alimony	18.6	26.9	29.4	44.0	45.5	97.0	33.9	37.4	38.8
Interest, dividends[3]	13.4	11.2	10.3	53.6	53.5	51.8	37.6	35.0	32.4
Food stamps	67.2	66.5	71.7	16.6	10.4	13.8	36.7	34.9	40.8
Housing assistance	21.6	29.9	32.0	6.0	6.0	7.8	12.2	16.4	19.1
Percent of total income from:									
Earnings[3]	24.8	27.8	27.5	74.2	79.1	79.9	64.9	69.7	68.9
OASDI, railroad retirement	5.7	5.9	4.9	6.8	4.6	4.4	6.6	4.8	4.5
Pensions	0.4	0.6	0.4	1.2	1.5	1.3	1.1	1.3	1.1
UC and other compensation	1.5	1.0	1.9	1.5	1.2	1.5	1.5	1.1	1.6
AFDC, SSI, general assistance	38.1	32.9	30.3	3.8	1.5	2.1	10.2	7.3	8.0

1145

Child support, alimony	4.8	5.8	6.5	8.1	8.1	8.0	7.5	7.7	7.7
Interest, dividends [3]	0.3	0.3	0.3	2.9	3.4	1.9	2.4	2.9	1.6
Food stamps [4]	16.5	16.5	18.4	0.9	0.4	0.7	3.8	3.4	4.4
Housing assistance [4]	8.0	9.2	9.8	0.7	0.2	0.3	2.1	1.9	2.3
Mean income per family member [5] (1992 dollars)	$2,611	$2,505	$2,586	$8,646	$9,839	$9,492	$6,047	$6,462	$6,014
Percent with 50 percent or more of income from public assistance [5]	58.8	55.2	56.6	4.5	1.6	2.0	26.1	25.0	27.4
Percent with 90 percent or more of income from public assistance [5]	39.0	37.4	36.9	1.3	0.4	0.3	16.3	16.6	17.4

[1] Based on census ("Orshansky") poverty levels.   [2] Includes "other races."   [3] Negative incomes (i.e. losses) set to zero.   [4] The cash values of food stamps and housing assistance were estimated using their market values. Their cash values are excluded from total income for purposes of determining poverty status. Cash values of food stamps and housing assistance are included in total income for calculating the percentage share of total income.   [5] Includes cash values of food stamps and housing assistance and includes negative incomes (i.e. losses). Mean income converted to 1992 dollars using the CPI–X1 price index.

Note: Details may not sum to totals due to rounding.

Source: March 1981, 1990, 1991, 1992, and 1993 Current Population Surveys (CPS). Table prepared by CRS.

TABLE G-33.—TRENDS IN DEMOGRAPHIC CHARACTERISTICS AND INCOME COMPOSITION OF MALE-PRESENT FAMILIES WITH CHILDREN, 1979, 1989, AND 1992

	Poor [1]			Nonpoor [1]			Total		
	1979	1989	1992	1979	1989	1992	1979	1989	1992
Number of families (in thousands)	1,663	2,142	2,542	24,315	24,761	24,829	25,978	26,903	27,371
Family characteristics:									
Percent with head age 15 to 19	1.1	1.3	6.4	0.3	0.2	1.4	0.4	0.3	1.9
Percent with head age 20 to 29	25.4	26.7	27.7	19.3	15.1	13.0	19.6	16.0	14.3
Percent with head age 30 and over	73.6	72.0	71.3	80.4	84.8	86.9	80.0	83.8	85.4
Percent white non-Hispanic [2]	66.2	59.4	58.0	86.1	83.9	83.6	84.8	81.9	81.3
Percent black non-Hispanic	18.0	17.0	16.2	7.7	8.1	8.0	8.3	8.8	8.7
Percent Hispanic	15.8	23.6	25.8	6.2	8.0	8.4	6.8	9.2	10.0
Average family size	4.8	4.6	4.5	4.2	4.1	4.1	4.3	4.1	4.1
Percent with income from:									
Earnings [3]	82.3	83.7	80.5	99.4	99.1	99.2	98.3	97.9	97.4
OASDI, railroad retirement	14.3	8.7	9.9	5.9	5.6	5.7	6.4	5.9	6.1
Pensions	2.1	1.7	2.1	4.1	4.7	4.8	4.0	4.4	4.5
UC and other compensation	16.8	15.7	19.5	17.2	12.9	16.1	17.2	13.2	16.4
AFDC, SSI, general assistance	24.3	25.0	28.3	3.2	2.7	3.7	4.5	4.5	6.0
Child support, alimony	7.4	12.0	13.5	11.3	15.3	16.6	11.0	15.0	16.3
Interest, dividends [3]	27.4	20.4	20.3	73.9	73.3	71.4	71.0	69.1	66.7
Food stamps	41.8	42.2	48.6	3.5	2.5	3.6	6.0	5.6	7.8
Housing assistance	7.3	10.2	9.7	1.1	0.8	1.0	1.5	1.5	1.8
Percent of total income from:									
Earnings [3]	62.5	66.8	62.5	93.2	92.7	92.5	92.2	92.2	91.8
OASDI, railroad retirement	8.1	5.3	5.7	1.0	0.9	1.0	1.1	1.0	1.1
Pensions	0.7	0.6	0.8	0.9	0.9	0.9	1.1	0.9	0.9
UC and other compensation	4.4	3.5	5.1	1.0	0.9	1.3	1.1	0.9	1.3
AFDC, SSI, general assistance	10.3	10.8	11.2	0.3	0.2	0.3	1.1	0.4	0.5
Child support, alimony	1.5	2.2	2.3	0.7	0.9	1.1	0.7	0.9	1.2
Interest, dividends [3]	1.7	1.3	1.1	2.8	3.5	2.9	2.8	3.5	2.8
Food stamps [4]	8.7	7.7	9.3	0.1	0.1	0.1	0.2	0.2	0.3
Housing assistance [4]	2.3	1.8	2.0	0.1	0.0	0.0	0.1	0.1	0.1

Mean income per family member [5] (1992 dollars)	$2,235	$2,419	$2,367	$11,640	$13,180	$12,719	$11,013	$12,217	$11,709
Percent with 50 percent or more of income from public assistance [5]	15.3	16.5	18.4	0.2	0.2	0.3	1.2	1.5	1.9
Percent with 90 percent or more of income from public assistance [5]	7.1	8.9	9.7	0.0	0.1	0.1	0.5	0.8	1.0

[1] Based on census ("Orshansky") poverty levels.

[2] Includes "other races."

[3] Negative incomes (i.e. losses) set to zero.

[4] The cash values of food stamps and housing assistance were estimated using their market values. Their cash values are excluded from total income for purposes of determining poverty status. Cash values of food stamps and housing assistance are included in total income for calculating the percentage share of total income.

[5] Includes cash values of food stamps and housing assistance, and includes negative incomes (i.e. losses). Mean income converted to 1992 dollars using the CPI-X1 price index.

Note: Details may not sum to totals due to rounding.

Source: March 1980, 1990, 1991, 1992, and 1993 Current Population Surveys (CPS). Table prepared by CRS.

TABLE G–34.—NUMBERS, PERCENT COMPOSITION, AND RATES OF CHILDREN BELOW POVERTY,[1] BY RACE, 1974–92

[Numbers in thousands]

	Total	Black	White	Hispanic [2]
1974	10,156	3,755	6,223	NA
1975	11,104	3,925	6,927	NA
1976	10,273	3,787	6,189	1,443
1977	10,288	3,888	6,097	1,422
1978	9,931	3,830	5,831	1,384
1979	10,377	3,833	6,193	1,535
1980	11,543	3,961	7,181	1,749
1981	12,505	4,237	7,785	1,925
1982	13,647	4,472	8,678	2,181
1983	13,911	4,398	8,862	2,312
1984	13,420	4,413	8,472	2,376
1985	13,010	4,157	8,253	2,606
1986	12,876	4,148	8,209	2,507
1987 [3]	12,843	4,385	7,788	2,670
1988	12,455	4,296	7,435	2,631
1989	12,590	4,375	7,599	2,603
1990	13,431	4,550	8,232	2,865
1991	14,341	4,755	8,848	3,094
1992	14,617	4,938	8,955	3,116
Percentage Composition				
1974	....	37.0	61.3	NA
1976	....	36.9	60.2	14.0
1980	....	34.3	62.2	15.2
1984	....	32.9	63.1	17.7
1988	....	34.5	59.7	21.1
1990	....	33.9	62.0	21.3
1991	....	33.2	61.7	21.6
1992	....	33.8	61.3	21.3
Rates				
1974	15.4	39.8	11.2	NA
1975	17.1	41.7	12.7	NA
1976	16.0	40.6	11.6	30.2
1977	16.2	41.8	11.6	28.3
1978	15.9	41.5	11.3	27.6
1979	16.4	41.2	11.8	28.0
1980	18.3	42.3	13.9	33.2
1981	20.0	45.2	15.2	35.8
1982	21.9	47.6	17.0	39.4
1983	22.3	46.7	17.5	38.1
1984	21.5	46.5	16.7	39.2
1985	20.7	43.6	16.2	40.3
1986	20.5	43.1	16.1	37.7
1987 [3]	20.3	45.1	15.3	39.3
1988	19.5	43.5	14.5	37.6
1989	19.6	43.7	14.8	36.2
1990	20.6	44.8	15.9	38.4
1991	21.8	45.9	16.8	40.4
1992	21.9	46.6	16.9	39.9

[1] Includes all persons under 18 below the poverty level, including unrelated children.
[2] Hispanic origin may be of any race; this category is not exclusive.
[3] The 1987 numbers have been revised.
NA—Not available.
Source: U.S. Bureau of the Census, Current Population Reports, Series P–60, No. 185, Poverty in the United States: 1992, table 3.

TABLE G–35.—COMPOSITION OF CHILD POVERTY POPULATION BY FAMILY TYPE AND RACE: 1966–92

[In thousands]

Year	Total poor	Female head				Per-cent of total	Male present				Per-cent of total
		Nonwhite	White	His-panic [1]	Total		Nonwhite	White	His-panic [1]	Total	
1966	12,146	2,150	2,112	NA	4,262	35.1	2,792	5,092	NA	7,884	64.9
1967	11,427	2,316	1,930	NA	4,246	37.2	2,382	4,799	NA	7,181	62.8
1968	10,739	2,334	2,075	NA	4,409	41.1	2,032	4,298	NA	6,330	58.9
1969	9,500	2,179	2,068	NA	4,247	44.7	1,655	3,598	NA	5,253	55.3
1970	10,235	2,442	2,247	NA	4,689	45.8	1,651	3,891	NA	5,546	54.2
1971	10,344	2,398	2,452	NA	4,850	46.9	1,605	3,889	NA	5,494	53.1
1972	10,082	2,821	2,273	NA	5,094	50.5	1,477	3,511	NA	4,988	49.5
1973	9,453	2,710	2,461	606	5,171	54.7	1,281	3,001	758	4,282	45.3
1974	9,966	2,678	2,683	621	5,361	53.8	1,209	3,396	793	4,605	46.2
1975	10,881	2,784	2,813	694	5,597	51.4	1,350	3,394	925	5,284	48.6
1976	10,080	2,870	2,713	636	5,583	55.4	1,176	3,321	789	4,497	44.6
1977	10,029	2,965	2,693	686	5,658	56.4	1,121	3,250	716	4,371	43.6
1978	9,722	3,060	2,627	663	5,687	58.5	988	3,047	692	4,035	41.5
1979	9,993	3,006	2,629	668	5,635	56.4	1,079	3,279	837	4,358	43.6
1980	11,114	3,053	2,813	809	5,866	52.8	1,244	4,004	909	5,248	47.2
1981	12,069	3,185	3,120	909	6,305	52.2	1,455	4,309	966	5,764	47.8
1982	13,139	3,447	3,249	990	6,696	51.0	1,411	5,032	1,127	6,443	49.0
1983	13,427	3,359	3,388	1,018	6,747	50.2	1,534	5,146	1,233	6,680	49.8
1984	12,929	3,395	3,377	1,093	6,772	52.4	1,448	4,709	1,223	6,157	47.6
1985	12,483	3,344	3,372	1,247	6,716	53.8	1,300	4,467	1,266	5,767	46.2
1986	12,257	3,421	3,522	1,194	6,943	56.6	1,121	4,192	1,219	5,313	43.3
1987	12,435	3,600	3,474	1,241	7,074	56.9	1,285	4,076	1,390	5,361	43.1
1987 [2]	12,275	3,586	3,433	1,250	7,019	57.2	1,291	3,966	1,356	5,257	42.8
1988	11,935	3,530	3,424	1,294	6,954	58.3	1,310	3,671	1,282	4,981	41.7
1989	12,001	3,553	3,255	1,158	6,808	56.7	1,285	3,908	1,338	5,193	43.3
1990	12,715	3,766	3,597	1,314	7,363	57.9	1,253	4,098	1,437	5,352	42.1
1991	13,658	4,125	3,941	1,398	8,065	59.1	1,217	4,376	1,579	5,593	40.9
1992	13,876	4,250	3,783	1,289	8,032	57.9	1,293	4,550	1,657	5,844	42.1

[1] Persons of Hispanic origin may be of any race.
[2] Revised.

NA: Not available.

Note: Includes only related children in families. 1987 revised through 1991 estimates are not comparable to prior years due to processing changes in the CPS.

Source: U.S. Department of Commerce. Bureau of the Census. "Characteristics of Low Income Population: 1983" P–60 No. 147; 1983 rev-1987 from U.S. Department of Commerce. Bureau of the Census. "Money Income and Poverty Status in the United States: 1987" P–60 No. 161; 1987 rev to 1992 figures from March Current Population Survey (CPS). Table prepared by CRS.

TABLE G–36.—POVERTY RATE OF CHILDREN BY FAMILY TYPE AND RACE, 1966–92

Year	Total	Female head				Male present			
		Black	White	His-panic	Total	Black	White	His-panic	Total
1966	17.4	76.6	46.9	NA	58.2	39.9	9.2	NA	12.6
1967	16.3	72.4	42.1	NA	54.3	35.3	8.7	NA	11.5
1968	15.3	70.5	44.4	NA	55.2	29.8	7.8	NA	10.2
1969	13.8	68.2	45.2	NA	54.4	25.0	6.7	NA	8.6
1970	14.9	67.7	43.1	NA	53.0	26.0	7.3	NA	9.2
1971	15.1	66.6	44.6	NA	53.1	25.5	7.4	NA	9.3
1972	14.9	69.5	41.1	NA	53.1	24.1	6.8	NA	8.6
1973	14.2	67.2	42.1	68.7	52.1	21.7	6.0	18.8	7.6
1974	15.1	65.0	42.9	64.3	51.5	20.0	6.9	20.0	8.7
1975	16.8	66.0	44.2	68.4	52.7	22.1	8.2	23.8	9.8
1976	15.8	65.6	42.7	67.3	52.0	19.4	7.1	20.8	8.5
1977	16.0	65.7	40.3	68.6	50.3	19.9	7.1	17.9	8.5
1978	15.7	66.4	39.9	68.9	50.6	17.6	6.8	17.2	7.9
1979	16.0	63.1	38.6	62.2	48.6	18.7	7.3	19.2	8.5
1980	17.9	64.8	41.6	65.0	50.8	20.3	9.0	22.9	10.4
1981	19.5	67.7	42.8	67.3	52.3	23.4	10.0	24.5	11.6
1982	21.3	70.7	46.5	71.8	56.0	24.1	11.6	27.8	13.0
1983	21.8	68.3	47.1	70.6	55.4	23.7	12.0	27.2	13.5
1984	21.0	66.2	45.9	71.0	54.0	24.3	11.0	27.5	12.5
1985	20.1	66.9	45.2	72.4	53.6	18.8	10.4	27.4	11.7
1986	19.8	67.1	46.3	66.7	54.4	17.0	9.8	25.8	10.8
1987	20.0	68.3	45.8	70.1	54.7	19.8	9.5	28.3	10.9
1987 [1]	19.7	66.9	45.0	69.8	53.7	19.1	9.3	27.7	10.6
1988	19.0	64.7	44.9	69.6	52.9	18.7	8.5	25.4	10.0
1989	19.0	63.1	42.5	64.3	51.1	20.3	9.1	25.5	10.4
1990	19.9	64.7	45.9	68.4	53.4	19.3	9.5	26.7	10.7
1991	21.1	68.2	47.1	68.6	55.5	17.3	10.1	29.1	11.1
1992	21.1	67.1	45.3	65.7	54.3	19.4	10.4	29.5	11.5

[1] Revised.

Note: Persons of Hispanic origin may be of any race.

NA—Not available.

Sources: U.S. Department of Commerce. Bureau of the Census. "Money Income and Poverty Status in the United States" P–60 No. 147 and 161; 1987 revised through 1992 data from March Current Population Survey (CPS). Table prepared by CRS.

TABLE G–37.—NUMBER OF CHILDREN POOR UNDER 6 AND FROM 6 TO 17 YEARS AND THEIR POVERTY RATES, 1966–92

Year	Total number of children under 18	Total number under 6	Total number of poor children under 6	Poverty rate of children under 6	Total number of poor children 6–17 years	Poverty rate of children 6–17 years
1966	70,218	23,779	4,304	18.1	8,085	17.4
1967	70,408	23,171	4,055	17.5	7,601	16.1
1968	70,385	22,249	3,659	16.6	7,295	15.2
1969	69,090	21,681	3,361	15.5	6,330	13.4
1970	69,159	21,556	3,601	16.7	6,839	14.4
1971	68,816	20,898	3,579	17.1	6,972	14.5
1972	67,930	20,510	3,388	16.5	6,896	14.5
1973	66,959	20,043	3,204	16.0	6,438	13.7
1974	66,134	19,887	3,361	16.9	6,795	14.7
1975	65,079	19,353	3,522	18.2	7,582	16.6
1976	64,028	18,971	3,358	17.7	6,915	15.3
1977	63,137	18,518	3,426	18.5	6,862	15.4
1978	62,311	18,789	3,344	17.8	6,587	15.1
1979	63,375	19,012	3,479	18.3	6,898	15.5
1980	62,914	19,974	4,054	20.3	7,489	17.4
1981	62,449	20,396	4,487	22.0	8,018	19.1
1982	62,345	20,789	4,899	23.6	8,748	21.1
1983	62,334	21,039	5,302	25.0	8,609	20.8
1984	62,447	21,196	5,066	23.9	8,354	20.3
1985	62,876	21,526	4,951	23.0	8,059	19.5
1986	62,948	21,656	4,796	22.1	8,080	19.6
1987	63,290	21,860	4,984	22.8	7,979	19.3
1988 (revised)	63,747	22,232	4,957	22.3	7,499	18.1
1989	64,144	22,505	5,071	22.5	7,518	18.1
1990	65,049	22,937	5,412	23.6	8,019	19.0
1991	65,918	23,206	5,702	24.6	8,639	20.2
1992	66,834	23,508	6,046	25.7	8,571	19.8

Source: "Money Income and Poverty Status in the United States: 1989," Current Population Reports, U.S. Department of Commerce. Data on children under 6 from "Five Million Children: A Statistical Profile of Our Poorest Young Citizens," National Center for Children in Poverty, 1990. 1990–92 data are estimates prepared by the Congressional Research Service (CRS), using data from the March 1991, 1992, and 1993 Current Population Surveys.

APPENDIX H. DATA ON POVERTY

When the Federal Government began measuring poverty in the early 1960's, the continued existence of poor people in a time of the "Affluent Society" seemed anomalous. Official concern soon translated into efforts to measure the size of the poverty population, and the search began for programmatic ways to alleviate poverty. The first rough estimates of the incidence of poverty were based on survey data indicating that families generally spent about one-third of their income on food. A poverty level income was then calculated by using as a yardstick the amount of money necessary to purchase the lowest cost "nutritionally adequate" diet calculated by the Department of Agriculture (roughly equivalent to the current Thrifty Food Plan). This price tag was multiplied by 3 to produce a poverty threshold. This procedure assumed, then, that if a family did not have enough income to buy the lowest cost nutritionally adequate diet, and twice that amount to buy other goods and services, it was "poor." Adjustments were made for the size of the family, the sex of the family head, and for whether or not the family lived on a farm. Farm families were assumed to need less cash income because their needs could be met partially by farm products, particularly food. The adjustments for sex of the family head and for farm-nonfarm residence were abolished in 1981. Policy officials made one change to the basic approach for calculating the poverty threshold in 1969. The current poverty threshold is established each year simply by increasing the previous year's threshold by the change in the Consumer Price Index (CPI), rather than multiplying the cost of the Thrifty Food Plan by three. The poverty thresholds for selected years are shown in table 2.

Note that the tables in this subsection provide poverty data calculated using the official Census definition of poverty. The Census definition of poverty has remained fairly standard over time and is useful for measuring progress against poverty. Under this definition, poverty is determined by comparing pretax cash income with the poverty threshold.

It should be noted that the Census Bureau revised its method of estimating the poverty threshold four times—in 1966, 1974, 1979, and 1981. These revisions changed the estimate of the poverty rate. The first two revisions slightly reduced the estimated number of poor, while the more recent revisions slightly increased the number. In 1984, the Census Bureau also revised its method of imputing missing values for interest income, which slightly lowered the estimated poverty rate.

Data on income and poverty after 1987 may not be comparable to data in earlier years because of changes in the methods used by the Census Bureau to process survey results. This new processing system was applied to 1987 data so that 1988 and 1987 data are comparable. Revised 1987 data are denoted as 1987R. The new processing system increased aggregate income by 0.9 percent and lowered the poverty rate for 1987 by 0.1 percent.

Table H–1 shows the population, number of persons in poverty and the poverty rate in 1992 by age, race, region and family type. In 1992, 14.5 percent (36.9 million persons) of the total U.S. population lived in poverty. Of all demographic groups shown, poverty was highest among female-headed families with children (48.3 percent). Among children under age 18, nearly 22 percent, or 14.6 million children, lived in poverty in 1992; this represents an increase of over 1 million since 1990.

Families with children represented a small fraction of the increase in poverty between 1991 and 1992. The increase in the number of poor individuals in families with children was 0.2 million, out of a total increase of 1.2 million. Poverty among female-headed families decreased by 0.2 million between 1991 and 1992 while poverty among married-couple families with children rose by 0.4 million.

TABLE H-1.—POVERTY STATUS OF PERSONS, 1992

	Poverty rate [percent]	Population [thousands]	Percent of total population	Number of poor [thousands]	Percent of poverty population	Poverty increase from 1991 [thousands]	Percent of increase
Age:							
Under 18	21.9	66,834	26.3	14,617	39.6	276	23.5
18 to 64	11.7	156,265	61.5	18,281	49.6	696	59.4
65 and over	12.9	30,870	12.2	3,983	10.8	202	17.2
Total	14.5	253,969	100.0	36,880	100.0	1,172	100.0
Race:							
White	11.6	211,820	83.4	24,523	66.5	776	66.2
Black	33.3	31,916	12.6	10,613	28.8	371	31.7
Hispanic[1]	29.3	22,720	8.9	6,655	18.0	316	27.0
Region:							
Northeast	12.3	50,655	19.9	6,227	16.9	50	4.3
Midwest	13.1	60,931	24.0	7,983	21.6	−6	−.5
South	16.9	87,422	34.4	14,763	40.0	980	83.6
West	14.4	54,961	21.6	7,907	21.4	148	12.6
Total	14.5	253,969	100.0	36,880	100.0	1,172	100.0
Family type:							
Unrelated individuals	21.8	36,734	14.5	7,991	21.7	218	18.6
Female-headed families with children	48.3	26,283	10.3	12,707	34.5	−200	−17
Married-couple families with children	9.6	107,107	42.2	10,247	27.8	427	36.4
Other families with children	22.9	4,598	1.8	1,054	2.9	131	11.2
All other families	6.2	79,247	31.2	4,481	12.2	197	16.8
Total	14.5	253,969	100.0	36,880	100.0	1,172	100.0

[1] Persons of Hispanic origin may be of any race.   Source: U.S. Bureau of the Census, Current Population Reports, Series P-60, No. 185, "Poverty in the United States: 1992" and special tabulations.

TABLE H-2.—WEIGHTED AVERAGE POVERTY THRESHOLDS FOR NONFARM FAMILIES OF SPECIFIED SIZE, SELECTED YEARS, 1959–92

Calendar year	Unrelated individuals			Families of 2 or more persons							
				2 persons							
	All ages	Under age 65	Aged 65 or older	All ages	Head under age 65	Head aged 65 or older	3 persons	4 persons	5 persons	6 persons	7 persons or more
1959	$1,467	$1,503	$1,397	$1,894	$1,952	$1,761	$2,324	$2,973	$3,506	$3,944	$4,849
1960	1,490	1,526	1,418	1,924	1,982	1,788	2,359	3,022	3,560	4,002	4,921
1965	1,582	1,626	1,512	2,048	2,114	1,906	2,514	3,223	3,797	4,264	5,248
1970	1,954	2,010	1,861	2,525	2,604	2,348	3,099	3,968	4,680	5,260	6,468
1975	2,724	2,797	2,581	3,506	3,617	3,257	4,293	5,500	6,499	7,316	9,022
1980	4,190	4,290	3,949	5,363	5,537	4,983	6,565	8,414	9,966	11,269	[1]12,761
1981	4,620	4,729	4,359	5,917	6,111	5,498	7,250	9,287	11,007	12,449	[1]14,110
1982	4,901	5,019	4,626	6,281	6,487	5,836	7,693	9,862	11,684	13,207	[1]15,036
1983	5,061	5,180	4,775	6,483	6,697	6,023	7,938	10,178	12,049	13,630	[1]15,500
1984	5,278	5,400	4,979	6,762	6,983	6,282	8,277	10,609	12,566	14,207	[1]16,096
1985	5,469	5,593	5,156	6,998	7,231	6,503	8,573	10,989	13,007	14,696	[1]16,656
1986	5,572	5,702	5,255	7,138	7,372	6,630	8,737	11,203	13,259	14,986	[1]17,049
1987	5,778	5,909	5,447	7,397	7,641	6,872	9,056	11,611	13,737	15,509	[1]17,649
1988	6,024	6,155	5,674	7,704	7,958	7,158	9,435	12,092	14,305	16,149	[1]18,248
1989	6,311	6,452	5,947	8,076	8,343	7,501	9,885	12,675	14,990	16,921	[1]19,162
1990	6,652	6,800	6,268	8,509	8,794	7,905	10,419	13,359	15,792	17,839	[1]20,241
1991	6,932	7,086	6,532	8,865	9,165	8,241	10,860	13,924	16,456	18,587	[1]21,058
1992	7,143	7,229	6,729	9,137	9,443	8,487	11,186	14,335	16,592	19,137	[1]21,594

[1] Poverty threshold for 7 persons, not 7 persons or more.

Source: Bureau of the Census, technical papers.

TRENDS IN THE OVERALL POVERTY RATE [2]

In the late 1950s, the overall poverty rate for individuals in the United States was 22 percent, representing 39.5 million poor persons (tables 3 and 4). Between 1959 and 1969, the poverty rate declined dramatically and steadily to 12.1 percent. As a result of a sluggish economy, the rate increased slightly to 12.5 percent by 1971. In 1972 and 1973, however, it began to decrease again. The lowest rate over the entire 24-year period occurred in 1973, when the poverty rate was 11.1 percent. At that time roughly 23 million people were poor, 42 percent less than were poor in 1959.

The poverty rate increased by 1975 to 12.3 percent, and then oscillated around 11.5 percent through 1979. After 1978, however, the poverty rate rose steadily reaching 15.2 percent in 1983. In 1992, the last year for which data are available, the poverty rate was 14.5 percent and 36.8 million people were poor.

POVERTY RATES FOR INDIVIDUALS IN SELECTED SUBGROUPS OF THE POPULATION

As table H–4 also illustrates, there are substantial differences between the overall poverty rate and the poverty rates of individuals in certain demographic subgroups. Most notably, blacks, individuals in female-headed households, and Hispanics have poverty rates that greatly exceed the average. The poverty rates for blacks and individuals in female-headed households remained above 30 percent over the 1959 through 1992 period. The poverty rate for all Hispanics has remained near 30 percent during the 1980s and early 1990s. The poverty rate for the aged, which exceeded the overall poverty rate in 1959, fell below the overall poverty rate beginning in 1982. It was 12.9 percent in 1992. The poverty rate for whites was below the overall poverty rate throughout the entire 1959–91 period. It was 11.6 percent in 1992. The poverty rate for children exceeds the average rate; it was 21.9 percent in 1992.

---

[2] All poverty trend information is based upon published Census Bureau data contained in Current Population Reports, Series P–60, Nos. 124, 140, 145, 149, 154, 157, 161, 166, 168, 174, 180, and 185. These figures may differ with other parts of this report which provide a more refined breakdown of this age category. Data for blacks, the aged, and nonaged population were not available for the years 1961 to 1965.

TABLE H-3.—NUMBER OF PERSONS IN POVERTY FOR INDIVIDUALS IN SELECTED DEMOGRAPHIC GROUPS, 1959-92

Year	Overall	Aged	Children [1]	Individuals in female-headed families [2]	Blacks	Hispanic origin [3]	Whites
			Number below poverty (thousands)				
1959	39,490	5,481	17,552	7,014	9,927	NA	28,484
1960	39,851	NA	17,634	7,247	NA	NA	28,309
1961	39,628	NA	16,909	7,252	NA	NA	27,890
1962	38,625	NA	16,963	7,781	NA	NA	26,672
1963	36,436	NA	16,005	7,646	NA	NA	25,238
1964	36,055	NA	16,051	7,297	NA	NA	24,957
1965	33,185	NA	14,676	7,524	NA	NA	22,496
1966	28,510	5,114	12,389	6,861	8,867	NA	19,290
1967	27,769	5,388	11,656	6,898	8,486	NA	18,983
1968	25,389	4,632	10,954	6,990	7,616	NA	17,395
1969	24,147	4,787	9,691	6,879	7,095	NA	16,659
1970	25,420	4,793	10,440	7,503	7,548	NA	17,484
1971	25,559	4,273	10,551	7,797	7,396	NA	17,780
1972	24,460	3,738	10,284	8,114	7,710	2,414	16,203
1973	22,973	3,354	9,642	8,178	7,388	2,366	15,142
1974	23,370	3,085	10,156	8,462	7,182	2,575	15,736
1975	25,877	3,317	11,104	8,846	7,545	2,991	17,770
1976	24,975	3,313	10,273	9,029	7,595	2,783	16,713
1977	24,720	3,177	10,288	9,205	7,726	2,700	16,416
1978	24,497	3,233	9,931	9,269	7,625	2,607	16,259
1979	26,072	3,682	10,377	9,400	8,050	2,921	17,214
1980	29,272	3,871	11,543	10,120	8,579	3,491	19,699
1981	31,822	3,853	12,505	11,051	9,173	3,713	21,553
1982	34,398	3,751	13,647	11,701	9,697	4,301	23,517
1983	35,303	3,625	13,911	12,072	9,882	4,633	23,984
1984	33,700	3,330	13,420	11,831	9,490	4,806	22,955
1985	33,064	3,456	13,010	11,600	8,926	5,236	22,860
1986	32,370	3,477	12,876	11,944	8,983	5,117	22,183
1987	32,341	3,564	12,963	12,278	9,577	5,442	21,249
1988	31,745	3,481	12,455	11,972	9,356	5,357	20,715
1989	31,534	3,369	12,590	11,668	9,305	5,430	20,788
1990	33,585	3,658	13,431	12,578	9,837	6,006	22,326
1991	35,708	3,781	14,341	13,824	10,242	6,339	23,747
1992	36,880	3,983	14,617	13,716	10,613	6,655	24,523

[1] All children including unrelated children.
[2] Does not include females living alone.
[3] Hispanic origin may be of any race; it is an overlapping category.

NA—Not available.

Source: Bureau of the Census, Current Population Reports series P-60-185.

1158

TABLE H–4.—POVERTY RATE FOR INDIVIDUALS IN SELECTED DEMOGRAPHIC GROUPS, 1959–92

Year	Overall	Aged	Children[1]	Individuals in female-headed families[2]	Blacks	Hispanic origin[3]	Whites
1959	22.4	35.2	27.3	49.4	55.1	NA	18.1
1960	22.2	NA	26.9	48.9	NA	NA	17.8
1961	21.9	NA	25.6	48.1	NA	NA	17.4
1962	21.0	NA	25.0	50.3	NA	NA	16.4
1963	19.5	NA	23.1	47.7	NA	NA	15.3
1964	19.0	NA	23.0	44.4	NA	NA	14.9
1965	17.3	NA	21.0	46.0	NA	NA	13.3
1966	14.7	28.5	17.6	39.8	41.8	NA	11.3
1967	14.2	29.5	16.6	38.8	39.3	NA	11.0
1968	12.8	25.0	15.6	38.7	34.7	NA	10.0
1969	12.1	25.3	14.0	38.2	32.2	NA	9.5
1970	12.6	24.6	15.1	38.1	33.5	NA	9.9
1971	12.5	21.6	15.3	38.7	32.5	NA	9.9
1972	11.9	18.6	15.1	38.2	33.3	22.8	9.0
1973	11.1	16.3	14.4	37.5	31.4	21.9	8.4
1974	11.2	14.6	15.4	36.5	30.3	23.0	8.6
1975	12.3	15.3	17.1	37.5	31.3	26.9	9.7
1976	11.8	15.0	16.0	37.3	31.1	24.7	9.1
1977	11.6	14.1	16.2	36.2	31.3	22.4	8.9
1978	11.4	14.0	15.9	35.6	30.6	21.6	8.7
1979	11.7	15.2	16.4	34.9	31.0	21.8	9.0
1980	13.0	15.7	18.3	36.7	32.5	25.7	10.2
1981	14.0	15.3	20.0	38.7	34.2	26.5	11.1
1982	15.0	14.6	21.9	40.6	35.6	29.9	12.0
1983	15.2	13.8	22.3	40.2	35.7	28.0	12.1
1984	14.4	12.4	21.5	38.4	33.8	28.4	11.5
1985	14.0	12.6	20.7	37.6	31.3	29.0	11.4
1986	13.6	12.4	20.5	38.3	31.1	27.3	11.0
1987	13.4	12.5	20.5	38.3	32.6	28.1	10.4
1988	13.0	12.0	19.5	37.2	31.3	26.7	10.1
1989	12.8	11.4	19.6	35.9	30.7	26.2	10.0
1990	13.5	12.2	20.6	37.2	31.9	28.1	10.7
1991	14.2	12.4	21.8	39.7	32.7	28.7	11.3
1992	14.5	12.9	21.9	38.5	33.3	29.3	11.6

[1] All children including unrelated children.
[2] Does not include females living alone.
[3] Hispanic origin may be of any race; it is an overlapping category.

NA—Not available.

Source: Bureau of the Census, Technical Paper 56, table 1; Current Population Reports series P–60.

CHART H–1. POVERTY RATES BY AGE: 1959–92

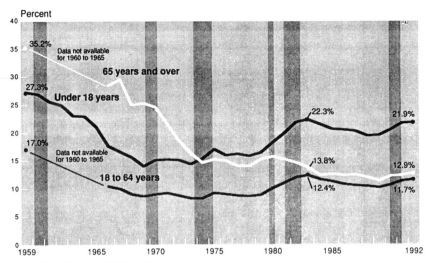

Shaded areas = Recessionary periods.

Source: U.S. Bureau of the Census.

POVERTY RATES FOR FAMILIES [3]

Table H–5 shows the composition of the poverty population for various demographic groups for selected years between 1959 and 1991. Table H–6 presents poverty data for families and unrelated individuals (individuals living alone). Female-headed families with children and unrelated individuals are more likely to be poor than other families with children or families with aged members. In 1992, 47 percent of female-headed families with children were poor, compared with 9 percent of male-present families. Although only about 7 percent of all families with an aged member were poor, 25 percent of all aged unrelated individuals were poor. About 21 percent of nonaged unrelated individuals were poor.

---

[3] Income figures reported in this subsection were from the March 1991 Current Population Survey (CPS) computer data tape. There is a tendency in surveys, such as the CPS, for respondents to underreport their incomes by both source and amount. Reporting of income from earnings is usually more accurate than reporting of income from other sources. In general, CPS estimates of amounts or numbers of recipients of various cash and noncash transfer programs tend to be lower than administrative program totals. As a result, the data are a better reflection of general trends and patterns than of absolute numbers with income from a particular source, or the amount received.

Unrelated subfamilies are included as families in this analysis. The Census Bureau excludes such families from its poverty counts.

TABLE H–5.—COMPOSITION OF POVERTY POPULATION FOR SELECTED DEMOGRAPHIC GROUPS [1]

[Percent of poverty population]

	1959	1966	1975	1982	1983	1985	1987	1988	1989	1990	1991	1992
Aged	13.9	17.9	12.8	10.9	10.5	10.5	10.9	11.0	10.7	10.9	10.6	10.8
Children	43.6	42.6	42.1	39.2	39.0	38.8	39.4	38.7	39.4	39.5	39.5	39.1
Nonaged adults	42.5	39.5	45.1	49.9	50.5	50.7	49.7	50.3	49.9	49.7	49.9	50.1
Individuals in female-headed families [2]	26.3	36.0	47.4	47.5	47.4	49.5	52.6	52.9	52.4	53.4	54.0	52.7
Individuals in all other families [2]	73.7	64.0	52.6	52.5	52.6	50.5	47.4	47.1	47.6	46.6	46.0	47.3
Blacks	25.1	31.1	29.2	28.2	27.8	27.0	29.8	29.5	29.5	29.3	28.7	28.8
Whites	72.1	67.7	68.7	68.4	68.1	69.1	65.6	65.3	65.9	66.5	66.5	66.5
Other races	2.8	1.2	2.1	3.4	4.1	3.9	4.7	5.3	4.6	4.2	4.8	4.7
Hispanic origin [3]	NA	NA	11.6	12.5	13.1	15.8	16.9	16.9	17.2	17.9	17.8	18.0
Individuals in families with children [4]	NA	NA	NA	NA	NA	NA	NA	NA	67.9	68.0	68.4	67.6
Male present	NA	NA	NA	NA	NA	NA	NA	NA	31.3	30.7	30.3	30.9
Female-headed	NA	NA	NA	NA	NA	NA	NA	NA	36.6	37.2	38.1	36.7
Individuals in all other families	NA	NA	NA	NA	NA	NA	NA	NA	32.1	32.0	31.6	32.4

[1] Data are for March of the following year.
[2] Includes unrelated or single individuals.
[3] Hispanic origin may be of any race; therefore numbers add to more than 100 percent.
[4] Family includes related children under 18.

NA—Not available.

Note: 1987, 1988, 1989, 1990, 1991 and 1992 estimates are not comparable to prior years due to processing changes in the CPS.

Source: 1959–1985 estimates based on data from "Money Income and Poverty Status of Families and Persons in the United States 1985," P–60 No. 154 and No. 157. 1986–1992 data from "March Current Population Survey." Table prepared by CRS.

TABLE H-6.—POVERTY RATES BY FAMILY TYPE, 1987-92, AND PERCENTAGE OF FAMILIES AND UNRELATED INDIVIDUALS BY RATIO OF TOTAL INCOME TO POVERTY THRESHOLD, 1992 [1,2]

	Poverty rate, 1987-92						Percentage distributions by ratio of total income to poverty threshold, 1992							1992 total (in thousands)
	1987R	1988	1989	1990	1991	1992	Under 0.50	0.50 to 0.99	1.00 to 1.24	1.25 to 1.49	1.50 to 1.99	2.00 to 2.99	3.00 and over	
Total:														
Families	11.0	10.8	10.6	11.1	11.8	12.1	5.1	7.0	4.1	4.3	9.1	18.2	52.2	68,852
Unrelated individuals	20.4	20.6	19.2	20.7	21.1	21.8	8.2	13.6	7.7	6.4	11.8	17.9	34.6	36,734
No members age 65 or over:														
Families	11.9	11.6	11.5	12.2	13.0	13.1	5.8	7.3	4.0	4.0	8.3	17.0	53.6	55,706
Unrelated individuals	19.1	19.3	18.1	19.1	19.6	20.6	10.1	10.5	5.5	4.9	10.1	18.3	40.6	26,693
Any member age 65 or over:														
Families	7.2	6.9	6.6	6.4	6.7	7.7	2.0	5.7	4.8	5.4	12.3	23.2	46.6	13,146
Unrelated individuals	23.9	24.1	22.0	24.7	24.9	24.9	3.2	21.7	13.5	10.4	16.1	16.7	18.4	10,041
Families with children:														
Female headed family, no husband present	46.3	45.5	43.7	45.3	47.6	46.5	24.8	21.8	8.2	6.5	11.7	14.3	12.8	8,787
Male present families	8.1	7.7	8.0	8.5	9.0	9.3	2.9	6.4	4.4	4.6	9.9	21.3	50.5	27,371

[1] Based on Census ("Orshansky") poverty levels.
[2] Unrelated subfamilies are treated as separate families; related subfamilies are not treated as separate families but as members of the family with whom they reside.

Source: March Current Population Survey for selected years. Table prepared by CRS.

POVERTY UNDER ALTERNATIVE MEASURES OF INCOME AND PRICE
INFLATION

The Census Bureau publishes data that reflect two adjustments
in the official definition of poverty. The first of these is an alternative inflation adjustment. The official poverty line is based on a
procedure developed in 1965 with yearly adjustments for inflation
using the Consumer Price Index (CPI). The Consumer Price Index,
in turn, is based on the yearly change in prices of goods used by
most Americans. Prior to 1983, the CPI measured housing prices
using a procedure that included changes in the asset value of
owned homes. Because the asset value of houses was growing so
much faster than the consumption value, the inflation rate that included asset values was excessive.

In 1983 the Bureau of Labor Statistics began using a rental
equivalence approach to measuring the value of housing. The official CPI–U inflation rate, then, is based on the asset value of housing prior to 1983 and rental equivalence in 1983 and thereafter. To
provide a consistent time series, the Bureau constructed an experimental series called the CPI–U–X1 for 1967 through 1982 based on
rental equivalence.

The general effect of using the CPI–U–X1 is to lower inflation in
past years which in turn has the effect of lowering poverty thresholds for those years. A lower threshold means that fewer people are
poor. As can be seen by comparing the first two columns in table
H–7, adjusting the poverty threshold using the CPI–U–X1 reduces
the official poverty rate by an average of about 1.5 percentage
points (or 11 percent) per year between 1979 and 1992. Using the
CPI–U–X1 to adjust the poverty threshold each year from 1967 to
1992 results in 3.2 million fewer poor persons in 1992.

The second adjustment in the official poverty rate made by the
Census Bureau is to expand the definition of income to take into
account some noncash income, including Government benefits.
Under the procedures by which the official poverty rate is calculated, only cash, including Government benefits, is counted in determining whether a family is poor; income from cash welfare programs counts, but benefits from food programs, medical care, social
services, education and training, and housing are not included in
the calculation. Moreover, because Government spending on
means-tested noncash benefits has increased more rapidly than
spending on means-tested cash benefits over the years, ignoring
noncash benefits may be an increasingly serious omission if we
want a broad picture of the impact of Government programs on
poverty.

The question of how to value noncash benefits raises a variety
of substantive and technical issues. The Census Bureau has been
working on these issues, consulting with academic experts, sponsoring conferences, and issuing technical reports. In 1992, the Bureau published a consistent historical data series, covering the
years 1979 to 1991, to trace the impact of variety of taxes and
noncash benefits on poverty and income. The measurement of
noncash benefits extended beyond Government spending for the
poor to include Government spending programs such as Medicare

that are not means-tested as well as to employer contributions to employee health plans.

To examine the impact on income and poverty of various State and Federal taxes, Government noncash programs, employer-provided benefits, and so forth, the Bureau has adopted a framework that includes 15 definitions of income. By comparing income under these multiple definitions, it is possible to estimate the impact of the various income sources on the average income and the poverty rates of individuals and families.

Income definition 14 is of interest to those concerned with the impact of Government means-tested, noncash benefits on poverty rates. Unlike the official poverty rate, which includes only cash Government benefits, definition 14 includes the effects of State and Federal taxes, employer-provided benefits, non-means-tested Government benefits, and means-tested noncash benefits including Food Stamps, housing, school lunch, and the fungible value of Medicaid.

By comparing the official poverty rate with the definition 14 poverty rate, we can determine the impact on poverty of noncash benefits and Government taxes. The fifth column in table H–7 is the poverty rate for years 1979 through 1992 based on definition 14 and using the CPI–U–X1 deflator. Compared with the rate based on CPI–U–X1 (column 2), including taxes and noncash benefits (and a few other types of income that have little impact on poverty) in the poverty calculation reduces the poverty rate by an average of 2.8 percentage points.

The combined impact of using the CPI–U–X1 and including noncash benefits can be determined by comparing the poverty rate in column 5 with the official rate in column 1. On average, the two Census Bureau adjustments reduce the poverty rate by over 4 percentage points or 30 percent across the years 1979–92 and by 4.2 percentage points or nearly 11 million persons in 1992.

The question of whether or not to include medical benefits when measuring poverty has great implications on poverty rates. The valuation of medical benefits is particularly difficult. Medical coverage should not by itself raise poor individuals above the poverty line or constitute a major portion of the poverty threshold. The development of the poverty thresholds did not take into account medical costs. Although poor persons are clearly better off with medical coverage, such benefits cannot be used by recipients to meet other needs of daily living. Also, since health insurance costs are not imputed to the incomes of those above poverty, it seems inappropriate to count health benefits as income for those below the poverty line.

Table H–7 illustrates that regardless of what measure of income or which price inflator is used, the trend is the same: poverty has increased substantially over the last decade. Using the official CPI–U definition, the poverty rate increased by 23.9 percent between 1979 and 1992. Using the CPI–U–X1 inflator and factoring in all noncash benefits (including health benefits), poverty has increased by 23.6 percent. Between 1979 and 1989, two peak years in the economic cycle, the increase in poverty has been smaller. Using the CPI–U–X1, the poverty rate increased by 7.5 percent over this time period. Including all noncash benefits yields a poverty increase of 12.7 percent. The relatively greater decrease in the poverty rate,

according to measures that include means-tested Government benefits, suggests that Government programs benefiting the poor have
not reduced poverty as much as they had in prior years.

TABLE H–7.—POVERTY UNDER ALTERNATIVE MEASURES OF INCOME AND PRICE
INFLATION, 1979–92

Year	Poverty rate			Percentage reduction in official poverty associated with:	
	Official (CPI–U)	Using CPI–U–X1	CPI–U–X1 w/noncash benefits [1]	CPI–U–X1	CPI–U–X1 w/noncash benefits [1]
1979	11.7	10.6	7.9	9.4	32.5
1980	13.0	11.5	8.6	11.5	33.8
1981	14.0	12.2	9.8	12.9	30.0
1982	15.0	13.2	10.6	12.0	29.3
1983	15.2	13.7	11.0	9.9	27.6
1984	14.4	12.8	10.4	11.1	27.8
1985	14.0	12.5	10.1	10.7	27.9
1986	13.6	12.2	9.8	10.3	27.9
1987	13.4	12.0	9.5	10.4	29.1
1988	13.0	11.7	9.5	10.0	26.9
1989	12.8	11.4	8.9	10.9	30.5
1990	13.5	12.1	9.5	10.4	29.6
1991	14.2	12.7	9.9	10.6	30.3
1992	14.5	13.1	10.3	9.7	29.0
Percent change:					
1979–89	9.4	7.5	12.7	NA	NA
1979–92	23.9	23.6	30.4	NA	NA

[1] Includes income from capital gains, health insurance supplements to wage or salary income, nonmeans-tested and means-tested government cash transfers, other means-tested government noncash transfers, the value of Medicare, the value of regulars-price school lunches, the value of Medicaid, the Earned Income Tax Credit (EITC), less Social Security payroll taxes, less Federal Income Taxes (excluding the EITC), less State income taxes.

Source: U.S. Bureau of the Census, Current Population Reports, Series P–60, No. 182RD, "Measuring the Effect of Benefits and Taxes on Income and Poverty: 1979 to 1992."

TABLE H–8.—POVERTY RATES IN NONMETRO AND METRO AREAS, 1978–92

[Percent of persons]

	Nonmetro	Metro	
		Total	Central cities only
1978	13.5	10.4	15.4
1979	13.8	10.7	15.7
1980	15.4	11.9	17.2
1981	17.0	12.6	18.0
1982	17.8	13.7	19.9
1983	18.3	13.8	19.8
1984	NA	NA	NA
1985	18.3	12.7	19.0
1986	18.1	12.3	18.0
1987	16.9	12.5	18.6
1989	15.7	12.0	18.1
1990	16.3	12.7	19.0
1991	16.1	13.7	20.2
1992	16.8	13.9	20.5
Percent increase, 1978–92	24.4	33.7	33.1

NA—Not available.

Source: U.S. Census Bureau, Poverty in the United States: 1992, Table 8.

TABLE H–9.—PERCENT OF PERSONS IN POVERTY BY RACE, BY METRO AND NONMETRO RESIDENCE, 1992

	Nonmetro	Metro	
		Total	Central cities only
1992:			
All races	16.8	13.9	20.5
White	14.2	10.7	15.6
Black	40.8	31.9	35.2
Hispanic	36.7	28.7	33.7

Source: Bureau of the Census, Poverty in the United States: 1992, Table 8.

TABLE H-10.—POVERTY STATISTICS BY STATE

State	Poverty rate							
	1969 [1]	1975 [2]	1979 [3]	1983 [4]	1989 [4]	1990 [4]	1991 [4]	1992 [4]
Alabama	25.4	16.4	18.9	22.9	18.9	19.2	18.8	17.1
Alaska	12.6	6.7	10.7	12.4	10.5	11.4	11.8	10.0
Arizona	15.3	13.8	13.2	16.5	14.1	13.7	14.8	15.1
Arkansas	26.8	18.5	19.0	21.6	18.3	19.6	17.3	17.4
California	11.1	10.4	11.4	14.9	12.9	13.9	15.7	15.8
Colorado	12.3	9.1	10.1	12.5	12.1	13.7	10.4	10.6
Connecticut	7.2	6.7	8.0	8.7	2.9	6.0	8.6	9.4
Delaware	10.9	8.2	11.8	8.5	10.0	6.9	7.5	7.6
DC	17.0	12.5	18.6	21.3	18.0	21.1	18.6	20.3
Florida	16.4	14.4	13.4	14.8	12.5	14.4	15.4	15.3
Georgia	20.7	18.0	16.6	18.8	15.0	15.8	17.2	17.8
Hawaii	9.3	7.9	9.9	13.4	11.3	11.0	7.7	11.0
Idaho	13.2	10.3	12.6	17.3	12.4	14.9	13.9	15.0
Illinois	10.2	10.5	11.0	14.4	12.7	13.7	13.5	15.3
Indiana	9.7	8.1	9.7	16.1	13.7	13.0	15.7	11.7
Iowa	11.6	7.9	10.1	16.7	10.3	10.4	9.6	11.3
Kansas	12.7	8.0	10.1	13.5	10.8	10.3	12.3	11.0
Kentucky	22.9	17.7	17.6	18.0	16.1	17.3	18.8	19.7
Louisiana	26.3	19.3	18.6	21.6	23.3	23.6	19.0	24.2
Maine	13.6	12.0	13.0	12.4	10.4	13.1	14.1	13.4
Maryland	10.7	7.7	9.8	8.6	9.0	9.9	9.1	11.6
Massachusetts	8.6	7.1	9.6	7.7	8.8	10.7	11.0	10.0
Michigan	9.4	9.1	10.4	16.8	13.2	14.3	14.1	13.5
Minnesota	10.7	8.3	9.5	12.3	11.2	12.0	12.9	12.8
Mississippi	35.4	26.1	23.9	26.9	22.0	25.7	23.7	24.5
Missouri	14.7	12.0	12.2	16.7	12.6	13.4	14.8	15.6
Montana	13.4	11.5	12.3	15.1	15.6	16.3	15.4	13.7
Nebraska	13.1	9.6	10.7	15.3	12.8	10.3	9.5	10.3
Nevada	9.1	8.8	8.7	9.8	10.8	9.8	11.4	14.4
New Hampshire	9.1	7.9	8.5	8.1	7.7	6.3	7.3	8.6
New Jersey	8.1	8.1	9.5	10.9	8.2	9.2	9.7	10.0
New Mexico	22.8	19.3	17.6	24.2	19.5	20.9	22.4	21.0
New York	11.1	9.4	13.4	15.8	12.6	14.3	15.3	15.3
North Carolina	20.3	14.7	14.8	15.9	12.2	13.0	14.5	15.7
North Dakota	15.7	10.6	12.6	15.1	12.2	13.7	14.5	11.9
Ohio	10.0	9.4	10.3	13.6	10.6	11.5	13.4	12.4
Oklahoma	18.8	13.8	13.4	16.9	14.7	15.6	17.0	18.4
Oregon	11.5	8.9	10.7	16.4	11.2	9.2	13.5	11.3
Pennsylvania	10.6	9.7	10.5	15.5	10.4	11.0	11.0	11.7
Rhode Island	11.0	8.7	10.3	14.8	6.7	7.5	10.4	12.0
South Carolina	23.9	17.2	16.6	20.9	17.0	16.2	16.4	18.9

TABLE H–10.—POVERTY STATISTICS BY STATE—Continued

State	Poverty rate							
	1969[1]	1975[2]	1979[3]	1983[4]	1989[4]	1990[4]	1991[4]	1992[4]
South Dakota	18.7	13.1	16.9	18.1	13.2	13.3	14.0	14.8
Tennessee	21.8	15.8	16.4	20.1	18.4	16.9	15.5	17.0
Texas	18.8	15.2	14.7	15.7	17.1	15.9	17.5	17.8
Utah	11.4	8.5	10.3	13.9	8.2	8.2	12.9	9.3
Vermont	12.1	13.5	12.0	15.6	8.0	10.9	12.6	10.4
Virginia	15.5	10.5	11.8	11.4	10.9	11.1	9.9	9.4
Washington	10.2	8.5	9.8	10.8	9.6	8.9	9.5	11.0
West Virginia	22.2	15.1	15.0	22.3	15.7	18.1	17.9	22.3
Wisconsin	9.8	7.7	8.7	10.6	8.4	9.3	9.9	10.8
Wyoming	11.7	8.7	7.9	12.7	10.9	11.0	9.9	10.3

[1] U.S. Bureau of the Census, Statistical Abstract of the United States: 1979, table 764, pp. 465 (110th edition), Washington, D.C. 1979, 1969 estimates are from the 1970 census.

[2] Data are also from the 1979 Statistical Abstract of the United States, but estimates are from the Survey of Income and Education.

[3] U.S. Bureau of the Census, Statistical Abstract of the United States: 1982–83, table 732, p. 443. (103d edition). Washington, D.C. 1982. 1979 estimates are from the 1980 census.

[4] U.S. Department of Commerce, Bureau of the Census. "Poverty in the United States: 1992." Series P–60, No. 181.

ANTIPOVERTY EFFECTIVENESS OF VARIOUS CASH AND NEARCASH INCOME SOURCES

The following tables provide estimates of the number and percentage of individuals removed from poverty by different social insurance programs (e.g., Social Security, Unemployment Compensation and Workers Compensation), means-tested cash and nearcash programs (e.g., Aid to Families With Dependent Children, Supplemental Security Income, General Assistance, Food Stamps, Housing, and School Lunch programs) and Federal payroll and income taxes. The analysis allows comparisons between 1979 and 1989 (peaks of economic cycles); 1979 to 1983 (peak of an economic cycle to a year when poverty was at its peak); and 1989 to 1992 (peak of an economic cycle to the latest year data are available).

METHODOLOGY

One way of measuring the antipoverty effectiveness of various income sources is to estimate the number of persons who would be counted as poor if a particular source of income were not received. Subtracting from this number the actual number of persons that are counted as poor after accounting for the effects of the income source provides an estimate of the number of people lifted out of poverty by that particular income source. For example, the effect of Social Security upon poverty can be seen by comparing the number who would be counted as poor if they did not receive Social Security with the number of poor remaining after Social Security income is counted.

A second way of assessing the effectiveness of various income sources upon poverty is to estimate the degree to which those sources reduce the gap between a poor family's income and the poverty threshold. This concept is known as the "poverty gap" or the "poverty income deficit." A cash transfer program which is highly targeted toward the poor may appear to do little to eliminate poverty—that is, to reduce the number who are counted as poor—but such a program may still have a very real impact by reducing the degree of poverty as measured by the poverty gap.

The number of persons who would be counted as poor (or the degree to which the poverty gap expands) if a particular governmental source of income were not received overstates the magnitude of the effect upon poverty because the methodology fails to account for any work disincentives that may be associated with that particular program. However, the analysis comparing different years does give reliable estimates of how a given program's antipoverty effectiveness changes over time.

There are also several reasons why the analysis does not capture all the changes in antipoverty effectiveness. The Census Bureau has noted that for many different reasons there is a tendency in household surveys for respondents to underreport their income. In addition, Federal law requires AFDC families to assign their child support rights to the State. While child support payments ought to be counted as private income, because they are administered by the State, recipients probably do not distinguish between AFDC benefit payments and child support payments. Therefore, the effect of governmental programs is slightly overstated as private income may appear to be a government benefit. At the same time, the decline in the effectiveness of governmental benefits in reducing poverty over time is probably slightly understated because AFDC child support payments have increased from $597 million in 1979 to $2.0 billion in 1991. Further, in 1979, the Comprehensive Employment and Training Act (CETA) spent some $5 billion on public service employment jobs. This program was terminated by 1983. These expenditures of monies and their antipoverty effects are not reflected in the analysis as a change in governmental policy.

All valuations of in-kind transfers are those estimated by the Bureau of the Census using a market-based valuation technique. The market value generally attempts to measure the private market cost of benefits provided in-kind. Food stamps are assigned their value, while school lunches are assigned the average amount of Federal subsidy per child. Housing assistance is valued as the difference between the estimated market rent (based on the American Housing Survey) and the reduced rent paid by subsidized households.

In this analysis, poverty is measured under five or six different income concepts. "Cash income before transfers" is all cash income prior to any governmental benefits or taxes (also referred to as "private cash income"). "Plus social insurance" adds to cash income all benefits from social insurance programs such as Workers' Compensation and Unemployment Compensation, as well as all benefits from the Social Security programs. On some of the tables, the Social Security program is separated from other social insurance programs. "Plus means-tested cash transfers" adds to cash income and social insurance all means-tested transfer income such as Aid to Families with Dependent Children, Supplemental Security Income, Veteran's pensions and General Assistance. "Plus food and housing benefits" adds to cash, social insurance and means-tested cash income all means-tested in-kind transfers received for food and housing. These would include food stamps, housing programs and school lunch programs. "Less Federal taxes" subtracts from income all Federal income taxes and the employee portion of Federal payroll taxes.

CHANGES IN POVERTY SINCE THE 1990–91 RECESSION

Total population

As a result of the 1990–91 economic recession, gross domestic product in 1987 dollars bottomed out at $4,821 billion in 1991. In 1992, the economy recovered to its 1990 level of $4,878 billion and began an expansion which has continued well into 1994. This section examines the impact of the economic recovery and expansion on poverty as of 1992, the latest year for which data are available.

As the economy fell into recession, the official rate of poverty rose from 12.8 percent in 1989 to 13.5 percent in 1990 and 14.2 percent in 1991. With the first full year of economic recovery and expansion, the rate of increase in poverty slowed dramatically to what is likely to be a cyclical peak of 14.5 percent. With continued economic expansion in 1993, the rate of poverty for 1993, which will be available late in 1994, is likely to be down from 14.5 percent.

Overall, the population grew by 1.1 percent in 1992 to nearly 253 million. Reflecting the lagging effects of the recession, the poverty population, before accounting for Federal income transfers and taxes, grew by 4.3 percent to over 57 million. After accounting for income transfers and taxes, the poverty population was still over 33 million, which was a 4.2 percent increase over 1991.

The proportion of individuals removed from poverty by Federal income transfers and taxes in 1992 remained unchanged from 1991 at 41.9 percent. Nearly three-fourths of this poverty reduction was due to social insurance programs and over one-fourth was attributable to means-tested welfare benefits. Poverty was increased by nearly one percent or 438,000 persons because of taxes, but with the large increase in the earned income tax credit enacted in 1993, this impact is likely to diminish when data for 1994 and subsequent years become available.

In contrast to the 4.3 percent rise in the poverty population, before accounting for Federal income transfers and taxes, the corresponding poverty gap jumped by 5.4 percent from 1991 to 1992 to over $169 billion. After accounting for taxes and transfers, the increase in the poverty gap was 6.8 percent at about $55 billion. While the poverty population was reduced by only 41.9 percent, the poverty gap was cut by 67.3 percent. Two-thirds of the reduction in the poverty gap stemmed from social insurance programs while one-third derived from means-tested welfare programs. Taxes had the minor effect of increasing the poverty gap by only 0.3 percent.

Without Federal income transfers and taxes, the poverty rate would have been 22.5 percent in 1992 compared to 21.8 percent in

1991. Social insurance programs reduced the 1992 poverty rate to 15.6 percent. Means-tested welfare programs reduced the poverty rate further to 14.5 percent, and when food and housing benefits were factored in, the poverty rate dropped to 12.9 percent. Federal taxes raised this rate to 13.0 percent.

Single-parent families

In 1992, there were over 32 million persons in single-parent families with related children under 18 years old. Nearly 17 million of these families or 51.5 percent of them were poor. After Federal taxes and transfers, about 12.5 million were still poor. Seventy percent of this reduction in poverty was due to means-tested welfare programs. None of these figures changed substantially from 1991.

The poverty gap before Federal transfers and taxes for single-parent families was $44.6 billion in 1992, up 2.8 percent from 1991. Federal transfers and taxes reduced this gap by 61.6 percent to about $17 billion in 1992. Eighty percent of this reduction was attributable to means-tested welfare programs.

Without Federal transfers and taxes, the poverty rate for single-parent families would have been 51.5 percent. After factoring in Federal transfers and tax benefits, the poverty rate of single-parent families fell to 38.5 percent.

Persons in housing units with all members 65 years old and older

Before Federal transfers and taxes, about 13 million elderly persons in these households were poor. After including Federal transfers and taxes, only 2.7 million elderly persons in these households were poor. Ninety-three percent of this reduction in poverty is due to social insurance. Federal taxes had virtually no impact. There was little change in these figures from 1991.

The poverty gap before Federal transfers and taxes for these elderly persons was nearly $52 billion in 1992. After Federal transfers and taxes, the poverty gap was reduced to only $4.5 billion. Ninety-five percent of this reduction was due to social insurance programs. There was little change in these figures from 1991.

The poverty rate before Federal transfers and taxes for these elderly would have been 57 percent. After Federal transfers and taxes, the poverty rate was only 11.8 percent. There was little change in these figures from 1991.

TABLE H-11.—ANTIPOVERTY EFFECTIVENESS OF CASH AND NEARCASH TRANSFERS (INCLUDING FEDERAL INCOME AND PAYROLL TAXES) FOR ALL PERSONS

	1979	1983	1989	1990	1991	1992
Total population (thousands)	222,893	231,140	246,492	248,054	251,179	253,969
Number of poor individuals (thousands):						
Cash income before transfers	42,783	52,700	49,052	50,851	54,679	57,021
Plus social insurance (other than Social Security)	40,867	49,468	47,377	49,052	52,164	54,367
Plus Social Security	28,604	36,928	33,825	35,928	38,131	39,717
Plus means-tested cash transfers	25,924	35,030	31,534	33,585	35,708	36,880
Plus food and housing benefits	21,546	31,697	27,642	29,377	31,129	32,680
Less Federal taxes	22,215	33,923	28,941	30,465	31,770	33,118
Number of individuals removed from poverty due to (thousands):						
Social insurance (other than Social Security)	1,916	3,232	1,675	1,799	2,515	2,654
Social insurance (including Social Security)	14,179	15,772	15,227	14,923	16,548	17,304
Means-tested cash, food, and housing benefits	7,058	5,231	6,183	6,551	7,002	7,037
Federal taxes	-669	-2,226	-1,299	-1,088	-641	-438
Total	20,568	18,777	20,111	20,386	22,909	23,903
Percent of poor individuals removed from poverty due to:						
Social insurance (including Social Security)	33.1	29.9	31.0	29.3	30.3	30.3
Means-tested cash, food, and housing benefits	16.5	9.9	12.6	12.9	12.8	12.3
Federal taxes	-1.6	-4.2	-2.6	-2.1	-1.2	-.8
Total	48.1	35.6	41.0	40.1	41.9	41.9

TABLE H-11.—ANTIPOVERTY EFFECTIVENESS OF CASH AND NEARCASH TRANSFERS (INCLUDING FEDERAL INCOME AND PAYROLL TAXES) FOR ALL PERSONS—Continued

	1979	1983	1989	1990	1991	1992
Poverty gap (millions of 1991 dollars):						
Cash income before transfers	122,875	151,930	143,907	149,149	160,355	169,050
Plus social insurance (other than Social Security)	114,537	139,817	137,082	141,845	150,704	158,534
Plus Social Security	63,624	85,642	79,050	84,527	91,123	94,317
Plus means-tested cash transfers	44,235	63,821	58,978	62,991	67,920	71,693
Plus food and housing benefits	34,630	50,846	45,631	47,630	51,161	54,814
Less Federal taxes	35,176	52,739	46,583	48,630	51,734	55,250
Percent reduction in the poverty gap due to:						
Social insurance (including Social Security)	48.2	43.6	45.1	43.3	43.2	44.2
Means-tested cash, food and housing benefits	23.2	22.9	23.2	24.7	24.9	23.4
Federal taxes	-0.4	-1.2	-0.7	-0.7	-0.4	-0.3
Total	70.9	65.3	67.6	67.4	67.7	67.3
Poverty rate (in percent):						
Cash income before transfers	19.2	22.8	19.9	20.5	21.8	22.5
Plus social insurance (other than Social Security)	18.3	21.4	19.3	19.7	20.8	21.4
Plus Social Security	12.8	15.9	13.8	14.4	15.2	15.6
Plus means-tested cash transfers	11.6	15.1	12.8	13.5	14.2	14.5
Plus food and housing benefits	9.7	13.7	11.2	11.8	12.4	12.9
Less Federal taxes	10.0	14.6	11.8	12.3	12.6	13.0
Total reduction in poverty rate	9.2	8.2	8.1	8.2	9.2	9.5

Source: Congressional Budget Office.

TABLE H–12.—ANTIPOVERTY EFFECTIVENESS OF CASH AND NEARCASH TRANSFERS (INCLUDING FEDERAL INCOME AND PAYROLL TAXES) FOR INDIVIDUALS IN SINGLE-PARENT FAMILIES WITH RELATED CHILDREN UNDER AGE 18

	1979	1983	1989	1990	1991	1992
Total population (thousands)	23,547	25,559	29,260	30,525	31,733	32,381
Number of poor individuals (thousands):						
Cash income before transfers	11,786	13,751	14,074	15,110	16,387	16,679
Plus social insurance (other than Social Security)	11,568	13,501	13,820	14,841	16,061	16,361
Plus Social Security	10,645	12,611	13,040	14,203	15,290	15,600
Plus means-tested cash transfers	9,491	12,063	12,388	13,324	14,573	14,647
Plus food and housing benefits	7,115	10,531	10,636	11,313	12,452	12,661
Less Federal taxes	7,141	10,800	10,648	11,234	12,263	12,461
Number of individuals removed from poverty due to (thousands):						
Social insurance (other than Social Security)	218	250	254	269	326	318
Social insurance (including Social Security)	1,141	1,140	1,034	907	1,097	1,079
Means-tested cash, food, and housing benefits	3,530	2,080	2,404	2,890	2,838	2,939
Federal taxes	−26	−269	−12	79	189	200
Total	4,645	2,951	3,426	3,876	4,124	4,218
Percent of poor individuals removed from poverty due to:						
Social insurance (including Social Security)	9.7	8.3	7.3	6.0	6.7	6.5
Means-tested cash, food, and housing benefits	30.0	15.1	17.1	19.1	17.3	17.6
Federal taxes	−0.2	−2.0	−0.1	0.5	1.2	1.2
Total	39.4	21.5	24.3	25.7	25.2	25.3

TABLE H-12.—ANTIPOVERTY EFFECTIVENESS OF CASH AND NEARCASH TRANSFERS (INCLUDING FEDERAL INCOME AND PAYROLL TAXES) FOR INDIVIDUALS IN SINGLE-PARENT FAMILIES WITH RELATED CHILDREN UNDER AGE 18—Continued

	1979	1983	1989	1990	1991	1992
Poverty gap (millions of 1991 dollars):						
Cash income before transfers	30,003	37,790	37,189	40,081	43,363	44,599
Plus social insurance (other than Social Security)	29,154	36,398	36,387	39,015	41,948	43,017
Plus Social Security	25,747	32,804	33,011	35,968	38,913	39,581
Plus means-tested cash transfers	14,856	21,552	22,593	24,418	26,659	27,982
Plus food and housing benefits	9,219	14,006	14,391	14,761	16,029	17,547
Less Federal taxes	9,153	14,095	14,221	14,588	15,643	17,106
Percent reduction in the poverty gap due to:						
Social insurance (including Social Security)	14.2	13.2	11.2	10.3	10.3	11.3
Means-tested cash, food and housing benefits	55.1	49.7	50.1	52.9	52.8	49.4
Federal taxes	0.2	-0.2	0.5	0.4	0.9	1.0
Total	69.5	62.7	61.8	63.6	63.9	61.6
Poverty rate (in percent):						
Cash income before transfers	50.1	53.8	48.1	49.5	51.6	51.5
Plus social insurance (other than Social Security)	49.1	52.8	47.2	48.6	50.6	50.5
Plus Social Security	45.2	49.3	44.6	46.6	48.2	48.2
Plus means-tested cash transfers	40.3	47.2	42.3	43.7	45.9	45.2
Plus food and housing benefits	30.2	41.2	36.4	37.1	39.2	39.1
Less Federal taxes	30.3	42.2	36.4	36.8	38.6	38.5
Total reduction in poverty rate	19.8	11.6	11.7	12.7	13.0	13.0

Source: Congressional Budget Office.

1175

TABLE H-13.—ANTIPOVERTY EFFECTIVENESS OF CASH AND NEARCASH TRANSFERS (INCLUDING FEDERAL INCOME AND PAYROLL TAXES) FOR ALL INDIVIDUALS IN MARRIED-COUPLE FAMILIES WITH RELATED CHILDREN UNDER AGE 18

	1979	1983	1989	1990	1991	1992
Total population (thousands)	109,888	106,182	105,876	106,092	106,058	107,241
Number of poor individuals (thousands):						
Cash income before transfers	10,302	15,184	11,117	11,564	12,454	13,071
Plus social insurance (other than Social Security)	9,538	13,447	10,521	10,918	11,510	12,047
Plus Social Security	8,453	12,644	9,665	10,191	10,617	11,092
Plus means-tested cash transfers	7,785	12,183	9,019	9,507	9,846	10,291
Plus food and housing benefits	6,528	11,205	7,813	8,412	8,628	9,127
Less Federal taxes	6,867	12,620	8,515	8,693	8,827	9,167
Number of individuals removed from poverty due to (thousands):						
Social insurance (other than Social Security)	764	1,737	596	646	944	1,024
Social insurance (including Social Security)	1,849	2,540	1,452	1,373	1,837	1,979
Means-tested cash, food, and housing benefits	1,925	1,439	1,852	1,779	1,989	1,965
Federal taxes	-339	-1,415	-702	-281	-199	-40
Total	3,435	2,564	2,602	2,871	3,627	3,904
Percent of poor individuals removed from poverty due to:						
Social insurance (including Social Security)	17.9	16.7	13.1	11.9	14.8	15.1
Means-tested cash, food, and housing benefits	18.7	9.5	16.7	15.4	16.0	15.0
Federal taxes	-3.3	-9.3	-6.3	-2.4	-1.6	-.3
Total	33.3	16.9	23.4	24.8	29.1	29.9

TABLE H–13.—ANTIPOVERTY EFFECTIVENESS OF CASH AND NEARCASH TRANSFERS (INCLUDING FEDERAL INCOME AND PAYROLL TAXES) FOR ALL INDIVIDUALS IN MARRIED-COUPLE FAMILIES WITH RELATED CHILDREN UNDER AGE 18—Continued

	1979	1983	1989	1990	1991	1992
Poverty gap (millions of 1991 dollars):						
Cash income before transfers	16,425	25,497	17,366	17,991	20,544	21,382
Plus social insurance (other than Social Security)	14,637	21,570	15,685	16,283	18,168	18,906
Plus Social Security	11,600	18,936	13,034	14,091	15,672	16,035
Plus means-tested cash transfers	9,228	15,150	10,123	10,836	12,395	12,563
Plus food and housing benefits	6,994	11,895	7,568	8,184	9,300	9,374
Less Federal taxes	7,045	12,705	7,676	8,249	9,076	9,065
Percent reduction in the poverty gap due to:						
Social Insurance (including Social Security)	29.4	25.7	24.9	21.7	23.7	25.0
Means-tested cash, food, and housing benefits	28.0	27.6	31.5	32.8	31.0	31.2
Federal taxes	-0.3	-3.2	-0.6	-0.4	1.1	1.4
Total	57.1	50.2	55.8	54.2	55.8	57.6
Poverty rate (in percent):						
Cash income before transfers	9.4	14.3	10.5	10.9	11.7	12.2
Plus social insurance (other than Social Security)	8.7	12.7	9.9	10.3	10.9	11.2
Plus Social Security	7.7	11.9	9.1	9.6	10.0	10.3
Plus means-tested cash transfers	7.7	11.5	8.5	8.9	9.3	9.6
Plus food and housing benefits	5.9	10.5	7.4	7.9	8.1	8.5
Less Federal taxes	6.2	11.9	8.0	8.4	8.3	8.5
Total reduction in poverty rate	3.2	2.4	2.5	2.5	3.4	3.7

Source: Congressional Budget Office.

TABLE H–14.—ANTIPOVERTY EFFECTIVENESS OF CASH AND NEARCASH TRANSFERS (INCLUDING FEDERAL INCOME AND PAYROLL TAXES) FOR ALL INDIVIDUALS IN FAMILIES WITH RELATED CHILDREN UNDER AGE 18 [1]

	1979	1983	1989	1990	1991	1992
Total population (thousands)	133,435	132,123	135,430	136,790	137,791	139,622
Number of poor individuals (thousands):						
Cash income before transfers	22,088	28,935	25,190	26,674	28,841	29,751
Plus social insurance (other than Social Security)	21,106	26,948	24,341	25,759	27,570	28,408
Plus Social Security	19,098	25,255	22,704	24,394	25,906	26,691
Plus means-tested cash transfers	17,276	24,246	21,408	22,832	24,419	24,939
Plus food and housing benefits	13,642	21,736	18,449	19,725	21,080	21,788
Less Federal taxes	14,008	23,420	19,163	20,197	21,090	21,627
Number of individuals removed from poverty due to (thousands):						
Social insurance (other than Social Security)	982	1,987	849	915	1,271	1,343
Social insurance (including Social Security)	2,990	3,680	2,486	2,280	2,935	3,060
Means-tested cash, food, and housing benefits	5,456	3,519	4,255	4,669	4,826	4,903
Federal taxes	–366	–1684	–714	–472	–10	161
Total	8,080	5,515	6,027	6,477	7,751	8,124
Percent of poor individuals removed from poverty due to:						
Social insurance (including Social Security)	13.5	12.7	9.9	8.5	10.2	10.3
Means-tested cash, food, and housing benefits	24.7	12.2	16.9	17.5	16.7	16.5
Federal taxes	–1.7	–5.8	–2.8	–1.8	0.0	.5
Total	36.6	19.1	23.9	24.3	26.9	27.3

TABLE H-14.—ANTIPOVERTY EFFECTIVENESS OF CASH AND NEARCASH TRANSFERS (INCLUDING FEDERAL INCOME AND PAYROLL TAXES) FOR ALL INDIVIDUALS IN FAMILIES WITH RELATED CHILDREN UNDER AGE 18 [1]—Continued

	1979	1983	1989	1990	1991	1992
Poverty gap (millions of 1991 dollars):						
Cash income before transfers	46,428	63,286	54,553	58,072	63,907	65,980
Plus social insurance (other than Social Security)	43,788	57,968	52,071	55,298	60,116	61,922
Plus Social Security	37,346	51,739	46,044	50,059	54,586	55,616
Plus means-tested cash transfers	24,085	36,702	32,717	35,254	39,054	40,545
Plus food and housing benefits	16,213	25,901	21,959	22,945	25,329	26,920
Less Federal taxes	16,198	26,800	21,896	22,836	24,719	26,171
Percent reduction in the poverty gap due to:						
Social insurance (including Social Security)	19.6	18.2	15.6	13.8	14.6	15.7
Means-tested cash, food and housing benefits	45.5	40.8	44.2	46.7	45.8	43.5
Federal taxes	0.0	-1.4	0.1	0.2	1.0	1.1
Total	65.1	57.7	59.9	60.7	61.3	60.3
Poverty rate (in percent):						
Cash income before transfers	16.6	21.9	18.6	19.5	20.9	21.3
Plus social insurance (other than Social Security)	15.8	20.4	18.0	18.8	20.0	20.3
Plus Social Security	14.3	19.2	16.8	17.8	18.8	19.1
Plus means-tested cash transfers	12.9	18.4	15.8	16.7	17.7	17.9
Plus food and housing benefits	10.2	16.5	13.6	14.4	15.3	15.6
Less Federal taxes	10.5	17.8	14.2	14.8	15.3	15.5
Total reduction in poverty rate	6.1	4.1	4.4	4.7	5.6	5.8

[1] This table is a summation of female-headed and married-couple families with children.

Source: Congressional Budget Office.

TABLE H-15.—ANTIPOVERTY EFFECTIVENESS OF CASH AND NEARCASH TRANSFERS (INCLUDING FEDERAL INCOME AND PAYROLL TAXES) FOR INDIVIDUALS IN UNITS WITH ALL MEMBERS AGE 65 OR OLDER

	1979	1983	1989	1990	1991	1992
Total population (thousands)	17,623	19,294	21,805	22,209	22,812	22,940
Number of poor individuals (thousands):						
Cash income before transfers	10,564	10,843	11,971	11,904	12,551	13,073
Plus social insurance (other than Social Security)	10,344	10,654	11,806	11,733	12,298	12,798
Plus Social Security	3,361	3,231	3,138	3,253	3,404	3,512
Plus means-tested cash transfers	3,008	2,928	2,810	3,038	3,157	3,239
Plus food and housing benefits	2,635	2,520	2,335	2,452	2,498	2,712
Less Federal taxes	2,641	2,533	2,354	2,458	2,505	2,715
Number of individuals removed from poverty due to (thousands):						
Social insurance (other than Social Security)	220	189	165	171	253	275
Social insurance (including Social Security)	7,203	7,612	8,833	8,651	9,147	9,561
Means-tested cash, food, and housing benefits	726	711	803	801	906	800
Federal taxes	−6	−13	−19	−6	−7	−3
Total	7,923	8,310	9,617	9,446	10,046	10,358
Percent of poor individuals removed from poverty due to:						
Social insurance (including Social Security)	68.2	70.2	73.8	72.7	72.9	73.1
Means-tested cash, food, and housing benefits	6.9	6.6	6.7	6.7	7.2	6.1
Federal taxes	−0.1	−0.1	−0.2	−0.1	−0.1	0.0
Total	75.0	76.6	80.3	79.4	80.0	79.2

TABLE H–15.—ANTIPOVERTY EFFECTIVENESS OF CASH AND NEARCASH TRANSFERS (INCLUDING FEDERAL INCOME AND PAYROLL TAXES) FOR INDIVIDUALS IN UNITS WITH ALL MEMBERS AGE 65 OR OLDER—Continued

	1979	1983	1989	1990	1991	1992
Poverty gap (millions of 1991 dollars):						
Cash income before transfers	41,873	43,678	47,473	47,453	50,015	51,932
Plus social insurance (other than Social Security)	39,890	42,106	46,083	46,268	48,471	50,238
Plus Social Security	7,166	6,814	6,505	6,788	7,560	7,054
Plus means-tested cash transfers	4,773	4,470	4,563	5,056	5,423	5,396
Plus food and housing benefits	4,114	3,887	3,766	4,105	4,515	4,527
Less Federal taxes	4,125	3,901	3,780	4,117	4,533	4,539
Percent reduction in the poverty gap due to:						
Social insurance (including Social Security)	82.9	84.4	86.3	85.7	84.9	86.4
Means-tested cash, food and housing benefits	7.3	6.7	5.8	5.7	6.1	4.9
Federal taxes	0.0	0.0	0.0	0.0	0.0	0.0
Total	90.1	91.1	92.0	91.3	90.9	91.3
Poverty rate (in percent):						
Cash income before transfers	59.9	56.2	54.9	53.6	55.0	57.0
Plus social insurance (other than Social Security)	58.7	55.3	54.1	52.8	53.9	55.8
Plus Social Security	19.1	16.8	14.4	14.7	14.9	15.3
Plus means-tested cash transfers	17.1	15.2	12.9	13.7	13.8	14.1
Plus food and housing benefits	15.0	13.1	10.7	11.0	11.0	11.8
Less Federal taxes	15.0	13.1	10.8	11.1	11.0	11.8
Total reduction in poverty rate	44.9	43.1	44.1	42.5	44.0	45.2

Source: Congressional Budget Office.

TRENDS IN FAMILY INCOMES, 1967–92

In the past 25 years, the level of and inequality among family incomes has changed significantly according to all income measures. Between 1967 and 1973, income increased for all quintiles, and income inequality went down. As measured by the Congressional Budget Office, over this time period, the lowest quintile experienced an increase in mean adjusted family income (family income divided by the poverty threshold for the appropriate family size) of 30 percent, while income for the highest quintile grew by 21 percent. Since, 1973, however, the trend has been markedly different. Income of the bottom quintile has declined, while the income for the highest quintile has risen.

While the general trends in families' economic well-being are similar regardless of how measured, varying results for the distribution of family incomes are obtained depending on which income measure is used. Three commonly used income measures (all adjusted for inflation) are family cash income, family cash income per capita, and adjusted family income. While no measure perfectly captures the economic well-being of families, adjusted family income most accurately accounts for differences in family size by incorporating the scale implicit in the official Federal poverty thresholds.

Family composition in the United States has undergone pronounced changes over the past two decades, as the number of families grew twice as fast as the population between 1973 and 1989.[7] The growth in families overall reflects very different trends among particular types of families. The number of married couples with children, for example, fell almost 2 percent between 1973 and 1989. In contrast, the number of families headed by a single mother grew over 70 percent during the same period.

Changes in family composition are also reflected in the number of persons and earners per family. The average family has become smaller, reflecting in part relatively fewer families with children (and fewer children in those families). The average family also had fewer earners in 1989 than in 1973.

Total family cash income grew over 50 percent in real terms between 1973 and 1989, before falling slightly as the recession that began in 1990 took hold. The real income of the average family rose during this period as well, but the magnitude and timing of the increase depends on the income measure used. For example, family cash income rose about 9 percent between 1973 and 1989, on average, with virtually all of the increase taking place between 1979 and 1989. In contrast, average pretax adjusted family income (AFI)—which takes into account changes in family size—rose about 20 percent, with the annual increase about equally divided between the two time periods shown. The larger increase in AFI reflects in part a decrease in average family size.

---

[7] In contrast to some measures of income from the Bureau of the Census, this analysis treats unrelated individuals as one-person families. Family types are defined in detail below.

TABLE H-16.—CHANGES IN POPULATION, FAMILY COMPOSITION, AND INCOME, 1973, 1979, 1989, AND 1992

	1973	1979	1989	1992	Percent change		
					1973–89	1979–89	1989–92
A. Distribution of families and persons by family type							
Number of families (in thousands)	73,166	84,229	101,663	105,460	38.9	20.7	3.7
Families with children	31,098	32,166	34,768	36,158	11.8	8.1	4.0
Married couples with children	24,798	24,166	24,378	24,640	-1.7	.9	1.1
Single mothers with children	4,126	5,650	7,123	8,041	72.6	26.1	12.9
Nonelderly childless units[1]	28,183	35,730	46,467	48,270	64.9	30.1	3.9
Elderly childless units[2]	13,884	16,331	20,428	21,032	47.1	25.1	3.0
Number of persons in different family types (in thousands)	207,525	217,718	245,846	253,843	18.5	12.9	3.3
Families with children	134,248	130,426	135,381	139,622	.8	3.8	3.1
Married couples with children	108,976	101,318	99,471	100,533	-8.7	-1.8	1.1
Single mothers with children	14,240	18,132	21,504	24,159	51.0	18.6	12.3
Nonelderly childless units[1]	50,148	60,514	77,025	79,496	53.6	27.3	3.2
Elderly childless units[2]	23,129	26,778	33,440	34,725	44.6	24.9	3.8
B. Size, age composition, and number of earners for all families							
Average number of persons per family:							
Total	2.87	2.59	2.40	2.41	-16.4	-7.3	0.5
Under 18	.94	.75	.64	0.63	-31.9	-14.7	-1.7
18 to 64	1.64	1.55	1.47	1.49	-10.1	-5.2	1.3
65 and older	.30	.28	.29	0.29	-1.9	3.6	.09

Average number of earners per family:

Total	1.39	1.34	1.29	1.29	-6.9	-3.7	-0.2
Male earners	.81	.75	.69	.69	-15.3	-8.0	0.2
Female earners	.57	.59	.60	.60	5.2	1.7	-0.7

C. Income trends for all families, by income measure

Income measure (in 1989 dollars):							
Total family cash income (billions)	2,220	2,591	3,353	3,272	51.0	29.4	-2.4
Mean family cash income	30,341	30,764	32,978	31,022	8.7	7.2	-5.9
Mean family cash income per capita [3]	10,718	11,922	13,743	12,888	28.2	15.3	-6.2
Adjusted pretax income [4]	19,096	20,592	23,025	21,776	20.6	11.8	-5.4
Adjusted posttax income [5]	NA	17,404	19,424	18,502	NA	11.6	-4.7
High adult male earner	NA	12,044	12,189	11,128	NA	1.2	-8.7
High adult female earner	NA	4,111	5,633	5,758	NA	37.0	2.2
Other earners in family	NA	923	894	718	NA	-3.1	-19.7
Other private income	NA	2,021	2,700	2,471	NA	33.6	-8.5
Cash transfer income (non-means-tested)	NA	1,190	1,429	1,492	NA	20.0	4.4
Cash transfer income (means-tested)	NA	302	180	197	NA	-40.4	9.7
Noncash transfer income	NA	145	139	170	NA	-4.0	21.8
Taxes	NA	-3,333	-3,740	(3,431)	NA	12.2	-8.3

[1] Families in which both the head and spouse are under age 65 and there are no children under 18, and unrelated individuals under age 65.

[2] Families in which either the head or spouse of head is 65 or older and there are no children under 18, and unrelated individuals 65 and older.

[3] Family cash income divided by the number of persons in the family.

[4] Pretax AFI (adjusted family income) is pretax family income divided by the poverty threshold. Thresholds are based on the 1989 distribution of family sizes, with no adjustment for the age of the head of household or the number of children. In this table only, pretax AFI is expressed in dollars by multiplying adjusted family income by the 1-person poverty threshold.

[5] Posttax AFI (adjusted family income) is posttax family income, plus the cash value of noncash food and housing benefits, divided by the poverty threshold. Thresholds are based on the 1989 distribution of family sizes, with no adjustment for the age of the head of household or the number of children. In this table only, posttax AFI is expressed in dollars by multiplying adjusted family income by the 1-person poverty threshold.

NA—Not available.

Source: Congressional Budget Office based on CPS data.

Definitions and methods

Analyzing trends in the distribution of family incomes over time requires making decisions about a number of variables: How should variation in incomes be measured? What is the appropriate time-frame over which to look at changes? How should inflation be taken into account? And, finally, what is the appropriate measure of income to use?

Measuring variation. Most of the data in this section are presented for income quintiles, each of which represents one-fifth of the income distribution (either families or persons, as indicated). Quintiles are calculated by ordering all relevant family units from that with the lowest income to that with the highest. For the analysis of changes in incomes among different types of families, quintiles are defined separately for each family type.

The analysis of changes in the distribution of family incomes over time is done by looking at average incomes, adjusted for inflation, by income quintile for specific types of families.

Timeframe. Most of the analysis focuses on data for 4 years: 1967, 1973, 1979, and 1989. These years reflect peaks in the business cycle, and allow comparisons to be made in a consistent fashion that holds constant general economic conditions. Data are also shown for 1992, the most recent year for which data are available.

Adjustment for inflation. To examine changes in family income over time, the dollar amounts must be adjusted for inflation to compare actual buying power. Adjustment for inflation is done here using the CPI–U–X1, a revised version of the official Consumer Price Index that provides a consistent treatment of the costs of homeownership over the years examined. The CPI–U–X1 is an index of the cost of a market basket of goods and services representing the average consumption of the urban population.[8]

Income measure. The purpose of looking at the distribution of family incomes over time is to analyze changes in family economic well-being. Two important issues in choosing an appropriate income measure are how to adjust for differences in family size and what to include as income.

One measure, used extensively by the Bureau of the Census, is real family cash income, which is the sum of wage, salary, and self-employment earnings, private pension and retirement income, interest and dividends, and government cash transfers received by each family member. By this measure, which takes inflation into account, but not changes in family size, noncash transfers, or taxes, the average income of all families increased 8.7 percent between 1973 and 1989, with most of the growth occurring between 1979 and 1989 (see A of table H–17). Family cash income also shows quite different trends among income quintiles: the average income

---

[8] The official CPI is viewed by many analysts as having overstated the growth in housing costs during the late 1970s. Prior to 1983, the housing component of the CPI reflected both the flow of services and the investment aspects of homeownership; only the former is appropriate in an index measuring consumption costs.

Since 1983, the Bureau of Labor Statistics (BLS) has used a rental-equivalence measure incorporating the consumption aspects of owning a home, not the investment aspects. The CPI–U–X1 series is used to calculate what the CPI would be had the rental-equivalence measure been in place since 1967. The BLS recommends using the CPI–U–X1 when a consistent treatment of homeowner costs is desired. See Bureau of Census; "Money Income of Households, Families, and Persons in the United States: 1991," Current Population Reports, Series P–60, No. 180 Appendices A and B.

of the lowest quintile fell 3.2 percent between 1973 and 1989, where as the average income of the highest quintile rose 17.1 percent.

Family cash income has several shortcomings as a measure of changes in economic well-being. Most notably, it fails to take into account changes in family size and composition: a family of one— i.e., a person living alone—with $30,000 in income is treated as being as well off as a family of four with $30,000 in income. This assumption is inappropriate, however, as a family of four requires more income to attain the same standard of living as a single person.

An alternative approach is to measure income on a per capita basis, by dividing total family income by the number of persons in the family. Using family cash income per capita yields quite different results (see C of table H–17). The growth in average per capita income among all families between 1973 and 1989 is much larger than the growth in average family cash income: 28.2 percent, compared with 8.7 percent. Moreover, average cash income per capita rose for each quintile between 1973 and 1989, whereas average family cash income rose only for the top two quintiles. These results reflect a decline in family size between 1973 and 1989.

In contrast to family cash income, which completely ignores differences in family size, using per capita family income as a measure of well-being assumes that a family of four requires exactly four times as much as a single person to attain the same standard of living. But four persons living together would generally require less than four times as much income because of the economies of scale reaped from increased family size. (For example, families with more children might require more bedrooms, but not more kitchens.) A measure that reflects such economies of scale would therefore provide a better method of taking family size into account.

TABLE H–17.—ALTERNATIVE MEASURES OF FAMILY INCOME, BY INCOME QUINTILE AND CHANGE OVER TIME, 1973, 1979, 1989, AND 1992 FOR ALL FAMILIES

[In 1989 dollars]

Quintile	1967	1973	1979	1989	1992	Percent change		
						1973–89	1979–89	1989–92
I. Pre-Tax Cash Income								
A. Mean family cash income (family weighted):								
Lowest	NA	6,061	5,994	5,866	5,256	−3.2	−2.1	−10.4
Second	NA	15,416	15,306	15,107	13,885	−2.0	−1.3	−8.1
Middle	NA	25,909	25,609	25,823	24,118	−.3	.8	−6.6
Fourth	NA	37,946	38,680	40,374	38,367	6.4	4.4	−5.0
Highest	NA	66,364	68,230	77,716	73,487	17.1	13.9	−5.4
Total	NA	30,341	30,764	32,978	31,022	8.7	7.2	−5.9
B. Mean adjusted family income (person weighted): [1]								
Lowest	.69	.90	.90	.86	0.77	−4.3	−4.3	−10.4
Second	1.54	1.94	2.06	2.09	1.95	7.7	1.3	−6.7
Middle	2.26	2.82	3.07	3.27	3.10	16.0	6.7	−5.2
Fourth	3.16	3.94	4.32	4.77	4.55	20.9	10.5	−4.5
Highest	5.67	6.87	7.39	8.84	8.36	28.7	19.6	−5.4
Total	2.66	3.29	3.55	3.97	3.75	20.4	11.8	−5.5

C. Mean family income per capita (person weighted):[2]

Lowest	NA	2,795	2,912	2,822	2,504	1.0	-3.1	-11.3
Second	NA	5,906	6,535	6,872	6,384	16.4	5.2	-7.1
Middle	NA	8,628	9,713	10,723	10,134	24.3	10.4	-5.5
Fourth	NA	12,386	14,046	16,058	15,145	29.6	14.3	-5.7
Highest	NA	23,875	26,405	32,237	30,274	35.0	22.1	-6.1
Total	NA	10,718	11,922	13,743	12,888	28.2	15.3	-6.2

D. Mean adjusted family income (post-tax income plus food and housing benefits) (person weighted):[1]

Lowest	NA	NA	.96	.93	.88	N/A	-2.1	-6.4
Second	NA	NA	1.89	1.90	1.80	N/A	0.5	-5.2
Middle	NA	NA	2.67	2.84	2.71	N/A	6.4	-4.6
Fourth	NA	NA	3.63	4.01	3.85	N/A	10.6	-3.9
Highest	NA	NA	5.85	7.04	6.69	N/A	20.4	-5.0
Total	NA	NA	3.00	3.35	3.19	N/A	11.6	-4.8

[1] Family income divided by the poverty threshold. Thresholds are based on the 1989 distribution of family sizes, with no adjustment for the age of the head of household or the number of children.

[2] Total family income divided by the number of persons in the family.

Source: Congressional Budget Office tabulations of data from the March Current Population Survey, 1974, 1980, 1990, and 1993.

Analysts disagree over the best method of making incomes comparable for families of different size, but one readily available candidate is the scale implicit in the official Federal poverty thresholds. This scale assumes, for example, that a family of four needs about twice as much income as a single person to attain an equivalent standard of living (see table H–18). The equivalence scale implicit in the poverty thresholds may not perfectly capture the disparate needs of families of different sizes, but it probably yields a better assessment of relative economic well-being than making no adjustment (mean family cash income) or assuming no economies of scale (mean family cash income per capita).

TABLE H–18.—POVERTY THRESHOLDS AND EQUIVALENCE VALUES FOR DIFFERENT FAMILY SIZES, 1992

	Official poverty threshold	Adjusted poverty threshold	Equivalence value (one person=1.00)
Family size (persons):			
1	$7,143	$6,572	1.00
2	9,137	8,407	1.28
3	11,186	10,292	1.57
4	14,335	13,190	2.01
5	16,592	15,266	2.32
6	19,137	17,608	2.68
7	21,594	19,869	3.02
8	24,053	22,131	3.37
9 or more	28,745	26,449	4.02

Note.—Poverty thresholds shown for 1- and 2-person families are a weighted average of the separate official thresholds for elderly and non-elderly individuals and families. Adjusted poverty thresholds are computed using the CPI–U–X1 (1967 equals 100) to adjust for inflation. The official poverty threshold is adjusted for inflation using the CPI.

Source: Congressional Budget Office.

CHART H-2. CHANGES IN POSTTAX ADJUSTED FAMILY INCOME BY QUINTILE, 1979–89

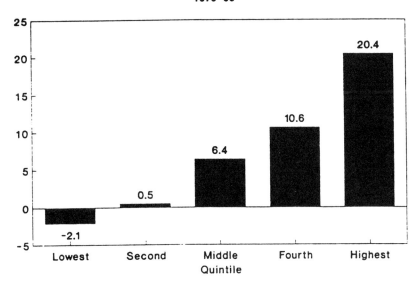

The adjusted family income (AFI) measure shown in B of table H-17 incorporates the equivalence scale underlying the poverty thresholds. Each family's pretax cash income is divided by its poverty threshold, yielding family income as a multiple of poverty. Thus, for example, the average family in the middle quintile in 1989 had an income of 3.27 times its poverty threshold.[9]

Adjusting for family size in this way yields results that are generally intermediate to those obtained for the family cash income and family cash income per capita measures. Between 1967 and 1973, income increased significantly for all quintiles, by 30 percent for the lowest quintile. On average, pretax AFI increased 20.4 percent between 1973 and 1989, with a 4.3 percent decline for the lowest quintile and a 28.7 percent increase for the highest quintile. Also like the other measures, average pretax AFI declined for the lowest quintile between 1979 and 1989 and rose for the highest quintile.

It must be remembered that there is no adjustment in these analyses for labor inputs. For example, if mean income increases by 10 percent over a given time period while family work hours also increase by 10 percent, the family's overall economic well-being may be qualitatively different than a 10-percent increase in income would suggest. For example, work expenses may have increased by an even larger amount, particularly if more family members are working, and leisure time would have decreased.

---

[9] Poverty thresholds for 1- and 2-person families in this section do not vary by the age of the family head. The 1989 weighted averages are adjusted for inflation using the CPI–U–X1.

Adjusting for noncash income and taxes. A family's economic well-being is determined not only by its pretax cash income, but also by the amount of any noncash income it receives. Analyses that ignore noncash benefits—whether received from employers in the form of fringe benefits or through social welfare transfer programs—understate how well-off families are. The understatement has grown over time, moreover, because in-kind income has increased as a share of personal income. Employer-provided benefits increased from about 7 percent of wages and salaries in 1973 to 10 percent in 1989. Adjusted for inflation and population growth, spending on the major government noncash transfer programs—food stamps, public housing, Medicare, and Medicaid—almost tripled over the same period.

Whereas the omission of noncash income understates economic well-being for most families, pretax measures of income overstate it. Both income and payroll taxes reduce disposable income, so that posttax income provides a better measure of the resources available to families at any point in time. Taking taxes into account is especially important for assessing income trends over time because Social Security tax rates increased by almost 30 percent, and the amount of annual earnings subject to the tax increased by nearly 70 percent in real terms between 1973 and 1989. And although individual income taxes as a share of income have been relatively constant, the share varies widely across income quintiles.

The income measure shown in D of table H–17 shows posttax AFI, plus the estimated cash value of food and housing benefits, for 1979, 1989, and 1992.[10] Food benefits reflect the value of food stamps and school lunches; housing benefits reflect subsidized public housing; and taxes include Federal income and payroll taxes, but not State income taxes. Being more comprehensive, posttax AFI is a better indicator of economic well-being than pretax AFI, and is used extensively in this study.[11]

The growth in average posttax AFI between 1979 and 1989 is generally similar to the growth in pretax AFI, both for families overall and for each income quintile. The most notable difference between the two measures is in their levels: average posttax AFI was about 8 percent higher than average pretax AFI for the lowest quintile in 1989, but about 20 percent lower for the highest quintile. The difference in the two measures reflects the addition of food and housing benefits to the incomes of families in the lowest quintile and the subtraction of taxes from incomes of families in the highest quintile.

Income shares. Another way of tracking income trends is to look at changes in the percentage share of income received by families in each quintile. Income shares measure whether families have gained or lost in relative terms. That is, a given quintile may receive a smaller share of real income even as its average income has increased.

---

[10] Data on noncash transfers are available only for 1979 and later years, as the Bureau of the Census did not collect this information until then. Similar information about the value of Medicaid and Medicare is also available, but the family-level data needed to allocate employer-provided health insurance benefits are not. The value of Medicaid and Medicare benefits is therefore excluded to avoid skewing the distribution of income toward low-income families.

[11] Unless stated otherwise, posttax AFI always includes the cash value of noncash food and housing benefits.

All four income measures show broadly similar trends in the share of income received by each quintile (see table H–19). Between 1973 and 1989, the shares of each of the lowest three quintiles fell, and the share of the top quintile rose. The measures show different patterns of shares at any point in time, however. In 1989, for example, the share of the top quintile was 47.1 percent when measured as family cash income, compared with 42.1 percent when measured as posttax AFI.

TABLE H–19.—SHARES OF FAMILY INCOME, BY INCOME QUINTILE FOR SELECTED YEARS, 1967–92 FOR ALL FAMILIES

[In percent]

Quintile	1967	1973	1979	1989	1992
I. Pretax Cash Income					
A. Mean family cash income (family weighted):					
Lowest	NA	4.0	3.9	3.6	3.4
Second	NA	10.2	10.0	9.2	9.0
Middle	NA	17.1	16.6	15.7	15.5
Fourth	NA	25.0	25.1	24.5	24.7
Highest	NA	43.7	44.4	47.1	47.4
B. Adjusted family income (AFI) (person weighted): [1]					
Lowest	5.2	5.5	5.1	4.3	4.1
Second	11.6	11.8	11.6	10.5	10.4
Middle	16.9	17.1	17.3	16.5	16.6
Fourth	23.7	23.9	24.3	24.0	24.3
Highest	42.6	41.7	41.7	44.6	44.6
C. Family cash income per capita (person weighted): [2]					
Lowest	NA	5.2	4.9	4.1	3.9
Second	NA	11.0	11.0	10.0	9.9
Middle	NA	16.1	16.3	15.6	15.7
Fourth	NA	23.1	23.6	23.4	23.5
Highest	NA	44.6	44.3	46.9	47.0
II. Posttax Income Plus Food and Housing Benefits					
D. Adjusted family income (AFI) (person weighted): [1]					
Lowest	NA	NA	6.4	5.6	5.5
Second	NA	NA	12.6	11.4	11.3
Middle	NA	NA	17.8	17.0	17.0
Fourth	NA	NA	24.2	24.0	24.2
Highest	NA	NA	39.0	42.1	42.0

[1] Family income divided by the poverty threshold. Thresholds are based on the 1989 distribution of family sizes, with no adjustment for the age of the head of household or the number of children.
[2] Total family income divided by the number of persons in the family.

Source: Congressional Budget Office tabulations of data from the March Current Population Survey, 1968, 1974, 1980, 1990, and 1993.

CHART H–3. RATIO OF AVERAGE ADJUSTED FAMILY INCOME OF HIGHEST QUINTILE TO AVERAGE INCOME OF LOWEST QUINTILE, 1967–92

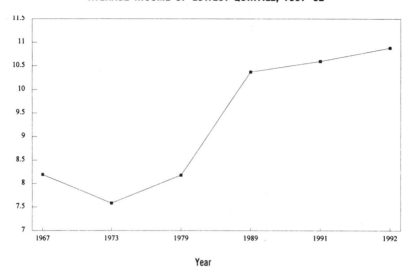

Year

Note: Data available only for points shown.

Source: Congressional Budget Office. Calculations and chart done by committee staff.

TRENDS IN PRETAX CASH INCOMES BY TYPE OF FAMILY

The composition of the typical family has changed over time. Compared with 1973 and 1979, there were fewer persons in each family in 1989, on average, and married couples with children made up a smaller fraction of all families. (See table H–20.) Additional insights can therefore be gained by looking at changes in incomes for specific family types. This analysis distinguishes seven types of family units:

—*Married couples with children,* which are families composed of a married couple living only with their own or related children, at least one of whom is under age 18;

—*Single mothers with children,* which are families composed of unmarried, divorced, separated, or widowed mothers living only with their own or related children, at least one of whom is under age 18;

—*Other families with children,* which are all other families with at least one related child under age 18;

—*Nonelderly childless families,* which are families composed of two or more related people living together, in which the family head and the spouse of the head are both under age 65 and there are no children under age 18;

—*Nonelderly unrelated individuals,* which are people over age 17 and under age 65 who are not living with relatives;

—*Elderly childless families,* which are families composed of two or more related people living together, in which either the family head or the spouse of the head is 65 or older and there are no children under age 18;

—*Elderly unrelated individuals,* which are people 65 or older who are not living with relatives.

In addition, results are also presented for four aggregates:

—*All families with children,* which comprises married couples, single mothers, and other families with children;

—*Nonelderly childless units,* which comprises nonelderly childless families and nonelderly unrelated individuals;

—*Elderly childless units,* which comprises elderly childless families and elderly unrelated individuals;

—*All families,* which comprises all families and unrelated individuals (i.e., the noninstitutional U.S. population).

Unless otherwise noted, the analysis of changes in income for each family type listed above is based on quintiles computed for that family type. This procedure permits comparisons within, but not across, family types; the quintile in which a particular family is found says nothing about its place among all families, but measures its position in relation to families of the same type. (For example, individuals in the middle quintile of single mothers with children may be in the lowest quintile of the all-families grouping.)

Comparisons over time show how the incomes of families of a given type compare with similar families at another time, not how incomes have changed for a particular type of family. Families may move among income quintiles as their incomes—or the incomes of other families—rise or fall; they may also change types as their members grow older, have children, marry, or divorce. In addition, the average number of members and earners within a given type of family may change over time, as may the characteristics of those persons.

TABLE H–20.—AVERAGE FAMILY SIZE AND NUMBER OF FAMILIES,[1] BY FAMILY TYPE, WEIGHTED BY FAMILIES, 1973, 1979, 1989 AND 1992

Family type and year	Persons per family	Number of families (thousands)	Percent of families
All families: [1]			
1973	2.84	73,166	100.0
1979	2.59	84,229	100.0
1989	2.42	101,663	100.0
1992	2.41	105,460	100.0
All families with children:			
1973	4.35	31,098	42.5
1979	4.09	32,166	38.2
1989	3.89	34,768	34.2
1992	3.89	36,158	34.3
Married couples with children:			
1973	4.42	24,798	33.9
1979	4.23	24,166	28.7
1989	4.08	24,378	24.0
1992	4.08	24,640	23.4
Single mothers with children:			
1973	3.50	4,126	5.6
1979	3.24	5,650	6.7
1989	3.02	7,123	7.0
1992	3.00	8,041	7.6
Nonelderly childless units:			
1973	1.76	28,183	38.5
1979	1.68	35,730	42.4
1989	1.66	46,467	45.7
1992	1.65	48,270	45.8
Nonelderly childless families:			
1973	2.32	16,363	22.4
1979	2.35	17,931	21.3
1989	2.44	21,257	20.9
1992	2.44	21,704	20.6
Nonelderly unrelated individuals:			
1973	1.00	11,820	16.2
1979	1.00	17,799	21.1
1989	1.00	25,210	24.8
1992	1.00	26,567	25.2
Elderly childless units:			
1973	1.64	13,884	19.0
1979	1.62	16,331	19.4
1989	1.64	20,428	20.1
1992	1.65	21,032	19.9

TABLE H–20.—AVERAGE FAMILY SIZE AND NUMBER OF FAMILIES,[1] BY FAMILY TYPE, WEIGHTED BY FAMILIES, 1973, 1979, 1989 AND 1992—Continued

Family type and year	Persons per family	Number of families (thousands)	Percent of families
Elderly childless families:			
1973	2.17	7,590	10.4
1979	2.16	8,676	10.3
1989	2.23	10,600	10.4
1992	2.25	10,990	10.4
Elderly unrelated individuals:			
1973	1.00	6,294	8.6
1979	1.00	7,655	9.1
1989	1.00	9,828	9.7
1992	1.00	10,041	9.5

[1] Corresponds more closely to census definition of household. Includes families of one person.

Source: Congressional Budget Office tabulations of data from the March Current Population Survey, 1974, 1980, 1990 and 1993.

Pretax AFI

Trends in incomes for different family types show more variation than trends for families overall. Between 1973 and 1989, adjusted family income grew 14.9 percent, on average, for families with children (see table H–21). This compares with an income gain of 20.4 percent for all families. Average AFI fell 16.1 percent during this period for the lowest quintile, from 88 percent of poverty to 74 percent of poverty. For the highest quintile, average AFI rose 25.6 percent, compared with 28.7 percent for all families.

Must of the divergence in incomes among families with children reflects compositional change, as families of single mothers with children became increasingly common. The lowest quintile of married couples with children has a 1.1 percent decline in average AFI between 1973 and 1989; the lowest quintile of single mothers with children fared much worse, with a 23.4 percent decline during the same period. These two family types as a whole, however, showed income gains: 20.6 percent for married couples with children and 16.9 percent for single mothers with children.

TABLE H-21.—AVERAGE PRETAX AFI (INCOME AS A MULTIPLE OF POVERTY) BY FAMILY TYPE AND INCOME QUINTILE, WEIGHTED BY PERSONS, 1967, 1973, 1979, 1989, AND 1992

Family type and quintile	1967	1973	1979	1989	1992	Percent change			
						1967–89	1973–89	1979–89	1989–92
All families:									
Lowest	0.69	0.90	0.90	0.86	0.77	25.1	–4.3	–4.3	–10.4
Second	1.54	1.94	2.06	2.09	1.95	35.5	7.7	1.3	–6.7
Middle	2.26	2.82	3.07	3.27	3.10	45.2	16.0	6.7	–5.2
Fourth	3.16	3.94	4.32	4.77	4.55	50.8	20.9	10.5	–4.5
Highest	5.67	6.87	7.39	8.84	8.36	56.0	28.7	19.6	–5.4
Total	2.66	3.29	3.55	3.97	3.75	49.0	20.4	11.8	–5.5
All families with children:									
Lowest	.74	.88	.84	.74	.65	.1	–16.1	–11.9	–12.2
Second	1.54	1.88	1.95	1.87	1.72	21.6	–.7	–4.2	–7.8
Middle	2.13	2.65	2.84	2.93	2.77	37.4	10.8	3.3	–5.5
Fourth	2.84	3.54	3.85	4.14	4.00	45.5	16.9	7.6	–3.4
Highest	4.77	5.73	6.15	7.20	6.86	50.9	25.6	17.1	–4.7
Total	2.40	2.94	3.13	3.38	3.20	40.4	14.9	8.0	–5.2
Married couples with children:									
Lowest	.89	1.16	1.18	1.14	1.07	27.9	–1.1	–2.9	–6.6
Second	1.66	2.12	2.29	2.34	2.25	40.9	10.1	2.2	–3.8
Middle	2.23	2.84	3.12	3.34	3.26	49.9	17.8	7.1	–2.6
Fourth	2.93	3.71	4.11	4.52	4.43	54.2	21.9	10.2	–2.0
Highest	4.88	5.94	6.41	7.67	7.36	57.3	29.2	19.8	–4.1
Total	2.52	3.15	3.42	3.80	3.67	51.1	20.6	11.2	–3.5
Single mothers with children:									
Lowest	.21	.33	.32	.25	.23	18.6	–23.4	–22.9	–9.2
Second	.59	.71	.75	.64	.58	9.3	–9.2	–13.8	–10.0
Middle	.91	1.03	1.22	1.14	1.06	26.0	10.7	–6.1	–7.3

Fourth	1.45	1.67	2.01	2.03	1.89	39.9	21.5	.6	−6.8
Highest	2.78	3.29	3.65	4.14	3.81	49.2	26.0	13.5	−8.2
Total	1.19	1.41	1.59	1.64	1.51	38.5	16.9	3.2	−7.9
Nonelderly childless units:									
Lowest	.80	1.22	1.24	1.19	1.07	49.3	−1.8	−3.9	−10.5
Second	2.19	2.81	2.91	2.94	2.75	34.0	4.5	.9	−6.6
Middle	3.28	4.09	4.27	4.45	4.24	35.6	8.9	4.2	−4.7
Fourth	4.47	5.49	5.78	6.29	6.00	40.8	14.5	8.8	−4.6
Highest	7.42	8.95	9.35	10.94	10.38	47.4	22.3	17.1	−5.2
Total	3.63	4.51	4.71	5.16	4.89	42.1	14.4	9.6	−5.3
Nonelderly childless families:									
Lowest	1.03	1.74	1.85	1.80	1.71	74.2	3.5	−2.8	−4.9
Second	2.47	3.31	3.59	3.68	3.55	49.1	11.1	2.5	−3.4
Middle	3.52	4.53	4.89	5.20	5.03	48.0	15.0	6.3	−3.4
Fourth	4.70	5.88	6.33	7.03	6.77	49.6	19.5	11.1	−3.7
Highest	7.65	9.33	9.94	11.72	11.19	53.3	25.7	17.9	−4.6
Total	3.87	4.96	5.32	5.89	5.65	52.0	18.8	10.7	−4.0
Nonelderly unrelated individuals:									
Lowest	.32	.51	.61	.61	.51	90.4	19.4	−.4	−16.4
Second	1.14	1.49	1.72	1.83	1.63	61.1	23.1	6.4	−11.3
Middle	2.12	2.53	2.78	3.00	2.74	41.5	18.8	8.0	−8.7
Fourth	3.23	3.82	4.03	4.46	4.15	37.9	16.9	10.6	−7.0
Highest	5.88	7.00	7.11	8.48	7.83	44.3	21.2	19.3	−7.7
Total	2.54	3.07	3.25	3.68	3.37	44.9	19.9	13.1	−8.4
Elderly childless units:									
Lowest	.48	.76	.84	.95	.90	96.8	24.7	13.4	−6.1
Second	.95	1.34	1.50	1.73	1.69	82.6	28.6	14.8	−2.0
Middle	1.48	1.97	2.26	2.64	2.52	78.1	34.1	16.9	−4.4
Fourth	2.40	3.02	3.38	4.02	3.73	67.3	33.2	19.1	−7.4
Highest	5.32	6.54	6.85	8.63	7.86	62.1	32.0	26.0	−8.9
Total	2.13	2.73	2.97	3.59	3.34	68.9	31.8	21.2	−7.1

TABLE H-21.—AVERAGE PRETAX AFI (INCOME AS A MULTIPLE OF POVERTY) BY FAMILY TYPE AND INCOME QUINTILE, WEIGHTED BY PERSONS, 1967, 1973, 1979, 1989, AND 1992—Continued

Family type and quintile	1967	1973	1979	1989	1992	Percent change			
						1967–89	1973–89	1979–89	1989–92
Elderly childless families:									
Lowest	.60	.96	1.06	1.20	1.13	100.2	25.3	13.5	-5.7
Second	1.16	1.63	1.86	2.15	2.09	85.9	31.5	15.2	-2.8
Middle	1.77	2.34	2.67	3.14	2.97	77.6	34.0	17.4	-5.3
Fourth	2.76	3.50	3.83	4.61	4.20	67.2	31.8	20.3	-8.9
Highest	5.73	7.12	7.37	9.54	8.58	66.7	34.0	29.4	-10.1
Total	2.40	3.11	3.36	4.13	3.79	72.0	32.7	22.9	-8.1
Elderly unrelated individuals:									
Lowest	.35	.54	.64	.73	.70	109.0	35.7	13.6	-4.0
Second	.63	.93	1.02	1.17	1.12	86.1	26.1	14.7	-4.5
Middle	.86	1.23	1.37	1.62	1.59	88.9	32.2	18.2	-2.4
Fourth	1.29	1.73	2.05	2.46	2.32	91.2	42.1	20.2	-5.8
Highest	3.44	4.08	4.83	5.58	5.41	62.3	36.8	15.5	-3.1
Total	1.31	1.70	1.98	2.31	2.23	76.3	36.0	16.7	-3.8

Note: Poverty thresholds are based on the 1989 distribution of family sizes, with no adjustment for the age of the head of household or the number of children. Quintiles are based on the number of persons.

Source: Congressional Budget Office tabulations of data from the March Current Population Survey, 1968, 1974, 1980, 1990, and 1993.

Elderly persons experienced income gains across the board between 1973 and 1989. For elderly childless units, which include
both single persons and married couples, average AFI rose 24.7
percent for the lowest quintile and 32.0 percent for the highest
quintile. Despite their gains, the elderly generally had much lower
incomes than the nonelderly. In 1989, for example, the average income of elderly childless units was about 3.6 times poverty; the average income of nonelderly childless units, by comparison, was
about 5.2 times poverty.

The effects of differences in rates of growth in incomes by quintile show up directly in data on income shares. The share of total
family income received by families in the lowest quintile declined,
while the share received by the highest quintile increased between
1973 and 1989 (see table H–22).

Average family cash income

For all families, average cash income grew more slowly than average pre-tax AFI between 1973 and 1989. This was also generally
true for specific family types. At the same time, those groups of
families whose average cash incomes declined, had more pronounced decreases than occurred in pretax AFI.

Average family cash income grew 5.8 percent for families with
children between 1973 and 1989, with most of the growth taking
place between 1979 and 1989 (see table H–23). The average for the
lowest quintile fell 26.7 percent during the 1973 to 1989 period,
while the average for the highest quintile rose 16.4 percent. As
with pretax AFI, compositional change is important for interpreting
changes in incomes among families with children. The 5.5 percent
decrease in average family cash income for the lowest quintile of
married couples with children was much smaller than the 26.9 percent decline for single mothers with children.

Because the change in family size among elderly persons was almost negligible over the period, their trend in average family cash
incomes is almost identical to the trend in average pretax AFI. Elderly childless units, which comprise married couples and unrelated individuals, experienced income gains in every quintile between 1973 and 1989.

In percentage terms, average family cash income increased
slightly less among nonelderly childless units between 1973 and
1989 than did pretax AFI: 10.4 percent, compared with 14.4 percent. Among both nonelderly childless families and individuals separately, average family cash income increased for every quintile between 1973 and 1989.

Table H–24 shows family cash income limits (the income cutoffs
between quintiles) by quintile and family type. Between 1973 and
1992, income limits among families with children have declined or
grown slowly while those for the elderly have increased, in some
cases significantly. Across all family types, income limits among
the higher quintiles have increased more than among the lower
quintiles.

For most family types, the share of average family cash income
received by the highest quintile is slightly higher than that
quintile's share of pretax AFI (see table H–25). The trend in these

shares between 1973 and 1989, and between 1979 and 1989 is generally similar.

Income trends year by year

Tables H–26 and H–27 show average pretax AFI and average family cash income by type of family and income quintile for selected years before 1979 and all years thereafter.

TABLE H–22.—SHARES OF PRETAX ADJUSTED FAMILY INCOME (AFI) BY FAMILY TYPE AND INCOME QUINTILE, 1967, 1973, 1979, 1989, AND 1992

Family type and quintile	1967	1973	1979	1989	1992
All families:					
Lowest	5.2	5.5	5.1	4.3	4.1
Second	11.6	11.8	11.6	10.5	10.4
Middle	16.9	17.1	17.3	16.5	16.6
Fourth	23.7	23.9	24.3	24.0	24.3
Highest	42.6	41.7	41.7	44.6	44.6
All families with children:					
Lowest	6.2	6.0	5.4	4.4	4.1
Second	12.8	12.8	12.5	11.1	10.8
Middle	17.8	18.0	18.2	17.4	17.3
Fourth	23.7	24.1	24.6	24.5	25.0
Highest	39.7	39.0	39.3	42.6	42.9
Married couples with children:					
Lowest	7.1	7.3	6.9	6.0	5.8
Second	13.2	13.5	13.4	12.3	12.2
Middle	17.7	18.0	18.2	17.6	17.7
Fourth	23.3	23.5	24.0	23.8	24.1
Highest	38.7	37.7	37.5	40.3	40.1
Single mothers with children:					
Lowest	3.5	4.6	4.1	3.0	3.0
Second	9.9	10.1	9.4	7.9	7.7
Middle	15.3	14.7	15.3	13.9	14.0
Fourth	24.4	23.7	25.3	24.7	25.0
Highest	46.8	46.8	45.9	50.5	50.3
Nonelderly childless units:					
Lowest	4.4	5.4	5.3	4.6	4.4
Second	12.1	12.5	12.4	11.4	11.2
Middle	18.1	18.1	18.1	17.2	17.4
Fourth	24.6	24.4	24.5	24.4	24.6
Highest	40.9	39.7	39.7	42.4	42.5
Nonelderly childless families:					
Lowest	5.3	7.0	7.0	6.1	6.1
Second	12.7	13.4	13.5	12.5	12.6
Middle	18.2	18.3	18.4	17.7	17.8
Fourth	24.3	23.7	23.8	23.9	24.0
Highest	39.5	37.6	37.4	39.8	39.6

1201

TABLE H–22.—SHARES OF PRETAX ADJUSTED FAMILY INCOME (AFI) BY FAMILY TYPE AND INCOME QUINTILE, 1967, 1973, 1979, 1989, AND 1992—Continued

Family type and quintile	1967	1973	1979	1989	1992
Nonelderly unrelated individuals:					
Lowest	2.5	3.3	3.8	3.3	3.0
Second	9.0	9.7	10.6	10.0	9.6
Middle	16.7	16.5	17.1	16.3	16.3
Fourth	25.5	24.9	24.8	24.3	24.6
Highest	46.3	45.6	43.8	46.1	46.5
Elderly childless units:					
Lowest	4.6	5.6	5.7	5.3	5.4
Second	8.9	9.9	10.1	9.6	10.1
Middle	13.9	14.4	15.2	14.7	15.1
Fourth	22.6	22.1	22.8	22.4	22.3
Highest	50.0	48.0	46.2	48.0	47.1
Elderly childless families:					
Lowest	5.0	6.1	6.3	5.8	6.0
Second	9.6	10.5	11.1	10.4	11.0
Middle	14.7	15.1	15.9	15.2	15.7
Fourth	23.0	22.5	22.8	22.4	22.1
Highest	47.7	45.8	43.9	46.2	45.2
Elderly unrelated individuals:					
Lowest	5.3	6.3	6.5	6.3	6.3
Second	9.6	10.9	10.3	10.1	10.1
Middle	13.1	14.4	13.8	14.0	14.2
Fourth	19.6	20.4	20.7	21.3	20.9
Highest	52.4	47.9	48.7	48.2	48.6

Note: Poverty thresholds are based on the 1989 distribution of family sizes, with no adjustment for the age of the head of household or the number of children. Quintiles are based on the number of persons.

Source: Congressional Budget Office tabulations of data from the March Current Population Survey, 1968, 1974, 1980, 1990, and 1993.

TABLE H–23.—AVERAGE FAMILY CASH INCOME BY FAMILY TYPE AND INCOME QUINTILE
1973, 1979, 1989, AND 1992

[In 1989 dollars]

Family type and income quintile	1973	1979	1989	1992	Percent change		
					1973–89	1979–89	1989–92
All families:							
Lowest	6,061	5,994	5,866	5,256	−3.2	−2.1	−10.4
Second	15,416	15,306	15,107	13,885	−2.0	−1.3	−8.1
Middle	25,909	25,609	25,823	24,118	−0.3	0.8	−6.6
Fourth	37,946	38,680	40,374	38,367	6.4	4.4	−5.0
Highest	66,364	68,230	77,716	73,487	17.1	13.9	−5.4
Total	30,341	30,764	32,978	31,022	8.7	7.2	−5.9
All families with children:							
Lowest	10,529	9,369	7,714	6,568	−26.7	−17.7	−14.9
Second	23,176	22,365	20,664	18,561	−10.8	−7.6	−10.2
Middle	32,616	33,317	33,067	31,038	1.4	−0.8	−6.1
Fourth	43,426	44,940	47,217	45,427	8.7	5.1	−3.8
Highest	70,420	72,971	81,966	78,057	16.4	12.3	−4.8
Total	36,034	36,592	38,127	35,929	5.8	4.2	−5.8
Married couples with children:							
Lowest	15,450	15,148	14,606	13,491	−5.5	−3.6	−7.6
Second	27,170	28,294	28,660	27,471	5.5	1.3	−4.1
Middle	35,513	37,693	39,683	39,023	11.7	5.3	−1.7
Fourth	45,783	48,616	53,106	52,147	16.0	9.2	−1.8
Highest	72,842	76,547	88,168	84,522	21.0	15.2	−4.1
Total	39,352	41,260	44,846	43,327	14.0	8.7	−3.4
Single mothers with children:							
Lowest	3,505	3,338	2,563	2,308	−26.9	−23.2	−9.9
Second	7,931	8,122	6,737	6,086	−15.1	−17.1	−9.7
Middle	11,922	13,136	11,803	10,736	−1.0	−10.1	−9.0
Fourth	17,867	19,904	19,427	18,201	8.7	−2.4	−6.3
Highest	33,430	35,714	38,394	35,263	14.8	7.5	−8.2
Total	14,930	16,043	15,792	14,517	5.8	−1.6	−8.1
Nonelderly childless units:							
Lowest	5,809	5,863	5,727	4,990	−1.4	−2.3	−12.9
Second	15,886	15,808	15,840	14,496	−.3	0.2	−8.5
Middle	25,562	25,397	26,154	24,570	2.3	3.0	−6.1
Fourth	37,670	38,217	40,549	38,624	7.6	6.1	−4.7
Highest	67,136	69,142	79,550	74,864	18.5	15.1	−5.9
Total	30,412	30,886	33,565	31,507	10.4	8.7	−6.1
Nonelderly childless families:							
Lowest	13,044	13,881	13,712	13,240	5.1	−1.2	−3.4
Second	25,352	27,773	28,880	28,100	13.9	4.0	−2.7

TABLE H–23.—AVERAGE FAMILY CASH INCOME BY FAMILY TYPE AND INCOME QUINTILE
1973, 1979, 1989, AND 1992—Continued

[In 1989 dollars]

Family type and income quintile	1973	1979	1989	1992	Percent change		
					1973–89	1979–89	1989–92
Middle	35,256	38,599	41,716	40,551	18.3	8.1	−2.8
Fourth	47,199	51,058	57,713	55,483	22.3	13.0	−3.9
Highest	76,867	83,026	98,413	93,304	28.0	18.5	−5.2
Total	39,543	42,867	48,093	46,127	21.6	12.2	−4.1
Nonelderly unrelated individuals							
Lowest	2,948	3,504	3,522	2,950	19.5	.5	−16.2
Second	8,620	9,957	10,621	9,437	23.2	6.7	−11.1
Middle	14,628	16,065	17,389	15,898	18.9	8.2	−8.6
Fourth	22,105	23,330	25,849	24,075	16.9	10.8	−6.9
Highest	40,555	41,215	49,182	45,457	21.3	19.3	−7.6
Total	17,770	18,814	21,315	19,563	20.0	13.3	−8.2
Elderly childless units:							
Lowest	4,148	4,632	5,221	4,945	25.9	12.7	−5.3
Second	7,556	8,367	9,665	9,410	27.9	15.5	−2.6
Middle	11,628	13,325	15,446	14,936	32.8	15.9	−3.3
Fourth	18,576	21,202	25,021	23,750	34.7	18.0	−5.1
Highest	45,276	47,577	59,036	54,327	30.4	24.1	−8.0
Total	17,436	19,021	22,880	21,473	31.2	20.3	−6.2
Elderly childless families:							
Lowest	7,083	7,864	8,940	8,514	26.2	13.7	4.8
Second	12,074	13,841	15,967	15,666	32.2	15.4	1.9
Middle	17,200	19,750	23,381	22,497	35.9	18.4	−3.8
Fourth	26,124	28,889	34,869	32,016	33.5	20.7	−8.2
Highest	56,136	57,963	75,091	67,731	33.8	29.5	−9.8
Total	23,723	25,661	31,657	29,282	33.4	23.4	−7.5
Elderly unrelated individuals:							
Lowest	3,108	3,717	4,221	4,061	35.8	13.6	−3.8
Second	5,393	5,932	6,806	6,513	26.2	14.7	−4.3
Middle	7,114	7,963	9,414	9,206	32.3	18.2	−2.2
Fourth	10,046	11,881	14,286	13,482	42.2	20.2	−5.6
Highest	23,626	27,984	32,331	31,387	36.8	15.5	−2.9
Total	9,857	11,495	13,414	12,925	36.1	16.7	−3.6

Note: Quintiles are based on the number of families.

Source: Congressional Budget Office tabulations of data from the March Current Population Survey, 1974, 1980, 1990, and 1993.

TABLE H-24.—FAMILY CASH INCOME LIMITS BY QUINTILE AND FAMILY TYPE

[In 1989 dollars]

Family type	Year				Percent change		
	1973	1979	1989	1992	1973–79	1979–89	1973–92
All families:							
Lowest	10,561	10,604	10,452	9,545	0	−1	−9.6
Second	20,595	20,099	20,005	18,560	−2	0	−9.9
Middle	31,540	31,679	32,050	30,306	0	1	−3.9
Fourth	45,759	46,951	50,319	48,212	3	7	5.4
All families with children:							
Lowest	17,778	16,749	14,472	12,621	−6	−14	−29.0
Second	28,049	28,063	26,944	24,659	0	−4	−12.1
Middle	37,353	38,583	39,400	37,719	3	2	1.0
Fourth	50,745	52,386	56,415	54,708	3	8	7.8
Married couples with children:							
Lowest	22,606	22,946	22,678	21,505	2	−1	−4.9
Second	31,540	33,230	34,110	33,408	5	3	5.9
Middle	39,934	42,350	45,524	44,810	6	7	12.2
Fourth	52,937	56,109	62,200	60,895	6	11	15.0
Single mothers with children:							
Lowest	6,150	6,080	4,770	4,266	−1	−22	−30.6
Second	9,909	10,391	9,000	7,954	5	−13	−19.7
Middle	14,456	16,317	15,000	13,699	13	−8	−5.2
Fourth	21,933	24,286	24,935	23,008	11	3	4.9
Nonelderly childless unit:							
Lowest	11,039	11,222	11,053	9,877	2	−2	−10.5
Second	20,737	20,137	20,551	19,267	−3	2	−7.1
Middle	31,182	31,011	32,100	30,693	−1	4	−1.6
Fourth	45,982	46,911	50,681	48,669	2	8	5.8
Nonelderly childless families:							
Lowest	20,209	22,058	22,500	21,600	9	2	6.9
Second	30,257	33,377	35,010	34,344	10	5	13.5
Middle	40,665	44,217	48,900	47,196	9	11	16.1
Fourth	55,194	59,638	68,739	65,793	8	15	19.2
Nonelderly unrelated individuals:							
Lowest	5,677	6,782	7,200	6,364	19	6	12.1
Second	11,617	13,064	14,000	12,556	12	7	8.1
Middle	18,348	19,285	21,020	19,462	5	9	6.1
Fourth	26,591	28,390	31,635	29,343	7	11	10.4

TABLE H–24.—FAMILY CASH INCOME LIMITS BY QUINTILE AND FAMILY TYPE—
Continued

[In 1989 dollars]

Family type	Year				Percent change		
	1973	1979	1989	1992	1973–79	1979–89	1973–92
Elderly childless units:							
Lowest	6,069	6,579	7,466	7,128	8	13	17.5
Second	9,330	10,562	12,215	11,803	13	16	26.5
Middle	14,230	16,473	19,249	18,477	16	17	29.8
Fourth	24,443	27,246	32,371	30,200	11	19	23.6
Elderly childless families:							
Lowest	9,967	11,284	12,767	12,565	13	13	26.1
Second	14,301	16,600	19,454	18,782	16	17	31.3
Middle	20,711	23,147	28,000	26,419	12	21	27.6
Fourth	33,353	36,412	43,400	39,294	9	19	17.8
Elderly unrelated individuals:							
Lowest	4,452	5,001	5,688	5,437	12	14	22.1
Second	6,274	6,860	7,904	7,645	9	15	21.9
Middle	8,129	9,493	11,368	10,924	17	20	34.4
Fourth	12,490	15,074	18,061	16,992	21	20	36.1
Other families with children:							
Lowest	18,713	16,556	14,008	11,638	− 12	− 15	− 37.8
Second	28,793	27,611	24,100	21,212	− 4	− 13	− 26.3
Middle	40,145	39,715	36,150	31,871	− 1	− 9	− 20.6
Fourth	55,066	55,759	55,075	49,455	1	− 1	− 10.2

Source: Congressional Budget Office tabulations of data from the March Current Population Survey, 1974, 1980, 1990, and 1993.

TABLE H–25.—SHARES OF FAMILY CASH INCOME, BY INCOME QUINTILE AND FAMILY TYPE, 1973, 1979, 1989, AND 1992

[In percent]

Family type and quintile	1973	1979	1989	1992
All families:				
Lowest	4.0	3.9	3.6	3.4
Second	10.2	10.0	9.2	9.0
Middle	17.1	16.6	15.7	15.5
Fourth	25.0	25.1	24.5	24.7
Highest	43.7	44.4	47.1	47.4
All families with children:				
Lowest	5.8	5.1	4.0	3.7
Second	12.9	12.2	10.8	10.3
Middle	18.1	18.2	17.3	17.3
Fourth	24.1	24.6	24.8	25.3
Highest	39.1	39.9	43.0	43.4
Married couples with children:				
Lowest	7.9	7.3	6.5	6.2
Second	13.8	13.7	12.8	12.7
Middle	18.0	18.3	17.7	18.0
Fourth	23.3	23.6	23.7	24.1
Highest	37.0	37.1	39.3	39.0
Single mothers with children:				
Lowest	4.7	4.2	3.2	3.2
Second	10.6	10.1	8.5	8.4
Middle	16.0	16.4	14.9	14.8
Fourth	23.9	24.8	24.6	25.1
Highest	44.8	44.5	48.6	48.6
Nonelderly childless units:				
Lowest	3.8	3.8	3.4	3.2
Second	10.4	10.2	9.4	9.2
Middle	16.8	16.4	15.6	15.6
Fourth	24.8	24.7	24.2	24.5
Highest	44.2	44.8	47.4	47.5
Nonelderly childless families:				
Lowest	6.6	6.5	5.7	5.7
Second	12.8	13.0	12.0	12.2
Middle	17.8	18.0	17.3	17.6
Fourth	23.9	23.8	24.0	24.1
Highest	38.9	38.7	40.9	40.4
Nonelderly unrelated individuals:				
Lowest	3.3	3.7	3.3	3.0
Second	9.7	10.6	10.0	9.6
Middle	16.5	17.1	16.3	16.3
Fourth	24.9	24.8	24.3	24.6
Highest	45.6	43.8	46.1	46.5
Elderly childless units:				
Lowest	4.8	4.9	4.6	4.6
Second	8.7	8.8	8.4	8.8
Middle	13.3	14.0	13.5	13.9
Fourth	21.3	22.3	21.9	22.1
Highest	51.9	50.0	51.6	50.6

TABLE H–25.—SHARES OF FAMILY CASH INCOME, BY INCOME QUINTILE AND FAMILY TYPE, 1973, 1979, 1989, AND 1992—Continued

[In percent]

Family type and quintile	1973	1979	1989	1992
Elderly childless families:				
Lowest	6.0	6.1	5.6	5.8
Second	10.2	10.8	10.1	10.7
Middle	14.5	15.4	14.8	15.4
Fourth	22.0	22.5	22.0	21.9
Highest	47.3	45.2	47.4	46.3
Elderly unrelated individuals:				
Lowest	6.3	6.5	6.3	6.3
Second	10.9	10.3	10.1	10.1
Middle	14.4	13.9	14.0	14.2
Fourth	20.4	20.7	21.3	20.9
Highest	47.9	48.7	48.2	48.6

Note: Quintiles are based on the number of families.

Source: Congressional Budget Office tabulations of data from the March Current Population Survey, 1974, 1980, 1990, and 1993.

TABLE H–26.—AVERAGE PRETAX AFI (INCOME AS A MULTIPLE OF POVERTY) BY FAMILY TYPE AND INCOME QUINTILE, 1973–92

	1973	1979	1989	1990	1991	1992
All families:						
Lowest	0.93	0.92	0.87	0.84	0.80	0.78
Second	1.97	2.09	2.10	2.04	1.98	1.96
Middle	2.85	3.09	3.28	3.18	3.12	3.11
Fourth	3.94	4.31	4.75	4.63	4.54	4.55
Highest	6.86	7.36	8.80	8.52	8.34	8.32
Total	3.31	3.55	3.96	3.84	3.76	3.74
All families with children:						
Lowest	0.91	0.85	0.74	0.71	0.66	0.65
Second	1.91	1.96	1.86	1.79	1.72	1.72
Middle	2.67	2.85	2.92	2.79	2.76	2.76
Fourth	3.55	3.84	4.12	3.97	3.96	3.98
Highest	5.72	6.11	7.14	6.89	6.76	6.82
Total	2.95	3.12	3.36	3.23	3.17	3.18
Married couples with children:						
Lowest	1.19	1.20	1.15	1.12	1.07	1.07
Second	2.15	2.30	2.34	2.27	2.24	2.25
Middle	2.86	3.13	3.34	3.22	3.23	3.26
Fourth	3.72	4.11	4.51	4.41	4.39	4.43
Highest	5.93	6.38	7.63	7.39	7.28	7.33
Total	3.17	3.42	3.80	3.68	3.64	3.67
Single mothers with children:						
Lowest	0.33	0.33	0.25	0.25	0.24	0.23
Second	0.72	0.75	0.64	0.61	0.59	0.58
Middle	1.05	1.22	1.13	1.07	1.02	1.05
Fourth	1.67	2.01	1.98	1.90	1.86	1.85
Highest	3.32	3.67	4.03	3.79	3.77	3.71
Total	1.42	1.60	1.61	1.52	1.49	1.48
Nonelderly childless units:						
Lowest	1.21	1.23	1.17	1.13	1.10	1.05
Second	2.79	2.88	2.89	2.84	2.76	2.70
Middle	4.04	4.22	4.38	4.30	4.20	4.18
Fourth	5.42	5.70	6.20	6.03	5.93	5.92
Highest	8.83	9.23	10.77	10.45	10.26	10.22
Total	4.46	4.65	5.08	4.95	4.85	4.81
Nonelderly childless familes:						
Lowest	1.73	1.84	1.77	1.78	1.74	1.68
Second	3.28	3.56	3.62	3.60	3.51	3.50
Middle	4.48	4.85	5.14	5.06	4.95	4.96
Fourth	5.82	6.26	6.94	6.77	6.66	6.69
Highest	9.22	9.84	11.55	11.26	11.05	11.03
Total	4.91	5.27	5.80	5.69	5.58	5.57

TABLE H–26.—AVERAGE PRETAX AFI (INCOME AS A MULTIPLE OF POVERTY) BY FAMILY TYPE AND INCOME QUINTILE, 1973–92—Continued

	1973	1979	1989	1990	1991	1992
Nonelderly unrelated individuals:						
Lowest	0.50	0.60	0.59	0.57	0.55	0.50
Second	1.47	1.69	1.79	1.70	1.65	1.59
Middle	2.49	2.73	2.93	2.86	2.78	2.68
Fourth	3.74	3.93	4.36	4.24	4.17	4.06
Highest	6.78	6.88	8.30	7.95	7.84	7.66
Total	3.00	3.17	3.60	3.46	3.40	3.30
Elderly childless units:						
Lowest	0.82	0.90	1.01	1.00	0.99	0.95
Second	1.44	1.61	1.84	1.86	1.84	1.80
Middle	2.11	2.42	2.80	2.83	2.73	2.68
Fourth	3.22	3.60	4.25	4.21	3.97	3.95
Highest	6.95	7.28	9.10	8.92	8.50	8.30
Total	2.91	3.16	3.80	3.76	3.60	3.53
Elderly childless families:						
Lowest	1.03	1.13	1.27	1.29	1.30	1.20
Second	1.76	2.00	2.28	2.33	2.29	2.22
Middle	2.51	2.85	3.32	3.37	3.20	3.15
Fourth	3.71	4.08	4.86	4.77	4.51	4.44
Highest	7.58	7.83	10.05	9.82	9.42	9.05
Total	3.32	3.58	4.36	4.31	4.15	4.01
Elderly unrelated individuals:						
Lowest	0.57	0.68	0.77	0.74	0.74	0.74
Second	0.99	1.09	1.25	1.21	1.19	1.19
Middle	1.31	1.46	1.72	1.73	1.69	1.68
Fourth	1.85	2.19	2.61	2.62	2.50	2.46
Highest	4.35	5.15	5.92	5.92	5.50	5.74
Total	1.81	2.12	2.45	2.44	2.32	2.36

Note: Adjusted family income equals pretax family cash income divided by the poverty threshold. Entries in this table are based on poverty thresholds that take age, gender, and rural residence into account, and are therefore not directly comparable with other tables in this section. Quintiles are based on the number of persons. In 1989, the Bureau of the Census revised its method of processing data from the Current Population Survey, which made the incomes of some families higher than what they would have been using the old method. For further discussion, see U.S. Bureau of the Census, "Money Income and Poverty Status in the United States: 1988," Current Population Reports, Series P–60, No. 166, October 1989.

Source: Congressional Budget Office tabulations of data from the March Current Population Survey, 1974–93.

TABLE H–27.—AVERAGE FAMILY INCOME BY INCOME QUINTILE AND FAMILY TYPE, 1973–1992

[In 1989 dollars]

	1973	1979	1989	1990	1991	1992
All families:						
Lowest	6,061	5,994	5,866	5,649	5,429	5,256
Second	15,416	15,306	15,107	14,781	14,241	13,885
Middle	25,909	25,609	25,823	25,191	24,387	24,118
Fourth	37,946	38,680	40,374	39,269	38,446	38,367
Highest	66,364	68,230	77,716	75,429	73,680	73,487
Total	30,341	30,764	32,978	32,063	31,236	31,022
All families with children:						
Lowest	10,529	9,369	7,714	7,317	6,730	6,568
Second	23,176	22,365	20,664	19,834	19,024	18,561
Middle	32,616	33,317	33,067	31,916	31,239	31,038
Fourth	43,426	44,940	47,217	45,964	45,285	45,427
Highest	70,420	72,971	81,966	79,427	77,681	78,057
Total	36,034	36,592	38,127	36,890	35,989	35,929
Married couples with children:						
Lowest	15,450	15,148	14,606	14,186	13,569	13,491
Second	27,170	28,294	28,660	27,960	27,497	27,471
Middle	35,513	37,693	39,683	38,810	38,583	39,023
Fourth	45,783	48,616	53,106	52,275	52,042	52,147
Highest	72,842	76,547	88,168	85,483	84,140	84,522
Total	39,352	41,260	44,846	43,741	43,163	43,327
Single mothers with children:						
Lowest	3,505	3,338	2,563	2,529	2,461	2,308
Second	7,931	8,122	6,737	6,499	6,247	6,086
Middle	11,922	13,136	11,803	11,238	10,785	10,736
Fourth	17,867	19,904	19,427	18,703	18,503	18,201
Highest	33,430	35,714	38,394	36,228	36,019	35,263
Total	14,930	16,043	15,792	15,036	14,797	14,517
Nonelderly childless units:						
Lowest	5,809	5,863	5,727	5,425	5,287	4,990
Second	15,886	15,808	15,840	15,448	14,985	14,496
Middle	25,562	25,397	26,154	25,518	24,961	24,570
Fourth	37,670	38,217	40,549	39,503	38,897	38,624
Highest	67,136	69,142	79,550	77,006	75,405	74,864
Total	30,412	30,886	33,565	32,578	31,903	31,507
Nonelderly childless families:						
Lowest	13,044	13,881	13,712	13,969	13,670	13,240
Second	25,352	27,773	28,880	28,802	28,067	28,100
Middle	35,256	38,599	41,716	41,203	40,572	40,551
Fourth	47,199	51,058	57,713	56,552	55,733	55,483
Highest	76,867	83,026	98,413	96,054	93,869	93,304

TABLE H–27.—AVERAGE FAMILY INCOME BY INCOME QUINTILE AND FAMILY TYPE,
1973–1992—Continued

[In 1989 dollars]

	1973	1979	1989	1990	1991	1992
Total	39,543	42,867	48,093	47,311	46,380	46,127
Nonelderly unrelated individuals:						
Lowest	2,948	3,504	3,522	3,362	3,273	2,950
Second	8,620	9,957	10,621	10,077	9,782	9,437
Middle	14,628	16,065	17,389	16,950	16,484	15,898
Fourth	22,105	23,330	25,849	25,189	24,776	24,075
Highest	40,555	41,215	49,182	47,167	46,520	45,457
Total	17,770	18,814	21,315	20,546	20,166	19,563
Elderly childless units:						
Lowest	4,148	4,632	5,221	5,060	4,984	4,945
Second	7,556	8,367	9,665	9,724	9,561	9,410
Middle	11,628	13,325	15,446	15,702	15,226	14,936
Fourth	18,576	21,202	25,021	25,097	23,771	23,750
Highest	45,276	47,577	59,036	58,134	55,280	54,327
Total	17,436	19,021	22,880	22,741	21,761	21,473
Elderly childless families:						
Lowest	7,083	7,864	8,940	9,138	9,096	8,514
Second	12,074	13,841	15,967	16,468	16,185	15,666
Middle	17,200	19,750	23,381	23,917	22,861	22,497
Fourth	26,124	28,889	34,869	34,665	32,736	32,016
Highest	56,136	57,963	75,091	73,345	70,387	67,731
Total	23,723	25,661	31,657	31,503	30,247	29,282
Elderly unrelated individuals:						
Lowest	3,108	3,717	4,221	4,038	4,022	4,061
Second	5,393	5,932	6,806	6,616	6,498	6,513
Middle	7,114	7,963	9,414	9,468	9,233	9,206
Fourth	10,046	11,881	13,973	14,286	13,692	13,482
Highest	23,626	27,984	32,331	32,398	30,106	31,387
Total	9,857	11,495	13,414	13,367	12,707	12,925

Note: Quintiles are based on the number of families. In 1989, the Bureau of the Census revised its methods of processing data from the Current Population Survey, which made the incomes of some families higher than what they would have been using the old method. For further discussion, see U.S. Bureau of the Census, "Money Income and Poverty Status in the United States: 1988," Current Population Reports, Series, P–60, No. 166, October 1989.

Sources: Congressional Budget Office tabulations of data from the March Current Population Survey, 1974–93.

APPENDIX I. SELECTED ECONOMIC, POPULATION, IMMIGRATION, INCOME AND FISCAL DATA FOR THE UNITED STATES AND BY STATE

TABLE I-1.—PRICE LEVELS, 1970–98

[1987=100]

Calendar year	GDP implicit price deflator	All items (CPI–U)	All items (CPI–U) (fiscal year)	Food and beverage [1]	Housing [2]	Medical care	CPI–X1	CPI–X1 (fiscal year)
1970	35.2	38.8	37.8	40.1	36.4	34.0	41.3	40.3
1971	37.1	40.5	39.7	41.4	38.0	36.1	43.1	42.2
1972	38.8	41.8	41.2	43.1	39.4	37.3	44.4	43.7
1973	41.3	44.4	42.8	48.8	41.2	38.8	47.2	45.5
1974	44.9	49.3	46.7	55.5	45.8	42.4	51.9	49.3
1975	49.2	53.8	51.8	60.2	50.7	47.5	56.2	54.2
1976	52.3	56.9	³55.5	62.1	53.8	52.0	59.4	³57.9
1977	55.9	60.6	59.7	65.8	57.4	57.0	63.2	62.2
1978	60.3	65.2	63.9	72.2	62.4	61.8	67.5	66.2
1979	65.5	72.6	70.4	79.9	70.1	67.5	74.0	72.1
1980	71.7	82.4	80.0	86.7	81.1	74.9	82.3	80.2
1981	78.9	90.9	88.9	93.5	90.4	82.9	90.1	88.2
1982	83.8	96.5	95.5	97.3	96.9	92.5	95.6	94.4
1983	87.2	99.6	98.8	99.5	99.5	100.6	99.6	98.7
1984	91.0	103.9	102.9	103.2	103.6	106.8	103.9	102.9
1985	94.4	107.6	106.7	105.6	107.7	113.5	107.6	106.7
1986	96.9	109.6	109.3	109.1	110.9	122.0	109.6	109.3
1987	100.0	113.6	112.5	113.5	114.2	130.1	113.6	112.5
1988	103.9	118.3	117.1	118.2	118.5	138.6	118.3	117.1
1989	108.5	124.0	122.7	124.9	123.0	149.3	124.0	122.7
1990	113.2	130.7	128.8	132.1	128.5	162.8	130.7	128.8
1991	117.8	136.2	135.3	136.8	133.6	177.0	136.2	135.3
1992	120.9	140.4	139.4	138.7	137.5	190.1	140.4	139.4
1993	124.2	144.5	143.5	141.6	141.2	201.4	144.5	143.5

TABLE I-1.—PRICE LEVELS, 1970–98—Continued

[1987=100]

Calendar year	GDP implicit price deflator	All items (CPI–U)	All items (CPI–U) (fiscal year)	Food and beverage[1]	Housing[2]	Medical care	CPI–X1	CPI–X1 (fiscal year)
1994[4]	126.7	148.6	147.6	....	....	....	148.6	147.6
1995[4]	129.6	152.6	151.6	....	....	....	152.6	151.6
1996[4]	132.6	156.7	155.7	....	....	....	156.7	155.7
1997[4]	135.5	161.0	159.9	....	....	....	161.0	159.9
1998[4]	138.5	165.3	164.2	....	....	....	165.3	164.2

[1] Includes alcoholic beverages, not shown separately.
[2] Housing data from the Economic Report of the President, February 1994, p. 335.
[3] In 1976, the fiscal year was moved from July–June to October–September. The 3-month period from July through September, 1976, is not represented in this table. The value for CPI–U during this period is 57.4; the value of CPI–X1 during this period is 59.8.
[4] Forecast.

Note: Data beginning 1978 are for all urban consumers; earlier data are for urban wage earners and clerical workers. Data for CPI–U beginning 1983 incorporate a rental equivalence measure for homeowners' costs (the measure used in determining CPI–X1) and therefore are not strictly comparable with earlier figures.

Source: Department of Labor, Bureau of Labor Statistics, and Congressional Budget Office.

TABLE I-2.—POPULATION ESTIMATES BY STATE

[In thousands]

	Resident population, 1993 [1]	Resident population, 1990 [2]	Resident population, 1980 [2]	Percentage change, total population, 1980–90 [2]	Population age 65 years and over, 1990 [2]	Percentage of population age 65 and over, 1990 [2]	Population ages 0–17, 1990 [2]	Percentage of population ages 0–17, 1990 [2]
Alabama	4,187	4,041	3,894	3.8	520	12.9	1,064	26.3
Alaska	599	550	402	36.8	22	4.0	173	31.5
Arizona	3,936	3,665	2,718	34.8	476	13.0	986	26.9
Arkansas	2,424	2,351	2,286	24.7	349	14.8	624	26.5
California	31,211	29,760	23,668	25.7	3,112	10.5	7,810	26.2
Colorado	3,566	3,294	2,890	14.0	328	10.0	864	26.2
Connecticut	3,277	3,287	3,108	5.8	444	13.5	754	22.9
Delaware	700	666	594	12.1	80	12.0	164	24.6
District of Columbia	578	607	638	-4.9	77	12.7	119	19.6
Florida	13,679	12,938	9,746	32.8	2,356	18.2	2,884	22.3
Georgia	6,917	6,478	5,463	18.6	651	10.0	1,736	26.8
Hawaii	1,172	1,108	965	14.8	124	11.2	282	25.5
Idaho	1,099	1,007	944	6.7	121	12.0	309	30.7
Illinois	11,697	11,431	11,427	0	1,429	12.5	2,961	25.9
Indiana	5,713	5,544	5,490	1.0	694	12.5	1,461	26.4
Iowa	2,814	2,777	2,914	-4.7	426	15.3	721	26.0
Kansas	2,531	2,478	2,364	4.8	342	13.8	663	26.8
Kentucky	3,789	3,685	3,661	.7	465	12.6	957	26.0
Louisiana	4,295	4,220	4,206	.3	466	11.0	1,233	29.2
Maine	1,239	1,228	1,125	9.2	163	13.3	310	25.2
Maryland	4,965	4,781	4,217	13.4	514	10.8	1,168	24.4
Massachussetts	6,012	6,016	5,737	4.9	815	13.5	1,361	22.6
Michigan	9,478	9,295	9,262	.4	1,104	11.9	2,468	26.6
Minnesota	4,517	4,375	4,076	7.3	546	12.5	1,170	26.7
Mississippi	2,643	2,573	2,521	2.1	319	12.4	750	29.1
Missouri	5,234	5,117	4,917	4.1	716	14.0	1,319	25.8
Montana	839	799	787	1.5	106	13.3	223	27.9
Nebraska	1,607	1,578	1,570	.5	223	14.1	430	27.2
Nevada	1,389	1,202	800	50.3	127	10.6	299	24.9
New Hampshire	1,125	1,109	921	20.4	125	11.3	280	25.2

TABLE I–2.—POPULATION ESTIMATES BY STATE—Continued

[In thousands]

	Resident population, 1993 [1]	Resident population, 1990 [2]	Resident population, 1980 [2]	Percentage change, total population, 1980–90 [2]	Population age 65 years and over, 1990 [2]	Percentage of population age 65 and over, 1990 [2]	Population ages 0–17, 1990 [2]	Percentage of population ages 0–17, 1990 [2]
New Jersey	7,879	7,730	7,365	5.0	1,025	13.3	1,811	23.4
New Mexico	1,616	1,515	1,303	16.3	162	10.7	449	29.6
New York	18,197	17,990	17,558	2.5	2,340	13.0	4,292	23.9
North Carolina	6,945	6,629	5,882	12.7	800	12.1	1,616	24.4
North Dakota	635	639	653	–2.1	91	14.2	176	27.5
Ohio	11,091	10,847	10,798	.5	1,403	12.9	2,808	25.9
Oklahoma	3,231	3,146	3,025	4.0	423	13.4	840	26.7
Oregon	3,032	2,842	2,633	7.9	390	13.7	727	25.6
Pennsylvania	12,048	11,882	11,864	.2	1,821	15.3	2,807	23.6
Rhode Island	1,000	1,003	947	5.9	150	15.0	227	22.6
South Carolina	3,643	3,487	3,122	11.7	394	11.3	926	26.6
South Dakota	715	696	691	.7	102	14.7	199	28.6
Tennessee	5,099	4,877	4,591	6.2	616	12.6	1,222	25.1
Texas	18,031	16,987	14,229	19.4	1,708	10.1	4,858	28.6
Utah	1,860	1,723	1,461	17.9	149	8.6	629	36.5
Vermont	576	563	511	10.2	66	11.7	144	25.6
Virginia	6,491	6,187	5,347	15.7	661	10.7	1,511	24.4
Washington	5,255	4,867	4,132	17.8	573	11.8	1,267	26.0
West Virginia	1,820	1,793	1,950	–8.1	268	14.9	445	24.8
Wisconsin	5,038	4,892	4,706	4.0	650	13.3	1,292	26.4
Wyoming	470	454	470	–3.4	47	10.4	136	30.0
United States	257,908	248,710	226,546	9.5	31,079	12.5	63,924	25.7

[1] Estimates for 1993 are for July 1.
[2] Estimates for 1990 and 1980 are for April 1.

Source: U.S. Department of Commerce, Bureau of the Census, Population Estimates and Projections, Series P-25.

TABLE I-3.—TOTAL U.S. RESIDENT POPULATION, BY AGE GROUP, SELECTED YEARS, 1940–2020

[In thousands]

Year	Total	Age						
		0–5	6–15	16–19	20–24	25–44	45–64	65 and over
1940 [1]	132,122	12,686	22,704	9,895	11,690	39,868	26,249	9,031
1945 [1]	139,928	15,224	21,663	9,362	12,036	42,521	28,630	10,494
1950	151,868	19,126	24,006	8,471	11,524	45,505	30,842	12,397
1955	165,069	22,014	29,231	8,601	10,299	46,904	33,493	14,525
1960	179,979	24,300	34,536	10,568	10,868	46,848	36,184	16,675
1965	193,526	23,913	38,848	13,412	13,404	46,609	38,889	18,451
1970	203,984	20,923	41,059	15,187	16,579	48,149	41,981	20,107
1975	215,465	19,667	38,962	16,953	19,317	54,074	43,794	22,696
1980	227,225	19,632	35,659	17,113	21,386	63,234	44,497	25,707
1985	237,924	21,360	33,930	14,969	21,265	73,387	44,595	28,416
1990	249,415	22,553	34,913	14,415	19,131	80,901	46,277	31,224
1993 [2]	257,927	23,698	36,613	13,764	19,201	83,193	48,864	32,594
1994 [2]	260,711	23,965	37,171	13,903	18,893	83,487	50,122	33,169
1995 [2]	263,434	24,144	37,746	14,136	18,473	83,820	51,465	33,649
2000 [2]	276,241	23,447	40,359	15,947	17,947	83,360	59,860	35,322
2010 [2]	300,431	23,974	40,797	18,090	20,976	77,838	78,651	40,104
2020 [2]	325,942	26,333	42,840	17,335	21,725	83,215	81,147	53,348
Percentage composition:								
1940	100	9.6	17.2	7.5	8.8	30.2	19.9	6.8
1950	100	12.6	15.8	5.6	7.6	30.0	20.3	8.2
1960	100	13.5	19.2	5.9	6.0	26.0	20.1	9.3
1970	100	10.3	20.1	7.4	8.1	23.6	20.6	9.9
1980	100	8.6	15.7	7.5	9.4	27.8	19.6	11.3
1990	100	9.0	14.0	5.8	7.7	32.4	18.6	12.5
1993	100	9.2	14.2	5.3	7.4	32.3	18.9	12.6
1994	100	9.2	14.3	5.3	7.2	32.0	19.2	12.7
1995	100	9.2	14.3	5.4	7.0	31.8	19.5	12.8
2000	100	8.5	14.6	5.8	6.5	30.2	21.7	12.8
2010	100	8.0	13.6	6.0	7.0	25.9	26.2	13.3
2020	100	8.1	13.1	5.3	6.7	25.5	24.9	16.4
Percentage growth:								
1990 to 2000	10.8	4.0	15.6	10.6	− 6.2	3.0	29.4	13.1
2000 to 2010	8.8	2.2	1.1	13.4	16.9	− 6.6	31.4	13.5
2010 to 2020	8.5	9.8	5.0	− 4.2	3.6	6.9	3.2	33.0

[1] Excludes Alaska and Hawaii.
[2] Projected High Immigration Series.

Note: Alaska and Hawaii are excluded in the years 1940 and 1945.

Source: U.S. Bureau of the Census, Current Population Reports Series P–25, Nos. 310, 311, 519, 917, 1092, 1095, and 1104.

TABLE I-4.—TOTAL U.S. RESIDENT POPULATION BY RACE AND HISPANIC ORIGIN, 1970–2000

Year	All races			White			Black			Hispanic [1]		
	Total	Male	Female	Total	Male	Female	Total	Male	Female	Total	Male	Female
1970	203,984	99,291	104,692	178,703	87,203	91,500	22,687	10,799	11,888	0	0	0
1975	215,465	104,876	110,589	187,216	91,408	95,807	24,696	11,727	12,969	0	0	0
1980	227,225	110,399	116,826	195,185	95,169	100,016	26,771	12,653	14,117	14,869	7,422	7,447
1985	237,924	115,730	122,194	202,031	98,635	103,396	28,569	13,505	15,064	18,368	9,275	9,093
1990	249,415	121,600	127,815	209,150	102,376	106,773	30,620	14,488	16,131	22,554	11,489	11,065
1993 [2]	257,927	125,921	132,006	214,778	105,305	109,473	32,137	15,230	16,907	25,085	12,757	12,329
1994 [2]	260,711	127,318	133,393	216,586	106,237	110,349	32,631	15,466	17,165	25,939	13,182	12,757
1995 [2]	263,434	128,685	134,749	218,334	107,140	111,195	33,117	15,697	17,420	26,798	13,610	13,188
2000 [2]	276,241	135,101	141,140	226,267	111,245	115,022	35,469	16,802	18,667	31,166	15,777	15,388
Percentage composition:												
1970	100	48.7	51.3	87.6	42.7	44.9	11.1	5.3	5.8	0	0	0
1975	100	48.7	51.3	86.9	42.4	44.5	11.5	5.4	6.0	0	0	0
1980	100	48.6	51.4	85.9	41.9	44.0	11.8	5.6	6.2	6.5	3.3	3.3
1985	100	48.6	51.4	84.9	41.5	43.5	12.0	5.7	6.3	7.7	3.9	3.8
1990	100	48.8	51.2	83.9	41.0	42.8	12.3	5.8	6.5	9.0	4.6	4.4
1993	100	48.8	51.2	83.3	40.8	42.4	12.5	5.9	6.6	9.7	4.9	4.8
1994	100	48.8	51.2	83.1	40.7	42.3	12.5	5.9	6.6	9.9	5.1	4.9
1995	100	48.8	51.2	82.9	40.7	42.2	12.6	6.0	6.6	10.2	5.2	5.0
2000	100	48.9	51.1	81.9	40.3	41.6	12.8	6.1	6.8	11.3	5.7	5.6
Percentage growth:												
1970 to 1980	11.4	11.2	11.6	9.2	9.1	9.3	18.0	17.2	18.8	0	0	0
1980 to 1990	9.8	10.1	9.4	7.2	7.6	6.8	14.4	14.5	14.3	51.7	54.8	48.6
1990 to 2000	10.8	11.1	10.4	8.2	8.7	7.7	15.8	16.0	15.7	38.2	37.3	39.1

[1] Hispanic origin date not available for 1970 and 1975.
[2] Projected.

Note: Hispanic origin may be of any race.

Source: U.S. Department of Commerce, Bureau of the Census, Population Estimates and Projections, series P-25, No. 917, 1092, 1095, and 1104.

TABLE I–5.—IMMIGRATION TO THE UNITED STATES: FISCAL YEARS 1820–1992

Year	Number
1820–1992	59,795,158
1820	8,385
1821–30	143,439
1821	9,127
1822	6,911
1823	6,354
1824	7,912
1825	10,199
1826	10,837
1827	18,875
1828	27,382
1829	22,520
1830	23,322
1831–40	599,125
1831	22,633
1832	60,482
1833	58,640
1834	65,365
1835	45,374
1836	76,242
1837	79,340
1838	38,914
1839	68,069
1840	84,066
1841–50	1,713,251
1841	80,289
1842	104,565
1843	52,496
1844	78,615
1845	114,371
1846	154,416
1847	234,968
1848	226,527
1849	297,024
1850	369,980
1851–60	2,598,214
1851	379,466
1852	371,603
1853	368,645
1854	427,833
1855	200,877
1856	200,436
1857	251,306
1848	123,126
1859	121,282
1860	153,640

TABLE I–5.—IMMIGRATION TO THE UNITED STATES: FISCAL YEARS 1820–1992—
Continued

Year	Number
1861–70	2,314,824
1861	91,918
1862	91,985
1863	176,282
1864	193,418
1865	248,120
1866	318,568
1867	315,722
1868	138,840
1869	352,768
1870	387,203
1871–80	2,812,191
1871	321,350
1872	404,806
1873	459,803
1874	313,339
1875	227,498
1876	169,986
1877	141,857
1878	138,469
1879	177,826
1880	457,257
1881–90	5,246,613
1881	669,431
1882	788,992
1883	603,322
1884	518,592
1885	395,346
1886	334,203
1887	490,109
1888	546,889
1889	444,427
1890	455,302
1891–1900	3,687,564
1891	560,319
1892	579,663
1893	439,730
1894	285,631
1895	258,536
1896	343,267
1897	230,832
1898	229,299
1899	311,715
1900	448,572

TABLE I–5.—IMMIGRATION TO THE UNITED STATES: FISCAL YEARS 1820–1992—
Continued

Year	Number
1901–10	8,795,386
1901	487,918
1902	648,743
1903	857,046
1904	812,870
1905	1,026,499
1906	1,100,735
1907	1,285,349
1908	782,870
1909	751,786
1910	1,041,570
1911–20	5,735,811
1911	878,587
1912	838,172
1913	1,197,892
1914	1,218,480
1915	326,700
1916	298,826
1917	295,403
1918	110,618
1919	141,132
1920	430,001
1921–30	4,107,209
1921	805,228
1922	309,556
1923	522,919
1924	706,896
1925	294,314
1926	304,488
1927	335,175
1928	307,255
1929	279,678
1930	241,700
1931–40	528,431
1931	97,139
1932	35,576
1933	23,068
1934	29,470
1935	34,956
1936	36,329
1937	50,244
1938	67,895
1939	82,998
1940	70,756

TABLE I–5.—IMMIGRATION TO THE UNITED STATES: FISCAL YEARS 1820–1992—Continued

Year	Number
1941–50	1,035,039
1941	51,776
1942	28,781
1943	23,725
1944	28,551
1945	38,119
1946	108,721
1947	147,292
1948	170,570
1949	188,317
1950	249,187
1951–60	2,515,479
1951	205,717
1952	265,520
1953	170,434
1954	208,177
1955	237,790
1956	321,625
1957	326,867
1958	253,265
1959	260,686
1960	265,398
1961–70	3,321,677
1961	271,344
1962	283,763
1963	306,260
1964	292,248
1965	296,697
1966	323,040
1967	361,972
1968	454,448
1969	358,579
1970	373,326
1971–80	4,493,314
1971	370,478
1972	384,685
1973	400,063
1974	394,861
1975	386,194
1976	398,613
1976, TQ	103,676
1977	462,315
1978	601,442
1979	460,348
1980	530,639

TABLE I–5.—IMMIGRATION TO THE UNITED STATES: FISCAL YEARS 1820–1992—
Continued

Year	Number
1981–90	7,338,062
1981	596,600
1982	594,131
1983	559,763
1984	543,903
1985	570,009
1986	601,708
1987	601,516
1988	643,025
1989	1,090,924
1990	1,536,483
1991–92	2,765,144
1991	1,827,167
1992	973,977

Note: The numbers shown are as follows: from 1820–67, figures represent alien passengers arrived at seaports; from 1868–92 and 1895–97, immigrant aliens arrived; from 1892–94 and 1898–1992, immigrant aliens admitted for permanent residence. From 1892–1903, aliens entering by cabin class were not counted as immigrants. Land arrivals were not completely enumerated until 1908.

Source: U.S. Department of Justice, Immigration and Naturalization Service, 1992 Statistical Yearbook of the Immigration and Naturalization Service. Issued October 1993.

TABLE I-6.—IMMIGRANTS ADMITTED BY TYPE AND SELECTED CLASS OF ADMISSION FISCAL YEARS 1985-92

Type and class of admission	1985	1986	1987	1988	1989	1990	1991	1992
Total, all immigrants	570,009	601,708	601,516	643,025	1,090,924	1,536,483	1,827,167	973,977
New arrivals	356,365	376,110	386,995	377,885	402,431	435,729	443,107	511,769
Adjustments	213,644	225,598	214,521	265,140	688,493	1,100,754	1,384,060	462,208
Total, IRCA legalization	NA	NA	NA	NA	478,814	880,372	1,123,162	163,342
Residents since 1982	NA	NA	NA	NA	478,814	823,704	214,003	46,962
Special Agricultural Workers	NA	NA	NA	NA	NA	56,668	909,159	116,380
Total, non-legalization	570,009	601,708	601,516	643,025	612,110	656,111	704,005	810,635
Preference immigrants	266,703	269,556	269,328	259,499	274,833	272,742	275,613	329,321
Family-sponsored immigrants	213,257	212,939	211,809	200,772	217,092	214,550	216,088	213,123
Unmarried sons/daughters of U.S. citizens[1]	9,319	10,910	11,382	12,107	13,259	15,861	15,385	12,486
Spouses of alien residents[1]	114,997	110,926	110,758	102,777	112,771	107,686	110,126	118,247
Married sons/daughters of U.S. citizens[2]	18,460	20,702	20,703	21,940	26,975	26,751	27,115	22,195
Siblings of U.S. citizens[2]	70,481	70,401	68,966	63,948	64,087	64,252	63,462	60,195
Employment-based immigrants[2,3]	53,446	56,617	57,519	58,727	57,741	58,192	59,525	116,198
Immediate relatives of U.S. citizens	204,368	223,468	218,575	219,340	217,514	231,680	237,103	235,484
Spouses	129,790	137,597	132,452	130,977	125,744	125,426	125,397	128,396
Children[4]	35,592	40,639	40,940	40,863	41,276	46,065	48,130	42,324
Orphans	9,286	9,945	10,097	9,120	7,948	7,088	9,008	6,536
Parents	38,986	45,232	45,183	47,500	50,494	60,189	63,576	64,764
Refugees and asylees	95,040	104,383	91,840	81,719	84,288	97,364	139,079	117,037

Refugee adjustments	106,379	116,415	92,427	79,143	76,274	86,840	99,383	90,040
Asylee adjustments	10,658	22,664	4,937	5,145	5,445	5,000	5,000	5,000
Other immigrants	128,793	52,210	54,325	35,475	82,467	21,773	4,301	3,898
Amerasians (P.L. 100–202)	17,253	16,010	13,059	8,589	319	NA	NA	NA
Children born abroad to alien residents	2,116	2,224	2,410	2,740	2,997	3,174	3,450	3,429
Cuban/Haitian entrants (P.L. 99–603) ..	99	213	710	2,816	29,002	4,634	NA	NA
Diversity transition	33,911	NA	NA	NA	NA	NA	NA	NA
Legalization dependents	52,272	NA	NA	NA	NA	NA	NA	NA
Nationals of adversely affected countries (P.L. 99–603)	1,557	12,268	20,371	7,068	6,029	3,037	NA	NA
Natives of underrepresented countries (P.L. 100–658)	880	9,802	8,790	NA	NA	NA	NA	NA
Parolees, Soviet Union or Indochina (P.L. 101–267)	13,661	4,998	NA	NA	NA	NA	NA	NA
Registered nurses and their families (P.L. 101–238)	3,572	3,069	2,954	NA	NA	NA	NA	NA
Registry, entered prior 1/1/72	1,293	2,282	4,633	10,570	39,999	8,060	25	32
Suspension of deportation	1,013	782	889	3,384	3,772	2,441	413	17
Other	1,166	562	509	308	349	427	413	420

[1] Excludes children.
[2] Includes spouses and children.
[3] Includes immigrants issued third preference, sixth preference, and special immigrant visas prior to fiscal year 1992, and immigrants issued employment-based preference visas during fiscal year 1992.
[4] Includes orphans.

Source: U.S. Department of Justice, Immigration and Naturalization Service, 1992 Statistical Yearbook of the Immigration and Naturalization Service. Issued October 1993.

TABLE I–7.—TOTAL IMMIGRANTS FOR TOP TEN COUNTRIES OF BIRTH IN
FISCAL YEAR 1992

Country of birth	Total		Non-legalization		IRCA legalization	
	Number	Percent	Number	Percent	Number	Percent
All countries	973,977	100.0	810,635	100.0	163,342	100.0
1. Mexico	213,802	22.0	91,332	11.3	122,470	75.0
2. Vietnam	77,735	8.0	77,728	9.6	7	(1)
3. Philippines	61,022	6.3	59,179	7.3	1,843	1.1
4. Soviet Union	43,614	4.5	43,590	5.4	24	(1)
5. Dominican Republic	41,969	4.3	40,840	5.0	1,129	.7
6. China, Mainland	38,907	4.0	38,735	4.8	172	.1
7. India	36,755	3.8	34,629	4.3	2,126	1.3
8. El Salvador	26,191	2.7	21,110	2.6	5,081	3.1
9. Poland	25,504	2.6	24,837	3.1	667	.4
10. United Kingdom	19,973	2.1	19,757	2.4	216	.1
Other	388,505	39.9	358,898	44.3	29,607	18.1

[1] Rounds to less than 0.05.

Source: U.S. Department of Justice, Immigration and Naturalization Service. Advance Report, Immigration Statistics: Fiscal Year 1992. Issued May 1993.

TABLE I–8. IMMIGRANTS ADMITTED (NON-LEGALIZATION) FOR TOP FIFTEEN COUNTRIES
OF BIRTH IN FISCAL YEARS 1991 AND 1992

Country of birth	1992	1991	Change	
			Number	Percent
All countries	810,635	704,005	106,630	13.2
1. Mexico	91,332	52,866	38,466	42.1
2. Vietnam	77,728	55,278	22,450	28.9
3. Philippines	59,179	55,376	3,803	6.4
4. Soviet Union	43,590	56,839	− 13,249	−30.4
5. Dominican Republic	40,840	30,177	10,663	26.1
6. China, Mainland	38,735	31,699	7,036	18.2
7. India	34,629	31,165	3,464	10.0
8. Poland	24,837	16,611	8,226	33.1
9. El Salvador	21,110	14,872	6,238	29.5
10. United Kingdom	19,757	12,807	6.950	35.2
11. Korea	18,983	21,628	−2,645	−13.9
12. Jamaica	16,820	18,025	−1,205	−7.2
13. Taiwan	16.232	12,548	3,684	22.7
14. Canada	14,958	12,200	2,758	18.4
15. Iran	12,808	18,019	− 5,211	− 40.7
Other	279,097	263,895	15,202	5.4

Source: U.S. Department of Justice, Immigration and Naturalization Service. Advance Report, Immigration Statistics. Fiscal year 1992. Issued May 1993.

TABLE I–9.—IMMIGRANTS ADMITTED BY COUNTRY OF BIRTH AND MAJOR CATEGORY OF ADMISSION IN FISCAL YEAR 1992

Region and country of birth	Total	Family-sponsored preferences	Employment-based preferences	Immediate relatives	Refugee and asylee adjustments	IRCA legalization	Legalization dependents	Diversity transition	Amerasians	Other
All countries[1]	973,977	213,123	116,198	235,484	117,037	163,342	52,272	33,911	17,253	25,357
Africa	27,086	3,749	4,967	10,630	4,480	2,260	332	322	....	346
Egypt	3,576	879	662	1,694	18	179	18	11	....	115
Ethiopia	4,602	210	110	806	3,268	191	4	3	....	10
Ghana	1,867	356	201	719	1	73	....	17	....	8
Nigeria	4,551	513	843	2,322	9	668	120	6	....	70
South Africa	2,516	151	1,657	570	33	31	5	45	....	24
Other Africa	9,974	1,640	1,494	4,519	1,136	771	41	254	....	119
Asia	356,955	87,575	63,107	102,414	53,422	8,402	5,271	6,724	17,253	12,787
Afghanistan	2,685	183	35	292	2,082	75	2	3	....	13
Bangladesh	3,740	1,258	134	923	10	588	71	5	....	377
Cambodia	2,573	134	20	430	1,695	4	....	1	46	243
China, Mainland	38,907	12,198	11,058	11,443	884	172	2,764	75	14	299
Hong Kong	10,452	5,705	2,800	1,249	193	43	140	58	1	263
India	36,755	14,468	9,686	9,796	34	2,126	352	34	....	259
Indonesia	2,916	224	438	387	13	24	27	1,497	....	306
Iran	13,233	1,682	2,434	4,582	3,093	425	76	10	....	931
Iraq	4,111	2,149	188	1,332	365	41	1	6	....	29
Israel	5,104	441	2,599	1,856	10	97	11	44	....	46
Japan	11,028	288	3,203	2,550	5	53	26	4,839	....	64
Jordan	4,036	1,168	262	2,491	15	57	....	2	....	41

TABLE I–9.—IMMIGRANTS ADMITTED BY COUNTRY OF BIRTH AND MAJOR CATEGORY OF ADMISSION IN FISCAL YEAR 1992—Continued

Region and country of birth	Total	Family-sponsored preferences	Employment-based preferences	Immediate relatives	Refugee and asylee adjustments	IRCA legalization	Legalization dependents	Diversity transition	Amerasians	Other
Korea	19,359	6,270	4,712	7,559	....	376	264	26	3	149
Laos	8,696	136	7	508	8,026	6	....	....	1	12
Lebanon	5,838	1,522	1,162	2,289	140	490	8	10	....	217
Malaysia	2,235	282	1,143	650	88	22	16	12	....	22
Pakistan	10,214	4,331	1,243	2,714	129	1,229	328	6	....	234
Philippines	61,022	14,435	9,708	30,572	221	1,843	677	15	4	3,547
Syria	2,940	541	415	1,230	2	11	....	6	....	406
Taiwan	16,344	4,610	8,368	2,812	10	112	345	32	....	55
Thailand	7,090	856	450	1,355	4,048	177	130	5	3	66
Turkey	2,488	230	750	1,144	16	71	20	6	....	251
Vietnam	77,735	12,133	142	11,306	32,155	7	1	6	17,181	4,804
Yemen	2,056	796	15	1,218	5	16	....	2	....	4
Other Asia	5,398	1,535	1,767	1,726	89	98	8	26	....	149
Europe	145,392	11,769	19,791	33,808	42,721	1,663	1,925	25,401	....	8,314
France	3,288	158	1,128	1,400	13	44	6	488	....	51
Germany	9,888	302	1,552	7,315	94	62	11	460	....	92
Greece	1,858	215	305	932	28	68	11	7	....	292
Ireland	12,226	180	712	908	2	59	6	10,066	....	293
Italy	2,592	207	583	1,286	105	42	24	314	....	31
Netherlands	1,586	101	662	650	2	24	7	119	....	21
Poland	25,504	7,054	1,575	3,174	1,512	667	1,552	9,383	....	587
Portugal	2,748	700	998	660	....	225	140	....	....	25
Romania	6,500	216	273	991	4,971	8	1	7	....	33

Region and country of birth	Total								
Soviet Union, former	43,614	220	572	2,796	33,504	24	10	35	6,453
Armenia	6,145	5	17	101	479				5,543
Azerbaijan	1,640	5	14	30	1,551				40
Belarus	3,233	11	9	185	3,008		2	1	17
Moldova	1,705	11	31	66	1,588				9
Russia	8,857	78	280	1,175	7,122		1	12	189
Ukraine	14,383	45	101	670	13,347		1	11	208
Uzbekistan	1,712	13	44	64	1,550				41
Other republics	1,286	8	37	99	1,035			1	106
Unknown republic	4,653	44	39	406	3,824	24	6	10	300
Spain	1,631	100	434	876	50	71	68	17	15
United Kingdom	19,973	1,322	7,572	7,358	7	216	14	3,261	223
Yugoslavia	2,604	482	619	1,267	58	94	65	5	14
Other Europe	11,380	512	2,806	4,195	2,375	59	10	1,239	184
North America	384,047	93,147	19,029	66,819	15,962	145,495	39,870	253	3,472
Canada	15,205	1,545	6,304	6,172	5	247	58	186	688
Mexico	213,802	33,361	3,226	24,440	29	122,470	28,449	23	1,804
Caribbean	97,413	42,636	3,945	25,422	9,969	12,873	2,013	25	530
Cuba	11,791	1,261	22	471	9,919	37	3	1	77
Dominican Republic	41,969	26,463	298	13,077	27	1,129	826	4	145
Haiti	11,002	680	78	1,422	16	8,591	141	1	73
Jamaica	18,915	8,996	1,482	5,446	1	2,095	792	3	100
Trinidad & Tobago	7,008	2,364	1,427	2,690		409	54	1	63
Other Caribbean	6,728	2,872	638	2,316	6	612	197	15	72
Central America	57,558	15,593	5,545	10,749	5,959	9,904	9,350	12	446
El Salvador	26,191	6,735	2,978	2,449	743	5,081	8,135	1	69
Guatemala	10,521	3,827	1,285	1,928	169	3,081	181	1	49

TABLE I–9.—IMMIGRANTS ADMITTED BY COUNTRY OF BIRTH AND MAJOR CATEGORY OF ADMISSION IN FISCAL YEAR 1992—Continued

Region and country of birth	Total	Family-sponsored preferences	Employ-ment-based preferences	Immediate relatives	Refugee and asylee adjust-ments	IRCA le-galization	Legaliza-tion de-pendents	Diversity transi-tion	Amerasians	Other
Honduras	6,552	2,346	389	2,342	105	852	492	4	....	22
Nicaragua	8,949	1,441	369	1,407	4,668	472	345	....	....	247
Panama	2,845	555	287	1,600	243	103	33	2	....	22
Other Central America	2,500	689	237	1,023	31	315	164	4	....	37
Other North America	69	12	9	36	....	1	....	7	....	4
Oceania	5,169	750	1,346	2,262	9	684	22	40	....	56
Australia	2,238	72	883	1,205	....	19	1	27	....	31
Other Oceania	2,931	678	463	1,057	9	665	21	13	....	25
South America	55,308	16,133	7,957	19,551	442	4,820	4,852	1,171	....	382
Argentina	3,877	375	1,148	932	15	203	88	1,062	....	54
Bolivia	1,510	300	397	543	3	154	82	4	....	27
Brazil	4,755	394	1,154	2,190	7	927	15	28	....	40
Chile	1,937	407	382	873	16	144	87	9	....	19
Colombia	13,201	3,667	1,273	4,956	74	1,357	1,784	8	....	82
Ecuador	7,286	2,543	794	1,940	6	500	1,443	1	....	59
Guyana	9,064	5,319	681	2,512	....	317	216	7	....	12

Peru	9,868	2,544	1,244	3,914	74	984	1,039	21	48
Venezuela	2,340	338	584	1,032	220	114	13	14	25
Other South America	1,470	246	300	659	27	120	85	17	16
Unknown or not reported	20	....	1	....	1	18	....	....	....

[1] Only countries with more than 1,500 immigrants are listed.

Source: U.S. Department of Justice, Immigration and Naturalization Service, Advance Report, Immigration Statistics: Fiscal Year 1992. Issued May 1993.

TABLE I–10.—IMMIGRANTS ADMITTED FOR TOP TWENTY METROPOLITAN AREAS OF INTENDED RESIDENCE IN FISCAL YEAR 1992

Metropolitan area of intended residence [1]	Total		Non-legalization		IRCA legalization	
	Number	Percent	Number	Percent	Number	Percent
Total	973,977	100.0	810,635	100.0	163,342	100.0
1. Los Angeles-Long Beach, CA	129,266	13.3	92,806	11.4	36,460	22.3
2. New York, NY	127,875	13.1	120,600	14.9	7,275	4.5
3. Chicago, IL	37,236	3.8	34,719	4.3	2,517	1.5
4. Anaheim-Santa Ana, CA	34,417	3.5	26,120	3.2	8,297	5.1
5. Miami-Hialeah, FL	31,627	3.2	25,774	3.2	5,853	3.6
6. Washington, DC-MD-VA	27,387	2.8	26,588	3.3	799	.5
7. Houston, TX	27,067	2.8	21,236	2.6	5,831	3.6
8. San Jose, CA	23,537	2.4	21,046	2.6	2,491	1.5
9. San Francisco, CA	21,276	2.2	19,033	2.3	2,243	1.4
10. San Diego, CA	20,936	2.1	13,394	1.7	7,542	4.6
11. Boston, MA [2]	18,259	1.9	16,927	2.1	1,332	.8
12. Oakland, CA	17,187	1.8	14,590	1.8	2,597	1.6
13. Riverside-San Bernardino, CA	16,535	1.7	9,089	1.1	7,446	4.6
14. Newark, NJ	13,734	1.4	12,828	1.6	906	.6
15. Bergen-Passaic, NJ	12,405	1.3	12,069	1.5	336	.2
16. Dallas, TX	12,312	1.3	9,082	1.1	3,230	2.0
17. Philadelphia, PA-NJ	11,882	1.2	11,649	1.4	233	.1
18. Nassau-Suffolk, NY	11,415	1.2	10,820	1.3	595	.4
19. Seattle, WA	9,855	1.0	9,660	1.2	195	.1
20. Sacramento, CA	9,564	1.0	8,286	1.0	1,278	.8
Other MSAs [1]	290,200	29.8	241,367	29.8	48,833	29.9
Non-MSA [1]	69,594	7.1	52,630	6.5	16,964	10.4
Unknown	411	(3)	322	(3)	89	.1

[1] Metropolitan statistical areas defined by the Office of Federal Statistical Policy, Office of Management and Budget.
[2] Includes Essex, Middlesex, Norfolk, Plymouth, and Suffolk counties.
[3] Rounds to less than 0.05.

Source: U.S. Department of Justice, Immigration and Naturalization Service. Advance Report, Immigration Statistics: Fiscal year 1992. Issued May 1993.

TABLE I-11.—NONIMMIGRANTS ADMITTED BY CLASS OF ADMISSION SELECTED FISCAL YEARS 1981–92

Class of admission	1981	1985	1988	1989	1990	1991	1992
All classes [1]	11,756,903	9,539,880	14,591,735	16,144,576	17,574,055	18,962,520	20,793,847
Foreign government officials and families ..	84,710	90,190	98,927	101,557	96,689	97,811	102,645
Ambassador, public minister, career diplomatic or consular officer (A1)	NA	21,168	22,182	22,165	22,018	22,750	23,533
Other foreign government official or employee (A2)	NA	67,084	74,723	77,491	72,511	72,926	77,087
Attendant, servant, or personal employee of A1 and A2 classes (A3) ..	NA	1,938	2,022	1,901	2,160	2,135	2,025
Temporary visitors	10,650,592	8,405,409	13,196,729	14,667,303	16,079,666	17,385,990	19,238,240
For business (B1)	1,135,422	1,796,819	2,375,565	2,552,719	2,661,338	2,652,202	2,788,141
Visa Waiver, business	NA	NA	3,854	99,665	294,065	370,138	527,932
For pleasure (B2)	9,515,170	6,608,590	10,821,164	12,114,584	13,418,328	14,733,788	16,450,099
Visa Waiver, pleasure	NA	NA	55,904	2,348,959	4,528,112	5,599,266	7,981,880
Transit aliens	214,218	236,537	299,138	293,364	306,156	364,187	345,610
Alien in transit (C1)	NA	138,957	153,811	152,623	153,801	174,426	168,053
Alien in transit to the U.N. (C2)	NA	1,804	1,381	874	1,296	992	1,055
Foreign government official and family in transit (C3)	NA	7,010	6,612	6,047	6,190	6,604	7,576
Transit without visa (C4)	NA	88,766	137,334	133,820	144,869	182,165	168,926
Treaty traders and investors and families ..	80,802	96,489	125,555	139,949	147,536	155,014	152,416
Treaty trader (E1)	NA	65,406	75,785	78,524	78,658	76,948	71,817
Treaty investor (E2)	NA	31,083	49,770	61,425	68,878	78,066	80,599
Students	240,805	257,069	312,363	334,402	326,264	282,077	241,093

TABLE I-11.—NONIMMIGRANTS ADMITTED BY CLASS OF ADMISSION SELECTED FISCAL YEARS 1981–92—Continued

Class of admission	1981	1985	1988	1989	1990	1991	1992
Academic student (F1)	NA	251,234	305,868	327,581	319,467	276,553	237,077
Vocational student (M1)	NA	5,835	6,495	6,821	6,797	5,524	4,016
Spouses and children of students	31,056	28,427	25,540	26,369	28,943	32,315	33,431
Academic student (F2)	NA	27,747	25,062	25,952	28,490	31,622	32,812
Vocational student (M2)	NA	680	478	417	453	693	619
Representatives (and families) to international organizations	54,223	57,203	58,947	61,406	61,449	64,470	69,985
Principal of recognized foreign government (G1)	NA	8,316	8,401	8,664	8,256	8,194	8,472
Other rep. of recognized foreign government (G2)	NA	6,989	8,101	8,260	8,110	7,277	8,909
Rep. of nonrecognized foreign government (G3)	NA	271	360	444	376	466	412
International organization officer or employee (G4)	NA	40,397	40,593	42,538	43,104	46,896	50,670
Attendant, servant or personal employee of rep. (G5)	NA	1,230	1,492	1,500	1,603	1,637	1,522
Temporary workers and trainees [2]	44,770	74,869	113,424	138,703	139,587	161,291	163,137
Registered nurses (H1A) [3]	NA	NA	NA	NA	NA	1,309	7,147
Specialty occupations (H1B) [4]	NA	NA	NA	NA	NA	116,729	110,193
Performing services unavailable in the U.S. (H2)	NA	24,544	32,966	46,570	35,973	39,972	34,414
Agricultural workers (H2A)	NA	NA	10,851	30,189	18,219	18,487	16,385
Nonagricultural workers (H2B)	NA	NA	22,115	16,381	17,754	21,485	18,029
Industrial trainee (H3)	NA	3,003	2,527	2,277	3,168	3,281	3,355

Workers with extraordinary ability/achievement (O1) [5]	NA	NA	NA	NA	NA	NA	448
Workers accompanying and assisting in performance of O1 workers (O2) [5]	NA	NA	NA	NA	NA	NA	252
Internationally recognized athletes or entertainers (P1) [5]	NA	NA	NA	NA	NA	NA	3,523
Artists or entertainers in reciprocal exchange programs (P2) [5]	NA	NA	NA	NA	NA	NA	89
Artists or entertainers in culturally unique programs (P3) [5]	NA	NA	NA	NA	NA	NA	1,126
Workers in international cultural exchange programs (Q1) [5]	NA	NA	NA	NA	NA	NA	7
Workers in religious occupations (R1) [5]	NA	NA	NA	NA	NA	NA	2,583
Spouses and children of temporary workers and trainees	10,110	12,632	19,673	23,807	28,687	34,418	39,921
Spouses and children of H1, H2, and H3 workers (H4)	10,110	12,632	19,673	23,807	28,687	34,418	39,080
Spouses and children of O1 and O2 workers (O3) [5]	NA	NA	NA	NA	NA	NA	NA
Spouses and children of P1, P2, and P3 workers (P4) [5]	NA	NA	NA	NA	NA	NA	144
Spouses and children of R1 workers (R2) [5]	NA	NA	NA	NA	NA	NA	697
Representatives (and families) of foreign information media (I1)	16,708	16,753	21,461	21,349	20,252	21,101	21,746
Exchange visitors (J1)	80,230	110,942	166,659	178,199	174,247	182,940	189,919

TABLE I-11.—NONIMMIGRANTS ADMITTED BY CLASS OF ADMISSION SELECTED FISCAL YEARS 1981–92—Continued

Class of admission	1981	1985	1988	1989	1990	1991	1992
Spouses and children of exchange visitors (J2)	27,793	30,271	36,267	39,259	40,397	41,217	42,031
Fiances(ees) of U.S. citizens (K1)	5,456	6,975	5,927	5,856	6,545	7,470	7,794
Children of fiances(ees) of U.S. citizens (K2)	742	832	688	625	673	754	775
Intracompany transferees (L1)	38,595	65,349	63,849	62,390	63,180	70,357	75,347
Spouses and children of intracompany transferees (L2)	26,449	41,533	37,846	38,335	39,375	42,541	45,501
NATO officials and families (N1–7)	7,124	8,323	8,545	8,783	8,333	8,695	8,888
U.S.-Canada Free-Trade Agreement (TC)[6]	NA	NA	NA	2,677	5,293	8,344	12,675
Spouses and children of U.S.-Canada Free-Trade Agreement (TC)[6]	NA	NA	NA	140	594	804	1,283
Unknown	142,520	77	197	103	189	724	1,410

[1] Excludes classes of admission processed as nonimmigrants in the following years: for all countries—1985—64,487 parolees (R1–3), 3,239 withdrawals (R4) and stowaways (R5), and 68,044 refugees (RF); 1988—94,918 parolees (R1–3), 17,060 withdrawals (R4) and stowaways (R5), and 80,382 refugees (RF); 1989—106,857 parolees (R1–3), 20,605 withdrawals (R4) and stowaways (R5), and 101,072 refugees (RF); 1990—90,265 parolees (R1–3), 19,984 withdrawals (R4) and stowaways (R5), and 110,197 refugees (RF); 1991—127,146 parolees (R1–3), 26,059 withdrawals (R4) and stowaways (R5), and 100,229 refugees (RF); 1992—137,478 parolees, 25,839 withdrawals (WD) and stowaways (ST), and 123,010 refugees (RE).

[2] Excludes entries under the U.S.-Canada Free-Trade Agreement (shown separately).

[3] Entries began October 1, 1990 (fiscal year 1991). Data for fiscal year 1991 are underreported; an unknown number of H1A entries were counted as H1B entries.

[4] Prior to October 1, 1991 (fiscal year 1992), H1B entries were termed "Distinguished merit or ability." Data for fiscal year 1991 are overreported; an unknown number of H1A entries were counted as H1B entries.

[5] Entries began in April 1992.

[6] Entries under the U.S.-Canada Free-Trade Agreement began in January 1989.

Note: "Family," "immediate family," and "spouse and children" are defined as spouse and unmarried minor (for dependent) children.

TABLE I–12.—MEDIAN MONEY INCOME OF HOUSEHOLDS BY STATE, 1984–92

[In 1992 dollars]

State	1984	1985	1986	1987 [1]	1988	1989	1990	1991	1992
Alabama	$22,691	$23,206	$23,775	$23,660	$22,966	$23,378	$25,073	$25,079	$25,891
Alaska	42,415	44,027	38,966	39,844	38,112	39,549	42,184	41,835	41,969
Arizona	28,085	30,223	31,689	32,071	30,435	31,361	31,371	31,662	29,593
Arkansas	20,547	22,089	23,276	22,572	23,224	23,542	24,460	24,140	23,893
California	33,148	34,153	36,051	36,143	34,870	36,257	35,735	34,677	35,173
Colorado	33,822	35,673	33,791	31,743	30,180	29,443	32,990	32,447	32,716
Connecticut	39,262	39,354	40,662	39,400	41,692	46,485	41,725	43,423	41,059
Delaware	33,845	29,088	31,845	35,062	35,121	35,223	33,067	33,566	35,739
District of Columbia	26,752	26,678	30,225	32,917	30,787	29,384	29,404	30,785	30,357
Florida	25,936	27,016	28,394	29,361	29,250	28,651	28,645	28,072	27,456
Georgia	26,197	26,644	30,285	32,029	30,586	30,252	29,585	28,031	28,889
Hawaii	37,854	36,659	35,042	41,989	38,021	38,482	41,780	38,367	42,171
Idaho	27,649	26,279	25,785	24,884	26,998	27,080	27,164	26,902	27,784
Illinois	31,136	31,480	32,945	32,472	33,991	34,380	34,932	32,844	31,707
Indiana	29,849	28,702	28,244	26,999	30,271	28,446	28,906	27,904	28,663
Iowa	26,038	26,489	27,910	26,605	27,983	28,849	29,292	29,413	28,880
Kansas	32,286	28,845	29,733	30,673	29,434	29,505	32,114	30,177	30,447
Kentucky	23,176	21,976	24,697	24,786	22,919	25,574	26,600	24,479	23,567
Louisiana	24,840	26,808	25,960	25,596	23,598	25,110	24,051	26,061	25,479
Maine	27,067	25,973	29,109	28,295	30,397	30,998	29,481	28,707	29,705
Maryland	38,943	38,146	38,032	41,927	42,083	39,560	41,711	38,064	37,287
Massachusetts	35,340	35,704	37,702	38,655	38,238	39,636	38,909	36,789	36,558
Michigan	30,104	30,685	33,062	33,213	33,931	33,803	32,136	33,084	32,347
Minnesota	32,033	30,197	32,861	33,669	33,488	33,155	33,776	30,366	31,077
Mississippi	20,227	20,776	20,521	22,196	20,915	21,877	21,660	20,061	20,585
Missouri	27,233	27,770	27,246	28,439	26,990	29,104	29,340	28,767	27,490
Montana	25,609	25,615	25,262	24,547	25,595	26,023	25,092	25,574	26,602
Nebraska	28,049	27,593	27,056	27,897	28,966	28,908	29,501	30,439	30,177
Nevada	33,789	29,460	32,580	32,225	32,217	32,227	34,375	33,929	32,026
New Hampshire	33,970	33,421	37,962	38,771	39,864	41,225	43,802	37,117	39,644

TABLE I-12.—MEDIAN MONEY INCOME OF HOUSEHOLDS BY STATE, 1984-92—Continued

[In 1992 dollars]

State	1984	1985	1986	1987[1]	1988	1989	1990	1991	1992
New Jersey	36,411	39,214	39,412	41,053	41,778	42,969	41,579	41,255	39,227
New Mexico	27,043	25,851	24,661	24,888	22,216	24,826	26,878	27,339	26,158
New York	28,875	29,922	31,099	31,633	33,290	34,595	33,911	32,751	31,254
North Carolina	26,963	27,153	27,167	27,288	28,109	29,004	28,263	27,661	27,835
North Dakota	27,228	26,841	26,728	27,067	27,737	27,711	27,120	26,671	27,105
Ohio	30,311	31,865	31,210	30,900	31,937	31,876	32,217	30,687	31,479
Oklahoma	27,722	26,841	26,032	26,006	27,248	25,996	26,175	26,228	25,363
Oregon	28,051	27,713	30,785	30,019	31,947	31,336	31,432	31,099	32,114
Pennsylvania	26,671	28,958	29,585	30,482	30,788	31,513	31,135	31,281	29,985
Rhode Island	28,331	31,170	32,981	33,920	34,357	33,088	34,316	31,764	30,636
South Carolina	26,623	25,362	27,300	30,032	29,396	26,139	30,846	28,290	27,667
South Dakota	25,443	22,964	24,727	25,359	25,667	26,480	26,376	25,381	26,351
Tennessee	21,999	22,503	22,687	25,392	24,012	24,836	24,251	25,189	24,339
Texas	30,182	30,054	30,026	29,639	28,740	28,433	30,301	28,568	28,282
Utah	30,225	31,946	32,659	31,807	30,294	33,739	32,356	28,859	34,433
Vermont	29,597	32,911	30,569	30,471	33,374	34,374	33,382	30,033	32,829
Virginia	34,771	35,985	36,927	35,963	37,588	37,475	37,649	37,225	38,223
Washington	32,794	30,379	33,405	32,754	37,218	35,106	34,471	34,993	34,064
West Virginia	22,079	20,231	20,460	20,630	22,281	23,810	23,763	23,844	20,301
Wisconsin	27,191	29,425	32,845	31,615	34,050	31,988	32,967	32,070	33,415
Wyoming	31,220	27,950	29,277	33,079	30,416	32,425	31,624	29,924	30,379

[1] Implementation of a new March CPS processing system.

Note: Dollars are adjusted for inflation using CPI-V-X1.

Source: Current Population Reports, Series P-60, No. 184, October 1993.

TABLE I-13.—STATE NOMINAL AND REAL ANNUAL BUDGET INCREASES, FISCAL 1979 TO FISCAL 1995

[In percent]

Fiscal year	State general fund	
	Nominal increase	Real increase
1995	3.1	−0.4
1994	5.1	1.6
1993	3.3	−0.2
1992	5.1	1.5
1991	4.5	−0.1
1990	6.4	1.7
1989	8.7	3.5
1988	7.0	2.9
1987	6.3	2.6
1986	8.9	3.7
1985	10.2	4.6
1984	8.0	3.3
1983	−0.7	−6.3
1982	6.4	−1.1
1981	16.3	6.1
1980	10.0	−0.6
1979	10.1	1.5
1979–1995 average	7.0	1.4
1980–1990 average	8.0	1.9

Note: The state and local government implicit price deflator was used for state expenditures in determining real changes. Figures for fiscal 1994 and fiscal 1995 are estimates.

Source: The fiscal survey of states, National Governors' Association, National Association of State Budget Officers, April 1994.

TABLE I–14.—RECOMMENDED FISCAL 1995 REVENUE ACTIONS BY TYPE OF REVENUE AND NET INCREASE OR DECREASE

[In millions of dollars]

State	Sales	Personal income	Corporate income	Cigarettes/ Tobacco	Motor fuels	Alcohol	Other taxes	Fees	Total
Alabama	....	....	....	....	....	....	....	....	$0.0
Alaska	....	....	....	$9.0	$82.2	$6.0	$21.9	$1.0	120.1
Arizona	....	−$100.0	....	....	....	....	....	....	−100.0
Arkansas	....	....	....	....	....	....	....	....	0.0
California	....	−95.0	....	....	....	....	....	....	−95.0
Colorado	....	....	....	....	....	....	....	....	0.0
Connecticut	....	−10.0	....	....	....	....	....	12.0	2.0
Delaware	....	....	....	....	....	....	....	....	0.0
Florida	....	....	....	....	....	....	....	33.7	33.7
Georgia	−$40.0	−140.0	....	....	....	....	....	....	−180.0
Hawaii	....	....	....	....	....	....	2.0	4.3	6.3
Idaho	....	....	....	....	....	....	....	....	0.0
Illinois	....	....	....	....	....	....	....	....	0.0
Indiana	....	....	....	....	....	....	....	....	0.0
Iowa	....	....	....	....	....	....	....	....	0.0
Kansas	....	....	....	....	....	....	....	....	0.0
Kentucky	....	....	....	....	....	....	....	....	0.0
Louisiana	....	....	....	....	....	....	....	....	0.0
Maine	....	....	....	....	....	....	....	....	0.0
Maryland	....	....	....	70.0	....	....	....	8.6	78.6
Massachusetts	....	−105.0	....	....	....	....	....	....	−105.0
Michigan [1]	1,883.0	−255.0	....	343.0	....	....	1,173.5	....	3,144.5
Minnesota	....	−11.3	....	....	....	....	....	−5.4	−16.7
Mississippi	....	−71.5	....	....	....	....	....	....	−71.5
Missouri	....	....	....	....	....	....	20.0	5.0	25.0
Montana	....	....	....	....	40.0	....	27.7	2.4	70.1
Nebraska'	....	....	....	....	....	....	−3.8	....	−3.8
Nevada	....	....	....	....	....	....	....	....	0.0
New Hampshire	....	....	−$14.0	....	....	....	....	....	−14.0

New Jersey		-549.0	-40.0		-40.2				64.0	-525.0
New Mexico	-12.0	-18.0							-58.2
New York		-65.0	-78.0				-38.0	10.8	-182.2
North Carolina									0.0
North Dakota									0.0
Ohio								5.0	5.0
Oklahoma						4.2		12.4	12.4
Oregon		3.7	-2.6	29.3			6.1		40.7
Pennsylvania		-52.0	-72.7				-2.0		-126.7
Puerto Rico				7.0					7.0
Rhode Island				5.5			-1.7	71.4	75.2
South Carolina		-9.0							-9.0
South Dakota									0.0
Tennessee									0.0
Texas	-191.0								-191.0
Utah	4.1								4.1
Vermont		-45.1					-8.8		-53.9
Virginia	-11.4	-32.4	-15.9						-59.7
Washington	-12.6		-9.3					2.4	-19.5
West Virginia									0.0
Wisconsin			4.8						4.8
Wyoming									0.0
Total	1,620.1	-1,554.6	-227.7	463.8	82.0	10.2	1,196.9	227.6	1,818.3

[1] In Michigan tax increases are accompanied by a decrease in local property taxes for elementary and secondary education. The net result is a $660 million decrease in combined state and local taxes in fiscal 1995.

Source: The fiscal survey of States, National Governors' Association, National Association of State Budget Officers, April 1994.

TABLE I-15.—FISCAL 1995 STATE GENERAL FUND, RECOMMENDED

[In millions of dollars]

Region/State	Beginning balance	Revenues	Resources	Expenditures	Ending balance	Budget stabilization fund
New England:						
Connecticut*	$0	$8,248	$8,248	$8,246	$2	$0
Maine	3	1,627	1,630	1,627	3	0
Massachusetts	14	12,734	12,748	12,700	48	325
New Hampshire	29	892	921	919	2	20
Rhode Island	0	1,577	1,577	1,576	2	44
Vermont	0	684	684	683	0	8
Mid-Atlantic:						
Delaware*	285	1,444	1,729	1,493	236	(*)
Maryland	19	6,948	6,968	6,967	1	220
New Jersey*	1,013	14,448	15,461	15,010	451	(*)
New York*	0	33,422	33,422	33,422	0	157
Pennsylvania*	267	15,400	15,667	15,665	2	160
Great Lakes:						
Illinois	200	13,489	13,689	13,489	200	0
Indiana*	0	6,705	6,705	6,595	110	297
Michigan	0	8,096	8,096	8,096	0	408
Ohio*	315	11,917	12,232	12,122	110	36
Wisconsin*	235	7,822	8,058	7,956	102	(*)
Plains:						
Iowa*	0	3,696	3,696	3,665	30	(*)
Kansas*	329	3,221	3,549	3,297	253	25
Minnesota*	777	8,435	9,212	8,532	680	(*)
Missouri	157	5,138	5,295	5,245	50	23
Nebraska	110	1,725	1,835	1,721	114	32
North Dakota*	21	626	657	641	16	0

South Dakota*	22	0	605	605	605	0

	Col1	Col2	Col3	Col4	Col5	Col6
South Dakota*	22	0	605	605	605	0
Southeast:						
Alabama	0	1	4,026	4,027	3,908	119
Arkansas	0	0	2,363	2,363	2,363	0
Florida	315	0	14,007	14,007	14,007	0
Georgia	123	0	9,396	9,396	9,396	0
Kentucky	130	6	4,995	5,001	5,001	0
Louisiana	0	0	4,740	4,740	4,740	0
Mississippi*	160	162	2,302	2,464	2,346	119
North Carolina*	141	880	9,246	10,126	9,530	596
South Carolina*	(*)	224	3,900	4,124	3,965	159
Tennessee*	(*)	125	4,967	5,092	4,928	164
Virginia*	(*)	1	7,371	7,372	7,179	193
West Virginia	0	11	2,247	2,257	2,217	41
Southwest:						
Arizona	0	30	4,235	4,265	4,073	192
New Mexico*	(*)	154	2,609	2,763	2,609	154
Oklahoma	46	223	3,377	3,600	3,472	128
Texas*	20	46	19,918	19,964	20,302	−339
Rocky Mountain:						
Colorado*	(*)	244	3,737	3,981	3,661	320
Idaho	36	0	1,286	1,286	1,258	28
Montana*	NA	24	622	642	619	27
Utah	62	0	2,267	2,267	2,254	13
Wyoming	0	11	438	449	427	22
Far West:						
Alaska	205	0	2,515	2,515	2,515	0
California*	(*)	488	38,788	39,236	39,929	−693
Hawaii	0	177	3,212	3,389	3,064	325
Nevada	0	61	1,104	1,164	1,098	66
Oregon	0	255	3,271	3,526	3,211	315
Washington*	125	291	7,946	8,238	8,269	−32

TABLE I-15.—FISCAL 1995 STATE GENERAL FUND, RECOMMENDED—Continued

[In millions of dollars]

Region/State	Beginning balance	Revenues	Resources	Expenditures	Ending balance	Budget stabilization fund
Territories:						
Puerto Rico	75	4,770	4,845	4,845	0	71
Total	5,691	335,240	340,938	335,157	5,826	3,140

Notes to Table I-15.—For all states, unless otherwise noted, transfers into budget stabilization funds are counted as expenditures and transfers from budget stabilization funds are counted as revenues.

California—Beginning balance and revenues include an off-budget eighteen-month payoff of prior year deficit. Ending balance includes a budget stabilization fund of $55 million and a $393 million reserve for liquidation.

Colorado—Ending balance includes a budget stabilization fund of $170.7 million.

Connecticut—Figures include federal reimbursements, such as Medicaid.

Delaware—Ending balance includes a budget stabilization fund of $78.3 million. Figures include federal reimbursements for Medicaid.

Indiana—Figures include property tax replacement fund, but do not include balance of the general fund tuition reserve, which will be $180 million in fiscal 1995. The impact of the Governor's deficit reduction plan and Medicaid reforms will reduce projected fiscal 1995 expenditures by $254.5 million.

Iowa—The ending balance, by law, is transferred to the cash reserve fund and, to the extent the balance in the cash reserve exceeds the required amount, the excess is transferred to the Generally Accepted Accounting Principles (GAAP) deficit retirement account. The budget stabilization fund includes balances in cash reserve and economic emergency at the end of the year and is currently $78.8 million.

Kansas—The budget stabilization fund includes $50 million that is recommended to be transferred to social services to offset reductions in disproportionate share funds.

Minnesota—Ending balance includes a budget stabilization fund of $500 million. The recommendation also includes creating a $180 million school aid reserve account dedicated to future funding for elementary and secondary education. Any future forecast improvement would be added to this account, up to a total of $300 million.

Mississippi—Fifty percent of the unencumbered ending balance, not to exceed 7.5 percent of current year appropriations, is transferred to a budget stabilization fund.

Montana—Figures include changes in earmarking of taxes for a school equalization increase of $125 million in expenditures and $134 million in revenues. These amounts had not been recorded in the general fund in previous years.

New Jersey—Reflects both the general fund and the Property Tax Relief Fund. Ending balance includes a budget stabilization fund of $147.8 million.

New Mexico—Revenues are adjusted for $58.2 million in executive-proposed recurring tax cuts. Ending balance includes a budget stabilization fund of $154 million.

New York—The state ended fiscal 1993 with a general fund surplus of $671 million and is estimated to end fiscal 1994 with a $299 million surplus. Because any general fund surplus is automatically deposited to the state's Tax Stabilization Reserve Fund (which can be used only in the case of a deficit), the state chose instead to deposit the excess monies into the personal income tax refund reserve account. As a result, state tax revenues in fiscal 1993 were reduced by $671 million; projected tax revenues in fiscal 1994 were artificially inflated by $671 million as well as reduced by $299 million; and projected tax revenues in fiscal 1995 were artificially inflated by $299 million. Additionally, the estimated fiscal 1994 disbursements include $314 million to be transferred from the general fund to the contingency reserve fund. These monies are projected to be disbursed from the contingency reserve fund in fiscal 1995 for litigation expenses.

North Carolina—Ending balance includes a budget stabilization fund of $140.5 million and a reserve for repairs and renovations of $60 million. Neither the budget stabilization fund nor the reserve for repairs and renovations has been adjusted to include any increases from the ending balance as of June 30, 1994. The fiscal 1995 expenditures reflect budget adjustments for the 1994 Special Session on Crime.

North Dakota—The beginning and ending balances represent the unobligated cash balance. Revenues include obligated cash carried forward from the prior year. Expenditures include obligations against cash and transfers out of the general fund.

Ohio—Fiscal 1995 figures are per the state's enacted biennial budget and not recommended figures. Fiscal 1995 expenditures include a planned transfer of $15 million to the rainy day fund. State law requires any amount in excess of $70 million at the end of fiscal 1995 to be transferred into the rainy day fund at the beginning of fiscal 1996.

Pennsylvania—Expenditures include a transfer to the rainy day fund, which will occur in the subsequent year.

South Carolina—Ending balance includes a budget stabilization fund of $110.1 million.

South Dakota—The beginning and ending balances represent the unobligated cash balance. Revenues includes obligated cash carried forward from the prior year. Expenditures include obligations against cash and transfers out of the general fund.

Tennessee—Ending balance includes a budget stabilization fund of $125.0 million.

Texas—Expenditures include a transfer of $31 million to the rainy day fund. (Texas is on a biennial budget. The general fund closes with a positive balance in odd-numbered years.)

Virginia—Ending balance includes a budget stabilization fund of $79.9 million and is appropriated in fiscal 1995.

Washington—Revenues include transfers to and from the state budget stabilization account.

Wisconsin—Ending balance includes a budget stabilization fund of $78.8 million.

Note: NA indicates data are not available.

Source: The fiscal survey of States, National Governors' Association, National Association of State Budget Officers, April 1994.

TABLE I–16.—NOMINAL PERCENTAGE EXPENDITURE CHANGE, FISCAL 1994 AND FISCAL 1995

[In percent]

Region/State	Fiscal year—	
	1994	1995
New England:		
Connecticut	3.6	6.7
Maine	− 1.2	2.7
Massachusetts	5.8	3.7
New Hampshire*	11.7	4.7
Rhode Island	− 4.4	1.0
Vermont	1.6	4.6
Mid-Atlantic:		
Delaware	8.3	9.5
Maryland	3.0	6.0
New Jersey	5.9	− 0.8
New York	5.4	2.6
Pennsylvania	7.2	4.7
Great Lakes:		
Illinois	6.0	5.5
Indiana	5.6	− 1.0
Michigan	1.9	2.5
Ohio	4.7	9.0
Wisconsin	6.3	7.8
Plains:		
Iowa	1.9	4.8
Kansas*	16.9	4.8
Minnesota	12.3	3.7
Missouri	11.1	9.8
Nebraska	− 1.9	5.8
North Dakota	− 5.7	4.1
South Dakota*	6.2	− 2.6
Southeast:		
Alabama	8.2	4.7
Arkansas	8.1	5.3
Florida	10.7	5.5
Georgia	8.9	6.6
Kentucky	5.1	5.1
Louisiana	6.1	6.3
Mississippi	7.3	8.1
North Carolina	13.6	1.2
South Carolina	7.8	2.8
Tennessee	6.7	1.1
Virginia	6.2	7.9
West Virginia	4.5	5.9
Southwest:		
Arizona	3.0	10.9
New Mexico	16.3	3.3
Oklahoma	− 0.5	2.3
Texas	8.2	0.0
Rocky Mountain:		
Colorado	3.8	4.4
Idaho	10.3	13.0
Montana*	− 5.2	25.4
Utah	6.8	7.4
Wyoming	− 2.6	6.8

TABLE I–16.—NOMINAL PERCENTAGE EXPENDITURE CHANGE, FISCAL 1994 AND FISCAL 1995—Continued

[In percent]

Region/State	Fiscal year—	
	1994	1995
Far West:		
Alaska	15.7	−21.6
California	−3.9	−1.4
Hawaii	0.3	4.6
Nevada	−5.1	7.9
Oregon	9.3	6.2
Washington	3.6	−1.9
Territories:		
Puerto Rico	9.3	5.9
Average	5.1	3.1

Notes to Table 1–16.

Kansas—Expenditures for fiscal 1994 reflect a state assumption of $325.9 million of local school spending as a result of school finance reform. Excluding school finance reform, which shifted significant responsibility for school spending from localities to the state, the growth for fiscal 1994 is estimated to be 3.4 percent.

Montana—Figures include changes in earmarking of taxes for school equalization increase of $125 million in expenditures and $134 million in revenues. These amounts had not been recorded in the general fund in previous year.

New Hampshire—Medicaid enhancement fund was not previously budgeted as general funds.

South Dakota—Fiscal 1995 expenditures reflect the fact that $29.5 million in higher education tuition and fees are no longer deposited in the general fund.

Source: The Fiscal Survey of States, National Governors' Association, National Association of State Budget Officers, April 1994.

APPENDIX J. BUDGET TABLES

TABLE J–1.—CBO BASELINE OUTLAY PROJECTIONS FOR MAJOR SPENDING CATEGORIES

[By fiscal year, in billions of dollars]

Spending category	1993	1994	1995	1996	1997	1998	1999
Defense discretionary	292	280	273	277	283	291	298
International discretionary	22	21	21	21	22	22	23
Domestic discretionary ...	228	246	260	267	273	282	290
Subtotal, discretionary	542	547	546	551	549	549	566
Mandatory spending excluding deposit insurance	762	802	847	897	963	1,028	1,100
Deposit insurance	− 28	− 3	− 12	− 14	− 6	− 5	− 4
Net Interest	199	201	214	230	241	252	264
Offsetting receipts	− 67	− 68	− 77	− 72	− 76	− 82	− 85
Total outlays	1,408	1,478	1,518	1,591	1,670	1,743	1,843
			As a percentage of GDP				
Defense discretionary	4.6	4.2	3.9	3.8	3.6	3.5	3.5
International discretionary	0.3	0.3	0.3	0.3	0.3	0.3	0.3
Domestic discretionary ...	3.6	3.7	3.7	3.6	3.5	3.4	3.4
Subtotal, discretionary	8.6	8.2	7.8	7.5	7.1	6.7	6.6
Mandatory spending excluding deposit insurance	12.1	12.1	12.1	12.1	12.4	12.6	12.8
Deposit Insurance	− 0.4	− 0.1	− 0.2	− 0.2	− 0.1	− 0.1	a
Net interest	3.2	3.0	3.0	3.1	3.1	3.1	3.1
Offsetting receipts	− 1.1	− 1.0	− 1.1	− 1.0	− 1.0	− 1.0	− 1.0
Total outlays	22.4	22.3	21.7	21.5	21.5	21.3	21.4

Source: Congressional Budget Office.

(1249)

TABLE J-2.—THE TEN-YEAR BUDGET OUTLOOK

[By fiscal year]

	1994	1995	1996	1997	1998	1999	2000	2001	2002	2003	2004
	In billions of dollars										
Revenues	1,251	1,338	1,411	1,479	1,556	1,630	1,706	1,783	1,868	1,958	2,054
Outlays:											
Discretionary	547	546	551	549	549	566	584	602	621	640	660
Mandatory:											
Social Security	318	335	352	370	388	408	429	450	473	497	523
Medicare	160	177	195	216	238	263	290	320	354	391	434
Medicaid	86	96	108	121	135	151	168	186	206	227	250
Civil Service and military retirement	62	65	68	71	74	79	82	86	90	94	99
Other	176	174	174	185	192	199	206	212	219	226	223
Subtotal	802	847	897	963	1,028	1,100	1,175	1,255	1,342	1,436	1,538
Deposit insurance	-3	-12	-14	-6	-5	-4	-2	-2	-1	-1	-1
Net interest	201	214	230	241	252	264	276	291	307	325	345
Offsetting receipts	-68	-77	-72	-76	-82	-85	-88	-92	-95	-99	-104
Total	1,478	1,518	1,591	1,670	1,743	1,843	1,945	2,054	2,173	2,300	2,439
Deficit	228	180	180	192	187	213	240	271	305	343	385
Debt held by the public	3,465	3,653	3,846	4,055	4,260	4,492	4,751	5,041	5,366	5,728	6,132
	As a percentage of GDP										
Revenues	18.8	19.1	19.1	19.0	19.0	19.0	18.9	18.9	18.8	18.8	18.8
Outlays:											
Discretionary	8.2	7.8	7.5	7.1	6.7	6.6	6.5	6.4	6.3	6.1	6.0

Mandatory:											
Social Security	4.8	4.8	4.8	4.8	4.8	4.7	4.7	4.8	4.8	4.8	4.8
Medicare	4.0	3.8	3.6	3.4	3.2	3.1	2.9	2.8	2.6	2.5	2.4
Medicaid	2.3	2.2	2.1	2.0	1.9	1.8	1.7	1.6	1.5	1.4	1.3
Civil Service and military retirement	0.9	0.9	0.9	0.9	0.9	0.9	0.9	0.9	0.9	0.9	0.9
Other	2.1	2.2	2.2	2.2	2.3	2.3	2.4	2.4	2.4	2.5	2.6
Subtotal	14.1	13.8	13.5	13.3	13.0	12.8	12.6	12.4	12.1	12.1	12.1
Deposit insurance	[1]	[1]	[1]	[1]	[1]	[1]	-0.1	-0.1	—	-0.2	-0.1
Net interest	3.2	3.1	3.1	3.1	3.1	3.1	3.1	3.1	3.1	3.0	3.0
Offsetting receipts	-0.9	-1.0	-1.0	-1.0	-1.0	-1.0	-1.0	-1.0	-1.0	-1.1	-1.0
Total	22.3	22.1	21.9	21.7	21.6	21.4	21.3	21.5	21.5	21.7	22.3
Deficit	3.5	3.3	3.1	2.9	2.7	2.5	2.3	2.5	2.4	2.6	3.4
Debt held by the public	56.1	55.0	54.1	53.3	52.7	52.3	52.1	52.1	52.1	52.1	52.2

[1] Less than 0.05 percent of GDP.

Source: Congressional Budget Office.

Notes to table 2.—

CBO expects that under current policies, revenues will remain just under 19 percent of GDP (see the table above), but spending growth will outstrip revenues. Outlays climb by 2 percent of GDP in the 1998–2003 period. Within the spending totals, some categories grow and others shrink. The Government's big health care programs—Medicare and Medicaid—continue to soar, and together they represent 7 percent of GDP in 2003 (compared with 5.2 percent in 1998). Net interest outlays inch up from 3.7 percent of GDP in 1998 to 4.5 percent in 2003. Social Security benefits stay at about 4.9 percent of GDP in 2003, the big demands that the baby-boom generation will place on Social Security and Medicare are still more than 5 years away. Most other spending programs roughly preserve their 1998 shares. A sole exception is discretionary spending—defense, international, and domestic. These programs are assumed in the baseline projections, to keep up with inflation once the Budget Enforcement Act's caps expire in 1995. They, therefore, dwindle gradually as a share of GDP, from 7.4 percent in 1998 (already a historic low) to 6.9 percent in 2003.

Economic assumptions are critical to these projections. In the 1999–2003 period, CBO posits that real economic growth will continue at about 2 percent a year. The unemployment rate remains at about 5.6 percent, down very slightly from 1998's level. Short-term interest rates (as measured by 3-month Treasury bills) and longer-term rates (such as 10-year Treasury notes) are also assumed to remain constant, at 4.9 percent and 6.4 percent, respectively. Inflation continues at 2.7 percent.

Five-year budget projections are highly uncertain, and 10-year extrapolations are even more so. Some key uncertainties surround the assumptions about economic performance (chiefly, real economic growth and interest rates), and others are more narrowly budget-related: uncertainty about the continued surge in medical care expenditures, the size and timing of outlays for deposit insurance, and so forth. CBO's projections, uncertain though they are, nevertheless call into question the comfortable notion that the deficit will eventually go away of its own accord.

TABLE J-3.—HOW TIGHT ARE THE DISCRETIONARY CAPS?

[By fiscal year, in billions of dollars]

	1995	1966	1997	1998
Budget Authority				
Discretionary caps	518	519	530	533
Amount needed to preserve 1994 real resources:				
Defense	269	278	287	295
International	21	22	22	23
Domestic	227	240	248	261
Total	517	540	557	579
Amount over or under (−) caps	−1	20	27	45
Amount needed to freeze 1994 dollar resources:				
Defense	260	260	260	260
International	20	20	20	20
Domestic	220	225	226	232
Total	501	506	507	513
Amount over or under (−) caps	−17	−13	−22	−21
Outlays				
Discretionary caps	546	551	549	549
Amount needed to preserve 1994 real resources:				
Defense	273	277	283	291
International	21	21	22	22
Domestic	260	267	273	282
Total	554	565	578	595
Amount over or under (−) caps	8	15	30	45
Amount needed to freeze 1994 dollar resources:				
Defense	267	264	261	261
International	21	20	21	20
Domestic	255	255	255	256
Total	543	539	536	537
Amount over or under (−) caps	−4	−11	−12	−13

Note.—Amounts needed to preserve 1994 real resources include adjustments for inflation of about 3 percent a year. Amounts needed to freeze 1994 dollar resources include no adjustment for inflation. Both paths include the budget authority necessary to renew expiring contracts for subsidized housing. The estimated caps are based on those published in Office of Management and Budget, "Budget Enforcement Act Preview Report," in "Budget of the United States Government: Analytical Perspectives" (February 1994), as modified by CBO for expected adjustments.

Source: Congressional Budget Office.

TABLE J–4.—CBO PROJECTIONS OF TRUST FUND SURPLUSES

[By fiscal year, in billions of dollars]

Trust fund	1994	1995	1996	1997	1998	1999
Social Security [1]	62	70	75	84	92	99
Medicare [2]	8	1	2	0	−3	−11
Military retirement	9	9	7	6	6	4
Civilian retirement [3]	29	30	31	33	34	36
Unemployment	3	5	5	5	6	4
Highway and Airport	−2	−3	−0	−1	−1	−1
Other [4]	4	3	3	4	4	4
Total trust fund surplus [5]	113	116	123	131	138	136
Federal funds deficit [5]	−341	−295	−303	−323	−325	−349
Total deficit	−228	−180	−180	−192	−187	−213
Memorandum: Net Transfers from Federal Funds to Trust Funds	213	214	230	252	273	295

[1] Old-Age and Survivors Insurance and Disability Insurance.
[2] Hospital Insurance and Supplementary Medical Insurance.
[3] Civil Service Retirement, Foreign Service Retirement, and several smaller funds.
[4] Primarily Railroad Retirement, employees' health insurance and life insurance, Superfund, and various veterans' insurance trust funds.
[5] Assumes that discretionary spending reductions are made in non-fund programs.

Source: Congressional Budget Office.

TABLE J–5.—TRUST FUND SURPLUSES, 1981–93

[In billions of dollars]

Account	1981	1982	1983	1984	1985	1986	1987	1988	1989	1990	1991	1992	1993
Social Security	-5	-8	(1)	(1)	9	17	20	39	52	58	54	51	47
Medicare	3	5	6	6	4	6	9	15	22	15	15	14	10
Military retirement					12	12	14	14	14	12	13	12	10
Civilian retirement[2]	11	12	14	15	18	19	18	19	20	22	24	26	28
Unemployment	-1	-4	-1	4	5	4	7	8	7	6	-3	-12	1
Highway and airport	-2	-1	1	4	2	1	2	2	4	2	4	2	-1
Other[3]	1	2	2	5	5	3	3	1	4	5	6	4	6
Total trust fund surplus	7	6	23	33	54	62	73	98	124	120	112	96	100
Federal funds deficit	-86	-134	-231	-218	-267	-283	-222	-253	-276	-342	-381	-386	-355
Overall deficit	-79	-128	-208	-185	-212	-221	-150	-155	-153	-221	-270	-290	-255

[1] Less than $500 million.
[2] Includes Civil Service Retirement, Foreign Service Retirement, and several smaller funds.
[3] Includes primarily Railroad Retirement, Employees' Health Insurance and Life Insurance, and Hazardous Substance Superfund.

Source: Congressional Budget Office.

TABLE J–6.—OUTLAYS FOR MAJOR SPENDING CATEGORIES FOR SELECTED YEARS IN NOMINAL DOLLARS, AND AS A PERCENTAGE OF GDP

[By fiscal year]

	1965	1970	1975	1980	1985	1990	1995
	In nominal dollars (billions)						
Defense discretionary	51.0	81.9	87.6	134.6	253.1	300.1	273.2
International discretionary	4.7	4.0	8.2	12.8	17.4	19.1	20.9
Domestic discretionary	26.1	38.7	66.7	129.1	145.7	182.5	259.7
Subtotal, discretionary	81.8	124.6	162.5	276.5	416.2	501.7	546.1
Social Security	17.1	29.6	63.6	117.1	186.4	246.5	334.8
Medicare	0	6.8	14.1	34.0	69.7	107.4	177.4
Medicaid	0.3	2.7	6.8	14.0	22.7	41.1	96.2
AFDC, SSI, Food Stamps	2.8	4.7	14.1	22.2	30.4	39.7	51.2
Deposit insurance	−.4	−.5	.5	−.4	−2.2	58.1	−12.1
Other entitlements and mandatories	8.0	13.3	47.5	75.0	93.7	73.1	110.6
Net interest	8.6	14.4	23.2	52.5	129.5	184.2	213.5
Total	118.2	195.6	332.3	590.9	946.4	1,251.8	1,517.7
Memo: GDP	671.4	985.6	1,511.0	2,644.5	3,970.9	5,459.5	7,005.5
	As a percentage of GDP						
Defense discretionary	7.6	8.3	5.8	5.1	6.4	5.5	3.9
International discretionary	.7	.4	.5	.5	.4	.3	0.3
Domestic discretionary	3.9	3.9	4.4	4.9	3.7	3.3	3.7
Subtotal, discretionary	12.2	12.6	10.8	10.5	10.5	9.2	7.8
Social Security	2.5	3.0	4.2	4.4	4.7	4.5	4.8
Medicare	.0	.7	.9	1.3	1.8	2.0	2.5
Medicaid	0	.3	.5	.5	.6	.8	1.4
AFDC, SSI, Food Stamps	.4	.5	.9	.8	.8	.7	0.7
Deposit insurance	−.1	−.1	0	0	−.1	1.1	−0.2
Other entitlements and mandatories	1.2	1.3	3.1	2.8	2.4	1.3	1.6
Net interest	1.3	1.5	1.5	2.0	3.3	3.4	3.0
Total	17.6	19.8	22.0	22.3	23.8	22.9	21.7
Memo: Social Security, Medicare and Medicaid	2.6	4.0	5.6	6.2	7.0	7.2	8.7
	As a percentage of budget						
Defense discretionary	43.1	41.9	26.4	22.8	26.7	24.0	18.0
International discretionary	4.0	2.0	2.5	2.2	1.8	1.5	1.4
Domestic discretionary	22.1	19.8	20.1	21.8	15.4	14.6	17.1
Subtotal, discretionary	69.2	63.7	48.9	46.8	44.0	40.1	36.0
Social Security	14.5	15.1	19.1	19.8	19.7	19.7	22.1
Medicare	0	3.5	4.2	5.8	7.4	8.6	11.7
Medicaid	.3	1.4	2.0	2.4	2.4	3.3	6.3
AFDC, SSI, Food Stamps	2.4	2.4	4.2	3.8	3.2	3.2	3.4
Deposit insurance	−.3	−.3	.2	−.1	−.2	4.6	−0.8
Other entitlements and mandatories	6.8	6.8	14.3	12.7	9.9	5.8	7.3
Net interest	7.3	7.4	7.0	8.9	13.7	14.7	14.1
Total	100.0	100.0	100.0	100.0	100.0	100.0	100.0

Source: Congressional Budget Office.

TABLE J–7.—MAJOR POLICY CHANGES IN WAYS AND MEANS COMMITTEE PROGRAMS (BUDGETARY SAVINGS ESTIMATES FOR FISCAL YEAR 1993)

	In billions of dollars	Percent [1]
Social Security:		
6-month COLA delay [2]	4.5	
Taxation of benefits	6.1	
Elimination of students benefits	2.6	
Elimination of certain mother/father benefits	.8	
Elimination of minimum benefits	.3	
Disability insurance:		
6-month COLA delay	.5	
Taxation of benefits	.2	
Limit on family maximum	1.1	
Assume 1971–80 award rate continued through 1993 [3]	10.7	
Subtotal—Social Security	26.8	8
Medicare:		
Provider reductions [4]	51.1	27
Deductible increases	2.3	
Part B premium increases [5]	8.1	
Subtotal	61.5	
AFDC:		
Real benefit decline since 1975 [6]	8.6	
Earnings disregard and other charges	.7	
Subtotal	9.3	36
Title XX (Social Services Block Grant):		
Real decline in budget authority [7]	3.3	54
Unemployment compensation:		
Decline in State coverage [8]	.9	
Taxation of benefits [9]	2.2	
Subtotal	3.0	
SSI:		
Benefit increase in July 1983 [10]	+1.1	
Child welfare services	NA	
Trade adjustment assistance	NA	
Total changes	102.8	
Total change in outlays	94.2	
Total changes in benefits to individuals	51.6	

[1] Calculated as savings/(savings plus fiscal year 1993 outlays).

[2] This illustrates that the provision to tax 50 percent of Social Security benefits above $25,000 for a single individual and $32,000 of a married couple filing jointly indirectly cut Social Security benefits.

[3] These savings are due mostly to administrative policy. The savings of $10.7 billion are derived by assuming that the new award rate that prevailed during the 1970's would continue throughout all of the 1980's.

[4] The Medicare provider reductions and the deductible increases are derived by assuming that the real increase in expenditures per Medicare beneficiary that prevailed from 1975 to 1980 would continue into the 1980's. See appendix B in the section entitled "Analyzing Trends in Medicare Spending, 1967–1997" for a more complete discussion of how this savings estimate was attained.

[5] This shows the increase in part B premiums that took place as a result of maintaining part B premiums at 25 percent of the total cost of the part B program. During the 1970's part B premiums increased at a rate equal to the increase in the Social Security COLA.

[6] This estimate is derived by assuming that States would have held their AFDC benefit level in real terms equal to that in 1975.

[7] This estimate is a result of the real decline in the title XX (Social Security Block Grant) program using the CPI–X1 price index. It compares 1977 real budget authority to that in 1993.

[8] This savings estimate is derived by assuming that the ratio of insured unemployed workers to job losers would be at the same ratio as that prevailing in 1979.

[9] This savings estimate shows the amount of money derived by taxing unemployment benefits.

[10] This number illustrates the additional cost in fiscal year 1993 of the $20-per-month increase in the SSI benefit for individuals and the $30-per-month increase for couples.

Note.—This table illustrates the savings for fiscal year 1993 for the major changes in policy that occurred between 1980 and 1990 for the entitlement programs under the jurisdiction of the Committee on Ways and Means. For example, if the 6-month cost-of-living allowance delay had not been enacted in the 1983 Social Security amendments, Social Security outlays would be $4.5 billion larger in fiscal year 1993. This table does not attempt to differentiate between legislative changes made at the Federal and the State level nor does it attempt to differentiate between regulation and law. It is an effort to illustrate precisely the magnitude of entitlement savings that actually occurred due to policy changes at the Federal and State level. It also makes no judgment about whether these policy changes were appropriate.

Source: Ways and Means Committee Staff based upon CBO technical assistance. Table created in March 1991.

TABLE J–8.—FEDERAL REVENUES BY SOURCE FOR SELECTED YEARS IN NOMINAL
DOLLARS, AS A PERCENTAGE OF GDP AND TOTAL REVENUES [1]

[By fiscal year]

	1965	1970	1975	1980	1985	1990	1995
	In nominal dollars (billions)						
Individual income	48.8	90.4	122.4	244.1	334.5	466.9	595.9
Corporate income	25.5	32.8	40.6	64.6	61.3	93.5	130.2
Social insurance	22.2	44.4	84.5	157.8	265.2	380.0	499.3
Excise	14.6	15.7	16.6	24.3	36.0	35.3	56.0
Estate and gift	2.7	3.6	4.6	6.4	6.4	11.5	13.9
Other	3.0	5.9	10.4	19.9	30.6	44.0	42.9
Total	116.8	192.8	279.1	517.1	734.1	1,031.3	1,338.2
	As a percentage of GDP						
Individual income	7.3	9.2	8.1	9.2	8.5	8.6	8.5
Corporate income	3.8	3.3	2.7	2.4	1.5	1.7	1.9
Social insurance	3.3	4.5	5.6	6.0	6.7	7.0	7.1
Excise	2.2	1.6	1.1	.9	.9	.6	.8
Estate and gift	.4	.4	.3	.2	.2	.2	.2
Other	.4	.6	.7	.8	.8	.8	.6
Total	17.4	19.5	18.3	19.4	18.6	19.1	19.1
	As a percentage of revenues						
Individual income	41.8	46.9	43.9	47.2	45.6	45.3	44.5
Corporate income	21.8	17.0	14.6	12.5	8.4	9.1	9.7
Social insurance	19.0	23.0	30.3	30.5	36.1	36.9	37.3
Excise	12.5	8.1	5.9	4.7	4.9	3.4	4.2
Estate and gift	2.3	1.9	1.7	1.2	.9	1.1	1.0
Other	2.6	3.0	3.7	3.9	4.2	4.3	3.2
Total	100.0	100.0	100.0	100.0	100.0	100.0	100.0

[1] Projected.

Source: Congressional Budget Office.

TABLE J-9.—CBO BASELINE REVENUE PROJECTIONS BY SOURCE, AND AS A PERCENTAGE OF GDP, 1993–1999

[By fiscal year, in billions of dollars]

	1993 actual	Projections					
		1994	1995	1996	1997	1998	1999
Individual income	509.7	546.6	595.9	635.0	667.7	707.9	747.5
Corporate income	117.5	128.0	130.2	132.7	138.0	143.5	148.3
Social insurance	428.3	468.5	499.3	525.5	551.1	578.1	603.8
Excise	48.1	55.4	56.0	56.8	57.7	58.7	59.7
Estate and gift	12.6	13.2	13.9	14.6	15.3	16.1	16.9
Customs duties	18.8	19.3	21.1	22.2	23.5	24.9	26.1
Other	18.6	19.5	21.8	24.0	25.5	26.7	27.6
Total	1,153.5	1,250.5	1,338.2	1,410.7	1,478.7	1,555.9	1,629.9
As a percentage of GDP							
Individual income	8.1	8.2	8.5	8.6	8.6	8.6	8.7
Corporate income	1.9	1.9	1.9	1.8	1.8	1.8	1.7
Social insurance	6.8	7.1	7.1	7.1	7.1	7.1	7.0
Excise	0.8	0.8	0.8	0.8	0.7	0.7	0.7
Estate and gift	0.2	0.2	0.2	0.2	0.2	0.2	0.2
Customs duties	0.3	0.3	0.3	0.3	0.3	0.3	0.3
Other	0.3	0.3	0.4	0.4	0.3	0.3	0.3
Total	18.3	18.8	19.1	19.1	19.0	19.0	19.0

Source: Congressional Budget Office.

TABLE J–10.—CBO BASELINE PROJECTIONS FOR SELECTED PROGRAMS WITHIN THE JURISDICTION OF THE COMMITTEE ON WAYS AND MEANS FOR FISCAL YEARS 1993–99

[By fiscal year, in billions of dollars]

	1993 actual	1994	1995	1996	1997	1998	1999
Social Security	301.6	318	334.8	353.4	370	388.6	408
OASI	268	281	294.6	309.7	322.9	337.9	353.6
DI	33.6	37	40.2	43.7	47.1	50.7	54.4
Medicare	124.2	160	177.3	195.1	215.6	237.8	263.4
HI	77.9	100.8	110.5	119.5	130.1	141.7	155.5
SMI	46.3	59.2	66.8	75.6	85.5	96.1	107.9
Trade adjustment	0.1	0.2	0.2	0.2	0.2	0.2	0.2
Unemployment insurance	36.3	27.8	24.6	25.4	25.7	26	27
Family support	16	17	18	18	19	20	20
EITC—outlays	8.8	9.9	15.3	18.1	20.1	20.1	21.7
SSI	21	25	24	24	29	32	35
Title XX—social services	2.8	2.9	3.2	3.3	2.8	2.8	2.8
Child welfare	0.3	0.3	0.3	0.3	0.3	0.3	0.3
Foster care and adoption assistance	2.6	3.	3.6	3.8	4	4.4	4.7
Child health insurance credit	0.6	0.7	0	0	0	0	0
Child care and development block grant	0.7	0.9	1.3	1.2	1.2	1	1
SMI premium	−16.1	−17.4	−19.9	−19.9	−22.5	−22.7	−27.4
Total	498.9	548.3	582.7	622.9	665.4	707.5	756.7

Source: Congressional Budget Office.

TABLE J-11.—WAYS AND MEANS PROGRAM OUTLAYS COMPARED WITH TOTAL FEDERAL GOVERN-
MENT OUTLAYS, IN NOMINAL DOLLARS, AND AVERAGE ANNUAL GROWTH RATES FOR SELECTED
YEARS

	Fiscal year					
	1970	1975	1980	1985	1990	1995
	In nominal dollars (billions)					
Social Security[1]	29.6	63.6	117.1	186.4	246.5	334.8
Medicare[1]	6.8	14.1	34.0	69.7	107.4	177.3
Unemployment compensation and trade adjustment assistance[1]	2.8	12.0	15.7	16.0	17.5	24.8
Public assistance and social services (Family Support Administration, SSI, Title XX, EITC, and Foster Care)	5.1	13.5	17.8	23.3	32.0	60.5
Nondefense discretionary spending and other entitlements	−55.5	117.8	219.6	270.6	306.0	446.1
Deposit insurance	−0.5	0.5	−0.4	−2.2	58.1	−12
National defense	81.9	87.6	134.6	253.1	300.1	273
Net interest	14.4	23.2	52.5	129.5	184.2	213.5
Total	195.6	332.3	590.9	946.4	1,251.8	1,518
Memo: CPI–X1 (1987=100)	40.3	54.2	80.2	106.7	128.8	151.6

	Average annual growth rates				
	1970–75	1975–80	1980–85	1985–90	1990–95
Social Security[1]	16.5	13.0	9.7	5.7	6.3
Medicare[1]	15.7	19.2	15.4	9.0	10.5
Unemployment compensation and trade adjustment assistance[1]	33.8	5.5	.4	1.8	7.2
Public assistance and social services (Family Support Administration, SSI, Title XX, EITC, and Foster Care)	21.5	5.7	5.5	6.6	13.6
Nondefense discretionary spending and other entitlements	16.2	13.3	4.3	2.5	7.8
Deposit insurance	NA	NA	NA	NA	NA
National defense	1.4	9.0	13.5	3.5	−1.9
Net interest	10.0	17.7	19.8	7.3	3
Total	11.2	12.2	9.9	5.8	3.9
Memo: CPI–X1	5.8	8.0	5.6	3.8	3.2

[1] Includes entitlement spending only.

Note: All growth rates were calculated using the LOTUS 1-2-3 formula @Rate =(Y/A)[1]/n=r.

Source: Congressional Budget Office.

TABLE J–12.—WAYS AND MEANS PROGRAM OUTLAYS COMPARED WITH TOTAL FEDERAL PROGRAM OUTLAYS IN PERCENTAGE TERMS FOR SELECTED YEARS

	1970	1975	1980	1985	1990[1]	1995[1]
Social Security (including Medicare)	18.6	23.4	25.6	27.1	28.3	33.7
Unemployment compensation and trade adjustment assistance	1.4	3.6	2.7	1.7	1.4	1.6
Public assistance and social services (AFDC, SSI, title XX, EITC, low-income energy assistance and child welfare programs)	2.6	4.1	3.0	2.5	2.6	4.0
Nondefense discretionary spending and other entitlements	28.4	35.4	37.2	28.6	24.4	29.4
Deposit insurance	−.3	−.2	−.1	−.2	4.6	−.8
National defense	41.9	26.4	22.8	26.7	24.0	18.0
Net interest	7.4	7.0	8.9	13.7	14.7	14.1
Total	100.0	100.0	100.0	100.0	100.0	100.0
Ways and Means programs as a percentage of total Federal Government outlays, less interest	24.4	33.4	34.3	36.2	37.8	45.8

[1] Based on CBO baseline current law projections.

Source: Ways and Means Committee staff based upon CBO data.

TABLE J-13.—HISTORICAL OUTLAYS FOR ENTITLEMENTS AND OTHER MANDATORY SPENDING

[In billions of dollars]

Category	1975	1980	1981	1982	1983	1984	1985	1986	1987	1988	1989	1990	1991	1992	1993
Means-tested programs:															
Stafford loans [1]	0.1	1.4	2.3	3.0	2.6	3.2	3.5	3.3	2.5	2.8	3.9	4.4	4.8	1.7	2.2
Medicaid	6.8	14.0	16.8	17.4	19.0	20.1	22.7	25.0	27.4	30.5	34.6	41.1	52.5	67.8	75.8
Food stamps	4.6	9.1	11.3	11.0	12.7	12.4	12.5	12.4	12.4	13.1	13.7	15.9	19.6	22.8	24.6
Child nutrition	1.5	3.4	3.4	3.0	3.3	3.5	3.7	3.8	4.0	4.3	4.6	5.0	5.5	6.1	6.6
Earned income tax credit	0	1.3	1.3	1.2	1.2	1.2	1.1	1.4	1.4	2.7	4.0	4.4	4.9	8.2	9.4
Supplemental security income	4.3	5.7	6.5	6.9	7.9	7.6	8.7	9.3	9.9	11.4	11.5	11.5	14.8	17.9	21.2
Family support	5.1	7.3	8.2	8.0	8.4	8.9	9.2	9.9	10.5	10.8	11.2	12.2	14.1	15.7	16.4
Veterans' pensions	2.7	3.6	3.8	3.9	3.9	3.9	3.8	3.9	3.8	3.9	4.0	3.6	4.0	3.7	3.5
Other	.3	.1	.3	.4	.3	.5	.8	.9	1.0	1.0	1.3	1.8	2.1	2.5	2.7
Total, means-tested programs	25.4	45.9	53.9	54.8	59.3	61.3	66.0	69.9	72.9	80.5	88.8	99.9	122.3	146.5	162.3
Non-means-tested programs:															
Medicare	14.1	34.0	41.3	49.2	55.5	61.0	69.7	74.2	79.9	85.7	94.3	107.4	114.2	129.4	143.2
Social Security	63.6	117.1	137.9	153.9	168.5	176.1	186.4	196.5	205.1	216.8	230.4	246.5	266.7	285.1	302.0
Subtotal	77.7	151.1	179.2	203.1	224.0	237.1	256.1	270.7	285.0	302.5	324.7	353.9	380.9	414.5	445.1
Other retirement and disability:															
Federal civilian [3]	7.4	15.5	18.6	20.6	22.1	23.3	24.6	25.0	27.6	30.3	31.8	33.7	36.9	37.0	38.8
Military	6.2	11.9	13.7	14.9	15.9	16.5	15.8	17.6	18.1	19.0	20.2	21.5	23.1	24.5	25.7
Other	4.7	4.7	5.1	5.2	5.2	4.9	5.1	4.9	5.1	4.9	5.2	4.7	4.4	5.1	4.2
Subtotal	18.3	32.1	37.4	40.7	43.2	44.7	45.5	47.5	50.8	54.2	57.2	59.9	64.4	66.6	68.7

TABLE J-13.—HISTORICAL OUTLAYS FOR ENTITLEMENTS AND OTHER MANDATORY SPENDING—Continued

[In billions of dollars]

Category	1975	1980	1981	1982	1983	1984	1985	1986	1987	1988	1989	1990	1991	1992	1993
Other programs:															
Unemployment compensation	12.8	16.9	18.3	22.2	29.7	17.0	15.8	16.1	15.5	13.6	13.9	17.5	25.1	36.9	35.4
Farm price supports	.6	2.8	4.0	11.7	18.9	7.3	17.7	25.8	22.4	12.2	10.6	6.5	10.1	9.2	15.6
Social services	2.9	3.7	3.9	3.4	3.5	4.4	3.5	4.0	4.1	4.2	4.6	5.1	5.6	5.2	5.1
Veterans' benefits [3]	10.2	11.0	12.2	12.5	12.7	12.8	12.9	12.9	13.0	14.8	14.9	13.4	14.4	15.7	17.0
General revenue sharing	6.1	6.8	5.1	4.6	4.6	4.6	4.6	5.1	.1	0	0	0	0	0	0
Other	10.4	21.2	26.6	19.8	15.8	17.1	27.9	7.7	6.4	12.3	12.5	10.4	13.1	16.7	11.4
Subtotal	30.2	45.5	51.8	52.0	55.5	46.2	66.6	55.5	46.0	43.5	42.6	35.4	43.2	83.7	50.6
Total, Non-means-tested programs	139.0	245.6	286.7	318.0	352.4	345.0	384.0	389.8	397.3	413.8	438.4	466.7	513.6	564.8	599.8
Total outlays	164.4	291.5	340.6	372.8	411.7	406.3	450.0	459.7	470.2	494.3	527.2	566.6	635.9	711.3	762.1

[1] Formerly known as Guaranteed Student Loans.
[2] Includes Civil Service, Foreign Service, Coast Guard, other retirement programs, and annuitants' health benefits.
[3] Includes veterans' compensation, readjustment benefits, life insurance, and housing programs.

Source: Congressional Budget Office.

TABLE J-14.—COMPARISON OF AVERAGE ANNUAL GROWTH RATES FOR MAJOR ENTITLE-MENT AND MANDATORY SPENDING PROGRAMS FOR SELECTED TIME PERIODS, BASED ON VARIOUS ADJUSTMENTS FOR INFLATION AND POPULATION GROWTH

Between years adjusted for	1975–93[1]	1975–93[2]	1975–93[2,3]	1975–81[2,3]	1981–92[2,3]	1992–93[2,3]
Means-tested programs:						
Medicaid	13.4	8.0	7.0	5.7	7.6	7.8
Food stamps[4]	9.3	3.9	2.9	5.6	1.3	3.9
Supplemental security income	8.9	3.5	2.5	−2.5	4.1	14.4
AFDC and child support enforcement	6.5	1.1	0.1	−1.5	0.8	0.5
Veterans' pensions	1.4	−4.0	−5.0	−3.7	−5.3	−9.4
Child nutrition	8.2	2.8	1.8	4.2	0.2	4.2
Guaranteed student loans	17.2	11.8	10.8	42.9	−7.8	25.4
Other and EITC	20.5	15.1	14.1	18.5	12.2	9.1
Total means-tested programs	10.3	4.9	3.9	3.1	4.0	6.8
Non-means-tested programs:						
Social Security	8.7	3.3	2.3	3.5	1.5	1.9
Medicare	12.9	7.5	6.5	8.5	5.3	6.7
Subtotal	9.7	4.3	3.3	4.5	2.5	3.4
Other retirement and disability:						
Federal civilian[5]	9.2	3.8	2.8	6.0	1.2	0.9
Military	7.9	2.5	1.5	3.8	0.2	1.3
Other	−.6	−6.0	−7.0	−8.0	−5.1	−21.6
Subtotal	7.3	1.9	.9	2.5	0.1	−0.8
Unemployment compensation	5.7	.3	−.7	−3.4	1.3	−8.1
Other programs:						
Veterans' benefits[6]	2.8	−2.6	−3.6	−6.4	−2.8	4.3
Farm price supports	18.1	12.7	11.7	22.2	2.5	65.5
Social services	3.1	−2.3	−3.3	−4.5	−2.5	−5.9
Other	.5	−4.9	−5.9	6.3	−9.3	35.7
Subtotal	2.9	−2.5	−3.5	−.4	−.7	43.5
Total, non-means-tested programs	8.1	2.7	1.7	2.7	1.1	2.2
Total outlays	8.5	3.1	2.1	2.7	1.6	3.1

[1] Nominal growth.
[2] Adjusted for inflation (based on the CPI–XI).
[3] Adjusted for overall population growth.
[4] Includes nutrition assistance for Puerto Rico.
[5] Includes Coast Guard retirement.
[6] Includes veterans' compensation, readjustment benefits, life insurance, and housing projects.

Note: All growth rates were calculated using the exponential growth function $Y=Ae^{rt}$.

TABLE J–15.—CBO BASELINE PROJECTIONS FOR MANDATORY SPENDING EXCLUDING DEPOSIT INSURANCE

[By fiscal year, in billions of dollars]

01–Mar–94	1993 actual	1994	1995	1996	1997	1998	1999
	Means-tested programs						
Medicaid	75.8	85.9	97.0	108.1	120.9	135.4	151.1
Food stamps [1]	24.6	25.4	25.9	26.5	27.6	28.9	30.0
Supplemental security income	21.2	24.7	24.5	24.5	29.3	32.1	35.1
Family support	16.4	17.3	17.9	18.5	19.0	19.5	20.2
Veterans' pensions	3.5	3.5	3.1	2.7	2.9	2.7	3.0
Child nutrition	6.6	7.0	7.4	7.9	8.4	8.9	9.5
Earned income tax credit	9.4	10.6	15.3	18.1	20.1	20.8	21.7
Student loans [2]	2.2	2.3	2.1	1.7	1.5	1.7	1.7
Other	2.7	3.0	3.4	3.8	4.1	4.4	4.7
Total, means-tested programs	162.3	179.5	195.8	211.8	233.8	254.5	276.9
	Non-means-tested programs						
Social Security	302.0	318.0	334.8	352.1	370.0	388.5	408.0
Medicare	143.2	160.0	177.4	195.1	215.6	237.7	263.4
Subtotal	445.1	478.0	512.1	547.2	585.5	626.2	671.3
Other retirement and disability:							
Federal civilian [3]	38.8	40.2	42.1	43.8	46.4	48.8	51.3
Military	25.7	26.5	27.5	28.9	30.5	32.1	34.6
Other	4.2	4.7	4.8	4.8	4.6	4.6	4.4
Subtotal	68.7	71.3	74.4	77.5	81.5	85.5	90.3
Unemployment compensation	35.4	27.2	24.0	24.9	25.2	25.5	26.5
Other programs:							
Veterans' benefits [4]	17.0	17.8	17.0	16.2	17.8	18.3	19.0
Farm price supports	15.6	10.6	7.4	7.8	8.2	8.4	8.7
Social services	5.1	5.9	5.9	5.8	5.5	5.6	5.4
Credit reform liquidating accounts	1.5	-1.2	-0.6	-4.3	-4.6	-5.5	-5.9
Other	11.4	12.7	10.9	9.6	10.0	9.9	8.3
Subtotal	50.6	45.8	40.7	35.2	37.0	36.7	35.5
Total, non-means-tested programs	599.7	622.3	651.2	684.8	729.2	773.9	823.6
Total outlays	762.1	801.8	847.0	896.7	962.9	1028.4	1100.5

[1] Includes nutrition assistance to Puerto Rico.
[2] Formerly known as Guaranteed Student Loans.
[3] Includes Civil Service, Foreign Service, Coast Guard, other retirement programs, and annuitants' health benefits.
[4] Includes veterans' compensation, readjustment benefits, life insurance, and housing programs.

Note.—Spending for major benefit programs shown in this table includes benefits only. Outlays for administrative costs of most benefit programs are classified as nondefense discretionary spending, and Medicare premium collections are offsetting receipts.

Source: Congressional Budget Office.

TABLE J–16.—CHANGES IN LOW INCOME DISCRETIONARY PROGRAM FUNDING, FISCAL YEARS 1982–94

[Budget authority, in millions of dollars]

	Fiscal year 1982 actual	Fiscal year 1982 inflated [1]	Fiscal year 1994	Fiscal year 1994— 1982 inflated	Percent change
Education					
Compensatory education	3,026	4,721	7,031	2,310	49
Education for the homeless [2][3]	0	0	35	35	NA
Financial aid	3,569	5,568	8,020	2,452	44
Head Start	912	1,423	3,326	1,903	134
Higher education (TRIOS)	150	234	419	185	79
Indian Education	341	532	579	47	9
Subtotal, education	7,998	12,477	19,410	6,933	56
Nutrition					
Commodity supplemental food program	29	45	95	50	110
Food donation programs	141	220	259	39	18
Temporary emergency food assistance	0	0	120	120	NA
WIC supplemental food program	905	1,412	3,210	1,798	127
Subtotal, nutrition	1,076	1,679	3,683	2,004	119
Housing					
Emergency food and shelter [2]	0	0	130	130	NA
Emergency shelter grants [2]	0	0	115	115	NA
Housing elderly/handicapped [4]	831	1,296	1,194	− 102	− 8
Public housing operating subsidies	1,491	2,326	2,621	295	13
Rural housing insurance fund [5]	3,455	5,390	1,135	− 4,255	− 79
Additional rural housing [6]	431	672	521	− 151	− 23
Section 8 homeless SRO's [2]	0	0	150	150	NA
Subsidized housing	13,275	20,709	8,244	− 12,465	− 60
Subsidized housing renewals	0	0	5,202	5,202	NA
Transitional and supporting housing [2]	0	0	334	334	NA
Subtotal, housing	19,483	30,393	19,646	− 10,747	−35
Health					
Community health centers	281	438	604	166	38
Health care homeless [2]	0	0	63	63	NA
Immunizations	35	55	528	473	867
Maternal and child health	374	583	695	112	19
Migrant health	38	59	57	−2	−4
Homeless mental health [2][7]	0	0	51	51	NA
Indian health	618	964	1,646	682	71
Indian health facilities	58	90	297	207	228
Subtotal, health	1,404	2,190	3,940	1,750	80
Employment					
Job training welfare recipients [8]	281	438	860	422	96
Older Americans employment	277	432	411	− 21	−5
Training and employment services	2,984	4,655	5,014	359	8
Subtotal, employment	3,542	5,526	6,285	759	14
Other					
Child welfare services	160	250	295	45	18
Community development block grant	3,456	5,391	4,400	− 991	− 18
Community services block grant [9]	366	571	464	− 107	− 19
Legal services	241	376	400	24	6
Low income energy assistance	1,875	2,925	2,037	− 888	− 30

TABLE J–16.—CHANGES IN LOW INCOME DISCRETIONARY PROGRAM FUNDING, FISCAL YEARS 1982–94—Continued

[Budget authority, in millions of dollars]

	Fiscal year 1982 actual	Fiscal year 1982 in-flated [1]	Fiscal year 1994	Fiscal year 1994— 1982 in-flated	Percent change
Low income weatherization	180	281	207	−74	−26
Runaway and homeless youth	11	17	36	19	110
VISTA	18	28	42	14	50
Subtotal other	6,307	9,839	7,881	−1,958	−20
Total, low-income discretionary	39,810	62,104	60,845	−1,259	−2
Total less subsidized housing	20,327	31,710	41,199	9,489	30

[1] Inflation from fiscal year 1982 to fiscal year 1994, calculated using CPI–XI price inflater.

[2] These programs are part of the Stewart B. McKinney Homeless Assistance Act.

[3] These programs include adult literacy, homeless children education grants, and exemplary grants.

[4] In fiscal year 1991, a new capital grants program replaced the direct loan program for housing assistance for the elderly and handicapped. Therefore, the fiscal year 1982 figure is a loan limitation, as loan limits provide the best measure of program activity for loan programs, and the fiscal year 1994 figure is budget authority.

[5] This is a loan program. Therefore, levels listed are loan limits instead of budget authority.

[6] These programs include domestic farm labor housing, mutual and self-help housing, very low income housing repair grants, rural housing preservation grants and rural rental assistance.

[7] These programs include the homeless block grant, mental health demonstrations, and alcohol and drug abuse demonstrations, administered by the Alcohol, Drug Abuse and Mental Health Administration.

[8] The fiscal year 1982 figure is budget authority for the discretionary WIN program. The fiscal year 1994 figure is the obligation level for the entitlement JOBS program, which replaced WIN. While $1.1 billion was appropriated for JOBS in fiscal year 1993, CBO estimates that States will only request $860 million.

[9] The fiscal year 1982 figure is budget authority of the Community Services Administration which was dismantled in fiscal year 1982 and replaced by the community services block grant. While these activities are similar, they are not identical.

NA—Not applicable.

Source: Congressional Budget Office.

TABLE J–17.—CONGRESSIONAL BUDGET OFFICE BASELINE, ADMINISTRATION, AND BLUE CHIP ECONOMIC PROJECTIONS, CALENDAR YEARS 1993–99

	Esti-mated [1] 1993	Forecast		Projected			
		1994	1995	1996	1997	1998	1999
Real GDP [2] (Percentage change, year over year):							
CBO	2.8	2.9	2.7	2.7	2.7	2.6	2.5
Administration	2.8	3.1	2.8	2.7	2.6	2.6	2.5
Blue Chip	3.0	3.6	2.8	2.6	2.5	2.4	2.8
GDP Deflator (Percentage change, year over year):							
CBO	2.6	2.7	2.7	2.6	2.5	2.5	2.5
Administration	2.6	2.6	2.8	2.9	3.0	3.0	3.0
Blue Chip	2.6	2.3	2.9	3.2	3.2	3.1	3.1
Consumer Price Index [3] (Percentage change, year over year):							
CBO	3.0	2.7	3.0	3.1	3.1	3.1	3.1
Administration	3.0	2.8	3.2	3.3	3.3	3.4	3.4
Blue Chip	3.0	2.8	3.3	3.4	3.5	3.4	3.4
Civilian Unemployment Rate (Percent): [4]							
CBO	6.8	6.8	6.5	6.3	6.2	6.1	6.1
Administration	6.8	6.9	6.5	6.3	6.1	5.9	5.9
Blue Chip	6.8	6.5	6.2	6.0	6.1	6.1	6.0
Three-Month Treasury Bill Rate (Percent): [5]							
CBO	3.0	3.5	4.3	4.6	4.6	4.7	4.7
Administration	3.0	3.4	3.8	4.1	4.4	4.4	4.4
Blue Chip	3.0	3.5	4.0	4.3	4.4	4.4	4.3
Ten-Year Treasury Note Rate (Percent):							
CBO	5.9	5.8	6.0	6.1	6.2	6.2	6.2
Administration	5.9	5.8	5.8	5.8	5.8	5.8	5.8
Blue Chip [6]	5.9	6.0	6.2	6.6	6.4	6.3	6.4

The Administration used CBO's economic forecast in its budget calculations. The forecast labeled "Administration" in this table reflects the Administration's own forecast and includes its estimate of its own programs' effects.

[1] The Blue Chip forecast was prepared two month later than the other forecasts, so the Blue Chip data for 1993 are actual.

[2] Based on constant 1987 dollars.

[3] Consumer price index for all urban consumers (CPI-U).

[4] The Bureau of Labor Statistics changed the unemployment survey in January 1994. The CBO and Administration forecasts for 1994 through 1999 originally used 1993 methodology. The forecast tables reported here have been adjusted upward 0.4 percentage points to make the forecasts comparable with currently published figures. Data for 1933, shown in italics, use pre-1994 methodology.

[5] Consumer price index for all urban consumers (CPI-U).

[6] The Blue Chip does not project a 10-year note rate. The values shown here are based on the Blue Chip projection of the Aaa bond rate, adjusted by CBO to reflect the estimated spread between Aaa bonds and 10-year Treasury notes.

Notes: The CBO forecast is based on data available through December 1992 and does not reflect fourth-quarter data for gross domestic product or the consumer price index published in January 1993. The Blue Chip forecasts are based on a survey of private forecasters published on March 10, 1993.

Sources: Congressional Budget Office; Office of Management and Budget; Eggert Economic Enterprises, Inc., Blue Chip Economic Indicators.

TABLE J–18.—EFFECTS ON CBO BUDGET PROJECTIONS OF SELECTED CHANGES IN ECONOMIC ASSUMPTIONS

[By fiscal year, in billions of dollars]

	1994	1995	1996	1997	1998	1999
Real growth: Effect of 1-percentage-point lower annual rate beginning January 1994						
Change in revenues	−8	−25	−46	−69	−93	−118
Change in outlays	1	4	8	14	22	31
Change in deficit	9	29	54	82	115	149
Unemployment: Effect of 1-percentage-point higher annual rate beginning January 1994						
Change in revenues	−33	−49	−50	−52	−54	−57
Change in outlays	4	8	12	15	20	24
Change in deficit	37	57	62	67	74	81
Inflation: Effect of 1-percentage-point higher annual rate beginning January 1994						
Change in revenues	7	20	35	51	68	87
Change in outlays	5	20	34	49	66	88
Change in deficit	−1	−1	−2	−2	−1	−1
Interest rates: Effect of 1-percentage-point higher annual rate beginning January 1994						
Change in revenues	0	0	0	0	0	0
Change in outlays	5	16	23	29	35	42
Change in deficit	5	16	23	29	35	42

Source: Congressional Budget Office.

TABLE J–19.—REVENUES, OUTLAYS, DEFICITS, AND DEBT HELD BY THE PUBLIC, FISCAL YEARS 1962–93

[In billions of dollars]

| | Reve-nues | Outlays | Deficit (−) or Surplus | | | | Debt held by the pub-lic[1] |
			On-Budget	Social Security	Postal Service	Total	
1962	99.7	106.8	− 5.9	− 1.3	0	− 7.1	248.0
1963	106.6	111.3	− 4.0	− .8	0	− 4.8	254.0
1964	112.6	118.5	− 6.5	.6	0	− 5.9	256.8
1965	116.8	118.2	− 1.6	.2	0	− 1.4	260.8
1966	130.8	134.5	− 3.1	− .6	0	− 3.7	263.7
1967	148.8	157.5	− 12.6	4.0	0	− 8.6	266.6
1968	153.0	178.1	− 27.7	2.6	0	− 25.2	289.5
1969	186.9	183.6	− 0.5	3.7	0	3.2	278.1
1970	192.8	195.6	− 8.7	5.9	0	− 2.8	283.2
1971	187.1	210.2	− 26.1	3.0	0	− 23.0	303.0
1972	207.3	230.7	− 26.4	3.1	0	− 23.4	322.4
1973	230.8	245.7	− 15.4	.5	0	− 14.9	340.9
1974	263.2	269.4	− 8.0	1.8	0	− 6.1	343.7
1975	279.1	332.3	− 55.3	2.0	0	− 53.2	394.7
1976	298.1	371.8	− 70.5	− 3.2	0	− 73.7	477.4
1977	355.6	409.2	− 49.8	− 3.9	0	− 53.7	549.1
1978	399.6	458.7	− 54.9	− 4.3	0	− 59.2	607.1
1979	463.3	503.5	− 38.2	− 2.0	0	− 40.2	639.8
1980	517.1	590.9	− 72.7	− 1.1	0	− 73.8	709.3
1981	599.3	678.2	− 74.0	− 5.0	0	− 79.0	784.8
1982	617.8	745.8	− 120.1	− 7.9	0	− 128.0	919.2
1983	600.6	808.4	− 208.0	.2	0	− 207.8	1,131.0
1984	666.5	851.8	− 185.7	.3	0	− 185.4	1,300.0
1985	734.1	946.4	− 221.7	9.4	0	− 212.3	1,499.4
1986	769.1	990.3	− 238.0	16.7	0	− 221.2	1,736.2
1987	854.1	1,003.9	− 169.3	19.6	0	− 149.8	1,888.1
1988	909.0	1,064.1	− 194.0	38.8	0	− 155.2	2,050.3
1989	990.7	1,143.2	− 205.2	52.4	0.3	− 152.5	2,189.3
1990	1,031.3	1,252.7	− 278.0	58.2	− 1.6	− 221.4	2,410.4
1991	1,054.3	1,323.8	− 321.7	53.5	− 1.3	− 269.5	2,687.9
1992	1,090.5	1,380.9	− 340.5	50.7	− 0.7	− 290.4	2,998.6
1993	1,153.5	1,408.2	− 300.0	46.2	− 0.9	− 254.7	3,247.2

[1] End of year.

Source: Congressional Budget Office.

TABLE J–20.—REVENUES, OUTLAYS, DEFICITS, AND DEBT HELD BY THE PUBLIC, FISCAL YEARS 1962–93

[As a percentage of GDP]

| | Reve-nues | Outlays | Deficit (−) or surplus | | | | Debt held by the pub-lic [1] |
			On-budget	Social Security	Postal Service	Total	
1962	18.0	19.3	−1.1	−0.2	0	−1.3	44.7
1963	18.2	19.0	−.7	−.1	0	−.8	43.4
1964	18.0	18.9	−1.0	.1	0	−.9	41.0
1965	17.4	17.6	−.2	(2)	0	−.2	38.8
1966	17.7	18.2	−.4	−.1	0	−.5	35.7
1967	18.8	19.9	−1.6	.5	0	−1.1	33.7
1968	18.0	21.0	−3.3	.3	0	−3.0	34.1
1969	20.2	19.8	−.1	.4	0	.4	30.0
1970	19.6	19.8	−.9	.6	0	−.3	28.7
1971	17.8	20.0	−2.5	.3	0	−2.2	28.8
1972	18.1	20.1	−2.3	.3	0	−2.0	28.1
1973	18.1	19.2	−1.2	(2)	0	−1.2	26.7
1974	18.8	19.2	−.6	.1	0	−.4	24.5
1975	18.5	22.0	−3.7	.1	0	−3.5	26.1
1976	17.7	22.1	−4.2	−.2	0	−4.4	28.3
1977	18.5	21.3	−2.6	−.2	0	−2.8	28.6
1978	18.5	21.3	−2.5	−.2	0	−2.7	28.2
1979	19.1	20.7	−1.6	−.1	0	−1.7	26.3
1980	19.6	22.3	−2.7	(2)	0	−2.8	26.8
1981	20.2	22.9	−2.5	−.2	0	−2.7	26.5
1982	19.8	23.9	−3.8	−.3	0	−4.1	29.4
1983	18.1	24.4	−6.3	(2)	0	−6.3	34.1
1984	18.0	23.0	−5.0	(2)	0	−5.0	35.2
1985	18.5	23.8	−5.6	.2	0	−5.3	37.8
1986	18.2	23.5	−5.6	.4	0	−5.2	41.1
1987	19.2	22.5	−3.8	.4	0	−3.4	42.4
1988	18.9	22.1	−4.0	.8	0	−3.2	42.6
1989	19.1	22.1	−4.0	1.0	(2)	−2.9	42.3
1990	18.8	22.8	−5.1	1.1	(2)	−4.0	44.0
1991	18.6	23.3	−5.7	.9	(2)	−4.8	47.4
1992	18.4	23.2	−5.7	.9	(2)	−4.9	0.5
1993	18.3	22.4	−4.8	.7	(2)	−4.0	51.6

[1] End of year.
[2] Less than .05 percent.

Source: Congressional Budget Office.

TABLE J–21.—REVENUES BY MAJOR SOURCE, FISCAL YEARS 1962–93

[In billions of dollars]

Fiscal year	Individ- ual in- come taxes	Cor- porate income taxes	Social insur- ance taxes	Excise taxes	Estate and gift taxes	Cus- toms duties	Mis- cella- neous re- ceipts	Total revenues
1962	45.6	20.5	17.0	12.5	2.0	1.1	0.8	99.7
1963	47.6	21.6	19.8	13.2	2.2	1.2	1.0	106.6
1964	48.7	23.5	22.0	13.7	2.4	1.3	1.1	112.6
1965	48.8	25.5	22.2	14.6	2.7	1.4	1.6	116.8
1966	55.4	30.1	25.5	13.1	3.1	1.8	1.9	130.8
1967	61.5	34.0	32.6	13.7	3.0	1.9	2.1	148.8
1968	68.7	28.7	33.9	14.1	3.1	2.0	2.5	153.0
1969	87.2	36.7	39.0	15.2	3.5	2.3	2.9	186.9
1970	90.4	32.8	44.4	15.7	3.6	2.4	3.4	192.8
1971	86.2	26.8	47.3	16.6	3.7	2.6	3.9	187.1
1972	94.7	32.2	52.6	15.5	5.4	3.3	3.6	207.3
1973	103.2	36.2	63.1	16.3	4.9	3.2	3.9	230.8
1974	119.0	38.6	75.1	16.8	5.0	3.3	5.4	263.2
1975	122.4	40.6	84.5	16.6	4.6	3.7	6.7	279.1
1976	131.6	41.4	90.8	17.0	5.2	4.1	8.0	298.1
1977	157.6	54.9	106.5	17.5	7.3	5.2	6.5	355.6
1978	181.0	60.0	121.0	18.4	5.3	6.6	7.4	399.6
1979	217.8	65.7	138.9	18.7	5.4	7.4	9.3	463.3
1980	244.1	64.6	157.8	24.3	6.4	7.2	12.7	517.1
1981	285.9	61.1	182.7	40.8	6.8	8.1	13.8	599.3
1982	297.7	49.2	201.5	36.3	8.0	8.9	16.2	617.8
1983	288.9	37.0	209.0	35.3	6.1	8.7	15.6	600.6
1984	298.4	56.9	239.4	37.4	6.0	11.4	17.0	666.5
1985	334.5	61.3	265.2	36.0	6.4	12.1	18.5	734.1
1986	349.0	63.1	283.9	32.9	7.0	13.3	19.9	769.1
1987	392.6	83.9	303.3	32.5	7.5	15.1	19.3	854.1
1988	401.2	94.5	334.3	35.2	7.6	16.2	19.9	909.0
1989	445.7	103.3	359.4	34.4	8.7	16.3	22.8	990.7
1990	466.9	93.5	380.0	35.3	11.5	16.7	27.3	1,031.3
1991	467.8	98.1	396.0	42.4	11.1	15.9	22.8	1,054.3
1992	476.0	100.3	413.7	45.6	11.1	17.4	26.5	1,090.5
1993	509.7	117.5	428.3	48.1	12.6	18.8	18.6	1,153.5

Source: Congressional Budget Office.

TABLE J–22.—REVENUES, BY MAJOR SOURCE, FISCAL YEARS 1962–93

[As a percentage of GDP]

Fiscal year	Individual income taxes	Corporate income taxes	Social insurance taxes	Excise taxes	Estate and gift taxes	Customs duties	Miscellaneous receipts	Total revenues
1962	8.2	3.7	3.1	2.3	0.4	0.2	0.2	18.0
1963	8.1	3.7	3.4	2.3	.4	.2	.2	18.2
1964	7.8	3.7	3.5	2.2	.4	.2	.2	18.0
1965	7.3	3.8	3.3	2.2	.4	.2	.2	17.4
1966	7.5	4.1	3.5	1.8	.4	.2	.3	17.7
1967	7.8	4.3	4.1	1.7	.4	.2	.3	18.8
1968	8.1	3.4	4.0	1.7	.4	.2	.3	18.0
1969	9.4	4.0	4.2	1.6	.4	.3	.3	20.2
1970	9.2	3.3	4.5	1.6	.4	.2	.3	19.6
1971	8.2	2.5	4.5	1.6	.4	.2	.4	17.8
1972	8.3	2.8	4.6	1.4	.5	.3	.3	18.1
1973	8.1	2.8	4.9	1.3	.4	.2	.3	18.1
1974	8.5	2.8	5.3	1.2	.4	.2	.4	18.8
1975	8.1	2.7	5.6	1.1	.3	.2	.4	18.5
1976	7.8	2.5	5.4	1.0	.3	.2	.5	17.7
1977	8.2	2.9	5.5	.9	.4	.3	.3	18.5
1978	8.4	2.8	5.6	.9	.2	.3	.3	18.5
1979	9.0	2.7	5.7	.8	.2	.3	.4	19.1
1980	9.2	2.4	6.0	.9	.2	.3	.5	19.6
1981	9.6	2.1	6.2	1.4	.2	.3	.5	20.2
1982	9.5	1.6	6.4	1.2	.3	.3	.5	19.8
1983	8.7	1.1	6.3	1.1	.2	.3	.5	18.1
1984	8.1	1.5	6.5	1.0	.2	.3	.5	18.0
1985	8.4	1.5	6.7	.9	.2	.3	.5	18.5
1986	8.3	1.5	6.7	.8	.2	.3	.5	18.2
1987	8.8	1.9	6.8	.7	.2	.3	.4	19.2
1988	8.3	2.0	7.0	.7	.2	.3	.4	18.9
1989	8.6	2.0	7.0	.7	.2	.3	.4	19.1
1990	8.5	1.7	7.0	.6	.2	.3	.5	18.8
1991	8.2	1.7	7.0	.7	.2	.3	.4	18.6
1992	8.0	1.7	7.0	.8	.2	.3	.4	18.4
1993	8.1	1.9	6.8	.8	.2	.3	.3	18.3

Source: Congressional Budget Office.

TABLE J-23.—OUTLAYS FOR MAJOR SPENDING CATEGORIES, FISCAL YEARS 1962-93

[In billions of dollars]

Fiscal year	National defense	Entitlements and other mandatory spending	Nondefense discretionary spending	Net interest	Offsetting receipts	Total outlays
1962	52.6	32.3	22.3	6.9	−6.8	106.8
1963	53.7	33.6	24.6	7.7	−7.9	111.3
1964	55.0	35.7	27.8	8.2	−7.7	118.5
1965	51.0	36.1	30.8	8.6	−7.9	118.2
1966	59.0	39.9	35.1	9.4	−8.4	134.5
1967	72.0	47.4	38.4	10.3	−10.2	157.5
1968	82.2	56.1	39.9	11.1	−10.6	178.1
1969	82.7	61.2	38.7	12.7	−11.0	183.6
1970	81.9	68.7	42.7	14.4	−11.5	195.6
1971	79.0	82.7	48.1	14.8	−14.1	210.2
1972	79.3	96.8	53.8	15.5	−14.1	230.7
1973	77.1	112.2	57.9	17.3	−18.0	245.7
1974	80.7	127.1	61.8	21.4	−21.2	269.4
1975	87.6	164.4	74.9	23.2	−18.3	332.3
1976	89.9	189.7	85.7	26.7	−19.6	371.8
1977	97.5	206.6	99.6	29.9	−21.5	409.2
1978	104.6	228.4	114.1	35.5	−22.8	458.7
1979	116.8	248.2	123.2	42.6	−25.6	503.5
1980	134.6	291.5	141.9	52.5	−29.2	590.9
1981	158.0	340.6	150.2	68.8	−37.9	678.2
1982	185.9	372.7	140.3	85.0	−36.0	745.8
1983	209.9	411.6	143.5	89.8	−45.3	808.4
1984	228.0	406.3	151.6	111.1	−44.2	851.8
1985	253.1	450.0	163.1	129.5	−47.1	946.4
1986	273.8	459.7	165.2	136.0	−45.9	990.3
1987	282.5	470.2	162.4	138.7	−53.0	1,003.9
1988	290.9	494.2	174.2	151.8	−57.0	1,064.1
1989	304.0	526.2	185.7	169.3	−63.9	1,143.2
1990	300.1	567.4	201.6	184.2	−58.8	1,252.7
1991	319.7	634.2	215.1	194.5	−106.0	1,323.8
1992	302.6	711.7	233.4	199.4	−68.8	1,380.9
1993	292.4	762.1	250.1	198.8	−67.1	1,408.2

Source: Congressional Budget Office.

TABLE J–24.—OUTLAYS FOR MAJOR SPENDING CATEGORIES, FISCAL YEARS 1962–93

[As a percentage of GDP]

Fiscal year	National Defense	Entitle- ments and other man- datory spending	Nondefense discre- tionary spending	Net interest	Offsetting receipts	Total out- lays
1962	9.5	5.8	4.0	1.2	−1.2	19.3
1963	9.2	5.7	4.2	1.3	−1.3	19.0
1964	8.8	5.7	4.4	1.3	−1.2	18.9
1965	7.6	5.4	4.6	1.3	−1.2	17.6
1966	8.0	5.4	4.7	1.3	−1.1	18.2
1967	9.1	6.0	4.9	1.3	−1.3	19.9
1968	9.7	6.6	4.7	1.3	−1.2	21.0
1969	8.9	6.6	4.2	1.4	−1.2	19.8
1970	8.3	7.0	4.3	1.5	−1.2	19.8
1971	7.5	7.9	4.6	1.4	−1.3	20.0
1972	6.9	8.4	4.7	1.4	−1.2	20.1
1973	6.1	8.8	4.5	1.4	−1.4	19.2
1974	5.8	9.1	4.4	1.5	−1.5	19.2
1975	5.8	10.9	5.0	1.5	−1.2	22.0
1976	5.3	11.3	5.1	1.6	−1.2	22.1
1977	5.1	10.8	5.2	1.6	−1.1	21.3
1978	4.9	10.6	5.2	1.6	−1.1	21.3
1979	4.8	10.2	5.1	1.8	−1.1	20.7
1980	5.1	11.0	5.4	2.0	−1.1	22.3
1981	5.3	11.5	5.1	2.3	−1.3	22.9
1982	6.0	11.9	4.4	2.7	−1.2	23.9
1983	6.3	12.4	4.4	2.7	−1.4	24.4
1984	6.2	11.0	4.1	3.0	−1.2	23.0
1985	6.4	11.3	4.1	3.3	−1.2	23.8
1986	6.5	10.9	3.9	3.2	−1.1	23.5
1987	6.3	10.6	3.7	3.1	−1.2	22.5
1988	6.0	10.3	3.7	3.2	−1.2	22.1
1989	5.9	10.2	3.6	3.3	−1.2	22.1
1990	5.5	10.3	3.7	3.4	−1.1	22.8
1991	5.6	11.2	3.8	3.4	−1.9	23.3
1992	5.1	12.1	3.9	3.4	−1.2	23.2
1993	4.6	12.1	4.0	3.2	−1.1	22.4

Source: Congressional Budget Office.

TABLE J–25.—FEDERAL FINANCES AND THE FEDERAL DEBT, 1955–93

[Dollar amounts in billions]

	Total deficit		Federal debt, end of year					
			Gross		Held by Government accounts		Held by the public	
	Amount	Per-centage of GDP	Amount	Per-centage of GDP	Amount	Per-centage of GDP	Amount	Per-centage of GDP
1955	− 3.0	− .8	274.4	71.5	47.8	12.4	226.6	59.0
1956	3.9	1.0	272.7	65.7	50.5	12.2	222.2	53.5
1957	3.4	.8	272.3	62.3	52.9	12.1	219.3	50.2
1958	− 2.8	− .6	279.7	62.6	53.3	11.9	226.3	50.6
1959	− 12.8	− 2.7	287.5	60.1	52.8	11.0	234.7	49.0
1960	.3	.1	290.5	57.4	53.7	10.6	236.8	46.8
1961	− 3.3	− .6	292.6	56.6	54.3	10.5	238.4	46.1
1962	− 7.1	− 1.3	302.9	54.7	54.9	9.9	248.0	44.7
1963	− 4.8	− .8	310.3	53.0	56.3	9.6	254.0	43.4
1964	− 5.9	− .9	316.1	50.4	59.2	9.5	256.8	41.0
1965	− 1.4	− .2	322.3	48.0	61.5	9.2	260.8	38.8
1966	− 3.7	− .5	328.5	44.5	64.8	8.8	263.7	35.7
1967	− 8.6	− 1.1	340.4	43.0	73.8	9.3	266.6	33.7
1968	− 25.2	− 3.0	368.7	43.4	79.1	9.3	289.5	34.1
1969	3.2	.4	365.8	39.5	87.7	9.5	278.1	30.0
1970	− 2.8	− .3	380.9	38.6	97.7	9.9	283.2	28.7
1971	− 23.0	− 2.2	408.2	38.8	105.1	10.0	303.0	28.8
1972	− 23.4	− 2.0	435.9	38.0	113.6	9.9	322.4	28.1
1973	− 14.9	− 1.2	466.3	36.5	125.4	9.8	340.9	26.7
1974	− 6.1	− .4	483.9	34.5	140.2	10.0	343.7	24.5
1975	− 53.2	− 3.5	541.9	35.9	147.2	9.7	394.7	26.1
1976	− 73.7	− 4.4	629.0	37.3	151.6	9.0	477.4	28.3
TQ	....	....	643.6	36.2	148.1	8.3	495.5	27.8
1977	− 53.7	− 2.8	706.4	36.8	157.3	8.2	549.1	28.6
1978	− 59.2	− 2.7	776.6	36.0	169.5	7.9	607.1	28.2
1979	− 40.2	− 1.7	828.9	34.1	189.2	7.8	639.8	26.3
1980	− 73.8	− 2.8	908.5	34.4	199.2	7.5	709.3	26.8
1981	− 79.0	− 2.7	994.3	33.5	209.5	7.1	784.8	26.5
1982	− 128.0	− 4.1	1,136.8	36.4	217.6	7.0	919.2	29.4
1983	− 207.8	− 6.3	1,371.2	41.3	240.1	7.2	1,131.0	34.1
1984	− 185.4	− 5.0	1,564.1	42.3	264.2	7.1	1,300.0	35.2
1985	− 212.3	− 5.3	1,817.0	45.8	317.6	8.0	1,499.4	37.8
1986	− 221.2	− 5.2	2,120.1	50.3	383.9	9.1	1,736.2	41.1
1987	− 149.8	− 3.4	2,345.6	52.7	457.4	10.3	1,888.1	42.4
1988	− 155.2	− 3.2	2,600.8	54.1	550.5	11.4	2,050.3	42.6
1989	− 152.5	− 2.9	2,867.5	55.4	678.2	13.1	2,189.3	42.3
1990	− 221.4	− 4.0	3,206.3	58.6	796.0	14.6	2,410.4	44.1
1991	− 269.5	− 4.8	3,599.0	63.9	911.1	16.2	2,687.9	47.7
1992	− 290.4	− 4.8	4,002.7	59.4	1,004.0	16.6	2,998.6	49.7
1993 [1]	− 322.0	− 5.1	4,396.7	69.0	1,092.8	17.2	3,308.8	51.9

[1] 1993 figures are estimates.

Source: Budget of the United States Government, Fiscal Year 1994, and Analytical Perspectives, Fiscal Year 1995.

TABLE J–26.—CBO PROJECTIONS OF INTEREST COSTS AND FEDERAL DEBT

[By fiscal year]

	Actual 1993	1994	1995	1996	1997	1998	1999
	Net interest outlays (billions of dollars)						
Interest on public debt (gross interest) [1]	293	299	312	331	348	365	385
Interest received by trust funds:							
Social Security	−27	−30	−34	−37	−42	−47	−52
Other trust funds [2]	−55	−58	−56	−57	−58	−60	−61
Subtotal	−82	−88	−89	−94	−100	−106	−114
Other interest [3]	−11	−9	−9	−7	−7	−7	−7
Total, net interest, outlays	199	201	214	230	241	252	264
	Federal debt, end of year (billions of dollars)						
Gross Federal debt	4,351	4,693	5,005	5,330	5,673	6,019	6,390
Debt held by Government accounts:							
Social Security	366	428	498	573	657	749	848
Other Government accounts [2]	738	801	854	910	961	1,011	1,051
Subtotal	1,104	1,229	1,352	1,483	1,618	1,759	1,899
Debt held by the public	3,247	3,465	3,653	3,846	4,055	4,260	4,492
Debt subject to limit [4]	4,316	4,657	4,968	5,292	5,634	5,980	6,350
	Federal debt as a percentage of GDP						
Debt held by the public	51.6	52.2	52.1	52.1	52.1	52.1	52.3

[1] Excludes interest costs of debt issued by agencies other than the Treasury (primarily deposit insurance agencies).

[2] Principally Civil Service Retirement, Military Retirement, Medicare, Unemployment Insurance, and the Highway and the Airport and Airway trust funds.

[3] Primarily interest on loans to the public and to the Resolution Trust Corporation and the Bank Insurance Fund.

[4] Differs from the gross federal debt primarily because most debt issued by agencies other than the Treasury (currently about $20 billion) is excluded from the debt limit.

Note: Projections of interest and debt assume compliance with the discretionary spending caps in the Budget Enforcement Act.

Source: Congressional Budget Office.

TABLE J–27.—STATUTORY DEBT LIMIT AND DEBT SUBJECT TO LIMIT, 1977–93

[In billions of dollars]

End of fiscal year	Statutory debt limit	Debt subject to limit
1977	700.0	700.0
1978	798.0	772.7
1979	879.0	827.6
1980	925.0	908.7
1981	1,079.8	998.8
1982	1,290.2	1,142.9
1983	1,389.0	1,378.0
1984	1,573.0	1,573.0
1985	1,823.8	1,823.8
1986	2,111.0	2,111.0
1987	2,800.0	2,336.0
1988	2,800.0	2,586.9
1989	2,870.0	2,829.8
1990	3,195.0	3,161.2
1991	4,145.0	3,569.3
1992	4,145.0	3,972.6
1993	4,900.0	4,315.6

Source: Budget of the United States Government, Historical Tables, fiscal year 1995, tables 7.2, 7.3.

TABLE J-28.—STATUTORY LIMITS ON FEDERAL DEBT: 1981—CURRENT

[Dollars in billions]

Date and act	History of legislation	Amount of limit
December 19, 1980, 94 Stat. 3261	Increased the total debt limit to $935.1 billion (composed of $400.0 billion of permanent ceiling, $535.1 billion of temporary ceiling).	$935.1
February 7, 1981, 95 Stat. 4	Increased the temporary portion of the debt limit to $585.0 billion (to a total debt ceiling of $985.0 billion) through September 30, 1980.	985.0
September 30, 1981, 95 Stat. 955	Increased the temporary portion of the debt limit to $599.8 billion for one day—September 30, 1981.	999.8
September 30, 1981, 95 Stat. 956	Increased the temporary portion of the debt limit to $679.8 billion through September 30, 1982.	1,079.8
June 28, 1982, 96 Stat. 130	Increased the temporary portion of the debt limit to $743.1 billion through September 30, 1982.	1,143.1
September 30, 1982, 96 Stat. 1156	Increased the temporary portion of the debt limit to $890.2 billion through September 30, 1983.	1,290.2
May 26, 1983, 97 Stat. 196	Eliminated the distinction between permanent and temporary limit with the enactment of a single permanent limit. Raised the debt limit to $1,389.0 billion.	1,389.0
November 21, 1983, 97 Stat. 1012	Increased the debt limit to $1,490.0 billion	1,490.0
May 25, 1984, 98 Stat. 211	Increased the debt limit to $1,520.0 billion	1,520.0
July 6, 1984, 98 Stat. 313	Increased the debt limit to $1,573.0 billion	1,573.0
October 13, 1984, 98 Stat. 475	Increased the debt limit to $1,823.8 billion	1,823.8
November 14, 1985, 99 Stat. 814	Increased the debt limit temporarily to $1,903.8 billion through December 6, 1985	1,903.8
December 12, 1985, 99 Stat. 1037	Increased the debt limit temporarily to $2,078.7 billion	2,078.7
August 21, 1986, 100 Stat. 818	Increased the debt limit to $2,111.0 billion	2,111.0
October 21, 1986, 100 Stat. 1874	Increased the debt limit temporarily to $2,300.0 billion through May 15, 1987	2,300.0
May 15, 1987, 101 Stat. 308	Increased the debt limit temporarily to $2,320.0 billion through July 17, 1987	2,320.0
July 30, 1987, 101 Stat. 542	Increased the debt limit temporarily to $2,320.0 billion through August 6, 1987	2,320.0
August 10, 1987, 101 Stat. 550	Increased the debt limit temporarily to $2,352.0 billion through September 23, 1987	2,352.0
September 29, 1987, 101 Stat. 754	Increased the debt limit to $2,800.0 billion	2,800.0

August 7, 1989, 103 Stat. 182	Increased the debt limit temporarily to $2,870.0 billion through October 31, 1989	2,870.0
November 8, 1989, 103 Stat. 830	Increased the debt limit to $3,122.7 billion	3,122.7
August 9, 1990, 104 Stat. 403	Increased the debt limit to $3,195 billion through October 2, 1990	3,195.0
October 2, 1990, 104 Stat. 878	Increased the debt limit temporarily to $3,195.0 billion through October 6, 1990	3,195.0
October 9, 1990, 104 Stat. 894	Increased the debt limit temporarily to $3,195.0 billion through October 19, 1990	3,195.0
October 19, 1990, 104 Stat. 1030	Increased the debt limit temporarily to $3,195.0 billion through October 24, 1990	3,195.0
October 25, 1990, 104 Stat. 1075	Increased the debt limit temporarily to $3,195.0 billion through October 27, 1990	3,195.0
October 28, 1990, 104 Stat. 1086	Increased the debt limit temporarily to $3,230.0 billion through November 5, 1990	3,230.0
November 5, 1990, 104 Stat. 1388	Increased the debt limit to $4,145.0 billion	4,145.0
April 6, 1993, 107 Stat. 42	Increased the debt limit temporarily to $4,370.0 billion through September 30, 1993	4,370.0
August 10, 1993, 107 Stat. 312	Increased the debt limit to $4,900.0 billion	4,900.0

Source: Historical table 7.3, Budget of the U.S. Government, Fiscal Year 1995.

TABLE J–29.—HISTORICAL TABLE: BUDGET RECONCILIATION BILLS

Reconciliation bills	Date of enactment
Omnibus Reconciliation Act of 1980 (H.R. 7765).	December 5, 1980 (P.L. 96–499).
Omnibus Budget Reconciliation Act of 1981 (H.R. 3982).	August 13, 1981 (P.L. 97–35).
Omnibus Budget Reconciliation Act of 1982 (H.R. 6955).	September 8, 1982 (P.L. 97–253).
Tax Equity and Fiscal Responsibility Act of 1982 (TEFRA) (H.R. 4961).	September 3, 1982 (P.L. 97–248).
Omnibus Budget Reconciliation Act of 1983 (H.R. 4169).	April 18, 1984 (P.L. 98–270).
Deficit Reduction Act of 1984 (H.R. 4170)	July 18, 1984 (P.L. 98–369).
Consolidated Omnibus Budget Reconciliation Act of 1985 (COBRA) (H.R. 3128).	April 7, 1986 (P.L. 99–272).
Omnibus Budget Reconciliation Act of 1986 (H.R. 5300).	October 21, 1986 (P.L. 99–509).
Omnibus Budget Reconciliation Act of 1987 (H.R. 3545).	December 22, 1987 (P.L. 100–203).
Omnibus Budget Reconciliation Act of 1989 (H.R. 3299).	December 19, 1989 (P.L. 101–239)
Omnibus Budget Reconciliation Act of 1990 (H.R. 5835).	November 5, 1990 (P.L. 101–508).
Omnibus Budget Reconciliation Act of 1993 (H.R. 2264).	August 10, 1993 (P.L. 103–66).

INDEX

Section 1. The Old-Age and Survivors Insurance Program (OASI)

Section 2. Disability Insurance Program

Section 3. Financing

Section 4. Railroad Retirement System

Section 5. Medicare

Section 6. Supplemental Security Income

Section 7. Unemployment Compensation

Section 12. Child Care

Section 17. The Pension Benefit Guaranty Corporation

Section 18. Description of Other Major Federal Assistance Programs not Within the Jurisdiction of the Committee on Ways and Means

Food Stamp Program

Medicaid

Federal Housing Assistance

Appendix E. Medicare Reimbursement to Physicians

Appendix F. Data on Employment, Earnings, and Unemployment

Appendix G. Data on Families

○